INTELLECTUAL PROPERTY
Commentary and Materials

Jill McKeough

Kathy Bowrey

Philip Griffith

FOURTH EDITION

Lawbook Co. 2007

Published in Sydney by

Lawbook Co.
   100 Harris Street, Pyrmont, NSW

First edition, J McKeough, M Blakeney 1987
Second edition, J McKeough...................................1992
Third edition 2002

National Library of Australia
   Cataloguing-in-Publication entry

McKeough, Jill.
   Intellectual property : commentary and materials.

   4th ed.
   Includes index.
   ISBN 0 455 22279 7.

   1. Intellectual property - Australia - Textbooks.
   2. Industrial property - Australia - Textbooks. 3. Copyright -
   Australia - Textbooks. I. Bowrey, Kathy. II. Griffith,
   Phillip B. C. III. Title.

346.94048

This edition is up to date as of September 2006.

Editor: Lara Weeks

Typeset in Stone Sans and Stone Serif, 9 on 12 point, by Midland Typesetters,
Australia

Printed by Ligare Pty Ltd, Riverwood, NSW

INTELLECTUAL PROPERTY
Commentary and Materials

HEAD OFFICE: 100 Harris Street PYRMONT NSW 2009
Tel: (02) 8587 7000 Fax: (02) 8587 7100
For all sales inquiries please ring 1800 650 522
(for calls within Australia only)

INTERNATIONAL AGENTS & DISTRIBUTORS

NORTH, CENTRAL & SOUTH AMERICA,
CARIBBEAN
Carswell Co
Ontario, Canada

HONG KONG
Sweet & Maxwell Asia
Hysan Avenue, Causeway Bay
Hong Kong

MALAYSIA
Sweet & Maxwell Asia
Petaling Jaya, Selangor

NEW ZEALAND, PACIFIC ISLANDS
Brooker's Ltd
Wellington

SINGAPORE
Sweet & Maxwell Asia
Battery Road

EUROPE, MIDDLE EAST AND AFRICA
ISM Europe, Middle East & Africa
Sweet & Maxwell Ltd
Andover, Hampshire

AUSTRALIA, PAPUA NEW GUINEA
Thomson Legal & Regulatory Ltd
Pyrmont, Sydney

JAPAN, KOREA, TAIWAN
ISM Asia Operations
Thomson Legal & Regulatory
Pyrmont, Sydney

AUTHOR'S ACKNOWLEDGMENT

Kathy Bowrey would like to include a big thank you to her research assistant: Amy Wootten.

PUBLISHER'S ACKNOWLEDGMENTS

The following extracts/graphics were reproduced with the kind permission of:

ABC Network: www.abc.net.au
- ABC Logo images. Courtesy of the Australian Broadcasting Corporation. All Rights Reserved.

Australia Council: www.ozco.gov.au/the_council
- David Throsby and Virginia Hollister, "Don't Give Up Your Day Job: An Economic Study of Professional Artists in Australia" (2003), Appendix Tables: 8.1.

CCH Australia: www.cch.com.au
- Australian Trade Practices Reporter (ATPR).

Commonwealth Attorney General's Department, Copyright Law Branch: www.ag.gov.au
- Department of Communications Information Technology and the Arts, *Copyright Collecting Societies in Australia.*
- Shape Simpson, *Review of Australian Copyright Collecting Societies*, Report to a Working Group of the Australian Cultural Development Office and the Attorney-General's Department (Department of Communication and the Arts, Canberra 1995).
- Australia-United States Free Trade Agreement: www.dft.gov.au/trade/negotiations/us.html
- Copyright Law Review Committee, "Simplification of the Copyright Act 1968, Part 2—Categorization of Subject Matter (September 1998).

Council of Law Reporting for New South Wales:
- New South Wales Law Reports (NSWLR). © Council of Law Reporting for New South Wales.

Incorporated Council of Law Reporting for England & Wales: www.lawreports.co.uk
- Appeal Cases (AC).
- Chancery Reports (Ch).
- Weekly News Reports (WLR).

IP Australia: www.ipaustralia.gov.au
- Australian Patent Office, "Manual of Practice and Procedure", Vol.2 "National"

- Australian Patent Office, "Manual of Practice and Procedure", Vol.2. www.ipaustralia.gov.au/resources/manuals_patents.shtml.
- Intellectual Property Competition Review Committee, "Review of Intellectual Property Legislation under the Competition Principles Agreement", Final Report (September 2000).
- IP Australia, "Patents for Business Schemes".

Lawbook Co. part of Thomson Legal & Regulatory Limited: www.thomson.com.au
- Australian Law Journal Reports (ALJR).
- Commonwealth Law Reports (CLR).
- Federal Court Reports (FCR).
- Federal Law Reports (FLR).
- State Reports of New South Wales (SR (NSW)).
- Weekly Notes New South Wales (WN (NSW)).

LexisNexis Australia: www.lexisnexis.com.au
- Australia Law Reports (ALR).
- Intellectual Property Reports (IPR).

Office of Public Sector Information (also HMSO): www.hmso.gov.uk
- Reports of Patent Design and Trade Mark Cases (RPC).

Parliament of Australia House of Representatives, Standing Committee on Legal and Constitutional Affairs: www.aph.ov.au
- House of Representatives, Standing Committee on Legal and Constitutional Affairs, *Don't Stop the Music*!, A Report of the Inquiry into Copyright, Music and Small Business (June 1998).

Sweet & Maxwell, London: www.sweetandmaxwell.co.uk
- Entertainment and Media Law Reports (EMLR).
- Fleet Street Reports (FSR).

Lawbook Co. part of Thomson Legal and Regulatory Limited and its authors are grateful to the publishers, agents and authors, who have allowed us to reproduce extracts of their work in this book. Every effort has been made to contact copyright holders and/or their agents, to establish and acknowledge copyright, however, Lawbook Co. tenders its apology for any accidental infringement. The publisher would be pleased to come to a suitable agreement with the rightful owners in each case.

SUMMARY OF CONTENTS

TABLE OF CONTENTS

TABLE OF CASES

TABLE OF STATUTES

Introduction

INTRODUCTION TO INTELLECTUAL PROPERTY AND THE INTERNATIONAL REGIME

WHAT IS INTELLECTUAL PROPERTY?

[1.05] The term "intellectual property" (IP) originally applied to the rights which protected literary and artistic creations. In its modern formulation the term embraces what has been called industrial or commercial property as well as literary and artistic property. Intellectual property laws seek to promote investment in, and access to, the results of creative effort, and extend to protecting the marketing of goods and services.

An overview of the separate origins of "industrial" and "intellectual" property reveals that the term "industrial property" is derived from the French term "propriete industrielle". This is probably an inexact translation for the purposes of our law, since "industrielle" has an extremely broad meaning, embracing all aspects of human labour. The French term "propriete" does not mean property in its common law sense, but merely refers to the right to restrain imitation or infringement. As Holmes J explained in a copyright case, *White-Smith Music Publishing Co v Apollo Co* 209 US 1 at 19 (1908):

"The right to exclude is not directed to an object in possession or owned, but is in vacuo, so to speak. It restrains the spontaneity of men when but for it there would be nothing of the kind to hinder their doing as they saw fit. It is a prohibition of conduct remote from the persons or tangibles of the party having the right."

The scope of industrial property can be seen in the *Paris Convention for the Protection of Industrial Property 1883*, the principal international Convention dealing with the subject. Article 1 provides:

"(2) The protection of industrial property has as its object patents, utility models, industrial designs, trademarks, service marks, trade names, indications of source or appellations of origin, and the repression of unfair competition.
(3) Industrial property shall be understood in the broadest sense and shall apply not only to industry and commerce proper, but likewise to agricultural and extractive industries and to all manufactured or natural products, for example, wines, grain, tobacco leaf, fruit, cattle, minerals, mineral waters, beer, flowers, and flour."

The *Convention Establishing the World Intellectual Property Organisation* (WIPO) *1967* first defined the scope of intellectual property. Australia is a member of this Convention, which has as its objectives the promotion of the protection of intellectual property throughout the world and the administration of a number of conventions and agreements concerning intellectual property. The term "intellectual property" is defined in Art 2(viii) as to:

> "include the rights relating to:
> * literary, artistic and scientific works,
> * performances of performing artists, phonograms and broadcasts,
> * inventions in all fields of human endeavour,
> * scientific discoveries,
> * industrial designs,
> * trade marks, service marks, and commercial names and designations,
> * protection against unfair competition'
> * and all other rights resulting from intellectual activity in the industrial, scientific, literary or artistic fields."

Intellectual property is a major tool of world trade. Since 1995, intellectual property law has largely been shaped by trade concerns, emanating from the *Agreement on Trade-Related Aspects of Intellectual Property Rights* (TRIPs), which is the most significant multilateral agreement on the range of intellectual property rights (IPR). It came into force on 1 January 1995. TRIPs is one agreement in the system of agreements which make up the World Trade Organisation (WTO). TRIPs links intellectual property rights to GATT or WTO rights and obligations. WTO Ministerial Conferences are held every two years, the most recent being in Hong Kong, December 2005. Intellectual property issues on the agenda in Hong Kong included TRIPS and public health; compulsory licensing of essential patented drugs; geographical indications (GIs) in general; a multilateral register for GIs related to wines and spirits; extending the "higher level of protection" for GIs beyond wines and spirits; patents and plants, animals, biodiversity and traditional knowledge; dispute settlement mechanisms.

The definition of IPR in TRIPs does not vary greatly in substance from the subject matter identified in the WIPO and Paris Conventions and is regarded as including:

* copyright and related rights (Arts 9-14);

* trade marks including service marks (Arts 15-21);

* geographical indications (or appellations) of origin (Arts 22-24);

* industrial designs (Arts 25-26);

* patents (including plant varieties rights) (Arts 27-34);

* layout (or designs of integrated circuits) (Arts 35-38); and

* undisclosed information (including trade secrets) (Art 39).

TRIPs also addresses the issue of control of anti-competitive practices in contractual licences, to allow members to legislate to control abuses of intellectual property rights which have an adverse effect on competition in a market (Art 40).

The general goals of TRIPs are set out in the Preamble, and formal objectives are found in Art 7. The general goals include:
* reduction of distortions and impediments to international trade;

* promotion of effective protection for IPR; and

* ensuring that measures to protect IPR do not become barriers to legitimate trade.

The objectives are that protection and enforcement of IPR should contribute to:

- promotion of technological innovation;

- dissemination of technology;

- the mutual advantage of producers and users of technological knowledge in a manner conducive to social and economic welfare; and

- a balance of rights and obligations.

The general provisions and basic principles underling TRIPs are found in Arts 1-8 and can be summarised thus:

- IPR are approached from a trade and commerce perspective, and IPR subject matters are seen as private property interests to be enforced principally through private civil action.

- TRIPs builds upon the existing WIPO treaties, that is, the Berne, Paris and Rome Conventions, and extends them.

- The Agreement adopts the existing WIPO principle of National Treatment (NT) for IPR (Arts 3, 5) which forbids discrimination between a member's own nationals and nationals of other members.

- TRIPs introduces the WTO principle of Most Favoured Nation Treatment (MFN) to the international IPR system (Arts 4, 5). MFN forbids discrimination between nationals of other members, that is, when a member extends a benefit to the nationals of another member they must extend that benefit to the nationals of all other members.

- Members may choose their own legal mechanisms for implementing TRIPs (Art 1). Members may adopt measures consistent with the Agreement necessary to protect public health and other sectors of vital importance to their development (Art 8(1)), and measures necessary to prevent abuse of IPR which unreasonably affect trade or international transfer of technology (Art 8(2)).

- There are general rules intended to ensure that the procedural technicalities of IPR do not interfere with the claimed substantive benefits of TRIPs.

- TRIPs is a minimum standards treaty and members may provide more, but not less, generous protection. The Agreement does provide for reservations under certain conditions. However, reservations not specifically provided for in the Agreement may not be entered into without the consent of other members (Art 72).

Articles 65 and 66 give all members transition periods to comply with TRIPS. Industrialised economies were required to comply in full by 1 January 1996. All members were required to comply with the NT and MFN principles by 1 January 1996. "Developing" and "transition" economies were required to comply by 1 January 2000, and "least developed" economies by 1 January 2005. Generally TRIPS has been very successful in globalising intellectual property rights, and linking these rights with global trade agendas. However, developing country compliance, especially with regard to the treatment of pharmaceutical patents and access to essential medicines, remains one of the most heated issues in contemporary intellectual property law.

Intellectual property rights have also been expanded by regional and bi-lateral Free Trade Agreements. Some intellectual property provisions in Chapter 17 of the Australia-United States Free Trade Agreement (AUS-US FTA) have generated significant debate about the justifications for and beneficiaries of stronger intellectual property laws. Controversial provisions concerning copyright extend the term of protection, provide greater protection for works that are technologically protected, change the conditions of ISP liability for infringement and create new performer's rights.

Controversial patents provisions affect the pharmaceutical industry and generic drug manufacturers (that is, makers of drugs in which patents have expired). There are provisions permitting term extensions for unreasonable delays in processing applications. Owners of pharmaceutical patents have a new right for compensation for unreasonable delays in marketing approval processes for drugs, and generic drug manufacturers have new obligations before they can market their drugs. These changes have consequences for the Australian Pharmaceutical Benefits Scheme (PBS) and its drug price fixing role for commonly prescribed drugs in Australia. There is also a strengthening of enforcement provisions.

SCOPE OF IP PROTECTION IN AUSTRALIA

[1.10] The term "intellectual property" was not especially current in common law jurisdictions at the time of Federation. Accordingly the Federal power to enact intellectual property laws was drafted as:

> "51 The Parliament shall, subject to this Constitution, have power to make laws for
> the peace, order, and good government of the Commonwealth with respect to:
> (xviii) Copyrights, patents of inventions and designs, and trade marks."

This specificity has led to a consideration of the constitutional limits of the provision. The constitutionality of "Union" trade marks, performer's rights and plant variety rights and plant breeder's rights has been debated. However in *The Grain Pool of WA v The Commonwealth* (2000) 202 CLR 479, the High Court supported a generous interpretative approach to s 51 (xviii), supporting *"fresh rights* in the nature of copyright, patents of inventions and designs and trade marks" (emphasis added). Potential to enact some intellectual property legislation by relying upon the postal and telegraphic power s 51(v) and the external affairs power s 51 (xxix) was also acknowledged. Given the High Court's support for "fresh rights" and the importance of treaty-making to contemporary intellectual property law reform, constitutional challenges are likely to remain uncommon.

The wide ambit of the industrial and intellectual property conventions mentioned above derives, in part, from the natural law theories popular in continental Europe that intellectual property rights are not created by law but have always existed. Consequently, suggestions have been made in common law countries for the development of a similarly broad prohibition of unfair trading.

This proposition attracted some judicial attention in the Supreme Court of New South Wales, being adverted to by Else-Mitchell J in *Willard King Organization Pty Ltd v United Telecasters Sydney Ltd* [1981] 2 NSWLR 547, and supported by Needham J in *Hexagon Pty Ltd v Australian Broadcasting Commission* (1975) 7 ALR 233 at 252, who declared "it seems to me that there is room in our jurisprudence for a concept such as 'unfair competition'". However, the existence of a remedy in unfair competition in Australia was laid to rest by the High Court in the following case.

▬▬▬ Moorgate Tobacco v Philip Morris (No 2) ▬▬▬

[1.15] *Moorgate Tobacco Co Ltd v Philip Morris Ltd (No 2)* (1984) 156 CLR 414 High Court of Australia

[Philip Morris was the assignee of rights under a trade mark licence agreement with the Lorillard Division of Loew's Theatres Inc (Loew's). This agreement permitted Philip Morris to make and sell KENT cigarettes. The agreement provided that in the event that the licensor decided to licence "the use of any of its other cigarettes or tobacco product trade marks" in the licence area, the licensor offered the licensee on such terms as the licensor "shall deem reasonable, the right of first refusal of such licence or licences". In the middle of 1975 Loew's decided to test the US market for a new type of tar-reduced cigarette under the brand name "KENT Golden Lights". In October and November 1975 the new brand was test-marketed in the US. Between November 1975 and November 1976 there were discussions between representatives of Loew's and Philip Morris about the possible manufacture and marketing by Philip Morris of the new brand. At this time Philip Morris had already been manufacturing and selling its own low-tar cigarettes under the name "Marlbro Lights".

The licence agreement between Loew's and Philip Morris was to terminate in late 1977 and the possibility of extending the licence to cover "KENT Golden Lights" became part of the negotiations for renewal of the agreement. In March 1977 negotiations commenced between Loew's and the British American Tobacco Company Group (BAT) for the acquisition by BAT of the "International Sales business" of Loew's in cigarettes and "the goodwill associated therewith". Included in the proposed sale was the Australian KENT trade mark. Philip Morris was not alerted to these developments until early June 1977 whereupon it offered to purchase the KENT brand. This offer was not taken up and on 22 June 1977 Moorgate and Loew's entered into a formal agreement for the sale to Moorgate of Loew's business outside the US. Three weeks later Philip Morris applied for registration in Australia of the trade mark "Golden Lights" and in December 1977 it assigned its interests in the mark to the second respondent PM Inc. From the beginning of 1978 PM Inc commenced the use of the name "Marlbro Golden Lights" for its cigarettes.

Declaratory, injunctive and consequential relief was sought by Moorgate in the Supreme Court of New South Wales for breach of contract, breach of confidence and for unfair competition. This action was dismissed by the trial judge in a decision upheld by the New South Wales Court of Appeal.]

DEANE J [with whom GIBBS CJ and MASON, WILSON and DAWSON JJ agreed]: **[439]** ... The phrase "unfair competition" has been used in judgments and learned writings in at least three distinct ways, namely, (i) as a synonym of the doctrine of passing off; (ii) as a generic name **[440]** to cover the range of legal and equitable causes of action available to protect a trader against the unlawful trading activities of a competitor; and (iii) to describe what is claimed to be a new and general cause of action which protects a trader against damage caused either by "unfair competition" generally or, more particularly, by the "misappropriation" of knowledge or information in which he has a "quasi-proprietary" right. The first and second of the above uses of the phrase are liable to be misleading in that they may wrongly imply that the relevant action or actions are restricted to proceedings against a competitor. The second use is also liable to imply that there exists a unity of underlying principle between different actions when, in truth, there is none. The third use of the phrase is, in an Australian context, simply mistaken in that "unfair competition" does not, in itself, provide a sufficient basis for relief under the law of this country. It is in that third and mistaken sense that "unfair competition" was called in aid of Moorgate's case in the present appeal.

■■■■■■■■ Moorgate Tobacco v Philip Morris (No 2) *continued*

The genesis of the notion of a general cause of action for "unfair competition" is to be found in the majority judgment of the US Supreme Court in *International News Service v Associated Press* 248 US 215; 63 Law Ed 211 (1918). As the name would indicate, that case was concerned with published news or information. The complainant, a co-operative association of newspaper publishers, gathered news which it telegraphed to its member publishers throughout the United States. The defendant was a corporation which was engaged in the business of gathering news for other publishers. The defendant made a practice of obtaining news from the early publications of the complainant's members and sending it by telegraph to its own customers thus enabling them, in some parts of the United States, to publish news gathered by the complainant for its members as soon or even earlier than it was published in the newspapers published by those members. The majority judgment, delivered by Pitney J, denounced (248 US 215 at 240; 63 Law Ed 211 at 221) the actions of the defendant as "an unauthorised interference with the normal operation of complainant's legitimate business precisely at the point where the profit is to be reaped, in order to divert a material portion of the profit from those who have earned it to those who have not; with special advantage to defendant in the competition because of the fact that it is not burdened with any part of the expense of gathering the news". That fulsome description of the defendant's actions was immediately followed by the conclusion that the "transaction speaks for itself and **[441]** a court of equity ought not to hesitate long in characterising it as unfair competition in business".

The majority judgment in *International News Service* assumed, rather than sought to establish, that such "unfair competition in business" was, in itself, an actionable wrong. The "underlying principle" was stated to be "much the same as that which lies at the base of the equitable theory of consideration in the law of trusts that he who has fairly paid the price should have the beneficial use of the property. (Pom Eq Jur para 981.) That equitable principle is, however, applicable to determine beneficial ownership of property which is capable of being the subject of a trust (see *Pomeroy's Equity Jurisprudence* (5th ed, 1941), Vol 3, para 981) and cannot logically either found a conclusion that published news, as distinct from copyright in its presentation or arrangement, itself constitutes property, or provides any basis for a general cause of action for unfair competition. The judgment went on to assert (248 US 215 at 242; 63 Law Ed 211 at 222) that the "news matter" should be regarded as "the mere material from which [the] two competing parties are endeavouring to make money" and be treated as "quasi-property for the purposes of their business because they are both selling it as such" and that, so regarded and treated, the "news material" had been "misappropriated" by the defendant. It is not explained why the information which had been published should have been regarded by the majority of the Supreme Court as "mere material from which" a party was endeavouring to make money, why that information should have been "treated" as "quasi-property" when it had long been the common law that, in the absence of rights of patent, trade mark or copyright, information and knowledge are not the property of an individual, or why a person who had gathered and published information about world events should be seen as owning the information in the sense that the "unfair" use of it by another in competition in a manner that was contrary to that party's business interests constituted "misappropriation". In addition to misappropriation, the judgment (at 242; Law Ed at 222) identified "elements of imitation of false pretense in defendant's practices" but stated that "these elements, although accentuating the wrong, are not the essence of it". It is difficult to know whether "misappropriation" of "news material" should be regarded as a separate basis of the decision or as but one instance of the general wrong of "unfair competition in business" to which the judgment had earlier referred. Either way, one searches in vain **[442]** in the majority judgment for any identification of the ingredients of that general wrong.

Not surprisingly in a court of which Holmes J and Brandeis J were members, the muddled birth of the new action was not an occasion for unanimity. Holmes J, in what was essentially a dissenting judgment, held that the complainant was entitled to but limited relief on the basis of inverse passing off and that any entitlement to wider relief was a matter for the legislature and not for the court. Brandeis J filed a strong dissent in which he considered relevant US and English authorities and concluded that the law did not recognise any general proprietary right in knowledge or information or any general action for unfair competition.

Subsequent decisions of United States courts have tended to isolate rather than develop the doctrine of a general action for unfair competition enunciated in the *International News Service* case. ... [443] ...

The notion of a general action for "unfair trading" or "unfair competition" has received little encouragement in either the House of Lords or this court. In so far as the House of Lords is concerned, it suffices to refer to the recent decision in *Warnink v Townend & Sons (Hull)* [1979] AC 731. In that case, their Lordships were concerned to decide whether the appellants had a cause of action against the respondents who had, in Lord Diplock's words (at 740), engaged in "unfair, not to say dishonest trading". It was held that the question fell to be answered not by reference to any [444] general notion of unfair trading or competition but by reference to what Lord Diplock (in a speech with which Viscount Dilhorne, Lord Salmon and Lord Scarman agreed) identified as the "five characteristics which must be present in order to create a valid cause of action for passing off" (at 742). Lord Diplock pointed out (at 742) that, while it is true that the presence of those five characteristics "indicates what a moral code would censure as dishonest trading", it did not follow that all factual situations which present them "give rise to a cause of action for passing off" in an "economic system which has relied on competition to keep down prices and to improve products". He added that

> "[T]he market in which the action for passing off originated was no place for the mealy mouthed; advertisements are not an affidavit; exaggerated claims by a trader about the quality of his wares, assertions that they are better than those of his rivals even though he knows this to be untrue, have been permitted by the common law as venial 'puffing' which gives no cause of action to a competitor even though he can show that he has suffered actual damage in his business as a result" (at 742).

In so far as this court is concerned, one need go no further than the decision in *Victoria Park Racing and Recreation Grounds Co Ltd v Taylor* (1937) 58 CLR 479. In that case, a majority of the court, in confirming the dismissal of an action to restrain a radio station broadcasting descriptions of horse races conducted on the plaintiff's land made from a platform erected on adjoining land for that purpose, expressed conclusions which correspond closely with those of Brandeis J in the *International News Service* case. Dixon J (at 509) commented that the reasons of Brandeis J substantially represented "the English view" which he described (at 508-509) in terms which involved a rejection of the reasoning underlying the majority judgment in *International News Service*:

> "The fact is that the substance of the plaintiff's complaint goes to interference, not with its enjoyment of the land, but with the profitable conduct of its business. If English law had followed the course of development that had recently taken place in the US, the 'broadcasting rights' in respect of the races might have been protected as part of the quasi-property created by the enterprise, organisation and labour of the plaintiff in establishing and equipping a racecourse and doing all that is necessary to conduct race meetings. But courts of equity have not in British jurisdictions thrown

███████ Moorgate Tobacco v Philip Morris (No 2) *continued*

the protection of an injunction around all the intangible elements of value, that is, value in **[445]** exchange, which may flow from the exercise by an individual of his powers or resources whether in the organisation of a business or undertaking or the use of ingenuity, knowledge, skill or labour. This is sufficiently evidenced by the history of the law of copyright and by the fact that the exclusive right to invention, trade marks, designs, trade name and reputation are dealt with in English law as special heads of protected interests and not under a wide generalisation."

His Honour added (at 509) that the judgment of Brandeis J contained "an adequate answer both upon principle and authority to the suggestion that the defendants are misappropriating or abstracting something which the plaintiff has created and alone is entitled to turn to value". Dixon J identified that answer as being that:

"[I]t is not because the individual has by his efforts put himself in a position to obtain value for what he can give that his right to give it becomes protected by law and so assumes the exclusiveness of property, but because the intangible or incorporeal right he claims falls within a recognised category to which legal or equitable protection attaches".

The rejection of a general action for "unfair competition" or "unfair trading" does not involve a denial of the desirability of adopting a flexible approach to traditional forms of action when such an approach is necessary to adapt them to meet new situations and circumstances. It has not, for example, prevented the adaptation of the traditional doctrine of passing off to meet new circumstances involving the deceptive or confusing use of names, descriptive terms or other indicia to persuade purchasers or customers to believe that goods or services have an association, quality or endorsement which belongs or would belong to goods or services of, or associated with, another or others: see, eg, *Warnink v Townend & Sons* at 739ff; *Henderson v Radio Corp Pty Ltd* [1960] SR (NSW) 576. The rejection of a general action for "unfair competition" involves no more than a recognition of the fact that the existence of such an action is inconsistent with the established limits of the traditional and statutory causes of action which are available to a trader in respect of damage caused or threatened by a competitor. Those limits, which define the boundary between the area of legal or equitable restraint and protection and the area of untrammelled competition, increasingly reflect what the responsible parliament and parliaments have determined to be the appropriate balance between competing claims and policies. Neither legal principle nor social utility requires or warrants the obliteration of that boundary by the importation of a cause of action whose main characteristic is the scope it allows, **[446]** under high-sounding generalisations, for judicial indulgence of idiosyncratic notions of what is fair in the market place.

██

[1.20] Another route which has been explored in the search for the protection of intellectual property rights outside the traditional heads of protection, has been by way of actions to enjoin breaches of the *Trade Practices Act 1974* (Cth), s 52(1). That provision proscribes conduct engaged in by persons in trade or commerce "that is misleading or deceptive or ... likely to mislead or deceive". Such actions were encouraged by the identification of an "additional jurisdiction" in the Federal Court of Australia to hear general law actions based on a "common substratum of fact" with those which could be brought under the *Trade Practices Act 1974* (Cth) and by the subsequent cross-vesting of jurisdiction in intellectual property matters between the State Supreme Courts and the Federal Court of Australia. However, the scope of *Trade Practices Act 1974* (Cth), s 52 to supplement the traditional intellectual property causes of action was circumscribed at an early stage by the High Court in the following case.

▰▰▰▰▰▰ Parkdale Custom Built Furniture v Puxu ▰▰▰▰▰▰

[1.25] *Parkdale Custom Built Furniture Pty Ltd v Puxu Pty Ltd* (1982) 149 CLR 191 High Court of Australia

[Puxu Pty Ltd (Puxu) since June 1978 manufactured and sold under the name "Post and Rail" furniture of distinctive appearance and design known as the "Contour" range. The furniture had been designed and sold by Puxu's predecessors in business since late 1976 or early 1977. It was advertised quite widely and had an established reputation, but the design had not been registered under the *Designs Act 1906* (Cth), as amended. From June 1978, Parkdale Custom Built Furniture Pty Ltd (Parkdale) manufactured and sold under the general names "Parkdale Custom Built Furniture" and "Custom Built Furniture" furniture known as the "Rawhide" range. The furniture made by Parkdale closely resembled that made by Puxu. There was sewn into the front of each piece of Parkdale furniture a label about 6.35 centimetres square which stated that the item was "Parkdale Custom Built Furniture" of the "Rawhide" range. The label could be tucked under the upholstery, and would then not be visible, and it might easily enough be removed by cutting it off. It was the practice of manufacturers to label such furniture in that way and Puxu's furniture bore labels of a similar kind but somewhat smaller.

Puxu sued Parkdale alleging that Parkdale was engaging in conduct that was misleading or deceptive, or which was likely to mislead or deceive, and sought injunctions and damages.]

GIBBS CJ: **[199]** ... Speaking generally, the sale by one manufacturer of goods which closely resemble those of another manufacturer is not a breach of s 52 if the goods are properly **[200]** labelled. There are hundreds of ordinary articles of consumption which, although made by different manufacturers and of different quality, closely resemble one another. In some cases this is because the design of a particular article had traditionally, or over a considerable period of time, been accepted as the most suitable for the purpose for which the article serves. In some cases indeed no other design would be practicable. In other cases, although the article in question is the product of the invention of a person who is currently trading, the suitability of the design or appearance of the article is such that a market has become established which other manufacturers endeavour to satisfy, as they are entitled to do if no property exists in the design or appearance of the article. In all of these cases, the normal and reasonable way to distinguish one product from another is by marks, brands or labels. If an article is properly labelled so as to show the name of the manufacturer or the source of the article its close resemblance to another article will not mislead an ordinary reasonable member of the public. If the label is removed by some person for whose acts the defendant is not responsible, and in consequence the purchaser is misled, the misleading effect will have been produced, not by the conduct of the defendant, but by the conduct of the persons who removed the label.

For these reasons I have reached the conclusion that the conduct of the appellant was not of the kind to which s 52 refers.

...

MASON J: **[205]** The relationship of s 52(1) with established statutory regimes dealing with related topics gives rise to an important question. Can it be inferred from the

██████ Parkdale Custom Built Furniture v Puxu *continued*

detailed treatment of limited monopolies of intellectual and industrial property in specific statutes that s 52(1) should be read down if it otherwise could facilitate the creation of new monopolies not subject to the limitations imposed by those statutes? In my view there are sound reasons for not construing s 52 in that way.

Clearly there is here no question of infringement of a trade mark. As a general proposition the *Trade Marks Act 1955* (Cth) is concerned with deception or confusion to the public as to the source of goods, whilst the *Trade Practices Act* is concerned with deception of the public as consumers of goods or services. Likewise, the operation of s 52 is not restricted by the common law principles relating to passing off. If, as I consider, the section provides the public with wider protection from deception than the common law, it does not follow that there is a conflict between the section and the common law. The statute provides an additional remedy.

To obtain a monopoly in a particular design under the *Designs Act* it is not sufficient merely to have a period of undisturbed **[206]** use. The necessary registration is only possible for a "new or original design, which has not been published in Australia before the lodging of an application for its registration" (s 17(1)). A certificate of registration remains in force for a limited period (s 26). Importantly a registered design is open to public inspection (s 27) so that others can assess whether they could be infringing the copyright in a registered design. Thus the statute seeks a balance between limited monopoly rights for traders with a novel design on the one hand and the stimulus of competition aided by access to information on the other hand. Similarly the *Patents Act 1952* (Cth) seeks to balance competing interests in connection with the grant of letters patent for a particular invention. Essentially, in return for the disclosure of his invention a patentee receives a limited monopoly at the expiration of which the invention is available to the public at large.

The case made by the respondent as a competing trader here is that it is entitled to an injunction to restrain the appellant from producing and selling goods which very closely resemble the respondent's product. Its claim in substance is that s 52 gives it the rights which it would have had if it had a registered design for the furniture.

On the other hand the appellant's case is that to forbid a manufacturer to manufacture a product because it too closely resembles a competitor's earlier product without subjected the resulting monopoly for the earlier product to the limitations imposed by the *Designs Act*, would be to create a monopoly in a design in circumstances in which that Act does not confer a monopoly. This, the appellant urges, is a result which would scarcely have been intended.

Mr Staff QC for the respondent submits that the *Patents Act* and the *Designs Act* are directed to a field of obligations and rights quite different from s 52. In one sense this is so. It is the object of the two statutes to create private property rights. They confer exclusive or monopoly rights in patents and designs respectively and prescribe the conditions according to which these rights come into existence. With s 52 it is different. Its primary purpose is not to create private property rights but to regulate the conduct of traders by prohibiting them from engaging in conduct which misleads or deceives consumers. Enforcement of this statutory prohibition may enable trader A to prevent trader B from manufacturing or marketing goods which closely resemble those of trader A because the marketing of them will mislead or deceive the public, but this result, if it occurs, will be incidental to the enforcement of the prohibition—it is an unavoidable consequence of protecting the **[207]** public from misleading or deceptive conduct. When s 52 is viewed in this light, there is no very strong reason for saying that the generality

▓▓▓▓▓▓ Parkdale Custom Built Furniture v Puxu *continued*

of its language should be restricted on the ground that it runs counter to the policy and purposes of the *Patents Act* and the *Designs Act*.

It would be otherwise if the policy and purpose of the two statutes were to prohibit all monopoly rights in patents and designs except those for which they provide. If the two statutes were anti-monopoly statutes then we might be justified in saying that the general words of s 52 should be read subject to the particular words of the *Patents Act* and the *Designs Act*—generalia specialibus non derogant. But it is not possible to say of them that they are anti-monopoly statutes—their object is to create exclusive rights.

The appellant attempts to turn this argument aside by asserting that the policy which underlies the two statutes is that there will be no monopoly rights in patents and designs except on the prescribed statutory conditions. Certainly this is the effect of the two statutes one can only obtain a grant of letters patent or registration of a design by complying with the statutory conditions. But I would not describe it as the policy of the statutes. Their emphasis is positive, it is on the grant of exclusive rights on stipulated conditions; it is not on the prohibition of similar rights except on stipulated conditions. Consequently, I would not read down the provisions of s 52 by reference to considerations of policy said to arise from the *Patents Act* and the *Designs Act*. As I have already said, the words of the section, though general, are reasonably plain. The argument based on the two statutes is not of sufficient strength to displace the ordinary meaning of the words.

However, I am inclined to the view that the evidence did not establish conduct by the appellant of the proscribed type.

BRENNAN J: **[224]** If s 52 of the *Trade Practices Act* authorised or required the granting of such an injunction, it would run counter to the intention of Parliament implied in the statutes which create or provide for the creation of monopolies. Those statutes define the conditions governing the creation of monopolies and thus chart the limits of the contemporary reservations from the freedom to manufacture and sell which the *Statute of Monopolies* assured. The notion that patent laws imply an intention to leave free the field of activity not covered by the grant of monopoly rights underlay the judgments of the Supreme Court of the United States in *Sears, Roebuck & Co v Stiffel Co* 376 US 225; 11 Law Ed 2d 661 (1964) and in *Compco Corp v Day-Brite Lighting Inc* 376 US 234; 11 Law Ed 2d 669 (1964). The Court of Appeals for the Seventh Circuit in *Sears, Roebuck* had held that a likelihood of confusion as to the source of products was sufficient, without passing off, to attract an Illinois law proscribing unfair competition and to warrant the granting of injunctive relief. The Supreme Court, assuming that the State law had the operation thus attributed to it, denied the competence of a State legislature to encroach upon federal patent laws. These cases were explained in *Goldstein v California* 412 US 546 at 569-570; 37 Law Ed 2d 163 at 181 (1973):

"In regard to mechanical configurations, Congress had balanced the need to encourage innovation and originally of invention against the need to insure competition in the sale of identical or substantially identical products. The standards established for granting federal patent protection to machines thus indicated not only which articles in this particular category Congress wished to protect, but which configurations it wished to remain free. The application of state law in these cases to prevent the copying of articles which did not meet the requirements for federal protection disturbed the careful balance which Congress had drawn and thereby necessarily gave way under the Supremacy Clause of the Constitution."

▧▧▧ Parkdale Custom Built Furniture v Puxu *continued*

It would be surprising if *Trade Practices Act* were to alter the "careful balance" of the *Patents Act* and the *Designs Act* by a side-wind and, after four centuries, open the way to the creation of prescriptive monopolies for the manufacture of goods. In my view, it does not have that effect.

THE FUTURE OF INTELLECTUAL PROPERTY

[1.30] The "careful balance" referred to by Brennan J in *Parkdale v Puxu* (above) is that between the interests of intellectual property owners on the one hand, and the interests of users or potential users of material embodying the rights, on the other, which may include downstream innovators. The creation of intellectual property involves intellectual effort and can entail substantial resource outlays. Producers need an incentive to make that effort and incur the costs of production, by receiving an appropriate return, usually through a period of exclusive rights to exploit the intellectual property. There are many challenges to intellectual property and the appropriate scope of protection is to be considered in the light of these challenges, which recently include issues of competition policy, privacy, health, biodiversity and public policy. The custodians of traditional knowledge, and those working on genetic resources, are making new claims for enfranchisement. Marketers are increasingly requiring protection for well-known trade marks, geographic indications, and domain names in circumstances where existing trade mark or copyright laws would not recognise proprietary rights. There are serious and subversive threats to the established order as the law continues to address the issues surrounding material on the internet. Here, open source, peer-to-peer file sharing systems and "copyleft" assist in returning to users what encryption, private contractual arrangements and legislative reform may take away. Despite the perception that intellectual property is at a "crisis point", the belief that intellectual property law is "outdated and obsolete" is challenged by those who see the law as able to draw on a long history of attempts to grant property status to intangibles.[1] This work challenges the notion that these laws have ever had clear, uncontested foundations or clear definitions of what ought to be protected, and to what extent.

The focus of international discussions on what is called the "Digital Agenda", resulting in the "internet treaties", illustrates the adaptation of intellectual property law at national and international level. The distribution of information by means of digital technology is revolutionising conditions of international trade and bringing into sharp focus the requirements of protection of intellectual property in a world with no physical boundaries. National differences in copyright protection are tolerable where physical objects embody the intellectual property. But a film (or other material) loaded onto the internet will, in the absence of a technical barrier, be available instantly and in full all over the world.

Intangible property moves differently to other goods, but does this mean that intangible property needs even stronger protection harmonised across the globe?

In the information technology industry "incentive theories" that lead to restricted access to computer code by "downstream" developers, are commonly challenged. The computing industry took off in the 70s and 80s with weak if any, intellectual property protection, but this

---

1   B Sherman and L Bently, *The Making of Modern Intellectual Property Law: The British Experience, 1760–1911* (Cambridge University Press, 1999), pp 1–5.

did not lead to any shortage of innovation. Rather it was a very vibrant time for development. Thus, many argue that patents and copyright protection may hinder, rather than sponsor these particular kinds of innovations. Justifying intellectual property rights is a complicated and difficult business, and recourse to general theories without address to the specifics of particular categories, their individual histories and mixes of policy objectives is quite problematic.

The politics of intellectual property law-making is more contested now than at any other stage of the development of the rights. This points to the fact that the "right" intellectual property rights are perceived to have a much greater impact on the future growth of the economy and on balances of trade.

Consideration of the "balance between owners and users" presupposes a world in which all creators, owners and users are equal in terms of capacity to create, disseminate and access the desired product or service comprising the intellectual property. In fact, apart from differences between individuals and corporations, another consideration is "Australia's ability to compete in world markets",[2] where the value of our imports of copyright material far outweighs the value of exports. The Australian Bureau of Statistics does not provide statistics on the value or cost of intellectual property rights per se, and lump sum figures are hard to calculate. However to give one example, longitudinal data on audio-visual trade reveals persistent significant imbalances. Our trade deficit with the United States for film, video and television for 2003/04 was $553 million.[3] Likewise, the impact of the AUS-US FTA on the cost of the PBS scheme, as applied to 2003 figures, is estimated to be an increase of $1.5 billion for prescription of the same drugs for the same level of use, with no added health benefit to Australian consumers.[4]

Intellectual property is not just about "incentives" and simple calculations of trade balances. Increasingly there has been international focus on treaties that deal with justice, equity and development issues. For example Art 8 (j) of the Convention of Biological Diversity establishes that:

> "each contracting party will ... subject to its national legislation, respect preserve and maintain knowledge, innovations and practices of indigenous and local communities embodying traditional lifestyles relevant for the conservation and sustainable use of biological diversity and promote their wider application with the approval and involvement of the holders of such knowledge, innovations and practices and encourage the equitable sharing of benefits arising from the utilisation of such knowledge, benefits and practices".

This can be the foundation for a capacity to impact on patents that seek to capitalise on traditional knowledge without engagement with traditional owners. In 2004, developing countries led by Brazil and Argentina launched an initiative to establish a Development Agenda in WIPO. The proposal notes,

> "[t]echnological innovation, science and creative activity in general are rightly recognised as important sources of material progress and welfare. However, despite the important scientific and technological advances and promises of the 20th and early 21st centuries, in many areas a significant 'knowledge gap' as well as a 'digital

2   A Mason, "Reading the Future" (1996) 9 AIPLB 138.
3   Australian Film Commission, "Total Value of Trade in Royalties Arising from Imports and Exports of Cinema Films, TV Content and Videos, 1987/88 to 2003/04", *Get the Picture*, available at www.afc.gov.au/gtp/atradetotal.html.
4   P Drahos, T Faunce, M Goddard and D Henry, *The FTA and the PBS: A Submission to the Senate Select Committee on the US-Australia Free Trade Agreement* (2004).

divide' continue to separate the wealthy nations from the poor ... Intellectual property protection cannot be seen as an end in itself, nor can the harmonisation of intellectual property laws leading to higher protection standards in all countries, irrespective of their levels of development".[5]

The proposal was accepted by the General Assembly which provides for new rounds of meetings seeking ways of addressing these issues and seeking to reconcile intellectual property protection with development agendas.

It is certainly an interesting time to be studying intellectual property laws, where the nature of the rights and concept of balance, and the complexity of interests that might feature in such discussions, continues to broaden.

SCOPE OF THIS BOOK

[1.35] This book contains a set of materials designed to teach undergraduate students the parameters of intellectual property within the constraints of a university semester. It focuses on Australian materials and will require close reference to relevant legislation, since this book does not contain lengthy extracts of statutory material; nor does it deal fully with remedies for breach of intellectual property rights, on the assumption that a one semester course may be complemented by a proper study of remedies as a separate topic.

---

5   *Proposal by Argentina and Brazil for the Establishment of a Development Agenda for WIPO*, WIPO General
     Assembly Document WO/GA/31/11.

Part 2

Copyright

PART **2**

CHAPTER 2

HISTORICAL AND CONCEPTUAL ISSUES

WHAT IS COPYRIGHT?

[2.05] See *Copyright Act 1968* (Cth), ss 8, 31, 85-88.

"It is often claimed or assumed that intellectual property laws are necessary to encourage individual creativity and inventiveness and that society would be worse off without such law. … [In] the field of copyrights and patents at least, such claims rest on myth and paradox rather than proof, and should be viewed sceptically."[1]

Copyright is commonly classified as "intellectual" rather than "industrial" property. This characterisation suggests that copyright is more concerned with sponsoring and protecting

---

1   D Vaver, "Intellectual Property Today: Of Myths and Paradoxes" [1990] 69 *Canadian Bar Review* 98.

intellectual or creative endeavours, and less interested in ways of protecting investments in commodity production, than other areas of intellectual property law. However, copyright is both a form of intellectual and industrial property.

Explanations of the origins of copyright law most commonly strive to show how and why creativity has come off "second best" in the law, with economic interests receiving a much more dedicated treatment by legislature and the courts. Vaver's scepticism about the function of copyright law is shared by many others, as can be seen by this overview of influential writings on the history of copyright dating from the late 1960s to the present.

■ Copyright and the rise of the modern author

[2.10] In early writings about copyright's history, including those of Benjamin Kaplan,[2] Lyman Ray Patterson,[3] Victor Bonham-Carter[4] and John Feather,[5] the primary concern was to explain why the priority of the law was not that of protecting the author's private property rights in the text. Though modern copyright law developed at the same time as the rise of the professional author (from the 17th-19th centuries), and the birth of the modern romantic author, the law was relatively unsympathetic to either professional or philosophical changes to the writer's social status.

Romanticism was a particularly influential philosophical movement in the late 18th and early 19th centuries. In romantic philosophy, artistic vision is explained in terms of a "natural" opposition to the "mechanical" world. In themes, 18th and 19th century romantic writers often expressed dismay at the natural, social and artistic consequences of industrialisation, and a desire to produce "original" works:

> "An Original may be said to be of a vegetable nature; it rises spontaneously from the vital root of genius; it grows, it is not made; Imitations are often a sort of manufacture, wrought up by those mechanics, art and labour, out of pre-existent materials not their own ...
>
> ... Modern writers have a choice to make ... they may soar in the regions of liberty, or move in the soft fetters of easy imitation."[6]

As a matter of history, romanticism can be read as a movement in opposition to the mechanical, commodity-oriented production of the developing marketplace.

As romantic texts express the unique personality of the author, it is argued that the proper meaning of an expression should be sought with reference to its source—the meaning of the text is to be found with unique person that gave birth to it. In this sense romantic claims that the author "owns" the text refers to ownership in both a moral and an economic sense. It is the original author's effort that gives rise to the meaning of the work and the right to profit from it as they see fit.

Poets and writers of erudite texts were in previous centuries dependent on patronage. In the 18th and 19th centuries, where patronage was a less reliable source of income and support, writers were also sceptical about the quality of the works that the market might reward and the balance of returns that authors might receive. Though freedom from the relations of patronage had meant:

---

2   *An Unhurried View of Copyright* (Columbia University Press, New York, 1967).
3   *Copyright in Historical Perspective* (Vandebilt University Press, Nashville, 1968).
4   *Authors By Profession* (The Society of Authors, London, 1978).
5   *Publishing, Piracy and Politics: An Historical Study of Copyright in Britain* (Mansell, London, 1994).
6   E Young, *Conjectures on Original Composition* (1759), as cited in R Williams, *Culture and Society, 1780-1950* (Penguin Books, Middlesex, 1971), p 54.

"There was an advance, for the fortunate ones, in independence and social status—the writer became a fully fledged 'professional man' ... the change also meant the institution of the market as the type of a writer's actual relations with society. Under patronage, the writer had at least a direct relationship with an immediate circle of readers, from whom, whether prudentially or willingly, as mark or as matter of respect, he was accustomed to accept and at times to act on criticism. It is possible to argue that this system gave the writer a more relevant freedom to that which he succeeded.

... [A]gainst the independence and the raised social status which success on the market commanded had to be set similar liabilities to caprice and similar obligations to please, but now, not liabilities to individuals personally known, but to the workings of an institution which seemed largely impersonal."[7]

In France and Germany romantic concerns led to the view that authors' rights were a natural property right, and continental copyright came to be defined in law in terms of a moral right of personality. Continental copyright laws attempted to strengthen the economic position of authors and in turn sponsor new "original", creative works that were expressive of the author's personality.

In the United Kingdom, however, though romantic property claims were socially influential, they had a lesser impact on the development of the law. The poor social and legal status of authors is precisely what most of the early writers of British copyright history have sought to account. Throughout the 17th-19th centuries, professional authors, including Ben Jonson (1573-1637), Robert Southey (1774-1843), William Wordsworth (1770-1850) and Charles Dickens (1807-1892), were politically active, advocating for reform of their legal rights. Clearly, not all of these writers ascribed to romantic theories of rights, but all shared gripes about miserly publishers and others unfairly profiting from their works. That there was little consensus about the nature of the rights deserved by the writer over time only complicated the legal cause of authors. Ultimately, case law determined that Anglo copyright had no space for "moral rights" comparative with those that developed elsewhere.

Feather[8] evaluates this history with reference to local circumstances, personal and political relationships, parliamentary instrumentalism and, in this environment, the inability to achieve political consensus. We should not expect copyright to reflect any *one* party's hopes or desires given this context. These writers of history emphasise the impact of political organisation, lobbying and petitioning Parliament on the "development" of copyright law. Authors lacked the level of organisation and political skill to put their interests firmly on the political agenda.

In tracing this history of author-publisher legal relations, these early works present copyright as an unfinished project. Though it is not necessarily stated, the early histories of copyright read as if the law's destiny would be fulfilled were copyright to better serve the first poets, and it could also better reward the scribes.

This kind of scholarship came under scrutiny in the 1980s and 1990s following the publication of Michel Foucault's work "What is an Author?".[9] This article interrogates the philosophical presuppositions related to the "rise to the author", including the juridical and institutional system that placed the author and her/his text in a system of property relations. The work has had a major influence on the telling of copyright's history. Many conferences

---

7   Young, n 6, p 51.
8   Feather, n 5.
9   In J V Harari (ed), *Textual Strategies: Perspectives in Poststructuralist Criticism* (Cornell University Press, Ithica NY, 1979), p 141.

were held in the 1980s and early 1990s to explore the relevance of Foucault's work and literary theory more generally to copyright law.[10] This marked a new stage in reading the history of copyright, seeking to refocus the relationship between law and authorship.

Mark Rose's paper, "The Author as Proprietor"[11] was one of the first to deal with the history of British copyright following Foucault's lead.[12] This paper centres on a discussion of the late 18th century case *Donaldson v Beckett*.[13] In this decision the Court addressed the question of the origins of copyright law and specifically the argument that the author was a proprietor—a claim justified by Locke's theory of labour and romantic theory. It was argued that:

> "Authors have ever had a property in their Works, founded upon the same fundamental maxims by which Property was originally settled, and hath since been maintained. The Invention of Printing did not destroy this Property of Authors, nor alter it in any Respect, but by rendering it more easy to be invaded.[14]

> Every man was entitled to the fruits of his labor, they argued, and therefore it was self-evident that authors had an absolute property in their own works. This property was transferred to the bookseller when the copyright was purchased and thereafter it continued perpetually just like any other property right."[15]

The majority of the Court failed to find any authoritative legal precedent that endorsed this purported theory of right and declared that, there being no common law literary property right, the power to define (and limit) copyright rested exclusively with Parliament. Statutory rights could not be beefed up in the interest of authors and publishers, by way of legal reference to rights that might be claimed as existing according to "natural law". Copyright was not concerned with the author's moral claims to own texts, and it was not a perpetual right.

Lord Camden rejected such a view because:

> "I find nothing in the whole that favours of Law, except the term itself, Literary Property. They have borrowed one single word from the Common Law. ... Most certainly every Man who thinks, has a right to his thoughts, while they continue to be his; but here the question again returns; when does he part with them? When do they become public juris? While they are in his brain no one indeed can purloin them; but what if he speaks, and lets them fly out in private or public discourse? Will he claim the breath, the air, the words in which his thoughts are cloathed? Where does this fanciful property begin, or end, or continue?"[16]

---

10 See, for example, the conference proceedings published in M Woodmansee and P Jaszi (eds), *The Construction of Authorship: Textual Appropriation in Law and Literature* (Duke University Press, Durham, London, 1994).
11 M Rose, "The Author as Proprietor: Donaldson v Becket and the Genealogy of Modern Authorship" (1988) 23 *Representations* 51. It was republished in B Sherman and A Strowel (eds), *Of Authors and Origins: Essays on Copyright Law* (Clarendon Press, Oxford, 1994), pp 23-55.
12 Woodmansee's article, "The Genius and the Copyright: Economic and Legal Conditions of the Emergence of the 'Author'" *Eighteenth Century Studies* 17 (1984) at 425 predated Rose's work; however, it is primarily about copyright and the development of a class of professional writers in 18th century Germany.
13 (1774) 4 Burr 2408; 98 Eng Rep 257.
14 *The Case of Authors and Proprietors of Books*, as quoted in Rose, n 11, at 57.
15 Rose, n 11.
16 Cited in S Parks (ed), *The Literary Property Debate: Seven Tracts, 1747-1773* (Garland Publishing, New York, 1974) at F32.

He rejected the claim that the common law had ever recognised such a right. It was noted that there was no record of it preceding the arrival of the Caxton printing press in England in 1476, thus it was not a legal right conferred by time immemorial. He then proceeded to discuss if it *should* recognise such a right, concluding that:

"Knowledge has no value or use for the solitary owner; to be enjoyed it must be communicated.

... Glory is the reward of science, and those who deserve it, scorn all meaner views ... It was not for gain, that Bacon, Newton, Milton, Locke instructed and delighted the world.

... Some authors are as careless for profit as others are rapacious of it; and what a situation would the public be in with regard to literature if there were no means of compelling a second impression of a useful work. ... All our learning will be locked up in the hands of the Tonsons and Lintons of the age, who will set what price upon it their avarice chuses to demand, till the public becomes as much their slaves, as their own hackney compilers are."[17]

In failing to endorse any specific philosophical theory of copyright, *Donaldson v Beckett* decided that copyright is a creature of positive law. Contemporary statutory recognition of this resonates in the *Copyright Act 1968* (Cth), s 8 which states: "[c]opyright does not exist otherwise than by virtue of this Act ...". The legislation that is consequently cited as the origin of our copyright law is the *Statute of Anne 1709*.[18]

As would be clear from its full title and from its date, the *Statute of Anne* was not concerned with romantic rights. It reflected the quite different philosophical concerns of the Enlightenment. The social purpose of the law was to promote broader public access to books by creating limited economic rights in literary texts. In reality it recognised, not the author's rights to own the text, but the longstanding economic interests of some publishers, as most ably represented by the guild organisation, the Stationers' Company of London. That the primary legal interest was protecting the economic interests of certain printers can be seen from a 1709 petition in support of the legislation:

"The poor distressed printers and bookbinders in London and Westminster; setting forth, that having served seven years apprenticeship, hoped to have gotten a comfortable livelihood by their trades, who are in number at least 5000; but by the liberty taken of some few persons printing books, to which they have no right to the copies, is such a discouragement to the bookselling trade, that no person can proceed to print any book without considerable loss, and consequently the petitioners cannot be employed; by which means the petitioners are reduced to very great poverty and want: And praying that their deplorable case may be effectively redressed."[19]

In effect, the Statute recognised the exclusive rights to print texts for a set term of years, arising through the action of registering a "copy" of the text. Historically speaking, the Copy Register that marked the "copy right" had been maintained by the Stationers' Company of London.

The legislation internally regulated the book trade and prevented cheaper versions of texts flooding the London market from printers in Northern England and Scotland. Though the

---

17 Cited in Parks, n 16, at fn 34.
18 "An Act for the Encouragement of Learning, by vesting the Copies of Printed Books in the Authors or Purchasers of such Copies, during the Times therein mentioned": 8 Anne c 19, 1710.
19 Reported in "Information for John Robertson, Defender against J Mackenzie ...", in *The Literary Property Debate*, n 16, at D35.

title of the Act implied that the first copy of the text was originally obtained from authors, the legislation said nothing explicitly about author-publisher legal relations. Though they could have, the majority in *Donaldson v Beckett* failed to fully explore the nature of these relations and especially the origin of the author's right in owning the text, purchased by the publisher. Presumably the author transferred to the publisher more than the rights to the manuscript as a chattel. They also sold a form of intangible property right, the exclusive right to reproduce those thoughts as expressed in the text. However, this was never clearly defined in early statute or case law. *Donaldson v Beckett* left copyright, as it was defined by its statutory origins, as a matter of limited "economic rights", and more concerned with publishers' than authors' interests.

Rose, following Foucault, is interested in *Donaldson v Beckett* because the decision demonstrates "the historicity of the seemingly 'solid and fundamental unit of the author and the work'".[20] That is, the case shows that there is no necessary connection between authors and texts. Such a relationship was only constructed in the 18th and 19th centuries. Rose argues that the view of "the author as proprietor" has been so widely circulated since then, that it is often assumed to be a universal, timeless truth. Uncritical histories such as Bonham-Carter's *Authors by Profession*,[21] in seeking to link copyright with the author's exclusive claims to rights, continue to advertise the "author myth". Rose's work tries to redress this ahistoricism.

In doing this Rose made a valuable contribution to the copyright story. However, what is troubling about his work is that it raises fundamental questions about the nature of the legal order, but fails to take them very far. If property arguments were so dominant in the late 18th century, why was the majority of the court in *Donaldson v Beckett* so unmoved by them? Rose suggests that the problem was that whilst Lockean ideas were current, romantic conceptions of authorship were still relatively new to Britain. Failing to appreciate what was, to the romantics, an essential difference between works of "art" and works of "industry", the courts could not see why literary works should be treated differently to mechanical works. Mechanical works were protected by patents. So the courts treated copyright as a kind of patent for literary works—hence it remained a statutorily limited property interest.

The problem with this is not what it says, but rather with the way the explanation leaves off at this point. By leaving off here, Rose implies that there was no acceptance of copyright as a natural right because the *Donaldson v Beckett* court was basically a conservative one, imprisoned in their time and space, and so unable to appreciate the significance of the artistic movement coming their way. In reading *The Author as Proprietor*, one is left with the feeling that if the test case for a common law right had come just a little bit later, when the romantic movement was stronger, there may have been a different result. "What if?" points are difficult to argue with. However, Rose's failure to link up here with an earlier point he had made about the 18th century ideal of an autonomous legal order causes some concern. In the 16th-18th centuries it was often argued that the importance of legal precedent was that it allowed law to rise above the rabble and their ever-changing fashions in ideas, and give law the authority that comes with "objectivity". Given this jurisprudence, there is no reason to presume a different result would follow a decade or so later, even though a romanticised civil society may have wanted it. To be caught by the past was no mere historical accident, it was an established strand of the politics of the common law courts.[22] On this reading of *Donaldson v Beckett*, the case was not just about the author's right to copyright, it was also about the

---

20   Rose, n 11, at 78.
21   Bonham-Carter, n 4.
22   18th century tensions over this tradition are discussed by Michael Lobban in "Blackstone and the Science of Law" (1987) 30 *The Historical Journal* 311.

authority of law and its relationship to society. Rose's account, however, is so preoccupied with the former issue that it fails to do justice to the latter.

Rose expanded upon this article in his book *Authors and Owners*.[23] Here Rose ties his critique of romantic notions of authorship to a critique of Lockean possessive individualism. He argues that this period was marked more by relations of *propriety* than *property*. Whilst authors were paid for their work, payment symbolised honour, virtue and reward for the writer, not recognition of ownership of the text.

This propriety/property distinction can create some confusion for the reader familiar with the history of property theory. Rose treats "property" as if it is fixed to a particular idiom of transhistorical relevance, derived from CB Macpherson's influential interpretation of possessive individualism.[24] It leaves 16th to mid-18th century literary property in a no man's land of "pre-property". This is unsatisfactory in a book that purports to map the links between economic and political theory and the realm of cultural production.

Further, whilst Rose is generally careful in his treatment of Locke, he tends to merge Locke's views on literary property with Blackstone's inventive reinterpretation of them in the literary property cases of the 18th century. This marginalises the significance of the Enlightenment philosopher's empiricist views. Whilst Locke's ideas contributed to the social construction of the author, he was uncertain about how far the private property right that belonged to the author of a work should extend. The exercise of extensive private ownership rights could conflict with the pursuit of truth. This created a philosophical impasse for Locke; however, Rose treats it more as an oversight. It is precisely the coincidence of the need for both public and private rights in a text that makes copyright a peculiar and indeterminate subject of private property, as troubled the court in *Donaldson v Beckett*. Much of the objection to acknowledging in law the social importance of "good works", by defining copyright as the natural right deserved by the creator of expressive works, related to concerns over the educational implications of this for society. The law that respected the natural property right of the author was also a law creating a "tax upon knowledge". There were competing social goals at stake in the literary property debates. This complexity should not be confused with the law's lack of development. Because of historical, philosophical and jurisprudential reasons, there could only be a very loose and uncertain connection between the romantic notion of authorship and possessive individualism.

Saunders' *Authorship and Copyright*[25] is, in a sense, a scholarly response to the work of Rose. His main purpose is to distinguish the author as a legal subject from the author as a cultural construct. Saunders wants to show that Anglo-American copyright, unlike the French, is not *organised* by the aesthetic figure of the "whole" human being, and hence to save it from postmodern criticisms like Rose's, "preoccupied" with the text and the subject. The French model was based upon a natural right of personality, whilst the Anglo model developed out of trade regulation of booksellers and publishers. He cites the works of Patterson and Feather as authority. He suggests that because of this, though Anglo-American law can in places reflect aesthetic concerns, such occurrences are simply "fortuitous" historical accidents.[26] So far as copyright is a body of law, aesthetics does not touch its heart. In fact, as a body that emerged from a myriad of pragmatic considerations, Saunders questions whether it follows any particular direction at all.

---

23 The full title is *Authors and Owners: The Invention of Copyright* (Harvard University Press, Cambridge, Massachusetts, London, 1993).
24 *The Political Theory of Possessive Individualism: Hobbes to Locke* (Clarendon Press, Oxford, 1962).
25 Published by Routledge, London, 1992.
26 Saunders, n 25, p 237.

Although in the Anglo-American legal world the received wisdom is that copyright is an economic right rather than a right of personality, if you move beyond concerns for legal form (the origins of the law), Lockean and romantic conceptions of property are clearly evident and intermingling in the substance of copyright cases. However, Saunders fails to appreciate this because he only considers British case law in any depth up to the decision in *Donaldson v Beckett*. His main preoccupation is with the early *legislative* period. Saunders' discussion of "authorship" is quite broad, but his analysis of law is quite narrow.

In reading copyright case law it is important to consider whether theories like romanticism have influenced judicial understandings. Though copyright is in the sense outlined above, a creature of positive law, despite *Copyright Act 1968* (Cth), s 8 not all important copyright principles are expressed in the text of the legislation. Further, in many places the legislation relies on the "ordinary" or "common sense" meaning of terms. There is ample space for romantic and other values coming into the body of copyright law. Therefore, understanding copyright law requires an interpretation of case law in view of many possible social and cultural influences and prejudices, including that of romanticism.

In her more recent work, *Literary Copyright Reform In Early Victorian England*,[27] Catherine Saville, like Saunders, focuses almost exclusively on copyright as defined in legislation. Her work picks up where Rose had left off. Though the modern author may not have been accorded great respect in the literary property debates of late 18th century, surely by the 1840s his prospects for a more favourable legal right must have improved? What happened to author's rights with the passage of the *Copyright Act 1842*? Saville considers why efforts to reform copyright law in the interest of professional authors, supported by literary elders like William Wordsworth and sponsored in Parliament by Serjeant Talfourd, were compromised. Saville's reading is influenced by Feather's approach; however, given her subject is the legislation, she focuses much more on parliamentary politics than the politics of the printing trade—degrees of influence in the House, party pragmatics as well as more philosophical perspectives that affected legislative decision making. This combination of factors led to important concessions such as an extension of the copyright term for authors, but, as with Saunders, not the adoption of any coherent rationale for copyright protection.

In theme, *all* these works are preoccupied with authors and their claims to own texts in law. They are engrossed in literary property legislation. Where case law figures, it is only considered in relation to how the courts interpreted the first copyright statute, the *Statute of Anne 1709*.

Ronan Deazley's, *On the Origin of the Right to Copy*,[28] is a welcome recent addition to the literature because it explains a lot more about the litigation strategies of the publishers in this early period. He argues that in the 18th century, legislative reforms in the form of stronger protections for author and publisher interests, were not forthcoming out of concern for a range of public interests. Copyright law was understood as a "social contract"—for the benefit of society as a whole. The reason for the outbreak of literary property cases in the mid-late 18th century occurred because publishers shifted their attention to the courts. However this was motivated not only for hope of a more favourable legal interpretation of author/publisher rights. It occurred also because of the remedies on offer through equity, which included a perpetual injunction and account of profits:

---

27 Published by Cambridge University Press, Cambridge, 1999.
28 The full title is *On the Origin of the Right to Copy: Charting the Movement of Copyright Law in Eighteenth Century Britain (1695-1775)* (Hart Publishing, Oxford, 2004).

"The possibility of securing such a decree in Equity, when added to the existing protections of the Statue of Anne, meant that, for the booksellers, it became something of a redundant exercise to lobby for a replacement for the Statute of Anne".[29]

His work points to a problem for the courts—in redressing claims of piracy inter-partes, is there space for a broader consideration of the public interest implications of the law?

Deazley's work is firmly tied to 18th century events, however the question of the public interest in copyright law—how it arises and can be taken into account in the existing legislative framework and by the courts, is very much of contemporary interest. Much new copyright scholarship is emerging around this theme today.

■ Copyright in theory

[2.15] In the "historical" approaches to copyright the story of literary property legislation is presumed as the model for all copyright law. However, quite diverse subject matter was protected in early 19th century legislation, similar to the literary property acts. These have been left relatively unexplored. It is presumed that the copyright story is primarily about the legal meaning of "literature". A second group of writings does not focus so narrowly on literature, and focuses in much more depth on the nature of law and legal rights.

Bernard Edelman's *Ownership of the Image*[30] draws on Marxist theory, specifically the work of Althusser. In relation to owning the image, here specifically the case for photography, Edelman traces its reclassification from a process involving manual labour and incapable of sustaining a copyright, to a creative endeavour deserving protection. When photography was a craft practised by small tradespersons and amateurs it was seen as a mechanical activity. There was no labour involved capable of attracting a copyright. However, with the cinema industry attracting investment, particularly after the development of the talkies, the court changed the way it interpreted photographic activity. They "corrected" the error of their previous classification and re-characterised photography as a creative endeavour. Edelman argues that the subject served by this was not the creative photographer because s/he automatically consented to the disposal of her/his rights in the image by way of a labour contract. It was "capital" that copyright created and rewarded. Copyright reduced the risk to investors of a "plagiarised" film competing with the "original". For Edelman, "creativity" is celebrated in copyright law not because of respect for art, but because it is a tool that can serve the interests of capital. Edelman's approach has influenced a number of works that works offer political readings of the development and practice of intellectual property law, including those by Celia Lury,[31] Ronald Bettig[32] and Jane Gaines.[33] These works tend to be ignored by mainstream copyright lawyers; Lury and Gaines usually dismissed as being of greater relevance to cultural studies, than law. Though they are all scholarly and complex works, perhaps lawyers are nervous about seriously addressing what the writers say about the economy of copyright practice.

On one level, Brad Sherman and Lionel Bently's, *The Making of Modern Intellectual Property*,[34] addresses similar political themes, but in terms of theory, it is written in the

---

29 Deazley, n 28, at 110.
30 The full title is *Ownership of the Image—Elements for a Marxist Theory of Law*, E Kingdom (transl) (Routledge and Kegan Paul, London, 1979).
31 *Cultural Rights: Technology, Legality and Personality* (Routledge, London, 1993).
32 *Copyrighting Culture: The Political Economy of Intellectual Property* (Westview Press, Colorado, 1996).
33 *Contested Culture: The Image, The Voice and The Law* (University of North Carolina Press, Chapel Hill, 1991).
34 Published by Cambridge University Press, Cambridge, 1999.

language of jurisprudence which is more familiar to lawyers. This work discusses the origins of copyright with reference to a distinction between pre-modern and modern intellectual property laws. Pre-modern laws are characterised as subject specific and geographically localised. Modern laws are abstract, forward looking and perceived as autonomous. The 18th century literary property debates are cast as a pre-modern struggle over the nature and legitimacy of intangible property rights. It is argued that the law was unable to effectively determine the metaphysical dimensions of intangible property—there was no universal philosophy to which the law could be confidently tied. Following the 18th century literary property debates, there was a jurisprudential shift away from a concern that the law reflect the "natural" property in mental labour, to a "consequential" analysis of the merits of granting a right. In the process it has been left up to the autonomy of law (largely expressed in statutes), rather than natural rights, to "create" the incorporeal property at stake in intellectual property laws.

With modern law making, protecting creative efforts of many forms is accepted as legitimate. The main interest of law reformers is not with cultural questions about the meaning or significance of works but with legal aesthetics—drawing simple, uniform and precise laws. Legal simplicity does not come from reliance on definition in terms of philosophical essences or principles, but from a high level of legal abstraction in definitions. It is argued that these abstractions serve to include but never clearly exclude various objects from protection. As a consequence of this, the property at the heart of intellectual property rights is now only partially defined in law. Further, it is mainly explained in terms of comparisons between different intellectual property rights. For example, copyright might still be cursorily distinguished from patents by reference to the essential creative activity at issue, patents cast as involving "discoveries" rather than creation. However, the unique expression at issue in patents would only be legally defined with reference to the technical requirements of the patent specification and the conditions of its registration, and thereby differentiated from a copyright expression that lacks these distinctions. The authors suggest that by the late 19th century any reference to creativity in intellectual property texts is superficial.

With the full modernisation of the law in the 20th century "the law moved its focus away from the labour used to create, for example, a book ... to focus instead on the book ... itself".[35] With echoes of Edelman's theoretical concerns, Sherman and Bently argue that rather than try to value the labour embodied in the book, modern law assesses value with reference to the (potential) macro-economic value of the book as a commodity, and in the main, tries not to value the work at all. The subject matter of intellectual property is decontextualised—seen as a "legal object", that is, represented as property in law by indicia such as legally significant drawings and writings, and as circumscribed by policy.

These more theoretical works draw out the implications of looking for creativity in copyright's history. They are most conscious of tracking what is left out when an inquiry is too single-minded in pursuit of the creative subject in the law. Ultimately they also lead to a questioning of the point of dwelling too much on reading copyright law with reference to its historically contingent origins. The law is too fluid, legislators too creative and economic interests too powerful to be caught by culture and the past.

Accordingly, and particularly in relation to copyright, this work suggests a concern for too much priority being given to the older rights now found in the *Copyright Act 1968* (Cth) as "Part III Subject Matter", simply because these rights are longer established than the others listed as "Part IV Subject Matter Other Than Works". In industry and legal terms, there is little

---

35 Sherman and Bently, n 34, p 174.

reason to presume that any one category of rights is the model for any other, or that any one category of interests is more important than any other. It is possible that, as a body of law, there is little philosophically in common amongst the various copyright interests beyond their aggregation in the one, unwieldy body of legislation. This needs to be kept in mind in studying the categories of copyright law.

■ Postmodern histories

[2.20] A third grouping of writings use a postmodern sensibility to inform their analysis of contemporary cultural and legal practice. Rosemary Coombe's, *The Cultural Life of Intellectual Property*,[36] explores the creativity inherent in cultural practices that confront intellectual property rights. Appropriative practices are considered as creative practices, often motivated by political objections to corporate power. The works are histories of the present, based on conclusions about copyright's past. The writers reflect on how particular social and economic relations and practices have been historically favoured by the law, and discuss how others have been constrained.

Coombe's work adopts Foucault's insights into authorship and authority in her reading of contemporary cultural practices. She makes explicit the cultural specificity of the subject privileged by the law, by examining postmodern and transgressive appropriation of corporate intellectual property and its legal consequences.

Coombe argues that we live in a postmodern society and our collective experience and memory is recorded with reference to mass media signs and symbols. To express ourselves we draw upon this experience. We treat it as our common heritage, and we use it individually, to affirm our identities. We are not necessarily passive consumers of meanings produced by the author and marketed by cultural and corporate elites. In viewing cultural texts we can generate new, personally meaningful identities that resist manufactured culture.

From an intellectual property point of view, the reference points or cultural symbols we draw upon are privately owned, and therefore access can be prohibited. She gives numerous examples of how corporate actors have used the intellectual property regime to ensure that only corporately appropriate (sanitised) messages circulate. She argues that this enables certain forms of political practice and constrains others. It permits the proliferation of "benign" identities, and silences others. For Coombe, copyright law is a great site for exploration of contemporary art and cultural practice, read in terms of production of and resistance to cultural power.

Coombe is an acute observer of "fringe" cultural practice in contest with the "mainstream". However, she treats creativity as a defining characteristic of those resisting the law. Mainstream copyright practice is not interested in sponsoring creative activity. It is preoccupied with commercial considerations.

■ Australian social histories

[2.25] The recent work by Matthew Rimmer[37] takes the form of microhistories of particular cultural disputes like Coombe, but he does not presume creativity to be the exclusive tool of any particular cause. Rimmer's work, drawing upon a different postmodern sensibility, looks

---

36 *The Cultural Life of Intellectual Properties. Authorship, Appropriation and the Law* (Duke University Press, Durham, London, 1998).
37 See, for example, "Shine: Copyright Law and Film" (2001) 12 AIPJ 129; "Heretic: Copyright Law and Dramatic Works", *Queensland University of Technology Law And Justice Journal*, Vol 2, No 1, pp 131-149; "Daubism: Copyright Law and Artistic Works", *Murdoch University Electronic Journal of Law*, Vol 9, No 4; K Bowrey, and M Rimmer, "Rip, Mix, Burn: The Politics of Peer to Peer" (2002) 7(8) *First Monday*.

at all cultural production as collaborative activity. As the product of collaborative activity, any mass-reproduced work at the heart of copyright is also a site of competing claims for artistic attribution and copyright ownership. He then accounts for how proponents advocate, contest, resist, litigate and lobby—manipulating cultural discourse, most especially surrounding relative claims to "creativity", in order to achieve desired legal outcomes. When viewed from this battleground, the law's mediations of creativity are complex and fluid. There is no creative subject universally favoured in law; nevertheless, there are numerous reasons that account for the success or failure of particular claims, such as historical privilege, money, professional organisation and support, access to and use of the media, effective legal counsel, political favour and personality.

Writer and legal academic Stephen Gray also explores creativity and contestations over authorship in the context of indigenous cultural property. His Vogel Literary Award winning novel, *The Artist is a Thief*,[38] is a detective novel about alleged Aboriginal art fraud. His tale explores western expectations about authorship and art market pressures on contemporary indigenous communities and their celebrated artists. His academic work considers the impact of new developments to protect indigenous culture such as protocols on western expectations of creative freedom, as well as more practical issues for film makers trying to use these emerging forms of regulation that sit alongside rights granted under the *Copyright Act 1968* (Cth).[39]

Because postmodern and social histories are deeply involved in the richness of contemporary cultural practice, these works are potentially of interest to a broader audience than many of the more theoretical or conventional historical legal works. To the student of copyright law, these new works act as a reminder of the need to consider how law is received in the community; to think about potential gaps between law in the books and in social practice; to consider how the copyright story is popularly expressed in the media and other places; and ultimately to consider how law and law makers should respond to the social challenges the law must face.

■ Knowledge economy critiques

[2.30] Similar questioning of the social and economic impact of copyright laws arises in debates about the wisdom and politics associated with the strengthening of intellectual property rights globally. While this is an international concern raised in law making bodies such as WIPO, overwhelmingly it is American academic work, most notably by Lawrence Lessig,[40] that has publicised these concerns. Australian perspectives on these developments are found in *Who Owns the Knowledge Economy?* by Peter Drahos and John Braithwaite.[41]

These are books that reach out far beyond traditional legal audiences, seeking to educate the broader public about the power of multinational media, entertainment and technology corporations and their industry consortium such as the Recording Industry Association of America, the Motion Picture Association of America and the Business Software Alliance. It is argued that TRIPS, new digital agenda copyright laws, copyright term extensions and free

---

38   Published by Allen and Unwin, Sydney, 2001.
39   S Gray, "Imagination, Fraud and the Cultural Protocols Debate: A Question of Free Speech or Pornography?" (2004) 9(1) *Media and Arts Law Review* 23.
40   *Free Culture: How Big Media Uses Technology and the Law to Lock Down Creativity* (Penguin Press, 2004); *The Future of Ideas: The Fate of the Commons in a Connected World* (Random House, 2001); *Code, and Other Laws of Cyberspace* (Basic Books, 1999).
41   Published by Earthscan, UK, 2002. Also K Bowrey, "Can we Afford to Think about Copyright in a Global Marketplace?" in F Macmillan (ed), *New Directions in Copyright Law, Volume 1* (Edward Elgar, Cheltenham, UK, 2005), pp 51-69.

trade agreements have advanced particular economic interests and upset the traditional public balances of intellectual property laws. A healthy public domain, where information circulates for free, is considered essential to a healthy democracy, innovation and education system.

Lessig argues that copyright struggles with creativity more than ever, with strong protections imperilling creative activity and detrimentally restricting consumer rights and access to works. New "public" licenses such as creative commons, open source, free software, and free for education licenses, are promoted to counter perceived erosions of the public domain. In 2003 one million web pages were published under creative commons licenses. In 2005 there were five million pages.[42]

Exploring the relationship between public and private rights in Australian copyright law and practice is an emerging area of interest in copyright law today.

■ Some important copyright concepts

[2.35] In light of this overview of historical and critical writings about copyright, it is important to think more about some important copyright concepts:

- the distinction between copyright as an "economic right" and copyright as a "moral right";

- the nature of copyright as an "incorporeal right";

- there is no "property in ideas" or a "property right in information";

- the precise meaning of moral rights, as recently introduced by the Australian Parliament; and

- the legal meaning of "author".

No rights at all arise until the ideas are expressed in a tangible medium, and this, combined with the concept of copyright as property which can be divided and transferred from one individual or group to another by a commercial transaction, makes the *Copyright Act 1968* (Cth) inept to protect certain material, even if of prime cultural significance. An important example is Aboriginal folklore. In 1981, a report of the Working Party on the Protection of Aboriginal Folklore was produced by the Federal Government, in co-operation with the Australia Council and the Australian Copyright Council. The report highlighted a number of reasons why the *Copyright Act 1968* (Cth) fails to protect Aboriginal folklore, one being the conception of property rights arising in material which, although sacred and traditional, is not amenable to being traded in the market place. The working party recommended an Aboriginal Folklore Act aimed at the preservation of the cultural heritage, with appropriate economic rights but without the usual requirements for the subsistence of copyright necessarily being present. In 2001 the Federal Government set up an Inquiry into contemporary visual arts and craft. The Myer Report included wide-ranging recommendations concerned with strengthening visual arts and craft in Australia, including several concerning taxation, superannuation, copyright protection, resale royalties and other proposals for administrative and legislative change.

---

42 See http://creativecommons.org.

NATURE OF THE PROPERTY RIGHT

▬ Pacific Film Laboratories v Commissioner of Taxation ▬

[2.40] *Pacific Film Laboratories Pty Ltd v Commissioner of Taxation* (1970) 121 CLR 154 High Court of Australia

[The plaintiff, a photograph processing company, objected to paying sales tax on prints processed by it and paid for by customers, arguing that there was no sale of goods as the customers owned the negatives and the plaintiff had no general property in them. The Court distinguished between the copyright in the negatives (owned by the customer) and property in the prints (owned by the plaintiff).]

BARWICK CJ: **[162]** ... But it is objected that there could not in any case be a sale of a print or duplicate either to the photographer or to any other person because of the provisions of the *Copyright Act 1912*. It has been assumed in argument that the person ordering the print was the owner of the copyright in the negative or transparency. This may or may not be so, but I am prepared to assume it as fact. Because the negative or transparency was the subject of copyright it is said that the appellant as the producer of the print or duplicate as a reproduction of the negative or transparency could not have any general property in the print which he could transfer by sale to any person including the owner of the copyright. It is submitted that it would have no more than a lien for the amount agreed to be paid for the production of the print **[163]** or duplicate. The fact that he owned the sensitised paper or the film on which the print or duplicate was made to appear and such of the chemicals as remained on the paper or film at the end of the process of making the print or duplicate did not give him any general property in the print or duplicate as reproductions of the copyright work, the negative or transparency as the case may be.

... [C]opyright shall be deemed to be infringed by any person who without the consent of the owner of the copyright does anything, the sole right to do which is by the Act conferred on the owner of the copyright. By s 7, all infringing copies of any work in which copyright exists shall be deemed to be the property of the owner of the copyright who accordingly may take proceedings for the recovery of possession thereof or in respect of the conversion thereof. But s 8 provides that where proceedings are taken in respect of the infringement of the copyright in any work and the defendant establishes that he was not aware nor had reasonable ground for suspecting that copyright existed in the work the plaintiff shall not be entitled to any remedy other than an injunction.

There are, in my opinion, several clear answers to this submission. In the first place, there is authority for the proposition that the property in a chattel may be in one person and the copyright in another: *Re Dickens; Dickens v Hawksley* [1935] Ch 267. In the second place, an authority to reproduce a copyright work given by the owner of the copyright allows the authorised person to produce the copy as his own property and indeed unless the authority to reproduce it provides otherwise, he is free to dispose of the reproduction. In the third place, whilst of course the *Copyright Act* enables the copyright owner to recover possession of infringing copies of the copyright work or damages **[164]** for the conversion of such infringing copies there were in this case no infringing copies, the owner of the copyright on the supposition made, authorised the making of the copy and its delivery to himself. It seems to me that even if the agreement between the owner of the copyright and the appellant had been no more than an agreement for the rendering of services the print produced by the

█████ Pacific Film Laboratories v Commissioner of Taxation *continued*

appellant could not have been claimed by the owner of the copyright as his own nor could he have recovered it in detinue before it had been delivered to him but if as I think the agreement was an agreement for the sale of the print or duplicate by the appellant to the owner of the copyright it seems to me necessarily to follow that not only was there no property in the owner of the copyright in the print viewed as a chattel at any time before the delivery of the print to the owner of the copyright but that it was intended that property in the print or duplicate should pass on delivery of the print or duplicate.

In my opinion, the appellant had general property in the print or duplicate when produced with the authority of the copyright owner: it was not an infringing copy of the negative or transparency as the case may be though possibly it might have become so if sold to some person other than the owner of the copyright: this was so because of the limited nature of the authority to reproduce given by the owner of the copyright. But the rights given by s 7 to recover infringing copies, though subject to s 8, only arise when the copy is the infringing copy: that is to say, it is the sale which attracts the operation of the section in the case supposed. But that conclusion denies that the authorised reproducer had no general property in the print or duplicate. As I have said, the appellant, in my opinion, had the general property in the print or duplicate which it manufactured out of its own materials and none the less so because the copyright in the negative or transparency was in some other person, or as has been supposed in the member of the public ordering the print or duplicate.

WINDEYER J: ... [165] Of course a man cannot buy something that is already his. And the Sale of Goods Acts in force in Australia, all copied from the *Sale of Goods Act 1893* (UK), it being itself a codification of the common law, treat a sale as a transaction effecting a transfer of "the general property in the goods". It was argued that, because the owner of a photographic negative has copyright in it as an artistic work, someone else who makes prints from it for him cannot have the general property in them as goods that he can sell to him. There is I think here a fallacy. [166] It lies in the failure to distinguish between the copyright as incorporeal property and property in the material thing which is the subject of the copyright. ... [168] ...

Academic purists in the use of jurisprudential language now say it is a mistake to speak of an incorporeal right. A right, they say, is essentially incorporeal: property is either corporeal or incorporeal. That may be so. Nevertheless the expression, an incorporeal right, can be defended as simply a transferred epithet which is a not uncommon figure of speech. But defence is not necessary for it would be a pedantic presumption to discard an expression that has long been used in connection with copyright by great lawyers, including Lord Mansfield in the 18th century and Lord Maugham in this.

... [169] Copyright under the Act is thus properly called an incorporeal right. ... It cannot be said that the owner of a copyright cannot buy a chattel made by his licence. It is not an infringing copy. It is a lawful copy. In this case the contract was for the sale to the owner of the copyright of future goods, namely copies of prints that he by implication licensed to be made for that very purpose. They could only be lawfully sold to him or by his authority because his licence to the copyist to make them [170] was only so that they might be sold to him. His incorporeal right to prevent infringement of his copyright could not prevent his right to have chattels he had agreed to buy delivered to him or absolve him from an obligation to pay for them on delivery as goods sold and delivered. I agree in the order that the Chief Justice proposes.

■ Property rights in information?

═══════════════════ Breen v Williams ═══════════════════

[2.45] *Julie Breen v Cholmondeley W Williams* (1996) 186 CLR 71 High Court of Australia

BRENNAN CJ

[77] ... The appellant, who has been a patient of the respondent medical practitioner, claims a legal right to reasonable access to the records kept by the respondent with respect to the appellant and a right to inspect and/or copy those records. Subject to certain admitted exceptions, the appellant submits that that right is enforceable by declaration and injunction. The right is submitted to be based variously on contract, property and fiduciary duty. ... **[78]**

Property

[80] ... The appellant concedes that the property in the records as chattels is in the respondent. The concession is rightly made. Documents prepared by a professional person to assist the professional to perform his or her professional duties are not the property of the lay client; they remain the property of the professional (*Leicestershire County Council v Michael Faraday & Partners Ltd* [1941] 2 KB 205 at 216; *Chantrey Martin v Martin* [1953] 2 QB 286). In the light of that principle, it is not easy to see what relevance the law of property has to the supposed right of the appellant to access to the respondent's records. If (as it was put during argument) the respondent is said to have no proprietary right that would entitle him to refuse access, the question whether the appellant has a right to be given access still remains. On that approach, the supposed right (if any) must find some basis other than property. But even on that approach, the argument is flawed. Absent some right to require, or the exercise of some power to compel, production of a document for inspection, its owner is entitled by virtue of the rights of ownership to refuse to produce it. As for copying, where the professional person is the owner of the copyright, **[81]** he or she has the sole right to copy or to permit the copying of the document (*Copyright Act 1968* (Cth), ss 13, 31, 36; *Commonwealth of Australia v John Fairfax & Sons Ltd* (1980) 147 CLR 39 at 58).

If the approach is that a right to access and to copy arises because the information contained in the records is proprietary in nature, the approach mistakes the sense in which information is described as property. The sense in which information is so described is stated by Lord Upjohn in *Phipps v Boardman* ([1967] 2 AC 46 at 127-128) in these terms:

> "In general, information is not property at all. It is normally open to all who have eyes to read and ears to hear. The true test is to determine in what circumstances the information has been acquired. If it has been acquired in such circumstances that it would be a breach of confidence to disclose it to another then courts of equity will restrain the recipient from communicating it to another. In such cases such confidential information is often and for many years has been described as the property of the donor, the books of authority are full of such references; knowledge of secret processes, 'know-how', confidential information as to the prospects of a company or of someone's intention or the expected results of some horse race based on stable or other confidential information. But in the end the real truth is that it is not property in any normal sense but equity will restrain its transmission to another if in breach of some confidential relationship."

As information is not property except in the sense stated by Lord Upjohn, the remedies which equity grants to protect against the disclosure of certain kinds of information do not have their source in notions of property. Deane J pointed this out in *Moorgate Tobacco Co Ltd v Philip*

■■■■■ Breen v Williams *continued*

Morris Ltd (No 2) ((1984) 156 CLR 414 at 438; see also *Smith Kline & French v Secretary, Department of Community Services & Health* (1990) 95 ALR 87 at 135-136 per Gummow J):

"Like most heads of exclusive equitable jurisdiction, its rational basis does not lie in proprietary right. It lies in the notion of an obligation of conscience arising from the circumstances in or through which the information was communicated or obtained."

Equity might restrain the respondent from disclosing without authority any information about the appellant and her medical condition that is contained in the respondent's records and, in that sense, it might be arguable that that information is the property of the appellant. Even if such a description were correct—and it is not necessary to consider that question—the description would provide no foundation for the existence of a right to access and to copy enforceable in equity. The mere possession by the respondent of his **[82]** records relating to the appellant breaches no obligation of conscience and thus it attracts no equitable remedy that might clothe the information with some relevant proprietary character. There is no obligation in conscience requiring the respondent to open his records to inspection and copying by the appellant. Whichever approach is taken to the relevance of the law of property, it fails to provide any basis for the appellant's claim.

...

The appeal should be dismissed.

GUMMOW J **[126]** ...

Property rights

The appellant also sought to draw support for the right she asserts from a complex of equitable institutions and doctrines dealing with fiduciary duty, confidential information, undue influence, and with unconscientious transactions of the nature considered in such authorities as *Louth v Diprose* ((1992) 175 CLR 621).

To some extent these submissions reflect an imperfect understanding of some basic matters of the law of personal property. Other submissions concern classification as "property" of the information contained in the records in question. As the submissions for the appellant appear to reflect some confusion of thought, it is appropriate, before proceeding further, to draw several basic distinctions.

First, as I understand the submissions, the appellant did not contend before us, and she had not contended before the Court of Appeal ((1994) 35 NSWLR 522 at 561), that she owned the relevant records "as such". That concession (as the Court of Appeal agreed (1994) 35 NSWLR 522 at 538, 559-561) was correctly made. The documents in question, including any photographs, are chattels, ownership and the right to exclusive possession of which appear to be enjoyed by the respondent. Access to those records would be an incident of those rights. They would be protected against invasion by the law of tort, in particular by actions for detinue and conversion. **[127]** Thus, in *Moorhouse v Angus & Robertson (No 1) Pty Ltd* ((1980) FSR 231 at 239-240), McLelland J held that a cause of action in detinue had been established by an author against his publishers by reason of their failure to comply with his demand for the return of his original manuscript.

...

Secondly, the appellant's submissions gave insufficient allowance to the operation in this field of copyright law, a matter of federal statute. The composition by the medical practitioner of the material shown on the records may have involved the authorship by him of what, whilst not of literary quality, were nevertheless literary works for the purposes of copyright

■■■■ Breen v Williams *continued*

law. This would vest in him various exclusive proprietary rights, including that to reproduce the work in a material form (*Copyright Act 1968* (Cth), s 31(1)(a)(i)). In *Pacific Film Laboratories Pty Ltd v Federal Commissioner of Taxation* ((1970) 121 CLR 154 at 165-170), Windeyer J referred to the fundamental distinction between copyright as incorporeal property and property in the material thing which is the subject of the copyright, the essence of the former being the power to prevent the making of a reproduction in material form. His Honour referred to authorities, including *Re Dickens* ((1935) Ch 267). This illustrates the distinction. On the proper construction of his will, Charles Dickens bequeathed the manuscript of an unpublished work to his sister-in-law and his residuary estate, including the copyright in the unpublished work, to his children. Ownership of the manuscript would not, of itself, carry with it the right to publish it and to reproduce it.

It is unlikely that the medical practitioner would have made the literary works in pursuance of the terms of his employment by the patient under what was classified as a contract of service, so that the patient was the owner of the copyright (s 35(6)). Ownership of the copyright in any photographs, as artistic works (see the definition of "artistic work" in s 10(1) of the *Copyright Act 1968* (Cth)) would, pursuant to s 35(5) of the *Copyright Act 1968* (Cth), vest in the patient only if within the meaning of that provision the patient had made for valuable [128] consideration an agreement for the taking of the photographs and they were taken in pursuance of that agreement.

The copyright of the respondent would not be infringed by anything done for the purposes of a judicial proceeding (s 43(1)). Nor would it be an infringement to act pursuant to a licence or permission (which might be express or implied) (*Avel Pty Ltd v Multicoin Amusements Pty Ltd* (1990) 171 CLR 88 at 103-106, 119-120; *Lorenzo & Sons v Roland Corporation* (1992) 23 IPR 376 at 380-383; *Devefi Pty Ltd v Mateffy Perl Nagy Pty Ltd* (1993) 113 ALR 225 at 237-242).

However, the circumstances of the present case, as disclosed in the evidence, do not provide support for the existence of any copyright licence or consent given to the appellant either expressly or by implication. Nor does it appear that such a licence is implied in the contract between medical practitioner and patient as a matter of law in the sense I have described earlier in these reasons.

...

The appeal should be dismissed with costs.

MORAL RIGHTS AND NEIGHBOURING RIGHTS

[2.50] It is only relatively recently in Australian law that there has been any consideration of copyright as encompassing personal, non-economic rights, known as moral rights. To a large extent, this reflection has been prompted by the requirements of international treaties to which Australia wishes to belong, beginning with (and in spite of) the fact that Australia is a signatory to the Berne Convention, which in Art 6*bis* sets up an obligation for members to protect the rights of "paternity" and "integrity". The enforcement of these rights and the mode of exercise is determined by the legislation of each member country. In December 2000 moral rights were finally introduced to Australian law after much debate. There are two separate moral rights, distinct from the economic rights in works or films. They are: the right of attribution of authorship—to be named in connection with one's work; and the right of integrity of authorship which is intended to allow authors to object to treatment of a work that demeans their reputation.

The moral rights now enacted into Australian law are:

- the right of an author or artist to be identified with his or her works—known as the right of attribution; and

- the right to object to alteration or other derogatory treatment of the work that would be prejudicial to the author or artist's honour or reputation—known as the right of integrity.

Moral rights apply to all works, except films, existing on 21 December 2000 and which are still protected by copyright, and to all works including films created after that date.

Under the right of attribution, the creator's right to recognition as creator of a work consists of four sub-rights:

- to be known as the creator of a work;

- to prevent others from claiming to be the creator of a work;

- to prevent the false attribution of works to the creator; and

- to prevent attribution to the creator of unauthorised altered versions of a work.

The right of integrity is the creator's right to object to derogatory treatment of a work, and covers both:

- changes made to the work itself (that is, distortion, mutilation or other modification of the work), or

- the manner in which the work is presented.

Moral rights are not full property rights in the sense of most rights exercised by copyright owners, but rather are personal to the creator and cannot be assigned (s 195AN). However, it is possible to consent to subsequent uses of copyright material which may offend against the moral rights, but the owner of a work may not have the right to alter a work against the wishes of the creator. This could have implications for the use of material written by academics in "electronic courseware" and other products where material is used and altered.[43] Generally, industry practice will provide a guide to what is acceptable use that will not infringe the moral rights in copyright material. More generally, in determining infringement of the rights of integrity and attribution in relation to works, ss 195AR and 195AS provide for consideration of the reasonableness of the acts or omissions done in relation to the work, as well as industry practice and voluntary codes of practice.

One of the recommendations in the Myer Report related to Indigenous Communal Moral Rights, and in 2003 the Government indicated it would introduce amendments to the *Copyright Act 1968* (Cth) to provide indigenous communities with the right to take action against inappropriate, derogatory or culturally insensitive use of creative works embodying traditional community knowledge and wisdom. The *Copyright Amendment (Indigenous Communal Rights) Bill 2003* was introduced but there has been criticism that it is unlikely to deliver the intended benefits to Indigenous communities.[44] Nonetheless legislation is scheduled for 2006.

---

43   L Wiseman, "Moral Rights in the Australia Academy: Where to Now?", (2005) 28(1) UNSWLJ 98-121.
44   J Anderson, "The Politics of Indigenous Knowledge: Australia's Communal Moral Rights Bill" (2004) 27(3) UNSWLJ 585-604.

Resale royalties or droit de suite is a scheme to remit visual artists a percentage of the sale price of their work each time it is resold. Creators of artistic works where the primary value is in the original work cannot always licence the reproduction of the work as other creators can. The Myer Report recommended the introduction of a resale royalty scheme in Australia, although this is not mandated under the Berne Convention. In 2004 DCITA (Department of Communications, Information Technology and the Arts) released the *Proposed Resale Royalty Arrangement Discussion Paper* (www.dcita.gov.au), which examined the issue and reviewed recent international developments as well as discussing the effects of different models of resale royalty schemes. Interestingly, the Discussion Paper concludes that "Outcomes for Indigenous artists do not seem to support introduction of a resale royalty scheme ... Non-Indigenous Australian artists dominate the royalty payments under all models".[45]

■ Performer's rights and performer's moral rights

[2.55] Performances of dramatic and other works are protected independently of any underlying work being performed. In Chapter 3 at **[3.90]-[3.175]**, there is discussion of copyright in dramatic, musical and literary works, works which may be created by someone who does not necessarily perform them. Since 1989, Part XIA has protected live performances from unauthorised recording and protection now extends to prohibiting communication and "public performance" of a performance or recording without authorisation. A performer's right is a "neighbouring right" to copyright or author's rights and was not originally a full property right in that the rights were personal to the performer and could not be assigned. Further the performer's right is not, in fact, a "copyright" in the traditional meaning since protection of an actual performance not fixed in some permanent form goes beyond the nature of protection conferred by the rest of the *Copyright Act 1968* (Cth).

Copyright in a sound recording of a live performance supplements the existing performer's rights to prevent unauthorised recordings of a performance of a dramatic, literary or musical work or improvisation thereof, a dance, circus act, variety act or similar presentation, and since 2004 the definition of "performance" has been expanded by s 248A(1)(f) to include an "expression of folklore".

In addition to copyright in performances, a new form of moral rights for performers in their live performances and recordings thereof has been introduced into Part IX of the *Copyright Act* as part of the AUSFTA amendments designed to ensure more perfect adherence to the WPPT (WIPO Performers and Phonograms Treaty 1996).[46] The *US Free Trade Implementation Act 2004* has also introduced the word "performership", which is participation in a performance as a performer (s 189). The performer's moral rights of attribution of performership, against false attribution and right to integrity of the performership mirror the moral rights applicable to other copyright material.

■ Film director's, screenwriters and producer's rights

[2.60] The ownership regime for copyright is covered at **[3.50]** and **[4.60]** but it is worth noting here that there is increasingly pressure to expand neighbouring rights to allow the creative effort in films to be recognised through vesting moral rights and indeed ownership of film copyright in directors and screenwriters as well as producers. To that end the

---

45 Department of Communications, Information Technology and the Arts, *Proposed Resale Royalty Arrangement Discussion Paper*, p 33. A copy can be reviewed at www.dcita.gov.au.
46 See K Weatherall, "'Pretend-y Rights': On the Insanely Complicated New Regime for Performers' Rights in Australia, and How Australian Performers Got Gypped" in (eds) F Macmillan & K Bowrey, *New Directions in Copyright Law, Volume 3* (Edward Elgar, Cheltenham, UK, 2005), pp 171-197.

Copyright Amendment (Film Director's Rights) Bill 2005 was passed to amend the *Copyright Act 1968* (Cth) to allow for film directors to be joint copyright owners of their films, along with producers, for the purposes of the retransmission statutory licence in Part VC of the Act. The amendments did not include screenwriters, however, and following referral of the Bill to the Senate Legal and Constitutional Legislation Committee the Committee recommended that the federal government, in consultation with relevant stakeholders, consider extending similar rights to provide for screenwriters to be joint copyright owners of films, along with producers and directors, for the purposes of the retransmission statutory licence in Part VC of that Act.[47] The Committee noted that:

> "the Bill will have little practical impact on the Australian film industry or on investment in that industry. The Bill will only confer a limited right on directors (that is, the right to retransmission in a free-to-air broadcast). This right only applies in respect of the retransmission scheme under Part VC, which is a new regime that has yet to generate an income stream. It does not extend to commissioned films, which are the overwhelming majority of films currently being made in Australia. Nor does it automatically extend to employed directors. Moreover, industry practice in Australia is for directors to assign any copyright they may have to the producers of the film they are to direct".[48]

■ When is a work "debased"?

▬▬▬ Schott Musik International v Colossal Records ▬▬▬

[2.65] *Schott Musik International GmbH & Co v Colossal Records of Australia Pty Ltd* (1997) 38 IPR 1 Federal Court of Australia

[This is not a moral rights case but provides some indication of the Federal Court's approach to the question of "debasement" and the "integrity" of a musical work.]

HILL J: [5]... In 1936 Carl Orff composed "Carmina Burana". The composition includes the well-known "O Fortuna" chorus (the work). The first appellant is the owner of the copyright in the work. The second appellant is the exclusive licensee of the copyright in the work in so far as it relates to the right to licence public performances, mechanical reproduction and synchronisation television performances of the work in Australia. The third appellant administers on behalf of its members the statutory licence scheme in s 55(1) of the Act. The respondents have recorded a compact disk known as "Excalibur" containing four remixed tracks of parts of the "O Fortuna" chorus. Each of these tracks is an adaptation, the making of which, subject to the provisions of s 55(2) of the Act, would constitute an infringement of the appellants' copyright. The remixed tracks adopt the style of what is referred to as "techno music", particularly favoured at all night dance sessions (raves) where loud, pulsating music is played. No distinction is drawn by the parties between any one of the four remixed tracks and any other. It is conceded that if the respondents infringe the appellants' copyright in respect of any one of those tracks, then they infringe the appellants' copyright in respect of the others.

It is agreed between the parties that the appellants are entitled to a declaration that the respondents have infringed the copyright in the work by the making of the adaptation and

■■■■■■ Schott Musik International v Colossal Records *continued*

are thus entitled to declarations and consequential relief as claimed, only if, in terms of s 55(2) of the Act, the adaptation is such as to "debase" the work constituted by the "O Fortuna" chorus. The substantial dispute between the parties is as to the meaning of s 55(2) and its application to the present facts.

...[11]

At the heart of the controversy between the parties are the following matters; whether the term "debases" in s 55(2) is dependent upon musicology; whether debasement is to be determined by reference to some section of the community; whether debasement is to be viewed purely economically; and whether debasement is to be looked at by reference to some value judgment to be made of the work.

Senior counsel for the appellants submits that the test of whether a work has been debased is largely objective. What is required is a comparison between the adaptation and the work to determine whether the adaptation affected the integrity, oneness or wholeness of the work, so as to destroy the form, nature, structure and message which the composer intended. [12] Thus, a work will be debased, it was submitted, if the work is so distorted that its fundamental character is changed, that is to say, its form, context and message have suffered change.

Senior counsel for the respondents rightly criticised this test for bringing subjectivity in through the back door in the guise of apparent objectivity. Debasement was said by the respondents to arise where, to a significant segment of the community, the original work was so devalued or lowered in esteem that real injury was or was liable to be caused to the owner of the copyright.

In my view, neither of these tests is satisfactory in the context of the legislation. The appellants' test comes perilously close to one of determining debasement by reference to the quantum or extent of the alterations constituting the adaptation. Indeed it was initially submitted that if the context or integrity of the work was affected, but to the musical benefit of the work, there would nevertheless have been a debasement.

The test of the respondents is equally unsatisfactory. If the test depends upon a significant segment of the community, there may well be different segments of the community having different views of debasement. There is no reason why a work should be held to have been debased merely because one section of the community regards it to have been, no matter how significant that section of the community might be....

For reasons I have already suggested, the focus in the present context can not solely be upon economic value of a copyright right since a work having no measurable commercial value might still be debased. Rather, I think that the test to be adopted is whether it is a consequence of the adaptation (taking into account that the adaptation differs from the original) that a reasonable person will be led to think less of the original work.

It will probably be rare for an adaptation of a work, no matter how different the adaptation from the original, to be a debasement of the original. One example might be an adaptation which brings into the original associations which to a reasonable person would be objectionable. So, for example, for a rearrangement of a work to incorporate within it notes associating the work with say a terrorist or racist body would constitute a debasement of the original. Perhaps a parody might bring about the result that one could not recall the original without the parody coming to mind in such a way as to diminish the value of the original: cf *Luther R Campbell v Acuff-Rose Music Inc* (1994) 127 L Ed 2d 500 (US Supreme Court).

So expressed, the test is objective. So expressed, it relieves the Court from the danger of artistic censorship or, of even more concern, from being an arbiter of taste. The Court in its conclusion may be assisted by evidence, but that evidence will not be directed as the evidence here was, to matters of musicology or taste.

▰▰▰▰ Schott Musik International v Colossal Records *continued*

On no view of the matter could it be said here that the techno adaptation debased the original. A reasonable person, in my view, would distinguish the [13] techno version from the original as different in style and approach, while recognising that the techno version in no way detracted from the original.

I would therefore dismiss the appeal with costs.

WILCOX J: [2] ... I agree with the orders proposed by Hill J but, regrettably, not his reasons. My regret extends beyond mere politeness; from the Court's point of view, there are advantages in Hill J's approach. If the operation of s 55(2) of the *Copyright Act* [3] *1968* is limited to cases where the adaptation causes a reasonable person to think less of the original work, as Hill J suggests, its application will be relatively easy. I am not sure this approach would wholly relieve the Court from involvement in artistic censorship or matters of taste, as Hill J suggests. If it was claimed that an adaptation debased an original work because it constituted a parody, or because it included material having a repugnant association, for example, with a person or an organisation widely regarded as abhorrent, the Court would be required to make a judgment of degree involving a measure of subjectivity. However, I agree that the task would be less difficult and invidious than that which the trial judge was invited to undertake.

... [4]

"Debase" is a strong term. It requires much more than an opinion, even an expert opinion, that the adaptation is musically inferior. For the term to be applicable, the adaptation must be so lacking in integrity or quality that it can properly be said to have degraded the original work. It is difficult to think an adaptation that has its own integrity could be so characterised, even if it is musically inferior and however radical or distasteful (to some) it may be.

Tamberlin J summarised his conclusions of principle in seven propositions:

1. The term "debase" does not call for substantial sameness or even similarity in style, instruments or performance. They are relevant but not conclusive considerations.
2. The only necessary similarity between the original work and the adaptation is that the latter must be an "arrangement" or "adaptation" of the work.
3. The term "debase" calls for a value judgment based on a significant lowering in integrity, value, esteem or quality of the work.
4. Regardless of which view is taken as to the meaning of "debase", there is, of necessity, a question of degree involved in deciding whether a work is 'debased' by an adaptation.
5. As musical tastes are so divergent and varied, ... it is necessary in approaching the question, to pay due regard to that broad spectrum of taste and values. It would be wrong to take a strictly analytical or pedantic view of individual changes made in the adaptation and simply find the sum of those changes to reach a conclusion. Rather, it is necessary to consider the overall impression which it is likely to make on a community with a wide range of tastes and attitudes in relation to adaptations and musical forms.
6. In forming a conclusion, it is necessary to determine and consider the nature and extent of the variations. [5]
7. While some guidance can be obtained from "expert" witnesses, the question is largely one of impression and the Court must decide on the evidence placed before it whether the adaptation is so extensive, detrimental or inferior, as a whole that it amounts to debasement.

Subject to proposition 3 being read in the light of the comments I have made, I respectfully agree with these propositions. Tamberlin J applied them to the facts of the present case and held none of the adaptations complained of by the appellants debased the original work. I respectfully agree. There are numerous differences between each of the adaptations and the original work. Some people may think those differences result in an inferior work; they may

━━━━━ Schott Musik International v Colossal Records *continued*

even scorn or despise them. But nobody has suggested that any of the adaptations lacks its own integrity or constitutes a mere travesty of the original. The decision of Tamberlin J to dismiss the application was correct.

I agree with Hill J that the appeal should be dismissed with costs.

━━━

━━━ Benchmark Building v Mitre 10 (New Zealand) ━━━

[2.70] *Benchmark Building & Anor v Mitre 10 (New Zealand) Ltd* [2003] NZCA 213 (29 August 2003), Court of Appeal, New Zealand.

GAULT P: [3] Mitre 10 (New Zealand) Ltd, the first respondent, under licence from the second respondent, an Australian company, franchised in New Zealand the name and style "Mitre 10" for large super-market outlets for hardware, tools and equipment for home maintenance and improvement. To promote these businesses in a price-sensitive competitive market the first respondent (hereafter Mitre 10) produces at regular intervals promotional brochures that are delivered to householder letter-boxes. They are illustrated brochures, printed in colour, and depict photographic illustrations of various products, each accompanied by a brief description and, in prominent print, the prices at which they may be purchased. Most of the products featured show, and are described by reference to, the brand names of the manufacturers. A small number appear unbranded and some others are identified by the trade name BUTLERS which is a trade mark of Mitre 10.

[It was found that there was no copyright infringement by copying or adaptation of the brochure]

... [32] In the present case the copyright works claimed by Mitre 10 are the original artistic and literary works reproduced in the printed brochures. By displaying Mitre 10's own brochures Benchmark has done nothing to reproduce the copyright works. Nothing has been copied. Even if a new work is created incorporating the brochures (and we very much doubt that applying stickers has that affect), the representations of the copyright works remained unchanged and no new representations of them were made...

Breach of authors' moral rights

[41] The claim for infringement of the right not to have a copyright work subjected to a derogatory treatment cannot succeed here. It is a right of the author not of the owner of the copyright. While Mitre 10 may be the owner of works embodied in the brochures, it is not the author. The evidence establishes that there were a number of contributors to the works. They were all individuals who are not parties to the proceeding.

[42] Mr Asher argued that a company may be the author of a work. He relied on s 29 of the *Interpretation Act 1999* providing that a reference in an enactment to a "person" includes a body corporate. He invoked that interpretation to construe s 5(1) of the *Copyright Act* which provides that the author of a work is the person who created it. He argued that the works in the brochures were created by Mitre 10.

[43] Section 4 of the *Interpretation Act* makes clear that the provisions of that Act apply unless the context on an enactment requires a different interpretation. We have no doubt that in the *Copyright Act* the word "person" in the definition of author, except where the contrary is expressly stated, does not extend to bodies corporate. The exceptions are found in s 5(2) and (3).

[44] Section 98(2) defining the author's right refers to "his or her work". Section 18 qualifies works for protection in New Zealand by reference to the status of the author in terms of

▋▋▋▋ Benchmark Building v Mitre 10 (New Zealand) *continued*

citizenship or domicile. In that section there is reference to a body corporate but that was introduced into the law at the same time as s 5(2) and (3) and plainly to provide for the exceptions they introduced. Section 22 prescribes the duration of copyright by reference to the life of the author. Again there are specific provisions in ss 22(2), 23, 24 and 25, providing for duration in respect of those works specified in s 5(2) of which the author may be a body corporate.

[45] The moral rights of authors are provided to enable authors to protect the integrity of their works even though ownership passes to others. It would be contrary to the very purpose of those rights if the author's right accrued to those employing or commissioning the authors or purchasing the copyright in their works.

[46] Although it is unnecessary to go further, we comment that we are not persuaded that displaying brochures in which copyright works are reproduced for comparative advertising purposes amounts to derogatory treatment of those works. They are being used for the very purpose for which they were created—to convey information about products Mitre 10 has for sale. That Benchmark is taking advantage from it cannot be said to be prejudicial to the honour or reputation of the authors whose identity is not disclosed.

[47] We conclude that there is no arguable case of infringement of copyright.

■ Moral rights in practice

[2.75] There are very few studies of attitudes of artists to copyright. However, a recent study by David Throsby and Virginia Hollister titled *Don't Give Up Your Day Job: An Economic Study of Professional Artists in Australia* (Australia Council, 2003) provides some empirical research reflecting on the adequacy of the law and moral rights in particular.

TABLE 2.1 ARTISTS' EXPERIENCE OF INFRINGEMENT OF THEIR MORAL RIGHTS (PER CENT)

	Writers	Visual artists	Craft practitioners	Actors	Dancers	Musicians	Composers	Community cultural development workers	All artists
Failure to be acknowledged as the author/creator of the work	60	50	47	52	50	56	67	65	55
Work was reproduced without permission	53	31	55	68	50	44	43	50	46
Work was altered without permission	64	39	25	40	33	27	50	57	41
Work was defaced or destroyed without permission	3	31	20	8	–	4	14	22	16
Other infringement	5	18	5	8	–	–	–	–	7
weighted n =	37	68	19	25	6	48	6	23	232
unweighted n =	47	72	25	27	14	23	14	14	236

(a) Proportions are of artists experiencing one or more kinds of moral right infringements. Columns do not sum to 100 because multiple responses permitted.
– indicated full response in this sample.

TABLE 2.2 ADEQUACY OF PROTECTION OF ARTISTS' COPYRIGHT AND MORAL RIGHTS (PER CENT)

	Writers	Visual artists	Craft practitioners	Actors	Dancers	Musicians	Composers	Community cultural development workers	All artists
Proportion of artist(s) who believe current provision for copyright protection is:									
Very effective	4	2	2	5	3	1	3	5	3
Adequate	54	31	29	34	38	39	68	37	39
Inadequate	25	30	31	35	25	32	23	21	30
Don't know/not sure	17	37	38	27	34	28	7	37	29
Total	100	100	100	100	100	100	100	100	100
Proportion of artist(s) who believe Australian legislation offers adequate protection against moral rights infringement:									
Yes	33	20	20	20	34	29	42	21	26
No	40	27	31	41	22	32	24	29	33
Don't know/no sure	27	53	49	40	44	39	33	51	42
Total	100	100	100	100	100	100	100	100	100
Weighted n =	170	223	96	149	32	297	32	64	1062
unweighted n =	219	239	123	160	75	142	66	38	1062

(a) Proportions are of all artists.

COMPARISON WITH OTHER INTELLECTUAL PROPERTY RIGHTS

▬▬▬ Corelli v Gray ▬▬▬

[2.80] *Corelli v Gray* (1913) 29 TLR 570 High Court of Justice (United Kingdom)

SARJANT J: [571] Before comparing the relative probability of these two rival cases I should like to make two observations, both of which tend in favour of the defendant. In the first place, it is fairly clear, and I assume in favour of the defendant, that under the new Act, as under the former law, no absolute monopoly is given to authors analogous to that conferred on inventors of patents that is to say, if it could be shown as a matter of fact that two precisely similar works were in fact produced wholly independently of one another, I do not think that the author of the work that was published first would be entitled to restrain the publication by the other author of that author's independent and original work. The right appears to be merely a negative right to prevent the appropriation of the labours of an author by another. The second observation is this, that the onus of establishing appropriation, of course, rests upon the plaintiff. With these two observations, I will now deal with the case in the order in

Corelli v Gray *continued*

which it was presented to me namely, first, by examining the extent of the similarities or coin-cidences between the two works; and next by investigating the story put forward by the defendant.

AMBIT OF PROTECTION: EXPRESSION, NOT IDEAS OR INFORMATION

Donoghue v Allied Newspapers

[2.85] *Donoghue v Allied Newspapers* [1938] Ch 106

[Several articles were published in the News of the World newspaper based on interviews between the plaintiff and a journalist. The articles had titles such as "Enthralling Stories of the King of Sports" and "Donoghue's Racing Secrets" and were based on the experiences of the plaintiff, a well-known character of the turf.]

FARWELL J: **[109]** The first question that I have to determine is whether the plaintiff is or is not either the sole or the joint owner of the copyright in the original articles which appeared in the News of the World. If the plaintiff has no copyright, either as sole owner or as joint owner, in these articles, this action necessarily fails, and it will be unnecessary for me to consider the further question which I shall have to consider if that is not the position namely, as to the effect of the agreement on 4 April 1931, and whether that agreement amounts to an equitable assignment of the plaintiff's copyright to the News of the World.

It is necessary, in considering whether the plaintiff is the owner or part owner of the copyright in this work, to see in what it is that copyright exists under the *Copyright Act 1911*. This at any rate is clear beyond all question, that there is no copyright in an idea, or in ideas. A person may have a brilliant idea for a story, or for a picture, or for a play, and one which appears to him to be original; but if he communicates that idea to an author or an artist or a playwright, the production which is the result of the communication of the idea to the author or the artist or the playwright is the copyright of the person who has clothed the idea in form, whether by means of a picture, a play, or a book, and the owner of the idea has no rights in that product.

On the other hand, and I think this is equally plain, if an author employs a shorthand writer to take down a story which the author is composing, word for word, in shorthand, and the shorthand writer then transcribes it, and the author has it published, the author is the owner of the copyright and not the shorthand writer. A mere amanuensis does not, by taking **[110]** down word for word the language of the author, become in any sense the owner of the copyright. That is the property of the author.

The explanation of that is this, that that in which copyright exists is the particular form of language by which the information which is to be conveyed is conveyed. If the idea, however, original, is nothing more than an idea, and is not put into any form of words, or any form of expression such as a picture, then there is no such thing as copyright at all. It is not until it is (if I may put it in that way) reduced into writing or into some tangible form that there is any copyright, and the copyright exists in the particular form of language in

██████ Donoghue v Allied Newspapers *continued*

which, or in the case of a picture the particular form of the picture by which, the information or the idea is conveyed to those who are intended to read it or to look at it.

[On the point of "material form"] ... In the present case, the ideas of all these stories, apart altogether from what one may call merely the embellishments which were undoubtedly supplied wholly by Mr Felstead the ideas of all these stories, and in fact the stories themselves, were supplied by the plaintiff; but in my judgment, upon the evidence it is plain that the particular form of language by which those stories were conveyed was the language of Mr Felstead and not of the plaintiff. Although many of the stories were told in the form of dialogue, and to some extent Mr Felstead no doubt tried to reproduce the story as it was told to him by the plaintiff, nevertheless the particular form of language in which those adventures or stories were conveyed to the public was the language of Mr Felstead and not the language of the plaintiff.

One case has been cited to me which is, I think, very near to the present one, and if I were to decide in favour of the plaintiff on this first point I think that I should be disregarding the decision of Tomlin J in *Evans v E Hulton & Co Ltd* [1924] Mac CC 51. The facts of that case are not quite on all fours with the present one; but the principle upon which that judgment rests is the same as that which I have to apply in this case.

[111] In that case the person who supplied the information was a foreigner, and no doubt he did not convey the information in a form which would have been suitable for an article in a newspaper, and to that extent it may be that the person who wrote it down and supplied the article had more to do than Mr Felstead in the present case; but the principle applicable is the same. What Tomlin J said was this (at 56):

> "One thing is reasonably plain, I think, that probably Mr Zeitun would not himself claim that he was capable of producing in the English tongue a literary work which would find a market. He certainly agreed that he has never attempted to do so, and I should doubt his capacity to do so. The fact that he is the subject matter of the production in the sense that it is an incident from his life, for which he provided the material, does not seem to me to make him in any sense the joint author with Mr Evans of the manuscript which was in fact written, and, upon the facts which I have stated, I find that he did not take any part in producing the express matter which is the original literary work, the subject matter of copyright."

What I understand the learned judge to mean by the "express matter" is that which I have endeavoured to define as the particular form of language in which the information is conveyed, and although it may be that in the present case the plaintiff could give more help to Mr Felstead than Mr Zeitun could give in the case of *Evans v E Hulton & Co Ltd* (at 51), to the author of the manuscript, nevertheless, although the plaintiff supplied all the substance of the articles, it was conveyed in language which was the language or Mr Felstead, and for which the plaintiff himself was not responsible.

Appeal dismissed.

Mono Pumps v Karinya Industries

[2.90] *Mono Pumps (New Zealand) Ltd v Karinya Industries Ltd* (1984) 4 IPR 505 High Court of New Zealand

CASEY J: [506] This is a motion for an interlocutory injunction to restrain the defendants from dealing with pump parts which are reproductions of drawings of "Mono" pump components in which the plaintiffs claim copyright.

... [508]

For the plaintiffs, Mr Judd analysed the position in this way. There can be no doubt that copyright exists in three-dimensional reproductions of drawings, and it is claimed by the plaintiffs in the drawings which they have produced themselves and in the pumps and the components which it manufactures from them. They say the parts imported by defendants are reproductions of corresponding Mono drawings and parts, and are interchangeable with them. To this the defendants assert that they are not reproductions of the latter, but of the French inventor's original drawings. Mr Judd says such an approach ignores the fundamental aspect of copyright law namely, its concern with the copying of physical material only and not with the reproduction of ideas. The idea can be taken, but the drawings embodying it cannot be copied. Those appearing in the patent specification and in the thesis submitted by counsel as a further exhibit are only intended to illustrate and explain the inventor's ideas. There is no doubt that copyright can subsist in such drawings, but this is not infringed by anybody producing drawings or three-dimensional articles applying the principles they illustrate, and using the idea exemplified by them. However, copyright is infringed if what is produced reproduces the form in which that idea is expressed.

... [511]

In *Plix Products Ltd v Frank M Winstone (Merchants) Ltd* (1984) 3 IPR 390 at 419 Prichard J embarked on an impressive analysis of what he described as "probably the most difficult concept in the law of copyright" that it exists not in the idea itself but in the concrete form in which it is expressed. Anyone is free to use the basic idea.

"But no-one can appropriate the forms or shapes evolved by the author in the process of giving expression to the basic idea. So he who seeks to make a product of the same description as that in which another owns copyright must tread with care. If he copies the details which properly belong to the expression and not to the basic concept, he will infringe the copyright. That is why, when the basic idea is expressed in a crude, or simplistic form, the potential plagiarist or business competitor can, without offending, come very close to an exact reproduction of the copyright work. But where the expression is ornate, complex or detailed, then he must keep his distance: the only product he can then make without infringing may bear little resemblance to the copyright work."

...

Injunction granted to plaintiff.

CHAPTER 3

CRITERIA FOR SUBSISTENCE
OF COPYRIGHT

[3.05] There are no formal requirements to obtaining copyright protection; protection arises upon the fulfilment of certain criteria and does not require a registration process. The *Copyright Act 1968* (Cth) protects:

* certain types of subject matter

* in a material form

* that has been created by a qualified person (as defined by the Act) or published in Australia.

Once these criteria are met the owner of the copyright gains certain exclusive rights which endure for a period of time and then finish.

SUBJECT MATTER

[3.10] The conceptual distinction between ideas and expressions is articulated in a number of statutory provisions that determine when copyright subsists and to whom it belongs.

Copyright only comes into being in relation to the particular cultural forms of expression for which there is a corresponding legal provision. Copyright lawyers often refer to these legally recognised forms of expressions as having "subject matter". Copyright has expanded considerably from its origins as a form of "literary property". The expansion in copyright subject matter in the 20th century was accommodated by the development of a distinction between protected expressions known as "works" and those that fall under the rubric of "subject matter other than works". The nuances associated with the many definitions of copyright subject matter will be considered later.

See s 32 (for works) and ss 89, 90, 91 and 92 (for subject matter other than works).

■ Exclusive rights

[3.15]

TABLE 3.1: PART III SUBJECT MATTER (WORKS)

Literary, dramatic and musical works	Artistic works
s 31(1)(a)(i) to reproduce the work in a material form	s 31(1)(b)(i) to reproduce the work in a material form
s 31(1)(a)(ii) to publish the work	s 31(1)(b)(ii) to publish the work
s 31(1)(a)(iii) to perform the work	—
s 31(1)(a)(iv) to communicate the work to the public	s 31(1)(b)(iii) to communicate the work to the public
s 31(1)(a)(vi) to make an adaptation of the work;	—
s 31(1)(a)(vii) to do in relation to an adaptation any of the acts mentioned in (i) to (iv)	—
s 31(1)(c) (where the work is other than a computer program) to enter into a commercial rental arrangement in respect of the work reproduced in a sound recording	—
s 31(1)(d) in the case of a computer program, to enter into a commercial rental arrangement in respect of the program	—

TABLE 3.2: PART IV SUBJECT MATTER (OTHER THAN WORKS)

Sound recordings	Cinematograph films	Television and sound broadcasts	Published editions
s 85(1)(a) to make a copy of the sound recording	s 86(a) to make a copy of the film	s 87(a) in the case of a television broadcast, in so far as it consists of visual images —to make a film of the broadcast, or a copy of the film	s 88 to make a facsimile copy of the edition

continues . . .

Sound recordings	Cinematograph films	Television and sound broadcasts	Published editions
s 85(1)(b) to cause the recording to be heard in public	s 86(b) to cause the film, in so far as it consists of visual images, to be seen in public, or in so far as it consists of sounds, to be heard in public	s 87(b) in the case of a sound broadcast, in so far as it consists of sounds—to make a sound recording of the broadcast, or a copy of the sound recording	—
s 85(1)(c) to communicate the recording to the public	s 86(c) to communicate the film to the public	s 87(c) to rebroadcast it or communicate it to the public other than by broadcasting it	—
s 85(1)(d) to enter into a commercial rental arrangement in respect of the recording	—	—	—

■ Duration of copyright

[3.20] Copyright was originally for a term of 14 years under the *Statute of Anne*—equal to two terms of an apprenticeship. It could be renewed for a further 14 years if the author remained alive. Under pressure from well connected romantic artists, such as William Wordsworth, who claimed they could not publish in their lifetime as they needed to reserve texts for their family to live off after their deaths, the *Literary Copyright Act 1842* (UK) introduced a life-plus term. This allowed copyright protection for life plus seven years, with a maximum of 42 years.

Since those times, the duration of terms have varied, however the life-plus model was established as the norm for most original works. In Australia, until recently, this has been a term of 50 years from the end of the year in which the author died. There are, however, some anomalies in the treatment of some artistic works, such as photography, which has been treated in the same way as film. Where the original work has joint authorship, the relevant date is the death of the last surviving author (s 80). The duration of copyright remains tied to the creator's lifetime, even though ownership may be transferred.

For subject matter other than works, such as film and sound recordings (s 181), and Crown copyright (ss 180(1)(b), 180(3)), protection has generally been a term of 50 years from the end of the year of first publication.

Unpublished works have indefinite copyright.

The European Union (EU), in 1995, extended the copyright term for its member states to life of the author plus 70 years. This extension does not apply to sound recordings. The change is a consequence of a Directive of the European Commission in 1993 requiring member states to increase their basic term of protection to this standard. Ostensibly the purpose of the Directive was to harmonise the laws of EU members on the matter of term, as national laws ranged from between life plus 50 years (the minimum Berne requirement), life plus 60 years (Spain) and life plus 70 years (Germany). The United States has also extended the term of copyright protection in line with the European move with the passing of the *Sonny Bono Copyright Term Extension Act 1998*. Sonny Bono, from the 1970s pop group and variety hour television show *Sonny and Cher*, believed copyright should last forever. As a Florida senator he introduced the American legislation.

Critics of the term extension argue that the effect of expanding the copyright term is to prevent valuable copyright works, for example, Disney's Mickey Mouse, from falling into the public domain, but without any "incentive" effect leading to greater creative activity. While expansion of the copyright term in the interest of "harmonisation" has a level of support within Australia, as a net importer of copyright material, this would have a detrimental effect on balance of trade figures as payment for material that would otherwise be in the public domain would be required.

The Australia-United States Free Trade Agreement came into effect on 1 January 2005. Under this agreement copyright duration is extended to 70 years from the end of the year the creator died or the material was first published. Copyright does not revive for works in which copyright had expired under the 1968 Act. However, photographs are now entitled to protection for the term of the life of the author plus 70 years. Performers now also have economic rights in relation to authorised sound recordings of their performances.

Determining whether a work is in or out of copyright can be very difficult. The term of protection for different kinds of works can vary depending on the applicable legislation. For example, it will require translating a piece of music into the respective rights that attach to the literary and musical works, and to the sound recordings. These will most likely belong to different parties. It will then require knowledge of the date of first publication or date of the death of the author for each of the rights, and knowledge of the various applicable statutory schemes that have applied. In some instances, some rights may have expired, but not all of them. As the Act affords post mortem protection, you may need to research the date of the death of the relevant author and trace who inherited that personal property by will.

There is no registry for copyright material that would allow users to check the status of the work. There are concerns that the administrative costs and complexity associated with rights clearance is a major stumbling block to locating and accessing what should be public domain material in Australia.

REDUCED TO MATERIAL FORM/MADE

[3.25] Historically copyright has not protected ideas unless there is some embodiment of the idea in a form of storage from which it can be retrieved (s 10). The "storage ... from which the work can be reproduced" includes the RAM of a computer: *Microsoft Corporation v Business Boost Pty Ltd* (2000) 49 IPR 573. This makes it necessary to decide what "making" a work or reducing it to material form consists of.

■ Subsistence issues

[3.30] Section 22(1) of the 1968 Act defines "making" as "the work ... reduced to writing or to some other material form" and s 22(2) further defines "reduced to material form" as including the recording of a work into "sounds embodied in an article or thing". Section 10(1) defines "writing" as meaning a mode of representing or reproducing words, figures or symbols in a visible form, and "written" has a corresponding meaning. In *Donoghue v Allied Newspapers* [1938] Ch 106 it was the journalist who took the interviewee's ideas and put them into writing, who provided the material form and therefore the copyright work. As *Mono Pumps v Karinya Industries* ([**2.90**]) illustrates, the reproduction of the pump parts amounted to taking the expression of the copyright work, rather than just the concept.

While publication is not essential to the existence of copyright, copyright will subsist, according to s 32(2), in published works. To be subject to copyright before publication, the work must have taken a material form within s 22(1). If not, s 29(1)(a) provides that a work is published if "reproductions of the work or edition have been supplied (whether by sale or otherwise) to the public". Obviously the publication of a work assumes it to be in a material form. Furthermore, s 31(1) gives the exclusive right of reproduction in a material form, and s 29(3) provides that publication does not take place where a work is performed or exhibited, thus ephemeral expression does not amount to "publication".

■ Enforcement issues

[3.35] Digitisation has created new problems in applying the material form requirement. The objection that copyright should not be used to protect something incapable of being seen or heard was fatal to the plaintiff's claim to establish copyright in a computer program in *Apple Computer Inc v Computer Edge Pty Ltd* (1983) ATPR 40-421. The High Court subsequently upheld this decision of Beaumont J in *Computer Edge Pty Ltd v Apple Computer Inc* (1986) 161 CLR 171. Sheppard J in the Federal Court (on appeal from Beaumont J ((1984) 53 ALR 225) was also of the opinion that, in the context of the existing *Copyright Act*, a literary work or an adaptation thereof needed to be capable of being seen or heard. Computer programs are a type of "literary work" under copyright law, now excused from the requirement of being perceptible by human senses.

Under the Australia-United States Free Trade Agreement there is a new definition of material form:

> "in relation to a work or an adaptation of a work, includes any form (whether visible or not) of storage of the work or adaptation, or a substantial part of the work or adaptation, (whether or not the work or adaptation, or a substantial part of the work or adaptation, can be reproduced)."

This provision applies to all reproductions, in any manner or form, permanent or temporary. Material may be regarded as having been "reproduced" if it is held in a form of storage (such as RAM), even though it may not be possible to reproduce it from that form of storage. However, under s 43B there is no infringement of copyright if the reproduction is "incidentally made as part of a technical process" in using a non-infringing copy of a work.

Even with traditional works, the dichotomy between an idea and its expression is not always easy to formulate.

■ When are ideas "expressed in material form"?

Tate v Thomas

[3.40] *Tate v Thomas* [1921] 1 Ch 503 Chancery Division (United Kingdom)

EVE J: [508] The plaintiffs in this action are three gentlemen accustomed to collaborate in the production of revues and dramatic pieces for stage purposes, one of them composing the music and the other two writing the words, and they claim damages from the defendants for an alleged infringement of their copyright in so far as it includes the right to produce a film version of a dramatic work called *The Lads of the Village*. It is admitted that if the plaintiffs are the owners of the copyright that which the defendants have done constitutes an infringement of their rights, and further that the defendants are in no better position as regards their claim to copyright in the said work than Mr Joseph Peterman through whom the claim would have been had he not parted with his interest. The real issue I have to determine is whether Mr Peterman ever had any interest in the copyright either as the author or one of the joint authors of the work. There is this further suggestion, that if he is not either the sole or joint author he may have acquired the copyright as assignee from the plaintiffs under an agreement to which I shall have to refer later on.

The evidence, which I do not propose to go through in detail, comes to this, that some few years ago in the early days of the war Mr Peterman conceived the idea of a play embodying incidents appropriate to the warlike atmosphere then subsisting, to which he contemplated attaching a name suggested by a prominent advertisement not unconnected with the assassination of spies. It was to be called *Kill that Spy*, [509] the spy being a German and the characters including a hero and a heroine, the latter of whom was to turn up in very unexpected places but at most opportune occasions.

The plot if such it can be called was outlined to Mr Roberts, the stage manager at the Oxford, and with the assistance of Mr Baldwin a rough sketch was later on reduced into writing.

Mr Peterman acting on the advice of his friends decided to postpone the production of the play for a period, but early in 1917 finding there was a demand for plays dealing with incidents connected with the war he decided to put his idea into a more concrete form and with that view he opened up communications with the plaintiffs in Manchester in January 1917. They were somewhat suspicious of Mr Peterman's ability to pay for their services and the matter languished a little until April, when Mr Peterman having obtained some financial assistance was in a position to enter into an agreement with the plaintiffs whereby they agreed to compose the music and write the lyrics and dialogue appropriate to the subject matter of the proposed work, and he agreed to make them certain payments for their services. The music was composed and the lyrics and dialogue duly written, and prima facie the production was one of which the plaintiffs were the joint authors and as such owners of the copyright.

But Mr Peterman contends that he was really the author or at least a joint author with the plaintiffs. It was not disputed that he suggested the name of the piece, and there is no doubt that in many parts of the work are introduced incidents suggested in his rough sketch or culled from works in which he has no copyright interest. One of the witnesses called for the defendants went so far as to say that the whole play was "pinched" from other people's productions. I had the opportunity of seeing Mr Peterman in the witness box and I can well understand that he is speaking the truth when he states that he was frequently making suggestions to the authors and indicating to them how they were to do the work they had undertaken. He is a gentleman of a fertile imagination and possessed of a fluency [510] and powers well qualifying him for communicating his views to the authors.

The plaintiffs do not deny that their work embodies some ideas and a few catch lines or words for which Mr Peterman may claim credit, but they dispute altogether his claim to a share in the authorship of the work and contend (and in my opinion rightly contend) that the sum total of his contribution does not amount to anything entitled to protection under the Act. His assistance, such as it was, was confined to accessorial matters such as scenic effects, or stage "business" not the subject matter of copyright.

When the work was completed the names of the plaintiffs were inscribed thereon as those of the authors. On all further copies of the work made for the use of the performers and actors the authorship was again attributed to these gentlemen, and in the poster and other literature

■■■■■■ Tate v Thomas *continued*

issued in connection with the production a statement was made to the effect that the play had been composed and written by the plaintiffs. Finally, when it became necessary to deal with the Colonial and American rights and for that purpose to obtain declarations as to the authorship of the work, the plaintiffs, at the instigation and at the request of the company who claim through Peterman, made declarations that they were respectively the authors and composer.

By these circumstances a strong presumption is raised that the plaintiffs were the authors and sole authors of this work, and as such are entitled to the copyright. To rebut this presumption two arguments have been advanced, the one that in a work of this class when the dialogue is of an ephemeral character and of little or no account compared with the scenes and action depicted, the real author is the man who so to speak stages the piece, arranges the scenes, and determines the appropriate action and the other that when the infringement complained of is the reproduction of the drama in the cinema, and therefore without the dialogue, the true owner of the copyright must be the individual responsible for the scenic effects, and not the musical composer, or the writers of the dialogue. I think the former of [511] these arguments is disposed of by the judgment of the Court of Appeal in *Tate v Fullbrook* [1908] 1 KB 821, and the latter by para (d) of subs (2) of s 1 of the *Copyright Act 1911*. In *Tate v Fullbrook* it was pointed out that the Act creates a statutory monopoly, and that there must be certainty in the monopoly so created in order that injustice may be avoided. To bring about this result there must be matter capable of being printed and published. Scenic effects may be protected as part and parcel of the drama, but they cannot in themselves be subject matter for the statutory protection. Even were I to give Mr Peterman credit for a much larger share than I am prepared to attribute to him in settling the scenes and accessories of this play, I could not hold his claim to be considered the author of the piece paramount to that of the plaintiffs. I am quite satisfied that he cannot be regarded as the author. Then it is said that if he is not the sole author, he is at least a joint author. A suggestion has been made that the play is a collective work, but I am not prepared to treat it as a collective work within the meaning of the Act. It is, however, a work in the production of which there could be joint authorship. The question whether Mr Peterman's claim to be a joint author of this work, so far as it is subject matter for protection under the Act, is one of fact; and having heard all the evidence I have come to the conclusion that his contributions to the matter capable of being printed and published were so insignificant and negligible as to make it quite impossible for me to hold him to have been in any sense a joint author within the Act. But then it is said that on the true construction of the agreement of 17 April 1917, he was to be treated from the beginning as a joint author, and that when Tate and Peterman agreed that Peterman should commission Tate to write the music and that Clifford, Harris and Valentine should collaborate on the libretto of this production and write the lyrics, it was, in substance, an agreement by Tate on behalf of himself and his two co-plaintiffs that the latter would collaborate not inter se but with Peterman. I think that is an impossible construction [512] to impose on the agreement, and as Mr Clayton pointed out it is one which, having regard to the later part of the agreement, would involve extraordinary results. On the agreement I hold that Mr Peterman has failed to establish any right in the authorship of this play.

Order for the plaintiffs.

Piracy of a good idea—not copyright infringement

▰▰▰ Green v Broadcasting Corporation of New Zealand ▰▰▰

[3.45] *Green v Broadcasting Corporation of New Zealand* [1988] 16 IPR 1 Court of Appeal of New Zealand

[The appellant, Green, had been the author, producer and compere of a television talent quest produced and broadcast in the UK under the name *Opportunity Knocks* from the early 1960s until 1978. Green's program was not broadcast in New Zealand. Between 1975 and 1978 the Broadcasting Corporation of New Zealand produced and broadcast a television talent quest with the title *Opportunity Knocks*. The Corporation's version included the repetition from show to show of features of Green's productions, in particular various catchphrases used by Green, the use of "sponsors" to introduce contestants and a "clapometer" to measure studio audience reaction, features which the trial judge held the Corporation had copied from Green. In 1979 Green brought an action for damages against the Corporation alleging that it had passed off its program as his, or as an adaptation authorised and approved by him. In the alternative, he alleged that the Corporation had infringed his copyright in the title *Opportunity Knocks*, and in the scripts and the dramatic format of his program.]

SOMERS J: ... [7] I think it may be said that each written script contained the skeleton outline or framework of the manner in which a type of talent quest would be conducted. The competitors, the sponsors and their interviews, would change from programme to programme but the general form or structure was, on the evidence set out in the script for the first and second programmes. The latter and subsequent programmes differed from the first for in these there was at the beginning a brief review of the immediately preceding programme, the announcement of its winner and a repetition of that winner's act as part of the current programme. Upon the evidence the format was adhered to thereafter in all future scripts. I think, however, that it would be necessary to see a show before its whole could be appreciated; in particular the essence of the sponsorship could not, as I understand the evidence, have been fully apprehended from the script. ...

The scripts, as I understand them, could not constitute a dramatic work. They could not themselves be acted or performed which I take to be the essence of such a work for they were no more than a general scheme for a proposed entertainment. The actual telecast programme to which each script was the guide may have been a dramatic work. But copyright in the performance (assuming it to have been reduced to material form) is not claimed by Mr Green nor was it suggested that any one of his many telecast productions was actually copied.

Nor can situations or scenic effects by themselves apart from the words and incidents of a dramatic work be the subject of dramatic copyright. That [8] topic is discussed in *Tate v Fullbrook* [1908] 1 KB 821 at 829, 832 and 834. They may be protected as part of a whole dramatic work and similarity may evidence an intention to steal a work.

I am of the opinion that Mr Green's script or scripts cannot support a claim of copyright in a dramatic work. Nor do I think there can be a claim for "format" which is not either a dramatic or literary work itself or perhaps a combination of both. The monopoly conferred by the *Copyright Act* can only be maintained where the condition of its grant are complied with.

...

CASEY J: ... [15] One can understand the sense of grievance felt by people in Mr Green's position when they witness the piracy of a good entertainment idea. Nevertheless, the overall interests of society in maintaining the free exchange and ability to develop ideas must also be

◼◼◼◼◼ Green v Broadcasting Corporation of New Zealand *continued*

considered. Any extension of the defined breadth of copyright protection must be approached with caution and is probably best left to the informed decision of the legislature.

I have referred to the situation in Australia where Mr Green sold his show to a television channel, but there was an important difference in that his name went with it and I understand he hosted the opening programme. One of his problems in New Zealand was the view held by the Corporation—whether rightly or wrongly—that his style would not be acceptable to New Zealand viewers ...

GALLEN J (dissent): [20] The concept of dramatic format is one which has assumed a considerable importance in the entertainment industry. Television as a medium lends itself to episodic repetition and most people would now be familiar with the kind of programme where the characters and the background situation are repeated, but each week's story content is different. While there can be no doubt that copyright would subsist in each particular individual performance, there has been much more controversy over whether or not the basic structural idea in the context of which each performance takes place, is itself capable of protection. Leaving aside for the moment the question of the existing form which must be established to satisfy the requirements of the Act, the initial question is whether or not an idea developed into an original continuing or repeated dramatic format, could be the subject of copyright protection. If the combination of material upon which the person seeking protection relies has a recognisable framework or structure and that framework is such as to impose a shape upon the other constituent parts of the show produced within it, then I should not have thought it contrary to principle to regard it as an original literary or dramatic work for the purposes of s 7 of the *Copyright Act 1962*. I do not think that a musical work which provides for ad libitum cadenzas or ornamentation which may be left to the taste or ability of the individual performer, would be any the less subject to copyright. That would no doubt be at one end of the spectrum. At the other, it would be difficult to contend a mere collection of unrelated features, even although some were repeated, could justify protection. That suggests that in the end the question is one of degree and it is a question which I think may be answered, at least for the purpose of this case, by considering whether or not there is a sufficient structure to be perceived in the series of shows ...

[21] The judge refers to "distinctive features" having been borrowed and imported into the New Zealand show. This recognises that there were features in common in both and undoubtedly there were, but the use of the term "distinctive" goes further than this. It carries the implication that those features were to some extent definitive or descriptive of the appellant's show and were certainly [22] associated with it. The judge considered that those features were copied from the English show and he considered that they made the New Zealand show readily identifiable with the appellant's show.

... In my view, on the findings of the Judge there was an established framework of the show *Opportunity Knocks* recognisable from the combination of repeated material identified and associated with the show and which justified copyright protection as a dramatic work.

Notes

[3.50] The notion that concepts and ideas are not protected means that directorial contributions generally do not possess sufficient material form to create rights in a literary or dramatic work. As noted in Chapter 2 at **[2.60]** the *Copyright Amendment (Director's Copyright)*

Bill 2005 creates a director's copyright with respect to a limited part of owner's rights concerning the retransmission statutory licence in Part VC of the Act. There is a proposal to extend this new ownership right to screenwriters as well as directors. However, as with the existing moral right for directors, the proposed new economic right attaches to the cinematographic film and does not affect entitlements to rights in the underlying literary or dramatic work.

The idea for a film or show at an early stage (that is, before there is any script in material form) may be regarded as confidential information. See *Fraser v Thames Television* [1983] 2 All ER 101; *Wilson v Broadcasting Corp of New Zealand* (1988) 12 IPR 173. Further copying of successful concepts may constitute passing off and deceptive conduct under s 52 of the *Trade Practices Act 1974* (Cth). See *Telstra Corporation Limited v Royal & Sun Alliance Insurance Australia Limited* [2003] 57 IPR 453.

Since the *Copyright Act 1968* (Cth) requires that a work be in a "material form" before being protected, issues of authorship could arise if the reporting of a speech or writing down of another's thoughts reduces those thoughts to material form, when this has not been done by the person supplying the intellectual content. Does such a transcription create an original work? In *Walter v Lane* [1900] AC 539 copyright was held to arise in the report of a speech written down in shorthand and transcribed, the reporter being the author. The *Copyright Act* at the time did not require originality as one of the criteria of copyright subsistence and the House of Lords could see no distinction between the labour of writing down a directory consisting of names and addresses (which would attract protection) and the labour of reproducing spoken words into writing or print. To some extent this is still relevant, if it is accepted that the sheer exercise of skill or labour may amount to an original work coming into existence. The question is probably whether or not sufficient skill has been demonstrated, or whether the person is a "mere amanuensis". It is possible that two or more people may combine to produce a physical embodiment of certain ideas resulting in them becoming joint authors. The question must be, therefore, where to draw the line between being a mere amanuensis and a contributor to the work.

Mere scribe or creator of original copyright work?

Cummins v Bond

[3.55] *Cummins v Bond* [1927] 1 Ch 167

[The plaintiff engaged in psychic research, acting as a spiritualist and medium at séances during which she practised automatic writing while in a trance state. The defendant was an architect who was interested in recent discoveries at the Abbey of Glastonbury, and automatic writings related to them. Séances with the defendant in attendance resulted in *The Chronicle of Cleophas*, which the plaintiff wrote in her automatic writing. The nature of the writing was archaic, of the 16th and 17th centuries. Cleophas is mentioned twice in the New Testament as one of the followers of Christ. A dispute arose as to the ownership of copyright in the *Chronicle*, the defendant claiming that the writings were addressed to him and inspired by his presence, or that they were not susceptible to copyright protection at all, being communicated in substance and form by a psychic agent.]

EVE J: **[172]** The issue in this action is reduced to the simple question who, if anyone, is the owner of the copyright of this work. Prima facie it is the author, and so far as this world is concerned there can be no doubt who is the author here, for it has been abundantly proved

■■■■■■ Cummins v Bond *continued*

that the plaintiff is the writer of every word to be found in this bundle of original script. But the plaintiff and her witness and the defendant are all of opinion and I do not doubt that the opinion is an honest one that the true originator of all that is to be found in these documents is some being no longer inhabiting this world, and who has been out of it for a length of time sufficient to justify the hope that he has no reasons for wishing to return to it.

According to the case put forward by those entertaining the opinion I have referred to the individual in question is particularly desirous of assisting in further discoveries relating to the ancient Abbey of Glastonbury, and he chooses the Brompton Road as the locality in which, and the plaintiff as the medium through whom, his views as to further works to be undertaken on the site of the Abbey shall be communicated to the persons engaged in the work of excavation. He is sufficiently considerate not to do so in language so antiquated as not to be understood by the excavators and others engaged in the interesting operations, but in order not to appear of too modern an epoch he selects a medium capable of translating his messages into language appropriate to a period some 16 or 17 centuries after his death. I am not impunging the honesty of persons who believe, and of the parties to this action who say that they believe, that this long departed being is the true source from which the [173] contents of these documents emanate; but I think I have stated enough with regard to the antiquity of the source and the language in which the communications are written to indicate that they could not have reached us in this form without the active co-operation of some agent competent to translate them from the language in which they were communicated to her into something more intelligible to persons of the present day. The plaintiff claims to be this agent and to possess, and the defendant admits that she does possess, some qualification enabling her, when in a more or less unconscious condition, to reproduce in language understandable by those who have the time and inclination to read it, information supplied to her from the source referred to in language with which the plaintiff has no acquaintance when fully awake.

From this it would almost seem as though the individual who has been dead and buried for some 1900 odd years and the plaintiff ought to be regarded as the joint authors and owners of the copyright, but inasmuch as I do not feel myself competent to make any declaration in his favour, and recognising as I do that I have no jurisdiction extending to the sphere in which he moves, I think I ought to confine myself when inquiring who is the author to individuals who were alive when the work first came into existence and to conditions which the legislature in 1911 may reasonably be presumed to have contemplated. So doing it would seem to be clear that the authorship rests with this lady, to whose gift of extremely rapid writing coupled with a peculiar ability to reproduce in archaic English matter communicated to her in some unknown tongue we owe the production of these documents. But the defendant disputes the plaintiff's right to be considered the sole author, alleging that he was an element and a necessary element in the production, and claiming, if the authorship is to be confined to persons resident in this world, that he is entitled to the rights incident to authorship jointly with the plaintiff.

In the course of the trial, after reading the correspondence, [174] and hearing the evidence of Miss Gibbes, I expressed an unfavourable opinion of the defendant's conduct in certain respects. For one thing he had at a very early stage of his acquaintance with that lady commenced to borrow money from her, and when at a later date he was called upon to repay the sums so borrowed he set up a wholly insupportable story that the moneys had been paid to him as a gift; and for another, when he was submitting a complicated agreement for the approval of the two ladies and inducing them to believe that he desired them to take legal advice thereon, he was at the same time urging a mutual friend to obtain their approval and

████ Cummins v Bond *continued*

execution of the same without taking any such advice. Since I expressed that unfavourable opinion I have seen and heard the defendant in the box, and although his conduct in the matters I have referred to cannot but be regarded as involving grave errors of judgment, I do not think he was actuated by the sordid motives which his conduct was certainly calculated to suggest. He is an individual upon whose memory little reliance can be placed, he is of an imaginative temperament and regards the alleged supernatural incidents connected with this work with a reverence that is almost fanatical, and he has, I think, in more than one incident shown that he is occasionally subject to hallucinations. His claim to be considered a joint author is suggestive of an hallucination, for it is based upon the assertion that by his presence at the séances where the writing took place he in some way transmitted from his brain to the unconscious brain of the medium the classical and historical references which are to be found in these documents. He frankly admits that he does not appreciate how it was done, or to what extent he did it; but he has evidently brought himself to believe that he did contribute materially to the composition of the work and that his contribution was made by means of some silent transfer from his brain to that of the unconscious medium of phrases and allusions with which he was familiar but of which she knew nothing. But inasmuch as the medium is credited with a power to translate language of which she knew nothing into archaic English, [175] of which she was almost equally ignorant, and at a phenomenal pace, it does not appear necessary to fall back on the defendant's presence in order to explain the classical and historical references which he maintains must have emanated from his brain. They may well have originated in the brain of the medium herself. In these circumstances I am quite unable to hold that the defendant has made out any case entitling him to be treated as a joint author. I think he is labouring under a complete delusion in thinking that he in any way contributed to the production of these documents.

Alternatively failing to establish any claim on his own behalf he submits that there is no copyright in the work at all, that it has come from a far off locality which I cannot specify, and that the plaintiff is the mere conduit pipe by which it has been conveyed to this world. I do not think that it is a fair appreciation of the plaintiff's activities, they obviously involved a great deal more than mere repetition; but, apart altogether from these considerations, the conclusion which the defendant invites me to come to in this submission involves the expression of an opinion I am not prepared to make, that the authorship and copyright rest with some one already domiciled on the other side of the inevitable river. That is a matter I must leave for solution by others more competent to decide it than I am. I can only look upon the matter as a terrestrial one, of the earth earthy, and I propose to deal with it on that footing. In my opinion the plaintiff has made out her case, and the copyright rests with her.

Upon the same footing it has been further contended on behalf of the defendant that an agreement was come to between him and the plaintiff under which he is beneficially interested in the copyright, or alternatively that the conduct of the plaintiff has been such as to estop her from denying that he has such an interest. In order to determine these questions the evidence and correspondence require some examination. [His Lordship proceeded to go through these in detail and concluded:] It is quite clear that no agreement was ever concluded, and I am quite unable to hold that the [176] plaintiff ever abandoned the position she took up in the latter part of the year 1925 or ever so conducted herself as to preclude her from insisting on the claims put forward in this action. Accordingly I hold she is entitled to the declaration for which she asks, that is to say, a declaration that she is the owner of the copyright in this work it must be identified in some way delivery up of such parts of the original manuscript as have not already been handed to her, and the defendant must pay

■■■■■■■ Cummins v Bond *continued*

the costs of the action. The counterclaim by which the defendant seeks a declaration that he is entitled to the copyright is dismissed with costs.

Order for the plaintiff.

■■

■ Other subject matter

[3.60] Subject matter other than works must also fulfil specific material form requirements: ss 22(3), (4), (5) and 24.

BY A QUALIFIED PERSON

[3.65] Works: s 32(1), (2), (4). Other subject matter: s 84.

There is provision for the making of original works at the direction of the Crown (Commonwealth or State) in which case copyright arises without the author needing to be a qualified person (s 176). Similar principles apply in regard to cinematograph films and sound recordings (s 178) and with respect to original works (s 187), or other subject matter (s 188), made or published by, or at the direction of, certain international organisations.

ORIGINALITY

[3.70] Although the *Copyright Act 1968* (Cth) does not require critical acclaim to attach to a literary, dramatic, musical or artistic work before protection will be afforded, s 32(1) requires that such a work be "original". To some extent the concept of what constitutes a "work" within the Act, and the concept of originality, are intertwined. It is difficult to discuss what amounts to a "work" without discussing originality, since without a sufficient degree of originality a "work" will not come into existence. There are general principles of "originality" which would seem to apply to all classes of works.

The requirement of originality for Part IV copyrights is implied rather than expressly required, in that copyright subsists for a period of 70 years after the expiration of the calendar year in which the first publication of a recording (s 93), or film (s 94) took place. The relevant term for broadcasts is 50 years after the year in which it took place (s 95). Rebroadcasts have the term limited to that of the first broadcast (s 95(2)). The term of copyright for a published edition of a work is 25 years from first publication (s 96).

■ Originating with the author

■ University of London Press v University Tutorial Press ■

[3.75] *University of London Press Ltd v University Tutorial Press Ltd* [1916] 2 Ch 601

PETERSON J [After stating the facts]: [608] The first question that is raised is, Are these examination papers subject to copyright? Section 1(1) of the *Copyright Act 1911* provides for copyright in "every original literary dramatic musical and artistic work", subject to certain conditions which for this purpose are immaterial, and the question is, therefore, whether these examination papers are, within the meaning of this Act, original literary works. Although a literary work is not defined in the Act, s 35 states what the phrase includes; the definition is not a completely comprehensive one, but the section is intended to show what, amongst other things, is included in the description "literary work", and the words are " 'Literary work' includes maps, charts, plans, tables and compilations". It may be difficult to define "literary work" as used in this Act, but it seems to be plain that it is not confined to "literary work" in the sense in which that phrase is applied, for instance, to Meredith's novels and the writings of Robert Louis Stevenson. In speaking of such writings as literary works, one thinks of the quality, the style, and the literary finish which they exhibit. Under the Act of 1842, which protected "books", many things which had no pretentions to literary style acquired copyright; for example, a list of registered bills of sale, a list of foxhounds and hunting days, and trade catalogues; and I see no ground for coming to the conclusion that the present Act was intended to curtail the rights of authors. In my view the words "literary work" cover work which is expressed in print or writing, irrespective of the question whether the quality or style is high. The word "literary" seems to be used in a sense somewhat similar to the use of the word "literature" in political or electioneering literature and refers to written or printed matter. Papers set by examiners are, in my opinion, "literary work" within the meaning of the present Act.

Assuming that they are "literary work", the question then is whether they are original. The word "original" does not in this connection mean that the work must be the expression of original or inventive thought. Copyright Acts are not concerned with the originality of ideas, but with the expression of thought, and, in the case of "literary work", with the expression of thought in print or writing. The originality which is required relates to the expression of the thought. But the Act does not require that the expression [609] must be in an original or novel form, but that the work must not be copied from another work that it should originate from the author. In the present case it was not suggested that any of the papers were copied. Professor Lodge and Mr Jackson proved that they had thought out the questions which they set, and that they made notes or memoranda for future questions and drew on those notes for the purposes of the questions which they set. The papers which they prepared originated from themselves, and were, within the meaning of the Act, original. It was said, however, that they drew upon the stock of knowledge common to mathematicians, and that the time spent in producing the questions was small. These cannot be tests for determining whether copyright exists. If an author, for purposes of copyright, must not draw on the stock of knowledge which is common to himself and others who are students of the same branch of learning, only those historians who discovered fresh historical facts could acquire copyright for their works. If time expended is to be the test, the rapidity of an author like Lord Byron in producing a short poem might be an impediment in the way of acquiring copyright, and, the completer his mastery of the his subject, the smaller would be the prospect of the author's success in maintaining his claim to copyright. Some of the questions, it was urged, are questions in book work, that is to say, questions set for the purpose of seeing whether the student has read and understood the books prescribed by the syllabus. But the questions set are not copied from the book; they are questions prepared by the examiner for the purpose of testing the student's acquaintance with the book, and in any case it was admitted that the papers involved selection, judgment, and experience. This objection has not, in my opinion, any substance; if it had, it would only apply to some of the questions in the elementary papers, and would have little, if any, bearing on the paper on advanced mathematics. Then it was said that the questions in the elementary papers were of a common type; but this only means that somewhat similar questions have been asked by other examiners. I suppose that most elementary books on mathematics may be said to be of a common type, but that fact would not give impunity to a predatory infringer. The book and the papers alike originate from the author and are not copied by him from another book or other papers. The objections with which I **[610]** have dealt do not appear to me to have any substance, and, after all, there remains the rough practical test that what is worth copying is prima facie worth protecting. In my judgment, then, the papers set by Professor Lodge and Mr Jackson are "original literary work" and proper subject for copyright under the Act of 1911.

■ The minimum level of originality

▬▬▬▬▬ Desktop Marketing Systems v Telstra ▬▬▬▬▬

[3.80] *Desktop Marketing Systems Pty Ltd v Telstra Corporation Limited* (2002) 119 FCR 491 Federal Court of Australia

SACKVILLE J: [comments on "originality"] **Subsistence of Copyright—Some preliminary points**

[572] The principal issue in this case concerns the "innovation threshold" which must be satisfied if a compilation of the names, addresses and telephone numbers of subscribers to a telephone service is to be accorded copyright protection: see S Ricketson, *The Law of Intellectual Property* (2001), at [7.35], citing a comment by Professor James Lahore. The resolution of this issue and the related question of infringement ultimately depends on the proper construction of the *Copyright Act* since, as noted earlier, copyright in Australia cannot subsist otherwise than by virtue of the Act: s 8. It is, however, difficult to approach the task of construction without reference to the older authorities which predate the passage of the first comprehensive copyright legislation, namely the *Copyright Act 1911* (UK) (the "1911 Act") declared to operate in Australia, subject to minor modifications, by the *Copyright Act 1912* (Cth) (the "1912 Act"). Indeed, the written and oral submissions on the appeal referred to numerous authorities decided both before and after 1911.

The earlier authorities may be important, especially if they have been followed or approved in more recent cases based on modern legislation. Telstra relied, for example, on the decisions of the House of Lords in *Walter v Lane* [1900] AC 539, upholding copyright in reporters' published records of speeches given by Lord Rosebery, and that of North J in *Collis v Cater Stoffell & Fortt Ltd* (1898) 78 LT 613, upholding copyright in a catalogue of medicines and other articles sold by a chemist. In *Sand McDougall Pty Ltd v Robinson* (1917) 23 CLR 49 Isaacs J (with whom Gavan Duffy and Rich JJ agreed) not only rejected the argument that the expression "original work" in s 1(1) of the 1911 Act implied inventive ingenuity, but stated that the principles stated by the House of Lords in *Walter v Lane* continued to apply to the new statutory regime (at 55). Similarly, the Court of Appeal in *Purefoy Engineering Co Ltd v Sykes Boxall & Co Ltd* (1955) 72 RPC 89 at 95, a decision post-dating the 1911 Act, remarked that *Collis v Cater* had never been doubted (see also *Ladbroke (Football) Ltd v William Hill (Football) Ltd* [1964] 1 WLR 273 at 278, per Lord Reid; at 287-288, per Lord Hodson; at 292, per Lord Pearce).

Even so, some caution is necessary when reading the earlier authorities. There are significant differences between the nineteenth century law of copyright and the more modern law. At the time the much-cited case of *Kelly v Morris* (1866) 1 LR Eq 697 was decided (upholding copyright in the "Post Office London Directory"), the legislation in the United

▨▨▨▨ Desktop Marketing Systems v Telstra *continued*

Kingdom made no explicit provision for a literary work to include a compilation. A provision to that effect was first introduced by s 35 of the 1911 Act. The reasoning in other cases depends, at least in part, on provisions that have no exact counterpart in modern legislation. In *Chilton v Progress Printing and Publishing Company* [1895] 2 Ch 29, for example, the Court of Appeal held that there was no copyright in a list of the plaintiff's selection of horses tipped to win at races to be held in the ensuing week. Lord Halsbury pointed out that the object of the *Literary Copyright Act 1842* (UK), as stated in the preamble, was "to afford greater encouragement to the production of literary works of lasting benefit to the world". That object was, in his Lordship's view (at 32), not served by regarding the plaintiff's opinion as to likely winners as a "literary composition [573] such as intended to be protected by the *Copyright Act*". The *Copyright Act* currently in force in Australia makes specific provision for copyright in compilations, but has no preamble or statement of objects corresponding to the provisions relied on by Lord Halsbury.

It is also important to bear in mind that copyright protection extends to many different kinds of work. Each particular category of copyright presents its own issues as to the subsistence and infringement of copyright. It ought not to be assumed that the concepts applicable to one form of copyright work necessarily apply, without modification, to others. In *Autospin (Oil Seals) Ltd v Beehive Spinning* [1995] RPC 683, the issue was whether the defendants, by manufacturing seals, had infringed the copyright in the plaintiff's drawings of seals and in a compilation of measurements included in the plaintiff's charts. Laddie J cautioned (at 700-701) against the assumption that the question of "substantial reproduction" must be decided without regard to the nature of the copyright work allegedly infringed:

> "When the court has to decide whether a particular act constitutes a substantial reproduction of a copyright work in my view it must have regard to the nature of the copyright work in issue. What amounts to a substantial reproduction of a particular type of artistic work may well not be a reproduction of a particular type of literary work. Indeed it should be remembered that the categories of copyright work created by copyright legislation are, in some cases, very broad and include materials which have little in common. Maps, charts and plans were protected as literary works under the 1911 Act but as artistic works under the 1956 and 1988 Acts. Therefore under the former Act they were treated as brethren to plays and novels while under the latter they are treated as being in the same category as paintings. ... When considering what amounts to infringement of the copyright in, say, a compilation, there is no compelling reason why the courts should pretend that the works covered by literary and artistic copyright form a coherent whole. It should be borne in mind that it is not enough to say that the defendant has 'used' the plaintiff's work. He must have **reproduced** it. In my view the court should ask the question 'is it accurate to say that the alleged infringer's article is, from a common sense point of view, a reproduction of this particular type of literary work?'" [emphasis added]

A similar point was made by an American commentator in relation to copyright in factual compilations (R C Denicola, "Copyright in Collections of Facts: A Theory for the Protection of Nonfiction Literary Works" (1981) 81 Colum L Rev 516 at 542):

> "the subject matter of copyright law is varied, and slogans and catchwords that produce rational results in one context cannot always be successfully transplanted to another. Non-fiction literary works pose a unique challenge. They heighten concern for access and dissemination, yet they underscore the necessity of preserving incentive."

▰▰▰▰ Desktop Marketing Systems v Telstra *continued*

As the present case demonstrates, policy tensions permeate the law of copyright, especially in the area of factual compilations. In *Skybase Nominees Pty Ltd v Fortuity Pty Ltd* (1996) 36 IPR 529, Hill J (with whom French J agreed) identified (at 531) the:

> "tension in policy between the monopoly rights which are conferred upon the owner of copyright in a literary, dramatic or artistic work on the one hand, and the freedom to express ideas or discuss facts on the other. [574] While there will be an infringement of the copyright of an owner in a literary, dramatic, musical or artistic work where there is a reproduction of that work or a substantial part of it, the fact that another work deals with the same ideas or discusses matters of fact also raised in the work in respect of which copyright is said to subsist will not, of itself, constitute an infringement. Were it otherwise, the copyright laws would be an impediment to free speech, rather than an encouragement of original expression."

It is this tension between "incentive and dissemination" (Denicola, supra, at 519) that underlies the difficulties raised by the present case. It also underlies the difficulty of distinguishing between expressions of ideas (which are the subject matter of copyright) and the ideas themselves (which, generally speaking, are not).

The Supreme Court of the United States pointed out in *Feist* that there is an "undeniable tension" between the "fundamental axiom" of copyright law, that no author may have copyright in the facts narrated (*Victoria Park Racing and Recreation Grounds Co Ltd v Taylor* (1937) 58 CLR 479 at 498, per Latham CJ), and the principle, enshrined in statute in Australia as elsewhere, that compilations of facts may be the subject matter of copyright. The present case provides a nice illustration. Since compilations, consisting exclusively of a record of facts, can be the subject matter of copyright, does it not follow that Telstra should be rewarded for its substantial investment of time and resources by being accorded copyright protection in the directory information recorded in the White Pages and Yellow Pages? And if that protection is to be meaningful, should it not protect Telstra not merely against a competitor who produces more or less identical publications, but also against one who uses Telstra's directory information to create a rather different commercial product? On the other hand, if Telstra is entitled to prevent use of its directory information by a competitor, regardless of whether the final product is structured and presented in the same way as the White Pages and the Yellow Pages, is this not, in effect, conferring copyright protection in respect of facts?

... [587] The *Copyright Act,* which came into force on 1 May 1969, did not make any significant changes to the provisions governing copyright in factual compilations. As I have noted, the legislation implemented many of the recommendations of the *Spicer Report*. The *Report* did not, however, specifically address the law relating to compilations, although it did include a section headed "Sporting Spectacles". Under that heading, the *Spicer Report* considered submissions from football bodies which had argued that copyright should exist in lists of players and the numbers allocated to them. The *Spicer Report* rejected the submission (at pars 483-484):

> "We are unable to see how copyright can be conferred merely in respect of the name of a player associated with his football number. It has been held that copyright may exist in various compilations such as an alphabetical list of railway stations, a list of railway stations, a list of fox-hounds and hunting dogs and lists of stock exchange prices and football fixtures. **In all these cases the question whether copyright exists depends to a large extent on the amount of labour, capital or skill expended in making the compilation. We think that the law in this regard should not be changed.**

▨▨▨▨ Desktop Marketing Systems v Telstra *continued*

It seems that the football clubs may have copyright in the lists they prepare as published in the various football publications (see *Football League Ltd v Littlewoods Pools Ltd* [1959] 3 WLR 42). Such copyright, however, does not prevent a person making his own list by attending a match." [emphasis added]

The *Spicer Report* seems to have taken the view that whether copyright existed in a compilation depended on the amount of labour, capital or skill expended in making the compilation and that the law in that respect should not be changed. ... **[591]**

The Berne Convention

Desktop argued that Australian law relating to originality should be construed in conformity with Australia's obligations under the *Berne Convention*. Although the contention was not developed at length, it appears to rest on art 2(5) of the *Berne Convention*, which provides as follows:

"Collections of literary or artistic works such as encyclopaedias and anthologies which, by reason of the selection and arrangement of their contents, constitute intellectual creations, shall be protected as such, without prejudice to the copyright in each of the works forming part of such collections."

Article 2(5) was introduced in its present form at the Brussels Conference of 1948 (and renumbered by the Paris Conference of 1971). It is true that art 2(5) refers to "intellectual creations". But, as Telstra pointed out, the *Berne Convention* prescribes only minimum standards in relation to copyright protection. As Professor Ricketson has observed (*The Berne Convention for the Protection of Literary and Artistic Works:* 1886-1986 (1987), p 303):

"Article 2(5), by definition, does not cover collections of subject matter that are not capable of attracting copyright protection, that is, because they are not literary or artistic works in their own right. Instances are the names and addresses in a telephone directory ... such collections of non-copyright material may involve selection and arrangement in the same degree as are required for collections of literary or artistic works, but there is no requirement to protect them under Article 2(5). **This, then, is a matter for national legislation. ...**" [emphasis added]

As I have noted, the requirement of originality was first introduced by statute into English law in 1911. At that time, the *Berne Convention* merely provided, in what was then art 2(2), that State parties were bound to protect "collections of different works". The 1909 *Gorell Report*, examined the extent to which English law was not in accord with the *Convention*. The *Gorell Report* did not, however, address the question of copyright in compilations. The legislation specifically dealt with the question of compilations only because of an amendment proposed by Lord Gorell himself.

It may be that the grant of copyright protection to compilations which are original in the sense accepted by the English and Australian authorities goes further than required by international law. But that does not place Australia in breach of its international obligations. Nor does the fact that Australian law goes further than the requirements of the *Berne Convention* justify modifying the law.

[532]

■■■■■ Desktop Marketing Systems v Telstra *continued*

LINDGREN J:

Conclusion on subsistence of copyright—The White Pages Directories and Yellow Pages Directories

While it is possible to distinguish particular cases on their facts, in my opinion the course of authority in England and Australia examined above supports the following propositions of relevance to the subsistence of copyright in compilations of factual information:

1. The concept of originality is correlative with that of authorship (*Sands & McDougall*).

2. Authorship (likewise originality) does not require novelty, inventiveness or creativity, whether of thought or expression, or any form of literary merit (cf *Walter v Lane; University of London Press; Sands & McDougall; Victoria Park; Ladbroke*).

3. Not all works, even literary works, are of the same kind and one must identify and keep in mind the particular kind of work within the Act in which copyright is claimed to exist—in the present case, a particular form of literary work, namely, a "compilation" (cf *Walter v Lane; Sands & McDougall*). (The Act's definition of "literary work" as including a "compilation" has made extended discussion of the meaning of "literary work" unnecessary, but it is noteworthy that the noun "work" has been defined to mean, in the word's relevant general sense, "A thing, structure or result produced by the operation, action, or labour of ... a person or other agent" (*OED*) and as "a product of exertion, labour, or activity" (of which an artistic, literary or musical work is given as an example) (*Macquarie*).)

4. It appears to be a necessary feature of a factual compilation that it supply "intelligible information" (cf *Real Estate Institute* discussed at [93], **[533]** *Canterbury Park* discussed at [101]-[102]; and cf *Exxon*). Accordingly, a totally random collection and listing of unrelated pieces of factual information would not be a compilation within the Act. (Apparently the position would be different if the compilation included a statement that it was a random selection, since that very statement would give the whole a significance it would otherwise lack.) A telephone directory satisfies the apparent requirement that a compilation convey a significance of its own which is independent of that of its component items considered individually and in isolation from one another. A telephone directory purports to be an alphabetical listing of particulars of all listable telephone subscribers within a given geographical area, and therefore to perform the function of providing access to the telephone number of every subscriber. It impliedly proclaims: "These are the names, addresses and telephone numbers of all listable subscribers within the stated geographical region, and if a name does not appear in its alphabetical position, there is no listable subscriber by that name".

5. One must apply the test of originality to the literary work, including a compilation, in which copyright is claimed to exist, as a whole, rather than dissecting it and applying the test to the individual parts (cf *Cambridge University Press; Ladbroke; Warwick Film; A-One*).

6. The test of originality is whether the work was not copied, but originated from the putative author (cf *Dicks v Yates; University of London Press; Mander v O'Brien; Victoria Park; Purefoy; Ladbroke; Ogden; Computer Edge; Kalamazoo; Erica Vale; Skybase; Harpur v Lambourne; Data Access*).

7. This test is not an "all or nothing" one but raises a question of fact and degree as to the extent of the putative author's contribution to the making of the particular literary work in question, in the present case, a compilation (cf *Macmillan v Cooper; Cramp; Ladbroke; Computer Edge; Interlego; Flanagan*). (In *Sampson v Brokensha and Shaw Ltd* (1935) 37 WALR 90 ("*Sampson*") it was decided that a person who merely bound into a book all the forms prescribed by a set of regulations did not have copyright in the compilation.)

8. For this purpose, no particular kind of antecedent work contributed by the putative author is, *a priori*, to be left out of account, except, perhaps, antecedent work which was undertaken for a purpose or purposes which did not include the making of the literary work at all (cf *Football League; Ladbroke; Mirror Newspapers; Autospin*).

9. It is not the law that where there is only one way of expressing and arranging a whole-of-universe factual compilation, the compilation cannot attract copyright protection (cf *Matthewson v Stockdale; Longman v Winchester; Kelly v Morris; Ibcos*).

10. Decisively for the present case, there is no principle that the labour and expense of collecting, verifying, recording and assembling (albeit routinely) data to be compiled are irrelevant to, or are incapable of themselves establishing, origination, and therefore originality; on the contrary, the authorities strongly suggest that labour of that kind may do so (cf *Matthewson v Stockdale; Longman v Winchester; Kelly v Morris; Scott v Stanford; Morris v Ashbee; Cox v Land and Water Journal Company; Morris v Wright; Hogg v Scott; Ager; Collis; Weatherby; ACP v Morgan; Autospin*; and the recent **[534]** Indian case, *Burlington's Home Shopping Ltd v Chibber* (1995) Patent & Trademark Cases 278 (noted in Pravin Anand, "*Burlington's Home Shopping Ltd v Chibber*" (1995) 6 Ent L Rev 159, in which the Delhi High Court, not following *Feist*, held that a computer database of mail order customers (names, addresses, telephone and fax numbers) was protected as a compilation within the definition of literary work).

To recognise copyright in compilations of factual data which do not involve selection or scope for variance in expression or arrangement may be seen, as a practical matter, to be an acceptance of the proposition that copyright can subsist in facts. No doubt policy reasons can be suggested for withholding, as for according, copyright protection in such cases. There are those who point to the advantages of permitting others to build on the first compiler's work, without first having to repeat that work independently. Others point out that to deny the first compiler copyright protection is to discourage research by would-be first compilers. The Act does not provide for the compulsory licensing of copyright for reasonable remuneration in aid of the commercial objectives of a would-be licensee. Accordingly, the situation in cases such as the present under Australian law is an "all or nothing" one.

Consideration has been given to some of the policy issues involved in Europe. In the United Kingdom the *Copyright and Rights in Databases Regulations 1997* (SI 1997 No 3022) ("the Regulations"), made pursuant to *Directive 96/9/EC of the European Parliament and Council of 11 March 1996 on the Legal Protection of Databases* ("the Directive"), has amended the definition of "literary work" in subs 3(1) of the 1988 UK Act by adding after the word "compilation", the words "other than a database", and including and dealing with databases as a special kind of literary work in their own right. A new s 3A of that Act defines "database" as:

"a collection of independent works, data or other materials which—
(a)   are arranged in a systematic or methodical way, and
(b)   are individually accessible by electronic or other means."

In *British Horseracing Board Ltd v William Hill Organization Ltd* (2001) 51 IPR 488, the parties agreed that the Regulations were to be construed consistently with the Directive and that, for the purpose of that proceeding, attention was to be paid only to the latter. By art 7(1) of the Directive, Member States undertook to provide:

"a right for the maker of a database which shows that there has been **qualitatively and/or quantitatively a substantial investment in either the obtaining, verification or presentation of the contents** to prevent extraction and/or re-utilization of the

▬▬▬ Desktop Marketing Systems v Telstra *continued*

whole or of a substantial part, evaluated qualitatively and/or quantitatively, of the contents of that database." [emphasis added]

Unlike its United Kingdom counterpart, the Commonwealth Parliament has not amended the legislation to give effect to a policy in respect of the issues raised by the present case.

The task of carefully identifying and listing all the units constituting a defined universe is usefully and commonly, undertaken. Moreover, alphabetical order is a common form of arrangement according to which such lists are made up. There are two special benefits offered by the compiler in such cases. The first is the assurance that the universe has been thoroughly explored, and that all members of it have been captured. "Whole-of-universe certification" gives value to the list. A compilation which can only profess to have captured [535] "nearly all" the members of a defined universe is not as valuable as one that can claim to have captured all of them. But whole-of-universe certification is a benefit only if the second special benefit to which I referred is also present: an intelligible arrangement of the data compiled. Who would want a telephone directory containing particulars of all subscribers listed randomly and therefore inaccessibly?

The making of accessible whole-of-universe compilations is arguably to be encouraged by the giving of copyright protection on account of the industrious collection, verification, recording and assembly necessarily undertaken for the purpose. But ultimately the weighing of the competing policy considerations is a matter for the legislature.

For reasons given above, and as a result of proposition (10) in [160], the First Issue should be resolved in favour of Telstra.

▬▬▬▬▬▬▬▬▬▬▬▬▬▬▬▬▬▬▬▬▬

■ Originality and selective copying

▬▬▬ A-One Accessory Imports v Off Road Imports ▬▬▬

[3.85] *A-One Accessory Imports Pty Ltd v Off Road Imports Pty Ltd* (1996) 65 FCR 478 Federal Court of Australia

DRUMMOND J: [470] ... The first applicant, in its statement of claim alleges that it is the owner of the copyright in a literary work comprising its 1991 motorcycle parts catalogue known as "A-One Parts", and that the respondents have infringed that copyright by producing the first respondent's 1993 parts [480] catalogue. A major issue for my decision is whether the applicants' 1991 catalogue is the product of copying of other catalogues, viz, the 1984 Phoenix Imports and the 1991 Link International catalogues and so cannot be an original work the subject of copyright.

... [487] In considering whether a compilation that wholly consists of or that includes existing material is itself an original work, the question is whether the compilation, looked at as an entity, is original: it is not proper to dissect the work into its parts, and by determining that the individual parts lack originality, to deny originality to the whole work. This issue is dealt with fully in *Ladbroke (Football) Ltd*, supra. The reason is that by s 32 of the Act, "copyright is a statutory right which ... would appear to subsist, if at all, in the literary or other work as one entity", per Lord Hodson at 285. See also *Ladbroke (Football) Ltd*, supra, at 276-277, 290 and 291.

▨▨▨▨▨ A-One Accessory Imports v Off Road Imports *continued*

... [I]t is clear that the effort expended by Rogers and Bennett in selecting the information to be used was directed to the preparation of a self-contained catalogue for use by A-One in its business, ie, an up-to-date, complete listing of information about sprockets for a wide range of motorcycles in service in Australia. Cf *Ladbroke (Football) Ltd*, supra, at 290 and 293.

Skill, judgment or labour expended in the process of copying a particular **[488]** work or portion of a particular work, as distinct from selecting material to be copied into a compilation, cannot confer originality; but even if the effort involved in producing a compilation is mostly devoted to copying another work or works, a relatively small alteration or addition quantitatively may suffice to convert that which is copied from an earlier work into a new and original work in which copyright will subsist. Whether it does or not is a question of degree having regard to the quality, rather than the quantity of the addition: *Interlego AG v Tyco Industries Inc* [1989] 1 AC 217 at 263.

[Note: For a consideration of the impact of infringement on the rights of the compilation owner see **[3.255]**.]

CATEGORIES OF WORKS

■ Literary works

[3.90] All manner of items have been regarded as literary works for copyright purposes, ranging from the original subject matter of copyright books, to computer selected numbers arranged in grid form (on a card published by a daily newspaper which enabled their readers to play a form of bingo): see *Express Newspapers Plc v Liverpool Daily Post & Echo Plc* [1985] FSR 306. Advertisements have not always but are now generally regarded as subject to copyright protection: see *O'Brien v Komesaroff* (1982) 41 ALR 255. The effect of the adjective "literary" in defining the types of original material in which copyright subsists would appear to be relevant possibly to the form in which the work appears, and the function it should perform.

The effect of this would seem to be that "literary" does not mean the work has to display any learning, but must simply amount to the exercise of sufficient effort, to effect a certain type of result. This result is the conveying of information, or perhaps instruction and pleasure in the form of literary enjoyment: *Exxon Corp v Exxon Insurance Consultants International Ltd* [1981] 2 All ER 495. In that case the invented word "Exxon" was not regarded as a literary work because:

> "It is a word which although invented and therefore original, has no meaning and suggests nothing in itself. To give it substance and meaning, it must be accompanied by other words or used in a particular context or juxtaposition. ... It is not in itself a title or distinguishing name and, as I have said, only takes on meaning or significance when actually used with other words. ..." (at 503 per Graham J).

The function of a literary work is to afford pleasure or instruction. Titles and single words from, for example, a poem or book are part of a "literary work" when embodied in the larger work, but questions of their protection by copyright when taken alone will revolve around whether such use amounts to taking a substantial part of the whole work so as to amount to an infringement: *Exxon* (at 504).

▓▓▓▓ Kalamazoo (Aust) v Compact Business Systems ▓▓▓▓

[3.95] *Kalamazoo (Aust) Pty Ltd v Compact Business Systems P/L* (1985) 84 FLR 101 Supreme Court of Queensland

THOMAS J: **[102]** The plaintiff company (Kalamazoo) claims that the defendant company (Compact Business Systems Pty Ltd) and its directors (Mr Crossley and Mr Spollen) have infringed the plaintiff's copyright in a number of business record systems. References to "the defendant" should be taken to refer to the defendant company unless otherwise indicated.

Six systems remain in issue, namely those described as:

(a) medical instant billing system;

(b) vertical payroll ten entry system;

(c) vertical payroll eighteen entry system;

(d) solicitors account system;

(e) real estate property **[103]** management and accounting system;

(f) combined purchases and cash payments system.

Although they have been described as "systems", the use of that term may be apt to mislead, especially as it is well known that there is no copyright in a system, method or idea. What is intended to be described by the plaintiff in each instance is a compilation of various blank accounting forms for intended use by customers in association with an apparatus known as a pegboard.

The plaintiff's forms were designed and published in combination with one another, and it is central to the plaintiff's case that they be viewed as a totality or single work. The plaintiff's counsel submits that copyright exists in the compilation of the various forms. Although conscious of the problems in use of the word "system", I shall use it in the sense relied on by the plaintiff, that is to say as referring to the group of documents upon which the plaintiff in each instance relies.

...

Pegboard systems

The pegboard holds the particular documents in certain positions in relation to one another by means of punched holes. The system, which is described as a "one-write" system, depends upon carbon or idem copies being made on the lower documents as an entry is written on the top document. General accounting systems of such kind have been in extensive use for many years, and there is evidence of application being made in the US for patent rights (no doubt in relation to the physical clamp-like apparatus and not in relation to the contents of the forms) as early as 1916.

To take the first-mentioned "medical instant billing system" as an example, there are three basic forms designed to be used within a single pegboard folder. Although given longer titles, the documents are respectively (from bottom to top) a journal page, a ledger page, and a receipt. When the patient pays for his service the appropriate part of the receipt is written out, and the headings and columns are so ordered that the same words and figures fill out the appropriate details in the underlying ledger and journal. The receipts are prepared in marginally overlapping bundles, so that as each one is torn off (and handed to the patient) the next one will be in the appropriate position one line further down in relation to the underlying documents. Thus the process is repeated until the underlying documents are sufficiently filled out, whereupon they are transferred to the appropriate loose-leaf journal or ledger. ... **[104]** ...

▨▨▨▨ Kalamazoo (Aust) v Compact Business Systems *continued*

Issues

The primary issue in the case is whether Kalamazoo is entitled to the copyright of the relevant systems. Kalamazoo claims that certain of its servants have spent considerable skill and care in the devising and drawing of the forms that comprise the systems, that they were the original works of such servants, and that as the employer of such persons it is entitled to such copyright as exists in such works. The defendants contended, inter alia, that the forms are insignificant variants of traditional accounting and bookkeeping forms, and that neither individually nor collectively are they original literary works under the *Copyright Act 1968*. ... **[120]** ...

Originality

The next vital question is whether such works were "original" literary works. ...

[124] ... If, as the defendants' counsel invited me to do, I looked piecemeal at various parts of the documents, it would be possible to say that such parts were either reproductions, paraphrases or minor variations of documents already in general use. Taken alone, the size of the page, the number of columns, the width of the column, the spacing of holes for the punch, the heading of a column, a direction or instruction, the use of the "one-write" system, and the provision of boxes which force the taking of the balance, are trivial variants of commonplace ideas and forms, or applications of a method to which copyright is not available. However, whilst I refuse to find that the authors showed great skill, I did find that their preparation required a degree of concentration, care, analysis, comparison, and a certain facility in using and adapting the altered forms to a composite "one-write" system. In each case, some awareness of contemporary developments and the marketability of such forms played a part in their creation. Looking at each system as expressed, there is sufficient originality of expression, shape and content to comprise an original literary work. Whilst the importance and ingenuity of much of the data on the forms was overstressed in evidence, I am satisfied that, as a whole, the documents are entitled to protection of copyright and that each one forms an integral part of a particular system.

Thus, on this piecemeal approach, there is nothing left justifying the protection of copyright. The present case is perhaps a good example of demarcation problems that afflict the law of intellectual property. The present "works" are partly diagramocatic, partly literary, and partly an apparatus designed for the use of customers. It presents problems in identifying work suitable for protection by copyright law as distinct from patent or design. But, in the end, I think that *Hollinrake's Case* must be distinguished. The documents have their own character, their own form of expression, and in a sense tell their own story to the user. Therefore, even though it is true that they form part of a tool or device, I do not think that this aspect of their character needs to be severed or disregarded when evaluating their literary and original qualities.

I acknowledge that it is central to my finding in favour of the existence of copyright that the documents be looked at compositely, and that the plaintiff's case gains (rather than loses) weight from the fact that they were prepared and intended for a utilitarian function. If these components should be viewed separately, then my conclusion is wrong because item by item there is negligible originality in the works.

Support for the need to look at the work as a whole may be found in *Ladbroke (Football) Ltd v William Hill (Football) Ltd*.

I conclude that each system comprised an original work.

[THOMAS J later discussed the concept of "literary work".]

■■■■■ Kalamazoo (Aust) v Compact Business Systems *continued*

Literary work

It is as well to repeat that the term "system" should be taken to refer to the respective groups of compatible documents upon which the plaintiff in each instance relies. The copyright asserted in the statement of claim is that of an original literary work, under s 32(2) of the *Copyright Act 1968*. ... **[118]** ... The relevant definition for present purposes is simply that "literary work" includes a written table or compilation. That in no way limits the ordinary meaning of the term, or the wide connotation given to it in decided cases. It will be noted that it expressly includes a compilation. Plaintiff's counsel submits that each particular group of forms is a compilation of such forms, pointing out that they are specifically designed for use in conjunction with one another, and that in each instance they are part of a cohesive system. They are a compilation just as much as if they were put together in the one book, which in a sense they are.

[119] ... Mr Cooper QC, for the defendants, submitted that a "literary work" requires, as a minimum, that information, instruction or pleasure in the form of literary enjoyment be conveyed. Reliance was placed upon *Exxon Corp v Exxon Insurance Ltd* [1981] 3 All ER 241; [1982] Ch 119 at 142-144. Courts have refrained from spelling out any particular degree of skill perceivable from the words of the publication, and it is clear that literary merit is irrelevant. The formulation in the *Exxon* case was not treated as definitive or exhaustive by the members of the Full Court of the Federal Court in *Apple Computer Inc v Computer Edge Pty Ltd* (1984) 53 ALR 225 at 234-235, 258-259. The approach taken in *Mirror Newspapers Ltd v Queensland Newspapers Pty Ltd* [1982] Qd R 305 at 307 and *Ladbroke (Football) Ltd v William Hill (Football) Ltd* [1964] 1 All ER 465; [1964] 1 WLR 273 at 285, seems to be inconsistent with the proposition derived from the *Exxon* case. In his valuable work *The Law of Intellectual Property*, Mr Ricketson considers the denial of copyright on such a ground to be an aspect of "insubstantiality", a problem which commonly arises in relation to titles of works, slogans, phrases and, sometimes, advertisements (paras 5.61-5.63). This is, I think, the true basis of the rejection of copyright for some works that obviously fail to provide information, instruction or pleasure.

The submission points out that the forms are in themselves meaningless, and that they acquire utility and meaning only by additions made by the user after sale. Whilst accepting the force of that submission, it is also apparent that there is intellectual input in the forms inasmuch as they are designed and presented in a way which will produce meaningful results for the user. A similar submission, that a newspaper bingo game lacked meaning and utility in isolation was rejected in *Mirror Newspapers Ltd v Queensland Newspapers Pty Ltd* (at 308). The submission alternatively described the forms as being concerned with well-known subject matter which, at best, could be set out in a limited way and in a limited number of combinations. The submission described the works as "obvious or commonplace", and suggested that copyright was being sought in the subject or method rather than in the expression. Reliance was placed upon *Kenrick & Co v Lawrence & Co* (1890) 25 QBD 99 at 103. That case concerned a voting form on which the publisher printed the representation of a hand holding a pencil in the act of completing a cross within a square. Wills J said, at 104:

> "The copyright must be confined to that which is special to the individual drawing over and above the idea in other words, the copyright is of the extremely limited character which I have endeavoured to describe. A square can only be drawn as a square, a cross can only be drawn as a cross, and for such purposes as the plaintiffs' drawing was intended to fulfil, there are scarcely more ways than one of drawing a pencil or the hand that holds it. If the particular arrangement of square, cross, hand, or pencil be relied upon it is nothing more than a claim of copyright for the subject, which in my opinion cannot possibly be supported."

████ Kalamazoo (Aust) v Compact Business Systems *continued*

The submission would be acceptable if the component parts of the forms were considered in isolation. But the present case is, in my view, distinguishable. The forms and the systems, if viewed as a whole, are not so commonplace that they cannot be presented in more that one way. Indeed, the evidence in the case indicates that such forms can be and have been presented in [120] different ways, and no doubt will continue to be presented in different ways from time to time, according to the needs of business and professional communities from time to time.

I therefore conclude that each of the systems was a literary work.

Note

[3.100] It should be noted that the *Copyright Act 1968* (Cth) provides, in s 22(2), that a literary work can subsist in a non-written form. For instance, sounds embodied in an article or thing may constitute the material form of a literary work (inter alia). Therefore, a film or sound recording may have a "literary work" copyright as well as copyright protection as subject matter other than a work.

■ Computer programs as literary works

[3.105] Internationally, copyright is the preferred vehicle for protecting the intellectual property in computer software. The *Copyright Act 1968* (Cth) defines a computer program as "a set of statements or instructions to be used directly or indirectly in a computer in order to bring about a certain result". The protection of computer programs in Australian copyright law came about following a High Court decision to the effect that computer programs were not literary works (or any other sort of subject matter known to copyright law) and could be copied with impunity. In *Apple Computer Inc v Computer Edge Pty Ltd* (1983) ATPR 40-421 it was held that computer programs in source code and object code were not literary works within the *Copyright Act 1968* (Cth) because they did not afford information, pleasure or instruction but merely drove a machine, that is, controlled the sequence of operations carried out by a computer, without performing those other functions. This was reversed on appeal to the Full Federal Court: *Apple Computer Inc v Computer Edge Pty Ltd* (1984) 53 ALR 225. On appeal, it was held that the source code was copyright as a literary work and the object code was an adaptation thereof within s 31(1)(a)(vi) of the *Copyright Act 1968* (Cth) since it could be viewed as a translation. The source code conveyed a meaning to suitably trained people and there is a distinction between the functioning of the machine due to electro-magnetic functions and the computer program itself which contained instructions for the storage and reproduction of knowledge: *Apple Computer Inc v Computer Edge Pty Ltd* (1984) 2 IPR 1 at 11.

The High Court, by a majority, restored the judgment of the trial judge. The majority held that the object code was not a literary work because, although original, they "were not visible or otherwise perceptible, and they were not, and were not intended to be, capable by themselves of conveying a meaning which could be understood by human beings" (Gibbs CJ).

Gibbs CJ, Mason, Wilson and Brennan JJ, held that Apple source codes were literary works within s 32.

The decision led to consternation in the software industry, and in 1984, following a national symposium, computer software was hastily given the status of "literary work" by amending the legislation.

The 1984 definition has achieved unexpected longevity and was subjected to fairly minor amendments as part of the "Digital Agenda" amendments in 2001. Those amendments also introduced ss 47AB-47H to the *Copyright Act 1968* (Cth), dealing with the issue of decompilation for the purposes of interoperability. The *Data Access* case (following) discusses the meaning of "computer program". However, the case was the subject of submissions to a review committee set up to examine problems arising out of intellectual property law which may need to be addressed in order to enhance the effectiveness of the law for users of the copyright system. The main problem remaining from the High Court's deliberations is the finding that the compression table could be a literary work.

▬▬▬ Data Access v Powerflex Services ▬▬▬

[3.110] *Data Access Corporation v Powerflex Services Pty Ltd* (1999) 202 CLR 1 High Court of Australia

GLEESON CJ, McHUGH, GUMMOW AND HAYNE JJ: Pursuant to the grant of special leave to appeal, Data **[9]** Access Corporation (Data Access) appeals to this Court against orders of the Full Court of the Federal Court (Black CJ, Hill and Sundberg JJ) which were based on a holding that copyright as original literary works did not subsist in commands in the Dataflex computer language contained in a computer program developed by Data Access in the US. The Full Court, reversing the judgment of the trial judge, Jenkinson J, held that those commands were not "computer programs" within the meaning of the definition in s 10 of the *Copyright Act 1968* (Cth) (the Act) and were not entitled to protection under that statute.

The provisions of the Act apply to the proceedings because, although Dataflex appears first to have been published in the US, the international arrangements implemented by s 184(1)(a) of the Act and by reg 4(1) of the *Copyright (International Protection) Regulations* (Cth) treat Dataflex as if it had been first published in Australia.

... **[12]** ...

The Dataflex system

Development of the Dataflex application development system commenced in 1979, and it was first published in 1981. Dataflex has been the subject of 18 revisions since that time, is well known, and has achieved a significant share of the market for programs of its kind. It is a system which allows a programmer or developer to develop customised database applications or databases.

...

Mr Cory Casanave, Executive Vice-President of Data Access, gave evidence as to the nature of the language used in computer programs. He said:

"A computer language defines the names of each word in the language and the rules governing the use of each word (syntax). Each word in a computer language is an instruction to the computer to invoke lower level processes, the word chosen to invoke those processes is generally chosen to suggest the nature of the process that will be invoked.

A computer language is comprised of a set of reserved words which are used in accordance with the rules of syntax governing their use. A computer language syntax, like the syntax of a human **[13]** language, comprises the rules by which the words can be combined to form statements which are correct for the language. For each command or function there is a specific syntax which describes how arguments may be applied to the command. Arguments can be likened to a noun phrase, they describe what the command will act on. Various documents also refer to 'functions' as well as commands. Functions are a type of command which perform a computation and return a result."

Two hundred and fifty-four words of the Dataflex language are listed in the Dataflex encyclopedia. However, 29 of those words, which express commands for developing graphics, are not used at all in the PFXplus language. Of the other 225, 192 are used in the PFXplus language in a way which eventually causes the computer to perform the same function as those words perform in the Dataflex language.

At first instance, the reasons of Jenkinson J suggest that he considered that copyright subsisted in each of these 192 common words and that the use of them in PFXplus infringed Data Access' copyright in them. However, the orders made by his Honour restrain the use of only 169 of the common words, three of which are "Macros". It may be that, after judgment but before the orders were made, Data Access conceded that the remaining 23 words (which include words such as "SHOW" and "ENTRY") were not protected by copyright. Perhaps a concession was made during argument and, in a complex case, overlooked when the reasons for judgment were being prepared. But whatever the reason for not dealing with these 23 words, the issue of copyright in this Court is confined to the 169 words the subject of the order made by his Honour.

We will deal with the three "Macros" separately from the remaining 166 common words which can conveniently be called the "Reserved Words". Of these Reserved Words, at least 55 are unique to the Dataflex program. But many are ordinary English words—such as "BOX", "CHART", and "RETAIN". Others are a combination of two English words such as "PAGEBREAK". Some are not only common English words but are used in most, if not all, computer programs. Examples are "DIRECTORY" and "SAVE".

The PFXplus system

Some years ago, the third respondent, Dr David Bennett (Dr Bennett), became familiar with the Dataflex system. He decided to create and market an application development system which would be compatible with the Dataflex language and the Dataflex database file [14] structure so that persons who were familiar with the Dataflex system would be able to use his new product.

The Full Court of the Federal Court found the following facts to be common ground between the parties to the appeal:

- by a process of reverse engineering and study of both the documentation and operation of the Dataflex system, Dr Bennett created a system of computer programs, which was originally known as "Powerflex", but is now known as "PFXplus", intending that the system would be compatible with the Dataflex system, ie that certain commands and "reserved words" (including the Macros) used as commands in the Dataflex system would operate in like manner in the PFXplus system;
- the source code in which the Dataflex system is written is quite different from the source code in which the PFXplus system is written; and
- there is not necessarily any similarity between the object code used in the Dataflex system and that used in the PFXplus system.

PFXplus achieved Dr Bennett's aim of being highly compatible with Dataflex. Dr Bennett and his wife subsequently incorporated a company, the second respondent, to sell PFXplus.

▬▬▬▬ Data Access v Powerflex Services *continued*

The issues

The only allegations of copyright infringement that are now in issue are the claims that by publishing PFXplus the respondents have infringed the copyright which Data Access has in:

A. The Reserved Words.

B. The Macros.

C. The Dataflex Huffman compression table, to which reference will later be made.

A. *The Reserved Words*

...

1. Is each of the Reserved Words a "computer program" within the meaning of s 10(1) of the Act?

The appellant contends that each of the Reserved Words is itself a "computer program" within the meaning of the definition in s 10(1) **[15]** of the Act. In order to determine the validity of the appellant's submissions, it is convenient to divide the definition of "computer program" into its component parts.

The definition of "computer program" requires that each Reserved Word be:

(i)   "an expression";

(ii) "in any language, code or notation";

(iii) "of a set of instructions (whether with or without related information)";

(iv) "intended, either directly or after either or both of the following:

(a)   conversion to another language, code or notation;

(b)   reproduction in a different material form;

to cause";

(v)   "a device having digital information processing capabilities to perform a particular function."

Each of the first four of these elements qualifies what follows and the scope of the definition is marked out by the requirement of an intention that the device be caused "to perform a particular function". In form, the definition of a computer program seems to have more in common with the subject matter of a patent than a copyright. Inventions when formulated as a manner of new manufacture traditionally fell within the province of patent law, with the scope of the monopoly protection being fixed by the terms of a public document, the patent specification. In Australia claims to computer programs which are novel, not obvious and otherwise satisfy the *Patents Act 1990* (Cth) and which have the effect of controlling computers to operate in a particular way, have been held to be proper subject matter for letters patent, as "achieving an end result which is an artificially created state of affairs of utility in the field of economic endeavour", within the meaning of *National Research Development Corporation v Commissioner of Patents*.

The amendment of the definition of "literary work"' in s 10(1) of the Act to include as item (b) "a computer program or compilation of computer programs" obviously marked a significant departure from what previously had been the understanding of what was required for subsistence of copyright in an original literary work. It is true that copyright may subsist in a literary work which is related to the exercise of mechanical functions. A set of written instructions for the assembly and operation of a domestic appliance is an example. However, it is not to the point in copyright law that, if followed, the instructions do not cause the appliance to function. The protection of the function performed by the appliance will be for the patent law, including the law as to inutility. This is what was indicated by Bradley J in a passage in *Baker v Selden* which was repeated by Brennan J in *Computer Edge*. Bradley J said that no one would contend that the exclusive right to the manner of manufacture **[16]**

▓▓▓▓ Data Access v Powerflex Services *continued*

described in a treatise would be given by the subsistence of copyright in that work, and continued:

> "The copyright of the book, if not pirated from other works, would be valid without regard to the novelty, or want of novelty, of its subject-matter. ... To give to the author of the book an exclusive property in the art described therein, when no examination of its novelty has ever been officially made, would be a surprise and a fraud upon the public. That is the province of letters-patent, not of copyright."

Further, the requirement in copyright law that a work be "original" is to be distinguished from the requirements that an alleged invention be novel and that it not be obvious. The question for copyright law is whether "the work emanates from the person claiming to be its author, in the sense that he has originated it or brought it into existence and has not copied it from another". If so, the work does not lack originality because of the anterior independent work of another, although, in such circumstances, an invention might lack novelty.

Finally, to say that the copyright law does not protect function and extends only to the expression of systems or methods does not deny that a work may serve utilitarian rather than aesthetic ends. A map and a recipe book are obvious examples.

There is, with respect, some oversimplification of these principles in the following statement by Dawson J in *Autodesk Inc v Dyason* (*Autodesk No 1*):

> "[W]hen the expression of an idea is inseparable from its function, it forms part of the idea and is not entitled to the protection of copyright".

The 1984 amendment departed from traditional principles by identifying for copyright purposes a species of literary work, the very subsistence of which requires an expression of a set of instructions intended to cause a device to perform a particular function. The difficulties which arise from accommodating computer technology protection to principles of copyright law have been remarked upon but the Act now expressly requires such an accommodation.

... [17] ...

In our opinion, none of the Reserved Words satisfies the statutory definition. Each Reserved Word is undoubtedly in "code or notation"—the Dataflex language. It follows that whether a Reserved Word is a "computer program" within the meaning of the definition depends on whether it is an "expression ... of a set of instructions ... intended ... to cause a device having digital information processing capabilities to perform a particular function". However, each of the Reserved Words is a single word; none is a set of instructions in the Dataflex language. Further, none of the Reserved Words intends to express, directly or indirectly, an algorithmic or logical relationship between the function desired to be performed and the physical capabilities of the "device having digital information processing capabilities".

... [20] ...

The relevant "set of instructions" executed by a computer

As the Full Court pointed out:

> "A computer system consists of hardware and software. The hardware includes a central processing unit which contains the electronic circuits which control the computer and perform the relatively simple arithmetical calculations and logical operations (ie comparing values to determine which is larger) of which the computer is capable. It is because the computer is able to perform millions of such operations each second that computers may be used to perform extremely complex calculations and functions."

████ Data Access v Powerflex Services *continued*

It is impossible to overemphasise the importance of the fact that a computer has no "intelligence" to execute instructions over and beyond the simple logical functions which are hard wired into its circuits. In order for the simple logical functions of a computer to translate into a useful result, it is necessary to express complex problems in terms of a sequence of a large number of these simple operations. A "set of instructions" will not cause a computer to execute a particular function unless that set of instructions can be ultimately expressed in terms of a sequence of the logical operations which are hard wired into the computer. No doubt it is very rare to express a complex computer program in terms of the simple logical operations [21] which are hard wired into a computer. That is because the process of writing programs becomes practically unmanageable unless the "set of instructions" is perceived at a high level of abstraction. Such a level of abstraction is required in order to express what are millions of simple logical operations in terms of a manageable number of more complex instructions which themselves are reducible to these simple logical operations.

An example of, and a commentary upon, the varying levels of abstraction at which a set of instructions can be viewed is given by Mr Prescott QC in "Copyright and microcomputers—Some current legal problems". Suppose we wished to write a computer program in a high level language such as BASIC to cause a "device having digital information processing capabilities" to perform the "particular function" of printing the character "*" in the middle position on the screen. The relevant set of instructions could be stated shortly and clearly in BASIC as follows:

```
10 PRINT @ 544 '*'
20 GOTO 20
```

If we view this set of instructions at a lower level of abstraction, in a lower level language known as Z-80 assembly language, however, the set of instructions would be:

```
ORG 7D00H
LD A,42
LD (3E20H),A
LOOP JP LOOP
END 7D00H
```

The following programming comments provide a description of the Z-80 commands in terms of the corresponding actions of the microprocessor:

ORG 7D00H	Assemble program to start at address 7D00H
LD A,42	Load 42 (=ASCII for "*") into the A-register
LD (3E20H),A	Copy contents to address 3E20H (=screen centre)
LOOP JP LOOP	Keep jumping to the address "LOOP" ad infinitum, ie wait
END 7D00H	Entry point

If we express the same "set of instructions" in object code, which is at a still lower level of abstraction and expresses the contents of [22] various "addresses" or "memory locations" in hexadecimal notation, the language would be:

Address	Contents
7D00	3E2A
7D02	32203E
7D05C3057D	

The object code, being at a low level of abstraction, is quite a close representation of the physical reality of what is occurring in the computer. Each address location is a label for a

■■■■■ Data Access v Powerflex Services *continued*

particular group of circuits in the computer. The hexadecimal number which sets out the content of the address expresses a binary number in hexadecimal notation. Each hexadecimal character 0-9 and A-F is the representation of a four-bit binary number in the range 0000 to 1111. The 0's and 1's themselves are a representation of the absence or presence, respectively, of electrical impulses in that circuit. The logic functions which are hard wired into the computer operate on these electrical impulses to eventually produce the result of printing an asterisk on the screen.

In practice, when the above set of instructions in BASIC is typed into a computer, a separate program known as a compiler program reads the instruction "PRINT". It recognises that this is a command to invoke a program in object code which provides the computer with a set of electrical impulses to feed into its hard wired logic functions which will have the effect of printing a character on the screen. The choice of the word "PRINT" in BASIC is arbitrary in the sense that it would be possible to change the BASIC compiler program so that the typing of the word "TYPE" caused the same program in object code to be invoked as had been previously invoked for the word "PRINT".

No doubt, at the highest level of abstraction, the word "PRINT" is an expression of *an instruction* which is intended to cause a device having digital information processing capabilities to perform a particular function. Thus, at the highest level of abstraction, each of the Reserved Words in Dataflex may likewise be regarded as an expression of *an instruction* which is intended to cause a device having digital information processing capabilities to perform a particular function.

However, the appellant must show that each Reserved Word is an "expression, in any language, code or notation, *of a set of instructions* ... intended, either directly or after ... conversion to another language, code or notation ... to cause a device having digital information processing capabilities to perform a particular function".

... [23] ...

Two competing interpretations of "computer program"
... [24] ...

The meaning of the phrase "expression ... of a set of instructions" was referred to in the Explanatory Memorandum to the *Copyright Amendment Bill 1984*:

> "The phrase 'expression ... of a set of instructions' is intended to make clear that it is not an abstract idea, algorithm or mathematical principle which is protected but rather a particular expression of that abstraction. The word 'set' indicates that the instructions are related to one another rather than being a mere collection."

It is the particular selection, ordering, combination and arrangement of instructions within a computer program which provide its expression. A computer program in a particular language may be relatively inefficient because it uses many instructions to achieve the function that a single instruction could achieve. A computer program in a particular language may also operate relatively inefficiently because of the way it is structured, in terms of the ordering of the instructions and the sequence in which they are executed. Considerations of efficiency are largely a function of the particular language which is used. It is the skill of the programmer in a particular language which determines the expression of the program in that language.

... [26] ...

In our opinion, whether what is claimed to be a "computer program" is an "expression ... of a set of instructions ... intended ... to cause a device having digital information processing capabilities to perform a particular function" must be answered separately for each language in which the item in question is said to be a computer program.

Moreover, something is not a "computer program" within the meaning of the definition in s 10(1) unless it intends to express, either directly or indirectly, an algorithmic or logical relationship between the function desired to be performed and the physical capabilities of the "device having digital information processing capabilities". Thus, in the sense employed by the definition, a program in object code causes a device to perform a particular function "directly" when executed. A program in source code does so "after … conversion to another language, code or notation".

Some support, by way of analogy, may be derived from considering the position in the US. In *Baystate Technologies Inc v Bentley Systems Inc*, it was held that whilst the computer program comprising "CADKEY" was protected, the particular "data structures" [27] with which the case was concerned "[did] not bring about any result on their own", so that they were protected, if at all, only as part of the whole computer program. This was because, as was later expressed in the judgment: "a computer cannot read data structures and perform any function".

Once these principles are applied to each Reserved Word in the Dataflex language, it is clear that they are not "computer programs". Each Reserved Word comprises but a single instruction in that language. Each Reserved Word, considered alone, is not a "set of instructions" in that language. It is not a "computer program" expressed in the Dataflex language.

Meaning and syntax

There remains to be addressed the further argument of the appellant that the relevant set of instructions at the level of the Dataflex language is the "meaning and syntax of the word or command in question". In response to questions from members of this Court during the argument of the appeal, counsel for the appellant was asked on a number of occasions to identify the relevant "set of instructions". His answer was that it was the "meaning and syntax of the word or command in question".

However, the function which will be executed by a particular Reserved Word depends entirely on the source code underlying the Reserved Word. Thus, its "meaning" depends on the source code underlying it. This is also the case with the "syntax". There are, of course, grammatical and syntactical rules for the use of the Reserved Words. These rules would be written in the source code underlying the Dataflex commands. Equivalent rules would be written in the source code underlying the PFXplus commands. The meaning of the Reserved Words, and the grammatical and syntactical rules for their use, are not an "expression" until they are reduced to the underlying source code. However, the appellant does not, and could not, contend that Dr Bennett's source code expression of the meaning of commands or of the grammatical and syntactical rules in PFXplus is a reproduction of the source code expression of those meanings or rules in the Dataflex language. There was a finding that the source code of PFXplus was dissimilar to the source code of Dataflex. … [29] …

2. Is the collocation of the Reserved Words a computer program?

Furthermore, the collocation of the Reserved Words is not a "computer program". Although the Reserved Words together form "an expression … of a set of instructions", their simple listing together, without more, does not cause a computer to perform any identifiable function. There is no interrelationship of the instructions with one another which is an expression of a logical or algorithmic relationship between an identifiable function and the physical capabilities of the computer via the medium of the Dataflex language.

It is no answer that there is a set of instructions with a single identifiable function in that it provides a programmer with the vocabulary to enable him or her to program in the Dataflex language. As in the case of each individual Reserved Word, this is a function which the author of the Reserved Words intended them to perform in relation to the user, not in relation to the computer. As we have indicated, the definition of a "computer program" requires that the set of instructions be intended to cause the computer to perform a particular function.

3. Does the collocation of the Reserved Words form a substantial part of a literary work (the Dataflex system)?

The Dataflex system is a computer program. Hence it is a literary work for the purpose of the Act. The appellant contends that the collocation of Reserved Words, even if it is not itself a literary work, constitutes a substantial part of the Dataflex system. Section 14(1)(b) of the Act provides that in the Act "a reference to a reproduction ... [30] of a work shall be read as including a reference to a reproduction ... of a substantial part of the work". A copyright owner's exclusive right to reproduce a work is therefore infringed if another person reproduces a "substantial part" of the work.

In *Autodesk No 1*, this Court held that it was not necessary that the reproduction of a substantial part of a computer program should itself be a computer program. Relying on that reasoning, the appellant contends that its copyright is infringed because the collocation of Reserved Words is a substantial part of the Dataflex system.

Substantiality

... [32] ... In *Autodesk No 2*, Mason CJ ... thought that the judgment in *Autodesk No 1* should be reopened in order to hear the respondent's argument as to whether the look-up table was a substantial part of Widget C. Mason CJ said:

> "It is clear that the phrase 'substantial part' refers to the quality of what is taken rather than the quantity. In *Ladbroke (Football) Ltd v William Hill (Football) Ltd*, Lord Pearce stated:
>
>> 'Whether a part is substantial must be decided by its quality rather than its quantity. The reproduction of a part which by itself has no originality will not normally be a substantial part of the copyright and therefore will not be protected. For that which would not attract copyright except by reason of its collocation will, when robbed of that collocation, not be a substantial part of the copyright and therefore the courts will not hold its reproduction to be an infringement. It is this, I think, which is meant by one or two judicial observations that "there is no copyright" in some unoriginal part of a whole that is copyright.'
>
> As this statement makes clear, in determining whether the quality of what is taken makes it a 'substantial part' of the copyright work, it is important to inquire into the importance which the taken portion bears in relation to the work as a whole: is it an 'essential' or 'material' part of the work?
>
>> In this case, it is argued by the appellants that such an inquiry compels an affirmative answer as the look-up table is essential to the operation of the AutoCAD locking mechanism. Such an argument, however, misconceives the true nature of the inquiry and seeks to reintroduce by another avenue an emphasis upon the copyright work's function. True it is that the look-up table is essential to the functioning of the AutoCAD lock. However, in the context of copyright law, where emphasis is to be placed upon the 'originality' of the work's expression, the essential or material [33] features of a work should be ascertained by considering

▬▬▬▬▬ Data Access v Powerflex Services *continued*

> the originality of the part allegedly taken. This is particularly important in the case of functional works, such as a computer program, or any works which do not attract protection as ends in themselves (eg, novels, films, dramatic works) but as means to an end (eg, compilations, tables, logos and devices)."

There is great force in the criticism that the "but for" essentiality test which is effectively invoked by the majority in *Autodesk No 2* is not practicable as a test for determining whether something which appears in a computer program is a substantial part of it. For that reason, we prefer Mason CJ's opinion that, in determining whether something is a reproduction of a substantial part of a computer program, the "essential or material features of [the computer program] should be ascertained by considering the originality of the part allegedly taken". [33]

In order for an item in a particular language to be a computer program, it must intend to express, either directly or indirectly, an algorithmic or logical relationship between the function desired to be performed and the physical capabilities of the "device having digital information processing capabilities". It follows that the originality of what was allegedly taken from a computer program must be assessed with respect to the originality with which it expresses that algorithmic or logical relationship or part thereof. The structure of what was allegedly taken, its choice of commands, and its combination and sequencing of commands, when compared, at the same level of abstraction, with the original, would all be relevant to this inquiry.

That being so, a person who does no more than reproduce those parts of a program which are "data" or "related information" and which are irrelevant to its structure, choice of commands and combination and sequencing of commands will be unlikely to have reproduced a substantial part of the computer program. We say "unlikely" and not "impossible" because it is conceivable that the data, considered alone, could be sufficiently original to be a substantial part of the computer program.

...

Substantiality and the collocation of the Reserved Words

[34] As they appear in the source code of the Dataflex system, the Reserved Words are irrelevant to the structure, choice of commands and combination and sequencing of the commands in source code. They are merely literal strings which, from the computer's perspective, could be replaced by any other literal string. Accordingly, they are not a substantial part of the Dataflex program as it appears in source code unless they have their own inherent originality.

In our opinion, even when the Reserved Words are considered as a collocation, they do not possess sufficient originality as data to constitute a substantial part of the computer program which is the Dataflex system.

4. Does copyright subsist in the table or compilation of the Reserved Words in the Dataflex User's Guide?

The Reserved Words are contained in the Dataflex User's Guide. The appellant did not submit that any of the Reserved Words [35] themselves were traditional literary works protected by copyright, no doubt because they would face significant hurdles in the form of originality and substantiality. Given that the Reserved Words are arranged in alphabetical order in the Dataflex User's Guide, very little skill or labour was involved in compiling the Reserved Words in the form in which they appear in the User's Guide over and above the sum of the skill and labour involved in devising each individual Reserved Word. As the Full Court said:

"This is not a case where disconnected words are used in a particular order so that the order becomes the linchpin for copyright."

Furthermore, as we have already said, each of the Reserved Words is suggestive of the function it performs. In many cases, it is an ordinary English word, or a concatenation of two or more ordinary English words.

Even if the skill and labour involved in devising each individual Reserved Word is combined and consideration given to the total skill and labour, there may still be a real question as to whether there is sufficient originality for copyright to subsist in the combination. This is so even allowing for the inclusion in the definition of para (b) of "literary work" of a "compilation of computer programs".

The totality of the Reserved Words cannot be protected as a "compilation" within the definition because it requires a "compilation of computer programs" and the Reserved Words are not themselves programs. This does not necessarily preclude them together from protection as constituting a single program, but the set of instructions said to constitute such a program would still require identification. For the reasons leading to the conclusion that each of the Reserved Words does not constitute programs, a collection thereof does not constitute a program. The English letters which make them up are never at any stage executed by the computer. They are not instructions. They never cause a computer to perform a function. Their totality might be considered a "set", but of labels or data, rather than of instructions as required by the definition.

In any event, even if copyright does subsist in the table or compilation of the Reserved Words, we do not think that the respondents have infringed this copyright. The Reserved Words appear in the PFXplus source code program not as an alphabetical list, but as literal strings to which certain commands are assigned. [36]

B. The Macros

The appellant also contends that copyright subsists in what are referred to as "Macros". It contends that each of these commands is a "computer program" within the statutory definition and that Dr Bennett made an adaptation of the Dataflex Macro commands. Consequently, it submits that Dr Bennett infringed the appellant's copyright in them.

Three particular commands in the Dataflex language, "REPORT", "ENTERGROUP" and "ENTER", are described as "Macros" because they cause the performance of a more complex function than any of the other Reserved Words. Executing a Macro command causes a sequence of other functions to be executed, so that the overall effect of performing a more complex function is achieved.

Are the macros computer programs in Dataflex?

It follows from the nature of a "computer program" as defined in s 10(1) of the Act that the words assigned to the Macros, comprising as they do one instruction in the Dataflex language, cannot qualify as a "computer program". However, the underlying source code of each Macro may qualify as a "computer program". In practice, the source code underlying each Macro is a small fragment of the source code of the overall Dataflex computer program (the relevant portion was said by the Full Court of the Federal Court to be some 229 lines).

The Full Court said that the question of whether a component part of a computer program is itself a computer program for the purposes of the Act is a question of fact. However, the Full Court went on to say that "[i]f a particular set of instructions is functionally separate from the entirety of the program, then ... there is no difficulty in treating that set of instructions as being a literary work separate from the balance of the program". Although it did not expressly say so, the Full Court must have considered that the particular set of instructions comprising each Macro was not functionally separate from the remainder of the Dataflex compiler program. This is because it said that "the relevant program to be considered here would not be that small fragment of program which causes the macro command to perform its function (some 229 lines), but the Dataflex compiler program itself".

... [37] ...

Reproduction or adaptation of the macros?

The learned trial judge found strong objective similarity between the underlying source code of the PFXplus Macros and the underlying source code of the Dataflex Macros. Jenkinson J did not find that Dr Bennett had reproduced the Dataflex Macros, but instead found that Dr Bennett had "made an adaptation of the expression in I-Code of each of the three sets of instructions". The finding of no reproduction was not challenged; the appellant contended that there was an adaptation.

The meaning of "adaptation" in relation to computer programs, as set out in s 10(1) of the Act, is "a version of the work (whether or not in the language, code or notation in which the work was originally expressed) not being a reproduction of the work". In examining the meaning of the word "version", the Full Court referred to the meanings of the word "version" given by the *Macquarie Dictionary*: "2. a translation. 3. a particular form or variant of anything". The Full Court also quoted the following passages from the Explanatory Memorandum:

11. "Copyright in literary works includes exclusive rights to reproduce or adapt such works and computer programs will be treated as literary works. However, the present definition of adaptation in relation to literary works only includes translation, conversion between dramatic and non-dramatic forms, and [38] conversion to a pictorial form.

12. Of these, only translation is likely to be relevant to adaptation of programs and there are legal doubts as to whether this refers only to translations between human languages.

13. The new definition is intended to cover translation either way between the various so-called 'high-level programming languages' in which the programs may be written by humans (often called 'source code') and languages, codes or notations which actually control computer operations (often called 'machine code' or 'object code'). Thus 'adaptation' is intended, for example, to cover the compilation of a FORTRAN program to produce machine code which will directly control the operation of a computer. Languages, etc of intermediate level would also be covered.

14. It is also possible for a program to be converted from object code into source code, or between different languages of similar level. In some circumstances this process will result largely in a substantial reproduction of the original program. In other cases, however, such as compilation followed by de-compilation, the differences may be so substantial that one cannot speak of a reproduction although the final product is clearly derived from the original. The new definition of adaptation is intended to cover such situations."

The Full Court said:

"The evidence is clear that while Dr D Bennett carefully studied the Dataflex program so as to ensure that the PFXplus commands in question performed the same functions as the Dataflex commands, the expression of the source program as written by him was an original expression, albeit having much which was objectively similar to the expression of the source code in the Dataflex program. But it is clear that the process involved no translation from one form or language to another, nor did it involve the kind of process referred to in para 14 of the Explanatory Memorandum involving compilation followed by decompilation, or vice versa. In our view, a process of devising a source code to perform the same function as is performed in some other source code expressed in original language does not involve creating a version of the original source code."

Thus, the Full Court was of the opinion that there needed to be "translation from one form or language to another", or, alternatively, "the kind of process referred to in para 14 of the Explanatory Memorandum involving compilation followed by decompilation, or vice versa" in order for there to be a "version" within the meaning of the statute. [39]

...

Paragraph 12 of the Explanatory Memorandum states that "only translation is likely to be relevant to adaptation of programs". This indicates that Parliament did not intend the word "version" to cover situations where, although the functionality of a computer program was copied, original code has been written to perform that function. The focus on translation indicates that Parliament was concerned to ensure that the different languages in which a computer program may be expressed did not provide a means by which copying could occur and infringement be avoided on the ground that the expression in the new language was not a "reproduction".

The use of the words "derived from the original" in para 14 of the Explanatory Memorandum also indicates that the focus is on copying. In accordance with the fundamental principle that copyright protects expression and not ideas, this must relate to the copying of the code (the "expression ... of a set of instructions"), rather than a copying of the idea or function underlying the code.

There was no adaptation of the Macros.

C. The Dataflex Huffman Compression Table

The respondents seek special leave to cross-appeal against the Full Court's finding that they infringed the copyright which the appellant held in the Huffman compression table embedded in the Dataflex program.

Usually, in storing data, all of the 256 characters which a computer recognises are stored in memory as bit strings which are eight bits in length. Huffman compression is a method of reducing the amount of memory space consumed by data files. It stores characters in a data file as bit strings which have a length which relates to the character's frequency of occurrence in the data file. If a character occurs frequently in the data file, it is stored as a bit string of shorter length than a character which occurs infrequently in a data file.

...

The Huffman algorithm, when expressed in source code, analyses a data file to determine the relative frequency of the occurrence of characters, and then assigns a bit string of appropriate length to each character, depending on its frequency of occurrence. There is no allegation in this case that Dr Bennett copied the source code of the Huffman algorithm from the Dataflex program. Dr Bennett states that he obtained "freely distributable" source code for this purpose.

...

███████ Data Access v Powerflex Services *continued*

The definition of "literary work" in the Act includes:

"a table, or compilation, expressed in words, figures or symbols (whether or not in a visible form)."

The Explanatory Memorandum to the *Copyright Amendment Bill 1984* stated:

"By removing the requirement that tables or compilations be in a visible form it is made clear that a computerised data bank, for example, may be treated as a compilation being a literary work. It is also important because data is often stored in a computer as a table. These changes are consistent with the definition of material form."

In our opinion, the Dataflex Huffman table is a table expressed in figures and symbols, and falls squarely within the statutory definition of a "literary work". The reference in the Explanatory Memorandum to "data ... stored in a computer as a table" clearly describes the Dataflex Huffman table. The Dataflex Huffman table is similar to the look-up table in Widget C which, in *Autodesk No 1*, Dawson J considered was a "literary work" within the meaning of the above definition. His Honour thought this was so even though no reliance was placed on that point by *Autodesk*.

For copyright to subsist in the standard Dataflex Huffman table, it must be an "original literary ... work". As we have indicated, the requirement that a work be "original" in copyright law is a requirement that "the work emanates from the person claiming to be its author, in the sense that he has originated it or brought it into existence and has not copied it from another". At first instance, Jenkinson J found that "[t]he use of the Huffman system [42] to produce a compression table requires the employment of substantial skill and judgment and a very great deal of hard work". The Full Court agreed with this finding.

The skill and judgment employed by Dataflex was perhaps more directed to writing the program setting out the Huffman algorithm and applying this program to a representative sample of data than to composing the bit strings in the Huffman table. Nevertheless, the standard Dataflex Huffman table emanates from Dataflex as a result of substantial skill and judgment. That being so, the Full Court was correct in holding that the standard Dataflex Huffman table constituted an original literary work.

In addition, in our opinion the Full Court was correct in holding that the process undertaken by Dr Bennett constituted a "reproduction" of the standard Dataflex Huffman table. The fact that Dr Bennett used an ingenious method of determining the bit string assigned to each character does not make the output of such a process any less a "reproduction" than if Dr Bennett had sat down with a print-out of the table and copy-typed it into the PFXplus program.

The finding that the respondents infringed the appellant's copyright in the Huffman table embedded in the Dataflex program may well have considerable practical consequences. Not only may the finding affect the relations between the parties to these proceedings, it may also have wider ramifications for anyone who seeks to produce a computer program that is compatible with a program produced by others. These are, however, matters that can be resolved only by the legislature reconsidering and, if it thinks it necessary or desirable, rewriting the whole of the provisions that deal with copyright in computer programs.

▬ Review of Intellectual Property Legislation under ▬ the Competition Principles Agreement

[3.115] Intellectual Property Competition Review Committee, *Review of Intellectual Property Legislation under the Competition Principles Agreement*, Final Report (September 2000) (References omitted.)

In September 1999 the High Court handed down judgment in the *Data Access v Powerflex* case. Perhaps the two most significant findings in this case were that:

- commands contained in a computer program did not constitute a computer program for the purposes of the *Copyright Act*; and
- a compression table contained in a system of computer programs could be a literary work for the purposes of the *Copyright Act*.

The first finding is largely consistent with the policy objectives behind the interoperability provisions introduced into the *Copyright Act* by the *Computer Programs Act*. However the finding with regard to the compression table may create problems for developers of inter-operable products in Australia.

The High Court found that the compression table contained in the Dataflex system was a protected literary work, and that Powerflex had reproduced it in breach of the *Copyright Act*, notwithstanding that it had not copied it but rather devised an ingenious process to replicate it.

The High Court commented on the potential impact of the decision regarding compression tables on the development of interoperable products in Australia. The Court stated:

> "The finding that the respondents infringed the appellant's copyright in the Huffman table embedded in the Dataflex program may well have considerable practical conse-quences. Not only may the finding affect the relations between the parties to these proceedings, it may also have wider ramifications for anyone who seeks to produce a computer program that is compatible with a program produced by others. These are, however, matters that can be resolved only by the legislature reconsidering and, if it thinks necessary or desirable, rewriting the whole of the provisions that deal with copyright in computer programs".

Consideration of issues

Submissions called for clarity in the protection afforded to computer technology and practical solutions—allowing decompilation of computer program to enable development of inter-operable products encourages competition in industry, and a restrictive approach in allow-ing such reverse engineering should ameliorate disincentive to produce first generation technology.

Some submissions put it to the Committee that the current *Copyright Act* (as amended by the *Computer Programs Act*) is too wide, and "may be widened for no other reason than that interoperability is the desired policy outcome". It was refuted that entire reproductions or adaptations of works should be permitted for achieving first generation product as this would "completely and irreparably undermine copyright in computer programs".

However the ADA rejected the submission that the amendments devalue the level of copyright protection in Australia, and stated that "the 1999 amendments now make it possible for Australian developers to create innovative, interoperable products without the risk of unreasonable claims of copyright infringement from existing dominant vendors in the software industry".

▄▄▄▄▄ Review of Intellectual Property Legislation under the Competition Principles Agreement *continued*

Some submissions raised the *Connectix* case as an illustration of some possible short-comings in the Australian legislation. That particular (US) case dealt with the reverse engineering of a product in order to make a substitute product (functional equivalent):

"[I]f the type of issues that arose in the *Connectix* case came before an Australian courts, it is possible that an emulator developer would have cause for concern. As the recent *Powerflex* case demonstrated, reverse engineering rights are very difficult to establish under Australian copyright law. It is doubtful whether recent amendments to the *Copyright Act* would change this situation.

Under s 47D of the amended Act, a person may reverse engineer copies of a program owned by someone else, but *only* if they intend to make a product that inter-operates with that program ... the right would not be available to Connectix in Australia because the VGS does not interoperate with the PlayStation console code. It is a substitute for it. ... In Australia, it would appear that the development of emulators such as the VGS is *not* fair play [sic] under current laws. This has serious implications for Australian software developers as they cannot compete in the international market in the same way as their overseas counterparts can."

Possible solutions to overcome the negative consequences of the High Court's finding in relation to the compression table in the *Powerflex* case include:

* amending s 47D(d) to cover program-to-file interoperability (which arose in the *Powerflex* case), not merely program-to-program interoperability;
* including a provision modelled on 17 USC 112(b) which confirms that, where idea and expression merge in a functional element of a computer program (eg, a compression table), that element is treated as unprotectable for copyright purposes.

The Committee is of the view, and has received submissions in support, that the Government should review the Computer Programs provisions to ensure that all legitimate acts necessary to achieve interoperability are permitted.

Definition of/ protection of compilations/ databases

In its Interim Report, the Committee posited the removal of compilations from the category of literary works. IBM has submitted that compilations should *not* be removed from the definition of literary works. Australia would otherwise be out of step with law in other juris-dictions. They argue that the definition of "compilation" is important to the development of databases and IP protection in ecommerce.

▄▄▄▄▄▄▄▄▄▄▄▄▄▄▄▄▄▄▄▄▄▄▄▄▄▄▄▄▄▄▄▄▄▄▄▄

■ **Are all digital files on a DVD considered to be "computer programs"?**

▄▄▄▄▄▄▄ **Australian Video Retailers Association** ▄▄▄▄▄▄▄
v Warner Home Video

[3.120] *Australian Video Retailers Association Ltd v Warner Home Video Pty Ltd* [2001] 53 IPR 242
Federal Court of Australia

EMMETT J : **[259]** The copyright protection of computer programs is not designed to extend to the original content that a computer program is capable of causing to be reproduced. On the other hand, the mere commands, by themselves, bring about no result at all. It follows that the material on the DVD discs in question that constitutes computer programs is limited to program instructions, including commands as identified by Dr Lambert. It does not extend to the audio, visual and caption content of the DVD discs.

Essential object of rental

It is common ground that Warner is the owner of the copyright in relation to the computer programs referred to in the answer to question 2. Under s 31(1)(d) of the Act, that copyright includes the exclusive right to enter into a commercial rental arrangement in respect of those programs, except for entering into a commercial rental arrangement where the programs are not "the essential object of the rental"—s 31(5).

    ... [260] ...

Section 31(5) is concerned with the "essential object of the rental". Warner's final contention on the point was that phrase refers to the subject matter of the rental rather than the purpose. The purpose of a rental or hiring arrangement is to obtain the use of the subject matter of the rental or hire. In the case of a DVD disc, the subject matter of the rental or hire must be the DVD disc itself. The hire or rental of the DVD disc may carry with it a licence (or precarium) to use the computer program embodied in the DVD disc. However, the subject matter of the rental or hire is the DVD disc that has digital information embodied in it. That digital information comprises both video and audio material as well as computer programs.

I consider that the phrase should be construed as meaning that s 31(1)(d) does not extend to entering into a commercial rental arrangement if the essential object of the rental is not to obtain the right or licence to make use of the computer program. Thus, where the essential object (in the sense of purpose) is to be able to experience both the video and audio aspects of a motion picture, albeit that the full benefit of the DVD technology cannot be experienced or obtained without use of the computer program embodied in the DVD disc, the essential object of the rental is not the computer program but video and audio content of the motion picture and other material consisting of special features, documentaries, etc.

■ Circuit layouts

Nature of integrated circuits

[3.125] Integrated circuits are also known as "circuit layouts", or "silicon chips" or "semi-conductor chips". They consist of an electrical circuit in which a connected arrangement of transistors in a three-dimensional design performs functions assigned by software and or hardware within a computer system. There is a constant process of technical advance in the integrated circuits industry, and the continued expansion and evolution of the "computer information age" depends upon continued innovation and development in the capacities of "chips". The creation of a new and original computer chip requires extensive research and development (and sometimes some trial and error experimentation) and then a complex design process to arrange the transistors. The earliest design process was achieved by hand drawing maps or plans of the circuit on sometimes-enormous pieces of paper and then painstakingly working out the distribution of transistors into layers. Modern designing utilises computer design programs and is a less cumbersome but remains a highly skilled and complex task. Design of the circuit is followed by complex process manufacturing technology. Despite the fact that integrated circuits are expensive and time consuming to create, they can be relatively cheap to produce and the final layout may be, relatively speaking, easy to copy.

During the early 1980s there was an assumption that there was a significant risk of copying of integrated circuit layouts in computer chips. It was considered that neither copyright nor design law provided appropriate protection for those aspects of chip design which required significant investment of creative skill, ingenuity, technical sophistication, hard work and finance. It was also thought that attempting to fit chip protection into either the copyright or design systems would be inconsistent with the normal principles of those regimes. Although an analogy could be made to argue that a drawing making up a plan for a circuit was an "artistic work", or the resultant object could be regarded as a sculpture and so an artistic work within the definition of the *Copyright Act 1968* (Cth), this was inconsistent with the normal application of copyright principles. Accordingly it was thought that a new sui generis form of protection for chip design was required.

International developments

[3.130] The first example of sui generis legislation for the new technology was the US *Semi-Conductor Chip Protection Act 1984*. Earlier attempts to pass such legislation failed because there had been disagreement about the form and content of the protection. Some had argued that there should be no protection at all and that open competition had provided a spur to American innovation leading to world leadership in the field. The eventual Act included attempts at some compromise positions and this is one of the reasons behind the recognition of a sort of fair use reverse engineering defence. A particular feature of the US *Semi-Conductor Chip Protection Act 1984* was that it did not grant national treatment to non-US integrated circuits. Reciprocal protection was extended to countries who put in place complementary legislation providing standards in keeping with the US legislation. There was clearly a need for a more comprehensive approach to international protection based on a multilateral treaty. WIPO was able to bring about the conclusion of the *Washington Treaty on the Protection of Intellectual Property in Respect of Integrated Circuits* in May 1989. Australia introduced a Bill for circuit layout protection in 1988 in anticipation of the diplomatic conference in Washington in 1989, which resulted in the Washington Treaty. Parliament enacted the *Circuit Layouts Act 1989* and it came into force on 1 October 1990. The legislation permitted Australia to join the Washington Treaty although it appears that Australia is not a formal signatory.

TRIPs Agreement, Art 35 now requires members to provide protection for layout designs in accordance with the Washington Treaty. TRIPs Agreement, Art 36 requires the scope of protection to address unauthorised "importing, selling or otherwise distributing for commercial purposes" of a layout design, a chip made in accordance with a layout design or an article incorporating a circuit "only in so far as it continues to contain an unlawfully reproduced layout design". TRIPs Agreement, Art 37 describes acts which do not require authorisation from the rights holder and which accordingly will not constitute an infringement. It deals with:

- innocent commercial dealing with an circuit or article containing an unauthorised circuit provided the defendant pays an equitable remuneration to the rights holder once there is sufficient notice of the unauthorised circuit; and
- compulsory licensing and use by or for the government.

TRIPs Agreement, Art 38 specifies a minimum term of protection of 10 years from registration (where required) or from the date of first commercial exploitation anywhere in the world.

Circuit layout litigation in Australia

[3.135] Australia is not a major manufacturer of computer chips. Indeed few countries are. It is generally said that 90 per cent of the world's chips are made in the US, Japan and Korea. However, Australian computer chips were used in some important innovative items such as bionic ears, heart pacemakers and photo-electric cell technology converting sunlight to electricity. These specialist chips are successfully and profitably exported. The Commonwealth Attorney-General, when introducing the legislation, said that although the industry was small, it was "nevertheless important and growing" (Second Reading Speech, *Hansard*, 3 November 1988, p 2392). It is also the case that Australia imports nearly all chips used in the country either already installed in products imported into the country or imported as chips for installation in items manufactured locally.

During the period in which the *Circuit Layouts Act 1989* (Cth) has been in force there have been seven relevant reported cases. These cases relate to only four fact situations and two were copyright cases. The cases are *Brooktree Corp v Advanced Micro Devices Inc* (1998) 14 IPR 85 (a copyright case); *Avel Pty Ltd v Jonathan Wells* (1991) 22 IPR 305; *Avel Pty Ltd v Wells* (1991) 23 IPR 353; *Nintendo Co Ltd v Centronics Systems Pty Ltd* (1991) 23 IPR 119; *Centronics Systems Pty Ltd v Nintendo Co Ltd* (1992) 24 IPR 481; *Nintendo Co Ltd v Centronics Systems Pty Ltd* (1994) 28 IPR 431; *Sega Enterprises Ltd v Galaxy Electronics Pty Ltd* (1996) 35 IPR 161. These cases involved either gambling machine chips or computer game chips.

There are several possible explanations for the low level of attempted enforcement through court action. One is that the possibility of litigation has discouraged infringement. Another is that rights owners are able to use the threat of litigation to successfully resolve any dispute. Yet another possibility is that it is simply not worthwhile to copy chips of leading manufacturers directly because of the costs and difficulty in reproducing the process technology. Genuine chips are readily available and cheap for nearly all applications. If the last of these is the major reason, it may be that the copying of chips is not in fact the significant problem it was feared it would become. Another possibility is that most protection for computer technology is achieved through the *Copyright Act 1968* (Cth).

Overlap with copyright and other legislation

[3.140] It is ordinarily said that there is no dual protection between the *Circuits Layouts Act 1989* (Cth) and the *Copyright Act 1968* (Cth) or *Designs Act 2003* (Cth). This is true in the sense that those aspects of the design for a circuit or the circuit itself which give rise to "eligible layout" rights are not the subject matter of the copyright or designs systems. However, a computer chip as a memory device can hold or store "embodiments" or "aggregations" of information which are "works" or "subject matter other than works" within the meaning of the *Copyright Act 1968* (Cth). This question was addressed by the Australian courts on two occasions. In *Avel Pty Ltd v Wells* (1992) 23 IPR 353 the Court said:

> "[A] chip, that is to say an integrated circuit, may embody two different subject matters of protection: a circuit layout and a copyright work. The subject of copyright protection, usually a computer program, has protection only under one Act, namely the *Copyright Act*. A person importing a chip into Australia having purchased it as a result of a commercial exploitation abroad does not obtain as a result of s 24 or any other section of the *Layouts Act* the right to reproduce the computer program. To do so would remain an infringement of the *Copyright Act*. All that subs (2) of s 24 ensures is that the commercial exploitation of the chip in Australia will not be hindered in such a case, provided that the making of a copy or adaptation of the work stored in the chip and otherwise the subject of copyright protection did not constitute a copyright infringement."

In *Sega Enterprises Ltd v Galaxy Electronics Pty Ltd* (1996) 35 IPR 161, Burchett J held that certain computer games, "Virtua Cop" and "Daytona USA" which were stored in integrated circuits imported into Australia, were "cinematographic films" within the meaning of the *Copyright Act 1968* (Cth). His Honour rejected an argument that the fact that these games were stored within a computer meant that they should find protection, if at all, in the *Circuits Layouts Act 1989* (Cth). His Honour said:

> "The fact that there are here integrated circuits and that these give rise to the application of particular statutory provisions, does not subtract from the further and relevant fact that the use of the integrated circuits is capable of bringing to the screen, so as to be shown as a moving picture, the aggregate of visual images making up Virtua Cop. That attracts the operation of the provisions of the *Copyright Act* in respect of cinematographic films."

■ Dramatic works

[3.145] These are not defined by the *Copyright Act 1968* (Cth), although s 10(1) states:

> " 'dramatic work' includes:
> (a)   a choreographic show or other dumb show ; and
> (b)   a scenario or script for a cinematograph film,
> but does not include a cinematograph film as distinct from the scenario or script for a cinematograph film."

The *Copyright Act 1905* (Cth) in s 4 defined a dramatic work as "any tragedy, comedy, play, drama, farce, burlesque, libretto of an opera, entertainment or other work of like nature, whether set to music or other scenic or dramatic composition". Many dramatic works may also be literary works: see *Zeccola v Universal City Studios Inc* (below). One of the difficulties here is distinguishing between the idea and the expression thereof. The question is to what extent the dramatic incidents or the plot of a play, for example, may be protected: see *Tate v Thomas* ([**3.40**]).

■ Is there any difference between a literary work and a dramatic work?

Zeccola v Universal City Studios

[3.150] *Zeccola v Universal City Studios Inc* (1982) 67 FLR 225 Federal Court of Australia

LOCKHART J: The judgment I am about to deliver is the joint judgment of [226] Fitzgerald J and myself. This is an appeal from a judgment of the Supreme Court of Victoria delivered on 4 August 1982 which granted interlocutory injunctions restraining the appellants until the final hearing of the action or further order from infringing the respondent's copyright in a novel, screenplay and film each entitled *Jaws* and from infringing the respondent's registered trade mark in the word *Jaws*.

A problem in these proceedings is that the parties tended to blur the distinction between final and interlocutory proceedings and the problem was exacerbated by the different copyrights asserted by the respondent as the basis of its claim. Many questions have been raised, some of which were dealt with by the learned primary judge, which may be of importance at the trial but do not fall for present decision and indeed are best left open at this juncture for later determination.

It is well-established that where the judgment appealed from involves the exercise of discretion by the trial judge this court will not interfere unless an error of the kind mentioned in various cases, including *House v The King* (1936) 55 CLR 499, is shown to have been made.

...

We will not trouble to recite all the findings of fact and law made by the primary judge in an extensive judgment. It is sufficient if we refer to them in summary form as follows.

The novel *Jaws* was written by Peter Benchley, a US citizen. It was first published in 1974 in the US. The *Jaws* screenplay was completed in the same year. The film *Jaws* was made in the US in 1975 and was first shown to the public there in July of that year. Since then it has been exhibited in most countries of the world, including Italy, where it was called *La Squalo* which, translated into English means "The Shark". **[227]**

The film *Jaws* has been a huge success and has made a lot of money for the respondent. Apart from exhibitions in motion picture theatres it has been shown under contract on television in the US and many other countries. Most of those contracts are still on foot. The sale of video cassettes and disks has also been widespread and is still proceeding. In 1977 the respondent arranged for the making of a sequel to *Jaws* which was called *Jaws II*. *Jaws II* concerns much the same subject matter and character as *Jaws*. *Jaws II* was first exhibited to the public in June 1978 and has also been a great success. Both films have been prominently featured as Universal films and some $20 million has been expended in promoting the films throughout the world.

Another film *Jaws 3-D* is presently being made by the respondent and the respondent has also obtained registration in Australia of the word *Jaws* and of a drawing depicting the head and open jaws of the shark as trade marks in respect of, among other things, cinema films and printed matter.

The film *Great White* was made by Italian film makers in early 1980. A full page advertisement in *Weekly Variety*, an American periodical, dated 7 May 1980 stated that the film was to be called *The Last Jaws*. When the film was first shown in Italy later in 1980 its name was *La Ultimo Squalo* which translated into English as *The Last Shark*. The appearance of the advertisement in *Weekly Variety* excited the interest of the respondent. Steps were taken in Italy to prevent the showing of the film *Great White* and litigation ensued which is still pending. Litigation followed in other countries.

The primary judge dealt at length with the various issues between the parties. The appellants do not dispute that the respondent has acquired and is entitled to sue in Australia to enforce any copyright which exists here in the novel, screenplay or film *Jaws*, but asserts that no such copyright exists. Counsel for the appellants made various submissions impunging the judgment from which they have appealed. Some of these submissions were disposed of in the course of discussion between counsel and the bench and need not be referred to further. Other submissions were put in various ways but in essence were the same as each other. We confine ourselves to the principal submissions made on behalf of the appellants.

Counsel for the appellants submitted that the primary judge erred in holding that the novel *Jaws* was an original work for the purposes of the *Copyright Act 1968* (the Act). It was submitted that there was no evidence or at least no sufficiently reliable evidence to support his Honour's conclusion. The hearing was conducted, as applications for interlocutory injunctions usually are, on evidence by affidavit supplemented where necessary by cross-examination. We see no purpose in analysing in detail the evidence before his Honour touching this question, but it is sufficient to say that there was evidence of the originality of the novel *Jaws* ... it was submitted by counsel for the appellants that the primary judge

▬▬▬▬ Zeccola v Universal City Studios *continued*

committed a fundamental error in his approach to the question whether the appellants had infringed the copyright of the respondent in the film *Jaws*. It was submitted that copyright in a film subsists only in those parts of the film capable of being the subject matter of copyright, that is, having the requisite character of originality, and that it is necessary to excise other parts from the whole. It was said that it is only the residue that can be the subject of copyright and thereby be protected from infringement. ... [228] ...

Counsel for the appellants submitted that both films *Jaws* and *Great White* are genre films based upon the idea of a savage monster menacing a community. Each is a film about a killer shark terrorising human beings and it was said that neither film was entitled to protection as there is no copyright in that general idea.

The difficulties involved in severing films into parts which are capable of characterisation as original works and other parts that are not is obvious. Indeed, it is the subject of only limited exploration by the laws of this country and the UK. We were referred to certain decisions of US courts where this question has been considered from time to time and we have found those cases helpful in resolving the questions before us. In general, there is no copyright in the central idea or theme of a story or play, however original it may be; copyright subsists in the combination of situations, events and scenes which constitute the particular working out or expression of the idea or theme. If these are totally different the taking of the idea or theme does not constitute an infringement of copyright.

Of necessity certain events, incidents or characters are found in many books and plays. Originality, when dealing with incidents and characters familiar in life or fiction, lies in the association, grouping and arrangement of those incidents and characters in such a manner that presents a new concept or a novel arrangement of those events and characters. We accept that where a story is written based on various incidents which, in themselves, are commonplace, a claim for copyright must be confined closely to the story which has been composed by the author. Another author who materially varies the incidents and characters and materially changes the story is not an infringer of the copyright. If a literary or dramatic work is not wholly original there is no copyright in the unoriginal part so as to prevent its use. Additional factors may fall for consideration where the alleged infringement is by cinematograph film.

The primary judge closely analysed the two films *Jaws* and *Great White*. Notwithstanding that the subject matter of the film *Jaws* was not particularly striking his Honour held the view, in essence, that the combination of the principal situations, singular events and basic characters was sufficient to constitute an original work that was susceptible of protection under the law of copyright in this country. In our opinion his Honour's finding has not been shown to be in error. It must be remembered that all his Honour did was make his findings on the basis that a prima facie case was established. [229] He did not make any final or definitive finding on this, or indeed any other question.

It was submitted that his Honour erred in holding that the question whether the respondent's copyright was infringed by the making and showing of the film *Great White* came down to a question of whether *Great White* was a substantial adaptation or reproduction of the book or screenplay *Jaws* or a substantial copy of the film *Jaws*. Counsel for the appellants submitted that the film *Great White* could not be said to constitute an infringement of any copyright of the respondents in the film *Jaws* unless it was an exact or facsimile copy of the film *Jaws*.

The argument was based on various matters including certain sections of the Act. Section 10 which defines the word copy and ss 86 and 101 are some of the sections referred to. No authority was cited for this proposition, but counsel adopted as part of his argument a passage from Lahore's *Intellectual Property in Australia*. We do not find it necessary to answer this question. It raises important and difficult questions which, if they are relevant on the final hearing, may be debated then.

At its narrowest, the major issue is whether or not the appellants' film *Great White* substantially reproduced the novel *Jaws* or the screenplay based upon that novel from which the respondents' film *Jaws* was made. In the resolution of that question it is appropriate to have regard to the operation of s 21 of the Act which deems cinematographic films to be reproductions of literary or dramatic works in certain circumstances. If the primary issue is so stated any problems of statutory interpretation arising out of the definition of "adaptation" in the Act, or as to what constitutes an infringement of one cinematographic film by another, can be avoided without risk of limiting the substance of the relief sought, which is to restrain the exhibition of the appellants' film *Great White*.

The primary judge correctly realised that two questions were involved in the resolution of what is the major issue: namely, the degree of objective similarity between the appellants' film and the respondent's novel and screenplay and, given sufficient objective similarity, whether copying was established. In relation to the question of copying, the appellants sought to show that the inspiration for the film *Great White* came partly from the imagination of its producer, Dr Tucci, and partly from a book by one Ramon Bravo called *Carnada* which is published only in Spanish.

His Honour was provided with a copy of the novel and screenplay *Jaws*, but did not have time to read them in the circumstances attending the claim for interlocutory relief. However, the proceedings before him were conducted on the basis that the screenplay closely followed the novel and that the film *Jaws* closely followed the screenplay. Thus the exercise of comparison between the novel and the screenplay *Jaws* on the one hand, and the film *Great White* on the other hand, was regarded as appropriately undertaken by a comparison of the two films. Further, all his Honour had of the book *Carnada* was a translation in condensed form. His Honour, with some degree of fortitude, viewed both films, one after the other.

The comparative exercise which his Honour undertook was central to his decision. He considered that there was such a marked degree of similarity between the two films that there was an inescapable inference of copying and that the respondent had an excellent chance of success at the trial. The strength of his views in relation to the similarity between the two films **[230]** influenced the attitude which he took to much of the evidence, including expert evidence, and to the appellant's denial of copying, most of which was held to be inadmissible.

Much criticism was levelled by the appellants at the approach which his Honour took to such evidence and at the inference of copying which he drew. While our own viewing of the films did not instill in us the same degree of conviction that his Honour felt, we are not persuaded that his Honour was wrong.

Appeal dismissed.

Note

[3.155] The copyright in a film script (as a work) should be distinguished from the copyright in the film itself, which may embody a work and also cinematograph film copyright (s 86).

■ Is a public spectacle a dramatic work?
Nine Network Australia v ABC

[3.160] *Nine Network Australia Pty Ltd v Australian Broadcasting Corp* (1999) 48 IPR 333 Federal
Court of Australia

HILL J: **[334]** ... Around 9 pm on 31 December 1999, and especially around 12 midnight and
half an hour thereafter into the year 2000, an event will occur in the City of Sydney focused
particularly on Sydney Harbour and the Harbour Bridge. There will be fireworks accompanied
by music displays on the Harbour Bridge. Eighteen barges will carry large lantern figures of sea
creatures promenading around the harbour. It promises to be an event of significance to the
city, to Australia and, indeed, to the world.

The event is being financed by the Council of the City of Sydney which is not at least at
present, a party to the current proceedings. To obtain some contribution to the cost of this
and previous New Year events the Council entered into an agreement with Nine Network
Australia Pty Limited (Channel Nine), the commercial television broadcaster which through
its network and affiliated TV stations effectively covers in its "footprint" mainland Australia
and Tasmania. That agreement takes the form of a letter written by the Council of the City of
Sydney to Channel Nine and concerned New Year celebrations in December 1997 through to
December 2000. Under it Channel Nine is required to contribute an amount to the costs in
accordance with a formula in the letter. According to the evidence before me, the estimated
contribution by Channel Nine to the 2000 event is in the order of $450,000. The total cost of
the event is estimated to be approximately $3 million.

In consideration of this contribution the city named Channel Nine the official television
broadcaster and granted to it the exclusive right to record all performances, the fireworks
spectacular and other entertainment organised by the city and connected with the event, and
televise the coverage it recorded throughout Australia and Papua New Guinea.

The respondent Channel Two is the public television broadcaster in Australia. It has made
arrangements with an international consortium of television stations led by the BBC for a
worldwide television coverage of some 25 hours illustrating the events which will occur in
various countries throughout the world to celebrate the arrival of what at least most people
refer to as the new millennium. It is contemplated that that coverage will include a coverage
of the happenings on Sydney Harbour. A confidential exhibit details the program as presently
scheduled. The Australian segment goes of course beyond Sydney and **[335]** includes other
state capitals, although Channel Two proposes to film the entire spectacle in Sydney Harbour
and parts of that will form the international coverage which Channel Two proposes to
broadcast in Australia and which will be broadcast internationally throughout a large part of
the world to what could be no doubt an audience of millions.

The fact that both channels propose to televise (Channel Nine the whole and Channel
Two at least part thereof) the Sydney celebrations is not something that has only become
known in the past few days. It has been known by the Council, Channel Nine and Channel
Two at least since 16 August 1999 when Channel Nine sought from the Council the international television rights for its coverage presumably to block Channel Two passing what
Channel Nine in the letter described as "stolen coverage" onto the BBC led international TV
consortium of which Channel Two was to be a member.

It is also clear that the shape, if I may call it that, of the event was settled by that
time, though subject no doubt to fine tuning which fine tuning may well continue until
31 December. However it took until 13 December of this year for Channel Nine to commence

Nine Network Australia v ABC *continued*

proceedings in this Court. It seeks now, but a few working days before the event is to take place, urgent interlocutory relief restraining Channel Two from broadcasting in Australia a television broadcast featuring what are referred to as the bridge face device, the bridge word design, the Sydney Harbour lanterns and the fireworks production at 9 pm and midnight, subject to a proviso that any conduct constituting a fair dealing under s 42 of the *Copyright Act 1968* (*Copyright Act*) would not be prohibited.

The original threat made by Channel Nine went much further than the current proceedings do. Indeed they initially seemed to want to restrain Channel Two filming any of these events for inclusion in an international broadcast, although it is clear that Channel Nine's rights, such as they are, extend only to Australia and Papua New Guinea and no further. However that has now been abandoned.

Channel Nine base its claim for relief on copyright rights which it alleges vest in the City Council in each of these "works" of which it claims to be the exclusive licensee for TV broadcasts in Australia. ...

In what is copyright alleged to exist?

... [337] ...

For Channel Nine its strongest case of copyright is with the drawing of the sea creatures and the lanterns which reproduce those drawings in a three-dimensional form. The drawings are on any view of the matter original and copyright exists, in my view, in those drawings and in the three-dimensional form the drawings take being, at the least, works of artistic craftsmanship.

In my view, the weakest copyright case for Channel Nine, on the other hand, is the claimed copyright said to exist in the dramatic work originating from the schedule dealing with the fireworks display and what written submissions of senior counsel for Channel Nine referred to as "the fireworks production". As I understand it, each type of firework produces a particular effect. Randomly set off the effect of those fireworks might be chaotic. It takes skill and artistry, perhaps, to determine the order in which particular kinds of fireworks are set off and to produce the spectacular effect which is hoped for to meet the occasion. The relationship between the music, its beat or rhythm, and the exploding fireworks is no doubt also of importance.

Having said that I have difficulty in the conclusion that if the schedule is itself followed precisely, because that would have to be a prerequisite of the copyright protection, (it is certainly contemplated that that will be the case although I suspect that fine tuning may still be possible between now and 31 December) the exploding fireworks display is a dramatic work within the definition of that expression in s 10(1) of the *Copyright Act*. That section defines dramatic work to include:

(a)   a choreographic show or other dumb show; and
(b)   a scenario or script for a cinematograph film;
but does not include a cinematograph film as distinct from the scenario or script for a
cinematograph film.

The expression of course has its ordinary English meaning in addition to the defined meaning to which I have referred.

The question really is whether the setting off of the fireworks spectacular, ephemeral as it is, is a "dramatic work" in the ordinary sense of those words. It is not a matter upon which I have formed a concluded view but there are certainly difficulties it seems to me with the argument. It is or will be if the matter goes to trial the case for Channel Nine, that because the fireworks show alone or in combination with other events such as the barge display is in the nature of a series of composed events and has dramatic unity and interest, it is therefore a dramatic work.

████████ Nine Network Australia v ABC *continued*

There is also the question whether the ultimate fireworks show is really a material form of what was planned. The requirement that it be scripted, directed and staged, assuming Sydney Harbour to be a gigantic outdoor stage for the present purposes may more readily be accepted to the extent that it is planned, but as I have already suggested there may be many a slip between the actual plan and the ultimate performance. It can be argued not to involve improvisation: *Karno v Pathé Frères Ltd* (1908) 24 TLR 588 at 590-591 affirmed on appeal (1909) 25 TLR 242 and see *Australian Olympic Committee Inc v The Big Fights Inc* [1999] FCA 1042 (3 August 1999) per Lindgren J at para 42.

It is, one would think, common place in at least a half of the present decade that firework shows with music are planned. It has never been suggested to my [338] knowledge, and there is no reported case in which the matter has been subjected to legal analysis which has suggested that copyright subsists in a fireworks show set to music just because the sequence of events is scripted. That does not mean that copyright might not exist. It may merely be the result either of difficulties of enforcing the non-filming of such events or it may be that no one has thought deeply about the issue. At the heart of the problem may well be that copyright is a monopolistic right existing not to protect ideas as such but the physical manifestation of some original literary, artistic or dramatic work.

Channel Nine's argument cannot be said to be doomed to failure although at the present I am inclined to the view that it is not strong. The question of subsistence of copyright in the bridge face or bridge word drawings and the related question of the photography, recording and then showing of images of the actual bridge with the lit designs constituting infringement also had difficulties for Channel Nine. In each case the drawing of the bridge is a substantial part of what is said to be the original artistic work. No doubt a drawing of the bridge is capable of being an original artistic work but what is photographed is the actual Harbour Bridge, on any view an object in the public domain, to which is affixed a representation in lights of either the face or the word "Eternity". The face itself is, on the evidence as it stands no doubt an original drawing, but I have reservations in whether copyright can subsist in a representation in copperplate in lights of the word "Eternity" made if not popular, at least prominent, as I have said, by Mr Stace ...

■ Performances of works: Part XIA Copyright Act 1968 (Cth)
See [2.55].

Performer/author of musical works

████████████ **Hadley v Kemp** ████████████

[3.165] *Hadley v Kemp* [1999] EMLR 589. Chancery Division, Court of Appeal (United Kingdom)

PARK J: **[593]** ... The plaintiffs, Mr Tony Hadley, Mr John Keeble and Mr Steve Norman, were three members of a former pop group, Spandau Ballet. In this case they are suing a fourth member, Mr Gary Kemp, and Reformation Publishing Company Ltd, a company owned by him. They have a main case, which I will call "the contractual claim", and an alternative case, which I will call "the copyright claim".

...

▬▬▬ Hadley v Kemp *continued*

The copyright claim, their alternative argument, was first advanced in 1998. The plaintiffs contend that, contrary to what everyone had believed before then, Mr Kemp and his company, Reformation, were not the sole owners of the copyrights in the band's songs. Rather they now say either that they were all joint owners with Mr Kemp of the copyrights in all the songs, or that one or more of them were joint owners with him of some or all of the copyrights. They also say that, if they are right, this gives them rights to receive large amounts of money from Reformation.

... [639] ...

N3. The copyright claim: the facts and the evidence

Records, CDs and other forms in which recorded songs are marketed to the public always identify the writers of the music and the lyrics. I believe that Spandau Ballet recorded something like 60 tracks, which were split between six albums and a number of singles. On all except one of them the credit for writing the music and the lyrics was accorded to Gary Kemp. All the plaintiffs thought at the time that that was right.

...

To describe Gary Kemp as the "writer" of the music could be misleading without adding a little explanation. As I have said once or twice already he did not write the music down on paper. We have all seen imaginative sketches of the great classical composers of the past sitting at their desks in what one imagines might be an attic, quill pens in hand and sheafs of musical paper before them, writing out their compositions by hand. Popular music is not usually created that way, and Gary Kemp did not create his music that way. He composed at home, with a guitar and sometimes a piano. In this way for each song he developed, and fixed in his musical consciousness, the melody, the chords, the rhythm or groove, and the general structure of the song from beginning to end. Usually at the same stage he wrote the entire lyrics for the song.

When Mr Kemp had created a song in this way, and not before then, he presented it to the other members of the band. Usually this happened in a rehearsal studio. Mr Kemp played the complete song on an acoustic guitar, and sang it. A process then followed of rehearsals leading into recording. At the rehearsal stage the members of the band [640] learned the song, interpreted it on their own instruments, practised and perfected the playing or (in Mr Hadley's case) the singing of their own parts, and rehearsed the performance of it as an ensemble. They did these things aurally, and without music sheets setting it all out in musical notation. As Mr Kemp said in evidence: "We can talk music to each other. All popular music is achieved in that way." At the recording stage they moved from the rehearsal studio into the recording studio (which was much more expensive). They were joined there by the record producer and technicians, and the definitive recording was made. Invariably there would be several takes of the same song, and the master recording to be delivered to the record company would be a composite put together by the record producer (or under his supervision) from the whole series of takes.

...

I need to say more about the rehearsals, but I think that it might be useful for me first to say what did not happen. What did not happen was a process such as was described by the judge (Thomas Morison QC, as he then was) in *Stuart v Barrett* [1994] EMLR 448 at p 455:

> "The plaintiff says that he can remember that there was a moment when they stopped playing and the second defendant played a riff on the guitar and looked towards him as though tacitly inviting the plaintiff to put something to support what he was playing. He tried different drum beats and ended up with an off-beat drum pattern which seemed to fit well; and the others joined in, embellishing and changing octave.

■■■■■■ Hacley v Kemp *continued*

By the end of the session they had a completed piece of music without words, which became the song 'The Outsider'."

This kind of collective creation of a song is often referred to as "jamming". It is not the way that Spandau Ballet did things. I suspect that, **[641]** before the evidence, Mr Sutcliffe entertained hopes on behalf of the plaintiffs that it might appear to me that, although Gary Kemp started the process off, the band's songs emerged from a process of collective jamming such as Mr Morison described.

In my view, however, that is not borne out by the evidence. There are two specific points which I wish to make.

First, both at rehearsals and in the recording studio Gary Kemp was in charge. His own evidence was that they were not a democratic band; they were a hierarchy and people would listen to him where music was concerned. Mr Keeble said that it was more organic than Mr Kemp said, but he accepted that Mr Kemp was a perfectionist and decisive. He was asked whether Mr Kemp was very definite about what he (Mr Keeble) should play, and he answered: "Gary often had very strong ideas, yes". Mr Norman accepted that Mr Kemp, the songwriter, had to have the last word (as Mr Norman had when the band recorded his own song 'Motivator' for the last album). There was a substantial body of evidence from witnesses who were not members of the band but who were present during rehearsals or recording sessions or both. All of them (including the witness called on behalf of the plaintiffs) gave evidence to the effect that Mr Kemp had definite ideas about how his songs should sound, and was clearly the person in charge. I give one other example, but could give more. Mr Gary Langan was involved on the first album (Journeys to Glory) as a recording engineer, and on the last two albums as producer. He said that Mr Kemp was a "control freak", and that the other members of the band went along with what he said.

Second, once Mr Kemp had presented his songs to the band with a view to them being rehearsed and recorded, there were very few changes made to them. Mr Norman could not remember an instance when the melody as presented by Mr Kemp was not complete, but added that "with any song you refine it. There were never radical changes to the melody but there were slight changes". No other witness went even that far. Mr Dagger said that, in terms of changing the songs, he never saw or heard of it happening. (In fairness I should add that Mr Dagger, being the band's manager, was commonly not present at rehearsals or recording sessions.) Richard Lengel, a recording engineer, said that in the recording studio nobody changed the melody. Toby Chapman (a session musician who was present at rehearsals as well as at recording sessions) gave evidence that Mr Kemp did not allow anyone to change his songs; Mr Kemp had very set ideas. Tony Swain, the record producer on the second and third albums, said that Mr Kemp was very sensitive about anyone changing his songs.

[642] N4. The copyright claim: authorities on joint authorship

I do not wish to review all the cases which over the years have examined the concept of joint authorship, but I would like to say something about two which have been concerned with pop music, and to quote briefly passages from other recent decisions.

I have already referred to the decision of Thomas Morison QC in *Stuart v Barrett* [1994] EMLR 448. He described the way in which the group created songs by a process of collective "jamming". He summed it up in these words (at 458):

"Someone started to play and the rest joined in and improvised and improved the original idea. The final piece was indeed the product of the joint compositional skills of the members of the group present at the time."

■■■■■ Hadley v Kemp *continued*

In those circumstances he held that all the members were joint authors of the songs. But he stressed that this was a conclusion on the particular facts and in no sense represented a rule of law:

> "It would not be sensible to try and lay down any general rules which would apply to all group compositions. One member of a pop group may have an idea which is so nearly perfected that the compositional input of any of the other members of the group would be regarded as insignificant … It may be that, within a group, only one member is the composer. It must depend entirely on the individual circumstances of the band."

Later he said:

> "Ultimately, as it seems to me, the question of whether a person is a joint author or not within the *Copyright Act* is simply a question of fact and degree."

Godfrey v Lees [1995] EMLR 307 is a decision of Blackburne J. The plaintiff was a classically trained musician who worked closely with the pop group Barclay James Harvest. On several tracks the band had an orchestral accompaniment. The plaintiff provided the orchestral arrangements and conducted the orchestra. And he contributed other musical ideas and material. He claimed to be a joint author of six of the recorded tracks, and the judge agreed on the facts. (It did not do the plaintiff any good in the end, as I will explain in N7 below).

Blackburne J stated the principle as follows:

> "What the claimant to joint authorship of a work must establish is that he has made a significant and original contribution to the creation of the work and that he has done so pursuant to a common design. See, for example, *Stuart v Barrett* [1994] EMLR 448. It is not necessary that his contribution to the work is equal in terms of either quantity, quality or originality to that of his collaborators. Nor, in the case of a **[643]** song, does it matter that his contribution is to the orchestral arrangement of the song rather than to the song itself."

In my view the crucial expression (with which I respectfully agree in every respect) is "a significant and original contribution to the creation of the work". There are four elements. (1) The claimant must have made a contribution of some sort. (2) It must have been significant. (3) It must have been original. (4) It must have been a contribution to the creation of the musical work. The last point is particularly important. There is an echo of it in the words of Laddie J in the more recent case of *Flyde Microsystems Ltd v Key Radio Systems Ltd* [1998] FSR 449 at 457 (a case about computer software): the putative author must have contributed "the right kind of skill and labour". In the present case contributions by the plaintiffs, however significant and skilful, to the performance of the musical works are not the right kind of contributions to give them shares in the copyrights. The contributions need to be to the creation of the musical works, not to the performance or interpretation of them.

In the second part of the passage which I have quoted Blackburne J says that the contribution to a song of a person claiming to be a joint author of it does not have to be equal in terms of quantity, quality or originality to that of his collaborators. However, it still has to be "significant". Further, all the cases (including *Godfrey v Lees*) agree that, if two or more persons are joint authors, they own the copyright in equal shares (unless of course they have made an agreement which specifies different shares). It would be surprising if a slight contribution was enough to make a person a joint author and thereby make him an equal owner with another or others who had contributed far more than he had.

…

██████ Hadley v Kemp *continued*

[645] N5. The copyright claim: conclusions. The claim for communal joint authorship

As I listened to Mr Sutcliffe's argument on this part of the case it appeared to me that he advanced two different theories in support of the plaintiffs' claim to be communal joint authors with Gary Kemp of the songs. The main theory contended for in the pleadings (at least as I read them) was that Gary Kemp came along with the bare bones of a song, but that thereafter all the members of the band contributed creatively and collectively to changes and developments to all parts of the song. The result was a whole new song of which they were all joint authors. On this theory it was rather like the jamming process described by Mr Morison QC in the passage from *Stuart v Barrett* [1994] EMLR at 448, which I quoted earlier. However, for the reasons which I gave in N3 above, I do not believe that the theory can survive the evidence. When Mr Kemp presented a song to the band the melody was complete, the chord structure was complete, the rhythm or groove was apparent in the song as presented, and the structure of the song from start to finish was already laid out. Very few changes were made in the process leading up to the recording of it, and Mr Kemp had the last word on such changes as were made.

The second theory is rather different. It seeks to claim joint authorship for all the members of the band by relying on the combination of three factors:

(i)   as a matter of law copyright did not arise when Mr Kemp first presented a song to the band, because the song was not then reduced to some material form (as required by s 49(4));

(ii)   copyright in the musical work arose when it was first recorded, and that was a recording made by all the members of the band, not by Mr Kemp alone;

(iii)   for the purpose of that first recording the members of the band sang or played their instruments in their own creative ways.

I comment on the three factors.

As to (i), the proposition that copyright does not exist in a musical work until it is first reduced to a material form does not mean that the musical work does not exist until it is first reduced to a material form. Quite the contrary: the Act assumes that a work may exist before it is reduced to material form. In my judgment a song devised by Mr Kemp and worked up by him in his own mind to the developed stage at which he presented it to the band was already a musical work. Further, at that stage he was undoubtedly the sole author of it.

As to (ii) the critical point is that, in my opinion, the songs in their recorded form were the same musical works as the songs which Mr Kemp had composed in his mind and his memory. Of course there was a marked difference between (a) the sound of the song sung by [646] Mr Kemp to the accompaniment of himself on an acoustic guitar, and (b) the sound of the song sung by Mr Hadley with the backing of the whole Spandau Ballet band. But that does not mean that the whole band were creating a new and different musical work. Rather they were reducing Mr Kemp's musical work to the material form of a recording. After all, when Mr Kemp devised the song he devised it for performance, not by himself as a solo artist, but by Mr Hadley and the whole band. A composer can "hear" the sound of his composition in his mind before he ever hears it played. Beethoven could hear his music in this sense even when he was deaf. When Mr Kemp was devising his songs the sound which he had in his musical consciousness must surely have been the sound they would have when performed by Spandau Ballet, not the sound they would have when sung by Mr Kemp alone to the accompaniment just of his own guitar.

...

Hadley v Kemp *continued*

As to (iii) (the members of the band sang or played their instruments in their own creative ways), there is a vital distinction between composition or creation of a musical work on the one hand and performance or interpretation of it on the other. Mr Protheroe's evidence frequently stressed this point. It is certainly true that the members of the band sang or played in their own ways (and, in so far as I am able to judge, did so excellently). But these are matters of performance, not matters which go to the creation of a new musical work. To repeat the words of Laddie J in the *Flyde Microsystems* case ([1998] FSR at 457), what the plaintiffs contributed was not 'the right kind of skill and labour'. The members of the band (and the session musicians, who cannot be differentiated from the other artists so far as this point is concerned) did what any good musician does: they performed the songs to the best of their considerable abilities, injecting elements of individuality and [647] artistry into their performances. That did not make them joint authors of the songs. In my judgment that remains so even if there were some elements of improvisation in their performances. Very interesting evidence was given on this by Mr Charlie Morgan, who was an expert witness for the defendants on the role of a drummer. He explained that a composer with an idea of how he wanted the drums to sound could, without writing it down, sing the rhythm part to the drummer. He agreed that the improvisation by the drummer with the beat in his head was a creative part of the compositional process, but he added:

> "Yes, but I think it is no more than the input that any musician would be expected to make: any musician of any kind. I think that is the area of expertise of the drummer, and certainly if I was present on a session I would be expected to inject something of my own persona, if you like, into the part."

For these reasons I do not accept either of the theories on which it is suggested that all of the plaintiffs became collective joint authors of the songs.

■ Musical works

[3.170] No definition of "musical work" is found in the *Copyright Act 1968* (Cth), and as with other categories, the description relates to the character of the work rather than merit. Where words are set to music, the two works (literary and musical) remain separate. Selections of existing music may attract copyright as such, separate from that in the original. This is distinct from the issue of infringement of an existing work The question of what degree of effort constitutes originality will depend upon general principles.

CBS Records Australia v Guy Gross

[3.175] *CBS Records Australia Ltd v Guy Gross* (1989) 15 IPR 385 Federal Court of Australia

[Colette, an Australian singer, re-recorded for CBS a song called "Ring My Bell", originally recorded during the 1970s by Anita Ward, an American singer. The original song was "in keeping with the black American 'funk' vocal tradition" (at 389) to which Anita Ward belonged. The Colette version was adapted to the style, range and capabilities of that singer resulting in a version which took "what may be called the line of least resistance to the song" (ibid). Colette had made a demonstration tape for CBS using an arrangement of "Ring My Bell" with instrumental parts supplied by Guy Gross, using a synthesiser. Gross claimed that the demonstration tape (the Trackdown version) embodied an original musical work, being an

■■■■■ CBS Records Australia v Guy Gross *continued*

arrangement of the song sufficiently different from the Anita Ward version, and that CBS had infringed that copyright by copying the arrangement.]

DAVIS J: ... **[392]** As to whether any copyright subsists in the Trackdown version is a point of difficulty. For copyright in an arrangement to subsist, the differences from the work arranged must be such that a new original work can be identified. Differences resulting from mere interpretation, particularly differences brought about by an arrangement of a work to suit the qualities of a particular singer's voice, do not result in the creation of an original work. Particularly is this so in the area of popular music where the latitude given to a performer may be much greater than that in classical works, where the notes, phrasing, emphasis and the like tend to be specified in great detail. Creational competition is required to bring into being an original work.

[The Trackdown version was considered by Davies J to be an original musical work.]

[394] ... But this is not a case where a particular feature stands out, where an opera score has been rewritten for piano or where important new harmonisations have been composed. In the present case, I am unable to identify any such element.

The work was a song having vocal lines and an instrumental backing. There were not two pieces of music. The vocal and instrumental parts were elements which combined together to form a single work. Whether there may be separate copyright in each map of a street directory, as discussed by Hill J in *Universal Press Pty Ltd v Provest Ltd & Brothers Publishing Pty Ltd* (1989) 14 IPR 623; 87 ALR 497, or in each chapter of a novel, as mentioned in *University of New South Wales v Moorhouse* (1975) 133 CLR 1; 6 ALR 193, the present is not such a case.

Notes

[3.180] In the event, CBS was found not to have infringed any copyright which subsisted in the "multitude of differences" between the two works.

Again, the requirement of "material form" means that improvised or traditional music will not attract copyright until and unless written down or otherwise embodied. Whether the person who effects this is the "author" of the work depends upon general principles, see *Report of the Committee appointed by the Attorney-General of the Commonwealth to consider what alterations are desirable to the copyright law of the Commonwealth* (Spicer Report) (22 December 1959, Canberra, 1965), paras 497-499.

■ Artistic works

[3.185] The question of what amounts to an artistic work for copyright purposes is, unusually, defined in the legislation rather than left to general principles. Also unusually, this definition imports aesthetic notions into the decision as to whether works of artistic craftsmanship, are protected. The *Copyright Act 1968* (Cth) provides:

"s 10 (1) 'artistic work' means:
 (a)   a painting, sculpture, drawing, engraving or photograph, whether the work is of artistic quality or not;
 (b)   a building or a model of a building, whether the building or model is of artistic quality or not; or

(c)   a work of artistic craftsmanship whether or not mentioned in paragraph (a) or (b); but does not include a circuit layout within the meaning of the *Circuit Layouts Act 1989.*"

Works of artistic craftsmanship are treated as "artistic" only if they have aesthetic appeal, whereas works encompassed within paras (a) and (b) of s 10(1) have only to exhibit the originality and substance generally required in order for copyright to subsist.

Painting

▬▬▬ Merchandising Corp of America v Harpbond ▬▬▬

[3.190] *Merchandising Corp of America Inc v Harpbond Ltd* [1983] FSR 32 Court of Appeal (United Kingdom)

LAWTON LJ: [42]...This is an appeal by the plaintiffs against an order of Walton J made on 25 November 1981, whereby he granted the plaintiffs some interlocutory relief by way of injunctions. But the plaintiffs, like Oliver Twist, have asked for more and, like Oliver Twist, they are not going to get it.

The appeal centres round what seems to me to be a novel and startling proposition, that there can be copyright in unusual facial make-up. Perhaps it is a sign of the times that it does not arise in connection with women's make-up but in connection with the make-up of the second plaintiff, Mr Stuart Leslie Goddard, it being make-up which he uses in the course of his performances as a pop star and in the publicity material with which he advertises himself to what no doubt is his adoring public.

The plaintiffs are four in number. The principal one is Mr Goddard. His stage name is Adam and he is the singer and the leader of a group which perform under the name of "Adam and the Ants". It is a matter within the knowledge of this court from another appeal a few weeks ago that, since 1979, the second plaintiff has arisen from comparative obscurity in the world of pop music to international fame. He has a large following in this country and it would appear from what we know of this case that he has followings outside the UK.

The plaintiffs are an American corporation called Merchandising Corporation of America. They specialise in exploiting the commercial opportunities which exist these days out of the reputations of persons in the public eye, particularly those in the world of pop entertainment.

The third and fourth plaintiffs are companies associated with Mr Goddard and they exist for various commercial purposes associated with his performances. One of the curiosities of the pop world is that there is a great deal of money to be made by putting on to the market what most of us would regard as garish material about pop stars. The first, second, third and fourth defendants are all concerned with publishing material of that kind. The fifth defendant, Mr Frank Langford, is a commercial artist. He comes into the story briefly but goes out again quickly. The reason he comes into the story is this, that at one stage, in the course of the activities of the first, second, third and fourth defendants, he was asked to paint a portrait of Mr Goddard, and he did so. That portrait was reproduced in various publications produced by the other defendants. The plaintiffs have taken exception to that portrait, alleging that it was published in breach of their copyright in the facial make-up of Mr Goddard. Mr Langford has, wisely, made his peace with the plaintiffs. So he is no longer involved in this litigation. He did, perhaps as part of making his peace (I know not), provide the plaintiffs with some information which he put into an affidavit to which I shall be

███████ Merchandising Corp of America v Harpbond *continued*

referring later, stating the circumstances in which he came to paint the portrait and how he went about it. ...

[46] ... Mr Wilson's bold submission at the beginning of his presentation of his clients' case was that the marks on Mr Goddard's face by way of facial make-up were painting. That caused me very considerable surprise, because, although there are various statutory provisions in the Act defining various words used in it, there is no statutory definition of a painting. "Painting" is a word in the ordinary usage of the English language and it is a question of fact in any particular case whether that which is under discussion is or is not a painting. It seemed to me, right at the beginning of Mr Wilson's submissions (and I want to be restrained in my language), that it was fantastic to suggest that make-up on anyone's face could possibly be a painting.

Mr Swift, in his succinct and concise reply, pointed out what had occurred to me and I had mentioned to Mr Wilson in the course of argument, that a painting must be on a surface of some kind. The surface upon which the startling make-up was put was Mr Goddard's face and, if there were a painting, it must be the marks plus Mr Goddard's face. If the marks are taken off the face there cannot be a painting. A painting is not an idea: it is an object; and paint without a surface is not a painting. Make-up, as such, however idiosyncratic it may be as an idea, cannot possibly be a painting for the purposes of the *Copyright Act 1956*.

The next submission made by Mr Wilson was that there had been indirect copying of the sketch. That indirect copying was alleged to have been partly in the kind of photographs which were reproduced in the defendants' magazines, to which I have already referred and clearly they were not reproductions of the sketch and partly (said Mr Wilson) in the portrait, because what had happened was that Mr Langford had used the concept of the make-up and, for the purposes of using that concept, had taken into account the photograph published in the Sun newspaper and had produced that which was remarkably like the photographs taken by Mr Ballard.

Mr Swift, in a careful analysis of the portrait and the sketch, showed that there were a number of dissimilarities. Clearly the portrait was not a copy of the sketch. It was something entirely different. Mr Wilson was no doubt alive to that way of looking at the problem, because he based his argument largely on the assertion that what Mr Langford had done in the portrait and what the first, second, third and fourth defendants had done by reproducing the portrait in their magazines was to use a substantial part of the sketch, the part which he had used being the lines on the face.

Mr Wilson relied upon part of the speech of Lord Reid in *Ladbroke (Football) Ltd v William Hill (Football) Ltd* [1964] 1 WLR 273. In [47] the course of his speech Lord Reid had referred to a "substantial" reproduction being something which was a "striking" part of the artistic work. But there are other passages in the case of Ladbroke which are of very considerable importance. The one which, in my judgment, is of particular importance occurs in the speech of Lord Pearce at 293. He asked this question:

> "Did the defendants reproduce a substantial part of it? Whether a part is substantial must be decided by its quality rather than its quantity. The reproduction of a part which by itself has no originality will not normally be a substantial part of the copyright and therefore will not be protected. For that which would not attract copyright except by reason of its collocation will, when robbed of that collocation, not be a substantial part of the copyright and therefore the courts will not hold its reproduction to be an infringement."

Two straight lines drawn with grease-paint with another line in between them drawn with some other colouring matter, in my judgment, by itself could not possibly attract copyright.

███ Merchandising Corp of America v Harpbond *continued*

It is only when they are put on Mr Goddard's face that anything particularly relevant to Mr Goddard comes into existence. When they are taken away from the sketch, as they must be taken away if their reproduction on anything else is said to be a reproduction of a striking part of the artistic work, then Lord Pearce's words apply.

Sculpture

[3.195] "s 10 (1) 'sculpture' includes a cast or model made for purposes of sculpture."

███ # Greenfield Products v Rover-Scott Bonnar ███

[3.200] *Greenfield Products Pty Ltd v Rover-Scott Bonnar Ltd* (1990) 17 IPR 417 Federal Court of Australia

PINCUS J: **[419]** The applicant and the respondent are competing manufacturers of ride-on mowers for use in parks and gardens. The applicant's substantial case is that it designed a new kind of drive mechanism for its mowers; the respondent later used the same basic design, having carefully inspected the applicant's. The suit seeks an injunction to restrain further breaches of copyright, damages for infringement of copyright, an account of profits and other relief.

... **[420]** ...

There being no doubt that the respondent imitated the applicant's design to a consider-able extent, taking advantage of the applicant's inventiveness and its development of that design over some years, some might have thought that the law would give the applicant some right of redress. The most obvious basis of a suit of that kind is the patent law, but the applicant had no patent for its invention (assuming it to be patentable) so that applicant has sued, as I have said, for breach of copyright, saying that the respondent copied its design.

In a very broad sense it did, and there are high authorities which suggest that such a claim as this is proved if copying is proved: *LB (Plastics) Ltd v Swish Products Ltd* [1979] RPC 551 at 619:

> "The protection given by the law of copyright is against copying, the basis of the protection being that one man must not be permitted to appropriate the result of another's labour. That copying has taken place is for the plaintiff to establish and prove as a matter of fact. The beginning of the necessary proof normally lies in the establishment of similarity combined with proof of access to the plaintiff's productions."

... **[426]** ...

Copyright in three-dimensional objects

There are no two-dimensional objects; the above heading is intended as a shorthand way of referring to the applicant's claim to copyright in certain moulds and in a drive mechanism, as opposed to its claim to copyright in drawings. The relevant parts of the statement of claim are paras 11(iii) (p 4) and 13 (pp 10, 11). These allege, in effect, that there is copyright in "moulds used in connection with the casting of" certain pulleys and clutch plates and in a certain drive mechanism.

It is argued on behalf of the applicant that the *Copyright Act*, as presently construed, is wide enough to encompass such objects.

Under Pt III of the Act, copyright may subsist in, inter alia, an artistic work and the applicant contends that the moulds and the drive mechanism **[427]** are artistic works. The expression "artistic work" is defined in s 10 to mean, inter alia:

"A painting, sculpture, drawing, engraving or photograph, whether the work is of artistic quality or not."

Each of the words "sculpture" and "engraving" is separately defined:

" 'Sculpture' includes a cast or model made for purposes of sculpture."

" 'Engraving' includes an etching, lithograph, product of photogravure, woodcut, print or similar work, not being a photograph."

It was argued on behalf of the applicant that copyright can subsist in the moulds and machine parts because they are "engravings" and that the drive mechanism is an "artistic work", being made up of its components which are themselves sculptures and therefore artistic works.

It is convenient to take the latter point first. Although the definition of "sculpture' is not exhaustive, in so far as the word remains undefined it must be given its ordinary meaning, in accordance with orthodox principles of construction. It is for that reason that I rejected evidence proffered on behalf of the respondent to prove what "sculpture" means in certain circles. The word "sculpture" is, at least in this context, not a technical term so as to make evidence admissible on the issue of statutory construction.

It appears to me clear that neither the moulds nor the drive mechanism, nor the parts of the latter, are sculptures in the ordinary case. It is true, as was pointed out in the course of argument, that some modern sculptures consist of or include parts of machines, but that does not warrant the conclusion that all machines and parts thereof are properly called sculpture, and similar reasoning applies to moulds. I respectfully agree with the conclusion arrived at in the New Zealand Court of Appeal, in *Lincoln Industries Ltd v Wham-O Manufacturing Co* (1984) 3 IPR 115 at 131 that frisbees are not sculptures under the *Copyright Act 1962* (NZ); that conclusion is consistent with mine.

I therefore reject the submission that there can be copyright in the drive mechanism. I do so with more confidence having regard to the concept of infringement by copying objects made from a copyright drawing; the development of that doctrine would have been unnecessary if machinery were itself the subject of copyright.

A submission which is not quite so easily disposed of is that moulds are "engravings" under the Act; this has some support from the Lincoln Industries case just referred to and from the reasons of the Court of Appeal of Hong Kong in *Interlego AG v Tyco Industries Inc* [1987] FSR 409 at 421 and 453. In the former case, there was evidence that the frisbee moulds were made by use of a tool, cutting medal blanks on a lathe. The court remarked (at 127):

"We see no reason why the process involved in the production of the die or mould, particularly the creation of the cuts to produce the ribs and rings should not be regarded as the act of engraving within the provisions of s 2(1)(a) of the Act, and the mould or die so created an 'engraving' just as a 'print' is an engraving in terms of the extended definition in s 2 of the Act."

The definition of "engraving" in issue there differed slightly from that with which I am concerned, but the difference is not of present significance.

■■■ Greenfield Products v Rover-Scott Bonnar *continued*

I do not well understand why the court thought that working at a lathe cutting into a rotating piece of metal with a tool is the work of engraving. One can use a tool fixed in a lathe to inscribe a pattern onto the surface of metal or other materials, but even that would not, perhaps, ordinarily be [428] called engraving. It is true that dictionary definitions of engraving refer to cutting, but it is not all cutting which is engraving; for example, to cut a piece of steel rod into lengths is not to engrave it. Nor, in my opinion, is the process of cutting metal from a block spinning of a lathe a process of engraving the block, in the ordinary sense of the word. The term does not cover shaping a piece of metal or wood on a lathe, but has to do with marking, cutting or working the surface typically, a flat surface of an object. The second edition of the *Oxford English Dictionary* cites usages of the word "engrave" which appear to support the New Zealand decision. For example, a translation of the *Metamorphoses* has: "The fatall steele ... he waues Deepe in his guts, and wounds on wounds ingraues." But that was published in 1626 and no modern similar example is given. More generally, the text under "engrave" supports the view that in current usage the physical meaning is confined to cutting, marking or otherwise working a surface. The same may be said of the dictionary's treatment of "engraving", except that "engraving" can mean the product as well as the process.

I note that the Court of Appeal went on to say (at 219) that each frisbee made from a mould is an "image produced from an engraved plate" and therefore a "print". I was urged by Mr Hanger QC to adopt what he described as the "flexible approach" evinced in this decision, particularly as it has at least the tentative approval of the Hong Kong Court of Appeal in the *Interlego* case.

No consideration of policy, or other orthodox approach, could justify straining the English language so far as to call the moulds engravings. Despite the respect which one must have for any decision of the New Zealand Court of Appeal, I find myself unable to follow the approach in the *Lincoln Industries* case. In particular, I cannot, with respect, agree with the view that a frisbee is an image or that it is a print. Similarly, in my opinion, the moulds from which these machine parts are made are not engavings. It is unnecessary to consider the question whether "engraving" in the Act includes such objects as were dealt with in *James Arnold & Co Ltd v Miafern Ltd* [1980] RPC 397.

I should add that I am by no means convinced that the New Zealand decision, even if correct, produces success for the applicant on this point; as was pointed out on behalf of the respondent, the basis of that decision appears to have been that operations which involve cutting to create a shape are properly called engraving. But here there was no evidence that the moulds were produced by any sort of cutting.

The applicant also contended that the machine parts are themselves "engravings". Counsel did not shrink from the proposition that a machined steel shaft, however enormous, is an "engraving". That seems to me preposterous.

I therefore arrive at the conclusion that the applicant's claim to copyright in the moulds and machine parts is ill-founded and cannot succeed, because they cannot be the subject of copyright.

Drawings

[3.205] "s 10(1) 'drawing' includes a diagram, map, chart or plan."

The question of whether a work amounts to a "drawing" is not usually in dispute. In view of the vast array of items which can begin life as a drawing in which copyright subsists, any difficulties are usually found when considering reproduction of the work in another dimension, which will amount to infringement. There may be a point at which a drawing is so close to an idea that copyright protection is of little value: *Kenrick & Co v Lawrence & Co* (1890) 25 QBD 99; *Beck v Montana* [1964-65] NSWR 229; *FAI Insurance Ltd v Advance Bank Aust Ltd* (1986) 7 IPR 217. Almost certainly, the main area of commercial activity, with respect to litigating copyright in drawings, concerns the "architect's plans" cases. See *Eagle Homes Pty Ltd v Austec Homes Pty Ltd* (1999) 43 IPR 1; (1999) 44 IPR 535; *LED Builders v Eagle Homes* (1999) 44 IPR 24; *Carlisle County Homes v Brown* [1999] QDC 284; *Clarendon Homes (Aust) Pty Ltd v Henley Arch Pty Ltd* (1999) 46 IPR 309; *Tolmark Homes v Paul* (1999) 46 IPR 321; *New England Country Homes Pty Ltd v Moore* (1998) 45 IPR 186.

Engravings

[3.210] "s 10(1) 'engraving' includes an etching, lithograph, product of photogravure, wood cut, print or similar work, not being a photograph.

'plate' includes a stereotype, stone, block, mould, matrix, transfer, negative or other similar appliance."

Photographs

[3.215] "s 10(1) 'photograph' means a product of photography or of a process similar to photography, other than an article or thing in which visual images forming part of a cinematograph film have been embodied, and includes a product of xerography, and 'photographic' has a corresponding meaning."

Buildings and models

[3.220] "s 10(1) 'building' includes a structure of any kind."

The copyright subsisting in a building is separate from any copyright in plans or drawings for that building. In *Half Court Tennis Pty Ltd v Seymour* (1980) 53 FLR 240 it was held that a half sized tennis court was a copyright work. Dunn J said (at 248):

"The plaintiffs' case was that Wills and K had, by using considerable industry and skill, produced an artistic work, namely a building, in which copyright subsists. The building in question, in my opinion, was a concrete slab with special markings upon it ...

The fact that a half court can scarcely be described as a thing of beauty does not matter. What does matter is that it is the result of skill and labour by Wills and K."

In *Darwin Fibreglass Pty Ltd v Kruhse Enterprises Pty Ltd* (1998) 41 IPR 649 it was held that a fibreglass swimming pool was a "structure" and therefore capable of being a building since it had the size, permanence and was substantial enough to be within copyright concepts. The mould from which the pool was cast was a model of a building, since "the mould stores the form, or a substantial part of the form of the pool in a three dimensional way, from which it would be relatively easy to copy the form of the ideas therein expressed" (at 656).

Works of artistic craftsmanship

[3.225] Despite the apparently narrow scope of protection offered under this heading, its importance lies in the fact that this is the only category of protection for three-dimensional objects, apart from sculptures, buildings and models of buildings. Many cases have sought protection as a "work of artistic craftsmanship" for what is otherwise an industrial mass-produced item.

This is the only category of work where there needs to be some assessment of the merits of the creative effort. "Artistic" in this context seems to connote some aesthetic element: see *Burke & Margot Burke Ltd v Spicers Dress Designs* [1936] Ch 400; *George Hensher Ltd v Restawile Upholstery (Lancs) Ltd* [1976] AC 64; [1975] RPC 31. The restriction placed on works of artistic craftsmanship reflects the law's anxiety not to protect for the duration of copyright objects which may be more readily regarded as items of commerce, at the same time recognising that artistic endeavour may be manifested in various media. The Gregory Committee (*Report of the Copyright Committee*, Cmnd 8662, HMSO, 1952) decided that the term should not be defined by statute but would include items crafted from silver, pottery, wood and embroidery (at para 260). A work of artistic craftsmanship must be fixed in material form to be protected, so moving sand landscapes are not protected by copyright: *Komesaroff v Mickle* (1986) 7 IPR 295.

The following extract considers whether a machine-made article is "artistic craftsmanship".

▬▬▬ Coogi Australia v Hysport International ▬▬▬

[3.230] *Coogi Australia Pty Ltd v Hysport International Pty Ltd* (1998) 41 IPR 593 Federal Court of Australia

DRUMMOND J: **[594]** ... The applicant has long been a designer and manufacturer of machine knitted fabrics and garments made up from its fabrics. In the early 1990s it made and **[595]** sold garments from a fabric it manufactured which embodied a design described as its "XYZ design". The first respondent (of which the second to sixth respondents are directors) is a competitor. The applicant claims that the first respondent has "since at least May 1992" made and sold three styles of knitted garments (together with variations of those styles) which are identified as HY95, HY82 and HY96. The applicant claims that, by doing this, the first respondent has infringed its copyright:

(1)   in two "artistic works", viz, its fabrics and its garments that bear the XYZ design. It is said that each piece of fabric and each garment is an "artistic work" for the purposes of ss 31 and 32 of the *Copyright Act 1911* because it is a "work of artistic craftsmanship" within the definition of "artistic work" in s 10 of that Act;

(2)   in a "literary work", viz, "the computer program and/or data comprised in the computer program, made in or about 1989, used for the manufacture by computerised knitting machines of garments bearing the XYZ design, including the print out of the programming codes, known as the XYZ control program, and the XYZ graph in symbol form contained therein".

It is said that this program is a "literary work" for the purposes of ss 31 and 32 of the Act because it is a "computer program" within the meaning of that term in the definition in s 10 of "literary work", ie, it is within the definition of "computer program" in that section of the Act. ...

While Coogi, in its pleading, identified the subject matter of the first of its copyright claims as works of artistic craftsmanship comprising "fabric and/or garments manufactured by the applicant since 1989 bearing the XYZ design", at trial it put this part of its case more narrowly. In the course of the hearing, Coogi's counsel limited the subject matter of its copyright claim in the XYZ fabric to the form of the stitch structure of the fabric: Coogi produced the fabric in a total of eight colour ranges, but it made no attempt to identify them and disavowed that its colour selections comprised any part of this particular copyright claim. At trial, Coogi put its claim that Hysport had infringed its copyright in the XYZ fabric on the basis that there were so many similarities between the stitch structures of the two fabrics that

━━━━ Coogi Australia v Hysport International *continued*

Hysport had reproduced not the whole, but a substantial part, of the structure of the XYZ fabric. ... [596] ...

The applicant's case, as refined in counsel's closing submissions, of infringement of copyright in its computer program is one of infringement by unauthorised adaptation, rather than reproduction. Counsel for the applicant also said that no claim was made to copyright in the data associated with the program, save in so far as that data actually forms part of the Coogi computer program. ... [601] ...

The XYZ fabric as a work of artistic craftsmanship

A substantial argument by Hysport against Coogi's claim that its XYZ fabric is a work of artistic craftsmanship turns on the proposition, which I accept, that Coogi's design effort was directed entirely to setting up a system for the mass production of fabric having particular features. The product of such a process, so Hysport says, is the antithesis of a work of artistic craftsmanship. In order to deal with this argument, it is first necessary to dispose of Coogi's contention that each of the many mass-produced runs of fabric embodying the XYZ design (and each of the many garments made from that fabric) is itself an "original work of artistic craftsmanship" within s 32.

Such a claim is not sustainable. Copyright only subsists, pursuant to s 32 of the Act, in an original work of which the author was a qualified person "when the work was made". It is clear from s 22 that, since a work is made for the purposes of s 32 when it "was first reduced to ... some ... material form", it is only the first expression or fixation of the author's skill and labour that can constitute the work in which copyright subsists. If the fact that Coogi produced fabric to the XYZ design in eight separate colour ranges is ignored for the moment, Coogi [602] can, at most, have copyright only in that portion of the first roll of fabric produced by it in which the XYZ design was first completely embodied: it cannot sustain its claim to copyright in every length of fabric bearing the XYZ design.

But the question remains: can Coogi claim copyright in the first embodiment of the XYZ design as a "work of artistic craftsmanship", given that it too was the result of Coogi's efforts in setting up a process for the mass production of fabric to that design. (If Coogi can make out this claim, it would be an infringement for Hysport to reproduce that copyright subject matter by indirectly copying it from any one of the 2,500 or so Coogi garments that incorporated it.)

The law as to what is a work of artistic craftsmanship is not in a very satisfactory state: cf Lord Kilbrandon's comment in *George Hensher Ltd v Restawhile Upholstery (Lancs) Ltd* [1976] AC 64 at 98. But current authority supports, I think, a number of propositions:

(1) The phrase "works of artistic craftsmanship" is a composite phrase that must be construed as a whole. There is nothing to suggest that any of the words is used in other than one of its ordinary senses: *Hensher,* per Lord Simon, at 91.

(2) As is suggested by a comparison of paras (a) and (b) with para (c) of the definition of "artistic work" in s 10, a work will qualify as one of artistic craftsmanship only if it has an element of real artistic, ie, aesthetic, quality, whether or not it is a utilitarian article: *Cuisenaire v Reed* [1963] VR 719 at 730 lines 30 to 35; *Hensher* at 77F and 78F-G, 81H, 85H and 86E, 96G-H; *Merlet v Mothercare PLC* (1984) 2 IPR 456 at 465 and *Bonz Group (Pty) Ltd v Cooke* (1994) 3 NZLR 216 at 224.

(3) Implicit in the proposition that the existence of utilitarian features will not disqualify an article from being a work of artistic craftsmanship is the further proposition that the article need not have such a high level of aesthetic quality as to make it a work of fine art. In *Hensher,* Lord Reid at 78H and Lord Simon at 90F-G said as much. Lord Simon explained why (at 90): the object of giving copyright protection to "works of artistic

craftsmanship", first conferred by the *Copyright Act* (UK), was to extend to works of applied art the protection formerly restricted to works of fine art, an extension made under the influence of the Arts and Crafts Movement.

(4) The level of aesthetic appeal required for a work of artistic craftsmanship is higher than mere visual appeal (one of the tests for design registrability); *Hensher* at 79C-F, 81E-F, 84F-G and 93E-F, 95F-H.

(5) In determining whether an article has sufficient aesthetic quality to be a work of artistic craftsmanship the Court is determining a question of fact on the basis of the evidence before it: *Hensher* at 82B, 87A-B, 94H and 97C-D.

It has been said that in deciding whether a work of craftsmanship has artistic quality the Court must not act on its own aesthetic judgment: *Hensher* at 78CD, 87BC, 94G and 96H-97A; *Bonz* at 224 lines 1-5. Accordingly, Laddie, Prescott and Vitoria, in *The Modern Law of Copyright and Designs* (2nd ed), p 208, favour Lord Reid's test in *Hensher* and suggest that the necessary artistic element in a work of artistic craftsmanship will be shown by evidence that the visual appearance of the article is such as to cause at least some members of the public to wish to acquire and retain the article "on especial account" thereof. That, the authors say, is a fact capable of objective ascertainment by the Court and the Court is not required to base its decision on its own aesthetic opinion. Viscount Dilhorne at 87D rejected this sort of test as did Lord Simon, at 93D-H. It cannot be right. The statute by its definition of "artistic work" requires that a work of artistic craftsmanship be "of artistic quality"; in this context, that seems clearly [603] to require that it have some aesthetic value. That a segment of the public can be found which may have been persuaded by advertising or by a transient fad to want to own the work because of its visual appeal does not necessarily mean that it must have the requisite minimum level of aesthetic value. I do not think the Court can, in determining whether a work is one of artistic craftsmanship, avoid the task of making a judgment, on the evidence before it, whether the work has a sufficient level of aesthetic appeal to be "of artistic quality". Forming a view, on conflicting evidence, as to what is essentially a matter of aesthetic taste is not a novel task for a court: see, eg, *Attorney-General for NSW v Trustees of the National Art Gallery of New South Wales* (1944) 62 WN(NSW) 212.

(6) Whether a work has the requisite aesthetic quality must be determined objectively: *Hensher* 81F-G (and cf 95B-C, where it was said that it is "the intent of the creator and its result" which will determine whether the work is one of artistic craftsmanship); *Cuisenaire* at 730 lines 50-55 and *Bonz* at 223-224.

(7) In determining whether an article has the requisite aesthetic quality, evidence that the creator intended to make an article possessing aesthetic quality is important, although not essential: *Hensher* 78F-G, 81G, 95B-C; *Merlet* at 465 ll 25-30 and *Cuisenaire* at 730 lines 50-55. Because the test is objective, whether the work has aesthetic quality cannot depend solely upon the subjective intent of the creator, since he may have failed to realise his intent, if it was an aesthetic one: *Bonz* at 223-224 and *Merlet* at 465.

In *Hensher*, Lord Kilbrandon, at 96F-H, appears to suggest that the presence of such an intention in the creator is determinative of whether the work will have the necessary artistic quality, although he also seems to say this is an objective test at bottom, in so far as he says that "[i]t must be possible to deduce the conscious purpose of artistic creation from the work itself or from the circumstances of its creation". But the way he then qualifies this statement makes it difficult to be certain just what he means.

(8) Expert evidence as to whether a work possesses the requisite aesthetic quality is admissible: *Hensher* at 78G, 82B-C, 87C, 94G-H (although the members of the House place differing emphases on the cogency of such evidence).

━━━━ Coogi Australia v Hysport International *continued*

(9) Beyond this, it is difficult to find any guidance as to the considerations relevant to identifying the existence of the requisite aesthetic quality. But one thing is clear enough: the presence of non-functional features cannot be the test since, as Lord Simon observes in *Hensher* at 93B-C, the anthesis between function and beauty is a false one, especially in the context of the Arts and Crafts Movement.

(10) Before a work will qualify as a work of craftsmanship, it must be a manifestation of pride in sound workmanship and the result of the exercise of skill on the part of its creator in using the materials of which the article is made and the devices by which those materials are turned into the article. Lord Simon in *Hensher* said, at 91:

> "A work of craftsmanship, even though it cannot be confined to handicraft, at least presupposes special training, skill and knowledge for its production: see *Cuisenaire v Reed* [1963] VLR 719; *Cuisenaire v South West Imports Ltd* [1968] 1 ExCR 493, 514. 'Craftsmanship', particularly when considered in its historical context, implies a manifestation of pride in sound workmanship—a rejection of the shoddy, the meretricious, the facile."

See also *Merlet* at 460, *Bonz* at 224 and *Cuisenaire* at 729. **[604]**

(11) There is a difference of judicial opinion as to whether craftsmanship connotes only something hand made. In *Hensher* Lord Reid at 77E referred to a work of craftsmanship suggesting "a durable useful handmade object" and Viscount Dilhorne at 84D said: "[a] work of craftsmanship is, in my opinion, something made by hand and not something mass produced". Pape J, in *Cuisenaire* at 729, spoke of craftsmanship as involving the display of manual skill.

In *Hensher*, Lord Simon, however, observed at 90F that Parliament deliberately used the words "artistic craftsmanship" not "artistic handicraft" and, in discussing the reason why copyright protection was given by the 1911 Act to works of artistic craftsmanship, viz, to give protection to works of applied art, in response to the influence of the Arts and Crafts Movement, said, at 91:

> "[A]lthough 'works of artistic craftsmanship" cannot be adequately construed without bearing in mind the aims and achievements of the Arts and Crafts movement, 'crafts-manship" in the statutory phrase cannot be limited to handicraft; nor is the word 'artistic" incompatible with machine production: see *Britain v Hanks Brothers and Co* (1902) 86 LT 765."

... Pape J, in *Cuisenaire*, found support for his view that manual involvement was necessary to craftsmanship in the 1952 UK Copyright Committee's comment that copyright protection given to works of artistic craftsmanship was not intended to be given to mass-produced articles, which could obtain protection under the registered designs legislation, even if they might otherwise qualify as works of artistic craftsmanship: s 22 of the *Copyright Act 1911* (UK) then in force (the legislation with which Pape J was concerned—[605] see [1963] VR at 725) denied copyright protection to designs capable of registration under the designs legislation. Pape J therefore read down the expression to cover only unique, handmade objects. ... **[605]** ...

Hysport put a similar argument to that which Pape J accepted. It contended that, since the object of Div 8 of Part III the *Copyright Act* was to deny copyright protection to artistic works applied in mass production and to permit only design protection for such works, achievement of that object would be impeded if the exemption of works of artistic craftsmanship from the general rule in Div 8 against dual protection for artistic works were widened by widening

██████ Coogi Australia v Hysport International *continued*

the meaning of the expression "a work of a artistic craftsmanship" to include mass-produced articles. But the *Copyright Act* treats works of artistic craftsmanship differently from other artistic works. Unlike the position reflected in s 22 of the 1911 UK Act and that which obtained under Div 8 of Part III the *Copyright Act 1968* prior to the 1989 amendments, protection under both the *Copyright Act 1968* and the *Designs Act 1906* (Cth) is now available to works of artistic craftsmanship. It matters not whether such a work is intended to be the subject of or used in mass production. Copyright protection is only lost for a work of artistic craftsmanship if the owner chooses to obtain design registration for that work. Otherwise, he can enforce his intellectual property rights in such a work by relying only on the *Copyright Act*, even though it was always his intention that the work would be industrially exploited. See ss 75 and 77 of the Act.

The Explanatory Memorandum to the Bill which became the 1989 amending Act suggests that the reason why works of artistic craftsmanship were exempted from the general rule in Div 8 that copyright should not be available to protect artistic works capable of industrial application was that, even though such works can embrace a wide range of works well capable of industrial application, they are a special case: "it is considered these articles are more appropriately protected under the [Copyright] Act whether industrially applied or not" (para 24). What may justify the special status conferred on works of artistic craftsmanship by ss 74-77 is recognition that the real artistic quality that is an essential feature of such works and the desirability of encouraging real artistic effort directed to industrial design is sufficient to warrant the greater protection and the accompanying stifling effect on manufacturing development that long copyright gives, in contrast to relatively short design-protection. Division 8 therefore provides no foundation for arguing that an expression "a work of artistic craftsmanship" should be narrowly construed.

(12)   There is also a conflict of judicial opinion whether a work can be one of artistic craftsmanship only if it is the product of a person who combines both artistic and craft skills in making it or whether it is enough that the work meets the two criteria of being a work of craftsmanship and a work possessing the requisite minimum degree of aesthetic quality.

In *Hensher* at 94E-F, Lord Simon said that whether a work was one of artistic craftsmanship depended on whether it was produced by a person who is an artist-craftsman, not on whether it had two separate characteristics, viz, first, that it was produced by a craftsman and, secondly, that it had artistic quality: see also 95B-C. Statements in *Cuisenaire* at 729 and 730 suggest Pape J was of the same opinion. I have difficulty in accepting what is said in *Cuisenaire* (at 730 [606] lines 25-30) to the effect that the word "artistic" refers to some quality in the acts performed by the maker in the physical operation of making the article as distinct from "earlier cogitation and thought which produced the idea upon which the work was based". It must be possible for many works of artistic craftsmanship to come into existence as a result of an artistic design fully realised before any of the skilled work to implement that design is undertaken, even where it is all the work of a single person. Despite what he said in *Bonz*, at 224, in apparent acceptance of Lord Simon's view on the point, Tipping J in the passage immediately following considered that a work could be one of artistic craftsmanship even "[i]f two or more people combined to design and make the ultimate product". He held that the garments there in question were works of artistic craftsmanship because "the designer of the garments can fairly be called an artist and the handknitters can fairly be described as craftsmen".

Once it is accepted, as I think it should be, that "works of artistic craftsmanship" are not confined to handmade objects, there is no reason why it should be essential for such a work to be the product of the efforts of a single person, ie, of an artist-craftsman. It is enough that it satisfies the two criteria of craftsmanship and aesthetic quality.

▬▬▬ Coogi Australia v Hysport International *continued*

It cannot be contended that the XYZ fabric does not have aesthetic value sufficient to show that it is "of artistic quality". The way Coogi has used stitch structures and colour to produce an unusual textured and multi-coloured fabric for fashion garments suggests this. The experts, Mr Sonday, Mr Buckingham and Dr Dutton, agree that the fabric has aesthetic quality.

Mass production is not inconsistent with the articles so produced each having aesthetic value. Many mass-produced articles, such as nails, screws, etc made as purely functional fasteners, will not be capable of being works of artistic craftsmanship simply because they lack any aesthetic element in themselves (even though their display by Marcel Duchamp might be said by some to transmute them into works of art). But other mass-produced articles (such as the works of Charles and Ray Eames, "American designers best-known for the beauty, comfort, elegance and delicacy of their mass-producible furniture": *New Encyclopaedia Britannica*, 15th ed, Vol 4, p 317) have real aesthetic quality.

Nor do I accept that the only article capable of attracting copyright here, viz, the first production run of the XYZ fabric that was the first piece of fabric that the Coogi design team accepted as realising their design objective, was not also a work of craftsmanship.

There is no necessary difference between a skilled person who makes an article with hand-held tools and a skilled person who uses those skills to set up and operate a machine which produces an article. Such an article can still be a work of craftsmanship even though the creator has used a highly sophisticated computer-controlled machine to produce it, if nevertheless it is a manifestation of the creator's skill with computer-controlled machinery, knowledge of materials and pride in workmanship. The expert witnesses, Dr Dutton, Mr Sonday and Mr Buckingham did not suggest the contrary. To hold otherwise would be to import a Luddite philosophy into copyright legislation enacted against a background of modern industrial organisation and intended to regulate rights of value to persons involved in that area of activity ... **[608]** ...

In my opinion, the first run of the XYZ fabric is a "work of artistic craftsmanship" for the purposes of the *Copyright Act,* notwithstanding that it was made as, and intended by those involved in its creation to be, the first of many identical runs of fabric bearing that design. None of the runs of the fabric subsequent to the first one to bear the XYZ design is, however, capable of being such a work (subject only to the consideration that needs to be given to the significance to its copyright claim of the fact that Coogi produced XYZ design fabric in a limited number of different colourways).

■ **The boundaries of statutory protection for copyright and designs**
See *Copyright Act 1968* (Cth), ss 74–77A.

▬▬▬▬▬▬▬ **Sheldon v Metrokane** ▬▬▬▬▬▬▬

[3.235] *Sheldon & Hammond Pty Ltd v Metrokane Inc* (2004) 135 FCR 34 Federal Court of Australia

CONTI J: **[36]** ... This litigation has its origins in a corkscrew product called Rabbit, the development whereof was initiated in the United States of America, in or about September 1997 by the Respondent/Cross-Claimant Metrokane Inc ("Metrokane"), a company established in 1983 in the United States. Metrokane conducts the business of designing and selling unique houseware products ...

■■■■ Sheldon v Metrokane *continued*

In about October 1997, Metrokane engaged Edward Kilduff, ("Mr Kilduff") being the second cross-claimant and a citizen of the United States, and then associated informally with Daniel Winigrad ("Mr Winigrad") ... to develop a new design for a corkscrew having a lever-action. His instructions were to produce a design which would be refined and elegant yet be "utilitarian and homely". It was also to have award winning aesthetics, with a distinctive design and an aesthetically visual appeal, rather than something merely utilitarian and functional...The mechanism of the corkscrew was to be based upon the technical principles of a patent for lever action corkscrews, owned by the multinational manufacturer Le Creuset, which was due to expire in July 1999. The trade name of the Le Creuset corkscrew was and apparently still is Screwpull. Mr Larimer informed Mr Kilduff that he expected that a number of lever-action corkscrews would be produced and arrive on the market after the expiry of that patent ... **[38]** ...

Mr Kilduff said that he oversaw the design and assembly in the factory in China, in order "... to make sure it is what I had in mind". Although the Rabbit corkscrew is a so-called "functional or utilitarian article", Metrokane's case was that the same had nevertheless "real aesthetic qualities".

The design of the Rabbit corkscrew received the following two awards in 2001:

(i) The IDSA 2001 Award for design excellence in consumer products, which was judged by the Industrial Designers Society of America, and sponsored by Business Week Magazine; and

(ii) The Good Design Award from the Chicago Athenaeum Museum for "The World's Best and Most Innovative New Product Designs".

The IDSA press release described the Rabbit corkscrew as having "... an ergonomic design that sets a new standard for ease of use without sacrificing beauty".
... **[47]** ...

The controversy as to boundaries of statutory protection of copyright and designs

S & H drew attention to what was described as the enigma of the so-called copyright/design "overlap" protection provisions, in support of a contention that s 77 could not sensibly have been intended, as a matter of legislative intention, to permit an article, said by S & H to be registrable under the *Designs Act*, to secure so much longer protection as an artistic work under the *Copyright Act*.

[49] ... It is ... apparent that the presence within s 77 of the undefined expression 'artistic craftsmanship' has left open for the Courts to determine its parameters. So much was in effect acknowledged by the Gregory Committee Report of 1953 in the following terms:

> "It is clear that some protection of this kind is required to cover works of art other than such things as works of painting, drawing and sculpture, which are mentioned by name. We are here concerned not with articles manufactured under conditions of ordinary industrial production (artistically meritorious as many of these are) which can secure their own appropriate protection under the Registered Designs Act, but with the works of craftsmen working in many media (silversmiths, potters, woodworkers, hand-embroiderers and many others) in circumstances for which that Act does not provide appropriate protection. We do not think it will be questioned that original works of the kind we have in mind are fully entitled to protection and but for the Copyright Act this would be lacking. We believe that copyright provides the proper basis for protecting these works and to ensure this protection we believe that it is necessary to retain the term 'works of artistic craftsmanship' in the Act. It is by no

means certain that full preliminary sketches or drawings are prepared for all kinds of articles made by the craftsman (in which case copying the article itself might infringe copyright as a reproduction of the sketch), or, even where there is a full design, that the finally finished article as it leaves the craftsman's hands would unquestionably be regarded in every case as a reproduction of that copyright design. In these circumstances the only safe way to ensure protection is by making specific mention of this class of work. In doing so, it will be necessary, we believe, to retain the word 'artistic' in conjunction with 'craftsmanship', but we do not believe it is practicable to draft a statutory definition equally applicable to each of the whole range of activities and of the varieties of materials used. Faced with these almost endless possibilities we feel that, as now, the decision in doubtful cases must be left to the courts to decide on the facts before them, and we recommend that while the protection given to 'works of artistic craftsmanship' should remain, the term should not be defined in the Act."

It would appear that the copyright protection which Metrokane seeks to enforce in the present proceedings is conceptually beyond the scope of what was envisaged by the Gregory Committee Report, unless Metrokane could establish its claim as one of the "doubtful cases" which the Report seemingly had in mind. To that observation I would add reference to dictum in *Interlego AG v Croner Trading Pty Ltd* (1992) 25 IPR 65 at 97, where Gummow J, with whom Black CJ and Lockhart J agreed, said as follows, in terms of the distinction between the principles of protection respectively afforded by the general law as to copyright, designs and patents:

"It is well established that in copyright law originality is a concept distinct from novelty in design law and patent law and from obviousness in patent law. Whilst the author of what is claimed to be an original artistic work must have expended a significant amount of his skill and labour, 'originality' does not mean novelty or uniqueness and does not require inventiveness in the sense of patent law ... The degree of skill and labour required of the artist will vary with the nature of the work."

... [64] ...

Whether Metrokane established the existence of authorship of any work of artistic craftsmanship

Unless inconsistent with the context, any reference in this segment to Metrokane should be taken to include reference to Mr Kilduff. No challenge was made to Mr Kilduff's credentials or qualifications as an industrial designer. A critical controversy concerning Mr Kilduff however arises as to whether he has been established by Metrokane as the craftsman of the Rabbit corkscrew. It [65] may be accepted that he was the artist, being the author of the Kilduff drawings. For Metrokane to qualify the Renshape prototype, CNC Model or Rabbit corkscrew as a work of artistic craftsmanship, it became necessary to establish the existence of the author or joint authors of such articles, and the craftsman so established, if Mr Kilduff alone, would have the consequence that he was empowered to enforce the alleged copyright appertaining to the Rabbit corkscrew as a cross-claimant.

S & H contended that Mr Kilduff was not the craftsman, or at least not the sole craftsman of the Rabbit corkscrew, as distinct from being merely the designer or architect, and thus the artist, in respect thereof. That was said to be because of the functions and activities of unknown and unidentified persons in the factory in China who engaged in whatever crafting of the Rabbit corkscrew might have occurred, such as to establish the existence of a work of artistic craftsmanship, and thus to sustain the cross-claim. As indicated in *Cuisenaire*, the craftsman must be identified, and to merely give instructions to the manufacturer is not to be

■■■■■ Sheldon v Metrokane *continued*

thereby constituted as a craftsman. The craftsman must be closely involved in the manufacture, as illustrated in Coogi.

... [69] ...

In light of the evidence of Mr Kilduff which I have reviewed, a factual conclusion is open to be drawn to the effect that Mr Kilduff was not the sole author of whatever copyright might exist in relation to the first manufactured Rabbit corkscrew as an alleged work of artistic craftsmanship. The contribution of an unidentified employee or unidentified employees of the unidentified manufacturer in China to the existence of any craftsmanship element of that work may be inferred from the evidence to have been not immaterial or insignificant, at least by reason of the apparent length of time taken up to, and so it would seem including, the occasion of the first run of manufacture of the Rabbit corkscrew, commencing perhaps from the time of Mr Kilduff's initial visit to China as far back as March 1999. I acknowledge that a work of artistic craftsmanship may be brought into existence jointly by the efforts of two or more authors. ... [70] ...

[His Honour set out the principles of joint authorship from *Bulun Bulun v R T Textiles Pty Ltd* (1998) 41 IPR 513. See [**4.65**].]

If Mr Kilduff was not the sole author of the artistic work within s 35(2) of the *Copyright Act*, by reason of some one or more persons in the factory in China having jointly contributed to the creation of such craftsmanship as may be inherent in the Rabbit corkscrew, it must follow in my opinion that Mr Kilduff as purported author, and therefore also Metrokane as his assignee, are not qualified to maintain their cross-claims for relief as copyright authors. ...

... [72] ...

If my resolution of the authorship issue be correct, the question as to whether the Rabbit corkscrew comprises a work of artistic craftsmanship does not arise. Nevertheless it remains appropriate that I resolve the same.

... [80] ...

My resolution of the issue as to whether the Rabbit corkscrew constituted a work of artistic craftsmanship

... There is something antithetical in the notion of a manufacturer gaining exclusive protection of a mass-produced article by way of copyright, for a period of time substantially longer than that provided by statute law in relation to designs and patents. The circumstances of the present case exemplify the kind of conceptual enigmas which may thus arise. Inferentially essential to the purpose of creation and distribution of this mass-produced Rabbit corkscrew is its function as a corkscrew based upon its lever-action mechanism being the same as or virtually identical to the celebrated Le Creuset mechanism the subject of recently expired international patent protection. No member of the public would have sensibly purchased the Rabbit corkscrew, I would infer, in the absence of its mechanism, or in other words, would have purchased the same merely to enjoy the sight and feel of its handle or body structure, attractive as they may be.

The emphasis of the Australian authorities, to which I have earlier referred, is upon the object of the author in purportedly creating a work of artistic craftsmanship, rather than upon the reaction of the viewer to the completed work, the merit or otherwise thereof being immaterial for qualification within that statutory description. That emphasis also appears from what I have cited from the speeches in the House of Lords in *Hensher* of Lord Reid and Lord Simon. Moreover the related theme as to the inappropriateness of the courts making aesthetic judgments also appears in what I have cited from the speeches in *Hensher* of

▬▬▬ Sheldon v Metrokane *continued*

Viscount Dilhorne, Lord Simon and Lord Kilbrandon, and has been similarly emphasised in the Australian authorities which I have reviewed, and to which I would add reference to the opening observation in the judgment of Hill J, as a member of a Full Federal Court, in *Schott Musik International GMBH & Co v Colossal Records of Australia Pty Ltd* (1997) 75 FCR 321 at 325.

I am unable to accept the submission of Metrokane that the object of Metrokane in creating the Rabbit corkscrew was for a sole or dominant purpose of creating a work of artistic craftsmanship per se. ... **[81]** ... As I have already inferred, the motivation of Metrokane in manufacturing the Rabbit corkscrew originated in the pending expiration of the Le Creuset patent relating to what appears to have been a somewhat sophisticated corkscrew mechanism. It could not sensibly be postulated, nor was it postulated, that consumers would buy the Rabbit corkscrew without that mechanism. The attraction to consumers, I would infer, has been to acquire an efficient corkscrew mechanism contained within an attractively presented framework.

The present circumstances are thus distinguishable from those in *Coogi*. The manufactured fabric there involved would have been purchased by consumers for use as clothing per se, and not as a framework for an every day consumer facility. ... What is here claimed to reflect "the main object of appealing to the aesthetic tastes of those who view it", to cite further from *Cuisenaire*, consists only of the body or framework of something which would not be acquired by a consumer, at least in the normal course, without the working parts installed within that framework. It is in that respect that I think there is something to be said in favour of the contention of S & H to the effect that the law of copyright should not be afforded an "overlapping" operation, notwithstanding that I have not given effect to that contention. The objective of Metrokane in creating the Rabbit corkscrew may be described, perhaps repetitively, as the reproduction in attractive clothing of the mechanism of an expired, and apparently well known patent earlier developed by a third party (Le Creuset), with a view to mass production for the sole purpose of substantial profit-making by sale. That objective appears to have been achieved.

... **[83]** ...

In the result, as a judge of fact at first instance, I would reject the characterisation of the Rabbit corkscrew as a work of artistic craftsmanship.

■ Adaptation of works

[3.240] The idea/expression dichotomy implies that certain kinds of uses of another's work are permissible so long as the forms of expression of the two works remain different. However, free access to a copyright work needs to be qualified in view of the exclusive right under *Copyright Act 1968* (Cth), s 31(1)(a)(vi) to "make an adaptation" of a literary, dramatic and musical work. Note there is no adaptation right for artistic works, or in relation to other copyright subject matter; see, however, s 21(3).

Section 10 defines the meaning of adaptation. In relation to literary works, the adaptation right includes an exclusive right to make dramatised versions of non-dramatic forms of literary works. For example, Peter Benchley, as author of the novel (literary work) *Jaws*, has an exclusive right to adapt it into the form of a film script (dramatic work) *Jaws*. The adaptation right also includes the reverse situation of making non-dramatic versions of a dramatic form of a literary work. There is also a right to make a version of a work where the story is conveyed solely or principally in pictures, such as in a printed format.

Translating a work is also included as part of the "adaptation" right for literary works, (whether or not the work is in dramatic or non-dramatic form). The adaptation right in relation to musical works is a right to make an arrangement or transcription of the work.

With respect to computer programs, "adaptation" means a right to make a version of a work, whether or not in the same language, code or expression as the original program. Thus, with literary works expressed as computer programs, an infringement may occur through reproducing the computer program and through making a different version of it, and in both instances the literary expression of an infringing computer work may differ from that of the original computer program. This has led to ongoing confusion over defining the role of the idea/expression dichotomy in relation to computer programs.

Adaptation of a computer program

▚▚▚▚▚ Coogi Australia v Hysport International ▚▚▚▚▚

[3.245] *Coogi Australia Pty Ltd v Hysport International Pty Ltd* (1998) 41 IPR 593 Federal Court of Australia

[The facts are outlined in the extract on p 113 above.]

DRUMMOND J ... [620] ...

Do the Hysport programs infringe Coogi's copyright in its XYZ program?

Hysport's major answer to the charge of infringement of copyright in the Coogi XYZ computer program, however, is that there is no objective similarity between the XYZ and the Hysport programs so Coogi cannot prove an essential element of its infringement claim. Alternatively, it was submitted that if there is such similarity between them, as Professor Goldschlager asserts, and which is revealed by his manipulation of the XYZ program in order to compare it with the Hysport programs, that must be the consequence of such form of expression as is common to both being entirely determined by function. That is, if there is any objective similarity between the forms of expression that constitute the two programs at a particular level of programming language, that is a consequence of it being impossible to write the instructions comprising a program to cause any computer-controlled knitting machine to knit fabric to the XYZ design in any other form because that particular form of expression is wholly dictated by that particular function.

... [621] ...

Despite the criticisms that have been made of the accuracy of the proposition, it is settled law in Australia that copyright protects not the underlying idea, but only the form of expression of the idea. See *Autodesk (No 1)* at 344-345 and *Powerflex Services* at 450. It is also the law in Australia that merely because one program performs the same function as another, that is insufficient to make the one an infringement of copyright in the other: *Autodesk (No 1)* at 344; *Autodesk (No 2)* at 304 and *Powerflex Services* at 455. Consistently with this, a computer program can only be an "adaptation" of another when it is "a version of the work", ie, a version of the particular form of expression of that other in which alone copyright can subsist, and not merely an expression of the idea or function of that other program.

In *Powerflex Services*, the Full Court placed a precise and limiting gloss on the statutory definition, holding, at 454, that, while the word "version" in the statutory definition of "adaptation" is used in its ordinary English sense, the legislature intended that it should bear one particular meaning of those which it has in ordinary speech, viz, a translation; at 457 it

███████ Coogi Australia v Hysport International *continued*

repeated that "the word 'adaptation', as used in s 10, means 'translation'". In ordinary usage, the term "version" is applicable to a wider range of renderings of the original literary work than is the term "translation": a version can apply to as literal as possible a [622] rendering of the original in another language, as well as to a work in the same or another language that is only recognisable as related to the original because that is the identifiable source of the theme of the version. The term "translation" has a much narrower reach. In ordinary speech, Piave's libretto in Italian for Verdi's opera "Macbeth" could fairly be called a version of Shakespeare's play; it could not, however, be properly described as a translation of the English original.

... [624] ...

Translation, as that term is ordinarily used, connotes more than conveying in a different language the same ideas expressed in another language. It describes a closer connection between the original and the translated text than that. I do not think an activity could be described in ordinary speech as a translation unless it involves the expenditure of effort on the original words or text to render them into words or text in a different language that conveys with precision the same meaning as that conveyed by the original. A person can probably be said to make a translation, in the ordinary meaning of that term, indirectly, eg, by translating into English from a French rendering of the original German text. But there can be no translation without the expenditure of effort, directly or indirectly, on the original text. Further, translation into a second language of instructions for achieving a result expressed in another language involves more than describing in the second language some method for achieving that same result: to be a translation, as that term is ordinarily used, of the original instructions, the new text would have to describe the particular sequence of steps for achieving the result that are expressed in the original text. Assume A writes in German a set of instructions for the making of a device, eg, a clock, and that someone uses those instructions to make a clock. B does not make a translation of A's original instructions by taking the clock, breaking it down into its parts and then writing his own set of instructions in English for reproducing the clock. The reason is that he has not produced his manual of instructions in English by working directly or indirectly (via a translation of the original in a third language) from the original text in German.

It is, I think, in this narrow sense which the word "translation" has in ordinary speech that the Full Court in *Powerflex Services* considered that the definition of "adaptation" applicable to computer programs should be understood. One computer program will therefore be an unauthorised "adaptation" of another firstly, only if the whole or a substantial part of the particular form of expression of the program in which copyright is claimed appears in the allegedly infringing program in a different computer language, either at the same language level or at a different language level and, secondly, only if the allegedly infringing program has been produced by direct or indirect use, in the sense described, of the copyright program. It is a meaning of "adaptation" that is supported by paras 13 and 14 of the Explanatory Memorandum and one which preserves, so far as concerns copyright in computer programs, the function/expression dichotomy that is currently entrenched in Australian copyright law.

... [625] ...

I consider that a computer program will be an infringing "adaptation", ie, translation, of an original program only if the Court can be convinced that, although the two programs are quite different so far as their forms of expression are concerned, use has been made of the original not just to identify the idea of the original or the function it performs, but as an aid to devising the descriptions of the activities (and any accompanying data) which together comprise the allegedly infringing program. Unless the expression "objective similarity" as used

███████ Coogi Australia v Hysport International *continued*

in copyright infringement law is to be given a new, highly artificial and technical meaning, instead of the ordinary usage meaning it has hitherto had, so that it will import into infringement law tests like that adopted in the American case, *Computer Associates International Inc v Altai Inc* (1992) 23 IPR 385 and favoured by the Copyright Law Review Committee Report (Canberra, 1995), para 9.27, it cannot sensibly be employed, in my opinion, in order to determine whether one program is an unauthorised adaptation of another.

In my opinion, the F823 program is not an adaptation, in the sense of a translation, of the particular form of expression of instructions that constitutes the Coogi XYZ program. ... [626] ...

I would therefore dismiss Coogi's claim against all respondents for this reason.

... Here, on the view I have taken of the evidence, Shima Seiki, and thus Hysport, never had access to any literary form in which the XYZ computer program was expressed, only to a garment manufactured by running that program in the computer control of a knitting machine. They could never therefore be in a position to make a translation, directly or indirectly, of the XYZ program. Instead, the F823 program and the Hysport programs based on it were the product of the extensive skill and effort of their own which they put into writing those programs.

In my opinion, it will never be possible to make out a case that one program constitutes an infringement of another computer program where the purpose of the original is to control the manufacture of an object and the alleged infringer has produced its own computer program to enable it to manufacture a like object by reverse engineering the original object, ie, by analysing it to see how it has been constructed and then by writing its own program to identify the steps that have to be gone through to make the object. I reject Coogi's submission to the contrary.

INFRINGING MATERIAL

[3.250] Authority on the issue of the subsistence of copyright in infringing material is scant. Ricketson has argued that, in view of the notion of a multiplicity of copyrights, the expenditure of sufficient skill and labour upon existing material so as to impart originality to the later work should result in a recognised copyright in that later work, subject perhaps to the owner of the first copyright. The copyright issues relevant to infringing material usually concern the extent to which infringement can be excused rather than copyright asserted for the infringing work.

■ Copyright in a work infringing or using other copyright material

████████ **A-One Accessory Imports v Off Road Imports** ████████

[3.255] *A-One Accessory Imports Pty Ltd v Off Road Imports Pty Ltd* (1996) 34 IPR 306 Federal Court of Australia

[This case involved the claim for copyright in a spare parts catalogue, where the originality of the compilation revolved around the claim to have selected and corrected entries copied from earlier versions. See p 70 above.]

▬▬▬▬ A-One Accessory Imports v Off Road Imports *continued*

DRUMMOND J: **[307]**

... [T]he fact that the 1986 A-One catalogue may be an infringement of the copyright in the 1984 Phoenix catalogue does not prevent A-One having copyright in its own 1986 catalogue ... **[318]** ...

In *Macmillan v Suresh Chunder Deb* (1900) 1 Ind LR, 17 C 951, a decision universally approved, the work of selecting poems, which included a group the subject of copyright (see *Macmillan & Co Ltd v K & J Cooper* (1924) 130 LT 675 at 680 RHC) for compilation into an anthology was held sufficient to confer originality and so copyright on the anthology: see 130 LT at 680 LHC. The compiler had the consent of the owners of the copyright in the group of copyright poems to include them in his compilation (see 130 LT at 680 RHC). Consent is obviously relevant to the question: does the compilation infringe the copyright that may exist in any of the material included in it? But the presence or absence of such consent cannot be relevant to whether the work of selecting from existing material, including existing copyright material, to make a compilation, is sufficient in the particular case to confer originality on the compilation. Consent cannot turn material in which someone else has copyright and which material is selected by the compiler into his original material.

In *Redwood Music Ltd v Chappell & Co Ltd* (1982) RPC 109, one of the issues was whether the owner of copyright in an original musical work could claim ownership of copyright in an arrangement of the original work because it was an adaptation of the original work made in breach of copyright in the original. Goff J held that the answer depended upon whether the infringing arrangement itself constituted an "original" work. He pointed out that the relevant section of the *Copyright Act* (UK), like s 32(1) of the Act, provided that copyright subsists in every original literary, dramatic, musical or artistic work and that this cannot be read as limited to lawful or non-plagiarised original works. So long as the arrangement involved sufficient originality to qualify it as an original work within the meaning of that term in the Act, it would not therefore matter that the **[319]** arrangement was, in part, an infringing reproduction of an earlier piece. While the author of the arrangement would be liable to the owner of copyright in the earlier piece for its infringement, he would himself own copyright in the infringing arrangement, given that the arrangement satisfied the test of originality. As Goff J observed at 120, to hold that copyright cannot subsist in a version of a work made in infringement of the copyright in the original work would mean that the original copyright owner would, in addition to his undoubted entitlement to restrain publication of an infringing work, be entitled to reap the benefit of the infringer's original work by exploiting it for his own benefit, however extensive such original work might be.

In *Warwick Film Productions Ltd v Eisinger* [1969] 1 Ch 508, the question was whether the defendant had infringed the copyright in what was called the "Hyde book", an account of the trials of Oscar Wilde, by copying extensive passages appearing in the Hyde book. Those same passages, however, had been copied by the author of the Hyde book from an earlier book. The plaintiff, who had copyright in the Hyde book, failed to prove that it also had copyright in the earlier book. Plowman J held that even though the Hyde book may have infringed the copyright in the earlier book because of the copying it included, it was itself an original literary work in which copyright subsisted, saying, at 524-525:

> "Although Hyde's account of the proceedings of the trials was substantially copied from the account in 'Three Times Tried', he himself did a good deal of editing. Certain portions of his account printed in square brackets were his own contribution, and he added material, omitted material, made verbal alterations, rearranged material, transposed material and abbreviated material. ... Moreover, Hyde frequently put into

oratio recta speeches which are reported in 'Three Times Tried' in oration obliqua.

Again, I take the view, after reading it, that the (Hyde) book as a whole is a literary work entitled to copyright in its own right."

Ladbroke (Football) Ltd, supra, *Redwood Music*, supra, and *Eisinger*, supra, proceed on the basis that a composite work made up of pirated material and original material produced by the compiler can itself be an original work possessing copyright, even though it may also infringe the copyright in the pirated material included in it.

In my opinion, a work can be an original work in which copyright will subsist, even though it is itself an infringement of the copyright in an earlier work because it is, in part, a copy of a substantial part of that copyright work. This will be the position provided the later work includes qualitatively significant changes to the copied material.

The 1986 A-One catalogue is an infringement of the copyright that may exist in the 1984 Phoenix catalogue, because of the substantial amount of material the A-One catalogue contains which was copied from the Phoenix catalogue. But that A-One catalogue is also in its entirety an original compilation in which copyright subsists because of the skill, judgment and effort that Rogers and his assistants expended in making the additions to and deletions from the information recorded in the Phoenix catalogue to which I have referred. In my opinion, it is also relevant to take into account, in assessing the originality of the 1986 A-One catalogue, that Rogers and Bennett corrected errors in the Phoenix catalogue, particularly in its recording of motorcycle model numbers. While the correction of, eg, spelling errors in a literary script could not be relevant to the question of the originality of the corrected script, the object of a sprocket catalogue is to provide an accurate compilation of information as to the various sprockets that can be used on a wide range of motorcycles. Work done to enhance [320] the accuracy of an existing compilation of that sort, intended to be put to such a use, involves skill and labour of the same quality as the effort expended in selecting new material for inclusion in the compilation and can therefore be relevant in determining whether the corrected compilation is itself an original work.

Because of this expenditure of effort on deciding upon and then making these changes, and on making the corrections to the Phoenix catalogue, the whole 1986 A-One catalogue is an original work within s 32 of the Act and is therefore copyright.

SUBJECT MATTER OTHER THAN WORKS

[3.260] Copyright in the Anglo-Australian world has traditionally been framed in response to technological change, originally commencing with the introduction of printing. The first statutory copyright was confined to books, and later extended to the other traditional categories of works. The *Copyright Act 1911* (UK) extended copyright to records to overcome problems of piracy unknown before the invention of the gramophone. (Records were defined as "mechanical contrivances to cover discs and rolls".) The *Copyright Act 1968* (Cth) introduced four categories of subject matter upon which copyright is conferred in order to protect entrepreneurial effort rather than authorship. These are sound recordings, cinematograph films, television and sound broadcasts and published editions of works (defined in s 10). These copyrights are additional to copyright in any underlying work, so one person may own the right to a song (as a musical work) while another owns the rights to the sound recording: see *CBS Records v Telmak* (1987) 9 IPR 440.

The extension of copyright to the subject matters under discussion was recommended by the Spicer Committee in its 1959 report, which in turn was based on the 1952 report of the Gregory Committee in the UK. The 1968 Act was obsolete before it was passed. Cornish stated that the extended protection is to allow recoupment of the risk taken in producing and marketing such industrial property. The Spicer Committee reported that, at least in the case of sound recordings, a great deal of artistic and technical skill was required (based on the decision in *Gramophone Co Ltd v Stephen Cawardine & Co* [1934] Ch 450 at 544 per Maugham J), thus implying that a degree of aesthetic creativity is being rewarded, rather than a commercial project protected. Cornish has suggested that when a "jumble of motives" leads to the legal protection of hitherto unprotected endeavours, incongruity results. The application of traditional concepts to new forms of creative or technical output may result in inappropriate protection, perhaps too long or short a period, with "gaps" where the subject matter is not covered by existing regimes and above all the loss of the balance which intellectual property law seeks to achieve between the interests of the public and the author. This is particularly apparent in the current debate concerning integrated circuits and communications. Tension is evident even within the *Copyright Act 1968* (Cth) which has separated out the "new" subject matter to be dealt with piecemeal in Part IV of the Act.

The difficulty in interpreting provisions designed specifically for the "new" subject matter, and reconciling these with the traditional principles of protection for works can be seen in *Galaxy Electronics Pty Ltd v Sega Enterprises Ltd*, and "The Panel" Full Federal Court and High Court appeal cases, below. Note that the Full Federal Court decision was overturned on appeal, however it is included below to assist in more fully understanding the legal issue under discussion in the High Court.

Galaxy Electronics v Sega Enterprises

[3.265] *Galaxy Electronics Pty Ltd v Sega Enterprises Ltd* (1997) 37 IPR 462 Federal Court of Australia

WILCOX J: **[469]** ... I agree with Burchett J [trial judge] that it would be wrong to interpret narrowly the definition of "cinematograph film" in s 10 and s 24. These provisions were intended to cover new technologies, the emphasis being on the end product—motion pictures—rather than the means adopted to create those pictures. Nonetheless, the definition will apply to any particular new technology only if that technology satisfies the words of the definition, liberally read.

[470] ... The definition of "cinematograph film" refers to "the aggregate of the visual images embodied in an article or thing". Section 24 sets out circumstances under which "visual images shall be taken to have been embodied in an article or thing". I also agree that the word "embodied" refers to the giving of a material or discernible form to an abstract principle or concept. The Lord Chancellor's "Iolanthe" song neatly illustrates this meaning. According to his Lordship, the abstract concept of excellence achieves material manifestation in the Law; and the Law, in turn, is manifested in his noble person.

It seems inherent in both the dictionary definition and the "Iolanthe" illustration that the abstraction must pre-exist the material manifestation. Counsel for the appellants argue that the images visible to players of the games do not exist before the moment of visibility; accordingly, it cannot be said that they represent an embodiment of pre-existing images. Counsel make the point that computer-generated images are fundamentally different to film or video images; in the latter case the images are fixed on celluloid or videotape before the moment of projection and viewing.

▬▬▬▬ Galaxy Electronics v Off Road Imports *continued*

This analysis is superficially attractive; but, I think, unsound. The visual images depicted in these video games did exist before the game was played. They existed in the minds of their creators and the drawings and models they made. The images were embodied in the computer program built into the video game machine so as to be capable, by the use of that program, of being shown as a moving picture. It does not matter that they were embodied in a different form; that is, three-dimension vertices of the polygon model, rather than a two-dimensional image. The statutory definition says nothing about the form of embodiment. Nor does it matter that the images seen by players are created by computer calculations only immediately before their appearance on the screen of the video game machine. Although that means, in a sense, that they are new, they are exact recreations of images previously devised by the graphic designers. Similarly, of course, it is unimportant that the images could not be seen on the screen as a moving picture until generated by the computer, any more than it matters that a length of video tape is incapable of being seen as a moving picture until passed through a video player.

...

Upon analysis, the present case seems to fall directly within the terms of the s 10 definition of "cinematograph film", without the necessity of resorting to s 24. However, that section puts the matter beyond doubt. The visual images that constitute the moving picture are taken to have been "embodied" in the computer program because the computer program was so treated in relation to those images as to be capable of reproducing them.

Counsel for the appellants argue it is not enough that a particular article was capable of producing particular sounds or visual images. If capability is the test, they say, every piano would have to be held a "sound recording" of Beethoven's "Moonlight Sonata". Every piano is capable of producing the notes that constitute that work. Counsel have in mind that the term "sound recording" is defined by s 10 as meaning "the aggregate of the sounds embodied in a record" and a "record" includes any "device in which sounds are embodied". ... [472] ...

I accept capability is not enough. It is important to note the requirement of s 24 that the article or thing "has been so treated in relation to those sounds or visual images" that they are capable of being reproduced from the article or thing. There must have been a treatment of the article or thing that is related to specific sounds or visual images. This can be said of a computer program, not of a piano. It is necessary to include a keyboard in a piano, if it is to be capable of reproducing the notes that constitute the "Moonlight Sonata". But the inclusion of a keyboard is not something done "in relation to" those particular sounds; it is done in relation to piano music generally.

I think Burchett J was correct in holding that the aggregate of the visual images generated by the playing of each of the two subject video games constituted a "cinematograph film" within the meaning of s 10 of the *Copyright Act*.

[Lockhart and Lindgren JJ concurred.]

▬▬▬▬▬▬▬▬▬▬

▬▬▬▬ "The Panel" Full Federal Court Decision ▬▬▬▬

[3.270] *TCN Channel Nine Pty Ltd v Network Ten Pty Limited* (2002) 55 IPR 112 Federal Court of Australia

FINKELSTEIN J: **[114]** It is usually apparent whether a particular work may be the subject of copyright. The precise identification of that work will also cause no difficulty in most cases. Speaking generally, copyright subsists in a work of a particular kind, generally a literary, dramatic, musical or artistic work. But a work cannot be copyright unless it is fixed in some material form: *Tate v Fullbrook* [1908] 1 KB 821 at 832-833. So the work can be seen and its character and scope identified. There are, however, some exceptions, and this case deals with one of those exceptions. This appeal is concerned with copyright in a television broadcast. The issue is whether Channel Ten has infringed copyright in a number of television broadcasts made by Channel Nine. To resolve this dispute it is necessary to identify the precise subject matter in which Channel Nine claims copyright. The reason why the subject matter must be identified with some precision is that copyright can be infringed if either the whole of the subject matter in which there is copyright or a substantial part of that subject matter has been copied: s 14 of the *Copyright Act 1968* (Cth). Thus the first step in a copyright infringement case is to identify the work or subject matter of copyright. The second step is to determine whether the whole or a substantial part of that work or subject matter has been copied without permission. In some cases there will be a third step. There are exceptions to the monopoly rights given to copyright owners. Fair dealing is one of those exceptions. The *Copyright Act* confers a privilege on third parties to use copyright material without the consent of the owner in certain circumstances. The doctrine developed to resolve the tension between, on the one hand, the monopoly granted to the owner and, on the other hand, the public interest.

A television broadcast differs from most other subject matter in which there is copyright because it does not exist in any tangible form. According to s 91 of the Copyright Act, copyright subsists in a television broadcast made from a place in Australia. Section 99 provides that the maker of the broadcast is the owner of that copyright. But what is a "television broadcast". The answer is to be found principally in two definitions in s 10. First there is the definition of "television broadcast" which means "visual images broadcast by way of television, together with any sounds broadcast for reception along with those images". The second is the definition of "broadcast" which means "a communication to the public delivered by a broadcasting service within the meaning of the *Broadcasting Services Act 1992*." Channel Nine is such a service.

I will return to these definitions in a moment, but before doing so I wish to draw attention to some other provisions in the *Copyright Act*. The first is s 101 which sets out what conduct will infringe copyright in a television broadcast. The section relevantly provides:

"(1) Subject to this Act, a copyright subsisting by virtue of this Part is infringed by a person who, not being the owner of the copyright, and without the licence of the owner of the copyright, does in Australia, or authorizes the doing in Australia of, any act comprised in the copyright.

[115] ...

(4) Subsection (1) applies in relation to an act done in relation to a television broadcast or a sound broadcast whether the act is done by the reception of the broadcast or by making use of any article or thing in which the visual images and sounds comprised in the broadcast have been embodied."

This takes us to s 87 where there is an explanation of the nature of copyright that subsists in a television broadcast. Section 87 provides that copyright in relation to television broadcast is the exclusive right:

"(a) in the case of a television broadcast in so far as it consists of visual images—to make a cinematograph film of the broadcast, or a copy of such a film;

(b)   in the case of a sound broadcast, or of a television broadcast in so far as it consists of sounds—to make a sound recording of the broadcast, or a copy of such a sound recording; and

███████ "The Panel" Full Federal Court Decision *continued*

(c) in the case of a television broadcast or of a sound broadcast—to re-broadcast it or communicate it to the public otherwise than by broadcasting it."

These provisions show that in so far as a television broadcast is concerned copyright subsists in visual images (and any accompanying sound). To understand what these images are, it is instructive to refer to another subject matter of copyright, namely a cinematograph film. Copyright in a cinematograph film is conferred by s 90. In s 10 a cinematograph film is defined to mean:

"[T]he aggregate of the visual images embodied in an article or thing so as to be capable by the use of that article or thing:
(a) of being shown as a moving picture; or
(b) of being embodied in another article or thing by the use of which it can be so shown;
and includes the aggregate of the sounds embodied in a sound-track associated with such visual images."

One can immediately see a distinction between what constitutes a television broadcast and what constitutes a cinematograph film. A television broadcast is defined by reference to the visual images that are broadcast, whereas a cinematograph film is more than a series of visual images. It is the aggregate of those images when they are embodied in an article or thing.

The distinction between, on the one hand, visual images and, on the other hand, an aggregate of visual images is important when one is attempting to identify precisely the visual images that constitute a television broadcast. It will be appreciated that what appears on a television screen is a sequence of still images of pictures which, when shown in rapid succession, give the appearance of a moving scene. Once it is seen that the visual images that constitute the broadcast need not be an aggregate of images it follows, in my opinion, that there is copyright either in each and every still image which is transmitted or in each and every visual image that is capable of being observed as a separate image on a television screen.

HELY J: [122]
To establish infringement of s 87(c) of the Act, Nine needed to show that Ten re-broadcast a "television broadcast" the copyright in which was owned by Nine. Alternatively, Nine needed to show that s 14(1)(a) of the Act applied, and that Ten re-broadcast a substantial part of a "television broadcast". The resolution of either of these questions required identification of the subject matter which constituted the relevant television broadcast.
... [125]

The operation of s 25(4) of the Act
The making of a cinematograph film of a television broadcast, insofar as it consists of visual images, or a copy of such a film, is an infringement of copyright in the television broadcast by virtue of s 87(a) and s 101. Section 25(4) of the Act provides as follows:

"(4) In this Act:
(a) a reference to a cinematograph film of a television broadcast shall be read as including a reference to a cinematograph film, or a photograph, of any of the visual images comprised in the broadcast; and
(b) a reference to a copy of a cinematograph film of a television broadcast shall be read as including a reference to a copy of a cinematograph film, or a reproduction of a photograph, of any of those images."

████████ "The Panel" Full Federal Court Decision *continued*

The catalyst for the enactment of s 25(4) was par 295 of the Spicer Report ... Paragraph 295 of that report explicitly recommended that the taking of a photograph "of any part of a television broadcast" should constitute an infringement of copyright, unless done for the private use of the photographer. Section 111(1) of the Act provides that the copyright in a television broadcast insofar as it consists of visual images is not infringed by the making of a cinematograph film of the broadcast, or a copy of such a film, for the private and domestic use of the person by whom it is made.

Section 25(4)(a) does not directly play a part in the definition of the subject matter of a television broadcast. The subsection is in the nature of a deeming provision, which gives an expanded meaning to the notion of a cinematograph film of a television broadcast beyond that which would otherwise flow from the s 10 definition of cinematograph film. This has the indirect effect of defining one of the exclusive rights in relation to a television broadcast.

Thus s 25(4) of the Act deems a photograph of any of the visual images comprised in a television broadcast to be a cinematograph film of that broadcast. Consistently with par 295 of the Spicer Report, the provisions of s 14(6) of the 1956 UK Act as to any "sequence of images sufficient to be seen as a moving picture" have not been taken up in s 25(4).

The effect of s 25(4) is thus that a cinematograph film or photograph of any of the visual images comprised in a television broadcast is an exclusive right of the copyright owner, subject to specific statutory exceptions such as s 111.

[126] ... It is true that the present case is not concerned with photographs. But the fact that s 25(4) applies to a photograph of any of the visual images comprised in the broadcast supports the view that the expression "any of the visual images" encompasses any one or more of those images, without any requirement that the images should amount to a substantial part of the broadcast.

... [129] ...

I conclude that a television broadcast in which copyright may subsist is made whenever visual images and accompanying sounds are broadcast by way of television. Re-broadcasting of any of the actual images and sounds so broadcast is an infringement of copyright under s 87(c), whether or not the subject matter of the re-broadcast is characterised as a programme, a segment of a programme, an advertisement, a station break or a station logo, or as a substantial part of any of those things.

Accordingly, I do not agree, with respect, with the primary judge's conclusion that whether or not there has been "re-broadcasting" of a television broadcast is to be measured against those benchmarks. For the same reasons I would also reject Ten's submission that the benchmark is a day's television, with the added comment that where broadcasting is continuous, there is no more logic in adopting a day's output than, for example, a week's.

On this view there may be many collocations of visual images and accompanying sounds broadcast during the space of a day all of which satisfy the definition of a "television broadcast". Thus, for example, the first minute of transmission may be a television broadcast as much as the first five minutes. If there is a re-broadcasting of the first minute by one competitor and of the first five minutes by another, then each has infringed the initial broadcaster's copyright in a television broadcast which is of one minute's duration in the first case, and of five minutes duration in the second.

The fact that there may be thousands of transmissions in any day which are [130] a television broadcast as defined does not lead to any inconvenience or absurdity given that copyright protection is confined to the actual images and accompanying sounds broadcast.

This conclusion allows for a limited role for s 14(1). If a broadcast consists of visual images and sounds, but the re-broadcast is of one, rather than the other, or if the re-broadcast is of

■■■■■ "The Panel" Full Federal Court Decision *continued*

images which have been cropped, then issues of substantiality may arise. In any event, s 14(1) applies "unless the contrary intention appears". One should therefore not approach the problem of identifying the interest protected by the copyright on the basis that resolution of that problem should necessarily accommodate s 14(1).

... Ten's submission overlooks, or pays insufficient regard to, the fact that the interest protected by the copyright is differently defined in the case of a television broadcast. It also overlooks, or pays insufficient regard to, the fact that there is no infringement of copyright in a television broadcast unless the actual sounds or images which were broadcast by the broadcaster are taken. A re-creation of those sounds or images may infringe copyright in some underlying work, but would not constitute an infringement of the copyright arising under Part IV of the Act. It is the actual visual images or sounds which comprise the television broadcast which are protected and not some imitation or reproduction thereof produced by collateral means: Laddie et al, *The Modern Law of Copyright and Designs,* 2nd Ed, 1995 at para 7.32.

"The Panel" High Court Decision

[3.275] *Network Ten Pty Limited v TCN Channel Nine Pty Limited* [2004] 59 IPR 1 High Court of Australia

McHUGH ACJ, GUMMOW AND HAYNE JJ: **[3]** ... Nine seeks to uphold the Full Court decision in its favour that each visual image capable of being observed as a separate image on a television screen and accompanying sounds is "a television broadcast" in which copyright subsists. The gist of Ten's complaint is that the term "a television broadcast" as it appears in the Act was misread by the Full Court, with the result that the content of that expression is so reduced that questions of substantiality have no practical operation and the ambit of the copyright monopoly is expanded beyond the interests the legislation seeks to protect.

Ten's submissions should be accepted and the appeal allowed.

... **[4]** ...

The context in which the broadcasting right was introduced, including well-established principles of copyright law, the inconvenience and improbability of the result obtained in the Full Court, and a close consideration of the text of various provisions of the Act relating to the broadcasting right, combine to constrain the construction given to the Act by the Full Court and to indicate that the appeal to this Court should be allowed.

... **[6]** ...

The legislative context

In 1968, at the time of the enactment of the Act, the predecessor of the Broadcasting Act, the *Broadcasting and Television Act 1942* (Cth) ("the 1942 Act"), was in force. As it stood in 1968, s 99(1) of the 1942 Act required the holder of a commercial television station licence to "provide programmes ... in accordance with standards determined by the [Australian Broadcasting Control] Board". With respect to what was then the Australian Broadcasting Commission, s 59 of the 1942 Act required the Commission to "provide, and ... broadcast or televise from transmitting stations made available by the Postmaster-General, adequate and comprehensive programmes". Section 121 of **[7]** the 1942 Act prohibited the broadcasting of programmes of other stations, and s 132 rendered an offence the contravention of any provision of the 1942 Act.

The Act was preceded by the Report ("the Spicer Report") delivered in 1959 of the

■■■■■   "The Panel" High Court Decision *continued*

Committee appointed by the Attorney-General of the Commonwealth to consider what alterations were desirable in the copyright law of the Commonwealth ("the Spicer Committee"). The Spicer Report had said it was significant that neither the Brussels Convention nor the Universal Copyright Convention recognised a copyright in sound broadcasts or television broadcasts (para 285). In the end, the Spicer Report concluded (paras 288, 289) that protection for broadcasters could properly be included in the copyright law with an adaptation of the provision then recently made by s 14 of the UK Act.

The introduction by s 14 of the UK Act of the new species of copyright protection followed Recommendation 31 in the *Report of the Copyright Committee* ("the Gregory Report") which had been presented in 1952. Recommendation 31 had been:

> "That a broadcasting authority should have the right to prevent the copying of its programmes either by re-broadcasting, or by the making of records for sale and subsequent performance. (Paragraph 117)"

Paragraphs 116 and 117 of the Gregory Report state the policy and objectives which were subsequently to find expression in the provisions of the Australian legislation upon which this appeal turns. Accordingly, pars 116 and 117 should be set out in full:

> "116. We now turn to the question whether a new right should be given to the broadcasting organisations in their own programme, additional to any copyright there may be in the individual items which go to make up those programmes, and we deal at this stage solely with a right to prevent other persons from copying the programme either by way of again broadcasting a programme (in the event of there being more than one broadcasting authority in the future) or by way of recording such programmes for subsequent performance in some other way.

> 117. On the question of copyright in the ordinary sense, *the position of* the [British Broadcasting Corporation (the *BBC*)], as we see it, *is not, in principle, very different from that of a gramophone company or a film company. It assembles its own programmes and transmits them at considerable cost and skill. When using copyright material it pays the copyright owner, and it seems to us nothing more than natural justice that it should be given the power to control any subsequent copying of these programmes by any means.* It has been represented to us that the absence of such a right [8] has already caused considerable embarrassment to the BBC. Apparently, indifferent reproductions both of sound and television programmes have been made, and sold to the public, to the detriment alike of the [BBC] and of those taking part. We consider that a right should be given to the BBC or any other broadcasting organisation to prevent this happening again. Any right so conferred would be additional to the right of the author or composer to prevent mechanical recording where copyright material is broadcast. It would also extend to prevent the mechanical recording of a broadcast of material which is either non-copyright, or of a nature in which a right to prevent recording may not, under the present law, subsist at all, eg news, talks, music-hall 'gags'." [emphasis in original]

In Australia, the Spicer Committee stressed the significance of the new head of copyright protection, saying (para 282):

> "The conception of copyright which has hitherto been accepted is one which extends protection against copying and performing in public any work insofar as it is reduced to a permanent form. Copyright has not been extended to confer such protection in relation to a mere spectacle or performance which is transitory of its very nature."

■■■■ "The Panel" High Court Decision *continued*

In *Victoria Park Racing and Recreation Grounds Co Ltd v Taylor*, the High Court had rejected the submission that by the expenditure of money the plaintiff had created a spectacle at its racecourse so that it had "a quasi-property in the spectacle which the law would protect" by enjoining the broadcast of a race-meeting there. The issue before the Spicer Committee was a different one, namely the protection of broadcasts themselves.

The Spicer Committee added (par 284):

> "It is true that in many cases the broadcast will be recorded on tape or film, in which case the record or film will enjoy its own copyright protection, but the copyright here being considered is one which attaches to the broadcast itself."

In the second reading speech on the Bill for the Act, the Attorney-General, Mr N H Bowen QC, said that the matters of records and broadcasts were dealt with in the UK Act and that it was appropriate to deal with them in the Bill. He also referred to the provisions of the Rome Convention which had postdated the UK Act but to which Australia was yet to accede. The Rome Convention also provided for the grant of "neighbouring rights" to various persons including broadcasters. Article 13 of the Rome Convention provided that "[b]roadcasting organisations [were to] enjoy the right to authorise or prohibit", among other things, "the rebroadcasting of their broadcasts", "the fixation of their broadcasts" and "the reproduction ... of fixations, made without their consent, of their broadcasts".

[On first Federal Court hearing of the dispute] Conti J noted that the Gregory Report had spoken of the right to prevent the copying of the "programmes" of broadcasting authorities, and the [9] broadcasting systems established by the 1942 Act spoke of the provision of "programmes" broadcast or televised from transmitting stations, and the Spicer Report spoke both of the protection of "broadcasts" and (in par 286) of "the programme received". The Rome Convention, like the Act, used the term "broadcast". There was no significant step taken with this shift in language. At this time, the use of "broadcast" as a noun indicated:

a   "Broadcasting as a medium of transmission.
b   The material, music, or pictures broadcast; also, a single program of such material".

The policy and objective in the recommendations of both Committees was to protect the cost to, and the skill of, broadcasters in producing and transmitting their programmes, in addition to what copyrights may have subsisted in underlying works used in those programmes. There is no indication, as Nine would have it, that, with respect to television broadcasting, the interest for which legislative protection was to be provided was that in each and every image discernible by the viewer of such programmes, so as to place broadcasters in a position of advantage over that of other stakeholders in copyright law, such as the owners of cinematograph films or the owners of the copyrights in underlying original works.

The television broadcasting right

Part III (ss 31-83) of the Act provides for copyright in original literary, dramatic, musical and artistic works. Part IV (ss 84-113) provides for copyright in subject-matter other than works, namely sound recordings, cinematograph films, television broadcasts and sound broadcasts, and published editions of works. Of Pt IV copyrights, it is accurately observed:

> "In general, these subject matters receive a lower level of protection than works, with shorter terms and more restricted exclusive rights."

... [10] ...

▬▬▬▬ "The Panel" High Court Decision *continued*

There are various points of contact made in the Act between the copyrights conferred by Pt III in respect of original works and the newer forms of copyright provided for in Pt IV....What is significant for present purposes is that the exclusive rights with respect to original literary, dramatic and musical works include the right to broadcast the works (s 31(1)(a)(iv)) whether by way of sound broadcasting or television (s 25(1)), and the exclusive rights with respect to original artistic works include the right to include the works in television broadcasts (s 31(1)(b)(iii)). The result is that a television broadcast may be more than a broadcast of some event or spectacle; it also in some cases may reproduce one or more works in which copyright subsists under Pt III and is vested in a different ownership to that of the broadcast.

... [11] ...

However, for this appeal ... what is comprehended by the "subject-matter" of the protection under Pt IV given to "a television broadcast"[?]. That is the phrase used in ss 91, 95, 99 and 101(4). It should be observed that s 101(4) uses the phrase "the visual images and sounds comprised in the broadcast". Likewise, for the purposes, for example, of fixing the commencement of the 50 year period specified in s 95(1), the television broadcast is treated by s 22(5) as having been made "by the person by whom, at the time when, and from the place from which, the visual images or sounds constituting the broadcast ... were broadcast". The decision which Ten challenges appears to discount the force of that phrase, redolent of plurality and interconnection of images and sounds, by treating as "a television broadcast" that which is capable of being observed as a separate image and (in an unexplained fashion) that capable of being heard and distinguished as the accompanying sounds (if any).

The medium of communication

Where the "subject-matter" of copyright protection is of an incorporeal and transient nature, such as that involved in the technology of broadcasting, it is to be expected that the legislative identification of the monopoly (eg, by s 87) and its infringement (eg, by s 101) of necessity will involve reference to that technology. But that does not mean that the phrase "a television broadcast" comprehends no more than any use, however fleeting, of a medium of communication. Rather, as the Gregory Report indicated, protection was given to that which had the attribute of commercial significance to the broadcaster, identified by the use of the term "a broadcast" in its sense of "a programme". In the same way, the words, figures and symbols which constitute a "literary work", such as a novel, are protected not for their intrinsic character as the means of communication to readers but because of what, taken together, they convey to the comprehension of the reader.

In fixing upon that which was capable of perception as a separate image upon a television screen and what were said to be accompanying sounds as the subject-matter comprehended by the phrase "a television broadcast", the Full Court appears to have fixed upon the medium of transmission, not the message conveyed by its use.

Because the medium is ephemeral, it is necessary to capture what a television broadcaster transmits if any practical use is to be made of the signal that is broadcast. ... [12] ...

Section 87 of the Act, in pars (a) and (b), identifies the nature of copyright in a television broadcast by reference to two methods by which what is transmitted can be captured and recorded in permanent or semi-permanent form. One method (s 87(a)) is to take a still visual image of what otherwise appears on a television set as part of a continuous visual trans-mission. In that context it may be sensible to speak of a single visual image that is broadcast. However, it by no means follows that it is sensible to confine the understanding of "a television broadcast" by basing the meaning that is given to the expression upon the capacity

■■■■■ "The Panel" High Court Decision *continued*

to capture and record singular visual images. Especially is that so when it makes little sense to speak of a single "moment" of sound accompanying that image. The instantaneous fixing of single visual images is familiar, but the instantaneous fixing of single sounds is not. When it is further observed that s 87(c), with its reference to re-broadcasting, at least encompasses the capture and simultaneous retransmission of a television broadcaster's signal, it is apparent that to understand "a television broadcast" as a singular and very small portion of the signal which a broadcaster transmits virtually continuously, and a person receiving is intended to receive continuously, is to give the expression a very artificial meaning. Yet that is what the Full Court did.

The reasoning of the Full Court

The conclusion of the Full Court with respect to s 87(a) rested largely upon a view taken of the significance of s 25(4). That sub-section treats the reference in s 87(a) to the making of "a cinematograph film" of "a television broadcast" as "including a reference to a cinematograph film ... of any of the visual images comprised in the broadcast". In that regard, Hely J held that "the expression 'any of the visual images' encompasses any one or more of those images, without any requirement that the images should amount to a substantial part of the broadcast" ...

[14] ... The outcome of the decision of the Full Court now under appeal is that the interests of broadcasters are placed by the Act in a privileged position above that of the owners of copyright in the literary, dramatic, musical and artistic works which may have been utilised in providing the subject of the images and sounds broadcast. This is because the diminished requirements in respect of infringement of television broadcasts for the taking of a substantial part of the subject-matter facilitate the proof of infringement there while leaving the owners of copyrights under Pt III with a heavier burden. Ten points to this apparent incongruity as favouring a construction of the Act contrary to that adopted by the Full Court.

[Their Honours discuss at length, and then reject, the Full Federal Court interpretation of s 87, its relation to s 25(4) and the relevance of substantial part].

... [19] ...

What is "a television broadcast"?

The definition given in s 10 is "television broadcast", which is drawn in terms of the technology of broadcasting which is to be utilised. But the phrase in the exclusive right provisions of s 87 (as also in ss 91, 95, 99 and 101(4)) is "a television broadcast" (emphasis added).

In the present case, Hely J focused attention not upon the statutory phrase "a television broadcast", but upon the use of technical language in the definition of "television broadcast". His Honour concluded:

"Here the interest protected by the copyright is the visual images broadcast by way of television and any accompanying sounds. It is the actual images and sounds broadcast which constitute the interest protected. The interest protected is not defined in terms of some larger 'whole' of which the visual images and sounds broadcast are but a part. The ephemeral nature of a broadcast, and the fact that copyright protection is conferred by reference to a broadcaster's output, rather than by reference to the originality of what is broadcast, may also help to explain why the interest protected is defined in this way."

That identification of the interest sought to be protected by the broadcast copyright should not be accepted.

███████ "The Panel" High Court Decision *continued*

The interest sought to be protected by the conferral of the television broadcast copyright was identified by the Spicer Committee with reference to the experience of the BBC and the Independent Television Authority. The latter was established by the *Television Act 1954* (UK) and charged by s 3 to "broadcast ... programmes" of a certain standard.

... [Their Honours set out the statutory obligations of the broadcasters TCN Ten and Channel Nine to provide free to air "programs" noting programs are defined under s 6(1) of the *Broadcasting Act* as:

"(a) matter the primary purpose of which is to entertain, to educate or to inform an audience; or

(b) advertising or sponsorship matter, whether or not of a commercial kind"]

... [21] ...

There can be no absolute precision as to what in any of an infinite possibility of circumstances will constitute "a television broadcast". However, the programmes which Nine identified in pars 5.1-5.11 of its pleading as the Nine Programs, and which are listed with their dates of broadcast in the reasons of Conti J, answer that description. These broadcasts were put out to the public, the object of the activity of broadcasting, as discrete periods of broadcasting identified and promoted by a title, such as *The Today Show*, *Nightline*, *Wide World of Sports*, and the like, which would attract the attention of the public.

However, Conti J was, with respect, correct in adding, with reference to *Copinger and Skone James on Copyright*, that:

"Television advertisements should be treated as discrete television broadcasts, particularly since 'A television or cinema commercial is typically the product of the creative and administrative work of many separate individuals' ... I would reject Ten's submission that because advertising is the 'life blood' of commercial television broadcasting, it is 'impossible for [Nine] to avoid the conclusion that these advertisements are part of that program'."

His Honour added:

"Moreover, where a given program divides into segments, it may be legitimate in the facts of a given case to use a segment of a program for measurement of the television broadcast, rather than the whole of the program."

We would reserve consideration of that proposition for a particular case where the point arises. However, the circumstance that a prime time news broadcast includes various segments, items or "stories" does not necessarily render each of these "a television broadcast" in which copyright subsists under s 91 of the Act.

... [22] ...

Conclusions
The appeal should be allowed with costs.

[The question as to what constitutes a "substantiality" under s 14(1) (a) of the Act was sent back to the Full Court for determination. See [6.170].

KIRBY J (dissent)
I agree in the conclusion reached by Callinan J. In my view, the approach adopted by the Full Court was correct.

... [25] ...

Criticisms of the ambit of copyright protection

I reach my conclusion without quite the same enthusiasm as Callinan J appears to feel for it. The opinion of the Full Court has been described as "highly literal". Perhaps it is; but the language of the Act leaves no scope for another approach. The most telling criticism voiced of the Full Court's interpretation is that it makes television broadcast copyright "an extraordinarily strong right, easily the strongest of all copyrights in Australia, able to be infringed by taking less than a substantial part of the broadcast". This, it is said, is counterintuitive given the ephemeral nature of television broadcasts and the original reasons for granting copyright in them.

If I were free of the constraints of the language of the Act, I would be happy to agree in the conclusion reached in this Court by McHugh ACJ, Gummow and Hayne JJ, whilst feeling anxiety about the lack of precision as to what, in any of an infinite range of circumstances, will constitute "a television broadcast" on that view. I also have some sympathy for the opinion expressed by Ms de Zwart in a comment upon the Full Court's opinion in these proceedings:

> "There are ... many circumstances in which the public interest lies in permitting the use of a work without the permission of the owner of copyright, with or without payment. The Panel decision provides a good example of circumstances in which a licence would not be granted (between competitors). ...
>
> It is vital to recognise the public interest element of copyright ... Copyright is not solely concerned with economic returns for the owner. Neither was copyright intended to enable owners to exploit all possible uses and derivations of the work. The public domain is an important legacy of copyright law and its existence should also be protected in the face of the growth of digital capture and licensing of works.
>
> ... The Panel serves as a vehicle for social comment and criticism, albeit in a relaxed, humorous fashion. ... Copyright is a social as well as a commercial construct and its role in facilitating new creations as well as protecting existing creations should not be forgotten." (de Zwart, "Seriously entertaining: The Panel and the future of fair dealing" (2003) 8 *Media & Arts Law Review* 1 at 16-17).

[26] ... The Act contemplated a form of copyright apt to the particular technology involved in television broadcasting. It therefore provided that copyright would attach to "the visual images comprised in the broadcast". Those who conceive the Parliament as confining the scope of the new copyright protection for television broadcasts to entire programmes (or defined and undefined sections and segments of a continuous day's broadcasting) must not watch much television. It is the very power of particular, and often quite limited (even fragmentary) portions of "visual images" on television that makes it such a potent and commercially valuable means of expressing thoughts and ideas: noble and banal, serious and humorous, uplifting and discouraging.

Everyone knows that still images or very brief segments in television broadcasts can constitute commercially valuable commodities, standing alone. The acquisition by a broadcaster of comparatively short filmed sequences will sometimes represent very important and commercially valuable rights that exist without the need of a surrounding context, let alone an extended programme or particular segment of a day's broadcast. The parties to the present appeal were in commercial competition with each other. That fact is itself also a consideration that generally favours the claim of a copyright owner.

... [27] ...

███████ "The Panel" High Court Decision *continued*

The proper approach to the meaning of the Act

It follows that the Parliament did not envisage the striking of a balance between public and private interests in the Act by the adoption of an unspecified and ultimately undefinable notion of "a television broadcast" in the sense of a "unit of programming". The Act does not refer to that notion of a "programme" or unit thereof. It might have done so. But it did not.

CALLINAN J (dissent) [39] ... The Act falls to be read therefore against the background of these indisputable facts. The parties compete with each other. The production of any programme, indeed each and every frame and segment of it, comes at a cost. It is produced in order to make money by inducing advertisers to pay to have their activities advertised in association with its broadcast one or more times. Further value may arise from the isolation, reproduction and broadcasting of an image or images, with or without sound, from it, and the licensing of it or an isolated image or images from it, whether by and in a photograph, a film or a video film. What is clear in this case is that value did lie in the copying, reproduction and rebroadcasting of segments, albeit generally fairly brief segments, of the respondents' programmes. That value had two aspects: it enabled the appellant to gain revenue from advertising associated with *The Panel*; and it relieved the appellant of the cost of buying or producing other matter to occupy the time taken by the rebroadcasting, during *The Panel*, of the copied and reproduced segments. The intention of Pt IV Div 2 of the Act was, as the Attorney-General said, broadly not only to place television footage on at least the same basis as other original work, particularly moving films, protected by the Act, but as appears from the language used in it, with necessary adaptations to suit the medium and the means available to competitors to exploit it, and in consequence to create new rights. Why should, it is reasonable to ask, the appellant, save to the extent that it deals fairly with any of the respondents' valuable broadcasted matter, get it and rebroadcast it for its own commercial benefit, for nothing? The question in this case is whether the Act prevents it from doing that.

The use by the appellant of excerpts from the respondents' broadcasts was blatant. And although blatant appropriation of the kind which has occurred here might not be such as to warrant an evangelical fervour in responding to it, in the nakedly commercial context of television broadcasting in Australia, the test of "what is worth copying is prima facie worth protecting" posed by Peterson J in *University of London Press Ltd v University Tutorial Press Ltd* has much to commend it, and provides at least a reasonable starting point. After all, in recognising the validity of the respondents' copyright in excerpts from their programmes, the Court would not be denying access to the general public of the golden words of a new Shakespeare. This is a case of blatant commercial exploitation, neither more nor less.

It has always been the respondents' case that the appellant has infringed both ss 87(a) and 87(c) of the Act. The appellant has never denied that it copied by reproducing in full the respondents' programmes. It has therefore infringed, on any view, s 87(a) of the Act.

As to s 87(c) however, the appellant argues that because it did not rebroadcast other than an excerpt from, that is to say, less, indeed much less than, [40] the whole of any of the programmes of the respondents, it did not rebroadcast "a television broadcast" of the respondents. In short the appellant submits that a television broadcast within s 87 of the Act cannot be less than the whole or a substantial part of a television programme, notwithstanding that the relevant sections do not anywhere use that term, and the Act attempts no definition of it. The appellant's proposition, it further argues, is correct because otherwise there is no, or little work for s 14 of the Act to do.

I am unable to agree. ...

That the appellant thought a few seconds of the respondents' broadcast worth rebroadcasting provides some indication of the understanding in the industry of what is sufficient to constitute a broadcast. Hely J was right to hold that "any of the visual images", the expression used in s 25(4) of the Act, means a visual image, that is something that can be isolated and fixated. The Act was not enacted in a vacuum of awareness as to how the industry operated, or without regard to practicalities. Those practicalities include the certain knowledge that one television licensee would only seek to use what would be of real value to it: it would have no interest, commercial or otherwise, in anything less than something complete enough in itself to be viewed, in short, a broadcast. In that sense the term "broadcast" is almost self-defining.

To regard a broadcast differently, as for example, a "programme", is not only to introduce a concept not reduced to concrete language or even implied anywhere in the Act, but is also to create a deal of uncertainty about its operation.

[41] ... Nothing turns, in my opinion, upon any perceived differences between the quality or nature of the copyright afforded by the Act to television broadcasts and other copyright holders. It was and was intended to be a new and unique right. The medium is very different from others. To exploit it, different and perhaps more expansive infrastructures, fees, techniques and resources are required. The industry is, and has always been in this country, a highly competitive, and, as this case shows, a highly commercialised one. There may have been good reason for the legislature to single it out for special treatment. It is for the Court to give effect to the language of the Act and not to speculate about that.

I would dismiss the appeal with costs.

Simplification of the Copyright Act 1968

[3.280] Copyright Law Review Committee, *Simplification of the Copyright Act 1968, Part 2— Categorisation of Subject Matter* (September 1998) (References omitted.)

Problems with the current Act

5.04 The main features that characterise the current legislation's approach to categorisation of protected subject matter and exclusive rights are the use of a relatively large number of categories of subject matter and rights, wherein those categories are defined in a relatively narrow and often technologically specific way. There are a number of consequences of this approach which, in the view of the majority of the Committee, are problematic. These consequences are an element of unnecessary legislative complexity, some instances of unjustifiable differential treatment of similar subject matter, and an undesirable degree of technological specificity of protected subject matter and exclusive rights. Each of these consequences are described in more detail, and illustrated by examples, below.

5.05 One consequence of the current legislation's approach to categorisation is that it is long and complex. This arises from the treatment of works and subject matter other than works in different parts of the Act. As a result, there is a degree of duplication within those two parts of provisions relating to the same issues—including, in particular, in relation to the exceptions and limitations to the exclusive rights granted. The majority of the Committee agrees with the general view contained in the submissions it received that there is a fundamental difference between the types of subject matter that fall within Parts III and IV of the Act. However, the majority of the Committee does not believe that it is necessary to recognise this difference through the current unwieldy structural distinction, and is of the view that the difference can continue to be maintained in a more efficient and simplified form.

5.06   Another consequence is that there is a difference in the protection granted to different categories of subject matter within the same part of the Act, even where the different categories of subject matter satisfy the same requirements for subsistence of protection. In certain instances at least, this difference in treatment seems, to the majority of the Committee, to be unjustified. An example is the lesser protection given to artistic works compared with other works in Part III of the Act. In contrast to other works, artistic works do not receive the exclusive right of adaptation. The majority of the Committee believes that this result has the appearance, and may have the practical effect, of artists being discriminated against in comparison to other creators.

5.07   To the majority of the Committee, however, the most problematic consequence of the current legislation's approach to categorisation is its technological specificity. This arises from the relatively narrow definitions used for both protected subject matters and exclusive rights, from the distinction drawn in those definitions between tangible and intangible embodiments, and from the requirement for Part III subject matter to be identified with a human "author". Technological developments have produced new means of creating copyright subject matter, and new means of exploiting that subject matter. The majority of the Committee is of the view that those new means are being utilised now, and are likely to be utilised with increasing frequency in the future, to produce subject matter of a type, and to exploit subject matter in a way, that does not easily or at all come within the existing categories. The majority of the Committee is concerned that without a significant change in approach to categorisation of subject matter and rights, there will be increasing uncertainty in the application of the Act in the digital environment, and an increasing pressure on the legislature to make ad hoc amendments to deal with these uncertainties. Both of these outcomes are undesirable.

5.08   One example of a new type of subject matter arising from technological developments, for which there is already uncertainty about the Act's application and calls for ad hoc legislative amendment, is the so-called "multimedia entity". As discussed in more detail in Section 2 of this report, it is unclear whether a multimedia entity as such, as distinct from its component parts, is protected at all under the Act. The majority of the Committee is of the view, however, that a sufficiently creative multimedia entity should receive protection in its own right. It is also of the view that any other new media material, including material that has not yet been identified as such, should also receive protection if it is sufficiently creative. In short, the majority of the Committee is concerned that the current Act discriminates against creative material on the basis of its physical (or non-physical) form, and hence fails to protect material that, as a matter of policy, is deserving of protection.

5.09   An example of a new act of exploitation of protected subject matter arising from technological developments, for which likewise there is uncertainty about the Act's application and calls for its amendment, is dissemination to the public by computer network. Uncertainty about the application of the current legislation lay behind the Copyright Convergence Group's 1994 recommendation for a new, broadly defined right of transmission to the public, to replace the technology-specific rights of broadcast by wireless telegraphy and transmission to subscribers to a diffusion service. By 1996, developments in communications technology, and in particular the Internet, resulted in the adoption in both the WCT and the WPPT of an even broader new right—the right of communication to the public by wire or wireless means, which is defined to include making available to the public by interactive means. While the Committee supports the Government's Digital Agenda decision to implement this new right in the current legislation, the majority of the Committee is concerned that these changes do not go far enough. In particular, the majority of the Committee considers problematic the fact that the provisions of the Act relating to exclusive rights will still distinguish between activities on the basis of whether they are carried out on a tangible or intangible embodiment of protected material. For example, it may be argued that the right of publication is confined to the first dissemination of a work to the public by distribution of physical copies of it. Yet a majority of the Committee believes that the publication right should embrace first dissemination of a work to the public by any means, including by distribution of intangible embodiments of the work.

5.10   The Act's distinction between tangible and intangible embodiments of copyright material is potentially problematic in another way. Currently the legislation requires a work to be in a tangible embodiment to qualify for protection under Part III. As a result, material that has only an intangible embodiment, such as an extempore speech, is not protected even though arguably as deserving of protection as a speech that is written down prior to recitation. Also of concern to the majority of the Committee is the extent to which the current legislation accommodates the increasing, indeed almost ubiquitous, use of computers in the creation of copyright subject matter. The Act currently requires the identification of a human as the "author" of a Part III work. While a majority of the Committee recognises there is an ongoing need for copyright legislation to connect a work with a human, it is concerned that the current requirement of "authorship" may preclude the grant of protection to material that is deserving of protection, simply because the extent to which a computer was utilised in its creation exceeds a particular (currently uncertain) level.

5.11   The majority of the Committee notes that there has been some discussion relating to the "overlapping" of the current exclusive rights when applied to the digital environment. In particular, the majority of the Committee notes that at the Sydney consultations it was stated by some interests that the overlapping of rights should be avoided, as it would unjustifiably allow for the creation of a number of separate licences and the collection of separate royalties for what was primarily the performance of the one activity. In this regard, the majority of the Committee also notes the comments made in the US report *Intellectual Property and the National Information Infrastructure* (1995). The US report stated:

> "The exclusive rights, which comprise the so-called bundle of rights that is copyright, are cumulative and may overlap in some cases … the fact that more than one right may be involved in infringing activity does not, and should not, mean that only the one right should apply. Each of the exclusive rights is distinct and separately alienable and different parties may be responsible for infringements or licensing of different rights—and different rights may be owned by different people."

5.12   On this issue the majority of the Committee agrees with what was stated in the US report. Although the majority of the Committee recognises that rights appear to be "overlapping" to an increasing extent as a result of digital technology, it does not believe that this fact alone will result in the overprotection of copyright material. In the majority of the Committee's view each right represents a specific and separately remunerable activity. The fact that the performance of an activity may involve the exercise of more than one right is justified. The majority of the Committee notes that the overlapping of rights is not peculiar to the digital environment—for example, the act of publication of a literary work in hard copy form traditionally involves the exercise of both the right of reproduction and the right of publication.

5.13   In summary, a majority of the Committee is of the view that the current legislation's technologically specific approach to categorisation of protected subject matter and of exclusive rights is suboptimal in a number of key respects. It considers that the Act

▬▬▬ Simplification of the Copyright Act 1968 *continued*

should be recast, in a manner that simplifies it and enables it better to deal with the challenges, both foreseen and as yet unforeseen, raised by the digital environment.

Note

[3.285] Since the CLRC report in 1998 many, many more provisions have been added to "update" the *Copyright Act 1968* (Cth), mainly dealing with aspects of the digital environment. There has been no "simplification". Finding and understanding the myriad of legal rights and obligations the Act now confers on owners, users and the public remains very difficult.

The organisation of the Act is widely acknowledged in practice, and especially in academia, as sub-optimal. One explanation for the lack of action to remedy the complexity is "law reform fatigue". There are too many smaller initiatives that have needed a more urgent response. Hence new provisions are drafted or old ones redefined within the existing structure, and the problem continues unabated.

Beyond a question of time, energy and resources, the bigger problem is that any restructuring of the legislation opens up jurisprudential debates about the fundamental purposes and objects of copyright law. From an historical perspective these have always been poorly expressed. For example, fundamental legal ideas like the idea/expression dichotomy and the public domain, and popular notions in public legal education like "piracy", have no clear or direct legislative reference. In addition, any larger reorganisation of the Act potentially interferes with established expectations of particular vested interests. There is little consensus and much disagreement about the politics of copyright, locally and globally, at this time. This political environment leads to ongoing piecemeal reform and continual deferral of legislative address to the structural complexity and incoherence of the Act.

CHAPTER 4

OWNERSHIP

[4.05] See *Copyright Act 1968* (Cth), s 35.

AUTHORSHIP OF WORKS

[4.10] The owner of copyright in a work and the author of the work are not necessarily the same person, but the basic rule is that the author is the first owner of copyright. "Author" is not defined by the *Copyright Act 1968* (Cth) (except in regard to photographs, the author of a photograph is the person who takes it (s 10(1)), but the concept is obviously focused upon the first reduction of ideas to material form (*Tate v Thomas*, **[3.40]** above).

In *Kenrick v Lawrence* (1890) 25 QBD 99 it was stated that a person who had an idea for a drawing could not be regarded as the author where it was actually drawn by another person. Compare *Mitchell v Brown* (1880) 6 VLR 168. In *Walter v Lane* [1900] AC 539 the reporters who took down verbatim speeches were regarded as authors, having exercised sufficient skill to bring into being an original work. This case may be of dubious authority today since it was decided under the *Copyright Act 1911* (UK), but it points out the connection between authorship and originality, which remains relevant. See *Donoghue v Allied Newspapers* [1938] Ch 106; *Cummins v Bond* [1927] 1 Ch 167 at **[3.55]**; *Express Newspapers Plc v News (UK) Ltd* (1990) 18 IPR 201.

■ Joint authorship
[4.15]

"s 10(1) 'work of joint authorship' means a work that has been produced by the collaboration of two or more authors and in which the contribution of each author is not separate from the contribution of the other author or the contributions of the other authors."

It is to be noted that not all jointly-produced works result in joint authorship, for example, separate copyrights exist in the words and the music respectively of a song (unless of course, two or more persons produced them together in such a way as to come within the definition of joint authorship): see *Hadley v Kemp* (**at [3.165]**). In *Mitchell v Brown* (1880) 6 VLR 168, the plaintiff, a veterinary surgeon, had spent many years making observations and taking notes in order to be able to produce a complete picture of the anatomy of the horse. He consulted with an artist who agreed to execute the drawing, based on the information and guidance provided by the plaintiff. The parties agreed to share equally any profits resulting from sale of copies of the picture. When the artist claimed that it was his work alone, Molesworth J held the picture to be the result of their "joint labour". The owners of such a work take as tenants in common anyone who can sue in respect of an infringement, and obtain an injunction and damages for a moiety without necessarily joining the other authors as plaintiffs.

Joint proprietorship of copyright may arise independently of authorship through an agreement between the creator and another person(s) (see below).

NON-AUTHORS

[4.20] Exceptions exist to the basic rule in *Copyright Act 1968* (Cth), s 35(2). These are found in Parts VII and X of the Act dealing with Crown use and assignment of copyright respectively.

■ Commissioned works

[4.25] One of the preliminary issues to ascertain is whether the agreement concerns the type of artistic work to which this exception applies. The limitations imposed by *Copyright Act 1968* (Cth), s 35(5) are apparently based on previous copyright legislation, and presumably relate to issues of privacy surrounding personal portraits, photographs and the like.

"Portrait"

Attorney General v Trustees of National Art Gallery of NSW

[4.30] *Attorney General v Trustees of National Art Gallery of NSW* (1944) 62 WN (NSW) 212 Supreme Court of New South Wales

[The issue arose not in the context of copyright but as a result of the award of the Archibald Prize for 1943 to William Dobell for his portrait of Joshua Smith. Objection was made to the payment of the prize to Dobell for what was termed a caricature and not a likeness of Joshua Smith, when the prize was to be awarded from the income of a trust established to award a prize for "the best portrait preferentially of some man or woman distinguished in Art, Letters, Science or Politics". As to the meaning of portrait Roper J said:]

ROPER J: [215] With the assistance of dictionaries and the many works to which I have been referred by counsel in this case, I think that the word "portrait" as used in this will, incorporating in its meaning the limitations imposed by its context, means a pictorial representation of a person, painted by an artist. This definition connotes that some degree of likeness is essential and for the purpose of achieving it the inclusion of the face of the subject is desirable and perhaps also essential.

▨▨▨ Attorney General v Trustees of National Art Gallery of NSW *continued*

The picture in question is characterised by some startling exaggeration and distortion clearly intended by the artist, his technique being too brilliant to admit of any other conclusion. It bears, nevertheless, a strong degree of likeness to the subject and is I think, undoubtedly, a pictorial representation of him. I find as a fact that it is a portrait, within the meaning of the word in this will, and consequently the trustees did not err in admitting it to the competition.

Whether as a work of art or a portrait it is good or bad, and whether limits of good taste imposed by the relationship of artist and sitter have been exceeded, are questions which I am not called upon to decide and as the expression of my opinions upon them could serve no useful purpose I refrain from expressing them. I mention those matters, however, because I think that the witnesses for the informant, whose competency to express opinions in the realm of art is very great, were led into expressing their opinions that the work was not a portrait because they held strong views against it upon those questions. They excluded the work from portraiture, in my opinion, because they have come to regard as essential to a portrait characteristics which, on a proper analysis of their opinions, are really only essential to what they consider to be good portraiture.

Finally I think that it is necessary to state my opinion on the claim that the picture cannot be included as a portrait because it is proper to classify it in another realm of art or work as caricature according to the information or as fantasy according to a witness for the informant. It is, I think, unnecessary to consider whether the picture could properly be classed as a caricature or a fantasy. If it could be so classed that would only establish to my mind that the fields are not mutually exclusive, because in my opinion it is in any event properly classed as a portrait. In the result I think that this suit must be dismissed. I make a decree accordingly and order that the relators pay the costs of the defendants.

Judgment for plaintiff.

Note

[4.35] As well as being a portrait, photograph or engraving, the work must have been commissioned: see *Leach v Two Worlds Publishing Co Ltd* [1951] Ch 393.

■ Journalists' copyright

[4.40] An employee journalist retains copyright for the purposes stated in s 35(4)(c), generally for reproduction in hard copy form. It would be possible to publish such material in a book, as a sound recording or to make a cinematograph film based on the work, in the absence of any agreement to the contrary (s 35(3)). The rights of journalists were redefined in amendments to the *Copyright Act 1968* (Cth) in 1997 intended to apportion ownership of material in electronic form, with publishers seeking amendments to the Act to ensure they retain electronic distribution rights. Accordingly, s 35(4)(d) provides the proprietor retains copyright for all other purposes than those set out in s 35(4)(c).

■ Contract of service or apprenticeship

[4.45] General employment law principles will determine the question of ownership of copyright material produced by employees. A number of the employment cases have also been concerned with copyright ownership. *Copyright Act 1968* (Cth), s 35(6) is the relevant statutory provision.

Are books written by academics produced pursuant to their terms of employment? This is a controversial question, the answer to which is by no means clear cut. The same question arises in respect of articles written by academics for publication in periodicals and materials produced for students and teaching purposes, although different considerations may apply. Most academics are employed under a contract of service, however the extent of their obligations to produce copyright works and other subject matter, and the ownership of that material, is in doubt. Employers and staff associations have different opinions, and it may be that different types of material published in various forms will belong to academics on some occasions and to the university on others. For example, books written by academic staff are usually produced by a commercial publisher, with royalties due to the author. This is a long-established and accepted practice. On the other hand, materials produced for teaching arguably belong to the institution, being centrally located within the terms of employment. Articles seem to occupy the middle ground and cause the most controversy due to the operation of the compulsory licence allowing copying of educational material. If the copyright owner of academic articles written for periodical publication is the employer institution, the licence fees collected for educational copying will be returned to the institution, having had the Copyright Agency Ltd's administrative expenses deducted and adding to the expense of tertiary education in the meantime. On the other hand, the academics or publishers, if found to be the copyright owners of such material, will be remunerated in circumstances where previously they were paid nothing (or a token fee) and indeed in some disciplines have actually paid to have their work published.

"Contract of service or independent contractor?"

▬ Redrock & Hotline Communications v Adam Hinkley ▬

[4.50] *Redrock Holdings Pty Ltd & Hotline Communications Ltd v Adam Hinkley* (2001) 50 IPR 565 Supreme Court of Victoria

HARPER J: [567] These proceedings concern an acrimonious dispute about the ownership of software written by Mr Adam Hinkley, the first defendant in each proceeding. Mr Hinkley's father, Mr Paul Hinkley, and Mr Paul Hinkley's business vehicle, Meta Consultants Pty Ltd (Meta Consultants), are also defendants to the proceedings.

There is no dispute that Mr Adam Hinkley was the author of the programs in question. Rather, the issues in contention concern the identity of the owner of the copyright in the programs.

...[568] ...

Adam Hinkley is a young man of great talent. He is a computer programmer. Before he left school, he had embarked on the development of a "library" (he referred to it as a "class library") as that expression is defined in the computer lexicon: that is, a collection of files, computer programs, or sub-routines; a collection of reference materials and software tools: see *Dictionary of Computer and Internet Terms* (6th ed) by Douglas Downing, Michael Covington and Melody Covington. Another definition, used in this case by Professor Justin Zobel, Associate Professor, Department of Computer Science, RMIT University, is "a collection of functions that a programmer can call upon when writing a piece of software". Mr Hinkley defines the expression "class library" as "a software tool that is used for making other software". One of the features of this library is that it comprises reusable code that can be used in many applications. Moreover, it was designed as a "cross-platform" program which is defined as being "applicable to more than one kind of computer (for example PC and Macintosh)": *Dictionary of Computer and Internet Terms* (supra). In this case, the library was used to write, or assist in writing, software that is indisputably owned by Redrock as well as software that was being developed by or on behalf of Mr Paul Hinkley and Meta Consultants. It was similarly used by Mr Adam Hinkley in writing software which according to him was exclusively his.

... **[570]** ...

By the last quarter of 1995 Redrock was ready to employ a programmer with Macintosh skills. Adam Hinkley had those skills, as he demonstrated during a meeting with Messrs Hamilton, Spearritt, and another Redrock director, Rohan Lean.

...

[571] Mr Hinkley brought with him to the interview his Macintosh prototype of WinPage. There was some dispute at trial about the degree of sophistication of this prototype, but it appears that it comprised a graphic representation of the user interface with limited functionality. ...

The interview achieved its purpose. Several days later, Redrock offered Mr Hinkley a position. Mr Hinkley accepted. In doing so, he assumed (he says) that the library would remain his; and there can be no doubt that, before he joined Redrock, it was with him that the copyright resided. For the purposes of the *Copyright Act 1968*, a computer program or compilation of computer programs is a literary work: s 10. By s 31(1) of that Act, copyright in relation to a literary work is (unless the contrary intention appears) the exclusive right to (among other things) reproduce the work in a material form, to publish it, to make an adaptation of it and, if it is an adaptation, to reproduce or publish that adaptation. Subject to s 35 of the Act, the author of a literary work is the owner of any copyright subsisting in it: s 35(2). Where, however, a computer program is made by its programmer in pursuance of the terms of his or her employment under a contract of service, the employer is the owner of any copyright subsisting in the program: s 35(6). ... **[572]** ...

Mr Hinkley relies upon the circumstance that there was no express agreement for the transfer of copyright in the library from him to Redrock. But if, having taken to his new employer a library which was then in embryonic form, Mr Hinkley in pursuance of the terms of his employment under a contract of service transformed that library into something that was qualitatively and quantitatively quite different, the copyright in the work will vest in Redrock by virtue of the operation of s 35(6) of the *Copyright Act 1968*. It is not necessary for there to be any transfer agreement or licence, either written or oral. In such circumstances, copyright in the qualitatively and quantitively different library vested in Redrock by operation of law.

Mr Hinkley submits that he was employed under a contract for services rather than under a contract of service. He relies on the so-called "control test", saying that he was given little, if any, direction or control by Redrock and cites passages from the judgment of Evershed, MR in *Stevenson Jordan & Harrison Ltd v MacDonald & Evans* [[1952] I TLR 101]. However, legal authority to control, while remaining relevant and indeed often decisive, is no longer the sole determining factor when assessing whether a person is employed under a contract of service, in particular where that person exercises a high degree of professional skill and expertise in the performance of his or her duties. So, in *Beloff v Pressdam Ltd* [[1973] 1 All ER 241]] Ungoed-Thomas J cited with approval a number of passages to this effect and then said at 250:

"It thus appears, and rightly in my respectful view, that, the greater the skill required for an employee's work, the less significant is control in determining whether the employee is under a contract of service. Control is just one of many factors whose influence varies according to circumstances. In such highly skilled work as that of the plaintiff it seems of no substantial significance. The test which emerges from the

◾◾◾◾◾ Redrock & Hotline Communications v Adam Hinkley *continued*

authorities seems to me, as Denning LJ said, whether on the one hand the employee is employed as part of the business and his work is an integral part of the business, or whether his work is not integrated into the business but is only accessory to it, or, as Cooke J expressed it, the work is done by him in business on his own account."

[573] In this case, there is no doubt that Mr Hinkley as a software programmer exercised a high degree of professional skill and expertise in the performance of his duties for Redrock. Moreover, as a skilled Macintosh technician employed to fill a gap in Redrock's technical staff, it could be expected that even as an employee he would be given a great deal of latitude. I therefore conclude that the evidence about control does not in the circumstances of this case establish that Mr Hinkley was employed under a contract for services.

In his judgment in *Stevenson Jordan & Harrison Ltd v MacDonald & Evans* [op cit at 111] Lord Denning expressed reservations about the control test, and instead enunciated the famous passage which was to become the "integration test":

"As [Evershed MR] has said it is almost impossible to give a precise definition of the distinction [between a contract of service and a contract for services]. It is often quite easy to recognise a contract of service when you see it, but very difficult to say wherein the difference lies. A ship's master, a chauffeur, and a reporter on the staff of a newspaper are all employed under a contract of service; but a ship's pilot, a taxi-man, and a newspaper contributor are employed under a contract for services. One feature which seems to me to run through the instances is that, under a contract of service, a man is employed as part of the business and his work, although done for the business, is not integrated into it but is only accessory to it."

The "integration" or "organisation" test has not been embraced by the High Court of Australia. However, it may be helpful in an appropriate case as one indicator of the totality of the relationship between the parties, all aspects of which must be considered: *Stevens v Brodribb Sawmilling Co Pty Ltd* [(1986) 160 CLR 16 at 27 per Mason J, and at 36-37 per Wilson and Dawson JJ]. In doing so, I find that Mr Hinkley's work as a software programmer was integrated into the business of Redrock. Mr Hamilton gave evidence in his witness statement that in the first four years of its business Redrock's emphasis was in developing the intellectual property in its products and that, after its staff, those products were the most significant asset of the company. Mr Hinkley's work as a programmer was therefore central to developing the business of Redrock.

There is other evidence which satisfies me that Mr Hinkley was employed under a contract of service. He was on a fixed salary, from which group tax was deducted. He signed an Australian Taxation Office Employee Declaration on 3 November 1995. He was entitled to annual leave, to sick leave and to long service leave. Superannuation contributions were made by Redrock on his behalf. Redrock provided Mr Hinkley with necessary equipment and with programs such as CodeWarrior all specially purchased to assist him in writing software for the company, together with access to the Internet to download manuals, information or software as needed. Indeed, in his written submissions Mr Hinkley states on the issue of the use of an external hard disk owned by him that it would be "unbelievable to suggest that I was expected to use my equipment for Redrock's work". All the indicia put forward in the evidence are consistent with the conclusion that Adam Hinkley became an employee of Redrock in or about November 1995. ... [574] ...

A very significant aspect of this case, already touched upon, must now be emphasised. The library was from November 1995 being developed not only to better serve as a tool with which to write software (a) for Adam Hinkley and his father, and (b) for the clients of Redrock,

▰▰▰▰▰ Redrock & Hotline Communications v Adam Hinkley *continued*

but also as a necessary component in the operating capacity of all the software in categories (a) and (b). In other words, the latter, as well as being built by means of the former (that is, with the class library being used as a tool), could not "run" without the class library.

In these circumstances, if Mr Hinkley proposed to fulfil his obligations to his employer by drawing upon the library by means which might in the absence of prior agreement blur the question of ownership of the copyright in the library, it fell to Mr Hinkley, as the only repository of the relevant information, to place his employer in a position from which employer and employee, both being fully informed of the relevant facts, could either negotiate a mutually satisfactory resolution to the copyright problem or go their separate ways. ...

By contrast, it was immaterial to Redrock whether Mr Hinkley developed the software that he was employed to write by resort to one "library" or another—or, indeed, if it was technically feasible, by resort to no library at all. It was similarly immaterial to Redrock whether Mr Hinkley so arranged the software he wrote that some part of an entire package could or could not function independently of another part of the package; if he chose to design a program in such a way that some part of it could not "run" without resort to another, that was his business. But he was employed to create a functional software package, and Redrock were entitled to such protection as was necessary to ensure that functionality. ... [580] ...

I turn now to the question of whether the library software was written during working hours at Redrock. This was an issue to which much time was devoted during the course of the trial. It is an important issue. It is nevertheless also important to record that the ultimate question—that concerning the ownership of copyright in the AW library—depends more on the relationship between the library and the programs written by Mr Hinkley for Redrock than on an identification of the times during which work on the library continued.

The plaintiffs contend that, while at work, Mr Hinkley wrote a significantly large part of the library for the purpose of developing software for use by customers of Redrock. Mr Hinkley says the library was developed "almost entirely" outside his life as an employee of Redrock. He says he frequently worked throughout the night and on the weekends making substantial changes to the library. He relies on the fact that he used a portable hard disk to carry the library to and from work, much as a builder might carry his toolbox to work. ... [583] ...

I have little doubt that Mr Hinkley spent some time, outside the hours of his employment, working on the class library as well as on Hotline and eText. I nevertheless find that something in the order of 90% of the development of the AppWarrior library occurred during ordinary business hours and while Mr Hinkley was physically present at the Redrock premises. Much of this time was used in refining AW to operate more effectively with software which Mr Hinkley was writing for Redrock; but, the library being a tool of general application, this work would have assisted, directly or indirectly, the development of the Hotline and eText software as well. This of itself, being a natural concomitant of work that directly benefited Redrock, could not have been the ground of any complaint by that company as Mr Hinkley's employer. On the other hand, neither could it found any viable claim by Mr Hinkley to copyright in anything. ... [584] ...

For all these reasons, I conclude that, on the balance of probabilities, a very significant proportion of the AW software was written by Mr Hinkley for work-related purposes and during work hours. I also conclude that all the Redrock software written by Mr Hinkley was written during the course of his employment and (with the possible exception of work done at home during transport strikes or other irregular and infrequent circumstances) during work hours. My additional finding that SPFS and other Redrock programs were dependent for their operational capacity upon the AW software leads me to the further conclusion that Redrock was the owner of the copyright in the AW library when Mr Hinkley, without any warning, left

████████ Redrock & Hotline Communications v Adam Hinkley *continued*

that company's employ in September 1997. During the period of his employment, moreover, the library had been transformed. The copyright which subsisted in November 1995 subsisted in the library as it then was. By September 1997, it was no longer that library. What little original material then remained had been absorbed into a much larger entity capable of performing altogether different tasks. The literary work of September 1997 was a new literary work, made by Adam Hinkley "in pursuance of the terms of his ... employment ... under a contract of service": *Copyright Act*, s 35(6).

██

■ Joint ownership

[4.55] See s 10(1) works of joint authorship; ss 78-83.

Joint ownership may arise from joint authorship, by agreement (*Stovin-Bradford v Volpoint Properties Ltd* [1971] Ch 1007; *Rebeschini v Miles Laboratories (Aust) Ltd* (1982) 1 IPR 159; *Acorn Computers Ltd v MCS Microcomputer Systems Pty Ltd* (1984) 57 ALR 389), assignment (*Murray v King* (1984) 55 ALR 559; *Greenfield Products Pty Ltd v Rover-Scott Bonnar Ltd* (1990) 17 IPR 417) or by will or devolution by operation of law (*O'Brien v Komesaroff* (1982) 41 ALR 255).

■ What conditions create co-ownership?

████████████ **Seven Network v TCN Channel Nine** ████████████

[4.60] *Seven Network (Operations) Ltd v TCN Channel Nine Pty Ltd* [2005] FCAFC 144 Federal Court of Australia, Full Court

[Facts: This dispute arose over the rights to film footage of troubled youths on a trek along the Kokoda Track. The trip was organised by Mr Murray, for the charity "Camp Dare". Filming was by a camera operator and a sound recordist provided by Channel Seven. It was agreed that the television station would have rights to produce and broadcast news and current affairs stories from the footage and that after these went to air the charity could use the raw footage to promote the charity. Channel Seven provided the raw footage to the charity. The charity subsequently provided the footage to Channel Nine who made a documentary of the trip. Channel Seven seeks an injunction to prevent that screening.

Mr Murray argued that the agreement with Channel Seven that he could access the footage, and his organisational efforts in making the trip possible, gave him a right to provide the raw footage to Channel Nine.

The significance of co-ownership is considered in a later extract at [5.25].]

LINDGREN J:
Who owned the copyright in the camera tapes film?

[10] I also agree with the primary Judge that Seven and Mr Murray were co-owners of the copyright in the Camera Tapes film.

[11] Subsections 98(2) and (3) of the *Copyright Act 1968* (Cth) ('the Act') provide:

"(2) Subject to the next succeeding subsection the maker of a cinematograph film is the owner of any copyright subsisting in the film by virtue of this Part.

(3) Where:

(a) a person makes, for valuable consideration, an agreement with another person for the making of a cinematograph film by the other person; and

(b) the film is made in pursuance of the agreement;

the first-mentioned person is, in the absence of any agreement to the contrary, the owner of any copyright subsisting in the film by virtue of this Part."

Subsection 22(4) of the Act provides:

"For the purposes of this Act:

(a) a reference to the making of a cinematograph film shall be read as a reference to the doing of the things necessary for the production of the first copy of the film; and

(b) the maker of the cinematograph film is the person by whom the arrangements necessary for the making of the film were undertaken."

[12] Professor Lahore (*Copyright and Designs*, at [20,145]) states in relation to s 22(4):

"The owner is therefore the producer who arranges the production of the first negative or tape of the film. The directors, actors and others involved in the making of the film have no copyright interests in the film unless they are 'makers' of the film."

Also in relation to s 22(4), Professor Ricketson states (*The Law of Intellectual Property: Copyright, Designs and Confidential Information* at [5.45]) that the subsection's reference to the doing of things that are necessary for the production of a film:

"... could include the business and financial 'things' that are necessary for the production of the first copy as much as the actual physical acts involved in its making, such as the direction, shooting and editing."

Professor Ricketson suggests that s 22(4) has the effect that ordinarily the owner of the copyright in a cinematograph film is the producer, rather than the camera operator or the director.

[13] His Honour, the primary Judge, referred to both learned authors but did not find either's exposition of great assistance in the unusual circumstances of the present case.

[14] Seven submits that while Mr Murray made the arrangements for the trip, Seven alone made the arrangements for the production of the Camera Tapes film.

[15] I disagree. In my opinion, both Seven and Mr Murray made the arrangements necessary for the production of the first copy of the Camera Tapes. I respectfully adopt his Honour's description of the arrangement as a "joint venture". The idea for the trek and for the filming of it was Mr Murray's. He arranged for the selection of the school boys to go on it and for the consent of their parents. Accordingly, he arranged for the subject matter of the film: ten troubled and troublesome schoolboys walking the Kokoda Track. He arranged for the funding of the return airfares, two nights' hotel accommodation in Port Moresby, insurance, and the supply of shoes, socks, sporting undergarments, backpacks, one-man tents, sleeping bags and food and drink, not only for them and the Camp Dare personnel, but also for Messrs Shannon and Lynch.

[16] Seven's contribution was:

(a) remunerating the freelance camera operator, Mr Shannon, who was already providing his services to Seven (Seven paid Mr Shannon's tax invoices for his services totalling $6,435);

(b) remunerating the freelance sound recordist, Mr Lynch, who was also already providing his services to Seven (Seven paid Mr Lynch's tax invoice of $3,850);

(c) supplying, through Mr Simond, a "script", in the sense of a list of the kinds of matters to be filmed, prepared by Mr Simond and given by him to Mr Shannon for use by him and Mr Lynch on the trip;

(d) providing one Sony camera;

(e) paying for the hire from Mr Shannon of a second Sony camera (Seven paid his invoice for $550);

(f) supplying the blank Sony Mini DV tapes which were, in due course, recycled;

(g) hiring the sound recording equipment for use by Mr Lynch from the Audio Sound Centre at Artarmon;

(h) supplying the batteries for the cameras and for the sound recording equipment;

(i) supplying the blank DV Pro tapes;

(j) through Mr Shannon and Mr Lynch, deciding upon scenes and sequences to be filmed but with suggestions from Mr Murray and others.

[17] The evidence was that the cost of Seven's contribution was of the order of $10,000. The "cost" of Mr Murray's contribution is difficult to identify. In one sense, he contributed nothing more than his own time. However, he obtained substantial cash and kind from others. Mr Murray estimated the total value at $150,000. The value of the cash, goods and services which Mr Murray obtained far exceeded the cost of Seven's contribution.

[18] No doubt a person's contribution may be too distant from the production of the first copy of a cinematograph film, for that person to be regarded as a "maker" of it, but that is not so in the present case. Mr Murray arranged for the trip and came to an arrangement with Seven for the filming of it. Without Mr Murray, there would have been no expedition, and, without his invitation to Seven, there would have been no filming of it by Messrs Shannon and Lynch, and therefore no Camera Tapes film. It is not as though Mr Murray was proposing only the trip, and Seven suggested the filming of it. The filming of it was Mr Murray's idea from the outset. Indeed, he had made or set in train arrangements for another camera operator (once, Honie Rowley and later Paul Croll) which, in the event, were not implemented.

[19] As was no doubt to be expected, in the course of the trek, various individuals made suggestions as to what should be filmed. For example, Mr Murray suggested a shot which included boys in the background, praying, with a view to showing that their Islamic faith was respected and that Camp Dare's work was applicable to those of all faiths, nationalities and races. Of course, Mr Shannon, as the camera operator, had the ultimate say as to precisely what filming took place, but this does not signify that Seven alone was the maker of the film.

[20] Although the circumstances may indicate otherwise, ordinarily co-owners of copyright hold as tenants in common, not as joint tenants: *Lauri v Renad* [1892] 3 Ch 402 at 412-413; *Cescinsky v George Routledge & Sons Ltd* [1916] 2 KB 325 ('*Cescinsky*'); *Prior v Lansdowne Press Pty Ltd* [1977] VR 65 at 68; *Prior v Sheldon* (2000) 48 IPR 301 at [79]. In the absence of the consent of the other co-owner, one co-owner is neither entitled to do an act comprised in the copyright, nor to grant a licence to a third party to do such an act, and the non-consenting co-owner is entitled to an injunction against the infringing co-owner or putative licensee: *Lauri v Renad*, above, at 413-3; *Cescinsky*, at 329-320.

[21] In my opinion, Mr Murray and Seven owned the copyright in the Camera Tapes film as tenants in common. We are not required to determine in what shares. The primary Judge said (at [59]) that "[c]opyright in the Camera Tapes was jointly held between DARE and Seven". I have little doubt that his Honour was not intending to distinguish between "joint" and "in common" co-ownership. The word "joint" is often used, even by the most highly respected writers, in a broad sense to refer simply to co-ownership; cf *Copinger and Skone James on Copyright* (13th ed), ch 7; *Prior v Sheldon*, above, at [79].

[22] Unless Seven assigned its interest in the copyright to Mr Murray, or the respondents enjoy the benefit of a licence, binding on Seven, to do what they propose, they threaten to infringe the copyright in the Camera Tapes film, and Seven is entitled to an injunction.

Note. Finkelstein J casts doubt over this reasoning however the Primary Judge's finding, with which Lindgren J is in agreement, was not overruled. See **[5.25]** at para [89].

■ Community ownership

▬▬▬▬▬ John Bulun Bulun v R & T Textiles ▬▬▬▬▬

[4.65] *John Bulun Bulun v R & T Textiles Pty Ltd* (1998) 41 IPR 513 Federal Court of Australia

VON DOUSSA J: **[515]** These proceedings arise out of the importation and sale in Australia of printed clothing fabric which infringed the copyright of the first applicant Mr Bulun Bulun, in the artistic work known as "Magpie Geese and Water Lilies at the Waterhole" (the artistic work).

The proceedings were commenced on 27 February 1996 by Mr Bulun Bulun and the second applicant, Mr George Milpurrurru. Both applicants are leading Aboriginal artists. The respondents were at that time, R & T Textiles Pty Ltd (the respondent) and its three directors. Mr Bulun Bulun sued as the legal owner of the copyright pursuant to the *Copyright Act 1968* (Cth) for remedies for the infringement, for contraventions of sections of Part V of the *Trade Practices Act 1974* (Cth) dealing with misleading or deceptive conduct, and for nuisance. Mr Milpurrurru brought the proceedings in his own right and as a representative of the traditional Aboriginal owners of Ganalbingu country which is situated in Arnhem Land, in the Northern Territory of Australia. He claims that the traditional Aboriginal owners of Ganalbingu country are the equitable owners of the copyright subsisting in the artistic work.

These proceedings represent another step by Aboriginal people to have communal title in their traditional ritual knowledge, and in particular in their artwork, recognised and protected by the Australian legal system. The inadequacies of statutory remedies under the *Copyright Act 1968* as a means of protecting communal ownership have been noted in earlier decisions of this Court: see *Yumbulul v Reserve Bank of Australia* (1991) 21 IPR 481 at 490 and *Milpurrurru v Indofurn Pty Ltd* (1994) 54 FCR 240 at 247. See also McKeough and Stewart "Intellectual Property and the Dreaming", published in *Indigenous Australia and the Law*, Johnston, Hinton & Rigney eds (1997); Henderson "What's in a Painting? The Cultural Harm of Unauthorised Reproduction" (1995) 17 Syd Law Rev 591 at 593; Ellison, "Unauthorised Reproduction of Traditional Aboriginal Art" (1994) 17 UNSWLJ 327; and "Stopping the Rip-Offs: Intellectual Property Protection for Aboriginal and Torres Strait Islander Peoples" (1994, National Capital Printing) where it was said at p 6:

> "While joint authorship of a work by two or more authors is recognised by the *Copyright Act*, collective ownership by reference to any other criterion, for example, membership of the author of a community whose customary laws invest the community with ownership of any creation of its members is not recognised."

[516] Mr Bulun Bulun's claim

As soon as the proceedings were served the respondent admitted infringement of Mr Bulun Bulun's copyright in the artistic work, and pleaded that the infringement had occurred in ignorance of the copyright. The respondent immediately withdrew the offending fabric from sale. At that time approximately 7,600 metres of the fabric had been imported and approximately 4,231 metres sold in Australia.

On 27 June 1996 an administrator of the respondent was appointed under Part 5.3A of the *Corporations Law*, and on 5 July 1996 receivers and managers were appointed.

On 20 January 1997 the applicants were granted leave by consent to proceed against the respondent pursuant to s 440D of the *Corporations Law*. The applicants informed the Court that the proceedings would be discontinued against the directors of the respondent, and leave

▬▬▬▬▬ John Bulun Bulun v R & T Textiles *continued*

was given to the applicants to file an amended application and statement of claim. The respondent then consented to final declarations and orders on the claim by Mr Bulun Bulun. These included a declaration that the respondent had infringed Mr Bulun Bulun's legal title to the copyright in the artistic work, and comprehensive permanent injunctions against future infringement.

The amended application and amended statement of claim continued to plead a claim by George Milpurrurru on his own behalf and in a representative capacity for the Ganalbingu people in respect of equitable ownership of the copyright in the artistic work. The claims under the *Trade Practices Act* were abandoned. A claim in nuisance was repleaded, but that claim was also abandoned before trial.

In its defence filed to the original statement of claim the respondent pleaded that Mr Bulun Bulun had full legal rights under the *Copyright Act* to recover in respect of any infringement of copyright in the artistic work, and that it was therefore unnecessary to consider whether the Ganalbingu people or any of them were equitable owners of the copyright. In any event the respondent did not admit the allegations concerning equitable ownership of the copyright.

Counsel for the applicants informed the Court that the artistic work incorporates within its subject matter much that is sacred and important to the Ganalbingu people about their heritage. Counsel emphasised that copyright infringements of artworks such as the artistic work affect interests beyond those of the copyright owner, and that the Ganalbingu people considered it to be of great importance that the Court recognise the rights of the Ganalbingu people and the injury caused to them by the respondent's infringement. Counsel said that Mr Milpurrurru therefore proposed to continue with his claim notwithstanding the consent orders in favour of Mr Bulun Bulun.

Accordingly, on 20 January 1997 directions were given for the filing of affidavit evidence, and generally to bring the claims pleaded by Mr Milpurrurru to readiness for trial.

Evidence in Mr Milpurrurru's claim

[517] ... The amended application in this case alleges that the Ganalbingu people are the traditional Aboriginal owners of Ganalbingu country who have the right to permit and control the production and reproduction of the artistic work under the law and custom of the Ganalbingu people. It is pleaded that the traditional owners of Ganalbingu country comprise:
(i) Members of the Ganalbingu people;
(ii) The Yolngu people (Aboriginal people of Arnhem Land) who are the children of the women of the Ganalbingu people;
(iii)The Yolngu people who stand in a relationship of mother's-mother to the members of the Ganalbingu people under Ganalbingu law and custom;
(iv)Such other Yolngu people who are recognised by the applicants according to Ganalbingu law and custom as being traditional Aboriginal owners of Ganalbingu country.

The amended statement of claim pleads that the Ganalbingu people are the traditional Aboriginal owners of the corpus of ritual knowledge from which the artistic work is derived, including the subject matter of the artistic work and the artistic work itself.

Mr Milpurrurru is the most senior person of all the Ganalbingu people. The Ganalbingu people are divided into "top"" and "bottom" people as is the Ganalbingu country. Mr Milpurrurru is a "top" Ganalbingu. Mr Bulun Bulun is the most senior person of the "bottom" Ganalbingu and is second in line to Mr Milpurrurru of the Ganalbingu people generally.

Djulibinyamurr is the site of a waterhole complex situated close to the eastern side of the Arafura Swamp between the Glyde and Goyder river systems and the Woolen River. Djulibinyamurr, along with another waterhole site, Ngalyindi, are [518] the two most important

████████ John Bulun Bulun v R & T Textiles *continued*

sites on Ganalbingu country for the Ganalbingu people. Mr Bulun Bulun describes Djuli-binyamurr as the ral'kal for the lineage of the bottom Ganalbingu people. In his affidavit evidence Mr Bulun Bulun says: ...

"Barnda not only created the place we call Djulibinuyamurr but it populated the country as well. Barnda gave the place its name, created the people who follow him and named those people. Barnda gave us our language and law. Barnda gave to my ancestors the country and the ceremony and paintings associated with the country. My ancestors had a responsibility given to them by Barnda to perform the ceremony and to do the paintings which were granted to them. This is a part of the continuing responsibility of the traditional Aboriginal owners handed down from generation to generation. Djulibinyamurr is then our life source and the source of our continuing totemic or sacred responsibility. The continuity of our traditions and ways including our traditional Aboriginal ownership depends upon us respecting and honouring the things entrusted to us by Barnda.

...

In the same way my creator ancestor formed the natural landscape and granted it to my human ancestors who in turn handed it to me. My creator ancestor passed on to me the elements for the artworks I produce for sale and ceremony. Barnda not only creates the people and landscape, but our designs and artworks originate from the creative acts of Barnda. They honour and deliberate the deeds of Barnda. This way the spirit and rule of Barnda is kept alive in the land. The land and the legacy of Barnda go hand in hand. Land is given to Yolngu people along with responsibility for all of the Madayin (corpus of ritual knowledge) associated with the land. In fact for Yolngu, the ownership of land has with it the corresponding obligations to create and foster the artworks, designs, songs and other aspects of ritual and ceremony that go with the land. If the rituals and ceremonies attached to land ownership are not fulfilled, that is if responsibilities in respect of Madayin are not maintained then traditional Aboriginal ownership rights lapse. Paintings, for example, are a manifestation of our ancestral past. They were first made, in my case by Barnda. Barnda handed the painting to my human ancestors. They have been handed from generation to generation ever since.

The creation of artworks such as 'at the Waterhole' is part of my responsibility in fulfilling the obligations I have as a traditional Aboriginal owner of Djulibinyamurr. I am permitted by my law to create this artwork, but it is also my duty and responsi-bility to create such words, as part of my traditional Aboriginal land ownership obligation. A [519] painting such as this is not separate from my rights in my land. It is a part of my bundle of rights in the land and must be produced in accordance with Ganalbingu custom and law. Interference with the painting or another aspect of the Madayin associated with Djulibinyamurr is tantamount to interference with the land itself as it is an essential part of the legacy of the land, it is like causing harm to the spirit found in the land, and causes us sorrow and hardship. The land is the life force of our people. It sustains and nurtures us, as it has done for countless generations. We are very troubled by harm caused to the carrying out of the rituals which are such essential part of the management of our land, like the making of paintings or perfor-mances of ceremony. It is very important that ceremonies are carried out precisely as directed by Barnda, and that the ceremonies are respected.

...

▆▆▆▆▆ John Bulun Bulun v R & T Textiles *continued*

Unauthorised reproduction of 'at the Waterhole' threatens the whole system and ways that underpin the stability and continuance of Yolngu society. It interferes with the relationship between people, their creator ancestors and the land given to the people by their creator ancestor. It interferes with our custom and ritual, and threatens our rights as traditional Aboriginal owners of the land and impedes in the carrying out of the obligations that go with this ownership and which require us to tell and remember the story of Barnda, as it has been passed down and respected over countless generations."

...

Mr Bulun Bulun explained that the classes of people, described earlier in these reasons, who comprise the traditional Aboriginal owners of Ganalbingu country have interests in Djulibinyamurr and also in the Madayin including paintings such as the artistic work. Many of these people would need to be consulted on any matter that concerned Djulibinyamurr. He went on to say:

"In ... cases where it has been agreed in principle that the types of uses in question are allowable direct consultation and approval may not be necessary. If Bulun Bulun wanted to licence 'at the Waterhole' so that somebody could mass produce it in the way that the Respondents have he would need to consult widely. If he wanted to licence 'at the Waterhole' to a publisher to reproduce the painting in an art book he probably would not need to consult the other traditional Aboriginal owners at all.

The question in each case depends on the use and the manner or mode of production. But in the case of a use which is one that requires direct consultation, rather than one for which approval has been already given for a class of uses, all of the traditional Aboriginal owners must agree. There must be total consensus. Bulun Bulun could not act alone to permit the reproduction of 'at the Waterhole' in the manner as was done."

[522] Intervention and amicus curiae

As the trial date approached it was plain that no one would appear on the respondent's behalf to act as a contradictor either on matters of fact or law. The applicants brought the proceedings to the notice of the Minister for Aboriginal and Torres Strait Islander Affairs (the Minister).

... [523] ...

The Minister and the Attorney-General were concerned that the pleadings claimed that (1) the intellectual property rights in the artistic work were an incident of native title; (2) being an incident of native title the intellectual property rights constituted an interest in land; and (3) the Ganalbingu people were entitled to a determination in these proceedings that they were the native title holders of the Ganalbingu country. The outline of submissions presented by the applicants at the commencement of the trial appeared to support this interpretation of their claim.

In the present case there is no application for determination of native title pursuant to s 74 of the *Native Title Act 1993*, and this Court is without jurisdiction to make a determination of native title in these proceedings.

The submissions of the Minister went on to contend that whilst native title to an area of land may exist without a judicial determination as to its existence (*Mabo [No 2]*) the necessary elements of proof of native title are not made out in this case in any event. As this Court does not have jurisdiction to make a determination of native title in land it is not appropriate to consider those submissions save to note that the evidence does not address at all a number of issues that would arise in a proceeding commenced and resolved in a State or Territory Court in accordance with the principles expressed in *Mabo [No 2]*.

▓▓▓▓ John Bulun Bulun v R & T Textiles *continued*

... [524] ...

However, it is not necessary to further consider these issues as the initial suggestion in the submissions that intellectual property rights are an incident of native title in land such that they constituted some recognisable interest in the land itself was not pressed. Rather, the submissions were modified to assert that the claimed equitable interests in the copyright subsisting in the artistic work were incidental to the applicants' claimed land ownership, and to their perception of their relationship with the land. Their traditional use and occupation of the land is the basis for the continuing existence of and adherence to Ganalbingu laws and customs concerning the creation, reproduction and use of traditional art. In their final form, the applicants' submissions did not seek to have the Court declare by some indirect route that the Ganalbingu people were the holders of native title in the Ganalbingu country.

Why the claim is confined to one for recognition of an equitable interest

The submissions of counsel for the applicants reflected a wide ranging search for a way in which the communal interests of the traditional Aboriginal owners in cultural artworks might be recognised under Australian law. This exercise was painstakingly pursued by counsel for the applicants (and later by counsel for the Minister). That the claim was ultimately confined to one for recognition of an equitable interest in the legal copyright of Mr Bulun Bulun is an acknowledgment that no other possible avenue had emerged from the researches of counsel.

While it is superficially attractive to postulate that the common law should recognise communal title, it would be contrary to established legal principle for the common law to do so. There seems no reason to doubt that customary Aboriginal laws relating to the ownership of artistic works survived the introduction of the common law of England in 1788. The Aboriginal peoples did not cease to observe their sui generis system of rights and obligations upon the acquisition of sovereignty of Australia by the Crown. The question however is whether those Aboriginal laws can create binding obligations on persons outside the relevant Aboriginal community, either through recognition of those laws by the common law, or by their capacity to found equitable rights in rem.

In *Mabo [No 2]* Deane and Gaudron JJ, after analysing the effects of the introduction of the common law of England into Australia in 1788 said, at 79:

> "The common law so introduced was adjusted in accordance with the principle that, in settled colonies, only so much of it was introduced as was 'reasonably applicable to the [525] circumstances of the colony'. This left room for the continued operation of some local laws or customs among the native people and even the incorporation of some of those laws and customs as part of the common law." (footnotes omitted).

In 1788 there may have been scope for the continued operation of a system of indigenous collective ownership in artistic works. At that time the common law of England gave the author of an artistic work property in unpublished compositions which lasted in perpetuity: *Mansell v Valley Printing Co* [1908] 1 Ch 567 and Laddie Prescott and Vitoria, *The Modern Law of Copyright* (1980), para 4.64. That property was lost upon publication of the artistic work. Exhibition for sale or sale constituted publication: *Britain v Hanks Bros* (1902) 86 LT 765. This property interest was separate from the right recognised in equity to restrain a breach of confidence, a right which continues and was invoked in *Foster v Mountford and Rigby Ltd* (1976) 14 ALR 71. The common law of England did not protect an author of an artistic work after publication. If the common law had not been amended in the meantime by statute, an interesting question would arise as to whether Aboriginal laws and customs could be incorporated into the common law. However, the common law has since been subsumed by statute. The common law right until first publication was abolished when the law of

▆▆▆▆ John Bulun Bulun v R & T Textiles *continued*

copyright was codified by the *Copyright Act 1911* in the UK. That Act, subject to some modifications, became the law in Australia by s 8 of the *Copyright Act 1912* (Cth). Copyright is now entirely a creature of statute: McKeough and Stewart, *Intellectual Property in Australia* (1991), para 504, *Copinger and Skone James on Copyright* (13th ed), para 1-43. The exclusive domain of the *Copyright Act 1968* in Australia is expressed in s 8 (subject only to the qualification in s 8A) namely that "copyright does not subsist otherwise than by virtue of this Act".

Section 35(2) of the *Copyright Act 1968* provides that the author of an artistic work is the owner of the copyright which subsists by virtue of the Act. That provision effectively precludes any notion of group ownership in an artistic work, unless the artistic work is a "work of joint ownership" within the meaning of s 10(1) of the Act. A "work of joint authorship" means a work that has been produced by the collaboration of two or more authors and in which the contribution of each author is not separate from the contribution of the other author or the contributions of the other authors. In this case no evidence was led to suggest that anyone other than Mr Bulun Bulun was the creative author of the artistic work. A person who supplies an artistic idea to an artist who then executes the work is not, on that ground alone, a joint author with the artist: *Kenrick & Co v Lawrence & Co* (1890) 25 QBD 99. Joint authorship envisages the contribution of skill and labour to the production of the work itself: *Fylde Microsystems Ltd v Key Radio Systems Ltd* (1998) 39 IPR 481 at 486.

In *Coe v The Commonwealth* (1993) 118 ALR 193 at 200 Mason CJ rejected the proposition that Aboriginal people are entitled to rights and interests other than those created or recognised by the laws of the Commonwealth, its States and the common law. See also *Walker v New South Wales* at 45-50 and Kirby J in *Wik Peoples v Queensland* at 214. To conclude that the Ganalbingu people were communal owners of the copyright in the existing work would ignore the provisions of s 8 of the *Copyright Act*, and involve the creation of rights in indigenous peoples which are not otherwise recognised by the legal system of Australia.

[526] Do the circumstances in which the artistic work was created give rise to equitable interests in the Ganalbingu people?

The statement of claim alleges "on the reduction to material form of a part of the ritual knowledge of the Ganalbingu people associated with Djulibinyamurr by the creation of the artistic work, the First Applicant held the copyright subsisting in the artistic work as a fiduciary and/or alternatively on trust, for the second applicant and the people he represents". The foundation for this contention is expanded in written submissions made on Mr Milpurrurru's behalf. It is contended that these rights arise because Mr Milpurrurru and those he represents have the power under customary law to regulate and control the production and reproduction of the corpus of ritual knowledge. It is contended that the customs and traditions regulating this use of the corpus of ritual knowledge places Mr Bulun Bulun as the author of the artistic work in the position of a fiduciary, and, moreover, make Mr Bulun Bulun a trustee for the artwork, either pursuant to some form of express trust, or pursuant to a constructive trust in favour of the Ganalbingu people. The right to control the production and reproduction of the corpus of ritual knowledge relating to Djulibinyamurr is said to arise by virtue of the strong ties which continue to exist between the Ganalbingu people and their land.

Was there an express trust?

The possibility that an express trust was created in respect of the artistic work or the copyright subsisting in it was not at the forefront of the applicants' submissions. In my opinion that possibility can be dismissed on the evidence in this case.

...

▬▬▬ John Bulun Bulun v R & T Textiles *continued*

The artwork, when completed, was sold by Mr Bulun Bulun to the Maningrida Arts and Crafts Centre. It is not suggested that he did not receive and retain the sale price for his own use. Moreover, the evidence indicates that on many occasions paintings which incorporate to a greater or lesser degree parts of the ritual knowledge of the Ganalbingu people are produced by Ganalbingu artists for commercial sale for the benefit of the artist concerned. ... [527] ...

Did Mr Bulun Bulun hold the copyright as a fiduciary?

In *Breen v Williams* (1996) 186 CLR 71 at 82, Brennan CJ identified two sources of fiduciary duties, the first being the circumstances in which a relationship of agency can be said to exist, and the other is founded in a relationship of ascendancy or influence by one party over another, or dependence or trust on the part of that other. The applicants' counsel did not seek to characterise the fiduciary relationship for which he contends as derived from either source in particular. The existence of a fiduciary relationship is said to arise out of the nature of ownership of artistic works amongst the Ganalbingu people. ... [528] ...

The factors and relationships giving rise to a fiduciary duty are nowhere exhaustively defined: *Mabo [No 2]*, at 200 per Toohey J, *Hospital Products v USSC* (1984) 156 CLR 41 at 68, 96-97, PD Finn, *Fiduciary Obligations* (1977), p 1, and *News Ltd v ARL* at 564. It has been said that the term "fiduciary relationship", defies definition: *Breen v Williams* at 106 per Gaudron and McHugh JJ, see also Gibbs CJ in *Hospital Products v USSC* at 69. For this reason the fiduciary concept has developed incrementally throughout the case law which itself provides guidance as to the traditional parameters of the concept. The essential characteristics of fiduciary relationships were referred to by Mason J in *Hospital Products* at 96-97:

> "The critical feature of [fiduciary] relationships is that the fiduciary undertakes or agrees to act for or on behalf of or in the interests of another person in the exercise of a power or discretion which will affect the interests of that other person in a legal or practical sense. The relationship between the parties is therefore one which gives the fiduciary a special opportunity to exercise the power or discretion to the detriment of that other person who is accordingly vulnerable to abuse by the fiduciary of his position ... It is partly because the fiduciary's exercise of the power or discretion can adversely affect the interests of the person to whom the duty is owed and because the latter is at the mercy of the former that the fiduciary comes under a duty to exercise his power or discretion in the interests of the person to whom it is owed".

In *Mabo*, Toohey J said at 200:

> "Underlying such relationships is the scope for one party to exercise a discretion which is capable of affecting the legal position of the other. One party has a special opportunity to abuse the interests of the other. The discretion will be an incident of the first party's office or position."

... [529] ...

The relationship between Mr Bulun Bulun as the author and legal title holder of the artistic work and the Ganalbingu people is unique. The "transaction" between them out of which the fiduciary relationship is said to arise is the use with permission by Mr Bulun Bulun of ritual knowledge of the Ganalbingu people, and the embodiment of that knowledge within the artistic work. That use has been permitted in accordance with the law and customs of the Ganalbingu people.

The grant of permission by the djungayi and other appropriate representatives of the Ganalbingu people for the creation of the artistic work is predicated on the trust and confidence which those granting permission have in the artist. The evidence indicates that if

▬▬▬ John Bulun Bulun v R & T Textiles *continued*

those who must give permission do not have trust and confidence in someone seeking permission, permission will not be granted.

The law and customs of the Ganalbingu people require that the use of the ritual knowledge and the artistic work be in accordance with the requirements of law and custom, and that the author of the artistic work do whatever is necessary to prevent any misuse. The artist is required to act in relation to the artwork in the interests of the Ganalbingu people to preserve the integrity of their culture, and ritual knowledge.

This is not to say that the artist must act entirely in the interests of the Ganalbingu people. The evidence shows that an artist is entitled to consider and pursue his own interests, for example by selling the artwork, but the artist is not [530] permitted to shed the overriding obligation to act to preserve the integrity of the Ganalbingu culture where action for that purpose is required.

In my opinion, the nature of the relationship between Mr Bulun Bulun and the Ganalbingu people was a fiduciary one which gives rise to fiduciary obligations owed by Mr Bulun Bulun.

The conclusion that in all the circumstances Mr Bulun Bulun owes fiduciary obligations to the Ganalbingu people does not treat the law and custom of the Ganalbingu people as part of the Australian legal system. Rather, it treats the law and custom of the Ganalbingu people as part of the factual matrix which characterises the relationship as one of mutual trust and confidence. It is that relationship which the Australian legal system recognises as giving rise to the fiduciary relationship, and to the obligations which arise out of it.

It is convenient at this point to dispose of an alternative submission raised as a possibility by the applicants in argument, although not seriously pressed. That is that the facts are open to the construction that there was a contract between Mr Bulun Bulun and those who gave him permission to create the artistic work (acting on behalf of the Ganalbingu people), and that the contract imposed obligations akin to fiduciary obligations, or even created an equitable interest, in the artwork. It is not inconceivable that contractual arrangements could be made between representatives of a clan and a particular artist as to the circumstances in which ritual knowledge could be incorporated into an artistic work. ...

The fiduciary obligation

Central to the fiduciary concept is the protection of interests that can be regarded as worthy of judicial protection: Glover, *Commercial Equity—Fiduciary Relationships* (1995), para 3.4. The evidence is all one way. The ritual knowledge relating to Djulibinyamurr embodied within the artistic work is of great importance to members of the Ganalbingu people. I have no hesitation in holding that the interest of Ganalbingu people in the protection of that ritual [531] knowledge from exploitation which is contrary to their law and custom is deserving of the protection of the Australian legal system.

Under the *Copyright Act*, the owner of the copyright has the exclusive right to reproduce the work in a material form, and to publish the work. The copyright owner is entitled to enforce copyright against the world at large. In the event of infringement, the copyright owner is entitled to sue and to obtain remedies of the kind actually obtained by Mr Bulun Bulun in this case.

Having regard to the evidence of the law and customs of the Ganalbingu people under which Mr Bulun Bulun was permitted to create the artistic work, I consider that equity imposes on him obligations as a fiduciary not to exploit the artistic work in a way that is contrary to the laws and custom of the Ganalbingu people, and, in the event of infringement by a third party, to take reasonable and appropriate action to restrain and remedy infringement of the copyright in the artistic work.

▆▆▆▆▆▆ John Bulun Bulun v R & T Textiles *continued*

Whilst the nature of the relationship between Mr Bulun Bulun and the Ganalbingu people is such that Mr Bulun Bulun falls under fiduciary obligations to protect the ritual knowledge which he has been permitted to use, the existence of those obligations does not, without more, vest an equitable interest in the ownership of the copyright in the Ganalbingu people. Their primary right, in the event of a breach of obligation by the fiduciary is a right in personam to bring action against the fiduciary to enforce the obligation.

In the present case Mr Bulun Bulun has successfully taken action against the respondent to obtain remedies in respect of the infringement. There is no suggestion by Mr Milpurrurru and those whom he seeks to represent that Mr Bulun Bulun should have done anything more. In these circumstances there is no occasion for the intervention of equity to provide any additional remedy to the beneficiaries of the fiduciary relationship.

However, had the position been otherwise equitable remedies could have been available. The extent of those remedies would depend on all the circumstances, and in an extreme case could involve the intervention of equity to impose a constructive trust on the legal owner of the copyright in the artistic work in favour of the beneficiaries. Equity will not automatically impose a constructive trust merely upon the identification of a fiduciary obligation. Equity will impose a constructive trust on property held by a fiduciary where it is necessary to do so to achieve a just remedy and to prevent the fiduciary from retaining an unconscionable benefit: *Muschinski v Dodds* (1985) 160 CLR 385 at 619-620 and *Baumgartner v Baumgartner* (1987) 164 CLR 137 at 148. By way of example, had Mr Bulun Bulun merely failed to take action to enforce his copyright, an adequate remedy might be extended in equity to the beneficiaries by allowing them to bring an action in their own names against the infringer and the copyright owner, claiming against the former, in the first instance, interlocutory relief to restrain the infringement, and against the latter orders necessary to ensure that the copyright owner enforces the copyright. Probably there would be no occasion for equity in these circumstances to impose a constructive trust.

On the other hand, were Mr Bulun Bulun to deny the existence of fiduciary obligations and the interests of the parties asserting them, and refuse to protect the copyright from infringement, then the occasion might exist for equity to impose a remedial constructive trust upon the copyright owner to strengthen the standing of the beneficiaries to bring proceedings to enforce the copyright. This may be necessary if the copyright owner cannot be identified or found and the [532] beneficiaries are unable to join the legal owner of the copyright: see *Performing Rights Society Ltd v London Theatre of Varieties* [1924] AC 1 at 18.

It is well recognised that interlocutory injunctive relief can be claimed by a party having an equitable interest in copyright: Laddie, Prescott and Vittoria, *The Modern Law of Copyright* (1995), para 11.79-11.81, although as a matter of practice injunctive relief will not be granted without the legal owner of copyright being joined: *Performing Rights Society Ltd v London Theatre of Varieties* at 19-20, 29, *Acorn Computers Ltd v MCS Microcomputer Systems Pty Ltd* (1984) 57 ALR 389 at 394. For an example of proceedings brought to establish the existence of an equitable interest in copyright based on a constructive trust imposed in consequence of a breach of fiduciary duty see *Missinglink Software v Magee* [1989] 1 FSR 361 at 367.

I do not consider Mr Milpurrurru and those he seeks to represent have established an equitable interest in the copyright in the artistic work. In my opinion they have established that fiduciary obligations are owed to them by Mr Bulun Bulun, but as Mr Bulun Bulun has taken appropriate action to enforce the copyright, he has fulfilled those obligations and there is no occasion to grant any additional remedy in favour of the Ganalbingu people. However, in other circumstances if the copyright owner of an artistic work which embodies ritual knowledge of an Aboriginal clan is being used inappropriately, and the copyright owner fails

▬▬▬▬ John Bulun Bulun v R & T Textiles *continued*

or refuses to take appropriate action to enforce the copyright, the Australian legal system will permit remedial action through the courts by the clan.

For these reasons, the proceedings by Mr Milpurrurru must be dismissed.

SUBJECT MATTER OTHER THAN WORKS

[4.70] The first owner of copyright in recordings, films, broadcasts and published editions is, subject to a contrary agreement and the rights of the Crown, the "maker" or publisher of the subject matter. See *Seven Networks v TCN Nine* at **[4.60]** and **[5.25]**. This is separate from and additional to any copyright in works which are incorporated in the other subject matter: *WEA Records Pty Ltd v Stereo FM Pty Ltd* (1983) 1 IPR 6 at 10; *CBS Records Australia Ltd v Telmak (Aust) Pty Ltd* (1987) 9 IPR 440. Numerous provisions elaborate who is the maker of the subject matter depending upon the nature of the recording medium. Note that a literary, dramatic or musical work can be embodied through the making of a sound recording of it, leading to two separate but related rights coming into being contemporaneously, one in the underlying literary, dramatic or musical work, and one in the sound recording of it. See *Copyright Act 1968* (Cth), ss 22, 97-100.

CROWN COPYRIGHT

[4.75] The Crown owns copyright of works, recordings and films "made by, or under the direction or control of, the Commonwealth or a State, as the case may be" (s 176(2)). "State" includes the administration of a Territory (s 10(3)(n)). Copyright may arise (and be owned by the Crown) in material that would not otherwise fulfil the criteria of the *Copyright Act 1968* (Cth) as to subsistence of copyright, for example, due perhaps to the author not being a qualified person. Thus, the Crown has copyright in material made under its direction or control, irrespective of the nationality or residence of the author, or the place of first publication, but of course it may arise in the normal way and belong to the Crown by virtue of s 35(6): see *Director-General of Education v Public Service Association of New South Wales* (1985) 4 IPR 552.

The *Copyright Act 1968* (Cth) makes it clear in s 8A(1) that no prerogative right or privilege of the Crown is affected by the legislation. The extent of this prerogative is unclear, but it seems to be a relic of the censorship and concern with public order evinced by the Crown in Anglo-Australian copyright law. In 2005 the Copyright Law Review Committee examined "Crown Copyright". The chief concern was whether government should be in a privileged position compared with other owners of copyright.

The CLRC recommended the repeal of special Crown copyright subsistence and ownership provisions in Part VII Division 1 of the *Copyright Act 1968* (Cth) (ss 176–179). The Committee preference was that the usual copyright ownership rules should apply, rather than special default provisions that advantage the government in negotiations, and mean that failure to conclude negotiations result in the creator losing copyright.

In the interest of the public domain, the Committee recommended retaining a fifty-year duration of copyright for published literary, dramatic and musical works, films, sound recordings and artistic works.

The CLRC also noted "new technology has improved the accessibility of information for many people, (but) it has also allowed the development of new protection measures which can restrict that access". Accordingly a general policy consideration in regard to Crown copyright should be recognition that "open access to government information is an essential characteristic of modern democracy" and "there is great danger in the possibility of government using copyright as an instrument of censorship".

The Committee also recommended that copyright in certain material produced by the judicial, legislative and executive arms of government be abolished, including that which currently applies to

- bills, statutes, regulations, ordinances, by-laws and proclamations, and explanatory memoranda or explanatory statements relating to those materials;

- judgments, orders and awards of any court or tribunal;

- official records of parliamentary debates and reports of parliament, including reports of parliamentary committees;

- reports of commissions of inquiry, including royal commissions and ministerial and statutory inquiries; and

- other categories of material prescribed by regulation.

CHAPTER 5

EXPLOITATION

[5.05] Despite the introduction of moral rights into Australian copyright law in late 2000, and although the branches of copyright may share some notion of non-utilitarian, cultural significance, it has been the case that in Australian law copyright is basically concerned with economic exploitation. The introduction of more recent "other subject matter" varieties of copyright in *Copyright Act 1968* (Cth), Part IV emphasises this commercial aspect. The rights in non-work subject matter derive from manufacturing and technological procedures, and engender discrete copyrights, while embodying concomitant author's copyrights in the works thus represented. The protection of economic rights which may be dealt with as a form of property may have emphasised one aspect of copyright at the expense of moral rights, which have long been recognised in Europe. The Berne Convention, of which Australia is a member, states in the Paris Revision, Art 6(1) that:

> "Independently of the author's economic rights, and even after the transfer of the said rights, the author shall have the right to claim authorship of the work and to object to any distortion, mutilation or other modification of, or other derogatory action in relation to, the said work, which would be prejudicial to his honour or reputation."

Although the 1968 Act provided that false attributions of authorship were an offence, this did not amount to a positive right to be acknowledged as the author.

The new regime of moral rights is regarded by many users of copyright work as a commercial problem. See, for example, *Wilson v Weiss Art Pty Ltd* (below), where the use of material by an advertising agency may be subject to moral rights. One of the most debated aspects of the moral rights regime was the issue of whether the rights could be waived; obviously no-one would contract with a writer who refused to waive their rights, and the view put forward was that the personal moral rights are inalienable and can never be waived. In the end, there are "consent" provisions in the legislation (ss 195AW-195AWA) allowing written permission to be given by an author to excuse acts or omissions which may otherwise contravene the author's moral rights.

The most lucrative copyright works are often exploited in a number of ways. A popular novel may be marketed as a volume (book), serial (in newspapers and magazines), translation, film, play, opera, musical or ballet. In addition, licensing for inclusion in electronic databases, and other digital uses are all within the copyright owner's rights. The *Copyright Act 1968* (Cth), s 196(2) allows these rights to be licensed or assigned separately. Furthermore, these rights can be confined geographically (s 196(2)(b)) and temporally (s 196(2)(c)).

ASSIGNMENT

[5.10] Formalities: s 196

▬▬▬▬▬▬▬ Wilson v Weiss Art ▬▬▬▬▬▬▬

[5.15] *Wilson v Weiss Art Pty Ltd* (1995) 31 IPR 423 Federal Court of Australia

HILL J: **[424]** Faye Ann Wilson, the applicant, is an artist and an illustrator. Between 1982 and 1987, at the request of McSpedden Carey, an advertising agency, she executed various drawings. At least at the outset, the Agency was the advertising agent for Peter Weiss Pty Ltd (PWPL), a clothing manufacturer and vendor. She claims in these proceedings that the respondent, Weiss Art Pty Ltd, without her licence, reproduced or procured the reproduction of some or all of these drawings, published them or sold articles which constituted an infringement of her copyright in the drawings. In consequence she claims, inter alia, a declaration that the respondent has infringed her copyright, injunctive relief and damages or an accounting of profits.

[425] ... Although there is some divergence of evidence, the basic facts are not really in dispute and may shortly be stated.

McSpedden Carey (the Agency) was, at relevant times, a rather small advertising agency. It was established in 1980 and its principals were Mr Bani McSpedden and Mr Peter Carey. Shortly after the Agency was established, PWPL became a client of it. One of the principals of PWPL, at that time, was Mr Peter Weiss who early approached the Agency for advice on establishing a recognisable image for clothing marketed under the Weiss brand.

The Art Director of the Agency, Mr Pavlovitch, and his then assistant, a Ms Uttinger, prepared some simple brush drawings using Indian ink on a white background and thereby created what may be called a recognisable style which was used to promote Weiss garments in a newspaper advertising campaign from 1980 onwards.

Ms Uttinger died suddenly in 1982 and Mr Pavlovitch had the task of locating alternative illustrators to prepare further "Weiss" illustrations for the Agency. It was in this context that he came to interview Ms Wilson. Mr Pavlovitch gave Ms Wilson a layout and asked her to prepare a drawing in the same style as that which Mr Pavlovitch and Ms Uttinger had devised using broad brush strokes of black ink on white paper.

There is little evidence of the initial commercial arrangement between Ms Wilson and the Agency. Mr Pavlovitch did not suggest in his evidence that he had any commercial discussions with Ms Wilson. He led her to believe that the Agency wished to have the right to cut up and change the illustrations if they were to be used. Most of the discussion probably centred upon the requirement that the drawings be in "the Weiss style". There was no discussion about copyright. Mr Pavlovitch made it clear to Ms Wilson that the drawings were for use in advertising products of Weiss and there was no discussion concerning the use of the drawings for merchandising purposes.

From 1982 Ms Wilson supplied drawings upon request. The initial procedure adopted where drawings were required was that the Agency would issue a work order indicating the subject or concept to be adopted. Ms Wilson would prepare a number of drawings and present them. It was clearly understood by the parties that not all of the drawings would be used and payment would be made only in respect of drawings which the Agency wished to use. Having made that decision, the Agency issued a purchase order to Ms Wilson in respect of the drawing to be used. She, in turn, then invoiced the Agency by reference to that purchase order.

Initial drawings were for use in advertisements to be placed in the media. According to Ms Wilson's evidence Mr Pavlovitch said to her, words to the effect, "these are for newspaper advertisements and when you invoice me make a note to that effect".

[427]... It seems clear enough that Ms Wilson was told nothing about the plans which Mr McSpedden had for a joint venture between the Agency and PWPL. The proposal for that joint venture appears to have been under way by about May 1986 when a shelf company was acquired, the shares in which were held as to one share by Mr McSpedden, one share by Mr Carey and two shares by Talbridge Pty Ltd, a company associated with Mr Peter Weiss. That company changed its name to Weiss Art Pty Ltd, the respondent, on 8 October 1986.

Although little is known of the circumstances surrounding the acquisition by Mr McSpedden and others of the respondent company, it is clear that its purpose was to engage in a merchandising activity, manufacturing or procuring the manufacture at a profit of various items on which appeared drawings in the Weiss style, including those of Ms Wilson. The venture was ultimately profitable.

Mr McSpedden had a further conversation with Ms Wilson on or about 25 August 1986. According to Ms Wilson, this was a shorter conversation in which Mr McSpedden said words to the following effect:

"Look, I've spoken to Weiss and they've agreed to the proposal we discussed when I last spoke to you. I'll send you out a cheque for $1000 for the 'other uses' rights for the old illustrations and a letter outlining the new terms of payment as discussed."

Mr McSpedden's version of the conversation was as follows:

"Mr McSpedden: Faye, I'm just following up our last conversation when I mentioned we would be using some of your drawings on various items.

Ms Wilson: What are they being used for?

Mr McSpedden: We are trying to put them on everything from towels to T shirts. What we're thinking is that we will pay you $1000 for merchandising rights for everything you have done to date. But we will also need additional drawings and for those we will pay you $500 for the drawing for advertising plus an additional $500 if we use it for merchandising.

▬▬▬▬▬   Wilson v Weiss Art *continued*

Ms Wilson: That sounds fine. Do you want me to invoice you for that or how will it happen?

[428] Mr McSpedden: Well, we'll send a cheque to you for the $1000, and you'll invoice us as usual for new drawings after we've advised you they're being used."

I think it is more probable than not that Mr McSpedden was not as open as he says he was in his conversation with Ms Wilson. In particular, I would not find that he made it clear that the drawings could be used for merchandising on anything from towels to T shirts. It is clear, however, that Ms Wilson was aware that the additional payment she was to get was to permit her drawings to be used on shopping bags, caps and T shirts which were promotional adjuncts to the clothes sold by Weiss. I do not think that the conversation went beyond this. I find that no reference was made to the proposal that the respondent would merchandise for a profit a large range of items incorporating Ms Wilson's drawings.

Shortly after that telephone discussion, Mr McSpedden wrote a letter, on the Agency's letterhead, to Ms Wilson. In that letter Mr McSpedden purported to confirm the two conversations of 11 June and 25 August "regarding costs".

The letter said, relevantly:
(1) We will pay you $1000 for all rights to all material to June 1986.
(2) We will pay $500 for each future illustration used for advertising.
(3) We will pay an additional $500 for all rights for these illustrations.

The letter enclosed a cheque for $1000 "for the rights to work up to June 1986".

... [429]

The respondent launched a large range of products at David Jones in May 1987. All the windows of the store displayed products bearing Ms Wilson's drawings and the fifth and sixth floors were taken up with all manner of merchandise bearing them. The merchandise included towels, sheets, pillowcases, beach towelling robes, large framed prints, deckchairs, greeting cards and paper, yo-yos, underwear, tissue holders, make-up purses and T-shirts. Drawings depicted on these products included drawings of a cello, musical notes, flowers, an emu, a cockatoo, a koala, a kangaroo, a kookaburra, a lyre bird, the Harbour Bridge and the Opera House. At the time no order had been placed for four of these illustrations, nor had any payments been made for rights other than advertising with respect to them.

Ms Wilson was away at the time of this launch but saw the display upon her return. Ms Wilson's recollection of the next conversation with Mr McSpedden is [430] "very vague". It seems that Mr McSpedden rang Ms Wilson after the David Jones launch to gauge her reaction to the display at that store.

There was some discussion of an article in *The Bulletin* written about the Weiss Art concept, in which no credit was given to Ms Wilson. That was the last time that Mr McSpedden and Ms Wilson spoke to each other.

There was, at the outset of the case, some dispute between the parties as to the usage of Ms Wilson's drawings on merchandise sold by the respondent.

There was also dispute as to the occasions upon which payments had been made to her. That dispute was largely resolved during the course of the hearing as a result of evidence given. ...

On 1 July 1987 solicitors instructed by Ms Wilson wrote to the Agency alleging copyright infringement and demanding undertakings, inter alia, to deliver up offending works. For its part, the Agency claimed that copyright in all relevant drawings vested in their client, by implication, the respondent. The correspondence led to the present proceedings.

▨▨▨▨ Wilson v Weiss Art *continued*

The issue between the parties is of relatively narrow compass. The respondent claims that the applicant has assigned or agreed to assign the copyright in the drawings, so far as that copyright extends to the right to reproduce the drawings on merchandise directly or indirectly, to it.

Alternatively, the respondent says that the agreements arranged by Mr McSpedden with Ms Wilson should be construed as a licence from her to use the drawings in the manner in which they have been used by the respondent. The applicant, on the other hand, denies that there has been an assignment or agreement to assign, and claims that the agreement entered into with the Agency should be construed as a personal licence operating in favour of PWPL, not the respondent.

Alternatively, the respondent submits that if otherwise there was no assignment but a licence which was personal to PWPL, that the applicant is estopped from asserting that she did not irrevocably give the rights identified to the respondent.

[431] ... Certain general propositions of copyright law may be shortly stated. They are not seriously in dispute.

It is clear that under the *Copyright Act 1968*, the author of an artistic work will be the first owner of the copyright in it: s 35(2). That ownership carries with it the exclusive right, inter alia, to reproduce the work. Copyright may be assigned: s 196(1), and that assignment may be of the whole of the author's rights, or there may be a partial assignment: s 196(2) and s 16. A legal assignment must be in writing under the hand of the copyright owner: s 196(3). An agreement to assign for consideration, not being a legal assignment, operates in equity as an equitable assignment.

Copyright may also be the subject of a licence given by the owner. Sections 36 and 37 dealing with direct and indirect infringement make it clear that a licence involves permission to do what would otherwise constitute an infringement: *British Actors Film Co Ltd v Glover* [1918] 1 KB 299; *Computermate Products (Aust) Pty Ltd v Ozi-Soft Pty Ltd* (1988) 20 FCR 46. A licence may be exclusive: s 10(1), or non-exclusive: cf s 196(4), and may be in respect of particular parts of the overall rights conferred upon the copyright holder. Exclusive licences, like assignments, are required to be in writing. However, an agreement binding upon the copyright owner to license another to do some act which otherwise would constitute an infringement need not be in writing signed by the copyright owner: cf s 15.

The onus in the present case lies upon the applicant to show that she is the owner of the copyright and that she has not licensed the respondent to use the drawings in the manner described: *Avel Pty Ltd v Multicoin Amusements Pty Ltd* (1990) 171 CLR 88.

Was there a partial assignment of Ms Wilson's copyright?

It is obvious enough that the questions whether there was an assignment, or equitable assignment, and the extent of the rights assigned, depend upon the construction of the agreement reached between the parties as reflected in the letter of 26 August 1986. That agreement was not wholly in writing, so the terms of the agreement must be found against the background of the two conversations of 11 June and 25 August to which reference has already been made. Nor does the parol evidence rule preclude reference to the way the parties subsequently acted for the purpose of ascertaining what their agreement was: *Australian Estates Ltd v Palmer* (New South Wales Court of Appeal, 22 December 1989, per Samuels JA, with whose judgment Kirby P and Meagher JA agreed).

It is clear that, prior to the letter of August 1986, payment for drawings from time to time related solely to the right to reproduce the drawings for advertising products of PWPL in the print media and perhaps in other media as well. I exclude from this payments made for reproduction of particular drawings in the promotional booklet intended to be taken to Japan, where the rights conferred on PWPL were limited to that purpose.

[432] ... Clearly Ms Wilson did not intend, when this initial arrangement was entered into, to assign to PWPL absolutely the right to reproduce the drawings in a material form, being one of the rights referred to in s 31(1)(b) of the *Copyright Act*. It is clear, also, that the relations between the Agency and Ms Wilson proceeded with some informality, particularly with reference to copyright, a topic of which it would seem Mr McSpedden had a somewhat inexact knowledge. Surprising as it might seem, the Agency never attempted to obtain formal assignments of copyright in copy or drawings for the benefit of its clients, nor did it seek to document in any formal way the rights which it, on behalf of clients, obtained in works the subject of copyright.

It was submitted for the respondent that the cases show that the courts "strive" to find that a particular contract operates as an assignment, rather than as a licence. This is said particularly to be the case where artistic works are concerned. I was referred to a number of cases, among which were *London Printing & Publishing Alliance Ltd v Cox* (1891) 3 Ch 291; *EW Savory Ltd v The World of Golf Ltd* [1914] 2 Ch 566; *Murray v King* (1984) 4 FCR 1; *Chaplin v Leslie Frewin (Publishers) Ltd* [1966] Ch 71; *Wintergarden Theatre (London) Ltd v Millennium Productions Ltd* [1948] AC 173; and *Greenfield Products Pty Ltd v Rover-Scott Bonnar Ltd* (1990) 17 IPR 417.

What these cases demonstrate, however, is merely that the question whether there has been an assignment is one of construction of the particular instrument in the light of the particular circumstances. It is true, as *Lacy v Toole* (1867) 15 LT 512, *Chaplin* and the *Rover-Scott Bonnar* cases demonstrate, that formal language will not be required to effect an assignment. It will not be necessary that an assignment use the word "assign" (cf *Chaplin*), nor will it be necessary for there to be specific reference to "copyright": *Murray v King* (supra), where the sale of "all right, title and interest in" a business was held to effect an assignment pursuant to s 196 of copyright owned by the vendors. The writing relied upon, if a legal assignment be asserted, may be in the form of a receipt: (see *The World of Golf* (supra)) or an invoice (*London Printing & Publishing Alliance* (supra)).

Ultimately, the question whether there has been an assignment, if a legal assignment is relied upon or, if not, whether there has been an equitable assignment will depend upon whether the writing or the terms of the agreement reached reflects or reflect an intention on the part of the assignor to effect an assignment of, or to agree to assign, copyright. In reaching a conclusion upon intention the commercial significance of the transaction to the parties will, no doubt, form part of the surrounding circumstances to be considered: *Messager v British Broadcasting Corporation Ltd* [1929] AC 151; *Loew's Inc v Littler* [1958] 2 All ER 200, both cases on facts wildly different, however, from the present.

[433] Although much was made in argument of the distinction between assignment and licence, I am of the view that in the present case nothing really turns upon that distinction. It is difficult to see for present purposes what difference there could be between an equitable assignment of a limited right and the irrevocable grant for consideration of an exclusive licence to use copyright limited in a particular way. The grant of an irrevocable and exclusive licence for consideration must create in equity in favour of the licensee an interest in the copyright, no different from that created in favour of an assignee by an equitable assignment, except for the right, in an appropriate case, to call for a legal assignment. An assignee under an assignment of limited rights has by force of that assignment the exclusive right to use the rights assigned the same way as a licensee has.

The important question in the present case is, if the matter is approached as an equitable

███████ Wilson v Weiss Art *continued*

assignment the extent or definition of the rights assigned or, if the matter is approached as a licence, the terms of that licence. It should be noted that no evidence was led of any assignment of rights from PWPL to the respondent.

In the present case it is clear that both parties believed that the effect of the initial transaction was to confer upon PWPL, as the Agency's client, a limited but clearly exclusive and irrevocable right to use the drawings in connection with the Weiss logo for the purposes of advertising Weiss fashion goods in the media.

The real dispute between the parties is as to the legal effect of the agreement relating to the "other rights". Although the letter from the Agency referred to "other rights", it is clear from the context of the discussion between Mr McSpedden and Ms Wilson that neither contemplated that Ms Wilson was assigning the residue of her rights in the drawings to the Agency's client ...

I would find that neither party to the agreement intended that the Agency's principal should have the exclusive right to use the drawings upon any merchandise unconnected with "Weiss" brand fashion goods, or indeed upon any merchandise of any merchandiser. As an example discussed in the evidence illustrated, it could hardly have been contemplated that Ms Wilson was authorising the use of the drawings by some assignee of the right upon products for use in a brothel. She was clearly content, however, to authorise use of her drawings by PWPL upon items to be separately merchandised by that company, in the context that these items could be seen to be related to advertising "Weiss" brand fashion goods. Although Ms Wilson wrote on her copy of an invoice (repeating what had been written upon the purchase order from the Agency delivered to her) the words "for merchandising rights", she did so in the context to which I have referred.

... [435]

Thus, if the arrangement be characterised as an equitable assignment it can be seen that Ms Wilson agreed to assign to PWPL a limited right, namely the right to reproduce the drawings in which copyright subsisted on articles to be merchandised by PWPL in connection with the Weiss logo, and as part of advertising the fashion goods which PWPL merchandised.

It might be added that no evidence was adduced of any assignment of relevant copyright from PWPL to the respondent. There was evidence of an agreement between the Agency and the respondent on the Agency ceasing to be a shareholder that the Agency would assign any copyright rights to the respondent, but that would be of no assistance to the respondent's case here. If the arrangement should properly be characterised as an exclusive licence, that licence is limited in the same way, namely, to use of the drawings on articles which would be merchandised by PWPL in connection with the Weiss logo and as part of advertising the fashion goods which PWPL merchandised.

The involvement of PWPL had, I would find, significance to Ms Wilson, over and above the association with "Weiss" brand fashion goods. Those goods were positioned, it can be inferred, at the higher end of the market and were clearly tasteful. It would be unlikely that an artist would consent to an arrangement where her designs could be used in conjunction with products which might detract from the artist's own reputation were the artist's involvement to become known.

Although, as I have said, I do not think the result in the present case differs depending upon the characterisation of the right conferred as an equitable assignment or irrevocable licence, I am inclined to the view that a licence was intended, particularly having regard to the close connection which the right conferred had to PWPL and the products which that company marketed.

██████ Wilson v Weiss Art *continued*

... **[436]**

I would thus conclude that the use by the respondent of the drawings, the copyright in which continued in Ms Wilson, involved an infringement of Ms Wilson's copyright without her licence.

██

[5.20] In the case below the informal relations that gave rise to co-ownership, created confusion over the scope of implied licenses, including the right to assign copyright.

████████████ **Seven Network v TCN Channel Nine** ████████████

[5.25] *Seven Network (Operations) Ltd v TCN Channel Nine Pty Ltd* [2005] FCAFC 144 Federal Court of Australia, Full Court

FINKELSTEIN J:

[72] The point we have to decide on this appeal lies in a narrow compass, but the matter is of some consequence to the parties. The issue is this. Who is the owner of the copyright in a cinematograph film, being footage taken on a trip to the Kokoda Trail? The judge decided (and his finding is not challenged) that the footage was made by the appellants (collectively "Seven") and Mr Murray, and therefore they were joint owners. In *Prior v Lansdowne Press Pty Ltd* [1977] VR 65 at 68, Gowans J held that co-authors hold copyright as tenants in common rather than as joint tenants and, in the absence of agreement to the contrary, in equal shares. Mr Murray contends that at a meeting held on 11 February 2004 Seven agreed to assign to him absolutely its then future interest (the film was taken the following month) in the copyright. Thus he says he was entitled to authorise the fifth and sixth respondents, production companies, to make from the footage a documentary to be shown in a broadcast by the first respondent, TCN Channel Nine Pty Ltd ("Nine"). The judge accepted these contentions. They are challenged on appeal.

[His Honour outlines conversations surrounding the making and usage of the footage.]

...

[87] The general approach taken by the [trial] judge adopts "top-down" reasoning. He inquired whether copyright had been assigned (and found that it had) and then investigated whether there was any exception to an absolute assignment. I would prefer a "bottom-up" approach and determine precisely what has been given over.

[88] In deciding exactly what has been agreed, we are confined to an examination of what the parties said and did. This examination is to be approached from the perspective of the reasonable person, who previously only had work in torts cases. What would the reasonable person think the parties meant?

[89] The discussion between the parties must be understood in the following context. I have already mentioned that the judge found that the footage was jointly owned by Seven and Mr Murray. He reached this conclusion in the following way. Copyright in a cinematograph film lies with the maker of the film: *Copyright Act 1968* (Cth), s 98(1). The maker is "the person by whom the arrangements necessary for the making of the film were undertaken": s 22(4). Mr Murray made the arrangements for the Kokoda expedition. The trip was filmed by Seven personnel. So, according to the judge, each was a maker of the film. This finding is probably incorrect, but was not challenged on appeal. Notwithstanding the finding of joint ownership, it is clear that at the meeting the discussion proceeded upon the assumption that the footage of the trip would, in the absence of some agreement to the contrary, belong to Seven. If anyone had turned their mind to the ownership of copyright (it is possible that

▨▨▨▨▨ Seven Network v TCN Channel Nine *continued*

Mr Townhill had copyright in mind but he made no mention of it), it seems also to have been assumed that copyright would belong to Seven.

[90] Turning then to what the parties said, the first thing the reasonable person would think having observed the discussion is that the parties implicitly agreed (that is the observer would be required to presume the existence of the agreement, for the topic was not discussed) that Seven could use the film for a program to be broadcast to the public through its network. Mr Murray wanted this broadcast to be a one-hour special program but even if it were not, the reasonable observer would implicitly understand that Seven could broadcast whatever section of the film it saw fit. In legal terms, the joint owners of the copyright, Seven and Mr Murray, conferred a licence on Seven to do an act that would otherwise be in breach of their jointly owned copyright.

[91] It is equally clear that Mr Murray was given some "right". What was the nature of that right? The proper approach is to examine what right Mr Murray requested. He asked for nothing more than to be given the footage so that he could use it for promotional purposes. He had made a similar request in the past. He confirmed in May 2004 that this is what he was seeking. Mr McPherson agreed to give Mr Murray what he wanted. Nothing that has been attributed to Mr McPherson can be taken by our reasonable observer as a promise to give Mr Murray any more than he had requested. Another way of looking at it is this. In negotiating a contract the language used by the parties is often imprecise. Then it is the duty of the court to give a common sense meaning to the words used: *Antaios Compania Naviera SA v Salen Rederierna AB* [1985] AC 191. The court's duty is to separate the "purposive sheep from the literalist goats": *Summit Investment Inc v British Steel Corporation (The "Sounion")* [1987] 1 Lloyd's Reps 230 at 235. The sheep must win the day.

[92] It will be necessary to further define the legal character of the "right" obtained by Mr Murray. But first I should say something about the content of the "right" to use the film. It had several aspects. First, the right was conferred on Mr Murray and him alone. Second, it was not a right that was capable of being passed on; it was personal to Mr Murray. Third, the right to use the film was for a limited purpose, namely to use the film for promotional purposes. That is, the film could not be used for commercial purposes. The distinction between the two types of use is important. It is, I think, clear that the parties intended that Mr Murray could use the footage to promote DARE's activities and thereby raise funds. Indeed that was the reason he sought the right in the first place. But the right to use the film for promotional purposes did not carry with it the right to lease, hire or assign the right to use the film to a third party for use by that third party, even if that use would promote the activities of DARE.

[93] Turning now to the legal character of the rights given to Mr Murray. On the view that I take, Seven did not assign copyright to Mr Murray. If copyright were assigned he would have the full power to deal with the footage in any way he chose. No such thing was intended by the parties to the agreement. It is perfectly clear that what was intended was the grant of permission (or to use the statutory term—a licence) to Mr Murray for him to use the footage for a limited purpose. Being for consideration, the licence was granted in perpetuity. In the absence of that licence Mr Murray could not make any use of the film although he is a co-owner: *Ray v Classic FM plc* (1998) 41 IPR 235. The licence granted protected Mr Murray from an action for infringement. Whether the permission is capable of protection by action by Mr Murray (as to which see *British Actors Film Company, Limited v Glover* [1918] 1 KB 299, 309) need not be decided.

[94] The next point is this. Nine's ability to broadcast the film to the public is dependent upon it having permission to do so from the copyright owner or owners: *Copyright Act*, ss 86, 101. It has Mr Murray's permission, but he is not the sole owner of the copyright. So Nine also requires the permission of Seven. It does not have that permission directly from Seven. It

███████ Seven Network v TCN Channel Nine *continued*

could only obtain that permission if the licence given to Mr Murray contained an implied term that it could be assigned. Here we look to the presumed intention of the parties and ask whether the putative implied term is necessary for the reasonable or effective operation of the licence: *Hospital Products Limited v United States Surgical Corporation* (1984) 156 CLR 41. The judge made a finding that is inconsistent with the implication of the supposed term. The finding is that "if the possibility of any part of the [film] being broadcast on Nine had been raised, it is likely that McPherson would not have agreed to that possibility".

LINDGREN J:

[35] ...For whatever agreement Seven made at the meeting, Mr Murray furnished consideration: he agreed to permit Seven's Mr Shannon and Mr Lynch to go on the trip and to record the moving images and accompanying sounds, to bear the cost of their fares, accommodation and other expenses, and to allow Seven first use of the raw footage for the purpose of the making of a story and the broadcasting of it on Today Tonight.

[36] Was the consideration furnished by Mr Murray furnished for a promise by Seven to him to assign to him Seven's interest in the copyright in the cinematograph film to be made, or was it furnished for the grant of a licence by Seven? The answer to this question is not obvious. As McCardie J observed in *Messager v British Broadcasting Co* [1927] 2 KB 543 at 550, whether an assignment or licence is created often gives rise to difficulty, and (at 551):

> "Intention must be the ultimate test for deciding whether an agreement be an assignment or a licence, and intention is to be gathered from the document itself and the surrounding circumstances."

[37] The primary Judge was persuaded to find a promise to assign. In support he referred to the facts that Seven and Mr Murray were to be co-owners of the copyright; that Seven had no continuing use for the Camera Tapes after the broadcasting of the story on Today Tonight; and that through Mr Simond, Seven handed over to Mr Murray the Camera Tapes, which were the only embodiment of the subject matter of the copyright.

[38] To my mind, the handing over of the Camera Tapes carries little weight: since they were the only embodiment of the Camera Tapes film and Seven had no further use for them, it was inevitable that they would be delivered to Mr Murray in order that he be able to do any act at all comprised in the copyright, no matter how minor. For example, if Seven had consented to Mr Murray's copying a substantial part of the Camera Tapes film for the purpose of screening it for his family, the Camera Tapes would have had to be handed over (cf the delivery of the electro blocks of illustrative drawings in *Cooper v Stephens* [1895] 1 Ch 567 and *W Marshall & Co Ltd v AH Bull Ltd* (1901) 85 LT 77). In any event, Mr Murray agreed in cross-examination that the basis on which he was handed the Camera Tapes at Soldiers Beach was the basis, whatever it was, that had been agreed at the meeting on 11 February 2004. The property in them passed from Seven to Mr Murray upon delivery; but in implementation of the contract of 11 February 2004.

...

[After considering the evidence in detail his Honour concluded]:

[69] Seven agreed, for valuable consideration, that Mr Murray was to have a non-assignable licence to do the acts comprised in the copyright for the promotion of Camp Dare.

[70] The proposed communication by Nine to the public of the documentary "DAREing the Kokoda", lies outside that licence, and would, for lack of a licence binding on Seven, infringe the copyright in the Camera Tapes film.

[71] The appeal should be allowed with costs, and there should be an injunction.

■ Effect of assignment

[5.30] Once an assignment of copyright is made, the assignee may exercise and enforce all relevant rights to the exclusion of the assignor. Areas of difficulty with regard to the assignment of copyright may arise in three ways; where the assignor seeks to continue to exercise moral rights, where a later work by the same creator may infringe that assigned (see s 72) and in respect of the trade practices implications of certain organisations wielding power due to the aggregation of assigned rights. All exercises of intellectual property rights, including copyright, are subject to the operation of *Trade Practices Act 1974* (Cth), Part IV. There are limited exemptions provided under s 51(3) of that Act in respect of certain dealings with statutory rights, but they do not extend to monopolisation or resale price maintenance, and tend to be related to the first material embodiment of the work, rather than the dealings associated with the exercise of copyright.

General principles applicable in cases of restraint of trade or undue influence will apply to assignments (and licensing arrangements) which are unduly restrictive and contrary to public policy as an unreasonable restraint of trade. See *Schroeder Music Publishing Co Ltd v Macauley* [1974] 1 WLR 1308; *Clifford Davis Management Ltd v WEA Records Ltd* [1975] 1 WLR 61; *Davidson v CBS Records* (1983) AIPC 90-106; *Elton John v Richard Leon James* [1991] FSR 397.

Recording company contract—pitfalls for young players

▬▬▬▬ Zang Tumb Tuum Records v Holly Johnson ▬▬▬▬

[5.35] *Zang Tumb Tuum Records Ltd v Holly Johnson* [1993] EMLR 61 Civil Division, Court of Appeal (United Kingdom)

DILLON LJ: **[64]** The plaintiffs in this action Zang Tumb Tuum Records Ltd (the recording company) and Perfect Songs Ltd (the publishing company) appeal against the Order made by Whitford J on 10th February 1988 after the trial of the action and counterclaim.

The issues argued before us on the appeal, not all of which have to be decided, raise questions—

(1) as to the true construction of certain clauses in

    (a) a recording agreement made on the 1 September 1983 between the recording company and five young men—the Defendant Mr Holly Johnson and Messrs Peter Gill, Mark O'Toole, Brian Nash and Paul Rutherford—who were the members of a pop group called Frankie Goes to Hollywood (the group) and

    (b) a publishing agreement dated the 11 May 1984 and made between the publishing company and the members of the Group other than Mr Rutherford.

(2) as to whether the recording agreement and the publishing agreement were or either of them was, unenforceable against the defendant as being in unreasonable restraint of trade

(3) as to whether the defendant had, before he purported to exercise such right, waived any right he might otherwise have had to object to the recording agreement or the publishing agreement on the grounds **[65]** of unreasonable restraint of trade and

(4) as to the basis for and scope of an enquiry as to damages which the judge awarded the defendant on his counterclaim.

Certain preliminary matters must be appreciated before I come to the terms of the recording agreement and the publishing agreement.

In the first place, though the publishing agreement is dated 11 May 1984, the agreement signed then merely replaced a publishing agreement in the same terms which had been made between the same parties on 1 September 1983, but had been lost. The publishing agreement

████████ Zang Tumb Tuum Records v Holly Johnson *continued*

can therefore be treated as if made on 1 September 1983. The publishing agreement is of course a separate agreement from the recording agreement, but before either agreement was entered into it was made plain to the Group that the recording company would not enter into the recording agreement with the Group, unless the members of the Group other than Mr Rutherford entered into the publishing agreement with the publishing company.

In the second place, the recording company and the publishing company are sister companies whose only directors and shareholders at all material times were Mr Trevor Horn and Miss Jill Sinclair, who were married to each other in 1980, though Miss Sinclair continues to use her maiden name for business purposes. By 1983 Mr Horn had considerable experience, and a very high reputation, as a producer of records of pop music but the recording company was newly formed and its recording of the Group under the recording agreement was Mr Horn's first independent venture in record production. Miss Sinclair had considerable administrative experience in relation to the production of records: her father and brother ran a recording studio and she had joined that on the administrative side in 1977.

In the third place, the members of the Group were in 1983 young men in fairly humble circumstances and of little business experience. Some of them were apprentices and others on supplementary benefit. They had however a manager, a Mr Bob Johnson, who was no relation to the defendant. They were little known to the general public, but had performed occasionally on television and radio, and it was as a result of seeing and hearing them that Mr Horn asked Miss Sinclair to get in touch with Mr Bob Johnson and she consequently did so. The defendant was lead singer of the Group, and there seems no doubt that he was the member of the Group with the greatest talent and potential.

To make a success in the world of pop music the Group needed to make records which would sell well. They therefore needed a recording company since, as the judge has explained in his judgment, the making of a [66] record is a highly complex matter, involving very sophisticated and expensive equipment. In view of Mr Horn's reputation, they very much wanted that he should produce their records, although it seems that there was at least one other small recording company which would have been prepared to do so. In the upshot, the approach by Miss Sinclair to Mr Bob Johnson led to negotiations and these led to the recording agreement and the publishing agreement. In the negotiations the Group were represented by Mr Bob Johnson, and they had the assistance, so far as it could go, of an experienced solicitor, Mr Gentle of Gentle Matthias & Co.

There is no suggestion in this case that Mr Horn and Miss Sinclair or anyone else exercised undue influence over the Group or acted fraudulently or in bad faith. What is said is that the terms of the recording agreement and publishing agreement put forward by the recording company and the publishing company, even after such concessions as were made during the negotiations, were so one-sided and unfair that consistently with the principles applied by the House of Lords in *Schroeder Music Publishing Co Ltd v Macaulay* [1974] 3 All ER 616, [1974] 1 WLR 1308 they cannot stand and cannot be enforced against the defendant.

In that case Lord Diplock at 1315H put the question to be answered as "Was the bargain fair?" He went on:

> "[T]he test of fairness is, no doubt, whether the restrictions are both reasonably necessary for the protection of the legitimate interests of the promisee and commensurate with the benefits secured to the promisor under the contract. For the purpose of this test all the provisions of the contract must be taken into consideration."

■■■■■ Zang Tumb Tuum Records v Holly Johnson *continued*

Lord Diplock also agreed with Lord Reid's analysis and conclusions. Lord Reid had said at 1310 A-B:

> "[I]n a case like the present two questions must be considered. Are the terms of the agreement so restrictive that either they cannot be justified at all, or they must be justified by the party seeking to enforce the agreement? Then if there is room for justification, has that party proved justification—normally by showing that the restrictions were no more than what was reasonably required to protect his legitimate interests."

Lord Reid's analysis of the agreement in *Macaulay's* case includes the following at 1313C-1314B:

> "The public interest requires in the interests both of the public and of the individual that everyone should be free so far as practicable to earn a livelihood and to give to the public the fruits of his particular abilities. The main question to be considered is whether and how far the operation of the terms of this agreement is likely to conflict with this objective. The respondent is bound to assign to the appellants during a long period the fruits of his musical talent. But what are the appellants [67] bound to do with those fruits? Under the contract nothing. If they do use the songs which the respondent composes they must pay in terms of the contract. But they need not do so. As has been said they may put them in a drawer and leave them there."

No doubt the expectation was that if the songs were of value they would be published to the advantage of both parties. But if for any reason the appellants chose not to publish them the respondent would get no remuneration and he could not do anything. Inevitably the respondent must take the risk of misjudgment of the merits of his work by the appellants. But that is not the only reason which might cause the appellants not to publish. There is no evidence about this so we must do the best we can with common knowledge. It does not seem fanciful and it was not argued that it is fanciful to suppose that purely commercial consideration might cause a publisher to refrain from publishing and promoting promising material. He might think it likely to be more profitable to promote work by other composers with whom he had agreements and unwise or too expensive to try to publish and popularise the respondent's work in addition. And there is always the possibility that less legitimate reasons might influence a decision not to publish the respondent's work.

It was argued that there must be read into this agreement an obligation on the publisher to act in good faith. I take that to mean that he would be in breach of contract if by reason of some oblique or malicious motive he refrained from publishing work which he would otherwise have published. I very much doubt this but even if it were so it would make little difference. Such a case would seldom occur and then would be difficult to prove.

I agree with the appellant's argument to this extent. I do not think that a publisher could reasonably be expected to enter into any positive commitment to publish future work by an unknown composer. Possibly there might be some general undertaking to use his best endeavours to promote the composer's work. But that would probably have to be in such general terms as to be of little use to the composer.

But if no satisfactory positive undertaking by the publisher can be devised, it appears to me to be an unreasonable restraint to tie the composer for this period of years so that his work will be sterilised and he can earn nothing from his abilities as a composer if the publisher chooses not to publish. If there had been in Clause 9 any provision for entitling the composer to terminate the agreement in such an event the case might have had a very different appearance. But as the agreement stands not only is the composer tied but he cannot recover the copyright of work which the publisher refuses to publish."

In the present case, the recording agreement defines the term "the Artist" as meaning the five members of the Group. But Clause 14.1 provides that although the recording agreement covered the engagement of the Artist [68] primarily as a group performing under the name "Frankie Goes to Hollywood" it shall nevertheless extend to and does include individually each and every person who was at the date of the recording agreement or might during the term thereof become a member of the Group. All provisions were to apply and be binding upon each member of the Group jointly and severally.

Further relevant provisions of the recording agreement are as follows:

By Clause 1 the Artist undertook as and when required by the recording company during the Term (as later defined) to perform record and deliver to the recording company fully edited and mixed Masters sufficient to constitute the Minimum Recording Commitment as specified in Clause 4. The Artist agreed to record such compositions at such time and studio as the recording company should designate after consultation with the Artist until in the recording company's opinion a commercially and technically acceptable Master should have been obtained. The Recording Budget, the producer and the composition to be recorded by the Artist were to be decided in consultation between the recording company and the Artist but in the event of any dispute the opinion of the recording company was to prevail.

By clause 2 the Artist granted and assigned to the recording company the sale and exclusive rights throughout the world in respect of the Masters to manufacture records therefrom and to sell/release and otherwise deal with the same or to refrain therefrom as the recording company should in its absolute discretion think fit. In addition the copyright in the Masters and all records therefrom throughout the world was vested solely in the recording company.

...

Under Clauses 8, 9 and 10 the Artist was to receive certain royalties and advances and there were to be half yearly accountings for royalties. The precise details do not matter, but it should be noted that the advances ranged from £250 on the signing of the recording agreement and £250 upon delivery by the Artist of the Masters constituting the first single to be recorded by the Artist under the recording agreement, to substantial sums, amounting from £5,000 to £30,000 on delivery of successive albums. It should also be noted that under Clause 9.1 the recording company was entitled to deduct and retain from all royalties (if any) payable to the Artist under the recording agreement all unrecouped advances and recording costs.

...

Against that very stringent background, the crucial provisions of the recording agreement are, in my judgment, Clause 3 which (as amplified by Clauses 13.3 and 17.12) provides for the length of the Term of the Agreement, Clause 4 which provides for the Minimum Recording Commitment, and the provisions in Clause 14 which attempt to deal with the situation where, as happened, a member of the Group left the Group.

...

The Group made an initial single "Relax" with the recording company which was highly successful. There was then a second single "Two Tribes" which was almost as successful. There was then a first album—in fact a double album—"Welcome to the Pleasure Dome", which was also highly successful. The recording company exercised its options under Clause 3. By then, July 1985, the defendant was unhappy at the high costs of the making of these records, which the recording company was recouping from the royalties due to the Group. The recording cost of the first single had been roughly £26,000 and the recording cost of the first album no less than £394,000. The point had been taken that the recording agreement and the publishing agreement were void and unenforceable on grounds of unreasonable restraint of trade and there had been some correspondence between solicitors. Against this background a second album was recorded, starting in mid-November 1985. At the same time the defendant's relations with the other members of the Group broke down. The Group's part in the making of the second album was completed by the end of April 1986, but Mr Horn continued reworking it from April to September 1986. It was finally released in November 1986. It had been the common hope that the recording costs of the second album would be approximately half the costs of the first, since the second was not a double album. In the event, however, the costs of the second album came out at approximately £760,000. In July 1986 there was a meeting and in September there was further correspondence between solicitors. Though a couple of singles (taken from tracks in the second album) were completed in February 1987, the Group had done no recording work since April 1986, and by March 1987 the Defendant had virtually ceased to be a member of the Group. Nothing further happened on either side until in July 1987 the defendant's solicitors wrote asserting that the recording agreement and the publishing agreement were unenforceable, in so far as unperformed, because in unreasonable restraint of trade. The appellants countered by issuing the Writ on 5th August 1987, claiming that both agreements are valid and enforceable and claiming also that the defendant, as the leaving member of the Group, was bound to enter into a fresh recording agreement with the recording company under Clause 14.2 of the recording agreement and on the terms, so far as unperformed, of the present recording agreement.

So far as the recording agreement is concerned, the judge held that it was indeed unenforceable as an unreasonable restraint of trade, and he also held that Clause 14.2 was void for uncertainty.

...

On the general validity of the recording agreement, I find its provisions as to the duration of the term grossly one-sided. The members of the Group are to be bound, collectively and individually, in the discretion of the recording company, for up to seven option periods after the seven month initial period, if the recording company chooses to exercise its options under Clause 3. Each option period is to be for at least one year and possibly for up to 120 days or a third of a year more. It is an agreement which could well last eight or nine years and during all that time, when their earning potential would be likely to be at its highest, the members of the Group would be bound to record only for the recording company. But the recording company itself is free to terminate its obligations at any time by not exercising the next option.

However much weight is put on the words "proper and reasonable judgment" of the recording company in Clause 18 and however much it is implicit in Clause 1 that the recording company will act not merely honestly but reasonably in approving compositions for the Group to record, in choosing the producer of the records and in deciding what is a commercially and technically acceptable Master, and in spending no more than is reasonable

▆▆▆▆▆▆ Zang Tumb Tuum Records v Holly Johnson *continued*

on recording costs, the last word is necessarily given to the recording company on all these important matters. The band of reasonableness on all such matters is likely to be wide. Moreover under Clause 2 the recording company is given a purportedly absolute discretion to refrain from releasing records, and even if they are not released the copyright in the records will remain in the recording company.

Though the members of the Group are exclusively bound to the recording company the recording company is not exclusively bound to them. It was obviously envisaged that the recording company would make and release records of other Artists. This could well affect the scope and timing of the promotion by the recording company of the Group's records, a factor recognised by Lord Reid in *Schroeder v Macaulay* [1974] 3 All ER 616, [1974] 1 WLR 1308, as cited above.

Pop musicians are promoted by the sales of their records, and obviously a recording company has difficulty in promoting a little known group when there are so many others seeking fame and fortune. Stringent provisions such as many of those in the recording agreement may be justifiable in an agreement of short duration. But the onus must, in my judgment, be on the recording company to justify the length of the Term and the one-sidedness of the provisions as to its duration in this recording agreement.

Two factors are mentioned by Mr Carr as justifications. First it is said that for every one record issued by a recording company which is a hit and a financial success there are nine issued which are failures. Consequently, it is submitted, it is reasonable and in the interests of the music industry and of all engaged in that industry, that the Artists whose records are successful should be tied to the recording company so that the recording company's share of the profits of these Artists' successful records should compensate the recording company for the costs of other Artists' unsuccessful records. Secondly it is said that a second record of an Artist's music will have better chances of success if a first record of another composition of that Artist was successful. So, it is submitted, the recording company will not truly get the full fruits of a successful first record unless the recording company has the right to make the second record and so on. These arguments can feed on themselves, and lead logically to a submission that every recording agreement should last, at the recording company's option, for the whole lifetime of the Artist. But the criterion of validity is the objective test of reasonableness, judged as at the date when the agreement was made. By that criterion such validity as there is in the two factors relied upon by Mr Carr does not justify, in my judgment, anything like so long and one-sided a Term as that provided for by this recording agreement.

I agree therefore with the conclusion of the judge that the recording agreement is void as an unreasonable restraint of trade. I stress again the points made by Lord Reid in *Schroeder v Macaulay* [1974] 3 All ER 616, [1974] 1 WLR 1308.

LICENSING

[5.40] Whereas an assignment is basically a transfer of ownership, a licence is simply permission to do what would otherwise amount to an infringement. If more than a bare permission, a licence may confer property rights which could interfere with revocation of the licence or the exercise of rights thereunder. The licensee may not be allowed to make alterations to the work or to assign or sub-license her or his interest. A licence granted in respect of a copyright by the owner thereof binds successors in title of the grantor to the same extent (s 196(4)). This is also the case in relation to licensing of future copyright (s 197(3)). Licences may be granted for the exercise of any of the rights comprised in the copyright, and may be compulsory (statutory) (ss 54-64); exclusive (ss 117-125); or implied, and can be verbal or written. See *Clune v Collins A&R* (1993) 25 IPR 246 for a discussion of the meaning of "licence" in copyright law.

■ Free software, open source and creative commons licences

[5.45] There are various forms of licenses that promote freedom from strong copyright restrictions and facilitate access to copyright works. These licences were originally developed in relation to the computing industry, however, more recently creative commons licensing has been developed for authors, artists and educators. There is a global movement to "unlock IP" and the new forms of licensing are pursuing a means of countering copyright maximalisation evident in recent treaty making and national law reform. See Lawrence Lessig, *Free Culture* (Penguin 2004), Kathy Bowrey, "Chapter 4", *Law and Internet Cultures* (Cambridge UP, 2005).

■ Exclusive licences

[5.50] See ss 117-125.

A licensor may retain the right to grant licences to others unless exclusivity has been promised to the licensee. Exclusive licence is defined under the *Copyright Act 1968* (Cth) as follows:

> "s 10(1) 'exclusive licence' means a licence in writing, signed by or on behalf of the owner or prospective owner of copyright, authorizing the licensee, to the exclusion of all other persons, to do an act that, by virtue of this Act, the owner of the copyright would, but for the licence, have the exclusive right to do, and 'exclusive licensee' has a corresponding meaning."

An exclusive licensee has the right to sue for infringement (s 119(a)), and to seek damages for conversion and detinue (s 116) subject to the discretion of the court as to the adequacy of the remedy under s 115.

■ Implied licences

[5.55] Implied licences frequently arise from the circumstances in which copyright material is to be used.

Architectural plans

Gruzman v Percy Marks

[5.60] *Gruzman Pty Ltd v Percy Marks Pty Ltd and Anor* (1989) 16 IPR 87 Supreme Court of New South Wales

[The plaintiff applied for an interlocutory injunction to restrain infringement of copyright. Note the "moral rights" argument.]

MCLELLAND J: **[88]** The plaintiff is a company which provides the architectural services of its director, Mr Neville Gruzman. The first defendant is a retailer of high quality jewellery.

In May 1989 the first defendant retained the plaintiff to provide Mr Gruzman's services in relation to the fitting out of new shop premises for the first defendant, at 70 Elizabeth Street,

████████ Gruzman v Percy Marks *continued*

Sydney. Thereafter Mr Gruzman prepared plans, and performed various other functions in connection with the proposal, including (i) the engagement on behalf of the first defendant, of the second defendant, a builder, to carry out the construction work, and (ii) the supervision of that work.

The work commenced on 13 July 1989, and is still in progress. However, differences arose between Mr Gruzman and the first defendant, and on 6 October 1989 the first defendant purported to terminate the plaintiff's retainer, alleging among other things, very substantial cost overruns, and claims for excessive fees. Negotiations followed which terminated on 3 November 1989 without resolution of the dispute. In the meantime, the defendants have been proceeding with the work, with various modifications designed to reduce cost.

The present proceedings were commenced on 6 November 1989, by summons in which the plaintiff claims a declaration that it is the owner of the copyright in the plans prepared by Mr Gruzman, an order restraining the defendants from using those plans in relation to the fitting out of the shop, an order for delivery up of the plans to the plaintiff, and damages. The substantial matter now before the court is whether the plaintiff should have an interlocutory injunction to prevent the defendants from using the plans for the purpose of completing the fitting out of the shop.

For the purpose of the present application, it is common ground that the plaintiff is the owner of the copyright in the plans. The plaintiff's case is based on the contention that use of the plans for the purpose of completing the fitting out work, would infringe the plaintiff's copyright therein.

[89] When an architect contracts with a building owner to produce plans for the purpose of their being used to carry out construction work at a particular site, there arises, subject to any contractual provision to the contrary, an implied licence from the architect for the use of the plans for that purpose: see *Beck v Montana Constructions Pty Ltd* (1963) 80 WN (NSW) 1578; *Blair v Osborne & Tomkins* [1971] 2 QB 78, and *Ng v Clyde Securities Ltd* [1976] 1 NSWLR 443. It was held in *Clyde Securities* that once granted and acted upon by the commencement of the work, the licence was irrevocable, notwithstanding any subsequent failure by the owner to pay the architect's fees.

The question whether the licence could be effectively revoked in the event of the repudiation by the building owner of a contractual right in the architect to continue employment on the project did not there arise, and was expressly left open. Although I doubt whether even such a repudiation would enable the licence to be revoked, time constraints have precluded proper argument on, or full consideration of, that question, and it is better left until the facts relating to the termination of the retainer have been established: see *Kolback Securities Ltd v Epoch Mining* (1987) 8 NSWLR 533 at 535. For present purposes I will treat the proposition as arguable.

It has been submitted for the plaintiff that even if there is an irrevocable implied licence of the kind already referred to, any departure from, or modification of, the plans in order to reduce costs would fall outside the licensed use, on the basis that the implied licence is for use of the plans in respect of construction work in accordance with the plans, and not otherwise. This submission proceeded by reference to the broad expression "use" of the plans, which occurs also in the claims for relief. However, architects' plans are, for the purposes of the *Copyright Act 1968* (Cth), to be classified as an "artistic work" (see definitions of "artistic work" and "drawing" in s 10), and what would relevantly constitute an infringement of the plaintiff's copyright, would be the "reproduction" of that work "in a material form" "without the licence of" the plaintiff: see ss 31(1)(b), and 36.

For the purposes of the Act, "an artistic work shall be deemed to have been reproduced ...

in the case of work in a two-dimensional form if a version of the work is produced in a three-dimensional form" (s 21(3)). ...

In the light of these provisions the plaintiff's submission based on a departure from, or modification of, the plans, has a paradoxical element in that the more the work departs from the plans, the less likely it is that it will reproduce those plans. However this may be, I do not consider that any arguable basis has been shown for restricting the implied licence in the manner contended for. Subject to any contractual provision to the contrary, such an implied licence would in my view extend to the use of the plans for the purposes of the construction work, to such extent as the owner may decide, and involves no implied restraint on the carrying out of work which **[90]** departs from those plans: see *Barnett v Cape Town Foreshore Board* (1960) 4 SA 430; [1978] FSR 176, and *Hunter v Fitzroy Robinson & Partners* [1978] FSR 167. It should be noted that the decision of the British Columbia Court of Appeal in *Netupsky v Dominion Bridge Co* referred to in Hunter was reversed by the Supreme Court of Canada: see (1972) 24 DLR (3d) 484. ...

In the circumstances of the present case, the course best calculated to achieve justice between the parties, is to refuse any interlocutory injunction. The plaintiff's claim of infringement of its copyright in the plans, although arguable, may very well fail. Even if that claim were ultimately to succeed, it may well be held that damages are an adequate remedy and final injunctive relief inappropriate: see for example *Hunter v Fitzroy Robinson & Concrete Systems Pty Ltd v Devon Symonds Holdings Ltd* (1978) 20 SASR 79.

There would be grave difficulties in framing the terms of any interlocutory injunction with sufficient precision to enable the defendants to know what they can, and what they cannot, do, and yet so as to confine any restraint to what, on the most favourable view of the plaintiff's case, would be justifiable. Moreover, in granting an interlocutory injunction there would be a serious risk that the court would be allowing itself to be used as an instrument of unjustified economic pressure on the defendants.

Finally, the adverse consequences to the first defendant of an injunction which ultimately turns out to be unjustified, would be far greater than the adverse consequences to the plaintiff, of refusing an injunction which ultimately turns out to have been justified. The loss to the first defendant of business and goodwill if completion of the fitting out work is further delayed, or interrupted, as would almost inevitably be the consequences of any injunction, is likely to be both very substantial and very difficult of assessment in monetary terms. The plaintiff asserts potential damage to Mr Gruzman's reputation if the fitting out is completed otherwise than in accordance with his plans, having regard to his known association with the project. This is a somewhat speculative claim in so far as it is based on what **[91]** is said to be the possibility of aesthetic deficiencies in the new shop, arising from departures from, or modifications of, Mr Gruzman's plans. Its legal basis appears slight, having regard to what I have held to be the right, subject to any contrary provision of an owner to depart from his architect's plans to such extent as he may wish. Even if there were a solid basis for such a claim it would not in my view swing the balance of potential injustice sufficiently to justify interlocutory relief.

Application for interlocutory relief dismissed.

Repair

[5.65] It is possible to reproduce a copyright work in another dimension (s 21(3)), therefore, many three-dimensional objects are reproductions of artistic works (drawings). If an object such as a pump, car exhaust system or solar hot water heater is closely examined by a competitor and "reverse engineered", then this, prima facie, is infringement of copyright in the underlying artistic works, being the plans and blueprints (drawings) for the machine or spare parts. A number of cases have held that the sale of machinery carries an implied licence to repair the machinery, in order to allow it to work and thus give business efficacy to the contract of sale. The point at which "repair" becomes replacement of a substantial part of the item (and therefore infringement of the underlying work) is a question of fact, depending upon the nature of the article.

This inroad into copyright protection under the implied licence to repair reached its peak in the House of Lord's decision in *British Motor Corp v Armstrong Patents Co Ltd* [1986] RPC 279 where the makers of British Leyland cars were unable to prevent the wholesale manufacturing of exhaust systems for those cars by the defendant. The basis of the majority decision was the implied right of car owners to repair their cars in the most economical way possible, unrestricted by monopoly. This was not necessarily based on an implied licence to repair, but also on non-derogation from grant: at 376 per Lord Templeman. The majority made little effort to hide their opinion that "the exploitation of copyright law has gone far enough" (at 377 per Lord Templeman J) and that the use of it to protect monopolies in the sale of functional items of commerce was inappropriate. The decision has led one commentator to state that the House of Lords has "opened up an avenue of startling legal innovation in the BL spare parts case which the dissenting Law Lord described as 'this untrodden path'. He was referring to the consumer's hitherto unknown right to repair his durables economically".

The 1989 amendments to the *Copyright Act 1968* (Cth) removed copyright protection for artistic works mass produced in a three-dimensional form. Before that time, copyright was lost only for artistic works which could be registered as designs. Because of these amendments, which seem to demonstrate legislative sympathy with the result of the *British Leyland* case, there is probably very little scope for the implied licence to repair operating as an exception to copyright infringement, since repair (indeed, wholesale reproduction) of mass-produced articles is no longer an infringement of copyright.

The owners of rights in machinery, spare parts and the like must now rely on patent or design protection if available. The implied licence to repair is, however, still relevant in respect of patented articles.

Parallel importing
[5.68] See *Copyright Act 1968* (Cth), ss 37, 44A-44F and ss 102, 112A, 112C, 112D, 112DA.

[5.70] It might be expected that purchasing quantities of books, cassette tapes, compact disks or computer software from a legitimate supplier would enable the purchaser to import and sell such items in Australia, since, unless the items are "pirated" the copyright owner gets the royalties on the sales and, since copyright is an "incorporeal" right it does not necessarily entail the right to control the physical movement of goods. See *Pacific Film Laboratories Pty Ltd v Commissioner of Taxation* (at [2.40]). The *Copyright Act 1968* (Cth) has, however, been construed in such a way as to allow authorised distributors to uphold territorial restrictions and maintain Australia as a closed market for the products mentioned. The importing of legitimate copies of copyright works and other subject matter by someone other than an authorised importer is known as "parallel importing".

In *Interstate Parcel Express Co Pty Ltd v Time-Life International (Nederlands) BV* (1977) 138 CLR 534 (the *Time-Life* case) the High Court held that *Copyright Act 1968* (Cth), s 37 requires that an importer must have a positive licence to import works for sale in Australia. When Angus and Robertson purchased supplies of a cookbook from a wholesaler in the US, with no restrictive terms as to the use to which the buyer might put the books including their resale anywhere in the world, this did not involve the grant of a licence by the copyright owner to Angus and Robertson to deal with the books in a manner inconsistent with the rights of an appointed distributor. *Time-Life* has been discussed and applied in subsequent cases, one point in issue being whether the purchase of quantities of books or other such product direct from the copyright owner (rather than a wholesaler, as in *Time-Life*) leads to the implication of a positive licence to resell.

Ozi-Soft v Wong

[5.75] *Ozi-Soft Pty Ltd v Wong* (1988) 10 IPR 520 Federal Court of Australia

[The first applicant was the exclusive licensee in Australia of the copyright in computer programs, mainly games and some educational software. The other 14 applicants were the owners of copyright in the programs. The respondents purchased commercial quantities of the programs embodied in disks in the UK, and imported them to sell in Australia.]

EINFELD J: **[520]** On 13 March 1987 Wilcox J ordered that the following question be tried separately upon the basis of a statement of agreed facts filed in court on 13 March 1987: "Whether the importation and sale by the respondents of the diskettes referred to in the statement of agreed facts was done with the licence of the respective applicants?"

[521] ... It is clear from the agreed facts that the importation and sale by the respondents of the diskettes was not done with the express consent of the applicants. If consent cannot be implied, s 37 of the *Copyright Act 1968* (the Act) forbids such importation and sale. Section 37 states:

> "The copyright in a literary, dramatic, musical or artistic work is infringed by a person who, without the licence of the owner of the copyright, imports an article into Australia for the purpose of
> (a) selling, letting for hire, or by way of trade offering or exposing for sale or hire, the article;
> (b) distributing the article
>   (i) for the purpose of trade; or
>   (ii) for any other purpose to an extent that will affect prejudicially the owner of the copyright; or
> (c) by way of trade exhibiting the article in public,
> where, to his knowledge, the making of the article would, if the article had been made in Australia by the importer, have constituted an infringement of the copyright."

The applicants submit that s 37 casts the onus upon the respondent to show that there was licence and not on them to prove that they have, or could have, imposed a restriction.

Legislation, case law and various international conventions have developed in this area favouring exclusivity of ownership for the copyright owner. Under s 13 of the Act, for example, the copyright owner has both the exclusive right to do or to authorise another person to do acts protected by the copyright.

There is no argument that the diskettes are encompassed in copyright legislation. A computer program is defined in s 10 of the Act as: "an expression in any language, code or notation of a set of instructions intended ... to cause a device having digital information

■■■■■ Ozi-Soft v Wong *continued*

processing [522] capabilities to perform a particular function." By s 10(1)(b), a literary work includes a computer program or compilation of computer programs.

...

The only issue to be determined here is whether there was an implied unrestricted licence to import and sell these diskettes.

Counsel for the applicants argued that the decision in *Interstate Parcel Express Co Pty Ltd (Ipec) v Time-Life International (Nederlands) BV* (1977) 138 CLR 534 (the *Time-Life* case) is a most profound statement by the High Court on facts alleged to be indistinguishable for present purposes. The proposition relied on is that in copyright law a licence cannot be implied from the mere fact that the copyright owner had sold the goods without any express restriction on their subsequent disposal.

It is necessary to consider this case in some detail as the success of either party in this matter depends on an understanding of the decision.

The *Time-Life* case was an appeal from a judgment of the New South Wales Supreme Court making certain declarations and orders in respect of copyright infringement, in favour of Time-Life against Ipec, which was then operating the Angus and Robertson bookshops. Time-Life, a Dutch company, was at the time the exclusive licensee of Time Inc, a New York company (Time Inc), in respect of certain books of which Time Inc was the copyright owner. The proceedings were originally instituted by both these companies but Time Inc discontinued, fearing that to proceed might involve advancing an argument that could be construed as an infringement of the anti-trust legislation of the US.

Time-Life's distributor, Little Brown & Co, sold books to an American company, Raymar Inc, without restriction. Raymar sold them to Ipec which imported the books to Australia and sold them. There was no express licence from Time-Life or Time Inc to do so, nor were there any restrictions placed on the sales to Raymar or Ipec.

The issue was whether Ipec imported the books into and sold them in Australia without the licence of the owner of the copyright. The High Court was of the view that the word licence as it appears in s 37 means no more than consent; and that a licence in this context may be given orally or be implied by conduct. As in the present case, there was no question in the *Time-Life* case of an express licence or of consent to the importation and sale.

Reliance was placed on a line of authorities in patent cases, the principle there being that when a patented article is bought, control is implied unless there is explicit indication by the vendor that the buyer cannot sell it. The High Court distinguished the patent cases from copyright because, under patent law, the patentee has the exclusive right to make, exercise and vend [524] the product. Therefore to avoid a licence being implied, an express restriction needs to be placed on resale.

Copyright differs. Gibbs J (1977) 138 CLR 534 at 542 said:

> "The owner of copyright has not the exclusive right to use or sell the work in which copyright subsists. The buyer of a book in which copyright subsists does not need the consent of the owner of the copyright to read the book. The necessity to imply a term in the contract which exists when a patented article is sold does not arise on the sale of a book the subject of copyright. It was not, and could not be, suggested that the sale of a copy of a book is a licence to do the acts comprised in the copyright."

His Honour continued that in some circumstances when the owner of copyright sells a book, his consent to a particular use may be implied. He said that in the *Time-Life* case, there were only the bare facts of a sale without restriction and no evidence put forward of the copyright owner knowing who the identity of the purchaser is.

▒▒▒▒▒ Ozi-Soft v Wong *continued*

Gibbs J continued (at 544):

"It would therefore appear that in the US, as in Australia, it is not necessary, in order to give business efficacy to the sale of a book in which copyright subsists, to imply a term of vendor's consent."

Gibbs J (at 544) held that a licence:

"means the consent of the owner to the importation of the articles into Australia for the purpose of selling them, or to their sale after importation, and such a licence cannot be inferred from the mere fact that the owner of the copyright has sold the goods without any express restriction on their subsequent disposal."

Stephen J (at 555) said:

"There is, then, no novelty in the view that indirect infringement of copyright may result from the importation of material which until imported infringed no copyright … Any undesirable economic or cultural effects which some may discern as flowing from this aspect of copyright protection are a matter for the legislature."

Jacobs J (at 556) said:

"The purpose of s 37 is to make it clear that a positive licence is required. But the section does not say that importation for sale is allowed unless a restriction is given."

It is thus obviously easier to argue an implied licence, Jacobs J said, if the copyright owner is selling the goods in commercial quantities direct to a purchaser in another country and does not impose any restriction on importation.

In this case, counsel for the respondent sought to confine *Time-Life* to its facts and relied on two matters to dictate a different result. The first was the absence of any self-imposed or agreed restriction falling upon the copyright owner in Australia. The second was that *Time-Life* was decided against the background that it would have been illegal under the *Sherman Antitrust Act* for an American company to impose a restriction on end use and export when it granted Time-Life its licence.

Counsel for the respondents by contrast placed reliance on *Polydor Ltd v Harlequin Record Shop* [1980] FSR 362.

This case involved an argument about whether there was an implied licence to import a recording into the UK. Polydor Ltd was the exclusive licensee in the UK from the copyright owner of a certain recording. The licensee in Portugal was a Polydor company. The records were bought **[524]** legally in Portugal by Harlequin but imported into the UK without the consent of Polydor.

Harlequin argued that the sale in Portugal implied a licence by every member of the Polydor group for the importing of records into the UK. This argument was rejected and the English Court of Appeal, following the High Court in the *Time-Life* case, held (at 366):

"The sale of records by the Portuguese licensees conferred ownership and possession on the defendants (Harlequin), but did not constitute a licence from anyone to import those records into the UK."

This was relied on by the respondents for the proposition that, just as it was not permissible to exercise territorial or national rights in the nature of copyright so as to delimit markets as between England and Portugal, arising from a prohibition of that type in the Treaty of Rome affecting the states in the European Community, so it should be in Australia.

Ozi-Soft v Wong *continued*

Counsel submitted that the effect of Art 30 of the Treaty of Rome is that in a member state of the European Community, no contractual right or copyright can be exercised that has the effect of limiting the trade use in the UK of a copyright item.

Notwithstanding the earnest submissions of counsel in this regard, I cannot see how this case assists the interpretation of the *Copyright Act* in Australia.

The High Court in *Time-Life* expressly recognised that it is a question of fact as to the nature of the contract as to whether any licence is to be implied. Nevertheless, the court made substantial pronouncements of law, and I must seek to apply them here.

The respondent argued that the fact that in *Time-Life* the US parent company did not have legal freedom to impose any restrictions forced the High Court to find a solution in the interests of commercial efficacy against a licence employing importation into Australia.

Despite developing thought that it is or may be impermissible to impose restrictions upon the resale of goods because they infringe European Community law or the Sherman Antitrust legislation, the result surely cannot be that there is necessarily a licence by implication.

However, as Murphy J observed in the *Time-Life* case, there is an element of public interest in copyright enforcement cases and, should the facts show a reasonable possibility of serious breach of the *Trade Practices Act* or injury to the public, the court can and should require the offending party to negate this before upholding its copyright.

In *Enzed Holdings Ltd v Wynthea Pty Ltd* (1984) 57 ALR 167 the Full Federal Court repeated (at 181) the well established principle that any uncertainty or ambiguity in the provisions of the *Copyright Act* would be resolved with regard to the Berne Convention of 1886. As already mentioned, this supports what has become known as the Doctrine of National Treatment, which means that foreign authors should have in Australia that which is granted to Australian nationals.

As both counsel conceded, this was regarded by both parties as a test case because, other than the *Time-Life* case, there is no apparently substantive authority directly in point.

[525] It may be that some other mechanism needs to be developed to resolve these issues, because the interests of the Australian people in having free access to literary, musical and artistic works, even computer video entertainment, are adversely affected if oppressive restrictions on importation and sale may be imposed by copyright owners who are not themselves importing or intending to import the works in question.

Nevertheless, despite the force of the respondent's argument, they have failed to persuade me that I ought not to follow the principles enunciated in *Time-Life* and its result.

There is no evidence of any serious breach of trade practices legislation, nor any allegations of grave injury being caused to the public if the diskettes cannot be marketed here at this time. Adapting the comments of Stephen J in *Time-Life* (at 555), any undesirable community or societal consequences which may flow from this aspect of copyright protection are matters for the legislature. I do not think that I am able to shape the result of this case to counter any that may appear to flow if the respondents fail here.

I answer the question posed by Wilcox J on 13 March 1987 in the negative.

Notes

[5.80] The Full Federal Court discussed the nature of a "licence" under s 37 in *Computermate Products (Aust) Pty Ltd v Ozi-Soft Pty Ltd* (1988) 12 IPR 487; *Avel v Wells* (1991) 22 IPR 305. See also *Lotus Development Corp v Vacolan Pty Ltd* (1989) 16 IPR 143; *Avel Pty Ltd v Multicoin*

Amusements Pty Ltd (1990) 18 IPR 443; *RA Bailey & Co Ltd v Boccaccio Pty Ltd* (1986) 6 IPR 279; *Ozi-Soft Pty Ltd v Wong* (1988) 12 IPR 487.

Einfeld J's comments in *Ozi-Soft* concerning the detriment to the Australian public caused by the prohibition on parallel importing were extensively discussed in the media, and the Copyright Law Review Committee (CLRC) made an extensive inquiry into the question of whether there should be changes to the law in order to increase the range of copyright material available, and to lower the prices of books and sound recordings in particular: CLRC, *The Importation Provisions of the Copyright Act 1968* (1988). The Prices Surveillance Authority also looked into the question, with particular reference to the price of books: Prices Surveillance Authority, *Inquiry into Book Prices: Interim Report* (No 24) (1989) and sound recordings. The *Copyright Amendment Bill 1990* (Cth) amended ss 37 and 38 (dealing with works) by making them subject to a new s 44A. Parallel importing restrictions for sound recordings were subsequently removed.

In February 2000 legislation was introduced to prevent owners of non-copyright products that incorporate copyright material from using the parallel importation provisions of the *Copyright Act 1968* (Cth) to prevent the importation of competitor's products. The use of artistic works such as labels can no longer have their copyright asserted to prevent the importation of such items as detergent, toys and indeed the whole range of consumer goods. Discussion of the issue of restrictions on parallel importing was a major focus of the Ergas Committee Report, which recommended the removal of all restrictions on parallel importation from copyright legislation (Intellectual Property Competition Review Committee, *Review of Intellectual Property Legislation under the Competition Principles Agreement*, Final Report, AGPS, September 2000.) The recommendations have proved controversial and subject to attack by major overseas copyright producer interests. The recommendations, to free up the market for all copyright material, are incorporated in the *Copyright Amendment Act 2002* (Cth), with the exception of cinematograph films. 2002 Amendments also closed a loop-hole where owners had prevented the parallel importation of sound recordings by relying on the copyright in secondary material (for example, computer programs or short video clips) included on a music CD. However following *Australian Video Retailers Association v Warner Home Video Pty Ltd* (2001) at **[3.120]**, an amendment was also made to the definition of feature film, preventing the parallel importation of DVDs with interactive components (and hence incorporating both a film and a computer program).

The right to import music CDs has led to litigation under sections 45, 46 and 47 of the *Trade Practices Act 1974* (Cth). The ACCC instigated proceedings arguing that the big labels, Universal and Warner, had ceased to supply certain retailers who had imported CDs from overseas. The Full Federal Court found that while neither Universal nor Warner had a substantial degree of power in the relevant market, the companies had engaged in exclusive dealing for the purpose of substantially lessening competition in breach of s 47. Each company was ordered to pay $1 million in penalties and half of the ACCC's costs of the appeal. *See Universal Music & Ors v Australian Competition and Consumer Commission* [2003] FCAFC 193.

■ Compulsory licences/collecting societies: s 135ZZB

[5.85] Conferred by statute, compulsory licences exist to draw a balance between the rights of the copyright owner and the interests of the public. This is most evident in the record, music and broadcasting industries where aggregation of market power is possible due to the licensing of organisations to act on behalf of copyright owners (See House of Representatives, *Debates*, Second Reading Debate on the Copyright Bill 1968, 16 May 1968, p 1527.) The use of copyright material in an educational context is also relevant here, recognising the inevitability of copying in the university context. The *Copyright Act 1968* (Cth) establishes various types of compulsory licences, for the exercise of which a royalty must be paid, as distinct from providing defences to infringement.

The various types of compulsory licences include copying by educational institutions or institutions assisting persons with a print or intellectual disability; recording of musical works; broadcasting sound recordings or causing them to be heard in public; recording or filming works for the purpose of ephemeral broadcast by another person, or copying such a recording; copying of broadcasts by educational institutions or institutions assisting persons with an intellectual disability; copying of artistic works and Crown use of copyright material.

Amendments introduced by the *Copyright Amendment Act 1989* (Cth) streamlined the system of granting compulsory licences, largely by recognising and giving statutory force to the licensing arrangements agreed upon between copyright owners and users, as well as introducing a statutory scheme to allow for copying of audio visual broadcast material by educational institutions and institutions assisting readers with a print or intellectual disability. In 1989 amendments were also passed to implement a "blank tape levy" to allow taping at home of sound recordings in return for a levy on blank media.

An important feature of the compulsory licence scheme is the role played by the Copyright Tribunal, established under Part VI of the 1968 Act with jurisdiction to settle disputes relating to fixing royalties or equitable remuneration and arbitrating disputes between parties to licence agreements.

There is a distinction to be drawn between the compulsory licensing and fair dealing provisions of the Act. In *Haines v Copyright Agency Ltd* (1982) 42 ALR 549 the Director-General of Education for New South Wales circulated a memorandum to school principals entitled "Further Information on the Copyright Act" in order to explain certain aspects concerning the copying of educational material for teaching purposes. The memorandum pointed out that s 40 (providing for fair dealing) "allows for virtually the same amount and type of copying without imposing any need to keep records or make payments. A teacher could use s 40, for example, in preparing his/her own materials and students could use s 40 for themselves simply by doing their own copying on the photocopying machine in the library or elsewhere." The Full Federal Court emphasised the distinction between fair dealing and copying under the compulsory licence, and denied that s 40 was "an attractive alternative" to the compulsory licence for multiple copying.

Copyright Collecting Societies in Australia

[5.90] Department of Communications, Information Technology and the Arts, *Copyright Collecting Societies in Australia* (www.dcita.gov.au)

The copyright collecting societies are non-governmental organisations administer(ing) statutory and voluntary licences for copying and communicating literary, dramatic and artistic works, ensuring that Australians are rewarded for their creativity. The societies negotiate licences with users and receive payments which they pass onto their members. Each collecting society represents a different aspect of copyright.

Collective administration has many benefits. For individual owners, it is often difficult to maximise the economic value of their rights and to protect those rights. Similarly, third parties who wish to use those rights must incur the trouble and expense of finding the appropriate rights owners, negotiating individual deals and administering and accounting to a vast number of such rights owners. The collective administration of copyright is often the most effective method of managing the rights, both for the owners of the rights and those who need access to them.

▆▆▆▆▆ Copyright Collecting Societies in Australia *continued*

Collecting societies have three common features. All societies:

- collect and distribute the income earned from the exploitation of copyrights;
- aim to advance the economic and creative interests of the owners that they represent; and
- fulfil their functions by means of collective administration.

List of Australian copyright collecting societies

[5.95] Australasian Mechanical Copyright Owners Society Ltd (AMCOS)
Administers the rights to reproduce a musical work in a material form.
www.apra.com.au/Amcosweb

Australian Performing Rights Association (APRA)
Administers the public performance, broadcasting and cable diffusion rights in musical works (such as music compositions and lyrics).
www.apra.com.au

Audio Visual Copyright Society (AVCS)/Screenrights
Administers the statutory scheme whereby educational institutions and institutions assisting intellectually handicapped people can copy programs from radio or television for educational purposes.
www.screen.org

Copyright Agency Limited (CAL)
Administers statutory and voluntary licences for copying and communicating literary, dramatic and artistic works.
www.copyright.com.au

Phonographic Performance Company of Australia Ltd (PPCA)
Administers broadcast and public performance vested in sound recordings and music videos.
www.ppca.com.au

Visual Arts Copyright Collecting Agency (VISCOPY)
Administers visual artists' rights over their artistic works.
www.viscopy.com/

Christian Copyright Licensing International
Administers a Church copyright licence scheme.
www.ccli.com/

▆▆▆ Review of Australian Copyright Collecting Societies ▆▆▆

[5.100] Shane Simpson, *Review of Australian Copyright Collecting Societies*, Report to a Working Group of the Australian Cultural Development Office and the Attorney-General's Department (Department of Communication and the Arts, Canberra, 1995)

1.3 Executive summary of findings

The procedures by which collecting societies operate are necessarily very complex. This is largely because of the complexity inherent in administering a wide range of rights on behalf of thousands of owners, for a wide range of uses and users. Achieving a satisfactory degree of accuracy in collecting, allocating and delivering the appropriate income to the appropriate rights owners, is an extraordinarily difficult task.

Given this complexity, all societies (throughout the world) must try to strike a balance between the administrative cost of achieving a perfectly accurate capture and delivery system and the maximisation of returns to rights owners. Generally, the societies make a determined effort to achieve this balance and the introduction of new Information Technology is assisting them to this end.

The workings of each of the Societies was examined in detail and the procedures by which the data is captured, income is collected, allocations are made and distributions are performed, is generally both efficient and equitable. That is not to say that there are not alternative approaches possible as to each of these matters and it is clear that each of the societies is continually trying to improve their mechanisms. The degree of commitment of the senior staff to such improvement is also evident.

The widespread belief that collecting societies are awash with unjustifiable undistributed funds was found to be without basis. The amounts vary according to the nature of the collecting scheme of each society and the stage of development of each society. Certainly, all are striving to minimise such sums and maximise the return to their members. One important qualification to this is the method by which such sums are redistributed and whether those methods are truly appropriate. As the Committee will see, the Report recommends that a greater proportion of the undistributables be allocated to the cultural purposes of the wider industry sector rather than merely redistributed as a windfall to future royalty recipients.

The Report recommends important changes to the *Copyright Act* and the extension of the role of the Copyright Tribunal to cover all copyright licensing schemes. It also recommends the establishment of the position of Ombudsman for collecting societies—a role that must be independent of, not a creature of, the societies.

Also recommended, is the establishment of a collecting society for the visual arts—one that is fully representative of the relevant rights owners. It is important that this organisation be established on a firm footing and to achieve this it has been recommended that it receive limited Government funding in its establishment phase, together with the repeal or amendment of s 135ZM.

▬▬

Note. VISCOPY was established in 1995 as a collection agency for visual artists.

■ Artists and copyright: Don't Give Up Your Day Job

[5.105] In November 2003, the Australia Council published *Don't Give Up Your Day Job—An Economic Study of Professional Artists in Australia* by Professor David Throsby and Virginia Hollister. Intellectual property issues were considered in relation to artist's professional practice.
    The study noted that

- If artists are to gain the full economic benefit to which their creative endeavour entitles them, their intellectual property in their work must be adequately protected against unauthorised exploitation or appropriation.

- The great majority of writers, visual artists and composers believe that they hold copyright in work that they produce (see Table 5.2). Craft practitioners and performing artists generally are somewhat less sure.

- Altogether, one-quarter of all artists are members of one or more collecting societies. The highest proportion, 93 per cent, is among composers, where collective copyright administration is long established and common practice. Around two in five writers are members of a society but fewer than one in five visual artists and craft practitioners are members, where a specialised collecting society has only existed for a short time (see Table 5.2).

TABLE 5.1: SOURCES OF CREATIVE INCOME (PER CENT)

	Writers	Visual artists	Craft practitioners	Actors	Dancers	Musicians	Composers	Community cultural development workers	All artists
Salaries, wages, fees	55	34	21	94	90	95	38	78	63
Gross sales of work, including commissions	13	54	68	3	1	2	25	12	22
Royalties, advances	18	2	2	2	1	1	22	–	6
Other copyright earnings	*	*	–	*	1	1	1	–	*
Grants, prizes, fellowships	5	10	7	1	7	1	11	6	6
Public lending right	4	*	–	–	–	*	–	–	1
Educational lending right	5	*	–	–	–	*	–	–	1
Other creative source	*	*	2	–	–	*	3	4	1
Total	100	100	100	100	100	100	100	100	100
weighted n =	158	202	84	127	23	264	28	57	943
unweighted n =	203	219	108	138	54	126	58	34	940

* indicates less than 1%. – indicates nil in this sample.

TABLE 5.2: ARTISTS' COPYRIGHT – OVERVIEW (PER CENT)

	Writers	Visual artists	Craft practitioners	Actors	Dancers	Musicians	Composers	Community cultural development Workers	All artists
Believe copyright held(a)	90	87	75	48	74	60	97	77	73
Is a member of one or more copyright collecting societies(a)	42	12	18	11	9	32	93	8	25
Has received copyright payment in the last 12 months(b)	37	14	14	41	17	57	84	–	45
Has ever assigned copyright to another party(a)	43	33	25	35	25	21	48	34	31
Has had copyright infringed(a)	24	28	31	24	19	18	22	31	24
Has taken action(c)	33	32	18	31	21	19	20	25	26
Action was successful(d)	59	62	29	83	33	40	67	67	59
weighted n(a) =	170	223	96	149	32	297	32	64	1062
unweighted n(a) =	219	239	123	160	75	142	66	38	1062

(a) Proportions are of all artists.
(b) Proportions are of artists who are members of one or more copyright collecting societies.
(c) Proportions are of artists who have had copyright infringed.
(d) Proportions are of artists who have taken action against infringement.

TABLE 5.3: ARTISTS' MEMBERSHIP IN COPYRIGHT COLLECTING
SOCIETIES(A) (PER CENT)

	Writers	Visual artists	Craft practitioners	Actors	Musicians	Composers	All artists
Screenrights	11	4	–	31	–	–	5
Viscopy	1	70	82	–	–	–	13
Copyright Agency Limited	49	7	–	–	–	–	14
Australian Performing Rights Association	9	15	12	63	98	100	58
Australasian Mechanical Copyright Owners Society	1	7	6	6	18	30	12
Other	47	11	11	13	2	–	16
weighted n =	71	27	17	16	96	29	264
unweighted n =	91	29	22	17	46	61	266

(a) Proportions are of artists belonging to one or more copyright collecting societies. Columns do not sum to 100 because multiple responses permitted.

TABLE 5.4: REASONS FOR ARTISTS' ASSIGNMENT OF THEIR COPYRIGHT(A)
(PER CENT)

	Writers	Visual artists	Craft practitioners	Actors	Dancers	Musicians	Composers	Community cultural development workers	All artists
Assignment was required by collecting society or agent	7	14	21	10	–	10	19	–	10
Assignment was a condition of contract for production or sale of work	75	65	63	60	63	79	75	55	69
Art work was produced as an employee	40	23	21	44	43	21	13	62	32
The artist wished to assign copyright to another party	3	10	8	6	–		13	14	8
Other reason	3	12	8	8	14	–	7	–	6
Not sure why copyright was assigned	6	–	4	2	–	3	–	–	2
weighted n =	73	74	24	52	8	63	15	22	331
unweighted n =	94	79	31	56	18	30	32	13	353

(a) Proportions are of all artists who have ever assigned copyright for one or more reasons. Columns do not add to 100 because multiple responses permitted. – indicates less than 1%.

- The collecting societies to which artists belong are shown in Table 5.3 for all except dancers and community cultural development workers for whom membership in collecting societies is too small to allow valid inference. The results in this table confirm the significance of artform-related collecting societies as a means of administering artists' rights.

- Artists only receive revenue from a collecting society if usage of a particular work that is covered by the society's operation is monitored, and if this usage triggers a payment. As indicated in Table 5.2, the majority of composers and musicians who are members of a collecting society have received payment in the last 12 months, but smaller proportions have received payment in other artforms.

- Sometimes artists yield their copyright to another party, by choice or by necessity. About one-third of artists reported assigning their copyright to someone else, at some point. In the vast majority of cases this has been because assignment of copyright was required by contract or was necessitated because the work in question was produced when the artist was an employee (see Table 5.4).

- About one-quarter of all artists claim that their copyright has been infringed on some occasion, but of these only one in four artists have actually taken action to seek restitution (see Table 5.2). Of the relatively small number of cases where action has been taken by an artist against copyright infringement, about 60 per cent have been successful.

- As shown in Table 5.5, which draws together the main indicators of the protection of artists' rights in Australia at the present time, fewer than half of all artists regard copyright protection as adequate and only one-quarter of artists believe current moral rights legislation is adequate. However, in considering these figures we have to remember that significant numbers of artists don't know or are unsure about the adequacy of protection in either of these areas, suggesting that education about artists' rights remains an important area to be addressed.

TABLE 5.5: PROTECTION OF ARTISTS' COPYRIGHT AND MORAL RIGHTS

	Are members of one or more copyright collecting societies	Have experienced infringement of:		Believe current legal protection is adequate for:	
		Copyright	Moral rights	Copyright	Moral rights
	%	%	%	%	%
Writers	42	24	21	58	33
Visual artists	12	28	30	33	20
Craft practitioners	18	31	20	31	20
Actors	11	24	17	39	20
Dancers	9	19	19	41	34
Musicians	32	18	16	40	29
Composers	3	22	22	71	42
Community cultural development workers	8	31	37	42	21
All artists	25	24	22	42	26

Don't Stop the Music!

[5.110] Australia, House of Representatives, Standing Committee on Legal and Constitutional Affairs, *Don't Stop the Music!*, A Report of the Inquiry into Copyright, Music and Small Business (June 1998)

Summary and recommendations
Chapter 7—The Copyright Tribunal as an avenue for review to small businesses

51. This chapter reviews the purpose of the Copyright Tribunal and its role in offsetting the power of collecting societies arising from their monopoly status. It examines the accessibility of the Copyright Tribunal to small businesses seeking review of licensing arrangements. The chapter also explores options for ensuring that small businesses have adequate avenues of review and for restricting collecting societies' ability to abuse their monopoly position when dealing with licensees.

52. APRA and PPCA exercise rights in relation to almost all music which is subject to copyright. Collecting societies enable parties which would ordinarily be competitors to jointly determine the price of a licence. Music users do not have a choice of suppliers from which to acquire a licence. The only option available to a person who does not want to take out a licence with PPCA and/or APRA is to not use music at all.

53. The evidence indicated that small business operators did not believe that the Copyright Tribunal was an effective avenue of review of the copyright royalty licensing schemes. The Committee was told that small business did not have the knowledge, time or financial resources to pursue issues in the Tribunal, particularly in light of the amount of the licence fees.

54. The evidence clearly demonstrated a need to ensure that in their efforts to act on behalf of their members, copyright collecting societies do not become overzealous in their licensing activities. In the case of small users of music, the Copyright Tribunal may not be achieving this outcome as successfully as it could. The Committee believes that improvements can be made to existing avenues of appeal, and that new mechanisms can be introduced to ensure that the rights of collecting societies and the rights of small music users are fairly balanced.

55. The Committee believes that the Copyright Tribunal's jurisdiction should be as broad as possible to ensure that those who have genuine disputes with copyright collecting societies have access to some form of review. The Committee agrees with the recommendations made in the Simpson Report with respect to the jurisdiction of the Copyright Tribunal.

56. Most witnesses supported the idea of establishing some form of independent dispute resolution process. The Committee agrees that an informal dispute resolution process carried out by the Copyright Tribunal would be more accessible to small businesses than formal proceedings before the Tribunal. The Committee also believes that licensees should be informed by collecting societies about options for review of licensing schemes, including review and/or mediation by the Copyright Tribunal.

57. The Committee believes that the implementation of a code of conduct for copyright collecting societies would be an effective way of outlining acceptable licensing practices and activities. The Committee agrees that the code should be voluntary. However, if collecting societies do not comply with the voluntary code, the Committee believes that the code should be made enforceable under legislation.

Recommendation 4

The Committee recommends that the Copyright Tribunal should have as wide a jurisdiction as possible in respect of licences and licence tariffs including the variation, approval and interpretation of all licensing schemes.

▨▨▨▨▨▨ Don't Stop the Music! *continued*

Recommendation 5
The Committee recommends that mediation between parties in dispute over a licensing scheme be available through the Copyright Tribunal.

Recommendation 6
The Committee recommends that a voluntary code of conduct for copyright collecting societies be developed in consultation with the collecting societies, relevant Commonwealth Government departments, user groups and other interested parties. The code of conduct should outline standards of acceptable licensing practices and activities.

The Government supported these recommendations. A preference was expressed for industry co-operation and self-regulation rather than mandatory provision. It was noted that "the Government will consider the development of a mandatory code if a voluntary code of conduct is not effectively implemented or if there is significant dissatisfaction amongst copyright users and members of collecting societies with the code and its operation."

■ Blank tape levy

[5.115] Copyright owners argue that home taping results in lost sales, and thus they require compensation. A levy or blank tape royalty was to be imposed on new blank tapes, the proceeds to be collected by a collecting society for distribution of the royalty to composers, publishers, record producers and part of it to be paid into a fund for the development of Australian contemporary music. This was ruled to be unconstitutional before ever being introduced (*Australian Tape Manufacturers Association v Commonwealth* [1993] 176 CLR 480). The scheme has not been resuscitated since.

As long as it is for private use, home taping of sound recording and film broadcast material for "time shifting" purposes is allowed under *Copyright Act 1968* (Cth), s 111. However more recently it has been argued that while this provision allows recording of the "broadcast" it does not permit a right to copy any underlying works. It is thus argued to be of limited use.

Several countries have introduced a levy on blank CDs, DVDs, hard drives and flash memory devices in return for legalisation of copying for private use. This suggests that if a private copying provision were to be introduced as part of reform to fair dealing law in Australia (see [6.180]), we may face a similar debate to that in France, Germany, Italy and Canada over an 'i-pod tax'.

■ Public lending right/educational lending right

[5.120] Although authors or other owners of copyright gain royalties on sales of their books to libraries, it is considered that organised borrowing eliminates the sale of copies to readers who would buy their own, could they not borrow, and who benefit from the book without the author receiving a correlative return. To remedy this, a Public Lending Right Committee was established by the *Australia Council Amendment Act 1976* (Cth), s 5. The *Public Lending Right Act 1985* (Cth) established a statutory basis for the scheme, administered by the Department of Arts, Heritage and Environment. The Act is designed to provide for payments in respect of Australian books held in Australian libraries.

Strictly speaking, this is not an exploitation of copyright as it is independent of the *Copyright Act 1968* (Cth) and authors remain eligible to receive their entitlement even after assigning away their copyright.

■ Other transmission of copyright

[5.125] Copyright may also change hands by will and by devolution by operation of law (s 196(1)). This latter mode of transmission has been discussed mainly in the context of partnerships where it has not been clear whether an assignment of the partnership and its assets (or part thereof) included copyright. See *O'Brien v Komesaroff* (1982) 150 CLR 310; *Murray v King* (1984) 55 ALR 559.

CHAPTER 6

INFRINGEMENT

[6.05] Acts amounting to infringement of copyright are described in *Copyright Act 1968* (Cth), ss 36-39B, 47A-47D and 100A-104B. Infringement of copyright may be direct (ss 13(2), 36(1), 101(1)) or indirect (ss 37, 38, 39(1), 102, 103), and since 2001, includes commercially dealing with circumvention devices or tampering with electronic rights management information (ss 116A-116D).

Direct infringement consists of doing or authorising an act comprised in the copyright, or allowing a place of public entertainment to be used to perform a work. The elements of copyright in works are set out in *Copyright Act 1968* (Cth), s 31(1) and 31(2), which make the right to authorise a person to do an act in relation to a work, or adaptation or other subject matter, one of the exclusive rights comprised in the copyright. Copyright in other subject matter is described in *Copyright Act 1968* (Cth), ss 85-88.

Indirect infringement consists of dealing with goods that are infringing reproductions, either because they are "pirated" copies or legitimate copies which become infringing articles due to the parallel importing provisions of the *Copyright Act 1968* (Cth).

Whereas most infringement involves doing something comprised within the owner's exclusive rights, the *Copyright Amendment (Digital Agenda) Act 2000* (Cth) introduced (by ss 116A-116D) a range of "para-copyright" measures to protect against accessing copyright protected material. Civil remedies and criminal offences in relation to the manufacture and supply of, and other dealings with, broadcast decoding devices where the use is for a commercial purpose have been introduced against persons using devices and services designed to circumvent the technological protection measures used by copyright owners to protect their material. It is illegal to manufacture, supply, commercially deal, import, make available online, advertise or promote activities for the purpose of circumventing technological protection methods for copyright material: see *Stevens v Kabushiki Kaisha Sony Computer Entertainment* (2005) 65 IPR 513. Similarly, the intentional removal and alteration of electronic rights management information or commercial dealing in material where a person knows or is reckless as to whether rights management information has been removed, attracts new criminal and civil remedies.

Reference to copyright in a work or other subject matter relates to a "substantial part" of that work or other subject matter (*Copyright Act 1968* (Cth), s 14(1)(a)).

SUBSTANTIAL PART

■ What is worth copying is worth protecting?
See *Copyright Act 1968* (Cth), s 14.

▰▰▰▰▰▰▰ Network Ten v TCN Channel Nine ▰▰▰▰▰▰▰

[6.10] *Network Ten Pty Limited v TCN Channel Nine Pty Limited* (2004) 218 CLR 273 High Court of Australia

McHUGH ACJ, GUMMOW AND HAYNE JJ: **[281]** ...

Copyright and copying
Counsel for Nine invoked a well-known statement made in *University of London Press Ltd v University Tutorial Press Ltd*. This was a case of infringement of copyright in an original literary work and Peterson J applied "the rough practical test that what is worth copying is prima facie worth protecting". But later authorities correctly emphasise that, whilst copying is an essential element in infringement to provide a causal connection between the plaintiff's intellectual property and the alleged infringement, it does not follow that any copying will infringe. The point was stressed by Laddie J when he said:

> "Furthermore many copyright cases involve defendants who have **[282]** blatantly stolen the result of the plaintiff's labours. This has led courts, sometimes with almost evangelical fervour, to apply the commandment 'thou shalt not steal'. If that has necessitated pushing the boundaries of copyright protection further out, then that has been done. This has resulted in a body of case law on copyright which, in some of its further reaches, would come as a surprise to the draughtsmen of the legislation to which it is supposed to give effect."

Professor Waddams, speaking of the use of terms such as "piracy", "robbery" and "theft" to stigmatise the conduct of alleged infringers of intellectual property rights, describes "the choice of rhetoric" as "significant, showing the persuasive power of proprietary concepts". He also remarks:

> "Against the merits of enlarging the property rights of one person or class of persons must always be set the loss of freedom of action that such enlargement inevitably causes to others."

In another English decision, Jacob J identified Peterson J's aphorism in *University of London Press* as an indication of the dangers in departing too far from the text and structure of the legislation; his Lordship said that the aphorism "proves too much" because if "taken literally [it] would mean that all a plaintiff ever had to do was to prove copying" so that "appropriate subject matter for copyright and a taking of a substantial part would all be proved in one go".

In Australia, the dangers in the use of the remarks in *University of London Press* were explained by Sackville J in *Nationwide News Pty Ltd v Copyright Agency Ltd* as follows:

> "[T]he test has a certain 'bootstraps' quality about it. The issue of substantiality, in relation to a literary work, arises only where the work has been reproduced or published, at least in part. If applied literally, the test would mean that all cases of copying would be characterised as reproducing a substantial part of the work. It is therefore unlikely to be of great assistance in determining whether a particular reproduction involves a substantial part of a work or subject matter of copyright."

▬▬▬ Network Ten v TCN Channel Nine *continued*

"Substantial part"

All the species of copyright enjoy a protection which is not limited **[283]** to infringement by the taking of the whole of the protected subject-matter. The taking of something less will do. That lesser degree of exploitation is identified in s 14(1) by the phrase "a substantial part". The decision in *Data Access Corporation v Powerflex Services Pty Ltd* with respect to infringement of the literary works in computer programs provides a recent example of the operation of s 14(1). The sub-section states:

> "In this Act, unless the contrary intention appears:
> (a)   a reference to the doing of an act in relation to a work or other subject-matter shall be read as including a reference to the doing of that act in relation to a substantial part of the work or other subject-matter; and
> (b)   a reference to a reproduction, adaptation or copy of a work shall be read as including a reference to a reproduction, adaptation or copy of a substantial part of the work, as the case may be."

...The term "substantial part" has a legislative pedigree. It appeared in s 1(2) of the *Copyright Act 1911* (Imp) ("the 1911 Act"). ... The scheme of the 1911 Act, as with the UK Act and the Australian legislation which succeeded it, keeps separate the concepts of substantial part and fair dealing. Accordingly:

> "acts done in relation to insubstantial parts do not constitute an infringement of copyright and the defences of fair dealing only come into operation in relation to substantial parts or more".

It would be quite wrong to approach an infringement claim on the footing that the question of the taking of a substantial part may be by-passed by going directly to the fair dealing defences.

▬▬▬

■ Quality, not quantity

▬▬▬▬▬Walt Disney v H John Edwards Publishing▬▬▬

[6.15] *Walt Disney Productions v H John Edwards Publishing Co P/L* (1954) 71 WN (NSW) 150 Supreme Court of New South Wales

[The plaintiff claimed copyright in Australia in drawings of certain characters, namely "Donald Duck", and three ducklings known as "Houey", "Dewey" and "Louie", a dog "Goofy" and a donkey "Basil". The defendant published in Australia children's comics known as "Super Duck Comics" featuring a duck named "Super Duck", a duckling, a dog and donkey, all alleged to infringe copyright in the plaintiff's drawings.]

MCCLELLAND J: **[160]** A colourable imitation is treated as one kind of copy, and, when I speak of copies, colourable imitations will be included.

The question then is: Are any of the drawings contained in "Super Duck" comics, Nos 1, 2, 3 and 4 copies of any of the drawings in the plaintiff's publications in respect of which copyright has been established or of any substantial part of any of such drawings? What is a substantial part of a drawing is, of course, a question of degree and in this respect the quantity taken may not be so relevant as the quality of that which is taken.

▄▄▄▄▄▄ Walt Disney v H John Edwards Publishing *continued*

It is immaterial that a defendant's drawing is a bad or inartistic copy, if it is a copy: cf *Hanfstaengl v Baines & Co Ltd* [1895] AC 20 at 26 per Lord Watson. It is also immaterial if a copy is made from a work which is a derivative of the original work.

Although there was considerable evidence before me in relation to the question of infringement, in relation to the alleged infringing drawings there was no evidence of the actual operations of copying or of its absence. In these circumstances, the plaintiff accepted the position that the approach to be made was similar to the approach which was made in *King Features Syndicate Inc v O & M Kleeman Ltd* [1941] AC 417 at 435, 436 by Lord Wright, who said:

> "The test to be applied is purely visual, the sketch and the brooch being compared
> oculis subjecta fidelibus. It is not material that the respondents were stealing the idea
> of 'Popeye the Sailor', or availing themselves for commercial profit of the popularity
> acquired by that figure. The appellants' copyright is in the actual sketch, not in the
> idea. There would be no infringement if the respondents had independently produced
> a similar figure without copying the sketch directly or indirectly. The question is
> whether there was copying of the actual sketch. Here the only evidence of actual
> copying, direct or indirect, is similarity with regard to the figure, which is a substantial
> part of the sketch, between the copyright work and the alleged infringement. I think,
> however, that, where there is a substantial similarity, that similarity is prima facie
> evidence of copying which the party charged may refute by evidence that, notwith-
> standing the similarity, there was no copying but independent creation. In the present
> case, on a careful comparison of the brooches and the sketch, I find substantial
> similarity between the different editions of the brooch and sketch No 3, sufficient to
> raise a prima facie case of actual copying. The respondents have called no evidence to
> rebut that prima facie case. I agree, accordingly, with Simonds J in finding that the
> copy is proved in respect of the brooches, equally with the dolls and toys."

The approach in the present case, however, must be made having in mind the general evidence which was given, and which may be put into four classes: (a) evidence of the history of the plaintiff's fanciful characters which was elicited on behalf of the defendant; (b) evidence of the past conduct of the defendant's predecessors in title relating to the publication of fanciful characters and, in particular, of the fanciful character "Super Duck" which was elicited on behalf of the plaintiff; (c) evidence of the publication prior to 1936 of fanciful characters being humanised animals and birds, elicited on behalf of the defendant; (d) evidence of experts who purported to point out similarities and differences between and from the drawings in the plaintiff's works and the drawings in the publications of the defendant. ...

[161] It remains to state the conclusions I have arrived at as a result of comparing each of the drawings in the "Super Duck" comics, Nos 1, 2, 3 and 4, with each of the drawings in which plaintiff has copyright.

[His Honour then referred to drawings which had been selected during the course of the case as disclosing most similarity between drawings of "Super Duck" and "Donald Duck", "The Three Nephews" and "Fauntleroy", and "Goofy" and "Hamburger" and in each of those cases found insufficient or no substantial similarity between the respective drawings to raise a prima facie case of actual copying of the drawings or of any substantial part thereof. His Honour then considered selected drawings of "Basil" and "The Donkey", and continued:]

[162] ...Upon making the appropriate comparisons, I find substantial similarity between each of the drawings in the "Super Duck" comic and each of the drawings of "Basil" sufficient to raise a prima facie case of actual copying. There being no evidence called to rebut that

prima facie case, I find that the drawings of "The Donkey" in the "Super Duck" comic have been proved to be infringements.

Declare that the defendant has infringed the copyright of the plaintiff in the works being representations of a fanciful character of a donkey named "Basil".

Notes

[6.20] Since ideas as such are not protected by copyright, the line must be drawn between the taking of a concept and the copying of the form of expression. See *Kenrick v Lawrence* (1890) 25 QBD 99. Borrowing an idea that has its origins in another's work but producing a new original work by sufficient independent effort does not amount to infringement. See *Joy Music Ltd v Sunday Pictorial Newspapers (1920) Ltd* [1960] 2 QB 60; cf *Krisarts SA v Briarfines Ltd* [1977] FSR 577. If the alteration is so slight that there is no independent work, then substantial reproduction will be found: *Dronpool Pty Ltd v Hunter* (1984) 3 IPR 310. This will always be a question of degree which must depend upon the circumstances of each particular case: *Blackie & Sons v Lothian Book Publishing Co* (1921) 29 CLR 396. For an example of a painting "inspired by" but not a substantial reproduction of a photograph, see *Bauman v Fussell* [1978] RPC 485.

The issue of substantiality has both a quantitative and qualitative aspect although "the question of whether a defendant has copied a substantial part depends much more on the quality than the quantity of what he has taken": *Ladbroke v William Hill* [1964] 1 WLR 273 at 276 per Lord Reid; *Greenfield Products Pty Ltd v Rover-Scott Bonnar Ltd* (1990) 17 IPR 417; *Dixon Investments Pty Ltd v Hall* (1990) 18 IPR 481. A substantial reproduction is not necessarily reproduction of a "substantial part", where that part by itself has no originality: *Klissers Bakeries v Harvest Bakeries* (1986) 5 IPR 533.

The question of what amounts to a substantial part of a work must depend upon the nature of the work itself, and the characteristics or essential features which may identify the work.

▬▬▬▬▬ Hawkes & Son v Paramount Film Service ▬▬▬▬▬

[6.25] *Hawkes & Son (London) Ltd v Paramount Film Service* [1934] Ch 593 Court of Appeal (United Kingdom)

[A news reel recording the opening of a new school also recorded a band playing a few bars of the march Colonel Bogey, copyright in which was held by the plaintiffs. At trial, Eve J held that there was no reproduction of a "substantial part" of the musical work.]

LORD HANWORTH MR: [603] ... It is plain that the second defendants have made a record, by the contrivance of which the Colonel Bogey march may be mechanically performed, and they have in so doing infringed the right of the owner of the copyright. But, it is said, first, that there is no substantial part of this musical work taken, and that the cases show that we must look into the question of degree and what was the nature of the reproduction. In one case to which Lindley LJ refers, he points out that in that case a worsted work copy of an engraving was held not to be an infringement of the copyright therein. On the other hand,

▓▓▓▓ Hawkes & Son v Paramount Film Service *continued*

photographs of pictures have been held to infringe the copyright, although there is a vast difference between a photographic reproduction and the picture itself. Therefore, when one deals with the word "substantial", it is quite right to consider whether or not the amount of the musical march that is taken is so slender that it would be impossible to recognise it. ...

Having considered and heard this film, I am quite satisfied that the quantum that is taken is substantial, and although it might be difficult, and although it may be uncertain whether it will be ever used again, we must not neglect the evidence that a substantial part of the musical copyright could be reproduced apart from the actual picture film. ... [605] ...

SLESSER LJ: I am of the same opinion. The learned judge has come to the conclusion that no substantial part of the work has been reproduced. He continues: "It appears that the whole work would take a band about four minutes to play, and that the part recorded on the news reel takes 20 seconds." The learned judge, no doubt, in coming to the conclusion that no substantial part of the film has been reproduced, was not unmindful of the history of the words "substantial part" which appear in the *Copyright Act 1911*, and which are an essential ingredient if the plaintiffs are to succeed or have judgment found in their favour. Those words, as Mr Macgillivray has pointed out, had not appeared before that time in any statute, but they are words which are derived from several of the cases in which learned judges have used either those particular words or language similar. It is to be observed that in the old *Copyright Act* (5 & 6 Vict c 45), under which *Bradbury v Hotten* (1872) LR 8 Ex 1 and *Chatterton v Cave* (1878) 3 App Cas 483 and other cases fell to be decided, there is no such distinction. It is there provided [606] by s 15 "That if any person shall in any part of the British dominions ... print or cause to be printed either for sale or exportation any book in which there shall be subsisting copyright": no distinction is there made between the whole of the book and a substantial part of it, and, of course, the literal reading of those words would of necessity have produced absurdities, and the learned judges in several cases were at pains to point out that where the statute says "any book", it means any essential, vital or substantial part of the book as words, all of which appear in different judgments. The matter is put perhaps most clearly, or as clearly as anywhere else, by Lord Hatherley in *Chatterton v Cave*, where he says: "if the quantity taken be neither substantial nor material, if, as it has been expressed by some judges, 'a fair use' only be made of the publication, no wrong is done and no action can be brought." The learned Lord in his speech there uses the words "neither substantial nor material," and the words "a fair use only be made," in apposition, and it is in that sense, I think, that before the Act of 1911 the matter has to be considered.

Mr Archer is perfectly right when he points out that the authorities indicate that other matters beyond mere quantity may and have to be looked at; indeed it is a criticism, I think, if I may respectfully make it, of the judgment in this case, that the only ground on which the learned judge held that no substantial part had been reproduced was that the whole work would take not more than four minutes to play, and the part recorded on the news reel took 20 seconds. I agree with my Lord that this reproduction is clearly a substantial part of Colonel Bogey, looked at from any point of view, whether it be quantity, quality, or occasion. Any one hearing it would know that it was the march called Colonel Bogey, and though it may be that it was not very prolonged in its reproduction, it is clearly, in my view, a substantial, a vital, and an essential part which is there reproduced.

Appeal allowed.

Notes

[6.30] This use would be considered fair dealing within *Copyright Act 1968* (Cth), ss 41(1)(b) and 42(2).

It may be particularly difficult to distinguish between the mere taking of an idea and the expression thereof so as to infringe copyright in a dramatic work. The plot or dramatic incidents of a play or film may not be literally copied in the sense of using the actual words of the script, but infringement can occur by the reproduction of sufficiently similar situations and incidents (*Hexagon Pty Ltd v Australian Broadcasting Commission* (1975) 7 ALR 233; *Zeccola v Universal City Studios Inc* (1982) 46 ALR 189), as long as these are in material form and substantial enough to warrant attention: *Tate v Thomas* [1921] 1 Ch 503; *Green v Broadcasting Corp of New Zealand* (1983) 2 IPR 191; (1989) 16 IPR 1.

Similar considerations apply to infringement by a dramatic work of another category of work. The matter is very much one for the trial judge's assessment and impression: *Corelli v Gray* (1913) 29 TLR 570.

A fertile area of litigation is found in the "architect's plan cases". However, the issues of subsistence of copyright in project home plans and the infringement of plans requires assessments at the very edges of copyright protection. Most cases depend almost entirely on their facts, and the judge must form an impression of the originality and infringement issues in circumstances where "the borderline area is clouded by a band of grey within which opinions and conclusions may differ" (*LED Builders v Masterton Homes (NSW) Pty Ltd* (1994) 30 IPR 447, citing the *Ancher Mortlock Murray* case).

▬▬▬▬▬▬ Half Court Tennis v Seymour ▬▬▬▬▬▬

[6.35] *Half Court Tennis Pty Ltd v Seymour* (1980) 53 FLR 240 Supreme Court of Queensland

[249] ...

DUNN J: In my opinion, the building which I have discussed is an artistic work, and copyright subsists in it; the first plaintiff is the assignee of the copyright. I have already referred to the definition of "artistic work"; I should have added that the definition provides that a building may be such a work "whether the building ... is of artistic quality or not". The fact that a half court can scarcely be described as a thing of beauty does not matter. What does matter is that it is the result of skill and labour by Wills and K.

In *Ancher, Mortlock, Murray & Woolley Pty Ltd v Hooker Homes Pty Ltd* (1971) 20 FLR 481 at 486 Street J said:

> "In a case such as the present, where copyright is claimed in an architect's plan, a cautious approach must be made to the considerations arising both on the aspect of existence of copyright and on the aspect of close resemblance between the original and the reproduction."

His Honour then pointed out that in *Beck v Montana Constructions Pty Ltd* (1963) 80 WN (NSW) 1578 at 1580 Jacobs J (as he then was) had said:

> "It is clear I think that the degree of protection of an architectural plan must of its nature be very limited and it seems to me that one of the reasons for the severe limitation in the degree of protection under the law of copyright is that in an architectural plan more than any other form of literary or artistic reproduction there is a

▰▰▰▰▰ Half Court Tennis v Seymour *continued*

greater element which may be described as common to all plans and that the particular portion of the plan which may be regarded as belonging to the owner of the copyright, the particular features of it and of the expression must consequently be more limited." [250]

Street J also referred to *Copinger and Skone James on Copyright* (12th ed, 1980), para 719:

"Copyright is infringed by the production of something which to the eye is a copy of the original ... it is naturally more difficult to prove infringement of copyright in a plain building than in one showing marked originality ... slight differences between buildings of no marked originality will prevent them from being held to be copies of each other, which would not be the case if the buildings were of an original character."

Those observations are in point in this case, because half courts and compact tennis courts and indeed the "mini" courts which the witness Cooper has built all copy (using that work in a general sense) "standard" tennis courts. This being so, no "mini" court merits description as a work of marked originality, and because the area of each "mini" court is comparatively small slight differences in the arrangements of lines on the courts and the heights of the net posts are not so telling as would be the case if Wills had for the first time invented the game of tennis or if larger areas had to be considered.

In *Ancher, Mortlock, Murray & Woolley Pty Ltd v Hooker Homes Pty Ltd* (1971) 20 FLR 481 at 488-489, a case which I have found of great assistance, the judgment reads thus:

"An architect may legitimately inspect an original plan or house and then, having absorbed the architectural concept and appreciated the architectural style represented therein, return to his own drawing board and apply that concept and style to an original plan prepared by him and in due course to a house built to such plan. There is a dividing line separating such a legitimate process from an inspection followed by a later copying of a substantial part of the physical object inspected, even though the copying be from memory; the latter exercise does infringe. In many instances it will be difficult to state categorically whether the dividing line has been crossed. Cases will not always be black or white where the alleged copying is from memory. The borderline area is clouded by a band of grey within which opinions and conclusions may differ. Within this grey band conflicting answers could without error be given to the question is that plan or house only a copy of the concept or style or the original and hence legitimate?, or is it a copy of the author's manifestation of that concept or style and hence an infringement?

In this grey band, in answering such questions as these, it can be of critical importance to know how the architect who is said to have infringed went about the preparation and drawing of his plan. It is only after making a finding, either on direct evidence or by inference, of copying, that is to say, of unfair or unconscientious use of the author's plan or building, that significance [251] will attach to the degree of similarity. In a practical sense, of course, the degree of similarity is frequently a most telling element on the question of copying. To some extent the two aspects overlap, but they are distinct in point of principle and they must be considered with this distinction in mind."

In this case, as I have said, Seymour gave evidence and was subjected to a searching cross-examination. As I have said, he impressed me, and I accept that he did not measure nor copy nor memorise the arrangement of lines which is in the part of the first plaintiff's copyright, nor did he copy the half court net posts; indeed, the net posts on a compact court are significantly higher that the "rival" net posts. There is no doubt that he took and used an idea, but there is no copyright in ideas. I accept as authentic the calculation sheet, Exhibit 15, upon which he recorded his workings when he decided to go into the business of constructing compact tennis courts; that is to say, I do not agree that that document was brought into existence for use in this litigation.

(The similarities and differences between the half court pattern of lines on a slab and the compact tennis pattern of lines are as follows: Whilst the base lines on each court are the same length (6.1 metres), the side lines of a compact tennis court as designed by Seymour are 12.4 metres long (.2 metre longer than half court sidelines). The "tramlines" on a compact tennis court are 700 millimetres wide, as compared with "tramlines" 750 millimetres wide on a half court. On a compact tennis court the distance from the net of the line marking the front of each service court is 3.4 metres (as compared with 3.35 metres). Some similarities are enhanced because the "rival" designers took measurements from different parts of the lines. The height of a compact tennis net is 900 millimetres at the net posts, as compared with 825 millimetres in the case of a half court net.)

My conclusion therefore is that the defendants have not infringed the first plaintiff's copyright.

REPRODUCTION

■ Causal connection

[6.45] The plaintiff must show that the alleged infringing material is derived from the work or subject matter in which copyright is claimed. In other words, there must be copying or reproduction within s 31(1) not just a similar result achieved by independent effort: *Corelli v Gray* (1913) 29 TLR 570; *Ainsworth Nominees Pty Ltd v Andclar Pty Ltd* (1988) 12 IPR 551.

If the evidence establishes sufficient similarity between the alleged infringing material and the original, and that the latter was earlier in time and that the defendant had access to the work, there appears to be a shift of onus to the defendant to explain away the similarity.

In *King Features Syndicate Inc v O & M Kleeman Ltd* [1941] AC 417, Viscount Maugham in the House of Lords held:

"I think, however, that, where there is substantial similarity, that similarity is prima facie evidence of copying which the party charged may refute by evidence that, notwithstanding the similarity, there was no copying but independent creation. In the present case, on a careful comparison of the brooches and the sketch, I find substantial similarity ... sufficient to raise a prima facie case of actual copying. The respondents have called no evidence to rebut that prima facie case. I agree, accordingly, with Simonds J in finding that copying is proved in respect of the brooches, equally with the dolls and toys."

The appeal was allowed. This reversal of onus is not an invariable rule. Proof of copying may be deduced from a composite of elements, and need not be confined to conscious imitation.

Francis Day & Hunter v Bron

[6.50] *Francis Day & Hunter Ltd v Bron* [1963] Ch 587 Court of Appeal (United Kingdom)

WILLMER LJ: **[608]** This is an appeal from a judgment of Wilberforce J, given on 27 July 1962, whereby he dismissed an action brought by the plaintiffs for infringement of their copyright in a song called In a Little Spanish Town (to which I will refer hereafter as Spanish Town). This was composed in 1926, and (as has been admitted by the defendants) was extensively exploited in the US and elsewhere by the publication of sheet music, by the distribution of gramophone records and by broadcasting. Unlike many popular songs, Spanish Town appears to have retained its popularity over the years. Records published in this country (some of them quite recently) were played to us during the course of the hearing; and, speaking for myself, I was readily able to recognise the tune as a familiar one which I had heard on frequent previous occasions.

The defendants are the publishers of another song called Why, which was composed in 1959 by Peter de Angelis. Spanish Town is written in 3/4 time, and Why in 4/4 time. There are a number of other differences between the two works which were the subject of a good deal of evidence by musical experts on both sides. But when the two songs were played to us, it was immediately apparent, to me at any rate, that the effect on the ear was one of noticeable similarity. This is a matter which is not without importance, for, as was pointed out by Astbury J in *Austin v Columbia Gramophone Co Ltd* [1923] Mac CC 398: "Infringement of copyright in music is not a question of note for note comparison" (at 415) but falls to be determined "by the ear as well as by the eye" (at 409).

Wilberforce J included in his judgment a detailed analysis of the musical structure of the two songs. I accept this as correct, and it is, I think, unnecessary for me to repeat it except in summary form. In each case the essential feature of the song is contained in the first eight bars, which constitute what has been **[609]** described as a musical sentence, and in which the main theme is stated. It is common ground that in the case of Spanish Town, these first eight bars of the chorus constitute a "substantial part" of the work within the meaning of s 49 of the *Copyright Act 1956*. In Spanish Town a subsidiary and contrasting theme is then introduced, after which there is a return to the original theme, which is then re-stated with variations. By way of contrast, Why is described as a "thematic" song; there is no subsidiary or contrasting theme, but, practically speaking, the whole song is devoted to the development of the original theme.

[610] ... Having stated these various points of similarity and difference (which I wholly accept) the judge expressed the view that, in relation to the aural appeal of the sentence as a whole, there is an undoubted degree of similarity between the two songs, the only question being what adjective to put before the word "degree". He expressed his conclusion as follows:

> "On the whole, I think Mr Palmer's word 'definite' or 'considerable' is the right weight
> to put upon the degree of similarity; it is such that an ordinary reasonably experienced
> listener might think that perhaps one had come from the other."

With that conclusion I entirely agree.

If the matter stopped there, I do not think it could be doubted that there was material on which to base the inference that the composer of Why deliberately copied from Spanish Town. Were that the right inference, I am satisfied that the degree of similarity would be sufficient to constitute an infringement of the plaintiff's copyright. But the composer of Why was called as a witness, and not only denied copying, but denied that he had ever seen the music of Spanish Town, or even consciously heard it. He was a man of 33 years of age, and had lived most of his life in the US. He stated that he had been composing music ever since

■■■■■ Francis Day & Hunter v Bron *continued*

he was 11, and had played various instruments in dance bands. In cross-examination he admitted that at a younger age he might have heard Spanish Town, because he had heard a lot of music, but he adhered to his statement that he had never consciously studied it, and said that he did not recall ever playing it. Wilberforce J accepted his evidence, and I do not think that we in this court could properly interfere with that finding even if we were invited to do so, which we were not.

But that, the plaintiffs say, is by no means the end of the case, for de Angelis could well have copied from Spanish Town subconsciously. The song having been extensively exploited in the US, the overwhelming probability **[611]** (it is said) is that he must have heard it; and the degree of similarity between Spanish Town and Why is such that an inference of, at any rate, subconscious copying should be drawn. That, it is contended, would be enough to constitute an infringement of the plaintiff's copyright. Wilberforce J, however, decided that there was not sufficient material to justify the inference that de Angelis copied the plaintiff's work, even subconsciously; and he accordingly dismissed the action. It is to this point that the present appeal has been mainly directed.

In approaching the suggestion of subconscious copying on the part of de Angelis, it is to be observed that the *Copyright Act 1956*, nowhere uses the word "copying". [His Lordship read s 2(5) and continued:] By subs (6)(b) "adaptation" in relation to a musical work is defined as meaning "an arrangement or transcription of the work". By s 48(1) "reproduction" is defined as including reproduction in the form of a record. There is no further relevant definition of the word, and it has been left to judicial decision to introduce the notion of copying.

Mr Arnold, in presenting his argument on behalf of the defendants, drew attention to the fact that in relation to musical copyright there are, under s 2 of the Act, only three forbidden processes, namely, "reproduction", "arrangement", and "transcription". Arrangement and transcription, he submitted, can be only the result of a conscious and deliberate process; a man cannot arrange or transcribe without knowing that he is doing so. Wilberforce J's acceptance of the evidence of de Angelis, therefore precludes the possibility of finding any infringement of the plaintiff's copyright by arrangement or transcription. This submission must, I think, be accepted.

Mr Arnold conceded that reproduction could possibly be the result of a subconscious process. But he went on to submit that reproduction within the section could mean nothing short of identity. Reproduction, under s 49, may be of a substantial part; but there is no suggestion in the Act of any such thing as a "substantial reproduction". In the present case it cannot be said that there is anything approaching identity between the plaintiff's work and that of de Angelis. Consequently, Mr Arnold submitted, there could be no infringement of the plaintiff's copyright, whether conscious or unconscious, by way of reproduction.

I find myself quite unable to accept this submission, for I can find no warrant for the suggestion that reproduction, within the **[612]** meaning of the section, occurs only when identity is achieved. This not only offends against common sense, but is, I think, contrary to authority. In *Austin v Columbia Gramophone Co Ltd* [1923] Mac CC 398 the headnote reads: "Infringement of copyright in music is not a question of note for note comparison, but of whether the substance of the original copyright work is taken or not." In the course of his judgment in that case Astbury J (at 409, 410), quoted from the earlier case of *D'Almaine v Boosey* (1835) 1 Y & C 288; 160 ER 117 where it was laid down that (at 302) "it must depend on whether the air taken is substantially the same with the original". I accept that as a correct statement of the principle.

On the other side, Mr Foster, for the plaintiffs, submitted in the first place that de Angelis's denial of copying was wholly irrelevant. For where, as was said to be the case here, a sufficient degree of similarity is shown, and it is further proved that the composer of the second work had access to the earlier work in the sense that he must probably have heard it, an irrebuttable presumption arises that the former has been copied from the latter. No authority was cited in support of this proposition, which, if well-founded, would eliminate the necessity for any further evidence once similarity coupled with access had been proved. In my judgment the proposition contended for is quite untenable; the most that can be said, it seems to me, is that proof of similarity, coupled with access, raises a prima facie case for the defendant to answer.

Mr Foster contended in the alternative that the degree of similarity found by Wilberforce J in the present case is such as to compel an inference of copying which, even if subconscious, is sufficient to give the plaintiffs a cause of action for infringement. I confess that I have found the notion of subconscious copying one of some difficulty, for at first sight it would seem to amount to a contradiction in terms, the word "copying" in its ordinary usage connoting what is essentially a conscious process. The textbooks on copyright make no reference to the subject, and English authority in relation to it is confined to a single dictum of Luxmore J in *G Ricordi & Co (London) Ltd v Clayton & Waller Ltd* [1930] Mac CC 154. Our attention was, however, called to a number of cases in the US in which the subject has **[613]** been discussed, and in some of which a decision in favour of the plaintiff has been based on a finding of subconscious copying.

It appears to me that the question must be considered in two stages, namely, (1) whether subconscious copying is a psychological possibility, and (2) if so, whether in a given case it is capable of amounting to an infringement of the plaintiff's copyright. ... **[614]** ...

The conclusion at which I arrive on this part of the case is that subconscious copying is a possibility which, if it occurs, may amount to an infringement of copyright. But in order to establish liability on this ground, it must be shown that the composer of the offending work was in fact familiar with the work alleged to have been copied. This view is, I think, not inconsistent with the submissions put forward by Mr Skone James. In the course of an argument which, for my part, I found convincing, he submitted that in considering whether there has been reproduction, so as to constitute an infringement within the Act, it is wholly irrelevant to inquire whether any copying has been conscious or subconscious. It is for this reason, he modestly suggested, that the textbooks are silent on the subject of subconscious copying. Mr Skone James presented his argument in four propositions which, if I understand him correctly, may be summarised as follows:

(1) In order to constitute reproduction within the meaning of the Act, there must be (a) a sufficient degree of objective similarity between the two works, and (b) some causal connection between the plaintiffs' and the defendants' work.

(2) It is quite irrelevant to inquire whether the defendant was or was not consciously aware of such causal connection.

(3) Where there is a substantial degree of objective similarity, this of itself will afford prima facie evidence to show that there is a causal connection between the plaintiffs' and the defendants' work; at least, it is a circumstance from which the inference may be drawn.

(4) The fact that the defendant denies that he consciously copied affords some evidence to rebut the inference of causal connection arising from the objective similarity, but is in no way conclusive.

If this is the right approach (as I think it is) it becomes a simple question of fact to decide whether the degree of objective similarity proved is sufficient, in all the circumstances of the particular case, to warrant the inference that there is a causal connection between the plaintiffs' and the defendants' work. This is the way in which, as it seems to me, Wilberforce J in the present case approached the question which he had to decide. In his judgment, he directed himself as follows:

███████ Francis Day & Hunter v Bron *continued*

"The final question to be resolved is whether the plaintiffs' work has been copied or reproduced, and it seems to me that the answer can only be reached by a judgment of fact upon a number of composite elements: The degree of familiarity (if proved at all, or properly inferred) with the plaintiffs' work, the character of [615] the work, particularly its qualities of impressing the mind and memory, the objective similarity of the defendants' work, the inherent probability that such similarity as is found could be due to coincidence, the existence of other influences upon the defendant composer, and not least the quality of the defendant composer's own evidence on the presence or otherwise in his mind of the plaintiffs' work."

In my judgment that was a proper direction, against which no criticism can fairly be brought. ... [616] ...

The devices used by the two composers for developing the phrase stated in the first bar are among the commonest tricks of composition and, I would add, exactly the sort to be expected from the composer of a popular song. I do not think, therefore, that in the circumstances of this case, the fact that de Angelis developed the opening phrase stated in the first bar by way of the same devises as were employed by the composer of Spanish Town can be taken as in any sense proof of copying. There is at least an equal probability that his choice of these devices was the result of coincidence.

In my judgment, no sufficient reason has been shown for interfering with Wilberforce J's decision, and I would, accordingly, dismiss the appeal.

DIPLOCK J: [622] This appeal seems to me to turn entirely upon a question of fact: was the judge entitled, notwithstanding the similarities between the melodies of the plaintiffs' song In a Little Spanish Town and the defendants' song Why, to refuse to infer that the composer of the latter work copied it from the former work? ...

First, as to the law; and for this purpose I will assume that it is established that the composer of Why did in fact use his recollection of "a substantial part of" the melody of In a Little Spanish Town as the model for his own composition, although he was unaware that he was doing so, and genuinely thought that Why was his own independent creation. The word "to copy" is not used at all in the *Copyright Act 1956*, nor was it in the *Copyright Act 1911*. Nevertheless, it is well established that to constitute infringement of copyright in any literary, dramatic or musical work, there must be present two elements: first, there must be sufficient objective similarity between the infringing work and the copyright work, or a substantial part thereof, for the former to be properly described, not necessarily as identical with, but as a reproduction or adaptation of the latter; secondly, the copyright work must be the source from which the infringing work is derived.

[627] ... The degree of objective similarity is, of course, not merely important, indeed essential, in proving the first element in infringement, namely, that the defendant's work can properly be described as a reproduction or adaptation of the copyright work; it is also very cogent material from which to draw the inference that the defendant has in fact copied, whether consciously or unconsciously, the copyright work. But it is not the only material. Even complete identity of the two works may not be conclusive evidence of copying, for it may be proved that it was impossible for the author of the alleged infringing work to have had access to the copyright work. And, once you have eliminated the impossible (namely, copying), that which remains (namely, coincidence) however improbable, is the truth; I quote inaccurately, but not unconsciously, from Sherlock Holmes.

No useful purpose can thus be served by seeking to classify degrees of similarity into categories which must be taken to be sufficient to prove unconscious copying where access to the copyright work by the author of the alleged infringing work is proved (1) as a certainty;

■■■■■ Francis Day & Hunter v Bron *continued*

(2) as a probability; (3) as a possibility, and (4) as an impossibility. That is not how questions of fact are decided in courts of law, or anywhere else.

[628] The answer, as Wilberforce J said at the conclusion of an impeccable summary of the evidence, "can only be reached by a judgment of fact upon a number of composite elements". Those elements on which the judge directed himself have already been read by my Lord, and I need not repeat them.

I agree it is impossible for this court, which has not heard the evidence or seen the witnesses, to say that Wilberforce J came to a wrong conclusion of fact.

Appeal dismissed.

Notes

[6.55] *Francis Day* was the only relevant authority in *EMI Music Publishing Ltd v Papathanasiou* [1993] EMLR 306, where the defendant, Vangelis, the composer of "Chariots of Fire" (the theme for a successful film of the same name), was alleged to have reproduced a substantial part of the plaintiff's earlier composed tune "City of Violets". The trial judge accepted the defendant's testimony that he did not copy the earlier tune; the appeal was on the basis that subconscious copying had occurred. Although there were some similarities between the two works, they were not similar enough to convince the judge that copying had occurred, conscious or otherwise. Furthermore, the similarities could be explained by the use of certain musical "commonplaces" or features often found in popular music.

In assessing reproduction for the purposes of finding copyright infringement, establishing similarity is only the first step, the next being the issue of access by the defendant to the work. As *Francis Day* makes clear, and is also the case in the US:

> "[B]ecause of the difficulties in proving copyright infringement by direct evidence, the law has established a burden shifting mechanism whereby plaintiffs can establish a prima facie case of infringement by showing possession of a valid copyright, the defendant's access to the plaintiff's work, and substantial similarity between the plaintiff's and defendant's works": *William L Dawson v Hinshaw Music Inc* (1990) 18 IPR 256 at 257 per Murnaghan J.

It is not always easy to distinguish between the first inquiry and the second. The question of whether something has been reproduced is easier to answer where there is a strong degree of similarity between the copyright work and the alleged infringing copy.

■ Indirect reproduction

[6.60] A work may be reproduced by copying a copy. Dolls and brooches were held to be reproductions in a material form of drawings of "that glaucomatous salt 'Popeye' ... and not the less so because they were not copied directly from any sketch of the plaintiffs, but from a reproduction in material form derived directly or indirectly from the original work": *King Features Syndicate Inc v O & M Keeman Ltd* [1941] AC 417 at 419. (Note that breach of copyright would no longer be relevant on the facts of this case due to the operation of *Copyright Act 1968* (Cth), s 77.) Thus, a dress copied from another dress may infringe copyright in a sketch of the garment even if the infringer has never seen the artistic work allegedly infringed: *Burke & Margot Burke Ltd v Spicers Dress Design* [1936] Ch 400; *Shanton*

Apparel Ltd v Thornton Hall Manufacturing Ltd (1989) 17 IPR 311. Similarly, building a boat copied from a model which is a reproduction of plans for the boat will infringe copyright in those plans: *Dorling v Honnor Marine* [1965] Ch 1.

▰▰▰▰▰ Frank M Winstone (Merchants) v Plix Products ▰▰▰▰▰

[6.65] *Frank M Winstone (Merchants) Ltd v Plix Products Ltd* (1985) 5 IPR 156 Court of Appeal of New Zealand

COOKE, RICHARDSON and SOMERS JJ: **[157]** This is a copyright and passing off case which produced in the High Court a three-week trial and (understandably) an 87-page judgment but in the end falls to be determined, we think, by quite simple application of basic principles. The defendants, whom it is convenient to refer to collectively as Lily, appeal from a judgment of Prichard J granting to the plaintiff, Plix, against them an injunction, an inquiry as to damages and an order for the delivery up or destruction of infringing copies.

During the years 1975 to 1977 Plix by its employees evolved designs for and made a range of containers intended for carrying kiwifruit, primarily for the dramatically increasing New Zealand export trade. They are known as pocket packs. They fit into wooden or cardboard trays which are stacked one above the other. On the appeal it has been accepted by Lily that Plix has copyright in the drawings, patterns, moulds and kiwifruit pocket packs for each of the eight counts in the Plix range. The count is the number of fruit held in each pack. The Plix range was successful. As a result the New Zealand Kiwifruit Authority and the New Zealand Kiwifruit Exporters Association laid down respectively specifications and instructions framed on and derived from the Plix range. These applied from the beginning of the 1982 season.

The defendant, Frank M Winstone (Merchants) Ltd, a plastics manufacturer, wished to move into the kiwifruit pocket pack market but was aware of the risk of infringing copyright claimed by Plix. It instructed a former employee, Mr Miller, who had never to his recollection seen a kiwifruit pocket pack, to design a range for Lily. He was furnished with a quantity of ungraded kiwifruit and copies of the Authority's specifications and the Association's instructions. He was told that he must work on his own without discussion with any person who had knowledge of kiwifruit pocket packs, and that he should on no account look at any existing pocket packs.

Working in this way for a period of about 260 hours spread over some six months, Mr Miller designed such a range. Lily manufactured it from his drawings. The range and the individual packs are on any view very similar to the Plix equivalents, though there are some differences of detail. The similarity to the eye is increased by the adoption by Lily of the same **[158]** colour green, as has been used by Plix from the outset. So far the Lily range has been on the market on a trial basis only. In the action aimed in effect at preventing Lily's incursion into the market, Plix alleges breach of copyright and passing off. ... **[160]** ...

Indirect copying

Describing this as the threshold question, Mr Smellie contended that the judge was wrong in holding that indirect copying can be perpetrated through the medium of a verbal description of the copyright work. In developing his argument in this court counsel modified the argument that he had presented in the High Court on this topic by adopting a suggestion in a recently published (1984) work on *Intellectual Property* by Staniforth Ricketson, paras 9.30 and 9.31. The suggestion is made in the interests of manufacturers or traders who, the author says, often unknowingly use intermediate versions of copyright works. It is suggested that there should be no infringement if the medium worked from was generically different from the copyright work. As we understand Mr Smellie, he invites us to see the verbal specifications and instructions in this case as generically different from the drawings, patterns, moulds and packs in which he acknowledges copyright to subsist.

Mr Smellie argues that copyright has already been taken beyond the intention of the framers of the original legislation and that to treat indirect copying as an infringement in a case like the present would be a further extension and of a kind which should only be made by parliament. Mr Crew retorts that the suggested limitation is inconsistent with basic principle and would amount to an infringer's charter.

Two decisions of the English Court of Appeal were the subject of particular discussion in argument. In *Solar Thomson Engineering Co Ltd v Barton* [1977] RPC 537 it was held—we do not think that the passage was obiter, but that does not matter for our purposes—that instructions given by the defendant to his designer afforded a sufficient causal link to give the designer's version of a rubber ring the quality of an indirect reproduction of a sectional drawing of the plaintiff's ring. Buckley LJ's judgment that this was a breach of the plaintiff's copyright was applied here by Prichard J and Mr Smellie accepts that it did afford the judge considerable support. He argued, however, as Mr Ricketson does in his book that Solar Thomson is inconsistent with the earlier decision in *Purefoy Engineering Co Ltd v Sykes Boxall & Co Ltd* (1955) 72 RPC 89.

In *Purefoy* the plaintiff and the defendant made similar standard parts to be used by customers in the manufacture of jigs. In making and offering for sale such parts the defendant did not infringe the plaintiff's copyright. Each party issued a catalogue illustrating its range of products. The question, so far as the case is relevant to the present argument, was whether the defendant's catalogue could be treated as an indirect copy of the plaintiff's catalogue and hence as infringing the copyright in that [161] catalogue. It was held not. That decision seems readily understandable. The defendant's catalogue was in no sense derived from that of the plaintiff, for the latter merely followed the making of and described the plaintiff's range of parts. The parts were not made from the catalogue. The case is distinguishable from the present on that point; what is more important is that as a general proposition the concept of indirect copying is accepted in the judgment of Sir Raymond Evershed MR.

There can be no doubt that in principle a reproduction may be the result of indirect copying. We see no sound reason for introducing a generic limitation; and in this and other cases it could be most difficult to apply. The question must always be whether the work alleged to be an infringement can fairly be said to be a reproduction of the copyright work or of a substantial part of that work. If words alone enable a drawing to be reproduced, it seems to us that copyright in the drawing is infringed. It would be dangerous to hold otherwise. And if words alone were capable of enabling a copyright painting to be reproduced, we see insufficient reason for a different conclusion, although that precise point need not now be decided. The textbook already mentioned refers to the possibility of a painting, based on a copyright literary work, enabling a person seeing only the painting to reproduce the literary work. Such a case can safely be left until it ever arises, but again we would be disposed to answer it by the same principle.

In the present case the written words were sufficient to enable the defendants to copy at least a substantial part of each of the plaintiff's copyright designs. Accordingly we hold that infringement is established. ...

Appeal dismissed.

Notes

[6.70] Is the fact of an oral communication enough or does it have to be of a particular character so that the result is confined by the communication and not the result of independent creation based on an idea? See *Solar Thomson Engineering Co Ltd v Barton* [1977] RPC 537; *Gleeson v H R Denne* [1975] RPC 471 at 487.

It is submitted that the substance of this infringement action is accurately framed by Prichard J in *Plix Products Ltd v Frank M Winstone (Merchants) Ltd* (1984) 3 IPR 390 at 419:

> "[N]o-one can appropriate the forms or shapes evolved by the author in the process of giving expression to the basic idea. So he who seeks to make a product of the same description as that in which another owns copyright must tread with care. If he copies the details which properly belong to the expression, and not to the basic concept, he will infringe the copyright. ... Where the expression is ornate, complex or detailed, then he must keep his distance: the only product he can then make without infringing may bear little resemblance to the copyright work."

Indirect copying will be relevant in the area of manufacturing spare parts by reverse engineering, without having used the original work.

Copyright protection for drawings may be lost if those drawings are used as blueprints for mass-produced items. See s 77 *Copyright Act* 1968 (Cth).

PERFORMING A WORK IN PUBLIC

[6.75] Literary, dramatic or musical works will have copyright infringed if they are performed in public. See ss 27, 28, 31(1)(a)(iii) and 39.

■ "Performance" has been strictly interpreted

APRA v Tolbush

[6.80] *Australasian Performing Right Association v Tolbush* (1985) 62 ALR 521 Supreme Court of Queensland

[A representative of APRA heard songs (for which APRA held performing rights) being played over car radios being displayed for sale in the first defendant's car accessory shops. The second defendant, a director of the shops, refused to apply for a licence from APRA, arguing (inter alia) that the works were not being "performed".]

DE JERSEY J: **[522]** On 3 April 1984 a representative of the plaintiff wrote to the second defendant asserting that the playing of radios and tapes in his retail outlets involved breach of the plaintiff's copyright, and seeking payment of a licence fee. The second defendant did not apply for a licence, and on 12 June 1984 confirmed that he did not intend to do so. The next day, the plaintiff's representative visited the first defendant's shop at the Brookside Shopping Centre. A car radio was playing from a display stand. The songs I've Been to Bali Too and Rain were heard. The plaintiff has copyright in those songs. On the same day, the representative visited the first defendant's Margate store, where he heard the song Cry playing from a car radio in similar circumstances. The plaintiff also owns the copyright in that. On 11 September 1984 the plaintiff's solicitors wrote to the directors of the first defendant complaining about breaches of copyright, and again raising the matter of a licence. The defendant's solicitors replied on 18 September 1984 denying any breach. By letter dated 26 November 1984 the plaintiff's solicitors threatened court proceedings. No proceedings were then instituted. Some months later, on 28 March 1985, the same representative visited the first defendant's Chermside store and heard Baby Don't Speak No Evil playing in similar circumstances again, one of the songs in which the plaintiff has copyright. On 12 September 1985 the plaintiff's solicitors wrote to the solicitors for the defendants, again threatening court proceedings. A writ was issued on 18 September 1985. On 4 October 1985 there was discussion between the solicitors about the legal basis for the plaintiff's claim, and the plaintiff's claims were confirmed by letter on 10 October. On 4 October 1985 the plaintiff's representative had heard A Beat for You playing in similar circumstances in the first defendant's Chermside store. The plaintiff has copyright in that song as well. ...

[523] An additional, perhaps rather subsidiary, submission made for the defendants was that any breach to date has been trivial, and should not therefore attract the court's intervention. I was referred to *Canterbury Park Racecourse Co Ltd v Hopkins* (1931) 49 WN (NSW) 27 at 29, citing *Copinger*. If a plaintiff's copyright has been breached, and that is likely to recur, I would ordinarily hesitate to describe the position as trivial. Especially so here where the plaintiff apparently provides a substantial service to local composers and publishers of music in the protection of copyright. As a matter of fact, I would not describe the situation here as "trivial". ...

[524] The defendant's major submission was that by having its radio sets, on display for sale in its shops, play songs copyright in which vested in the plaintiff, the first defendant could not be said to "perform" the songs (in public). To perform the works in public would amount to infringement of copyright: cf s 31(1)(a)(iii). Counsel for the defendants did not argue that those shops were not public places. The evidence was that the public had free access to them, and that some members of the public (although few) were within them at the times of the alleged offences. I have little hesitation concluding as a matter of fact, that any performance has taken place "in public". In my view, the character of the audience is the decisive factor. Consistently with the decision in *Performing Right Society Ltd v Harlequin Record Shop Ltd* [1979] 1 WLR 851, "a performance given to an audience consisting of the persons present in a shop which the public at large were permitted, indeed encouraged, to enter without payment or invitation with a view to increasing the shop owner's profit, could only be described as a performance in public": cf Copinger (12th ed), para. 573.

The term "perform" is not comprehensively defined in the Act. Section 27(1) does however say that a reference to performance should be read as including a reference to "any mode of ... aural presentation, whether the presentation is by the operation of wireless telegraphy apparatus ... or by any other means". Now read literally, that would of course be amply wide to include what has occurred here. The decision of the Court of Appeal in *Performing Right Society Ltd v Hammonds Bradford Brewery Co* [1934] Ch 121 is strong authority if authority be needed that there has here been a performance within s 27(1), taken alone, in that the first defendant has utilised a "mode of ... aural presentation". But counsel for the defendants contends, in effect, that it is unlikely that copyright would have been intended to cover these situations, which he would describe as relatively innocuous. Of course, some situations are specifically excepted from the prohibition on performance other than by the copyright owner. There is, for example, an exception in relation to educational situations (s 28), covering amenities provided within hotels and the like (s 46), and of course domestic situations are excluded because of the reference in s 31(1)(a)(iii) to performance "in public". Counsel nevertheless would contend that unless read down, the extremely wide words of s 27(1) would give the copyright a scope which could never have been intended.

▬▬▬ APRA v Tolbush *continued*

He argued most forcefully that these situations could not amount to a "performance" by contrasting, in s 27, the references to "performance" with the references to "causing ... sounds to be heard". He submitted that in this case, there has been no performance merely a causing of sounds to be heard by means of the radio sets.

Of course, s 27(1) cannot be read alone, and the real question is whether the prima facie wide ambit of the reference to "any mode of ... aural presentation" should be restricted by the subsequent references in the section, arguably by way of contrast with the concept of "performance", to the situation of "causing ... sounds to be heard".

[525] The authorities offer no definitive assistance in resolving the point. I was referred to *Australian Performing Right Assn Ltd v Canterbury-Bankstown League Club Ltd* (1964) 5 FLR 415, but it concerned other points. I do note with some interest that in *Ernest Turner Electrical Instruments Ltd v Performing Right Society Ltd* [1943] 1 Ch 167, playing music over public address systems to a workforce in a factory, as "background music", was held to constitute a public performance of the relevant works, although it seems not to have been suggested in that case that there was not a "performance".

In *Performing Right Society Ltd v Hammonds Bradford Brewery Co*, Romer LJ said that (at 137) "a man performs a musical composition when he causes it to be heard". That of course is precisely what happened here. I note that *Copinger* (12th ed), para 597 suggests that the 1934 decision of the Court of Appeal in that case remains good authority, notwithstanding the subsequent inclusion in the 1956 English *Copyright Act* of similar separate references to "performance" and "causing sounds to be heard": cf the English s 48(5) and (6). Indeed, *Copinger* suggests a clear view, based on the English legislation comparable with the Australian legislation, that this sort of situation involves a "performance": cf for example para 584.

[526] ... On the material before me, the plaintiff owns copyright in "practically all copyright musical works in current use throughout Australia". At present, according to its records, the plaintiff has copyright in some two million individual musical compositions. In these circumstances, I am prepared to infer that there is a risk sufficient to warrant the granting of an injunction that ordinary radio broadcasts, over the radios on display in the stores, would result in the playing of songs in which the plaintiff owns copyright.

There will therefore be an injunction.

Note

[6.85] This is modified by *Copyright Act 1968* (Cth), s 28 when the work is being performed in the course of educational instruction. The infringer will not necessarily be the person (or group) which physically performs the work. Section 39 provides that a person permitting a place of public entertainment to be used for a public performance will be an infringer. See *Australasian Performing Right Association Ltd v Miles* (1961) 3 FLR 146; *Australasian Performing Right Association Ltd v Jain* (1990) 18 IPR 663.

▪ In public

[6.90] The concept "to the public" is an essential element of infringement where the use of copyright material takes the form of performance or transmission. The new right of "communication to the public" has only recently been introduced, but it is expected that the wide concept of "the public" developed by the courts will continue to be relevant. See *Telstra*

Corporation v APRA Ltd (1997) 38 IPR 294 (below). In *APRA v Commonwealth Bank of Australia* (1992) 25 IPR 157 the playing of a few seconds of music on a staff training tape was held to be a performance in public. Playing music in a record shop is also "in public" and is actionable, despite the fact that the purpose of the performance is to promote the sale of copyright material. See *Performing Right Society v Harlequin Record Shops* [1979] FSR 233; *Rank Film Production v Colin S Dodds* [1983] 2 NSWLR 553.

Telstra v APRA

[6.95] *Telstra Corporation Ltd v Australasian Performing Right Association* (1997) 38 IPR 294 High Court of Australia

DAWSON AND GAUDRON JJ: **[302]** The concept of the copyright owner's public was developed in a series of cases which, however, were concerned with the distinction between a performance in public and a private or domestic performance. Section 31(1)(a)(iii) speaks of the right to perform a work "in public", but the definition of "broadcast", with which we are concerned, speaks of transmission "to the public". If anything, the use of the words "to the

public" conveys a broader concept than the use of the words "in public" since it makes clear that the place where the relevant communication occurs is irrelevant. That is to say, there can be a communication to individual members of the public in a private or domestic setting which is nevertheless a communication to the public. A broadcast by a radio station is just such a communication.

A performance or broadcast to the world at large is obviously a performance or broadcast to the public. But the situation becomes a little more difficult in the case of a performance or broadcast to a limited class of persons. In that context, in considering what constitutes a performance in public, the cases recognise that the relationship of the audience to the owner of the copyright is significant in reaching a conclusion. It is from this that the notion of the copyright owner's public developed. In *Duck v Bates* Brett MR said:

> "[T]he representation must be other than domestic and private. There must be present
> sufficient part of the public who would go also to a performance licensed by the author
> as a commercial transaction; otherwise the place where the drama is represented will
> not be a 'place of dramatic entertainment' within the meaning of the statute."

In *Harms (Incorporated) and Chappell & Co v Martans Club* Lord Hanworth MR said:

> "In dealing with the tests which have been applied in the cases, it appears to me that
> one must apply one's mind to see whether there has been any injury to the author. Did
> what took place interfere with his proprietary rights? As to that, profit is a very
> important element."

The idea of the copyright owner's public first explicitly emerged in *Jennings v Stephens* where Greene LJ said:

> "The question may therefore be usefully approached by inquiring whether or not the
> act complained of as an infringement would, if done by the owner of the copyright
> himself, have been an exercise by him of the statutory right conferred upon him. In
> other words, the expression 'in public' must be considered in relation to the owner of
> the copyright. If the audience considered in relation to the owner of the copyright may
> properly be described as the owner's 'public' or part of his 'public', then in performing
> the work before that audience he would in my opinion be exercising the statutory

right conferred upon him; and any one who without his consent performed the work
before that audience would be infringing his copyright."

The view expressed by Greene LJ in *Jennings v Stephens* was repeated by him [303] in *Ernest
Turner Electrical Instruments Ltd v Performing Right Society Ltd* and was adopted by Luxmoore
and Goddard LJJ, the latter adding that the relevant question is: "Is the audience one which
the owner of the copyright could fairly consider a part of his public?" In *Performing Right
Society Ltd v Harlequin Record Shops Ltd* Browne-Wilkinson J also adopted the view of Greene
LJ, saying that it is important to see whether the performance is given to an audience for
performances to which the composer would expect to receive a fee, this being what he
understood Greene LJ to have meant by the copyright owner's public.

In this country, the concept of the copyright owner's public was adopted in *APRA v
Canterbury-Bankstown League Club Ltd* and *Rank Film Production Ltd v Colin S Dodds*. In the
latter case the playing of films transmitted by a video cassette recorder to television sets in
motel rooms was held to be "in public". Rath J observed:

> "In the present case the motel guest in his room may easily be envisaged as part of the
> copyright owner's public. It is not the restricted size of the audience, or the privacy of
> the surroundings, that is decisive on the issue; the critical matter is the presentation of
> the movie by the occupier of the motel to his guest in that capacity."

The distinction between what is "in public" and what is "in private" is of little assistance in
determining what is meant by transmission "to the public". The transmission may be to
individuals in private circumstances but nevertheless be to the public. Moreover, the fact that
at any one time the number of persons to whom the transmission is made may be small does
not mean that the transmission is not to the public. Nor does it matter that those persons in a
position to receive the transmission form only a part of the public, though it is no doubt
necessary that the facility be available to those members of the public who choose to avail
themselves of it. In *Rank Film Production Ltd v Colin S Dodds* the number of guests playing films
in their rooms may not have been large, but the motel was open to the paying public. Similarly,
those members of the public who choose to call a relevant number on their mobile telephone
may be relatively small, but the facility is available to members of the public generally.

What is important is the nature of the audience constituted by those who receive music
on hold. Lying behind the concept of the copyright owner's public is recognition of the fact
that where a work is performed in a commercial setting, the occasion is unlikely to be private
or domestic and the audience is more appropriately to be seen as a section of the public. It
is in a commercial setting that an unauthorised performance will ordinarily be to the
financial disadvantage of the owner's copyright in a work because it is in such a setting that
the owner is entitled to expect payment for the work's authorised performance. In this case
it is not so much the preparedness of the audience of music on hold to pay to hear the works
were it not for their unauthorised performance that is significant. That simple analysis
belongs to an age where communications were less technologically advanced and business
and marketing techniques were less [304] developed. Rather, it is the preparedness of those
who wish the music on hold to be played to bear the cost of the arrangement which provides
the key, for it reveals the commercial character of the broadcast and the commercial
deprivation suffered by the copyright owner. Callers on hold constitute the copyright
owner's public, not because they themselves would be prepared to pay to hear the music, but
because others are prepared to bear the cost of them having that facility. For the performance
of the music to that audience the copyright owner would expect to receive payment, even if
not from the members of the audience. For these reasons, we conclude that when the works

were transmitted to persons using mobile telephones when placed on hold, in each of the three situations revealed by the evidence, they were broadcast within the meaning of s 31(1)(a)(iv).

▰▰▰▰ Don't Stop The Music! ▰▰▰▰

[6.100] Australia, House of Representatives, Standing Committee on Legal and Constitutional Affairs, *Don't Stop the Music!*, A Report of the Inquiry into Copyright, Music and Small Business (June 1998)

Summary and recommendations
Chapter 2—The public performance right
6. Relevant to the inquiry is the right to perform a literary or musical work (or cause a sound recording to be heard) in public. These are separate rights which are set out in the *Copyright Act* 1968. Case law has established that music played in the presence of more than one person, other than in private or domestic circumstances, will generally amount to a public performance.

7. This interpretation of public performance is consistent with the international obligations which arise out of Australia's membership of the Berne Convention for the Protection of Literary and Artistic Works (the Berne Convention), International Convention for the Protection of Performers, Producers of Phonograms and Broadcasting Organisations (the Rome Convention) and the Agreement on Trade-Related Aspects of Intellectual Property Rights (TRIPs).

8. In Australia, the public performance right is administered by two separate collecting societies—the Australasian Performing Right Association (APRA) and the Phonographic Performance Company of Australia (PPCA). These collecting societies are non-profit organisations which collect royalties on behalf of their members, the copyright owners.

9. APRA administers rights which exist in musical and literary works. Its members are composers and publishers. It collects royalties for the use of recorded music played directly (for example music played on a CD or cassette player) as well as for the indirect playing of music (for example, music played on a radio or television).

10. The PPCA administers the copyright which exists in sound recordings. The right which exists in sound recordings is additional to that which exists in musical and literary works. It collects royalties for the use of directly played recorded music (for example, music played on a CD or cassette player). It does not collect royalties for the playing of music on a radio or television. This is because a provision in the *Copyright Act* exempts the playing of a sound recording via a broadcast in public from infringing copyright.

Chapter 3—Information provided to small business by copyright collecting societies
15. The Committee concludes that there is a high level of confusion and misunderstanding about the nature of the public performance right and the collecting societies which administer the right.

16. Information sent to small businesses:
- in the case of APRA, did not have a customer focus or take a business friendly approach;
- in some cases, failed to clearly explain the nature of copyright and of the obligations of small businesses to pay copyright royalties;

▬▬▬▬ Don't Stop The Music! *continued*

- in the case of APRA, failed to acknowledge that small businesses may be required to obtain licences from more than one collecting society;
- in the case of APRA, was highly legalistic and focused on compliance rather than explanation. The material seemed to be based on an underlying presumption that the business was using music, demanding that either a licence or exemption form be completed immediately, rather than making an initial inquiry about whether music was being used at all.

17. Many small business operators had been playing music for years without a licence and without the knowledge that a licence was required. A large proportion of these people had little or no knowledge of copyright before receiving correspondence demanding either the payment of money or the completion and return of an exemption form. In these circumstances, it is not surprising that many of those receiving the information thought that the licences were a hoax, or construed it to be threatening. A prudent organisation may have considered placing a greater emphasis on preliminary education and communication with industry bodies prior to sending out such demanding and compliance based correspondence.

Recommendation 1

The Committee recommends that the Australasian Performing Right Association and the Phonographic Performance Company of Australia, in consultation with the Council of Small Business Organisations of Australia and other relevant peak industry organisations develop an information campaign designed to educate the small business community about the law in relation to public performance of music and the obligations of those people who play music in public.

Chapter 4—Whether licences take sufficient account of the number of listeners
19. This chapter outlines the royalty licence schemes for the use of background music—the licences most relevant to small businesses. The problem was not so much one of cost. The fees, were not excessive. The issue was more one of principle. The fees were considered to be an unfair imposition because of the perceived "non-commercial" way in which music was being used and in light of the small numbers of people actually hearing the music. The chapter reviews a number of arguments put to the Committee by business representatives for various forms of exemption from paying licence fees.

20. APRA issues a blanket licence in return for an annual fee. This enables the licensee to play any music that is within APRA's repertoire. The annual fee for playing recorded music, is $55.59 with an additional 92c per extra speaker. For the use of a radio or television receiver, the fee is $37.09 per year with an additional 92c per extra speaker.

21. The PPCA also issues an annual licence. There are different tariffs for different types of premises. The fees are based on factors such as the size and seating capacity of the premises. The fees vary between about $45.00 and $105.00.

22. The Committee understands that APRA's flat rate annual licence fee for background music may lead to some anomalies, with different types of venues and uses of music not being taken into account. The Committee also notes that the PPCA takes a variety of factors into account when issuing a licence, such as floor space or, in the case of cafes and restaurants, seating capacity.

23. However, the Committee does not recommend that APRA should take into account the number of employees or the size of the premises into account when determining the appropriate licence fee. The Committee believes that this would make the licensing system more complicated and could increase the administrative burden on small business.

24. For many business people, the purpose for which the music was being used was as important an issue as the potential audience size. There was a perception amongst many

business operators that their use of music was not generating any profits or creating any commercial advantage—that the playing of music was incidental to their business. Most of those arguing this point were playing music (usually the radio) for the benefit of staff. In these cases the intended audience was so small and benefit so minimal that a fee should not be required.

25. The Committee notes that many businesses believed that licences should distinguish between music which is played for the purpose of entertaining customers and that which is being used for staff. The Committee understands the argument that music used for staff has a less direct commercial value to a business than music which is for the benefit of customers. However, determining the purpose for which music is being played is a highly subjective process. The Committee believes that to base a licence scheme exclusively on such a subjective factor would increase uncertainty and confusion amongst the business community and would be cumbersome to manage. This would place an unreasonably high administrative burden on APRA.

Chapter 5—Distinguishing between direct and indirect playing of music
34. One of the main issues during the inquiry was the perception amongst those who use music of a difference in the commercial value of using recorded music compared with music heard via radio or television broadcasts. Copyright owners believed that they should be paid for the public performance of their work, regardless of the means through which the music was heard. During the course of the inquiry, a number of options were put to the Committee about ways to limit the licensing of small businesses playing a radio for the benefit of employees. The three main options are examined in this chapter. These options can be distinguished from the general exemptions sought by some businesses which were explored in the previous chapter.

35. The principal focus of the concern and anger of small businesses was on having to pay a fee in order to listen to the radio. For a number of reasons, business people believed that music played on the radio was far less likely to make a commercial contribution to their businesses than using recorded music. It was put to the Committee that many businesses tune into talkback, news and sporting programs which have little or no music content. The radio was said to be a vital source of information to small businesses, particularly in times of emergency. Many business people were aware that musicians received royalties from radio stations. There was a firm belief that to require that an additional fee from businesses listening to a "free to air broadcast" was "double dipping".

36. On the other hand, copyright owners believe they should continue to receive royalties for the public performance of their work via radio and television. Attributing a lower value to the music because it was being played on the radio rather than a CD or tape was considered to be inconsistent with the principle of copyright and unjust to composers.

37. The Committee believes that there are compelling practical and philosophical arguments in favour of relaxing the licensing requirements for those listening to radio. The Committee considers that businesses playing a radio for the benefit of small groups of employees should be exempt from having to pay a licence fee. This is consistent with APRA's informal policy of not licensing certain common sense cases as discussed above. The Committee recognises the difficulties in making a subjective assessment of whether the music is being played for the benefit of staff or for the benefit of customers. However, the Committee believes that there are many situations where it would be clear that the radio was being used exclusively for the benefit of staff.

...

▬▬▬▬ Don't Stop The Music! *continued*

Recommendation 2

The Committee recommends that the Australasian Performing Right Association implement as soon as practicable after the release of this report a policy under which complimentary licences will be issued to small businesses causing public performances of copyright music in the following circumstances:

- the means of performance is by the use of a radio or television set; and
- the business employs fewer than 20 people; and
- the music is not intended to be heard by customers of the business or by the general public. That is, neither the radio or television set nor any speakers are located in an area that is accessible to customers or the general public and any performance inadvertently heard by customers or the general public is manifestly unintentional.

Note. APRA now issues a complimentary licence to businesses with fewer than 20 staff which play music by either radio or television for the enjoyment of employees, if the radio and television sets and speakers are not located in an area accessible to customers or the general public.

■ Paracopyright measures

[6.105] Electronic rights management (ERM) (also called digital rights management (DRM)), and technological protection measures (TPMs) can provide effective "self-help" mechanisms for owners keen to restrict access to works in the digital environment. However allowing owners to use technology to determine the practical scope of rights has the potential to upset the legislative copyright balance and interfere with the (otherwise) legitimate rights of users to access works.

The current provisions, drafted to address this compromise of interests, are found in *Copyright Act 1968 (Cth)*, Division 2A—Actions in relation to circumvention devices and electronic rights management information. The policy reasoning and politics behind them is discussed in *Stevens v Sony* below.

Under the Australia-US Free Trade Agreement, Article 17.4.7, parties to the agreement are required to create a liability scheme for certain activities relating to the circumvention of "effective technological measures". The Standing Committee on Legal and Constitutional Affairs "Inquiry into technological protection measures (tpm) exceptions" (2005) was established to consider whether the new liability scheme should include new exceptions to liability, in particular noting the activities of libraries, educational and research institutions, open source software developers and regional coding of digital technologies. Submissions to this inquiry closed before the High Court handed down its views on TPMs below.

What is a circumvention device?

▬▬▬▬▬▬▬▬▬▬ **Stevens v Sony** ▬▬▬▬▬▬▬▬▬▬

[6.110] *Stevens v Kabushiki Kaisha Sony Computer Entertainment* [2005] HCA 58 High Court of Australia

[1] GLEESON CJ, GUMMOW, HAYNE AND HEYDON JJ: With effect from 4 March 2001, the *Copyright Amendment (Digital Agenda) Act 2000* (Cth) ("the Amendment Act") made significant amendments to the *Copyright Act 1968* (Cth) ("the Act"). This appeal concerns a dispute as to the construction of the "circumvention device" provision ...

[5] This litigation turns upon the construction of provisions in the Amendment Act which expand neither the existing categories of copyright works and other subject-matter protected by the Act nor the categories of infringement. Rather, the legislation in question deals with "anti-spoiler devices" which would allow the side-stepping of technical barriers to copying.

Anti-spoiler devices

[6] There is considerable controversy in Australia and elsewhere concerning the proper scope of such legislation: Kell, Maurushat and Tacit, "Technical Protection Measures: Tilting at Copyright's Windmill" (2002-2003) 34 *Ottawa Law Review* 7. However, the task of the Court on this appeal is to construe the particular compromises reflected in the terms of the *Amendment Act*.

[7] The development of technical barriers to copying and the escalation of a struggle between those who design such barriers and those who devise means of surmounting them is not new. Professor Cornish writes (Cornish, *Intellectual Property: Omnipresent, Distracting, Irrelevant?* (2004) at 54):

> "Back in the 1970s and 1980s, the answer to analogue copying on photocopiers, cassette decks, and video recorders was pronounced to lie in the machines themselves: but the eternally springing hopes were often enough dashed. Every locked door seemed to produce a hacker with a jemmy. With the Internet, technical control remains the core objective, because it seems the *only* hope for preserving the copyright industries in something resembling their present form." (original emphasis) ...

[10] The *Amendment Act* inserted Div 2A (ss 116A-116D) in Pt V of the Act. Part V is headed "Remedies and offences". Division 2A is headed "Actions in relation to circumvention devices and electronic rights management information". The *Amendment Act* also introduced additions to the offence provisions contained in Div 5 (ss 132-133A) so as to create new offences for contravention of the new Div 2A. The *Amendment Act* further introduced new definitions into s 10 of the Act. The Act has been further amended on five occasions, the last set of changes being those made with effect from 1 January 2005 by the *US Free Trade Agreement Implementation Act 2004* (Cth) ("the 2004 Act"). This litigation is concerned with the statute in what is to be taken as its form at the date of commencement of the *Amendment Act*, 4 March 2001. ...

The facts

[19] The present respondents (collectively described as "Sony") produced and sold computer games on CD-ROMs for use with PlayStation consoles. Sony as owner or exclusive licensee controls the copyright in the computer programs (as literary works under the Act) and in the cinematograph films (as subject-matter other than works) embodied in the CD-ROMs for the games.

[20] On two occasions after the commencement of the *Amendment Act*, the appellant, Mr Stevens, sold unauthorised copies of PlayStation games. The games were titled "Croc 2", "Medi Evil", "Motor Races World Tour" and "Porsche 2000". Mr Stevens was not sued for any acts on his part that might have constituted infringements of Sony copyright in any computer program or cinematograph film. Nor were the makers of the unauthorised copies, whether Mr Stevens or others.

[21] However, the PlayStation software contained access restrictions described as follows by Sackville J in his judgment at first instance: *Kabushiki Kaisha Sony Computer Entertainment v Stevens* (2002) 200 ALR 55 at 65:

Stevens v Sony *continued*

> "The PlayStation software incorporates an access code, or a number of encrypted sectors of data that cannot be reproduced by conventional CD recording or copying devices (usually referred to as 'burning' mechanisms). The access code is stored on an encrypted portion of the CD-ROM and essentially consists of a string of characters. This string must be read by the boot ROM located within the PlayStation console if the particular game is to be played. The boot ROM recognises whether there is an access code and specifically what kind of access code it is. The access code is inaccessible to standard CD-ROM 'burners' or standard CD replication manufacturing parts."

Sony contended that, in this state of affairs, a "technological protection measure" could be said to exist in the boot ROM, or the access code in the PlayStation software, or the two in their combined operation.

[22] In addition to supplying the unauthorised copies, Mr Stevens on three occasions sold and installed "mod chips" into PlayStation consoles. The unauthorised copies could not be played upon an "unchipped" or unmodified PlayStation console because they did not have the requisite access code. However, these copies could be played upon the "chipped" PlayStation consoles which Mr Stevens had modified.

[23] By proceedings instituted in the Federal Court, Sony alleged that contrary to s 116A (inserted in the Act by the *Amendment Act*) Mr Stevens without permission had knowingly sold or distributed a "circumvention device" which was capable of circumventing or facilitating the circumvention of a "technological protection measure" which protected Sony's copyright in literary works (computer programs) and cinematograph films.

...

The litigation

[25] The Full Court enjoined Mr Stevens from selling circumvention devices for use in association with those computer consoles and CD-ROMs in contravention of s 116A of the Act. It remitted the matter to the primary judge for determination of the claims for damages pursuant to s 116D of the Act.

[26] Against those orders, Mr Stevens appeals by special leave to this Court. By Notice of Contention, Sony seeks to re-agitate the issues on which it did not succeed in the Full Court. At first instance, Sackville J had permitted the Australian Competition and Consumer Commission ("the ACCC") to appear as amicus curiae and to press for a construction of the relevant provisions of the Act at odds with that favoured by Sony: *Kabushiki Kaisha Sony Computer Entertainment v Stevens* (2001) 116 FCR 490. An application to this Court by the ACCC was withdrawn. However, the Court granted leave to appear as amici curiae to the Australian Digital Alliance Ltd and the Australian Libraries Copyright Committee.

Section 116A

[27] Section 116A(1), so far as immediately material, states that the section applies if "a work or other subject-matter is protected by a technological protection measure" and a person without the permission of the owner or exclusive licensee thereof makes, sells or offers for sale or hire or otherwise promotes or advertises "a circumvention device" which is capable of circumventing, or facilitating the circumvention of, that "technological protection measure". Making and importing are also proscribed by s 116A(1), but the mere use of a circumvention device is not proscribed. Supplying, making and importing are excused if "for use" for a "permitted purpose".

[28] The terms "circumvention device" and "technological protection measure" are defined in s 10(1) (the definitions shown in these reasons are in their form as amended with effect from 4 March 2001 by the *Copyright Amendment (Parallel Importation) Act 2003* (Cth), s 2, Sched 3, Items 1, 3). Save as to what follows, it was not disputed that Mr Stevens had sold "circumvention devices". The definition is as follows:

▓▓▓▓▓▓ Stevens v Sony *continued*

"circumvention device means a device (including a computer program) having only a limited commercially significant purpose or use, or no such purpose or use, other than the circumvention, or facilitating the circumvention, of an [sic] technological protection measure."

[29] What was in issue was the existence of the "technological protection measure" identified in the concluding words of the definition of "circumvention device". It is upon the following definition of "technological protection measure" that the appeal by Mr Stevens turns. The definition states:

"technological protection measure means a device or product, or a component incorporated into a process, that is designed, in the ordinary course of its operation, to prevent or inhibit the infringement of copyright in a work or other subject-matter by either or both of the following means:

(a) by ensuring that access to the work or other subject matter is available solely by use of an access code or process (including decryption, unscrambling or other transformation of the work or other subject-matter) with the authority of the owner or exclusive licensee of the copyright;

(b) through a copy control mechanism."

...

Statutory construction

[33] There is force in the statement by one commentator: Weatherall, "On Technology Locks and the Proper Scope of Digital Copyright Laws—Sony in the High Court" (2004) 26 *Sydney Law Review* 613 at 637 :

"The definition of 'technological protection measure' is a compromise, which was neither as restrictive as some copyright users had hoped, nor as broad as copyright owners sought—and parts of the legislative history are opaque."

[34] The result is that in the present case to fix upon one "purpose" and then bend the terms of the definition to that end risks "picking a winner" where the legislature has stayed its hand from doing so. In the selection of a sole or dominant "purpose", there is a risk of unintended consequences, particularly where, as here, the substratum of the legislation is constantly changing technologies.

"Technological protection measure"

[35] These considerations indicate the approach to construction evident in the reasoning of Sackville J, with its close attention to text and structure. Of the expression "technological protection measure", his Honour said (at 80):

"The definition has a number of elements, as follows:

• a device or product, or a component incorporated into a process that is designed

• in the ordinary course of its operation

• to prevent or inhibit the infringement of copyright in a work [or other subject-matter]

• by either or both of two particular means.

The two particular means of preventing or inhibiting the infringement of copyright are these:

• ensuring that access to the work is available solely by use of an access code or process with the authority of the owner or licensee; or

• a copy control mechanism."

[36] Sackville J did not accept the construction advanced by Sony which was to be accepted in the Full Court and which is urged again on this appeal. His Honour rejected the proposition that: (at 81):

"the definition is concerned with devices or products that do not, by their operations, prevent or curtail specific acts infringing or facilitating the infringement of copyright in a work [or other subject-matter], but merely have a general deterrent or discouraging effect on those who might be contemplating infringing copyright in a class of works, for example by making unlawful copies of a CD-ROM".

Rather, Sackville J said (at 80):

"It can be seen that the focus of the definition, as the expression 'technological protection measure' itself implies, is on a technological device or product that is designed to bring about a specified result (preventing or inhibiting the infringement of copyright in a work) by particular means. Each of the specified means involves a technological process or mechanism. The means identified in par (a) is an access code or process that must be used to gain access to the work. The means identified in par (b) is a 'copy control mechanism'."

[37] That latter expression is not defined in the legislation. However, the distinction between devices or means designed to prevent any copying at all and those designed to impair the quality of copies that are made has a provenance in s 296 of the 1988 UK Act... Consistently with this and with reference to the Australian legislative history, Sackville J concluded that the phrase "copy control mechanism" encompassed a mechanism restricting the extent (and, one might add, the effectiveness) of copying of a work that otherwise could be undertaken by someone with "access" to the copyright material: (at 80).

[38] Sackville J concluded that (at 81):

"a 'technological protection measure', as defined, must be a device or product which utilises technological means to deny a person access to a copyright work [or other subject-matter], or which limits a person's capacity to make copies of a work [or other subject-matter] to which access has been gained, and thereby 'physically' prevents or inhibits the person from undertaking acts which, if carried out, would or might infringe copyright in the work [or other subject-matter]".

That construction should be accepted.

[39] It is important to understand that the reference to the undertaking of acts which, if carried out, would or might infringe, is consistent with the fundamental notion that copyright comprises the exclusive right to do any one or more of "acts" primarily identified in ss 31 and 85-88 of the Act. The definition of "technological protection measure" proceeds on the footing that, but for the operation of the device or product or component incorporated into a process, there would be no technological or mechanical barrier to "access" the copyright material or to make copies of the work after "access" has been gained. The term "access" as used in the definition is not further explained in the legislation. It may be taken to identify placement of the addressee in a position where, but for the "technological protection measure", the addressee would be in a position to infringe.

[40] This construction of the definition is assisted by a consideration of the "permitted purpose" qualifications to the prohibitions imposed by s 116A(1). First, s 116A(3) provides that, in certain circumstances, the section does not apply in relation to the supply of a circumvention device "to a person for use for a permitted purpose". The term "supply" means selling the circumvention device, letting it for hire, distributing it or making it available online (s 116A(8)). Secondly, s 116A(4) states that the section in certain circumstances does not apply in relation to the making or importing of a circumvention device "for use only for a permitted purpose".

[44] There are three other considerations which support Sackville J's construction of the definition.

▬▬▬▬ Stevens v Sony *continued*

[45] The first is that, in choosing between a relatively broad and a relatively narrow construction of legislation, it is desirable to take into account its penal character. The present litigation does not arise from the institution of criminal proceedings under the offence provisions now contained particularly in s 132 of the Act. However, a person who makes or sells a circumvention device (s 132(5B)) is liable to imprisonment for not more than five years (s 132(6A)). An appreciation of the heavy hand that may be brought down by the criminal law suggests the need for caution in accepting any loose, albeit "practical", construction of Div 2A itself.

[46] The second consideration is that the true construction of the definition of "techno-logical protection measure" must be one which catches devices which prevent infringement. The Sony device does not prevent infringement. Nor do many of the devices falling within the definition advanced by Sony. The Sony device and devices like it prevent access only after any infringement has taken place.

[47] The third consideration is that in construing a definition which focuses on a device designed to prevent or inhibit the infringement of copyright, it is important to avoid an overbroad construction which would extend the copyright monopoly rather than match it. A defect in the construction rejected by Sackville J is that its effect is to extend the copyright monopoly by including within the definition not only technological protection measures which stop the infringement of copyright, but also devices which prevent the carrying out of conduct which does not infringe copyright and is not otherwise unlawful. One example of that conduct is playing in Australia a program lawfully acquired in the United States. It was common ground in the courts below and in argument in this Court that this act would not of itself have been an infringement: (2002) (at 75, 79-80).

...

[49] ...if one thing appears from a consideration of the Australian and international materials it is that in Australia there was a reluctance to give to copyright owners a form of broad 'access control". Indeed, this reluctance is manifest in the inclusion in the definition of "technological protection measure" of the concept of prevention or inhibition of infringe-ment.

[50] This outcome dissatisfied copyright owners. Yet other "stakeholders" with their own interests did not achieve all they may have desired. To those, such as the ACCC, concerned with the operation of restrictive trade practices law, it was significant that the access code for Sony products differed in various markets, so that a PlayStation game purchased in the United States could not be played on an unmodified PlayStation console purchased in Australia: (2002) (at 65). Users of copyright material such as those represented in the amici curiae in this Court were dissatisfied by the exclusion from the permitted purpose provisions of the general provisions protecting fair dealing. Other users were dissatisfied by the failure to include in the permitted purpose provisions the specific protection given by s 47C for back-up copies of computer programs. All of these considerations suggest no particular support for the "broad" approach to the definition of "technological protection measure".

...

McHUGH J:

Construing the legislation

[124] In determining issues of statutory construction, the text of the relevant statutory provision must be evaluated not only by reference to its literal meaning but also by reference to the purpose and context of the provision. And context is not limited to the text of the rest of the statute. For purposes of statutory construction, context includes the state of the law

▬▬▬▬ Stevens v Sony *continued*

when the statute was enacted, its known or supposed defects at that time and the history of the relevant branch of the law, including the legislative history of the statute itself...

[126] Much modern legislation regulating an industry reflects a compromise reached between, or forced upon, powerful and competing groups in the industry whose interests are likely to be enhanced or impaired by the legislation. In such cases, what emerges from the legislative process is frequently not a law motivated solely by the public interest. It reflects wholly or partly a compromise that is the product of intensive lobbying, directly or indirectly, of Ministers and parliamentarians by groups in the industry seeking to achieve the maximum protection or advancement of their respective interests. The only purpose of the legislation or its particular provisions is to give effect to the compromise. To attempt to construe the meaning of particular provisions of such legislation not solely by reference to its text but by reference to some supposed purpose of the legislation invites error.

[129] Against this background, the best—and certainly the preferable—guide to the meaning of the relevant provisions is the text of those provisions. ...

[139] In my opinion, for the purpose of s 10(1), a device is a device that is "designed ... to ... inhibit" copyright if the device functions, "in the ordinary course of its operation", so as to make the doing of an act of copyright infringement—not impossible—but more difficult than it would be if the device did not operate.

[140] This interpretation does not render the term "inhibit" redundant because it applies to at least two categories of devices that do not have an absolute preventative effect on copyright infringement. Thus, there are protective devices that regulate a user's access, not to the work itself, but to the appliance through which works are accessed. For example, "device binding" is a measure through which the decryption key of a work is linked to the "unique identifier" of the computer of a person who is licensed to download and copy a work: Kerr, Maurushat and Tacit, "Technical Protection Measures: Tilting at Copyright's Windmill" (2002-2003) 34 *Ottawa Law Review* 7 at 16. The work may only be downloaded and saved (and thus, copied) onto a computer with this identifier. The fact that access to the work is available solely by use of a decryption key that is linked to the computer's identifier does not make it impossible for another user of the same computer—who has not been licensed to reproduce the material—to download and save the work. Nonetheless, in disenabling the access of all other computers to the work, "device binding" mechanisms function to make it more difficult for users—who are not licensed to download the work—to have access to an appliance that will enable the copying and infringement of copyright in the work. In this way, "device binding" inhibits, but does not prevent, copyright infringement.

[141] Other devices are designed to make it impossible to do an act of copyright infringement by a particular method or methods, but are ineffective to prevent the doing of the same infringing act by other, more complex, methods. Online access controls are an example. They are measures that decrypt a work that is delivered to the computer through the Internet— "streamed"—when it is delivered to the computer. The work is then immediately re-encrypted, so as to enable only a small portion of the work to be decrypted at any given time. The result is that the work cannot be digitally copied onto the computer to which it is being delivered: Kerr, Maurushat and Tacit, "Technical Protection Measures: Tilting at Copyright's Windmill" (2002-2003) 34 *Ottawa Law Review* 7 at 16. However, the re-encryption of the work, after it has been delivered and played, does not restrain the user from reproducing the work on other recording devices while the work is being played. In making it impossible to do an act of copyright infringement (ie reproduction) using one method, but not making it impossible to do the same act of copyright infringement using a more tedious method, online access controls make it more difficult to reproduce the work.

▰▰▰▰▰▰ Stevens v Sony *continued*

[142] Acts of copyright infringement include not only acts that are comprised in the copyright but also acts of dealing with infringing copies of copyrighted works (for example by selling or importing). As French J observed: (2003) (at 40), it may be that the function of a protective device will rarely make it impossible, or even more difficult, to engage in the latter category of acts. But this is not an illogical result that ought to compel an alternate reading of the statutory definition....the s 10(1) definition of "technological protection measure" ought to be read according to its ordinary meaning and not artificially stretched to include within its scope acts of copyright infringement that are not comprised in the copyright.

[143] On the interpretation of the s 10(1) definition of "technological protection measure" that I favour, Sony's device of the Boot ROM chip and the access code or either of them does not constitute a "technological protection measure" by virtue of the device's deterrent effect on the copying of computer games. That is because the console's inability to load the software from an infringing copy does not make it impossible or more physically difficult to make an infringing copy.

KIRBY J:

[168] Conformably with authority (including the *Acts Interpretation Act 1901* (Cth), ss 15A and 15AB), this Court must identify, and explain, the interpretation that it prefers. It must do so by reference to established sources and tools: by close examination of the statutory text, its language, context and structure; by identification of the purposes suggested by that text (*Re Bolton; Ex parte Beane* (1987) 162 CLR 514 at 517-518); and by the use of the statutory history, including available background materials that cast light on the meaning of the text: *Palgo Holdings Pty Ltd v Gowans* (2005) 79 ALJR 1121 at 1129; 215 ALR 253 at 262-264. Yet, in construing the *Copyright Act* there are peculiar difficulties that, in my view, may be traced, ultimately, to the constitutional head of power (Constitution, s 51(xviii)) by which the Federal Parliament enjoys the legislative authority to make laws with respect to "copyrights, patents of inventions and designs, and trade marks". That power is granted in a constitutional and legal setting in which competing legal interests must also be upheld by the law, including, generally, free expression and the normal interest of property owners in the undisturbed enjoyment of their property: Constitution, s 51(xxxi). See *Pacific Film Laboratories Pty Ltd v Federal Commissioner of Taxation* (1970) 121 CLR 154; *Australian Tape Manufacturers Association Ltd v The Commonwealth* (1993) 176 CLR 480.

[169] "Copyright", it has been rightly declared, "is one of the great balancing acts of the law. Many balls are in play and many interests are in conflict": Ricketson, "Copyright", in Blackshield, Coper and Williams (eds), *The Oxford Companion to the High Court of Australia* (2001) 152 at 154. To the traditional problems of resolving such conflicts must be added, in the present age, the difficulties of applying the conventional model of copyright law to subject matters for which that model is not wholly appropriate; adjusting it to the "implications of the online environment"; and adapting it to international pressures that may reflect economic and legal interests that do not fit comfortably into the local constitutional and legal environment. "The dance proceeds", as Professor Ricketson has observed: Ricketson, "Copyright", in Blackshield, Coper and Williams (eds), *The Oxford Companion to the High Court of Australia* (2001) 152 at 154; but the multiplicity of participants and interests now involved in its rhythms inevitably affect the contemporary judicial task of resolving contested questions of interpretation of the *Copyright Act*.

[170] Where, as both sides effectively conceded in this appeal, alternative views are available as to the meaning of the disputed provisions of the *Copyright Act*, the resolution of the task of interpretation is bound to lie (even more than in most cases) in considerations additional to those that can be extracted directly from the statutory text. Although I agree in

■■■■■ Stevens v Sony *continued*

the conclusion stated in the reasons of Gleeson CJ, Gummow, Hayne and Heydon JJ ("the joint reasons") and of McHugh J as to the issues in, and outcome of, this appeal, it is to clarify and elaborate the range of considerations that affect my reasoning that I write separately.

[207]...Had it been the purpose of the Parliament, by the enactment of the *Digital Agenda Act*, to create a right to control access generally, it had the opportunity to say so. It even had overseas precedents upon which it could draw. The Australian Government was pressed to provide protection for all devices that "control access". This is evident in the definition of TPM suggested to the Australian Parliamentary Committee by the International Intellectual Property Alliance: the definition proposed by the International Intellectual Property Alliance was: "'effective technological protection measure' means any technology, device or component that, in the normal course of its operation, controls access to a protected work, sound recording, or other subject matter, or protects any copyright as provided by this Act": see International Intellectual Property Alliance submission to House of Representatives Standing Committee on Legal and Constitutional Affairs, 7 October 1999 at 5. Such a definition would effectively have mirrored the provision adopted by the Congress of the United States in the *Digital Millennium Copyright Act* of 1998, 17 USC §1201. By the time the Australian definition of TPM was enacted, the United States Act had been in force for two years. Nevertheless, the propounded definition of wider ambit was not accepted. Instead, in Australia, the Parliament chose to focus its definition upon protection from infringement of copyright as such.

[208] The preference inherent in the Australian Act has been viewed as one which "favours the use of protected works" (Kerr, Maurushat and Tacit, "Technological Protection Measures: Tilting at Copyright's Windmill" (2002-2003) 34 *Ottawa Law Review* 7 at 58. See also Linsday, "A Comparative Analysis of the Law relating to Technological Protection Measures" (2002) 20 *Copyright Reporter* 118 at 124), by limiting the operation of TPMs in terms of control over infringement of copyright rather than a potentially broader control over access. When the competing legislation of other jurisdictions, giving effect to the relevant international treaties, is contrasted, it appears clear that the distinctive statutory formula adopted in Australia was a deliberate one. It was less protective of copyright than the legal regimes adopted in the United States, the United Kingdom and elsewhere: *Digital Millennium Copyright Act* of 1998 17 USC §1201; *Copyright and Related Rights Regulations 2003* (UK), reg 24 amending s 296 and inserting ss 296ZA, 296ZB, 296ZD and 296ZF. In the face of such a formula, accepted after a long inquiry and contrary submissions made by affected interest groups, the safer course for this Court, in giving meaning to the definition of TPM in s 10(1) of the *Copyright Act*, is to stick closely to the more restricted language of the Act. This approach has a textual foundation. It lies in the meaning to be attributed to the words "designed" and "inhibit" appearing in the definition of TPM in the *Copyright Act*: cf reasons of McHugh J at [133]-[138].

[209] If the definition of TPM were to be read expansively, so as to include devices designed to prevent access to material, with no inherent or necessary link to the prevention or inhibition of infringement of copyright, this would expand the ambit of the definition beyond that naturally indicated by the text of s 10(1) of the *Copyright Act*. It could interfere with the fair dealing provisions in Div 3 of Pt III of the *Copyright Act* and thereby alter the balance struck by the law in this country.

[210] As the amici submitted to this Court, Sony's interpretation of s 116A would enable rights holders effectively to opt out of the fair dealing scheme of the Act. This would have the potential consequence of restricting access to a broad range of material and of impeding lawful dealings as permitted by Div 3 of Pt III of the *Copyright Act*. The inevitable result would be the substitution of contractual obligations inter partes for the provisions contained in the *Copyright Act*—the relevant public law. Potentially, this could have serious consequences for the operation of the fair dealing provisions of that Act. This is not an interpretation that

███████ Stevens v Sony *continued*

should be readily accepted. Especially so where the language of the definition of TPM presents the perfectly acceptable, apparently intentional, and more confined construction expounded by the primary judge: See generally Dellit and Kendall, "Technological Protection Measures and Fair Dealing: Maintaining the Balance Between Copyright Protection and the Right to Access Information" (2003) 4 *Digital Technology Law Journal* 1 at 51-53; Vinje, "Copyright Imperilled?" (1999) *European Intellectual Property Review* 192 at 198-200; Gasaway, "The New Access Right and its Impact on Libraries and Library Users" (2003) 10 *Journal of Intellectual Property Law* 269 at 298-299.

[211] Avoiding over-wide operation: There is an additional reason for preferring the more confined interpretation of the definition of TPM in the *Copyright Act*. This is because the wider view urged by Sony would have the result of affording Sony, and other rights holders in its position, a de facto control over access to copyrighted works or materials that would permit the achievement of economic ends additional to, but different from, those ordinarily protected by copyright law. If the present case is taken as an illustration, Sony's interpretation would permit the effective enforcement, through a technological measure, of the division of global markets designated by Sony. It would have the effect of imposing, at least potentially, differential price structures in those separate markets. In short, it would give Sony broader powers over pricing of its products in its self-designated markets than the *Copyright Act* in Australia would ordinarily allow: Weatherall at 624-625. This consideration gave rise to arguments of inconsistency with the provisions of the *Copyright Act* concerning parallel importation. It is unnecessary to consider these.

[213] Upholding fundamental rights: A further reason, not wholly unconnected with the last, is relevant to the choice to be made in selecting between the competing interpretations of the definition of TPM. The interpretation favoured by the primary judge confines that definition and hence the operation of s 116A of the *Copyright Act* and the civil remedies which that section provides. The Full Court's broader view gives an undifferentiated operation to the provisions of s 116A that clearly impinges on what would otherwise be the legal rights of the owner of a Sony CD ROM and PlayStation console to copy the same for limited purposes and to use and modify the same for legitimate reasons, as in the pursuit of that person's ordinary rights as the owner of chattels.

[214] Take, for example, the case earlier mentioned of a purchaser of a Sony CD ROM in Japan or the United States who found, on arrival in Australia, that he or she could not play the game on a Sony PlayStation console purchased in Australia. In the case postulated, there is no obvious copyright reason why the purchaser should not be entitled to copy the CD ROM and modify the console in such a way as to enjoy his or her lawfully acquired property without inhibition. Yet, on Sony's theory of the definition of TPM in s 10(1) of the *Copyright Act*, it is able to enforce its division of global markets by a device ostensibly limited to the protection of Sony against the infringement of its copyright.

[215] Ordinary principles of statutory construction, observed by this Court since its earliest days, have construed legislation, where there is doubt, to protect the fundamental rights of the individual: see Fitzgerald, "The Playstation Mod Chip: A Technological Guarantee of the Digital Consumer's Liberty or Copyright Menace/Circumvention Device?" (2005) 10 *Media and Arts Law Review* 85 at 95 citing such cases as *Potter v Minahan* (1908) 7 CLR 277 at 304; *Plaintiff S157/2002* (2003) 211 CLR 476 at 492. See also *Al-Kateb v Godwin* (2004) 78 ALJR 1099 at 1105, 1136 , 1144; 208 ALR 124 at 130, 173-174, 184; *Coleman v Power* (2004) 78 ALJR 1166 at 1199, 1212; 209 ALR 182 at 227, 245-246. The right of the individual to enjoy lawfully acquired private property (a CD ROM game or a PlayStation console purchased in another region of the world or possibly to make a backup copy of the CD ROM) would ordinarily be

a right inherent in Australian law upon the acquisition of such a chattel. This is a further reason why s 116A of the *Copyright Act* and the definition of TPM in s 10(1) of that Act should be read strictly. Doing so avoids an interpretation that would deprive the property owner of an incident of that person's ordinary legal rights.

[216] The provisions of the Australian Constitution affording the power to make laws with respect to copyright (Constitution, s 51(xviii). cf *MGM Studios* 73 USLW 4675 at 4688 (2005) per Breyer J) operate in a constitutional and legal setting (see for example Constitution, s 51(xxxi)) that normally upholds the rights of the individual to deal with his or her property as that individual thinks fit. In that setting, absent the provision of just terms, the individual is specifically entitled not to have such rights infringed by federal legislation in a way that amounts to an impermissible inhibition upon those rights constituting an acquisition. This is not the case in which to explore the limits that exist in the powers of the Australian Parliament, by legislation purporting to deal with the subject matter of copyright, to encumber the enjoyment of lawfully acquired chattel property in the supposed furtherance of the rights of copyright owners. However, limits there are: Lessig, *Code and Other Laws of Cyberspace* (1999) at 131, 133-134; Fitzgerald, "The Playstation Mod Chip: A Technological Guarantee of the Digital Consumer's Liberty or Copyright Menace/Circumvention Device?" (2005) 10 *Media and Arts Law Review* 85 at 96; cf *Grain Pool of Western Australia v The Commonwealth* (2000) 202 CLR 479 at 529-530, 531 fn 266.

[217] In *Wilson v Anderson* (2002) 213 CLR 401 at 457 [139] I said, in words to which I adhere, that fundamental rights will persist in the face of legislation said to be inconsistent with them "'unless there be a clear and plain intention' to extinguish such rights". These remarks were made in the context of a suggested extinguishment of rights ordinary to the ownership and possession of property. I added (at 457-458 [140]):

> "It is an old, wise and beneficial presumption, long obeyed, that to take away people's rights, Parliament must use clear language. The basic human right to own property and to be immune from arbitrary dispossession of property is one generally respected by Australian lawmakers. This fundamental rule attributes to the legislatures of Australia a respect for the rights of the people which those legislatures have normally observed, being themselves regularly accountable to the electors as envisaged by the Constitution. In some circumstances, at least in respect of federal legislation depriving people of established property rights, the presumption to which I have referred is reinforced by constitutional imperatives."

[218] To the extent that attempts are made to push the provisions of Australian copyright legislation beyond the legitimate purposes traditional to copyright protection at law, the Parliament risks losing its nexus to the constitutional source of power. That source postulates a balance of interests such as have traditionally been observed by copyright statutes, including the *Copyright Act*.

[219] In the present case, it is legitimate to say that, had it been the purpose of the Parliament to push the provisions of the *Copyright Act* attaching offences and sanctions to circumvention of TPMs in a way that deprived chattel owners of ordinary rights of ownership, such a provision would have been spelt out in unmistakable terms. In the definition of TPM in s 10(1) of the *Copyright Act*, such unmistakable language does not appear. This fact affords a further reason for preferring the more restricted interpretation that is compatible with the ordinary incidents of ownership of lawfully acquired chattels. ...

[223] In the Australian context, the inevitability of further legislation on the protection of technology with TPMs was made clear by reference to the provisions of, and some legislation already enacted for, the Australia-US Free Trade Agreement: Fitzgerald, "The

▰▰▰▰ Stevens v Sony *continued*

Playstation Mod Chip: A Technological Guarantee of the Digital Consumer's Liberty or Copyright Menace/Circumvention Device?" (2005) 10 *Media and Arts Law Review* 85 at 89 fn 18. As the author notes, Art 17.4.1 of the Australia-US Free Trade Agreement obliges Australia to enact laws giving copyright owners the right to prohibit all copies, in any manner or form, permanent or temporary. This change will be implemented under the *US Free Trade Agreement Implementation Act 2004* (Cth) which came into effect on 1 January 2005. That Act includes amendments to the definition of "material form" in s 10(1) of the *Copyright Act* and creates an exception to infringement where the reproduction is made as part of a technical process of using a non-infringing copy of the copyright material (see ss 43B and 111B). Provisions in that Agreement, and likely future legislation, impinge upon the subject matters of this appeal. Almost certainly they will require the attention of the Australian Parliament in the foreseeable future: the undertaking of a further review of the legislation was foreshadowed at the time the *Digital Agenda Act* was enacted: see Revised Explanatory Memorandum, *Copyright Amendment (Digital Agenda) Bill 2000* (Cth) at 17. A report from this review process was released on 28 April 2004: Phillips Fox, *Digital Agenda Review, Report and Recommendations* (2004). This is under consideration: see Weatherall at 615.

[224] In these circumstances, it is preferable for this Court to say with some strictness what s 10(1) of the *Copyright Act* means in its definition of TPM, understood according to the words enacted by the Parliament. If it should transpire that this is different from the purpose that the Parliament was seeking to attain (or if it should appear that later events now make a different balance appropriate) it will be open to the Parliament, subject to the Constitution, to enact provisions clarifying its purpose for the future. Moreover, the submissions in the present case, as it progressed through the courts, called to attention a number of considerations that may need to be given weight in any clarification of the definition of TPM in the *Copyright Act*. Such considerations included the proper protection of fair dealing in works or other subject matters entitled to protection against infringement of copyright; proper protection of the rights of owners of chattels in the use and reasonable enjoyment of such chattels; the preservation of fair copying by purchasers for personal purposes; and the need to protect and uphold technological innovation which an over rigid definition of TPMs might discourage. These considerations are essential attributes of copyright law as it applies in Australia. They are integrated in the protection which that law offers to the copyright owner's interest in its intellectual property.

[225] A court, not fully aware of the compromises that have been struck nationally and internationally and of the large debates that have addressed so-called super or "übercopyright" (Vinje, "Copyright Imperilled?" (1999) *European Intellectual Property Review* 192; Cornish, Intellectual Property: Omnipresent, Distracting, Irrelevant? (2004), Ch 2; Ginsburg, "Essay: From Having Copies to Experiencing Works: The Development of an Access Right in US Copyright Law" (2003) 50 *Journal of the Copyright Society of the USA* 113), is well advised, in the end, to confine itself to offering its best solution to the contested task of statutory interpretation. Whether that construction properly reflects the purpose that the Parliament had when it adopted its definition of TPM, or needs modification, is a decision that must be left to others in the Executive Government and the Parliament itself, assisted by the many contesting interests.

[6.112] The *Copyright Amendment (Technological Protection Measures) Bill 2006* supplements existing prohibitions on the manufacture and commercial supply of devices or services which circumvent TPMs by creating new offences for circumventing TPMs and new exceptions to those offences.

Section 10(1) of the Bill proposes new definitions for :

- access control technological protection measure;
- circumvention device;
- circumvention service; and
- technological protection measure.

TPMs solely designed for other purposes, such as market segmentation (eg region coding) or the protection against competition in aftermarket goods (eg spare parts) where the TPM does not have a connection with copyright are not covered.

There are limited exceptions included for:

- interoperability between computer programs;
- encryption research;
- computer security testing;
- online privacy;
- law enforcement and national security, and
- acquisitions by libraries and other related institutions.

There are new civil and criminal penalties for circumventing an access control measure, and criminal penalties for dealing in circumvention devices and services.

AUTHORISING AN INFRINGEMENT OF COPYRIGHT

[6.115] *Copyright Act 1968* (Cth), s 36(1) states that authorising the doing in Australia of any act comprised in the copyright of a work, without the licence of the owner, is an infringement of the copyright. The corresponding provision for subject matter other than works is s 101. Authorising others to do an act in relation to a copyright in a work is one of the owner's exclusive rights (s 13(2)).

Provisions related to the issue of authorisation specifically refer to copying in educational institutions, home taping, performing works in public, and responsibility for internet transmissions of infringing files.

■ Authorisation of educational copying

[6.117] *The Digital Agenda Act 2000* inserted a new s 36(1A) into the *Copyright Act 1968* (Cth) specifying a list of matters to be included in determining whether or not a person has authorised the doing in Australia of any act comprised in a "work" copyright. Section 87 deals with other subject matter. The Explanatory Memorandum to the *Digital Agenda Act* states that the legislation essentially codifies the principles drawn from the main Australian case on authorisation: *University of New South Wales v Moorhouse* (1975) 133 CLR 1. In this case the High Court of Australia declared that the university had authorised the breach of copyright by providing an unqualified supply of books and photocopying machines, amounting to an invitation to users of the library to make such use of the machines as they saw fit. Any steps taken to supervise machine use and exclude excessive copying were inadequate and directed towards giving students access to machines rather than safeguarding copyright owner's rights.

As a result of this case a new s 39A was inserted into the *Copyright Act 1968* (Cth) by the *Copyright Amendment Act 1980* (Cth) to the effect that a library providing photocopying services will not be taken as having authorised the making of infringing copies if a notice bringing the provisions of the Act to the attention of users of the machine is put up near the machine. This has the effect of making it very easy for universities to avoid "authorising" copyright infringements perpetrated by students and staff. The *Moorhouse* case is discussed below at **[6.130]** in the extract from *Australasian Performing Right Association v Jain* (1990) 18 IPR 663.

Note that libraries also have other special exceptions in relation to circumventing techno-logical protection measures. See also *Copyright Act 1968* (Cth), Part III, Division 5.

■ Authorisation of home taping

[6.120] Since the 1970s attempts have been made to make the suppliers of blank tapes or copying equipment liable to copyright owners for the illegal home taping of sound recordings that such equipment is inevitably used for, but these attempts had been unsuc-cessful. In *CBS Songs Ltd v Amstrad Consumer Electronics Plc* (1988) 11 IPR 1 the first respondents manufactured twin-deck tape-recording machines which were sold by the second respondent. These machines had a double tape-deck which allowed tapes to be reproduced directly onto another blank tape. The appellants were three record companies suing on behalf of themselves and other copyright owners in the music business. It was argued that the sale of twin-deck tape-recording machines capable of reproducing tapes directly onto blank tapes, was an authorisation of the practice, and therefore an infringement of copyright on the part of manufacturers and sellers of such equipment. The appellants also alleged that the machinery was advertised in such a manner as to encourage home taping and copying of copyright material, although the advertising warned that "recording and playback of certain material may only be possible by permission".

Lord Templeman (at 3) characterised the conflict as one between the electronic equip-ment industry and the entertainment industry, each one being interdependent on the other:

> "Without the public demand for entertainment, the electronic industry would not be able to sell its machines to the public. Without the facilities provided by the electronic equipment industry the entertainment industry could not provide entertainment in the home, and could not, for example, maintain orchestras which fill the air with 20th century cacophony or make gratifying profit from a recording of a group without a voice singing a song without a tune."

In discussing the meaning of authorisation Lord Templeman (with whom the other Law Lords agreed) applied the definition adopted in previous cases (*Falcon v Famous Players Film Co* [1926] 2 KB 474; *Monckton v Pathe Freres Pathephone Ltd* [1914] 1 KB 395; *Evans v Hutton* (1924) 131 LT 534; *University of New South Wales v Moorhouse* (1975) 133 CLR 1) that "authorise" means "sanction, approve or countenance" and this was not the situation since there was no control over the use to which machines were put once sold. Furthermore, there was no incitement to commit a tort, namely procuring copyright infringement (see *Amstrad Consumer Electronics Plc v British Phonographic Industry Ltd* [1986] FSR 159) nor were Amstrad negligent since there was no duty to prevent or discourage infringement by others.

This earlier relatively relaxed attitude that arose in the context of analogue recording has not carried over to the digital environment.

The legitimacy of home recording is also acknowledged in s 111 of the *Copyright Act 1968* (Cth), which permits filming or recording broadcasts for private and domestic use. However, new encryption and DRM technologies are designed to restrict such copying. Paracopyright protection assists in managing technologies that otherwise might be taken to authorise infringement. These extensions of the rights of owners may be balanced with new time and format shifting rights, currently being considered in relation to reform of fair dealing provisions related to a possible new right to make some personal uses of digital files.

■ Authorisation of performances in public

[6.125] Although clubs and other venues where live music is played may be directly liable for performing works in public through the musicians engaged to play (*Australasian Performing Right Assn Ltd v Miles* (1961) 3 FLR 146), the defendants in such actions are inevitably sued for authorising infringement as well. See *Australian Performing Right Assn Ltd v Canterbury-Bankstown League Club Ltd* (1964) 5 FLR 415.

See *Copyright Act 1968* (Cth), s 39.

APRA v Jain

[6.130] *Australasian Performing Right Association Ltd v Jain* (1990) 18 IPR 663 Federal Court of Australia

[Mr Jain, the principal executive officer of a company which owned the Old Windsor Tavern, Sydney, was alleged by APRA to have authorised infringement of copyright in works played by bands and on the jukebox at the tavern. APRA had written to Mr Jain advising him that a licence for the tavern should be obtained from them.]

SHEPPARD, FOSTER and HILL JJ: [663] ... This is an appeal from a judgment of a judge of the court (Davies J) in which his Honour dismissed an application brought [664] by the appellant against the respondent for injunctive and other relief in relation to an alleged infringement of copyright. ...

Early in his judgment his Honour said that it was conceded by the respondents before him that musical works, in respect of which the appellant, Australasian Performing Right Association Ltd (APRA), was the proprietor of the copyright (really the performing right), had been performed or played at the Old Windsor Tavern without the appellant's authority, that is, licence. In those circumstances Valamo Pty Ltd did not contest the proceedings and orders were made against it accordingly. It was contended, however, that the respondent to this appeal, Mr Jain, was not personally responsible for any of the infringements of copyright which had occurred and that the application, in so far as it related to him, should be dismissed with costs. That submission was upheld by his Honour and it is from that decision that this appeal is brought. ...

His Honour found that the day to day operations of the tavern, which is a licensed hotel, were controlled by the licensee, a Mr John Morgan, who is an employee of Valamo. Mr Morgan, his Honour found, was the day manager and another person was employed as night manager. Music was played at the tavern both through a jukebox and by live bands. His Honour found that Mr Morgan and the night manager were the persons who selected and engaged the bands for evening performances. But he also said that they were presumably the persons who selected the music videos for playing in the jukebox. His Honour found that Mr Morgan maintained the day to day financial records of the company including its cheque and receipt books. Almost all payments were made in cash. The bands were paid 10 per cent of the night's takings.

Mr Jain said he took no part in the selection of the bands or of the music which they performed. He was concerned with a band only if it [665] appeared that the takings of a night were bad, in which case he would advise the licensee to engage another band. ... [666] ...

On 2 August 1989 solicitors, who said that they acted for the proprietors of the tavern, replied to the letter. They said they had been asked to advise generally on the licence agreements which had been submitted. They said that their clients took "note of the APRA claims" and that a considered reply would be furnished within a short time. Nothing further was heard about the matter and these proceedings were instituted on 1 February 1990. The amended application sought orders restraining the public performance of the musical and literary works which have been earlier specified in these reasons. It also sought an injunction restraining the performance in public of the musical and literary works referred to in the schedule to the application and the authorising of the performance in public of those works. The works referred to in the schedule were the whole of the appellant's repertoire. ...

Before us counsel for the appellant put the case in two alternate ways. He submitted, first, that Mr Jain was in breach of s 36 of the Act because Mr Jain had, without the licence of the owner of the copyright, authorised the doing in Australia of an act comprised in the copyright. Counsel secondly submitted that Mr Jain was jointly or concurrently liable along with Valamo as a tortfeasor.

... So the question is whether the appellant has established that Mr Jain authorised the public performance of the musical works in question without the appellant's licence. His Honour thought that that question should be answered in the negative. He relied upon the decision of the Court of Appeal in England in *Performing Right Society Ltd v Ciryl Theatrical Syndicate Ltd* [1924] 1 KB 1. That is a relevant authority, but, in so far as it deals with authorisation as distinct from the question of liability as a joint or concurrent tortfeasor, it has been overtaken by later authorities to many of [667] which his Honour was not referred. The history of the development of the law in relation to authorisation is recounted by Gummow J in *WEA International Inc v Hanimex Corp Ltd* (1987) 10 IPR 349 at 358-363. His Honour, after referring to *Ciryl's Case*, said (at 359) that it was clear after *Ash v Hutchinson & Co (Publishers) Ltd* [1936] Ch 489 that the *Copyright Act 1911* (UK) (in force in Australia by virtue of the *Copyright Act 1912*) gave, for example, the owner of copyright in a literary work both the sole right of reproducing it and the sole right of authorising such reproduction and that those rights were separate and distinct so that infringement of each was a distinct tort. His Honour said (at 359) that the same was true of authorisation in respect of the current Act. So much was accepted by the High Court in *University of New South Wales v Moorhouse* (1975) 133 CLR 1. The relevant requirements of the 1968 Act were the provisions of s 13(2) and ss 31 and 36 to which reference has been made. Gummow J went on to say (at 359) that the circumstance that the concept of "authorisation" in the legislation had its own independent operation from what might be called primary infringement did not exclude the general law principles relating to joint tortfeasors from operation upon primary infringement.

We indicate our general agreement with Gummow J's account of the development of the law in relation to authorisation. But we feel it necessary to refer to some of the authorities ourselves. The starting point is the *Moorhouse* case. That case concerned unauthorised photocopying of copyright material (literary works) in a university library. The plaintiff relied upon a cause of action based on the university's having authorised the infringement which occurred when a person in the library used the photocopier to copy pages of a book. In the course of his judgment Gibbs J (as he then was) said (at 12-13; at 200):

> "The word 'authorise', in legislation of similar intendment to s 36 of the Act, has been held judicially to have its dictionary meaning of 'sanction, approve, countenance': *Falcon v Famous Players Film Co Ltd* [1926] 2 KB 474 at 491; *Adelaide Corp v Australasian Performing Right Assn Ltd* (1928) 40 CLR 481 at 489, 497. It can also mean 'permit', and in *Adelaide Corp v Australasian Performing Right Assn Ltd* 'authorise' and 'permit' appear to have been treated as synonymous. A person cannot be said to authorise an infringement of copyright unless he has some power to prevent it: *Adelaide Corp v Australasian Performing Right Assn Ltd* at 497-498, 503. Express or formal permission or sanction, or

active conduct indicating approval, is not essential to constitute an authorisation. 'Inactivity or "indifference, exhibited by act of commission or omission, may reach a degree from which an authorisation or permission may be inferred"': *Adelaide Corp v Australasian Performing Right Assn Ltd* at 504. However, the word 'authorise' connotes a mental element and it could not be inferred that a person had, by mere inactivity, authorised something to be done if he neither knew nor had reason to suspect that the act might be done. Knox CJ and Isaacs J referred to this mental element in their dissenting judgments in *Adelaide Corp v Australasian Performing Right Assn Ltd*. Knox CJ (at 487) held that indifference or omission is 'permission' where the party charged (amongst other things) 'knows or has reason to anticipate or suspect that the particular act is to be or is likely to be done'. Isaacs J apparently considered [668] that it is enough if the person sought to be made liable 'knows or has reason to know or believe' that the particular act of infringement 'will or may' be done (at 490-491). This latter statement may be too widely expressed: cf *Sweet v Parsley* [1970] AC 132 at 165."

Later his Honour said (at 13-14; at 201):

"In the present case the university made available to a section of the public the books in its library at least those in the open shelves and provided in the library the machines by which copies of those books could be made. It seems to me that the university must have known that it was likely that a person entitled to use the library might make a copy of a substantial part of any of those books. It is true that the machines were not used exclusively for the purpose of copying books; they were extensively used to copy lecture notes and other private documents. Moreover, not all of the books which might be copied were subject to copyright. However, in the nature of things it was likely that some of the books which were subject to copyright and which were in the open shelves might be copied by use of the machines in a manner that would constitute an infringement of copyright unless some means were adopted to prevent that from being done. It could not be assumed that persons making copies of works in which copyright existed would do so only in circumstances which amounted to a fair dealing for the purpose of research or private study, at least in the absence of any effective measures to ensure that any other copying of copyright works was forbidden. The university was aware of the assertions of the Australian Copyright Council that 'unlawful and undesirable practices are commonplace within the universities' and although it may have regarded these claims as exaggerated, it had been given enough information to raise the suspicion that some infringing copies were likely to be made."

Jacobs J (in whose judgment McTiernan ACJ agreed (at 7)) said (at 207-208):

"It is established that the word ['authorise'] is not limited to the authorising of an agent by a principal. Where there is such an authority the act of the agent is the act of the principal and thus the principal himself may be said to do the act comprised in the copyright. But authorisation is wider than authority. It has, in relation to a similar use in previous copyright legislation, been given the meaning, taken from the Oxford Dictionary, of 'sanction, approve, countenance': see *Falcon v Famous Players Film Co Ltd* [1926] 2 KB 474 which was approved in *Adelaide Corp v Australasian Performing Right Assn Ltd* (1928) 40 CLR 481. I have no doubt that the word is used in the same sense in s 36(1). It is a wide meaning which in cases of permission or invitation is apt to apply both where an express permission or invitation is extended to do the act comprised in the copyright and where such a permission or invitation may be implied. Where a general permission or invitation may be implied it is clearly unnecessary that the authorising party have knowledge that a particular act comprised in the copyright will be done.

The acts and omissions of the alleged authorising party must be looked at in the circumstances in which the act comprised in the copyright is done. The circumstances will include the likelihood that such an act will be done ... 'the court may infer an authorisation or permission from acts which fall short of being direct and positive; ... indifference, exhibited by acts of commission or omission, may reach a degree from which authorisation or [669] permission may be inferred. It is a question of fact in each case what is the true inference to be drawn from the conduct of the person who is said to have authorised': per Bankes LJ in *Performing Right Society Ltd v Ciryl Theatrical Syndicate Ltd* [1924] 1 KB 1 at 9."

In the course of his judgment in the *Moorhouse* case, Gibbs J referred to *Winstone v Wurlitzer Automatic Phonograph Co of Australia Pty Ltd* [1946] VLR 338. It was there held by Herring CJ that the owner of a gramophone installed in a shop authorised the public performance of musical works played on it. Herring CJ said (at 345):

"It is, of course, a question of fact in each case what is the true inference to be drawn from the conduct of the person said to have authorised the act complained of. And as the acts that may be complained of as infringements of copyright are multifarious, so, too, the conduct that may justify an inference of authorisation may take on an infinite variety of differing forms. In these circumstances any attempt to prescribe beforehand ready-made tests for determining on which side of the line a particular case will fall, would seem doomed to failure. So, too, will it be impossible to determine any particular case by reference merely to the relationship that may exist between the person said to have authorised the act complained of and the actual infringer, though no doubt in the case of principal and agent an authorisation may be more readily inferred than in the case of vendor and purchaser. In the end the matter must in each case depend on a careful examination of all the relevant facts."

In his judgment in the *Hanimex* case, Gummow J, having said that "sanction, approve, countenance" was the meaning ascribed by members of the High Court in the *Moorhouse* case to the word "authorisation", said (at 362):

"This meant that express or formal permission or active conduct indicating approval was not essential to constitute an authorisation. That view has not always been accepted in England in recent times. In *Amstrad Consumer Electronics Plc v British Phonographic Industry Ltd* [1986] FSR 159 at 207, Lawton LJ, speaking of the current UK legislation (*Copyright Act 1956*), said that the concept of granting or purporting to grant to a third person the right to do the act complained of came much nearer to the meaning of the word 'authorise' than the synonyms approved by the High Court of Australia in *University of New South Wales v Moorhouse*. Be that as it may, the position in Australia with respect to the 1968 Act is presently settled by *Moorhouse's* case."

... [670] ...

None of the authorities to which we have made reference deal with situations in which directors or employees of a company are themselves said to have authorised an infringement. There have been, however, some cases in which reference has been made to the position of directors or employees. In *Australasian Performing Right Assn v Tolbush Pty Ltd* (1985) 62 ALR 521, a decision of de Jersey J of the Supreme Court of Queensland, his Honour said (at 523-524; at 55):

■■■■■■ APRA v Jain *continued*

"If I enjoin the first defendant, I consider that I should also enjoin the second and third defendants, who are directors of the first defendant. The third defendant is also its secretary. Under s 36(1), those who 'authorise' infringements of copyright are liable for the infringement. The material before me suggests that the second and third defendants control and operate the first defendant. I consider that I should infer that they effectively run it. That being so, I consider that I should take the view that they, as the natural operatives of the first defendant, have authorised any infringement of copyright of which the first defendant has been guilty. My approach is similar to that of Thomas J in *Kalamazoo* ..."

His Honour's reference to *Kalamazoo* is a reference to the decision of Thomas J of the Supreme Court of Queensland in *Kalamazoo (Aust) Pty Ltd v Compact Business Systems Pty Ltd* (1985) 84 FLR 101.

It is necessary, in light of these authorities, to consider the circumstances of this case to see whether, upon the findings made by his Honour and upon inferences that may be drawn, the appellant has established its case. [671]

It is unnecessary to repeat the detail of the account of the evidence given earlier in these reasons. Mr Jain was effectively the chief executive officer of the company. But, as so often happens, he entrusted the running and day to day management of the tavern to Mr Morgan. He knew, however, that music would be played by live bands albeit he did not concern himself with the actual items of music which would be played by them. In this respect he was in a position similar to that of the university in the *Moorhouse* case. It may be that some of what the bands would play would not be the subject of copyright (although this seems unlikely) and it may have been that despite the extensive repertoire which it has, the appellant did not have the public performance right in some of the music which would be played. But the likelihood was that music would be played which would be part of the appellant's repertoire. The matter was brought to Mr Jain's attention by the appellant's solicitors' letter of 12 July 1989. The evidence of his reaction to that letter may be sketchy, but it may clearly be inferred that he read it. His solicitors said in their letter of 2 August 1989 that he had taken "note of APRA's claims". He did not claim to have procured a licence from the appellant to play the music and there is, in any event, the positive evidence of both Mr O'Neill and Ms Callaghan that no such licence existed. Plainly Mr Jain had the power to control what music was played at the tavern and also to determine whether a licence from the appellant would be applied for. He did nothing about the matter at all. He allowed a situation to develop in which bands went on playing the appellant's music night after night. Despite assurances that his solicitors would consider the matter and get in touch either with the appellant itself or its solicitors, nothing of this kind occurred.

The judgment of the members of the High Court in the *Moorhouse* case establishes that one of the meanings of the word "authorise" in the context in which it is here used is "countenance". It may be that not every act which amounts to the countenancing of something is an authorisation. Every case will depend upon its own facts. Matters of degree are involved. But the evidence in the present case reveals, in our opinion, a studied and deliberate course of action in which Mr Jain decided to ignore the appellant's rights and to allow a situation to develop and to continue in which he must have known that it was likely that the appellant's music would be played without any licence from it. It was within his power to control what was occurring but he did nothing at all. In those circumstances we have reached the conclusion that the appellant established that Mr Jain authorised the infringement of copyright in question contrary to s 36 of the Act. Our conclusion in this respect makes it unnecessary for us to consider the alternative argument based on the submission that Mr Jain was a joint tortfeasor. It does not arise for consideration and we express no view about it.

APRA v Jain *continued*

It follows that we allow the appeal and set aside his Honour's order dismissing the application brought against Mr Jain.

Contracting out of responsibility for authorisation?

APRA v Metro on George

[6.135] *Australasian Performing Right Association Limited v Metro on George Pty Limited* [2004] FCA 1123 Federal Court of Australia

BENNETT J:

The evidence

[12] The following facts were not in dispute:

(h) APRA usually grants licences with respect to the whole of its repertoire on a "blanket" basis.

(i) APRA grants different kinds of licences, for example, a venue licence (which it claims is the licence appropriate for Metro), a Promoter's licence (granted to certain "national promoters" (approximately 33) who deal directly with APRA), a Halls and Function Centre licence and a licence for Recorded Music for Dancing. ...

(l) APRA recognises that, in relation to any given performance, it may directly licence the promoter or licence the venue and has developed different schemes to accommodate these situations.

(m) A venue licence is a blanket licence that covers all performances of music in APRA's repertoire by live performers at the venue.

(n) Since 31 May 2002, Metro has not entered into any venue licence with APRA.

(o) Metro has taken promoter's licences for performances where Metro was itself the promoter.

(p) Subsistence and ownership of copyright by APRA in the musical works performed at Metro on George on dates between 26 June 2002 and 12 September 2002, as specified in the schedule to the statement of claim ('the eleven performances').

(q) In the eleven performances various artists performed works the subject of APRA's copyright.

(r) The eleven performances were performances in public.

(s) The eleven performances required an APRA licence.

(t) No applications for promoter's licences were received by APRA in respect of the eleven performances and APRA did not grant promoter's licences for those performances.

(u) Four promoters, not national promoters, did approach APRA for licences for other performances to be held at Metro on George. APRA issued a licence in each case.

(v) On 3 October 2002, Metro offered to advise APRA of all details of events held at Metro on George where they were promoted by others. Other licences required for events held at Metro on George, such as events where Metro was itself the promoter or where a Recorded Music for Dancing licence was appropriate, were obtained and payment made.

(w) There is no evidence of any relevant industry code of practice as referred to in s 36(1A)(c) of the Act.

[13] The respondents rely on the Metro Theatre Hire and Box Office Contract ("the Metro contract"), which Metro adopted on 17 April 2002. The respondents also assert that, although the format and wording of the Metro contract have changed since 1999, Metro's method of doing business has remained the same. The Metro contract included the following:

"Metro requires to know the description and details of events to enable Metro to maintain the image and reputation of Metro as a venue. The Hirer must obtain written approval to any change to the description and details provided which Metro may in its discretion refuse to consent.

Metro does not authorise or permit any particular performance whether containing copyright material or otherwise. The Hirer warrants that it will ensure all performances at the event will comply with the *Copyright Act* and the licence requirements of the Australian Performing Right Association ("APRA").

Metro agrees to provide ticketing services to the Hirer in the form of box office sales. This does not constitute a joint venture agreement or business partnership between the parties."

[14] This first sub-paragraph of this was subsequently amended to:

"Metro requires the Hirer to advise the name and description of the event. The Hirer warrants that the event so named and described will be the event that takes place."

[15] The Metro contract also included clauses 2.4, 5 and 6:

"2.4 The Hirer acknowledges that nothing in the Master Terms or the Hire Contract or otherwise amounts to Metro authorising or giving legal power for the doing of any act.

...

5.   Copyright

5.1   The Hirer acknowledges the provisions of section 39 of the *Copyright Act* and that Metro is unaware of the arrangements between the Hirer and the artist(s) performing at the Event.

5.2   The Hirer warrants in favour of Metro that all performances conducted at the Metro Theatre will comply with the *Copyright Act* (including without limitation the obtaining of all appropriate licences from and the approval of the Australian Performing Right Association ("APRA") and the Phonographic Performance Co of Australia Limited ("PPCA") and all other bodies relevant to ensuring broadcasting of music and performance of musical works comply with lawful and statutory requirements.

6.   Warranties by the Hirer

6.1   The Hirer warrants that the Event(s) shall comply with all relevant laws and regulations (including but not limited to those regarding copyright, intellectual property and entry into Australia) and with any relevant union requirement relating to local content of the Event(s), and that the Hirer shall not infringe or breach, or permit to suffer to be infringed or breached any copyright, performing right or any other protected right in connection with the Event(s) during the period of this licence or user or users of the Theatre.

6.2   The Hirer acknowledges that it is and will be at all times responsible for ensuring that the Event(s) and the actions of all persons involved in the Event(s) comply with the terms of this Agreement where applicable, and otherwise comply with the reasonable requests of Metro with respect to the staging of the Event(s).

6.3   The Hirer hereby indemnifies and agrees to keep Metro indemnified against all liabilities arising out of any breach of a warranty under Clause 5 and 6 hereof."

██████ APRA v Metro on George *continued*

...

Consideration

Date of termination of Metro's APRA licence

[24] In 1994, Metro obtained a Recorded Music for Dancing licence and the venue licence from APRA for the live performance of works in APRA's repertoire. Since June 1999, Metro has refused to pay licence fees. On 22 September 1999 Metro notified APRA that it believed that it had been wrongly classified by APRA and requested a reassessment of licence fees for the period 1 August 1994 to 30 June 1998. Metro asserted that it did not require a venue licence. APRA did not agree. From that time, the parties have been in correspondence but have not resolved the dispute.

[Various correspondence is considered]

[37] ... it is clear that, by 31 May 2002, Metro had refused to pay licence fees for almost three years and had demanded repayment of licence fees previously paid. In adopting that stance, Metro evinced an intention not to be bound by the licence, amounting to repudiation. That repudiation was not accepted by APRA prior to 31 May 2002, as the May letter affirms that the licence remains current. However, it is clear from the May letter that APRA, noting that Metro maintained that it was not the appropriate holder of the venue licence, accepted Metro's repudiation.

[38] Accordingly, there was no venue licence in place when the alleged infringements occurred.

General

[39] In detailed correspondence between the parties, the respondents assert:
- Metro does not arrange or provide performances or entertainment by "live artist performers" or by recorded means. It simply hires out its theatre to third parties so that those third parties can then promote or arrange live artists or dance parties. Metro does not retain any "gross sums paid for admission" to Metro on George. If the theatre has not been hired out to a third party, it does not open for business.
- Metro does not exercise any artistic judgment in the decision to hire the venue to potential bands and has no control over what performances will be given at any event.
- Metro does not authorise or permit the performance of any copyright material at Metro on George.
- Licence fees paid to APRA from 1 August 1994 to 30 June 1998 were incorrectly paid, as no venue licence was required.

[40] APRA rejects the assertion that Metro has been incorrectly licensed as a venue for live performance. It contends that the fact that Metro entered into contracts with agents, such as concert promoters, to organise events does not absolve Metro of legal responsibility under the Act. APRA points to the operation by Metro of a bar within the theatre and of the box office, as well as the advertisement of and reputation of Metro on George as a venue suitable for the performance of live music. ...

Approval, sanctioning or countenancing

[42] The Metro contract states that Metro does not authorise or permit any particular performance, whether containing copyright material or otherwise and that the hirer warrants that it will ensure that all performances comply with the Act and the licence requirements of APRA.

[43] The inclusion of these clauses in the Metro contract is said by Metro to bring it within s 36(1A)(c) of the Act, being a reasonable step to prevent or avoid the doing of the act, being the act comprised in the copyright.

[44] The inclusion of the warranty in the Metro contract was a reasonable step to take which, if implemented by the hirer, would have prevented an unlicensed performance. However, s 36(1A)(c) does not address steps to prevent or avoid infringement generally, rather it addresses steps to prevent or avoid the doing of the act itself, that is the act comprised in the copyright in a work. Metro did not take steps to prevent or avoid the performances.

[45] Further, the inclusion of the warranty in the Metro contract was not, in the majority of cases, implemented. It did not result in the hirer obtaining an APRA licence, although some hirers did. APRA informed Metro that unlicensed performances had taken place and there is no evidence that Metro took any action. Metro did not take steps to inquire whether a licence had been obtained or to ensure that it had. From the evidence, it is apparent that Metro took the view that it need do nothing further. While the warranty under the Metro contract amounted to more than a warning, to the extent that it notified the hirers of their obligations it was, in the circumstances, insufficient to exonerate Metro.

...

[48] Metro has not established that it was not aware or had no reasonable grounds for suspecting that performances would be an infringement of copyright... Metro was either aware of or was indifferent to the occurrence of unlicensed performances at Metro on George. The failure to make an inquiry of the hirer, in the face of APRA's assertions, can at best be described as a wilful disregard of whether the performance of works which it knew or ought reasonably to have known would include works within APRA's copyright were performed with APRA's authorisation or not. As was said by Kiefel J in *Golden Editions Pty Ltd v Polygram Pty Ltd* (1996) 34 IPR 84 at 93, "a deliberate choice not to inquire, in such circumstances, may enable a further finding, since it may suggest a mind in which real suspicion resided" and a failure to put such a question operated "to his peril". It is inconsistent with the application of s 39(2) of the Act.

...

Control

[63] APRA asserts that Metro was in a position to prevent infringements of works in APRA's repertoire. ...

[64] The respondents' case is that the elements of control are not present and that the only authorisation was of performances which either did not need or did have the necessary licences from APRA. If those licences were not held, according to Mr Bannon there was nothing the respondents could do, as they did not have the requisite control. It was, he asserted, up to APRA to licence the promoters. APRA did issue licences to promoters, so that the respondents did not know and could not be expected to know which promoters were and which were not licensed nor which particular works would be performed.

[65] The evidence does not directly establish Metro's power to prevent a performance. The relationship between Metro and the hirer was that of independent contractor and Metro had no direct relationship with the bands that perform at Metro on George. Metro had no control or input into the choice of songs. It could, however, refuse to hire out Metro on George to unlicensed hirers. APRA points out that Metro could take the simple step of either asking APRA in advance whether a licence has been granted for a particular performance or asking hirers for a copy of a relevant APRA licence. ...

[68] Clearly, the performances took place on Metro's premises, which were premises routinely used for live performances of music. It is not in dispute that Metro did not provide the material to be performed, exercised no control over the choice of material to be performed, nor over the range of material from which the particular works were chosen. As the choice of material was for the band, it cannot be said that Metro actively gave permission

for the performance of any particular work but it is the case that Metro was aware, knew or suspected that the bands would perform material the subject of copyright. ...

[73] The question is whether Metro had any control. In my view, it did. Unlike the circumstances in *Australian Tape Manufacturers Association Ltd v The Commonwealth of Australia* (1993) 176 CLR 480 where the infringements did not take place on the vendor's premises, Metro was in control of the premises. Metro advertised the performances. It operated the box office, provided refreshments and provided and operated the electricity necessary for the performances to take place. The Metro contract formed the basis of the hiring of the premises. This may not have amounted to control over the content of the performances but, in my view, it gave a measure of control over the use of the premises in circumstances where Metro knew or had grounds to believe that unlicensed performances were to take place or were in fact taking place at Metro on George. ...

Defences

[82] The respondents have not made out the defences under ss 36(1A)(c) or 39(2)(a) of the Act. It is clear from the above consideration that the Metro contract did not, on its own, constitute "reasonable steps to prevent or avoid the doing of the act" under s 36(1A)(c). There is no evidence that Metro checked whether the promoters were licensed, nor that it took any action once aware that unlicensed performances had taken place.

[83] Metro cannot, after the notification in the letter of 15 July 2002, avail itself of the defence afforded by s 39(2). The correspondence concerning the need for a venue licence, pre-dated the first of the eleven performances. This correspondence establishes that Metro was indeed aware, or at least had reasonable ground for suspecting, that unlicensed performances of work subject to APRA's copyright might occur. Accordingly, I am not satisfied that Metro has established that s 39(2) applies to the pre-15 July 2002 performances.

■ Authorising infringing internet file sharing

[6.140] See *Copyright Act 1968* (Cth), ss 39B, 112E.

MP3 file sharing has proven one of the biggest challenges for copyright law. The cases below deal with liability for authorising infringement by website operators and peer-to-peer technology makers who facilitate unauthorised file sharing. These actions follow similar litigation in the US such as *Metro-Goldwyn-Mayer Studios Inc v Grokster Ltd* 73 USLW 4675 (2005).

The Australia-US Free Trade Agreement provided for further amendments to this area. See *Copyright Act 1968 (Cth)*, Part V, Division 2AA—Limitation on remedies available against carriage service providers (ss 116AA-116AI). These "safe harbour" provisions, which came into force 1 January 2005, apply to "carriage service providers" as defined in s 87 of the *Telecommunications Act 1997 (Cth)*.

Comparable provisions overseas are drafted more broadly to include "online service providers" which may include others who also facilitate online communications such as libraries, educational institutions or search engine providers. The Attorney General is conducting an inquiry to address whether the new, current limitations in Part V, Division 2AA to carriage service providers should be redrafted.

The changes arising from the free trade agreement are noted in the first extract below.

▬▬▬ Universal Music Australia v Cooper ▬▬▬

[6.145] *Universal Music Australia Pty Ltd v Cooper* [2005] FCA 972 Federal Court of Australia

TAMBERLIN J:

[1] These proceedings are brought by thirty-one applicants. The first to sixth applicants are Australian record companies that claim to be owners or exclusive licensees in Australia of the copyright in large catalogues of music sound recordings, some of which are identified in Schedules A to F to the Amended Statement of Claim. The remaining twenty-five applicants are foreign corporations or entities that own copyright in those specifically identified music sound recordings, in addition to other recordings within the catalogues of the first to sixth applicants.

[2] The principal claims are based on infringement of copyright in the music sound recordings. In addition to the infringement of copyright, relief is sought under s 52 of the *Trade Practices Act 1974* (Cth) ("the TPA"), s 38 of the Queensland *Fair Trading Act 1989* ("the QFTA") and s 42 of the *Fair Trading Act 1987* (NSW) ("the FTA") on the ground of misleading and deceptive conduct based on implied misrepresentations concerning the legality of downloading copies of the music sound recordings from the internet. The QFTA is said to apply because the respondents are resident in Queensland. ...

The parties

[5] The first respondent, Stephen Cooper ("Cooper"), was the registered owner of the domain name mp3s4free.net ("the domain name") and the originator, owner and operator of the MP3s4FREE website ("the website"). The evidence indicates that Cooper did not charge visitors to the website any sum of money for the downloading of music sound recordings but that he derived income from the website through advertising arrangements.

[6] The second and third respondents, E-Talk Communications Pty Limited and Com-Cen Pty Limited (referred to together as "E-Talk/Com-Cen"), conducted an Internet Service Provider ("ISP") business which hosted the website. The second and third respondents derived benefits from an advertising and traffic sharing arrangement with Cooper, whereby the Com-Cen logo was displayed on the website with a hyperlink to the Com-Cen website. In return for the display of the Com-Cen logo on the website, Cooper received free web hosting from Com-Cen.

[7] The fourth respondent, Liam Francis Bal ("Bal"), and the fifth respondent, Chris Takoushis ("Takoushis"), are the principal and an employee respectively of E-Talk/Com-Cen. Bal is a director and the controlling mind of both companies and Takoushis was Cooper's primary contact at Com-Cen and provided assistance from time to time in relation to the establishment and operation of the website.

The claims

[8] In relation to the allegations of copyright infringement, the applicants allege that by means of or via or in the course of operating the website, Cooper has infringed the applicants' copyright in the music sound recordings. First, the applicants allege that Cooper has directly infringed the applicants' exclusive rights to make copies of the music sound recordings and to communicate the music sound recordings to the public. Secondly, the applicants allege that Cooper has authorised internet users, including those internet users who submitted MP3s to the website and who downloaded MP3s via the website, to make copies of the music sound recordings and has authorised both internet users and E-Talk/Com-Cen to communicate these music sound recordings to the public. Thirdly, the applicants allege that Cooper has infringed copyright as a joint tortfeasor by entering into a common design with internet users and

E-Talk/Com-Cen to make copies of the music sound recordings or to communicate them to the public. Finally, the applicants make a claim of secondary infringement pursuant to s 103 of the Act arising from Cooper's alleged exhibition and distribution of infringing digital music files.

[9] The applicants allege that E-Talk/Com-Cen directly infringed copyright in the music sound recordings by communicating them to the public and/or authorised Cooper and the internet users to make copies of the music sound recordings and to communicate them to the public. The applicants also allege that E-Talk/Com-Cen infringed copyright as a joint tortfeasor by entering into a common design with internet users and Coopers to engage in the above acts and, similarly to Cooper, infringed copyright by exhibiting and distributing the music sound recordings.

....

The Cooper website and hyperlinking

[16] The home page of the website is headed "MP3s4FREE". There are, of course, numerous other web pages on the Cooper website. The home page contains statements concerning the availability of free songs and albums on the website and numerous references to MP3 files and downloads. On the right hand side of each of the web pages on the website, the Com-Cen logo appears beneath a reference to "Best Server". The numerous pages of the website include thousands of music files organised by artist name and song title and hyperlinks are provided directly to those music files.

[17] Mr Speck gave evidence that the music files on the website are accessible in three main ways. First, the lists of music files are organised on the website in the form of charts which reproduce current Australian and international recording industry music charts, which reflect commercially successful recorded music. These charts include the Australian Top 40, Billboard 50 and a number of European charts. The evidence is that the Australian Top 40 chart corresponds exactly to the first 40 singles that appear in the Aria Top 50 chart for each relevant week. The charts on the website replicate the order of the singles, the names of the artists and the titles of the singles. Secondly, there are search mechanisms such as "Popular Artists", "Top 50 Downloads" and "Latest 50 Additions" which reflect the most popular files which can be downloaded through the website and the latest music files that have been added to the website via hyperlink. Finally, website maintains an archive of files arranged in alphabetical order by song title or artist name. These archived files can be located using the main search mechanism, entitled "Search for Artist or Title", at the top of each of the web pages on the website.

[18] Hypertext links, often referred to as "links" or "hyperlinks", are a standard internet technology that is used to enable internet users to move between web pages, which are usually displayed in ".html" code, and other information. A hyperlink is a means by which an internet user is able to access files in which he or she is interested. Hyperlinks are frequently identified in a user's internet browser by coloured, usually blue, and underlined text. However, this is not always so. In some cases, hyperlinks may be different colours or otherwise identified. A hyperlink notifies an internet user that by using an electronic mouse to click on the link, they will be able to receive information that does not appear on the web page they are currently viewing.

[19] Linking is a central feature of the World Wide Web. One way in which links are used is to direct internet users to another web page, whether that page is located on the same website or is part of a totally different website. Moving between web pages by activating hyperlinks on the website is a process typically known as "browsing". These other web pages may themselves contain hyperlinks to further web pages or to specific files or documents. The hyperlinks on the Cooper website are used to direct internet users to other pages of the

website or to the remote websites from which the music files are downloaded. A further way in which hyperlinks are used is to enable internet users to download a specific file or document of interest. This type of hyperlink is used to activate a download of a discrete data file, such as a document or a music file, to the internet user's computer. The hyperlink sends a command to the remote computer on which the file is stored to release the file to the person who has activated the hyperlink on the website. Without this command to release the file, and the communication from the website's software, the file would not be available to the user who has requested it.

[20] The above principles apply in the case of digital music files, with each file being a discrete set of data, usually with associated information such as file size, file title and other information, often described as metadata. This data can be transmitted to other computers and reproduced on the user's computer as an identical discrete set of data, usually with the same or virtually identical metadata. Therefore, when a link to a music file is activated, the remote computer on which the file is stored is directed to, and does automatically, transfer a copy of the file from the host server directly to the computer of the user activating the link. In the present case, the music file is not sent to, downloaded on or saved to the Cooper website or the host server of the Cooper website. The digital music files are stored on remote computers which are linked to the website and are accessed in the above way.

[21] The ultimate location of the data file from which the download occurs is often arbitrary and frequently unknown to the internet user. It is possible that the file could be stored on the same computer server on which the webpage files are stored. But it could equally be stored on another computer with no physical proximity to the computer on which the webpage files are stored. The physical location of a data file can be, and often is, entirely independent from the location of the web pages visible to the internet user. ... Professor Sterling gave evidence that in his opinion, in the case of the Cooper website, the presence of Java script code meant that an internet user is unlikely to know where a digital music file that is listed on the website, and capable of being directly downloaded by an activating hyperlink, was located. For example, Professor Sterling said that there were no messages or signs to inform internet users that they were leaving one website and going to another.

[22] In broad terms, there are two ways in which a hyperlink can be established on a website. They can be created by the operator of a website or, alternatively, the link can be created by software tools which are made available by the website to internet users to enable them to create hyperlinks that are visible on the website. The latter is what occurred in the case of the Cooper website. Professor Sterling gave evidence that a person cannot create a hyperlink between a file and website without the permission of the operator of the website, because access to the code required to create the link must occur at the website. In order for Cooper to enable files to be automatically linked to his website by internet users, he must have given permission for that access to occur. This process of adding hyperlinks to the website could not have occurred without Cooper's permission.

[23] In the case of hyperlinking, it is not the physical location of the computer that is relevant but rather the network address, internet provider address and the URL address associated with the computers. If Cooper did not know this information, he could have obtained it by relatively standard technical measures which are available to any operator of a website. This information must be incorporated into the website because without that information it would not have been possible for the links to work and internet users enabled to access the files. Cooper could, if he wanted to, have asked contributors of the hyperlinks to disclose their identity by adding an extra field in the form he used without any additional complex coding being required. ...

[25] In the present case, the hyperlinks on the website function in a variety of ways. There are hyperlinks which transfer the user to a web page on a remote website that contains information of various types. In such a case, the hyperlinks take the internet user directly, or via a series of other web pages, to another page on the same remote website that posts the software. It is up to the user to follow the hyperlink, or series of hyperlinks, on the remote site in order to arrive at the page that contains the hyperlink to the music recording and commence the download of the software. The download of the software takes place directly to the user. Other hyperlinks take the user to a page on a remote website on which there appears a direct link to the software, which may or may not contain links in addition to the music file. The user has only then to click on the link to the music file to commence the download. Finally, the hyperlinks may transfer the user to a music file on the remote website such that the download automatically commences without further user information being required. ...

[30] At the bottom of each page of the website, there are hyperlinks to the website's "Privacy Policy", "Terms and Conditions" and "Disclaimer". The "Terms and Conditions" contains the following statement which emphasises the linking function provided by the website:

> "Set forth below are the terms and conditions ... governing the MP3s4FREE.NET website located at, or linked to through, the route url www.mp3s4free.net, which may expand or change from time to time (the "Website").
>
> ...
>
> Sites *Linked* from the Website: Links to third-party websites from the Website are not necessarily under MP3s4FREE's control ... and MP3s4FREE does not intend any such *links* to third-party websites to imply MP3s4FREE's sponsorship or endorsement thereof." (Emphasis added)

The "Disclaimer" acknowledges the linking function of the website in the following terms:

> "... When you download a song, you take full responsibility for doing so. None of the files on this site are stored on our servers. *We are just providing links to remote files."* (Emphasis added)

The linking function of the website is also acknowledge in the Privacy Policy in the following terms:

> "*External Links:*   This site contains links to other sites.
>
> ...
>
> *Disclaimer:*   ... This site only provides links to the according sites and no songs are located on our servers. ... We are not responsible for any damage caused by downloading these files, or any content posted on this website or linked websites."

...

Infringement of copyright

[49] Section 85 of the Act provides that the owner of the copyright has the exclusive right to engage in certain acts. Pursuant to s 85(1), these acts include, first, "to make a copy of a sound recording" and, second, "to communicate the recording to the public". The applicants submit that both of these exclusive rights have been infringed in the present case.

[50] The expression "sound recording" is defined in s 10(1) to be "the aggregate of the sounds embodied in a record". The expression "record" is defined as "a disc, tape, paper or other device in which records are embodied". ...

[53] In my view, it can be accepted that an MP3 file is a record from which an aggregate of sounds can be reproduced.

███████ Universal Music Australia v Cooper *continued*

Making a copy of a sound recording

[54] The applicants submit that Cooper has directly infringed the applicants' copyright in the music sound recordings by making copies of these recordings. ...

[56] In view of the failure of Cooper to give any evidence from the witness box and to offer an alternative explanation for the existence of the MP3s on the hard drive of his computer, I am satisfied that the available inference that Cooper made these copies of the copyright sound recordings on the hard drive himself, most likely by downloading them from his website, can more safely and confidently be drawn. Accordingly, I find that Cooper has infringed the applicants' copyright by making copies of the music sound recordings.

The communication right—"to make available online" and/or "electronically transmit"

[57] The applicants allege that Cooper has directly infringed the applicants' copyright in the music sound recordings by communicating these recordings to the public.

[58] "Communicate" is defined in s 10(1) of the Act as including:

"to make available on-line or electronically transmit ... a work or other subject matter."

This definition covers circumstances where the transmission is over a path, or a combination of paths, provided by a material substance or otherwise.

[59] The applicants point to both of the limbs of the definition of "communicate", namely, "to make available on-line" and "to electronically transmit the subject matter". ...

[63] I am not satisfied that the Cooper website has "made available" the music sound recordings within the meaning of that expression. It is the remote websites which make available the sound recordings and from which the digital music files are downloaded as a result of a request transmitted to the remote website.

...

Authorisation of copyright infringement

[77] Section 101(1) of the Act provides that copyright is infringed by a person who, not being the owner of the copyright, authorises the doing in Australia of any act that infringes the copyright. ...

[81] Subsection 101(1A) was introduced into the Act by the 2000 Amendment. This provision states that in deciding whether a person has authorised the doing in Australia of any act comprised in the copyright, the matters that must be taken into account by the Court include:

"(a) the extent (if any) of the person's power to prevent the doing of the act concerned;

(b)   the nature of any relationship existing between the person and the person who did the act concerned;

(c)   whether the person took any other reasonable steps to prevent or avoid the doing of the act, including whether the person complied with any relevant industry codes of practice."

These factors are not exhaustive and do not prevent the Court from taking into account other factors, such as the respondent's knowledge of the nature of the copyright infringement.

[82] Among the objectives expressed in s 3 of the 2000 Amendment are to provide a practical enforcement regime for copyright owners and to promote access to copyright material online. These broadly expressed objectives conflict to some extent, however, in the present case, I consider that the reference to a practical enforcement regime is of some significance.

[83] Item 39 of the "Explanatory Memorandum" to the 2000 Amendment explains that the object of the Amendment was to "essentially codif[y] the principles in relation to authorisation that currently exist at common law". However, the applicants submit that the 2000

Amendment has strengthened and broadened the concept of infringement by authorisation. For example, the applicants refer to s 101(1A)(a), which they say contemplates that even a person with no power to "prevent" the doing of the act may nevertheless authorise infringement, and s 101(1A)(c), which requires that the Court take into account whether the person "took any other reasonable steps".

[84] The Cooper website is carefully structured and highly organised and many of its pages contain numerous references to linking and downloading. The website also provides the hyperlinks that enable the user to directly access the files on, and activate the downloading from, the remote websites. The website is clearly designed to, and does, facilitate and enable this infringing downloading. I am of the view that there is a reasonable inference available that Cooper, who sought advice as to the establishment and operation of his website, knowingly permitted or approved the use of his website in this manner and designed and organised it to achieve this result. In view of the absence of Cooper from the witness box, without any reasonable explanation apart from a tactical forensic suggestion that he was not a necessary or appropriate witness to be called in his own case, I am satisfied that the available inference of permission or approval by Cooper can more safely and confidently be drawn. Accordingly, I infer that Cooper has permitted or approved, and thereby authorized, the copyright infringement by internet users who access his website and also by the owners or operators of the remote websites from which the infringing recordings were downloaded.

[85] The words "sanction" and "approve" are expressions of wide import. Cooper, in my view, could have prevented the infringements by removing the hyperlinks from his website or by structuring the website in such a way that the operators of the remote websites from which MP3 files were downloaded could not automatically add hyperlinks to the website without some supervision or control by Cooper. The evidence of Professor Sterling, who was called on behalf of the applicants, is unchallenged to the effect that a website operator is always able to control the hyperlinks on his or her website, either by removal of the links or by requiring measures to be taken by the remote website operator prior to adding a hyperlink. A person cannot create a hyperlink between a music file and a website without the permission of the operator of the website because access to the code that is required to create the link must occur at level of the website. The Cooper website employed a "CGI-BIN" script to accept hyperlink suggestions from visitors to the website. By virtue of this script, such suggestions were automatically added to the website without the intervention of Cooper. The evidence is that alternative software was in existence that would have enabled a third party to add a hyperlink to a website but which required the consent or approval of the website operator before such hyperlinks were added. ...

[87] The Cooper website included a number of disclaimers indicating that MP3s could be both legal and illegal and that the downloading of MP3s would be legal only when the song's copyright owner had granted permission for the internet user to download and play the music sound recording. It is acknowledged by counsel for the first respondent that the disclaimers on the website inaccurately reflected copyright law in Australia. In my view, these statements do not, in the terms of s 101(1A)(c) of the Act, amount to reasonable steps to prevent or avoid the doing of the act. The disclaimers in fact indicate Cooper's knowledge of the existence of illegal MP3s on the internet and the likelihood that at least some of the MP3s to which the website provided hyperlinks constituted infringing copies of copyright music sound recordings. However, no attempt was made by Cooper, when hyperlinks were submitted to the website, to take any steps to ascertain the legality of the MP3s to which the hyperlinks related or the identity of the persons submitting the MP3s. In the words of Knox CJ in *Adelaide Corporation v Australasian Performing Right Association Ltd* (1928) 40 CLR 481 at 488,

▮▮▮▮▮▮ Universal Music Australia v Cooper *continued*

as approved by Gibbs CJ in *Moorhouse* at 13, Cooper "abstained from action which under the circumstances then existing it would have been reasonable to take, or ... exhibited a degree of indifference from which permission ought to be inferred."

[88] Accordingly, I find that Cooper has authorised the infringement of copyright in the music sound recordings, both by the internet users who downloaded the recordings and the operators of the remote websites. ...

Section 112E defences

[97] The 2000 Amendment provided for the protection of persons who make, or facilitate the making of, a communication. Section 39B applies to infringement of copyright in works and s 112E, which is in substantially similar terms, applies to infringement of copyright in subject matter other than works. Section 112E provides that a person, including a carrier or carriage service provider, who provides facilities for making, or facilitating the making of, a communication is not taken to have authorised any infringement of copyright in an audio-visual item merely because another person uses the facilities so provided to do something the right to do which is included in the copyright.

[98] ... The defence under s 112E applies only to infringement by authorisation.

[99] ... In my opinion, the circumstances of this case are taken outside the protection afforded by s 112E of the Act because Cooper has offered encouragement to users to download offending material, as evidenced by the numerous references to downloading material on the website, and has specifically structured and arranged the website so as to facilitate this downloading.

...

The US Free Trade Agreement Implementation Act 2004 (Cth)

[103] The second to fifth respondents seek to rely on the amendments to the Act effected by the *US Free Trade Agreement Implementation Act 2004* (Cth) ("the FTA Act"), which came into effect on 1 January 2005 after the initial hearing of this matter had taken place.

[104] The FTA Act inserted Div 2AA into Part V of the Act. The effect of these amendments was, broadly speaking, to provide a defence for internet service providers which excluded liability for damages for copyright infringement upon certain conditions.

[105] The applicants submit that these amendments constitute substantive amendments to the law, as opposed to procedural amendments, and therefore the Act should not, unless clearly indicated otherwise, be read to operate retrospectively. The applicants refer to the statement of Dixon CJ in *Maxwell v Murphy* (1957) 96 CLR 261 at 267:

> "The general rule of the common law is that a statute changing the law ought not, unless the intention appears with reasonable certainty, to be understood as applying to facts or events that have already occurred in such a way as to confer or impose or otherwise affect rights or liabilities which the law had defined by reference to the past events."

[106] I agree with the applicants' submission. In the present case, the amendments are substantive and accordingly the provisions do not apply to the present case.

[107] However, independently of that consideration, in order for the respondents to avail themselves of the protection, it is necessary under s 116AG(1) of the FTA Act for the respondents to satisfy the Court of the conditions set out in s 116AH, including that the carriage service provider has adopted and reasonably implemented a policy that provides for termination, in appropriate circumstances, of the accounts of repeated infringers. The evidence indicates that despite the respondents' awareness that copyright material was likely to be infringed, they have not taken any steps to implement such a policy. As counsel for the

applicants points out, Bal and Takoushis emphasised that they were indifferent to the use that Cooper made of the facilities provided by E-Talk/Com-Cen. This falls far short of demonstrating that they had adopted a policy to sanction infringers.

[108] Section 116AH imposes further conditions depending on the specific category of activity that was engaged in by the carriage service provider. The category of activity engaged in by E-Talk/Com-Cen was what is referred to in s 116AF as a "Category D activity", that is, "referring users to an online location using information location tools or technology." In the present case, the second to fifth respondents have not satisfied the particular conditions that apply to Category D activities under s 116AH. These conditions include that the provider must not have received a financial benefit directly attributable to the infringing activity if the service provider has the right and ability to control the activity. As I have found that the infringing activity is the triggering, and consequential downloading, of the music files from the website, I am satisfied that E-Talk/Com-Cen received a financial benefit from the infringing activity on the website because it obtained free advertising on the website. Further, the second to fifth respondents did not act expeditiously to remove or disable access from the hyperlinks and facilities hosted on its network notwithstanding that the circumstances made it apparent that copyright material was likely to be infringed.

[109] Accordingly, I do not accept the submissions of the second to fifth respondents that their liability for damages is excluded pursuant to the FTA Act.

...

Authorisation
[115] The evidence is that E-Talk/Com-Cen was, at all relevant times, a small, tightly-knit operation under the direction of Bal, employing in the order of eight persons working out of the same premises at Camperdown in close physical proximity to each other. In these circumstances, it is likely that the persons working in that office would have been aware of, and discussed, the offer made by Cooper, its subsequent acceptance and implementation. Moreover, it is in accordance with reasonable expectations as to the behaviour and experience of Bal in hosting as a commercial operator that he would have been keen to ensure that E-Talk/Com-Cen was receiving some benefit in return for hosting the website for free. The provision of these hosting services was a significant source of the revenue for Com-Cen Internet Services. It is noteworthy that Bal is named as the "Sales Person" in a series of Tax Invoices issued by Com-Cen to Cooper during the relevant period. ...

[119] I do not accept that Bal and Takoushis were unaware of the contents of the site or that they failed to take any steps to inform themselves as to the volume of traffic that the website would be likely to attract.

[120] ... In such a tight-knit operation as E-Talk/Com-Cen, it is unlikely, in my view, that Bal and Takoushis were unaware of the copyright problems that were said to arise from the operation of the website. However, no further steps were apparently taken by Bal or Takoushis on learning of these possible problems and the failure of Cooper to address these problems.

[121] Pursuant to s 101(1A) of the Act, in determining whether a person has authorised an infringement of copyright, the Court must take into account the extent of that person's power to prevent the doing of the act concerned and whether that person took any other reasonable steps to prevent or avoid the doing of the act. E-Talk/Com-Cen were responsible for hosting the website and providing the necessary connection to the internet and therefore had the power to prevent the doing of the infringing acts. They could have taken the step of taking down the website. Instead, they took no steps to prevent the acts of infringement. ...

[124] I do not accept that Takoushis, Bal or Georgiopoulos made no investigations regarding, or were uninterested to check, whether the amount of traffic attracted to the host

site was as initially suggested by Cooper. The records indicate there were a very high number of hits recorded over a 12 day period on the Cooper website in circumstances where there is no reason to suspect that this period was atypical. ...

[126] I should add that even if the version of events provided by Takoushis and Bal was accepted (which it is not) to the effect that it was a practice of E-Talk/Com-Cen not to make inquiries in relation to the contents of websites by reason of their title or name or other circumstances, this amounted to unreasonable conduct in relation to the provision of hosting services and to turning a blind eye to possible contraventions of copyright which could take place on the hosting site. Accordingly, within the meaning of s 112E it could not be said that they were doing no more than "merely" hosting the website involved in the present circumstances. Where a host is on notice of an irregularity and deliberately elects not to investigate the operation and contents of a site and turns a blind eye to such indications, even having regard to the possible indication afforded by the title of the website, then, in my view, there are additional factors called into play beyond merely hosting the site....

[131] For the same reasons given earlier in relation to Cooper, I am not satisfied that the second to fifth respondents can invoke the protection of s 112E of the Act. They have done more than merely provide facilities for the making of the communications. The word "merely" must be given its full force and effect. The second to fifth respondents have assumed an active role by agreeing to host the website and assisting with the operation of the website, which are necessary steps to effectively trigger the downloading of the copyright material. The reciprocal consideration passing between them, namely, the free hosting in return for the display of the Com-Cen logo on the website, is an additional matter which takes the situation beyond the protection afforded by s 112E.

▬▬▬▬▬▬▬▬▬▬▬▬▬▬▬▬▬▬▬▬▬▬▬▬▬▬▬▬▬▬

▬▬▬▬ Universal Music Australia v Sharman ▬▬▬▬

[6.150] *Universal Music Australia Pty Ltd v Sharman License Holdings Ltd* [2005] FCA 1242 Federal Court of Australia

[Facts: There were over 30 applicants, associated with ownership of music and sound recording rights. The case involves liability arising from use of the Kazaa website and Fast Track file sharing technology. The respondents included Sharman Networks and LEF Interactive who controlled Kazaa, and Altnet who provided search technology that allowed Kazaa users to access "gold files" which were files made available under license from copyright owners. The majority of Kazaa users would search and access "blue files", which would allow users to download files from another online user. The majority of this material would include infringing files.

Kazaa were found to have authorised the copyright infringement of users. The reasoning in relation to ss 112E and 101(1A) is extracted below.]

WILCOX J:

(iii) The application of s 112E
[395] The qualifying elements of s 112E apply to Sharman.

"(i)   Sharman is '[a] person' (it does not matter whether or not it is a carriage service provider);

(ii)   Sharman provides facilities (it does not matter they are not physical facilities);

(iii) the facilities are 'for making, or facilitating the making of, a communication' (an Internet file-sharing transaction)."

[396] It follows that Sharman is a person to whom s 112E may apply. Therefore, the effect of s 112E is that Sharman is "not taken to have authorised any infringement of copyright in a [sound recording] merely because [a Kazaa user] uses the facilities" to infringe the copyright. If the most that can be said against Sharman is that it has provided the facilities used by another person to infringe copyright, Sharman is not to be taken to have authorised the infringement. So understood, s 112E operates as a legislative reversal of the High Court's decision in *Telstra Corporation Limited v Australasian Performing Right Association Limited* (1997) 191 CLR 140 ('*Telstra*').

[397] There is good reason to believe such a reversal was the purpose of enacting s 112E. In July 1997, two Commonwealth Ministers, the then Attorney-General and the then Minister for Communications and the Arts, published a Discussion Paper entitled "Copyright Reform and the Digital Agenda". That paper made reference to the then recent decision of the Full Federal Court in *Telstra*. Paragraphs 4.87 and 4.88 of the Discussion Paper read:

"On the basis of the scheme proposed in this paper, it is intended that Telstra would as a carrier not be liable to APRA for the playing by others of music on-hold to users of mobile telephones, contrary to the result under the current law (in the Full Federal Court decision in *APRA v Telstra*).

No proposals are made in relation to providing carriers or carriage service providers with a statutory exception from liability for infringement of the new rights proposed in this paper on the basis that the case law on the authorisation of copyright infringement is better able to adapt to developments in this area. We do, however, invite comment on whether the *Copyright Act* should be amended to provide that ISPs would be exempt from copyright liability in any circumstances in which they provided notices to their subscribers about copyright rights and the nature of permitted use of copyright material under the *Copyright Act*."

[398] As counsel for Mr Rose noted, the first published draft Bill included the provision that is now s 112E, but with the word "facilities" qualified by the word "physical". That qualification was abandoned in the final Bill. In his Second Reading Speech to the Bill, the then Attorney-General said:

"The amendments in the bill also respond to the concerns of carriers and carriage service providers, such as Internet service providers, about the uncertainty of the circumstances in which they could be liable for copyright infringements by their customers. The provisions in the bill limit and clarify the liability of carriers and Internet service providers in relation to both direct and authorisation liability. The amendments also overcome the 1997 High Court decision of *APRA v Telstra* in which Telstra, as a carrier, was held to be liable for the playing of music-on-hold by its subscribers to their clients, even though Telstra exercised no control in determining the content of the music played.

Typically, the person responsible for determining the content of copyright material online would be a web site proprietor, not a carrier or Internet service provider. Under the amendments, therefore, carriers and Internet service providers will not be directly liable for communicating material to the public if they are not responsible for determining the content of the material. The reforms provide that a carrier or Internet service provider will not be taken to have authorised an infringement of copyright

◼◼◼◼ Universal Music Australia v Sharman *continued*

merely through the provision of facilities on which the infringement occurs. Further, the bill provides an inclusive list of factors to assist in determining whether the autho-risation of an infringement has occurred."

[399] A statutory provision to the effect that a person is not to be taken to have authorised an infringement merely because another person does a particular thing leaves open the possibility that, for other reasons, the first person may be taken to have authorised the infringement. Such a provision does not confer general immunity against a finding of autho-risation. Consequently, s 112E does not preclude the possibility that a person who falls within the section may be held, for other reasons, to be an authoriser. Whether or not the person should be so held is to be determined, in the present context, by reference to s 101 of the Act.

...

The application of s 101 to LEF and Ms Hemming

[421] LEF is wholly owned and controlled by Ms Hemming. It is a "one-woman" company, Ms Hemming's *alter ego*. Consequently, no distinction should be made between the position of these two respondents.

[422] Counsel for the Sharman respondents disputed that any of their clients authorised copyright infringement by Kazaa users. However, they also argued that, in any event, Ms Hemming should not be made liable for any authorisation by Sharman. They referred to an observation by Gummow J in *Hanimex* at 283:

"Where the infringer is a corporation questions frequently arise as to the degree of involvement on the part of directors necessary for them to be rendered personally liable. Those questions are not immediately answered by principles dealing with "authorisation" or joint tortfeasance. Rather, recourse is to be had to the body of authority which explains the circumstances in which an officer of a corporation is personally liable for the torts of the corporation."

[423] Gummow J went on to cite several cases. I need not deal with those cases. There is more recent authority on the point.

[424] In *King v Milpurrurra* (1996) 66 FCR 474 at 494, Beazley J said:

"It will be recalled that in [*Hanimex*], Gummow J stated that the principles dealing, inter alia, with joint tortfeasance, did not directly apply when determining whether a director was liable for a company's infringement of copyright. This must be so. The essence of joint tortfeasance is 'concerted action to a common end': *The Koursk* [1924] P 140 at 156. This notion does not fit easily with the liability of a director for the company's wrongs. This is because, as Lord Reid said in *Tesco Supermarkets Ltd v Nattrass* [1972] AC 153] at 170-171, the person who is the directing mind and will of the company:

'is an embodiment of the company ... and his mind is the mind of the company ...

Normally, [a] board of directors ... carry out the functions of management and speak and act as the company.'"

...

[426] Beazley J identified two competing lines of authority: cases that held "a director is personally liable for a tortious act committed by the company which the director has ordered or procured to be done" ("the *Performing Right Society* test") and cases that applied a higher test ("the *Mentmore* test"), whether the director (or officer) made "the tortious act his own". Although Beazley J acknowledged that the test usually applied in Australian intellectual

██████ Universal Music Australia v Sharman *continued*

property cases was the *Performing Right Society* test, she thought that test was unsatisfactory; it failed to "pay sufficient regard, either to the separate legal existence of the company, or to the fact that the company acts through its directors". Her Honour preferred the *Mentmore* test.

[427] In *Microsoft Corporation v Auschina Polaris Pty Ltd* (1996) 71 FCR 231 ("*Auschina Polaris*") at 239, Lindgren J also accepted the statement of principle of Gummow J in *Hanimex*. He went on to refer to the conflict of authority discussed by Beazley J, but he preferred the *Performing Right Society* test.

[428] The same issue was discussed, in the context of a claimed patent infringement, by Finkelstein J in *Root Quality Pty Ltd v Root Control Technologies Pty Ltd* [2000] FCA 980 ("*Root Quality*").

[429] Finkelstein J rejected the *Performing Right Society* test. He thought it presented a number of difficulties. At [125], his Honour said:

> "The first arises from the nature of corporate personality and the liability of a corporation for the acts of its agents. A corporation is an abstraction; a creature of statute. It can carry out acts only because the law attributes to the corporation certain actions of its directors and officers. Thus a corporation can interfere with the rights of a third party only when the acts constituting the unlawful interference are attributed to the corporation. There is a reason why, in that circumstance, the law should not impose liability both on the corporation for unlawful interference and separate liability on the director or officer for procuring that interference."

[430] On the other hand, Finkelstein J was uncomfortable with the *Mentmore* line of cases under which, he thought, "it would not always be easy to identify the circumstances under which a director could 'make that tort his own'". He concluded, at [146]:

> "All that can be said confidently is that if a director decides that his company should carry out an act that results in an infringement of the rights of a third party, the director does not, without more, render himself personally liable at the suit of the third party ... The director's conduct must be such that it can be said of him that he was so personally involved in the commission of the unlawful act that it is just that he should be rendered liable. If a director deliberately takes steps to procure the commission of an act which the director knows is unlawful and procures that act for the purpose of causing injury to a third party, then plainly it is just that liability should be imposed upon him. Lesser conduct may suffice. For example, if the director is recklessly indifferent as regards whether his company's act was unlawful and would cause harm, that may also suffice. In the end it will depend upon the facts of each particular case. Where the boundary lies, between the non-tortious conduct of a director who acts bona fide within the course of his authority and the tortious conduct of a director who acts deliberately and maliciously to cause harm, cannot be stated with any precision."

[431] The issue of the proper test was inconclusively noted in two recent Full Court judgments. In *Allen Manufacturing Co Pty Ltd v McCallum & Co Pty Ltd* [2001] FCA 1838; 53 IPR 400, at [43]–[44], the Court said:

> "The difference between the two tests may be more apparent than real. We are not aware of any case in which it has been held that a director or officer of a company directed or procured the company's infringing act, yet that person escaped liability because he or she did not deliberately, wilfully or knowingly pursue a course of conduct that was likely to constitute infringement or that reflected indifference to the risk of infringement. This may be because, in practice, an act of direction or

██████ Universal Music Australia v Sharman *continued*

procurement will generally meet the *Mentmore* test. It is notable that, in *Mentmore* itself, the Canadian Federal Court of Appeal declined (at 204) to 'go so far as to hold that the director or officer must know or have reason to know that the acts which he directs or procures constitute infringement'. The Court declined to do this because that 'would be to impose a condition of liability that does not exist for patent infringement generally'. To the extent there is a real difference between the tests, each has eloquent supporters. One day it may be necessary, in a practical sense, to choose between them. But it is not necessary to do so in this case."

[432] In *Sydneywide Distributors Pty Ltd v Red Bull Australia Pty Ltd* [2002] FCAFC 157 at [160]–[161], Weinberg and Dowsett JJ mentioned the two lines of authority. However, the issue went off on a pleading point.

[433] It will be apparent that the authorities are in some disarray. There are numerous cases, some of them recent, that would support a decision to adopt the *Performing Right Society* test and ask whether Ms Hemming procured and directed the acts and omissions of Sharman that constituted authorisation of users' infringements of the applicants' copyrights. There could be only an affirmative answer to that question.

[434] However, in recent years, several members of this Court have expressed dissatisfaction with the *Performing Right Society* test and have argued for the adoption of something more rigorous. Some judges have favoured the *Mentmore* test and asked whether the person 'made the tort his own'. My difficulty is that, like Lindgren J in *Auschina Polaris* and Finkelstein J in *Root Quality*, I am not sure what that test means. Like their Honours, I prefer to eschew any catchphrase and consider the justice of the case. In *Root Quality*, Finkelstein J said: 'The director's conduct must be such that it can be said of him that he was so personally involved in the commission of the unlawful act that it is just that he should be rendered liable'. I am happy to adopt that test, with the qualification that the person need not be a director of the company. I adopt that approach the more readily because I believe it encapsulates the approach which has in fact been taken, although perhaps not articulated in those words, in many intellectual property cases in this Court. See, for example, *Jain* at 53; *Auschina Polaris* at 246; *Metro* at 593; and *Cooper* at [130].

[435] *Jain* is particularly interesting. In that case the Full Court imposed personal liability for 'a studied and deliberate course of action in which Mr Jain decided to ignore the appellant's right and to allow a situation to develop and to continue in which he must have known that it was likely that the appellants' music would be played without any licence from it. It was within his power to control what was occurring be [sic] he did nothing at all'....

[445] In the present case, it may be open to the Court to do more than find that Ms Hemming, having the power to control what was happening, did nothing at all. A combination of the two possible inferences suggested above would lead to a conclusion that Ms Hemming (alone or with others) purchased the Kazaa system from Kazaa BV and then caused, or allowed, its structure to be changed away from the use of a Kazaaserver; presumably, to enable Sharman to argue (as it has done in this case) that it has no control over the copyright infringing conduct of Kazaa users.

[446] In the absence of rebutting evidence on either of the points, I am inclined to the view that I should reach that conclusion. However, it is not necessary to determine that matter. At the very least, the case is on all fours with *Jain*. See also *Auschina Polaris* at 246 and *Metro* at 593.

[447] LEF and Ms Hemming should be held to have authorised the Kazaa users' infringements of copyright in the applicants' sound recordings...

▓▓▓ Universal Music Australia v Sharman *continued*

(x) Conclusions on authorisation

[489] I have found that three of the Sharman parties (Sharman, LEF and Ms Hemming) and three of the Altnet parties (Altnet, BDE and Mr Bermeister) authorised infringement of the applicants' copyright by Kazaa users. They did this both individually and as joint tortfeasors pursuant to a common design. There is no doubt as to the close collaboration of Sharman and Altnet in developing and operating the system, and the involvement in that collaboration of Ms Hemming and Mr Bermeister on behalf of LEF and BDE respectively.

[Wilcox J also commented on the potential of the applicants to reduce piracy by broader licensing of works to make them available legitimately online, and by recourse to technological protection measures. This discussion, his orders requiring reprogramming of Kazaa to deter infringement, and a summary of the reasoning supporting the orders follow.

Universal Music v Sharman

[6.155] *Universal Music Australia Pty Ltd v Sharman License Holdings Ltd* [2005] FCA 1242

[In recognition of the "public interest" aspects of this case, and in response to the amicus brief of the Australian Consumers' Association Pty Ltd, Electronic Frontiers Australia Inc and New South Wales Council for Civil Liberties Inc Wilcox J provided a Summary in addition to his decision. This is extracted below.]

■ Summary

WILCOX J:

Before I indicate my conclusions about that claim, I wish to identify two matters that this case is **not** about.

First, many people (including the respondents) argue that the Internet is here to stay, it is being used by an ever increasing number of people and peer-to-peer file-sharing is one of its most valuable potential uses. They say that copyright owners, such as the present applicants, could eliminate (or at least substantially reduce) infringement of their copyrights if they were willing to make copyright works available on a licensed basis for a fee, in the way in which Altnet offers gold files. Second, it was suggested at one stage of this case that it would have been possible for the applicants to have made their compact discs less vulnerable to being "ripped" into a computer program by issuing them in a digital rights managed, rather than open, format.

Neither of these matters fall for decision in this case. I understand the argument in favour of more widespread licensing of copyright works. No doubt that course would have commercial implications for sound recording distributors. Whether or not they should take it is a matter to be determined by them. Unless and until they do decide to take that course, they are entitled to invoke such protective rights as the law affords them. Similarly in regard to making compact discs less susceptible to ripping; although, in regard to that matter, I add the evidence is insufficient for me to reach any conclusion about the feasibility of doing this.

I return to the true issue in the case: the applicants' copyright claim. Here again, the applicants overstated their case. It cannot be concluded, as the applicants claimed in their pleadings, that the respondents themselves engaged in communicating the applicants' copyright works. They did not do so. The more realistic claim is that the respondents authorised users to infringe the applicants' copyright in their sound recordings. Section 101 of the Australian *Copyright Act* provides that copyright is infringed by a person who, not being the owner of the copyright and without the licence of the copyright owner, authorises another person to do in Australia an infringing act.

I have concluded that this more limited claim is established against six of the ten respondents. My reasons may be summarised in this way:

(i) despite the fact that the Kazaa website contains warnings against the sharing of copyright files, and an end user licence agreement under which users are made to agree not to infringe copyright, it has long been obvious that those measures are ineffective to prevent, or even substantially to curtail, copyright infringements by users. The respondents have long known that the Kazaa system is widely used for the sharing of copyright files;

(ii) there are technical measures (keyword filtering and gold file flood filtering) that would enable the respondents to curtail—although probably not totally to prevent – the sharing of copyright files. The respondents have not taken any action to implement those measures. It would be against their financial interest to do so. It is in the respondents' financial interest to maximise, not to minimise, music file-sharing. Advertising provides the bulk of the revenue earned by the Kazaa system, which revenue is shared between Sharman Networks and Altnet.

(iii) far from taking steps that are likely effectively to curtail copyright file-sharing, Sharman Networks and Altnet have included on the Kazaa website exhortations to users to increase their file-sharing and a webpage headed 'Join the Revolution' that criticises record companies for opposing peer-to-peer file-sharing. They also sponsored a "Kazaa Revolution" campaign attacking the record companies. The revolutionary material does not expressly advocate the sharing of copyright files. However, to a young audience, and it seems that Kazaa users are predominantly young people, the effect of this webpage would be to encourage visitors to think it 'cool' to defy the record companies by ignoring copyright constraints.

A question arose as to the form of relief that might be made against the six respondents that I hold to have authorised infringement of the applicants' copyright. The applicants are entitled to declarations as to past violations of their rights and the threat of future violations. They are also entitled to an order restraining future violations. However, I have had to bear in mind the possibility that, even with the best will in the world, the respondents probably cannot totally prevent copyright infringement by users. I am anxious not to make an order which the respondents are not able to obey, except at the unacceptable cost of preventing the sharing even of files which do not infringe the applicants' copyright. There needs to be an opportunity for the relevant respondents to modify the Kazaa system in a targeted way, so as to protect the applicants' copyright interests (as far as possible) but without unnecessarily intruding on others' freedom of speech and communication. The evidence about keyword filtering and gold file flood filtering, indicates how this might be done. It should be provided that the injunctive order will be satisfied if the respondents take either of these steps. The steps, in my judgment, are available to the respondents and likely significantly, though perhaps not totally, to protect the applicants' copyrights.

[His Honour's orders included]

4. The infringing respondents be restrained, by themselves, their servants or agents, from authorising Kazaa users to do in Australia any of the infringing acts, in relation to any

■■■■■ Universal Music v Sharman *continued*

sound recording of which any of the applicants is the copyright owner, without the licence of the relevant copyright owner.

5. Continuation of the Kazaa Internet file-sharing system (including the provision of software programs to new users) shall not be regarded as a contravention of order 4 if that system is first modified pursuant to a protocol, to be agreed between the infringing respondents and the applicants or to be approved by the Court, that ensures either of the following situations:

(i): that:

    (a) the software program received by all new users of the Kazaa file-sharing system contains non-optional key-word filter technology that excludes from the displayed blue file search results all works identified (by titles, composers' or performers' names or otherwise) in such lists of their copyright works as may be provided, and periodically updated, by any of the applicants; and

    (b) all future versions of the Kazaa file-sharing system contain the said non-optional key-word filter technology; and

    (c) maximum pressure is placed on existing users, by the use of dialogue boxes on the Kazaa website, to upgrade their existing Kazaa software program to a new version of the program containing the said non-optional key-word filter technology; or

(ii) that the TopSearch component of the Kazaa system will provide, in answer to a request for a work identified in any such list, search results that are limited to licensed works and warnings against copyright infringement and that will exclude provision of a copy of any such identified work.

[Notes

The context of Wilcox J's orders can be gleaned from the summary and quotes below. The questions do not appear in the judgement.]

1. What was the relevance of some downloads involving non-infringing uses?

"I do not doubt that some people use Kazaa only in a non-infringing way. However, it seems unlikely that non-infringing uses would sustain the enormous Kazaa traffic claimed by the respondents. The explanation of that volume of traffic must be a more populist use." at [184].

2. What was the relevance of the commercial model?

The corporate logic of Kazaa is advertising: "It is a fundamental of advertising marketing that price is sensitive to the exposure likely to be achieved by the advertisement. The more shared files available through Kazaa, the greater the attraction of the Kazaa website. The more visitors to the Kazaa website, the greater its advertising value and the higher the advertising rate able to be demanded by Sharman. And what is more likely to attract large numbers of visitors to the website than music, especially currently popular 'hits'?" at [191].

Altnet benefited two ways. The gold file service fed off searches for blue files. Secondly, Altnet shared the advertising revenue received by Kazaa, the value of which must have been influenced by the volume of blue file sharing.

3. Can there be control without a centralised server?

He noted with some frustration a lack of direct evidence from those responsible for establishing and operating the Kazaa system, with its adjunct Altnet technology. Wilcox J was sceptical of evidence by Sharman's experts suggesting a lack of centralized control, but other experts were unable to locate it or conclusively identify a central server. He found that this made it impossible to implement a system of identifying user identities. However he found that:

> "TopSearch is capable of monitoring and controlling the conduct of Kazaa users in relation to gold files. TopSearch is a central server, in the relevant sense, but (at the present time) only in respect of gold files." at [235]

Accordingly technical measures (gold file flood filtering and keyword filtering) would enable the respondents to curtail—although probably not totally to prevent—the sharing of copyright files.

4. What is gold file flood filtering?

It is technically possible to flood search results page with gold files as an effective means of inhibiting the downloading of unauthorised blue files. This may include blank pages or "Don't steal copyright" messages. Gold flood filering has the advantage of affecting users even if they do not upgrade to a new version of FastTrack.

5. What is keyword filtering?

The Kazaa system already incorporated "advanced searches" limiting search results to particular categories of files: audio, video, software, archives and play lists. There are also filters for viruses which removes files with suspicious extensions such as .scr or .bat. An mp3 extension could thus be searched for, but this would block any mp3 files, including ones owners allow to download for free. File extension filtering and file icon filtering was accepted an unfeasible.

However Sharman had "the most comprehensive" adult filter and monitored for child pornography that looks through metadata such as the file title. This shows keyword filtering is feasible.

Wilcox J accepted "that a keyword filter system that was tied to the title of the sound recording or the name of the artist would not be 100% effective. However, counsel for the applicants argued this was no reason to reject the view that the respondents could have used this technique substantially to inhibit copyright infringement." at [280].

6. Who would be responsible for the lists of material to be filtered?

> "It would be necessary for the applicants, and other copyright owners, to co-operate in the creation of such a list. To the extent they refused or neglected to do so, they would deny themselves such copyright protection as keyword filtering might provide to them. It would also be necessary for the list regularly to be updated. This would be an onerous ongoing task. However, to the extent that copyright owners neglected to do this, it would be they (not the respondents) who would suffer." at [287].

7. What about filtering resulting in "false positives", that is blocking more than infringing files?

> "There is no evidence that suggests this would be a frequent occurrence. The impression I have gained from the evidence is that the predominant use of the blue files is the sharing of popular music. Such material may be expected to be overwhelmingly subject to copyright. If that impression is incorrect, the respondents have themselves to blame." at [288].

Thus Kazaa's history of identifying with downloading infringing material means it has to bear overreaching.

Users can devise methods of evading a keyword filter; for example, by the adoption of nickname for the artist or a codeword for a particular song but "this technique would allow

██████ Universal Music v Sharman *continued*

file-sharing of the relevant works only as between people who were privy to the adopted nicknames or codewords".

8. How do you make users upgrade to the filtering version of the technology?
New users could be made to include the necessary filtering elements. Existing users will not want to upgrade to filtering technology but "there are practical means of forcing an update on users even if it is only by force of rendering the existing version impracticable to use by incessant update offers" at [304]. The description sounds like a "mouse-trap" technique of incessant pop-up windows of messages that "drive the user mad".

9. Doesn't filtering Kazza affect users in other jurisdictions?
"If it is reasonable for the respondents (or any of them) to adopt a filtering mechanism in order to avoid an infringement of Australian copyright law, it is immaterial whether that step would also have been necessary in order to avoid infringement of the copyright law of some other country." at [330].

10. Why not make owners rely on technological protection, instead of forcing others to filter?
"It is not a defence to an action for copyright infringement for a respondent to point to failings in self-protection by the copyright owner. Copyright law contains no equivalent of the doctrine of contributory negligence." at [419].

INDIRECT INFRINGEMENT

■ Parallel importation and allowing a performance in a public place
[6.160] One of the main problems for enforcement of copyright with regard to indirect infringement is the requirement that the importer (s 37) or trader (s 38) knows that the material would infringe if made in Australia. See also ss 102 and 103. Allowing a place of public entertainment to be used for the performance of a work in public is also an infringement, unless the permission is given gratuitously or the consideration merely covers costs (s 39(1)).

INFRINGEMENT OF COPYRIGHT IN SUBJECT MATTER OTHER THAN WORKS: SECTIONS 101-103

[6.165] Direct infringement of Part IV copyrights is much more restricted than that in relation to works, being confined to a reproduction of the article embodying the subject matter, or else causing the content to be communicated, broadcast, rebroadcast, seen or heard in public. In *CBS Records Australia Ltd v Telmak Teleproducts (Aust) Pty Ltd* (1987) 9 IPR 440 the respondents had made a record entitled "Chart Sounds 16 Hit Songs No 1" using artists to re-record "cover versions" of popular songs. One of the issues between the parties was whether a "sound alike" (that is, a later sound recording by other performers which is an imitation of the original) was within the description of a "copy of a sound recording" referred to in *Copyright Act 1968* (Cth), s 10(3)(c). Bowen CJ held (at 444) that only "an actual embodiment of the very sounds on the original record" falls within the definition. Bowen CJ said (at 446):

"In the present case the question is whether, having regard to the terms of the statutory provisions including the definitions, the imitation sounds produced by different performers at a later point of time embody the sounds in the original sound recording in the sense used in the Act."

Indirect infringement through sale or importation of infringing material is, in Australia, far more prevalent, due to the activities of offshore record and video pirates. Part of the debate surrounding the question of repealing restrictions on parallel importing concerns s the alleged effect that freeing up the market will have in terms of opportunities for importation of illegally copied (directly infringing) sound recordings, etc. In a regime where only the authorised distributor may import copyright goods, it is easier to track the movement of pirated material.

■ Substantial part and Part IV copyright

━━━━━ TCN Channel Nine v Network Ten (No 2) ━━━━━

[6.170] *TCN Channel Nine Pty Limited v Network Ten Pty Limited (No 2)* (2005) 145 FCR 35 Federal Court of Australia

FINKELSTEIN J: [37] ...   Section 91 of the *Copyright Act 1968* (Cth) provides that copyright subsists in a "television broadcast" made from a place in Australia by the holder of a licence under the *Broadcasting Services Act 1992* (Cth). In this case there was a dispute as to the meaning of "television broadcast". Was it each single image shown on a television set, or was it the programme constituted by an aggregation of those images? The dispute was resolved by the High Court: *Network Ten Pty Ltd v TCN Channel Nine Pty Ltd* (2004) 78 ALJR 585. The High Court (by majority) pointed out (at 599) that the interest to be protected by this particular form of copyright (being copyright in non-original subject matter) is the cost and skill in assembling or preparing and transmitting the programme to the public. The nature of this interest, as well as the enacting history of s 91, led the High Court (at 593) to the conclusion that "broadcast" means "programme". In reaching this conclusion the High Court said (at 593) that the contrary view "fixed upon the medium of transmission, not the message conveyed by its use". Implicitly the High Court rejected the idea that the medium is the message, an idea popularised by Marshall McLuhan in *Understanding Media: The Existence of Man* (1st ed, McGraw-Hill, New York, 1964).

[38] The High Court did not resolve the entire dispute between the appellants ("Nine") and the respondent ("Ten"). Ten's weekly television programme, The Panel, used 20 short extracts (between eight and 42 seconds) from programmes previously broadcast by Nine, extracts which had previously been recorded on video tapes. Nine alleges that those extracts infringe its copyright in the programmes. At trial ((2001) 108 FCR 235) and on appeal ((2002) 118 FCR 417) Ten made out a fair dealing defence in respect of nine extracts. The dispute still to be resolved is whether the remaining 11 extracts that were copied and re-broadcast were "substantial" parts of the programmes from which they were taken. Only if they were "substantial" parts of those programmes will Nine's copyright be infringed.

The first thing to be done is to resolve a different dispute. When deciding whether a part of a programme is a substantial part of that programme for copyright purposes it is necessary to compare what has been taken with the copyright work. In the case of broadcast copyright it is necessary to identify with precision the particular programme in which it is

▓▓▓▓▓ TCN Channel Nine v Network Ten (No 2) *continued*

alleged the copyright has been infringed. This task is not as easy as it seems. Nine says that each programme identified in its statement of claim (the programmes ranged in duration from approximately 30 minutes to approximately five hours) is a separate television broadcast. Both Nine and Ten say that any advertisement shown during the course of a programme should be treated as a separate and discrete broadcast. According to the High Court those propositions are correct. On the other hand, and this is where a dispute has arisen, Nine claims that if a particular programme can be divided into separate and distinct parts in terms of theme, story and impact each segment should be treated as a separate broadcast. This is an important point. If a copyright owner is able to confine a programme in terms of length and subject matter, it will be easier for the owner to establish that the part that is taken is "substantial". The parties are at odds as to whether the High Court has determined that the programmes in this case are those described in Nine's statement of claim (where they are not broken into segments) or whether, for the purposes of determining infringement, the High Court left open the possibility that they may be segmented.

On this aspect the High Court first said ((2004) 78 ALJR 585, 600) that "a television broadcast" cannot be defined with "precision". Nevertheless it said the programmes that Nine identified in its pleading do answer that description, subject to the qualification that advertisements should be treated as discrete and separate programmes. The High Court referred to the judge's view that in an appropriate case it may be possible to treat a segment of a programme as the measure of a television broadcast. The majority (at 600) said as to this: "We would reserve consideration of that proposition for a particular case where the point arises." They added, no doubt by way of caution, that even if the judge's proposition is correct, a news broadcast made up of various segments, items or stories did not "necessarily render each of [them] a television broadcast in which copyright subsists". For a similar view see *Television New Zealand Ltd v Newsmonitor Services Ltd* [1994] 2 NZLR 91, 108.

... [39] ...

The principal issue that confronted the judge on the issue of substantiality was whether he should adopt the approach that applied to original works or whether a different test was required for non-original subject matter. Copyright in an original work will be infringed if there is an unauthorised reproduction of the work or if a person purports to be the author of the work by illegally appropriating the fruits of the author's labour by reproducing his work with colourable alterations. In *Dicks v Yates* (1881) 18 Ch D 76, 90, James LJ referred to the first kind of infringement as "open piracy" and to the second as "literary larceny".

Piracy is not committed only when the defendant has published the whole of the copyright work. If that happens it is immaterial in what form and for what purpose the work has been reproduced: *Scott v Stanford* (1867) LR 3 Eq 718, 723. There will also be piracy if the defendant reproduces a part of an original work because copyright protects the whole and all parts of the work: *White v Gerock* (1819) 2 Barn & Ald 298 [22 RR 786]; *Cary v Longman and Rees* (1801) 1 East 358. When part of the plaintiff's work is reproduced there will be an infringement of copyright if the part is an essential or material part of the original work. This was the position under the early *Copyright Acts*: *Sweet v Shaw* (1839) 3 Jur 217; *Sweet v Cater* (1841) 11 Sim 572, 573 [59 ER 994]; *Bohn v Bogue* (1846) 7 LT (OS) 277, 278; *Jarrold v Houlston* (1857) 3 K & J 708, 719 [69 ER 1294, 1299]; *Tinsley v Lacy* (1863) 1 H & M 747, 751 [711 ER 327, 329]. The rule had become so well entrenched that when s 2 of the *Dramatic Copyright Act 1833* (3 & 4 Will 4 c 15) for the first time enacted that there would be an infringement of copyright (in that case in a dramatic work) if there had been an unauthorised reproduction of "any part of the work", this was construed to mean a material or substantial part of the work:

Chatterton v Cave (1878) 3 App Cas 483, 492. Section 2 of the *Copyright Act 1911* (UK), which was in force in Australia from 1912 until its repeal by the *Copyright Act 1968* (Cth), made express provision for the reproduction of a substantial part of a copyright work to constitute an act of infringement. See now *Copyright Act 1968*, s 14.

There is no fixed rule for determining how much of a copyright work must be taken for it to be a substantial part of the work. The area of substantial similarity is at the heart of copyright law, yet it remains one of its most elusive aspects. The general rule is that substantiality depends on quality not quantity: *Ladbroke (Football) Ltd v William Hill (Football) Ltd* [1964] 1 WLR 273, 293. Often it will be obvious whether or not a substantial part of the copyright work has been taken from a visual or, if appropriate, an oral comparison between the copyright work and the allegedly infringing work: see *Hanfstaengl v Empire Palace* [1894] 3 Ch 109, 129 per Lindley LJ: ("the degree of resemblance is all important"). In the United States the visual comparison that is required is referred to as the "ordinary observer test" and is derived from *Daly v Palmer* 6 Fed Cas 1132, 1138 (2nd Circ, 1868). Following the decision in *Arnstein v Porter* 154 F 2d 462, 473 (2nd Circ, 1946) the approach is sometimes referred to as the "audience test". The test invites that a comparison **[40]** be conducted between the two works for the purpose of deciding substantial similarity: see by way of example *Henry Holt & Co Inc v Liggett & Myers Tobacco Co* 23 F Supp 302, 304 (3rd Circ, 1938); *Concord Fabrics Inc v Marcus Brothers Textile Corp* 409 F 2d 1315, 1316-1317 (2nd Circ, 1969); *Miller Brewing Company v Carling O'Keefe Breweries of Canada Ltd* 452 F Supp 429, 440 (2nd Circ, 1978); *American Greeting Corporation v Easter Unlimited Inc* 579 F Supp 607, 615-616 (2nd Circ, 1983).

There will be cases where a visual or oral comparison will not enable the tribunal to decide whether the part taken is indeed substantial. This is especially so when the amount copied is small. There will be an infringement if the defendant has reproduced something that is of aesthetic significance. Sometimes, however, "[w]hen it comes down to a question of quantity [the answer] must be very vague": *Bramwell v Halcomb* (1836) 3 My & Cr 732, 738 [40 ER 1110] per Lord Cottenham LC. In a doubtful case other factors must be considered.

One factor is the economic significance of that which has been taken. In *Bramwell v Halcomb* (1836) 3 My & Cr 732, 738 [40 ER 1110] Lord Cottenham said that it is the "value [to the plaintiff of what has been taken] that is always looked to." See also *Bell v Whitehead* (1839) 8 LJ Ch 141, 142 per Lord Cottenham LJ: ("Here, the value of the extract is very minute and trifling, and if there were nothing else in the case, the extreme minuteness of the value in the extract, and of the injury sustained by the plaintiff, would be sufficient to induce the Court not to interfere"); *Scott v Stanford* (1867) LR 3 Eq 718, 723 per Sir W Page Wood VC: ("But if, in effect, the great bulk of the Plaintiff's publication—a large and vital portion of his work and labour—has been appropriated and published in a form which will materially injure his copyright, mere honest intention on the part of the appropriator will not suffice as the Court can only look at the result, and not at the intention in the man's mind at the time of doing the act complained of, and he must be presumed to intend all that the publication of his work effects."); *Bradbury v Hotten* (1872) 8 LR Ex 1, 6 per Kelly CB: ("The principle of [the authorities] is, that where one man for his own profit puts into his work an essential part of another man's work, from which that other may still derive profit, or from which, but for the act of the first, he might have derived profit, there is evidence of a piracy upon which a jury should act"); *Weatherby & Sons v International Horse and Agency and Exchange Limited* [1910] 2 Ch 297, 305 per Parker J: ("[In utilising the plaintiff's labour and industry] they have appropriated the result of [his] labour and expense to their own use, and even if they have injured the plaintiffs in no other way, they have at any rate deprived them of the advantage, which their copyright conferred on them, of being able to publish such a book as the defendant's

▬▬▬▬ TCN Channel Nine v Network Ten (No 2) *continued*

book at much less labour and expense than any one else."). See also *Cambridge University Press v University Tutorial Press* (1928) 75 RPC 335, 343-344.

It should be noted, however, that if there is no damage to the plaintiff he will not necessarily fail in this action, for the right protected by the *Copyright Act* is not dependent upon proof of damage: see *Kipling v Genatosan Ltd* (1920) Mac Cop Cas 203, 205 per Peterson J: ("It was said that there was no competition or damage. But the judgment of Lord Parker in *Weatherby v International Horse Agency* ... showed that there might be infringement without either of these elements in the case"); *Hawkes and Son (London) Limited v Paramount Film Service Limited* [1934] 1 Ch 593, 603 per Lord Hanworth: ([41] "[T]he right of the owner of a copyright is not determined or measured by the amount of actual damage to him by reason of the infringement; copyright is a right of property, and he is entitled to come to the Court for the protection of that property even though he does not show or prove actual damage").

Another factor is the use which the defendant makes of the copied portion of the plaintiff's work. An unfair use, as when the defendant intends to go into competition with the plaintiff, may be a determining factor: *Bradbury v Hotten* (1872) 8 LR Ex 1, 6 per Kelly CB: ("Is [the defendant] by so doing applying to his own use and for his own profit what otherwise the plaintiffs might have turned, and possibly may turn, to a 'profitable account'? The pictures are of great merit, and no doubt were largely paid for, and by inserting these copies the defendant has unquestionably added to the value of his publication. Why should this not be an infringement?"); *Chatterton v Cave* (1878) 3 App Cas 483, 498 per Lord O'Hagan: ("In all, quantity and value are both the subjects of consideration, and in none of them has an infringement been established without satisfactory evidence of an appropriation, possibly involving a substantial loss to one person and a substantial gain to another; although as was observed by Lord Chief Justice Tindal in *Planche v Braham*, 'the damage to the Plaintiff is not the test of the Defendant's liability,' and the penalty is to be paid 'even if there is no actual damage'"); *Cooper v Stephens* [1895] 1 Ch 567, 572 per Romer J: ("But, in considering a question of infringement like this, it is important to consider the intent of the copyist and the nature of his work as was observed by Lord Chief Baron Kelly in *Bradbury v Hotten*. In the present case I observe that the Defendants are using the five drawings complained of for the very purpose for which the originals were made by the Plaintiffs, and so as to escape making any payment to the Plaintiffs in respect of their right in the drawings. And I cannot help seeing that, if the Defendants are allowed to do with impunity what they have done, the Plaintiff's copyright will be rendered practically valueless, and, in fact, destroyed"). Once again, as several of these passages indicate, the defendant's intention to profit from competition with the plaintiff is not necessarily decisive. See also *Football League Ltd v Littlewoods Pools Ltd* [1959] Ch 637, 656.

This whole area is neatly summed up by Storey J in *Folsom v Marsh* 9 Fed Cas 342, 348 (Mass, 1841):

"It is certainly not necessary, to constitute an invasion of copyright, that the whole of the work should be copied, or even a large portion of it, in form or in substance. If so much is taken, that the value of the original is sensibly diminished, or the labors of the original author are substantially to an injurious extent appropriated by another, that is sufficient, in point of law, to constitute a piracy pro tanto. ... Neither does it necessarily depend upon the quantity taken ... [i]t is often affected by other considerations, the value of the materials taken, and the importance of it to the sale of the original work. ... In short, we must often, in deciding questions of this sort, look to the nature and objects of the selections made, the quantity and value of the materials used, and the degree in which the use may prejudice the sale, or diminish the profits, or supersede the objects, of the original work."

▓▓▓▓▓ TCN Channel Nine v Network Ten (No 2) *continued*

The effect of the authorities seems to be this. The test of substantiality—that is the notion of quality—is not confined to an examination of the intrinsic elements of the plaintiff's work. The test of substantiality may involve a broader enquiry, an enquiry which encompasses the context of the taking. The key ideas here are first that copyright is granted to protect the owner's financial interest in **[42]** his property. The second idea links financial harm to the rationale of unfair use or the injurious appropriation of the plaintiff's skill and labour. The level of financial harm may indicate that the use of that labour is unfair. In *Blackie & Sons Limited v The Lothian Book Publishing Company Proprietary Limited* (1921) 29 CLR 396 Starke J (at 402-403) said that the question was "[whether] the defendant, to use the words of the statute, reproduced a substantial part of the plaintiff's book...or...has an unfair or undue use been made of the work protected by copyright?" One of the factors upon which Starke J relied to conclude (at 403) that the defendant "[appropriated] a substantial and valuable portion" of the plaintiff's work was that the defendant's books were intended to be, and were, in direct competition with the plaintiff's. The third idea draws on the paradigm of piracy. The "clear case" of copyright infringement is where the defendant sells a cheaper version of the plaintiff's work, causing the plaintiff financial harm. The fourth idea is the concept of "value", which denotes more fully than the word "quality" a financial dimension as well as the notion of originality or artistic merit.

Evidence of the harm caused by the defendant's conduct is potentially relevant in a number of ways. First, and most importantly, it might indicate that the financial interest protected by copyright has been interfered with. Its absence might indicate the contrary. Second, it may indicate that the extent of the taking has been unfair, for example when it causes the plaintiff injury by reducing his profits. Third, it may be evidence of a straightforward piracy, being an intentional "stealing" for profit of the author's skill or labour. Last, it might highlight that the part taken is important, vital or material in the sense that the part gives the work its financial value. As Lord Herschell LC said in *Leslie v J Young & Sons* [1894] AC 335, 342: "[i]t may be the very thing that the presence or absence of which would most largely promote or retard the sale of the work."

When the judge came to decide the issue of substantiality it was by no means clear how the principles applicable to original works should be applied to broadcast copyright. There were only two decisions that had considered substantiality in the case of copyright in non-original subject matter, *Nationwide News Pty Ltd v Copyright Agency Limited* (1996) 65 FCR 399, a decision of the Full Federal Court, and *Newspaper Licensing Agency Ltd v Marks and Spencer plc* [2001] Ch 257, a decision of the English Court of Appeal. Each case concerned copyright in a published edition. In *Nationwide News Pty Ltd v Copyright Agency Limited* it was held that published edition copyright was in the typographical arrangement or composition of the whole published edition. The leading judgment was delivered by Sackville J. On the question of substantiality he said that it was necessary to apply the test derived from cases on infringement of original works, where substantiality refers to the quality of what is taken. Applying that test to published edition copyright he said (at 418):

> "In relation to a published edition, the quality of what is taken must be assessed by reference to the interest protected by the copyright. That interest ... is in protecting the presentation and layout of the edition, as distinct from the particular words or images published in the edition."

He further went on to say (at 419) that "since [the key issue is to determine] the quality of the material taken ... the quantity is not the only nor necessarily the principal criterion". He then referred with obvious approval to a passage in *Copinger and Skone James on Copyright* (13th ed, 1991) where the authors said (at 8-27) that **[43]** "[i]n deciding [the quality or importance of

▰▰▰▰▰ TCN Channel Nine v Network Ten (No 2) *continued*

the part taken] regard must be had to the nature and objects of the selection made, the quantity and value of the materials used, and the degree to which the use may prejudice the sale, or diminish the profits, direct or indirect, or supersede the object of the original work."

A different view of substantiality in relation to published edition copyright was taken in *Newspaper Licensing Agency Ltd v Marks and Spencer plc* [2001] Ch 257. The Court of Appeal decided that substantiality could be determined quantitatively. ...

The quantitative test has not, however, survived. It was rejected when *Newspaper Licensing Agency Ltd v Marks & Spencer plc* [2003] 1 AC 551 was taken to the House of Lords. The leading speech was given by Lord Hoffman. He said (at 560) that, as with original works, substantiality is to be tested by quality rather than quantity. "But", asked Lord Hoffman (at 559), "what quality is one looking for?" In the case of original works it is in the originality of the skill or labour in producing the work. In the case of a published edition it is in the skill of designing the arrangement and the labour and cost of setting it up and keeping it running. As regards quantity, Lord Hoffman said (at 561) that

> "[t]he test is quantitative in the sense that as there can be infringement only by making a facsimile copy, the question will always be whether one has made a facsimile copy of enough of the published edition to amount to a substantial part. But the question of what counts as enough seems to be qualitative, depending not upon the proportion which the parts taken bears to the whole but on whether the copy can be said to have appropriated the presentation and layout of the edition."

In *Network Ten Pty Ltd v TCN Channel Nine Pty Ltd* (2004) 78 ALJR 585 the High Court decided that this approach is to be followed in Australia. The court said (at 595) that: "Questions of quality ... as well as quantity arise both in respect of [non-original subject matter copyrights] and ... copyrights in original works".

... **[45]** ...

It is now clear that the starting point for any enquiry into substantiality is not, as the judge (in *Panel No 1*) would have it, "primarily quantitative". Nor is the principal enquiry whether harm has been caused to the plaintiff's commercial interests. The first thing that must be done is to look at the part taken, compare it with the copyright work and ask whether it is possible to conclude from that comparison whether that part is a "substantial part" of the plaintiff's programme. The question will often boil down to one of the following (dependent on the type of programme): Does what has been taken amount to "essentially the heart" of the copyrighted work?: *New Era Publications International v ApS Carol Publishing Group* 904 F 2d 152, 158 (2nd Circ, 1987). Is what has been taken "the essential part of the copyright work?": *Cable/Home Communications Corporation v Network Productions Inc* (902) F 2d 829, 844 (11th Circ, 1990). Is what has been taken "at least an important ingredient" of the copyright work?: *Salinger v Random House* 881 F 2d 90, 99 (2nd Circ, 1987). Have the best scenes been taken from the programme?: *Hi-Tech Video Productions Inc v Capitol Cities/ABC* 804 F Supp 950, 956 (W D Mich, 1992). Are the excerpts "highlights" from the programme?: *New Boston Television Inc v Entertainment Sports Programming Network Inc* 215 US PQ 755, 757 (D Mass, 1981). Are the excerpts central to the programme in which it appeared?: *Roy Expert Company Establishment of Vaduz Liechtenstein, Black Inc v Columbia Broadcasting System Inc* 503 F Supp 1137, 1145 (2nd Circ, 1980). Does the portion used **[46]** "constitute the 'heart'—the most valuable and pertinent portion—of the copyright material?": *Los Angeles News Service v CBS Broadcasting, Inc* 305 F 3d 924, 940 (9th Circ, 2002).

If what has been taken does not meet any of those descriptions that will often be the end of the enquiry. There will, however, be borderline cases where an enquiry based on a visual comparison will not yield a result. Take as an example a programme that has no "core" or "heart". Here I have in mind two cinematograph films by the 1960s icon Andy Warhol. The films are "Sleep" and "Empire", films that few people have seen. "Sleep" has been described as "one of the most famous of unseen films": F Camper, "The Lover's Gaze", *Chicago Reader Movie Review*, section 1, 28 April, 2000. It is a six-hour (some say longer) film taken by a stationary 16 mm camera of a man sleeping. The reviewer Jonas Mekas writing in the Village Voice (September, 1963) queried whether the film was: "An exercise in hypnosis? Test of patience? A Zen joke?" "Empire" is a single shot from late dusk to early morning of the Empire State Building taken from the 44th floor of the Time-Life Building. Mr Koch described "Empire" as "the most profoundly mute motion picture ever filmed": S Koch, *Stargazer: Andy Warhol's World and His Films* (2nd ed, M Boyars, New York, 1985) at 60. The film has no plot and only two things happen. The sun moves through the sky and, at dusk, floodlights are turned on to illuminate the upper floors of the Empire State Building. If part of "Sleep" or "Empire" is taken, no amount of visual comparison would enable a tribunal to determine whether that part is a substantial part of the film. It would be necessary to consider factors such as the plaintiff's financial interest as well as the defendant's purpose to resolve the issue.

There is one other aspect of the judge's test for substantiality which, with respect, I think is wrong. It is the judge's acceptance of Ten's submission that "matters of technical significance ... to the broadcast may also be relevant". According to the judge (at 273) those matters encompass the "technical considerations associated with the infrastructure of production". If by accepting Ten's submission the judge meant that it is either necessary or permissible to enquire into the means by which a programme is created and broadcast then in my view he is in error. It cannot make any difference to the test of substantiality if, say, there is a live broadcast of a sporting event using several television cameras and microphones near the scene that send their signals to a control room where they are combined and then transmitted to television sets or whether the broadcast is of a video recording of the event. At any rate "matters of technical significance" is not the interest protected by the copyright.

The final thing that remains to be done is to apply the correct test to the extracts taken from Nine's programmes....Ten infringed Nine's copyright in the television broadcast when it broadcast the following extracts.

The Inaugural Allan Border Medal Dinner: Ten copied 10 seconds of the programme. The programme centred upon the dinner and presentation of the inaugural [47] Allan Border Medal for the Australian cricket player of the year. The extract was of Glen McGrath's reaction to the announcement that he was the winner of the award, his displayed emotion and the congratulations from his surrounding team mates. The cameras were trained on the winner to capture that moment. The cameras then followed Mr McGrath as he moved towards the stage. The excerpt was plainly a material and important part of the programme. The evidence of Mr Burns was that the announcement of Glen McGrath as the Australian cricketer of the year was "the highlight of the dinner".

Midday (Prime Minister singing Happy Birthday): Ten copied 17 seconds of the programme. The presence of the Prime Minister on the Midday show was a key part of that day's programme. The footage of the Prime Minister singing Happy Birthday to Australian cricketing legend, Sir Donald Bradman, was a key and memorable feature. One of the panellists, Mr Gleisner, said the footage should be included in the Midday's shows "best of" special.

Wide World of Sports (Grand Final Celebration/Glen Lazarus cartwheel): Ten copied eight seconds of the programme. The footage of the Glen Lazarus cartwheel was, on any view, a "highlight". Mr Lazarus was a prop (affectionately known as "the brick with eyes"). He was playing his very last game of rugby league and was able to celebrate it with a win in the 1999 grand final.

▬▬▬ TCN Channel Nine v Network Ten (No 2) *continued*

Australia's Most Wanted (re-enactment of stabbing by party gatecrashers): Ten copied 26 seconds of the programme. "Australia's Most Wanted" is a programme directed at unsolved crimes and seeking public assistance in relation to particular crimes that are the subject of re-enactments on the programme. The re-enactment was of a gang of youths who gatecrashed a party. The gatecrashers intimidate the innocent partygoers. The gatecrashers then force entry into the house and one of them stabs a young man. The intimidation and break-in sequence coupled with the climactic stabbing scene is very dramatic and clearly central to the programme in which it appeared.

Pick Your Face (Keri-Anne Kennerley): Ten copied 20 seconds of the programme. This programme is a game show for children. The identification by contestants of the faces they have assembled is an important part of the show. One of the Panel members, Mr Gleisner described the excerpt of the child who wrongly identified Keri-Anne Kennerley (from faces shown on a board) as a "little highlight".

The Today Show (child yawning): Ten copied nine seconds of the programme. The footage rebroadcast involved part of an interview by Richard Wilkins with Alex Breden, and his mother. Alex was a child celebrity who featured on the HBA health insurance advertisements. The extract showed Alex yawning while being interviewed. It is a memorable part of the interview.

There has been no infringement by taking extracts from the following programmes: A Current Affair (brothel masquerading as introduction agency); The Today Show (Boris Yeltsin); The Crocodile Hunter (scuba diving); The Today Show (Prasad interview); and Nightline (Kevin Gosper interview). In each case the extracts were very short, but as I have previously said quantity does not dictate the answer. I have found that these extracts have not infringed Nine's copyright because the extracts were insignificant (de minimis is another description) in the context of Nine's programme (or, if it be relevant, the segment of the programme from which they were taken). Moreover, as the judge pointed out, the taking of these extracts caused absolutely no injury to Nine's interests.

HELY J: [50]

Substantiality

The term "substantial" is imprecise and ambiguous. It takes its meaning from the context. Ten submits that in the present context, "substantial" is a reference to taking 'the substance of' the source television broadcast. That submission pays insufficient regard to the statutory language, which is expressed in terms of 'a substantial part' of a television broadcast, which is a different thing. There may be many parts of a television broadcast which qualify as a substantial part of that broadcast.

Both parties accepted that in determining whether a substantial part of a copyright work or other subject matter is taken, the relevant comparison is between the part taken and the copyright work or subject matter: see *Auto Desk Inc v Dyason (No 2)* (1993) 176 CLR 300 ("*Auto Desk (No 2)*") at 305. The issue is not the importance of the part taken to the defendant's product: *Designers Guild Ltd v Russell Williams (Textiles) Ltd* [2001] 1 All ER 700 at 709.

At first instance, Conti J accepted Ten's submission that a primarily quantitative approach should be taken to the issue of substantiality. His Honour said (at [67]):

"... ascertainment of what constitutes a substantial part of a program or a segment of a program will require consideration of both the quantity and quality of what has been taken from a television broadcaster's commercial interest in relation to its program or program segment, with the ultimate emphasis to be placed, whether on quantity or quality, depending on the particular circumstances of the particular case; a primarily quantitative approach will usually be the most practical starting point of any enquiry ..."

■■■■■■ TCN Channel Nine v Network Ten (No 2) *continued*

Ten's submission was based upon the decision of the Court of Appeal in *Newspaper Licensing Agency Ltd v Marks & Spencer plc* [2001] Ch 257. That approach did not meet with approval when the matter went to the House of Lords: [2003] 1 AC 551 at 561.

The High Court has also confirmed that an approach to the assessment of **[51]** substantiality in the case of Part IV subject matter involves taking into account questions of quality (which could include the potency of particular images or sounds, or both, in a broadcast) as well as the quantity of the material taken: 78 ALJR 585 at [47] (McHugh ACJ, Gummow and Hayne JJ). A small portion in quantitative terms may constitute a substantial part having regard to its materiality in relation to the work as a whole: at [100] (Kirby J).

... Whether the part taken is a substantial part of the source broadcast thus involves an assessment of the importance of the part taken to the source broadcast. In some cases the issue has been expressed in terms of whether what is taken is an "essential" or "material" part of the total work: *Autodesk (No 2)* at 305; *Nationwide News Pty Ltd v Copyright Agency Ltd* (1996) 65 FCR 399 ("*Nationwide News*") at 418. In other cases the issue has been expressed in terms of whether the part taken is recognisable as part of the original work (see *Hawkes & Son (London) Ltd v Paramount Film Services Ltd* [1934] Ch 593 at 604), or distinctive of it (see *Nationwide News* at 420). In *The Modern Law of Copyright* (H Laddie, P Prescott et al, 3rd ed, Butterworths, London, 2000 at [7.59]) the matter is put in the context of substantial part and films, as follows:

> "... The Act does not attempt to define what it means by a 'substantial part', so Parliament must be taken to have left it to the courts to apply a commonsense value judgment, having regard to the facts of each individual case. An approach which is frequently useful for the traditional subjects of copyright law (ie original literary, dramatic, musical and artistic works) is to enquire whether the aspect of the work which has been taken required a substantial amount of skill and labour for its origination. It is submitted that this approach is not satisfactory in the case of films. Films can be made which are copyright even though no skill and labour at all were expended in their making: they do not have to be 'original'. *Nor would it be correct to approach the question on the basis of some crude mathematical apportionment: the Act says* **[52]** *'a substantial part' not 'a substantial percentage'. It is suggested that a better approach is to enquire whether the taking amounts to something real and consequential, as opposed to that which is trifling or insignificant.*" (emphasis added)

Whether a substantial part has been taken of subject matter in which copyright subsists is to be assessed by reference to the interest protected by the copyright: *Nationwide News* at 418. It is settled in the case of Part III works, that the quality or importance of what has been taken must be understood in terms of the features of the work which made it an original work: *Copinger & Skone James on Copyright* (K Garnett, J James et al, 14th ed, Sweet & Maxwell, London, 1999 at [7-30]). Originality goes to the heart of the interest that the copyright protects, namely authorship. Thus, in the case of Part III copyright, reproduction of non-original matter will not ordinarily involve a reproduction of a substantial part of the work in which copyright subsists: *Ladbroke (Football) Ltd v William Hill (Football) Ltd* [1964] 1 All ER 465 at 481.

Broadcast copyright protects the sounds and images embodied in a television broadcast or programme. It protects the cost to, and the skill of, broadcasters in transmitting their programmes: 78 ALJR 585 at [29]. There is no requirement for originality in the case of Part IV copyright, a fact which leads Ten to submit that it is wrong to look to the originality of content as a touchstone for assessing substantiality in relation to Part IV subject matter. Nine's focus on whether the Panel Segments were "distinctive" of, or were "recognisable" as having come from Nine's broadcasts is, in Ten's submission, to do just that.

▓▓▓▓▓▓ TCN Channel Nine v Network Ten (No 2) *continued*

In the case of Part IV copyright, "originality" is not a touchstone for the assessment of substantiality as originality forms no part of the identification of the interest protected by the copyright. For that reason, the notion that reproduction of non-original matter will not ordinarily involve a reproduction of a substantial part of a copyright work can have no application in the case of Part IV copyright. Nonetheless, the High Court's observation that the element of "quality" bears on the substantiality question, and may involve consideration of the "potency of particular images or sounds, or both", invites an assessment of the relative significance in terms of story, impact and theme conveyed by the taken sounds and images relative to the source broadcast as a whole. Whether the part taken represents one of the highlights of the source broadcast has a bearing on that assessment as does whether the Panel Segments were "distinctive of" or were "recognisable" as having come from Nine's broadcast. Ten's submission to the contrary should be rejected.

At first instance, Justice Conti appears to have taken a narrower view of what is involved in a qualitative comparison, as his Honour said, at [67]:

"... quality is concerned with the considerations associated with infrastructure of production, and in consequence with the technicalities of presentation and appearance of the visual images rather than what may be involved in terms of program theme, story, information or other program content ..."

Consistently with that view, his Honour's judgment does not embark upon a consideration of the significance or materiality in terms of visual and sound content of the images of the Panel Segments compared to the Nine programmes from which they derived. His Honour does not identify how it is that "technicalities of presentation and appearance of the visual images" are evident [53] other than in the form of visual images and sounds broadcast. However, it is the message conveyed by use of the medium of transmission which is protected: 78 ALJR 585 at [38]–[39], rather than the techniques deployed in the production of the images and sounds in question. I do not agree, with respect, that "quality" is confined in the manner which his Honour suggests.

The third of the factors (ie, in addition to quantity and quality) which influenced his Honour in coming to the conclusion that the Panel Segments were not a substantial part of Nine's source broadcasts was the factor of Ten's object or purpose of copying. His Honour said, at [17]:

"... apart from quantity and quality considerations per se, a further guide as to whether a substantial part of the program or segment of the program has been taken may be the object or purpose of the re-broadcaster in so taking; an object or purpose of satire, comedy or light entertainment, will not normally involve infringement because it will not involve imitation and thus copying, whereas the same cannot be said in relation to the contrasting notions of parody and burlesque, the essence of which is imitation and thus copying ..."

His Honour found that the Panel Segments were used by Ten for different objects or purposes than those targeted by Nine, being in Ten's case purposes essentially of satire, light humour or light entertainment. Ten's object or purpose in taking by way of re-broadcasting has not been to create anything resembling the Nine programmes from which Ten has taken footage or excerpts.

Whether the part taken is a substantial part of the source work is to be determined objectively. Infringement of copyright does not have a mental element of purpose or intention. However, there are statements in the cases (see, for example, *Nationwide News* at 419) which indicate that in deciding the quality or importance of the part taken, regard must be had (inter alia) to the nature and objects of the selection made. In some cases and in some

▬▬▬▬ TCN Channel Nine v Network Ten (No 2) *continued*

circumstances evidentiary assistance favourable to the copyright owner may be gained from a consideration of the alleged infringer's conduct. One of the considerations sometimes put forward as helping to decide whether a substantial part has been taken was described by the authors of *Copinger & Skone James* (supra), at [7.31], as follows:

> "Are the two works in competition? Has the value of the plaintiff's work been diminished? Is the market for the plaintiff's work likely, or unlikely to be affected? Tests of these kind are sometimes applied but it is suggested that today they need to be used with caution. Obviously, if it can be seen that the market for lawful reproductions of the plaintiff's work has been adversely affected, this may be because a substantial part has been taken, particularly if the reason for this is that the public regard the defendant's work as an adequate substitute for the plaintiff's. Care needs to be taken, however, since this decline may simply be the result of lawful (ie non-infringing) competition. Conversely, it is possible to imagine many cases where the businesses of the plaintiff and the defendant do not compete but unfair advantage of the plaintiff's skill and labour may yet have been taken. In such a case it is difficult to see why the absence of competition should help answer the question in favour of the defendant. Where, however, the two works are clearly in the same market and compete, and the plaintiff's work would be expected to suffer if a substantial part had been taken, the absence of any injury may be a helpful indication."

In the present case, Ten submitted that the evaluation of what constitutes a material part of a television broadcast is a classic jury question. One takes into **[54]** account all the circumstances. Accepting that to be so, the fact that the Panel Segments were used by Ten for the purpose of satire or light entertainment strikes me, with respect, as throwing little, if any, light on whether the parts taken were a substantial part of the source broadcasts.

No doubt Ten used the Panel Segments because it considered that the Panel Segments would contribute to Ten's programme, even though the contribution made to that programme may be quite different from the contribution made by the Panel Segments to the source broadcast. But that says little, if anything, about whether those segments are a material part of the source broadcast.

Individual consideration of the Panel Segments

It remains for me to consider whether individual Panel Segments represent a substantial part of the source programmes. Subject to the foregoing discussion, this is largely a matter of impression as the text of "substantial part" under the Act imparts criteria of 'fact and degree': 78 ALJR 585 at [100] (Kirby J). As is apparent from the table set out above, quantitatively each of the Panel Segments is but a small proportion of the source programme.

Nonetheless, in my opinion, three of the Panel Segments are a substantial part of the television broadcast from which they have been taken. The first is "Midday" (Prime Minister singing). Programmes such as "Midday" which extend over a significant period of time are often punctuated by highlights. The footage of the Prime Minister singing Happy Birthday to Australia's cricketing legend, Sir Donald Bradman, is one such highlight. The re-broadcast of this potent footage provided entertainment in its own right, apart altogether from any additional contribution made by members of the panel.

The second is "Australia's Most Wanted" (Aria Award). The footage taken is part of a re-enactment of an unsolved stabbing that had taken place at a residential home. The crux of the re-enactment is the intimidation of the innocent partygoers and the forcible entry into the home culminating in the stabbing, all of which are shown on the footage taken. The footage shown is highly dramatic, and reproduces the essence of the original story, rather than something which is merely incidental to the originating broadcast. The fact that the Panel used the footage as the foundation for a humorous assertion that the boys dancing in another piece of footage shown were the same gang that stabbed the partygoer does not negate substantiality.

The third is "Pick Your Face" (Kerri-Anne Kennerley). Pick Your Face is a game show for children, in which child contestants are asked to identify a celebrity from a partial picture. The particular portion shown in the Panel Segment is a child mistakenly identifying a partial picture as depicting Ms Kerri-Anne Kennerley. In my opinion, the Panel Segment provided a substantial part of the entertainment value of the programme from which it is taken, and the footage re-broadcast is funny in its own right. The member of the Panel who introduced the footage, Mr Gleisner, described the excerpt as a "little highlight" from the programme.

In my opinion, the following Panel Segments are not a substantial part of the source programme:

- "A Current Affair" (Masquerade of Introduction Agency): the original programme is an exposé of questionable business practices conducted by an introduction agency. The Panel Segment relates to disguises worn by alleged victims of the introduction agency who were interviewed during [55] the programme. The Panel Segment strings together disconnected parts of the source broadcast, without conveying anything of significance in relation to the original story. The extracts are trivial, inconsequential or insignificant in the context of the source broadcast.
- "The Inaugural Allan Border Medal Dinner" (Prime Minister embarrassed): this Panel Segment takes a portion of a live Nine broadcast during which a number of awards are presented. The particular segment re-broadcast shows the passage of the winner of the inaugural Allan Border medal, Mr Glen McGrath, from his seat to the stage. The Panel re-broadcast 10 seconds of a source work that was 2 hours 11 minutes 44 seconds in length. The portion taken does not include any critical moments or highlights of the original broadcast such as Mr McGrath receiving the award or giving his acceptance speech. The material used by the Panel is only incidental to the source broadcast, and the part taken is trivial, inconsequential or insignificant in terms of the source broadcast.
- "The Today Show" (Boris Yeltsin): this Panel Segment takes a portion of the Today Show, a Nine program that presents a series of magazine-style segments. The particular portion taken is footage of successive Russian Prime Ministers who had been dismissed by President Boris Yeltsin. The footage taken is incidental to the source broadcast and is trivial, inconsequential or insignificant in terms of that broadcast.
- "Wide World of Sports" (Grand Final celebrations): this Panel Segment takes a portion of Nine's live broadcast of the National Rugby League grand final. The particular portion taken features one of the players, Mr Glen Lazarus, performing a cartwheel as part of the post-match celebrations. He was not the only player to do so, and the footage taken does not show that there were other players following suit doing cartwheels of their own. The part taken is fleeting in character, and is not in any sense a highlight of the broadcast. Even if it be accepted that the original broadcast had as its subject matter both the grand final itself as well as the post-match presentations, the footage taken was only incidental to the source broadcast, and was trivial, inconsequential or insignificant in terms of that broadcast.
- "The Today Show" (Child yawning): this Panel Segment takes another portion of the Today Show. The particular part taken is nine seconds in length during which a child is shown yawning in an interview with the presenter, Mr Richard Wilkins. The part taken is fleeting in nature and on the periphery of the original broadcast, making little, if any, contribution to the subject matter of that broadcast. The footage taken is only incidental to the source broadcast, and is trivial, inconsequential or insignificant in terms of that broadcast.

▬▬▬▬ TCN Channel Nine v Network Ten (No 2) *continued*

- "Crocodile Hunter" (Scuba diving): this Panel Segment takes a portion of a show featuring Mr Steve Irwin, who is promoted by Nine as the 'Crocodile Hunter'. During the programme Mr Irwin is filmed in various marine environments, and the show climaxes with him swimming in the open ocean with sharks. The particular portion shown in the Panel Segment depicts Mr Irwin in a large tank in which various marine creatures are swimming. The dialogue during the footage is Mr Irwin's [56] description of a wobbegong shark that is also in the picture. The Panel Segment is humorous, but there was nothing funny about the original broadcast. The footage taken is used in an entirely different context from the original broadcast, and in that broadcast it is trivial, inconsequential or insignificant.

- "The Today Show" (Prasad interview): the part taken is from an interview with the manager of a hostel for homeless people, in which a number of homeless people can be seen gesticulating in the background. The source broadcast is a human interest story. The Panel's focus is on matters which are no more than background in the source broadcast, and barely noticeable. Again, the footage taken is trivial, inconsequential or insignificant in terms of the source broadcast.

- "Nightline" (Kevin Gosper interview): Nightline is a late night news and current affairs programme broadcast by Nine. The particular part taken shows Mr Kevin Gosper, an Australian Vice President of the International Olympic Committee, expressing relief at being cleared of all corruption allegations. The part taken is fleeting in nature, and so taken out of context that it does not give the impression of a reproduction of a material part of the original story. Again, the footage taken is trivial, inconsequential or insignificant in terms of the source broadcast.

Note

[6.175] The High Court refused special leave to appeal. In response to the complaint that what amounts to the taking of a substantial part of Part IV subject matter still remains undetermined, the following comments are of relevance:

KIRBY J: "That might be because it cannot be determined any more than the statutory words. It is a matter of fact and degree. It is just a matter of fact and degree and that is what the judges in the majority in the Full Court said."

McHUGH J: "That is what copyright lawyers have to learn, just as income tax lawyers have to learn. They think every question under a statute is a question of law. It is not, it is a question of fact. It is a question of applying the statutory formula to the facts of the case." at [2205] HCA Trans 842 (7 October 2005).

EXCEPTIONS TO INFRINGEMENT

■ Fair dealing: ss 40-43, 103A-103C, 104-104A

[6.180] Copyright is usually discussed in terms of balancing owner and user interests. While this is borne out in concepts such as the idea/expression dichotomy, the need for material form, and the need for an infringement to constitute a substantial part of a work, the fair dealing exceptions provide an indication of more particular social interests that are awarded preferential treatment in copyright: for example, research and study, criticism and review, reporting news, and judicial proceedings.

Whilst conceptually fair dealing forms part of the copyright balance, these provisions have been interpreted quite narrowly in application. Whether they are too restrictive in ambit has led to much discussion over the past decade. See Copyright Law Review Committee, *Simplification of the Copyright Act. Part One: Report Examining Exceptions to the Exclusive Rights of the Copyright Owners* (1998); Robert Burrell and Alison Coleman, *Copyright Exceptions: The Digital Impact* (Cambridge University Press, 2005); Michael Handler and David Rolph, "A Real Pea-Souper: The Panel Case and the Development of the Fair Dealing Defences to Copyright Infringement in Australia" (2003) 27 MULR 381.

In 2005 the Attorney General Philip Ruddock conducted an inquiry into "Fair Use and Other Copyright Exceptions". Submissions were sought as to whether a more open-ended approach to exceptions, as exemplified by a US "fair use" right, would be better suited to contemporary Australian circumstances. The Attorney General acknowledged,

> "The Government is aware some common personal uses of copyright material infringe copyright. Examples include transferring music from a CD onto an MP3 or iPod player or copying a television broadcast to view later.
>
> Those engaged in such uses do not believe they are or should be considered copyright pirates.
>
> Many observers believe copyright law should be reformed to reflect public attitudes and practices."

The adoption of a US-style fair use right was subsequently rejected.

[6.183] The *Copyright Amendment Bill 2006: Exceptions and Other Digital Agenda Review Measures* provides for new exceptions including:

- *Timeshifting.* Section 111 is amended to allow a person to record a radio or television broadcast to permit private and domestic viewing in domestic premises at a more convenient time;

- *Format shifting.* Sections 43C, 47J, 109A, 110AA permit particular kinds of format shifting by the owner of an original article for private and domestic use. For example, dubbing VHS to DVD, or copying music files to an MP3 player;

- *Flexible fair dealing.* Section 200AB permits some non-commercial uses by libraries, archives and educational institutions; uses by or on behalf of a person with a disability; and parody or satire.

The Bill also contains new deeming provisions (ss 40(3), (4)) for interpreting what constitutes a "fair dealing" and "reasonable portion" in relation to research and study.

Reporting the news (rights to a spectacle)

Nine Network v ABC

[6.185] *Nine Network Australia Pty Ltd v Australian Broadcasting Corporation* (1999) 48 IPR 333
Federal Court of Australia

The relevant facts are extracted at **[3.160]**.

HILL J

... [339] ...

The proposed defences of Channel Two if copyright subsists

By its defence filed in court Channel Two relies on ss 65 and 67 and s 42 of the *Copyright Act*. These sections provide a more likely defence for Channel Two than [340] the other one to which I have already referred. I shall deal first with s 42. That section provides relevantly in subpara (1):

> "A fair dealing with a literary, dramatic, musical or artistic work or with an adaptation
> ... does not constitute an infringement of the copyright in the work if ... (b) it is for
> the purpose of, or is associated with, the reporting of news by means of broadcasting
> or in a cinematograph film."

Two issues arise if s 42 is to be relied upon by Channel Two. First is the question whether the extent of its coverage could be said to be in the context of the section a fair dealing of any work in which copyright subsists, and second whether what it proposes to show can be said to be for the purpose of or associated with the reporting of news by means of broadcasting.

In my view there is a strong argument that what Channel Two proposes to do falls within s 42 although there are questions of degree involved. No doubt the whole event is newsworthy, so much was conceded by Channel Nine. The question is whether the showing of this newsworthy event in the course of a program designed to cover New Year's Eve cele-brations around the world in many cities and countries can be said to be news or at least that part of it which deals with the coverage of what happens on Sydney Harbour.

A suggestion was made arising from cross-examination of a witness from Channel Two that because HG Nelson and Roy Slaven (to use their stage names) will be anchors of the ABC coverage but with Mr George Negus as well meant that hyperbole and humour would reign and impliedly negate any possibility of the program being treated as news. I should say that the evidence did not suggest that these two gentlemen were required to treat their anchoring role in quite that way although perhaps given their particular style it might well be the case.

For my part I find the distinction between news and entertainment a very difficult one. It is not one I think which can be resolved by looking at the dictionary definition of the word. In some ways it may well be as difficult as the issue that has dominated the news press over the last few months of some suggestion of difference between commentary and infotainment or entertainment.

In my view the fact that humour is used does not necessarily negate the fact that what is being broadcast may be news. Hopefully the fact that news coverage is interesting or even to some entertaining likewise does not negate the fact that it could be news. As I have already said the celebrations of the City of Sydney this New Year's Eve are of both national and inter-national significance. The reporting and showing of a part of them on TV by Channel Two as national broadcaster could well fall within s 42.

One difficulty of course in deciding this at the present stage lies in not really knowing the extent of the coverage or indeed what actually will happen apart from the confidential schedule to which I have referred. It suffices merely to say at the moment that the argument of Channel Two on this point is not a weak one.

Defences based on ss 65 and 67 of the *Copyright Act*, again involve issues that may be of substance depending ultimately on what happens. Those sections provide relevantly—s 65 which bears the heading "Sculptures, and certain other works in public places":

> "(1) The section applies to sculptures and to works of artistic craftsmanship of the kind
>   referred to in paragraph (c) of the definition of artistic work in section 10. [341]

(2) The copyright in a work to which this section applies that is situated … in a public place … is not infringed by the making of a … photograph of the work or by the inclusion of the work in a cinematographic film or in a television broadcast."

Section 66 is concerned with buildings or models of buildings and I have some difficulty in seeing any building necessarily involved, though perhaps it is said that the structures erected on the Sydney Harbour Bridge could be a building.

Section 67 provides without prejudice to the last two preceding sections, that copyright in an artistic work is not infringed by the inclusion of the work in a cinematographic film or in a television broadcast if its inclusion in the film or broadcast is only incidental to the principal matters represented in the film or broadcast.

As I have already indicated some of the so called works are capable of being referred to as works of artistic craftsmanship to which s 65 could apply if they are included in a television broadcast. Section 67 has more difficulties factually because of the requirement that the inclusion in the broadcast be only incidental to the principal matters represented in the broadcast. As I have said there are matters of degree involved in this which clearly at the moment could not be resolved.

However, these sections demonstrate I suppose that it does not follow that the filming or inclusion of the filming in a television broadcast is necessarily an infringement. It may or may not be depending on whether the defences in those sections can be ultimately availed of …

Balance of convenience

The evidence shows that Channel Nine is likely to make a contribution to the cost of staging the celebration, spectacular, or event, in the order of $450,000—a not insignificant but on the other hand perhaps not large amount and but a fraction of the actual cost of staging the actual event. On its evidence of course its real interest is in sponsorship for the broadcast and perhaps attracting or luring away from other channels non Channel Nine viewers. It has incurred costs to date of some $400,000 in its staging and advertising of its coverage. If there is a shortfall under the agreement between the City Council and Channel Nine it may be that Channel Nine has to pay more than the figure I have indicated. [342]

Channel Two has likewise incurred expenditure in its participation with the consortium in preparation for its telecast in Australia of the events of the 25 hours. If enjoined of course Channel Two would be unable to broadcast in Australia that part of the segment of what happens on Sydney Harbour. There would presumably be a blank screen in its presentation subject of course to s 42 which Channel Nine acknowledges would have to be excised from any injunctive relief.

Channel Two is not a commercial station; it obtains no direct sponsorship income so the loss to it may not be financial except so far, perhaps, as government funding may be measured by ratings which might include the New Year's event. However, there is no evidence that this is the case at this stage. On the other hand it is a public broadcaster to whom many look for reporting of significant events without the interruption of paid commercials. There is some evidence that those with poor Channel Nine reception but better Channel Two reception may perhaps miss out viewing the celebration if the available choice was only Channel Nine.

There is also in my view in this case a public interest. True it is not as strong as it would have been had Channel Nine maintained its position that it could stop Channel Two filming and providing to overseas countries, footage of what might show much to the world Australia's ability to celebrate an important occasion and indeed promote the country. However, the public interest is there in ensuring that the nation's public broadcaster be able

━━━ Nine Network v ABC *continued*

to show segments of the celebration to those who choose to watch it. As I have said it has made a financial commitment which in real terms is not recouped merely by providing film for showing by others around the world leaving Australian screens blank.

For Channel Nine it is submitted that good will with sponsors will be lost and that this is not compensable by way of damages. I accept that there can be difficulties in proving loss of good will. Such difficulties arise in many cases but there is no reason why such a loss cannot be proved at least sufficiently to demonstrate damage which is capable of being compensated. It is commonplace that proof of damages is controversial and Judges regularly have to do the best they can in trying to assess damages that are suffered if any are. That does not mean to say that in such a case injunctive relief should be not granted nor does it mean that injunctive relief should be refused just because of difficulties with proving damage. It is necessary to weigh up all relevant factors in coming to that conclusion.

It is further submitted on behalf of Channel Nine that it has a strong prima facie case. If that is true of course it is relevant to the question of balance of convenience. As the above discussion indicates I think that the case of Channel Nine ranges from strong to weak depending upon which particular copyright is said to be infringed. It is also true I think that to some extent again depending on the facts that Channel Two may have a strong defence to any infringement claim.

These matters do not persuade me that the balance of convenience favours Channel Nine particularly as injunctive relief could frustrate as well the preparations which Channel Two has put in place for its broadcast at some expense.

Discretionary matters

Finally there is the question of whether I should take into account the delay of Channel Nine in commencing the proceedings. It was I think at the end [343] conceded by Senior Counsel for Channel Nine that the ultimate action could be brought for infringement of copyright in works not yet completed, subject of course to the facts of a particular case. However I think that there has been delay in the present case and that it is a factor that I should take into account particularly where the issues in the present case both as to infringement and balance of convenience are quite difficult.

The fact is that the drawings and the so-called script, whether or not the subject of any adjustment which occurs thereafter and may continue to occur before New Year, were all in existence by August of this year. That Channel Two intended to broadcast was a fact well known to Channel Nine yet no action was taken until just a couple of weeks before Christmas Day. The only explanation for the delay that is given through counsel is the suggestion that there may be a difficulty of copyright not yet being in existence. A suggestion made by counsel for Channel Nine that Channel Nine thought Channel Two would film for the international consortium but not broadcast the program in Australia was to say the least, fanciful.

It is for these reasons that I propose to refuse interim injunctive relief. I am fortified also by the fact that framing an injunction so as to ensure that Channel Two has the advantage of s 42 of the *Copyright Act* presents difficulties. To issue an injunction restraining in terms conduct other than that which falls within s 42 would lead the respondent to that injunction liable to a charge of contempt of court if it gets wrong its interpretation of s 42, a section which appears to have had very little judicial attention and on which it seeks to rely for its defence against infringement.

■ Criticism and review

▬▬▬ Commonwealth v John Fairfax & Sons ▬▬▬

[6.190] *Commonwealth v John Fairfax & Sons Ltd* (1980) 147 CLR 39 High Court of Australia

MASON J: **[44]** … This is a motion to continue ex parte injunctions which I granted at about 12.45 am on Saturday, 8 November 1980, restraining the defendants from publishing (a) a book entitled *Documents on Australian Defence and Foreign Policy 1968-1975* or the contents thereof or excerpts or extracts therefrom; and (b) documents entitled *The Strategic Basis of Australian Defence Policy* written by the Department of Defence in 1968 and "The Regional Outlook in Southeast Asia" produced by the Department of Foreign Affairs in 1975 or the contents of either of them or any excerpts or extracts therefrom.

The circumstances in which the injunctions came to be granted were unusual. The plaintiff became aware for the first time on the afternoon of Friday 7 November that the book was to be published shortly and that its contents were to be serialised in *The Age* newspaper published in Melbourne by the second and third defendants commencing in the morning issue on Saturday 8 November. Although the plaintiff did not obtain a copy of the book before the afternoon of Monday 10 November, it did obtain a copy of the front page of the dust jacket and a "flier" on the Friday afternoon. They provided some indication of the contents **[45]** of the book, enough to reveal that the documents to be published included the two already referred to as well as unpublished government "memoranda, assessments, briefings and cables" relating to such topics as "the East Timor crisis seen largely through the cables which passed between Djakarta and Canberra at the time, the renegotiations of the agreements covering US military bases in Australia, the presence of the Soviet Navy in the Indian Ocean, Australia's support for the Shah of Iran and the predictions for the future of his regime, the security of the Butterworth base, outlines of the structure of the US and UK intelligence services and other matters, including the ANZUS Treaty.

[46] … As its title suggests, the book sets out a large number of government documents. The book does not contain technical information of military significance; it does not deal with weaponry, armaments, military technology, logistical information or dispositions of forces. It is not affected by the "D" Notice procedures. Even the two documents referred to in the ex parte injunction contain no material of value to a hostile power. The appreciations made of Australia's strategic situation and of the outlook in Southeast Asia are based on information which is generally known. The judgments made are fairly elementary and they are now quite out of date. The official documents contain comments on leaders and representatives of foreign countries to which I shall refer later. The book also contains general information taken from official documents relating to intelligence services.

The book consists of 437 pages; nine pages are biographical notes, no more than 50 pages are observations and comments by the authors (including an Introduction). The balance of the book **[47]** comprises government documents, the plaintiff having copyright in the great bulk of them. Much of the authors' comment is by way of background at the beginning of the chapters, placing documents in their correct setting so as to enable the reader to understand them. …

The plaintiff's case is that it is the owner of the copyright in most of the documents in the book, that they are classified documents which contain confidential information the disclosure of which will in a number of instances prejudice Australia's relations with other countries, especially Indonesia, and that it has not authorised or consented to publication.

██████ Commonwealth v John Fairfax & Sons *continued*

The plaintiff also claims that publication will involve the commission [49] of an offence against s 79 of the *Crimes Act 1914* (Cth). The defendants do not dispute that the plaintiff has copyright in most of the documents; nor do they allege that the plaintiff has consented to publication. They do, however, contest the view that the documents contain confidential information and that disclosure will be prejudicial to the national interest. They also contend that there is no point in preventing further disclosure when limited publication has taken place and the book has fallen into the hands of those foreign countries which are most likely to react adversely to its contents. They rely on the answer given by Mr Henderson, the Secretary of the Department of Foreign Affairs, that "It is much more likely to facilitate our future relations if the government has been seen to try its utmost to prevent that [disclosure] happening". The suggestion is that the plaintiff is maintaining the proceeding merely to demonstrate its bona fides to foreign governments. ...

The plaintiff is the owner of the copyright in those documents which have been brought into existence by the relevant departments and by public servants. Publication of the three instalments by the defendant will infringe the plaintiff's copyright unless the defendants can establish defences under ss 41 and 42 of the *Copyright Act 1968* (Cth), as amended, or the so-called common law defence of "public interest" ... [54]

To bring themselves within s 41 the defendants must show that what they proposed to publish is "a fair dealing" with the plaintiff's documents "for the purpose of criticism or review" and that "a sufficient acknowledgment of the work" was made. It has been suggested that s 41 does not provide a defence in the case of unpublished literary works, as distinct from unpublished dramatic or musical work, on the ground that criticism or review of an unpublished literary work could never amount to "a fair dealing": *Copinger and Skone James on Copyright* (11th ed, 1971), para 463. This suggestion is based on the remarks of Romer J in *British Oxygen Co Ltd v Liquid Air Ltd* [1925] Ch 383 at 393, where his Lordship said that it would be unfair that an unpublished literary work should, without the consent of the author, be the subject of public criticism or review.

In *Hubbard v Vosper* [1972] 2 QB 84 at 94-95 Lord Denning MR qualified these remarks by observing that a literary work not published to the world at large might be circulated to such a wide circle, for example, a circular sent by a company to its shareholders, as to make it "a fair dealing" to criticise or review it. With this qualification I agree.

To my mind the absence of consent, express or implied, or such circulation by the author of an unpublished literary work as to justify criticism or review is ordinarily at least an important factor in deciding whether there has been "a fair dealing" under s 41.

There has been no such consent or conduct on the part of the plaintiff here. As I have said, the defendants knew on the Friday evening that the plaintiff objected to any publication at all and knew or ought to have known that the documents had been "leaked" without the plaintiff's authority. There is a difficulty in saying that a publication of leaked documents, which could not without the leak have been published at all, is "a fair dealing" with unpublished works in the circumstances to which I have referred: see *Beloff v Pressdram Ltd* [1973] 1 All ER 241 at 264.

However, there is another possible approach to the concept of "fair dealing" as applied to copyright in government documents, an approach which was not spelled out in argument by the defendants. It is to say that a dealing with unpublished works which would be unfair as against an author who is a private individual may nevertheless be considered fair as against a government merely because that dealing promotes public knowledge and public discussion of government action. This would be to adopt a new approach to the construction of ss 41 and 42 and it would not be appropriate for me on an interlocutory application to proceed on the footing that its is a construction that will ultimately prevail. Situations such as the present case would scarcely have been within the contemplation of the draftsman when the two sections and their ancestors were introduced.

There is another obstacle in the way of a s 41 defence. The presentation to readers which the newspapers planned to publish was a presentation of hitherto unpublished documents from the secret files of the government. The attraction offered to the [56] reader was that, by courtesy of the newspapers, he was able to read for the first time documents which were so important that the government had maintained a secrecy blackout on them. The accompanying comment, which was significant only in the case of the first instalment, appears to have been designed to place the documents in their appropriate setting, to enable them to be understood and to highlight the more dramatic features. To speak of the publication of the three instalments as having been undertaken for the purpose of criticism or review is to add a new dimension to criticism and review. If there was criticism or review of the documents by the newspapers it was merely a veneer, setting off what is essentially a publication of the plaintiff's documents. The defendants did not propose to make any reference at all to the question raised on pp 2 and 3 of the Introduction to the book.

I put to one side the plaintiff's objection that there was not a "sufficient acknowledgment" of the work as defined by s 10. Certainly there was no express acknowledgment of the Commonwealth's copyright in the documents. There was an acknowledgment of the copyright of Messrs Walsh and Munster in the book which was the only acknowledgment of copyright which the defendants published or proposed to publish. But the defendants identified the documents as government documents and described them. In reality the plaintiff's complaint is that there has been an excessive acknowledgment of the work.

Similar problems surround the defendants' endeavour to mount a defence under s 42. The defendants seek to show that there has been "a fair dealing" with a literary work "for the purpose of, or ... associated with, the reporting of news in a newspaper ... and a sufficient acknowledgment of the work is made". The arguments advanced scarcely went beyond a bold assertion, and an equally stern denial, that what the defendants proposed to publish was "for the purpose of ... the reporting of news".

I am inclined to allow that "news", despite its context of "the reporting of news" "in a newspaper, magazine or similar periodical" is not restricted to "current events". Even so, the concept of "a fair dealing" with a literary work in the circumstances mentioned in s 42(1)(a) again presents a difficulty for the defendants. As things presently stand, it will not be easy for the defendants to bring their use of the plaintiff's documents, particularly in the two unpublished instalments, within the subsection. I refer to the East Timor cables and the "profiles".

It has been accepted that the so-called common law defence of public interest applies to disclosure of confidential information. [57] Although copyright is regulated by statute, public interest may also be a defence to infringement of copyright. Lord Denning MR considered that it is: see *Fraser v Evans* [1969] 1 QB 349 at 362-363, as did Ungoed-Thomas J in *Beloff v Pressdram Ltd* at 260; cf *Hubbard v Vosper* at 96-97. Assuming the defence to be available in copyright cases, it is limited in scope. It makes legitimate the publication of confidential information or material in which copyright subsists so as to protect the community from destruction, damage or harm. It has been acknowledged that the defence applies to disclosures of things done in breach of national security, in breach of the law (including fraud) and to disclosure of matters which involve danger to the public. So far there is no recorded instance of the defence having been raised in a case such as this where the suggestion is that the advice given by Australia's public servants, particularly its diplomats, should be ventilated, with a view to exposing what

▬▬▬▬ Commonwealth v John Fairfax & Sons *continued*

is alleged to have been the cynical pursuit of expedient goals, especially in relation to East Timor. To apply the defence to such a situation would break new ground.

Action remitted to Supreme Court of New South Wales.

■ Adjudication

▬▬▬▬▬ TCN Channel Nine v Network Ten ▬▬▬▬▬

[6.195] *TCN Channel Nine v Network Ten* (2001) 50 IPR 335 Federal Court of Australia

[The facts are outlined in the extract on [6.170] above.]

CONTI J:

Authorities relating to fair dealing for the purpose of criticism or review and for the purpose of reporting news

[372] ... The fair dealing provisions of ss 103A and 103B of the Act relating to audio-visual items came into force in 1986, in the context of the Explanatory Memorandum later referred to and partly extracted. Prior to that time, there was already in force s 41 of the Act relating to fair dealing with literary, dramatic, musical or artistic work (and an adaptation of any of the first three of such works) for the purpose of reporting news, and s 42 relating to fair dealing for the purpose of reporting news. No corresponding or similar provisions have been incorporated into Part IV of the Act, so that the matters to which regard should be had are at large, subject of course to such assistance as can be obtained from the authorities.

An appropriate starting point for review of authorities relating to fair dealing is the decision of this court in *De Garis v Neville Jeffress Pidler Pty Ltd* (1990) 37 FCR 99 (Beaumont J), where consideration was given to the common law origins of the defences of fair dealing, and to the subsequent Australian and UK authorities upon the respective Australian and UK statutory provisions until the handing down of the judgment in 1990. After referring to the common law origins of the doctrine of fair dealing, Beaumont J at 107, set out the *Macquarie Dictionary* definitions of "criticism" as follows:

> "1. The act or art of analysing and judging the quality of a literary or artistic work, etc: literary criticism. 2. The act of passing judgment as to the merits of something ... 4. A critical comment, article or essay; a critique."

and of "review" as follows:

> "1. A critical article or report, as in a periodical, on some literary work, commonly some work of recent appearance; a critique."

Such definitions have not changed over the past decade. Then his Honour continued at 107:

> "It would seem that the word 'review' in the sense in which it is to be understood in s 41 is cognate with the word 'criticism'. It may be said that one is the process and the other is the result of the critical application of mental faculties."

One of the reasons for his Honour's conclusion that the Neville Jeffress activities could not be characterised as either "criticism" or "review" for the purposes of s 41 was that the same did "not appear to extend to the passing of a judgment as to the merit of the articles identified".

As to the meaning of "fair" in relation to a dealing within s 41 of the Act, his Honour found assistance in the following often cited passage appearing in *Hubbard v Vosper* [1972] 2 QB 84 at 94 (per Lord Denning MR):

"It is impossible to define what is 'fair dealing'. It must be a question of degree. You must consider first the number and extent of the quotations and extracts. Are they altogether too many and too long to be fair? Then you must consider the use made of them. If they are used as a basis for comment, criticism or review, that may be fair dealing. If they are used to convey the same information as the author, for a rival **[373]** purpose, that may be unfair. Next, you must consider the proportions. To take long extracts and attach short comments may be unfair. But, short extracts and long comments may be fair. Other considerations may come to mind also. But, after all is said and done, it must be a matter of impression. As with fair comment in the law of libel, so with fair dealing in the law of copyright. The tribunal of fact must decide."

Thus, it will be appreciated that factors relevant to the notion of substantiality may overlap with those relating to fair dealing.

...

To the judicial dicta cited in *De Garis*, I would add reference to the dictum of Ungoed-Thomas J in *Beloff v Pressdram Ltd* [1973] 1 All ER 241 at 262 (also [1973] RPC 765 at 786):

"The relevant fair dealing is thus fair dealing with the memorandum for the approved purposes. It is fair dealing directed to and consequently limited to and to be judged in relation to the approved purposes. It is dealing which is fair for the approved purposes and not dealing which might be fair for some other purpose or fair in general. Mere dealing with the work for that purpose is not enough; it must also be dealing which is fair for that purpose; whose fairness, as I have indicated, must be judged in relation to that purpose."

That passage in Beloff has since been frequently cited since, for instance, in *British Broadcasting Corporation v British Sky Broadcasting Ltd* (1991) 21 IPR 503 at 514, where Scott J also added reference to what had been much earlier said in *Johnstone v Bernard Jones Publications Ltd* [1938] 1 Ch 599 at 607 as follows:

"I think there is much force in the contention of counsel for the plaintiff that any oblique motive, as he expressed it, would render the publication of the letter in question an unfair dealing."

Subsequent to the decision of this Court in *De Garis*, there has been, first in point of time, an important decision of the Court of Appeal in the United **[374]** Kingdom in *Time Warner Entertainment Co Ltd v Channel 4 Television Corporation PLC* (1993) 28 IPR 459, which related to copyright in a well known cinematograph film. The passage from *Vosper* extracted above was approved by Neill LJ (with whose judgment Farquharson LJ agreed), as was the following further passage from Vosper at 94:

"A literary work consists, not only of the literary style, but also of the thoughts underlying it, as expressed in the words. Under the defence of 'fair dealing' both can be criticised. Mr Vosper is entitled to criticise not only the literary style, but also the doctrine or philosophy of Mr Hubbard as expounded in the books."

And after referring to a further passage from *Beloff* at 263 that "fair dealing is a question of fact and impression", Neill LJ added at 467: "One has to consider whether the allegedly infringing material may amount to an illegitimate exploitation of the copyright holders' work". Henry LJ agreed with the other members of the Court of Appeal in *Time Warner*, and added the following further observations and analysis at 468-9:

> "The mischief at which the Act is aimed is to prevent copyright owners of works which they have put in the public domain from picking and choosing as to who may review their works, when they may do so, and what clips they may use.
>
> But even if it is assumed that the infringing excerpts were arguably not fairly representative, would that defeat the fair dealing defence? In my judgment as a matter of law it would not. As Lord Atkin said in a different context: 'The path of criticism is a public way: The wrong-headed are permitted to err therein ...': *Ambard v AG for Trinidad and Tobago* [1936] AC 322 at 335. 'Fair dealing' in its statutory context refers to the true purpose (ie good faith, the intention and the genuineness) of the critical work—is the program incorporating the infringing material a genuine piece of criticism or review, or is it something else, such as an attempt to dress up the infringement of another's copyright in the guise of criticism, and so profit unfairly from another's work? As Lord Denning said in *Hubbard v Vosper* ... 'it is not fair dealing for a rival in the trade to take copyright material and use it for his own benefit'.
>
> If it is the former, in a genuine criticism of the decision or to withdraw that work from the public domain, it seems to me that the defence is not lost if the offending excerpts might arguably be thought to be (in relation to the original film) unbalanced or unrepresentative ... If satisfied that the theme and purpose of the criticism was genuinely as summarised above, I would not regard such imbalance as raising an arguable case that the fair dealing defence was not available. Likewise, the other side of the same coin, if the intention was to profit from the breach of copyright ... under the pretence of criticism, then no matter how fair or balanced or representative the infringing excerpts might be, the purpose would not be that of criticism and review, and so would not have the protection of the s 30 defence."

... [375] ...

Sufficient acknowledgment

I come then to the requirement of "sufficient acknowledgment" for the purpose of Ten's s 103A defence. As earlier indicated above, the definition of that expression in the Australian Act applies only to Part III works, so that "sufficient acknowledgment" in relation to a Part IV subject matter is at large, subject to the observations I have already made above, and must be a question of fact in each case in relation to whatever "subject matter" is the subject of consideration. The following extract from [*Pro Sieben Media AG v Carlton UK Television Ltd* [1999] 1 WLR 605] at 618 provides a measure of guidance for the purposes of assessing what may constitute a "sufficient acknowledgment" within s 103A in relation to a Part IV work such as a television broadcast: [376]

> "Mr Silverleaf accepted that identification of an author would normally and naturally be achieved by communicating, by spoken works or writing or both, his correct name or, if the author wrote under a pseudonym, the name by which he was known as an author. But Mr Silverleaf submitted that the television transmission of a logo could also constitute identification for the purposes of section 178, especially if the logo was the means by which the author of a television programme was accustomed to identify itself, and if the use of the correct name was unlikely to have

▬▬▬▬ TCN Channel Nine v Network Ten *continued*

any particular significance to the bulk of the audience. In this case there was evidence, from Mr Michael von Dessauer, a vice president of Pro Sieben, that his company used the logo (of a stylised '7') as an identification. ... I would accept Mr Silverleaf's submissions and hold that the defendants succeed in making good a defence under s 30(1)."

... [380] ...

Conclusion upon fair dealing principles emerging from authorities

It is now appropriate to condense below the principles emerging from the authorities involving the fair dealing defences:

(i) Fair dealing involves questions of degree and impression; it is to be judged by the criterion of a fair minded and honest person, and is an abstract concept.

(ii) Fairness is to be judged objectively in relation to the relevant purpose, that is to say, the purpose of [381] criticism or review or the purpose of reporting news; in short, it must be fair and genuine for the relevant purpose, because fair dealing truth of purpose;

(iii) Criticism and review are words of wide and indefinite scope which should be interpreted liberally; nevertheless criticism and review involve the passing of judgment criticism and review may be strongly expressed;

(iv) Criticism and review must be genuine and not a pretence for some other form of purpose, but if genuine, need not necessarily be balanced;

(v) An oblique or hidden motive may disqualify reliance upon criticism and review, particularly where the copyright infringer is a trade rival who uses the copyright subject matter for its own benefit, particularly in a dissembling way; "the path of criticism is a public way";

(vi) Criticism and review extends to thoughts underlying the expression of the copyright works or subject matter;

(vii) "News" is not restricted to current events; and

(viii) "News" may involve the use of humour though the distinction between news and entertainment may be difficult to determine in particular situations.

...

Conclusions on fair dealing defence issues in relation to the subject programmes

[386] ... I am conscious of the circumstance that individual tastes and appraisals can readily intrude upon the views that may be adopted in relation to what is fair dealing in particular contexts, as well as what may reasonably be characterised as a purpose of criticism or review of a particular audio-visual item in the form, as here of course, of a television broadcast, or any other audio-visual item or a "work" included in the first-mentioned television broadcast (s 103A). I am also conscious of the further circumstances, first, that Ten and Nine are rivals or competitors for contemporary television audiences, and that The Panel programmes the subject of challenge have been broadcast concurrently with unrelated television broadcasts being then undertaken by Nine, and further that the burden of establishing ss 103A and 103B(1)(b) defences lies upon Ten. I am further conscious of the circumstance that as has been earlier emphasised, the object or purpose of a rebroadcast is material to establishing whether "a substantial part" of a rebroadcast has occurred, and that an object or purpose of satire light [387] entertainment may also intrude conceptually into a consideration of issues concerning purposes of criticism or review, and perhaps also of issues concerning purposes of reporting of news.

(i) "The Today Show" (Boris Yeltsin)

Ten submits that its rebroadcast here of footage concerning certain activities of Boris Yeltsin constituted fair dealing for the purpose of reporting news within s 103B(1)(b), being news relating to the conduct of President Boris Yeltsin in dismissing the Russian Cabinet on several occasions. What supposedly introduced this topic was the pending Australian Referendum on the Republic. Two issues of principle are involved, first that news is not necessarily to be restricted to current events, a principle which Nine's submissions have tended to disregard (see John Fairfax cited above), and secondly that the relevant news being rebroadcast need not wholly inhere in the audio-visual item being rebroadcast for the purposes of s 103B(1)(b). The rebroadcast here contains the following comments of members of The Panel which might arguably be thought, individually or cumulatively, to constitute "news" within s 103B(1)(b):

> "President Yeltsin dismissed the Russian cabinet every eighteen months.
> Prime Minister Putin is an 'ex KGB spy'.
> President Reagan (implicitly) was so old he could not 'take himself to the toilet', and was 'too old to be running the country'.
> President Yeltsin's disadvantage in holding office was not 'an age limit' but a 'blood alcohol limit'.
> President Clinton 'is all there but he's also all there and that has led to problems where Ronald (Reagan) wasn't about to do anything with an intern.' "

As I have earlier pointed out above, news may involve the use of humour, but that there can nevertheless be considerable difficulty in distinguishing news from entertainment ... As a matter of judgment and impression, I prefer the conclusion that the purpose of this rebroadcast, evident from The Panel discussion, was that of entertainment rather than the reporting of news, or was so rebroadcast in association with the reporting of news. I would therefore have rejected Ten s 103B(1)(b) defence, had Ten not succeeded in the first place on the issue of infringement. No issue arises as to sufficient acknowledgment.

(ii) "Midday"

Ten contends that its rebroadcast constituted fair dealing for the purpose of criticism or review of the "Midday" programme, and of the role of the presenter Ms Kennerley in that programme, and Ten relied on the principle in *Vosper, supra* at 94, to the effect that criticism or review may extend to ideas underlying the subject matter of copyright (see the later elaboration on that principle in *Pro Sieben* at [52(v)] above). I extract below the following on-screen remarks of various members of "The Panel", in order to illustrate the major thrust of The Panel's comments of relevance:

> "[D]id anyone see when Kerri-Anne got the Prime Minister John Howard to sing Happy Birthday to Don Bradman?"
> "That will get him back in."
> "Its not right to mock someone's stature but he really looks like he should have a hand up his a ... moving his mouth when he sits on that little stool ..."
> ...
> "Well I reckon if he didn't sing it, she would have put her hand up his a..."
> "Kerri-Anne will not take no for an answer."
> "She is essentially a Labour voter cause she got Costello to do the macarena ... and made him look like an idiot and now she's done it with John Howard." [388]
> "It is interesting with Midday because it was funny at the Logies this year (be)cause she was hot favourite for the Gold Logie. And I remember a conversation. I'll never forget this. A Nine executive coming up to me and saying 'Hey does Kerri-Anne win?' And I said "Oh no, she doesn't actually". He goes "Thank God". And I was like 'Why's that?' And he goes 'Mate, she would be unbearable'".
> "Leave Kerri-Anne alone. She does a good job I reckon."

"She resurrected it."

"You think about that though, what is it five hours."

"Five days a week."

"She is an ideal Midday host. It is interesting when Derryn Hinch was hosting it, the rating(s) aren't much better with Kerri-Anne, yet Derryn was looked upon as a Midday failure."

"A total failure."

"Whereas Kerri-Anne like on Monday, she was beaten by Judge Judy in Adelaide and Perth."

I have encountered difficulty in deciding whether the purpose of Ten in re-broadcasting the subject material was that of criticism and review, despite the somewhat disparaging remarks made concerning Ms Kennerley and the "Midday" programme which she had been hosting for some time. Ten has submitted that the purpose of the criticism or review related to both the programme and Ms Kennerley's role in it, but I think that the submission is not sufficiently supported by what I have extracted above. I would conclude that the purpose of Ten's dealing with the subject footage of "Midday" was to satirise aspects of Ms Kennerley's performance as presenter of "Midday", and certain supposed personality traits and political allegiances. I do not think that on balance, and as an issue of fact and degree, it can rightly be postulated that The Panel here engaged in criticism or review of "Midday", and that such was its purpose. If it had become necessary to determine Ten's reliance upon s 103A in relation to what would have otherwise constituted breach of copyright constituted by this rebroadcast, I would have rejected such basis of defence. I would also have rejected Ten's entitlement to have relied upon s 103B(1)(b), upon the purported basis that the Prime Minister's singing of "happy birthday" to Sir Donald Bradman was "newsworthy". It is unrealistic and inapposite to characterise Ten's rebroadcast of such event as having the purpose of or being associated with "the reporting of news". Such event involving the Prime Minister singing had been of course wholly broadcast by Nine in the full context of the earlier "Midday" presentation, and there is no suggestion from Ten to the effect that the same had been treated as newsworthy in whole or in part. Ten's purpose in rebroadcasting the event was rather to satirise the Prime Minister's already well-known admiration for Sir Donald Bradman. If I am wrong in my conclusion as to Ten's 103A defence as to criticism and review, I would have found in favour of Ten on the issue of "sufficient acknowledgment". I am unable to understand why Ten's use of the so-called "on screen watermark 'Ch 9'" was not sufficient identification of the fact that the "Midday" programme footage had been originally broadcast by Nine. To the average viewer, the material re-broadcast would have identified to him or her the source of the rebroadcast footage to Nine, without even the need to add Nine's logo (cf the dictum extracted from *Pro Sieben* at [54] above where a German television company had broadcast to the UK). I should add that where the on-screen watermark "Ch 9" has been used elsewhere in Ten's rebroadcasts the subject of the proceedings (see iv-vii, xi, xiii-xvi, xviii-xx), there was constituted a sufficient acknowledgment with s 103A.
    ... [389] ...

(iv) "A Current Affair" (Masquerade of Introduction Agency)

Ten contends that this rebroadcast was a fair dealing for the purpose of criticism or review of "A Current Affair" episode, by reference to such programme's use of "poor disguises", who appeared thereon, first of a member of the public who unwittingly visited a brothel in the belief that it was an introduction agency, and secondly of a person employed at the brothel as a receptionist. The Executive Producer of "A Current Affair" admitted in cross-examination that "a disguise is a disguise and if you had known the person well I'd reckon by and large they're not hard to see through". Ten was able to make entertaining mileage out of its rival's unsuccessful efforts in seeking to adequately disguise these two members of the public who had apparently volunteered to appear on Nine's programme. After the rebroadcast by Ten of the Nine episode had occurred, one member of The Panel put on a replica of the facial disguise of the male person interviewed on the Nine episode the subject of the rebroadcast, which occasioned further mirth to The Panel members and their studio audience. Whilst bearing in mind that this rebroadcast by Ten was made in purported derogation of its business rival's practices, albeit in an entertaining way and in circumstances involving an element of public interest, the essence of the theme the subject of the Ten rebroadcast seems to me to marginally weight the balance in favour of Ten's establishment of the statutory purpose of criticism or review. It is legitimate to criticise a rival telecaster for inadequately protecting the anonymity of its interviewees, even if the criticism takes advantage of humorous incidents to the rival's inadequacy. Nine has further contended that there was nevertheless absent fair dealing, because the "Simply the Best" rebroadcast on the part of Ten addressed in subpara (xv) below occurred in the same evening's programme of The **[390]** Panel, but I do not think that such circumstance is material to the issue of fair dealing purpose, such as deprive the otherwise availability of the defence. Accordingly had Ten not succeeded on the issue of substantiality, I would have ruled in its favour on the issue of criticism or review.

   ... **[391]** ...

(viii) "Days Of Our Lives" (Marlena Standing)
The evidence discloses that "Days Of Our Lives" has been broadcast by Nine since about 1962 or 1963, and for probably the last fifteen years, the programme has been Nine's highest rating day time show. Nine's Director of Programmes agreed to the description of the programme as "a dramatic soap opera", and as containing "elements of melodrama", and "a lot of tongue in cheek scenes". Its television audience is indicated in the evidence to be mainly female. The female character Marlena has been displayed on the programme as devil possessed, and the rebroadcast scene shows her on a balcony in that condition. Ten raised the s 103A defence of criticism and review, upon the basis that the footage demonstrates that the script writers of "Days Of Our Lives" are undertaking recourse to rather desperate and pathetic measures to prolong the life of an already protracted and attenuated daytime television programme. Part of The Panel commentary includes the following:

> "The writers sit around and they go ... they've gone after 10 or 11 years and they've gone guess we've got to make someone possessed."

The commentary of The Panel, and the way in which the visual images are re-broadcast, undoubtedly involve a measure of satire and humorous entertainment, but they are relevantly more than that. As a matter of fact and impression, the commentary and the visual images imply a purpose of criticism and review, in the sense of the dictionary definitions reproduced ... above, and do so on the footing of an innuendo of loss of originality and novelty of theme. My conclusion is that the rebroadcast was undertaken for the purposes of criticism and review, and in the circumstances such criticism and review was fair for such purposes, albeit that the same emanated from a rival television station.

   ... **[392]** ...

(xiii) "The 72nd Academy Awards" (Artificial Fog)
The defence here raised by Ten is fair dealing for the purpose of criticism or review. The purpose of the Academy Awards programme is to choose the best male actor and the best female actress. That part rebroadcast featured the well known US singer Isaac Hayes, and the

▰▰▰▰ TCN Channel Nine v Network Ten *continued*

same focused for purposes of humour upon him becoming mistakenly enveloped in an artificially contrived fog by reason of accidental misuse of the studio's fog machines. The Panel's point is that the televising of such a premier event should have been better controlled technically in order to avoid the mishap which occurred to Isaac Hayes in the course of his performance. Its dialogue concerning this brief mishap was as follows:

"Did you see that? ... Have a look at this. Isaac Hayes comes out ...

"This is great."

"Okay, okay Ken is going to stop the fog machine now. ... He's distracted by the girls ... oop ... the fog machine. We've lost Isaac Hayes. Isaac Hayes is in the middle of that fog. Do they go the wide shot they go ... okay the fog machine ... back again."

"Oh no."

"This is."

"That's really bad."

"That's a pea souper."

"That's a real pea souper. It is like an early Countdown." **[393]** ...

"Can I say."

"It is."

Because of the humorous, if not hilarious, treatment by The Panel of this footage, an initial reaction may well be that the purpose of this rebroadcast was light satire in the nature of entertainment proffered by a rival television station, and did not involve the passing of judgment on the merits of Nine's television presentation (see again the dictionary definitions and commentary extracted from *De Garis* above). My conclusion is that criticism or review do not necessarily exclude notions of comedy or satire, even though expressed lightly. As was said in *Vosper*, "But after all is said and done, it must be a matter of impression", and my impression on a somewhat precarious balance is in favour of a justifiable Ten purpose here involved of criticism and review. Consequently had I not found in favour of Ten upon the issue of substantiality, I would have found that the defence of fair dealing for the purpose of criticism or review had been made out.

In the result, I dismiss the causes of action for breach of television broadcast copyright brought by Nine based upon s 87(c) of the Act.

■ Other exceptions

[6.200] Amendments introduced by the *Copyright Amendment (Computer Programs) Act 1999* (Cth) allow an exception to the copyright reproduction right. Under s 47D where interface information about other programs is not readily available to a software producer, the producer is allowed to decompile another program to the extent necessary to get the required interface information to make the interoperable product. Decompilation for the correction of errors in a commercial program (s 47E), and decompilation to test the security of a computer program (s 47F) is also allowed. These amendments make Australian law similar to US and EU legislation allowing interoperability, error correction and security testing.

There are certain other uses of copyright material which will be excused from infringing although such use would prima facie be caught. These include the making of a backup copy of a computer program for use in case of the original copy being lost, destroyed or rendered unusable (s 43C). Use of the Part IV copyrights will be excused if the purpose is to report or facilitate a judicial proceeding, or for the purpose of seeking professional legal advice (s 104). An authorised officer of a parliamentary library may use Part IV material to assist members of Parliament in the performance of their duties as such (s 104A). Making a record embodying a sound recording for the purpose of broadcasting is permissible (s 107) and so is the public performance (s 108) or broadcast (ss 105, 109) of sound recordings in certain circumstances. Playing music at a guesthouse or club will not infringe unless admission is charged (s 106). Some of these uses overlap with compulsory licensing provisions. These exceptions largely continue in the digital environment; the *Copyright Amendment (Digital Agenda) Act 2000* (Cth) provides for digital copies to be made without infringing copyright under the library exceptions for document supply, and archives exceptions allow for preservation and administration.

In addition to the free uses of material permitted under the fair dealing provisions and uses subject to compulsory licensing provisions, there are numerous minor additional statutory exceptions to infringement. These concern both Part III and Part IV subject matter. The exceptions are hard to classify although they generally reflect established policy objectives.

They include:

- Some exceptions that permit certain uses in furtherance of educational, library and archival, judicial and parliamentary interests. With respect to these exceptions it could be argued there is a public interest in favour of free access to works by these qualified individuals. See ss 43, 44, 48A, 49, 50, 51, 51AA, 51A, 52, 53, 53A, 104, 104A, 104B.

- Others provisions exempt what might otherwise arise as a "technical" infringement. Here given the parliamentary objective as defined in associated legislative provisions, it could be argued that there is no real prejudice to the legitimate interests of the copyright owner at stake. See ss 43A, 44A, 44B, 44C, 44D, 111A, 112B, 112C, 112D, 112E.

- Many provisions seem to recognise non-commercial uses of copyright works as well as acknowledge that detection of an infringement is unlikely. See Exceptions relating to performances of works, ss 28, 45, 46; broadcasts, ss 47, 47AA, 47A; Permitted uses of sound recordings, ss 105-109; films and broadcasts, ss 110-111; artistic works, ss 65-70, 72-73, 75.

- The copyright/design overlap provisions are required to maintain the general order and division of intellectual property rights. See ss 75-77.

- There are specific exceptions relating to certain uses of computer programs. These generally facilitate access to computer programs in line with prescribed policy objectives. See Part III, Division 4A, ss 47AB-47H.

■ Relevance of evidence of industry practice as a defence in infringement proceedings

▬▬▬▬▬ TCN Channel Nine v Network Ten ▬▬▬▬▬

[6.205] *TCN Channel Nine v Network Ten* [2001] FCA 841 Federal Court of Australia

[In this Panel decision, Conti J considers the relevance of industry practice in relation to the taping of rival station's television broadcasts. His finding that Network Ten had not infringed copyright was overturned on appeal. See [3.270], [3.275], [6.170].

CONTI J

Whether Ten was authorised to contravene s 87(a) by implied license

[21] Ten's pleading of this alternative defence was in the following terms:

> "9B ... the making of the video tapes of parts of the Nine Programs for subsequent rebroadcast by [Ten] in the course of The Panel program was carried out with the implied license of [Nine] based upon trade practice and usage in Australia.
>
> *Particulars*
>
> Australian television stations including [Nine] and [Ten] regularly make video tapes of television broadcasts on BETA format cartridges as a step in preparation for possible rebroadcast of such material for the purposes of criticism, review or the reporting of news. The making of those video tapes without more is within the implied license constituted by the usage and practice of the television industry."

... Senior Counsel for Ten accepted in any event that Ten had to establish that up until the moment of rebroadcast, the technical steps which must necessarily be in position for rebroadcasting are by consent of the television industry treated as "innocuous copyings". Up until that time, so Ten contended, there was no competitive advantage to be obtained by making and holding for the time being such in-house tapings, and it was only after that time that infringement was otherwise to be evaluated. Moreover thus far, so the contention continued, no unilateral notice had been given by any Australian television station to bring this asserted usage to an end.

[22] Nine's position was ... that contrary to Mr Carroll's assertion, Nine did not copy the news programmes of television stations other than those produced by Channel Seven. Cross-examination of Mr Carroll confirmed and/or revealed the following circumstances:

(i)   His experiences at Channel Seven and Nine in relation to copying were confined to the areas of news and current affairs, usually of a sporting nature.

(ii)   All "feeds" or "splits" with which he was personally involved at Seven and Nine involved the use of Beta equipment, and took place in the context of obtaining "the specific consent of the rival network for the split".

(iii) It was not uncommon in his experience for television stations to make complaints to other television stations "about improper use of material" (transcript p 31).

(iv)   The quantities of footage of news the subject of "feeds" were only obtained "in small quantities".

(v)   He was not fully conversant with the current practices of Seven, ABC and SBS concerning Beta recordings of other programmes.

(vi)   He was unsure of Ten's precise current practices concerning the recording of the programmes of other networks on at least a daily basis.

(vii) Whilst he had been involved at Nine with the use of footage provided on an agreed "split feed" basis by other networks, he had understood that such use "was constrained by fair-dealing requirements" based upon "a news judgment factor".

(viii) He had recognised that if he involved Nine "beyond the fair dealing requirements, the station could be in trouble for copyright infringement".

...

[25] Nine has referred me to a number of authorities concerning implied licensing of copyright material, but many of which are of marginal assistance because their context was a prior contractual relationship, and the issue was one of implication of a contractual term, rather than as trade usage per se. *Copinger and Skone James on Copyright* (14th ed, 1999), p 321 encapsulates the principle potentially here applicable as follows:

▬▬▬▬ TCN Channel Nine v Network Ten *continued*

"It is clearly possible that a trade custom or practice may exist whereby works are accepted on all sides as being liable to be copied etc. The usual difficulty will be to show that the usage or custom is invariable, certain and general, as opposed to mere common practice."

In a passage often cited from *Walter v Steinkopff* [1892] 3 Ch 489 at 499, the foregoing precept is illustrated:

"The attempt to show that the Times agreed to this journalistic practice of copying, from the fact of its having taken extracts from other papers than the St James' Gazette, is a ludicrous failure; for the Times has shewn that in thirteen out of sixteen instances adduced by the Defendants the explanation is complete, most of them being cases in which the matter was inserted in the Times at the express request of the other papers, specially communicated to them in order that they might insert it; and the few others are trivial matters, doubtless susceptible of easy explanation at the time."

Further in *Avel Pty Ltd v Multicoin Amusement Pty Ltd* (1990) 171 CLR 88 at 123, McHugh J relevantly observed to not dissimilar effect as follows:

"[I]n the context of the correspondence between the distributor, its lawyers and Williams, I think that the proper conclusion to draw is that Williams had no objection to the importation of its machines into Australia.

It is another question, however, whether lack of objection to the importation of Williams machines into Australia constitutes a license from the owner to import those machines into Australia. No doubt indifference may reach a stage where authorisation or permission may be inferred ... But a failure to object or even an intention not to take any action to object to the importation of articles does not necessarily constitute a license to import them."

[26] Another illustration of the potential shortcomings of common business practice in relation to the copyright is the case of *Banier v News Group Newspapers Ltd* [1997] FSR 812, which involved a photograph of Princess Caroline of Monaco taken by the plaintiff, being a photographer of international repute, which was published in The Times under license but in circumstances as to dispute of the terms of the licence. News for its part published the photograph without any asserted license or permission, not having been able to make contact with the plaintiff's agent before the deadline for publication. Lightman J at 815 observed:

"This may be common newspaper practice and one which newspapers normally get away with. The risk of infringement proceedings may from a business and circulation point of view be worth taking: it may be economic to 'publish and be damned'. But it is plainly unjustified and unlawful and the sooner this is recognised the better for all concerned. The adoption of this practice is not a passport to infringe copyright."

[27] The conclusionary inferences which may be drawn from the evidentiary material adduced in the proceedings are as follows:

(i) It is the practice of at least the majority of the major Australian television broadcasters, if not all of them, to make video-tape recordings (which may be taken to equate with the statutory description of cinematograph films) of televised broadcasts made by their respective competitors, and to store such recordings in their respective libraries; there is insufficient material to establish implied mutual agreements between telecasters to such effect, which is understandable, since in the absence of any subsequent use made of such video-tapes of the broadcasts of one station by another station which was recorded the same, the television station copyright owners' basis for complaint would presumably be academic.

(ii) It is also the practice of at least the majority of Australian television broadcasters, if not all, to occasionally rebroadcast some relatively minor parts (in terms of length) of such video-tape recordings, being a practice to which I would refer by the description "excerpt rebroadcasting", upon the footing that by so doing, the rebroadcast would fall or be likely to fall, in the view of the rebroadcaster, within one or more of the fair dealing defences stipulated by the Act.

(iii) By undertaking the rebroadcasting step described in (ii) above, the television broadcaster would be likely to recognise and appreciate that there was some risk of not sustaining a fair dealing defence if its conduct was to be subsequently challenged by the copyright holder of the television broadcast, though in the case of rebroadcasting for the purpose of or in association with the reporting of news, such risk would tend to be less than the circumstance where the only defence conceivably open to be established was that of having a purpose of criticism of review.

(iv) There does not exist in Australia, at least among the major television broadcasters, such as those the subject of the present proceedings, any established trade practice or custom constituting a mutually implied license to the effect that a television broadcaster is entitled to make a video tape of a programme, or an excerpt of a programme, previously broadcast by another television broadcaster, for any purpose, and that the second-mentioned television broadcaster would consider itself uninhibited from making complaint or seeking redress, unconstrained by any supposed existence of any custom or usage to the contrary, by such processes as it may judge to be appropriate in the circum-stances of the case, where the infringement of copyright has occurred in circumstances outside what it may consider to be the perceptibly justifiable protection of applicable fair dealing defences.

[28] I therefore would have held that had Nine been able to sustain its cause of action against Ten for breach of s 87(a) of the Act (and also of s 87(c)), a defence of implied license or usage would not have been rightly available to Ten.

REMEDIES AND PENALTIES FOR INFRINGEMENT OF COPYRIGHT

■ Locus standi

[6.210] Actions for infringement of copyright may be brought by an owner (s 115) without the need to join other owners of copyright: *Prior v Lansdowne Press Pty Ltd* [1977] VR 65. Exclusive licensees have the same rights of action (except against the owner) as they would have if the licence had been an assignment (s 119), but the owner or exclusive licensee may be required to join the other party as plaintiff or defendant in the action where they have concurrent rights (s 120(1)), except in an application for an interlocutory injunction (s 120(2)). Equitable owners may also apparently obtain relief without joining the legal owner: *Acorn Computers Ltd v MCS Microcomputer Systems Pty Ltd* (1984) 4 IPR 214 at 220 per Smithers J.

■ Civil remedies

[6.215] Remedies awarded may include injunctions, account of profits and ex parte relief including Anton Piller orders (by which delivery up is usually effected). The plaintiff may elect between an account of profits or damages (s 115(2)) but damages are not appropriate for an infringement of which the defendant is unaware (s 115(3)). In addition to damages awarded on the usual basis, the plaintiff asking for conversion damages under s 116 is entitled to the value of an entire article of which an infringing copy is only a part, for example, a computer containing an infringing literary work in the form of a chip. On the other hand, where infringing items might be the only assets the defendant has, an award of damages will be of no benefit if the plaintiff cannot apply the infringing goods to their own purposes.

■ Criminal penalties

[6.220] The number and types of criminal offences in copyright have increased to combat digital piracy. The main provisions relate to s 132. Selling, offering for trade, or importing infringing copies, or copies that a person ought to know are infringing, are offences. There are also offences relating to circumvention devices and services, interfering with electronic rights management information, and converting a hard copy into digital format.

Though uncommon, criminal penalties may apply where infringements have a substantial prejudicial impact on the owner of the copyright; or occur on a commercial scale. Liability can arise without the need for money to change hands. In 2003 in an unreported case, *MP3 WMA Land*, three students Le, Ng and Trau who operated a file sharing website were each sentenced to 18 months imprisonment, suspended for three years on a $1,000 good behaviour bond. Tran was fined $5,000. Ng, who lacked Tran's medical certificate, was sentenced to 200 hours community service. The maximum penalty for an individual is five years imprisonment in respect of each infringing article.

While offences only relate to infringements within Australia, in *Griffiths v United States of America* [2005] FCAFC 34, the Federal Court found that Mr Griffith, an Australian citizen associated with a American based file trading network, could be extradited to face criminal charnges relating to alleged copyright infringements in the United States.

Copyright matters are usually heard in the Federal Court. The recent emergence of a role for local courts in criminal matters in relation to copyright infringement is discussed in Anon, "If You Go Down to the Woods Today: Tales from the Front Line of Criminal Copyright Enforcement" (2005) 16 AIPJ 165.

In May 2006 the Federal Government reaffirmed the priority of promoting co-operation between law enforcement agencies, the States and industry to tackle the problem of copyright piracy. The Government has set up an Interdepartmental Committee on Enforcement to consider intellectual property enforcement issues to encourage closer cooperation between Australian Government agencies, federal and State law enforcement bodies, Customs and industry through the work of the Intellectual Property Enforcement Consultative Group. A proposal to establish a law enforcement body based on a United States model that would specialise in investigating internet piracy is also being considered.

New legislative measures announced include police being able to issue on-the-spot fines and access and recover profits made by copyright pirates.

Patents

Part 3

Patents

CHAPTER 7

CONTEXT OF PATENT LAW

INTRODUCTION

[7.05] There are two forms of patent in Australia. A standard patent is a grant of exclusive rights to commercially exploit a novel, inventive and industrially applicable advance in forms or uses of technology for a term of years. An innovation patent is a second level form of patent where exclusive rights are granted for a shorter term. In an innovation patent the advance in forms or uses of technology must still be novel and industrially applicable, but it is required to be "innovative" rather than inventive.

An applicant for a patent must supply a complete specification that describes the nature of what has been invented, explains the best method of performing the invention known to the inventor and ends with definitions of those embodiments or uses of the invention for which the applicant/patentee claims the exclusive rights.

The subject matter of a patent should not be "available to the public" before the day of filing the application with the Patent Office but the patent system has a policy of "early publication" in order to make useful information publicly known. Standard patent specifications are published during the application process no later than 18 months after the earliest priority date except in the case of inventions concerning "associated technology" (or nuclear information) which may be subject to restrictions in publication. An innovation patent specification will be published when an application in a proper format is filed and accepted by the Commissioner.

A patent specification is a teaching document that must be written in a way that can be understood by a person skilled in the technology to which the invention relates. The public can discover from the publicly-available specification what has been invented, how to make or carry out what has been invented and which embodiments or uses of this invention have been reserved to the patentee. Furthermore, patent specifications are classified, identified and filed according to a system established by a multilateral international treaty (the *Strasbourg Agreement Concerning International Patent Classification 1971*). Patent documentation constitutes an important publicly available collection of technological information. The documents also contain information of potential commercial value about the owners and licensees of patents. The classification system makes it possible to systematically search domestic and international patent documents. One possible justification of the patent system is that it makes available to the public, as of right, technological and commercial information which might otherwise remain secret, or in limited circulation.

HISTORICAL BACKGROUND

■ Early history

[7.10] The origins of a system of monopoly rights granted in respect of inventions has been traced back to classical times.[1] However, the modern system of patent protection was developed in Venice in the mid-15th century. A 1474 Venetian statute provided:

> "Be it enacted that, by the authority of this Council, every person who shall build any new and ingenious device in this City, not previously made in our Commonwealth, shall give notice of it to the office of our General Welfare Board when it has been reduced to perfection so that it can be used and operated. It is forbidden to every

---

1 For example, see Fox, *Monopolies and Patents* (1947), Ch 1.

other person in any of our territories and towns to make any further device conforming with and similar to said one, without the consent and licence of the author, for the term of 10 years. And if anybody builds it in violation hereof, the aforesaid author and inventor shall be entitled to have him summoned before any magistrate of this City, by which magistrate the said infringer shall be constrained to pay him hundred ducats; and the device shall be destroyed at once. It being, however, within the power and discretion of the Government, in its activities, to take and use any such device and instrument, with this condition however that no-one but the author shall operate it.

We have among us men of great genius, apt to invent and discover ingenious devices; and in view of the grandeur and virtue of our City, more such men come to us every day from diverse parts. Now, if provision were made for the works and devices discovered by such persons, so that others who may see them could not build them and take the inventor's honor away, more men would then apply their genius, would discover, and would build devices of great utility and benefit to our Commonwealth."[2]

This statute exhibits many similarities to a typical, modern Patents Act. Familiar features include the requirement of newness (novelty) and ingenuity (inventiveness), registration with the State, exclusive rights to make and use, rights limited to a definite term, alleged infringements heard by a judicial officer, remedies for infringement including payment to the right holder and destruction of the infringing device, and a system of compulsory licence to the State. The objective of this patent system was as much to encourage the inflow of technology as to stimulate indigenous invention.

England's monarchs have extended protection to foreign craftsmen from as early as the 14th century, but this protection consisted of protection against interference by local guilds, rather than in the recognition of inventors' rights.[3] However recipients of these privileges were expected to live in England and teach local craftsmen the relevant art. The policy appears to have been intended as a form of incentive to "technology transfer" to assist in the development of English skills and crafts.[4]

A system of Crown grant of monopoly privilege to inventors and importers of new technology commenced in England during the reign of Mary as an exercise of Royal Prerogative and enforced by petition to the Star Chamber. The system involved an initial lump sum and then annual payments to the Crown known as "Royalties". Elizabeth I and James I both utilised the sale of patents as a valuable source of revenue, occasioning strong parliamentary protest.[5] In Elizabeth's last Parliament (1601), the protests were strong enough to move the Queen to issue a proclamation against the most offensive monopolies and more importantly, to give jurisdiction to the common law courts to determine the validity of the remaining monopolies.

The first case concerning the validity of a monopoly to be heard by a common law court was *Darcy v Allen* (1602) 11 Co Rep 84 (the *Case of Monopolies*). Edward Darcy, a groom of the Privy Chamber to Elizabeth I, had been granted letters patent in 1598 to "enjoy the whole traffic and merchandising of all playing cards" in England for which he paid one hundred marks per annum. One Thomas Allen, a haberdasher of London, had ordered a large number of playing cards to be manufactured and sold. Darcy sued for damages.

2   Quoted in Mandich, "Venetian Patents (1450-1550)" (1948) 30 JPOS 166 at 176-177.
3   See Hulme, "The History of the Patent System under the Prerogative and at Common Law" (1896) 12 LQR 141.
4   See Hulme, n 3.
5   For example, see Foster, "The Procedure of the House of Commons against Patents and Monopolies, 1621-1624" in Aiken and Henning, *Conflict in Stuart England* (1960), pp 59-85.

The Court found the monopoly was invalid and in doing so expressed their view of the proper basis for grant:

"[W]here any man does by his own charge and industry or by his own wit or invention doth bring any new trade into the realm, or any engine tending to the furtherance of a trade that never was used before—and that for the good of the realm—that in such cases the King may grant to him a monopoly patent for some reasonable time until the subjects may learn the same in consideration of the good that he doth bring by his invention to the Commonwealth otherwise not."

James I continued to use the monopoly system as part of his revenue struggle with the Commons and faced opposition from the courts and Commons. In the King's *Book of Bounty*, published in 1610, James declared his rights to reserve certain things for his pleasure and privilege, including the right to grant monopolies. Sir Edmund Coke regarded his judgment in *Darcy v Allen* as "the principal motive of the publishing of the King's Book".[6]

Eventually, the Commons moved to abolish monopolies except for the grant of "Patents for Inventions" for a limited term subject to the public interest. The *Statute of Monopolies* was introduced in the 1623-1624 session of Parliament "to reassert the law which was being neglected, evaded, and defied".[7] The *Statute of Monopolies* (21 Jac 1 c 3 1623) was passed by both Houses in May 1624. The Statute made a general abolition of the grant or continuance of monopolies but created a special limited exception in s 6.

"Section VI Provided also and be it declared and enacted that any declaration before mentioned shall not extend to any letters patent and grants of privilege, for the term of 14 years or under hereafter to be made of the sole working or making of any manner of new manufacture within this realm to the true and first inventor and inventors of such manufactures which others, at the time of making such letters patent or grant, shall not use, so as also they be not contrary to the law nor mischievous to the state by raising prices of commodities at home or hurt trade or generally inconvenient ... ."

This section continues to be of great importance in the question of patentability. See the *Patents Act 1990* (Cth) definition of "invention" in Schedule 1, ss 18(1)(a) and 18(1A)(a).

Despite this section the Crown continued to grant monopolies that conflicted with the intention of the legislature using a device that prevented the Crown enforcing a penalty against itself. This continued until 1688 and the Bill of Rights. There appear to have been no grants of Patents during the Commonwealth but the practice resumed after the Restoration.

The *Statute of Monopolies* established what could be the subject of a valid grant but did not address procedure for grant nor patent administration. Grant was a particularly convoluted process.[8]

Furthermore the grant, when made, was usually in very vague terms. From 1700 onwards attempts were made to require the clear definition of the invention itself and the scope of the monopoly granted. With the growth of British industry in the 17th and 18th centuries, conflicts between patents led to the development of patent specifications "giving the fullest and most sufficient description of all the particulars on which the effect depends". The development of the patent specification which included a clear description of the subject

---

6   See S Davies, "Further Light on the Statute of Monopolies" (1932) 48 LQR 394.
7   Davies, n 6 at 395, quoting Price, "The English Patents of Monopoly" (1913) 1 *Harvard Economic Series* 24.
8   See K Boehm, *The British Patent System*, "I: Administration", pp 18-19; OW Hulme, "On the History of Patent Law in the Seventeenth and Eighteenth Centuries" (1901) 18 LQR 280; C Dickens, *A Poor Man's Tale of a Patent* (Household Words, 19 October 1850); D Pascoe (ed), *Selected Journalism 1850-1870* (Penguin Modern Classics (USA); www.readbookonline.net/readOnLine/2530/).

matter of the patent and the method of its production changed the patent system to one in which new and useful information was "taught" to the public in exchange for the grant of the temporary monopoly. During the 18th century judges began to express the idea that the object of patent law was to secure the revelation of beneficial secrets that could be generally exploited when the inventor's monopoly expired.

This kind of thinking can be found in this extract from an early 20th century case.

▰▰▰ Attorney-General (Cth) v Adelaide Steamship Co ▰▰▰

[7.15] *Attorney-General (Cth) v Adelaide Steamship Co* (1913) 18 CLR 30 House of Lords

LORD PARKER: At common law every member of the community is entitled to carry on any trade or business he chooses and in such manner as he thinks most desirable in his own interests, and inasmuch as **[32]** every right connotes an obligation no-one can lawfully interfere with another in the free exercise of his trade or business unless there exists some just cause or excuse for such interference. Just cause or excuse for interference with another's trade or business may sometimes be found in the fact that the acts complained of as an interference have all been done in the bona fide exercise of the doer's own trade or business and with a single view to his own interests: *Mogul Steamship Co v McGregor Gow & Co* [1892] AC 25. But it may also be found in the existence of some additional or substantive right conferred by letters patent from the Crown or by contract between individuals. In the case of letters patent from the Crown this additional or substantive right is generally described as a monopoly. In the latter case the contract on which the additional or substantive right is founded is generally described as a contract in restraint of trade. Monopolies and contracts in restraint of trade have this in common, that they both, if enforced, involve a derogation from the common law right in virtue of which any member of the community may exercise any trade or business he pleases and in such manner as he thinks best in his own interests.

The right of the Crown to grant monopolies is now regulated by the *Statute of Monopolies* but it was always strictly limited at common law. A monopoly being a derogation from the common right of freedom of trade could not be granted without consideration moving to the public, just as a toll being a derogation from the public right of passage could not be granted without the like consideration. In the case of new inventions the consideration was found either in the interest of the public to encourage inventive ingenuity or more probably in the disclosure made to the public of a new and useful article or process. In the case of sole rights of trading with foreign parts it might be found in the interest of the public in new countries being opened to trade. But for the validity of every monopoly some consideration moving to the public was necessary. Many of the monopolies purported to be granted by the Tudor or Stuart Sovereigns were bad for want of such consideration, and it was the vexatious interference with trade under cover of these invalid grants that led to the passing **[33]** of the *Statute of Monopolies*. Further, monopolies were in the eyes of the lawyers of that time attended with the following evils: first, increase in the price of the wares, and secondly, deterioration of the wares themselves, both evils being due to the want of healthy competition.

[7.20] The "consideration moving to the public" Lord Parker refers to is revealed in the specification. Much patent litigation revolves around issues of whether the invention is of a kind that complies with the restrictions of the *Statute of Monopolies*, whether it is novel, inventive, useful and not previously secretly used. These are all aspects of the consideration moving to the public. Further questions concern whether the specification adequately describes the nature of the invention and the method of implementing it and whether the monopoly claimed is supported by the disclosure. These issues are all relevant to the desired balance between encouraging invention while at the same time not inhibiting areas of industry and technology by indiscriminately granting exclusive monopoly rights.

The 19th century saw demands for reform of the system including a proposal to abandon the system altogether.[9] Select Committees were appointed to consider reform of patent law in 1829 and 1851 and new Patents Acts were passed: *Patents Act 1835* (UK) (5 & 6 Wm IV, c 83); *Patents Act 1839* (UK) (2 & 3 Vict c 67); *Patents Act 1852* (UK) (15 &16 Vict c 83).

■ Reform of UK patent law

[7.25] The most important of these was the *Patents Law Amendment Act 1852* (UK) (15 & 16 Vict. C 65) which established the British Patent Office, appointed Commissioners of Patents to administer the system, established a uniform and single patent for the whole United Kingdom, established provisional protection from the date of application, simplified the system of grant and greatly reduced costs through the establishment of standard fees.

The *Patents, Designs & Trademarks Act 1883* (UK) (46 & 47 Vict c 57) is regarded as the model for the Australian *Patents Act*. The Act was an initial response to the newly created international treaty, the *Paris Convention for the Protection of Industrial Property 1883*. Some of the features of the Act were the introduction of an examination system, a description of the invention was required as a condition of grant rather than ground for invalidity, application was to be for one invention only, a compulsory licence system was introduced to prevent abuse of monopoly by non working of the patent and the term of monopoly was set at 14 years.

Further reforms were effected by:

* *Patents Act 1902* (UK) (2 Ed 7, c 34)—included applications examined for novelty;

* *Patents & Designs Act 1919* (UK) (9 & 10 Geo 5 c 80)—increased the term to 16 years;

* *Patents & Designs Act 1932* (UK) (22 & 23 Geo 5 c 32)—the major grounds for revocation were set into the legislation and the *Writ of Scirea Facias* provided other grounds of revocation;

* *Patents Act 1949* (UK) (12,13 & 14 Geo 6 c 87)—a complete list of revocation grounds were set out in the Act.

The *Patents Act 1977* (UK) (1977, c 37) gave effect to the recommendations of the Banks Committee and contained fundamental changes to UK law and practice to accommodate UK membership of the European Economic Community (EEC). The Act provides that its provisions should be interpreted to give effect to the European Patent Convention (EPC) that came into operation on 1 June 1978, and the decisions made under it. UK patent law is now "a hybrid mixture of national, European and international factors"[10]

■ Patent law in Australia

Colonial Acts

[7.30] Most Australian colonies had a *Patents Act* (for example, *Patents Act 1852-95* (NSW), *Patents Act 1890* (Vic)) based on the UK Act of 1883. The Colonial Acts continued in force

9   See Machlup and Penrose, "The Patent Controversy in the Nineteenth Century" (1950) 1 *Journal of Economic History* X.

10   L Bently and B Sherman, *Intellectual Property Law* (OUP, 2001), p 315.

until the Commonwealth Parliament exercised its power under the *Commonwealth of Australia Constitution Act* (Cth) (63 & 64 Vict c 12), s 51(xviii) and enacted the *Patents Act 1903* (Cth). The definition of patent under the 1903 Commonwealth Act included patents granted under the State Act.

Commonwealth Acts

Patents Act 1903 (Cth)
[7.35] The Act was in force for nearly 50 years and amended from time to time. It was reviewed by the Knowles Committee, appointed in 1935, and the Dean Committee, appointed in 1950. Following recommendations in both reports it was replaced in 1952.

Patents Act 1952 (Cth)
[7.40] The Act was strongly influenced by the reforms of the *Patents Act 1949* (UK). It was amended by 23 Acts during its currency. Important amendments included the *Patents Act 1969* which introduced a system of deferred and modified examinations, the *Patents Amendment Act 1978* (Cth) provided for early publication of complete specifications and the *Patents Amendment Act 1979* (Cth) introduced a petty patent system.

Petty patents were an Australian version of the German or Japanese "utility model" or the French "patent brevet". The object of the system was to provide protection for smaller scale inventions with a shorter potential market life that did not require or justify full patent term protection. Petty patents were easier to obtain, cheaper, quicker, granted without examination, and limited to an initial one year of protection renewable for a further five, giving a maximum of six years. The prior art base for testing novelty of petty patents was domestic prior art information. However, the standard of inventiveness was the same or similar for petty and standard patents.

Patents Act 1990 (Cth)
[7.45] The Industrial Property Advisory Committee produced a report in 1984, *Patents, Innovation and Competition in Australia*, in which reform of the patent system was recommended. The recommendations can be found in *Hansard* for 28 November 1986, as tabled by Barry Jones as Minister for Science. In response to the recommendations, the government introduced the *Patents Bill 1989* (Cth) and then, with some changes, the *Patents Bill 1990* (Cth). The Bill was a "plain English" Bill with a more systematic ordering of provisions. The major differences comprehended by the Bill are to be found in the Second Reading Speech in the House of Representatives, *Hansard*, 1 June 1989, p 3479.

The Act came into force on 30 April 1991. The *Patents Regulations 1991* (Cth) were notified in the Gazette on 26 April 1990 and came into force on 30 April 1991.

Transitional provisions (*Patents Act 1990* (Cth), ss 231-240; *Patents Regulations 1991* (Cth), Chap 23) provide that any patent granted under the *Patents Act 1952* (Cth) or applied for under that Act is treated as if it had been granted or applied for under the *Patents Act 1990* (Cth). However, no ground or objection available under the 1990 Act but which could not be raised against a patent or application under the 1952 Act can be raised against the transition patent or application (*Patents Act 1990* (Cth), s 233(4)).[11]

---

11   For discussion of the application of these provisions, see *NV Philips Gloeilampenfabrieken v Mirrabella International Pty Ltd* (1993) 26 IPR 513; *Re Franke and Commissioner of Patents* (1993) 29 ALD 801; *Murrex Diagnostics Australia Pty Ltd v Chivon Corp* (1995) 30 IPR 277; D Speagle and M Dowling, "The 1990 Patents Act: Unfinished Reform" (1993) 4 AIPJ 166.

Important amendments to the principal Act include:

- *Patents (World Trade Organization Amendments) Act 1994*—extended the term of a standard patent from 16 to 20 years in accordance with Australia's obligations under the TRIPS Agreement.

- *Patents Amendment (Innovation Patents) Act 2000*—ceased to allow new applications for Petty Patents and introduced a system of Innovation Patents (see below)

- *Patents Amendment Act 2001*—raised threshold requirements of novelty and inventive step and made amendments responding to recommendations in Final Report of the *Review of Intellectual Property Legislation under the Competition Principles Agreement* (The Ergas Report) (see below).

- *US Free Trade Agreement Implementation Act 2004*—This Act makes a number of amendments to meet the requirements of Australia-United States Free Trade Agreement.

The innovation patent

[7.50] The Advisory Council on Industrial Property (ACIP) and the Australian Law Reform Commission noted that the petty patent system did not protect "functional innovations that are not sufficiently inventive under the present standard or petty patent system to warrant protection and are not protectable under the designs system which protects the appearance of articles but not the way they work." ACIP recommended that petty patents be replaced by a new "second tier" form of protection to be called the "innovation patent".[12]

The innovation patent system was intended to be suitable for small and medium business entities to obtain relatively simple, quick and cheap patent-style protection for minor inventions or incremental variations, for a maximum term of 8 years considered sufficient to encourage research and development of the innovation. Innovation patents are available for most forms of invention patentable under a standard patent, but not for inventions which are plants, animals or essentially biological processes for the generation of plants and animals. Innovation patents are available for inventions involving micro-organism products or processes.

Australia-United States Free Trade Agreement[13]

[7.55] The Australia-United States Free Trade Agreement was concluded on 8 May 2004 and came into force on 1 January 2005. Chapter 17 of the Agreement deals with Intellectual Property.[14] Points of agreement in Chapter 17 specifically relating to patent law[15] are:

- the scope of patentability (17.9.1)

- scope of limitations and exclusions from patentability (17.9.2)

- freedom to adopt limitations and exceptions which do not unreasonably conflict with normal exploitation of the patent and do not unreasonably prejudice the legitimate interests of the patent owner taking into account the legitimate interests of third parties

---

12   See Advisory Council on Industrial Property, *Review of the Petty Patent System* (AIPO, October 1995); *Introduction of the Innovation Patent: Government Response to the Recommendations of the Advisory Council on Industrial Property Report Review of the Petty Patent System* (AGPS, 1997).
13   www.dfat.gov.au/trade/negotiations/us.html
14   C Arup, "The United States-Australia Free Trade Agreement—The Intellectual Property Chapter" (2004) 15 AIPJ 205.
15   See also R Cooper and M Swinson, "US and Australia Agree on Patent Basics" (2004) 138 *Managing Intellectual Property* 52.

(17.9.3 and 17.9.6 applies this to permitting a third party generate information necessary to support an application for marketing approval of a pharmaceutical product)

- parallel importation principles (17.9.4)

- limitations on revocation and extension of opposition grounds (17.9.5)

- limitations on compulsory licensing (17.9.7)

- extension of term for unreasonable delay in issuance of patents (17.9.8)

- grace period (17.9.9)

- opportunity for amendments (17.9.10)

- sufficiency of disclosure (17.9.11 and 17.9.12))

- requirement of specific substantial and credible utility (17.9.13)

- parties to endeavour to reduce differences in law and practice between their systems (17.9.14)

- parties to endeavour to establish a cooperative framework between their respective patent offices (17.9.15)

- extended protection for pharmaceutical and agricultural pharmaceutical products and the marketing approval process (17.10)

Generally speaking the principles agreed do not require major change to Australian patent legislation. However, such changes as are required to the patent system have been enacted by the *US Free Trade Implementation Act 2004* (*Cth*) and in particular by schedule 8 of that Act. The Act also brought about significant changes to the *Therapeutic Goods Act 1989*.

PATENT PROTECTION—EVALUATION

[7.60] From the commencement of the Industrial Revolution, opponents of the patent system have questioned the rationale of patent protection. In 1979, the Senate Standing Committee on Science and the Environment, in its report on Industrial Research and Development in Australia, expressed the view that "Australia's present patent system may well be acting against the country's best interests". Pursuant to that report, the Industrial Property Advisory Committee (IPAC) was commissioned to examine how patent protection could be made to serve the national interest.

IPAC's report, *Patents, Innovation and Competition in Australia*, was released in late 1984 and recommended that the patent system continue to operate in Australia, including participation in the international patent scheme. A number of changes and improvements were suggested. IPAC noted the tension between the patent monopoly and the proscription of monopolisation in the *Trade Practices Act 1974* (Cth) (s 46). It was recommended that the *Trade Practices Act* (Cth) be amended and *Patents Act* (Cth), s 112 (now s 144) be repealed, with "patent-related conduct" being subject to a "lessening of competition" test, rather than the piecemeal regulation of licensing etc arrangements which presently exist. To complement this competition law approach, an additional discretionary power to grant compulsory licences by an appropriate court was also recommended. Other recommendations by IPAC concerned the organisation of the Patent Office and its record keeping and information services, and the storage, access and dissemination of patent information by computerisation of data. Many of the suggested reforms have been made by the *Patents Act 1990* (Cth), but the trade practices issues have not yet been addressed.

▰▰▰ Review of Intellectual Property Legislation under ▰▰▰ the Competition Principles Agreement

[7.65] Intellectual Property Competition Review Committee, *Review of Intellectual Property Legislation under the Competition Principles Agreement*, Final Report (September 2000) (References omitted)

Description of patent rights and the patent system
Under current Australian patent law (*Patents Act 1990*) and associated regulations and case law), a patent may be granted on a new, non-obvious and useful invention, including improved products and processes. A patent gives the patentee the exclusive right, during the term of the patent, to "exploit" the patented invention in Australia, including the right to make, hire, sell, use or import the invention, and/or authorise another person to do so. In Australia, a standard patent lasts for 20 years, although annual renewal fees are payable from its fifth year. A petty patent may last up to six years, and the proposed innovation patent will have a maximum term of eight years.

Applications for patents must be filed with the Patent Office, which forms part of IP Australia. The application in its "specification" must fully describe the invention, and state the scope of the desired patent right. This often involves a lengthy description of the problem the invention is trying to solve. In contrast to the situation in some other countries, applicants for Australian patents are not currently required to disclose all previous attempts they know have been made to solve the specific problem or related problems involved (the "prior art").

The description of the invention included in the application must also describe the applicant's solution to the problem, in sufficient detail that a person familiar with ("skilled in") the technology (the "art") could perform the invention without undue experimentation. The description must include the best method known to the applicant for performing the invention. These requirements are often characterised as part of the bargain (quid pro quo) between the applicant and society—in return for the applicant's limited exclusive right, society gains through the disclosure of the invention which allows others to build on it or work around it during the exclusion period and to use it directly after the exclusion period expires.

The area of exclusivity ("scope") of the patent is defined by the claims of the specification. To be patentable, the claims must satisfy threshold tests required by the Act, the most important of which are:
(a) the invention must be a "manner of new manufacture" within the meaning of s 18 of Act and relevant case law;
(b) the invention must be novel in the sense that someone else should not have performed or published it; and
(c) the invention must be inventive and not merely an advance that would be obvious to a person skilled in the field of the invention.

These tests set a higher level of threshold to obtain patent rights than that required for other IP rights, because the scope of the patent right is generally greater. Patents allow the right holder to claim more than one manifestation of an idea, unlike copyright, which protects only a particular expression of an idea.

The Patent Office acts as the initial broker in forming the contract between the applicant and society for the grant of exclusive patent rights. The threshold tests are used as a rough proxy for the benefits of the claimed invention to society, since it is usually not possible to do a detailed cost benefit analysis for each patent, partly because the value of new inventions is generally difficult and expensive to predict. Patent examiners frequently reject an application at least once, usually because the scope of the claim is either unclear or too broad (usually because it is not "fairly based" on what is disclosed in the description or because it transgresses what is already known in the prior art). Applications may also be rejected because they are not sufficiently inventive, although this can be difficult to prove during examination, particularly when an applicant disputes that the examiner is a person suitably skilled in the art. Applicants may modify their specification, provided it is fairly based on what was originally disclosed, and resubmit the application up until 18 months from the beginning of the examination process ...

If the application is nonetheless finally rejected by an examiner, the applicant can appeal to the Commissioner for re-examination. The Commissioner appoints a senior examiner not previously involved in the case to re-examine the application ex parte. Recently, there have been only a small number of re-examinations (typically two or three per year).

If accepted by an examiner, the granting of the patent is delayed for three months after notification in the Patent Office *Gazette*, to allow third parties to lodge oppositions on grounds such as:

- lack of novelty and inventive step;
- insufficient disclosure of the invention; and
- claims which are not sufficiently clear or fairly based on what is disclosed in the description.

Opposition hearings are conducted by the Patent Office by a delegate of the Commissioner, usually a senior patent examiner who has knowledge of the technology but has not been involved in the prior examination process, and who has been trained in the process of managing hearings. These hearings are inter parte and have prescribed time periods to prevent either party from benefiting from delays. There are normally fewer than 100 such hearings per year.

Decisions of the Patent Office, depending on their type, can be appealed to the courts or to administrative tribunals. The courts, generally presided over by a single judge of the Federal Court, also hear cases alleging infringements of granted patents. Because of the technical issues involved, such cases usually require calling expert witnesses who act as "persons skilled in the art". These court proceedings are often very costly. The full bench of the Federal Court and the High Court only hear matters of law when appeal is allowed. Very few court cases involve IP Australia as a party.

Objectives of the patent system

The main objectives of the patent system can be summarised by the following quote from the Second Reading Speech on the *Patents Amendment Bill 1981*:

> "The main purpose of a patent system is to stimulate industrial invention and innovation by granting limited monopoly rights to inventors and by increasing public availability of information on new technology. Patent procedures must achieve a balance among competing interests while remaining administratively workable."

Furthermore:

> "The essence of the patent system is to encourage entrepreneurs to develop and commercialise new technology ... Since a patent confers a limited monopoly over the

▬▬▬▬▬ Review of Intellectual Property Legislation ... *continued*

use of the patented technology, the patent owner has the opportunity to make a profit from it, gaining a return on investment in innovation. The international character of the patent system makes a patent a useful tool in penetrating export markets."

Overall, the patent system aims to promote investment in innovation by providing the inventor with temporary exclusivity over the use of an invention. For the purposes of the patent, the invention is defined by reference to a series of claims, set out in the patent, that specify the advance made by the inventor over the prior art, while "use" is the broad set of exclusive rights the patentee obtains. As a counterpart to this protection, the inventor is required to disclose the invention to the public.

Problems patent rights attempt to address

As with other types of intellectual property, the principle problem which patents attempt to address is the threat of free riding on investment of intellectual effort. Unless kept secret, inventions and ideas can often be cheaply copied or imitated by competitors. Without patent protection it would be impossible to prevent freeriding by persons who did not contribute to the original investment. This makes it impossible for the investor to recoup the cost of the investment required to secure the advance. Market incentives for investment in invention would consequently be deficient. As discussed in more detail under the section on Alternatives, the patent system attempts to solve these market failures through an essentially market-oriented mechanism, unlike possible alternatives such as direct government subsidy.

As with patents, contracts and trade secret laws can be used to reduce free riding by making it a breach to disclose confidential knowledge. Trade secret laws can also reduce transaction costs by reducing the protective measures which knowledge owners must expend to maintain control over an invention. However, trade secret law cannot reduce transaction costs to zero, for at least two reasons. Firstly, there is still the cost to both parties of acquiring information about the current state of knowledge before entering the contract. (The lack of disclosure making this cost all the greater). Secondly, trade secret law can only be used where the bargainers (producers and users of the knowledge) are well-defined.

In addition, such contractual arrangements are in many situations very difficult and/or costly to make and enforce—for example, where the population of potential users is widely dispersed (for example, as between possible cancer patients and cancer researchers). In these situations, transactions and bargaining costs are likely to be high, and private negotiations cannot solve the problems free riding creates for efficient resource allocation.

Patent laws try to solve these problems by assigning the first producer exclusive rights for a limited period. By making patent law similar to real property law, the rights may be traded (sold or licensed) so that the knowledge can be transferred to its most efficient users. Bargaining issues are reduced and transaction costs are likely lower than with pre-production contracts or trade secrets. This is because the cost of identifying owners of knowledge and negotiating agreements with these owners is likely to be reduced and also because the cost of detecting violations is likely to be smaller (since all unauthorised users are violators).

The standard optimal conditions of welfare economics require equalisation between marginal social costs and marginal social benefits in every market, including that for innovation and knowledge. If marginal social cost in this market is less than the marginal social benefit, then increasing the amount of innovation will increase overall economic welfare, and conversely. However, the actual level of production of innovation in a market system will occur where the *marginal* private cost to an innovator (individual or company) equals the marginal *private* benefit. Assuming that private and social costs are equal (the opportunity costs of resources to their production) but that the marginal private benefit (value) of invention is less than its marginal social value, too little innovation will be produced. This is likely to be the case in the absence of a system of IP rights, as investors in creative effort could not prevent others from appropriating the fruits of that investment.

Research quoted by Revesz suggests that the private value of research and development (R & D) is much less than the social return ...

The social return on R & D generally far exceeds the private return. If returns are measured at the margin, it can be assumed that investment in innovation may be suboptimal for the innovator. Revesz concludes that by and large "the main economic problem that has been identified is one of inadequate rewards rather than excess windfall gains from patent protection".

Provided patents are granted for real innovations (as stipulated in the legislation) there is no conflict between patents and competition from the welfare economics perspective, because patents stimulate inventive activity that usually would have been more costly to induce by other means.

Under a patent system, it is unlikely that private and social costs will be equal. Indeed, the social costs will more often exceed the private costs (though both of these should be no greater than the resulting social benefits) because of:

- administrative costs of the Patent Office, though these can be internalised by fees;
- enforcement costs where the court system is subsidised by the public; and perhaps most importantly
- social costs due to the temporary market distortions caused by the exclusive right.

The patent system is not the only incentive to innovation (as further detailed in the Alternatives section below). Governments use other systems in parallel, including subsidy of knowledge production costs, either through direct grants and/or through indirect taxation relief. These systems interact, often pulling each other in different directions, making the economic and benefits analysis of the private and social costs more difficult.

Nature of the restrictions on competition

A patent excludes others from the area of technology defined by the scope of the claims for the duration of the grant. This exclusivity may enable the patentee to charge higher prices and make greater profits than would be possible if the ideas were freely available. Also, efficiencies gained as a result of the invention will be temporarily less widely available in society. Granting patents can therefore lead to losses in allocative and productive efficiency—the extent of these losses depends on the market power of the patentee and on the patentee's ability to price discriminate. In practice, however, a patent holder can rarely act as a pure monopoly, because of the availability of alternative and substitute products and processes, and also because some scope for imitation almost always exists.

Another effect of the temporary exclusive patent right is that it may inhibit innovation based on the ideas involved—this is because these ideas are not freely available for others to use. Kauffer suggests that these "dynamic" costs are potentially greater than the "static" deadweight costs, though they are likely to occur only when the scope of the patent is broad.

Similarly, Scotchmer states that until recently "economic theories of IP have assumed that innovations are isolated events with no bearing on future innovations". That view limits how well the theory can be applied to modern controversies, especially those involving biotechnology and computing hardware and software. These technologies have a high degree of "cumulativeness". This has implications for the social value of innovations and the ease with which firms can be given incentives to create them. Scotchmer continues by saying that cumulativeness "makes it especially difficult to turn social value into private value as must be

316   **PART 3** Patents

████ Review of Intellectual Property Legislation ... *continued*

done if firms are to have incentives to innovate. Later products can supplant the earlier ones, reducing their profitability. A solution is to give broad protection so that licensing is necessary. However, this may stifle the second-generation products."

To some extent dynamic losses are counteracted by the disclosure of ideas as part of the quid pro quo of granting a patent and by the fact that the patent system itself (by defining an assignable and enforceable property right) facilitates the use of licensing (in this case the use of cross-licensing between the original inventor and those that improve upon the invention).

International obligations

As the world economy becomes increasingly integrated, the international characteristics of the patent system are becoming more important. For innovation to play a major role in Australia's future, the ability of Australian innovators to gain property rights in export markets such as the US and Europe is crucial. By the same token, innovators in other countries will increasingly seek patents in Australia. Indeed, the majority of applications for standard patents made in Australia are from overseas. The Committee notes that the balance between the social benefits generated by the patent system and this system's cost to the community, is affected by whether the beneficiaries of the patents granted are in Australia or overseas. If the income transfers resulting from the system stay within Australia, then (all other things being equal) the social cost to the Australian economy of the system is potentially less and the net benefit correspondingly greater.

It might be simple to infer from this that Australia ought to seek easily obtainable protection in foreign markets while maintaining a system that restricts the availability of patent protection domestically. However, given the long term reciprocal nature of the patent system, a "beggar thy neighbour" approach is unlikely to be sustained—indeed, preferential treatment of domestic applicants has long been prohibited by the *Paris Convention for the Protection of Industrial Property*, and recently reinforced by TRIPs.

No less important is the fact that effective patent protection facilitates trade in technology, both domestically and internationally. An effective patent system, accessible to foreign technology suppliers, allows Australian firms to import technology that would otherwise be unavailable, or would only be available at higher cost. This increases productivity and enhances competition in the Australian economy. The importance of technological imports is illustrated by the more than 90 per cent of patents registered in Australia, which are owned by foreigners. In addition, there are more indirect cross-border spill overs through importing of goods which embody innovations and which may be used as intermediate inputs or sold directly to end users.

Reflecting the important international dimension of the patent system, Australia has entered into a number of international legal instruments that impose obligations with respect to the patent system.

These include:

Paris Convention for the Protection of Industrial Property 1883

This treaty applies to "industrial property" in the widest sense, including inventions, trade marks, industrial designs, utility models, trade names, geographic indications and the repression of fair competition. It covers national treatment (preventing discrimination against non-residents), right of priority provisions (for subsequent applications in contracting states) and some common rules. For patents, the most significant of the common rules cover independent assessment of patent eligibility by contracting states; maintaining national administrations including a special industrial property service with a central office for the communication with the public of patents, marks and industrial designs; and limitations on compulsory licensing provisions with respect to patents.

Patent Cooperation Treaty (PCT) 1970

The PCT enables patent protection for an invention to be sought simultaneously in member states designated by the applicant. An international search is conducted by one of the 10 major patent offices, of which Australia is one, and the report lists citations of prior art which are relevant to the novelty and inventiveness of the application. The applicant can optionally ask for an "international preliminary examination report", which gives a preliminary but non-binding opinion about the patentability of the claimed invention. However, after time periods specified by the PCT, the application must be filed with national offices where they are processed against the same national standards as any other application, though taking into account the results of the PCT search and examination.

Agreement on Trade-Related Aspects of Intellectual Property Rights 1995

The main features of TRIPs relevant to patents are:

(a) the requirement to have a patent system to be a member of the WTO;

(b) a minimum patent term set at 20 years;

(c) the requirement to protect artificially developed new varieties of micro-organisms through patents

(d) no areas of technology are to be excluded from patent protection, with the optional exceptions of medical methods for the treatment of humans, and of new life forms above the micro-organism level;

(e) the requirement to protect new plant varieties, within the patent system or with a separate system of breeder's rights, or both;

(f) the imposition of limitations to the application of compulsory licensing and government use of patents, and the

(g) requirement for adequate compensation;

(h) reversal of the burden of proof for process patents, and prohibition of any distinction in patent rights based on whether goods are locally produced or imported; and

(i) the requirement to develop a legal system for protecting trade secrets from unfair disclosure in accordance with

(j) principles of fair competition.

Australia was complying with most of the current requirements of TRIPs before they were adopted and so only relatively minor adjustments to the *Patents Act* were required to make it TRIPs compliant, the most important being the extension of the maximum patent term from 16 to 20 years.

Patent Law Treaty 2000

Recently, WIPO has been discussing the need for a *Patent Law Treaty*. After long negotiations, it was agreed that for the time being the treaty will not harmonise substantive issues such as the threshold tests of novelty and inventive step but will harmonise mainly administrative issues such as filing procedures. The treaty was adopted on 1 June 2000 by a Diplomatic Conference, including Australia, but has yet to be ratified.[16]

Alternatives to patents, including non-legislative means

Apart from patents there are other mechanisms for commercial appropriation of the benefits of innovation. An empirical survey by Levin et al found that the following methods were used by firms to protect their competitive advantage from innovations:

---

16 Since this Report was written 10 states have ratified the Treaty and it came into force in respect of those States on 28 April 2005. Australia has not yet ratified the Treaty.

■■■■■ Review of Intellectual Property Legislation ... *continued*

- patents;
- secrecy;
- lead time;
- moving quickly down the learning curve; and
- distinctive sales and service to customers.

A report by the OECD quoted similar findings from more recent studies. A study of American manufacturing [Cohen et al, 1996], for example, showed that secrecy was ranked first in terms of importance (over patents, lead time, service etc) in 14 out of 43 industries (33 per cent) among the means adopted to protect product innovation, and among 28 industries out of 43 (65 per cent) for product innovation. Similarly, in a 1994 survey of German small to medium enterprises with inhouse R & D [Fest, 1996], only about one third of respondents used patents to protect their IP. Another third relied on secrecy, pointing to the high cost of litigation. The remaining third introduced innovations faster than their competitors, indicating that the life cycle of their products is not much longer than the time it would take to obtain an European Patent Office (EPO) patent (2.5 to 3.5 years). Another survey, carried out in France by the Industry Ministry, revealed that only 10 per cent of innovating firms regarded patents as very important.

The main alternative to the patent system is trade secrets. Trade secret law is dominated by the common law action of breach of confidence. A successful action of breach of confidence requires that the disclosed information had sufficient quality of confidence, that it must have been imparted in circumstances giving rise to an obligation of confidence, that the disclosure must have been authorised and that some detriment must have been suffered as a consequence. Trade secrets and know-how may also be protected contractually. Unlike patents, there is no registration system involved for trade secrets.

In contrast to patents, where the innovator has exclusive rights, trade secret law allows others to duplicate an innovation, provided they do it independently or by reverse engineering. This puts a limit on the value of trade secrets. On the other hand, trade secrets have the potential to protect an innovation indefinitely, while patents give a maximum protection of 20 years.

Patents require sufficient disclosure. This disclosure provides social benefits by promoting diffusion of knowledge, but by the same token, it imposes a private cost on innovators by alerting competitors of the new ideas and facilitating "inventing around". Compared to patents, a primary social cost associated with trade secret law is the reduced diffusion of information. In addition, the property right associated with trade secret is less certain and may severely discourage trade in the innovation being protected. This in turn may impede or slow the transfer of new ideas to those who can put them to best use. Finally, because trade secret does not rule out independent invention, it may encourage duplicative investment in invention, resulting in some element of pure waste.

Thus the two systems—patents and trade secrets—have different advantages and disadvantages and can be seen as complementary. They give innovators a choice. Levin et al found that trade secrets are preferred when the innovation is a method of manufacture or a product that cannot be reverse engineered. Patents are preferred by innovators for product innovation that can be easily copied. Each system has its cost and benefits, both from society's and from the innovators' point of view. In practice, many licensing agreements rely on both systems.

Other incentive mechanisms have been used by governments to encourage innovation, by reducing the gap between private and social benefits. By and large, these centre on providing direct incentives to invention and innovation, through some combination of subsidies and of intra-mural conduct of R & D.

In theory, direct incentives to invention and innovation should allow for greater efficiency than the grant of exclusive rights. Thus, one of the pioneers of modern economics, Frank Knight, viewed patents as an "exceedingly crude way of rewarding invention". He concluded that "it would seem to be a matter of political intelligence and administrative capability to replace artificial monopoly with some direct method of stimulating and rewarding research". The Nobel laureate in economics, Kenneth Arrow, echoed this view some 40 years later in his classic article on the economics of R & D.

These arguments, compelling though they may be, rest on the assumption that governments, in implementing Knights' "direct method" of stimulation, will make fewer or less costly errors in allocating resources to creative effort than are caused by the market oriented mechanism of intellectual property rights. This assumption has merit when applied to pure research, but must surely fail at the application end of the spectrum. To begin with, it requires a greater degree of omniscience (and perhaps of omnibenevolence) from public decision makers than is safe to assume. Additionally, it underestimates the incentives even owners of monopoly rights have to expand output, say through price discrimination, and therefore likely overstates the costs of an alleged monopoly. Finally, it wrongly assumes that intellectual property rights serve only to fund investment in creative effort. In practice, they also act to promote the disclosure of new ideas (particularly where secrecy is a viable alternative), and by allowing well-defined rights to be traded, they facilitate the allocation of the ownership of creative works to those who can put them to their most highly valued use. Since no "direct method" of stimulation has yet been found that comes close to matching these effects, calls for a wholesale retreat from patents are poorly based.

Conclusions

In the Committee's view, there is little doubt that the social gains from investment in new ideas can exceed the private gains investors would secure from that investment in the absence of public intervention. The patent system does not, and cannot, provide a perfect or complete answer to this problem. However, it has strong advantages relative to alternatives—such as trade secret and government subsidisation—even though these alternatives have an important role to play in promoting innovation.

Overall, the Committee agrees with Scherer that "the patent system is recognised to be an imperfect instrument. Nevertheless, it may be the best solution policy man can devise to the difficult trade-off between, on the one hand, maintaining incentives for investment and, on the other hand, fostering the diffusion of new technology's benefits to consumers and to those who might make leapfrogging inventions. Its imperfections include uncertainty as to which of several contending parties will receive patent protection and how much protection patents will afford, the costs of concomitant legal services, and the ease in most cases (but not in pharmaceuticals) of "inventing around" existing patents.

The issue then is how to maximise the net social benefits that can be obtained from the patent system. This involves carefully examining the system itself, and identifying areas where benefits can be increased or costs reduced.

Two areas are of particular importance in this regard:

(a) The Committee is convinced that Australia would gain from ensuring, to a greater degree than is currently the case, that patents are not granted where it is likely that reasonable threshold tests for securing a valid patent will not be met. The Committee accepts that there are costs involved in screening applications, but believes, for reasons discussed below in this section, that these costs are outweighed by the costs society bears when patents that ought not to be granted, are granted.

(b) The Committee believes that subject to greater and more stringent control over their grant, those to whom a patent has been granted should have a reasonable degree of confidence in the validity of the rights they have obtained.

PROCEDURE FOR OBTAINING A PATENT

[7.70] The *Patents Regulations 1991* (Cth) and Schedules have detailed prescriptions of the format and presentation of the documentation required by the Patent Office. The patent specification has also been the subject of substantive law, and that is the subject of this part of the casebook. The formalities of application are only briefly described in this section in order to help students understand the legal obstacles to patentability. Statutory references throughout Chapters 7-10 are, unless otherwise indicated, references to the *Patents Act 1990* (Cth) and *Patents Regulations 1991* (Cth).

■ Types of patent:
[7.75] Sch 1, Dictionary "patent" means a standard patent or an innovation patent.

A standard patent is a form of personal property in which exclusive rights to make use or commercially exploit an invention in ways claimed by the patentee are granted after a successful application process. The subject matter must be an invention which is a manner of manufacture within the meaning of *Statute of Monopolies*, s 6, must be novel, involving an inventive step, is useful and has not been secretly used in the patent area with the consent of the patentee before the priority date. The invention must be adequately described in a patent specification and the claims of monopoly must be clear, succinct and fairly based on the invention disclosed in the specification. There are no specific limitations on the number of claims of monopoly that may be granted. The normal term of the patent is 20 years but in the case of certain patents relating to pharmaceutical inventions there may be an extension of term for an additional five years.

The *Patents Amendment (Innovation Patents) Act 2000* (Cth) introduced an innovation patent. An innovation patent requires that the subject matter be a manner of manufacture within the meaning of *Statute of Monopolies*, s 6. Innovation patents are available for most forms of invention patentable under a standard patent, including inventions involving micro-organism products or processes, but not for inventions that are plants, animals or essentially biological processes for the generation of plants and animals. Innovation patents are available where the subject matter is novel and involves an innovative step, is useful and has not been secretly used in the patent area before the priority date. The innovative step is a new threshold requirement different from the requirement of inventive step required for a standard patent. An innovation patent will be granted without first being subjected to substantive examination, although the Commissioner of Patents, the inventor or a third party may initiate examination after grant. An innovation patent can only be enforced once it has been "certified" and before it can be certified it must be examined. An innovation patent must contain at least one claim with a maximum of five claims and has a maximum term of eight years.

There are sometimes references to a "patent of addition" This is not a separate type of patent but a way of extending protection to improvements on the invention in an existing patent. See Improvements ([7.150]).

■ Who may apply for a patent?

[7.80] Any person, including a body of persons whether incorporated or not, may apply for a patent (s 29(1)). However, a patent can only be granted to an "eligible person", defined in *Patents Act 1990* (Cth), Sch 1 as a person to whom a patent may be granted under *Patents Act 1990* (Cth), s 15. Section 15 refers to the inventor and person deriving from the inventor. Where an application is filed on or after 24 May 2001 the applicant is taken to be the person nominated to be the "eligible person" (reg 3.1A).

Two or more persons may make a joint application (s 31) and the Commissioner has some powers to resolve disputes between joint applicants (s 32). See also ss 33, 34, 35 and 36.

■ Application

[7.85] The application must be made in the prescribed form (s 29(1), reg 3.1). An application may be a provisional or a complete application (s 29(2)). A provisional application must include a description of the invention (s 40(1)). A complete application or international application must be accompanied by a complete specification and an abstract that summarises the invention to be disclosed (reg 3.1). Where a provisional application is filed for a standard patent the applicant has 12 months to file a complete specification. However, an application for a patent can be withdrawn (s 141). A provisional application may be withdrawn before the 12 months has expired and refiled at a later time. If a complete application is withdrawn prior to publication of the application, and the invention has not otherwise been made publicly available, the applicant may file another application.

An application for a standard patent will be examined for formalities of drawings and specification (*Patents Regulations 1991* (Cth), Sch 3) and given a filing date (s 30, regs 3.5, 3.5A). The application will be classified according to the International Patent Classification system and allocated a filing number.

■ Role of the patent attorney

[7.90] See *Patents Act 1990* (Cth), Part 1 (Registration, privileges and professional conduct), ss 198, 200; Part 2 (Offences, ss 201-204).

Patent attorneys are given a statutory monopoly to prepare applications, specifications, claims and other documents relating to patent applications and amendment. The exception in s 202(b) refers to an amendment to a patent ordered by a court under s 105. Solicitors may have the carriage of patent litigation (see s 200(3)) and advise on patent law but are not to engage in the highly technical business of drafting patent applications. Although it is not unusual for solicitors to also be qualified as patent attorneys, a patent attorney is primarily someone with a scientific, engineering or technical background who has obtained passes or exemptions in a set of subjects concerned with intellectual property theory and practice. *Patent Regulations 1991* (Cth), Chap 20, Div 2 prescribes the required academic qualifications and Sch 5 lists the prescribed topics.

■ From application to acceptance

[7.95] The *Patents Act 1990* (Cth) comes with an illustration, notably the flow chart that "explains some difficult procedures in graphic form" (Second Reading Speech, *Patents Bill 1989* (Cth)). An understanding of the procedural aspects of obtaining a patent is important to understanding the law. See the flow chart (Table 1, at the beginning of the Act) illustrating the procedure for obtaining and maintaining a standard patent. Table 2, which once set out steps for obtaining a petty patent, is now omitted. Apparently the simplicity of grant for an innovation patent means that no Table 3 is necessary. If there is any inconsistency between any matter contained in the chart and a provision of the Act or Regulations, the provision prevails.

■ Applications for international patent protection

[7.100] One of the aims of the *Patents Act 1990* (Cth) is to enable Australia to participate fully in international developments in the field of patenting and technology transfer. Chapter 8 of the Act provides for applications made pursuant to the *Patent Cooperation Treaty* (PCT) and the *Paris Convention* or *European Patent Convention*. For the text of the PCT, see *Patents Regulations 1991* (Cth), Sch 2. Under the PCT a single patent application can be made in respect of any or all countries that are members of the PCT. The World Intellectual Property Organisation (WIPO), which administers the PCT, does not grant patents but searches existing literature, assesses claims and publishes its findings. Filing a PCT application secures an international priority date, even if patents are not ultimately registered in every country that is a signatory to the PCT. The majority of patents applied for or granted in Australia are based upon Convention or PCT applications.

■ The specification

[7.105] A patent application must be in approved form and accompanied by a specification (s 29). The specification is the document that reveals the consideration moving to the public that Lord Parker required in the *Adelaide Steamship* case ([7.15]). Specifications may be provisional or complete. The function of a specification is to describe the invention and delineate the monopoly being claimed. Much of patent law concerns issues surrounding the adequacy of the specification to fulfil the tasks it is called upon to perform. It is because the drafting of specifications is so technical that only patent attorneys may do it (s 202). *Patents Act 1990* (Cth), s 40 proscribes the requirements for specifications.

■ Inventions involving micro-organisms

[7.110] *Patents Act 1990* (Cth), ss 41 and 42 provide for special procedures to fulfil the requirement of full disclosure in s 40(2)(a) for inventions based on micro-organisms. Where the invention is a new micro-organism the applicant may attempt a written description or may deposit a sample of the micro-organism with a specialised depository institution recognised under the *Budapest Treaty on the International Recognition of the Deposit of Micro-organisms for the Purposes of Patent Procedure*. Where the invention involves the use, modification or cultivation of a micro-organism, and the micro-organism is not reasonably available to a person skilled in the relevant art and a sample is required for the performance of the invention, the applicant must deposit a sample with the deposit agency. The *Patents Act 1990* (Cth), ss 6, 41 and 42 provides for the fulfilment of Australia's obligations under the Budapest Treaty.

■ Priority date

[7.115] The priority date proscribed in s 43 is vitally important as it quite literally determines who won the race to the patent office. This is even more important now "prior claiming" as a ground of objection to a slightly later patent application has been abolished.

The *Patents Regulations 1991* (Cth) also provide that the priority date of a specification is the date of filing of a complete specification (reg 3.12(1)(a)), or the filing of a recognised priority document in the case of a Convention (international) application (regs 3.12(1)(b), 3.12(2)(a)(b)) or a PCT application (regs 3.12(2)(b), 3.12(2)(c)). It is possible to file a provisional specification that may be made complete later. A priority date may be secured by filing a provisional application as long as the later material is "fairly based" on matters earlier disclosed (reg 3.12(1)(b)). Other matters concerning the determination of priority dates are in regs 3.12-3.14.

■ Examination of an application for a standard patent

[7.120] An application for a standard patent will be examined prior to grant to see if it complies with the requirements of s 45. A report will be prepared recommending either acceptance or refusal of the application. Applications for innovation patents are not examined prior to grant. Many patent applications do not proceed. Inventors may change their ideas and withdraw the current application and file afresh, or fail to obtain commercial backing or simply lose interest. Examination will not be done automatically and must be requested in the "approved form" (reg 3.15(2) "within the prescribed period" (s 44(1)) which is five years from the filing date of a complete application (reg 3.15(1)). The Commissioner of Patents may direct that a request for examination be made (s 44(2), reg 3.16).

Normal examination of an application is conducted under ss 45 and 50.

If an applicant is hoping to get a patent from a prescribed foreign country (countries that are signatories to the *European Patent Convention*, Canada, New Zealand and the United States: (reg 3.21), they may delay full examination by the Australian Patent Office (s 46) and get a modified examination on certain basic points once the overseas patent is granted (ss 47, 48).

Under s 49 the Commissioner must either accept or refuse a patent request. Where an application is refused the applicant must be informed in writing of the reasons and a notice must be published in the *Official Journal*.

■ Formalities check and acceptance of innovation patents

[7.125] A "formalities check" is defined in *Patents Act 1990* (Cth), Sch 1. The formalities required are set out in reg 3.2B. The formalities check is the only assessment of an application for an innovation patent prior to grant. If the application complies with the regulations the Innovation patent must be granted.

■ Publication

[7.130] Publication of a complete specification for a standard patent occurs on or very shortly after 18 months from the earliest priority date for that application (s 54(3), reg 4.2(3)). Notice of availability for public inspection will be advertised in the *Official Journal* (for a standard patent, s 54(1), (3), (4), (5), (6), reg 4.2; for an innovation patent, s 62(2)). Section 55 and reg 4.3 set out the documents to be made available for public inspection. Once a complete specification for a standard patent is open to public inspection, "the applicant has the same rights as he or she would have had if a patent for the invention had been granted on the day when the specification became open to public inspection" (s 57(1)), but may not commence infringement proceedings until the patent is in fact granted (s 57(3)).

Documents are not to be published or made available for public inspection, nor are they normally to be produced in legal proceedings (s 56) until notification in the *Official Journal* provided for in s 54. *Patents Act 1990* (Cth), Chap 5 provides that certain material is not to be made available to the public even after examination and acceptance by the Patent Office (s 152). The prohibition on publishing information in specifications concerning "associated technology" is to prevent the dissemination to the public of documents concerning the enrichment, processing or production of nuclear material.

■ Opposition

[7.135] The Minister, or any person, may oppose the grant of a standard patent on the grounds exhaustively set out in s 59. These are: that the nominated person is not entitled to grant, or only entitled with another; that the invention is not a patentable invention; the specification does not comply with s 40(2) or (3). These grounds apply for applications for a standard patent made on or after 16 August 2004 and for applications made before that date where a patent has not yet been granted.

The previous s 59 was narrower in that the ground in s 59(b), concerning issues of validity of the patent, did not then, as it does now, encompass all of the requirements of s 18. Previously the opponent could only raise validity issues concerning lack of novelty, lack of inventive step and the restriction on the patenting of human beings or processes for their generation in s 18(2).

The grounds of opposition have been widened by the amendments to the *Patents Act* brought about by the *US Free Trade Agreement Implementation Act 2004*. The *Patents Regulations* have been amended by the *Patents Amendment Regulations 2004 (No 3)* (Cth) to provide procedures for opponents to rely upon the new grounds. In practice, the change means that an opponent may also rely on the grounds that the invention lacks utility or has been secretly used before the priority date. These grounds are both likely to raise contested issues of fact and, in the past, it was thought that such issues would be better tried in a court rather than by an officer of IP Australia exercising quasi judicial powers.

Notice of opposition must be filed within three months of the notice of acceptance of the application (reg 5.3) The Commissioner must hear and decide the opposition in accordance with the *Regulations* (s 60). See *Patents Regulations 1991* (Cth), Chap 5.

"Opposition" to an innovation patent is a different procedure. See s 101M.

■ Sealing of patent

[7.140] If there is no successful opposition of an application for a standard patent, the Commissioner grants the patent, by causing it to be sealed with the seal of the Patent Office (s 61). The time for sealing of a standard patent is usually not more than three months from the date of advertisement of acceptance of the application and complete specification (reg 6.2). If the Commissioner accepts an application for an innovation patent and there is no prohibition order under ss 152(1) or 173(3), the Commissioner grants the innovation patent by sealing it in the approved form (s 62). The patent will usually date from the date upon which the complete specification was lodged (s 65). After sealing, the patentee has the exclusive rights set out in s 13.

■ Term of a patent

[7.145] The term of a standard patent is 20 years from the date of the patent (s 67). While the previous term had been 16 years, the *Patents (World Trade Organisations) Amendment Act 1994* (Cth) extended the term to 20 years for all standard patents granted after 1 July 1995 or granted prior to that date for a 16-year term that had not expired on 1 July 1995. The term of an innovation patent is eight years from the date of the patent (s 68). The date of the patent is usually the date of filing of the complete specification (s 65).

There have been several regimes to allow for applications to extend the term of a patent. The current regime is set out in ss 70-79A. The *Patents Act 1990* (Cth) was amended by the *Intellectual Property Laws Amendment Act 1998* (Cth) to allow for extensions of term of up to five years for "pharmaceutical substances". To be eligible for extension the standard patent must satisfy the conditions of s 70.

During the period of extension, the patentees rights are limited so that it is not an infringement for a person to exploit the pharmaceutical substance disclosed, where that exploitation is solely for the purpose of having goods intended for therapeutic use included on the Australian register, or for obtaining regulatory approval outside Australia (ss 78 and 79). This permits the manufacturer of generic substitutes to meet regulatory requirements for marketing approval of the generic pharmaceutical relatively quickly after the standard patent expires. This system is sometimes called "springboarding".

■ Improvements

[7.150] Where an invention is protected by a standard patent, modifications of and improvements to the invention may be protected by a "patent of addition" (s 81). The patent of addition will generally remain in force for as long as the patent for the main invention (s 83(1)), although there can be exceptions where either the patent for the main invention or the patent of addition is extended independently of the other (s 81(2), (3), (4)). If the patent for the main invention is revoked the improvement may still be protected independently (s 85). Patents of addition are not available for innovation patents (s 80).

■ Revocation

[7.155] The validity of a patent is always subject to the risk of a successful revocation claim. A patentee claiming infringement will usually be challenged by the defendant counterclaiming for revocation under s 121 on all or any of the grounds listed in s 138(3). The grounds for refusing or revoking a patent, while derived from the common law, were eventually codified in legislation. See *American Cyanamid Co v Upjohn Co* [1970] 1 WLR 1507, Lord Guest discussing the *Patents and Designs Act 1932* (UK). Apart from a counterclaim to infringement, revocation may be ordered if a patent is not being worked (s 134), because the reasonable requirements of the public have not been met (s 135) or if a patentee surrenders a patent (s 137).

An innovation patent may not be revoked until it has been "certified" (s 138(1A)) which means that it must first be subjected to examination under s 101B. As a consequence of examination by the Commissioner, an innovation patent may be revoked on a number of grounds (s 101B(2), (4), (5)-(7)). The grounds of revocation are:

- that the specification does not comply with s 40,

- that the invention is not novel,

- that the invention does not involve an innovative step,

- that the invention is for a human being, animal or plant,

- that the invention is capable of being used as a food or medicine for humans or animals and is a mere mixture of known ingredients, or a process of producing such a substance by mere admixture,

- that the invention includes the name of a person as the name of the invention or is already patented by the same inventor with the same priority date.

These grounds reflect those which would lead the Commissioner to refuse an application for a standard patent. An innovation patent surviving examination may still be subject to revocation under s 138.

The grounds for claiming revocation of either a standard or an innovation patent in a counter-claim to infringement are found in s 138. Following amendments to the *Patents Act* made by the *US Free Trade Agreement Implementation Act,* sch 8 item 5, the grounds for revocation for patents are:

(a) that the patentee is not entitled to the patent;

(b) that the invention is not a patentable invention;

(c) repealed

(d) that the patent was obtained by fraud, false suggestion or misrepresentation

(e) that an amendment … was made or obtained by fraud, false suggestion or misrepresentation

(f) that the specification does not comply with subsection 40(2) or (3).

Ground (c), that is now repealed, provided for revocation if the patentee breached a condition in the patent.

CHAPTER 8

REQUIREMENTS OF VALIDITY

THRESHOLD MATTERS

Agreement on Trade-Related Aspects of Intellectual Property Rights

[8.05] Article 27 Patentable Subject Matter

1. Subject to the provisions of paragraphs 2 and 3, patents shall be available for any inventions, whether products or processes, in all fields of technology, provided that they are new, involve an inventive step and are capable of industrial application. Subject to paragraph 4 of Article 65, paragraph 8 of Article 70 and paragraph 3 of this Article, patents shall be available and patent rights enjoyable without discrimination as to the place of invention, the field of technology and whether products are imported or locally produced.

▬▬▬   Agreement on Trade-Related Aspects of Intellectual Property Rights *continued*

2. Members may exclude from patentability inventions, the prevention within their territory of the commercial exploitation of which is necessary to protect order public or morality, including to protect human, animal or plant life or health or to avoid serious prejudice to the environment, provided that such exclusion is not made merely because the exploitation is prohibited by their law.

3. Members may also exclude from patentability:

    (a) diagnostic, therapeutic and surgical methods for the treatment of humans or animals;

    (b) plants and animals other than micro-organisms, and essentially biological processes for the production of plants or animals other than non-biological and microbiological processes. However, Members shall provide for the protection of plant varieties either by patents or by an effective sui generis system or by any combination thereof. The provisions of this subparagraph shall be reviewed four years after the date of entry into force of the WTO Agreement.

Note

[8.10] Article 27 is likely to be the subject of discussion in the WTO Doha Development Round if and when negotiations recommence. In particular, para 27(3) will be contentious with developing and least developed countries seeking to widen the range of exceptions and exclude patenting for micro-organisms, and with industrialised countries pushing for removal of the possible exemptions altogether. Meanwhile an example of the approach likely to be taken can be seen in the Australia-United States Free Trade Agreement

▬▬▬ **Australia-United States Free Trade Agreement** ▬▬▬

[8.15] Australia-United States Free Trade Agreement at www.dfat.gov.au/trade/negotiations/us.html

Article 17.9: Patents

1. Each Party shall make patents available for any invention, whether a product or process, in all fields of technology, provided that the invention is new, involves an inventive step, and is capable of industrial application. The Parties confirm that patents shall be available for any new uses or methods of using a known product. For the purposes of this Article, a Party may treat the terms "inventive step" and "capable of industrial application" as synonymous with the terms "non-obvious" and "useful", respectively.

2. Each Party may only exclude from patentability:

    (a) inventions, the prevention within their territory of the commercial exploitation of which is necessary to protect order public or morality, including to protect human, animal, or plant life or health or to avoid serious prejudice to the environment, provided that such exclusion is not made merely because the exploitation is prohibited by law; and

    (b) diagnostic, therapeutic, and surgical methods for the treatment of humans and animals.

AUSTRALIAN VALIDITY REQUIREMENTS

[8.20] The requirements for a valid grant of a standard patent are set out in s 18(1). There must be an "invention" which is a "manner of manufacture", is "novel", involves an "inventive step", is "useful" and has not been "secretly used". The requirements for the valid grant of an innovation patent (s 18(1A)) differ only in that the invention must involve an "innovative step" rather than an inventive step.

Some inventions are specifically excluded from patentability. Human beings and biological processes for their generation, are not patentable in either standard or innovation patents (s 18(2)). Plants and animals, and biological processes for their generation, are not patentable in an innovation patent (s 18(3)), although this does not exclude an innovation patent for a microbiological process or product of such a process (s 18(4)).

■ Inventions

[8.25] Patents are granted for inventions. *Patents Act 1990* (Cth), Sch 1 defines invention:

> "'invention' means any manner of new manufacture the subject of letters patent and grant of privilege within section 6 of the *Statute of Monopolies*, and includes an alleged invention."

The Commissioner has discretion to refuse to grant for a standard patent for inventions contrary to law, or for a food or medicine consisting only of a mixture of known ingredients, or where a claim includes the name of a person as the name of the invention (see s 50). An innovation patent may be revoked after examination for certification on similar grounds (see s 101B(2)(d), (4)).

■ Invention: A threshold test?

[8.30] The meaning of the word "invention" as it appears in the opening words of s 18 has been considered in a number of cases. In the case of *NV Philips Gloeilampenfabricken v Mirabella International Pty Ltd* (1995) 32 IPR 449 the High Court, by a majority, considered that the words introduced a threshold test of general inventiveness or newness which was independent of the separate requirements imposed by the specific paragraphs of *Patents Act 1990* (Cth), s 18. This is a difficult, and with respect apparently regressive, decision and detailed extracts are provided at **[8.365]**.

■ Manner of manufacture

[8.35] Section 18(1) and (1A) of the *Patents Act 1990* (Cth) requires that a patent application be made only in respect of a "manner of new manufacture" within the *Statute of Monopolies*. An application for a standard patent may be opposed under s 59(b) or a granted standard patent may be revoked under s 138(3)(b) on the ground that it is not a "manner of manufacture". An innovation patent may be revoked by the Commissioner in the course of an examination for certification on the ground that it is not a "manner of manufacture" (s 101B(2)(b)). A certified innovation patent may be revoked by a court under s 138(3)(b) on the ground that it is not a "manner of manufacture".

NRDC v Commissioner of Patents

[8.40] *National Research Development Corporation v Commissioner of Patents* (1959) 102 CLR 252
High Court of Australia

[This case was an appeal from a direction by the Commissioner of Patents that three claims
be deleted from an application for a patent. The complete specification included six claims.
Three of them were "product" claims to selective herbicidal compositions and were not in
dispute. The three disputed claims were "method" claims involving the use of the selected
herbicidal compositions to chemically weed certain kinds of legume crop. Claim one, for
example, read:

> "1.   A method for eradicating weeds from crop areas containing a growing crop
> selected from leguminous fodder crops of the genera Trifolium and Medicago, celery
> and parsnip, which comprises applying to the crop areas a herbicide of the class
> consisting of the 9 (2: 4-dichlorophenoxy) butyric and caproic acids, their salts, esters,
> nitriles and amide."

Claims 2 and 3 were in similar terms but specifying different weeds and crop plants.
Although the chemical compositions were known it was not previously known that they
would interact with the enzymes of non leguminous plants causing those weeds to wither and
die while not affecting the legume crop plant. The Commissioner objected that these claims
were not directed to an "invention". Three objections to the patentability of these claims were
put in argument. The first was the objection that these were, in the words of the examiners
report "not therefore directed to any manner of manufacture in that they are claims to the
mere use of known substances which use also does not result in any vendible product". The
second was that what was revealed in the specification was not an invention but a mere
discovery and accordingly not patentable. The third was that agricultural and horticultural
processes should be excluded as unsuitable subject matter for the grant of a patent.]

DIXON CJ, KITTO and WINDEYER JJ: **[268]** The central question in the case remains. It is
whether that process that is claimed falls within the category of inventions to which, by
definition, the application of the *Patents Act* is confined. The definition, it will be
remembered, is exclusive: invention means any manner of new manufacture the subject of
letters patent and grant of privilege within s 6 of the *Statute of Monopolies*. The Commissioner,
adopting certain judicial pronouncements to which reference will be made, emphasises the
word "manufacture" and contends for an interpretation of it which, though not narrow, is
restricted to vendible products and processes for their production, and excludes all agricultural and horticultural processes. On the grounds both of the suggested restriction and of the
suggested exclusion he denies that a process for killing weeds can be within the relevant
concept of invention. The appellant, on the other hand, urges upon us a wider view: that
there is a "manufacture" such as might properly have been the subject of letters patent and
grant of privilege under s 6 of the *Statute of Monopolies* whenever a process produces, either
immediately or ultimately, a useful physical result in relation to a material or tangible entity.

Section 6 of the *Statute of Monopolies* provides that the declarations of invalidity contained
in the preceding provisions of the Act "shall not extend to any letters patents and graunts of
privilege ... **[269]** hereafter to be made of the sole working or makinge of any manner of new
manufacture within this realme, to the true and first inventor and inventors of such manufactures, which others at the tyme of makinge such letters patents and graunts shall not use,
soe as alsoe they be not contrary to the lawe or mischievous to the state by raising prices of

comodities at home, or hurt of trade, or generallie inconvenient": *Halsbury's Statutes of England* (2nd ed), Vol 17 (1950), p 619. It is of the first importance to remember always that the *Patents Act 1952-1955* (Cth), like its predecessor the *Patents Act 1903* (Cth) and corresponding statutes of the UK (see the *Patents, Designs & Trade Marks Act 1883*, s 46; the *Patents Act 1907*, s 93; and the *Patents Act 1949*, s 101), defines the word "invention", not by direct explication and in the language of its own day, nor yet by carrying forward the usage of the period in which the *Statute of Monopolies* was passed, but by reference to the established ambit of s 6 of that statute. The inquiry which the definition demands is an inquiry into the scope of the permissible subject matter of letters patent and grants of privilege protected by the section. It is an inquiry not into the meaning of the word so much as into the breadth of the concept which the law has developed by its consideration of the text and purpose of the *Statute of Monopolies*. One may remark that although the statute spoke of the inventor it nowhere spoke of the invention; all that is nowadays understood by the latter word as used in patent law is comprehended in "new manufactures". The word "manufacture" finds a place in the present Act, not as a word intended to reduce a question of patentability to a question of verbal interpretation, but simply as the general title found in the *Statute of Monopolies* for the whole category under which all grants of patents which may be made in accordance with the developed principles of patent law are to be subsumed. It is therefore a mistake, and a mistake likely to lead to an incorrect conclusion, to treat the question whether a given process or product is within the definition as if that question could be restated in the form: "Is this a manner (or kind) of manufacture?" It is a mistake which tends to limit one's thinking by reference to the idea of making tangible goods by hand or by machine, because "manufacture" as a word of everyday speech generally conveys that idea. The right question is: "Is this a proper subject of letters patent according to the principles which have been developed for the application of s 6 of the *Statute of Monopolies*?"

It is a very different question. A perusal of the definitions and quotations appearing in the Oxford English Dictionary under "manufacture" will show that the word has always admitted of applications beyond the limits which a strict observance of its etymology would suggest, and, as the present Chief Justice said **[270]** in *Maeder v Busch* (1938) 59 CLR 684 and 706, a widening conception of the notion has been a characteristic of the growth of patent law. As early as 1795 it was possible for Eyre CJ to say that "the exposition of the statute as far as usage will expound it, has gone much beyond the letter" (*Boulton v Bull* (1795) 1 H Bl 463 at 492; 126 ER 651 at 666), and the width of the meaning that had already been accepted may be gauged from the statement of the same learned judge that "manufacture" extended "to any new results of principles carried into practice ... new processes in any art producing effects useful to the public": *Boulton v Bull* (1795) 1 H Bl 463 at 492; 126 ER 651 at 666. By 1842 it was finally settled that "manufacture" was used in the *Statute of Monopolies* in a dual sense which comprehends both a process and a product: *Crane v Price* (1842) 1 Web PC 393; 4 Man & G 580; 134 ER 239. But a question which appears still to await final decision is whether it is enough that a process produces a useful result or whether it is necessary that some physical thing is either brought into existence or so affected as the better to serve man's purpose. In some of the cases it is suggested that the process must issue in some "vendible matter" or a "vendible product". The former expression was used by Heath J in *Boulton v Bull* (1795) 1 H Bl 463 at 482; 126 ER 651 at 661 in the course of maintaining the opinion, which must now be considered heretical, that there could not be a patent for a method; but no such expression appears in the powerful judgment in which Eyre CJ maintained the opposite view and reached the conclusion in the particular case which was ultimately upheld in *Hornblower v Boulton* (1799) 8 TR 95; 101 ER 1258. Abbott CJ in *R v Wheeler* (1819) 2 B & Ald 345 at 349; 106 ER 392, having spoken of a "thing made, which is useful for its own sake, and vendible as such", went on to show that he did not find in such expressions as those any absolute test. He said: "Something of a corporeal and substantial nature, something that can be made by man from the matters subjected to his art and skill, or at the least some new mode of employing practically his art and skill is requisite to satisfy this word.": (1819) 2 B & Ald 345 at 350; 106 ER 392 at 395. It is of course not possible to treat such a statement as conclusive of the question. The need for qualification must be confessed, even if only in order to put aside, as they apparently must be put aside, processes for treating diseases of the human body: see *Re C & W's Application* (1914) 31 RPC 235; *Maeder v Busch* (1938) 59 CLR 684. When appearing as counsel in the case **[271]** last cited, Sir George Ligertwood (at 696) made a helpful suggestion which in effect amended the statement of Abbott CJ to read "or at least some new method of employing practically the art and skill of the workman in a manual art". But even so comprehensive a statement needs to be given a somewhat flexible meaning to allow for longstanding authorities such as *Forsyth v Riviere* (1819) 1 Web PC 95 (where the patent was for a method of discharging firearms), and *The Electric Telegraph Co v Brett* (1851) 10 CB 838; 138 ER 331 (where the patent was for a method of giving duplicate electric signals). The truth is that any attempt to state the ambit of s 6 of the *Statute of Monopolies* by precisely defining "manufacture" is bound to fail. The purpose of s 6, it must be remembered, was to allow the use of the prerogative to encourage national development in a field which already, in 1623, was seen to be excitingly unpredictable. To attempt to place upon the idea the fetters of an exact verbal formula could never have been sound. It would be unsound to the point of folly to attempt to do so now, when science has made such advances that the concrete applications of the notion which were familiar in 1623 can be seen to provide only the more obvious, not to say the more primitive, illustrations of the broad sweep of the concept.

In a case which has been much cited in recent times, *Re GEC's Application* (1942) 60 RPC 1 at 4, Morton J, as he then was, while disclaiming the intention of laying down any hard and fast rule applicable to all cases, put forward a proposition which, if literally applied, would have a narrowing effect on the law and indeed has already been found to stand as much in need as the statute itself of a generous interpretation. The proposition was that "a method or process is a manner of manufacture if it (a) results in the production of some vendible product or (b) improves or restores to its former condition a vendible product or (c) has the effect of preserving from deterioration some vendible product to which it is applied". Any criticism to which this is open, as Lord Jenkins remarked in *Samuel Reitzman v Grahame-Chapman & Derusuit Ltd* (1950) 68 RPC 25 at 32, is certainly not on the score of its being too wide. It is valuable for its insistence that in patent law at the present day a process may be within the concept of "manufacture" notwithstanding that it merely improves, restores, or preserves some antecedently existing thing; but in so far as it may appear to restrict the concept by its use of the expression "vendible product", it must be considered now as substantially qualified by the comments made upon it by Evershed J (as he then **[272]** was) in *Re Cementation Co Ltd's Application* (1945) 62 RPC 151 and in *Re Rantzen's Application* (1946) 64 RPC 63 at 65, and by Lloyd-Jacob J in *Re Elton and Leda Chemicals Ltd's Application* [1957] RPC 267.

[Their Honours then discussed and drew upon each of the last named cases and continued:] **[275]**

The point is that a process, to fall within the limits of patentability which the context of the *Statute of Monopolies* has supplied, must be one that offers some advantage which is material, in the sense that the process belongs to a useful art as distinct from a fine art (see *Re Virginia-Carolina Chemical Corp's Application* [1958] RPC 35 at 36) that its value to the country is in the field of economic endeavour. (The exclusion of methods of surgery and other processes for treating the human body may well lie outside the concept of invention because the whole subject is conceived as essentially non-economic: see *Maeder v Busch* (1938) 59 CLR 684 at 706.) **[276]**

But the judgment in the *Elton and Leda Chemicals* case [1957] RPC 267 is also valuable for present purposes by reason of a suggestion which it contains as to the true office of the word "product" in such contexts as that of Morton J's "rule". The learned judge said (at 268, 269):

> "There has been no question, at any rate since before the year 1800, that the expression 'manner of manufacture' in the statute of James I must be construed in the sense of including a practice of making as well as the means of making and the product of making. It has thus been appreciated that, although an inventor may use no newly devised mechanism, nor produce a new substance, none the less he may, by providing some new and useful effect, appropriate for himself a patent monopoly in such improved result by covering the mode or manner by means of which his result is secured. Seeing that the promise which he offers is some new and useful effect, there must of necessity be some product whereby the validity of his promise can be tested."

[277] Notwithstanding the use of the word "making", which but for the context might have been taken to indicate the narrow view that an article or material must result if a process is to be a "manufacture", the tenor of the passage seems to be that what is meant by a "product" in relation to a process is only something in which the new and useful effect may be observed. Sufficient authority has been cited to show that the "something" need not be a "thing" in the sense of an article; it may be any physical phenomenon in which the effect, be it creation or merely alteration, may be observed: a building (for example), a tract or stratum of land, an explosion, an electrical oscillation. It is, we think, only by understanding the word "product" as covering every end produced, and treating the word "vendible" as pointing only to the requirement of utility in practical affairs, that the language of Morton J's "rule" may be accepted as wide enough to convey the broad idea which the long line of decisions on the subject has shown to be comprehended by the statute.

... [T]he view which we think is correct in the present case is that the method the subject of the relevant claims has as its end result an artificial effect falling squarely within the true concept of what must be produced by a process if it is to be held patentable. This view is, we think, required by a sound understanding of the lines along which patent law has developed and necessarily must develop in a modern society. The effect produced by the appellant's method exhibits the two essential qualities upon which "product" and "vendible" seem designed to insist. It is a "product" because it consists in an artificially created state of affairs, discernible by observing over a period the growth of weeds and crops respectively on sown land on which the method has been put into practice. And the significance of the product is economic; for it provides a remarkable advantage, indeed to the lay mind a sensational advantage, for one of the most elemental activities by which man has served his material needs, the cultivation of the soil for the production of its fruits. Recognition that the relevance of the process is to this economic activity old as it is, need not be inhibited by any fear of inconsistency with the claim to novelty which the specification plainly makes. The method cannot be classed as a variant of ancient procedure. It is additional to the cultivation. It achieves a separate result, and the result possesses its own economic utility consisting in an important improvement in the conditions in which the crop is to grow, whereby it is afforded a better opportunity to flourish and yield a good harvest.

Note

[8.45] When the "Morton Rules" (from *Re GEC's Application* (1942) 60 RPC 1) were first enunciated they were regarded as widening the area of patentable subject matter. As *NRDC* shows at [8.40], however, the range has been widened further.

■ Public policy considerations

[8.50] The *Statute of Monopolies*, while allowing patents for new manufactures, would not allow a grant for manufactures "contrary to the law nor mischievous to the State ... or hurt of trade, or generally inconvenient".

"Generally inconvenient"

[8.55] The term "generally inconvenient" is undefined, but an invention may be regarded as generally inconvenient where it presents some danger to the public, or where it would preclude the undertaking of normal activities: *Rolls Royce Ltd's Application* [1963] RPC 251; *Re Application by Beecham Group Ltd* (1984) 3 IPR 26. It is generally inconvenient to allow a monopoly over a set of mere working directions for operating a machine or the more efficient deployment of a workforce (*Re Quigley's Application* [1977] FSR 393), since this could deny others the right to use existing things or techniques in an efficient or normal manner. In *Telefon A/B LM Ericsson's Application* [1975] FSR 49 at 54, the Commissioner Delegate, Mr Ashman, on hearing an opposition proceeding in the Patent Office, concluded that it was generally inconvenient to allow a patent for a computer program. His decision illustrates the danger of relying upon such an assessment without fully understanding the implications of the technology under review.

In the Full Federal Court in *Anaesthetic Supplies Pty Ltd v Rescare Ltd* (1994) 28 IPR 383, Sheppard J (in dissent) considered that it was generally inconvenient to allow a patent for a method of treatment of a disease of the human body. In *Bristol-Myers Squibb Co v FH Faulding & Co Ltd* (2000) 46 IPR 553 at 556, two members of the Full Federal Court considered that such an invention was patentable.

The Court of Appeal of New Zealand has reconfirmed that patents for methods of the medical treatment of human beings are "generally inconvenient" in New Zealand. *Pfizer Inc v Commissioner of Patents* [2004] NZCA 104; (2004) 60 IPR 624. Interestingly, it was said that apart from inventions that were methods of the medical treatment of human beings, there was little scope for exclusions under this heading (see [7], [57]-[58]). It was also noted that a wider application of "generally inconvenient" could conflict with the requirements of Article 27 of the TRIPs Agreement ([57]- [58]).

The Australian Patent Office, *Manual of Practice and Procedure, Vol 2: "National"*, observes at [2.9.3] that: "There is really no clear guidance as to when an invention may or may not be regarded as 'generally inconvenient'. Hence examiners should refrain from taking this objection".

"Contrary to law"

[8.60] The Commissioner has discretion to refuse to accept a specification for an invention which would be contrary to law (s 50(1)(a); previously s 51(1)(a)). This seems to have been interpreted as allowing rejections of inventions which have no lawful use. For a discussion of the phrase "contrary to law", see *Dow Chemical v Ishihara Sangyo Kaisha Ltd* (1986) 5 IPR 415. An invention which can be used unlawfully but which has a lawful use may be accepted:

Pressers and Moody v Haydon & Co (1909) 26 RPC 58 and Australian Patent Office, *Manual of Practice and Procedure, Vol 2: "National"* at [2.9.6]. In a recent decision by the Australian Patent Office where an application was rejected, one of the reasons given for the rejection was that the invention was "contrary to law".

Woo-Suk Hwang

[8.65] *Woo-Suk Hwang* [2004] APO 24

[The applicant had applied for a patent for a method of producing a hybrid embryo created by transferring the nucleus of a human cell into a bovine ovum and then activating the ovum. The application was found to contravene s 18(2) as a biological process for the generation of a human being (see below) but was also found to be an application where the invention was "contrary to law" and should be refused on that ground as well.]

HERALD (Deputy Commissioner):
Section 50(1)(a) considerations
[11] Section50(1)(a) of the *Patents Act 1990* provides

"The Commissioner may refuse to accept a request and specification relating to a standard patent, or to grant a standard patent;

(a)   for an invention the use of which would be contrary to law."

[12] I note that this provision is rarely invoked, and there is little precedent for its operation. The entire guidance provided by the *Patent Office Manual of Practice and Procedure* is as follows:

"8.6.1 Under s 50(1)(a) the Commissioner may refuse to accept a patent request and specification, or to grant a patent, for an invention the use of which would be contrary to law. It should be noted that this is a discretionary power, and should only be applied in the clearest of circumstances.

Section 50(1)(a) is to be understood as covering broadly statute law, including regulations and ordinances, and case law.

8.6.2 Some guidance as to the meaning of "contrary to law" can be obtained from Official Rulings 1923 C, (1923) 40 RPC Appendix iv, where it was said that:

"An invention 'contrary to law' may be either (1), one the primary use of which would be a criminal act, punishable as a crime or misdemeanour, or, (2), one the use of which would be an offence by reason of its being prohibited under by-laws or regulations made for police and administrative purposes.

Inventions belonging to the former class would always be refused protection. As regards the latter class, the nature and possible uses of the invention and the exact terms of the prohibition would have to be considered in each case."

8.6.3 Where the invention could be used both for lawful and for unlawful purposes, there is authority in *Pessers and Moody v Haydon & Co*, (1909) 26 RPC 58, for saying that a patent in respect of it would not necessarily be bad.

In any particular case, regard must clearly be had to the main purpose of the invention, that is to the consideration whether the invention is primarily devised or intended for a lawful, or for an unlawful, use. For example, an invention which in the United Kingdom has been refused on this basis is an explosive safe designed to kill or injure a burglar

■■■■■■   Woo-Suk Hwang *continued*

8.6.4 Objections under s 50(1)(a) should be taken only against claims where an unlawful use and no lawful use has been described.

Where a claim is objectionable under s 50(1)(a), an objection to this effect is to be included in the report under s 45(1)(c) or s 48(1)(b). If the objection is disputed by the applicant and the examiner considers it should be maintained, the file should be referred to the supervising examiner before the next report is made."

[13] The relevant legislation that is said to render the claims contrary to law is the *Prohibition of Human Cloning Act 2002*. Section 20 of that Act provides:

"20 Offence—creating a chimeric or hybrid embryo

(1) A person commits an offence if the person intentionally creates a chimeric embryo.
Maximum penalty: Imprisonment for 10 years.

(2) A person commits an offence if the person intentionally creates a hybrid embryo.
Maximum penalty: Imprisonment for 10 years."

[14] The Act includes the following definition of a *hybrid embryo*:

"(d) an animal egg into which the nucleus of a human cell has been introduced; or
 ..."

[15] Prima facie, the product of the present method is a hybrid embryo within the meaning of this Act. Furthermore, a person performing the claimed method in Australia is prima facie liable to the penalty provided by that Act—of imprisonment for up to 10 years. Clearly this fits within the first category of laws contemplated by the aforementioned Official Rulings 1923 C.

[17] The Manual suggests that a relevant consideration is whether there are any uses of the invention that would not be contrary to law. While it might be thought that the method might have application in mammals other than humans, both the description and claims are specific in the application of the invention to humans only.

[18] Finally, the provision is a discretionary provision. It is noteworthy that the grounds for refusal to accept such an application are not available as a ground of opposition or of revocation. In my view, this suggests that refusal should only occur in the clearest of circumstances. Furthermore, it seems to me that a relevant consideration is whether the relevant law is of an ephemeral nature—that is, whether it is reasonable to expect that what is illegal today will be illegal throughout the term of the patent. The invention claimed in the present case is very clearly contrary to the *Prohibition of Human Cloning Act 2002*. Furthermore, in my view the prohibitions in s 20 of that Act are of a nature such that the prohibition is unlikely to be ephemeral. Accordingly I am satisfied that this application should be refused under s 50(1)(a) of the *Patents Act 1990* by reason of it being contrary to law.

Food or medicines being mere admixtures

[8.70] The Commissioner has discretion under *Patents Act 1990* (Cth), s 50(1)(c) to refuse to accept a patent request on the basis that the invention claimed is a substance capable of being a food or medicine for humans or animals, whether for internal or external use, and is a mere mixture of known ingredients, or is a process producing such a substance through mere admixture. Patent Office guidelines may be found at Australian Patent Office, *Manual of Practice and Procedures, Vol 2: "National"*, 2.9.7. Where the mixture produces an unexpected synergistic result there will be a patentable invention.

CONTROVERSIAL SUBJECT MATTER

■ Discoveries of principles

[8.75] The general dictate that the public requires consideration in return for the grant of letters patent means that "mere discoveries" will not be patentable, since even an original idea will not "add to the sum of human art" without some practical means of carrying out the idea: *Neilson v Minister of Public Works (NSW)* (1914) 18 CLR 423 at 429 per Isaacs J. In *Lane-Fox v Kensington & Knightsbridge Electric Lighting Co* (1892) 9 RPC 413 at 416, Lindley LJ pointed out that the *Statute of Monopolies* was concerned with promoting "useful arts" in the national economic interest.

The reluctance to grant patents for mere discoveries is also due to a desire to leave areas of research open to others in the field, and it may be difficult to delimit precisely the area of a "discovery" so that a patent will be valid.

Intellectual information is not, by itself, a vendible product: see *Slee & Harris' Application* [1966] RPC 194. Despite the expansion in *NRDC* of the meaning of "manner of new manufacture" beyond a vendible product, there must still be practical economic application of the subject matter of a patent application before the discovery can be an invention, since discovery only discloses something but invention necessarily involves also the suggestion of something to be done. See *Reynolds v Herbert Smith* (1902) 20 RPC 123 at 126 per Buckley J, and also *Otto v Linford* (1882) 46 LT 35.

▬▬▬▬▬▬▬ NRDC v Commissioner of Patents ▬▬▬▬▬▬▬

[8.80] *National Research Development Corporation v Commissioner of Patents* (1959) 102 CLR 252 High Court of Australia

[The facts of this case were stated at **[8.40]**.]

[263] This, we consider, differs not at all from the view which Lindley LJ expressed in the passage in his judgment in the case of *Lane Fox v Kensington & Knightsbridge Electric Lighting Co* [1892] 3 Ch 424 at 428, 429; (1892) 9 RPC 413 at 416 which is often cited and was referred to more than once in the argument of the present case, namely that a man who discovers that a known machine (his Lordship might equally have said a known substance) can produce effects which no-one before him knew could be produced by it has made a discovery, but has not made a patentable invention unless he so uses his knowledge and ingenuity as to produce either a new and useful thing or result, or a new and useful method of producing an old thing or result. His Lordship went on to say that the discovery how to use a known thing for a new purpose will be a patentable invention if there is novelty in the mode of using it as distinguished from novelty of purpose, or if any new modification of the thing or any new appliance is necessary for using it for its new purpose, and if such mode of user, or modification, or appliance involves any appreciable merit. But the whole passage is directed to the case of a thing which is known—not only the existence of which is known—as a scientific fact, but the characteristics and properties of which are understood, so that the "appreciable merit" (at

429; at 416), which is requisite for a patentable invention must be found, if it is to be found at all, exclusively in something which the alleged invention has superadded to the existing knowledge concerning the thing. There is nothing in the judgment of Lindley LJ to justify a denial that, in respect of a process for achieving a useful result by the employment of a substance to produce effects which antecedently it was not understood to be capable of producing, the inventiveness which is essential for a valid grant of a patent may be found in the step which consists of suggesting the use of the thing for the new purpose, notwith-standing that there is no novelty or "appreciable merit" in any suggested mode of using the thing, or any modification of the thing or of an appliance necessary for using it for the new purpose. It is not decisive it is not even helpful to point out in such a case that beyond discovery of a scientific fact nothing has been added except the suggestion that nature, in its newly ascertained aspect, be allowed to work in its own way. Arguments of this kind may be answered as Frankfurter J answered them in *Funk Bros Seed Co v Kalo Inoculant Co* 333 US 127 at 134, 135 (1948) [92 Law Ed 588 at 589]:

> "'It only confuses the issue', the learned Justice said, 'to introduce such terms as "the work of nature" and "the laws of [264] nature". For these are vague and malleable terms infected with too much ambiguity and equivocation. Everything that happens may be deemed "the work of nature", and any patentable composite exemplifies in its properties "the laws of nature". Arguments drawn from such terms for ascertaining patentability could fairly be employed to challenge almost any patent'."

The truth is that the distinction between discovery and invention is not precise enough to be other than misleading in this area of discussion. There may indeed be a discovery without invention either because the discovery is of some piece of abstract information without any suggestion of a practical application of it to a useful end, or because its application lies outside the realm of "manufacture". But where a person finds out that a useful result may be produced by doing something which has not been done by that procedure before, his claim for a patent is not validly answered by telling him that although there was ingenuity in his discovery that the materials used in the process would produce the useful result no ingenuity was involved in showing how the discovery, once it had been made, might be applied. The fallacy lies in dividing up the process that he puts forward as his invention. It is the whole process that must be considered; and he need not show more than one inventive step in the advance which he has made beyond the prior limits of the relevant art. This is perhaps nowhere more clearly put than it was by Fletcher Moulton LJ in *Hickton's Patent Syndicate v Patents & Machine Improvements Co Ltd* (1909) 26 RPC 339 at 347-348 when he said of Watt's invention for the condensation of steam, out of which the steam engine grew:

> "Now can it be suggested that it required any invention whatever to carry out that idea when once you had got it? It could be done in a thousand ways and by any competent engineer, but the invention was in the idea, and when he had once got that idea, the carrying out of it was perfectly easy. To say that the conception may be meritorious and may involve invention and may be new and original, and simply because when you have once got the idea it is easy to carry it out, that that deprives it of the title of being a new invention according to our patent law, is, I think, an extremely dangerous principle and justified neither by reason nor authority".

■ Agricultural and horticultural processes

[8.85] Note the comments in *NRDC* (at **[8.90]**) on Patent Office practice toward inventions with an agricultural or horticultural application. The problem in the case was not just that the application concerned a process, but also that its use lay in an area where patents were traditionally not obtainable. The practice arose as a result of a combination of factors. In the agricultural or horticultural realm, there may more readily be confusion between an invention and a "mere discovery" of the laws of nature, which is not patentable. It may be easier to establish that a product or process lacks novelty when the area of use is one with a long history of human endeavour leading to an impression that such inventions are generally not patentable. Furthermore, there is a reluctance (partly based on the statute) to allow monopolies in areas concerned with human or animal foodstuffs (*Patents Act 1990* (Cth), s 50). The result of these overlapping concerns was to establish a principle that agricultural or horticultural processes could not be a "manner of new manufacture", "a generalisation not supported by the reasons leading to the conclusions in the particular instances from which the generalisation is drawn".

▬▬▬▬▬▬ NRDC v Commissioner of Patents ▬▬▬▬▬▬

[8.90] *National Research Development Corporation v Commissioner of Patents* (1959) 102 CLR 252 High Court of Australia

[The facts of this case were stated at **[8.40]**.]

[277] There remains for consideration the Commissioner's contention that, even apart from the considerations which have been discussed, agricultural or horticultural processes are, by reason of their nature, outside the limits of patentable invention. Only in comparatively recent times have statements appeared which explicitly support the contention. In *Re Rau Gesellschaft's Application* (1935) 52 RPC 362, an application for a patent in respect of the production by selective cultivation of lupin seeds having certain characteristics was rejected. Luxmoore J approved a statement by the examiner in terms which seem to run together the question whether such a process can be novel and the question whether it can be a "manufacture'. It reads:

> "Selective breeding of animals and cultivation of plants for the obtainment of improved stocks by the rigorous selection of and breeding from the few individuals which are nearest the ideal has, as is well-known, been practised from the earliest times as a part of agriculture or horticultural development, as for example in the production of **[278]** improved flowers or fruit with desired characteristics in the progeny, and the exercise of art or skill in these directions has not been regarded as coming within the term 'manufacture'."

(There had been earlier cases in which applications relating to agriculture had been refused on other grounds; for instance, *Re Hamilton-Adam's Application* (1918) 35 RPC 90, where the process was one for rotation of crops, and the ground taken was that although there was a discovery there was no improvement in the method of carrying out any agricultural operations.) It must often happen in a sphere of human endeavour as old as that of primary production that a newly devised procedure amounts to nothing more than an analogous application of age-old techniques; and where that is the case, want of novelty is a fatal objection to a patent. It may be conceded, moreover, that if there were nothing that could properly be called a "product" of the process, even an ingenious new departure would be

NRDC v Commissioner of Patents *continued*

outside the limits of patentability. In *Re RHF's Application* (1944) 61 RPC 49 Morton J approved a statement of the examiner which had been made to illustrate that the vendible product test enunciated in the *GEC* case (1942) 60 RPC 1 was not definitive. The statement was that fruit and other growing crops, although the assistance of man may be invoked for their planting and cultivation, do not result from a process which is a "manner of manufacture". This may be agreed. However advantageously man may alter the conditions of growth, the fruit is still not produced by his action. But in the *Standard Oil Development Co's* case (1951) 68 RPC 114, where a patent was sought for a selective herbicidal process it emerged from the examiner's report that an "established Office practice" had grown up of denying that any agricultural or horticultural process could be a "manner of manufacture". Upon this, Lloyd-Jacob J made no comment, and the office view has since been adhered to: *Re Dow Chemical Co's Application* [1956] RPC 247; *Re Canterbury Agricultural College's Application* [1958] RPC 85. The proposition seems an example of a generalisation not supported by the reasons leading to the conclusions in the particular instances from which the generalisation is drawn. If it means that there is some consideration wrapped up in the label "agricultural or horticultural" which necessarily takes a process outside the area of patentability even though it is a novel process and of sufficient inventiveness, the consideration is not easy to identify. There seems to be here a classic illustration of thinking in terms of the everyday concept of manufacture **[279]** instead of following the lines along which, over a long period, the courts have given effect to the real purpose and operation of s 6 of the *Statute of Monopolies*. The cases of *Lenard's Application* (1954) 71 RPC 190 (pruning to reduce mortality from disease in clove trees) and *NV Philips' Gloeilampenfabrieken Application* (1954) 71 RPC 192 (a method for producing a new form of poinsettia) both seem to depend on the view that the process in question was only one for altering the conditions of growth, so that the contemplated end result would not be a result of the process but would be "the inevitable result of that which is inherent in the plant" (as it was expressed in the case last cited (at 194)). A distinction has necessarily to be drawn between cases of this class and cases of methods employing micro-organisms; see the *Commercial Solvents Corp v Synthetic Products Co Ltd* (1926) 43 RPC 185 and *Adhesives Pty Ltd v Aktieselskabet Dansk Gaerings-Industri* (1935) 55 CLR 523; *Virginia-Carolina Chemical Corp's Application* [1958] RPC 35 at 37, for in the latter class of cases the process is analogous to a chemical process in that, given the micro-organisms and the appropriate conditions, the desired result inevitably follows from the working of the process: see *Re Joseph Szuecs Application* [1956] RPC 25.

We are here concerned with a process producing its effect by means of a chemical reaction, and the ultimate weed-free, or comparatively weed-free condition of the crop-bearing land is properly described as produced by the process. The fact that the relevance of the process is to agricultural or horticultural enterprises does not in itself supply or suggest any consideration not already covered which should weigh against the conclusion that the process is a patentable invention.

Note

[8.95] The High Court appears to be requiring some form of technical intervention in *NRDC*. It is unclear why the resulting disease-free clove tree in *Lenards Application* or the new form of Poinsettia in *Philips Application* should not to be regarded as an acceptable "product" of the process, which in turn could then be regarded as a "manner of manufacture".

■ Biotechnological inventions

[8.100] Biotechnology involves the production of new and useful products using living organisms and cell culture. Living things are not unpatentable per se. See *Ranks Hovis McDougall Ltd's Application* (1976) 46 AOJP 3915; *Re Chakrabarty* (1978) 571 F 2d 40; 197 USPQ 73; *Diamond v Chakrabarty* 447 US 303 (1980). Standard patents may be available for new plants and animals excepting human beings and the biological processes for their generation, which are excluded by *Patents Act 1990* (Cth), s 18(2). Innovation patents are not available for plants, animals or the biological processes for their generation (s 18(3)), but may be available for a microbiological process or the product of such a process (s 18(4)).

In recent years it has been possible to produce entirely new plants and animals through "genetic engineering". Questions of patent system protection for such technology are complicated by legal and ethical problems, and by differing attitudes among Australia's trading partners. See, for example, the *EU Directive on the Legal Protection of Biotechnological Inventions 1998* and the *Convention on Biological Diversity 1993*. Australia is a world leader in genetic engineering and has opportunities for production and export. The literature on this topic is extensive and will not be reviewed here but a few pointers for students will be identified.

Plants

[8.105] Australia has the *Plant Breeder's Rights Act 1994* (Cth), designed to protect plant "inventions" and also new varieties originating through traditional breeding techniques. Dual protection under the *Patents Act 1990* (Cth) and the *Plant Breeders Rights Act 1994* (Cth) is possible. Patent protection may be more suitable for new plants produced by high technology, while plant breeders rights protection will be more suitable for plants derived from traditional techniques. The Act protects new varieties of trees, shrubs, vines, fruit, vegetables, flowers and ornamental plants, algae and fungi, but not bacteria. The Act was based on the *International Convention for the Protection of New Varieties of Plants*, first adopted in 1961 and revised in 1972 and 1978. Australia became a signatory in 1989. The Convention was substantially revised in 1991 to incorporate new technological developments, and the Australian 1994 Act complies.

Micro-organisms

[8.110] Micro-organisms have been employed by humans since bread was first baked using yeast. Processes using micro-organisms (for example, to produce antibiotics) are patentable if the usual requirements of patent legislation are fulfilled. See *American Cyanamid Co (Dann's) Patent* [1971] RPC 425; *American Cyanamid Co v Berk Pharmaceuticals Ltd* [1976] RPC 231. In *Ranks Hovis McDougall's Application* (1976) 46 AOJP 3915, the Commissioner of Patents allowed the patenting of a process for isolating a micro-organism and the variations in the organism induced by the inventor. However, the organism itself could not be protected because it occurred naturally and lacked novelty. The Patent Office originally set out its attitude to patenting micro-organisms (based on the decision in the *Ranks Hovis* case) in an official notice which points out that the criteria to be satisfied are exactly the same as for any other application: see (1980) 50 AOJP 1162. See also *Australian Patents for: Micro-organisms; Cell Lines; Hybridomas; Related Biological Materials and their Use; and Genetically Manipulated Organisms*, <www.ipaustralia.gov.au/pdfs/patents/specific/biotech.pdf> (IP Australia, February 1998). This position is summarised in the *Examiners Manual* at **[8.115]**.

▬▬▬ Manual of Practice and Procedure, Vol 2 ▬▬▬

[8.115] Australian Patent Office, *Manual of Practice and Procedure*, Vol 2 available at www.ipaustralia.gov.au/resources/manuals_patents.shtml

2.9.2.14 Micro-Organisms and Other Life-Forms

For a full treatment of this topic see 2.7 Micro-Organisms and Other Life Forms.

In its judgement on the NRDC case (above), the full bench of the High Court of Australia expanded the ambit of "manner of manufacture" by clarifying Morton J's definition of a vendible product:

- vendible – the requirement of "utility in practical affairs"
- product – is "an artificially created state of affairs"

Thus a biological entity may be patentable if the technical intervention of man (ie. manufacture) has resulted in an artificial state of affairs which does not occur in nature.

The question of patents directed to living organisms was considered in *Ranks Hovis McDougall Ltd's Application*, (1976) AOJP 3915. The hearing officer decided that:

- no objection can be taken to a claim to a new organism on the ground that it is something living;
- any new variants claimed must have improved or altered useful properties and not merely have changed morphological characteristics which have no effect on the working of the organism; and
- naturally occurring micro-organisms per se are not patentable as they represent a discovery and not an invention, but a claim to a pure culture in the presence of some specified ingredients would satisfy the requirement of a technical intervention.

Patent Office practice is that the isolation and cultivation of naturally occurring micro-organisms satisfy the requirement of a technical intervention. A claim to a biologically pure culture of the naturally occurring micro-organism is also acceptable.

[8.120] The *Patents Act 1990* (Cth), ss 41 and 42 sets out the requirements of disclosure of an invention in compliance with the *Patents Act 1990* (Cth), s 40 where the invention is a micro-organism. See also *Australian Patent Office Manual of Practice and Procedure – Volume 2* at 2.7.

Higher order life forms not including humans

[8.125] In 1987, the US Patent Office announced that it would allow non-naturally-occurring non-human multicellular living organisms (including animals) to be patentable subject matter. The first patent applied for was for the "Harvard Mouse" or "oncomouse", a rodent with a modified gene making it very susceptible to carcinogens, and a valuable research tool and lucrative source of revenue for the patent owner with a monopoly on supply of the mouse (valued at approximately US$100 each). In 1988, the Australian Patent Office received its first patent application from a German company, Transgene, for a new method of producing animals through recombinant DNA technology. A transgenic pig containing an extra growth hormone gene developed by researchers at Adelaide University has been granted patent protection and is in commercial production. Despite controversy in Europe and the United Kingdom about patentability of such inventions, the Australian attitude has been to allow patents for animals if the newly created subject matter conforms to the definition of "manner of manufacture". See K Ludlow, "Genetically Modified Organisms and their Products as Patentable Subject Matter in Australia" [1999] EIPR 298; "The Patenting of Animal Forms with New Traits" (1987) 61 ALJ 324.

Higher life forms: Humans and processes for their generation

[8.130] The *Patents Act 1990* (Cth), however, in s 18(2) expressly prohibits the patenting of human beings and processes for their generation, and claims to mammals, mammalian foetuses, embryos or fertilised ova should disclaim human application.

━━━━━━━ Fertilitescentrum AB and Luminis ━━━━━━━

[8.135] *Fertilitescentrum AB and Luminis Pty Ltd* [2004] APO 19; (2005) 62 IPR 420

[Re: Patent Application 44916/99 in the name of Luminis Pty Ltd and Fertilitescentrum AB, and a proposed direction under s.107 to delete certain claims

An application included claims for a method of growing pre-blastocyst human embryos in a specified medium. The medium was called "granulocyte-macrophage colony-stimulating factor" (referred to as GM-CSF) and is naturally present in a human fallopian tube. The invention involved using GM-CSF during in vitro fertilisation techniques in order to better simulate the natural environment and reduce the decay or death of cells in the developing blastocyst leading to more successful implantation and babies of greater body weight with fewer complications than IVF process outcomes not using the method. The examiner objected to the claims relating to the process of growing.]

HERALD (Deputy Commissioner):

[4] Claims 10 to 23 are said (by the examiner) to infringe against s 18(2). Claims 11 to 23 are all dependent claims. Claim 10, the sole independent claim in respect of this subject matter, is:

> "10. A method of growing preblastocyst human embryos, the method including the step of incubating the embryos *in vitro* in a culture medium containing an effective amount of human GM-CSF to increase the chance of implantation of the embryos, the amount of the GM-CSF being sufficient to increase the proportion of blastocysts formed from the preblastocyst embryos when compared to embryos incubated in a medium lacking GM-CSF."

[5] Fundamental to the present matter is the interpretation of s 18(2) of the *Patents Act 1990*, which provides:

> "(2) Human beings, and the biological processes for their generation, are not patentable inventions."

The position taken by the examiner is that the claimed method was a step along the path of generating a human being, and is therefore covered by the exclusion. The primary submission of the applicant (which was amplified at the hearing) is that a human being is created at the time the pronucleii of the fertilised ovum have coalesced so as to obtain mixing of the genetic materials from the respective parents. And since the method of the invention is applied after that stage, it cannot be a method of generating a human being—rather it is merely a treatment of a human being.

Some practical issues relevant to the application of s 18(2)

[12] Section 18(2) has not been the subject of any judicial consideration, nor any decisions by the Commissioner. Standard texts on patents in Australia (for example, Lahore on *Patents, Trademarks and Related Rights* by Butterworths, and *Australian Industrial & Intellectual Property* by CCH) provide no elucidation other than a brief reference to what is in the Patent Office Manual of Practice and Procedure. This section, which superficially looks very simple, has the inherent difficulty of defining the exclusion by reference to "human beings", without any definition of what constitutes a "human being". Reproductive technology exposes a range of fundamental issues concerning the nature of human life vis-à-vis human beings—issues that are essentially ethical or moral in nature, with no clear scientific answer. Illustrative of the issues are:

- In the context of human reproduction, when is a human being created? Is a human being created at a single step along the path from fertilisation to birth—and if so, where along the path? Or is it something that evolves along the path, with there being no clear beginning or end?

- The divergent societal values inherent in the debates concerning abortion, and the right to life of an unborn child; and in the rights of children to seek damages for adverse events that occurred before they were born.

- Societal concerns about the disposal of excess human embryos from *in vitro* fertilisation processes, and the natural disposal (in mensae) of human embryos that fail to implant in the uterus (a natural, very commonly-occurring process).

- Is there a difference between a human life form, and a human being? Is a human being in full existence in the human life form that exists at fertilisation, or does it entail extra characteristics that are imparted during some part of the gestation (or even after birth)?

- The requirement for a funeral in the event of miscarriage, but only if the miscarriage occurs after 20 weeks gestation or the foetus exceeds 400 grams weight (with there being differences between the States on the application of the 400 gram criterion).

- As technology and our knowledge of biochemical processes increase, our "technical" perceptions of when a human being/life form is created can change. For example, one can talk about life being created "at the moment of fertilisation"—but does that mean when the sperm enters the ovum, when the two pronucleii form, the two pronucleii fuse, or when the chromosomes within the two pronucleii mix [which is typically about 15 hours after the sperm enters the ovum]? And while this process is relevant to diploid embryos, is it compatible with haploid embryos (where there is only a single copy of each chromosome). [My understanding is that technology has not yet enabled haploid growth in animals beyond a few weeks, but the generation of a haploid "human being" cannot be said to be impossible in the future.]

- Cloning processes that entail the removal of nuclear DNA from an ovum and inserting the nuclear DNA from a cell of an existing human being, are *prima facie* incompatible with a concept of defining a human being by the bringing together of the DNA from different parents.

- Cloning processes that occur around the 4-cell stage, where the embryo is split in half, are incompatible with a concept of defining a human being by the bringing together of the DNA from different parents—as this cloning process does not affect the nuclear DNA in any manner. Rather it takes an existing life and physically divides the cells into two or more groups—so that two or more lives are created from the original one. Presumably such techniques are (only) viable before cell differentiation occurs—in which case the number of possible "human beings" derivable from a single fertilised ovum is not determinable until after cell differentiation has occurred.

Fertilitescentrum AB and Luminis *continued*

- What is entailed by "generating" a human being? In the "natural" environment, is it copulation, gestation, or both? Are the considerations different when the process is considered at a microbiological level? If one considers a fertilised ovum to be a human being, are the "processes for generating" a human being necessarily confined to events that occur before fertilisation? Is a process that is applied to an embryo such that it will properly grow a process of medically treating a human being or a process of generating a human being?
- Certain diseases and medications can affect the development of a foetus. Notorious examples are rubella (German Measles), and Thalidomide. Thalidomide administered in the first trimester can severely affect the growth of foetal limbs (arms, legs, hands, feet), and puts the foetus at risk of other injuries, including eye and ear defects and severe internal defects of the heart, genitals, kidneys, and digestive tract. Rubella can cause eye defects (resulting in vision loss or blindness), hearing loss, heart defects, mental retardation and, less frequently, cerebral palsy, if the infection occurs before ~16 weeks [*sic* about] gestation. This suggests that the process of generation (if viewed in the context of producing a "normal" offspring) extends to at least the end of the first trimester of gestation. Is the administration of a pharmaceutical to a mother for the express intention of treating the foetus a process for generating a human being, or merely medical treatment of the foetus? [For example, if without treatment the foetus would have severe abnormalities or defects, and the treatment ensured that the foetus grew without such abnormalities or defects.] Is treatment of a mother to prevent a disease from taking hold during pregnancy and affecting the foetus (for example vaccination against rubella) a treatment of the mother or part of a process for generating a human being?
- Is sorting to preferentially select sperm of a particular sex (or other genetic characteristics) part of a process of generating a human being? Is selection of fertilised ovum for implantation, on the basis of (for example) greatest viability or of sex, part of a process of generating a human being? Is genetic treatment of sperm or ovum such that the fertilised ovum will not be affected by a genetic defect, part of the process for generating a human being?
- In the context of gene therapy, how much "non-human" DNA can be present in a foetus before it is considered to be non-human?

Historical background to s 18(2)

[13] Section 18(2) did not exist in the exposure draft of the Bill that was released as the *Patents Bill 1989*, which lapsed when Parliament was prorogued. The subsequent *Patents Bill 1990* took into account the public consultations following from the 1989 Bill; the Bill as tabled in the Senate did not include s 18(2). And there is no reference to such a provision contained in the IPAC report that led to the *Patents Act 1990*, nor in the report of the Streamlining Working Party that made a number of recommendations for streamlining the Act. Accordingly there is nothing to be found in any of the materials leading up to the tabling of the Bill to indicate any relevant government policy concerning this subsection.

[The decision then discusses at some length the implications of an amendment moved by Senator Coulter and one proposed by Senator Harradine and the ensuing debate in both houses of parliament.]

[25] From this history, it might be inferred that s 18(2) owes its existence more to political process than to detailed policy deliberation. Nevertheless, several points can be gleaned from the Parliamentary debates:

- Much of the debate was a contrary reaction to Senator Coulter's amendment, which would have had the effect of excluding genetic material and life forms from patentability;

- There was a clear intention to continue to allow the patentability of life forms—with a recognition that research into medical issues was very important;
- There was unanimous agreement that human beings (whatever might be encompassed by the term) were not patentable;
- There was a clear intention to exclude not just human beings, but also of the "biological processes for their generation"; and
- While the scope of "biological processes for their generation" was queried by Senator Coulter, there was no detailed elaboration. Senator Harradine gave techniques for cloning at the four-cell stage as an "extreme example"—which suggests the exclusion relates primarily to reproductive technologies of much lesser significance than cloning. The opposition thought the exclusion was "essentially" of in-vitro fertilisation and cloning for reproduction purposes. But they also thought that there should not be patenting of "any human production process for generation in any way, shape or form". The government merely stated that the biological processes for their generation would not be patentable inventions—without any indication of scope, nor disagreement with the views of the opposition or Senator Harradine.

Interpretation of s 18(2)

[26] Section 18(2) involves two components: Human beings, and the biological processes for their generation. If it can be said that a human being comes into existence at a particular stage in the reproductive process, then prior to the "point" where a human being has come into existence processes are excluded—but any "thing" is not a human being and is patentable. After that "point", the "thing" is excluded for being a human being, but any process cannot be for generating that thing—as it occurs after the human being has been generated. [In the context of the present application, the allowability of the method claims would depend upon whether or not a fertilised ovum is a human being.] The grammatical construction of s 18(2) superficially invites a construction based on this premise, but I note that there is in fact nothing in the language of s 18(2) that requires that a human being comes into existence at a particular point.

[27] A first approach to interpreting s 18(2) is to ask the question—at what point in the reproductive process does a human being come into existence? The fundamental problem with this question is the absence of any legislative or agreed societal definition of what constitutes a human being. As is clear from the Senate report discussed above, while there would seem to be little disagreement that a fertilised ovum is a human life form, there is no agreement about when that life form takes on the characteristics of a human being.

[28] Having regard to the absence of any legislative or agreed societal definition of what constitutes a human being, I fail to see how s 18(2) can be interpreted on the basis that a human being comes into existence at some particular point in the reproductive process. Any effort to do that seems to me to lead inexorably to disagreement about where the point is, with no way of reconciling the divergent views.

[29] A second approach to interpreting this provision is to try to focus on the "wrong" that Parliament was addressing. This is difficult having regard to how this provision came into existence. One could infer that a primary concern of Parliament at the time was cloning, or other processes that controlled the genetic makeup of the entity—all occurring near the time of fertilisation. Notionally, the exclusion would then be interpreted as applying to the creation of any "self-contained entity that has everything needed to multiply and grow into a (human being)", and such entities. In practical terms, the exclusion of processes would be limited to the pre-blastocyst stage of development.

█████   Fertilitescentrum AB and Luminis *continued*

[30] This approach has the advantage of being deterministic, and excludes the cloning methods explicitly referred to in the parliamentary debates. In particular, cloning by division, and cloning by replacing the nuclear DNA, would both be excluded. However the parliamentary debates suggest that the intention was not to be limited to cloning as such—with one senator referring to cloning as being an "extreme" example of what was excluded. Most significantly, this approach completely ignores the question of what is a human being—which is the primary subject of the exclusion—and an interpretation that in effect ignores express words used in a provision is *prima facie* incorrect. This difficulty can be avoided by interpreting this self-contained entity as a human being. But this differs from the first approach only by allowing for the asserted time of creation of a human being to depend upon the method used [fertilisation for normal reproduction; time of splitting, or of nuclear transfer (etc), for cloning.] That is, it would merely be the first approach—with an asserted point of creation of a human being that is dependant upon its method of creation—and is therefore subject to exactly the same criticisms as the first approach.

[31] A third approach is to explicitly recognise that there is no agreement about when in the reproductive process a human being comes into existence. That is, the generation of a human being (as distinct from a human life form) occurs over a substantial period of time. I think it is important to note that this could arise in two ways — either as a general belief that the status of human being does in fact arise over a period of time; or as a reflection of the divergent views in society about when a human being comes into existence, with none being more right than others.

[32] To deal with this approach, it is necessary to specify the start and end points of the period in which a human being is generated. In my view, there is little doubt that a human life form is created at fertilisation. Further, I have little doubt from the parliamentary debates that Parliament intended to exclude a fertilised ovum from patentability. And as a human life form that has the inherent capacity to grow to a mature human being, I consider it has at least SOME of the characteristics that go to make up a human being—such that it properly falls within the ambit of the term "human being". And to the extent that there can be a significant difference in time between when a sperm enters an ovum, and the entanglement of the DNA, I think it is appropriate to take the starting point as being when the sperm enters the ovum— for at that time the ovum has all it needs to go on and develop as a human being.

[33] Defining the end point of when a human being is generated is less clearcut. In my view, the fact that rubella can cause defects if the infection occurs prior to the 16th week, and thalidomide causes serious deformities if administered in the first trimester, is clear indication that (at least in the physical sense) the human life form is still being generated up to at least the 16th week. I note the legislative regimes in the States for the distinction between abortions and still-births, which occurs at the 20th week. This suggests that by this stage of its development there is both a legislative and societal recognition that the foetus has significant aspects of being a human being—sufficient to require "proper" disposal rather than as hospital waste.

[34] On the other hand, subsequent to birth there is ongoing development of the human, including the major physical changes that occur during puberty. But I think that no-one would seriously argue that a pre-pubescent child was not a human being—which clearly indicates that the status of human being is not dependant upon maturity, or on obtaining completion of growth.

[35] The other significant stage in the development of a human is birth—where the foetus ceases to have physical dependency on the mother. Furthermore, a foetus does not have the same legal rights as a child that has been born (for example right to sue for damages; criminal

━━━━━━ Fertilitescentrum AB and Luminis *continued*

charges that are available in the event of its death)—even if they are at the same stage of development from conception. This to me suggests that the *full* status of human being is not acquired until birth.

[36] It seems to me that of these three approaches, only the third approach provides a satisfactory interpretation of s 18(2). Accordingly, in my view the correct interpretation of s 18(2) is ascertained by recognising a human being as being in the process of generation (in either of the two ways I refer to in paragraph 31) from the time of the processes that create a fertilised ovum (or other processes that give rise to an equivalent entity) up until the time of birth.

[37] The prohibition of "human beings" in my view is a prohibition of patenting of any entity that might reasonably claim the status of a human being. Clearly a person that has been born is covered by this exclusion. But to the extent that there is a process of generation of a human being that lasts from fertilisation to birth, I consider that a fertilised ovum and all its subsequent manifestations are covered by this exclusion.

[38] The prohibition of "biological processes for (the generation of human beings)" clearly covers all biological processes applied from fertilisation to birth—so long as the process is indeed one that directly relates to the generation of the human being. I also consider the exclusion of biological processes includes the processes of generating the entity that can first claim a status of human being. For example, processes for fertilising an ovum; processes for cloning at the 4-cell stage by division; processes for cloning by replacing nuclear DNA.

Decision

[39] Having considered the scope of the exclusion proscribed by s 18(2), I can now proceed to determine whether there is a lawful ground of objection to the present application such that the proposed direction under s 117 should be made.

[40] Claims 10 to 23 are directed to a method of growing preblastocyst human embryos. It is a method applied to a human embryo. The method has clear advantages in better simulating the natural environment, and reducing apoptosis of cells in the blastocyst, resulting in greater success in implantation, and babies of greater body mass and having fewer complications compared to IVF babies born without the benefit of the method—all of which demonstrates that the process is one that directly relates to the generation of a human being. The process is a biological process—it is a process involving the presence of a chemical such that the *in vitro* environment better simulates the natural fallopian tube environment. I am satisfied that these claims fall within the ambit of "biological processes for (the generation of human beings)" as proscribed by s 18(2).

━━

━━━━━━ **Manual of Practice and Procedure, Vol 2** ━━━━━━

[8.140] Australian Patent Office, *Manual of Practice and Procedure*, Vol 2 "National" available at <www.ipaustralia.gov.au/pdfs/patentsmanual/WebHelp/patent_examiners_manual.htm>

2.9.5 Human Beings and Biological Processes for their Generation

Human beings and the biological processes for their generation are specifically excluded from patentability under s 18(2) of the *Patents Act*.

■■■■   Manual of Practice and Procedure, Vol 2 *continued*

An interpretation of s 18(2) is given in *Fertilitescentrum AB and Luminis Pty Ltd's application* [2004] APO 19, and the decision gives guidance as to which inventions would be excluded from patentability. *Fertilitescentrum AB and Luminis Pty Ltd's application* addresses what constitutes a "human being" and thereby, what constitutes "biological processes for their generation". In his decision, the Deputy Commissioner reasoned that:

> "The correct interpretation of s 18(2) is ascertained by recognizing a human being as being in the process of generation from the time of the processes that create a fertilized ovum (or other processes that give rise to an equivalent entity) up until the time of birth."

and

> "The prohibition of 'human beings' is a prohibition of patenting any entity that might reasonably claim the status of a human being, including a fertilized ovum and all its subsequent manifestations."

and further

> "The prohibition of biological processes for the generation of human beings covers all biological processes applied from fertilisation to birth-so long as the process directly relates to the generation of the human being."

It follows that the exclusion under s 18(2) of human beings from patentability extends *inter alia* to:

> "fertilised human ova and equivalents, zygotes, blastocysts, embryos, fetuses, and totipotent human cells including those cells that are the products of nuclear transfer procedures."

Biological processes for generating human beings which would be excluded from patentability include *inter alia*:

> "methods of *in vitro* fertilisation, processes for intracytoplasmic sperm injection, processes for cloning at the 4-cell stage, processes for cloning by replacing nuclear DNA, processes or methods of growing or culturing fertilised ova, zygotes or embryos etc, and processes or methods for introducing transgenes and donor genetic or donor cytoplasmic material into fertilised ova, zygotes or embryos etc."

Methods and processes that involve the creation of a human embryo are also excluded from patentability. For example, methods for obtaining embryonic stem cells which comprise a step/s for making an embryo would contravene s 18(2). The exclusion applies regardless of the manner in which the embryo is generated. That is, the exclusion extends to methods in which an embryo is generated by fertilisation of gametes, or nuclear transfer, or activation of gametes, or parthenogenesis etc.

Examiners should also be aware that in some instances, inventions relating to human embryos and methods of using human embryos which contravene s 18(2), may also be in breach of the *Prohibition of Human Cloning Act* (Commonwealth of Australia, 2002) and/or the *Research Involving Human Embryos Act* (Commonwealth of Australia, 2002). For example, it is unlawful to create a human embryo by a process other than by fertilisation of a human egg by human sperm and it is unlawful to create an embryo for any purpose not related to assisted reproductive technology (ART). In Australia, embryonic stem cells may only be lawfully obtained from surplus ART embryos under the provisions of a licence granted by the National Health and Medical Research Council Licensing Committee.

In situations where an invention also contravenes the *Prohibition of Human Cloning Act* and/or the Research Involving Human Embryos Act, the invention is objectionable under s 50(1)(a) as being 'contrary to law' and examiners should include an objection to this effect in their report.

Additional guidance as to exclusions under se18(2) is provided in *Woo-Suk Hwang's application* [2004] APO 24 which relates to patentability of an inter-species hybrid embryo. In the decision it was deemed that activation of an ovum by non-natural means is in principle, analogous to fertilisation by natural means, and also, the presence of mitochondrial DNA from a non- human donor did not override the essential 'human' characteristic of a hybrid embryo wherein the nuclear DNA was human DNA.

Examples of inventions considered not to contravene s 18(2) include:

processes for cryopreservation of gametes, methods for preimplantation genetic analysis of gametes, and processes or methods for determining the developmental progress or viability of a fertilised ovum, blastocyst or embryo, by analysis of culture or incubation media.

Note: Within the above range of inventions there will inevitably exist a 'grey area' where it is not clear whether an invention falls foul of s 18(2).

If an examiner is unclear whether an invention constitutes a human being or a biological process for the generation of a human being and whether such a being or process is also contrary to law, they **must** refer the matter to their supervising examiner. The supervising examiner should then discuss the matter with a Deputy Commissioner.

2.9.5.1 Stem Cells

Recent developments and research into stem cell technology have generated questions regarding the relationship between human stem cells and subs 18(2).

The approach to be taken deals with whether the cells have an inherent capability to produce a human being.

Human totipotent cells are cells present in the earliest stages of development, up until the 8 cell stage. These cells possess the ability to form the entire range of cell types present in a human being, in the placenta and in other supporting tissues necessary for development of an embryo in utero. As a consequence of their inherent capability to give rise to all of the cell types necessary for the development of a human being totipotent cells are excluded under s 18(2).

Although these cells are similar to stem cells in that they have the ability to give rise to a wide range of cells types there is controversy over whether they are stem cells and they are not generally accepted as such.

Human stem cells are generally pluripotent or multipotent and unlike totipotent cells do not have the inherent capability to produce a human being.

Human embryonic stem cells are pluripotent cells derived from the inner cell mass of the blastocyst 4-5 days after fertilisation. Although they have the ability to develop into a broad range of specialised cell types they do not have the capability to develop into an entire human being, as they are not capable of producing cells for the placenta or other supporting tissues necessary for foetal development. Therefore isolated pluripotent human embryonic stem cells per se are not excluded under s 18(2).

Adult stem cells are multipotent cells found in a range of differentiated tissues such as bone marrow, neural tissue, fatty tissue and blood. These cells only have the potential to differentiate into a limited range of cell types. For example neural stem cells can give rise to neurons, astrocytes and oligodendrocytes. Therefore isolated multipotent human adult stem

▬▬▬   Manual of Practice and Procedure, Vol 2 *continued*

cells are also not excluded under s 18(2). Thus the key issue with respect to s 18(2) when considering inventions that relate to human stem cells is whether the stem cells are inherently capable of forming a human being.

For patent applications that relate to methods of using stem cells consideration should be given to the legality of the method. The *Patents Act 1990* provides a provision that allows the refusal of an application for a standard patent on the basis that the invention is contrary to law, s 50(1)(a). Some stem cell technology applications may fall within this category. Relevant legislation includes the *Prohibition of Cloning Act 2002* and *Research Involving Human Embryos Act 2002*. For further explanation relating to contrary to law issues under s 50(1)(a) see 2.9.6 Contrary to Law.

[8.145] For patent applications that relate to methods of using stem cells consideration should be given to the legality of the method. The *Patents Act 1990* provides a provision that allows the refusal of an application for a standard patent on the basis that the invention is contrary to law, s 50(1)(a). Some stem cell technology applications may fall within this category. Relevant legislation includes the *Prohibition of Cloning Act 2002* and *Research Involving Human Embryos Act 2002*.

Patenting of genes

[8.150] Another vexed issue is the one of patenting of gene sequences, particularly those identified as a result of the human genome project. It is argued that the sequences are information derived from observation (albeit using highly sophisticated techniques, skill and equipment) and not patentable as lacking the "manner of manufacture" requirement. However genetic materials which are more than a mere discovery, are novel, not obvious, useful, not secretly used before the priority date and are properly disclosed in the specification, will be patentable: *Kirin-Amgen Inc v Board of Regents of University of Washington* (1995) 33 IPR 557. For an analysis of many issues surrounding gene patents see Australian Law Reform Commission "*Genes and Ingenuity: Gene Patenting and Human Health*" (ALRC 99, 2004) <www.alrc.gov.au/publications/publist/dp.htm>.

Despite the remarkable achievements of biotechnology in producing new plants, animals, and drugs, the products and processes used to achieve the results may not be protected by patent law where an established technique is used to achieve a desired result. In *Genentech Inc v Wellcome Foundation Ltd* (1989) 8 RPC 147; (1988) 15 IPR 423, the first case involving the patenting of genetically engineered products, the Court of Appeal upheld the English High Court's decision to revoke patents relating to a genetically engineered drug, human tissue plasminogen activator (t-PA). The patents were held invalid on several grounds, one being that the gene-splicing technique used to produce the t-PA was obvious since the discovery of the amino acid and DNA sequences for t-PA was achieved by known technology. Although the work was painstaking, time-consuming and required great skill, no inventive step was disclosed, all the judgments were based on different grounds although the result was unanimously in favour of revocation. In Australia, *Genentech* might have been held to have claimed too widely in asking for a patent over the product however manufactured (*Patents Act 1990* (Cth), s 40(3)) but "lack of fair basis" is not a ground of revocation in the United Kingdom. The question of "obviousness" requires sophisticated analysis and the approach taken in *Genetech* will not necessarily be followed in Australia: see *Aktiebolaget Hassle v Alphapharm Pty Limited* [2002] HCA 59; (2002) 194 ALR 485; (2002-20003) 56 IPR 129 at **[8.340]**.

■ Methods of treatment of the human body

▰▰▰▰▰▰▰▰▰▰ Bristol-Myers Squibb v FH Faulding ▰▰▰▰▰▰▰▰▰▰

[8.155] *Bristol-Myers Squibb Co v FH Faulding Ltd* (2000) 97 FCR 524 Federal Court of Australia

BLACK CJ AND LEHANE J: **[526]**
This appeal concerns two petty patents for methods of administering taxol. Taxol has been known, for about three decades, to have anticarcinogenic properties. It inhibits the division of cancer cells. **[527]** Other drugs used in the treatment of cancer have that effect also; taxol, however, does so by a mechanism that differs from the way in which other drugs inhibit cell division. Consequently, taxol has for many years been recognised as potentially efficacious where other drug treatments have failed.

...

This is an appeal from a decision of a judge of the Court (Heerey J) in proceedings in which the appellant claimed that the respondent, in circumstances which we shall describe later in these reasons, infringed both patents. The respondent, by cross-claim, sought orders that the patents be revoked on the grounds that they disclosed no invention, that the method claimed was not a "manner of manufacture", that the alleged invention lacked novelty and an inventive step and that the claims were not fairly based on the complete specifications ...**[528]**

Manner of manufacture: "generally inconvenient"?

As the learned trial judge pointed out, the question whether a method of medical treatment of the human body is patentable was discussed extensively by each of the members of the Full Court in *Anaesthetic Supplies Pty Ltd v Rescare Ltd* (1994) 50 FCR 1 (*Rescare*). The examination of the question in that case included a review by Lockhart J of cases in Australia, New Zealand, the United Kingdom, Canada, the United States, Germany and Israel.

Having reviewed the authorities, Lockhart J concluded (at 18):

"I am not aware of any case in Australia where a process for the treatment of a human ailment or disease has arisen for consideration. In the *NRDC* case [*National Research Development Corporation v Commissioner of Patents* (1959) 102 CLR 252] the judges expressed in very tentative language their doubts about its patentability. The English cases, particularly *Schering, Eli Lilly* and *Upjohn* do not provide a satisfactory basis on which to halt the development of the law relating to patentability and processes for medical treatment. In Schering a distinction was drawn between a contraceptive process and medical treatment. In *Joos* [*Joos v Commissioner of Patents* (1972) 126 CLR 611] Barwick CJ distinguished the application of a substance to improve the strength of the hair and nails on the ground that it was not treatment to arrest or cure disease or a diseased condition or the correction of some malfunction or amelioration of some incapacity or disability. I agree with Davison CJ [in *Wellcome Foundation Ltd v Commissioner of Patents* [1979] 2 NZLR 591] that in both cases the courts established distinctions without a difference, in order to allow a patent. Both cases were ones where clinical substances were applied to the human body, in one case externally and in the other internally. In both cases the chemical produced a result in a changed condition of the body.

In my opinion, there is no justification in law or in logic to say that simply because on the one hand substances produce a cosmetic result or a functional result as opposed

███████   Bristol-Myers Squibb v FH Faulding *continued*

to a curative result, one is patentable and the other is not. I see no reason in principle why a method of treatment of the human body is any less a manner of manufacture than a method for ridding crops of weeds as in *NRDC*. Australian courts must now take a realistic view of the matter in the light of current scientific development and legal process; the law must move with changing needs and time. I agree with Davison CJ that the test enumerated in the *NRDC* case is whether the invention is a proper subject of letters patent according to the principles which have been developed for the application of s 6 of the *Statute of Monopolies.*"

Lockhart J also observed that there is no statutory provision in Australia prohibiting the grant of a patent for a process of medical treatment, and that it was noteworthy that Parliament had the opportunity to exclude methods of **[529]** treating the human body when it enacted the 1990 Act, but that the limit of the exclusion was s 18(2), namely:

"Human beings and the biological processes for their generation, are not patentable inventions".

Wilcox J (at 42) agreed with the reasons for judgment of Lockhart J and added comments of his own explaining why he considered that "in the unusual circumstances of this case", dicta of members of the High Court in *Maeder v Busch* (1938) 59 CLR 684 at 705-706 and 707, and *NRDC* at 270, should not be given the weight they would ordinarily command. He pointed out, too, that there had never been an actual decision by an Australian court to the effect of *Re C & W's Application* (1914) 31 RPC 235 and that Patent Office practice in this country had been to grant patents for methods of medical treatment. We should note here that, in his judgment at first instance, Gummow J also gave careful consideration to what had been said by members of the High Court before he rejected the submission that claims for a method of medical treatment of the human body were not patentable: see *Anaesthetic Supplies Pty Ltd v Rescare Ltd* (1992) 111 ALR 207 at 233-239.

On the appeal in *Rescare*, Sheppard J also gave full consideration to the question, but he came to a conclusion contrary to that of Lockhart J and Wilcox J In the present case the trial judge agreed with, and adopted as a matter of principle, much of what Sheppard J said in *Rescare* at 40-41.

Accepting for present purposes that the conclusions of Lockhart J and Wilcox J in *Rescare* are not part of a ratio of the case, so that the primary judge was free to depart from them and that this Full Court is also free to decide the question on that basis, we are nevertheless of the opinion that we should act in accordance with the views of the majority.

In the only substantial consideration of this important question in Australia, prior to its consideration in the present case, four members of this Court gave very close attention to whether a method of medical treatment of the human body is patentable according to Australian law, and three of them concluded that it is. That is the clear preponderance of opinion at appellate level. The consideration given to the question in this Court is quite recent and it has not been suggested to us that cases decided since 1994, here or elsewhere, throw further light on the controversy. The passing reference to the question in *Advanced Building Systems Pty Ltd v Ramset Fasteners (Aust) Pty Ltd* (1998) 194 CLR 171 at 190 does not, we think, do so.

It is in those circumstances that we consider that we should adopt and apply the view of the majority in *Rescare*: a view reached after a close and persuasive analysis of principle authority. In taking this course, we are fortified by two **[530]** considerations. The first of these is what seems to us to be the insurmountable problem, from a public policy viewpoint, of drawing a logical distinction which would justify allowing patentability for a product for treating the human body, but deny patentability for a method of treatment: see per Davison CJ in *Wellcome Foundation Ltd v Commissioner of Patents* (above) at 620 and per Gummow J in *Rescare* 111 ALR 205 at 238. This seems particularly the case where, as here, the claim is for an invention for the administration of a product.

The second compelling consideration is the very limited extent to which the Parliament dealt with patents with respect to the human body when it enacted the 1990 Act, bearing in mind, too, that it did so at a time when the longstanding practice in Australia was (as we are informed it still is) to grant patents for methods of medical treatment of the human body.

It is perhaps tempting to posit a possible special area in which, for example, an entirely novel and simple procedure, capable of saving many lives by its application as first aid, might be denied patentability even though otherwise meeting the requirements for a valid patent. It may be that the "certain methods of treatment of the human body" to which passing reference is made in *Ramset* (at 190) would fall into this category. Even here, however, although at first sight it is easy to see how it could be argued that it was "generally inconvenient" for a simple, novel and dramatically life-saving method of treatment to be denied patentability on the footing that such a thing should be available universally and without restriction, the difficulty remains of drawing any logical distinction between a method of treatment and a patentable pharmaceutical product that produces the same beneficial result. More specifically, if (say) an antivenene for spider bite is patentable, on what ground can a new form of treatment for the same life-threatening bite be denied? The second consideration, referred to above, would also seem to remain as an obstacle.

For those reasons, in our view the learned primary judge was in error in holding that the petty patents in suit were invalid on the ground of general inconvenience.

...

FINKELSTEIN J: [559]

...

A principled approach to the question whether a medical or surgical process is patentable requires the resolution of two separate issues. First, is such a process "a manner of new manufacture" within s 6 of the *Statute of Monopolies*? [567] Secondly, if such a process is "a manner of new manufacture", does it fall within the proviso so as to be excluded from patentability?

In stating the first question in this way, I do not mean to suggest that the answer depends upon an interpretation of the word "manufacture" or the words "new manufacture" in s 6. The true question is whether, in the developing concepts of patent law, a medical or surgical process is a proper subject of letters patent under the 1990 Act: see *NRDC* at 269. However, I have adopted the form of the first question in order to distinguish between an inquiry into subject matter, strictly so-called, and the operation of the proviso. I do not believe it is likely that in separating the two issues in the way that I have that, for that reason, I will arrive at an incorrect conclusion.

The answer to the first question admits of no doubt and must be in the affirmative. In the first place in *NRDC* the High Court confirmed what had already long been established: that the word "manufacture" comprehends a process that produces a useful result and that it is not necessary for that process to bring into existence or relate to a vendible product. In this connection reference might also be made to *Cementation Co Ltd's Application* (1945) 62 RPC 151 and *HB Rantzen's Application* (1946) 64 RPC 63. This then disposes of one ground of objection to patentability put forward by *C & W's Application*. In the second place, most medical or surgical processes do have commercial application. In *Joos v Commissioner of Patents* (1972) 126 CLR 611 at 618 Barwick CJ said in relation to this issue:

■■■■■   Bristol-Myers Squibb v FH Faulding *continued*

"The national economic interest in the product of good surgery—and therefore in the advancement of its techniques—if in no other respect than the repair and rehabilitation of members of the work force, including management in that grouping, is both obvious and may be regarded as sufficiently proximate, in my opinion, as to be capable of satisfying the economic element of an invention, if other elements are present and no impediments exist to the grant. One has only to recall the economic impact of workers' compensation, invalid pensions and repatriation costs to recognise that proximity."

Thus, the other objection to patentability raised by *C & W's Application* disappears.

I can now consider the second, and that which appears to me to be the critical, question on this aspect of the case, namely whether a medical or surgical process should be excluded from patentable subject matter because it falls within the proviso to s 6. Such a process is not of course contrary to law or mischievous to the State by raising the price of commodities. However, to grant a patent for such a process may be "generally inconvenient", that is to say, it may be contrary to public policy and be excluded for that reason. It is to this issue I now turn.

There now appears to be general consensus that medical and surgical products are appropriate subject matter for patent. The *General Agreement on Tariffs and Trade, Agreement on Trade-Related Aspects of Intellectual Property Rights*, Art 27 provides, in part, that "patents shall be available for any inventions, whether products or processes, in all fields of technology, provided they are new, [are non-obvious] and are capable of an industrial application" subject to the proviso that member States may exclude from patentability "diagnostic, therapeutic and surgical methods for the treatment of humans or animals". This is so notwithstanding the fact that many patients (perhaps **[568]** millions around the world) are denied access to new pharmaceuticals, because of the price charged by the monopolist or its licensee. No doubt it is the ever-increasing cost of developing new and more effective pharmaceuticals and surgical products that underlies the support for medical and surgical product patents. That is to say, the investment needed for the research and the development of these products justifies patent protection. The support may also be explained, in part at least, by the fact that it is usually a commercial organisation rather than a physician that is the inventor of pharmaceuticals and surgical products.

The opponents to the grant of a monopoly in respect of medical and surgical processes raise objections that can be put into two broad groups: (i) the adverse effects on the provision of medical care; and (ii) the adverse effects on medical progress and education. In addition there is the related "ethical" question whether a medical practitioner (medical and surgical processes are usually invented by a medical practitioner) should be entitled to patent her invention consistent with her obligation to provide medical services to humanity.

Perhaps the most powerful argument against patenting is the idea that a patient may be denied medical treatment that she needs. It is certainly the most emotive of the arguments. It presumes that a medical practitioner may be unable to obtain the right to use a particular process, or may not be able to do so within due time, and therefore will be unwilling to undertake the process on her patients for fear of legal action.

It is also said that the traditional commitment of medical practitioners to develop, share and disseminate new knowledge will be repressed. That is to say, the medical practitioner who is seeking to discover a new medical or surgical process will deliberately withhold new medical knowledge from her colleagues so as to protect her discovery and enhance her ability to obtain patent protection for financial reward. Another aspect of this argument is the potential conflict of interest which could arise when a medical practitioner has an economic interest in a patent: a conflict that might result in the practitioner not acting in the best interests of her

■■■■■■   Bristol-Myers Squibb v FH Faulding *continued*

patient. A further aspect of this argument is the suggestion that the existence of a patent is a disincentive to further invention.

On the other side of the debate is the underlying objective of patents, namely the promotion of science and the advancement of the arts for the general welfare of the State. As a general principle there can be no doubt that patent protection is desirable to encourage new medicines and surgical methods. It is an inescapable fact that inducement is necessary to encourage the great expense that is now required to evaluate and investigate the utility of many new medical processes and surgical method

As regards accessibility of information, there are of course the compulsory licensing procedures that are to be found in s 133 and s 134 of the 1990 Act. It is true that they may be cumbersome and expensive to apply. However, in relation to accessibility it may be thought that those who have obtained patent protection will seek to exploit their monopoly rights by granting licenses when appropriate.

On the issue of disclosure it has been a feature of the patent system since its inception that full disclosure of the invention is required as the consideration for the grant. Indeed publication with a specification of the means of working a patent may in many respects result in a much wider dissemination of the [569] information therein contained than would be the case if the same information is published in a medical journal or at a medical convention.

Thus, patent protection provides some measure of guarantee that the public and not just the inventor will benefit from the invention. Further, it may be expected that providing patent protection to medical or surgical procedures will expedite the development of improved medical or surgical processes and will avoid the duplication of research efforts and expenditure. It may also be that publication of a patent will act as an incentive for others to break new ground and thus improve medical technology.

How is a court able to resolve these competing contentions? None of them are supported by evidence. Some may not even be capable of proof. Even if evidence was called to make good the unsubstantiated assertions, on what basis is the court to decide how the public interest will best be served? In *Diamond v Chakrabarty* 447 US 303 (1980) the US Supreme Court was asked to rule on whether a live human-made micro-organism is patentable subject matter. The argument against patentability raised the spectre of a serious threat to the human race posed by genetic research. The Supreme Court said, in relation to the dangers of allowing the patent (at 318):

> "[W]e are without competence to entertain these arguments—either to brush them aside as fantasies generated by fear of the unknown, or to act on them. The choice we are urged to make is a matter of high policy for resolution within the legislative process after the kind of investigation, examination, and study that legislative bodies can provide and courts cannot. That process involves the balancing of competing values and interests, which in our democratic system is the business of elected representatives. Whatever their validity, the contentions now pressed on us should be addressed to the political branches of the Government, the Congress and the Executive, and not to the courts."

I do not believe that in a controversial issue such as is raised by the present argument, I would be abandoning my responsibility as a judge to follow this approach and to hold that if public policy demands that a medical or surgical process should be excluded from patentability, then that is a matter that should be resolved by the Parliament.

It is likely that few of the arguments admit of a definitive answer. The area of controversy is great. Public interest groups, medical and professional associations, medical scientists and

▬▬▬▬   Bristol-Myers Squibb v FH Faulding *continued*

the pharmaceutical industry, among others, would need to be approached and their views ascertained before a court could ever hope to arrive at a reasoned conclusion, if it could ever do so. Indeed a court might well be asked to take account of ethical and moral considerations to arrive at a decision. This is not the function of a court on an issue such as this. In my opinion, medical treatment and surgical process are patentable under the legislation and, if public policy requires a different result, it is for the Parliament to amend the 1990 Act.

Pfizer v Commissioner of Patents (NZ)

[8.160] *Pfizer Inc v Commissioner of Patents (New Zealand)* (2004) 60 IPR 624; [2004] NZCA 104

HAMMOND J: **[642]**
I agree that this appeal should be dismissed. In my view the present law in New Zealand is that claims to the medical treatment of human beings are, in general, not patentable. For public policy reasons, methods of medical diagnosis, therapy and surgery should be available to all participants in the medical profession and the public health system, and to the public.

[The] matters raised on the appeal are not just straightforward matters of statutory construction, but raise difficult and complex matters of public policy which should be reviewed—if there is to be a review—in the Parliament of New Zealand, and which are for that forum to resolve.

O'Regan J has dealt with the arguments of statutory construction which were advanced to this Court. For myself, I do not find it necessary to re-traverse or comment further on those matters. I do think it useful however, to put the appeal in context, to explain how the present public policy dimensions arise and why they are not appropriate for curial resolution, even if it were thought appropriate to disturb the longstanding principle against the patentability of subject-matter of the character in issue before us.

Patents on medical methods of treatment [644]
The term "medical treatment" is itself somewhere loose. For both functional and analytical purposes, it can usefully be broken out into diagnosis, therapy and surgery. This is the analytical scheme employed in the *Patents Act 1977* (UK), s 4(1).

Until a quarter of a century or so, ago the received wisdom was that patent claims to any of these elements ought not to be supportable. One of two bases was commonly advanced to support that conclusion. First, the inherent patentability of methods of medical treatment was treated as turning on the black letter question of the nature of an "invention". Secondly, behind that technical issue, in the view of some jurists, lay a very large moral and policy issue: whether, on the one hand, the undoubted public interest in encouraging research and innovation in the medical arena through patent incentives for the creation of new and therapeutic methods is outweighed, on the other hand, by the various public policy objections to permitting the monopolisation of those methods.

These objections include such things as hindering medical research by restricting the free availability of knowledge; inconsistency with the ethical [645] standards of medical practitioners and students; exposing medical practitioners who use and accept the use of a patented method without a licence to a liability for patent infringement; and enabling patentees to exact unreasonable payments for lifesaving or potentially lifesaving techniques (see, for a selection of the various views, Feros, "Patentability of Methods of Medical Treatment" [2001]

EIPR 79, 84-85; Gocyk-Farbr, "Patenting Medical Procedures: A Search for a Compromise Between Ethics and Economics" (1977) Cardozo L Rev 1527; American Medical Association Council on Ethical and Judicial Affairs, "Ethical issues in the Patenting of Medical Procedures" (1998) 53 *Food and Drug Law Journal* 341).

Increasingly however courts have come, more candidly and in my view more appropriately, to see the normative question as being the central issue. That is, as one Australian commentator put it: "[The issue is] to what extent (if any) legal constructions of the term 'invention' and patent eligibility generally can legitimately and openly accommodate ethical and other public policy considerations." (See Pila, "Methods of Medical Treatment within Australian and United Kingdom Patents Law" (2001) 24 UNSW L J 420, 421.) This is also the view taken by Ricketson, *The Law of Intellectual Property* in the last edition (1984) of that work which still included a section on patents. He said, and I agree, "the real question in relation to the patentability of such methods is not whether they can regarded as methods of manufacture, but whether, as a matter of policy, such subject matter should be patented at all" (para 48.53).

In fact, most countries still prohibit medical "method" patents of the character still in issue in this case. Writing in 1998, Kulbert in "Patents on Methods of Medical Treatment: Where Should the Balance Lie?" (1998) 1 NZIPJ 136, 143, suggested that "over 80 countries prohibit patents on methods of medical treatment". And in England, under the *Patent Act 1977* (UK), any invention that is claimed as a "method of treating the human or animal body by surgery or therapy or of diagnosis practised on the human or animal body" is unpatentable (s 4(2)). Hence the new English statute itself confirmed the historic prohibition on patentability of methods of medical treatment.

The traditional reason for exclusion from patentability is essentially a concession or exception that the protection of life and health are overarching human objectives which transcend what Jeremy Phillips once described as "the sordid realm of proprietary rights" (*Introduction to Intellectual Property Law* (1986) para 5.22). The proposition is that every individual should be able to expect a medical professional to be able to attend to his or her craft so as to serve the paramount aims of restoring health and decreasing pain. It would be unthinkable, it is said, by virtue of a patent grant, to prevent a health professional from performing her or his roles to the best of that person's knowledge and ability. It is worth adding here that the traditional reasoning was also that, since man is but one humble species of animal, it is only logical to extend the concession to read, for the treatment or diagnosis of man or beast.

There was overt judicial support for these propositions in the judgment of Cooke J in *Wellcome Foundation Limited v Commissioner of Patents* [1983] NZLR 385 at 338; (1982) 2 IPR 156 at 75, in this Court:

> "There remains … a deep-seated sense that the art of the physician or the surgeon in alleviating human suffering does not belong in the area of economic endeavour or trade and commerce."

[646] The changing conditions of medical treatment

However, times change, and this general issue cannot be considered in isolation from the realities of modern day medicine. Essentially what happened as the 20th Century advanced, is that pharmaceutical therapy of one kind and another has become hugely significant, and has supplanted much traditional medicine. A number of wonder drugs for a wide range of human afflictions from heart conditions, through cancer, to every day burdens such as arthritis, have been developed—and to the general benefit of mankind.

These drugs are enormously expensive to develop. The professional literature suggests that even an average drug can take ten years to bring to market, costs $1 billion dollars, and has about a 10 percent chance of attaining commercial success. Generic equivalents have been suggested, generally, to be about 66 percent of the original price (see Rose, <www.debatabase.org>, Topic 232). And the General Counsel to Pharmaceutical Research and Manufacturers of America has recently said:

> "The pharmaceutical research and development process is long, risky, and expensive. It typically takes from ten to fifteen years from drug discovery to approval by the Food and Drug Administration (FDA). Of every five thousand medicines tested, only one ultimately receives FDA approval. The average cost of developing a new drug has been estimated at $802 million. Only three out of every ten marketed drugs generate revenues that match or exceed average research and development costs (Kuhlik, "The Assault on Pharmaceutical Intellectual Property" (2004) 71 U Chicago L Rev 93, 94, footnotes omitted)."

Given the pronounced movement of medicine towards drug therapies, patent offices, judges, and legislatures world-wide have had to confront a voracious demand by the pharmaceutical industry for patent protection on the one hand, and the very real concerns of the medical profession and associated health systems, on the other. In turn, legal systems have had somehow to "mediate" this conflict (as Cornish and Llewellyn, *Intellectual Property: Patents, Copyright, Trade Marks & Allied Rights* (5 ed, 2003), p 215 term it).

What the pharmaceutical industry is interested in, is new therapeutic compounds—particularly the so called "wonder drugs"—which promise very significant returns. These drugs as such can be patented. But the research leading to a patent is very expensive. This is largely because very large numbers of compounds have to be synthesised and tested to locate a single compound that is worth putting to clinical use, to which must be added substantial advertising costs. The costs of testing and introducing alternatives are also extremely high, and are normally such that, from the point of view of a competitor, they outweigh the actual production costs of the product, thus leaving a gap between production costs and practicable selling price. This inhibits a search for alternatives. (See, Blanco White, *Patents for Inventions and the Protection of Industrial Designs* (4 ed, 1974), pp 1-103). And, there is also the complication that in an extremely price sensitive industry like medicine, there will almost always be political intervention in some form. (The literature on the economics of patents is difficult. Kitch, "The Nature and Function of the Patent System" (1977) 20 JL & Econ 256 is still very useful; see also, Landes and Posner, *The Economic Structure of Intellectual Property Law* (2003)).

[647] All of that said, it may be thought that the pharmaceutical companies have done relatively well in the legally mediated contest between the various competing interests. As in this case, there is no question that the drug compound itself can be patented. And the device of the allowing of Swiss-type claims in the northern hemisphere, and now in this country, has permitted drug manufacturers to gain extended patent protection, following the discovery of a known substance's second or subsequent medical use. (See *Pharmaceutical Management Agency v Commissioner of Patents* [2000] NZLR 529 (CA) and the discussion in Frankel and McClay *Intellectual Property in New Zealand* (2002) at 6.3.4).

In the simplest terms, Swiss-type claims are a variety of "subsequent medical use" claims, made when someone discovers that a known drug has a previously unknown medical use. The term "Swiss" patent claim is, as the name suggests, derived from the country of Switzerland and the importance to the pharmaceutical and chemical industries of those countries. The names Novaris and Hoffman la Roche spring readily to mind. The allowance of Swiss-type claims even in this country, by this Court, has not gone unchallenged (see, for instance, the sharp criticism by Armstrong, "The Arguments of Law, Policy and Practice Against Swiss-type Patent Claims" (2001) 32 VUWLR 201). But I emphasise that counsel for all parties before us was not anxious—for rather obvious reasons—to see disturbed the settled law: that Swiss-type claims are permissible in New Zealand.

The crux of the appeal

This brings me directly to the crux of this appeal. Once a pharmaceutical manufacturer can patent the compound; and also get Swiss-type protection, the question does then have to be asked "well, what is left?" One argument is, why should the law not go the full distance, as it were, and make all aspects of medical treatment fully patentable? Another is that a line does have to be drawn somewhere, and, all things considered, the present law is sensible.

Attempts have in fact been made elsewhere to draw other dividing lines. For instance, Australian law struggled with endeavouring to say that only applications in respect of methods of treatment of disease or ailments of the human body would be refused. This, on a so-called economic/non-economic distinction. But with all due respect the distinction is, as the leading Australian commentator noted, "tenuous". (Ricketson *The Law of Intellectual Property* at 48.52.)

In the end, as Professor Cornish has succinctly put it:

> The exception covering the methods of medical treatment may be regarded as a last redoubt against the sweep of the patent system into the territory of health care. Previously many countries precluded patenting for chemical substances as a whole, or pharmaceutical substances. The obligation in the TRIPS Agreement to allow such patents demonstrates the lobbying power of the pharmaceutical industry in much of the world (para 5-73).

What this present appeal urges is that the last redoubt should be breached. And, with all respect to the skill with which the arguments were advanced for the appellants by counsel of great experience in this subject area, the technique which is sought to be employed is to effect the breach by saying that, by a side-wind, and really without appreciating it, the Parliament of New Zealand has itself already brought down the walls.

[648] For myself, I think that Parliament would have to legislate in the clearest and most unequivocal terms before New Zealand law could be taken as having gone any further in the direction of unlimited protection of pharmaceutical patents, than the allowance of Swiss-type claims (which, in fairness to Parliament, are really a Court generated device). And whether it should do so, strikes me as a particularly difficult problem of public policy which lies well beyond the institutional competence of this Court.

This brings me to some short points about the practical difficulties of this particular application. I begin by noting that the drug at issue here is Ziprasidone (as specified). I again emphasise that the pharmaceutical company has already received (without any objection) protection for the actual drug itself. That is as it should be, as a result of the admirable and doubtless expensive research efforts of the appellant company. What the dispute is about are the claims—for it is the specification which is the foundation of the all litigation of this type—whereby methods of administration of the drug are put in issue.

I pressed Mr Andrew Brown QC in argument as to whether "a method" meant "any method". He confirmed that was the proper construction of the claim. If that is so, I am greatly troubled by the proposition that a health professional (particularly in the mental health area) might, in effect, have to be glancing over his or her shoulder at the possibility of a claim of patent infringement whilst trying to do his or her level best for a patient in a particularly fraught field of therapy. Even if, therefore, it was somehow possible to discriminate on some basis (and the evolution of appropriate tests would be very difficult) it seems to me that the subject matter of this particular method claim is not particularly happy for an extension to the law.

The standard answer—which was in fact advanced by the appellants—to this kind of concern, is that this sort of litigation would not in fact arise. But what is at stake in any suggested extension of the law is principle, not incidence. And there has certainly been at least one dramatic incident in North America which suggests that not all medical professionals view their traditional code of ethics in the traditional way. This is the case of Dr Pallin. He is an ophthalmologist who patented a method of "no stitch" eye surgery, and then sued another ophthalmologist for patent infringement. Dr Pallin said he intended to seek "millions of dollars" for royalties from other doctors. Two thousand doctors faced prosecution for patent infringement. Fortunately, the patent was found to be invalid, for technical reasons. (*Pallin v Singer and Hitchcock Associates of Randall* 36 USPQ 2d 1050 (D Vt 1995).)

I must say that I was troubled too by the answers given to the Bench in response to questions in oral argument, as to what precisely is the need for the extended form of protection sought by these claims, in this case. The answers could conceivably have been of two kinds. First, they might have been "positive", in the sense that they pointed out some practical gap in the protection available to a pharmaceutical company. Or, they might have been "defensive", in the sense that for tactical reasons (that is, to protect the drug patent itself) some greater protection is required. Perhaps I have not sufficiently grasped the point, but I could not discern a sound reason—indeed really any reasons at all—for the extended protection being presently "necessary" in New Zealand.

I appreciate that, historically, the traditional justification for intellectual property rights is ex-ante. That is, the object of intellectual property law is to influence behaviour that occurs before rights come into being, whereas there is **[649]** a contemporary school of thought that says that it is what happens to rights after they are developed (ex-post behaviour) which may be more important. This is an argument redolent, in economic terms, of Swiss-type claims. But even against that recognition, I cannot see the argument being pressed before us. Indeed the consequence of extending patent protection to what amounts to protection of information about how to use the drug would intuitively be very anti-competitive.

Finally, for my part I find it difficult to conceive how what I see to be the distinct extension of patent protection suggested by the appellant in this country could ever be countenanced without subjecting medical treatment patents to a regime of compulsory licensing. That would require legislation. And I also have great difficulty in seeing how the suggested undertakings not to sue would be fungible, for the protection of the greater public interest.

[Judgements rejecting the patentability in New Zealand of methods of treatment of humans were delivered by Anderson P, and Glazebrook, William Young and O'Reagan JJ.]

■ "Swiss style" claims

[8.165] Inventions known as "Swiss style" claims in the form "The use of substance X in the manufacture of a medicament for a new therapeutic use" will be accepted. See Australian Patent Office, *Practice Note*, 20 August 1998 (withdrawn). Swiss style claims are explained in *Bristol Myers Squibb Co v Baker Norton Pharmaceuticals Inc* [1999] RPC 253 at 271 per Jacob J.

PACKAGE CLAIMS

[8.170] In *Wellcome Foundation Ltd v Commissioner of Patents* (1980) 54 ALJR 397; 1A IPR 261, the High Court recognised the validity of claims for a process of treatment of cattle by administration of low doses of a chemical butt rejected the package claims, which were needed to give practical strength to the process claim. Many package claims were disguised attempts to get around what was then considered to be the exclusion of methods of treatment of the human body.

▬▬ Wellcome Foundation v Commissioner of Patents ▬▬

[8.175] *Wellcome Foundation Ltd v Commissioner of Patents* (1980) 145 CLR 520; 54 ALJR 397; 1A IPR 261, 30 ALR 510

GIBBS, STEPHEN, MASON, MURPHY AND WILSON JJ: **[526]**
The problems raised by claims to an old substance in a container, frequently accompanied by directions for use, have been examined in a number of cases in England, notably *Ciba-Geigy AG (Durr's) Applications* [1977] RPC 83; *Organon Laboratories Ltd's Application* [1970] RPC 574; *L'Oreal's Application* [1970] RPC 565. In the *Ciba-Geigy* case, Russell LJ, who delivered the opinion of the Court of Appeal, upheld the decision of Graham J that the package claim there under consideration was not valid. After reviewing earlier authorities, his Lordship stated (at 89):

> "There seems to us to be nothing inventive about parcelling up the known material in any and every convenient package or container having written thereon the information that it can be used for the stated purpose in the stated *loci*. There is no interaction between the container with its contents and **[527]** the writing thereon. The mere writing cannot make the contents in the container a manner of new manufacture. There is nothing novel in the mere presentation of information by ordinary writing or printing on a container."

For there to be novelty in a package claim there must be an interaction between the container with its contents and the writing so that the instructions or directions are novel by virtue of their link with the process. Needless to say, novelty is not often found in a package claim. *Organon* provides a striking illustration of a successful claim. There, the directions consisted of a card with the pills so arranged on it that it indicated that the pills were to be taken in a certain sequence, the sequence being part of the applicant's inventive improvement. Graha J said (at 578):

> "The discovery of a new method of treatment, which may itself be very meritorious even though not patentable, may it seems to me give subject matter to a pack or card of pills suitable for the carrying out of that method if, first, there is something novel in the constitution of the pack or card itself."

On the other hand, the *L'Oreal* case provides a more typical example, though the claims did not rest on the existence of instructions. There, the claim for a package of two components for use in a process for treatment of hair was refused. Graham and Whitford JJ said (at 572):

> "In substance the present applicants are really seeking to secure an extension of the protection they have already got or may get for their process."

Here, counsel conceded that the essence of the invention is the dosage (which is much lower than previously administered dosages of the chemicals) resulting in its suitability for a new use. An examination of the specification discloses that the instructions are merely directions as to use. They do not interact with the container and its contents. There is admittedly nothing novel about the container, nor its contents. The placement and design of the instructions are not novel.

■ Computer program inventions

▬▬▬▬▬▬▬▬▬▬▬▬   **CCOM v Jiejing**   ▬▬▬▬▬▬▬▬▬▬▬▬

[8.180] *CCOM Pty Ltd v Jiejing Pty Ltd* (1994) 51 FCR 260 Federal Court of Australia

SPENDER, GUMMOW AND HEEREY JJ: [286]

Manner of manufacture

As we have indicated, the primary Judge found against the appellants on this issue. His holding appears in the following passage (27 IPR at 594):

> "The material feature of the claimed combination is the means by which Chinese characters are categorised by stroke-type category and stroke order as defined in the specification of the petty patent in suit and the use of such criteria to retrieve and display Chinese characters. That is, the procedures used to organise and process the data. The other integers of programming and computer hardware are merely a conventional means to produce the desired result. Taking the claim as a whole, that which is sought to be made the subject matter of a monopoly is the use of stroke-type categories and stroke order as defined in the specification to organise and process data relevant to Chinese characters in a database and to retrieve and display Chinese characters on a computer screen. The formulation of such criteria and their use as rules to organise and process data stored in a database in a conventional computer are the product of human intellectual activity lying in the fine arts and not the useful arts. The claim discloses no method of manufacture within the meaning of s 6 of the *Statute of Monopolies* and therefore discloses no patentable invention."

The appellants challenge that holding. They renew their submission, rejected by the primary Judge, which his Honour had restated as follows (27 IPR at 583):

> "The (appellants) submit the claim in the petty patent was a combination claim for a new apparatus. The apparatus was a computer processing apparatus for assembling text in Chinese language characters [287] which produces a particular result, namely, the retrieval and display of Chinese characters on screen for assembly in text. Although a number of the integers represented conventional and known computer hardware, display, and processing systems including standard processing programs, the combination of those integers was a computer program or programs supplying the Chinese character database, stroke-type category criteria and graphic display of Chinese characters created, when programmed, a new machine which operated in accordance with the steps detailed in the claim. It was submitted that the production

of some useful effect, in this case the assembly of Chinese characters on a visual display unit, was sufficient to constitute the computer as programmed an invention under the (1990 Act)."

... [292]

What then of patent law in Australia? Professor Lahore pointed out (supra at 22-3):

"Some matter has never been considered to constitute a patentable invention. This matter includes a method of calculation or a process of mathematical operations, (including ways of solving mathematical problems), business, commercial and financial schemes, schemes of operation, and printed sheets, cards, tickets or the like which are mere records of intelligence."

A distinction also has been drawn between the discovery of laws or principles of nature and the application thereof to produce a particular practical and useful result. A reason why the former has not been treated as a proper subject of patent according to the principles developed pursuant to the *Statute of 1623* was considered as long ago as 1852 in Carpmael, *The Law of Patents for Inventions* (5th ed), pp 42-43:

"Let it not however be supposed that the minds of the individuals making such discoveries of principles are underrated, on the contrary, the highest respect is due to both, but it will be evident that their discoveries are not of that kind which should secure to them the right of toll on all future practical applications of such principles; such a course would lead to endless difficulties, and tend to prevent those rapid strides to improvements by which the existence of the present law has been marked."

The last case relating to computer programs decided in the UK before the commencement of the 1977 Act was that of the two Patent Judges, Graham and Whitford JJ, sitting as the Patents Appeal Tribunal in *International Business Machines Corp's Application* (1980) FSR 564. This was an appeal on an unsuccessful revocation application. The software was a program designed to calculate automatically the selling price of stock or shares by comparing a set of buying and selling orders. It was accepted that the scheme was not itself novel, and that a completely standard computer could be programmed to perform it. Nevertheless, their Lordships, speaking as specialist judges of long experience in the field, held that the patent was good. They said (at 572) that what the inventor sought to claim was a method involving the operation or control of a computer, such that it was programmed in a particular way to operate in accordance with the inventor's method. More than "intellectual information" was involved because the method was involved in the program and in the apparatus in physical form.

What had been happening elsewhere in the meantime is described as follows by Mr Colin Tapper in his work *Computer Law* (4th ed, 1989), p 9:

"It is somewhat ironic that the original impetus behind a strong movement to limit, or even to eliminate, the patenting of computer programs came from the US in the report of President's Commission ('To Promote The Useful Arts') in 1966. This view, largely inspired by practical considerations, was speedily echoed in France where it was implemented in new legislation explicitly excluding computer programs from patentable subject matter, a provision widely construed by the Court. This same approach seeped into international [293] provisions by way of the *Patent Co-operation Treaty 1970* which provided in rules 39 and 67 that computer programs were not required to be the subject of search by the appropriate international searching agency to the extent that such bodies were not equipped to search the prior art. These

▬▬▬   CCOM v Jiejing *continued*

definitions were then repeated in a slightly modified form as Art 52 of the *European Patent Convention*, a form in all relevant respects to that enacted (in the UK as the 1977 Act, subs 1(2))." ...

However, as we have pointed out, in Australia the legislature made no such provision when enacting the 1990 Act. Thus, in our view there is significant guidance to be obtained from the course of decisions in Britain before the new legislation with the application in this field of the principles expounded in the *NRDC* case.

Moreover, in this Court, in *International Business Machines Corp v Commissioner of Patents* (1991) 33 FCR 218, Burchett J followed the earlier decision of the Patents Appeal Tribunal in *Burroughs Corp (Perkin's) Application* (1974) RPC 147 at 161. There, Graham J, delivering the decision of himself and Whitford J, had expressed the view that computer programs which have the effect of controlling computers to operate in a particular way, where such programs are embodied in physical form, are proper subject matter for letters patent. His Lordship had also pointed out (at 158):

"[I]t is not enough to take a narrow and confined look at the 'product' produced by a method. Of course, if a method is regarded purely as the conception of an idea, it can always be said that the product of such a method is merely intellectual information. If, however, in practice the method results in a new machine or process or an old machine giving a new and improved result, that fact should in our view be regarded as the 'product' or the result of using the method, and cannot be disregarded in considering whether the method is patentable or not."

Burchett J held that the application of a mathematical formula to achieve an end, namely the production of an improved curve image, was a method entitled to the protection of the patent law. His Honour cited the statement of Rehnquist J in *Diamond, Commissioner of Patents & Trade Marks v Diehr & Lutton* 209 USPQ 1 (1981) that "an application of a law of nature or mathematical formula to a known structure or process may well be deserving of patent protection" (at 8).

In *International Business Machines Corp's Application*, supra, Graham and Whitford JJ accepted as a manner of new manufacture a claim as follows:

"A data handling system suitable for establishing prices for a given kind of fungible goods as hereinbefore defined in an auction market as hereinbefore defined, comprising data storing means suitable for storing data representing buy orders for the goods and representing sell orders for the goods, order entering means suitable for entering data representative of individual buy and sell orders including price information in said data storage means, comparing means which in use read out and compare the prices of buy and sell orders from the data storage means, by pairs chosen by progressing sequentially and simultaneously through a descending sequence of the buy orders and an ascending sequence of the sell orders by price, and means arranged to [294] be controlled by said comparing means so as to select the price at which the goods are to be sold in dependence on the price or prices of the last compatible pair of orders which are matched so as to select each pair of said buy and sell orders to be executed as a sale at a transaction price."

The claim of the petty patent may usefully be compared with the text of this claim.

In the present case, Counsel for the respondents submitted that what is involved is the storage of the result of linguistic tasks undertaken "outside the computer"; what the patentees claim is no more than a desirable characteristic of the computer program, the ability to search,

■■■■■■ CCOM v Jiejing *continued*

in the manner described, a data base of the type described. We accept that in a given case objections of this type might found an attack for obviousness or lack of novelty, or for failure to comply with s 40 in one or other of its aspects.

... [295]

Once full weight is given to the reasoning in the *NRDC* case and to other decisions, including those of the Patents Appeal Tribunal in England before the commencement of the 1977 Act, it follows that the petty patent should not have been held invalid on the footing that the claim was not for a manner of manufacture within the meaning of para 18(1)(a) of the 1990 Act.

The *NRDC* case (102 CLR at 275-277) requires a mode or manner of achieving an end result which is an artificially created state of affairs of utility in the field of economic endeavour. In the present case, a relevant field of economic endeavour is the use of word processing to assemble text in Chinese language characters. The end result achieved is the retrieval of graphic representations of desired characters, for assembly of text. The mode or manner of obtaining this, which provides particular utility in achieving the end result, is the storage of data as to Chinese characters analysed by stroke-type categories, for search including "flagging" (and "unflagging") and selection by reference thereto.

Conclusion

The appellants have succeeded in their challenge to the finding of invalidity based on non-compliance with s 18(1)(a) of the 1990 Act ("manner of manufacture").

■■■■■■■ **Manual of Practice and Procedure, Vol 2** ■■■■■■

[8.185] Australian Patent Office, *Manual of Practice and Procedure*, Vol 2, "National", <www.ipaustralia.gov.au/pdfs/patentsmanual/WebHelp/patent_examiners_manual.htm> at 2.9.27

2.9.2.7 Computer Software Related Inventions and Mathematical Algorithms

The Full Federal Court decision *CCOM v Jiejing* 28 IPR 481, (1994) AIPC 91-079, is the most recent authority on the patentability of computer software related inventions in Australia.

CCOM v Jiejing emphasises that the basic law on patentability of any invention in Australia is as set out in the NRDC case (above). The NRDC case and *International Business Machines Corporation v Commissioner* (1991) 22 IPR 417, both state that

> "a process, to fall within the limits of patentability ..., must be one that offers some advantage which is material, in the sense that the process belongs to a useful art as distinct from a fine art ... that its value is in the field of economic endeavour."

The particular statement of this test, formulated in *CCOM v Jiejing*, for determining the patentability of computer software related inventions is whether there is:

> "a mode or manner of achieving an end result which is an artificially created state of affairs of utility in the field of economic endeavour."

It is clear that each of the following will almost always be such a "mode or manner" as referred to in *CCOM v Jiejing*:

• source code for patentable computer software

- executable code for patentable computer software, which is in a machine readable form, and
- a computer, when programmed to achieve any result which has utility in the field of economic endeavour.

In *Data Access Corp v Powerflex* (1999) AIPC 91-514, the High Court gave apparent endorsement to the CCOM decision, saying:

> "In form, the definition of a computer program seems to have more in common with the subject matter of a patent than a copyright."

A mathematical algorithm is a procedure for solving a given mathematical problem. In the field of computer software related inventions, there will be cases in which it is not clear cut whether a mathematical algorithm is either or both of:

- "an artificially created state of affairs", and
- "of utility in the field of economic endeavour"

A mathematical algorithm per se is neither "an artificially created state of affairs" nor is it something having "utility in the field of economic endeavour". It will not have "utility in the field of economic endeavour" until it has been implemented.

Although a mathematical algorithm per se is not a manner of manufacture, the presence of such an algorithm as one of the steps in an otherwise patentable method does not exclude the claim from patentability. The test for manner of manufacture has to be applied to the claim as a whole. See, for example, *Diamond, Commissioner of Patents and Trademarks v Diehr and Lutton* (1981) 209 USPQ 1 at 9 where it was said:

> "It is inappropriate to dissect the claims into old and new elements and then to ignore the presence of the old elements in the analysis."

See also in *re Walter* (1980) 205 USPQ 397 at 406, *CCOM v Jiejing* 28 IPR 481 and the comments of the EPO Technical Board of Appeal in *Vicom Systems Inc's Application* (1987) 2 EPOR 74.

(See also 2.9.2.5 Discoveries, Ideas, Scientific Theories, Schemes and Plans).

Re Innovation Patent by Peter Szabo & Associates Pty Ltd [2005] APO 024, the Hearing Officer observed that in all the controversy surrounding the issue of algorithms, *"the important issue is not the presence of an algorithm or formula per se. Rather it is—what does the formula represent?"* (See paragraph 57, page 13 of the decision).

The Hearing Officer concluded that the mathematical relation which gives rise to the invention does not relate to a property of the universe, or the application of a law of nature. Thus "a prescription of the basis of a contractual agreement between parties, based on a mathematical expression formulated ... arrangement." (the subject of the Szabo application) *without any (material)* application of *science or technology*, did not constitute a manner of manufacture as defined by s.6 of the *Statute of Monopolies*.

Some illustrative instances where inventions involving mathematical algorithms would be patentable are:

- any otherwise-patentable process which uses a specific algorithm or mathematical formula, eg a claim to a method of annealing a tungsten alloy where:
   the heating time (seconds) = 6.78 mass of ingot/temperature (C)
- an applied algorithm or mathematical formula, eg a claim to a method of determining the length of a road (L) in metres by applying the formula:
   $L = \cos x \ N \ x \ g2$,
   where is the gradient of the road;
   N is the number of litres of fuel used by a car travelling on that road;
   and

▬▬▬▬▬   Manual of Practice and Procedure, Vol 2 *continued*

g is the acceleration due to gravity.

Note: The variables in the above formulae all describe physical entities in the real world.

• a method of operating a computer which makes the computer faster or requires less hardware resources by using a mathematical algorithm, eg a claim to a computer that calculates frequency spectrum values using a new fast Fourier transform.

An illustrative instance where inventions involving mathematical algorithms would not be patentable is:

• a pure mathematical formula (unapplied), eg a claim to a method of calculating a value c, where:

c = ex sin (t)

Note: c, x, and t are pure variables with no defined significance to the real world.

■ Schemes, methods and arrangements

[8.190] Schemes and systems for the working of machinery or carrying out an industrial process have not been granted patents (*Rolls Royce Ltd's Application* [1963] RPC 251), nor for the more efficient deployment of a workforce (*Quigley Co Inc's Application* [1977] FSR 393). Nor have plans, for example, for the layout of houses (*ESP's Application* [1945] RPC 86) or the arrangement of coloured buoys for navigation (*W's Application* (1914) 31 RPC 141). A system of numbering dressmaking patterns to facilitate assembly was rejected in *Millard v Commissioner of Patents* (1918) 24 CLR 331. Mere presentation of information on a sheet or tape or the like where the only "newness" is in the information itself has been regarded as unpatentable (*Fishburn's Application* (1938) 57 RPC 245). However, where the arrangement is for a functional or mechanical purpose it may be patentable. In *Moore Paragon Australia Ltd v Multiform Printers Pty Ltd* (1984) 3 IPR 270, marking sheets of paper with contrasting coloured bands to allow easier accurate recognition and readability of computer printouts onto the paper was held to result in an article having a functional purpose.

It has been traditional to assert that arrangements for the presentation of information, where the only novelty lies in the information itself, scientific or mathematical methods of calculation and methods of doing business, are not patentable inventions. The *Patents Act 1977* (UK), s 2 specifically excludes such subject matter from the definition of "invention". TRIPs Agreement, Art 27 may require reconsideration of these exclusions. There is no specifically expressed statutory exclusion in the *Patents Act 1990* (Cth) and patentability must be considered in light of the broad definition of "manner of manufacture" found in the *NRDC* case.

▬▬▬▬▬▬ **Welcome Real-Time v Catuity** ▬▬▬▬▬▬

[8.195] *Welcome Real-Time SA v Catuity Inc* (2001) 51 IPR 327; FCA 445 Federal Court of Australia

HEEREY J: [330]

I Introduction

The applicant Welcome Real-Time SA is the proprietor of Australian Patent No 712925 (the Patent). The invention disclosed is for a process and device for the operation of smart cards in connection with traders' loyalty programs. Smart cards are cards which contain a micro-processor or chip with the capacity for receiving and storing information. With loyalty programs a trader promotes goods or services by offering rewards based on prior transactions, for example according to the value of goods or services previously acquired or the frequency of such transactions. Rewards may take the form of a price discount or a free supply of goods or service.

...

The respondents have also cross-claimed seeking revocation of the Patent. They say that the invention the subject of the Patent is not a matter of manufacture: s 18(1)(a) of the Act. They say further that it is generally inconvenient within the meaning of s 6 of the *Statute of Monopolies*, ...

[331] II Construction

1. The field of the invention

Loyalty programs have been a feature of retail trading for many years. It is an incentive for a customer to deal with a particular trader if, after a specified number or value of transactions, a free benefit will be received. Earlier examples included Green Shield stamp ... Another example began in the early 1980s when airlines ... introduced frequent flyer programs. A passenger flying for a certain mileage became entitled to a specified free fare.

The operation of such programs involved cost and inefficiency. Typically, information about customers' entitlements had to be sent to some central repository and maintained in a retrievable form. Evidence of entitlement had to be sent by post or some other means to the customer who would in turn have to send off a claim for a benefit. The trader would then have to check the entitlement and forward the reward. All this was a cost. Moreover, documents evidencing entitlement might be lost or fraudulently duplicated.

With the advent of smart cards it became apparent that some of these problems could be overcome. If the information relating to the customer's entitlement could be stored on the card and read at a point of sale (POS) terminal, benefits to which the customer became entitled could be provided immediately at the retail outlet.

But, easier said than done. The more particular problems encountered in applying smart card technology to loyalty programs can be illustrated by the development of the invention the subject of the Patent by its inventors M Aneace Haddad and M Bernard Chevalier.

[His Honour explained difficulties encountered in the use of smart cards to manage loyalty reward programs and continued:] [332]

These examples illustrate the difficulty in developing a system which linked together many diverse traders with different technical infrastructures and promotional methods. Since a universal scheme-wide currency proved impractical, attention turned to exploring systems operated by single chains where points accumulated within the chain did not mingle with points accumulated elsewhere and where specific rewards could be provided for specific merchants or groups of merchants. To implement multiple distinct merchant programs on a single chip card, the inventors became aware that the chip card based system needed to be capable of using multiple counters within the chip, each counter dedicated to an individual merchant or chain of merchants.

[His Honour outlined further attempts to solve problems and the recognition of new technical difficulties and continued:] [333]

The solution arrived at by the inventors, which is said to be the invention of the Patent, is to "dynamically" store each merchant's loyalty program in a separate record of a file called

████████   Welcome Real-Time v Catuity *continued*

the Behaviour file. The merchant's loyalty program is added to the Behaviour file by the POS terminal the first time the cardholder uses the card at that merchant's store. Behaviour information and a points counter for merchants that the card holder never visits are never added to the chip card. There is not a preallocated memory slot for such non-visited merchants. Any chip card can still have only just a few points counters but the first points counter of any one card would be allocated to one merchant, while the same points counter on another card could be allocated to another merchant. The approach of the invention was to allow chip cards with a small memory capacity to be used across thousands of merchants each operating their own proprietary loyalty program. M Haddad knew of no other system before the priority date of the Patent that dynamically supported a plurality of different merchants each operating a different loyalty program within the chip card's memory, and each program being added only to those cards actually participating in the loyalty program. This was because all the previous systems lacked a Behaviour file indicating which merchant loyalty programs the customer was involved in, within a much larger pool of merchant loyalty programs available on the same chip card network.

[349] V Manner of manufacture

1.The respondents' case
The respondents argued that the alleged invention the subject of the Patent covered material that had never been previously held to be within the concept of "manner of manufacture" for the purposes of s 6 of the *Statute of Monopolies 1623*, which is adopted as part of the definition of "patentable invention" by s 18(1)(a) of the Act.

...

The respondents argued that working directions and methods of doing things fell outside the concept. Directions as to how to operate a known article or machine or to carry out a known process so as to produce an old result were not patentable, even though they may be a different and more efficient method of doing things.

In the present case it was said that the Patent was no more than a method or system for using well-known integers—a chip card, the memory space on that card, various computer programs, readers and printers—to operate familiar kinds of loyalty and incentive schemes for customers. Counsel argued that the recent Federal Court decisions in *International Business Machines Corp v Commissioner* [350] *of Patents* (1991) 33 FCR 218 (Burchett J) and *CCOM Pty Ltd v Jiejing Pty Ltd* (1994) 51 FCR 260 (Full Court) should be distinguished. Although like the present case in that they occurred in an environment of computing, in each case there was a physically observable effect that met the manner of manufacture requirement: the screen curve in *IBM* and the retrieval to graphical representations of desired characters for the assembly of text in *CCOM*.

As a variation of this argument it was also said that the invention fell within the principle stated in *Commissioner of Patents v Microcell Ltd* (1959) 102 CLR 232 at 249:

> "Many valid patents are for new uses of old things. But it is not an inventive idea for which a monopoly can be claimed to take a substance which is known and used for the making of various articles, and make out of it an article for which its known properties make it suitable, although it has not in fact been used to make that article before."

2. Principles
[110] The leading authority in this area is the decision of the High Court in *National Research Development Corp v Commissioner of Patents* (1959) 102 CLR 252 which has been described as

a "watershed" (*Joos v Commissioner of Patents* (1972) 126 CLR 611 at 616 per Barwick CJ) and a decision which "changed the direction of the case law not only in Australia but also in the UK" (*CCOM* at 287) ...

[His Honour closely discussed the meaning of the term "manner of manufacture" as explained in *NRDC*. See the extract above at **[8.40]**. His Honour then considered the application of that reasoning to computer program inventions and the reasoning in *CCOM*. See the extract from *CCOM* above at **[8.180]**.] [353]

The conclusion of the Full Court in *CCOM* on this issue was expressed in the following terms (at 295):

"The *NRDC* case at 275-277 requires a mode or manner of achieving an end result which is an artificially created state of affairs of utility in the field of economic endeavour. In the present case, a relevant field of economic endeavour is the use of word processing to assemble text in Chinese language characters. The end result achieved is the retrieval of graphic representations of desired characters, for assembly of text. The mode or manner of obtaining this, which provides particular utility in achieving the end result, is the storage of data as to Chinese characters analysed by stroke-type categories, for search including 'flagging' (and 'unflagging') and selection by reference thereto."

An issue analogous to that in the present case was considered by the US Court of Appeals for the Federal Circuit in *State Street Bank & Trust Co v Signature Financial Group* 149 F 3d 1368 (1998). The relevant US statute (35 USCA s 101) refers to four categories of statutory subject matter for patentability: "Any new and useful process, machine, manufacture or composition of matter". The case concerned a patent for a data processing system for implementing an investment structure. Mutual funds ("Spokes") pooled their assets in an investment portfolio ("Hub") organised as a partnership This system allowed for consolidation of costs of administering the funds combined with the tax advantages of a partnership In particular, it provided means for a daily allocation of assets for two or more Spokes that were invested in the same Hub. The system determined the percentage share that each Spoke maintained in the Hub, while taking into consideration daily changes both in value of the Hub's investment securities and the concomitant amount of each Spoke's asset.

Previous decisions of the US Supreme Court had held that mathematical algorithms are not patentable subject matter to the extent that they are merely abstract ideas. However, in *State Street* the Court of Appeals held (at 1373) that the transformation of data representing discrete dollar amounts by a machine through a series of mathematical calculations into a final share price constituted a practical application of a mathematical algorithm formula and calculation because it produced "a useful, concrete and tangible result" in the form of a final share price momentarily fixed for recording and reporting purpose.

[125] Reliance had been placed on the judicially created "business method" exception to statutory subject matter. The Court's response (at 1375) was terse, to the point of brutality:

"We take this opportunity to lay this ill-conceived exception to rest".

Their Honours considered that business methods should be subject to the same legal requirements for patentability as applied to any other process or method.

3. Conclusion

In my opinion the Patent does produce an artificial state of affairs in that cards can be issued making available to consumers many different loyalty programs of different traders as well as different programs offered by the same trader. All this can be done instantaneously at each retail outlet. So what is involved here is not just an abstract idea or method of calculation. Moreover this result is beneficial in a field of economic endeavour—namely retail trading— because it enables many traders (including small traders) to use loyalty programs and thereby compete more effectively for business. Such competition is in turn beneficial to consumers, both in the general sense that competition is good and in the sense that they can obtain benefits in the form of discounts and free goods and service.

What is disclosed by the Patent is not a business method, in the sense of a particular method or scheme for carrying on a business—for example a manufacturer appointing wholesalers to deal with particular categories of retailers rather than all retailers in particular geographical areas, or Henry Ford's idea of stipulating that suppliers deliver goods in packing cases with timbers of particular dimensions which could then be used for floorboards in the Model T. [354] Rather, the Patent is for a method and a device, involving components such as smart cards and POS terminals, *in* a business; and not just one business but an infinite range of retail businesses. *CCOM* and the English decisions referred to therein are in my opinion indistinguishable. The respondents' argument for distinguishing *CCOM*—the supposed lack of "physically observable effect"—turns on an expression not found in *CCOM* itself. Nor does such a concept form part of the Full Court's reasoning. In any event, to the extent that "physically observable effect" is required (and I do not accept that this is necessarily so) it is to be found in the writing of new information to the Behaviour file and the printing of the coupon.

The *State Street* [*State Street Bank & Trust Co v Signature Financial Group* 149 F 3d 1368 (1998)] decision is persuasive. It may be true, as the respondents argue, that US patent law has a different historical source owing little or nothing to the *Statute of Monopolies*. The Constitution of the US, Art 1, s 8, cl 8 confers power on Congress "To promote the Progress of Science and useful Arts, by securing for limited Times to Authors and Inventors the exclusive Right to their respective Writings and Discoveries". But the social needs the law has to serve in that country are the same as in ours. In both countries, in similar commercial and technological environments, the law has to strike a balance between, on the one hand, the encouragement of true innovation by the grant of monopoly and, on the other, freedom of competition.

As to the *Microcell* point, it cannot amount to the *mere* new use of a known article in a manner for which the known properties of that article make it suitable to have devised a particular method of processing data using a chip card, the properties of which (particularly its limited memory space) presented difficulties which were overcome only after much time and effort.

VI General inconvenience

The respondents argued that the Patent was, within the meaning of the Statute of Monopolies, generally inconvenient as it placed a restraint on traders in developing and operating loyalty and incentive schemes which were "a commonplace way of doing business and had been so for many years in both the real and on line worlds". It was said that the applicant was seeking to monopolise a series of known integers for the purpose of a particular kind of loyalty scheme and was thereby preventing other traders from seeking to use those integers or the same composition of them in their own customer loyalty schemes.

But if an invention otherwise satisfies the requirement of s 18 it can hardly be a complaint that others in the relevant field will be restricted in their trade because they cannot lawfully infringe the patent. The whole purpose of patent law is the granting of monopoly.

Note

[8.200] The US Patent Office grants patents for business methods used in "e-commerce". The most famous is US Patent No 5960411 being the Amazon.com "one click" sale system. The patentability of business methods has been confirmed in the US by *State Street Bank & Trust Co v Signature Financial Group Inc* 149 F3d 1368 (1998). The Current Australian Patent Office practice on business method patents is summarised in following note found on the IP Australia website.

▬▬▬▬▬ Patents for Business Schemes ▬▬▬▬▬

[8.205] IP Australia, *Patents for Business Schemes*, <www.ipaustralia.gov.au>

Developments in Australia and overseas are enabling schemes, particularly business schemes, to gain patent protection as long as certain criteria are met. We suggest you obtain the advice of a patent attorney, and consider seeking patent protection if your invention meets these criteria.

Essentially a patent may be granted for a scheme where there is a means for putting the scheme into effect. Any such scheme must also be new and inventive.

The means of effect requires the interaction of a physical system or process with the scheme. The means of effect must also include detail about the specific operation of the system or process to implement the scheme. For instance, business schemes may involve associated accounting, monitoring, reporting or analysis systems. Patent applications combining business schemes with such types of systems, and defining the specific operation of those systems, are acceptable because the systems are a means of effect. A further example of a means of effect may be electronic commerce systems. It is however inappropriate to regard a person, implementing the scheme or any component thereof, as a means of effect.

The following are examples of suitable subject matter in this field:

* A method of analysing business performance by operating a computer system to set specified parameters and thresholds in accordance with preselected criteria and to compare business performance against the parameters and thresholds.
* A method of raising funds by seeking sponsors to donate products, and programming a computerised random number generator to operate in a specified way to conduct a raffle of those products.

In the above examples the patentability of the schemes resides in artificially putting the schemes into effect. Note that the newness of the inventions may be a separate issue. The above examples are simply indicative of the patentability of the subject matter.

On the other hand a scheme (including a business scheme), by itself, is not suitable for a patent because it does not specifically give rise to a physical, artificially created end result. Some examples of schemes that are not acceptable are:

* A method of raising funds by seeking sponsors to donate products, and conducting a raffle of those products.
* A method of conducting a racing competition by causing each competitor to run the race alone, timing each competitor's time for the race, and designating the competitor with the fastest time as the winner.
* A method of analysing the performance of an investment by creating a benchmark, and comparing the investment to the benchmark.

There may be many patentable inventions in this field that are not covered by the examples above.

Note

[8.210] Consider the approach taken by the Australian Patent Office Hearing Officer in the two decisions discussed below in the APO Examiners Manual with the first being decided on the basis that it did not reveal an artificially created state of affairs and the second, more particular explanation that the invention must have "material application of science or technology".

▬▬▬ Manual of Practice and Procedure, Vol 2 ▬▬▬

[8.215] Australian Patent Office, *Manual of Practice and Procedure*, Vol 2, "National" at <www.ipaustralia.gov.au/pdfs/patentsmanual/WebHelp/patent_examiners_manual.htm>

2.9.2.10 Business Methods

In *Welcome Real-Time SA v Catuity Inc* [2001] FCA 445 at [129]; 51 IPR 327 at 354, Heerey J stated that the US Court of Appeals for the Federal Circuit decision, *State Street Bank & Trust Co v Signature Financial Group* 149 F 3d 1368 (1998) is persuasive. That court criticised the US judiciary's creation of the business method exclusion to statutory subject matter.

Their Honours considered that business methods should be subject to the same legal requirements for patentability as applied to any other process or method.

The *Welcome Real-Time SA v Catuity Inc* decision involved a patent for a process of operating smart cards in connection with traders' loyalty schemes. Heerey J. provides some scope of what is meant by a business method:

> "What is disclosed by the Patent is not a business method, in the sense of a particular method or scheme for carrying on a business—for example a manufacturer appointing wholesalers to deal with particular categories of retailers rather than all retailers in particular geographical areas, or Henry Ford's idea of stipulating that suppliers deliver goods in packing cases with timbers of particular dimensions which could then be used for floorboards in the Model T. Rather, the Patent is for a method and a device, involving components such as smart cards and POS terminals, in a business..."

Business methods that claim a technical solution or technical advantage, for example, computerised accounting, monitoring, reporting or analysis systems generally satisfy the criteria of a manner of manufacture, as do business methods involving electronic commerce systems. The artificially created state of affairs resides in the technological implementation.

In *Re Innovation Patent by Steven John Grant* [2004] APO 11, it was decided that the invention did not relate to an artificially created state of affairs. That case related to a business scheme taking advantage of a law of Parliament to protect an asset against loss of ownership as a result of a legal liability. The hearing officer noted the alleged invention did not involve the application of a newly discovered law of nature, nor the application of any technology to implement the scheme. Rather the alleged invention was a discovery in relation to a law of the Australian Parliament. The hearing officer stated the law is for the populace at large: it is not for the use of one individual to the exclusion of all others who desire to follow the law.

The Grant decision also affirmed that the traditional concept of a mere scheme or plan for doing business, *Cooper's Application* (1902) 19 RPC 53, in so far as it relates to subject matter issues, is not an additional exclusion from patentability over the principles set out in the NRDC decision. While it may be a convenient way of indicating subject matter that may not be a manner of manufacture, the true scope of a subject matter exclusion must be determined by reference to the NRDC principles.

■■■■■   Manual of Practice and Procedure, Vol 2 *continued*

In *Re Innovation Patent by Peter Szabo and Associates Pty Ltd* [2005] APO 024; the hearing officer decided that the invention did not have any material application of science or technology.

The application related to a method for providing an appropriate rebate for a mortgagee in the event of an early death under a 'reverse mortgage.' It pertained to a contractual agreement between parties, based on mathematical expressions formulated to produce a more equitable arrangement. At examination, the examiner objected that the subject matter of the application was not for a manner of manufacture.

The Hearing Officer observed that the type of subject matter which is patentable must be according to the principles which have been developed for the application of section 6 of the Statute of Monopolies; and noted that the scope of patentable subject matter has historically extended in relation to 'new areas of application of science and technology,' however the continued expansion of those areas did not mean that the scope extended to 'all endeavours of mankind.' (See paragraph 34). That is, the phrase 'artificially created state of affairs' requires an invention to be artificial 'through the application of science or technology – not through the mere involvement of human endeavour in any manner or form. The phrase should not be taken out of context in the NRDC judgement, and must be used in the context of the proper interpretation of Morton's rules. (See paragraph 36).

The decision further observes that 'the mere presence of science or technology in a claimed invention may not [be] sufficient; and concludes that patentable subject matter requires 'some materiality in the inter-relationship between the science or technology element and the remaining features of the claim. (See paragraph 46).

Examples where there is a prima facie lack of materiality in an interrelationship between features include:

- a method of acquisition of a house within a contractual relationship, which includes the step of 'building a house

Examples where there is prima facie some materiality in an inter-relationship between features include:

- a board for a board game and the rules for playing the game; and
- a computer and its software.

Another ground raised in *Welcome Real-Time SA v Catuity Inc* was that of general inconvenience, because others were restrained from using commonplace ways of doing business that had been so for many years in both the real and on line worlds.

This was rejected:

> "But if an invention otherwise satisfies the requirement of s 18 it can hardly be a complaint that others in the relevant field will be restricted in their trade because they cannot lawfully infringe the patent. The whole purpose of patent law is the granting of monopoly."

It is important not to confuse the issues of novelty and inventive step with the issue of manner of manufacture. This is especially the case when the examiner's initial impression is that the method should not be patentable; care must be taken that a subjective assessment of the novelty/obviousness of the invention is not mistaken or substituted for a consideration of traditional principles that have developed for manner of manufacture.

For a business method, the way of putting it into effect may be very simple or self-evident once the idea or concept behind the invention has been identified. This may give rise to a novelty or inventive step objection if the claim as a whole is not novel or is obvious, but is not on its own a relevant consideration when deciding manner of manufacture.

▬▬▬▬▬ Grant v Commissioner of Patents ▬▬▬▬▬

[8.220] *Grant v Commissioner of Patents* [2005] FCA 1100; AIPC 92-126

[In the appeal to the Federal Court which followed the refusal by the Deputy Commissioner to accept the application in *Re Innovation Patent by Steven John Grant* [2004] APO 11, Her Honour made the following observations.]

BRANSON J:

15 In *Re Innovation Patent No 2004100848 in the name of Peter Szabo and Associates Pty Ltd* [2005] APO 24 (*Szabo*), a decision of the Deputy Commissioner of Patents issued 5 May 2005, the Deputy Commissioner at [38] identified the subject matter of most of the *manner of manufacture* cases referred to in *NRDC* as well as in certain other decisions dealing with the same question. The table prepared by the Deputy Commissioner includes 59 decisions. At [39] he observed:

"What is readily apparent from this table is the general involvement of science and technology in patent cases. Indeed, this is particularly illustrated by reference to the so-called 'Ticket cases', where mere presentation of information does not constitute a manner of manufacture, whereas an arrangement that serves a 'mechanical purpose' is a manner of manufacture ..." (citations omitted)

16 It is clear that a *manner of manufacture* need not result in the production of a "product" in the sense of a physical thing. It is sufficient, as the High Court pointed out in *NRDC* at 276, that a new and useful effect may be observed in something such as a building, a tract or sub-structure of land, an explosion or an electrical oscillation. A method and device for the operation of "smart cards" may be a *manner of manufacture* (*Welcome Real-Time SA v Catuity Inc* (2001) 51 IPR 327). The application of a mathematical formula to achieve the production of an improved curve image on a computer screen may be a *manner of manufacture* (*International Business Machines Corporation v Commissioner of Patents* (1991) 33 FCR 218).

17 I conclude that a principle which has been developed for the application of s 6 of the *Statute of Monopolies* is that the notion of what is patentable must remain flexible in order for patent law to keep pace with scientific and technological developments.

18 However, the invention the subject of the Patent is unrelated to any new scientific or technological development. The novelty that attends the contention that the invention is patentable does not derive from the nature of the invention. There is nothing novel in the concept of structuring a financial transaction to achieve a desired outcome such as the protection of financial assets. Yet it seems that there is no reported case in which it has previously been argued that a method of structuring a financial transaction may be the subject matter of a patent. Presumably methods (or inventions) of this kind have previously been assumed to fall within the ambit of the authorities that hold that financial schemes and schemes of operation that are mere records of intelligence are not patentable (see J Lahore, "Computers and the law: the protection of intellectual property" *Federal Law Review*, vol 9, 1978, pp 15-41).

19 It may be that a principle has been developed for the application of s 6 of the *Statute of Monopolies* that patent protection is only available in respect of inventions which reflect scientific or technological developments. I interpolate that if a principle so expressed has been developed it may give rise to debate as to the true boundaries of science and technology; for this reason the principle may prove to be of little more assistance than the presently accepted dichotomy between useful arts and fine arts. It may also be that a narrower principle has or

will be developed that patent protection is not available for any invention that consists of a method of applying the law. I need not reach a concluded view here about either of these possible principles. This case can, in my view, be decided on another ground.

20 The principle which has been developed for the application of s 6 of the *Statute of Monopolies* that seems to me to be critical in this case is the principle that an invention should only enjoy the protection of a patent if the social cost of the resulting restrictions upon the use of the invention is counterbalanced by resulting social benefits. This principle is derived from the theoretical justification for the grant of a patent; that is, the assumed value of inventive ingenuity to the economy of the country. The monopoly granted by a patent to an inventor is assumed to serve the public interest both by rewarding, and thus encouraging, inventive ingenuity and by ensuring the disclosure to the public of a new article or process. As the High Court observed in *NRDC* at 275:

> "a process, to fall within the limits of patentability which the context of the *Statute of Monopolies* has supplied, must be one that offers some advantage which is material, in the sense that the process belongs to a useful art as distinct from a fine art — that its value to the country is in the field of economic endeavour." (citation omitted)

21 The Deputy Commissioner did not think that there could be any argument about the invention the subject of the Patent being of economic utility because of the number of financial advisers in society charged with looking after their client's assets. This was, in my view, to adopt the wrong approach to the question of whether the method has *'value to the country in the field of economic endeavour'* within the meaning of the above excerpt from *NRDC*. The economic utility identified by the Deputy Commissioner is not a utility of value to the country; it is a utility of value only to those whose assets are ultimately protected – and possibly to their professional advisers. The performance of the invention will not add to the economic wealth of Australia or otherwise benefit Australian society as a whole. For this reason, in my view, the invention the subject of the Patent is not a proper subject of letters patent according to the principles which have been developed for the application of s 6 of the *Statute of Monopolies*.

22 Moreover, the law of Australia assumes that the public interest is served by individuals paying their debts as and when they fall due. The *Bankruptcy Act 1966* (Cth) reflects a legislative policy that creditors may ultimately have recourse to a debtor's assets should the debtor not otherwise be able to pay his or her debts. The invention of a *'method for protecting an asset owned by an owner'* within the meaning of claim 1 of the Patent is thus the invention of a method by which the owner may be insulated from the operation of laws intended to serve the public interest. In my view, this is an additional reason why the invention the subject matter of the Patent is not a proper subject of letters patent according to the principles which have been developed for the application of s 6 of the *Statute of Monopolies*. A court of law must assume that the performance of the invention will not advance the public interest but merely advance private interests. The social cost of conferring on the invention the protection of a patent would therefore not be counterbalanced by any resultant benefit to the public.

Conclusion

23 For the above reasons I conclude that the invention the subject of the Patent is not a proper subject of letters patent according to the principles that have been developed for the application of s 6 of the *Statute of Monopolies*.

Note

[8.225] This appears to be a new and broad interpretation of the *NRDC* requirement of "economic utility" stated by Branson J. The Deputy Commissioner appears to be drawing upon the approaches of the European Patent Office under the European Patent Convention. Which reason for rejecting the application seems more persuasive? Might a concept of "generally inconvenient" have served?

■ Combinations

[8.230] Combinations of known integers can produce a new result and this is a patentable invention as long as the combination is more than a mere collocation of parts, each performing its own function to produce an aggregate result: *Williams v Nye* (1890) 7 RPC 62. A combination patent is subject to all the normal requirements and is not a separate species of patent, but much technology consists of combinations of existing elements or integers and determining the difference between a "mere collocation", and a true combination is where the "manner of manufacture" element is found.

▰▰▰▰▰▰ Fallshaw v Flexello Castors & Wheels ▰▰▰▰▰▰

[8.235] *Fallshaw Holdings Pty Ltd v Flexello Castors & Wheels Plc* (1993) 26 IPR 565 Federal Court of Australia

WILCOX, BURCHETT AND FOSTER JJ: **[566]**
The issue in this appeal is whether the Judge at first instance rightly rejected the appellant's cross-claim, brought in a patent infringement suit, for an order revoking the grant of the patent on the ground of obviousness (*Patents Act 1952*, s 100(1)(e)—cf *Patents Act 1990*, ss 7(2) and 18(1)(b)). The nub of that question is the appellant's contention that it was wrong to regard the matter as governed by those principles applicable to an invention consisting of a new combination of integers, some or all of which may be old. In truth, the appellant says, no more was involved than the selection, for quite straight forward reasons, of a well-known variant in substitution for one only of the integers of an already existing combination.

Both sides agreed, at the trial and on appeal, that the governing statute is the *Patents Act 1952*.

The patent relates to a device for fixing a castor to the tubular (or otherwise hollow) leg of a piece of furniture or other article to be mounted on castors. An outer hollow plastic cone is caused to expand when an inner plastic cone is forced into it, so that the device, to which the castor is attached, will lock firmly into the tubular or hollow leg. The method by which the inner cone is forced into the outer cone is by rotation of a threaded bolt or pintle which engages a threaded bore in the inner cone (in the manner of a bolt engaging in a nut). The bolt is of steel.

... **[567]**

The learned primary Judge identified seven integers in [Claim 1] ...

The evidence showed that, apart from the seventh integer, ie, the three-start thread, this combination was already known at the priority date, and available in the market. A castor known as the Shepherd castor had all these features, except that its thread was not a three-start thread; and there were possibly others also. But what was urged for the respondent, both at the trial and before us, was that the patent was a combination patent, and that this combination, utilising a three-start thread, was inventive. His Honour acceded to the

▬▬▬▬▬   Fallshaw v Flexello Castors & Wheels *continued*

argument. He noted that counsel "placed reliance upon the necessary level of inventiveness required to sustain a patent, especially a combination patent". He accepted a submission: "Perceiving the need to use a three-start thread is but one part of the combination and it is all parts which must be shown to be obvious to the non-inventive worker." His Honour stated his view in the following terms:

> "Even if one were to accept that the first six integers were present in the Shepherd Castor, the final integer, the three-start thread, had never been used in connection with a castor expander. None of the experts said that they had even considered this use. To say, as the respondent does, that any non-inventive worker in the field could have seen the use of plastic on the Shepherd Castor then realised the problem of the thread-stripping or the need to remove [568] plastic components from the mould quickly, and then come up with the solution of a three-start thread, is, in my opinion, to undertake a post facto dissection and to overlook the very inventiveness that often exists in a combination patent.
>
> A new combination of old integers is often patentable. ...
>
> It is the entire combination of the features of the Flexello device that are not obvious."

But why should attention be directed to "the entire combination of the features of the Flexello device"? Save for the use of a multi-start thread, in the place of a single-start thread, or some other type of thread, that particular combination, as a device to achieve the very end the patent contemplates, was familiar to the relevant industry at the priority date. The advance which the patent could be claimed to have achieved was the substitution of a more suitable type of thread—more suitable, it seems, because of the tendency of a single-start thread in plastic to be stripped when used with a steel bolt, and also because of the greater speed in fitting achieved with a multi-start thread. Whether the perception of the problems, or the provision of their solution, required an inventive spark is not to be answered by reference to the difficulties which once may have confronted the inventor of the combination. They did not confront the patentee. He has come later to the task, and refined one aspect of a device by then well-known. The critical question, as it seems to us, is whether the decision to add to the known combination a multi-start thread involved an inventive step.

Of course, patent law recognises that a combination patent may be granted in respect of a combination every integer of which may be both old and simple. But in such a case the combination is new. What is involved was stated by Dixon CJ, Kitto and Windeyer JJ in their joint judgment in *Welch Perrin Pty Ltd v Worrel* (1961) 106 CLR 588 at 611, as follows:

> "That is to say, what is described is a machine, the elements of which are all well-known and simple mechanical integers, but combined so that they are not a mere collocation of separate parts, but interact to make up a *new thing*." (Emphasis added.)

In *Minnesota Mining & Manufacturing Co v Beiersdorf (Australia) Ltd* (1980) 144 CLR 253 at 266, Aickin J said:

> "The patent thus claimed is a combination patent in the proper sense of that term, ie, it combines a number of elements which interact with each other to produce a new result or product. Such a combination may be one constituted by integers each of which is old, or by integers some of which are new, the interaction being the essential requirement."

...

■■■■■ Fallshaw v Flexello Castors & Wheels *continued*

What Griffith CJ said (with the agreement of Barton and Rich JJ) in *May v Higgins* (1916) 21 CLR 119 at 121-122 shows clearly the distinction between a new combination and an improvement in one integer of an old combination:

[569]

"It was sought to support the claim as being one for a combination, and it can only be supported as a combination. A combination is not an invention unless the combination is substantially a new thing. In this case the only new thing is the substitution in one integer of an old machine of a slightly different mode of applying power. ... The machine for which the patent is claimed is not new; it is old, but it is alleged that one of the parts has been improved. It is possible that that alteration is both valuable and novel, and so may be patentable. It is fair, therefore, that, although the applicant is not entitled to the patent which he claims, he should be allowed to put forward a claim for what may be patentable."

In the same case Isaacs J said (at 122-123):

"A true combination of parts, whether the parts be old or not, is a new unit, and is patentable, other requisite being present. It is the combination itself that is the novelty. ... I am assuming that there was invention here. Then comes the question whether the presence of this feature makes the whole thing a combination. It appears to me that it is a mere improvement of one previously existing integer. ... It is, I think, at best an improvement upon a prior integer not altering the essential character of the machine. Then, if that is the case, the whole machine as claimed is not a true combination, and, if the inventor has a meritorious invention, it is in respect of the improvement only, and that should be separately claimed."

May v Higgins was cited in *Sami Svendsen Incorporated v Independent Products Canada Ltd* (1968) 119 CLR 156, which was concerned with an alleged invention of a unit for holding a sausage skin so as to facilitate the introduction of sausage meat into it by means of a nozzle, known as a stuffing horn. The idea of such a holder was old, and what was actually new was the provision of a tab, referred to as an "ear", utilised in drawing the holder onto the stuffing horn. Kitto J said (at 164-165):

"The provision of the tab or ear was at best an improvement on a known device, not making the device a new thing but merely facilitating the use of an old thing in the old way for the old purpose. It seems to me impossible to regard the claims of the specification as being for a new combination of old integers; they are for the known device of a sausage casing holder (or unit) with an improvement in a particular part of it, consisting of an extension of the walls with a cut-out or cut-outs made in it so that what remains of the extension, namely the tab or ear, may be used for gripping to pull the holder (or unit) onto the stuffing horn more easily and therefore more quickly than before."

May v Higgins and *Sami S Svendsen* were not revocation cases. However their reasoning depends upon an appreciation of the nature of a combination patent, and an appreciation that a mere improvement of one integer of an existing combination does not, as the unsuccessful counsel had contended in *May v Higgins*, and as counsel for the respondent contended here, involve the creation of a new combination. At all events, this reasoning has been applied to a revocation suit in *Elconnex Pty Ltd v Gerard Industries Pty Ltd* (1991) 32 FCR 491 at 509-510, and that decision was affirmed on appeal by the Full Court: *Elconnex Pty Ltd v Gerard Industries*

▬▬▬   Fallshaw v Flexello Castors & Wheels *continued*

Pty Ltd (1992) 25 IPR 173 at 180, 184, 194 and 196. More recently, a similar view has been taken by Cooper J in *Winner v Ammar Holdings Pty Ltd* (1993) 25 IPR 273 at 294-295 (and see also, per Davies J, with whom Morling J agreed, at 284-285). It cannot be said, in these cases, that the question of obviousness concerned, as it did, for example, in *Rescare Ltd v Anaesthetic Supplies Pty Ltd* (1992) 25 IPR 119 at 141, "the problem solved [570] by the whole apparatus"; it concerned a new and narrower problem, confined to the operation of a part of an existing apparatus, and solved by an alteration of that part.

11. Another aspect of the point was put succinctly by Dixon J in *Palmer v Dunlop Perdriau Rubber Co Ltd* (1937) 59 CLR 30 at 73, when he said:

"But the characteristic which a combination of known integers must possess in order to afford subject matter is mutual relation in the operation of such integers."

In this context, of course, "subject matter" refers to inventiveness in contradistinction to obviousness: *Terrell on the Law of Patents* (13th ed, 1982), para. 5.82. There can be no subject matter, in that sense, in a mutual relation which is already well-known; inventiveness must lie, if at all, in the improvement which is claimed to have been effected in respect of one of the integer. Only if a change to an integer so transforms the combination as to establish what is truly a new mutual relation in the operation of the integers will it be correct to see the improved result as a new combination.

▬▬▬

▬Minnesota Mining & Manufacturing v Tyco Electronics▬

[8.240] *Minnesota Mining & Manufacturing Company v Tyco Electronics Pty Limited* (2002) 53 IPR 32; [2001] FCA 1359

SACKVILLE J: [75]

A combination patent, whether constituted by integers each one of which is old, or by integers some of which are new, may be patentable if the combination produces a new result or product: *Minnesota Mining v Beiersdorf,* at 266, per Aickin J. If the claimed combination is "simply the application of well known and well understood things to an analogous use", it will not amount to a new result or product: *Elconnex Pty Ltd v Gerard Industries Pty Ltd* (1992) 25 IPR 173 (*Elconnex (No 2)*), at 180, per Lockhart J, citing *Morgan & Co v Windover & Co* (1890) 7 RPC 131, at 134, per Lord Halsbury; see also *Fallshaw Holdings Pty Ltd v Flexello Castors & Wheels plc* (1993) 26 IPR 565, at 568-569, *per curiam*. Where questions of inventiveness arise in respect of a combination patent, it is the inventiveness of the combination as a whole that must be examined; inventiveness is not to be determined by a "piecemeal examination integer by integer": *Elconnex (No 2)*, at 184, per Lockhart J.

▬▬▬

■ Selection patents
[8.245] Sometimes a patentable invention results from applying skill and knowledge to isolate particular substances or products with particular advantages from a larger group of known substances or products. An invention which selects out a group of members from a previously-known class is called a selection patent. The main area where selection patents

occur is in finding new uses and applications for chemical compounds. The leading authority on selection patents is *IG Farbenindustrie AG's Patent* (1930) 47 RPC 289, a case concerning chemical selection patents, based on a selection of related compounds described in general terms in a previous originating patent. Maugham J held (at 322-323) that to be valid, a selection patent must be based on some substantial advantage to be secured by the use of the selected members; the selection of the components must not be obvious. A selection patent does not differ in nature from any other patent and is open to attack on the usual grounds of want of subject matter, utility and novelty. However there is some suggestion that in relation to chemical selection patents a more specific and so higher level of disclosure is required to prove anticipation. In *American Home Products Corporation* [1994] APO 58, the Delegate said that "A selection patent will only be anticipated by a specific disclosure of a compound. A non selection patent can be anticipated by a disclosure which is both clear and unmistakable and enabling. A higher degree of disclosure is needed to anticipate a selection patent". See Gummow J in *Nicaro Holdings Pty Ltd v Martin Engineering Co* (1990) 16 IPR 545 at 562. See contra Lord Evershed MR in *"Shell" Refining and Marketing Coy Ltd's Patent* [1960] RPC 35 at 54. If the selection embraces selected members which do not possess the alleged advantages the selection is defective; the patent could be misleading and also fail for insuffi- ciency and non-utility. Furthermore, the quality for which the selection is made must be of a special character, not one which those skilled in the art would expect to find in a large number of the members. See also *Kendall's Application* (1948) 65 RPC 323; *Re Shell Refining Co's Patent* [1960] RPC 35 at 47, 55; *Re Electric Co's Patent* [1964] RPC 413 and *Ethyl Corp (Cook's) Patent* [1970] RPC 227 at 232.

■ Improvements

[8.250] Improvements to part of a patented item may be protected but the claims must be limited to the improvement, otherwise the effect would be the grant of another patent for a known article or combination. Note the provisions for obtaining a patent of addition in respect of modification of or improvement to an invention for which a patent has been applied for or granted (*Patents Act 1990* (Cth), Chap 7).

Mere variations from a known device without any inventive step will not be patentable. See *Fallshaw Holdings Pty Ltd v Flexello Castors & Wheels Plc* (1993) 26 IPR 565; *Griffin v Isaacs* (1938) 12 AOJP 739; *Dennison Manufacturing Co v Monarch Marking Systems Inc* (1983) 1 IPR 431.

New uses of known articles or substances will not usually be patentable, unless an inventive step is shown. A classic example of this situation is the *NRDC* case where known chemicals were put to a new use, and a patent was allowed for the hitherto unsuspected properties. This is to be distinguished, however, from claims to a monopoly in a known substance when used as an ingredient in a process (rather than claims to a new process).

Finding a new use for an existing substance or article may be patentable if it goes beyond a mere "analogous use". In *Re Application by Shell Internationale Research Maatschappij BV* (1985) 4 IPR 439 an application was lodged in respect of a dispenser of pyrethroid insecticide. The device claimed was similar to a felt tip pen. Since the dispenser was known and the insecticidal properties of pyrethroids were known this could not be a "new" manner of manufacture, neither was the method of controlling insects (by depositing a line of insecticide) novel.

The *Statute of Monopolies* in s 6 refers to a "manner of new manufacture", and most of the issues in regard to "newness" of combination, selection, method and process patents also concern the requirements that the invention be novel and involves an inventive step (*Patents Act 1990* (Cth), s 18(1)(b)(i), (ii)) discussed below.

NOVELTY

■ Introduction

[8.255] The invention must be something new. If it is not new the applicant will not have provided sufficient consideration to justify the grant of a monopoly. No patent system allows monopolies for inventions that are already known to the public. The invention must be novel when compared with the prior art base (standard patent, s 18(1)(b)(i); innovation patent, s 18(1A)(b)(i)). What is meant by "novelty" is set out in the requirements of s 7(1) and the definitions of "prior art base" and "prior art information" in Sch 1.

══════ Patents Act 1990 (Cth), s 7 ══════

[8.260] 7 Novelty

(1) For the purposes of this Act, an invention is to be taken to be novel when compared with the prior art base unless it is not novel in the light of any one of the following kinds of information, each of which must be considered separately:

    (a) prior art information (other than that mentioned in paragraph (c)) made publicly available in a single document or through doing a single act;

    (b) prior art information (other than that mentioned in paragraph (c)) made publicly available in 2 or more related documents, or through doing 2 or more related acts, if the relationship between the documents or acts is such that a person skilled in the relevant art would treat them as a single source of that information;

    (c) prior art information contained in a single specification of the kind mentioned in subparagraph (b)(ii) of the definition of *prior art base* in Schedule 1.

Schedule 1 Definitions

"prior art information" means:

    (a) for the purposes of subsection 7(1)—information that is part of the prior art base in relation to deciding whether an invention is or is not novel;

"prior art base" means:

    (a) in relation to deciding whether an invention does or does not involve an inventive step or an innovative step:

        (i) information in a document that is publicly available, whether in or out of the patent area; and

        (ii) information made publicly available through doing an act, whether in or out of the patent area.

    (b) in relation to deciding whether an invention is or is not novel:

        (i) information of a kind mentioned in paragraph (a); and

        (ii) information contained in a published specification filed in respect of a complete application where:

            (A) if the information is, or were to be, the subject of a claim of the specification, the claim has, or would have, a priority date earlier than that of the claim under consideration; and

            (B) the specification was published after the priority date of the claim under consideration; and

            (C) the information was contained in the specification on its filing date and when it was published.

"Document" is defined by reference to s 25 of the Acts Interpretation Act1901:

    (a) any paper or other material on which there is writing;

(b) any paper or other material o which there are marks, figures, symbols or perfora-tions having a meaning for persons qualified to interpret them, and

(c) any article or material from which sounds, images or writings are capable of being reproduced with or without the aid of any other article or device.

"Patent area" means

(a) Australia and

(b) The Australian continental shelf

(c) The waters above the Australian continental shelf; and

(d) The airspace above Australia and the Australian continental shelf

[8.265] Section 45(3) provides that the applicant must inform the Commissioner of the results of any documentary searches carried out by or on behalf of the applicant, or the applicants predecessor in title, prior to the grant of a patent, whether conducted in Australia or elsewhere, for the purposes of assessing the patentability of an invention disclosed in the complete specification or in a corresponding application filed outside Australia.

A standard patent application must be examined before grant and the examiner is to report whether the invention is novel on the priority date of each claim (s 45(1)(c)). An allegation of lack of novelty can also be raised at the opposition stage (s 59(b)) and at the revocation stage (s 138(3)(b)). When re-examining a standard patent under s 97, the Commissioner must report on whether the invention is novel (s 98(1)(a)).

An innovation patent is granted without prior examination as to substance and without being subject to pre-grant opposition proceedings, but if the patentee wishes to enforce the patent and requests examination for certification of the patent, or another person requests examination, or if the Commissioner decides to examine the patent (s 101A), the Commissioner must determine if the patent is invalid and should be revoked for, amongst other grounds, lack of novelty (s 101B(2)(b)). If the innovation patent is in the process of being certified, any person may oppose the patent and seek revocation of it, and one ground of opposition is that the innovation patent lacks novelty (s 101M(b)). An innovation patent may be re-examined (s 101G) and the grounds for revocation include lack of novelty (s 101G(3)(a)). The Minister or any other person may apply to a court to have an innovation patent revoked on a ground that it is not novel (s 138(3)(b)).

When considering whether a standard patent or application has been "anticipated" by the prior art, a distinction must be made between objections based on want of novelty (s 18(1)(b)(i)), and those based on lack of inventive step (s 18(1)(b)(ii)) (or, that the invention is "obvious"). The *Patents Act 1952* (Cth) separated the two types of "newness" and the 1990 Act continues this differentiation. However, the two issues are closely allied and the same evidence may support both heads of opposition or revocation. Similarly, when considering an innovation patent a distinction must be drawn between the requirements of novelty (s 18(1A)(b)(i)) and "innovative step" (s 18(1A)(b)(ii)).

The 1990 Act (in force from 30 April 1991) introduced a key change from a domestic or national standard of novelty and inventiveness to a universal standard. Whereas previously the 1952 Act assessed novelty against what was public in Australia (and invention against what was known or used in the trade in Australia), now any publicly-available document throughout the world is relevant to the assessment of novelty for standard patents. If a standard patent was said to have been anticipated by some act, for example, using the invention in public, only domestic use within the patent area was relevant, not international use. Petty patents were judged against a domestic prior art base to protect minor inventions which were unlikely to be exported and thus not required to meet international patent standards.

The *Patents Amendment (Innovation Patents) Act 2000* (Cth) (in force from 24 May 2001) and the *Patents Amendment Act 2001* (Cth) (in force from 1 April 2002) continue the internationalisation of the Australian patent system. The innovation patent (which replaced the petty patent), when first introduced was required to be novel against the same prior art base as a standard patent, which then included documents publicly-available anywhere in the world and domestic acts. The *Patents Amendment Act 2001* (Cth) now requires extension of the prior art base to include actions which take place anywhere in the world.

■ Mode of anticipation: Publication by knowledge or use

Public knowledge

[8.270] For the purposes of novelty, publication is adding to the stock of knowledge which the public has or can acquire: *Gadd & Mason v Manchester Corp* (1892) 9 RPC 516 at 527. There is a difference between the "public knowledge" which is relevant in objections based on want of novelty as compared with the "common general knowledge" relevant to want of invention. See the passage from *Sunbeam Corp v Morphy-Richards (Aust) Pty Ltd* (1961) 35 ALJR 212 quoted by Gummow J in *RD Werner Inc v Bailey Aluminium Products Pty Ltd* (1989) 13 IPR 513.

The *Patents Act 1990* (Cth) refers to inventions being "made publicly-available", through documents or acts. The case law indicates that an invention becomes public knowledge when it has been revealed even to only a small number of people or is merely available for inspection if required.

Documentary anticipation

[8.275] The *Patents Act 1990* (Cth) provides for a three-pronged inquiry. The tests for lack of novelty are:

- disclosure in information made publicly-available in a document anywhere in the world;

- disclosure in information made publicly-available through doing an act anywhere in the world;

- and information in a specification filed but not published at the time of the priority date claimed in the application being considered for want of novelty (s 7(1) and definitions of "prior art information", "prior art base").

Disclosure by document or act may result from a combination of documents, or a combination of acts but not by a combination of documents and acts. Combination of documents or acts is only permitted if the relationship between the documents or the acts is such that a person skilled in the art would regard them as a single source of information (s 7(1)(b)). Presumably, this is a question of fact to be assessed on a case-by-case basis. The *Patents Act 1952* (Cth) had no express statutory provision for combination of documents, but in *Warner (George) Laboratories Pty Ltd v Chemspray Pty Ltd* (1967) 41 ALJR 75, a combination was permitted where at least one of the documents referred to the other.

In combination patents, cross-references in one specification containing some of the elements of a combination patent to another specification which has other elements, do not disclose the combination. The essential point is that it is the combination which must be disclosed in the case of a combination patent: *Blanco White*, para. 4.107.

"Document" is defined in *Acts Interpretation Act 1901* (Cth), s 25, and includes information stored in computer databases. In *C Van der Lely NV v Bamfords Ltd* [1963] RPC 61 a photograph was the document disclosing an invention.

Windeyer J pointed out in *Sunbeam Corp v Morphy-Richards (Aust) Pty Ltd* (1961) 180 CLR 98 at 111: "A description in an obscure journal would suffice to destroy novelty provided that … the document whether or not it was read generally by the public, had been available to the public". In *Dennison Manufacturing Co v Monarch Marking Systems Inc* (1983) 1 IPR 431 at 445, a French specification "resting quietly in the French language" in the Patent Office in Canberra was "available for public inspection" and resulted in the lack of novelty of a claim. In *Bristol-Myers Co's Application* [1969] RPC 146 a sole copy of a foreign specification held in a private library was held to be published, but may not be publicly-available under the 1990 Act. This was the case in *Tecalemit's Application* [1967] FSR 387 at 390 where a pamphlet in a private library was available to staff who were not restricted from disclosing it. Lloyd-Jacob J said that members of staff are members of the public but they did not have the right to inspect the document in their capacity as members of the public and thus it was not available to the public. However, in *Monsanto Co (Brignacs) Application* [1971] RPC 153 at 156 salesmen to whom a document was handed for distribution to customers were "considered as members of the public".

Acts disclosing an invention to the public

[8.280] Doing an act which makes an invention publicly-available includes using a product or working a process in public, telling someone about it or selling, displaying or giving the invention to some member of the public (but not experimenting with or dealing with an invention in a confidential, non-commercial way: see below. Furthermore, since 1 April 2002 there has been a general one-year "grace period" for disclosures made prior to filing a complete application where the disclosure was made by, or with the consent of, the patentee: see below). In *Griffin v Isaacs* (1938) 12 AOJP 739 disclosure to five people working for the opponent was public use. *Acme Bedstead Co Ltd v Newland Bros Ltd* (1937) 58 CLR 689 concerned anticipation of an invention consisting of a hospital bed which could be raised or lowered with a lever, which had been revealed to persons in a hospital. In *Fomento v Mentmore* [1956] RPC 87 a few ballpoint pens embodying the plaintiff's invention were given to a member of a government department to distribute to colleagues. This was held to be publication, in the absence of an obligation to preserve confidentiality. These revelations, confined as they were, amounted to the invention becoming "public knowledge". In *Bristol-Myers Co v Beecham Group* [1974] AC 646 at 680 the sale of a drug was held to be public use even though there was no way that the inherent information could be known. Lord Diplock said, "[W]here the invention claimed was a new product it was never doubted that any dealing with that product by way of trade whether by buying it or selling it with a view to profit or making it for the purposes of sale constituted such 'public use'".

Test of want of novelty

████████████████ **Nicaro v Martin Engineering** ████████████████

[8.285] *Nicaro Holdings Pty Ltd v Martin Engineering Co* (1990) 16 IPR 545 Federal Court of Australia

LOCKHART J: [549]

The generally accepted test for anticipation is the "reverse infringement" test: *General Tire & Rubber Co v Firestone Tyre & Rubber Co Ltd* [1972] RPC 457 at 485-486; *Meyers Taylor Pty Ltd v Vicarr Industries Ltd* (1977) 137 CLR 228; *Minnesota Mining & Manufacturing Co v Beiersdorf (Aust) Ltd* (1980) 144 CLR 253; 29 ALR 29; *RD Werner Inc v Bailey Aluminium Products Pty Ltd* (1989) 13 IPR 513 at 517.

▬▬▬▬   Nicaro v Martin Engineering *continued*

It is well established that the prior art must disclose all features of the invention embodied in the patent in suit and must do so in clear, unequivocal and unmistakable terms. The prior art must enable the notional skilled addressee at once to perceive and understand and be able practically to apply the discovery without the necessity of making further experiments. Whatever is essential to the invention must be read out of or gleaned from the prior publication: see *Hill v Evans* (1862) 31 LJ Ch 457 at 466; *General Tire & Rubber Co v Firestone Tyre & Rubber Co Ltd* at 486; *Washex Machinery Corp v Roy Burton Pty Ltd* (1974) 49 ALJR 12 at 18 and *C Van der Lely NV v Bamfords Ltd* [1963] RPC 61 at 72-73.

In revocation proceedings the prior publication must disclose all of the integers with the possible exception of the substitution of "mechanical equivalents to perform analogous purposes": *Sunbeam Corp v Morphy-Richards (Aust) Pty Ltd* (1961) 35 ALJR 212 at 220, per Windeyer J; *RD Werner Inc v Bailey Aluminium Products Pty Ltd*; *Dennison Manufacturing Co v Monarch Marking Systems Inc* (1983) 66 ALR 265 at 273, 274, 276 and 286. Although nothing turns on it in this case, I accept the correctness of the submission of counsel for the respondents that the term "mechanical equivalents" is properly used in cases of want of novelty and the term "workshop improvement" is essentially a term applicable to cases of obviousness: see Blanco White, *Patents for Inventions* (5th ed), para 4.212, and Terrell, *The Law of Patents* (13th ed), para 5.108; cf Terrell, para 6.52.

GUMMOW J: [555]
[His Honour's judgment contains much learned discussion of issues of novelty but two points are extracted here.]

... Much of the submissions before us concerned the construction of claim 1 in the patent and the interpretation of documents each said to amount to prior publication of the claimed invention. ...

The task of the court in such a situation was explained by the English Court of Appeal in *General Tire & Rubber Co v Firestone Tyre & Rubber Co Ltd* [1972] RPC 457 at 485, as follows:

"The earlier publication and the patentee's claim must each be construed as they would be at the respective relevant dates by a reader skilled in the art to which they relate having regard to the state of knowledge in such art at the relevant date. The construction of these documents is a function of the court, being a matter of law, but, since documents of this nature [556] are almost certain to contain technical material, the court must, by evidence, be put in the position of a person of the kind to whom the document is addressed, that is to say, a person skilled in the relevant art at the relevant date. ...

When the prior inventor's publication and the patentee's claim have respectively been construed by the court in the light of all properly admissible evidence as to technical matters, the meaning of words and expressions used in the art and so forth, the question whether the patentee's claim is new ... falls to be decided as a question of fact."

It is not for the court by its own efforts to put itself in the position of a person skilled in the relevant art at the priority date of the patent on 10 January 1977. Upon the hearing of the appeal, both counsel tended to encourage the court to do just that.

[560]... [T]here was some discussion before us as to the significance of the reverse infringement test as a criterion for judging anticipation. In the *Meyers Taylor* case Aickin J was dealing with alleged anticipation of a combination patent; none of the alleged anticipations incorporated all of the integers of any one of the claims. Therefore, as his Honour said (137 CLR at 235) none of them "could therefore possibly constitute an infringement". In such a situation,

the adequacy of the reverse infringement test will be readily apparent, given the fatal effect upon an infringement suit of omission from an alleged infringement of an essential integer. But Aickin J described this test as only "generally" applicable. Where the alleged anticipation is a paper publication, particularly a prior patent specification, there may be ground for debate in a comparison with the specification in suit as to the presence of inessential integers and mechanical equivalents ... There may also be dispute whether what has been disclosed sufficiently reveals an essential integer in the light of the principles in *Hill v Evans* (1862) 4 De GF & J 288: see *Werners Case* at 683 per Lockhart J.

▰▰▰ MJA Scientifics v SC Johnson & Son ▰▰▰

[8.290] *MJA Scientifics International Pty Ltd v SC Johnson & Son Pty Ltd* (1998) 43 IPR 287; [1998] 1466 FCA Federal Court of Australia

SUNDBERG J: **[289]**

[The first three paragraphs of the judgment contain a short description of cockroach species and includes a recipe for an edible cockroach paste described as a "succulent dish".]

... [T]he applicants (MJA) allege that they were at all material times the proprietors of patent number 557130, ... and that the respondent (SCJ) has infringed the patent. In the particulars of infringement it is said that after publication of the letters patent on 9 April 1987 SCJ had manufactured and sold in Australia SC Johnson New Raid Roach Mats (Raid Roach mats), which were cockroach insecticide mats made in accordance with the method claimed in the patent of proofing an item against **[290]** crawling insects, in that the pesticide contained in the Raid Roach mats is dispersed in printer's ink and the dispersed pesticide is applied to a carrier by a printing method. By its defence SCJ admits the proprietorship of the patent, ... but denies the infringement, and cross-claims for revocation on the ground that the invention claimed in the complete specification when compared with the prior art base as it existed before the priority date of the patent was not novel in the light of the publication of UK Letters Patent No 1360802 (the ICI patent). ...

The MJA patent

The invention the subject of the patent in suit is titled "Pesticidal Sheets or Containers". The priority date is 20 December 1982. The specification first sets out the prior art and its shortcomings. The prior art is said to consist of the spraying of insecticide and the use of pest strips. Spraying insecticide onto a surface is said not to produce a uniform distribution, so that a relatively high toxicity level must be used. Pest strips containing a vaporising pesticide are also said to involve fairly high toxicity levels in order to ensure that the pesticide is diffused throughout the area to be protected. Under the heading "Detailed Description of the Preferred Embodiments" it is said that in one embodiment the pesticide is applied by printing the pesticide dispersion onto the item using a flexopress, offset press or letterpress technique. The pesticide is preferably a residual contact pesticide, retained on the material of the item as a residue of fine crystals, uniform in size and distribution over the material. Instead of printing the pesticide dispersion directly onto the item to be proofed, it may first be applied to sheets which are placed in the target zone to protect it against crawling insects. Suitable sheets include paper or paper like materials, papiermache, thin felt, cloth, plastics or

■■■■■■   MJA Scientifics v SC Johnson & Son *continued*

other similar liquid-absorbent materials. The sheets can be cut to size and shape to enable them to be fitted to a particular surface. Other preferred embodiments are then described. In one of them, wettable residual pesticide powder is mixed in a water-based printer's ink in the ratio of approximately 30-70 per cent by weight. The resultant dispersion is printed onto a [291] sheet by conventional offset printing, and then dried to leave pesticidal-bearing ink on the sheet, the pesticide being in the form of fine crystals substantially uniformly distributed through the ink. The sheets may be cut to size and shape, and placed under a kitchen sink, bathroom vanity unit or laundry tub unit. It is said that if a cockroach is exposed to the pesticide for two minutes, it will be incapacitated in 45 minutes and will die in less than an hour. The sheets may be semi-rigid, and can be supplied in the form of mats or pads. These may be applied to the floor of ship holds, or may be provided as a lining for shipping containers.

The specification concludes with ten claims. The first is:

1. A method of proofing an item against crawling insects, the method including the steps of:
    dispersing a pesticide in a solvent, said solvent comprising a water-or alcohol-based printer's ink or ink/solvent mixture, and said pesticide comprising a wettable powder or liquid pesticide dispersible in the solvent;
    applying the pesticide dispersion to the surface of the item by a printing method; and drying the dispersion to remove the volatile solvent constituents and to leave the pesticide on the item to be contacted by the crawling insects.

Then follow the subsidiary claims: ...

The ICI patent

The complete specification was published in the UK on 24 July 1974. It became open for inspection in the Patent Office, Canberra, on 1 October 1974. The introductory part of the specification states that the invention relates to "bags", and more particularly to bags made of flexible plastics sheet material. The word "bags" includes sacks and the like, open or closed at either or both ends. The bag is coated or impregnated with an organo-phosphorous insecticide. Suitable insecticides are DDVP (dichlorvos) and pirimiphos ethyl. Especially preferred insecticides are those of low mammalian toxicity, such as malathion and fenitrothion. The most preferred is pirimiphos methyl, but diazinon is also very useful.

The bags are preferably made by first forming the selected plastics material into flexible sheets and then coating or impregnating the sheets or parts thereof with the selected insecticide. Sheet may be made by the "bubble" method [292] in which a tube of polyethylene is extruded and then caused to expand by the application of internal air pressure to form a tubular "bubble". The cooled tubular film may, after flattening, be sealed transversely at intervals of one bag length, and the separate bags severed from the length.

Coating or impregnation of the flexible plastics sheet material is generally done by treating it with a solution or dispersion containing the insecticide. The outside of the bag, or that surface of the material which subsequently becomes the outside of the bag, should be treated. This may be done by passing the flattened tubular film continuously through a bath of a solution or dispersion of the insecticide. This is preferably done by applying the insecticide to the bag surface in a lacquer or printing ink base. This lacquering or printing step should be carried out before the tubular film is transversely sealed and severed to form bags. It is not necessary to lacquer or print the whole of the exterior of the bag. Lacquer may be used to make the bag a pleasing or distinctive colour. Printing ink may be used to print indicia, including trade marks, the intended function of the bag, the presence of the insecticide, and precautions which should in consequence be observed.

It is said to be a "surprising feature" of the invention that, in favourable circumstances, the application of the insecticide to the exterior of a bag may be effective to kill insects inside the bag. Bags made according to the invention have a variety of uses. They may be used to hold refuse, for example as dustbin liners. When so used they may kill houseflies and like pests both in the bin and subsequently when the liner is removed to the refuse tip

Then follow six examples illustrating the invention. ... [These examples are referred to by Sundberg J when comparing the two patents and that comparison is set out below.] [293]

There are twenty claims, only three of which need be set out.

"1. A bag of flexible plastics sheet material coated or impregnated with an organophosphorus insecticide.

...

8. A bag as claimed in any of Claims 1 to 7 which has been coated or impregnated with an insecticide by the application thereto of printing ink containing an insecticide.

...

13. In a process for making a bag claimed in any of Claims 8 to 10, the steps which comprise forming a length of tubular plastics film and printing at least part of the exterior surface thereof with a printing ink comprising an insecticide." ... [302]

Revocation

...

The cross-claim for revocation is to be decided under the provisions of the *Patents Act*: *Patents Act 1990* (Cth), s 233(4). Under s 100(1)(g) of the [303] 1952 Act a standard patent may be revoked on the ground "that the invention, so far as claimed in any claim of the complete specification ... was not novel in Australia on the priority date of that claim".

The following propositions are supported by authority:

1. Whether a prior publication is an anticipation so as to destroy the novelty of the patented invention involves a three-step inquiry: the claims of the patent must be construed, the import of the alleged anticipation must be ascertained, and the claim must be compared with the alleged anticipation.

2. The comparison is between the prior publication and the claims of the patent in suit. Except in so far as the body of the specification of the patent in suit bears on the construction of ambiguous claims, it is irrelevant to the construction of the claim.

3. The construction of the claims and the prior document is a matter of law for the court. But where the claims contain, or the prior document contains, technical matter, expert evidence is admissible to put the court in the position of a skilled addressee at the date of the claims or of the alleged anticipation. Where there is more than one art involved, the notional skilled addressee may be a team rather than an individual.

4. Whether the prior document anticipates the claims is a question of fact. The usual test is the "reverse infringement" test, the question being whether, assuming the patent to be valid, the alleged anticipation would infringe it.

5. In order for a claim to lack novelty, the prior document must disclose all the essential integers of the claim. If it does, it is irrelevant that there are differences between the two which might be described as mere mechanical equivalents.

6. Where the alleged anticipation does not disclose all the essential integers of the patent in suit, the fact that the skilled addressee could come from the alleged anticipation to the patent in suit without the exercise of inventive ingenuity in the light of common general knowledge does not establish lack of novelty.

▬▬▬   MJA Scientifics v SC Johnson & Son *continued*

7. Where the alleged anticipation is a paper publication, particularly a prior patent specification, there may be uncertainty as to whether what has been disclosed sufficiently reveals an essential integer. In such cases, the alleged anticipation does not have to amount to a full description of the invention allegedly anticipated. There will be a sufficient disclosure to constitute anticipation if the prior document describes an effective means by which the combination claimed in the patent in suit might be produced, so long as the skilled addressee is not required to exercise any inventive ingenuity or take any inventive step.

8. Where a claim contains words denoting a particular object or purpose for the invention, a distinction exists between words which merely define the field of application of the claimed invention and words which import some limitation or special quality or characteristic of the invention and consequently constitute an essential integer of the claim. Whether the words fall into one category or the other is a question of construction. If they fall into the first category, they will not serve to distinguish the invention claimed from a prior document which otherwise discloses all the integers of the claim. If they fall into the second category, they may constitute a vital distinction between the invention as claimed and the prior disclosure which will defeat anticipation.

9. There is no novelty in a claimed invention which is nothing but a claim for a new use of an old method.

[304] 10. A foreign specification which has become open to public inspection in the Australian Patents Office has been published in Australia.

See *General Tire & Rubber Co v Firestone Tyre & Rubber Co Ltd* [1972] RPC 457 at 481-486; *Meyers Taylor Pty Ltd v Vicarr Industries Ltd* (1977) 137 CLR 228 at 235; *Werner Inc v Bailey Aluminium Products Pty Ltd* (1989) 85 ALR 679; *Nicaro Holdings Pty Ltd v Martin Engineering Co* (1990) 91 ALR 513 at 527-532; *GI Marketing CC v Fraser-Johnston* 1996 (1) SA 939 at 948; *Linotype Co Ltd v Mounsey* (1909) 9 CLR 195 at 203, 210-213; *Harris v Rothwell* (1887) 35 Ch D 416; *Merrilees v Rhodes* (1895) 16 ALT 219.

As I have said, the ICI specification became open to public inspection in the Patents Office, Canberra, on 1 October 1974. It was thus published in Australian on that date.

Claim 1

The essential integers of claim 1 are:

- dispersing a pesticide in a solvent comprising a water—or alcohol—based printer's ink
- applying the pesticide dispersion to the surface of the item by a printing method
- drying the dispersion to remove the volatile solvent leaving the pesticide on the item to be contacted by the crawling insect.

The ICI patent describes the first integer. Thus it is said that coatings or impregnation of the sheet material is generally done by treating it with a solution or dispersion containing the insecticide. The relevant surface is preferably treated by applying the insecticide to the bag surface in a lacquer or printing ink base. In the first example the surfaces were sprayed with solutions of pirimiphos methyl (insecticide) in industrial methylated spirits (solvent). In the second example the surfaces were treated with pirimiphos methyl in isopropyl alcohol (solvent). In the third, fourth and fifth examples the surfaces were treated with a printing ink formulation consisting of pirimiphos methyl, solvent and printing ink. Some of the sacks in the sixth example were treated with pirimiphos methyl in solvent/printing ink mixture.

The ICI patent also describes the second integer. Thus it is said that the lacquering or printing step is preferably carried out before the tubular film is sealed and severed to form bags. It is not necessary to lacquer or print the whole of the bag. Printing ink may be used to print indicia (trade marks, warnings etc) on the bag. In the third example the dispersion was applied to the bags using a hand operated printing roller. In the fourth example the film was passed through a multi-stage printing press which printed a pattern on one side and indicia on the other. In the fifth example a three-stage printing press was used to print a pattern on the film. In the sixth example the dispersion was printed on the face of a number of the sacks.

The third integer is described in the first example, where the bags were left open for five minutes to allow the solvent (methylated spirits) to evaporate. Although the example does not expressly so state, it is clear that the insecticide remained on the sides of the bags and that, in the case of the first set of bags, the flies died as a result of coming into contact with it. In the third example the dispersion (containing a solvent) was allowed to dry after being printed on the bags. ...

The first two integers are expressly disclosed by the ICI patent, and although the ICI patent does not expressly state that the insecticide remains on the item after the solvent had evaporated, a skilled addressee would know that it does, and be able to produce the invention the subject of claim 1 without the need to exercise any inventive ingenuity or take any inventive step.

MJA contends that claim 1 is not anticipated by ICI's patent because the claim is aimed at the elimination of crawling insects while ICI's patent is aimed at flying insects. It was pointed out that the steps of claim 1 are preceded by the words "A method of proofing an item against crawling insects", and that the third step concludes with the words "to be contacted by the crawling insects". The ICI examples, on the other hand, deal exclusively with flies. The fourth example, unlike the others, did not involve introducing flies into bags, though the outside of the bags in that example bore the words "kills flies". In order to deal with this submission it is necessary to ascertain what the MJA patent means by "crawling insects". .... . In the circumstances, resort can be had to the body of the specification to ascertain the ambit of the ambiguous expression "crawling insects". The specification mentions pests, cockroaches, fleas, ticks and termites. Fleas do not crawl in any sense of the word. Nor do cockroaches. Many cockroaches can fly, though their customary mode of progress is a quick run. Termites are white ants. They walk in a speedy fashion. So it is clear that in claim 1 the expression "crawling insects" is used in a very general sense to identify insects that proceed, whether by dragging, walking, running or hopping, across a surface rather than by flying over it.

Although the ICI examples deal with flies, it is clear that the invention is not restricted to the elimination of flies. The insecticides used or appropriate for use (malathion, fenitrothion, pirimiphos methyl and diazinon) are not flying insect specific. Reference is made to the killing of "insects" and "houseflies and like pests". Aphids on rose bushes are mentioned. A typical use of the bags is as dustbin liners. Here they may kill houseflies and other pests, both in the dustbin and when the liner is removed to the tip Mr Peters' evidence was that crawling insects such as cockroaches are common pests of dustbins, and that dichlorvos, diazinon, fenitrothian and malathion were commonly used insecticides in [306] Australia against public health crawling insect pests such as cockroaches prior to 1982. He said that many flying insects pick up insecticide when they crawl over a surface. He gave the example of flies crawling on garbage which has been sprayed. And many flying insects have a stage in life when they crawl, for example, maggots of the house fly. Mr Peters did not read the ICI patent as being limited to killing flying insects. Given that the ICI patent is not restricted to flies (but extends to aphids, insects, pests which frequent dustbins, and fly-like pests), and that the "crawling insects" to which MJA refers include insects that hop, walk or run, I am of the view that the ICI patent teaches a skilled addressee that the invention is suitable for use in killing crawling insects within the meaning of claim 1 as well as flying insects.

███████ MJA Scientifics v SC Johnson & Son *continued*

Even if I were of the view that the ICI patent describes proofing items against flying insects only, there is no novelty in the MJA claim to proof items against crawling insects within the meaning of the MJA claim. Although flies fly, they also walk. Apart from those in the ICI muslin cage examples, walking across the insecticide is what caused the flies' demise. What is claimed is at best a new use for a known method. It is a mere application of an old contrivance in the ordinary way to an analogous subject, without any novelty in applying that old contrivance to the new purpose: *Riekmann v Thierry* (1897) 14 RPC 105 at 121; *Linotype Co Ltd v Mounsey* (1909) 9 CLR 195 at 210. A device for the killing of flying insects (which also walk) is applied to crawling insects (ie, insects which hop, walk or run) without any novelty. In view of what I have said, it is unnecessary for me to examine the applicability to the claim of proposition 8 under the heading Anticipation.

Applying the reverse infringement test, one assumes that claim 1 of the MJA patent is valid, and asks whether the ICI patent would infringe the claim. For the reasons I have given, it would. The ICI invention involves dispersing a pesticide in an ink/solvent mixture, applying the dispersion to the surface of the item by a printing method, and drying the dispersion to remove the solvent, leaving the pesticide on the item to be contacted by the insects, including crawling insects within the sense of that expression in the MJA patent.

██

Measure of disclosure

███████ **Advanced Building Systems v Ramset Fasteners** ███████

[8.295] *Advanced Building Systems Pty Ltd v Ramset Fasteners (Aust) Pty Ltd* (1993) 26 IPR 171 Federal Court of Australia

[Advanced Building Systems was registered proprietor of a patent for an invention entitled "Lift Systems for Tilt-Up Walls". The invention related to apparatus and attachments for crane lifting prefabricated concrete wall sections into position on building sites. The apparatus was a combination of cable, shackles and an opening and closing ring clutch which could be locked closed with a bolt which included a lever arm attached to a release cable which would allow rapid disengagement of the apparatus from an anchor point emplaced in the wall to be positioned ... Advanced alleged that Ramset had infringed the patent by selling or hiring two competing lifting apparatus systems known as the "Ramset Frimeda Rapid Lift System" and the "Ramset Face-Lift Tilt-Up System". Ramset cross-claimed that the Advanced patent was invalid on a number of grounds but in particular that it lacked novelty having been anticipated by documents published in Australia.]

HILL J: **[179]**

Anticipation

In *Minnesota Mining & Manufacturing Co v Beiersdorf (Australia) Ltd* (1980) 144 CLR 253, Aickin J discussed in some detail (at 289 ff) the history of the English and Australian patents legislation. As his Honour points out, s 86(3) of the *Patents Act 1903* (Cth) provided for revocation of a patent on the same grounds as those upon which a patent might at common law be repealed by scire facia. The 1952 Act, for the first time in Australia, set out in statutory form the grounds upon which a patent might be revoked. It seems clear that s 100(1)(g) merely reproduced in statutory form the ground of novelty upon which a writ of scire facias might be granted.

By 1862 at the latest, in the judgment of the Lord Chancellor, Lord Westbury, in *Hill v Evans* (1862) 4 De GF and J 288, 45 ER 1195, it was established that where it was alleged that the invention had been anticipated by antecedently published works, it had to be shown that the information as to the alleged invention given by the prior publication was, for the purposes of practical utility, equal to that given by the subsequent patent. As his Lordship said at 301; at ER 1200.

> "The invention must be shewn to have been before made known. Whatever, therefore, is essential to the invention must be read out of the prior publication. If specific details are necessary for the practical working and real utility of the alleged invention, they must be found substantially in the prior publication."

To put it in another way, the subsequent invention must be found within the four corners of the prior publication relied upon as anticipation. Thus, the **[180]** cases make clear that it is not permissible, where want of novelty is asserted, to find a number of independent disclosures and make a mosaic from those disclosures purporting to show that the claimed new invention was earlier known. The expression "the making of a mosaic" was explained by Aickin J in *Minnesota Mining* (at 292-293) as being:

> "[T]he picking out of individual items of information from prior publications or prior and assembling them together so as to give them an appearance of unity and then alleging that such mosaic reveals the very thing claimed. That is an understandable, though not a permissible, process."

So in 1971 the Court of Appeal, comprising Sachs, Buckley and Orr JJ, writing of anticipation in the context of s 32(1)(e) of the *Patents Act 1949* (UK), said in *General Tire & Rubber Co v Firestone Tyre & Rubber Co Ltd* (1972) RPC 457 at 485:

> "To determine whether a patentee's claim has been anticipated by an earlier publication it is necessary to compare the earlier publication with the patentee's claim. The earlier publication must, for this purpose, be interpreted as at the date of its publication, having regard to the relevant surrounding circumstances which then existed, and without regard to subsequent events. The patentee's claim must similarly be construed as at its own date of publication having regard to the relevant surrounding circumstances then-existing. If the earlier publication, so construed, discloses the same device as the device which the patentee by his claim, so construed, asserts that he has invented, the patentee's claim has been anticipated, but not otherwise. In such circumstances the patentee is not the true and first inventor of the device and his claimed invention is not new within the terms of s 32(1)(e)."

As the judgment thereafter points out, the question of construction is to be determined having regard to what a reader skilled in the art to which the invention relates would understand and having regard to the relevant state of knowledge at the relevant date. The Court is put in the position of a person of the kind to whom the document is addressed by relevant expert testimony. In the present case, that clearly includes construction engineers and, although I do not think anything turns upon it, extends to include those who use the method of tilt-up operation such as builders and others engaged in the construction industry involved in or with onsite concrete construction.

Anticipation will be shown where carrying out the directions contained in the prior publication inevitably results in something which would infringe the subsequent patent. By way of contrast, as their Lordships said (at 486):

■■■■■   Advanced Building Systems v Ramset Fasteners *continued*

"If, on the other hand, the prior publication contains a direction which is capable of being carried out in a manner which would infringe the patentee's claim, but would be at least as likely to be carried out in a way which would not do so, the patentee's claim will not have been anticipated, although it may fail on the ground of obviousness. To anticipate the patentee's claim the prior publication must contain clear and unmistakable directions to do what the patentee claims to have invented ... A signpost, however clear upon the road to the patentee's invention will not suffice. The prior inventor must be clearly shown to have planted his flag at the precise destination before the patentee."

Later in the page, their Lordships deal with the impermissibility of the making of a mosaic in the following terms:

"Each of the documents (ie, those that were alleged to involve an anticipation) must be considered separately. For this purpose it is not permissible to combine [181] earlier unconnected publications to show anticipation, for, if combination of earlier unconnected publications is necessary to assemble all the elements of the invention said to have been anticipated, it follows that no-one man has previously made that invention and that the combination is novel."

In *RD Werner Inc v Bailey Aluminium Products Pty Ltd* (1989) 85 ALR 679, a question arose as to whether, where an invention represented an improvement on that which was disclosed in a prior publication, lack of novelty, so far as concerns that improvement, was a relevant matter. In the course of his judgment in that case, Lockhart J traced the history of the grounds of objection to validity of a patent and in particular the grounds now encompassed by "obviousness" or "invention" and "novelty". His Honour pointed out that the courts have not been consistent in distinguishing between novelty and obviousness, and that while the concepts are distinct, they do interact or overlap Both, in one sense, are to be found in the general concept that for there to be an invention there must be some manner of "new" manufacture. From the historical analysis and review of the case law, his Honour extracted the principle that although the claimed new invention was not totally disclosed by a prior publication, yet if that which was not disclosed represented merely a workshop improvement", there would be an absence of invention sufficient to support an objection on the ground of want of novelty. A ground of obviousness would, in such a case, also be made out. As his Honour said (at 698):

"'Workshop improvement' is a convenient expression to encompass a mechanical improvement to an invention disclosed in a prior specification which involves no inventive quality or ingenuity."

Put in another way, while it is clear that lack of inventiveness could not ordinarily be raised where the issue was novelty, it could be where the case was a clear one where the invention claimed obviously possessed no inventive merit whatever. ...

Gummow J, in his judgment, referred to the comment of Windeyer J *in Sunbeam Corp v Morphy-Richards (Aust) Pty Ltd* (1961) 35 ALJR 212 at 217-8, that the separate grounds of attack of novelty and obviousness were "logically precise". In that passage, his Honour had said:

"When want of novelty was asserted, the thing or process claimed as an invention was assumed to be an invention that is the product of the inventive faculties; but it was said that it was not now at the date of the patent, having been earlier invented and disclosed to the public. When want of subject matter, or lack of inventiveness, was

▄▄▄▄▄   Advanced Building Systems v Ramset Fasteners *continued*

asserted the thing or process claimed as an invention was assumed to be a new thing or process not previously disclosed to the public; but it was said that it was not really an invention and thus not a proper subject matter for the grant of a patent."

While Gummow J was of the view that obviousness had no part to play when the issue was novelty, his Honour said that a workshop improvement coming about by ordinary methods of trial and error would not bring about the result that the earlier anticipation ceased to be an anticipation; so too, where there was a substitution of a mechanical equivalent for an inessential integer. His Honour's conclusion is expressed at 716 of the report as follows:

[182] "In my view, in construing the grounds of opposition under the present Act it is not an element in the objection on the ground of lack of novelty that whilst there was no anticipation in the necessary sense, nevertheless the difference in the two is to be disregarded because to come from the alleged anticipation to the alleged invention would not have involved the exercise of inventive ingenuity in the light of common general knowledge."

The same Court heard the appeal in *Nicaro Holdings Pty Ltd v Martin Engineering Co* (1990) 91 ALR 513.

Again in this case a submission was made that where the difference in the prior art consisted in matters which made no substantial contribution to the working of the thing claimed, or involved no ingenuity or inventive step so that those variations amounted to mere workshop improvements, the patent was invalid for want of novelty. Again, the majority judgment is that of Gummow J, with whom Jenkinson J agreed. Again, I do not think that there is much practical difference between the views expressed by Gummow J and those of Lockhart J.

Gummow J took as a starting point a proposition from the judgment of Aickin J in *Minnesota Mining* that a prior publication will not amount to an anticipation of an invention claimed as a combination if it discloses some but not all of the integers of that combination. Thus, as his Honour said, it is important to determine what are the essential integers in a combination and to distinguish them from those integers which are not essential. His Honour said (at 527-8):

"Further, where what is in question is an inessential integer, a device which contains the essential integers will fall within the claim, whether or not an inessential integer is replaced by an obviously equivalent device or omitted altogether; hence the expression 'mechanical equivalent'."

As both Lockhart and Gummow JJ observed, the expressions "workshop adjustments" or "workshop improvements" are expressions used in relation to obviousness rather than novelty. In summarising the law in Australia, Gummow J said (at 531):

"It follows from the English authorities as they have been applied in Australia that, whilst *Hill v Evans* does not require a literal disclosure and something less may suffice, and whilst an alleged paper anticipation is to be treated as read by a skilled addressee, a disclosure will fall short of an anticipation by description of an effective means by which the combination claimed in the patent in suit might be produced, if what is required of the skilled addressee is the exercise of any inventive ingenuity and the taking of any inventive step.

Any references in this context to workshop improvements or variations should not be understood as importing into this field of novelty concepts of obviousness. There

━━━   Advanced Building Systems v Ramset Fasteners *continued*

may be room for disagreement upon the English authorities as to what degree of activity by the skilled addressee may be called for in respect of an alleged anticipation for it still to suffice to destroy novelty."

It seems clear, from his Honour's judgment, that the task is to be approached by determining what are the essential integers of the prior publication and what are the essential integers of the alleged invention. If the difference between the two arises from an inessential integer, then there will have been anticipation. The mere replacement of an inessential integer by something which is a mechanical equivalent will not result in the claimed **[183]** new invention being treated as novel. To that extent, the question whether the difference between the two is merely one involving a mechanical equivalent may have some bearing on the question of whether the integer in question, which is replaced by a mechanical equivalent, is inessential. The emphasis on what is an essential or inessential integer ultimately derives from the generally accepted test for anticipation or want of novelty, enunciated, for example, by Aickin J in *Meyers Taylor Pty Ltd v Vicarr Industries Ltd* (1977) 137 CLR 228 at 235, namely:

"[W]hether the alleged anticipation would, if the patent were valid, constitute an infringement."

The determination of what is an essential or inessential integer in an invention will involve, where the question arises in relation to a patent specification, the interpretation of the patent itself. The rules for interpretation of patents are conveniently set out by Sheppard J in *Décor Corp Pty Ltd v Dart Industries Inc* (1988) 13 IPR 385 at 400 and need not be repeated. See too *Populin v H B Nominees Pty Ltd* (1982) 41 ALR 471 at 476 and *Acme Bedstead Co Ltd v Newlands Brothers Ltd* (1937) 58 CLR 689 at 700.

The question that must therefore be addressed in the present case is what are the essential features of the invention the subject of the patent? In answering that question, the specification must be read and interpreted in light of what was known at the date of the patent: *Marconi v British Radio Telegraph & Telephone Co Ltd* (1911) 28 RPC 181 at 218. That case is instructive because the question whether a transformer, on the one hand, or an auto-transformer, on the other, was used for the purpose of securing the linkage between two circuits so that the cumulative effect of resonance might come into play between them, was held to be, in all the circumstances, a matter of indifference, it being said to be a well-known rule of patent law that no-one who borrows the substance of a patented invention can escape the consequences of infringement by making immaterial variations. The test to determine what is an inessential integer can thus be formulated in the language of Lord Diplock in *Catnic Components Ltd v Hill & Smith Ltd* (1981) 7 FSR 60 at 66 as being:

"[W]hether persons with practical knowledge and experience of the kind of work in which the invention was intended to be used, would understand that strict compliance with a particular descriptive word or phrase appearing in a claim was intended by the patentee to be an essential requirement of the invention so that any variant would fall outside the monopoly claimed, even though it could have no material effect upon the way the invention worked."

For Ramset, it was submitted that the provision of a cable to the distal end of the lever to facilitate release of the locking bolt was not an essential feature or integer of the invention the subject of the Australian patent. Emphasis was given to the fact that the essential feature of the invention was the length of the lever arm, it being a requirement that the lever arm be many times longer than that shown in the US patent. When the safety feature emphasised in the Australian patent was considered, it was submitted, the invention should be seen as one designed to prevent premature release of the clutch, not to facilitate release once the concrete had been lifted into position and, accordingly, the provision of the cable was an inessential feature.

For the cross-respondents, on the other hand, it was submitted that the essential ingredients of the patent comprised a combination of a hoisting **[184]** cable, a shackle, an anchor emplaced in the wall section, a ring clutch, essentially the same as that in the US patent save that it had an elongated lever arm extending generally parallel to the wall section during lifting and in the direction of the upper end, and significantly, for the present case, a release cable attached to the distal end of the lever arm to remotely operate the lever arm by rotating it outwardly and downwardly to a predetermined degree.

With respect, I agree with the cross-respondent. At the very outset of the specifications, emphasis is placed not merely on the issue of safety of use but also on the fact that the invention is "quickly releasable". That this is so is reinforced by the fact that the claims defining the invention themselves stipulate that the invention is to have a release cable attached to the distal end of the lever arm. It seems to me impossible to say that the provision of a release cable is not an essential integer of the invention the subject of the patent.

It is now necessary to turn to the various documents relied upon as anticipations to determine whether any of the apparatus described in them would have infringed the patent. [His Honour found that none of the documents disclosed all of the essential integers of the Advanced Patent.]

■ Publicly-available enabling disclosure

[8.300] In *Stanway Oyster Cylinders Pty Ltd v Marks* (1996) 35 IPR 71 at 74 Drummond J said:

> "It follows from the definition of prior art base in Sch 1 to the 1990 Act and s 7(1) that the prior art information will be sufficient to defeat a patent for want of novelty only where the prior art information discloses the invention in the subject of the patent. Prior disclosure of a physical embodiment or a written description of the patented invention will not therefore destroy the novelty of the invention unless the disclosure makes publicly available all of the essential features of the invention."

See the special circumstance of *Merrell Dow Pharmaceuticals Inc v NH Norton Ltd* (1995) 33 IPR 1. See also *Jupiters Ltd and Others v Neurizon Pty Ltd* (2005) 65 IPR 86 at 113-115; [2005] FCAFC 90 at [135]-[147].

■ Whole contents

■■■■■ Alcatel v Commissioner of Patents ■■■■■

[8.305] *Alcatel NV v Commissioner of Patents* (1996) 35 IPR 255 Federal Court of Australia

BURCHETT J: **[255]** This is an appeal pursuant to s 51 of the *Patents Act 1990* (the Act) from a decision of a Deputy Commissioner of Patents. The matter is wholly governed by the provisions of the Act.

The circumstances that give rise to the question debated in this court are easily stated. After the priority date claimed in the applicant's patent application (2 October 1991), and after the date of the filing of the application (29 September 1992), there was published (on 3 December 1992) a prior patent application, which had been filed earlier and had an earlier priority date. It had been filed on **[256]** 25 May 1992, and its priority date was 31 May 1991. The question thus raised relates to the material to which regard may legitimately be had when the novelty of the invention claimed in the present application is examined. Are disclosures made in the prior patent application to be taken into account, notwithstanding that its publication was delayed until after both the priority date and the date of filing of the application under consideration?

...

[His Honour set out ss 18(1)(b)(i) and 7(1)(c).]

... Both of these sections make reference to "the prior art base", and s 7 also makes reference to "prior art information". Schedule 1 contains, subject to any contrary intention appearing, definitions of those expression "Prior art information" is defined to mean "for the purposes of s 7(1)—information that is part of the prior art base in relation to deciding whether an invention is or is not novel". "Prior art base" is similarly defined so as to include:

"(b) in relation to deciding whether an invention is or is not novel:

...

(ii) information contained in a published specification filed in respect of a complete specification where:
    (A) if the information is, or were to be, the subject of a claim of the specification, the claim has, or would have, a priority date earlier than that of the claim under consideration; and
    (B) the specification was published after the priority date of the claim under consideration; and
    (C) the information was contained in the specification on its filing date and when it was published ..."

... **[257]** ...

Certainly, and unfortunately, the section is not a model of the draftsman's art. But although the logic of the construction may be defective, the meaning is reasonably plain. In such a situation, mere logic must give way to the true legislative intent: *Busby v Chief Manager, Human Resources Department, Australian Telecommunications Commission* (1988) 20 FCR 463 at 468. The interconnected language of s 7 and the definitions in Sch 1 would make no sense unless the word "novel" in s 7 is to be read as referring to the modified concept of novelty that those provisions introduce. Applying para (b) of the definition of "prior art base" to the question to which the definition itself purports to relate (it is a definition "in relation to deciding whether an invention is or is not novel"), the reader is required to take account of information of the kind specified in subpara (ii). Thus the existence of information of that kind may determine whether the invention is or is not novel.

It must be admitted that this conclusion involves the recognition of a small shift, effected by the Act, in the meaning of novelty. ...

If, contrary to my opinion, the verbal and logical infelicity with which s 7 is constructed should be regarded as making the section ambiguous, then resort could be had to the 1984 report of the Industrial Property Advisory Committee on Patents, *Innovation and Competition in Australia*, on which the relevant provisions of the Act were based. That report makes plain the intention to subsume the doctrine of prior claiming, as understood under the 1952 legislation, within an expanded doctrine of novelty. See para 7.3. The committee thought the "prior claiming approach has proved to be unsatisfactory in practice and, in our opinion, it is too narrow". It thought the law should be that a claim to an invention might be anticipated by "any disclosure contained in an earlier specification", that is a specification having an earlier priority date, "notwithstanding that at the priority date of the claim in question, the earlier specification was unpublished and its contents were not publicly available". This was to expand the notion of prior claiming, which was limited to the specific claims made in the earlier specification.

■ Permissible uses

[8.310] The *Patents Act 1990* (Cth) provides that certain uses of an invention will not constitute prior use amounting to anticipation of the patent. Use or publication on or after the priority date will not render it invalid (s 23). Even before the priority date, use or publication in the "prescribed circumstances" will not affect validity if a patent application is made within the prescribed period (s 24(1)(a)). These circumstances are set out in reg 2.2, and include disclosures at a recognised exhibition, in a paper written by the inventor and read before or published by a learned society, and public working of the invention for reasonable trial.

The Regulations have been amended to provide a general 12-month "grace period". From 1 April 2002, where information is disclosed before the priority date of a patent application with the consent of the patentee, either by documentary publication or use, it will not affect the novelty of a subsequently granted patent provided a complete specification is filed within 12 months of the disclosure: see Reg 2.2(1A). This benefit to patent applicants is balanced by an amendment to s 119(3) which now permits a person who makes use of the information disclosed prior to filing a complete specification, by or with the consent of the subsequent patentee, within the prescribed circumstances of s 24(1)(a), to rely upon a "prior use" defence to a claim of infringement.

Experimental use must be limited to a reasonable trial of the invention. In *Longworth v Emerton* (1951) 83 CLR 539 the High Court referred to *Re Newall & Elliot* (1858) 4 CB (NS) 269; 140 ER 1087 and noted that the essential conditions of fact which led to finding that there had been experimental use where (1) the experiment in an open area was necessary to determine the utility of the invention; (2) the performance of the experiment involved unavoidable disclosure; (3) the profit or advantage of the working was accidental; (4) the use was genuinely experimental. In *Longworth's Case* the court did not consider that the public use was in fact experimental. In other cases commercial advantages derived from the use or sale of the test product have been found to defeat a claim of experimental use exemption.

INVENTIVE STEP

[8.315] Where the applicant is seeking a standard patent, the alleged invention must include an inventive step to provide sufficient consideration for the grant of a monopoly. The nature of the requirement of inventive step is set out in s 7(2) and (3) and the definitions of "prior art base" and "prior art information" in Sch 1 (see **[8.260]**).

"*Inventive step*
(2) For the purposes of this Act, an invention is to be taken to involve an inventive step when compared with the prior art base unless the invention would have been obvious to a person skilled in the relevant art in the light of the common general knowledge as it existed in the patent area before the priority date of the relevant

claim, whether that knowledge is considered separately or together with the information mentioned in subsection (3).

(3) The information for the purposes of subsection (2) is:

(a) any single piece of prior art information; or

(b) a combination of any 2 or more pieces of prior art information;

being information that the skilled person mentioned in subsection (2) could, before the priority date of the relevant claim, be reasonably expected to have ascertained, understood, regarded as relevant and, in the case of information mentioned in paragraph (b), combined as mentioned in that paragraph."

Patent monopolies should not be granted for advances which, while technically new and novel, are no more than plain and logical extensions of the prior art, or mere workshop improvements, which could be accomplished by an unimaginative skilled person working in the area who has typical knowledge of the field in question. There must be some imaginative leap. An invention failing to meet the inventive step requirements is termed "obvious".

At examination of a standard patent application, the Examiner is to report whether the invention involves an inventive step on the priority date of each claim (s 45(1)(c)(ii)). An allegation of obviousness or lack of inventive step can also be raised at the opposition stage (s 59(b)) and at the revocation stage (s 138(3)(b)). When re-examining a standard patent under s 97, the Commissioner must report on whether the invention involves an inventive step (s 98(1)(b)).

An innovation patent does not require an inventive step, the requirement is for an innovative step (s 7(4)).

■ Inventive step in Patents Act 1990 (Cth)

[8.320] Making the qualitative assessment of whether there is an inventive step involves:

• classifying the relevant field of technology to which the alleged invention belongs;

• constructing a relevant hypothetical person skilled in the art in that field, or fields, of technology;

• establishing from evidence the common general knowledge of such a person;

• adding to that common general knowledge such additional information as is permitted by s 7(3) and the definition of prior art base;

• assessing what such a person could do with such knowledge; and,

• assessing whether in the light of such knowledge and ability the hypothetical person would consider the alleged invention to be obvious.

In the cases which follow note that the previous wording of Patents Act 1990 (Cth), s 7(3) is cited. This has now been amended, by the Patents Amendment Act 2001 (Cth), Sch 1, cl 4.

■ Overview of the inventiveness requirement

▬▬▬▬▬▬▬ Flexible Steel Lacing v Beltreco ▬▬▬▬▬▬▬

[8.325] Flexible Steel Lacing Co v Beltreco Ltd (2000) 49 IPR 331; [2000] FCA 890 Federal Court of Australia

[Flexible Steel Lacing Co was registered proprietor of two patents related to "pulley lagging". "Lagging material" or "lagging" is a term used in the conveyor industry to describe a material

■■■■■■   Flexible Steel Lacing v Beltreco *continued*

used to cover pulleys, both to protect the pulleys from wear and to increase the friction between the pulley and the conveyor belt and so improve grip and drive. Many lagging materials used in the industry included metal backing plates and sheets which required specific attachment to the pulley. Replacing such lagging was time consuming and expensive and was often difficult or expensive to repair or replace in situ. The applicant claimed to have invented a lagging material and a method of attachment which gave a number of advantages.

Claim one of the first patent read:

> "lagging material for application to the surface of a pulley, said material being in substantially elongate strip form; an upper surface being formed of a predetermined pattern and including a plurality of longitudinally spaced apart, elongate and transversly extending cutting sipes, defining raised portions there between; elongate trim lines being integrally formed or provided at each side of said cutting sipes ..."

A sipe is a groove cut into the surface of the material. The applicants claimed infringement. The defendants cross-petitioned for revocation of the patents on a number of grounds including that the invention was obvious in the light of the prior art relating to lagging materials and methods of attachment. The case was decided on the basis that the patent was invalid for failure to meet the requirements of s 40(3) (see below on issues of sufficiency and clarity). However, his Honour Justice Hely did provide useful discussion of the requirement of inventiveness. Note that this case is being considered in the light the *Patents Act 1952* (Cth). The *Patents Act 1990* (Cth), s 7(3) permits material to be added to common general knowledge.]

HELY J: [365]

Inventive step/obviousness

...

Inventive step is to be judged by reference to the state of common general knowledge in the industry in 1984: *Advanced Building Systems Pty Ltd v Ramset Fasteners Ltd* (1998) 194 CLR 171 [10]. Common general knowledge is "that which is part of the ordinary equipment of all persons engaged in the relevant art, ie, part of their general background knowledge which they put to use in the exercise of that branch of industry or manufacture" (per Aicken J in *Graham Hart (1971) Pty Ltd v SW Hart Pty Ltd* (1978) 141 CLR 305 at 329). The question is whether the invention would have been obvious to a non-inventive worker in the field, equipped with [366] the common general knowledge in that particular field as at the priority date, without regard to documents in existence, but not part of such common general knowledge: *Wellcome Foundation Ltd v VR Laboratories (Aust) Pty Ltd* (1981) 148 CLR 262 at 270.

The process which I have referred to as strip lagging was well-known in the industry prior to 1984. The applicant relied upon that fact in support of its submission as to the proper construction of the patent in suit. But the applicant contends that this patent is new and innovative in its combination of features, particularly the raised portions, plurality of cutting sipes and trim lines in lagging to be applied in strip form. Those features were not to be found in products which had been on the market at June 1984.

However, as Windeyer J pointed out in *Sunbeam Corp v Morphy-Richards (Aust) Pty Ltd* (1961) 180 CLR 98 at 111, when want of subject matter, or lack of inventiveness is asserted, the thing or process claimed as an invention is assumed to be new. It is clear that the fact that something has not been done before is not an answer to a plea of obviousness: *Preston Erection Pty Ltd v Speedy Gantry Hire Pty Ltd* (1998) 43 IPR 74 at 85. As Cotton LJ said in *Britain v Hersch* (1885) 5 RPC 226 at 232:

"I do not agree with the view ... that when anything is done which has not been done before, that is sufficient to justify a patent being obtained for it. In my opinion, it must be a question of whether there is sufficient invention to justify a monopoly being granted by the Crown for the particular thing."

In *Acme Bedstead Co Ltd v Newlands Brothers Ltd* (1936) 58 CLR 689 a well-designed bed containing new features compared with all known previous beds was a good and effective article, but not a patentable invention, since the plaintiff merely applied well-known things to an article to which they had not formerly been applied. At 709 Dixon J said, of the inventor:

"[H]e was not employed in invention but in supplying out of an embarrassing number of choices open to him that which in its practical application would prove most useful and commercially successful."

Invention means more than novelty. There must be an element of invention or inventive ingenuity, although even a very small advance over what is known may qualify as an inventive step: *Winner v Ammar Holdings Pty Ltd* (1993) 25 IPR 273 at 280-281. An improvement which does not go beyond ordinary skilled designing work or mere workshop improvements cannot be considered as having required the exercise of any invention: *Safveans Aktie Bolag v Ford Motor Co (England) Ltd* (1927) 44 RPC 49 at 61. However, in *Samuel Parkes Ltd v Cocker Bros Ltd* (1929) 46 RPC 241 at 248 Tomlin J said:

"Nobody, however, has told me, and I do not suppose that anybody ever will tell me, what is the precise characteristic or quality the presence of which distinguishes invention from a workshop improvement ... ."

The quantum of inventiveness required to establish that the invention is other than obvious has been expressed by various other formulations: the difference between the simple idea which really breaks new ground and an unimaginative extension of well-known techniques into a closely similar area: *Elconnex* (1991) 32 FCR 491 at 507 per Burchett J; whether the subject of the patent "was so obvious that it would at once occur to anyone acquainted with the subject, and desirous of accomplishing the end, or whether it required some invention to [367] devise it": *Vickers, Sons Ltd v Siddell* (1890) 15 AC 496 at 502; (to the same effect, whether if one wished to achieve a particular result, the means of doing so were obvious to persons skilled in the trade: *Acme Bedstead*; whether there is some difficulty overcome, some barrier crossed: *RD Werner v Bailey Aluminium Products Pty Ltd* (1989) 85 ALR 679 at 689 per Lockhart J; whether there is "such an addition to the stock of human knowledge as to entitle the patentee to a monopoly": *Blakey v Latham* (1889) 6 RPC 184 at 189 per Lopez LJ, cited with approval by Cooper J in *Winner* at 293; whether the invention was "beyond the skill of the calling": *Allsop Inc v Bintang Ltd* at 701. Something will be obvious (and hence the patent invalid) if it would appear to anyone skilled in the art but lacking inventive capacity, that to try the step or process would be worthwhile to solve some recognised problem or meet some recognised need: *Coopers Animal Health Australia Ltd v Western Stock Distributors Ltd* (1986) 6 IPR 545 at 565, and the cases there cited.

Whether or not the claimed invention involves an inventive step is ascertained on an objective basis. Because the test is objective, it is irrelevant whether the invention was a matter of chance or luck or the result of long experiment or great intellectual effort.

An inventive step may lie in the choice and management of integers in a combination patent. However, where one starts with a known article or thing and merely substitutes or adds a known device or means to facilitate the better use of the thing, there is a risk of want of inventive step "unless the combination is substantially a new thing": see *Winner* at 294; *Fallshaw Holdings Pty Ltd v Flexello Castors & Wheels PLC* (1993) 26 IPR 565 at 568. But it is the inventiveness of the combination as a whole that must be examined; it is impermissible to determine inventiveness by a piecemeal examination, integer by integer: *Elconnex* (1992) 25 IPR 173 at 184.

The applicant contends that neither of the respondent's experts expresses an opinion that the invention claimed is obvious, or that it is a solution to a problem which a skilled worker would have reached as a matter of routine. It will be necessary to return to the expert evidence in due course. The respondent submits that such evidence would be inadmissible on the basis of the statement in *British Celanese Ltd v Courtaulds Ltd* (1935) 52 RPC 171 at 196 that whilst an expert witness is entitled to give evidence as to the state of the art at any given time, and is entitled to explain the meaning of technical terms, he is not entitled to say whether any given step or alteration is obvious, that being a question for the Court. ...

In Blanco White, *Patents for Inventions* (5th ed) at 4-228 it is said: [368]

> "Apart from evidence directed to establishing the technical facts and the conditions and circumstances of the art and industry concerned, it is customary to adduce upon the question of obviousness evidence from expert witnesses as to whether (had they been faced with the alleged inventor's problem) the invention would at the relevant date have been obvious to them. There is usually a conflict of evidence as to this ... ."

It is, however, noted that the balance of the paragraph, which I have not quoted, suggests that this type of ad hoc expert evidence may have its problems and is not as useful or cogent as other evidence which might be called on the point, such as people being faced with a problem, and solving or failing to solve it.

In my view, whatever may have been the position when *British Celanese* was decided, expert evidence that a particular step or alteration would have been obvious to a skilled worker in the field, is admissible on the issue of inventive step In some cases it may be difficult to reach a conclusion on that issue without evidence on that matter.

In *British Celanese Ltd v Courtaulds Ltd* (1933) 50 RPC 63, 90 (at first instance), Clauson J said:

> "I have a man properly informed in the art who knows so and so. I can infer that everybody properly informed in the art will have some knowledge, because they have exactly the same opportunity as he has ... I must be satisfied that he has not an excess of any peculiar or special sort of knowledge, but that what he is telling me is what he has acquired in his ordinary practice as a man engaged in the art."

A body of evidence was placed before me as to the lagging products available in Australia prior to June 1984 and as to publications which described the features of those products. Of the products referred to in the evidence, those which assumed the greatest significance in submissions were: Bandag Lagging: Exhibit GW4 Gortread: Exhibit GW5 ETR70 : Exhibit GW7. There was some evidence that skilled people in the field of conveyor systems regularly had recourse to certain publications before June 1984 (for example, Norrish 6/12/99 at [33]), and there was evidence as to the general availability of some products. Except to the extent that specific reference is made hereafter, the common general knowledge amongst skilled people in the field of conveyor systems in 1984, was sought to be established by inference from the disclosures contained in the products and publications to which I have referred.

[His Honour considered evidence about these products and publications in some detail and continued:] [380]

▬▬▬▬   Flexible Steel Lacing v Beltreco *continued*

I accept that the [applicant's] product has been a commercial success. I accept that it is a well-designed product, which is user friendly and attractively [381] priced. There may be many explanations of commercial success. It may demonstrate a long felt want which is suggestive of invention. But there may be many other explanations such as, for example, good workmanship, price or qualities outside the claims of the invention.

...

In the circumstances of the present case I cannot infer from the fact of commercial success that the combination of features to be found in the patent is a substantially new thing. The remarks of Lord Herschell in *Longbottom v Shaw* (1891) 8 RPC 333, 336 are apposite:

"... If it were shown that the defects which this apparatus is designed to remedy, or does remedy, were defects which had been felt, and the knowledge of which had come to the public so that there was a demand for a new apparatus which did not possess those defects, and if it were shown that that demand had lasted for a considerable time, so that men's minds were likely to have been engaged upon a mode of remedying those defects, and they were not remedied until the apparatus was devised for which the patent is taken out, no doubt that would have afforded considerable evidence that the adaptation or arrangement of the patentee was not obvious, inasmuch as you would then have a demand for some considerable time not met although known, and the fact that it was not met for a considerable time though known would indicate that the mode by which it was ultimately met could not have been so obvious as otherwise might have been supposed."

The commercial success is not shown to have been due to having overcome some defect in the prior art where the need for a solution was long felt. Lagging may not have been manufactured in that form before, because to use the words of Mr Masters "nobody had bothered to do it because the call was not necessarily there" (T 187 lns 8-12).

I am conscious of the "seductive clarity of hindsight": *Allsop Inc v Bintang Ltd* at 701, that "a scintilla of inventiveness is sufficient" and that "no smallness or simplicity will prevent a patent being good": *Meyers Taylor Pty Ltd v Vicarr Industries Ltd* (1977) 137 CLR 228, 249. Nonetheless it seems to me that the lagging the subject of the claims of the patent [382] in suit was not the product of invention, and added nothing to the stock of knowledge about pulley lagging, or materials for use in pulley lagging as at the relevant time.

■ "Mosaicing"

▬▬▬▬▬▬▬▬▬▬ **Firebelt v Brambles Australia** ▬▬▬▬▬▬▬▬▬▬

[8.330] *Firebelt Pty Ltd v Brambles Australia Ltd* (2000) 51 IPR 531; [2000] FCA 1689 Federal Court of Australia

SPENDER, DRUMMOND, MANSFIELD JJ: [532]
This is an appeal from orders made by a single judge of this Court (Dowsett J) on 10 June 1999 in proceedings involving an invention which is the subject of Australian Letters Patent No 657082. The patentee is Firebelt Pty Ltd (Firebelt). The description in the provisional specification for the invention is:

"This invention relates to a refuse vehicle and in particular, to a sideloading refuse vehicle and more particularly, but not limited to, an automated sideloading refuse vehicle for simultaneous collection, but separate storage of garbage and/or recyclable wastes in the one vehicle."

Firebelt brought proceeding ... against Brambles Australia Lt ... and Cooloola Shire Council alleging infringement of the petty paten ... By a defence and further amended cross-claim ... Brambles denied infringement, and by the cross-claim alleged that the invention defined in claims 1, 2 and 3 of the petty patent is not a patentable invention within the meaning of s 138(3) of the *Patents Act 1990* (the Act). Five grounds [of invalidity] were alleged: including, want of inventive step ... In the cross-claim, Brambles sought, inter alia, revocation of the petty patent.

... [534]

Lack of inventive step

It is common ground that this petty patent is governed solely by the Act. The lack of inventive step depends upon a consideration of s 18 of the Act and related definition.

[The Court set out the text of ss 138 and 18 and Sch 1, definition of "prior art base".] [535]

The learned primary judge held that there had been certain disclosures in July and November 1991 by a company TWT Formark Pty Ltd (TWT Formark), a company associated with an inventor called Mr Colin Joseph Hickey. At that time Mr Hickey had filed, but there had not been published, a provisional specification for a Hickey invention, which invention was entitled "A System for Collecting Recyclable Products". The proposal on which Mr Hickey was working was very similar in effect to that of the claimed invention. It will be necessary to make detailed consideration later as to the nature of the disclosures and of the differences between what was known by a skilled but non-inventive worker in the field as a result of those disclosures, together with the common general knowledge of such a person, and the claimed invention. The complete specification into which Mr Hickey's provisional specification matured was filed after the 1992 priority date, and so is not an anticipation within subpara (a) (i) of the definition of "prior art base" in the Act.

[The Court set out the text of s 7(2) and (3).] [536]

The extent to which the prohibition of "*mosaicing*" various pieces of documentary or other prior disclosures for the purpose of determining common general knowledge, as established by the High Court in *Minnesota Mining & Manufacturing Co v Beiersdorf (Australia) Ltd* (1980) 144 CLR 253 (the *3M* case), has been relaxed by the provisions in s 7 of the Act, may be a matter of some interest. Burchett J in *Tidy Tea v Unilever* (1995) 32 IPR 405 suggested that the provisions in s 7 seemed to be designed to overcome the rejection in the *3M* case of the availability, when obviousness is being considered, of specifications of prior patents not actually proved to be part of the common general knowledge at the relevant time. Burchett J noted that before mosaicing might be carried out, the mosaic has to be one that can be put together by a skilled worker with no inventive capacity. The extent to which evidence is necessary is a matter of some debate, and the issue is by no means determined.

The contention for the appellant here was that there was insufficient evidence to enable his Honour to conclude what was within common general knowledge in respect of the skilled or notional addressee. This issue has to be determined on the basis of the provisions of s 7(2) of the Act.

It is necessary to have regard to the patent in respect of which want of inventiveness is alleged. ... Under the heading "Background Art" is a statement concerning the necessity of

■■■■■■   Firebelt v Brambles Australia *continued*

"new, convenient and economical approaches to garbage collection and recycling". It says that "sorting of recyclables from domestic garbage after collection is generally uneconomical", and as an "Outline of the Invention" it is said that:

> "The present invention has, as its primary object, to provide a useful alternative to the aforementioned prior art."

In summary, the contention is that the invention permits the collection and separate storage of pre-sorted garbage and recyclables.
    ... [537]
    As the consistory clause in the claim makes clear, there is no particular type of lid-opening device claimed.

    It is important, particularly in this case, not to ignore the true nature of a patentable combination. A patentable combination involves, as a matter of language in the claims, a cooperation of features, each of which may be known, to produce a new result or a known result in a more useful way. In *Palmer v Dunlop Perdriau Rubber Co Ltd* (1937) 59 CLR 30, Dixon J said at 73:

> "[T]he characteristic which a combination of known integers must possess in order to afford subject matter is mutual relation in the operation of such integers."

And at 75:

> "[T]he combination contained in the patentee's machine falls outside the class where the integers continue, so to speak, their independence and within that where a new [538] co-operation is established so that by an adaptation of each integer to the working of every other integer an entirety is provided which is new and implies invention. In saying this, I am speaking of the machine described in the specification as distinguished from the combination or combinations stated in the various claims. This actual machine does, I think, bring the integers sufficiently into relation in the production of the one article as an entirety."

In a well-known passage in the *3M* case, Aickin J said at 292:

> "The notion of common general knowledge itself involves the use of that which is known or used by those in the relevant trade. It forms the background knowledge and experience which is available to all in the trade in considering the making of new products, or the making of improvements in old, and it must be treated as being used by an individual as a general body of knowledge. I do not with respect think that it is correct to describe that process as the making of a mosaic although it has often been so described, a usage which however may be misleading. The process of applying such common general knowledge to the solution of a problem is not a process of picking out individual pieces of information and combining them, including inferences from known facts and known principles, as well as the application of such principles. The making of a mosaic prohibited in the case of an allegation of want of novelty is the picking out of individual items of information from prior publications or prior objects and assembling them together so as to give them an appearance of unity and then alleging that such mosaic reveals the very thing claimed. That is an understandable, though not a permissible, process.
>
>   In the case of alleged lack of an inventive step the question of making a mosaic must operate (if at all) in a very different matter. An allegation of want of inventive step is not made out by saying you may take one or two, or twenty one or twenty two,

■■■■■■ Firebelt v Brambles Australia *continued*

prior publications and then select from them appropriate extracts or pieces of information, which will add up to the invention claimed and so demonstrate that it was obvious. So to proceed is to mistake the nature of an invention and the nature of the objection of obviousness. *The question is, is the invention itself obvious*, not whether a diligent searcher might find pieces from which there might have been selected the elements which make up the patent. If this were not so, there could never be a valid patent for a new combination of old integers. The proper question is not whether it would have been obvious to the hypothetical addressee who was presented with an ex post facto selection of prior specifications that elements from them could be combined to produce a new product or process. It is rather whether it would have been obvious to a non-inventive skilled worker in the field to select from a possibly very large range of publications the particular combination subsequently chosen by the opponent in the glare of hindsight and also whether it would have been obvious to that worker to select the particular combination of integers from those selected publications. In the case of a combination patent the invention will lie in the selection of integers, a process which will necessarily involve rejection of other possible integers. The prior existence of publications revealing those integers, as separate items, and other possible integers does not of itself make an alleged invention obvious. It is the selection of the integers out of, perhaps many possibilities, which must be shown to be obvious." (Emphasis added.)

We have set out this extensive passage, because it is particularly apposite to the present issue.

It was submitted on behalf of the appellant that the primary judge failed to appreciate the essence of a combination patent and, as a consequence, failed to apply the proper test on the issue of want of inventive step.

Despite the usual industry and learning of the submissions by Mr Garnsey QC, senior counsel for Firebelt, those submissions and the criticisms made of the primary judge's dealing with, and conclusion on, the issue of inventiveness fail **[539]** properly to recognise that the test for want of novelty is not the same as the test for want of inventive step. The test for want of inventive step, which is expressed in s 7(2) of the Act, is not by any means the same as whether there has been infringement of one invention by another, nor is it appropriate to approach the matter on the basis of any "reverse infringement". Yet the submissions on behalf of Firebelt appear to fall into this type of error. The error into which the primary judge fell, according to the appellant, is "the error of saying you can take some of the features of Hickey, which were known, exclude others, add on two of the features of Richards, and say therefore there is no invention to the Richards' combination." It was submitted for the appellant:

"It is impermissible ... to say out of a different combination we take these bits of known features, and if I tried to do this I would have added these other two bits in just as a matter of course ... ."

In the course of submissions it was put by Drummond J to Mr Garnsey:

"What you've done is devised a combination that does exactly the same thing but you've addressed something that Mr Hickey didn't address, namely, how are you going to open the lid. Why does that make the whole of your combination inventive? I can see why you might be able to get a patent—indeed I think you've applied for a patent for the device that will open the lid, but why does that step, against a background of Hickey's combination, make the whole of your combination inventive?"

██████   Firebelt v Brambles Australia *continued*

The answer to this question, according to the appellant, was:

> "[W]e say what the law says one must compare is this combination as a whole with all its essential features as against that combination as a whole with all its essential features."

When one looks at what the primary judge did and what test he applied, it is clear that his Honour approached the issue of inventiveness correctly, and his conclusion on want of inventiveness was open to him on the evidence.

It is trite, of course, that where one has an invention that is a combination of well-known integers, the inventive step in the invention lies in the combination. The primary judge was fully alive to this central question on the issue of obviousness. His Honour said:

> "It is not disputed that each of the integers of the petty patent claims was known in the patent area before the priority date. The issue of absence of an inventive step requires an examination of the obviousness or otherwise of the combination."

The primary judge correctly observed:

> "Section 7(2) dictates a consideration of what would have been obvious to a person skilled in the relevant art in the light of two matters, namely common general knowledge as it existed before the priority date, and prior art information made publicly available, being information that the skilled person in question could, before the expiry date, be reasonably expected to have ascertained, understood and regarded as relevant to work in the relevant art. A person skilled in the relevant art is said to be a 'non-inventive skilled worker in the field'. See *Minnesota Mining & Manufacturing Co v Beiersdorf (Australia) Ltd* (1979-80) 144 CLR 253 at 293 per Aickin J."

The contention by Brambles, both at trial and before us, is that when one has regard to the disclosures at two presentations made by TWT Formark in July and November of 1991, and common general knowledge of a non-inventive skilled worker in the field, the Firebelt invention was obvious, applying the test imposed by s 7(2) of the Act. His Honour found that what was disclosed on each **[540]** of those occasions had the consequence that such information was publicly available for the purposes of ss 7 and 18. His Honour found:

> "It seems clear that such disclosures would be widely distributed in the waste management industry. It is also reasonable to infer that this would include distribution to the relatively small number of companies engaged in building trucks for waste collection."

Dealing with the issue of novelty, his Honour found that the disclosure at those presentations did not extend to a disclosure of each of the integers of the combination patent of Firebelt. What his Honour did find was that, having regard to what was disclosed on those earlier occasions, and having regard to the evidence of witnesses concerning not only the features in the TWT Formark proposal as revealed at the two presentations in 1991, but also concerning the common general knowledge of a skilled worker in the field about those features which were not part of the TWT Formark proposal, the combination of the old integers which constitutes the claimed invention of Firebelt was obvious.

■ Persons skilled in the art and common general knowledge

▭▭▭▭▭▭   ICI Chemicals & Polymers v Lubrizol   ▭▭▭▭▭▭

[8.335] *ICI Chemicals & Polymers Ltd v Lubrizol Corp Inc* (1999) 45 IPR 577; [1999] FCA 345
Federal Court of Australia

[This case concerned chemicals used in refrigeration equipment, CFC's (Chlorofluorocarbons) and HCFC's (which use a combination of hydrogen, chlorine, fluorine and carbon) were often used as a refrigerant but are now accepted to have a detrimental effect on the ozone layer of the Earth's stratosphere. There were demands from environmentalists and governments for a reduction or ban in use of CFC's as refrigerants and lubricants. This was reflected in the *Montreal Protocol on Substances that Deplete the Ozone Layer*, an international treaty to which Australia is a signatory. Attention turned to the possible use of refrigerants which used only hydrogen, fluorine and carbon known as HFCs. Refrigeration technology however requires the use of a particularly flexible lubricant and the traditional mineral oil based lubricants used with CFCs and HCFCs were not suitable for use with HFCs.

Lubrizol was the registered proprietor of a patent for a soluble organic lubricant suitable for use with HFCs. ICI brought proceedings under s 128 for a declaration that communications between Lubrizol and Woolworths and others, who were customers of ICI, were unjustifiable threats, and further under s 138, seeking revocation of the Lubrizol patent alleging inter alia that there was no inventive step. Lubrizol brought proceedings under s 120 seeking injunctions to prevent Woolworths and others making a composition of two products manufactured by ICI or operating refrigeration systems using the composition of the two products. Lubrizol alleged that making or using this composition would infringe its patent.]

EMMETT J: [596]

Obviousness

I have referred above to s 138(3)(b). In the context of obviousness, s 18(1)(b)(ii) of the 1990 Act relevantly provides that a "patentable invention is an invention that, so far as claimed in any claim ... when compared with the prior art base as it existed before the priority date of that claim ... involves *an inventive step*". Section 7(2) then provides that an invention is to be taken to involve an inventive step when compared with the art base "unless the invention would have been obvious to a person skilled in the relevant art in the light of the common general knowledge as it existed in the patent area before the priority date of the relevant claim".

In considering the question of whether the alleged invention of Lubrizol involved an inventive step, it is necessary to:
(a) determine the nature of the alleged invention and the alleged inventive step;
(b) identify the relevant art or field;
(c) ascertain the common general knowledge in that art or field at the priority date;
(d) determine whether the alleged invention would have been obvious to a hypothetical non-inventive person or persons skilled in the relevant art or field, equipped with the common general knowledge so ascertained.

In determining whether the invention would have been obvious, the following circumstances may also be of relevance:
• whether the work involved in the invention was a matter of routine;
• whether the invention satisfied a long felt need;

▬▬▬▬   ICI Chemicals & Polymers v Lubrizol *continued*

- the commercial success of the invention;
- whether others sought but failed to find the invention;
- whether the invention has been copied.

...

The relevant art and the skilled worker

The relevant art or field is, clearly enough, the manufacture and supply of hydrocarbons and lubricants suitable for combination and use together for purposes such as refrigeration and air conditioning. The skilled worker in that field could be expected to have practical knowledge of the chemical and other properties required of a lubricant, knowledge of the likely introduction of R-134a to replace CFCs and HCFCs and knowledge of the unsatisfactory nature of mineral oils as lubricants in that context.

The notional skilled reader may not be limited to a single person but may be a team whose combined skills would normally be employed in that art—Sachs LJ in *General Tire & Rubber Co v Firestone Tyre & Rubber Co Ltd* [1972] RPC 457 at 485, cited with approval in *Leonardis v Sartis No 1 Pty Ltd* (1996) 67 FCR 126 at 146. ICI contended that the skills of Mr Dobney and Mr Harrington would have been available to the hypothetical skilled worker. ICI also contended that if chemical matters went beyond the expertise of Mr Harrington, an academic or organic chemist, such as Professor Rae could be consulted. Accordingly, ICI contended, the skills of somebody in the position of Professor Rae should also be regarded as available to the hypothetical skilled worker.

However, there is no evidence that skilled practitioners in the field in fact consulted academic organic chemists for the purposes of devising refrigerant and lubricant compositions. Neither Mr Harrington nor Mr Dobney said that that was his practice and Professor Rae accepted that he had never made such a composition or advertised his ability to do so. Nor had he been asked to do so. Neither Lubrizol nor ICI had academic organic chemists as part of their team. There is no basis for concluding that a chemist having skills beyond that of an industrial chemist such as Mr Harrington would be regarded as a practitioner in the field which I have identified above. I do not consider, therefore, that the particular academic skills of Professor Rae should be regarded as being available to a hypothetical skilled worker for the purposes of this question.

[598] Common general knowledge

Professor Rae advanced the proposition that, from the point of view of a chemist, materials that are likely to show the greatest compatibility, in terms of solubility and miscibility, are those that are similar in terms of polarity. Polar materials are miscible with each other but not with non-polar materials. A simple example is water and oil. Water is a highly polar material and does not mix to any extent with oil which is non polar. ...

[His Honour then reviewed further elaboration by Professor Rae concerning the measurement of polarity by considering the interaction of molecular dipoles with an electric field. This measurement and some known properties of existing lubricants and refrigerants led Professor Rae to conclude that synthetic esters may have been suitable as lubricants for R-134a because he knew them to be polar substances. He said that he would have readily expected that polar refrigerants such as R-22 would be miscible with polar lubricants and that a mixture of R-22 and a non polar refrigerant such as R-115 would also be miscible with polar lubricants. His Honour then continued:] [599]

ICI contended that the relevance of polarity with respect to miscibility, as described by Professor Rae, was part of the common general knowledge as at April 1989. Dr Jolley acknowledged that it is drummed into a chemist from the beginning of his learning that "like dissolve in like", that "high polarity likes high polarity" and that "low polarity likes low polarity". The kinds of general chemical structures that give higher polarity and so forth were also part of that learning. He said that those matters were a "general thing that one learns as basic knowledge" as a chemist. He acknowledged that, in the course of his experimentation, he was considering polarity as one of the possible indicia of a suitable lubricant. Indeed, in an internal Lubrizol memorandum, Dr Jolley said the following:

> "[The lubricant] should ideally be compatible with neoprene, nitrile, and nylon elastomer. It is expected that a high amount of polarity will be needed in order to give the material a reasonable chance to be soluble in the refrigerant."

The question, however, is whether common knowledge of principles of polarity within the field of refrigeration engineering rendered the choices found in the Claims for the Patent *obvious* to a person skilled in that field. While polarity might be a starting point, it was not a self-evident basis for choosing an appropriate lubricant to use in conjunction with HFC's generally or R-134a in particular.

The notion of common general knowledge involves the use of that which is known or used by those who are in the relevant field or area. It forms the background knowledge and experience which is available to all in that field in considering the making of new products or making of improvements in old products. It must be treated as being used by an individual as a general body of knowledge—*Minnesota Mining & Manufacturing Co Pty Ltd v Beiersdorf (Australia) Ltd* (1980) 144 CLR 253 at 292.

The common general knowledge is the technical background to the hypothetical skilled worker in the relevant art. It is not limited to material which might be memorised and retained at the front of the skilled workers mind but also includes material in the field in which he is working which he knows exists and to which he would refer as a matter of course. It might, for example, include:

- standard texts and handbooks;
- standard English dictionaries;
- technical dictionaries relevant to the field;
- magazines and other publications specific to the field.

[His Honour set out a detailed list of products, processes, knowledge and an article which he found was part of the common general knowledge in the field.] [600]

Inventive step

A distinction must be drawn between an inventive step on the one hand and the trial and error which forms part of the normal industrial function of a skilled worker in the relevant field. If it would be apparent to the skilled worker in the relevant field that a proposal is "worth trying" there is no inventive step in so trying—see, for example, *Coopers Animal Health Australia Ltd v Western Stock Distributors Ltd* (1986) 6 IPR 545 at 569-70. If, in the state of knowledge to be attributed to the notional skilled worker, he should have been put on the track of such a solution, and would have recognised that the combination would be worth trying, the solution may be considered to be obvious in the relevant sense—per Buckley LJ in *Tetra Molectric Ltd v Japan Imports Ltd* [1976] RPC 547 at 583.

However, the test of whether something was "worth trying" involves [601] questions of degree—*Beecham Group Ltd (Amoxycillin) Application* [1980] RPC 261 at 291. If something is obvious then one can go straight to it. An inventive step, however, does not necessarily have to be a flash of inspiration. It may equally involve something which it might be predicted

████████   ICI Chemicals & Polymers v Lubrizol *continued*

could possibly be found down some generally defined track by a patient enough searcher. However, the question may be as to how much research a searcher may have to do if he is to achieve the desired result. A patient searcher is as much entitled to the benefits of a monopoly as someone who hits upon an invention by some lucky chance or an inspiration. If the expectation of success is sufficiently predictable, and the effort involved is not going to be very great, it may well be that there is no inventive step. On the other hand, if the expectation of ultimate success is doubtful and the effort involved is great, the person undertaking the work should be entitled to a monopoly—*American Cyanamid Co v Berk Pharmaceuticals Ltd* [1976] RPC 231 per Whitford J at 257. A patent monopoly is awarded, not to reward genius but to encourage the disclosure of information which is of value to the public in that it takes the store of knowledge ahead by the requisite "inventive step".

Several considerations are indicative of an inventive step in the present case. The finding of a composition of refrigerant and lubricant which was non-harmful to the ozone layer was a matter of significance. To identify a composition that met the requirements of the Montreal Protocol would be to satisfy a public need. The need was urgent. ... The fact that the problem had not been solved in Europe and America during that three year period is strongly indicative of invention.

Where a problem awaits solution for some time and the invention is novel and superior to what has gone before and is subsequently widely used, it is very difficult to say that there is not present that scintilla of invention necessary to support a patent—*Commonwealth Industrial Gases v MWA Holdings Pty Ltd* (1970) 180 CLR 160 at 164-5 and *Minnesota Mining & Manufacturing Co v Beiersdorf (Australia) Ltd* (1980) 144 CLR 253 at 298.

[His Honour then conducted a thorough review of evidence about the methodologies of attempts to solve the problem of selection of a suitable lubricant made by ICI, Lubrizol and others and concluded:] [607]

In all the circumstances outlined above, I am satisfied that the isolation of the categories of esters identified in the Lubrizol patent was not obvious to the skilled worker in the refrigeration and air conditioning field in Australia in April 1989. Accordingly, the ground of revocation contemplated by the combination of s 138(3)(b) and 18(1)(b)(ii) has not been made out.

Notes

[8.340] The appropriately-skilled addressee will clearly need to be identified in each case depending upon the relevant field of invention and the sophistication and skill level appropriate to a worker in that field. Depending upon the particular field of invention this could be:

- "highly qualified scientists" (*American Cyanamid Co v Ethicon* [1979] RPC 215);
- a number of technical specialists in different fields (*Osram Lamp Works Ltd v Popes Electric Lamp Co Ltd* (1917) 34 RPC 369);
- a team (*General Tire & Rubber Co Ltd v Firestone Tyre & Rubber Co Ltd* [1972] RPC 457); or
- in areas where the practice is to combine skills from different disciplines a notional skilled worker made up from the combination of skills: (*Olin Mathieson Chemical Corp v Biorex Laboratories Ltd* [1970] RPC 157).

See also the Australian Patent Office, *Manual of Practice and Procedure*, Vol 2: "National", para 4.2.5.3.

▰▰▰▰ Manual of Practice and Procedure, Vol 2 ▰▰▰▰

[8.345] Australian Patent Office, *Manual of Practice and Procedure*, Vol 2, "National"
See also electronic version of manual Volume 2 "National" 2.7 **Inventive Step**.

4.1.4 Assessing inventive step in examination
The procedure of courts relies upon the evidence of expert witnesses when seeking an answer to the question "is it obvious?". Unlike courts, examiners do not have access to evidence from the person skilled in the art, and so must assess "obviousness" based on their own knowledge.

Such assessment can be difficult. The examiner's initial consideration of whether a claim is obvious can be coloured by:
(a) ex post facto analysis;
(b) judging the merit of the invention;
(c) the motivation for the invention;
(d) failing to recognise that an inventive step requires no more than a scintilla of invention;
(e) failing to determine the common general knowledge appropriate to the person skilled in the art; and
(f) failing to consider all relevant issues.

Courts have also discussed the problem of ex post facto dissection of the invention. In *Meyers Taylor Pty Ltd v Vicarr Industries Ltd* (1977) 137 CLR 228 at 242, Aiken J said that "subsequent analysis of the invention—'the dissection of the invention'—is not helpful in resolving the question of obviousness".

4.1.4.1 The problem solution approach
An approach used by the courts to avoid this problem is the problem/solution approach. See *HPM Industries Pty Ltd v Gerard Industries Ltd* (1957) 98 CLR 424 at 437, where Williams J said:

"If the invention were novel it would nevertheless fail for want of subject matter if in the light of what was common general knowledge in the particular art, it lacked inventive ingenuity because the solution would have been obvious to any person of ordinary skill in the art *who set out to solve the problem*."

Other examples are *Hart v Hart* (1978) 141 CLR 305, *Allsop Inc & Another Inc v Bintang Ltd* (1989) AIPC 90-615 and *Winner v Ammar Holdings,* (1993) AIPC 90-971.

The problem/solution approach is based on the question of whether the claimed invention would have been obvious to a person skilled in the relevant art when faced with a particular problem.

This approach, as applied to examination for inventive step, ensures that the examiner's consideration of whether a claim lacks an inventive step:
(a) is valid and sustainable; and
(b) identifies all the issues relevant to establishing lack of inventive step.

4.1.4.2 The problem/solution approach involves the following steps:
(a) construe the specification under examination and determine the problem the claimed invention solves (see para 4.2.4 below);
(b) identify the person skilled in the art in the field of the problem (see para 4.2.5 below);
(c) determine whether, *in the context of the problem*, the citation is one that the person skilled in the art could be expected to have ascertained, understood, and regarded as relevant (see para 4.2.6 below);
(d) determine the disclosure of the citation, and the common general knowledge;
(e) determine whether, *in the context of the problem*, the claimed invention is one of:

▬▬▬▬   Manual of Practice and Procedure, Vol 2 *continued*

- a technical equivalent of the citation;
- a workshop improvement of the citation;
- an obvious selection or special inducement; or
- an obvious combination of features of common general knowledge;

(f) consider whether the claimed invention involves:
- the citation teaching away from the solution;
- practical difficulties overcome in seeking the solution;
- identifying the "real nature" of the problem (see para 4.3.7 below);

(g) if relevant, consider whether there has been a prior perceived need using the tests of:
- long felt need;
- failure of others;
- copying of invention in preference to prior art;
- commercial success;

(h) an objection of lack of inventive step only arises where it can be shown that a person skilled in the art would, in solving the problem, have taken the necessary steps to reach the claimed solution. In practice, this will be the case if the requirements under (c) and (e) are met, and those under (f) and (g) are not met.

4.1.5 Ex post facto analysis

... However examiners should remember that the question of obviousness is to be answered by adopting the position of the person skilled in the art and looking forward to finding a solution to the problem, and not by ex post facto reasoning which involves taking the known solution and working backwards to the problem by a succession of apparently easy steps. As stated in *Palmer v Dunlop Perdriau Rubber Co Ltd* (1937) 59 CLR 30 at 61:

> "It is frequently possible to take, as it were, a patent to pieces, and then, beginning with one piece, to show how, in order to obtain one result, step A must be taken; in order to obtain another particular result, step B must be taken—and so on until one has the whole combination for which inventive quality is claimed. If the analysis is taken into sufficient detail, every single step in the development of an invention, taken separately, can be shown to be obvious."

[8.350] See also *Minnesota Mining & Manufacturing Co v Beiersdorf (Aust) Ltd* (1980) 144 CLR 253; *Meyers Taylor v Vicarr Industries Ltd* (1977) 137 CLR 228; *British Acoustic Films Ltd v Nettlefold Productions* (1936) 53 RPC 221; *British Westinghouse Electric & Manufacturing Co Ltd v Braulik* (1910) 27 RPC 209.

▬▬▬▬▬ **Aktiebolaget Hässle v Alphapharm** ▬▬▬▬▬

[8.355] *Aktiebolaget Hässle v Alphapharm Pty Limited* (2002) 212 CLR 411

GLEESON CJ, GAUDRON, GUMMOW AND HAYNE JJ: **[418]**

The appellants appeal from a decision of the Full Court of the Federal Court *Aktiebolaget Hässle v Alphapharm Pty Ltd* (2000) 51 IPR 375; ... It is convenient to refer to the appellants without distinction as "Astra".

■■■■■■   Aktiebolaget Hässle v Alphapharm *continued*

The Patent
The Patent claims an oral pharmaceutical preparation in the form of a tablet, capsule or pellet containing omeprazole as the active ingredient ..... When absorbed in the upper part of the small intestine it inhibits gastric fluid secretions, and is useful in the treatment of gastric and duodenal ulcers. Astra held Standard Patent No 529,654 under the 1952 Act for this compound ("the compound patent"). This patent has expired and was not in suit in the present litigation.

... There was a problem in the administration of the drug which was answered with the formulation claimed in the Patent.

...

[The objective was to formulate omeprazole to allow it to be administered orally. To be effective if taken orally the omeprazole compound would have to be protected from moisture and stomach acids when swallowed but be able to disperse in the top of the lower intestine. A useful technique used in such formulations was to employ an enteric coating. However omeprazole was found to degrade in direct contact with an enteric coating. The final solution for which Astra had obtained their patent was to combine three integers, first the active ingredient omeprazole, second an inert covering layer separating omeprazole from the enteric coating and third an enteric coating] **[419]**

The tablet or pellet thus claimed is a combination in the proper sense of that term, combining three elements which interact with each other to produce the new product; it is the interaction which is the essential requirement of invention and such a combination may be constituted by integers each of which is old or some of which are new *Commonwealth Industrial Gases Ltd v MWA Holdings Pty Ltd* (1970) 180 CLR 160 at 163; *Minnesota Mining and Manufacturing Co v Beiersdorf (Australia) Ltd* (1980) 144 CLR 253 at 266; *Firebelt Pty Ltd v Brambles Australia Ltd* (2002) 76 ALJR 816 at 819-820 [21]; 188 ALR 280 at 285.

Thus, for example, in the present case, it is not to the point that of the three integers it may be said that omeprazole was known as an acid labile compound and that it was known that enteric coatings were resistant to acids. The question for decision concerns the ingenuity of the combination, not of the employment of any one or more integers taken individually. Astra complains that this analysis by dissection is what the Patent has wrongly been subjected to by the Full Court.

...**[420]**

The litigation
The respondent ("Alphapharm") markets "generic" drug formulations. In 1998, as the term of the compound patent neared its end, Alphapharm commenced steps to import and sell in Australia a pharmaceutical preparation containing omeprazole for therapeutic use in the treatment of gastrointestinal diseases. ....

...

The primary judge (Lehane J) held (1999) 44 IPR 593 that, assuming validity, the acts threatened by Alphapharm would constitute infringement of several of the claims of the Patent. However, his Honour ... made an order for revocation, with the result that the claim for infringement failed. The ground upon which his Honour determined that there should be revocation was obviousness. ....

...

An appeal by Astra to the Full Court (Wilcox, Merkel and **[421]** Emmett JJ) ((2000) 51 IPR 375) was dismissed. The Full Court upheld the finding of Lehane J as to obviousness, but its reasoning in some significant respects differed from that of his Honour. ... The issue on the

███████   Aktiebolaget Hässle v Alphapharm *continued*

appeal to this Court by Astra is whether the Full Court erred in not rejecting the finding by the primary judge with respect to obviousness. Were Astra to succeed in this Court, that would leave unresolved the balance of the issues before the Full Court. ...

The Australian legislation
Section 100(1) of the 1952 Act relevantly stated:

"A standard patent may be revoked, ... on one or more of the following grounds, but on no other ground:

(e) that the invention, ... was obvious and did not involve an inventive step having regard to what was known or used in Australia on or before the priority date of that claim".

...

The 1952 Act was repealed by s 230 of the *Patents Act 1990* (Cth) ("the 1990 Act"). The 1990 Act commenced on 30 April 1991. The 1990 Act deals with obviousness in terms which differ from those found in the 1952 Act, ... Lehane J ... concluded that, whilst the Patent might now be revoked only under the 1990 Act, for Alphapharm to succeed it would have to bring its case on obviousness within the terms of that ground as expressed in s 100 of the 1952 Act (1999) 44 IPR 593 at 601; ...**[422]** the appeal to this Court has been conducted on the same basis.

...

Nevertheless, the Amended Particulars of Invalidity filed by Alphapharm were framed in terms drawn from the text of the 1990 Act. ... Both the primary judge and the Full Court emphasised that it was the 1952 Act which was applicable. Nevertheless, as will appear, their treatment of the issues does suggest the intrusion of considerations adverse to Astra which may have had a firmer footing in the 1990 Act.
...**[423]**

Hindsight and combinations
The defendant to an infringement action who cross-claims for revocation on the ground of obviousness bears the onus of establishing that case. This obliges the defendant to lead evidence looking back to the priority date, sometimes, as here, many years before trial. In those circumstances, the warnings in the authorities against the misuse of hindsight are not to be repeated as but prefatory averments and statements of trite law. The danger of such misuse will be particularly acute where what is claimed is a new and inventive combination for the interaction of integers, some or all of which are known. It is worth repeating what was said by Lord Diplock in *Technograph Printed Circuits Ltd v Mills & Rockley (Electronics) Ltd* [1972] RPC 346 at 362. (See also *Olin Corporation v Super Cartridge Co Pty Ltd* (1977) 180 CLR 236 at 262-263.)

"Once an invention has been made it is generally possible to postulate a combination of steps by which the inventor might have **[424]** arrived at the invention that he claims in his specification if he started from something that was already known. But it is only because the invention has been made and has proved successful that it is possible to postulate from what starting point and by what particular combination of steps the inventor could have arrived at his invention. It may be that taken in isolation none of the steps which it is now possible to postulate, if taken in isolation, appears to call for any inventive ingenuity. It is improbable that this reconstruction *a posteriori* represents the mental process by which the inventor in fact arrived at his invention, but, even if it were, inventive ingenuity lay in perceiving that the final result which it was the object of the inventor to achieve was attainable from the particular starting point and in his selection of the particular combination of steps which would lead to that result."

The present invention

The case presented by Astra in opposition to the attack on validity was that the formulation claimed in the Patent had been arrived at by the exercise of scientific ingenuity, based upon knowledge and experimental research cf *National Research Development Corporation v Commissioner of Patents* (1959) 102 CLR 252 at 268.

[Their Honours outlined evidence by Astra pointing to perceived complexities, uncertainties, experiments and trial and error approaches to solving certain problems in formulating an acceptable oral preparation of omeprazole.]

The judgment at trial

... [427]

[Their Honours then referred to a number of positions and approaches taken by Lehane J which they considered to be correct and also observations which they considered made it "at first blush surprising that the primary judge held that Alphapharm had made out its case for revocation". Their honours continued]

However, the primary judge erred in his further identification of the legal concept of obviousness against which the facts were measured. The Full Court also fell into error in this respect. ...[428]

The law respecting obviousness

...

It is at this stage that further and for this appeal acute difficulties commence. They may be introduced by observations by Diplock LJ in a passage frequently cited in the English authorities. In *Johns-Manville Corporation's Patent* [1967] RPC 479 Diplock LJ remarked at 493-494:

> "I have endeavoured to refrain from coining a definition of 'obviousness' which counsel may be tempted to cite in subsequent cases relating to different types of claims. Patent law can too easily be bedevilled by linguistics, and the citation of a plethora of cases about other inventions of different kinds. The correctness of a decision upon an issue of obviousness does not depend upon whether or not the decider has paraphrased the words of the Act in some particular verbal formula. *I doubt whether there is any verbal formula which is appropriate to all classes of claims.*" (emphasis added)

This last point is borne out by a consideration of the judgment of Aickin J in *Wellcome Foundation Ltd v VR Laboratories (Aust) Pty* Ltd (1981) 148 CLR 262. In the course of that judgment, his Honour emphasised (i) inventions may be the result not only of long experiments and profound research but also of chance, sudden lucky thought or mere accidental discovery; (ii) not all inventions are to be classified as successful solutions to a problem which had presented a "long-felt want"; (iii) to the contrary, inventions which are an advance of contemporary expectations and thus reveal an "unfelt want" may well involve

■■■■■■ Aktiebolaget Hässle v Alphapharm *continued*

an inventive step; and (iv) in cases falling within (iii), experiments and research would throw no light on the quality of what was claimed as an inventive step.

Proposition (i) certainly also represented the law under the 1949 UK Act. In *Dow Corning Corporation's Application*, [1969] RPC 544 Graham J said at 560.:

> "An inventor may well arrive at his invention by a flash of genius which causes him no difficulty or concentrated thought at all, but the invention may still be a most brilliant one which would never have occurred to the notional skilled man in the art at all or only after prolonged **[429]** investigation and the concentrated exercise of his, perhaps lesser, inventive faculty. In such a case, though it is in a sense obvious to the inventor, nevertheless the invention is undoubtedly worthy of patent protection."

...

Biogen was the first case in which the House of Lords considered obviousness under the *Patents Act 1977* (UK) ("the 1977 UK Act"). What was said may reflect the "problem and solution" approach which is apparently mandated by the European Patent Convention which requires European patent applications to disclose the claimed invention "in such terms that the technical problem (even if not expressly stated as such) and its solution can be understood": Paterson, *The European Patent System* (2nd ed, 2001), §12-04; Cole, "Inventive Step: Meaning of the EPO Problem and Solution Approach, and Implications for the United Kingdom—Part I" (1998) *European Intellectual Property Review* 214 at 215-216. It will be necessary to return to the significance of the 1977 UK Act. However, earlier in *Amoxycillin* [1980] RPC 261 at 290, decided under the 1949 UK Act, Buckley LJ had spoken of the solution of "some recognised problem" and the meeting of "some recognised need".

In any event, the consistory clause in the Patent states that the invention claimed therein is designed to obtain a pharmaceutical dosage form of omeprazole which answers the problems referred to earlier in the body of the specification ... The claim is for a combination, the interaction between the integers of which is the essential requirement for the presence of an inventive step. It is the selection of the integers out of "perhaps many possibilities" which must be shown by Alphapharm to be obvious, bearing in mind that the selection of the integers in which the invention lies can be expected to be a process necessarily involving rejection of other possible integers. This expression of the issue follows what was said by Aickin J in *Minnesota Mining*. (1980) 144 CLR 253 at 293.

Divergence between Australian and United Kingdom law

In the argument in this Court, as in the Federal Court, reliance was **[430]** placed upon various decisions in the United Kingdom. Reference has already been made to some divergence between the case law concerning the 1952 Act and the United Kingdom legislation in 1949 and 1977. There are further areas of divergence, the failure in an appreciation of which was of determinative significance for the decisions both of Lehane J and the Full Court

The first concerns "mosaics" ... and related issues. The holding for which *Minnesota Mining* is celebrated is the rejection, as inapplicable to the terms of the 1952 Act, of the reasoning in certain English decisions. This might have permitted the basing of an argument of obviousness upon prior publicly available publications, without evidence that they had become part of the common general knowledge at the priority date.

... **[432]**

The result in Britain of the shift in grundnorm is exemplified in the observation by Laddie J *Cairnstores Ltd v Aktiebolaget Hässle* [2002] EWHC 309 (Ch) at [94] that the skilled worker (identified in s 3 of the 1977 UK Act):

▬▬▬ Aktiebolaget Hässle v Alphapharm *continued*

"is assumed to have read and understood all the *available* prior art". (emphasis added)

The treatment of the point by Aickin J in *Minnesota Mining*, as indicated above, expressly rejected any assumption as to what in such a way may be expected of and attributed to the hypothetical addressee. That distinction is important in considering the path taken by Lehane J in his judgment. It is convenient, before doing so, to refer to the notion of "routine" which also played a significant part in that reasoning.

"Matter of routine"

In *Wellcome Foundation*, Aickin J referred to the taking of a series of routine steps and the making of a series of routine experiments and continued (1981) 148 CLR 262 at 286:

> "The test is whether the hypothetical addressee faced with the same problem *would have taken as a matter of routine whatever steps* might have led from the prior art to the invention, whether they be the steps of the inventor or not." (emphasis added)

Lehane J, in critical passages in his reasoning (1999) 44 IPR 593 at 626, 629; referred to and applied what he understood to follow from this passage. ...

What Aickin J had in mind as "routine" appears from an earlier passage in his judgment in which he was discussing the question whether evidence of the steps taken by the patentee was relevant and therefore admissible in a revocation action. His Honour said (1981) 148 CLR 262 at 280-281

> "Evidence of what he did by way of experiment may be another matter. It might show that the experiments devised for the purpose were part of an inventive step. Alternatively it might show that the experiments were of *a routine character* which the uninventive worker in the field *would try as a matter of course*. The latter could be relevant though not decisive in every case. It may be that the perception of the true nature of the problem was the inventive step which, once taken, revealed that straightforward experiments will provide the solution. It will always be necessary to distinguish between experiments leading to an invention and subsequent experiments for checking and testing the product or process the subject of the invention. The latter would not be material to obviousness [433] but might be material to the question of utility." (emphasis added)

There are distinct strands of thought in this passage which may now be considered in terms applicable to the issues in this litigation. First, the working trials of which Dr Cederberg gave evidence may be (it is not necessary to determine the point) an example of the "subsequent experiments for checking and testing", to which Aickin J referred at the end of the above passage. Secondly, the invention claimed in the Patent lay not in perceiving "the true nature of the problem" to which "straightforward experiments" then would provide the solution; the invention was in the interaction between the integers of the compound, to answer the known problem. Thirdly, in a case such as the present, the relevant question was that posed in the first part of the passage. Were the experiments "part of" that inventive step claimed in the Patent or were they "of a routine character" to be tried "as a matter of course"? If the latter be attributable to the hypothetical addressee of the Patent, such a finding would support a holding of obviousness.

That way of approaching the matter has an affinity with the reformulation of the "Cripps question" by Graham J in *Olin Mathieson Chemical Corporation v Biorex Laboratories Ltd* [1970] RPC 157. ...

■■■■■   Aktiebolaget Hässle v Alphapharm *continued*

"*Would* the notional research group at the relevant date, in all the circumstances, which include a knowledge of all the relevant prior art and of the facts of the nature and success of chlorpromazine, *directly be led as a matter of course to try* the -CF$_3$ substitution in the '2' position in place of the -C1 atom in chlorpromazine or in any other body which, apart from the -CF$_3$ substitution, has the other characteristics of the formula of claim 1, *in the expectation that it might well* produce a useful alternative to or better drug than chlorpromazine or a body useful for any other purpose?" (emphasis added)

That approach should be accepted.

The reasoning of the primary judge

Lehane J did not treat "routine" in that way. He erred by giving it an operation more favourable to Alphapharm's case. What his Honour **[434]** did was in line with the position which now apparently obtains in England, that "all of the courses of action which present themselves without the exercise of invention are obvious" (*Pharmacia Corp v Merck & Co Inc* [2002] RPC 775 at 818). His Honour did not assess what was said by the expert witnesses concerning the procedures they would have followed by making findings whether they would have been led directly as a matter of course to pursue one avenue in the expectation that it might well produce the claimed compound.

His Honour also attributed to the hypothetical addressee the assistance to be gleaned from publications which had not been found to be part of the common general knowledge in Australia at the priority date. He correctly rejected the Alphapharm submission that the common general knowledge of the skilled formulator in Australia included material the formulator might find by conducting research, even if the information thus disclosed had not been generally assimilated and accepted by formulators (1999) 44 IPR 593 at 606; But Lehane J then took a wrong turning in his reasoning process. His Honour said (1999) 44 IPR 593 at 606:

"It may not necessarily follow, however, that documents which would have been found on search, but do not form part of the common general knowledge, are simply irrelevant. Common general knowledge is, after all, the stock of knowledge on the basis of which one asks whether what is claimed to be an invention was obvious and did not involve an inventive step. It may be that to make use of the result of a *routine literature search* is no different in concept from making use of *a series of routine experiments* where common general knowledge would have suggested either to the hypothetical formulator attempting to formulate omeprazole." (emphasis added)

Later in his judgment, his Honour accepted Dr Story's evidence that he would have regard to the literature revealed by this process "not ... only for the purpose of finding precise directions" but "for more general ideas" ((1999) 44 IPR 593 at 629); as a step in the statement of his conclusion that the Patent was bad for obviousness. That was an error. Further, the equating in this passage of "a routine literature search" with "a series of routine experiments" as something suggested by common general knowledge to the hypothetical formulator conflated two further errors. This came about as follows.

Lehane J held that the claimed combination had not been obvious "considered at the *commencement* of a hypothetical attempt" ((1999) 44 IPR 593 at 626); (original emphasis). However, he continued [Their Honours quoted several passages from the judgment of Lehane J which have been omitted here.] **[435]**

This led to the finding (1999) 44 IPR 593 at 627:

██████   Aktiebolaget Hässle v Alphapharm *continued*

"I have no difficulty with the proposition that a formulator asked, in April 1986, to formulate omeprazole would have done a literature search at least in order to discover what learning there was about omeprazole itself and its characteristics. Clearly enough such a search would have uncovered the compound patent, the omeprazole salts patent and Pilbrant and Cederberg. Pilbrant and Cederberg both indicated a number of the characteristics of omeprazole and pointed the formulator in a particular direction: an enteric coated dosage form seemed most likely to be the best possibility. That being so, there can be no surprise that the witnesses would have first tried directly enteric coating an omeprazole core, or that the particular 'controlled release' dosage form that Dr Marshall would have tried was an enteric coated one. I accept that that is what the hypothetical formulator would have done."

One flaw in this reasoning is that it treats what was "known or used" within the meaning of par (e) in s 100(1) of the 1952 Act as if it was directed to information which, whilst accessible, had not been assimilated into common general knowledge. ...

There follows the further conclusion (1999) 44 IPR 593 at 627 (later endorsed by the Full Court (2000) 51 IPR 375 at 406):

"I accept also that the process which would then have followed would have been a complex, detailed and laborious one, involving a good deal of trial and error, dead ends and the retracing of steps; and it is easy to fall into the twin traps of hindsight and over simplification. But there is no reason to doubt that the hypothetical formulator would, having tried the first simple formulation, have done substantially what Astra did: submitted it to appropriate tests, including tests for stability on manufacture and on storage and for acid resistance."

The tracing of a course of action which was complex and detailed, as well as laborious, with a good deal of trial and error, with dead ends and the retracing of steps is not the taking of routine steps to which the hypothetical formulator was taken as a matter of course. In *In re Farbenindustrie AG's Patents* (1930) 47 RPC 289 at 322, Maugham J had said that while "mere verification is not invention", what he likened to the citadel of invention:

"may be captured either by a brilliant *coup-de-main* or by a slow and laborious approach by sap and mine according to the rules of the art; the reward is the same".

Further, the routine, which Lehane J accepted, took as its starting point that which was attributed from the reading of information which he had not found to be part of the common general knowledge.

The result is that the reasoning by which the trial judge concluded that the Patent was to be revoked was flawed by errors of law.

The Full Court

There is a particular temptation to rely on hindsight by imprecisely identifying the issue which arises in determining an allegation of obviousness. To this, with apparent encouragement from English authorities upon which Alphapharm relies, the Full Court succumbed as support for its rejection of Astra's appeal. To this we now turn.

... Their Honours correctly held, contrary to what had been decided by the trial judge, that it was impermissible to have regard to documents that **[437]** would have been read merely for "general ideas" ((2000) 51 IPR 375 at 392). However, the Full Court passed around that difficulty by accepting Dr Rowe's evidence that the information in the manufacturer's literature, respecting "the basic characteristics of omeprazole", "could, and would" be readily

■■■■■   Aktiebolaget Hässle v Alphapharm *continued*

obtained by a formulator carrying out "a series of routine tests"((2000) 51 IPR 375 at 392, 409-410). That would instruct the formulator that omeprazole was an acid labile compound, which would need to be stabilised, so that "[t]he first integer selects itself" ((2000) 51 IPR 375 at 392-393). In this Court, Astra disputes the statement then made by the Full Court that Astra did not dispute that proposition. It is necessary here to take that point further.

This is because, in proceeding as it did, the Full Court considered each integer separately. It went on to say that it had been obvious to use an enteric coating and then said that ((2000) 51 IPR 375 at 393):

> "[t]he only integer whose presence raises a doubt about obviousness is the subcoat. Was it obvious, within the sense of the relevant legal authorities, for the hypothetical formulator to try out the idea of a subcoat? And, if so, was it *obvious* for the hypothetical formulator *to try out* a subcoat falling within the description contained in the patent? These are the questions critical to the claim of lack of inventive step. They overlap and may be addressed together." (emphasis added)

The Full Court stated as a proposition of law that, to make out a case of obviousness ((2000) 51 IPR 375 at 382-383):

> "[i]t is enough that it be apparent to [a non-inventive skilled worker] that it would be *worthwhile to try each of the integers* that was ultimately successfully used." (emphasis added)

Their Honours then said that this was the point made in what they identified as a classic statement by Buckley LJ in *Amoxycillin* ([1980] RPC 261 at 290). That was to the effect that, for "a particular step or process" to be obvious, it will suffice if it be shown that to a person skilled in the art but lacking an inventive capacity it would appear that "to try" the step or process would be "worthwhile" in solving the recognised problem or meeting the recognised need.

Astra points to several errors of law in this approach which deprive the Full Court decision of any support it might otherwise give to the decision at trial. The errors are interrelated.

First, the focus upon each integer rather than the interaction between them in combination went against the teaching in authorities such as **[438]** *Minnesota Mining*, to which reference has been made. Secondly, the reference to "worthwhile to try" led the Full Court into the following reasoning ((2000) 51 IPR 375 at 393):

> "[W]e reject the submission made by counsel for Astra that the finding made by Lehane J (1999) 44 IPR 593 at 626-627; logically concluded the issue of obviousness in their clients' favour. It will be recalled that his Honour said that *'considered at the commencement of a hypothetical attempt* ... the combination claimed in the patent was not obvious'. That finding would dispose of the issue only if the concept of obviousness was restricted, in the case of a combination patent, to a situation where the hypothetical formulator could foresee, at the commencement of his or her task and without the necessity for testing or any process of trial and error, which particular integers (out of all those 'worth a try') would be most appropriate. However, that is not the law, as was made clear by Buckley LJ in the extract from *Amoxycillin* quoted above ((2000) 51 IPR 375 at 383); Once it is accepted that it is sufficient that it be obvious to the hypothetical formulator that a particular possibility is worth trying (perhaps among many possibilities), it must follow that it is incorrect to say that an invention lacks obviousness simply because the hypothetical formulator would, or might, have been unable to say in advance which (if any) of the possibilities worth trying would prove most satisfactory." (emphasis added)

▓▓▓▓▓▓   Aktiebolaget Hässle v Alphapharm *continued*

The Full Court added ((2000) 51 IPR 375 at 393):

> This reasoning applies even where (as here) a problem unexpectedly appears during
> the course of routine steps undertaken for the purpose of creating a new product.
> Although the existence of the problem may not have been apparent at the outset, its
> solution (when it does appear) may be obvious, as distinct from inventive, depending
> on whether or not it would immediately be apparent to a skilled worker in the field to
> try the solution that in fact proved effective."

"Obvious" or "worthwhile" to try

It is by no means apparent that what was said by Buckley LJ in *Amoxycillin* was adapted to the
purpose to which the Full Court put it.

[There follows an examination of passages in judgments by Buckley LJ in *Amoxycillin*; of
Diplock LJ in *Johns-Manville* ([1967] RPC 479 at 494); of Reid LJ in *Technograph Printed Circuits
Ltd v Mills & Rockley (Electronics) Ltd* [1972] RPC 346 at 356 and Graham J in *American
Cyanamid Co v Ethicon Ltd* [1979] RPC 215.] [**440**]

Later English decisions (see, for example, *Boehringer Mannheim GmbH v Genzyme Ltd* [1993]
FSR 716 at 725; *Chiron Corporation v Murex Diagnostics Ltd* [1996] RPC 535 at 557; *Brugger v
Medic-Aid Ltd* [1996] RPC 635 at 661. See further *Pharmacia Corp v Merck & Co Inc* [2002] RPC
775 at 818-819; *Lilly Icos Ltd v Pfizer Ltd* [2002] EWCA Civ 1 at [57]) applying the 1977 UK Act
to chemical and biotechnological patents treat what was said by Diplock LJ in *Johns-Manville*
as synonymous with "worth a try" and "well worth trying out". On that basis, a number of
patents have been held invalid for obviousness. These cases include *Genentech Inc's Patent*
[1989] 8 RPC 147 upon which Alphapharm relied. The outcome may reflect the approach in
European law that "the assessment of inventive step depends upon the extent to which a
skilled person would have been technically motivated towards the claimed invention"
(Paterson, *The European Patent System,* 2nd ed (2001), §12-43). But cases such as *Genentech*
mark a divergence from the treatment of obviousness in the decisions of this Court. The Full
Court of the Federal Court recognised this in *ICI Chemicals & Polymers Ltd v The Lubrizol
Corporation Inc* (2000) 106 FCR 214 at 240; their Honours referred in particular to *Genentech
Inc's Patent* [1989] 8 RPC 147 at 278, and see further Torremans, *Intellectual Property Law* (3rd
ed, 2001), pp 68-78.

However, in the present case, a differently constituted Full Court, after setting out the
passage from *Amoxycillin* to which reference has been made above, noted that ((2000) 51 IPR
375 at 383):

> "Alphapharm does not suggest that the combination of integers disclosed in the patent
> would have been apparent to the skilled worker in the field prior to that worker
> attempting to formulate omeprazole",

[**441**] but stated that the critical question in relation to the appeal was whether Alphapharm
was correct in its further assertion ((2000) 51 IPR 375 at 383):

> "*each of the integers* was at least worthwhile trying; therefore *the combination* itself was
> 'obvious', in the sense in which that word is used in this area of the law" (emphasis
> added).

In so expressing the critical question and then proceeding to answer it favourably to
Alphapharm, the Full Court fell into various errors of law. Several points are to be made. First,
the statute does not ask whether a particular avenue of research was obvious to try so that the

▬▬▬   Aktiebolaget Hässle v Alphapharm *continued*

result claimed therefore is obvious; the adoption of a criterion of validity expressed in terms of "worth a try" or "obvious to try" and the like begs the question presented by the statute. In a sense, any invention that would in fact have been obvious under the statute would also have been worth trying. Paragraph (e) of s 100(1) of the 1952 Act, applied to the present case, asks whether the combination claimed in claim 1 was obvious. The paragraph does not fix upon the direction to be taken in making efforts or attempts to reach that particular solution to the problem identified in the Patent. Nor does it direct an inquiry respecting each integer of the claimed combination. The paragraph asks whether "the invention ... as claimed", here the combination, was obvious, not each of its integers.

In the United States, any criterion which adopts a notion of "obvious to try" has been rejected in a long series of decisions upon §103 of the 1952 US Act [93] Cooper, *Biotechnology and the Law,* (2001 rev), vol 1, §4.03[1][a][v]. The judgment in a number of these was given by Judge Rich, first as a member of the United States Court of Customs and Patent Appeals and latterly as a member of the United States Court of Appeals, Federal Circuit. In 1966, in *Application of Tomlinson* (363 F 2d 928 at 931(1966)), his Honour wrote:

> "Slight reflection suggests, we think, that there is usually an element of 'obviousness to try' in any research endeavour, that it is not undertaken with complete blindness but rather with some semblance of a chance of success, and that patentability determinations based on that as the test would not only be contrary to statute but result in a marked deterioration of the entire patent system as an incentive to invest in those efforts and attempts which go by the name of 'research.'"

... **[442]**

The reasoning in these and other United States authorities (including *Application of Antonie* 559 F 2d 618 (1977); *Application of Goodwin* 576 F 2d 375 (1978); *In re Geiger* 815 F 2d 686 (1987); *In re Fine* 837 F 2d 1071 (1988); *Merck & Co Inc v Biocraft Laboratories Inc* 874 F 2d 804 (1989); *In re Vaeck* 947 F 2d 488 (1991); and *In re Nunberg* 33 United States Patent Quarterly 2d 1953 (1994)) should be accepted in preference to the path apparently taken in the English decisions, particularly after the 1977 UK Act, upon which Alphapharm **[443]** relied. The United States decisions reflect an approach to the subject closer to that adopted in *Minnesota Mining* and *Wellcome Foundation*.

Conclusions

Astra complains that the Full Court denied it procedural fairness. The Full Court took the view that Lehane J may have had in mind a possible rather than a probable result of the hypothetical formulator's activity; if so, then, in the Full Court's view, Lehane J had erred ((2000) 51 IPR 375 at 389; [2000] AIPC ¶91-636 at 38,174). The Full Court then set out on a detailed review of the expert evidence. ...

... After its review of the evidence, the Full Court concluded ((2000) 51 IPR 375 at 406; [2000] AIPC ¶91-636 at 38,189) that Astra's "development" of the formulation "was essentially an exercise *in trying out* various known *possibilities* until the correct solution emerged" (emphasis added). That view of the matter wrongly takes as the starting point the assumed result. It succumbs immediately to the seduction of hindsight. Also, the notion of trying out possibilities invites the repetition of criticisms made earlier in these reasons.

The result is that the Full Court erred in the grounds upon which it supported the outcome at trial. ...

[444] There are obvious advantages in a substantial measure of uniformity between the patent laws of countries with which Australia maintains international arrangements under its

█████ Aktiebolaget Hässle v Alphapharm *continued*

patents legislation. But these reasons reveal that the law respecting obviousness in various jurisdictions currently diverges and that the extent of this divergence changes from time to time. There is no universal view of a matter which at bottom reflects a range of attitudes to the balance of interests at stake in patent law. Nor is it to the point that had the obviousness of the claims of the Patent fallen for decision solely under the 1990 Act, whether in its initial or amended form, the law may have favoured Alphapharm's case more than did the 1952 Act.

Orders

The appeal should be allowed with costs.

McHUGH J:

(In dissent) The issue in this appeal is whether "the invention, so far as claimed in any claim of the complete specification ... was obvious and did not involve an inventive step having regard to what was known or used in Australia on or before the priority date of that claim" (s 100(1)(e), *Patents Act 1952* (Cth)). This issue raised a question of fact that had to be determined by applying a statutory expression. A summary of some of the extensive evidence adduced in the case is contained in the joint judgment of Gleeson CJ, Gaudron, Gummow and Hayne JJ.

I would dismiss the appeal on the ground that there are concurrent findings of fact by Lehane J and the Full Court of the Federal Court that should not be disturbed by this Court. They were findings that were open to them on the evidence, they involved the application of a flexible, indeterminate expression and they were not flawed by any legal error.

The meaning of ordinary English words in a statute is a question of fact. "Obvious" is an ordinary English word whose primary meaning is "very plain" (*The General Tire & Rubber Company v The Firestone Tyre & Rubber Company Ltd* [1972] RPC 457 at 497). The question for Lehane J, therefore, sitting as a juror, was whether the inventive step claimed was "very plain". That involved making a judgment concerning a large volume of evidence. Different minds could reasonably have come to different conclusions about the effect of the evidence. If I had been the trial judge, I suspect that I would have applied the approach to the issue of "obviousness" **[445]** that Gleeson CJ, Gaudron, Gummow and Hayne JJ follow in their joint judgment and if I had done so, I would probably have reached the same result as their Honours do. But, as a matter of law, I would not have been bound to use the approach that their Honours outline. Despite the many judicial statements to which their Honours refer, the issue in this case involved a factual conclusion (*Société Technique de Pulverisation Step v Emson Europe Ltd* [1993] RPC 513 at 519 per Hoffmann LJ; *Chiron Corporation v Murex Diagnostics Ltd* [1996] RPC 535 at 557 per Aldous J) whose resolution could legitimately give rise to a number of differing approaches and answers. *Johns-Manville Corporation's Patent* ([1967] RPC 479 at 493-494 per Diplock LJ), Willmer LJ agreeing (In *Johns-Manville Corporation's Patent* 1967] RPC 479 at 493-494), Diplock LJ refrained from providing a definition of "obviousness" so that it could not be cited in later cases concerning different types of claims. Diplock LJ said that patent law "can too easily be bedevilled by linguistics" and that "obviousness" does not depend upon the use of a particular verbal formula or reliance upon cases about other inventions of different kinds.

A judge trying the obviousness issue is not bound, as a matter of law, to determine that issue by reference to persons who are not "particularly imaginative or inventive" (*Aktiebolaget Hässle v Alphapharm Pty Ltd* (1999) 44 IPR 593 at 604). Nor is the judge, in a case like the present, bound to ask "whether the hypothetical addressee faced with the same problem would have taken as a matter of routine whatever steps might have led from the prior art to the invention, whether they be the steps of the inventor or not" (*Wellcome Foundation Ltd v*

■■■■   Aktiebolaget Hässle v Alphapharm *continued*

VR Laboratories (Aust) Pty Ltd (1981) 148 CLR 262 at 286 per Aickin J). Nor is the judge bound to ask whether a notional research group would be directly led, as a matter of course, to try the approach of the "inventor" in the expectation that it might well produce a useful result or alternative (*cf Olin Mathieson Chemical Corporation v Biorex Laboratories Ltd* [1970] RPC 157 at 187-188 per Graham J). These statements, and similar ones, have been made by judges, highly experienced and eminent in patent law, and applied by many other judges. ... Nevertheless, all such judicial statements merely reflect reasoning processes concerning factual issues. They do not lay down any legal principles and they [446] have no precedent value. They are not binding upon judges hearing future cases.

In many fields of law governed by statute, such as income taxation, workers' compensation, environmental planning and patents, judges and practitioners, who specialise in those fields, have a tendency to treat judicial statements, determinative of particular cases, as principles of law. Few of them are. Most of the time, they simply reflect how experienced judges have resolved particular factual situations...

When a trial judge has made, and an intermediate court of appeal has affirmed, a finding or findings of fact, this Court will almost invariably refuse to grant special leave to appeal against that finding or those findings. Unless the lower courts have misapplied the law in making the factual findings, the case is not "special" enough to warrant the grant of special leave to appeal.

....[447]

I am not persuaded that the learned trial judge and the judges of the Full Court misunderstood the law or the issue that they had to decide. Nor am I persuaded, after taking into account the advantages of the trial judge, that he erred in his conclusion concerning the issue for decision.

I would dismiss the appeal with costs.

INNOVATIVE STEP

[8.360] An innovation patent must reveal an innovative step (s 7(4), (5) and (6)).

"*Innovative step*
(4) For the purposes of this Act, an invention is to be taken to involve an innovative step when compared with the prior art base unless the invention would , to a person skilled in the relevant art, in the light of the common general knowledge as it existed in the patent area before the priority date of the relevant claim, only vary from the kinds of information set out in subsection (5) in ways that make no substantial contribution to the working of the invention.
(5) For the purposes of subsection (4), the information is of the following kinds:
    (a) prior art information made publicly available in a single document or through doing a single act;
    (b) prior art information made publicly available in 2 or more related documents, or through doing 2 or more related acts, if the relationship between the documents or acts is such that a person skilled in the relevant art would treat them as a single source of that information.
(6) For the purposes of subsection (4), each kind of information set out in subsection (5) must be considered separately."

An innovation patent is granted without prior examination as to substance and without being subject to pre-grant opposition proceedings. However, if the patentee wishes to enforce the patent and requests examination for certification of the patent, or another person requests examination, or if the Commissioner decides to examine the patent (s 101A), the Commissioner must determine if the patent is invalid and should be revoked for, amongst other grounds, lack of an innovative step (s 101B(2)(b)). If the innovation patent is certified, any person may oppose the patent and seek revocation of it, and one ground of opposition is that the innovation patent lacks an innovative step (s 101M(b)). An innovation patent may be re-examined (s 101G), and the grounds for revocation include lack of novelty (s 101G (3)(b)). The Minister or any other person may apply to a court to have an innovation patent revoked on a ground that it does not involve an innovative step (s 138(3)(b)).

In deciding upon a requirement of innovative step, the government accepted recommendation 2 (para 5.1) made by the Advisory Council on Industrial Property (ACIP) in the *Review of the Petty Patent System* (AIPO, October 1995) in the following terms:

*   The inventive level for innovation patents should be lower than for standard patents

*   The test for this inventive level should be a modified form of the expanded novelty test set out in *Griffin v Isaacs*. The test would be worded something along the lines of:

    - an innovation patent should not be granted if the innovation is not novel and

    - if an innovation varies from a previously publicly available article, product or process, only in ways which make no substantial contribution to the effect of the product or working of the article or process, then it cannot be considered novel.

The *Griffin v Isaacs* test is found in *Griffin v Isaacs* (1938) 12 ALJ 169; (1942) 12 AOJP 739 per Dixon at 740:

"Where variations from a device previously published consist in matters which make no substantial contribution to the working of the thing or involve no ingenuity or inventive step and the merit if any of the two things, considered as inventions, is the same, it is, I think impossible to treat the differences as giving novelty".

This is a contentious formulation and Gummow J has commented upon the difficulties it presents in *RD Werner Inc v Bailey Aluminium Products Pty Ltd* 13 IPR 513 at 537-539. It is perhaps unfortunate that the ACIP report resurrected this troublesome spectre into yet another contentious area of patent theory. However, the statutory wording now falls to be interpreted on its own merits and without direct reference to *Griffin v Isaacs*.

The Revised Explanatory Memorandum discusses the test in *Patents Act 1990* (Cth), s 7(4) in items 6 and 7.

"6. This item adds new provisions which set out the test for innovative step. It requires a level of inventiveness that is greater than the invention simply being "new". The test requires that the invention is not only new but that it also differs from what was already known in a way that is not merely superficial or peripheral to the invention. The variation must be of practical significance in the way the invention works. However in contrast to a standard patent there is no requirement that an invention claimed in a innovation patent must be non-obvious. Therefore the test for innovative step will require an inventive contribution lower than that required to meet the inventive step threshold set for standard patents.

7. Innovative step is determined taking into account the prior art base. The prior art base is the same as that used to determine inventive step in relation to standard patents. The person assessing the innovative step is a person skilled in the art who assesses the invention in the light of common general knowledge in the field of the invention as it existed before the priority date."

It is generally said in relation to inventive step for a standard patent that a "scintilla" of inventiveness will suffice. The test for innovative step in *Patents Act 1990* (Cth), s 7(4) requires a "substantial contribution" while the Explanatory Memorandum refers to something "not merely superficial or peripheral" and "of practical significance". This seems to require more than a "scintilla".

INVENTION: A THRESHOLD TEST?
(Voodoo Child – Slight Return)

[8.365] Having considered the meaning of "manner of manufacture", "novelty" and "inventive step" it is now possible to consider the threshold requirement of "invention" as it appears in the opening words of s 18 has been considered in a number of cases. In *NV Philips Gloeilampenfabricken v Mirabella International Pty Ltd* (1995) 32 IPR 449 the High Court, by a majority, considered that the words introduced a threshold test of general inventiveness or newness which was independent of the separate requirements imposed by the specific paragraphs of *Patents Act 1990* (Cth), s 18. The matter is discussed in the following extract.

Bristol-Myers Squibb v FH Faulding

[8.370] *Bristol-Myers Squibb Co v FH Faulding & Co Ltd* (2000) 97 FCR 524 Federal Court of Australia

BLACK CJ, LEHANE J: [530]

Invention; "manner of new manufacture"; inventive step

A "patentable invention" must be an "invention" as defined, and thus a "manner of new manufacture the subject of letters patent and grant of privilege within s 6 of the *Statute of Monopolies*". The primary judge held, following *NV Philips Gloeilampenfabrieken v Mirabella International Pty Ltd* (1995) 183 CLR 655, that the opening words of s 18(1) impose a threshold requirement of inventiveness: a requirement independent of the specific provisions of s 18(1)(b) as to novelty and an inventive step, judged by comparison with the prior art base as it existed before the priority date. His Honour held that the claimed invention (we use that expression to refer to the invention claimed in each of the petty patents in suit) did not meet that threshold requirement. He held also that it did not involve an inventive step when compared with the prior art base. His Honour's conclusions were based upon two findings. One of them involved an application of the well-known principle which denies patentability to a claimed invention which is "nothing but a claim for the use of a known material in the manufacture of known articles for the purpose of which its known properties make that material suitable": *Commissioner of Patents v Microcell Ltd* (1959) 102 CLR 232 at 251. His Honour said at 477: [531]

"At the priority date the material (taxol) had been known for many years. It is a naturally-occurring compound and thus in itself unpatentable. In the words of the

███████ Bristol-Myers Squibb v FH Faulding *continued*

specification, taxol had 'shown great promise as an anticancer drug' and 'been found to be an active agent against drug-refractory ovarian cancer' ... The properties which made taxol effective against cancer, that is to say its biological mechanism, were well-known. They had been discussed in the articles referred to in the specification which were 'incorporated by reference as if reproduced in full below' ... Thus the specification is not merely a claim of a 'new use of an old substance' (*Re BA's Application* (1915) 32 RPC 348 at 349, Mirabella, 183 CLR at 661) but a claim for the same use of an old substance."

The primary judge, at 477, expressed his other finding as follows:

"Further, the specifications disclose that the claimed inventions were the product of routine testing which merely verified a hypothesis arising from analysis of reports of earlier trials: see *WR Grace v Asahi Kasei Kogyo Kabushiki Kaisha* (1993) 25 IPR 481 at 497-498.

... On their face they claim a particular dosage over a particular period of a substance known to be effective, in a known way, for the treatment of cancer, a dosage and a period arrived at by the 'ordinary methods of trial and error which involve no inventive step ...': *Van der Lely NV v Bamfords Ltd* [1963] RPC 61 at 71 per Lord Reid, cited with approval in *Nicaro Holdings Pty Ltd v Martin Engineering Co* (1990) 91 ALR 513 at 530 per Gummow J (with whom Jenkinson J agreed)."

Nothing in the more recent decision of the High Court in *Advanced Building Systems Pty Ltd v Ramset Fasteners (Aust) Pty Ltd* (1998) 194 CLR 171 detracts from the binding effect, in this Court, of the decision in *Philips v Ramset* fell to be decided under the *Patents Act 1952* (Cth) (the 1952 Act); the Court distinguished *Philips* on the basis that there were significant differences between the 1990 Act and its predecessor, so that *Philips* was not determinative of a question arising under s 100 of the 1952 Act. It is necessary, therefore, to ascertain precisely what was decided in *Philips*. The essence of the decision is, we think, to be found in the following passage in the judgment of the majority, at 663, 664 (omitting citations of authority):

"The effect of those opening words of s 18(1) is that the primary or threshold requirement of a 'patentable invention' is that it be an 'invention'. Read in the context of s 18(1) as a whole and the definition of 'invention' in the Dictionary in Sch 1, that clearly means 'an alleged invention', that is to say, an 'alleged' 'manner of new manufacture the subject of letters patent and grant of privilege within s 6 of the Statute of Monopolies'. In the light of what has been said above about what is involved in an alleged manner of new manufacture, that threshold requirement of 'an alleged invention' will, notwithstanding an assertion of 'newness', remain unsatisfied if it is apparent on the face of the relevant specification that the subject matter of the claim is, by reason of absence of the necessary quality of inventiveness, not a manner of new manufacture for the purpose of the *Statute of Monopolies*. That does not mean that the threshold requirement of 'an alleged invention' corresponds [532] with or renders otiose the more specific requirements of novelty and inventive step (when compared with the prior art base) contained in s 18(1)(b). It simply means that, if it is apparent on the face of the specification that the quality of the inventiveness necessary for there to be a proper subject of letters patent under the *Statute of Monopolies* is absent, one need go no further."

The majority, at 663, rejected an argument:

"that the fact that a claimed use is 'nothing but … a new use of an old substance' and therefore 'outside the whole scope of what is known as an invention' under traditional principles of patent law will not of itself preclude it from being a proper subject of letters patent under the Act."

Secondly, at 664, 665, the majority said:

"It is true that it can be argued that there is internal tension in an overall legislative scheme which imposes a threshold requirement of inventiveness reflecting the effect of the saving clause in s 6 of the *Statute of Monopolies* and then proceeds, if that threshold requirement be satisfied, to impose more specific requirements of novelty and inventive step. It seems to us, however, that there are several answers to that argument. One is that there is no construction of s 18(1) of the Act which is not susceptible of some legitimate criticism. Another is that traditional patents law under s 6 of the *Statute of Monopolies* long recognised cumulative requirements of an element of invention (as distinct, from, for example, mere discovery or analogous use) in the subject matter as described by the specification and novelty or newness as disclosed by comparison with a prior art base. The distinctive requirements of novelty and inventive step required by s 18 of the Act are emphasised by their elaboration in s 7. In that regard it may be noted that in the 1952 Act one of the grounds for revocation of a patent was that the invention 'was obvious and did not involve an inventive step, having regard to what was known or used in Australia' (s 100(1)(e)). More important, it seems to us to be highly unlikely that it was the legislative intent that there should be a significant alteration of the law as explained in *Microcell* by extending the ambit of a patentable invention so as to include what is 'nothing more' than 'the use of a known material in the manufacture of known articles for the purpose of which its known properties make that material suitable'. In that regard, we do not accept the argument on behalf of Philips that *Microcell* was decided on the question of newness and not on manner of manufacture."

Thirdly, their Honours observed, at 667, that "it would border upon the irrational if a process which was in fact but a new use of an old substance could be a 'patentable invention' under s 18 if, but only if, that fact were not disclosed by the specification". But, as the majority explicitly acknowledged, at 666, that observation was unnecessary to their decision. Fourthly, and finally, special leave to appeal had been granted on the basis that the sole issue on the appeal was the true construction of s 18(1)(a), including the opening words of s 18(1). Thus, the Court was not called upon to consider the correctness of the finding of the Full Court of this Court, that the claims of the patent in suit were indeed for nothing but a use of a known product for a purpose for which its known properties made it suitable.

It is important also to remember that the effect of the decision of the High Court in *Philips* was to affirm the decision of the Full Court (*NV Philips Gloeilampenfabrieken v Mirabella International Pty Ltd* (1993) 44 FCR 239). [533] There is no doubt that the majority of the Full Court (Lockhart J, with whom Northrop J agreed) drew what they perceived to be a clear distinction between obviousness or want of inventive step (s 18(1)(b)(ii)) and want of inventiveness sufficient to characterise the subject matter of a patent as a manner of new manufacture. So, at 263, Lockhart J said:

"Although grounds of objection in patent law sometimes overlap, objections of want of novelty and obviousness are nevertheless essentially distinct from each other. Likewise, the requirement that a patentable invention be a manner of new manufacture is inherently distinct from the requirements of novelty, lack of obviousness, involving an inventive step and utility as required by s 18 of the 1990 Act."

And the point emerges clearly from the following observation of Lockhart J at 265:

"Many of the submissions made by counsel for the appellants on this point blurred the distinction between the requirement that the invention be a manner of new manufacture and obviousness. The respondent did not press its case at the trial (nor therefore on appeal) on obviousness, no doubt, at least in part, because the respondent could not establish that what is described in the evidence as the Vrenken Article was common general knowledge in Australia."

In other words, what cannot be established not to involve an inventive step, by reference to common general knowledge in Australia at the priority date, may nevertheless exhibit a want of the quality of inventiveness which is part of the concept of manner of new manufacture.

Four comments may be made. First, the proposition that "inventiveness" means in one context something quite distinct from the connotation, in the other, of "inventive step" (or lack of obviousness) is not easy to reconcile with the analysis of Gummow J, with whom Jenkinson J agreed, in *RD Werner Inc v Bailey Aluminium Products Pty Ltd* (1989) 25 FCR 565 at 593, 599-601. Secondly, so far as the reasoning of Lockhart J depended (see at 263) upon regarding the 1990 Act as having made no relevant change in the law (a view with which it is easy to sympathise, given s 100(d) of the 1952 Act), the distinction between the two aspects of inventiveness having existed under the 1952 Act, that foundation appears to have been removed by *Ramset*. Thirdly, Lockhart J (upholding the primary judge) appeared to have looked solely at the specification in order to ascertain what was "known", for the purposes of the *Microcell* principle, though his Honour appears to have relied on other evidence as to aspects of the quality of inventiveness. Fourthly, and perhaps most importantly, little guidance is offered as to how one ascertains whether a claimed invention has the quality of inventiveness necessary to characterise it as a manner of new manufacture.

Just as it is not easy to see how one can describe something as new or novel except by reference to what has previously been made, done or published, we cannot see how inventiveness can be judged except by reference to a body of prior knowledge and from the standpoint of someone who has that knowledge. The question, then, is what knowledge, in whose possession, is relevant to the question whether the "inventiveness" component of "manner of new manufacture" is present?

...In *Philips*, Lockhart J said at 265:

"As mentioned earlier the expressions 'manner of new manufacture' and 'manner of manufacture' in this branch of law under the 1990 Act mean the same thing and involve the same concepts as they have been understood and developed since 1623 when the *Statute of Monopolies* was passed."

But, with respect, that begs the question, which are the developments referred to? The modern notions of novelty and obviousness represent, as we have said, developments of the concepts in the Statute. Is there a tertium quid? If so, what precisely is it? It might, perhaps, be supposed that, by preserving the requirement of inventiveness incorporated in "manner of new manufacture", Parliament intended that there be two cumulative requirements, one reflecting the law as it had developed up to some statutory intervention—perhaps in 1952, perhaps in 1990—the other reflected in the elaborate provisions of s 7(2) and s 7(3), read with

████████   Bristol-Myers Squibb v FH Faulding *continued*

the dictionary in Sch 1, of the 1990 Act. Where, however, the judicial and statutory development of the law are as interwoven as they have been in patent law, such a suggestion encounters great difficulty.

Philips, as we read it, does not provide a comprehensive answer to the question, by reference to what body of knowledge is that inventiveness judged? It holds, clearly, that the requirement of inventiveness is not satisfied in a case where the claims are for nothing more than the use of a known material in the manufacture of known articles for a purpose for which that material's known properties make it suitable. The majority judgment of the High Court in *Ramset* points out, at 192, two aspects of that proposition which are, we think, relevant to the present case. One is that the principle that "a claim for 'nothing but' a new use of an old substance lacked the quality of inventiveness" had emerged in the course of the development, during the nineteenth century, of "the doctrine with respect to obviousness and lack of inventive step"; the other is that, if an application for a patent claiming nothing but a new use of an old substance (to adopt the majority's shorthand) proceeded to grant, the grant—under the 1952 Act—would have been liable to revocation under s 100(e) (obviousness) not s 100(d) (not an invention: that is, not a manner of new manufacture). ...

Microcell was an appeal from a refusal by the Commissioner of Patents to accept an application and complete a specification. The Court held, at 246, that **[535]** "[it] must be enough to warrant rejection that it should be clear on its face that the specification discloses no inventive step". Their Honours proceeded to hold that the specification in suit disclosed no such step. It is interesting to note, in passing, that their Honours used the phrase "inventive step", the terminology both of s 100(e) of the 1952 Act (which did not apply to the application before the Court: it was required to be considered under the *Patents Act 1903* (Cth)) and s 18(1)(b)(ii) of the 1990 Act. The claims were for the manufacture of self-propelled rocket projectors, using synthetic resinous plastic material reinforced with mineral fibre. The Court's conclusion was expressed at 251 as follows:

> "We have in truth nothing but a claim for the use of a known material in the manufacture of known articles for the purpose of which its known properties make that material suitable. A claim for nothing more than that cannot be subject matter for a patent, and the position cannot be affected either by the fact that nobody thought of doing the thing before, or by the fact that, when somebody did think of doing it, it was found to be a good thing to do."

The foundation of that conclusion, however, appears in the following paragraph, at 250:

> "Here the specification does not on its face disclose more than a new use of a particular known product. To use Lord Buckmaster's words, no new product is obtained, and there is no new method of manufacture suggested or an old one improved. Tubular self-propelled rocket projectors were at the relevant time well-known articles of manufacture. Synthetic resinous plastics reinforced with mineral fibres, and in particular polyester plastics reinforced with glass or asbestos fibres, were well-known material. These things are to be gathered from the specification itself, which contains no suggestion of novelty in relation to the article to be manufactured or the material to be used. It further appears from matter published in Australia as early as 1946 that the reinforced plastic materials referred to in the specification had been used in the manufacture of a wide variety of articles. The properties of those materials were known generally, and in particular it was well-known that they possessed that combination of great strength and lightness wherein, according to the specification itself, lies their virtue for the purpose in hand. The matter published in 1946 refers to their 'extraor-

dinary strength in relation to weight'—they are 'stronger for their weight than steel'—and to their high tensile strength—another quality which the specification regards as a virtue for the purpose in hand. It was well-known too that they possessed high impact strength and high resistance to heat. In these circumstances we do not think it can be said, merely because it does not seem previously to have occurred to anyone to make a rocket projector out of reinforced plastic, that any inventive idea is disclosed by the specification."

That passage makes it quite clear that the lack of inventive step appeared on the face of the specification. It makes it clear also that the conclusion that there was no inventive step was reinforced by a consideration of material earlier published in Australia, information in which was "well-known" and "known generally". Although the language used by the Court differs somewhat from the formulation adopted by Aickin J in the *Minnesota* case, the substance of the Court's finding was that what was apparent on the face of the specification was reinforced by proof that particular information had passed into common general knowledge, in the relevant field, in Australia. **[536]**

The majority of the High Court in *Philips* explicitly say that their observations about a case where want of the threshold requirement of inventiveness is not apparent on the face of the specification are not necessary to their decision. And, in discussing the commencement point (what is "known") of the inquiry about inventiveness, their Honours refer only to the *Microcell* principle. In our view, in the light of the authorities to which we have referred, *Philips* stands for the proposition (as a matter of construction of the 1990 Act) that if, on the basis of what was known, as revealed on the face of the specification, the invention claimed was obvious or did not involve an inventive step—that is, would be obvious to the hypothetical non-inventive and unimaginative skilled worker in the field (*Minnesota* at 260 per Barwick CJ)—then the threshold requirement of inventiveness is not met. Some elaboration, however, is required in relation to what the specification reveals as "known". If a patent application, lodged in Australia, refers to information derived from a number of prior publications referred to in the specification or, generally, to matters which are known, in our view the Court—or the Commissioner—would ordinarily proceed upon the basis that the knowledge thus described is, in the language of s 7(2) of the 1990 Act, part of "the common general knowledge as it existed in the patent area". In other words, what is disclosed in such terms may be taken as an admission to that effect. In substance, we think, that is what happened, both in *Microcell* and in *Philips*. If, however, the body of prior knowledge disclosed by the specification is insufficient to deprive what is claimed of the quality of inventiveness, then the only additional knowledge or information which will be taken into account is knowledge or information of a kind described in s 7(2) of the 1990 Act. That again, in our view, is consistent with the approach taken in *Microcell*. It is also, with respect, the only approach which does not, in practical terms, render s 18(1)(b)(ii) otiose. Of course, once that additional knowledge is taken into account, one is applying s 18(1)(b)(ii), not the opening words of s 18(1)—unless, perhaps, one might apply either, there being, in this respect, no difference between them.

The findings of the trial judge as to the failure of the claims to meet the threshold requirement of inventiveness relied, as to what was known and as to the studies leading to the claimed invention, only upon what is disclosed in the specifications. The specifications reveal, as his Honour pointed out, that both the efficacy of taxol as an anticarcinogenic (particularly in relation to drug-refractory ovarian cancer) and the mechanism of its action were known. His Honour found, accordingly, that the claimed invention was not merely a claim for a new use for an old substance (his Honour's shorthand) but a claim for the same

━━━   Bristol-Myers Squibb v FH Faulding *continued*

use of an old substance, thus failing the *Microcell* test. In our opinion, however, that formulation overlooks two things. One is that the claim is for a method, not a product; the other is the importance of the phrase "nothing but" in the *Microcell* principle: as to both points, see *National Research Development Corporation v Commissioner of Patents* (1959) 102 CLR 252, especially at 262. Taxol may, if used in accordance with the claimed invention, be used for a purpose for which its known properties make it suitable; it does not follow that the method claimed does not involve an inventive step. Nor, if the method was proved to be efficacious by a routine process of trial and error (the authorities cited by his Honour have to do with how much, in order to destroy novelty, an anticipation must reveal), does it follow that the claimed invention is obvious or does not involve an inventive step: what matters is whether, to the skilled but unimaginative worker in the field, the claimed method was obvious in the sense [537] that the worker, not necessarily seeing that the method was likely to be safe and efficacious, would have seen that it was one which justified investigation.

Because, for the reasons we have given, we respectfully disagree with the primary judge's approach to this part of the case, it is now necessary that we consider the specifications for ourselves.

━━━━━━━━━━━━━━━━━━━━

[8.375] After a close review of the invention as described in the specification, their Honours were not prepared to hold that the quality of inventiveness was lacking. However, the patents were found to lack the novelty required by *Patents Act 1990* (Cth), s 18(1)(b)(ii).

The general issue of use of known substances for purposes consistent with known properties and the effect this has on upon patentability was also discussed by the court in *NRDC* (**[8.380]**). The following comments are generally useful to an understanding of the point discussed in the extract from *Bristol Myers Squibb*.

━━━━━ NRDC v Commissioner of Patents ━━━━━

[8.380] *National Research Development Corporation v Commissioner of Patents* (1959) 102 CLR 252 High Court of Australia

[The facts of this case were stated at **[8.40]**.]

[261] The principles which govern the power to refuse a patent have been discussed recently in the case of *Commissioner of Patents v Microcell Ltd* (1959) 102 CLR 232. It is shown in that case that in the portion of the definition of invention which includes in the meaning of the word an alleged invention, the word "alleged" goes only to the epithet "new" in the expression "a manner of new manufacture", and that accordingly the Commissioner may properly reject a claim for [262] a process which is not within the concept of a "manufacture". But the case cited shows also that even if the process is within the concept the Commissioner is not bound to accept the allegation of the applicant that it is new, if it is apparent on the face of the specification, when properly construed, that the allegation is unfounded: see also *Re Johnson's Patent* (1937) 55 RPC 4 at 19. It is therefore open to the Commissioner in a proper case to direct the deletion of a claim for a process which may be seen from the specification, considered as a whole, to be "outside the whole scope of what is known as invention" because, in the words of Lord Buckmaster, when Solicitor-General, in *Re BA's Application* (1915) 32 RPC 348 at 349 it is "nothing but a claim for a new use of an old substance".

▰▰▰▰▰ NRDC v Commissioner of Patents *continued*

But, as the *Microcell* case (1959) 102 CLR 232 emphasises, it must always be remembered how much is wrapped up in the "nothing but". Lord Buckmaster did not use the words without explanation: "when once a substance is known," he said, "its methods of production ascertained, its characteristics and its constituents well-defined, you cannot patent the use of that for a purpose which was hitherto unknown": *Re BA's Application* (1915) 32 RPC 348 at 349. And why? Because in the postulated state of knowledge the new purpose is no more than analogous to the purposes for which the utility of the substance is already known, and therefore your suggestion of the new purpose lacks the quality of inventiveness: see per Bowen LJ in *Elias v Grovesend Tinplate Co* (1890) 7 RPC 455 at 468. Unless invention is found in some new method of using the material or some new adaptation of it so as to serve the new purpose, no valid patent can be granted: see *Moser v Marsden* (1893) 10 RPC 350 at 358; *Pirrie v York Street Flax Spinning Co Ltd* (1894) 11 RPC 429 at 452. If, however, the new use that is proposed consists in taking advantage of a hitherto unknown or unsuspected property of the material, the situation is not that to which Lord Buckmaster's language refers. In that case there may be invention in the suggestion that the substance may be used to serve the new purpose; and then, provided that a practical method of so using it is disclosed and that the process comes within the concept of patent law ultimately traceable to the use in the *Statute of Monopolies* of the words "manner of manufacture", all the elements of a patentable invention are present: see the *Microcell* case (1959) 102 CLR 232 at 248, 249.

[264] No-one reading the specification in the present case can fail to see that what it claims is a new process for ridding crop areas of certain kinds of weeds, not by applying chemicals the properties of which were formerly well understood so that the idea of using them for this purpose involved no inventive step, but by applying chemicals which formerly were supposed not to be useful for this kind of purpose at all. There is a clear assertion of a discovery that a useful result can be attained by doing something which the applicant's research has shown for the first time to be capable of producing that result. This is not a claim which can be put aside as a claim for a new use of an old substance, true though it be that the chemicals themselves were known to science before the applicant's investigations began. It is a claim which denies that the chemicals are old substances in the sense in which the expression has been used in such cases as *Re AF's Application* (1913) 31 RPC 58; *Re BA's Application* (1915) 32 RPC 348 and *Re CGR's Application* (1924) 42 RPC 320. It treats them as substances which in the relevant sense are new, that is to say as substances which formerly were known only partially and, so far as weed-killing potentialities are concerned, were unknown ...

[There follows an analysis of the claims and the judgment continues:]

[268] The purpose of going thus fully into the contents of the specification is to show that it is out of the question to hold that on the face of the document, properly construed, the process the subject of the first three claims appears as nothing but a new use of an old substance.

SECRET USE

[8.385] One ground of invalidity of a patent is secret use in the patent area before the priority date (s 18(1)(d)). The *Patents Act 1990* (Cth), s 9 gives examples of what is not a secret use of an invention in the patent area.

There has been much confusion over what amounts to "secret" use such as will invalidate a patent for want of novelty. It seems that touting an invention about in order to see whether it will be a success in the market place may not be public use in the sense that the invention is revealed but will be an invalid secret use within s 9. See *Re Wheatley's Patent Application* (1984) 2 IPR 450; also *Bioglan Laboratories (Aust) Pty Ltd v Crooks* (1989) 17 IPR 328; *Riekie & Simpfendorfer v MJ McGrath Pty Ltd* (1985) 7 IPR 120; *A & K Aluminium Pty Ltd v Lidco Systems Sales Pty Ltd* (1990) 18 IPR 597; *Graf v Milward-Bason* (1990) 18 IPR 566; *Clafton Pty Ltd v Forbes Engineering Holdings Pty Ltd* (1990) 19 IPR 29.

Old Digger v Azuko

[8.390] *Old Digger Pty Ltd v Azuko Pty Ltd* (2000) 51 IPR 43; [2000] FCA 676 Federal Court of Australia

[The applicant alleged that the defendants had infringed two patents related to percussive hammers used in drilling equipment in the mining industry. The defendants counterclaimed for revocation of the patents alleging, amongst other things, a number of prior disclosures which they argued constituted either anticipation leading to lack of novelty or amounted to impermissible secret use.]

VON DOUSSA J: [81]
Under the 1990 Act revocation may be ordered on the ground that the invention is not a patentable invention: s 138(3)(b). An invention will not be a patentable invention if the invention has been:

> "secretly used in the patent area before the priority date of that claim by, or on behalf of, or with the authority of, the patentee or nominated person or the patentee's or nominated person's predecessor in title to the invention." (s 18(1)(d))

By s 9 of the 1990 Act the following acts are not to be taken to be secret use of the invention in the patent area:

> "(a) any use of the invention by or on behalf of, or with the authority of, the patentee or nominated person, or his or her predecessor in title to the invention, for the purpose of reasonable trial or experiment only;
>
> (b) any use of the invention by or on behalf of, or with the authority of, the patentee or nominated person, or his or her predecessor in title to the invention, being use [82] occurring solely in the course of a confidential disclosure of the invention by or on behalf of, or with the authority of, the patentee, nominated person, or predecessor in title; ..."

Thus the questions which the allegations of prior use of the inventions pose are:

> (a) whether the alleged use disclosed to a person skilled in the relevant art all the essential features or integers of each of the inventions; and if so
> (b) whether the use was a use in public; or
> (c) whether the use was a secret use by, or on behalf of, or with the authority of, the patentee or nominated person or the patentee's or nominee's predecessor in title to the invention, not being acts protected by s 9 of the 1990 Act. (This question is posed in terms of the 1990 Act as the 1952 Act is not more favourable to the applicant in its treatment of secret use: see [76] above).

███████   Old Digger v Azuko *continued*

The onus of proof is on the respondents to establish a clear case of invalidity: see *Montecatini Edison SpA v Eastman Kodak Co* (1971) 45 ALJR 593 at 595-596 per Gibbs J. The evidence adduced by the respondents as to the prior use of the invention is the oral evidence of witnesses to the alleged use based on their recollections of events years beforehand. The alleged use is said to have taken place in the course of trialling reverse circulation percussive hammers incorporating prototype face sampling drill bit assemblies. The particular assemblies have not been produced in evidence. Oral evidence led in these circumstances must be viewed with particular caution, partly for the reason that the memory of the witnesses is likely to have been influenced by other products seen in the meantime, and to reflect reconstruction on the basis of these later observations: see *Commonwealth Industrial Gases Ltd v MWA Holdings Pty Ltd* (1970) 180 CLR 160 at 165-166, and *Nicaro Holdings Pty Ltd v Martin Engineering Co* (1990) 91 ALR 513 at 525 per Gummow J.

[His Honour found that these uses were indeed secret uses of the hammers, which accordingly did not deprive the invention of novelty, and because made for the purpose of reasonable trial and experiment came within s 9(a). His Honour then considered other allegations of prior user including secret use.] [92]

The respondents also allege that the manufacture of the fifteen to twenty hammers before the priority date was a secret use which prevented the invention from being a patentable invention on 19 April 1990. One of the historical bases for the secret user ground of revocation was to prevent a patentee from gaining a longer monopoly than the statutory period of sixteen years by enjoying a period of de facto monopoly through the secret user without meeting the corresponding obligation attaching to such a monopoly, namely the public disclosure of the invention. It is against this rationale that the exemption in respect of use for the purpose of reasonable trial and experiment only is to be understood. There is authority that a prior secret use, if it is to invalidate a patent, must be a commercial use, although not every commercial use will necessarily be outside the concept of a reasonable trial and experiment only: see Ricketson, *The Law of Intellectual Property* (1984) at 49.27 and *International Paint Co Ltd's Application* [1982] RPC 247 at 274. Whether or not a particular secret use is for the purposes of reasonable trial and experiment only is a question of fact and degree in each case, depending on all the circumstances including the nature of the invention in question: see *Harrison v Project & Design Co (Redcar) Ltd* [1978] FSR 81 at 89 and *Young et al Terrell on the Law of Patents* (14th ed, 1994) at 5.41. In the present case the trial and experimentation conducted in Darwin in March 1990 was of a single prototype hammer. In my opinion reasonable trial and experiment of the invention would extend to the use of the invention in proceeding from that prototype to the production of commercial quality hammers for sale. Without actual manufacture of a commercial quality product, it would be difficult to know whether the invention would be economically viable, and whether other modifications were required to perfect the invention. I consider the manufacture of fifteen to twenty hammers in the period of less than one month following the trials in Darwin is within the scope of reasonable trial—at least that view is open on the very limited evidence elicited from Mr Giehl about the manufacture, which did not inquire of him what was involved in proceeding from prototype to commercial production, and why fifteen to twenty hammers were made when they were. I am not satisfied that the respondents [93] have made out a case for revocation of the Giehl patent on the ground of secret use not being for the purpose of reasonable trial or experiment only.

However, whether or not that view be correct, in my opinion the manufacture of the fifteen to twenty units, none of which was exposed for public view, or offered for sale before the priority date, comes within the exception from secret use provided in s 9(b) of the 1990 Act.

■■■■■   Old Digger v Azuko *continued*

In the manufacture of those units the invention was used by and on behalf of the predecessor in title of the invention, that use being a confidential use which did not involve disclosure of the invention to anyone other than employees of Mr Giehl engaged upon the manufacture.

Azuko v Old Digger

[8.395] *Azuko Pty Ltd v Old Digger Pty Ltd* (2001) 52 IPR 75; [2001] FCA 1079.

[The issue of "secret use" was one of the grounds for appeal from the previous case. Gyles J, with whom Beaumont J agreed held that there was no relevant "use" of the patented invention, while Heerey J took a more comprehensive view of the word use considering it be co-extensive with the term exploit, and so found that an invalidating secret use had occurred.]

GYLES J: [133]
The pleadings raise issues of both "use" as anticipation and "secret use". The trial judge sensibly looked at them together. The first issue on the pleadings is whether the acts in question are "use" under either limb: public or secret.

In my opinion, the trial judge was plainly right to reject the argument reflected in pars 2(10)(b) and 3A(b) of the particulars of objection, namely, that the receipt of an unsolicited order from the person who had been involved in testing of the prototype was use by Mr Giehl of the invention in any sense. It did not involve Mr Giehl in any relevant activity at all. There is no challenge to this finding.

The question left is as to the significance of the facts alleged in pars 2(10)(a) and 3A(a) of the Particulars of Objection which amount to manufacture simpliciter but with a view to eventual sale after application was made for the patent. There was, and could be, no finding that the appellants had proved that what was done was public. The evidence does not disclose any third party being involved in the manufacture. Even if employees were involved, it could be assumed that they would be bound by confidence. It can also be taken that, leaving aside consideration of uses within s 9 of the 1990 Act, what was done was intended to be, and was, secret, in the sense of being confidential. Indeed, it is plain enough that Mr Giehl had received advice as to patent law and practice and was concerned to ensure that there was no public disclosure before the priority date.

Counsel for both parties have made comprehensive written and oral submissions as to whether what occurred was "use" of the invention. Having considered these submissions, I have come to the conclusion that making the items in question was not "use" of the invention for relevant purposes. In my opinion, this follows from an understanding of the principle involved.

The trial judge drew attention to the relevant historical basis for the secret use ground of revocation, namely, to prevent a patentee from gaining a longer monopoly than the statutory period by enjoying a period of *de facto* monopoly through the secret use before the priority date, without meeting the corresponding obligation attaching to such a monopoly, namely, the public disclosure of the invention. This can be traced back (at least) to the informative case of *Morgan v Seaward* (1837) 2 M & W 544, 150 ER 874 ("*Seaward*"), where Parke B said (at 559):

> "... if the inventor could sell his invention, keeping the secret to himself, and, when it was likely to be discovered by another, take out a patent, he might have, practically, a monopoly for a much longer period than fourteen years."

In *Bristol-Myers Co v Beecham Group Ltd* [1974] AC 646 ("*Bristol-Myers*") Lord Diplock said (at 680-681):

> "... For the other mischief against which that statute was directed was that even monopolies of new manufactures should not extend beyond 14 years. If the inventor had already *reaped commercial benefit* from a de facto monopoly in his discovery owing to his concealment from all other traders of the way in which the new substance could be made, he was not to be permitted to prolong his monopoly for an additional 14 years. [134] So "public use" in the sense of commercial dealing in a product claimed as an invention, by any trader even though it were by the inventor himself, rendered invalid any patent for the product claimed.
>
> In the case of use by traders, at any rate, the expression 'public use' was not employed to mark the contrast between public and secret use but to distinguish commercial from experimental use in the course of discovering, perfecting and trying out the invention so as to test its suitability for commercial use. As the expression 'manufactures' in the *Statute of Monopolies* indicates, it was the commercial usefulness of the new inventions that provided the reason for encouraging them by grants of temporary monopolies to their inventors, and this object of the statute would be defeated if mere experimental uses of this kind either by the applicant for the patent or by others who had worked privily on the same discovery were to be a bar to the grant of a patent to him who first publicly disclosed the way in which the invention could be carried out." (emphasis added)

This passage suggests a practical test: has what occurred amounted to a *de facto* extension of the patent term? The answer to this will usually depend upon whether the patentee reaped commercial benefit from what was done before the priority date. In the present case, in my opinion, there has been no *de facto* extension of the term of the patent by making the articles in question.

The test of illegitimate extension of the patent term yields satisfactory results in differing circumstances. If the invention is a process or method, to secretly use the process or method to make goods for sale can readily be seen as a secret commercial use of the invention which would extend the patent if done prior to the priority date. Another example of secret commercial use of that character is if the product which is manufactured according to a product claim is then secretly used as part of a manufacturing process to make other goods before the priority date. Another example would be the use of a device made according to the SDS patent as part of a drill rig engaged in commercial drilling, but in conditions of secrecy, prior to the priority date. To make an article for ultimate [135] sale has, no doubt, a commercial aspect, but it does not amount to use of the product made and does not involve any *de facto* extension of the term of a patent claiming the product. The manufacturing of goods is not, in my opinion, commercial use of those goods.

...

My conclusion on this issue does not depend upon "use" being exclusive of the other aspects of the monopoly granted to a patentee which are reflected in the definition of "exploit" in the 1990 Act. It may be accepted that the various kinds of exploitation may overlap in different circumstances. I would accept, for example, that to sell goods might be seen as commercial use of the goods. However, reference to the different kinds of exploitation goes back to words in the original form of letters patent "to make, use, exercise and vend the invention" and the distinctions cannot be ignored (cf Heerey J in *Welcome Real-Time SA v Catuity Inc* [2001] FCA 445 at [101]-[103]).

▇▇▇▇▇   Azuko v Old Digger *continued*

If I were wrong concerning secret use, I would have difficulty with the conclusions of the trial judge as to the application of s 9(a) and (b) of the 1990 Act, substantially for the reasons advanced by the appellants and accepted by Heerey J. However, it is not necessary for me to come to a final view as to that.

HEEREY J (In dissent): [116]

4. Whether invention secretly used

...

The terms "use", "secret use", and "secretly used" are not defined in the Act. The rights conferred by a patent are the exclusive rights, during the term of the patent, "to exploit the invention and to authorise another person to exploit the invention": s 13(1). "Exploit" is defined in sch 1 in these terms:

In my opinion "not ... used" in s 18(1)(d) is referring compendiously to the exercise of any of the rights which would be conferred by a patent for the invention in question. True it is the drafters of s 18(1)(d) might have used the new term "exploit", but since English is a language rich in synonyms (being [117] historically a combination of two languages) the fact that one word is chosen instead of another often will carry little weight if the intended meaning is otherwise clear.

...

In s 100(1)(k) of the 1952 Act, prior secret use was dealt with in terms not relevantly different from s 18(1)(d) of the present Act. There is no obvious reason for imputing to the drafters of the present Act an intention that the change from "make, use, exercise and vend" to "exploit" should, by a sidewind, substantially narrow the range of conduct which might constitute prior secret use. Nor is there any discernible policy reason why "secret use" should exclude manufacture but, as the respondent concedes, include sale.

The definition of "exploit" in the present Act is not exhaustive; it "includes" the matters specified. In the case of a product, those matters amount to twenty alternatives, one of which is "use". The respondent's argument would mean that "secretly used" in s 18(1)(d) is referring to only one of the myriad ways in which an invention may be exploited. This seems contrary to the underlying rationale of the concept, which is that the prior secret user

"... should invalidate any patent subsequently granted, since patentees might otherwise postpone indefinitely the communication of their inventions to the public, and might in practice obtain a monopoly not only for the ordinary period of 16 years under the Statute but also for any prior period during which they had contrived to retain the secret of their inventions." (*Sargent Committee Report* (1931) par 305)

The monopoly there spoken of is the monopoly to enjoy the exclusive rights which a patent confers. There is a natural symmetry between what patentees can do with the invention after grant and what they could do secretly before grant, were it not for the doctrine of prior secret use.

Counsel for the respondent argued that there was no "use" within [118] s 18(1)(d) because there was no "taint of commerciality". Mr Giehl's making and keeping the hammers for later use or sale "stopped well short of a relevant commercial dealing and there (was) no evidence that his conduct resulted in the reaping of a commercial benefit".

It may be that "commerciality" is relevant to the question whether a particular activity involves using an invention: see *Re Wheatley's Application* (1984) 2 IPR 450 at 451, discussed infra. However, in the Act this aspect may shade into s 9(c) which excludes what would otherwise be prior secret use where there is use of the invention by the patentee "for any

▰▰▰ Azuko v Old Digger *continued*

purpose other than the purpose of trade or commerce". (The first legislation as to prior secret use in the UK, *Patents and Designs Act 1932* (Imp), s 3, inserting s 25(2)(o) in the 1907 Act, spoke of an invention being secretly worked "on a commercial scale". This qualification disappeared in the 1949 Act. As to the position under the 1977 Act, see *Terrell on the Law of Patents* (15th ed), p 159). Counsel for the respondent did not rely on s 9(c), and understandably so. Plainly Mr Giehl had a purpose of trade or commerce. This is probably sufficient in itself to answer the commerciality point, but I shall return to this aspect.

I turn now to authorities bearing on the point. (His Honour discussed passages from the following authorities: *R v Patents Appeal Tribunal, Ex parte Beecham Group Ltd* [1974] AC 646; *Fomento Industrial SA v Mentmore Manufacturing Co Limited* [1956] RPC 87 at 115; *Re Wheatley's Patent Application* (1984) 2 IPR 450 at 451- 453 apparently to demonstrate the comprehensive nature of the word "use" in these cases.)

... 122]

Before leaving this issue, the facts of the present case should be recalled. This was not, as the respondent submitted, "bare manufacture". Mr Giehl, before the priority date, manufactured fifteen or twenty hammers. It was his intention to sell them, doubtless at a profit. Some of those hammers were destined to fill Mr Gaden's order for five or six. There is no evidence that any of the hammers had been appropriated to Mr Gaden so that property passed to him: *Sale of Goods Act 1895* (SA) s 18 rule 5(1). However, there may well have been a binding contract constituted by Mr Gaden's order and Mr Giehl accepting that order by his conduct in manufacturing hammers: Cheshire and Fifoot *Law of Contract* (7th Australian ed) 95, Chitty on Contracts (28th ed) 101. Had the market for hammers collapsed and Mr Gaden refused to take delivery, Mr Giehl may well have had an action in damages. Whether this be so or not, the present case is a far cry from *Morgan v Seaward*. When one asks why Mr Giehl made these fifteen or twenty hammers, the answer must be that he proposed to sell them, including some five or six to Mr Gaden to fill an order already received. This has a distinctly commercial look about it. No philanthropy or hobby was involved. Mr Giehl's activity was, in the words of counsel in *Beecham*, something done for gain or for industrial or commercial purposes. When one asks how he made the hammers, the answer must be that he employed and applied the idea embodied in the Giehl patent and the detailed specification contained therein.

Looked at another way, on the priority date Mr Giehl had fifteen or twenty hammers ready for sale and delivery (subject to Mr Gaden's right in relation to five or six of them). This was a new and inventive product. Mr Giehl could immediately go into the market with this new, and presumably superior, product and thus obtain an immediate advantage over his competitors, who could not lawfully copy his product. How had he obtained this advantage? Because he had manufactured the hammers before the priority date employing the information of the Giehl patent.

In my opinion this was a use of the invention of the Giehl patent. The element of secrecy not being in dispute, the appellants established that the invention was secretly used before the priority date of the patent within the meaning of s 18(1)(d).

5. Whether reasonable trial and experiment—s 9(a)

The evidence permitted of only one conclusion. Production of fifteen or twenty hammers in a condition ready for commercial sale, an order having been received for five or six, cannot be considered a matter of trial and experiment, let alone *only* trial and experiment. .... In any event, the manufacture of fifteen or twenty hammers in a condition ready for sale (or of [123] "commercial quality" as his Honour put it) indicates that trial and experiment had concluded

███████ Azuko v Old Digger *continued*

in Darwin and commercial production commenced in Adelaide. As Mr Giehl accepted, the hammers were "ready to work".

There is a total lack of evidence from Mr Giehl as to what trials or experiments were carried out on the Adelaide hammers. The reasonable inference is that there were none. Even if he were making a limited number to see if production was commercially viable, I do not think that would be the kind of trial and experiment of which s 9(a) speaks. The provision is limited to trial or experiment to see how the product of an invention performs and whether any improvements are needed, as distinct from commercial or marketing assessments. But in any event Mr Giehl did not suggest his manufacture was for the limited purpose found by his Honour. The inference to be drawn is simply that Mr Giehl manufactured hammers because he proposed to sell them.

6. Whether in the course of confidential disclosure – s 9(b)

While it was accepted Mr Giehl's employees would be under obligations of confidence, s 9(b) speaks of use of the invention "solely in the course of a confidential disclosure". This suggests some larger transaction, properly characterised as a confidential disclosure of the invention, in the course of which the invention is "used". An example would be a demonstration to a patent attorney or potential purchaser or investor. Here there was no such disclosure. The hammers were simply manufactured for the purpose of sale. Such disclosure of the invention as there may have been by Mr Giehl to his employees—and he gave no evidence as to this— was not a disclosure in the course of which the invention was used. It was the other way around. He disclosed the invention to them so they could manufacture a product of the invention and thus "use" the invention. In any event, the use was not solely in the course of confidential disclosure—it was also for the purpose of sale.

Note

[8.400] For a discussion of the burden of proof in cases where secret use is relied upon as a ground of revocation see the discussion by Dowsett J in *Grove Hill Pty Ltd v Great Western Corporation Pty Ltd* (2002) 55 IPR 257 at 313-316; [2002] FCAFC 183.

USEFUL

[8.405] A patentable invention must be useful (s 18(c)). This term has a technical meaning in patent law. It is a requirement that the patent must actually produce the results which are promised, either expressly or by implication, in a fair reading of the specification. Lack of utility, as the objection is put, is not a matter for consideration at the examination stage or at re-examination nor is it a ground of opposition. Lack of utility is a matter which can only be raised in revocation proceedings (ss 18(c) and 138 (3)(b)). The date for assessing utility is at the date of the invention. The concept of usefulness or utility in patent law overlaps the s 40 requirements discussed in **[8.405]**.

In the Matter of Alsop's Patent

[8.410] *In the Matter of Alsop's Patent* (1907) 24 RPC 733

PARKER J: The letters patent granted to JN Alsop in 1903 which are attacked in these proceedings are for a process only. That processes are good subject matter of letters patent was finally decided in 1842 in the case of *Crane v Price* (1842) 134 ER 239; 1 Web PC 393. ... But a process to be patentable must be a process which leads to some result and the result arrived at must be useful, though it need not be an article at all; for example, a new process for chemically cleaning dirty linen would be good subject matter, but a process of treating material, of which no result at all could be predicated, would not be patentable.

In considering the validity of a patent for a process, it is therefore material to ascertain precisely what the patentee claims to be the result of the process for which the patent has been granted; the real consideration which he gives for the grant is the disclosure of a process which produces a result, and not the disclosure of a process which may or may not produce any result at all. If the patentee claims protection for a process for producing a result, and that result cannot be produced by the process, in my opinion the consideration fails. Similarly if the patentee claims for a process producing two results combined and only one of these results is in fact produced by the process, there is a partial failure of consideration, just as there is in the case of a patent containing one valid and one invalid claim; and such partial failure of consideration is sufficient to avoid the patent, "If" said Buller J in *Turner v Winter* (1787) 1 Web PC 82; 99 ER 1274 "the Patentee says that by one process he can produce three things and he fails in any one, the consideration of his merit, and for which the patent was granted, fails, and the Crown has been deceived in the grant".

An analogous principle applies to patents for improvement. Of course the patentee must in such a case state the nature of the improvement, or in other words, the result which he claims to have secured by his invention. If no such result is in fact secured by following the directions given in the specification there is a failure of consideration and the patent is void.

Objections to patents on the grounds above referred to are sometimes treated as objections for want of utility, and when so treated the well-known rule is that the utility of an invention depends upon whether, by following the directions of the patentee, the result which the patentee professed to produce can in fact be produced: see Lindley LJ in *Lane Fox v Kensington* (1892) 9 RPC 413 at 417. Want of utility in this sense must however, in my opinion, be distinguished from want of utility in the sense of the invention being useless for any purpose whatever. In the case of an invention not serving any useful purpose at all, the patent would no doubt be void, but not entirely for the same reason. It would be probably void at common law on the ground that the king's prerogative could not be properly exercised unless there were some consideration moving to the public, and the public could not be benefited by the disclosure of something absolutely useless. It would certainly be avoided as mischievous to the state and generally inconvenient within the meaning of the *Statute of Monopolies*. But it may well be that an invention, which is void because it does not produce the result, or one of the results claimed, may nevertheless be useful as producing other results. Further, there may be cases in which the result which the patentee claims to have produced can in fact be produced, but the patentee has gone on to detail the useful purposes to which such result can be applied, and that in fact the result produced cannot be applied to one or more of such purpose. In such a case I do not think the patent is necessarily void, provided there are purposes for which the result is useful. If it be avoided it can only be because it contains a misrepresentation so material that it can be said the Crown has been deceived. The importance of drawing a distinction between what the patentee claims to have effected by the invention for which he claims protection, and a statement of the additional purposes to which the invention can be applied, is well illustrated by the case of *Lyon v Goddard* (1893) 10 RPC 121 at 334; 11 RPC 354.

Such being, in my opinion, the law, I must, before I can properly apply it, construe Alsop's specification, and determine what, according to its true construction, are the results claimed by the patentee to be produced by the patented process ...

The patent according to the title is for "an improved process of treating flour to purify the same and increase the nutritive qualities thereof", and the patentee commences his specification by stating that his invention:

"relates to a novel process of treating flour to purify the same and increase the nutritive qualities thereof, and to this end resides broadly in subjecting flour to the action of a gaseous medium which will operate to bleach or purify the flour, and cause a reduction in the quantity of carbohydrate contents, and an increase in the quantity of the protein contents thereof."

...

[His Honour reviewed the patentees' explanation of the apparatus used to carry out the process and then set out the patent claims and continued:]

I do not think it is necessary, for the purpose of the point I am considering, to attempt to distinguish or define the precise ambit of these claiming clauses, for I am satisfied, on the construction of the specification, that the process referred to in each clause is a process resulting in the bleaching of the flour and in increasing its proteids and diminishing its carbohydrates as suggested in the title and detailed and emphasised in the body of the specification. I cannot read the statements in the specification on these points merely as laudatory of the results obtained by the process. They are themselves the results of the process for which protection is claimed. I arrive at this conclusion without the assistance of the disclaimer contained in the specification, though such disclaimer, as will appear presently, strongly confirms the conclusion at which I have arrived. It being now admitted by everyone that the treatment of the flour in the manner described does not and cannot increase its proteids or diminish its carbohydrates, I am of opinion that, on the principles of law already referred to, the patent is invalid.

Martin Engineering v Trison Holdings

[8.415] *Martin Engineering Co v Trison Holdings Pty Ltd* (1989) 14 IPR 330 Federal Court of Australia

BURCHETT J: **[331]**
The evidence shows that conveyor belts used in the mining industry and elsewhere for the transport of materials require to be cleaned, generally by some form of scraping, at a point at or near the commencement of the **[332]** return run of the belt after discharge of its load. Various problems are associated with this operation. The load may leave a residue which may build up on the scraper or scrapers, and on the means by which they are applied to the belt. Maintenance may be rendered more difficult by constriction of space under and in the

■■■■■■■   Martin Engineering v Trison Holdings *continued*

vicinity of the belt, and particularly at the point of discharge of its load. The minimisation of loss of the productive operation of the belt during any stoppage for maintenance of scraping equipment is a consideration of some importance.

It appears that a number of devices have been adopted from quite primitive scrapers knocked up in a mine workshop to relatively complex equipment. Patents obtained in respect of such equipment span a period of over 40 years up to 1977.

The Martin patent is in respect of an invention entitled "Belt Cleaner Mounting Arrangement", being, as it is described in the abstract of the disclosure,

"a track mounted conveyor belt cleaner wherein individual belt scraper blades are affixed to sleeve members which slide linearly along a support member positioned generally transverse to the direction of travel of the belt to be cleaned. The sleeves are slidably mounted on the support member such that they may freely slide from one end to the other but are fixed against either rotational or vertical movement and provide for repair or replacement of wiper blades without requiring conveyor belt shutdown".

There is in the specification a recital of the prior art, suggesting that many arrangements "have presented certain problems with respect to repair or replacement of individual blade elements". It is stated:

"Sometimes the wiper blades are carried on one end of a torsion spring. The other end of the spring is affixed to a transverse support. Such an arrangement is illustrated in US Patent 3,342,312. As the wiper blades wear, periodic replacement is required. Occasionally a wiper blade becomes damaged during regular use and the individual blade must be replaced. In either of these situations the conveyor belt must be shutdown [sic] and one of two alternatives is presented to the belt operator. If access permits, the operator may be able to disconnect the individual wiper blades from the support shaft and replace them as needed. In the majority of situations however, access to the underside of the conveyor belt is limited and the entire support shaft must be removed from the side of the conveyor housing. This is often difficult to accomplish because of limited space. The time lost for conveyor shutdown due to wiper blade replacement is a critical factor to be considered.

It is therefore an object of the present invention to provide a belt cleaner mounting arrangement which will obviate or minimise the foregoing disadvantages in a simple yet effective manner or which will at least provide the public with a useful choice."

...[334]

The cross-claimants' first ground of attack on the patent is the ground referred to in s 100(1)(h) of the *Patents Act 1952* (Cth), [see now s 18(1)(c)] "that the invention, so far as claimed in any claim of the complete specification ... is not useful". The cross-claimants draw attention to the words in the complete specification: "It is therefore an object of the present invention to provide a belt cleaner mounting arrangement which will obviate or minimise the foregoing disadvantages in a simple yet effective manner or which will at least provide the public with a useful choice". The "foregoing disadvantages" are conveyor shutdown, difficulty of disconnection of individual wiper blades from the support shaft, and "in the majority of situations" limited access to the underside of the conveyor belt and necessity to remove the entire support shaft from the side of the conveyor housing, which is "often difficult to accomplish because of limited space". The ultimate disadvantage is "time lost". ... [336]

The question, of course, is not whether the particular version or versions of the invention in fact marketed will work; the question is whether any version constructed in accordance

■■■■■   Martin Engineering v Trison Holdings *continued*

with claim 1 will work. There was no suggestion that any such embodiment of the invention would not work, if that means that it would not provide an effective belt cleaner the appropriate maintenance of which would be practicable. In other words, there was no challenge to utility in the sense that the invention is capable of making "the wheels ... go round", to use the often quoted metaphor of Maugham LJ in *Mullard Radio Valve Co Ltd v Philco Radio & Television Corp of Great Britain Ltd* (1935) 52 RPC 261 at 287. It has been said that this is what is required for immunity against attack on the ground of inutility not that an invention is commercially practicable: *Lane Fox v Kensington & Knightsbridge Electrical Lighting Co* [1892] 3 Ch 424 at 431.

[The cross-claimants argued it would be possible, following the instructions given in the specification to build a conveyer belt cleaner which took up a lot of space and was slow to disassemble and clean, both disadvantages claimed to be overcome by the present invention.] [337]

It is true that, for the purposes of utility, it is necessary to consider what on their correct construction is specified in the claims; if on their correct construction they assert a monopoly, not only in respect of something useful, but also in respect of something not useful, the patent is bad: Blanco White, *Patents for Inventions* (5th ed, 1983), paras 4.408-4.412. In *Norton & Gregory Ltd v Jacobs* (1937) 54 RPC 271 at 276-277 Lord Greene MR, speaking for the Court of Appeal, held that a claim for a process which included the words "wherein there is present ... a reducing agent" could not be cut down to avoid inutility by limiting it to those processes in which there was present a reducing agent that would work. It was held not to be enough that "a skilled chemist would avoid working in part of the area which the words in their ordinary meaning are wide enough to include". But Lord Greene was not eschewing the ordinary processes of construction of a document; he was asserting that the claims have to be read in the light of their function, that is "to define with clarity the area of [the] monopoly". He emphasised: "It is illegitimate to whittle away clear words in a claim by reading into them glosses and limitations extracted from the body of the specification whose function is in its essence different from that of the claim".

This reasoning, of course, cannot be applied where the words in the claim are not "clear words", nor does the reference to the peculiar purpose of the claims mean that they are to be construed without regard to the [338] specification of which they form part: see Blanco White, *Patents for Inventions* (5th ed, 1983), paras 2.101-2.104, and see *Henriksen v Tallon Ltd* [1963] RPC 329 at 335. In *British Thomson-Houston Co Ltd v Guildford Radio Stores* (1937) 55 RPC 71 at 88, Luxmoore J affirmed the necessity "to remember that the claims of a specification must be considered in the light of what an intelligent person skilled in the particular art to which they relate and desirous of making use of the invention would do ... to introduce into every claim limitations dictated by common sense after a perusal of the whole of the specification including the claim; and ... that a claim is not to be invalidated for vagueness or ambiguity by reason of the fact that it is possible to imagine debatable territory where the advantages of the invention may not be obtained". In *Welch Perrin Pty Ltd v Worrel* (1961) 106 CLR 588 at 601-602 Menzies J, as to whose decision on the point the Full Court (at 622) had "no doubt", said:

> "The lack of utility alleged did not go beyond the suggestion that the claims were so general that an unworkable machine could be made in conformity therewith. ... The principle that all within the scope of the claim must be useful if the claim is not to fail for inutility was invoked and reference was made to *Norton* and *Gregory Ltd v Jacobs* and other cases which show that a claim is bad if it covers means that will not produce the desired result even if a skilful person would know which means to avoid."

After referring to a particular suggestion of a useless machine that could be constructed according to the claim, he said:

> "I consider, however, that no-one reading the specification would so understand it and that a very ordinary person would know what was a workable angle. What I have quoted from the Master of the Rolls [this was a reference to the *Norton and Gregory* case] does not mean that a specification should be construed in a way that any sensible person would appreciate would lead to unworkability when by construction it could be given a more limited meaning."

It will be noted that in this passage Menzies J said "no-one reading the specification would so understand it", thus making it plain that he regarded the specification as legitimately throwing light on the true meaning of the claim. This decision was cited by Stephen J in *Washex Machinery Corp v Roy Burton Pty Ltd* (1974) 49 ALJR 12 at 18-20, where he also distinguished the *Norton and Gregory* case, dismissing a suggested type of useless machine, constructed according to the claim, as one which would only be produced "by a quite purposeful adoption of such a form ... as would obviously malfunction". He commented: "To postulate such a happening is not an appropriate mode of testing validity of a patent specification".

In my view, it is quite apparent from a reading of the whole specification in the present case how the invention enables the number of sleeves to be related to the width of the belt to be cleaned and the space available. To adapt the words of Stephen J, only by a quite purposeful selection of an inappropriately large sleeve could the result for which the cross-claimants contend be produced. Even if, in deference to the *Norton and Gregory* case, attention is focused singlemindedly on the claim, the words "at least one sleeve" must direct the attention of the skilled reader to the fact that a selection has to be made of the appropriate number for the job; in other words, he is inevitably cast back to the specification which makes plain the criteria of appropriateness. In terms of Lord Greene's formulation of the [339] principle, this is to narrow the claim by a process of construction in the light of the rest of the document of which it forms part, and not impermissibly to place a gloss upon it.

[The claim was found to reveal a useful invention.]

■■

■■■■■■■■ Rescare v Anaesthetic Supplies ■■■■■■■■

[8.420] *Rescare Ltd v Anaesthetic Supplies Pty Ltd* (1992) 25 IPR 119 Federal Court of Australia

[The applicant was registered proprietor of a standard patent for an invention entitled "device for treating snoring sickness" or obstructive sleep apnoea and alleged infringement of each of claims 1, 3, 6, 7, 8, 9 and 11. The inventor was Professor Sullivan, Professor of Medicine at the University of Sydney. Obstructive sleep apnoea (OSA) is a syndrome associated with an extreme form of snoring in which the sufferer chokes on his or her tongue and soft palate repeatedly whilst asleep. The invention consisted of a combination of integers permitting air at slightly above a normal atmospheric pressure to be introduced into the patients' upper respiratory passage. In this case and in subsequent litigation there was dispute about the precise form of the device but in broad it consisted of a source of pressurised air, tubes and an attachment (either nasal tubes or a mask) to the patients nose.]

▬▬▬▬   Rescare v Anaesthetic Supplies *continued*

GUMMOW J: **[142]**

Utility

I have referred already to the concept embodied in s 40 of insufficiency. The distinction between insufficiency and ambiguity on the one hand, and inutility on the other, is said to be that insufficiency occurs when the apparatus cannot be made, and inutility occurs when the apparatus can be made but, when made, does not work. However, as has been pointed out, the distinction is often less clear in practice: *Blanco White*, supra para 4-404. The result in this case is that there has been some overlapping in the submissions on these topics.

It is also important to bear in mind two related proposition. The first is that a claim may have utility even though the promised advantage is not achieved in all cases and the second is that there may be infringement of an apparatus claim if the machine can be used in a manner which infringes even though it can also be used in a manner which does not infringe: *Martin Engineering Co v Nicaro Holdings Pty Ltd* (1991) AIPC 90-799 at 37,582-3, per Burchett J.

Section 100(1) provides that a standard patent may be revoked either wholly or insofar as it relates to any claim of the complete specification on the ground that: **[143]**

> "(h) that the invention, so far as claimed in any claim of the complete specification ... is not useful; ..."

The ground of inutility is not concerned with the question of whether, in the present case, the apparatus to be used by following the directions in the Patent would not be commercially viable; rather, the question is whether the invention as claimed does not attain the result promised for it by the patentee: *Decor Corp Pty Ltd v Dart Industries Inc* supra at 38,829 per Lockhart J. A distinction is to be drawn between cases where the invention claimed is not useful unless an additional integer or integers be added (such claims being invalid) and those cases where qualifications and expedients necessary to make work the article which has been claimed can be, and on a proper construction of the claim are, left to the skilled reader to supply for himself; *Welch Perrin Pty Ltd v Worrel* supra at 601, 2, *Blanco White*, supra para 4-409. See also *Washex Machinery Corp v Roy Burton Pty Ltd* (1974) 49 ALJR 12 at 18-19.

Thus, in the present case, whilst claim 1 and some of the dependent claims do not claim an apparatus including a blower (an absence relied upon by the respondent) this does not mean that there is a lack of utility. The need for a particular air source would be apparent to the skilled addressee. If it be necessary, resort to the body of the specification shows that the air supply in a preferred form consists of a high volume air pump and one particular proprietary product is described as having been found to be ideal (p 3, ll 16-20).

The respondent also complains that claim 1 does not specify the appropriate weight, size or degree of comfort in the apparatus nor the appropriate means by which the nose piece is to be sealingly attached to the face of the patient in an airtight manner. However, it must borne in mind that it is not the task of the claims to teach the application of the invention; the task of the claims is to define the invention and mark out the area of the monopoly. Claims should not be construed in a way which the skilled addressee would appreciate would lead to unworkability. The Court should be reluctant to place a construction upon a claim so as to include embodiments which to the qualified reader would appear useless. A different result may obtain where the terms of a claim positively point to some useless construction, as in *Cincinnati Grinders (Inc) v BSA Tools Ltd* (1931) 48 RPC 33 at 73. Claim 1 and the dependent apparatus claims are not within this category.

[His Honour considered a number of other allegations of inutility against the evidence and concluded that the allegations of inutility had not been made out.]

Notes

[8.425] Some other cases in which the requirement of utility has been adjudicated include *Searle (GD) v Commissioner of Patents* (1987) 8 IPR 376; *Townsend Controls Pty Ltd v Gilread* 16 IPR 469; *Rehm Pty Ltd v Websters Security Systems (International) Pty Ltd* (1988) 11 IPR 299; *NV Philips Gloeilampenfabrieken v Mirabella International Pty Ltd* (1993) 26 IPR 513 at 540; *Patent Gesellschaft AG v Saudi Livestock Transport & Trading Co* (1996) 33 IPR 426; *Wimmera Industrial Minerals Pty Ltd v RGC Mineral Sands Ltd* (1996) 34 IPR 367; *Pracedes Pty Ltd v Stanlite Electronics Pty Ltd* (1995) 35 IPR 259; *Nesbit Evans Group Australia Pty Ltd v Impro Ltd* (1997) 39 IPR 56; *Old Digger Pty Ltd v Azuko Pty Ltd* (2000) 51 IPR 43.

The Australia-United States Free Trade Agreement requires at Art 17.9.5 that "each party shall provide that a claimed invention is useful if it has a specific, substantial and credible utility". The phrase "specific, substantial and credible" is also found in United States *Revised Utility Guidelines 2001.*

There has been discussion of the requirement of usefulness in the Australian Law Reform Commission Report, *Genes and Ingenuity*, Report 99 (June 2004).

"Recommendation 6-3

The Commonwealth should amend the *Patents Act 1990* (Cth) ...to:

(a) include "usefulness" as a requirement in the examination of an application for a standard patent and in the certification of an innovation patent;

(b) provide that the invention will satisfy the requirement of "usefulness" only if the patent application discloses a specific, substantial and credible use;

(c) require the Commissioner of Patents to be satisfied on the balance of probabilities that the requirement of "usefulness" is made out in order to accept an application for a standard patent or to certify an innovation patent; and

(d) include "lack of usefulness" as a basis upon which an accepted application for a standard patent may be opposed in addition to its current role as a ground of revocation.

Recommendation 6-4

IP Australia should develop guidelines, consistent with the *Patents Act*, the *Patents Regulations 1991* (Cth) and existing case law, to assist patent examiners in applying the "usefulness" requirement. The guidelines should outline factors relevant to determining whether a use disclosed in a patent application is specific, substantial and credible to a person skilled in the art."

CHAPTER 9

SPECIFICATIONS—THE INTERNAL OBJECTIONS

PRINCIPLES OF CONSTRUCTION OF SPECIFICATIONS

[9.05] Since the consideration for the grant of a patent monopoly depends on what is revealed by the applicant, the patent specification must include three essential parts. First, it must fully describe the nature of what has been invented; secondly, it must describe the best method known to the inventor of making or performing that which has been invented; and thirdly, having taught what has been invented and how to achieve that invention, it must set out clearly the embodiments or applications of the invention which the patentee claims to reserve for his or her exclusive use. Those claims must not seek to monopolise more than is described or taught.

These requirements were originally demanded by the common law and are now found in the *Patents Act 1990* (Cth), s 40. The requirements are sometimes referred to as the "internal objections" and are called insufficiency—being an insufficient description of the invention or best method of performance; ambiguity—having to do with clarity of the claims; and fair basis—being a matter of comparing the monopolies claimed with the invention described.

Flexible Steel Lacing v Beltreco

[9.10] *Flexible Steel Lacing Co v Beltreco Ltd* (2000) 49 IPR 331 Federal Court of Australia

[The facts are outlined in the extract at **[8.325]**.]

HELY J: **[347]**

Some principles of construction

A patent is a public instrument which grants the right to protection of a defined monopoly, for the consideration of the disclosure of the invention to the general knowledge base of society. It is the need for balance between these symbiotic, yet competing interests which underscores the rules of patent construction.

Section 40 of the 1990 Act relevantly provides that a complete specification must describe the invention fully, that it must end with a claim or claims describing the invention and that the claim or claims must be clear and succinct, and fairly based on the matter described in the specification.

Further, to be valid the patent must define a monopoly in such a way that it is not reasonably capable of being misunderstood: *Martin v Scribal Pty Ltd* (1954) 92 CLR 17 at 59, *Welch Perrin Pty Ltd v Worrel* (1961) 106 CLR 588 at 610, *Populin v HB Nominees Pty Ltd* (1982) 41 ALR 471 at 476, *Fisher & Paykel Healthcare Pty Ltd v Avion Engineering Pty Ltd* (1991) 103 ALR 239 at 255, *Decor Corp Pty Ltd v Dart Industries Inc* (1988) 13 IPR 385 at 400.

When determining the nature and extent of the monopoly claimed, the specification must be read as a whole. But as a whole it is made up of several parts, and those parts have different functions: *Welch Perrin* at 610, *Decor* at 391, 398. The claim, cast in precise language, marks out the legal limits of the monopoly granted by the patent. What is not claimed is disclaimed: *Walker v Alemite Corp* (1933) 49 CLR 643 at 656, *Electric & Musical Industries Ltd v Lissen Ltd* (1939) 56 RPC 23 at 35 and 39. The specification describes how to carry out the process claimed and the best method known to the patentee of doing that.

Hence, although the claims are construed in the context of the specification as a whole, it is not legitimate to narrow or expand the boundaries of monopoly as fixed by the words of a claim, by adding to those words glosses drawn from other parts of the specification: *Welch Perrin* at 610, *Decor* at 391, 398, *Braas GmbH v Humes Ltd* (1993) 26 IPR 273 at 284. If a claim is clear and unambiguous, it is not to be varied, qualified or made obscure by statements found in other parts of the document: *Welch Perrin* at 610, *Interlego AG v Toltoys Pty Ltd* (1973) 130 CLR 461 at 478-479, *Electric & Musical Industries* at 41, *Rosedale Associated Manufacturers Ltd v Carlton Tyre Saving Co Ltd* [1960] RPC 59 at 69, *Cooper Industries Inc v Metal Manufactures Ltd* (1994) 29 IPR 106 at 113, *Lantech Inc v First Green Park Pty Ltd* (1995) 31 IPR 327 at 333.

It is legitimate, however, to refer to the rest of the specification to explain the background to the claims, to ascertain the meaning of technical terms and resolve ambiguities in the construction of the claim. Where the language of the claim is "obscure or doubtful" (*Martin v Scribal* at 97 per Taylor J) the doubt was sometimes resolved by referring to words in the body of the document to explain it: see *Welch Perrin* at 610-611; *Electric & Musical Industries* at 41-42, *Interlego* at 478-479, *Decor* at 400, *Melbourne v Terry Fluid Controls Pty Ltd* (1994) 28 IPR 302 at 308, *Freeman v TJ & FL Pohlner Pty Ltd* (1994-1995) 30 IPR 377 at 383-384, *Sartas No 1 Pty Ltd v Koukourou & Partners Pty Ltd* (1994-1995) 30 IPR 479 at 486.

In *Decor* at 410, Sheppard J rejected the notion that the claims are first to be construed without reference to the body of the specification, and it is only if **[348]** ambiguity is exposed by that process that reference to the body of the patent is permissible. In his Honour's view, that approach ignores the "fundamental rule of construction" that the specification must be

██████   Flexible Steel Lacing v Beltreco *continued*

read as a whole, and the modern approach to interpretation, which requires that the context be considered in the first instance, and not merely at some later stage when ambiguity might be thought to arise. In addition, Sheppard J enunciates that "if there is disclosed in the specification an intention on the part of the draftsman that words used elsewhere are to have a particular meaning, that meaning must be given those words because the draftsman has used his own dictionary" (Sheppard J at 410-411).

The decision of Aickin J, in *Minnesota Mining & Manufacturing Co v Beiersdorf (Aust) Ltd* (1980) 144 CLR 253 exemplifies that approach. Focusing on the "essence of the invention" (at 267), Aickin J proceeded to construe various terms in the claim which were in dispute. In the course of so doing, his Honour made repeated reference to the body of the specification in order to understand the context in which words had been used. His Honour did this even though the specification did not provide a "dictionary" for such terms, and without first making a finding that any of the terms or questions were ambiguous. At 272 his Honour said:

> "This is not a case where the specification supplies its own dictionary meaning but it is legitimate to look at the specification to see whether it shows the word to have been used in some special sense. In fact it shows that it was not so used."

I do not think that there is any conflict between the decision of Sheppard J in *Decor* and the other authorities to which I have referred. Sheppard J's distillation of the rules of construction at 400, and in particular rule 5, make that clear. Rather, as I read his Honour's decision, he was seeking to convey that one reads the specification as a whole as part of the process of determining whether the terms of the claims are clear and unambiguous, or to use the language of the High Court in *Interlego* at 478-479, whether only one particular meaning is "necessarily" conveyed by the expression in question.

Once purely verbal or grammatical questions have been resolved according to ordinary principles of construction, there is no residual uncertainty as to the extent of the monopoly claimed: *Welch Perrin* at 610. However, it is open to a court to conclude that the terms of a specification are so ambiguous that its proper construction must always remain a matter of doubt in which case the patent is invalid (*Martin v Scribal* at 59), subject, perhaps, to the possibility of amendment under s 105 of the 1990 Act. In the present case, it was common ground that if I came to the conclusion that I was unable to choose between the competing constructions of the patent advanced by the applicant and the respondent, I should make a finding to that effect, but should afford the applicant the opportunity to make application under s 105.

In Blanco White, *Patents for Inventions* (5th ed) at 4-701 the matter is put in this way:

> "Thus a claim is bad if no reasonably certain construction can be given to it, or it is fairly and equally open to diverse meanings. But the rule goes further than this. A court is not bound to find a meaning for a claim, nor to approach a claim with the 'conviction that its language is capable of a reasonable construction when carefully examined' that is the due of an Act of Parliament. Thus a claim may be bad for uncertainty although the court could find its true meaning (and would do so if the words concerned appeared in a commercial contract) if it is so obscure that 'its proper construction must always [349] remain a matter of doubt'. On the other hand, what matters is not the grammar of the claim, but whether a reader would be left in doubt whether any given apparatus or method fell within the claim or not; the purpose of the rule is to enable the public to rely upon the words of the claim as defining the rights of the patentee. Accordingly, a mere grammatical ambiguity, not affecting the scope of the monopoly, will not invalidate.

███████   Flexible Steel Lacing v Beltreco *continued*

Thus far, the rule is clear; but it is not an easy rule for the practitioner to apply. The difficulty lies in deciding just how much doubt as to the meaning of a claim will invalidate it; for the standard of clarity required by the courts changes markedly from time to time. In the past, the standard of clarity required has indeed been put as high as this, that there must be 'no serious difficulty' in construing the claims, and that the claims must be capable of construction by rival manufacturers without the assistance of experienced counsel. Claims have, however, habitually been held valid, by all courts, that could not pass such a stringent test. Certainly a claim is not invalid merely because it might have been better drafted, nor merely because the patentee puts forward a construction that the court is not prepared to adopt; nor merely because it is capable of more than one construction, even though it be difficult to decide which is the right one."

Other principles of construction which may be of assistance in the resolution of the present matter include:

- A patent specification should be given a purposive construction rather than a purely literal one: *Catnic Components Ltd v Hill & Smith Ltd* [1982] RPC 183, per Diplock LJ at 243, cited in various Australian cases including *Decor* at 400—Rule (6); although it is noted by Gummow J in *Nicaro Holdings Pty Ltd v Martin Engineering Co* (1989-1990) 16 IPR 545 at 560-561, that a purposive approach was adopted in the pre-Catnic decision of *Commonwealth Industrial Gases Ltd v MWA Holdings Pty Ltd* (1970) 44 ALJR 385 at 388
- The hypothetical addressee of the patent specification is the non-inventive person skilled in the art before the priority date (*Welch Perrin* at 610, *Populin* at 476, *Fisher & Paykel* at 254, 260, *Decor* at 397, *Stanway Oyster Cylinders Pty Ltd v Marks* (1996) 66 FCR 577 at 582-583). The words used in a specification are to be given the meaning which the hypothetical addressee would attach to them, both in the light of his own general knowledge and in the light of what is disclosed in the body of the specification: *Decor* at 391—per Lockhart J.
- There is a fine line between, on the one hand, reading down the words of a patent claim to reflect how a person skilled in the art would understand it in a practical and commonsense way, and, on the other hand, impermissibly limiting the clear words of a claim because a reader skilled in the art would be likely to apply those wide words only in a limited range of all the situations they describe: *Stanway Oyster Cylinders* at 585—per Drummond J.
- It is permissible for an invention to be described in a way which involves matters of degree. Lack of precise definition in claims is not fatal to their validity, so long as they provide a workable standard suitable to the intended use: *Stanway Oyster Cylinders* at 585; *Minnesota Mining* at 274. The consideration is whether, on any reasonable view, the claim has meaning (*Elconnex Pty Ltd v Gerard Industries Pty Ltd* (1991) 32 FCR 491 at 512-513, *Tye-Sil Corp Ltd v Diversified Products Corp* (1991) 20 IPR 574 at 585). In determining this, the expressions in question must be understood in a practical, commonsense manner (*Nesbit Evans Group Australia Pty Ltd v Impro Ltd* (1997) 39 IPR 56 at 95, *Martin Engineering Co v Trison* **[350]** *Holdings Pty Ltd* (1989) 14 IPR 330 at 338). Absurd constructions should be avoided (*Stanway Oyster Cylinders* at 582-583) and mere technicalities should not defeat the grant of protection (*Tye-Sil* at 585).
- As a general rule, the terms of a specification should be accorded their ordinary English meaning: *Electric & Musical Industries* at 41, *Elconnex* (1991) 32 FCR 491 at 512-513, *Interlego* at 478, *Minnesota Mining* at 270.
- Evidence can be given by experts on the meaning which those skilled in the art would give to technical or scientific terms and phrases and on unusual or special meanings given by

██████   Flexible Steel Lacing v Beltreco *continued*

such persons to words which might otherwise bear their ordinary meaning: *Sartas No 1 v Koukourou* at 485-486, *NV Philips Gloeilampenfabrieken v Mirabella International Pty Ltd* (1993) 26 IPR 513 at 531-532, *Leonardis v Sartas No 1 Pty Ltd* (1996) 67 FCR 126 at 137-138, *Patent Gesellschaft AG v Saudi Livestock Transport & Trading Co* (1996) 33 IPR 426 at 455.

- However, the construction of the specification is for the Court, not for the expert witness. Insofar as a view expressed by an expert depends upon a reading of the patent, it cannot carry the day unless the Court reads the patent in the same way: *Allsop Inc v Bintang Ltd* (1989) 15 IPR 686, 697. See also *Glaverbel SA v British Coal Corp* [1994] RPC 443 at 486, *Sartas No 1 v Koukourou* at 485-486, *Patent Gesellschaft* at 455.

- Section 116 of the 1990 Act provides that the Court may, in interpreting a complete specification, refer to the specification without amendment. However, it is neither useful nor legitimate to do so where the amended specification is clear: *Martin & Biro Swan Ltd v H Millwood Ltd* [1956] RPC 125 at 135.

Minnesota Mining & Manufacturing v Tyco Electronics

[9.15] *Minnesota Mining & Manufacturing Co v Tyco Electronics Pty Ltd* (2001) 53 IPR 32; [2001] FCA 1359 Federal Court of Australia

SACKVILLE J: **[57]**

Principles of construction

The first task of the Court in infringement proceedings is to construe the patent in suit in order to determine the precise nature and extent of the rights claimed by the patentee. The principles of construction of patent claims were helpfully summarised by Hely J in *Flexible Steel Lacing Co v Beltreco Ltd* (2000) 49 IPR 331, at 347-350. I do not think it necessary to set out that passage in full. [See **[9.10]** above.] It is enough to say that I agree with the principles stated by his Honour. In particular, I agree with Hely J's observation that the specification must be read as a whole to see how words have been used and as part of the process of determining whether the terms of the claim are clear and unambiguous. This is consistent with a passage from the judgment of Lockhart J in *Décor Corp Pty Ltd v Dart Industries Inc* (1988) 13 IPR 385, at 391 put at the forefront of 3M's submissions:

> "It is well established that there are no special rules for the interpretation of patent specifications, which are to be interpreted in the same way as any other document upon ordinary principles of interpretation. The words used in a specification are to be given the meaning which the normal person skilled in the art would attach to those words, both in the light of his own general knowledge and in the light of what is disclosed in the body of the specification."

I would add four comments. First, as Hely J notes (at 349), the hypothetical addressee of the patent specification is the non-inventive person skilled in the art before the priority date. Accordingly, as the Full Court said in *Populin v HB Nominees Pty Ltd* (1982) 41 ALR 471, at 476-477:

> "The complete specification must not be read in the abstract but in the light of common knowledge in the art before the priority date, bearing in mind that what is

███████   Minnesota Mining & Manufacturing v Tyco Electronics *continued*

being construed is a public instrument which must, if it is to be valid, define a monopoly in such a way that it is not reasonably capable of being misunderstood. ... The essential features of the product or process for which it claims a monopoly are to be determined not as a matter of abstract uninformed construction but by a commonsense assessment of what the words used convey in the context of then-existing published knowledge. As **[58]** Lord Diplock (with whom the other members of the House of Lords agreed) commented in *Catnic Components Ltd v Hill & Smith Ltd* (1981) 7 FSR 60 at 65-6:

> '[A] patent specification is a unilateral statement by the patentee, in words of his own choosing, addressed to those likely to have a practical interest in the subject matter of his invention (ie, 'skilled in the art'), by which he informs them what he claims to be the essential features of the new product or process for which the letters patent grant him a monopoly. It is those novel features only that he claims to be essential that constitute the so-called 'pith and marrow' of the claim. A patent specification should be given a purposive construction rather than a purely literal one derived from applying to it the kind of meticulous verbal analysis in which lawyers are too often tempted by their training to indulge....'"

Second, the High Court recently addressed, albeit briefly, the approach to construction in *Kimberley-Clark Australia Pty Ltd v Arico Trading International Pty Ltd* (2001) 177 ALR 460, at 466:

> "Where the question concerns infringement of a claim or the sufficiency of a claim to 'define' the invention, it has been held in this court under the 1952 Act that the plain and unambiguous meaning of a claim cannot be varied or qualified by reference to the body of the specification (*Welch Perrin Pty Ltd v Worrel* (1961) 106 CLR 588 at 610). However, terms in the claim which are unclear may be defined or clarified by reference to the body of the specification (*Interlego AG v Toltoys Pty Ltd* (1973) 130 CLR 461 at 479)."

The well-known passage from *Welch Perrin,* a case involving an alleged failure to define an invention, is as follows:

> "If it is impossible to ascertain what the invention is from a fair reading of the specification as a whole, that, of course, is an end of the matter. But this objection is not established by reading the specification in the abstract. It must be construed in the light of the common knowledge in the art before the priority date. The general principles governing the construction of specifications are well-known, and no lengthy reference to them is necessary. It is, however, fitting that we remind ourselves of the criterion to be applied when it is said that a specification is ambiguous. For ... we are not construing a written instrument operating inter parties, but a public instrument which must, if it is to be valid, define a monopoly in such a way that it is not reasonably capable of being misunderstood. Nevertheless, it is to be remembered that any purely verbal or grammatical question that can be resolved according to ordinary rules for the construction of written documents, does not, once it has been resolved, leave uncertain the ambit of the monopoly claimed. The specification must be read as a whole. But it is a whole made up of several parts, and those parts have different function. Courts have often insisted that it is not legitimate to narrow or expand the boundaries of monopoly as fixed by the words of a claim by adding to those words glosses drawn from other parts of the specification. Similarly, if a claim be clear it is

■■■■■■ Minnesota Mining & Manufacturing v Tyco Electronics *continued*

not to be made obscure simply because obscurities can be found in particular sentences in other parts of the document." (Citations omitted.)

As Mr Catterns noted, this passage twice indicates that the specification must be read "as a whole". I do not understand either *Welch Perrin* or its endorsement in *Kimberley-Clark* as inconsistent with the approach taken by Hely J in *Flexible Steel*.

Third, as Hely J noted (at 350), evidence can be given by experts as to the meaning which those skilled in the art would give to technical or scientific terms and phrases and as to unusual or special meanings given by such persons to words which otherwise might bear their ordinary meaning. But the construction of the specification is ultimately for the Court. [59]

Fourth, it is important to bear in mind that it is the claim that defines the invention. Moreover, a "claiming clause operates as a disclaimer of what is not specifically claimed, and for such disclaimer there may be reasons known to the inventor but not to the Court": *Fellows v Thomas William Leech Ltd* (1917) 34 RPC 45 at 55, per Lord Parker, cited by Dixon J in *Walker v Alemite Corp* (1933) 49 CLR 643, at 656. The limitations on using the body of the specification as a basis for construction of the claims were stated by Lord Russell of Killowen in *Electrical & Musical Industries Ltd v Lissen* (1939) 56 RPC 23, at 39:

> "It is not permissible, in my opinion, by reference to some language used in the earlier part of the specification, to change a claim which by its own language is a claim for one subject matter into a claim for another and a different subject matter, which is what you do when you alter the boundaries of the forbidden territory. A patentee who describes an invention in the body of a specification obtains no monopoly unless it is claimed in the claims. As Lord Cairns said, there is no such thing as infringement of the equity of a patent: *Dudgeon v Thomson* (1877) 3 App Cas 34."

Sachtler v RE Miller

[9.20] *Sachtler GMBH & Co KG v RE Miller Pty Ltd* (2005) 65 IPR 605; [2005] FCA 788

BENNETT J: [608]

Terminology of the patent

The terminology used in the patent is not totally consistent. Some of the words and expressions are explained in the patent specification. There was some agreement on the meaning of terms of art as used by skilled workers in the art. [609] This agreement did not extend to the connotations of those words in the context of the claims. Accepting that the construction of the claims was a matter for the Court, each party called evidence as to the meaning of technical terms and terms of art and as to how the skilled reader would read the claims. There was no challenge to the qualifications of the experts to give evidence as persons of skill in the art.

Evidence can be given by experts on the meaning which those skilled in the art would give to technical or scientific terms and phrases and on unusual or special meanings given by such persons to words which might otherwise bear their ordinary meaning (*Sartas No 1 Pty Ltd v Koukourou & Partners Pty Ltd* (1990) 30 IPR 479 at 485-486 ('*Sartas*'); *NV Philips Gloeilampen-fabrieken v Mirabella International Pty Ltd* (1993) 26 IPR 513 at 531-532; *Leonardis v Sartas No 1*

━━━━   Sachtler v RE Miller *continued*

Pty Ltd (1996) 67 FCR 126 at 137-138 ('*Leonardis*'); *Patent Gesellschaft AG v Saudi Livestock Transport and Trading Co* (1996) 33 IPR 426 at 455 ('*Patent Gesellschaft*')). Where the patent contains technical material, the Court must, by evidence, be put in a position of a person of the kind to whom the patent is addressed, a person acquainted with the surrounding circumstances of the state and the art and at the relevant time (*General Tire & Rubber Co v Firestone Tyre & Rubber Co Ltd* [1972] RPC 457 at 485, cited in *Nicaro Holdings Pty Ltd v Martin Engineering Co* (1990) 91 ALR 513 at 523-524 per Gummow J ('*Nicaro*'); *Kimberley-Clark Australia Pty Ltd v Arico Trading International Pty Ltd* (2001) 207 CLR 1 at [24] ('*Kimberley-Clark*')). However, if the evidence does not establish that such a technical meaning exists, words used in a patent specification should be given their ordinary meaning (*PhotoCure ASA v Queen's University at Kingston* [2005] FCA 344 at [170] ('*Photocure*') and the cases cited therein).

As Branson J said in *EI Dupont De Nemours & Co v Imperial Chemical Industries PLC* (2002) 54 IPR 305 at [59], the evidence of the skilled reader is not determinative of the construction of the document. It is evidence of how a skilled reader would have read the document at the relevant time. It is then for the Court to construe the document, giving such weight to the evidence as it sees fit.

The construction of the specification is for the Court, not for the expert witness (*Allsop Inc v Bintang Ltd* (1989) 15 IPR 686 at 697. See also *Glaverbel SA v British Coal Corp* [1994] RPC 443 at 486, *Sartas* at 485-486, *Patent Gesellschaft* at 455; *Jupiters Ltd v Neurizon Pty Ltd* [2005] FCAFC 90 at [67] ('*Jupiters*')).

Note

[9.25] For a similar setting out of the principles see *Photocure ASA v Queen's University at Kingston and anor* [2005] FCA 344, (2005) 64 IPR 314 at [168]–[175].

■ Sufficiency of description

[9.30] The *Patents Act 1990* (Cth), s 40(2)(a) requires a *description* of the invention. A specification will contain a sufficient description if a person skilled in the relevant art on reading that specification as a whole, and in the light of the general common knowledge of those skilled in the relevant art, can understand the nature of what has been invented and a method of bringing that invention into practice.

━━━━ **Edison & Swan Electric Light v Holland** ━━━━

[9.35] *Edison & Swan Electric Light Co v Holland* (1889) 6 RPC 243

LINDLEY LJ: ... **[280]** On the one hand, the Patentee must make the nature of his invention, and how to perform it, clear and intelligible; on the other hand, it is not necessary for him to instruct persons wholly ignorant of the subject matter to which his invention relates, in all that they must know before they can understand what he is talking about. The Patentee is adding something to what was known before, and he does all that is necessary as regards the language he uses, if he makes the nature of his invention, and how to perform it, clear and intelligible to persons having a reasonably competent knowledge of what was known before on the subject to which his patent relates, and having reasonably competent skill in the practical mode of doing what was then known.

■■■■■■ Edison & Swan Electric Light v Holland *continued*

In complying with the first condition, ie, in describing the nature of his invention, the Patentee does all that is necessary, if he makes the nature of his invention plain to persons having a reasonably competent knowledge of the subject, although from want of skill they could not themselves practically carry out the invention. In complying with the second condition ie, in describing in what manner the invention is to be performed, the Patentee does all that is necessary, if he makes it plain to persons having reasonable skill in doing such things as have to be done in order to work the patent, what they are to do in order to perform his invention. If, as may happen, they are to do something the like of which has never been done before, he must tell them how to do it, if a reasonably competent workman would not himself see how to do it on reading the Specification, or on having it read to him. The principle to be applied to the language used to comply with the two conditions is the same for both; but one class of persons may understand only one part of the Specification and another class only the other, and yet the patent may be valid. In a well-drawn Specification, the two conditions that have to be complied with are kept distinct; but in many Specifications this course is not pursued. The nature of the invention and the manner of performing it are often described together.

Note

[9.40] This passage was cited with approval in the case of *Samuel Taylor Pty Ltd v SA Brush Co Ltd* (1950) 83 CLR 617 at 624-625 (see [9.50]).

■ Section 41 and micro-organism inventions

[9.45] It is difficult and sometimes impossible to provide accurate descriptions of micro-organisms and so it may be difficult or impossible to comply with the requirements of *Patents Act 1990* (Cth), s 40(2)(a) if using traditional descriptive techniques. However, biotechnology involving micro-organisms is an exceptionally important area of technological research and development. There are special provisions applying to micro-organism inventions; these are now ss 41 and 42. Previously, these provisions were s 40(3)-(7) of the 1952 Act as amended. The provisions were introduced in 1984 to give effect to ways of allowing sufficiency of description when the claimed invention is a micro-organism, or involves the use modification or cultivation of a micro-organism. Prior to the introduction of the provisions, written descriptions of micro-organisms were required and in many instances these proved ineffective or useless. Sections 41 and 42 allow the operation of the Budapest Treaty by which an international deposit system of micro-organisms is established. An inventor or applicant may deposit a sample of the micro-organism with a recognised depository under the treaty and receive international receipts and documents which the *Patents Act 1990* (Cth) provides will then meet the description requirement.

■ Best method of performance

══════════ Samuel Taylor v SA Brush ══════════

[9.50] *Samuel Taylor Pty Ltd v SA Brush Co Ltd* (1950) 83 CLR 617 High Court of Australia

LATHAM CJ: [620]

.... The patent was granted in Australia under s 121 of the *Patents Act 1903-1921*. The complete specification stated that the invention related to "wood-headed sweeping brooms or brushes, in which long bristles, hairs, fibres or mixture of these are employed, and has for its object to improve the construction of such class of brush so as to cheapen the cost of production".

...[622]

The invention claimed is not a claim for a process. No process of manufacture is described. It is a claim for a product—a broom head which possesses certain characteristics—long bristles set in a recess with their root ends inward, the recess containing cement, the bristles arranged either in tufts or otherwise. As already stated, all the features mentioned were well-known except that long bristles had not successfully been set in cement. The specification gives no direction as to how to bring about the improved result which it describes. It is contended for the defendant that the description of the broom in the specification is such that a competent workman would be able with the use of ordinary skill to make a broom according to the specification. Much evidence was given upon this aspect of the case. It appeared that when the plaintiff company was in treaty with one of the patentees in England for an assignment of the patent the patentee informed it that the patent itself was not very important. It was the secret technique of manufacture which was important and it was stated by the patentee that if the plaintiff company knew this technique they ought not to be greatly concerned if the application for the grant of the patent in Australia should fail. The witnesses for the defendant, when giving evidence, refused to disclose the method so successfully adopted by the defendant for making the "Dustmaster" broom. It was suggested by these [623] witnesses that any workman could make a broom in accordance with the specification by arranging bristles between cardboard or other slips with the ends projecting, holding the cardboard slips with the interposed bristles in position by some means and merely inserting the ends of the contained bristles into waiting cement in a recess. The learned trial judge was not satisfied that an effective broom with the necessary splayed ends and edges could be so manufactured, and there is no evidence that such means were practical or that they would in any circumstances, to use the words of the specification, "improve the construction of the brooms" so as to "cheapen the cost of production". The method suggested by the defendant's witnesses as obvious to a skilled workman would not, as one of the plaintiff's witnesses said, produce anything that could be called a broom "if one wishes to sell it".

The evidence for the plaintiff was to the effect that persons who were expert in broom manufacturing had conducted a long series of experiments in order to produce a broom with bristles held in position by cement, that they had not succeeded in producing such a broom with all the bristles set in tufts, The learned trial judge accepted this evidence and accordingly held that the patent was invalid because the specification was insufficient to enable the invention properly to be carried into effect.

In my opinion his Honour's decision was correct. ... The objection which in my opinion is fatal to the patent is that no method whatever of carrying out the invention is disclosed by the specification. A result is disclosed. The description of the result does not provide, expressly or impliedly, to a skilled workman any information as to a method of carrying out the invention. Even now no persons other than those employed by the defendant have been able to arrange bristles in tufts in cement in a broom. The specification contains the statement that "the bristles, hairs, fibres or mixtures may be formed into separate [624] tufts or not as desired". There is no indication whatever as to how this is to be done so as to hold them in position in a recess filled with cement.

I am therefore of opinion that the patent is invalid upon the ground that the specification is insufficient to enable the invention properly to be carried into effect and that therefore the appeal should be dismissed.

█████ Samuel Taylor v SA Brush *continued*

McTIERNAN J: [625]

I agree that the appeal should be dismissed. ...

In regard to the present specification Abbott J very correctly said: "It seems to me that the Specification of the defendant's patent describes with crystal clarity the nature of the invention, but fails entirely to describe the manner of performing it." There was no known practical method of doing the things that constituted the inventive step.

His Honour made this finding: "I am satisfied that the inventors discovered not only a broom, the nature of which they have disclosed, but also a manner of manufacturing it, which they not only have not disclosed, but which they have intentionally avoided disclosing, so as to keep it secret".

The specification does not convey to persons of reasonable skill in the trade what they are to do in order to make a sweeping brush or broom with long bristles secured by setting their root ends in cement, rubber or other retaining agent in a recess in its stock. [626]

In my opinion the learned trial judge was right in upholding the objection that the specification was insufficient.

[Webb J agreed with the judgment of the Chief Justice.]

███████████████ **Firebelt v Brambles Australia** ███████████████

[9.55] *Firebelt Pty Ltd v Brambles Australia Ltd* (2000) 51 IPR 531; [2000] FCA 1689   Federal Court of Australia

[See the extract above at [8.330] for the facts and discussion of the requirement of inventive step in this case].

SPENDER, DRUMMOND, MANSFIELD JJ: [543]

Non-disclosure of best method of performing the invention

Section 40(2)(a) provides that a complete specification must:

"describe the invention fully, including the best method known to the applicant of performing the invention".

Of this requirement, his Honour's findings were particularly terse:

"There is no indication of *which of the contemplated lid-opening devices was considered to be the best at the relevant time, nor of the preferred timing.* The specification indicates that different methods had been considered and that, at least in some embodiments, timing was thought to be of importance in determining the quality of outcome, that is the degree of maintenance of separation of waste. In view of the importance of this matter, it cannot be said, in the absence of such information, that the best method of performing the invention as a whole has been disclosed." (Emphasis added.)

This holding by the primary judge involves, in our respectful view, a misunderstanding of what is required by s 40(2)(a) of the Act concerning a description of the best method known to the applicant of performing the invention. In *Vidal Dyes Syndicate Ltd v Levenstein Ltd* (1912) 29 RPC 245 in the Court of Appeal, Fletcher Moulton LJ said at 269:

■■■■■   Firebelt v Brambles Australia *continued*

"It is settled law that a patentee must act towards the public uberrima fide, and must give the best information in his power as to how to carry out the invention. He is **[544]** therefore bound to tell the public all the steps that can advantageously be taken in carrying out the invention. But he is not limited to claiming only the best way of carrying it out."

This requirement is to ensure good faith on the part of the patentee, and to protect the public against a patentee who deliberately keeps to himself something novel and not previously published which he knows of or has found out gives the best results, with a view to getting the benefit of monopoly without giving to the public the corresponding consideration of knowledge of the best method of performing the invention.

Blanco White in *Patents for Inventions* (4th ed) at para 4-502 notes:

"To be proper and sufficient, the complete specification as a whole (that is, read together with the claims [*Evans v Hoskins & Sewell* (1907) 24 RPC 517 at 522 (CA)], and in the light of the drawings, if any [*Bloxam v Elsee* (1827) 1 C & P 558 at 564]) must in the first place contain such instructions as will enable all [*Knight v Argylls* (1913) 30 RPC 321 at 348 (CA)] those to whom the specification is addressed to produce something within each claim 'by following the directions of the specification, without any new inventions or additions of their own' [*R v Arkwright* (1785) 1 WPC 64 at 66; *Otto v Linford* (1882) 46 LT 35 at 41 (CA); *No-Fume v Pitchford* (1935) 52 RPC 231 at 243 (CA)] and without 'prolonged study of matters which present some initial difficulty'. [*Valensi v BRC* [1972] FSR 273 at 311 (CA)]."

Of the objection based on the provisions of the UK legislation, *Blanco White* says at para 4-516:

"There would seem to be no obligation under this provision to include information not strictly relating to 'the invention', however necessary to anyone needing to work the invention."

The learned author continues:

"Thus it would seem unnecessary to disclose how starting materials for a process are to be obtained [*American Cyanamid's (Dann) Patent* [1971] RPC 425, ante, §4-507]; whilst it has been held that the patentee of a new article need not disclose the best method of making it, 'performing' here going only to the design of the article and not to techniques for manufacturing it. [*Illinois Tool Works v Autobars* [1972] FSR 67 at 71-72. But cf ante, §4-502]

It is relevant in this case to recognise that the statutory obligation is an obligation to disclose the best method of *performing the invention* known to the applicant.

The invention claimed is not of a particular type of lid-opening device operating at any particular time. There is therefore no statutory obligation to describe which of the contemplated lid-opening devices was considered to be the best, nor the preferred timing, contrary to his Honour's understanding of the section.

The requirement of s 40(2) of the Act is that the patentee is required to give the best information in his power as to how to carry out *the invention*. That requirement is ordinarily satisfied by including in the specification a detailed description of one or more preferred embodiments of the invention offered, with reference to drawings of specific mechanisms or structures or examples of specific process conditions or chemical formulations, depending on the field of the invention and the nature of the instruction to be conveyed. It is necessary to have regard to what is the invention claimed in the petty patent. The invention **[545]** here claimed is not a particular type of lid-opening device operating at any particular time. It is only if it were such a claim that there might be a failure such as the primary judge found.

The text of the complete specification of the petty patent leaves no doubt that the figures 4, 5 and 8 referred to in that specification depict an embodiment of the lid-opening device, and the description of figures 4 and 5 includes:

> "[A] jet of water shown at 30 fired from nozzle 31 on the loading mechanism 19 opens the lid 32 of the bin 20 prior to the contents of the bin 20 being discharged. This will be slightly delayed due to the inertia of the bin being raised through its arc of movement to the final stop position illustrated in figure 5. In other words, the combined effect of the movement of the bin through its arc followed by the jet of water discharged from nozzle 31 followed by raising of the ramp into the aligned position illustrated in Figure 5 will ensure that minimum recyclables from compartment 27 end up in the wrong tank section. As an alternative to the jet of water, other mechanically equivalent contrivances can be employed including air jets or directly acting mechanical lid openers."

In our respectful view there has been no failure of the duty to disclose the best method of performing the invention known to the applicant, as required by s 40(2) of the Act.

...

The appellant has been successful on the issue of disclosure of the best method of performing the invention, but has failed on the issue of want of inventive step. The appeal should therefore be dismissed.

Note

[9.60] The requirement is, that such a best method of performance must be disclosed in the specification, not that the patentee has actually used it: *New England Biolabs, Inc v H Hoffmann-La Roche AG* [2004] FCA 1651; (2005) 63 IPR 524 at [33] Emmett J.

CLAIMS

[9.65] The requirements in the *Patents Act 1990* (Cth), ss 40(2)(b) and (c), (3) and (4) relate to the claims.

■ Defining the invention—the function of the claims: s 40(2)(b)

[9.70] While the specification as a whole must *describe* the invention, the claims must *define* the invention.

▆▆▆▆ EMI v Lissen ▆▆▆▆

[9.75] *Electric & Musical Industries Ltd v Lissen Ltd* (1938) 56 RPC 23

LORD RUSSELL OF KILLOWEN: [39] ... The function of the claims is to define clearly and with precision the monopoly claimed so that others may know the exact boundaries of the area within which they will be trespassers. Their primary object is to limit and not to extend the monopoly. What is not claimed is disclaimed. The claims must undoubtedly be read as

▬▬▬▬   EMI v Lissen *continued*

part of an entire document, and not as a separate document; but the forbidden field must be found in the language of the claims and not elsewhere. It is not permissible, in my opinion, by reference to some language used in an earlier part of the specification to change a claim which by its own language is a claim for one subject matter into a claim for another and different subject matter, which is what you do when you alter the boundaries of the forbidden territory. A patentee who describes an invention in the body of a specification obtains no monopoly unless it is claimed in the claim. As Lord Cairns said there is no such thing as infringement of the equity of a patent.

Note

[9.80] The *Patents Act 1990* (Cth), s 40(2)(c), which refers to the requirement for at least one but not more than five claims in an innovation patent, does not specifically require such claims to define the invention.

■ "Clear"— "lack of" ambiguity: s 40(3)

Kauzal v Lee

[9.85] *Kauzal v Lee* (1936) 58 CLR 670 High Court of Australia

DIXON AND MCTIERNAN JJ: **[685]** Vagueness of description, want of particularity and evident indistinctness of thought may be the source of so much uncertainty as to the scope of the monopoly that the claim fails to fulfil the requirement of stating with definiteness to what the patentee is exclusively entitled. In such a case the grammatical construction of the language may present no difficulty. Such indefiniteness has a deeper cause than an accident in the formal arrangement of a sentence which leaves it open to attribute an expression to either of two possible antecedents. When that happens a true question of construction arises. The language is open to two meanings. Each may be as definite as the other. The only doubt is which of the two was meant and doubt springs from verbal order, position, or the like. In such a case it is not likely that the scope of the claim would be so obscure **[686]** as to disentitle the patentee to protection for what he meant to claim

An ambiguity in a claim incapable of resolution by a skilled addressee by the application of common sense and common knowledge will invalidate the claim.

Manual of Practice and Procedure

[9.90] Australian Patent Office, *Manual of Practice and Procedure National* available at

2.11.7.2 Clarity and Succinctness
In order to comply with s 40(3), claims must be clear and succinct. Accordingly, technical terms, legal terms circumscribing the monopoly sought, and the grammatical construction must be clear and precise.

▬▬▬▬   Manual of Practice and Procedure *continued*

The addressee of the specification is the person skilled in the art; claims are frequently the province of persons trained in law. Thus a standard of clarity which may be adequate for the body of the specification is not necessarily adequate for the claims. The description in the body of the specification has the practical purpose of instructing the person in the art how to perform the invention when free to do so, ie after the patent has expired, while the claims define the monopoly — what must not be done during the life of the patent (see, for example, *British United Shoe Machinery Co Ltd v A Fussell and Sons Ltd* (1908) 25 RPC 631). In the body of the specification, the words used may be quite adequate to enable the invention to be performed, while the same words used in the claims may leave competitors uncertain as to what they may not do, and thus, vis-à-vis the quality standards for patent examination, affect the overall scope of the monopoly — see, for example, *AMP v Utilux*, (1971) 45 ALJR 123, in which McTiernan J stated:

"... the degree of particularity of the language required in the claims should not be expected in the body (of the specification)."

Thus, general terms of uncertain ambit may be objectionable in the claims even when they are terms which the addressee might be expected to be able to interpret for purposes of performance.

In *British Celanese Ltd.'s Application*, (1934) 51 RPC 192 at page 195, it was said:

"It is certainly dangerous for a patentee to seek to obtain a monopoly by reference to such general terms as 'known methods' or 'general methods', or equivalent phrases of that kind. I think that puts a burden on the public which should not be put upon them; it must necessarily lead to ambiguity and doubt ..."

▪ "Succinct": s 40(3)

[9.95] The now discontinued print version of the Examiners manual had this to say about the term "succinct".

▬▬▬▬   **Manual of Practice and Procedure, Vol 2**   ▬▬▬▬

[9.100] Australian Patent Office, *Manual of Practice and Procedure*, Vol 2, "National"

10.8.3 "Succinct" means compressed, brief or concise. Occasionally, a claim is set out in a number of paragraphs and subparagraphs, giving an appearance of size but which is not objectionable. On other occasions, claims are built up by superfluous verbiage to an extent of creating the impression of something of a rather complicated construction and a rather limited scope; such claims require careful scrutiny. Generally, it is Office practice not to object if the length of the claim does not obscure its meaning or create a false impression. It is important to appreciate that the requirement of succinctness applies not only to individual claims, but also to the statement of claims as a whole. Where two or more claims claim the same thing in substantially the same words the statement of claims as a whole is not succinct.

[9.105] The new "on line" web based version of the manual (at <www.ipaustralia.gov.au>) now includes the following comment.

"2.11.7.2 Clarity and Succinctness

A claim is not objectionable on the basis of its length per se, provided the length of the claim does not obscure its meaning or create a false impression, thereby resulting in a lack of clarity and succinctness. When an examiner considers this situation may apply, the matter should be referred to the relevant supervising examiner.

It is customary for a claim to consist of one sentence. The necessity for one-sentence claims was tested in *Leonard's Application*, (1966) RPC 269. The tenor of the decision was that one-sentence claims are highly desirable, but may not be enforceable in all instances. A claim in the form of disjunctive sentences was held to be ambiguous and not allowable, but an amended claim in nine sentences was ultimately allowed.

Claims consisting of more than one sentence are allowable on the basis of the decision in Leonard's Application, provided that it is clear from the wording of the claim that all the features of all the sentences of the claim must be read in combination."

■ "Fairly based": s 40(3)

━━━━━━ Leonardis v Sartas No 1 ━━━━━━

[9.110] *Leonardis v Sartas No 1 Pty Ltd & Anor* (1996) 35 IPR 23 Federal Court of Australia

[The invention in this case related to construction of concrete foundation. Cardboard form work in a complex box construction including "spacers" was laid so as to provide channels into which concrete could be poured and so create a grid pattern of beams under the slab. The invention provided a solution to the problem of movement of the relatively light cardboard form work by fixing or securing the box elements at the intersections of the channel. The appellant patentee claimed a priority date for certain claims based on the date of filing of two provisional specifications. These provisional specifications made references to drawings to indicate features of the invention. To claim priority from the date of the provisional specifications the claims had to be "fairly based" on the invention disclosed in the provisional specification. The appeal discussed at length whether the drawings could provide a relevant disclosure and provide a fair basis for the patentees claim and concluded that drawings were capable of providing an adequate disclosure. In the course of judgment the Court provided detailed discussion of the principles applicable to "fair basis" for the purposes of determining priority dates for claims based upon provisional applications and the related but different requirement in *Patents Act 1990* (Cth), s 40(3) that the claims in a specification be fairly based on the description of the specification.]

BURCHETT, HILL and TAMBERLIN JJ: **[38]**
In interpreting the expression "fair basis", one should not understand the word "fair" as connoting any idea of equity. "What is required to be fair is not the applicant's claim to priority but the basis which one document affords for a claim in the other": *Re Stauffer Chemical Company's Application* (1977) RPC 33 at 52, per Buckley LJ. Later in his judgment, Buckley LJ said (at 54):

Leonardis v Sartas No 1 *continued*

"If a new feature were a development along the same line of thought which constitutes or underlies the invention described in the earlier document, it might be that that development could properly be regarded as fairly based on the matter disclosed in the earlier document, and that the new process described in the later document which incorporates that development could as a whole be regarded as fairly based upon the matter disclosed in the earlier document. If, on the other hand, the additional feature involves a new inventive step or brings something new into the combination which represents a departure from the idea of the invention described in the earlier document, it could not, I think, be properly described as fairly based upon the earlier document."

Roskill LJ (as Lord Roskill then was), who said (at 63) that he agreed "entirely" with the reasons of Buckley LJ, also said (at 61) ...

"We were referred by both learned counsel to a number of authorities on 'fairly based', all decisions at first instance but, having regard to the experience of the judges respectively concerned, of high persuasive authority. None the less, what matters is whether the particular claim before the court is fairly based on the particular priority document. I respectfully question the use of paraphrases, synonyms and the like where Parliament has used a single and simple phrase in a statute with which alone the court is concerned. One does not answer the question whether a claim is fairly based by substituting another phrase such as 'plainly foreshadowed'. I respectfully agree with the comment made by Gibbs J in the High Court of Australia in *Hoffmann-La Roche (sic) v The Commissioner of Patents* (1973) RPC 34 at 42, that other phrases are no substitute for the statutory test though they may well and often do point to factors to be considered in the application of that test."

See also *Vax Appliances Ltd v Hoover plc* (supra) at 311.

The remark made in the judgment of Gibbs J in *F Hoffman-La Roche & Co Aktiengesellschaft v Commissioner of Patents* is reported in (1971) 123 CLR 529 at 539. The passage actually commences at 538, as follows:

"The question whether a claim in a complete specification is fairly based on matter disclosed in the provisional specification was considered by the Patents Appeal Tribunal, **[39]** constituted by Lloyd-Jacob J, in *Re Mond Nickel Company Ltd's Application* (1956) RPC 189 at 194 and *Imperial Chemical Industries Ltd's Application* (1960) RPC 223 at 228. The test to be applied is expressed in the Act in identical language in relation to provisional specifications and basic applications and what was said in those cases is applicable to the question that arises under ss 141 and 142 of the Act. Lloyd-Jacob J did not attempt to define all that is meant by the phrase 'fairly based' but he gave a guide to the approach that should be made in deciding a question of this kind. In his opinion it is necessary to investigate three questions which, if one substitutes a reference to the basic application for a reference to the provisional specification, he finally formulated as follows:

(1) Is the alleged invention as claimed broadly (ie, in a general sense) described in the basic application?

(2) Is there anything in the basic application which is inconsistent with the alleged invention as claimed?

(3) Does the claim include as a characteristic of the invention a feature as to which the basic application is wholly silent?

Leonardis v Sartas No 1 *continued*

It is needless to say that these questions are intended to assist the Court in applying the test laid down by the Act itself, viz whether the claim in the complete specification is fairly based on matter disclosed in the basic application, but are not a substitute for that test. In *Societe des Usines Chimiques Rhone-Poulenc v Commissioner of Patents* at 11, Fullagar J held that s 45(5) of the Act cannot be limited to cases where the subject matter of the later application has been made the subject of a specific claim in the earlier application, and further expressed the view that there must be 'a real and reasonably clear disclosure'."

Having regard to the comment made by Roskill LJ questioning the substitution for the statutory test of the phrase "plainly foreshadowed", it is interesting to note that in *Hoffman-La Roche* (at 540) the expression used by Gibbs J, who was summarising the submission of the then Mr KR Handley, is "fairly within, or fairly foreshadowed by" the first basic application.

In *CCOM v Jiejing* (supra, at 275 et seq), the Full Court provided what, with respect, must be seen as a valuable survey of the law in this area. The judgment (at 281) refers to the statement of Fox J in *Coopers Animal Health Australia Ltd v Western Stock Distributors Pty Ltd* (1987) 15 FCR 382 at 389:

"Where the holder of the provisional specification proceeds with a complete specification with a view to the grant of a patent, it is recognised that greater definition, as a result of further experimentation or otherwise, may be achieved before the later step is taken and the result expressed therein. Some generality of expression in the provisional specification is accepted."

In his judgment, Fox J (with whom Spender J agreed) went on to refer to the statement of Lloyd-Jacob J in *Imperial Chemical Industries Ltd* (supra, at 583) that the function of a provisional specification is "a description of the general nature of the invention, its field of application and the anticipated result", and to the statement in Blanco White, *Patents for Inventions* (4th ed, 1974) at 44:

"Thus the provisional specification should contain as clear a statement as possible of the principles upon which the success of the invention depends (foreshadowing as far as possible the broader claims) together with discussion of its field of application and some indication of what results the inventor hopes it will achieve."

In the same case (at 399), Beaumont J adopted expressions (to some of which reference has already been made) appearing in *Hoffman-La Roche* when, having noted that judicial tests "are not a substitute for the test laid down by the Act itself", he said: [40]

"It is convenient to proceed, as Gibbs J did in *Hoffman-La Roche* (at 539) by stages: (1) Was the claim based on matter disclosed in the provisional? (2) If so, was it 'fairly' so based, in the sense of something 'fairly within' or 'fairly foreshadowed' by the provisional (see *F Hoffman-La Roche and Co AG v Commissioner of Patents* at 540), that is, something appearing on a 'fair reading' of that specification (at 541)?"

To return to *CCOM v Jiejing*, the Court concluded its survey of the law in this area by saying (at 281-282):

"In *Rhone-Poulenc* (supra) at 11 Fullagar J emphasised that disclosure without claim is enough. Hence, it is wrong to proceed as if testing for infringement and to seek to isolate in the body of the complete specification, or in the provisional specification, 'essential integers' or 'essential features' of an invention disclosed therein and to ask

■■■■■■ Leonardis v Sartas No 1 *continued*

whether they correspond with the essential integers in the claim in question: cf *Coopers Animal Health Australia Ltd v Western Stock Distributors Pty Ltd* (1986) 6 IPR 545 at 560-561, the decision at first instance. Nor would it be applying the statute to ask whether the earlier specifications fairly described the essential features of the invention disclosed in the later specification: cf *Interact Machine Tools (NSW) Pty Ltd v Yamazaki Mazak Corp* (1993) 27 IPR 83 at 93, 97 Fullagar J also pointed out that the requirement of 'fair basing' on matter disclosed in an earlier specification would be senseless if what was required was that the subject matter of the claim must have been actually claimed in the earlier specification; rather, there must be 'a real and reasonably clear disclosure'. This passage was adopted and applied by Gibbs J in *Hoffman-La Roche* at 537-539, where the claims were for chemical compounds forming part of a very large class disclosed in the basic application."

But, although this passage, rightly it is respectfully suggested, took the statutory expression "fair basing" to refer to what Fullagar J had called "a real and reasonably clear disclosure", as Gibbs J did in *Hoffman-La Roche*, the Court made a comment (at 281) which is perhaps capable of being misunderstood. It said:

"In *Imperial Chemical Industries Ltd (Clark's) Application* at 584, Lloyd-Jacob J asked whether the claim was 'plainly foreshadowed' in the disclosure in the provisional application."

This seems to suggest that Lloyd-Jacob J had used the quoted expression as a synonym for fair basis, or as a statement of the legal test for fair basis. What Lloyd-Jacob J actually laid down as a matter of principle is stated at 583 of his judgment as follows:

"All it (ie, the provisional specification) needs to contain is a description of the general nature of the invention, its field of application and the anticipated result."

The passage at 584 contains a statement of what in fact was shown by the provisional specification under consideration in that case, and the logic is that it went well beyond what was required. Referring to certain chemicals the subject of an aspect of the argument, Lloyd-Jacob J said:

"The production of both types is plainly foreshadowed and the applicants are entitled to monopolise in the complete specification so much of the disclosure in the provisional specification as they are minded to retain."

With great respect, this offers no support to the proposition that the language used by Fullagar J should be qualified by a requirement of plain foreshadowing. That would be to erect an ambiguous test (depending whether the emphasis is placed on a mere foreshadowing, or upon its being done plainly) as some kind of **[41]** gateway to be passed through. It is better to adhere to the statutory language, as expounded in simple terms by Fullagar J and accepted in a number of the passages we have already cited.

Perhaps it should be added that the Court in *CCOM v Jiejing* probably intended to place the emphasis on the word "foreshadowed", and did not really intend to depart from the earlier statements of the law. The effect of those statements was put in general terms by Lockhart J (with whom Wilcox J agreed) in *Anaesthetic Supplies Pty Ltd v Rescare Ltd* (1994) 50 FCR 1 at 20:

"All that the provisional specification needs to do is to describe generally and fairly the nature of the invention, and not to enter into all the minute details as to the manner

▬▬▬ Leonardis v Sartas No 1 *continued*

in which the invention is to be carried out. It is a mode of protecting an inventor until the time of filing the final specification. It is not intended to be a complete description of the invention, but simply to disclose the invention fairly, though in its rough state. The interval of time between the provisional and the final is intended to provide an opportunity for the development and precise expression of the invention foreshadowed in the provisional."

This proposition is consistent with the language used by Gummow J in *Rehm Pty Ltd v Webster's Security Systems (International) Pty Ltd* (1988) 81 ALR 79 at 95, where he said that:

"[T]he question is whether there is a real and reasonably clear disclosure in the body of the specification of what is then claimed, so that the alleged invention as claimed is broadly, that is to say in a general sense, described in the body of the specification."

See also the same judgment at 93-94.

If the matter is tested according to these principles, the only conclusion that can be reached is, to borrow a metaphor employed by Barwick CJ in *Olin Corp v Super Cartridge Co Pty Ltd* (1977) 180 CLR 236 at 240, that the claims as expressed do not travel beyond the matter disclosed in the provisional specification.

...[42]

It follows from the conclusions reached so far that the Court should hold the first and second provisional specifications to have provided fair basis for the claims in question.

Lockwood Security v Doric

[9.115] *Lockwood Security Products Pty Ltd v Doric Products Pty Ltd* (2004) 217 CLR 274, (2004) 62 IPR 461, [2004] HCA 58,

[Lockwood was the owner of a patent for a key controlled latch and the appellant. Doric, the respondent, was a manufacturer and supplier of door locks. In the course of an action alleging infringement in which the defendant raised many differing grounds of invalidity, the trial judge concluded that the claims were not fairly based and that while Doric's activities infringed some of the claims they did not infringe others. The issue in this appeal to the High Court was whether the claims defining the scope of the patentees exclusive rights under the patent were "fairly based" on the matter described in the specification or were wider than the matter described. Lockwood argued that the invention was described in a general consistory clause which included some words identical to those found in Claim 1, with various other preferable or illustrative embodiments or examples. Doric argued that the invention was described by reference to the drawings.

The High Court made a number of useful observations concerning the requirement of "fair basis"...]

GLEESON CJ, MCHUGH GUMMOW HAYNE AND HEYDON JJ: [290]

The construction of s 40(3): Separate consideration of each ground of invalidity

The language of the legislation suggests that it is wrong to employ reasoning relevant to one ground of invalidity in considering another.

█████ Lockwood Security v Doric *continued*

Section 18 compared with s 40. Section 18 of the Act is in Ch 2, headed "Patent rights, ownership and validity". Section 18 sets out requirements which go to the nature and subject-matter of patents. In contrast, s 40 appears in Ch 3, which is headed "From application to acceptance", and which deals with the filing, examination and acceptance of patent applications. Section 40 sets out requirements that are certainly important: in the specification, patentees give the public directions about how the advantages of the invention may be obtained after the patent expires, while in the claims, patentees warn their rivals what they must not do before the patent expires: *Rehm Pty Ltd v Websters Security Systems (International) Pty Ltd* (1988) 81 ALR 79 at 94-95 per Gummow J; *CCOM Pty Ltd v Jiejing Pty Ltd* (1994) 51 FCR 260 at 277 per Spender, Gummow and Heerey JJ. The requirements of s 40, however, unlike those of s 18, say nothing about the nature or subject-matter of patents, and go more to the form that specifications must take. Both the differences in the requirements which s 18 and s 40 impose, and their respective locations in the Act, suggest that s 18 issues have no relevance to s 40. ...

The distinctness of the grounds of invalidity. It is common in patent infringement litigation for invalidity to be alleged, and for more than one ground of invalidity to be relied on. Certain matters of fact and construction may be relevant to more than one issue. Thus common general knowledge is relevant not only to issues of construction by the skilled addressee, which underlie the infringement inquiry and interact [291] with issues of validity (*Welch Perrin & Co Pty Ltd v Worrel* (1961) 106 CLR 588 at 610 per Dixon CJ, Kitto and Windeyer JJ) but also to obviousness: *Firebelt Pty Ltd v Brambles Australia Ltd* (2002) 76 ALJR 816 at 821-823 [31]-[36] per Gleeson CJ, McHugh, Gummow, Hayne and Callinan JJ; 188 ALR 280 at 287-289. Other factual matters may be relevant to more than one ground of invalidity: *Sunbeam Corporation v Morphy-Richards (Aust) Pty Ltd* (1961) 180 CLR 98 at 111-112 per Windeyer J. The issues may "intersect and overlap". *Kimberly-Clark Australia Pty Ltd v Arico Trading International Pty Ltd* (2001) 207 CLR 1 at 19 [34]. However, as Doric conceded in this Court, the grounds of invalidity themselves are, and must be kept, conceptually distinct. In particular, as Doric also conceded, a lack of fair basing is a distinct ground for revocation. Hence the "inventiveness" or "meritoriousness" of, or the technical contribution made by, the specification are issues to be examined if there is an objection under s 18(1)(b) of the Act for want of novelty or absence of an inventive step (ie, obviousness). There is no reason to introduce them into the fair basing question.

[The Court emphasised that the test under s 40(3) does not require a comparison between the claims and the inventive step, or a comparison between the claims and the merit of the invention or a comparison between the claims and the technical contribution to the art made by the patent [293]-[294].]

The approach required by s 40(3)
[300]
Erroneous principles. The comparison which s 40(3) calls for is not analogous to that between a claim and an alleged anticipation or infringement. It is wrong to employ "an over meticulous verbal analysis" (*CCOM Pty Ltd v Jiejing Pty Ltd* (1994) 51 FCR 260 at 281 per Spender, Gummow and Heerey JJ). It is wrong to seek to isolate in the body of the specification "essential integers" or "essential features" of an alleged invention and to ask whether they correspond with the essential integers of the claim in question: *CCOM Pty Ltd v Jiejing Pty Ltd* (1994) 51 FCR 260 at 281 per Spender, Gummow and Heerey JJ.

"Real and reasonably clear disclosure". Section 40(3) requires, in Fullagar J's words (the expression was used by Fullagar J in *Société des Usines Chimiques Rhône-Poulenc v Commissioner*

■■■■■   Lockwood Security v Doric *continued*

of Patents (1958) 100 CLR 5 at 11 in relation to s 45 (5) of the 1952 Act, which required that a claim in a specification lodged under the 1952 Act be "fairly based on matter disclosed" in a specification lodged under the 1903 Act. The expression has been applied to s 40(3): *CCOM Pty Ltd v Jiejing Pty Ltd* (1994) 51 FCR 260 at 281-282 per Spender, Gummow and Heerey JJ) "a real and reasonably clear disclosure. But those words, when used in connection with s 40(3), do not limit disclosures to preferred embodiments.

> "The circumstance that something is a requirement for the best method of performing an invention does not make it necessarily a requirement for all claims; likewise, the circumstance that material is part of the description of the invention does not mean that it must be included as an integer of each claim. Rather, the question is whether there is a real and reasonably clear disclosure in the body of the specification of what is then claimed, so that the alleged invention as claimed is broadly, that is to say in a general sense, described in the body of the specification" (*Rehm Pty Ltd v Websters Security Systems (International) Pty Ltd* (1988) 81 ALR 79 at 95 per Gummow J).

Fullagar J's phrase serves the function of compelling attention to the construction of the specification as a whole, putting aside particular parts [309] which, although in isolation they might appear to point against the "real" disclosure, are in truth only loose or stray remarks. ... [302]

In assessing whether the invention claimed by a patentee is fully described or fairly based, it is necessary to take into account, apart from common general knowledge so far as it casts light on questions of construction, only what is said about it in the specification, independently of whether it is a "patentable invention", and, in particular, independently of whether it is a patentable invention on the ground that it is not obvious. ... [310]

Doric submitted that *Olin Corporation v Super Cartridge Co Pty Ltd* ((1975) 49 ALJR 135 (Jacobs J); (1977) 180 CLR 236 (FC)) decided that a claim based on a consistory clause cannot be fairly based. It did not. Rather, as the Patentee submitted, the correct position is that a claim based on what has been cast in the form of a consistory clause is not fairly based if other parts of the matter in the specification show that the invention is narrower than that consistory clause. The inquiry is into what the body of the specification read as a whole discloses as the invention (*Welch Perrin & Co Pty Ltd v Worrel* (1961) 106 CLR 588 at 612-613). An assertion by the inventor in a consistory clause of that of which the invention consists does not compel the conclusion by the court that the claims are fairly based nor is the assertion determinative of the identity of the invention. The consistory clause is to be considered by the court with the rest of the specification.

These points are reflected in the statements in an Australian text (*Lahore, Patents, Trade Marks and Related Rights*, (2001), vol 1 at ¶15,345 (footnote omitted)):

> "Claims found to be inconsistent with the general description of the invention may be invalid as being not fairly based on the matter described in the specification. In order to avoid this possibility a well drawn specification will usually include in the body of the specification one or more formal 'consistory statements' setting forth what the patentee considers to be the scope of the invention, such statements often quoting the exact wording of the broadest claims in the specifications. ... Such statements will generally [311] follow an introductory portion of the specification, which may describe the technical field of the invention and the problems with the prior art which are to be addressed by the invention. It is important that the introductory part of the specification be worded so as to be consistent with the scope of the invention as defined in the claims and any formal consistory statements.

Lockwood Security v Doric *continued*

A statement implying that the invention has a limited field of application or requires as an essential feature something which is not required by the claims may result in a finding that the claims are wider than the invention disclosed in the specification, and are accordingly invalid for lack of fair basis on the matter described in the specification."

■ Interpretation of the claims

[9.120] Interpreting the claims is fundamental to decisions about their ambit, what is actually being claimed as the invention, and whether another person is infringing a patent by trespassing inside the patentee's claimed monopoly. Some of the principles of law relevant to the construction of patent specifications generally are found in the extracts from the *Flexible Steel Lacing Co v Beltreco Ltd* and *Minnesota Mining & Manufacturing Co v Tyco Electronics Pty Ltd*. Those cases referred with some approval to principles of construction in the *Decor* case.

CHAPTER 10

INFRINGEMENT AND EXPLOITATION

INFRINGEMENT

■ Introduction

[10.05] The *Patents Act 1990* (Cth) does not define infringement but the patentee is granted "exclusive rights" by s 13 which provides:

"(1) Subject to this Act, a patent gives the patentee the exclusive rights, during the term of the patent, to exploit the invention and to authorise another person to exploit the invention.

(2) The exclusive rights are personal property and are capable of assignment and of devolution by law.

(3) A patent has effect throughout the patent area."

The word "exploit" is defined, in a non-exclusive manner, in *Patents Act 1990* (Cth), Sch 1:

"'*exploit*', in relation to an invention, includes:

(a) where the invention is a product—make, hire, sell or otherwise dispose of the product, offer to make, sell, hire or otherwise dispose of it, use or import it, or keep it for the purpose of doing any of those things; or

(b) where the invention is a method or process—use the method or process or do any act mentioned in paragraph (a) in respect of a product resulting from such use;"

The patentee may commence an action for infringement under s 120(1). Infringement proceedings cannot be commenced for an innovation patent unless the patent has been certified (s 120(1A)). An exclusive licensee may commence infringement proceedings but if the patentee is not joined as a plaintiff he or she must be joined as a defendant (s 120(2)). However, the exclusive licensee will not incur costs unless entering an appearance and taking part in the proceedings (s 120(3)).

Although there is no obligation to do so, a plaintiff will often give notice to a suspected infringer, identifying the patent, describing the acts of the defendant the patentee considers infringement, and demanding the cessation of the activity and payment of a sum to cover the patentees losses. However, care must be taken because a person aggrieved by unjustifiable threats of infringement proceedings may themselves commence proceedings seeking a declaration that the threats are unjustifiable, an injunction against continued threats and recovery of damages (s 128). Mere notification of the existence of a patent is not an unjustifiable threat (s 131), and s 132 protects a legal practitioner or patent attorney in respect of an act done in his or her professional capacity on behalf of a client. A patentee may justify a threat and defend proceedings brought under s 128 by showing that the patent is valid and the threats relate to activities which are an infringement (s 129). A person defending an action under s 128 may counterclaim for infringement (s 130). Threats in relation to an innovation patent where the application has not been determined or where the innovation patent is not certified are always unjustifiable (s 129A).

In a claim for infringement the court must carefully interpret the claims according to the principles of construction (see below Principles of construction at **[10.10]**). The defendant's embodiment or actions must then be compared with the invention defined in the claims. If the defendant is acting with an embodiment or process which falls within the proper construction of the patentee's claims, and is doing so in relation to one (or more) of the activities given to the patentee as an exclusive right to "exploit", there is prima facie infringement. There are several statutory defences to infringement (ss 118, 119) and relief from certain remedies for innocent infringement (s 123). A very common form of defence to an infringement action is for the defendant to allege that the patent is invalid and counterclaim under s 121 seeking revocation of the patent on any of the grounds set out in s 138(3).

While judges agree that infringement is found where the defendant takes all of the essential integers of the plaintiff's claim, there have been different approaches to the task of assessing which are the essential integers. Some judges have taken what is called a "literal construction" or "textual construction", arguing that the patentee chooses the wording of the claim and so must have chosen the precise words to convey a particular meaning, so that any integer found clearly expressed in the words of the claim must be a deliberately chosen essential integer (see, for exampe, *C Van Der Lely NV v Bamfords* [1963] RPC 61). Other judges have allowed wider interpretations, and these approaches have been termed "pith and marrow" infringement, "non-textual" infringement or "purposive construction" (see below Principles of infringement **[10.15]**). It may be the case that judges are more generous in cases where the defendant has deliberately copied the plaintiff's patent and then makes minor alterations apparently outside the "literal construction" of the claims in an attempt to avoid infringement.

■ Principles of construction

▬▬▬ Sachtler v RE Miller ▬▬▬

[10.10] *Sachtler GMBH & Co KG v RE Miller Pty Ltd* (2005) 65 IPR 605; FCA 788

BENNETT J: **[613]**

Principles for construing claims

In a number of decisions, courts have noted that the principles of claim construction are not in dispute and have then restated those principles. Those courts have drawn on different expressions in order to assist in construing the scope of the claimed monopoly under consideration to take into account different submissions in the individual case on the permitted use of the body of the specification and the evidence of expert witnesses.

The underlying principles are clear and have been enunciated by the High Court in cases such as *Welch Perrin & Co Pty Ltd v Worrel* (1961) 106 CLR 588 ("*Welch Perrin*"); *Walker v Alemite Corporation* (1933) 49 CLR 643; *Interlego AG v Toltoys Pty Ltd* (1973) 130 CLR 461 ("*Interlego*"); *Kimberly-Clark*. Those principles, together with consideration of them by Full Courts in cases such as *Nicaro*; *Décor Corporation Pty Ltd v Dart Industries Inc* (1988) 13 IPR 385 ("*Décor*"); *Allsop; Patent Gesellschaft* and *Jupiters*; have been restated and summarised in recent decisions such as *Flexible Steel Lacing Company v Beltreco Ltd* (2000) 49 IPR 331 ("*Beltreco*") (by Hely J); *Photocure* (by Merkel J); and *Baygol Pty Ltd v Foamex Polystyrene Pty Ltd* [2005] FCA 624 ("*Baygol*") (by Tamblerlin J).

I draw with gratitude on those analyses and note some of the principles that are apposite to the issues in the construction of the claims in this patent:

- When determining the nature and extent of the monopoly claimed, the specification must be read as a whole. As a whole it is made up of several parts and those parts have different functions. The claim, cast in precise language, marks out the legal limits of the monopoly granted by the patent. What is not claimed is disclaimed. The specification describes how to carry out the process claimed and the best method known to the patentee of doing that (*Beltreco* at [73]).

██████   Sachtler v RE Miller *continued*

- Although the claims are construed in the context of the specification as a whole, it is not legitimate to narrow or expand the boundaries of monopoly, as fixed by the words of a claim, by adding to those words glosses drawn from other parts of the specification. If a claim is clear and unambiguous, it is not to be varied, qualified or made obscure by statements found in other parts of the document (*Beltreco* at [74]). **[614]**
- Terms in the claim which are unclear may be defined or clarified by reference to the body of the specification (*Welch Perrin* at 610; *Interlego* at 479, both approved in *Kimberly-Clark* at [15]).
- Reference may be made to the body of the specification to understand the context in which words have been used (*Beltreco* at [77] following *Minnesota Mining & Manufacturing Co v Beiersdorf (Aust) Ltd* (1980) 144 CLR 253 at 272 ("*3M*")).
- It is legitimate to refer to the rest of the specification to explain the background to the claims, to ascertain the meaning of technical terms and to resolve ambiguities in the construction of the claims. Where the language of the claim is obscure or doubtful the doubt is sometimes resolved by referring to words in the body of the document to explain it (*Beltreco* at [75]).
- It is not necessary first to construe the claims without reference to the specification and then to determine whether or not ambiguity exists (*Décor* at 410; *Beltreco* at [76]; *PhotoCure* at [174].
- There is a fine line between, on the one hand, reading down the words of a patent claim to reflect how a person skilled in the art would understand it in a practical and commonsense way and, on the other hand, impermissibly limiting the clear words of a claim because a reader skilled in the art would be likely to apply those wide words only in a limited range of all the situations they describe (*Stanway Oyster Cylinders Pty Ltd v Marks* (1996) 66 FCR 577 at 585 per Drummond J).
- The construction of the claim determines infringement, on both textual and substantive bases (*Catnic Components Limited v Hill & Smith Limited* [1982] RPC 183 at 242 ("*Catnic*") at 242; *PhotoCure* at [158]). It is a question of whether the alleged infringement is covered by the language of the claim (*Improver Corporation v Remington Consumer Products Limited* [1990] FSR 181 at 189-190 cited in *Photocure* at [158]).
- A patent should be given a purposive construction (*Catnic* at 242-243). However, that does not involve extending or going beyond the definition of the technical matter for which the patentee seeks protection in the claims. The question is always what the person skilled in the art would have understood the patentee to be using the language of the claim to mean. For this purpose, the language chosen is usually of critical importance (*Kirin-Amgen Inc v Hoeschst Marion Roussel Ltd* [2005] 1 All ER 667 at [34] ("*Kirin-Amgen*")).
- Purposive construction, permitting consideration of whether the person skilled in the art would understand a variant that does not strictly comply with the particular descriptive word used in the claim may still fall within the monopoly, does not arise where the variant would in fact have a material effect upon the way the invention worked (*Catnic* at 243; *Kirin-Amgen* at [50]).

■ Principles of infringement

============================ **Sachtler v RE Miller** ============================

[10.15] *Sachtler GMBH & Co KG v RE Miller Pty Ltd* (2005) 65 IPR 605; FCA 788,

BENNETT J: **[614]**

Principles of infringement

As with principles of construction of claims, emphasis has been placed on different expressions of the principles that apply in determining whether there has been infringement of the claims of a patent. In particular, some attention in this Court has recently been directed to decisions in the United Kingdom which **[615]** have developed from *Catnic*, such as *Improver* which have, in turn, been marshalled recently for that jurisdiction in *Kirin-Amgen*.

The *Improver* questions, as put by Hoffman J (as he then was) at 189, designed to give effect to the *Catnic* principle, are:

> "If the issue was whether a feature embodied in an alleged infringement which fell outside the primary, literal or a contextual meaning of a descriptive word or phrase in the claim ("a variant") was nevertheless within its language as properly interpreted, the court should ask itself the following three questions:
>
> (1) Does the variant have a material effect upon the way the invention works? If yes, the variant is outside the claim. If no –
>
> (2) Would this (ie that the variant had no material effect) have been obvious at the date of publication of the patent to a reader skilled in the art? If no, the variant is outside the claim. If yes –
>
> (3) Would the reader skilled in the art nevertheless have understood from the language of the claim that the patentee intended that strict compliance with the primary meaning was an essential requirement of the invention. If yes, the variant is outside the claim.
>
> On the other hand, a negative answer to the last question would lead to the conclusion that the patentee was intending the word or phrase to have not a literal but a figurative meaning (the figure being a form of synecdoche or metonymy) denoting a class of things which included the variant and the literal meaning, the latter being perhaps the most perfect, best-known or striking example of the class."

In *Root Quality Pty Ltd v Root Control Technologies Pty Ltd* (2000) 49 IPR 225 (*Root Quality*), Finkelstein J said at [45]: "when the Improver questions are posed and answered, it is difficult to see what can be achieved by recourse to the 'pith and marrow' approach". Merkel J in *Photocure*, in a section of the reasons headed "infringement in substance" said at [207]:

> "[207] However, in a case such as the present the *Improver* questions are useful guidelines because they can be of assistance in determining whether a reasonable person skilled in the art, reading the claims in context, would think that the patentee was not intending to employ the primary meanings of the relevant phrases used in claims 1 and 9 but, rather, was intending that the meaning of those phrases would include the use of an equivalent."

In *Baygol* (at [15]), Tamberlin J considered *Catnic* and its application in *Improver*. His Honour also considered the application of the purposive approach in Australian cases and the application of the *Improver* questions.

▬▬▬▬   Sachtler v RE Miller *continued*

While *Catnic* is often cited for its reference to "purposive construction", that reference must be read in context.

As stated by Lord Diplock at 242-3:

"My Lords, a patent specification is a unilateral statement by the patentee, in words of his own choosing, addressed to those likely to have a practical interest in the subject matter of his invention (ie, 'skilled in the art'), *by which he informs them what he claims to be the essential features of the new product or process for which the letters patent grant him a monopoly. It is those novel features only that he claims to be essential that constitute the so-called 'pith and marrow' of the claim.* A patent specification should be given a purposive construction rather than a purely literal one derived from applying to it the kind of meticulous verbal analysis in which lawyers are too often tempted by their training to indulge. The question in each case is: whether persons with practical knowledge and experience of the kind of work in which the invention was intended to be used, would understand that strict compliance with a particular descriptive word or phrase [616] appearing in a claim was intended by the patentee to be an essential requirement of the invention so that any variant would fall outside the monopoly claimed, even though it could have no material effect upon the way the invention worked.

The question, of course, does not arise where the variant would in fact have a material effect upon the way the invention worked. Nor does it arise unless at the date of publication of the specification it would be obvious to the informed reader that this was so. Where it was not obvious, in the light of then-existing knowledge, the reader is entitled to assume that the patentee thought at the time of the specification that he had good reason for limiting his monopoly so strictly and had intended to do so, even though subsequent work by him or others in the field of the invention might show the limitation to have been unnecessary. It is to be answered in the negative only when it would be apparent to any reader skilled in the art that a particular descriptive word or phrase used in a claim cannot have been intended by the patentee, who was also skilled in the art, to exclude minor variants which, to the knowledge of both him and the readers to whom the patent was addressed, could have no material effect upon the way in which the invention worked." (emphasis added)

In *Populin v HB Nominees Pty Ltd* (1982) 41 ALR 471 at 476-477 ("*Populin*"), Bowen CJ, Deane and Ellicott JJ cited *Catnic* as standing for the proposition that the essential integers are determined by a common sense assessment of what the words of the claims convey in the context of then-existing published knowledge (see also *Rehm Pty Ltd v Websters Security Systems (International) Pty Ltd* (1988) 81 ALR 79 at 92 per Gummow J (*Rehm*).

In *Populin* (at 475), the Full Court reiterated the fundamental proposition that, to establish infringement of a combination patent, the patentee must show that the defendant has taken each and every one of the essential integers of the claim. If, on its true construction, the claim is for a particular combination of integers and the alleged infringer omits one of the essential integers, the infringer escapes liability (*Populin* at 475). A defendant will not escape liability if an inessential integer is omitted or replaced by an equivalent (*Populin* at 475).

In *Populin* (at 475) the Full Court discussed the taking of the substantial idea disclosed by the specification and infringement of the claims:

"...it is whether the substantial idea disclosed by the specification *and made the subject of a definite claim* has been taken and embodied in the infringing thing" (emphasis added)

■■■■■■ Sachtler v RE Miller *continued*

This is the "pith and marrow" test which is based on a statement by James LJ in *Clark v Adie* (1875) LR 10 Ch App 667 that one should look to whether the allegedly infringing article is the same in substance and effect or is a substantially new or different combination. This principle applies to immaterial variations where an inessential part or step is omitted or substituted. A modification may be so small as to be insignificant and to have no material effect on the way the invention works (*Commonwealth Industrial Gases Ltd v MWA Holdings Pty Ltd* (1970) 180 CLR 160 at 168; *Rehm* at 92 per Gummow J).

This is consistent with the principle in *Catnic,* as discussed in *Kirin-Amgen* at [50], that there is no infringement if a variant has a material effect on the way the invention works. Put another way, if the variant were of an inessential integer, it would not be a mechanical equivalent.

This does not mean that there is infringement where there has been no taking of all the essential integers of the claim (*Olin Corporation v Super Cartridge Co Pty Ltd* (1977) 180 CLR 236 at 246 per Gibbs J) or where the wording of the claims make it clear that the [617] relevant area has been deliberately left outside the claim (*3M* at 286). *Catnic* is clear authority for the proposition that it is the essential integers of the claim that constitute the "pith and marrow" of the claim (at 243).

Although in *Nicaro* Gummow J (with whom Jenkinson J agreed) was considering anticipation rather than infringement, his Honour traced the application of the *Catnic* principle in Australia (at 528-529). *Nicaro* sets out the approach to construction of a claim for a combination for the purposes of infringement and anticipation. Gummow J expressed the view that *Catnic* and purposive construction did not propound a novel principle. His Honour referred to the Full Court decision in *Populin* where (at 476) the Court commented that the essential features 'are to be determined not as a matter of abstract uninformed construction but by a common-sense assessment of what the words used convey in the context of then-existing published knowledge' and cited *Catnic* as espousing the same principle.

To the extent that recent judgments of this Court have suggested that there may be infringement by taking what is determined to be the substantial idea disclosed by the specification but not the essential integers of the claim, I must respectfully disagree. To the extent that cases such as *Olin* are relied upon as authority for the proposition that there is infringement by taking the "pith and marrow" or substance of an invention, untrammelled by the form of the claims, in my view those cases stand for the opposite test. An examination of "non-textual" infringement raises the question whether *"the substance of the invention as claimed has been taken"* (emphasis added) (*Rehm* at 92).

Catnic has not changed the law as applied in Australia. Indeed, it did not purport to change the law in the United Kingdom. In any event, the applicable law is as set out by the High Court and the Full Court of this Court which have made clear the way in which *Catnic* is to be applied.

Before turning to *the Improver* questions, it is useful to consider the context in which they were framed and their applicability. Both of those issues were recently discussed by Lord Hoffman, the framer of the questions, in *Kirin-Amgen.* His Lordship discussed the fact that Article 69 of the *Convention on the Grant of European Patents 1973* ("European Patent Convention") and the *Protocol on the Interpretation of Article 69* ("the Protocol") were perceived to be a compromise between the principles of construction applied by United Kingdom courts, which were perceived as having sometimes resulted in claims being given an unduly narrow and literal construction and the principles applied in Europe which are based on the "essence of the invention" rather than the actual terms of the claims (at [23]-[25]).

▬▬▬▬▬ Sachtler v RE Miller *continued*

Lord Hoffman set out the principles applied to construction prior to the European Patent Convention. At [27]-[28] he traced the early approach applied in *Electric & Musical Industries v Lissen Ltd* [1938] 4 All ER 221; 56 RPC 234 in which meaning was assigned to the claims by their words and grammar and was adopted without regard to the context or background unless the words were ambiguous, in which case the Court could have regard to the context provided by the specification and drawings. As his Lordship points out at [30], by the time the Protocol was signed, English courts had adopted the approach of construing the language of the claims as it would be understood by the people to whom it was **[618]** addressed (see, for example, *Catnic*). As in Australia, the words were given the meaning that the notional addressee, the person skilled in the art, would have understood the author to have meant.

Lord Hoffman sounded a caution about the "purposive construction" of Lord Diplock in *Catnic* at [33]:

> "[33]…But there is, I think, a tendency to regard it as a vague description of some kind of divination which mysteriously penetrates beneath the language of the specification. Lord Diplock was in my opinion being much more specific and his intention was to point out that a person may be taken to mean something different when he uses words for one purpose from what he would be taken to mean if he was using them for another…"

The example in *Catnic* was the use of the word "vertical" as used in the building trade which was not to be construed in a strictly mathematical sense.

Lord Hoffman rejected the suggestion that one construes the patent claims in some way to be "fair to the patentee". As his Lordship points out at [33] "…There is no presumption about the width of the claims. A patent may, for one reason or another, claim less than it teaches or enables".

His Lordship described the question as what the person skilled in the art would have understood the patentee to be using the language of the claim to mean (at [34]). To that end, one looks to the words and syntax used which, it is assumed, were chosen with skill and care. It would not be often, as pointed out at [34], that it will be obvious to the skilled reader that the patentee has departed from conventional use of language or included in the description of the invention some element which was not meant to be essential.

Lord Hoffman then examined the way in which the courts of the United Kingdom and the United States have dealt with the difficulties of applying a literal or textual approach to construction of patent claims. In the United States, the courts have adopted the doctrine of equivalents. That has given rise to its own problems with regard to uncertainty and predictability (*Festo Corp v Shoketsu Kinzoku Kogyu Kabushiki Co Ltd* (2000) 234 F 3d 558). In the United Kingdom the courts adopted *Catnic* as a solution which, according to Lord Diplock (at [43]) was "a principle of construction which actually gave effect to what the person skilled in the art would have understood the patentee to be claiming".

It can be seen that the approach of courts in the United Kingdom mirrors that in the Australian cases. In *Kimberly-Clark* at [24], for example, the High Court articulates the familiar principle that the patent specification is to be construed in the light of common general knowledge and the art at the priority date.

Article 69 of the European Patent Convention, according to Lord Hoffman in *Kirin-Amgen* at [44], precludes a doctrine which extends protection outside the claims. At [48], his Lordship concludes that the *Catnic* principle of construction is precisely in accordance with the Protocol. Such a principle also, in the view of his Lordship, provides fair protection to the patentee (at [48]).

■■■■■■ Sachtler GMBH & Co KG v RE Miller *continued*

As Lord Hoffman pointed in *Kirin-Amgen* out at [69], there is no point in going through the motions of answering the *Improver* questions when you cannot sensibly do so until you have construed the claim. In such cases, they simply provide a justification for a conclusion that has already been reached on other grounds, namely on the construction of the claims. "They are not a substitute for trying to understand what the person skilled in the art would have understood the patentee to mean by the language of the claim" (at [71]). **[619]**

I am mindful of what was said in *Aktiebolaget Hassle v Alphapharm Pty Ltd* (2002) 212 CLR 411 ("*Alphapharm*") at [42] by Gleeson CJ and Gaudron, Gummow and Hayne JJ as to the consequence of the divergence between the case law of Australia and that of the United Kingdom, in particular after "the 'Europeanisation' of British law" (at [48]). In *Alphapharm*, the High Court was considering differences in the approach to obviousness but, as can be seen, the European Patent Convention has also affected the approach to claim construction.

Taking into account the observations of Lord Hoffman as to the usefulness of the *Improver* questions, which have been labelled "the Protocol questions", I do not consider that utilisation of those questions is helpful other than, perhaps, as a "check" on the conclusion reached as to the characterisation of essential or inessential integers present in the allegedly infringing article. They are no substitute for construction of the claim to ascertain the essential and inessential integers and a determination regarding the presence of those integers for infringement.

■ Purposive construction

■■■■■■■■■■■ Catnic Components v Hill & Smith ■■■■■■■■■■

[10.20] *Catnic Components Ltd v Hill & Smith Ltd* [1982] RPC 183 House of Lords

LORD DIPLOCK **[242]**: This appeal concerns a claim by the appellants (Catnic) for infringement of a simple but successful patent of which they are the registered proprietors for galvanised steel lintels for use in spanning the spaces above window and door openings in cavity walls built of bricks or similar constructional unit. In the patent in suit the necessary strength and rigidity was obtained by adopting a box-girder structure with consequent lightness, economy of material, and ease of handling.

The simplest way of explaining the invention is by reproducing Fig 1 of the complete specification, which is of a vertical section through the lintel, showing the outer and inner courses of the cavity wall. The lintel can be made in two modules, a three-course module (as shown) where the height between the upper and lower horizontal plates is equivalent to three courses of bricks and mortar and a two-course module which [sic] the height is equivalent to two courses only.

Of the claims in the specification it is only necessary for present purposes to reproduce the first.

"1. A lintel for use over apertures in cavity walls having an inner and outer skin comprising a first horizontal plate or part adapted to support a course or a plurality of superimposed units forming part of the inner skin and a second horizontal plate or part substantially parallel to the first and spaced therefrom in a downward vertical direction and adapted to span the cavity in the cavity wall and be supported at least

━━━━━   Catnic Components v Hill & Smith *continued*

at each end thereof upon courses forming parts of the outer and inner skins respectively of the cavity wall adjacent an aperture, and a first rigid inclined support member extending downwardly and forwardly from or near the front edge adjacent the cavity of the first horizontal plate or part and joining with the second plate or part at an intermediate position which lies between the front and rear edge of the second plate or part and adapted to extend across the cavity, and a second rigid support member extending vertically from or from near the rear edge of the first horizontal plate or part to join with the second plate or part adjacent its rear edge."

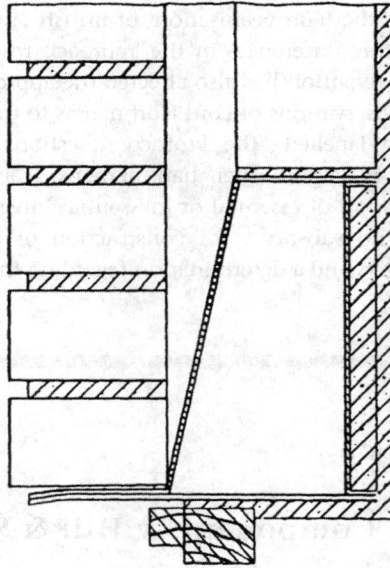

The complete specification was filed on 29 December 1969 and published on 6 December 1972. Lintels manufactured in accordance with the patent quickly achieved considerable success upon the market. At about the beginning of 1974 the respondents (Hill and Smith) ... decided to prepare to enter the market for builders' products and, in particular, for galvanised steel lintels ... [T]hey examined trade brochures issued by various manufacturers of steel lintels, including one published by Catnic. They decided that the Catnic lintel was the best; they were unaware that it was the subject matter of a patent; so they copied it and manufactured it.

[His Lordship then explained that Catnic brought a successful action for infringement and obtained injunctions and damages against Hill and Smith who subsequently decided to produce a second but altered version based upon box girder construction and continued:]

Hill and Smith then produced a modified design (referred to in the courts below as "DH4") which became the subject of the second writ. It was substantially in the form sketched below.

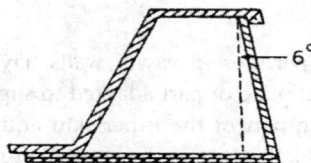

■■■■■■ Catnic Components v Hill & Smith *continued*

Between this design and that described in claim 1 of the patent the difference which is relied upon by Hill and Smith to save it from being an infringement is that the back plate is not precisely vertical but is inclined at a slight angle to the vertical, 6° in the case of the three-course module and 8° in the case of the two-course module. … Did the substitution of a back plate that was slightly inclined to the true vertical for one that was precisely vertical change what the patentee by his specification had made an essential feature of the invention claimed having regard to the patentee's description of the back plate in claim 1 as "extending vertically"?

The invention is a simple one; to understand what it does and how it works calls for no great technological or scientific expertise. It is designed for use by builders engaged in ordinary building operations; they constitute the readers to whom the specification is addressed. As any knowledgeable builder would know, indeed as would be known even by one of Lord Macaulay's schoolboys who had reached the triangle of forces in his study of elementary mechanics, a slight inclination from the vertical of an upright support reduces its load bearing capacity proportionately to the cosine of the angle of such inclination. Where that angle is 6° as in the Hill and Smith three-course module DH4 the reduction is 0.6%, where it is 8° as in the two-course module the reduction is still only 1.2%. From the point of view of function a reduction of this order in vertical support provided for the upper horizontal plate is negligible.

… My Lords, a patent specification is a unilateral statement by the patentee, in words of his own choosing, addressed to those likely to have a practical interest in the subject matter of his invention (ie, "skilled in the art"), by which he informs them [of] what he claims to be the essential features of the new product or process for which the letters patent grant him a monopoly. It is those novel features only that he claims to be essential that constitute the so-called "pith and marrow" of the claim. A patent specification should be given a purposive construction rather than a purely literal one derived from applying to it the kind of meticulous verbal analysis in which lawyers are too often tempted by their training to indulge. The question in each case is: whether persons with practical knowledge and experience of the kind of work in which the invention was intended to be used, would understand that strict compliance with a particular descriptive word or phrase appearing in a claim was intended by the patentee to be an essential requirement of the invention so that *any* variant would fall outside the monopoly claimed, even though it could have no material effect upon the way the invention worked.

The question, of course, does not arise where the variant would in fact have a material effect upon the way the invention worked. Nor does it arise unless at the date of publication of the specification it would be obvious to the informed reader that this was so. Where it is not obvious, in the light of then-existing knowledge, the reader is entitled to assume that the patentee thought at the time of the specification that he had good reason for limiting his monopoly so strictly and had intended to do so, even though subsequent work by him or others in the field of the invention might show the limitation to have been unnecessary. It is to be answered in the negative only when it would be apparent to any reader skilled in the art that a particular descriptive word or phrase used in a claim cannot have been intended by a patentee, who was also skilled in the art, to exclude minor variants which, to the knowledge of both him and the readers to whom the patent was addressed, could have no material effect upon the way in which the invention worked.

… Put in a nutshell the question to be answered is: Would the specification make it obvious to a builder familiar with ordinary building operations that the description of a lintel in the form of a weightbearing box girder of which the back plate was referred to as

▬▬▬   Catnic Components v Hill & Smith *continued*

"extending vertically" from one of the two horizontal plates to join the other, could *not* have been intended to exclude lintels in which the back plate although not positioned at precisely 90 ° to both horizontal plates was close enough to 90 ° to make no material difference to the way the lintel worked when used in building operations? No plausible reason has been advanced why any rational patentee should want to place so narrow a limitation on his invention. On the contrary, to do so would render his monopoly for practical purposes worthless, since any imitator could avoid it and take all the benefit of the invention by the simple expedient of positioning the back plate a degree or two from the exact vertical.

It may be that when used by a geometer addressing himself to fellow geometers, such expressions descriptive of relative position as "horizontal", "parallel", "vertical" and "vertically" are to be understood as words of precision only; but when used in a description of a manufactured product intended to perform the practical function of a weightbearing box girder in supporting courses of brickwork over window and door spaces in buildings, it seems to me that the expression "extending vertically" as descriptive of the position of what in use will be the upright member of a trapezoid-shaped box girder, is perfectly capable of meaning positioned near enough to the exact geometrical vertical to enable it in actual use to perform satisfactorily all the functions that it could perform if it were precisely vertical; and having regard to those considerations to which I have just referred that is the sense in which in my opinion "extending vertically" would be understood by a builder familiar with ordinary building operation. Or, putting the same thing in another way, it would be obvious to him that the patentee did not intend to make exact verticality in the positioning of the back plate an essential feature of the invention claimed.

It follows that I have reached the same conclusion as the trial judge and Sir David Cairns, although not by the route of drawing a distinction between "textual infringement" and infringement of the "pith and marrow" of the invention. Accordingly I would allow the appeal.

[The other members of the House of Lords concurred.]

▬▬▬▬▬▬▬▬▬▬▬▬▬▬▬▬▬▬▬▬

Notes

[10.25] In *Nicaro Holdings Pty Ltd v Martin Engineering Co* (1990) 16 IPR 545 at 560-561 Gummow J said:

> "The appellants sought, somewhat tentatively, to pray in aid the principles of 'purposive' construction of patent specifications, described by Lord Diplock in *Catnic Components Ltd v Hill & Smith Ltd* [1982] RPC 183 and discussed in several decisions of this court. The House of Lords found infringement. One may observe that such a result in an Australian court would have caused no great surprise to the reader of *Commonwealth Industrial Gases Ltd v MWA Holdings Pty Ltd* (1970) 44 ALJR 385 at 388. I would not treat the House of Lords as having propounded any novel principle or new category of 'non-textual infringement', and this court has treated the decision in that light: *Populin v HB Nominees Pty Ltd* (1982) 59 FLR 37 at 42-43; *Rehm Pty Ltd v Websters Security Systems (International) Pty Ltd* (1988) 11 IPR 299; 81 ALR 79 at 91-92."

In *Comonwealth Industrial Gases Ltd v MWA Holdings Pty Ltd* (1970) 44 ALJR 385 the invention related to mixer tubes in gas burners like oxyacetylene welding torches and was designed to reduce the danger of "flashback" explosion. One of the features of the invention was a reflector plate described as "flat". The defendant had at first copied the plaintiff's invention and on being found to be in infringement consulted attorneys and produced a new version with the reflector plate slightly curved. Menzies J said:

> "Patent rights are not to be set at nought by such a subterfuge which I am satisfied added nothing to the equipment and was made merely in an attempt to take full advantage of the invention while avoiding infringement of the plaintiffs letters patent by a modification so small as to be insignificant. ... The cases do establish that if the alleged infringement differs materially from an essential feature of the plaintiff's claim there can be no infringement. ... In the present case the normality of the reflector is made an essential feature of the plaintiff's patent. ... [H]owever the modified manufacture since 1966 does not avoid that essential feature because the reflector as made thereafter is so close to being flat that the defendants manufacture and sale still takes the plaintiff's invention"

See also *Old Digger Pty Ltd v Azuko Pty Ltd* (2000) 51 IPR 43 at 56-57.

Populin v HB Nominees

[10.30] *Populin v HB Nominees Pty Ltd* (1982) 41 ALR 471; 59 FLR 37 Federal Court of Australia

[The appellants are the owners of Letters Patent No 487810 which created patent rights to an invention relating to a machine and a method for planting sugar cane. The respondents, after the date of the appellants' patent, manufactured and sold a machine which the appellants argued was an infringement of their patent. There was a physical difference between the two machines. The appellants' patent described a machine with two separate containers, a large storage bin and a small feeder bin above the planting head. The respondents' machine had a single large container which included a trough-like depression in the base near the planting head which performed a similar function to the small bin on the appellants' machine.]

BOWEN CJ, DEANE and ELLICOTT JJ: ...[41] It has often been said that the claims operate as a disclaimer of what is not specifically claimed: eg, *Walker v Alemite Corp* (1933) 49 CLR 643 at 656 per Dixon J. They therefore determine the extent of the patentee's monopoly. The patentee must be vigilant to claim only the essence of the invention. This is particularly so in relation to a combination patent. It is important to claim only the essential integers in the combination or to distinguish what is essential from what is inessential. For to establish infringement of a combination patent, the patentee must show that the defendant has taken each and every one of the essential integers of the patentee's claim. Therefore if, on its true construction, the claim in a patent claims a particular combination of integers and the allowed infringer of it omits one of them he will escape liability.

At the same time, however, the courts have avoided too technical or narrow a construction of claims. In *Radiation Ltd v Galliers & Klaerr Pty Ltd* (1938) 60 CLR 36 at 51 Dixon J said:

> "But, on a question of infringement, the issue is not whether the words of the claim can be applied with verbal accuracy or felicity to the article or device alleged to infringe, it is whether the substantial idea disclosed by the specification and made the subject of a definite claim has been taken and embodied in the infringing thing."

It is in reliance on this approach that the courts have held that a defendant will not escape infringement by adopting what are immaterial variations, eg, by omitting an inessential part

■■■■■   Populin v HB Nominees *continued*

or step and substituting another part or step as its equivalent: see *Marconi v British Radio Telegraph & Telephone Co Ltd* (1911) 28 RPC 181 at 217 per Parker J. It was considerations such as this that led early in the history of patent law to the development of what has been termed the **[42]** "pith and marrow" or "pith and substance" test. The classic statement of it is found in the judgment of James LJ in *Clark v Adie* (1875) LR 10 Ch App 667 at 675, where he said:

"The patent is in the entire combination, but there is, or may be, an essence or substance of the invention underlying the mere accident of form; and that invention, like every other invention, may be pirated by a theft in a disguised or mutilated form, and it would be in every case a question of fact whether the alleged piracy is the same in substance and effect or is a substantially new or different combination."

The existence of this doctrine is still recognised by the High Court. But its limitations must be borne in mind. Thus in *Olin Corp v Super Cartridge Co Pty Ltd* (1977) 14 ALR 149 at 157, Gibbs J (as he then was) after referring to the above passages said:

"The statements in these passages are still good law; see *C Van der Lely NV v Bamfords Ltd* [1963] RPC 61 at 75. However, as was pointed out in Van der Lely at 78 and 80, the principle that there may be infringement by taking the 'pith and marrow' or the substance of an invention does not mean that there will be an infringement where the patentee has by the form of his claim left open that which the alleged infringer has done. And it does not affect the fundamental rule that there will be no infringement unless the alleged infringer has taken all of the essential features or integers of the patentee's claim: see *Rodi & Wienenberger AG v Henry Showell Ltd* [1969] RPC 367 especially at 383-384."

In *Minnesota Mining & Manufacturing Co v Beiersdorf (Aust) Ltd* (1980) 29 ALR 29 at 52-53, Aickin J with whose judgment Barwick CJ, Stephen, Mason and Wilson JJ all expressed agreement, wrote:

"Notwithstanding the undoubted fact that the doctrine of *Clark v Adie* (1875) LR 10 Ch App 667 concerning the taking of the pith and substance of an invention, but none the less staying outside the express words of the claim, is less often applicable at the present time than it was at the time of that decision, it remains the law that a defendant may not take the substance of an invention unless the wording of the claims makes it clear that the relevant area has been deliberately left outside the claim."

The authorities which demonstrate this to be so are collected in the judgment of Gibbs J in *Olin Corp v Super Cartridge Co Pty Ltd* (1977) 51 ALJR 525 at 530; 14 ALR 149 at 157, and need not be repeated here." See also *Beecham Group Ltd v Bristol Laboratories Ltd* [1978] RPC 153 at 200.

The complete specification must not be read in the abstract but in the light of common knowledge in the art before the priority date, **[43]** bearing in mind that what is being construed is a public instrument which must, if it is to be valid, define a monopoly in such a way that it is not reasonably capable of being misunderstood: see generally *Welch Perrin Pty Ltd v Worrel* (1961) 106 CLR 588 at 610. The essential features of the product or process for which it claims a monopoly are to be determined not as a matter of abstract uninformed construction but by a commonsense assessment of what the words used convey in the context of then-existing published knowledge. As Lord Diplock (with whom the other members of the House of Lords agreed) commented in *Catnic Components Ltd v Hill & Smith Ltd* [1987] FSR 60 at 65-66:

"[A] patent specification is a unilateral statement by the patentee, in words of his own choosing, addressed to those likely to have a practical interest in the subject matter of his invention (ie, 'skilled in the art'), by which he informs them [of] what he claims to be the essential features of the new product or process for which the letters patent grant him a monopoly. It is those novel features only that he claims to be essential that constitute the so-called 'pith and marrow' of the claim. A patent specification should be given a purposive construction rather than a purely literal one derived from applying to it the kind of meticulous verbal analysis in which lawyers are too often tempted by their training to indulge."

In the light of these principles it is necessary to construe the claims and to see whether the respondents' machine has taken the essential integers of what the patentees saw fit to claim. For the purpose of this appeal it is, we think, sufficient to consider in detail only claim 1.

[The Court then analysed Claim 1 in some detail and continued:] [**46**]

In the Supreme Court, Connolly J held there had been no infringement because the Binder machine does not have two quite separate containers ... His Honour's view as to the importance of the quite separate nature of the small bin and the supply container appears from the following passage from his judgment: "One must read the claim as a whole and so read, together with the body of the specification, it defines, on its proper construction, an invention in which the containers are deliberately separated for the purpose of ensuring that an unacceptable weight of billets is not held in the small bin from which the billets are taken up by the discharge conveyor."

There can be no doubt that reading claim 1 as a whole it describes an invention in which there are two containers quite distinct and separate. The relatively small bin is part of the planting unit. The relatively large supply container is described as having walls and a floor and is represented as being capable of being moved on wheel means when towed by an associated vehicle being connected with a small bin by conveyor means operable selectively and being mounted for cooperation with the planting unit which as has been said includes the small bin.

On the present state of authority, it appears to us that the outcome of the appeal ultimately depends upon whether the quite separate nature of the small bin as part of the planting unit and the large container as an associated receptacle should properly be seen as an essential feature of the invention described in the claim which the patentees formulated. If it is not essential, the use of an equivalent mechanism to produce similar results to those claimed for the patented invention will not prevent the respondents from being held to have infringed. On the other hand, if it be an essential feature and is not present in the machine adopted by the respondents, there will be no infringement. Their machine will be outside the area of the monopoly which the patentees saw fit to claim, notwithstanding that it adopts and uses concepts and ideas which are incorporated in the patented invention. [**47**]

The respondents' machine uses a good deal more of the concept of the appellants' invention than was conceded by the respondents' counsel. It, nevertheless, appears to us that the separate nature of the small bin and the supply container is an essential feature of the patented invention. As has been seen, the separate and distinct nature of the two appears plainly from the words of the patentees' claim and is emphasised and underlined by the nature and description of some of its elements. We agree with Connolly J's conclusion that the separation is a deliberate and essential feature of the actual concept of the patented invention. We are satisfied that the respondents have not adopted that particular feature. It is true that the trough at the front of the defendant's hopper, on the one hand, and the rear part

■■■■■■   Populin v HB Nominees *continued*

of it with an upwardly moveable floor and rear side, on the other, might if they existed quite separately be properly described as two separate containers. However, when combined as they are in the defendant's machine, they lack this quality. They are, instead, elements of one large container.

It follows that the respondents have not infringed the patent and that the appeal should be dismissed with costs

■ The "Improver questions"

■■■■■■■■■ Baygol v Foamex Polystyrene ■■■■■■■

[10.35] *Baygol Pty Ltd v Foamex Polystyrene Pty Ltd* (2005) 66 IPR 1; FCA 624,

TAMBERLIN J: [5]

Construction—Principles

In considering the appropriate approach to the construction of the claim, a useful starting point is the decision of the House of Lords in *Catnic Components Ltd v Hill & Smith Ltd* [1982] RPC 183 (*Catnic*), where the House of Lords held that the word "vertical", in relation to a lintel of a box girder structure, should be read to cover a situation where the relevant member was 6 to 8° off the vertical. Lord Diplock delivered the decision of the House and made a number of well-known observations. [His honour then quoted the well-known passages from *Catnic* at 242-243.] [6]

Catnic was considered and applied by Hoffman LJ in *Improver Corporation v Remington Consumer Products Limited* [1990] FSR 181 (*Improver*). His Lordship's approach to the application of the principles in *Catnic* is set out at 188-189 in the following terms:

> "If the issue was whether a feature embodied in an alleged infringement which fell outside the primary, literal or a contextual meaning of a descriptive word or phrase in the claim ('a variant') was nevertheless within its language as properly interpreted, the court should ask itself the following three questions:
> (1) Does the variant have a material effect upon the way the invention works? If yes, the variant is outside the claim. If no –
> (2) Would this (ie, that the variant had no material effect) have been obvious at the date of publication of the patent to a reader skilled in the art. If no, the variant is outside the claim. If yes –
> (3) Would the reader skilled in the art nevertheless have understood from the language of the claim that the patentee intended that strict compliance with the primary meaning was an essential requirement of the invention. If yes, the variant is outside the claim."

The three questions posed by his Lordship have subsequently been applied in many cases where they are referred to as "the Improver questions". At 189, his Lordship noted that the question is always whether the alleged infringement is covered by the language of the claim, thereby emphasising the importance of the language as the Court's primary focus. At 190, his Lordship pointed out that the answers to the first two questions do not involve questions of construction. The answers to these questions are used to provide the factual background against which the specification must be construed and it is the third question which raises the question of construction. In his Lordship's view, even a purposive construction of the language may lead to a conclusion that, although the variant made no material difference, it would have been obvious that the patentee was confining the claim to the primary meaning in excluding the variant. Otherwise, there would be no point in asking the third question.

The status in Australia of the purposive approach as formulated in *Catnic* is not settled.

In *Populin v HB Nominees Pty Ltd* (1982) 41 ALR 471 at 475-7, the Full Federal Court affirmed the well-settled "pith and marrow" approach. However, in *Rhone-Poulenc Agrochimie SA & Anor v UIM Chemical Services Pty Ltd & Anor* (1986) 12 FCR 477 (*Rhone-Poulenc*), the Full Federal Court did not draw any distinction between the "pith and marrow" approach and the approach taken in *Catnic*. Their Honours applied both approaches to reach their conclusion and did not analyse any differential application of the two approaches: see, for example, Lockhart J in *Rhone-Poulenc* at 498.

[7] In *Prestige (Australia) Group Pty Ltd v Dart* (1990) 26 FCR 197 at 208-9, Gummow J expressed the view that the "purposive approach" had received an uneven reception in the Federal Court: see also *Nicaro Holdings Pty Ltd v Martin Engineering Co* (1990) 91 ALR 513 at 528-9 and *Rehm Pty Ltd v Websters Security Systems (International) Pty Ltd* (1988) 81 ALR 79 (*Rehm*). In *Rehm*, Gummow J stated that *Catnic* did not propound any novel principle or new category of "non-textual" infringement. At 92, he agreed that what is called for in the construction of claims is a common sense assessment of what the words used convey, in the context of the published knowledge at the priority date. The emphasis is on the language used to express the claim. It is the meaning of this language which must be ascertained.

In *Olin Corporation Ltd v Super Cartridge Co Pty Ltd* (1977) 180 CLR 236 at 246, Gibbs J accepted that the approach described by James LJ in *Clark v Adie* (1875) 10 Ch App 667 at 675 was good law. The statement of James LJ at that reference is as follows:

"The patent is for the entire combination, but there is, or may be, an essence or substance of the invention underlying the mere accident of form; and that invention, like every other invention, may be pirated by a theft in a disguised or mutilated form, and it will be in every case a question of fact *whether the alleged piracy is the same in substance and effect, or is a substantially new or different combination*." (Emphasis added)

Justice Gibbs then went on to say:

" ... However, as was pointed out in *C Van Der Lely NV v Bamfords Ltd* [1963] RPC 61 at 78, 80, *the principle that there may be infringement by taking the 'pith and marrow' or the substance of an invention does not mean that there will be an infringement where the patentee has by the form of his claim left open that which the alleged infringer has done*. And it does not affect the fundamental rule that there will be no infringement unless the alleged infringer has taken all of the essential features or integers of the patentee's claim." (Emphasis added)

The respondents both rely on the qualification to the "pith and marrow" approach referred to by his Honour to support their submission that, in the present case, the patentee has, by the form of the claim, in selecting the adjective "concrete" as a criterion, left open the use of plastic spacers.

An overview of the patent construction principles is set out by Finkelstein J in *Root Quality Pty Ltd v Root Control Technologies Pty Ltd* (2000) 177 ALR 231 at [27] ff (*Root Quality*). That case was concerned with a patent for a container suitable for growing plants which were later to be transplanted. His Honour considered that the "purposive" approach set out in *Catnic* had

▰▰▰▰   Baygol v Foamex Polystyrene *continued*

been adopted in Australia but that cases such as *Populin* implied that the "pith and marrow" approach can still have application. His Honour considered that the "pith and marrow" approach is no longer necessary where the Improver questions are posed and answered and proceeded to analyse the facts on the basis of those questions.

In *Root Quality*, his Honour warned that the Courts should act with care before broadening a claim by applying a purposive construction because elements of the claim which would not appear to be essential for the invention may nevertheless have been regarded by the patentee as essential for some reason that is not evident.

At [47], his Honour said:

[8]

"If the language of the claim is clear, then the meaning of that language cannot change by reference to what appears in the specification. But the words of the claim must be read in light of the specification as a whole and be given a meaning in that context. Once construed it is not permissible to extend or narrow the ambit of the claim by reference to the specification." (Emphasis added)

At [48], in relation to the use the Court may make of amendments to the specification, which is an important matter in this case, his Honour said:

"The approach that I will adopt is to consider the claim in its unamended form to discern what was intended and then to consider whether the meaning has changed following the amendments. *Usually, the task of construction is best undertaken by taking the claim as it currently stands and ascertaining its meaning, having regard to the nature of any amendments made.* In this case, for reasons which will become apparent, a different approach is called for." (Emphasis added)

At [50], in relation to expert evidence, his Honour said:

"There will be cases, however, where expert evidence is not admissible on the question of construction. *Sometimes the text of the specification will be couched in language with which all lawyers are familiar,* containing no technical or trade terms calling for explanation. In that event *the court of construction can determine for itself, unassisted by experts,* the relevant meaning, as it does with any other instrument. In its unamended form the specification of the patent in suit falls into this category at least so far as concerns the issue presently under consideration."

In the present case, the respondents correctly submit that the word "concrete" is not a technical term. They submit that the Complete Specification is couched in words with which all lawyers are familiar and that these words should be given their natural meaning in the absence of any ambiguity. It is obvious that "concrete", whether used as an adjective or a noun, is not a word which is capable of including "plastic". The exercise in the present case is quite different from that undertaken in *Catnic* in relation to the word "vertical", which was clearly capable of being read differently depending on the experience and understanding of the practical reader. In *Catnic*, the expression was sufficiently ambiguous to include a member that was almost vertical so long as it provided sufficient support and strength to fulfil its purpose. In the present case, there is no such range or spectrum of permissible interpretation which could permit the word "concrete" to mean material other than concrete.

In *Root Quality*, Finkelstein J applied the *Improver* questions. In relation to the first question, his Honour thought it was evident that the variants would not affect the way in which the invention would facilitate the growth of the root ball in the desired fashion. On

▒▒▒▒▒ Baygol v Foamex Polystyrene *continued*

the second question, his Honour's conclusion was that it would have been obvious to a person who wanted to use the invention, namely, a horticulturist or nurseryman, that the variants did not have a material effect on the working of the invention. However, on the third question, particularly having regard to the amendments which had been made to the claim, his Honour reached the firm conclusion that the variants were not intended to be excluded from the claim, notwithstanding that they did not affect the working of the invention.

In *Societe Technique de Pulverisation v Emson Europe Ltd & Ors* [1993] RPC 513 at 522, Hoffman LJ, with whom Ralph Gibson and Leggatt LJJ agreed, rejected the evidence of witnesses as to the meaning of the expression "conduit means", saying:

> "... one has to construe the *language* of the claim. The judge allowed counsel to ask the expert witnesses what they understood words like 'conduit means'. These are not [9] technical words having a special trade meaning and in my judgment the *opinions of witnesses on their meaning were inadmissible*. Construction was a matter for the judge. 'Conduit' is in my view a word which expresses a function. It is not merely something through which liquid flows but of which at least one purpose is to convey liquid from one point to another, however close those points may be." (Emphasis added)

In that case, his Lordship applied the clear and unambiguous meaning of the expression "conduit means" and found that there was no infringement because the ring in question was not "conduit means". No such appeal can properly be applied when considering the meaning of "concrete spacer". It is a spacer made of concrete. It is not something which can bear another meaning.

In *Kirin-Amgen v Hoeschst Marion Roussel Ltd* [2004] UKHL 46 (21 October 2004) (*Kirin Amgen*), Hoffman LJ sounded a caution as to the limitations on the use of the Improver questions as a formula for all cases, rather than as guidelines which will, in appropriate cases, help to determine how the skilled man would understand the patentee's intention. The limitations on the utility of the guidelines are most clearly illustrated by the complex pharmaceutical patent under consideration in *Kirin-Amgen*.

Lord Walker, with whom Hope LJ and Rodger LJ agreed, reinforced that qualification in the following terms:

> "[138] ... I particularly welcome Lord Hoffman's detailed explanation of the real significance of the *Improver* (or protocol) questions ... and how they fit in with recent developments in continental patents jurisprudence. There is always a danger that any judicial summary of principle may, precisely because it is concise, practical and repeatedly cited, take on a life of its own, as if it were a statutory text with its own problems of construction to be resolved ('the way the invention works' in the first question is a striking example of this).
>
> [139] The fact is that neither *Catnic Components Ltd v Hill and Smith Ltd* [1982] RPC 183 nor *Improver* was concerned with anything approaching high-technology science Lord Hoffman has demonstrated that in a rapidly-developing, high-technology field the *Improver* questions may have no useful function, and may be a distraction from the one compulsory question set by Article 69 and its protocol."

I do not consider that the reference to Article 69 in the above remarks diminishes the force of the observations made by their Lordships as to the limitations on the utility of the *Improver* questions and the making of a decision as to the type of case in which the questions are appropriate.

Lord Hoffman in *Kirin-Amgen* reaffirmed the purposive approach to the construction of

■■■■■ Baygol v Foamex Polystyrene *continued*

patent claims. At [34] his Lordship points out that the reference is not to purpose in a vague generalised sense. Rather, Lord Diplock in *Catnic* was pointing out that a patentee may be taken to mean something different when he uses words for one purpose from what he would be taken to mean if he was using the words for another purpose. In the *Catnic* case itself, the question was what was meant by the word "vertical" and the distinction was between the meaning of the term "vertical" in a mathematical theory and the practical functional use of a lintel in the building trade.

In the present case, this question does not arise as the words "concrete spacer" are clear and unambiguous and do not admit of any definitional enlargement.

[10] The principles relating to the construction of claims were recently considered and applied by Merkel J in *PhotoCure ASA v Queen's University at Kingston* [2005] FCA 344. At [168]-[175] and [195]-[208], his Honour carried out a comprehensive review of the relevant authorities. At the conclusion of this consideration, his Honour decided to consider the case on the basis of the Improver questions within the framework outlined by Lord Hoffman in *Kirin-Amgen*. His Honour was of the opinion that the first *Improver* question should be answered in the negative and accordingly proceeded to consider the second question, namely, the obviousness to a reader skilled in the art of the lack of material effect of the variant at the date of publication. His Honour concluded that the second question should be answered in the negative. In relation to the third *Improver* question, his Honour expressed the opinion that it may not be strictly necessary to address this question, as the answer to the second question has the consequence that, applying the purposive approach to the construction of the claims, there was no proper basis for concluding that the primary meanings of the phrases under consideration in the claims were not the intended meanings. In any event, his Honour considered that the answer to the third *Improver* question was that the reader skilled in the art would have understood that compliance with the primary meaning of the phrases was an essential requirement. As a consequence, his Honour dismissed the infringement claim.

■ Exclusive rights of the patentee

[10.40] In *Bedford Industries Rehabilitation Association Inc v Pinefair Pty Ltd* (1998) 40 IPR 438, von Doussa J said at 449:

"The grant of an exclusive right to 'exploit' the invention provided by s 13 of the *Patents Act 1990* replaced the traditional formulation of the exclusive right granted by a patent 'to make, use exercise or vend'. The Explanatory Memorandum to the 1990 Act says in relation to s 13 and the definition of 'exploit':

"This definition, when read with clause 13, constitutes a codification of the scope of patent rights. It avoids some obscure language in the present Act which refers to the right to 'make, use, exercise and vend' the invention."

As the author observes in Lahore, *Patents, Trade Marks and Related Rights*, at para 24,000, the definition attempts to encapsulate the decisions in which these words 'make, use, exercise and vend' have been interpreted. It is not necessary in this judgment to explore the full meaning and extent of the total definition. For present purposes it is sufficient to observe that there seems to be no reason to doubt that in the definition the words 'make' and 'use' carry the same meaning as has been given to those words in the former legislation ..."

"Make"

[10.45] The extract quoted above continues:

> "The word 'make' is an ordinary English word with wide meaning. Terrell on *The Law of Patents* (14th ed, 1994), p 176 observes that for this reason, no difficulty should arise with the word. Where the invention is a product, what must be made is the whole product, not constituent parts, and the *'making'* is not complete until the final step is carried out which results in the complete infringing article: see *Lahore* at para 18,205."

This principle is often illustrated by reference to the case of *Dunlop Pneumatic Tyre Co v David Moseley & Sons Ltd* [1904] 1 Ch 616. The patent in that case was for a combination of integers to make up a bicycle wheel with a tubeless tyre. Broadly speaking, the combination of integers involved (a) a hub (b) spokes (c) a wheel rim and (d) a special tubeless tyre which fitted within the rim. The combination was not "made" by a person who manufactured and sold only the tyre (integer (d)). However, the combination would be made by a customer who obtained the tyre and fitted it to a wheel consisting of hub, spoke and rim. (See below for discussion of contributory infringement.)

To be an infringement, the "making" should be for a commercial purpose which in some way, whether by sale or otherwise, deprives the patentee of the commercial benefit of the invention. See *British Motor Syndicate v John Taylor & Sons* (1900) 17 RPC 723. Non-commercial uses, like pure experimentation, should not amount to infringement: *Freason v Loe* (1878) 9 Ch D 48 at 66-67. However, courts have seldom found that the defendant's use was truly experimental. See also discussion of "experiment principle" cases in *Smith Kline & French v Attorney General (NZ)* (1991) 22 IPR 143, Hardie Boys J at 149.

See also *Patents and Experimental Use* (Advisory Council on Intellectual Property Report (ACIP) Oct 2005, released 9 November 2005 which can be accessed through www.acip.gov. au/reviews.htm#expuse); the Australian Law Reform Commission Discussion Paper, *Gene Patenting and Human Health*; (Experimental and Research Use Defences Feb 2004); *The Research Exceptions to Patent Infringement: A Doctrine in Search of a Principle* (IPRIA Working Paper no 10/04 Sept 2004).

There is apparently an implied licence to a purchaser of patented goods to repair those particular goods without infringement, but such an activity must be a genuine repair to prolong the life of the article and not be so extensive a reconstruction as to be the making of a new one. The question is one of fact and must be judged in the light of the nature of the article. See *Solar Thompson Engineering Co Ltd v Barton* [1977] RPC 537 at 554; *Sirdar Rubber Co Ltd v Wallington Weston* (1907) 24 RPC 539 at 543; *Dunlop v Holborn Tyre Co* (1901) 18 RPC 222. A different explanation was offered in the United Kingdom in *United Wire Ltd v Screen Repair Services (Scotland) Ltd* [2000] 4 All ER 353 where Lord Hoffman said that the right of repair was a residual right being part of the right to do whatever does not constitute making the product.

"Sell" etc

[10.50] The terms "sell or otherwise dispose of the product, offer to make, sell, hire or otherwise dispose of it" seem straightforward and were intended to reduce the uncertainty in the old terms "exercise and vend". Mere possession coupled with an intention to trade with the product protected by patent rights amounts to infringement. See *Morton-Norwich Products Inc v Intercen Ltd* [1978] RPC 501. Where a patentee places a patented product on the market without a restrictive condition restricting dealing with the product a purchaser has an implied licence to resell or otherwise deal with the particular items. *Betts v Wilmott* (1871) 2 Ch LR 6; *National Phonograph Co of Australia v Menck* [1911] AC 336

"Use"

[10.55] The term "use" applies to both product and process patents. Again, the use must be one which interferes with the commercial interest of the patentee. It has been suggested that for a patented device the use should be within the purpose of the patent while in the case of substances or raw materials patented "per se" any commercial use will suffice.

The facts of *Bedford Industries Rehabilitation Association Inc v Pinefair Pty Ltd* (1998) 40 IPR 438 present an interesting application of infringement through use. Bedford were the owners of a patent for a garden edging product. The product was made of cut lengths of half round treated pine logs arranged side by side into a strip and joined by two strands of what was described in claim 1 as "elongated band means". In the preferred embodiment sold by Bedford the "band means" were two strands of wire attached by staples allowing for long sections of continuous edging strip, but the "elongated bands" could have been plastic strips, or metal bands or any other material and still have been within the claim. The respondent, Pinefair had made a product for all practical purposes identical to the patented product. An infringement action was settled and the respondent altered their manufacture to produce a different final result in which there was no elongated banded means of connection in an elongated strip. Pinefair now used long plastic strips stapled to the logs but these were then severed between the staples at the middle of each post to prevent there being continuous plastic strips. The logs were left connected by what were now separate small plastic hinges. However, Bedford complained that in the course of this new approach the respondent was making a product which infringed the patent. They alleged that as an intermediate step in the Pinefair's manufacture prior to the cutting of the plastic strips they made edging material which was connected by "elongated band means". So the allegation was that although the defendants final product did not infringe the plaintiff's patent there was an intermediate stage in which there was an product in existence which included every integer of the Bedford patent and this constituted infringement.

At trial von Doussa J considered that Pinefairs were exploiting the Bedford patent and found infringement. His Honour found Pinefairs activities involved a "use" of the Bedford patent because Pinefairs were taking commercial advantage of the Bedford product as an intermediate step in the manufacturing process to give themselves an advantage in the marketplace even though by the time of sale the Pinefair product was sufficiently altered that it no longer included all of the integers of the Bedford patent. His Honour considered reasoning in *Smith Kline & French v Attorney General (NZ)* (1991) 22 IPR 143, *Pfizer v Ministry of Health* [1965] AC 512, *Saccharin Corp Ltd v Anglo Continental Chemical Works Ltd* (1900) 17 RPC 307 and *Beecham Group Ltd v Bristol Laboratories* [1978] RPC 153 to assist him in reaching this conclusion.

Pinefair appealed to the Full Federal Court. In *Pinefair Pty Ltd v Bedford Industries Rehabilitation Association Inc* (1998) 87 FCR 458 Foster and Mansfield JJ agreed with von Doussa J, found infringement and dismissed the appeal. However Golberg J concluded that it was significant that the Bedford patent was for a product and not a process and that he did not "consider that the appellants have made or used the invention in the course of their manufacturing process in the sense in which those terms are used in the dictionary definition of 'exploit' in Sch 1 of the 1990 Act". His Honour said "In my opinion the appellants (Pinefairs) product was not 'made' at the point of time the respondent says its patent was infringed. At the point at which the post elements emerge from the saw the manufacturing process is not complete, further work is to be carried out and at that point I am satisfied that the applicants product has not yet been made, … Because the appellants have not made the product it follows … that they have not used it". This is predicated on the view that Pinefair's was merely in a transitory manufacturing phase when the patented combination came into existence and that the Pinefairs product should only be compared with the claims in the patent when the Pinefair manufacturing process was at an end … at which point the then completed Pinefairs product did not contain all of the Bedford patent integers. Is this the correct approach?

Where a patentee places patented goods upon the market without conditions or restrictions as to use a purchaser of the goods acquires an implied licence to use the goods. See *Interstate Parcel v Time-Life International* (1977) 138 CLR 534 and *National Phonograph Co of Australia v Menck* [1911] AC 336.

Import

[10.60] The rules about infringement by import are sometimes referred to as the "Saccharin Importation" doctrine after *Saccharin Corp v Anglo-Continental Chemical Works Ltd* (1900) 17 RPC 307. In that case the patentee owned a patent in the UK for a process for the manufacture of the chemical known commercially as Saccharin. The product itself could not be patented because as an existing and known chemical entity it was not novel. The defendants obtained saccharin manufactured in France. The manufacturing process used in France fell within the claims of the United Kingdom patent and if done in the United Kingdom would have constituted an infringement. The defendant then imported the product made by the process into England. The plaintiff alleged infringement. The defendant argued that the patent was for a process and that no process had been worked in the jurisdiction and that what was imported was a product and not covered by a patent for a process. The Court disagreed and found that the importation of a product which was made by a process which would be an infringement, if performed within the jurisdiction, would be an infringement of a process patent. The principle is now given statutory force in para (b) of the definition of exploit.

▬▬ Pinefair v Bedford Industries Rehabilitation Assoc ▬▬

[10.65] *Pinefair Pty Ltd v Bedford Industries Rehabilitation Assoc Inc* (1998) 87 FCR 458 Federal Court of Australia

MANSFIELD J [In the course of his judgment his Honour referred to the "importation" cases.] [466] The "infringing importation" cases are generally concerned with the question of whether that which is done or proposed to be done within the jurisdiction in respect of an imported product constitutes an infringing "use" of the imported product within the jurisdiction: *Smith Kline & French Laboratories Ltd v Attorney-General (New Zealand)* [1991] 2 NZLR 560; *Saccharin Corp v Anglo-Continental Chemical Works Ltd* (1900) 17 RPC 307; *Dunlop Pneumatic Tyre Co Ltd v British & Colonial Motor Car Co* (1901) 18 RPC 313; *Pfizer v Ministry of Health* [1965] AC 512. In those cases, the [467] manufacture of the imported product, if effected within the jurisdiction, would itself infringe the patent in suit.

In *Saccharin*, the Court also addressed whether the manufacture of the product itself, if done within the jurisdiction, would constitute infringement of the patent in suit. Buckley J said (at 319):

"If the patented process were the last stage in the production of the article sold, the importation and sale of the product would, in my opinion, plainly be an infringement.

████████   Pinefair v Bedford Industries Rehabilitation Assoc *continued*

Does it make it any the less an infringement that the article produced and sold is manufactured by the use of the patented process which is subjected to certain other processes? In my opinion it does not. By the sale of saccharin, in the course of the production of which the patented process is used, the Patentee is deprived of some part of the whole profit and advantage of the invention, and the importer is indirectly making use of the invention."

In *Beecham Group Ltd v Bristol Laboratories Ltd* [1978] RPC 153, similar issues were addressed. In that case, one particular issue was whether the use within the jurisdiction of the imported article infringed a particular product patent because, in the course of manufacture of the imported article, the article which was the subject of the product patent was made as an inter-mediate product in that manufacture. Russell LJ delivering the judgment of the Court of Appeal (Russell and Stamp LJJ and Brightman J) concluded that the defendants' production of a certain chemical made use of two patented products of the plaintiff and one patented process of the plaintiff, and so infringed the relevant product patents and process patent. Their Lordships did not regard legislative changes to have altered that conclusion, and said (at 185-186):

"The truth of the matter, as we see it, is that the law, in applying the language of the grant by letters patent of the monopoly to protect the invention of a new process for producing an article or substance, has found it, and established it as, a commonsense necessity to embrace in that language the product without which the process is a meaningless exercise. In our judgment, the cases relied upon by the plaintiff remain good law, and a claim to the product of a claimed process is not necessary. (We do not, of course, refer to a case in which the product per se is novel but might be produced by a different process: there a product claim would be valuable)."

That case went on appeal to the House of Lords. The appeal was dismissed. The speech of Lord Diplock, with which Viscount Dilhorne, and Lords Simon of Glaisdale, Salmon and Fraser of Tullybelton agreed, recognised the particular issues in the following terms (at 200):

"In the instant case Beechams have invited your Lordships to extend it from claims for processes for manufacturing products to claims for new products in themselves; so that if a patented product is used as a starting point in the manufacture of the imported article or formed as an intermediary at any stage in the course of its manufacture, this constitutes an infringement of the claim to the patented product, even though no part of the process of manufacture of the imported article infringed any claim to a new process by the patentee, and even though the imported article is wholly different in composition, characteristics and usefulness from the patented product."

His Lordship then affirmed the conclusion of the Court of Appeal (at 203), but with the reservation that the lawful use overseas of a product in the [468] manufacture of a different product, then imported and sold, should not, within the jurisdiction, constitute infringement of a product patent for the first product. Lord Simon addressed that issue in his short additional speech in the following terms (at 204):

"I would have thought that some formula might be devised whereby the Saccharin doctrine could be extended so as to cover, say, 6-APA playing a significant part in the manufacture of a semi-synthetic penicillin, but not of a wholly different product like, say, glue."

"Authorise"

[10.70] While *Patents Act 1990* (Cth), s 13 grants the patentee the exclusive right to "authorise" another to exploit the invention there is no definition of the term in the Act. One possibility is that it bears a similar meaning to the concept in the law of copyright of sanction approve or countenance and another is that to authorise means to "grant or purport to grant a third person the right to do the act complained of". (These possibilities were put by Gummow J in *Rescare Ltd v Anaesthetic Supplies Pty Ltd* (1992) 25 IPR 119 at 155.) In *Bristol-Myers Squibb Co v FH Faulding & Co Ltd* (1998) 41 IPR 467 at 488, Heerey J commented that it should not be assumed that copyright principles applied to patent infringement and that the term should be given a dictionary meaning "to give authority or legal power to". However, on appeal in *Bristol-Myers Squibb Co v FH Faulding & Co Ltd* (2000) 97 FCR 524, Black CJ and Lehane J at 585 said:

> "[C]ontrary to the view expressed by the trial judge we agree with the view on which Gummow J proceeded in *Rescare* that the word authorise in s 13(1) of the 1990 Act should be taken by analogy to have the meaning it has in the *Copyright Act*. The context of s 13(1) is analogous to that of ss 36 and 101 of the *Copyright Act*, and there is nothing novel in finding similar concepts behind aspects of patents and copyright law: *Ramset Fasteners (Aust) Pty Ltd v Advanced Building Systems Pty Ltd* (1999) 44 IPR 481 at [37] and [38]."

■ Contributory infringement

[10.75] It was sometimes said that there was no general concept of "contributory infringement" of a patent. There are two approaches to contributory infringement. One is found in s 117 and the other in the general principles of the common law as to concurrent tortfeasors.

▬▬▬▬ Bristol-Myers Squibb v FH Faulding ▬▬▬▬

[10.80] *Bristol-Myers Squibb Co v FH Faulding & Co Ltd* (2000) 97 FCR 524 Federal Court of Australia

[Bristol Myers were owners of two petty patents for methods of administration of an anticarcinogenic agent known as Taxol. The invention was a method of safe administration of taxol within a time period previously thought to pose unacceptable risks to the patient and which had the advantage of removing the need for overnight hospitalisation. These were not product patents since Taxol was a naturally-occurring known substance. Fauldings supplied Taxol as a substance to hospitals with product information guides and protocols. Bristol Myers claimed that administration of Taxol in accordance with these instructions would infringe their patent.]

BLACK and LEHANE JJ: [553]

Infringement

Because the facts relied on to establish infringement were those set out in an agreed statement of facts, it is convenient to start with the trial judge's summary, at 485, 486:

> "Those facts concern Faulding's conduct in Australia in relation to a drug it marketed under the name Anzatax. The active ingredient of that drug is admitted to be taxol, which is also referred to as paclitaxel. To avoid confusion I shall continue to use the term 'taxol', except for direct quotation from document.
>
>   Since 23 January 1995 Faulding sold and supplied taxol to doctors and hospitals in Australia, together with a product information guide. ..."

████████   Bristol-Myers Squibb v FH Faulding *continued*

Use of taxol in accordance with the method recommended in the [555] respondent's product information guide, and use in accordance with the protocols, would (assuming validity) infringe the petty patent. The question, in those circumstances, is whether the respondent infringed them.

The 1990 Act does not define infringement (cf *Copyright Act 1968* (Cth), s 36 and s 101). Section 13(1), however, provides that:

> "Subject to this Act, a patent gives the patentee the exclusive rights, during the term of the patent, to exploit the invention and to authorise another person to exploit the invention."

The word "exploit" is defined in the dictionary in Sch 1:

> " 'exploit', in relation to an invention, includes:
> (a) where the invention is a product—make, hire, sell or otherwise dispose of the product, offer to make, sell, hire or otherwise dispose of it, use or import it, or keep it for the purpose of doing any of those things; or
> (b) where the invention is a method or process—use the method or process or do any act mentioned in paragraph (a) in respect of a product resulting from such use."

Part 1 of Chapter 11 contains provisions which in some respects expand, and in others limit, the concept of infringement (that is, generally, the doing of an act, without the authority of the patentee, which the patentee has the exclusive right to do). Of those provisions, only s 117 is relevant for present purpose. It provides:

> "117(1) If the use of a product by a person would infringe a patent, the supply of that product by one person to another is an infringement of the patent by the supplier unless the supplier is the patentee or a licensee of the patent.
> (2) A reference in subsection (1) to the use of a product by a person is a reference to:
> > (a) if the product is capable of only one reasonable use, having regard to its nature or design—that use; or
> > (b) if the product is not a staple commercial product—any use of the product, if the supplier had reason to believe that the person would put it to that use; or
> > (c) in any case—the use of the product in accordance with any instructions for the use of the product, or any inducement to use the product, given to the person by the supplier or contained in an advertisement published by or with the authority of the supplier."

The respondent supplied taxol in the ways stated in the agreed statement of facts. The question to be decided is whether the supply was an infringement. In submitting that an affirmative answer should be given to that question, the appellant relied both on para (b) and para (c) of s 117(2), though oral argument concentrated on para (c). There is a textual difficulty—which, given our conclusion about para (c), we do not need to resolve—with the suggested application of para (b). The use to which the appellant had reason to believe that the taxol which it supplied would be put was, in part, use in the treatment of patients with cancer and, in part, use in clinical trials involving patients suffering from cancer. It is not clear, we think, that the particular method by which it was expected to be used is properly to be described as the use to which it was to be put. If one were to ask, to what use is a therapeutic drug, prescribed for a patient, put, the answer might be: "It is to be taken to cure the patient's [556] condition". It would not, perhaps, be: "It is to be taken three times daily, before meals."

■■■■■■ Bristol-Myers Squibb v FH Faulding *continued*

Paragraph (c) raises a more complex question. The appellant's argument commenced with the uncontroversial proposition that use of taxol in accordance with the product information guide or the protocols would infringe the petty patents; the next step was that the guide and the protocols were instructions (in the sense of directions or recommendations) given by the respondent for the use of the taxol which it supplied, and we accept that proposition. Then, it was said, s 117(1) applied, having regard to the dictionary in subs (2), as follows:

"If the use of [taxol] by a [medical practitioner], in accordance with any instructions for the use of taxol ... given to the [medical practitioner] by the [respondent] ... , would infringe [either of the petty patents], the supply of that [taxol] by [the respondent] to [the medical practitioner] is an infringement of the [petty patent] by the [the respondent] unless [as was not the case] the [respondent] is the patentee or a licensee of the [petty patent]."

It may be said immediately that there is considerable force in that way of looking at it. It involves, after all, a literal application of the words of s 117. The respondent, however, contended for a different approach, the one adopted by Heerey J. According to that approach, the starting point is not s 117 but the definition of "exploit". Where an invention is a method or process, use of a product exploits the invention only if the product is one which results from use of the method or process. Section 117, the argument proceeds, is concerned only with a case where the use of a product by a person would infringe a patent (because the person, not the patentee or a licensee, exploited it); and, where the patent is for a method or process, that will not be so unless the product is one which results from the use of that method or process.

Authority favours the construction for which the respondent contends. Gummow J considered the point in *Rescare*. It was submitted, in that case, that the supply of certain devices (themselves allegedly infringing products), with instructions for use, was itself an infringement of a method claimed by the supplier. Gummow J said, at 154:

"The difficulty with that proposition is that a pre-condition to the operation of s 117 in relation to a method claim such as claim 9, is that there is a product the use of which by the respondent would infringe claim 9. In other words, that user would have to amount [to] an 'exploitation' within the monopoly conferred by s 13, which is to be read with para (b) of the definition of 'exploit'.

As I have indicated, where the invention relevantly claims a method or process, exploitation occurs, other than by use of the method or process, only by the doing of an act mentioned in para (a) of the definition of 'exploit'. There must be an act done 'in respect of a product resulting from such use'. Here, the respondent urges, and I agree, there is no such product with the result that, in a case such as the present, s 117 has no operation."

Gummow J compared the position with that which arises under the rather different provision of the 1977 UK legislation.

It was submitted by the appellants that Gummow J's reasoning was limited to the particular type of case with which he was dealing (one where the device supplied was an "allegedly infringing device" and where the apparatus supplied might be used to alleviate either of two conditions, one falling within the claims, the other not), was not of general application and could be [557] distinguished. We do not accept that argument. Gummow J expressed himself in general terms. The relevant claim (claim 9 of the patent of which his Honour was concerned) was not distinguishable, for present purposes, from the claims of the petty patent: claim 9 read:

▓▓▓▓▓   Bristol-Myers Squibb v FH Faulding *continued*

"A method of treating snoring and/or obstructive sleep apnoea in a patient comprising: applying air through a nose piece at a pressure maintained slightly greater than atmospheric substantially continuously throughout the breathing cycle."

Thus, as here, the method claimed involved using an article or product, not one resulting from the use of the method, in a particular way.

On appeal, the Full Court held that the patent was wholly invalid and, therefore, it was not necessary to consider questions of infringement. Sheppard J, accordingly, did not consider the construction of s 117. Lockhart J said, at 24:

"The last remaining point is whether the primary judge erred in holding that s 117 of the 1990 Act did not apply in relation to the alleged infringement of claims 9 and 11 in that he held that it was a precondition to the operation of that section in relation to a method claim that there be a product the use of which would infringe that method claim. In my opinion his Honour decided that question correctly."

Wilcox J, in this respect, simply agreed with the reasons given by Lockhart J. In *Sartas No 1 Pty Ltd v Koukourou & Partners Pty Ltd* (1994) 30 IPR 479 Gummow J reiterated, at 495, the view which he had expressed in *Rescare*.

In those circumstances the trial judge followed the view expressed by Gummow J and affirmed by the Full Court in *Rescare*. However, there can be no doubt that the observations of Lockhart J, with which Wilcox J agreed, were unnecessary to the decision in *Rescare* and they were made without elaboration and in passing: they are obiter in the true sense of the word. In the circumstances, and as the matter has been argued before us, we think it is open to us to examine the question of construction for ourselves and, because of the importance of the matter, desirable that we do so. The first thing to be said is that if the views expressed in *Rescare* are right, s 117 has a very limited operation: perhaps, no practical operation at all. If the invention is a product, then to hire, sell, or otherwise dispose of it is to "exploit" it and therefore exclusively the right of the patentee. It is not easy to imagine circumstances in which the supply of a product is not a sale, hire, or disposal of it. If so, the supplier who, by operation of s 117, is an infringer is an infringer in any event, as one who "exploits". It is equally difficult to see what practical operation s 117 would have in relation to an invention which is a method or process, the use of which results in a product. If the product supplied is that which results from the use of the method or process, then the position is exactly the same as that where what is supplied is a patented product. If, on the other hand, the product supplied is one the use of which in the patented method or process results in some new product, then the case is no different from that where use of a patented method or process does not result in any product; an application of the construction preferred in *Rescare* would, as a matter of logic, require the conclusion that s 117 could not make the supply an infringement. Hence our opening comment: the *Rescare* construction leaves s 117 virtually, if not completely, otiose.

The second thing to be said is that it seems clear that s 117 was not meant by its framers to have the limited meaning given to it in *Rescare*. The report of the [558] Industrial Property Advisory Committee, *Patents, Innovation and Competition in Australia* (1984), dealt with contributory infringement in para 14.2. That paragraph begins as follows:

"A patentee may encounter serious difficulty in enforcing his patent where it is prone to infringement by an eventual consumer who is supplied by an unauthorised person with the means to infringe.

For example, a process patent for using a selective herbicide which is a known chemical would be infringed by a farmer who bought a container and followed instructions for use which, when followed, unknown to the farmer, resulted in infringement of the patent. Even if the patentee were prepared to bear the high cost of detecting infringement by the farmer and then to bring infringement proceedings, the result would almost certainly be unsatisfactory. The farmer would ordinarily be unaware of the patent and an award of damages would therefore be most unlikely. The farmer would be left with a stock of herbicide he was forbidden to use, and the patentee would find himself with no damages and a dissatisfied potential customer. To complicate the matter, there may be hundreds or thousands of such ultimate consumers.

It is unreasonable and wasteful of resources for a patentee to have to sue all of the direct infringers with so unsatisfactory a result in each case, when the supplier is, in a real sense, far more responsible for the commission of the infringing act

We believe that it would be far more effective, realistic and just for the patentee to be able to take action against the supplier or middleman who facilitates the commission of the infringing act by the ultimate consumer. The most common example of indirect, secondary or contributory infringement is where goods, materials or parts are supplied to a consumer with the intention that they be used, consumed or assembled in a way which constitutes an infringement of a patent. The intention might be evident, for example, from the provision of brochures containing instructions on how to make a product or use a process which would infringe a patent, or by advertisements soliciting the commission of an act which would infringe."

The explanatory statement which accompanied the Bill for the 1990 Act stated (para 170 and para 171) that the purpose of the then cl 117 was to give effect to the Committee's recommendation.

In her article "Contributory Infringement of a Process Patent under the Patents Act 1990: Does it Exist after Rescare?" (1995) 6 AIPJ 217, Ms Ann Monotti discusses s 117 and its construction in *Rescare* and *Sartas No 1*, and comes, as we do, to the conclusion that that construction substantially deprives s 117 of effective operation. She concludes as follows, at 228:

"In conclusion, the section can extend and clarify the common law and there is no justification for interpreting s 117 in a way that prevents the implementation of the policy decision made to incorporate contributory infringement in Australian Patent Law."

We agree with that conclusion. We may say, with all the advantages of hindsight, that the drafting of s 117 is less than felicitous: we have already pointed to a possible difficulty with subs (2)(b) and, more generally, it is perhaps a pity that the drafter chose to use the phrase "use of a product", which contains such a clear reference to the terminology of para (a) of the definition of "exploit". But s 117 provides its own dictionary, in subs (2). And **[559]** our paraphrase of s 117(1), incorporating subs (2)(c), shows, in our view, that the construction urged by the appellant is not only a possible construction but a literal one. That literal construction being consistent with the apparent purpose of the provision, it is, in our view, plainly to be preferred.

It follows that, assuming validity of the petty patents and taking what is contained in the statement of agreed facts as findings of fact, infringement is established, both in relation to taxol supplied with the product information guide and to that supplied for the purposes of the clinical trial.

▬▬▬   Bristol-Myers Squibb v FH Faulding *continued*

Because, in our view, s 117 applied to the supply of taxol by the appellant, it is unnecessary to consider in detail the other bases on which, it was said, the appellant infringed the petty patent. We make two comments only. First, contrary to the view expressed by the trial judge, we agree with the view on which Gummow J proceeded in *Rescare* that the word "authorise" in s 13(1) of the 1990 Act should be taken, by analogy, to have the meaning it has in the comparable context of the *Copyright Act*. The context of s 13(1) is analogous to that of s 36 and s 101 of the *Copyright Act*; and there is nothing novel in finding similar concepts behind aspects of patent and copyright law (*Ramset Fasteners (Aust) Pty Ltd v Advanced Building Systems Pty Ltd* (1999) 44 IPR 481 at paras 37 and 38). Secondly, the concepts of procurement of and participation in infringement, discussed in cases such as *Walker v Alemite Corp* (1933) 49 CLR 643, were considered in some detail by the Full Court in *Ramset*. It may well be that there is little distinction, in principle, between what happened here and what was found to have occurred there: see at para 41.

▬▬ Ramset Fasteners (Aust) v Advanced Building Supply ▬▬

[10.85] *Ramset Fasteners (Aust) Pty Ltd v Advanced Building Supply Pty Ltd* (1999) 44 IPR 481; FCA 898 Federal Court of Australia

[For the facts see the extract at **[8.295]** above.]

BURCHETT, SACKVILLE and LEHANE JJ: **[495]**

The issue of infringement

Logically, the next issue in the case is one of the issues raised by the cross-appeal, that is, whether Ramset is liable for infringement of the patent. Ramset did not itself erect pre-cast concrete walls or panel. It supplied, for profit, face-lift anchors and ring clutches which conformed to the patent and were used by those to whom they were supplied in face-lift tilt-up construction in accordance with the method disclosed by the patent. That, Ramset argued, did not involve any infringement by it.

There are certain principles of law which it is convenient to set out before the evidence is examined in detail. In *Walker v Alemite Corp* (1933) 49 CLR 643, Rich J referred (at 650) to "the authorities which establish that the sale of a component part of a combination claim for an entire machine is not an infringement of a combination". Starke J (with whom Evatt J agreed) said (at 654):

> "[W]hen a patent is for a combination of various parts, the manufacture of the single parts is no infringement. Such a manufacture is in itself lawful, and knowledge, even on the part of the manufacturer, that the single parts will be used for the purposes of infringement is not enough to render him liable as an infringer".

Dixon J (with whom McTiernan J agreed) said (at 658):

> "[I]t is settled law that the exclusive property in a combination invention is not infringed upon by the sale of the components (*Townsend v Haworth* (1875) 12 Ch D 831(n)); that selling articles to persons to be used for the purpose of infringing a patent is not an infringement of the patent (per Fry J, *Sykes v Howarth* (1879) 12 Ch D, at p 833); and that sale with a knowledge that the purchaser will use the articles for

infringement is not itself an infringement although the vendor gives the purchaser an indemnity: the vendor must have made himself a party to the act of infringement (per Mellish LJ, *Townsend v Haworth* (1875) 48 LJ Ch, at p 773(n); *Dunlop Pneumatic Tyre Co v David Moseley & Sons Ltd* [1904] 1 Ch, at pp 616, 620). Further, in the opinion of Vaughan Williams LJ, it is not enough that the article sold has no other use than a use in the course of what amounts to infringement ([1904] 1 Ch, at pp 616, 618, 619). The basis upon which these rules rest is that whatever is not included in the monopoly granted is publici juris and may be freely used as of common right. Narrow as this view of what constitutes participation in infringement may appear, it requires us, in my opinion, to hold that the claims 4 to 11 of the specification were not infringed."

It will be observed that Dixon J based these rules on a proposition confining the patentee's monopoly to the precise area claimed. In the case of a combination patent, that area does not extend to each constituent element of the combination, or to several of them, provided the combination itself is not involved. It does not follow that the public right of which Dixon J spoke extends beyond a dealing in a mere part of the combination, as a separate item, so as to include a dealing that embraces participation in the assembly and use of the whole combination.

What is required, and will suffice, for the establishment of liability, according to the statement of principle by Dixon J, is that "the vendor must have made himself a party to the act of infringement". A party to an act is a "person who takes part or is implicated in" that act: The *New Shorter Oxford English Dictionary* (1993) Vol 2, "party". That Dixon J was using the expression (which he partially borrowed from Mellish LJ) in this sense is confirmed by his **[495]** reference, later in the same paragraph, to "participation in infringement". Similarly, Pennycuick VC in *Re Maidstone Buildings Provisions Ltd* [1971] 1 WLR 1085 at 1092 construed a company law provision referring to "any persons who were knowingly parties to the carrying on of the business [in a particular manner]" on the basis that "the expression 'party to' must on its natural meaning indicate no more than 'participates in', 'takes part in' or 'concurs in'." He added this "involves some positive steps of some nature". The propositions excluding a vendor from liability must therefore refer to a vendor who does not participate in the infringement.

As Dixon J pointed out (Gummow J has remarked that he "emphasised": *Rescare Ltd v Anaesthetic Supplies Pty Ltd* (1992) 111 ALR 205 at 243), the authorities to which reference was made in *Walker v Alemite* exemplify a narrow view of what participation in infringement requires. But the stringency of that view should not be exaggerated by a failure to appreciate how confined was the issue examined in the cases cited. *Walker v Alemite* itself involved, in the words of Dixon J (at 657), an asserted infringement of a patent relating to an "appliance considered as a whole" by the mere "manufacture and sale of the grease-cup or nipple" forming part of it, the infringement being alleged "because the grease-cup would or must inevitably be used with the other parts of the respondent's invention". This is a far cry from a case of participation in an infringement actually committed by the person who brought together the grease-cup and the other parts for sale or use. The first decision in the series to which reference was made (by Starke J at 654) in the judgments in the High Court, *McCormick v Gray* (1861) 7 H & N 25; 158 ER 377, raised a precisely similar question. As Bramwell B pointed out (at 38-39; 384), the patent related to an entire reaping machine, while the alleged infringement consisted of the making of a blade which could have been used either in the patented or in some other machine.

The next decision, *Townsend v Haworth*, involved a demurrer to the plaintiff's bill. As it was a demurrer, the question was whether the particular allegations made in that bill showed a good cause of action for infringement of a patent. The patent was concerned with the preservation of cotton from mildew by treating it with a solution made up from well-known chemical compounds. The action was brought against the supplier of some of the chemical Jessel MR said (at 772) "that the mere making, using or vending of the elements ... which afterwards enter into the combination, is not prohibited by the patent". He concluded:

> "This bill treats the company as proper defendants solely and simply on the ground of their bona fides in endeavouring to sell for their own profit, but as selling to a person who would not have bought of them without an indemnity, and therefore would not have infringed in that way without they had given him an indemnity."

On appeal, Mellish LJ said (at 773):

> "Selling materials for the purpose of infringing a patent to the man who is going to infringe it, even although the party who sells it knows that he is going to infringe it and indemnifies him, does not by itself make the person who so sells an infringer. He must be a party with the man who so infringes, and actually infringe."

(The words "by itself" were later emphasised in decisions of the Court of Appeal to which reference will be made: see *Dow Chemical AG v Spence Bryson Ltd* (infra) at 403-404.) **[476]**

These principles were applied in the later case *Dunlop Pneumatic Tyre Co Ltd v David Moseley & Sons Ltd* [1904] 1 Ch 616. There, infringement was alleged of two patents, each for a combination, relating to tyres and rims for cycles and vehicles. The defendants did not put the components of the combination together, but dealt (as appears at 615-616) in "an outer detachable cover", capable of being used in the manner described in the patent. Even if it was capable of no other use, Vaughan Williams LJ considered there would be no infringement. As was pointed out by Buckley LJ (with whom Goff and Eveleigh LJJ agreed) in the later case *Belegging*-en (infra) at 65, this must be right because "goods which cannot be used otherwise than in an infringing manner may nevertheless be disposed of without any infringement. They may, for example, be exported." Vaughan Williams LJ, in his judgment in *Dunlop Pneumatic Tyre Co*, also said (at 616):

> "Now it is plain that what the plaintiffs allege is that there has been an infringement by the defendants, and that the infringement consists in the sale of these covers, which are constituent parts of one or other of the methods the subject of the combination patents ... In my opinion the sale of these covers does not amount to nor is evidence of an infringement of either of those patents. In truth and in fact, veil it as you like, the plaintiffs do not complain of any infringement in which the defendants have taken part as actors. All that they complain of is the sale of these covers to persons who the defendants must have known intended to commit an infringement of one or other of the patents."

The Lord Justice added (at 618):

> "It cannot be said on these facts that [the defendants] have aided or abetted any one in the commission of an act of infringement."

He also added (at 619) an important clarification:

> "If you are in substance selling the whole of a patented machine, I do not think that you can save yourself from liability for infringement, because you sell it in parts which are so manufactured as to be adapted to be easily put together. But that is not the present case. What is complained of here is merely the sale of one or other of the parts of the tyres patented by the plaintiffs."

■■■■■■■ Ramset Fasteners (Aust) v Advanced Building Supply *continued*

This observation accords with a number of other decisions: in particular, it was followed by Waddell J in *Windsurfing International Inc v Petit* [1984] 2 NSWLR 196 at 204-207 in respect of a kit sale of a windsurfer to be assembled by the buyer.

A case analogous to the example given by Vaughan Williams LJ, and cases of that kind, where in substance what is sold is the whole of a patented machine, although it is not actually put together, is *Innes v Short* (1898) 15 RPC 449. That case involved a patent for an "improved method of preventing corrosion and encrustation in steam boilers" by the introduction into the boilers of zinc in a powdered state, so that it would be held in suspension by the boiling water. The defendants sold ordinary zinc powder, sending to each customer a copy of a circular containing directions for the use of the powder in a manner which would infringe the patent. Bigham J held (at 451-452):

"I come to the conclusion, as a matter of fact, that Short has invited and requested many people to use the powder in such a way as to infringe the patent rights which I find the Plaintiff has, and I think for that reason that this case is distinguishable from [*Townsend v Haworth*]. ... That case, in my opinion, is quite different from this one. It [497] would be nonsense to say that a person is to be restrained from perfectly legitimate trade, namely, selling an article of commerce, because he happens to know when the buyer buys it from him that the buyer intends to put it to some improper purpose. The seller has nothing to do with the purpose to which the buyer is going to put it, and he cannot be said to infringe any patent because he simply knows that the buyer is going to use it—that is to say, he expects it. ... But I think it is a different case where the vendor himself asks and invites the purchaser to use the article so as to infringe somebody's patent, and I think, as a matter of fact, that Mr Short did invite the persons who bought this article of commerce, powdered zinc, from him, and hereby led them to infringe this patent at the time that he was selling the powdered zinc to them. That, I think, is a violation of the Plaintiff's rights. There is no reason whatever why Mr Short should not sell powdered zinc, and he will not be in the wrong, though he may know or expect that the people who buy it from him are going to use it in such a way as will amount to an infringement of Mr Innes' patent rights. But he must not ask the people to use it in that way, and he must not ask the people to use it in that way in order to induce them to buy his powdered zinc from him."

This case was described as being "of somewhat doubtful authority" in *Adhesive Dry Mounting Co Ltd v Trapp* (1910) 27 RPC 341 at 353, a decision of Parker J. However, in *CBS Songs Ltd v Amstrad Consumer Electronics Plc* [1988] AC 1013 at 1056, it was cited by Lord Templeman, whose speech received the assent of the House. His Lordship there accepted it, in a passage to which we shall have occasion to refer again, as a case where "the vendor and the purchaser had a common design to carry out an infringing act".

Innes v Short is discussed by Blanco White, in his *Patents for Inventions* (4th ed (1974)) in para 3-210. He suggests:

"[I]t would seem on general principles that it should not be very difficult, in cases of the sale of materials or apparatus accompanied by instructions to use what is sold in what the seller knows to be an infringing way, to persuade a court that the seller had caused the infringement to take place; and it would further seem, again on general principles, that the patentee should in such a case have a cause of action against the seller. The authorities on this point, however, are in an extremely unsatisfactory state. In one case, *Innes v Short*, the court did intervene to stop the sale of materials, with an

▬▬▬▬   Ramset Fasteners (Aust) v Advanced Building Supply *continued*

> instruction to infringe (and no warning that following the instructions would lead to infringement). Taken by itself, the decision seems unexceptionable as a simple application of general principles."

Despite this statement of his own opinion, the learned author referred to the doubt expressed by Parker J as that of "a very eminent Judge", and to the decision in *Townsend v Haworth*. He put forward the view that in *Innes v Short* the "real question was whether [the seller] was inducing numerous innocent purchasers of his materials to infringe", and that it was rightly decided. As to *Townsend v Haworth*, *Blanco White* points out a conspiracy to infringe may well have been involved, since there the purchaser knew of the patent and intended to act on the assumption that it was invalid, but no such case was pleaded.

In *Rotocrop International Ltd v Genbourne Ltd* (1982) FSR 241, Graham J dealt with an allegation of infringement of a patent claims 6 and 14 of which were concerned, respectively, with a "method of producing compost from decomposing vegetable matter" and a "compost bin" of a particular description. His Lordship said (at 258-259) that the defendants sold—

> "kits of parts for their customers to build into bins. They issue full instructions ... with every kit to enable the customer to do so. By virtue of these actions, in my judgment, the defendants are joint tortfeasors with their customers who erect and use their bins in [498] accordance with the defendants' instructions. When a customer does so and makes compost, as he is told to do, he is in my judgment a joint tortfeasor with the defendants and they are similarly joint tortfeasors with him. Both have a common design ... [I]t is quite clear from their advertisements that the defendants invited their customers to make bins from the kits they sold and to use them for making compost. It is a fair inference that at least some of them did so and the defendants knew quite well that they would do so as alleged in the particulars of infringement. ... That being so I find the defendants to be joint tortfeasors with their customers ... in infringing claim 6."

His Lordship went on to hold also (at 260):

> "[T]here is certainly infringement of claims 6 and 14 by the defendants who have procured their customers to infringe as alleged, knowing quite well that the customer would assemble the bin and use it in accordance with the defendants' instructions and thereby would infringe at least those claims. In any event therefore, even if joint tort-feasance [on the basis of a common design] ought not to be inferred, there is infringe-ment by the defendants by way of procuring customers to infringe and I so hold."

This case, as well as *Innes v Short*, was referred to by Lord Templeman in *CBS Songs Ltd* (ubi supra) in terms suggesting approval of the proposition that "the vendor and the purchaser had a common design to carry out an infringing act". Lord Templeman went on to refer (at 1056-1057) to the decision of the Court of Appeal in *Belegging-en Exploitatiemaatschappij Lavender BV v Whitten Industrial Diamonds Ltd* [1979] FSR 59, where the defendants were alleged to have sold diamond grit for the sole purpose of making grinding tools, in which it was to be embedded in a resin bond as part of a patented material. Lord Templeman said:

> "Buckley LJ held, at p 66, that the defendants could not be infringers unless they 'sold the grits in circumstances which in some way made them participants in their subsequent embodiment in resin bonded grinding wheels, or that they induced someone so to embody them ...'"

Later, Lord Templeman added (at 1058):

> "My Lords, I accept that a defendant who procures a breach of copyright is liable jointly and severally with the infringer for the damages suffered by the plaintiff as a result of the infringement. The defendant is a joint infringer; he intends and procures and shares a common design that infringement shall take place. A defendant may procure an infringement by inducement, incitement or persuasion."

In reading this passage, which refers to a breach of copyright, it is necessary to bear in mind that his Lordship treated the patent cases as involving the same principle.

In further remarks, Lord Templeman made a statement on which the cross-respondent Ramset strongly relies:

> "Sales and advertisements to the public generally of a machine which may be used for lawful or unlawful purposes, including infringement of copyright, cannot be said to 'procure' all breaches of copyright thereafter by members of the public who use the machine. Generally speaking, inducement, incitement or persuasion to infringe must be by a defendant to an individual infringer and must identifiably procure a particular infringement in order to make the defendant liable as a joint infringer."

Counsel appeared to suggest that this proposition was based on a legal necessity that there be a meeting of the minds of the parties to a common design in such a way as would involve some direct contact between them. But this is not true of the paradigm example of a common design in the law—the crime of conspiracy. **[499]** In *Commonwealth of Australia v Riley* (1984) 5 FCR 8 at 27, the joint judgment of the Full Court (Smithers, Sheppard and Wilcox JJ) accepts the statement of principle of the English Court of Criminal Appeal in *R v Griffiths* [1966] 1 QB 589 at 597:

> "[A]ll must join in the one agreement, each with the others, in order to constitute one conspiracy. They may join in at various times, each attaching himself to that agreement; any one of them may not know all the other parties, but only that there are other parties; any one of them may not know the full extent of the scheme to which he attaches himself. But what each must know is that there is coming into existence, or is in existence, a scheme which goes beyond the illegal act or acts which he agrees to do."

In *Smith and Hogan* on *Criminal Law*, 4th ed (1978) at 237, the rule is put tersely:

> "Provided that the result is that they have a common design—for example, to rob a particular bank—[several parties] may properly be indicted for conspiring together though they have never been in touch with one another until they meet in the dock."

But, in any case, the law as declared by Lord Templeman is concerned with more than what is involved in a common design; it extends to procurement through inducement or persuasion. His Lordship's remarks must be understood in the context of the case he was considering. The impugned transactions involved the sale of tape recorders which could be used for recording generally. Unless appropriate individual circumstances were proved, the mere advertising of their capabilities could not amount to a general invitation, inducement or persuasion to the carrying out of acts in breach of copyright. If, on the other hand, as in *Innes v Short*, purchasers or would-be purchasers of goods are not merely told their properties or capabilities, but are told how to use them to infringe a specific right, then, depending on the circumstances, there seems no reason why inducement should not be found.

It is to be observed that Lord Templeman lays down no rule for all cases; he says "Generally speaking ...". In the context of authorisation of breach of copyright, Jacobs J (with

▬▬▬▬   Ramset Fasteners (Aust) v Advanced Building Supply *continued*

whom McTiernan ACJ agreed) said in *University of New South Wales v Moorhouse* (1975) 133 CLR 1 at 21:

> "Where a general permission or invitation may be implied it is clearly unnecessary that the authorising party have knowledge that a particular act comprised in the copyright will be done."

Gibbs J took a similar view at 13, and, having regard to *R v Griffiths*, the equivalent proposition must be true also of the law of combination.

The principle was expounded by Dillon LJ (with whom Woolf and Leggatt LJJ relevantly agreed) in *Molnlycke AB v Procter & Gamble Ltd* [1992] 1 WLR 1112 (a case the authority of which has been accepted in Australia: see *Murrex Diagnostics Australia Pty Ltd v Chiron Corp* (1995) 55 FCR 194 at 207) at 1118, where his Lordship said:

> "For a very long time there has been a dichotomy applied between 'procuring' and 'facilitating' an infringement of a patent: see *Townsend v Haworth; Dunlop Pneumatic Tyre Co Ltd v David Moseley & Sons Ltd* and *Belegging-en Exploitatiemaatschappij Lavender BV v Whitten Industrial Diamonds Ltd* [at] 65, where Buckley LJ said: 'Facilitating the doing of an act is obviously different from procuring the doing of the act.' A person who merely facilitated, but did not procure, the infringement was not a joint tortfeasor with the infringer and so was not liable if, for instance, he sold articles which could be used for infringing or non-infringing purposes even though he knew that they would probably be used and were intended to be used for the infringing purposes.
>
> [500] More recently, however, a new concept has been developed. Parties will be regarded as joint tortfeasors if on the facts they have a common design to market in the UK articles which in truth infringe a UK patent."

The *Belegging-en* case had been the subject of some elaboration in a unanimous decision of the Court of Appeal in *Dow Chemical AG v Spence Bryson Ltd* (1982) FSR 397. The question related to an amendment of the plaintiff's pleading in an infringement action, which had been refused by reference to the principle of *Townsend v Haworth* and *Dunlop Pneumatic Tyre Co Ltd v David Moseley & Sons Ltd*. Lawton LJ (with whom Brightman and Fox LJJ agreed) referred to the judgment of Buckley LJ in the *Belegging-en* case, and continued (at 404):

> "Had the pleading merely alleged that the second defendants knew that the first defendants were going to use their latex for the purposes of infringing the second plaintiffs' patent, there would have been no difficulty about this case and Falconer J's decision, in my opinion, would have been right. But more was alleged, because the pleading avers that not only did they know but they procured the first defendants to infringe the second plaintiffs' patent. It is that allegation of procuring which is the material allegation for the purposes of founding a case against the second defendants. That becomes clear when one reads the rest of Buckley LJ's judgment in [the *Belegging-en* case], because he pointed out that it is persuading someone to do something which is a very important factor in the tort of procuring someone else to do an unlawful act. It may well be that at the trial the plaintiffs will not succeed in showing that there was any procuring in the sense of persuading, but that is a matter not of allegation but of evidence."

These authorities show that liability for infringement may be established, in some circumstances, against a defendant who has not supplied a whole combination (in the case of a combination patent) or performed the relevant operation (in the case of a method patent).

██████ Ramset Fasteners (Aust) v Advanced Building Supply *continued*

The necessary circumstances have been variously described: the defendant may "have made himself a party to the act of infringement"; or participated in it; or procured it; or persuaded another to infringe; or joined in a common design to do acts which in truth infringe. All these go beyond mere facilitation. They involve the taking of some step designed to produce the infringement, although further action by another or others is also required. Where a vendor sets out to make a profit by the supply of that which is patented, but omitting some link the customer can easily furnish, particularly if the customer is actually told how to furnish it and how to use the product in accordance with the patent, the court may find the vendor has "made himself a party to the [ultimate] act of infringement". He has indeed procured it. So to hold is not in any way to trespass against the established line of authority which, as Dixon J made clear in *Walker v Alemite*, is based upon the need to confine a monopoly to the precise area in which it operates. That protects the mere vendor of an old product, though selling with knowledge of the purchaser's intention to infringe a combination patent; but it affords no excuse to the person who sets out to induce customers to do what falls fairly within the area of the monopoly.

In the present matter, the evidence establishes, Ramset determined to enter into competition with Advanced, which was supplying ring clutches and face-lift anchors conforming to the patent for use in the manner described in the patent. Ramset, which, the trial judge found, was aware of the patent by August 1987, did not produce a different ring clutch or anchor, or propose a different manner of use. It is a large corporation, employing technical staff to advise on the use of its products. The relevant products were promoted through its sales staff and advisers to building contractors and those who direct their activities, such as [501] engineers. The nature of the product supplied by Ramset, the nature of the work in connection with which it was to be used, and the circumstances of the sales, all pointed to the probability that it would be so used as to infringe the patent. At about the time Ramset commenced marketing these products, it produced six thousand copies of a brochure, for distribution to contractors and engineers, copies also being held available over a period of several years to be handed out on request or utilised in marketing efforts. The trial judge found:

> "The Ramset brochure demonstrated use of clutches with extended lever arms in a way which infringed the patent."

His Honour also found, with reference to the cardinal feature of the invention, "that the use of rope releases was promoted by Mr Finlay [Ramset's Manager of Research and Development] in seminars given by him to potential users as part of Ramset's marketing programme".

... [504]

On the evidence and the findings of the trial judge, the conclusion is inescapable that when Ramset supplied the equipment complete with release ropes and instructions for use, it procured the infringements which followed.

... [506]

The appellant, of course, relies on the well-known proposition that a combination patent will not be infringed unless all the integers of the patent are taken by the alleged infringement: *Meyers Taylor Pty Ltd v Vicarr Industries Ltd* at 235; *Olin Corp v Super Cartridge Co Pty Ltd* (1977) 180 CLR 236 at 246; *Allsop Inc v Bintang Ltd* (1989) 15 IPR 686 at 698. Counsel claim an elongated lever arm, long enough to be blocked by the shackle, is an essential integer of the patent. However, it is necessary to bear in mind the words of Viscount Dunedin in *British Thomson-Houston Co Ltd v Metropolitan-Vickers Electrical Co Ltd* (1928) 45 RPC 1 at 25:

▬▬▬   Ramset Fasteners (Aust) v Advanced Building Supply *continued*

"[I]t is, I think, clear that you cannot avoid infringement by taking a patented machine and then making it work a little worse than it naturally would and then remedying that worseness by another device, and that is just what the Defendants have done." [507]

Aickin J took up the same point in the course of his well-known judgment in *Minnesota Mining & Manufacturing Co v Beiersdorf (Australia) Ltd* at 286 ...

See also *Elconnex Pty Ltd v Gerard Industries Pty Ltd* (1991) 32 FCR 491 at 515. What Ramset has done, without eliminating an elongated lever arm, has made the ring clutch a little worse, in so far as the reduction in the length of the lever arm has lost a degree of mechanical advantage in the rope release operation (there was evidence that contractors inserted extensions to overcome this), and in so far as safety was affected by the possibility of the arm passing through the bail of the shackle. However, Ramset could be confident that previous experience would enable contractors to remedy the former defect by the insertion of the extensions, and Ramset remedied the latter by the attachment of the chain, which would be heavy enough to drag the lever arm into a blocking relationship with the shackle, for practical purposes, even if it were not extended by the user.

Furthermore, as Aickin J made clear in the passage just cited, the "substance" of the invention may be taken, in respect of a particular integer, by the substitution of something that has the same qualities. Aickin J went on to say:

"[I]t remains the law that a defendant may not take the substance of an invention unless the wording of the claims makes it clear that the relevant area has been deliberately left outside the claim."

Far from deliberately leaving outside the claims any device, other than one depending solely on the length of the lever bare of all attachments, the drafting of the patent uses the wider language which has been quoted. See also *Sunbeam Corp v Morphy-Richards (Aust) Pty Ltd* (1961) 180 CLR 98 at 109-110; *Leonardis v Sartas No 1 Pty Ltd* (1996) 67 FCR 126 at 148; *Olin Corp v Super Cartridge Co Pty Ltd* (ubi supra). Having regard to all these considerations, the modifications to the Ramset shackle and ring clutch did not avoid infringement.

■ Liability under Trade Practices Act 1974 (Cth)

▬▬▬ Ramset Fasteners (Aust) v Advanced ▬▬▬ Building Supply

[10.90] *Ramset Fasteners (Aust) Pty Ltd v Advanced Building Supply Pty Ltd* (1999) 44 IPR 481; FCA 898 Federal Court of Australia

[The Court in *Ramset* (above) continued at a later point:]

BURCHETT, SACKVILLE and LEHANE JJ: [510]

The issue of contravention of s 52 of the Trade Practices Act

Having regard to the conclusions reached earlier in these reasons, it is unnecessary to say much about this issue. Even if damages should have been awarded under s 82 of the *Trade*

███████   Ramset Fasteners (Aust) v Advanced Building Supply *continued*

Practices Act 1974, in respect of the contravention of s 52, it would have involved a doubling up to have awarded such damages in addition to the larger damages for infringement of the patent. But his Honour did make a finding that s 52 had been contravened, and the appellant challenges that finding. His Honour said:

> "I am of the view that the failure of Ramset to warn its customers that use of clutches or components in a particular way might constitute an infringement of Advanced's patent, does constitute conduct in trade or commerce which is misleading or deceptive or likely to mislead or deceive users."

We agree with the reasons his Honour gave for this conclusion, and accordingly shall confine ourselves to some brief remarks.

Section 52 requires that a "corporation shall not, in trade or commerce, engage in conduct that is misleading or deceptive or is likely to mislead or deceive". Attention has been drawn, in a number of cases, to the fact that the section is not limited to "representations", a word that does not appear in it, although contravening conduct is generally apt to involve representations: *Henjo Investments Pty Ltd v Collins Marrickville Pty Ltd* (1988) 79 ALR 83 at 93; *Pacific Dunlop Ltd v Hogan* (1989) 23 FCR 553 at 585-586; *Demagogue Pty Ltd v Ramensky* (1992) 39 FCR 31 at 32, 40-41. Whether or not Ramset's conduct should be analysed as conveying an implicit misrepresentation, it acted misleadingly when it promoted and sold face-lift tilt-up equipment in the way that it did, without informing its customers of the liability it was inducing them to incur. This was conduct calculated to cause a mistaken impression about a significant consequence of the transaction proposed to those customers. In our opinion, in such a case, it is unnecessary, and may be artificial, to speak of a representation. The orthodox theory would find one, but it is more realistic to see the conduct as misleading, without resorting to a sophisticated analysis in which no-one would have engaged at the time.

It is plain, on the evidence and the findings of the trial judge, that Ramset's conduct was engaged in for the purpose of persuading customers to purchase the various forms of equipment it supplied for face-lift tilt-up operations. Many persons did so. For example, Mr Nightingale gave evidence, to which reference has been made, of a big change in the source of supply upon which Brambles Cranes drew to obtain ring clutches. In *Como Investments Pty Ltd v Yenald Nominees Pty Ltd* (1997) ATPR 43,617 at 43,619-43,620, a full court jointly stated:

> "Where a representation is relevant to the decision in question, and in its nature persuasive to induce the making of that decision, it accords with legal notions of causation to hold that it has a causative effect. And where a respondent, who may be taken to know his own business, has thought it was in his interests to misrepresent the situation in a particular respect, the Court may infer that the misrepresentation was persuasive. These inferences arise from the making of the representation followed by the respondent doing the thing it was calculated to induce him to do."

Those observations may be applied equally to the effect of the misleading conduct of Ramset upon its customers. See also *Gould v Vaggelas* (1985) 157 CLR 215 at 236; *Commission for the New Towns v Cooper (Great Britain) Ltd* [1995] Ch 259 at 282; *Sibley v Grosvenor* (1916) 21 CLR 469 at 473, [511] 478, 481; *Krakowski v Eurolynx Properties Ltd* (1995) 183 CLR 563 at 578; *Hanave Pty Ltd v LFOT Pty Ltd* (1999) FCA 357 at paras 37, 45. In the present case, the inference should be drawn that Ramset's misleading conduct did cause damage to Advanced, but it is unnecessary to pursue this point further.

DEFENCES AGAINST INFRINGEMENT

■ The so-called "Gillette defence"

▬▬▬ Woodbridge Foam v AFCO Automotive ▬▬▬ Foam Components

[10.95] *Woodbridge Foam Corporation v AFCO Automotive Foam Components Pty Ltd* (2002) 58 IPR 56; FCA 883

FINKELSTEIN J: **[57]**

The applicant is the proprietor of Australian Patent 728093 for methods of producing foamed articles in a mould and for moulds for producing foamed articles. ...

In this action the applicant claims that its monopoly in the patented methods and products has been infringed. Its statement of claim takes the usual form, describing the parties in paragraphs 1 and 2, claiming proprietorship and asserting the validity of the patent in paragraphs 3 and 4 and alleging infringement in paragraph 5. According to its amended defence, to which detailed reference will be made in a moment, the respondent denies infringement, alleges that the patent is invalid upon the grounds set out in the particulars of invalidity (which were separately delivered), gives notice that it will rely on s 123 of the *Patents Act 1990 (Cth)* (that is, the defence of innocent infringement) and pleads the equitable defences of estoppel and acquiescence. There is a cross-claim in which the respondent asks for revocation of the patent on the ground of invalidity.

[58] I now turn to the applicant's complaints. The first matter concerns paragraph 4 of the defence. Having denied the applicant's allegation that the patent is "subsisting and of full force and effect", paragraph 4.2 of the amended defence provides (with irrelevant portions omitted) "that the alleged infringements ... were not novel at the earliest priority date of any claim of the patent". This is the so called "Gillette Defence" and is based on the observations of Lord Moulton in *Gillette Safety Razor Company v Anglo-American Trading Company Ltd* (1913) 30 RPC 465. The plea is followed in paragraph 4.3 by the allegation, which is repeated in the cross-claim, that in any event the patent is invalid for the reasons set out in the particulars of invalidity. Reference must be made to those particulars. The grounds of invalidity sought to be established are that the specification does not meet the requirements of ss 40(2) or (3), that the claimed invention is not novel when compared with the prior art, that the claimed invention is obvious and did not involve an inventive step, that the claimed invention is not a manner of manufacture and that it is not useful. Paragraph 4.3 is then followed by a general denial of infringement in paragraph 5.

The applicant says that the Gillette Defence is embarrassing because it adds nothing to the respondent's general denial of infringement and its allegation of invalidity for want of novelty or, if it is intended to add something, that something is not spelt out. It is not without some hesitation that I propose to reject this submission. My reason requires me to state what I understand to be the point of the Gillette Defence. This takes me to Mr Frost's textbook *Patent Law and Practice*, the third edition of which was published in 1906. In a passage which appears to anticipate (if I might borrow a word that has a special meaning in this area) the Gillette Defence Mr Frost wrote (vol 1 p. 56):

> "Sometimes in a patent case a conclusion may be arrived at in favour of the defendant by considering the infringement apart from the patent. If it can be shown that the alleged infringement is an act which, having regard to the state of public knowledge

■■■■■ Woodbridge Foam v AFCO Automotive Foam Components *continued*

prior to the date of the patent, the public actually did or had the right to it (ie, passing from what was actually known or done to the act complained of involved no inventive step), the patentee cannot complain. He is in this dilemma, either the patent includes that which was actually done before or that which the public had the right to do—that is, something which involved no invention—in which the case is bad for want of novelty; or it does not include it, in which case the defendant is not an infringer."

What Lord Moulton said in *Gillette* is to the same effect. He pointed out that it is permissible for a patent case to be decided without regard to the patent in suit. That is really the important point. A plea of invalidity for want of novelty can only be resolved after there has been a close examination of the patent in suit [59] and the claimed invention has been compared with prior disclosures. Issues of infringement begin with a construction of the claims, which may also involve a close examination of the patent, and then the alleged infringing product or process must be compared with the claims. The Gillette Defence avoids these steps and the complexities that usually will result.

[10.100] Note the relationship between this defence and the concept of the reverse infringement test for anticipation establishing want of novelty. This relationship was noted by Gummow J in *R D Werner & Co Inc v Bailey Aluminum Products Pty Ltd* (1989) 13 IPR 513; 25 FCR 565 in paragraph 10 of his judgment in that case.

■ Prior use of invention by defendant

■■■■■ Welcome Real-Time v Catuity ■■■■■

[10.105] *Welcome Real-Time SA v Catuity Inc* (2001) 51 IPR 327; FCA 445 Federal Court of Australia

[For the facts see the extract at **[8.195]** above.]

HEEREY J: **[346]**

IV Definite steps to make or use

1. The construction of s 119
Section 119 of the Act provides as follows:
>   (1) Where, immediately before the priority date of a claim, a person:
>   (a) was making a product or using a process claimed in that claim; or
>   (b) had taken definite steps (whether by way of contract or otherwise) to make that product or use that process
>   the person may, despite the grant of a patent for the product or process so claimed, make the product, or use the process, (or continue to do so) in the patent area, without infringing the patent.
>   (2) Subsection (1) does not apply if the person:
>   (a) derived the subject-matter of the invention concerned from the patentee or the patentee's predecessor in title in the invention; or
>   (b) before the relevant priority date, had stopped making the product or using the process (other than temporarily), or had abandoned (other than temporarily) the steps mentioned in paragraph (1)(b).

■■■■■■ Welcome Real-Time v Catuity *continued*

[347] The respondents rely on s 119(1)(b).

The product or process referred to in s 119(1) is the product or process claimed in the claim of the patent: *CCOM Pty Ltd v Jiejing Pty Ltd* (1993) 27 IPR 577 at 627 per Cooper J. For s 119 to be applicable, it must be possible to say that immediately before the priority date the product or process of the patent was being made or used by the infringer or he or she had taken definite steps to make or use that particular product or that particular process.

The concept of which s 119 speaks may be illustrated by the following example. Assume a patented product consisting of components A, B and C. Immediately before the priority date an infringer: has drawings depicting the product; has actually made A; has on his premises the raw materials for component B; and has ordered the raw materials for component C. It can then be said that the infringer had taken definite steps to make that product. Conversely, it would not be sufficient that immediately before the priority date, the infringer has made A, has received the raw materials for B but is investigating whether C, D or E would be the preferable final component. And the infringer would be in no better position if, after the priority date, he in fact decided that C was preferable and then proceeded to manufacture a product consisting of A, B and C.

Reference was made in the course of argument to s 64 of the *Patents Act 1977* (Imp) which provides:

> "Where a patent is granted for an intention, a person who in the United Kingdom before the priority date of the invention
> (a) does in good faith an act which would constitute an infringement of the patent if it were in force, or
> (b) makes in good faith effective and serious preparations to do such an act
> has the right to continue to do the act or, as the case may be, to do the act, notwithstanding the grant of the patent, but this right does not extend to granting a licence to another person to do the act."

In *Helitune Ltd v Stewart Hughes Ltd* [1991] FSR 171 the production of prototypes before the priority date was held not enough to show effective and serious preparation. In *Lubrizol Corp v Esso Petroleum Ltd* [1998] RPC 727 the patent related to a lubricating oil. The first batch of the defendants' product was imported into the UK before the priority date and the defendants had given consideration to appropriate pricing. The defendants had also contemplated manufacturing the product in the UK. It was held that the defendants had not undertaken effective and serious preparations. Aldous J said (at 770) that the preparations must be "so advanced as to be about to result in the infringing act being done".

Thus the English courts have adopted a strict interpretation of s 64, a provision which, on its face, seems more favourable to infringers that s 119. Assuming for the moment that doing an act which would constitute infringement in the UK Act can be equated to making a product or using a process claimed in the claim of the patent in the Australian Act (but as to which, see below), in the normal course of events making preparations for the making of a product would be something that occurs prior to steps in the actual making.

2. Evidence

Mr Garton deposed that in August 1995 the respondents began work developing an upgraded system to make the Wizard/Transcard system suitable [348] for full scale production use. Work continued on the upgrade throughout August and by mid September 1995 the respondents had formulated "the rollout requirements for the upgrade system". Mr Garton produced a copy of the rollout commencement requirements dated 14 September 1995. He deposed that this was the "first and most critical document developed for the project". It described the "functionality expected (and finally delivered) by" the respondents' system. He further deposed that the "technical design of the (respondents') system was substantially completed by 21 January 1996".

Mr Ben-Meir considered the documents referred to by Mr Garton. In Mr Ben-Meir's opinion, those documents did not show that the technical design of the respondents' system was substantially completed by 21 January 1996. From a review of those documents Mr Ben-Meir opined that the development of the respondents' system had started but was in the early stage of development by that date. Seven of the documents referred to by Mr Garton in his affidavit were not completed by then. Mr Ben-Meir noted that the respondents' system became operational in August 1996.

3 Conclusion

Neither Mr Garton nor Mr Ben-Meir was cross-examined on their evidence on this issue. The onus is on the respondents. I am not satisfied that, within the meaning of s 119(1)(b), the respondents had taken definite steps to use their system by 21 January 1996. Quite apart from questions of onus, I note that in terms of Mr Garton's evidence the design of the respondents' system was only "substantially completed" by 21 January 1996. The fact that the respondents' system did not become operational until seven months later confirms the impression that what the respondents were doing as at the priority date was engaging in the ongoing development of a system.

Although this was not mentioned in argument, it is worth noting that s 119 may have a quite limited effect. If an infringer comes within the section, it by no means follows that it can act as though the patent did not exist. As Ann Monotti points out in her article "Balancing the Rights of the Patentee and Prior User of an Invention; The Australian Experience" (1997) 7 EIPR 351, s 119 in its terms appears to limit its protection to the act of making a product or using a process and does not extend to other acts which would constitute exploitation, and hence infringement, such as sale or importation of a product: see s 13(1) and the definition of "exploit" in Sch 1.

Another point is whether the making or using referred to in s 119 must be secret. If the making or use is public, whether by the patentee or anyone else, there will be an anticipation of the patent and thus ground for revocation for want of novelty: ss 7, 18(1)(b)(i), 138(3)(b). Secret use by or on behalf of the patentee is also a ground for revocation: ss 9, 18(1)(d), and 138(3)(b). In *Dyno Nobel Asia Pacific Ltd v Orica Australia Pty Ltd* (1999) 99 FCR 151 at [222] Dowsett J, in dealing with a prior use which was found to be not secret, expressed the obiter view that

> "[I]t (is) at least arguable that s 119 prescribes the protection to be afforded to a person who has previously used the process or product in question. If such prior use were sufficient to deprive an invention of novelty, there would be little purpose in express protection of a person who has previously used it."

A possible rationale is that s 119 applies to all prior making or using, whether public or secret. The section may have value for an infringer who has **[349]** engaged in a public making or using but does not wish to engage in the risk and expense of a revocation suit. It seems a reasonable reading of the section that such an infringer obtains relatively clear cut protection over a limited area leaving the patentee otherwise free to exploit the patent. Of course this would not prevent third parties relying on such making or using in their revocation claims. But the whole purpose of s 119 (and its UK counterpart) is to confer a personal right on somebody who would otherwise be an infringer rather than to interfere with the validity of the patent.

Notes

[10.110] Since the decision in this case a general "grace period" has been introduced. See *Patents Act 1990* (Cth), s 24(1)(a) and *Patents Regulations 1991*(Cth), reg 2.2 (1A). Where a patentee reveals information before the priority date and relies on the "grace period" to avoid that disclosure constituting an anticipation which negates the novelty of the invention, a defendant who learned the information from the patentee's disclosure may rely upon a defence to infringement under s 119(3).

Even more significantly the *Intellectual Property Laws Amendment Bill 2006*, sch 6 proposes amendments to s 119 to provide some clarification of the prior use exception. There are three major reforms. They appear to be directed to assisting research organisations, which are vulnerable to being excluded from use and exploitation of their own independent research if another is first to patent. The first change proposed is that the exemption is only available in relation to prior use in Australia. This then excludes what has been termed "obscure use overseas" from forging rights in Australia. Secondly, it is made clear that any use that "exploits a product, method or process and would infringe a patent" is covered by the exemption. This has a number of implications. It has been argued that the present s 119 allows a prior user to continue to make and use a product but not to commercially deal with it. This amendment clarifies that situation. It also makes it clear that non-commercial research use is protected. Thirdly, the Bill proposes that the holder of a right to continue to use the invention should be capable of assignment, but not of being licensed. This will benefit research institutions, such as Universities, which do not have manufacturing capacity and rely upon their capacity to assign their research. Interestingly the proposed amendments do not include a specific reference to "experimental use" as recommended by the IPCRC and the Explanatory Memorandum at p 8 comments that "experimental use is not generally regarded as consti-tuting infringement in other circumstances within ... the Patents Act". This should not be seen as a definitive statement on the status of experimental use but is perhaps a pointer to current government thinking.

■ Other defences under Patents Act 1990 (Cth)

Extensions of term—"springboarding"

[10.115] Where a patent for a pharmaceutical substance has been extended under the provisions of ss 70-77, it is not an infringement during the period of extension for a person to exploit the pharmaceutical substance disclosed in the specification. Claims where that exploitation is solely for the purpose of having goods intended for therapeutic use included on the Australian register, or for obtaining regulatory approval outside Australia (ss 78 and 79) are also not an infringement.

A broader exemption is proposed by sch 7 of the *Intellectual Property Laws Amendment Bill 2006*. Under the Bill there will not be an infringement of a pharmaceutical patent at any time during the patent term where there is an exploitation of the pharmaceutical substance disclosed in the patent solely for the purpose of obtaining regulatory approval for goods in Australia. Nor will there be an infringement of a pharmaceutical patent where there is an exploitation of the pharmaceutical substance disclosed in the patent for the purpose of obtaining regulatory approval in an overseas country, although this protection only applies during a period of extension of term. These proposed amendments follow an Interdepart-mental Committee (IDC) report in 2002 which concluded, amongst other things, that the current "springboarding" provisions were less generous that those pertaining in the laws of Australia's competitors such as the United States of America, Canada and New Zealand and that this posed an inhibition on research and development of generic pharmaceuticals in Australia. While it seems that the Government considered a broader approach for uses related to overseas approval to allow an exemption at any time during the term, it considered itself constrained by obligations in the TRIPS Agreement and the Australia-US Free Trade Agreement. See Explanatory Memorandum, p 20.

Lapse

[10.120] A patent may cease or lapse due to failure to pay renewal fees or file the prescribed documents (s 143). The patentee may apply for an extension of time for payment of the renewal fee of filing documents and, if granted, the patent will be restored (s 223). Infringement actions cannot be brought for activities which took place between the date of cessation and restoration (s 223(10)).

Crown use

[10.125] Use of the invention by the Commonwealth or a State or a person authorised in writing by them where the exploitation is for the service of the Commonwealth or a State is not an infringement (s 163). Remuneration must be paid and terms for the exploitation must be agreed or can be set by the court (s 165). See *Stack v Brisbane City Council* (1995) 32 IPR 69

Use on ships, aircraft and vehicles temporarily in Australia

[10.130] It is not an infringement to use a patented invention in or on a foreign vessel from another Paris Convention country, temporarily or accidentally in the patent area provided the use is only for the needs of the vessel. Similarly it is not an infringement to use a patented invention in the construction or working of a foreign aircraft or land vehicle from another Convention country where the aircraft or vehicle is temporarily or accidentally in the patent area (s 118).

Innocent infringement

[10.135] Where a defendant can satisfy the court that at the time of the infringement the defendant was "not aware, and no reason to believe" that there was a patent for the invention,the court has a discretion to decide not to award damages or an account of profit (s 123 (1)). However the defendant will be taken to be aware of the existence of the patent if products are marked to indicate that they are patented and have been sold or used to a substantial extent in Australia (s 123(2)). A court has discretion to grant an injunction (s 123 (3)).

■ Action for unjustified threats of infringement proceedings

▬▬▬ U and I Global Trading (Australia) v ▬▬▬ Tasman-Warajay

[10.140] *U And I Global Trading (Australia) Pty Ltd v Tasman-Warajay Pty Ltd* (1995) 32 IPR 494 Federal Court of Australia

COOPER J: **[499]**
The applicant's claim for injunctive relief to restrain threatened proceedings is based on s 128 of the *Patents Act 1990* (Cth) ("the Act") which provides:

"128(1) Where a person, by means of circulars, advertisements or otherwise, threatens a person with infringement proceedings, or other similar proceedings, a person aggrieved may apply to a prescribed court, or to another court having jurisdiction to hear and determine the application, for:

■■■■■   U and I Global Trading (Australia) v Tasman-Warajay *continued*

    (a) a declaration that the threats are unjustifiable; and
    (b) an injunction against the continuance of the threats; and
    (c) the recovery of any damages sustained by the applicant as a result of the threats.
  (2) Subsection (1) applies whether or not the person who made the threats is entitled to, or interested in, the patent or a patent application."

[500] Section 129 of the Act provides:

"129. The court may grant an applicant under s 128 the relief applied for unless the respondent satisfies the court that the acts about which the threats were made infringed, or would infringe:
    (a) a claim that is not shown by the applicant to be invalid; or
    (b) rights under s 57 in respect of a claim that is not shown by the applicant to be a claim that would be invalid if a patent had been granted."

Section 131 of the Act provides:

"131. The mere notification of the existence of a patent, or an application for a patent, does not constitute a threat of proceedings for the purposes of s 128."

For the purposes of this application I will treat the applicant as a person aggrieved within the terms of s 128.

The respondent submits that the letter in question contains no threats but merely states, as was the fact, that the respondent then had no right to issue proceedings for infringement and merely conveyed by way of information that it reserved its rights which are the rights given by s 57 of the Act.

Whether or not the letter of 13 January 1995 contains a threat within the terms of s 128 depends upon the construction to be given to the sentence:

"However, upon the registration of the patent, we reserve our right to sue for any past infringements of the patent that have occurred since April 1991 (being the date of publication of the patent application)."

The test is whether the language would convey to any reasonable person that the author of the letter in the present case intended to bring proceedings for infringement against the person said to be threatened. It is not necessary that there be direct words that action would be taken. There is some similarity between the present case and *Lido Manufacturing Co Pty Ltd v Meyers and Leslie Pty Ltd* (1964) 5 FLR 443. There McClelland CJ in equity said (at 450-451):

"Mr Meyers said that he had a provisional patent in circumstances which would have suggested to an ordinary person that he had the rights which the holder of a patent had and which would become enforceable when the `full patent' was issued, and what was said was more than a mere notification of the existence of an application for a patent. However, the fact that s 121(2) is inapplicable does not necessarily mean that what was said amounted to a threat or threats within the meaning of s 121(1).

    Mr Ramsden agreed that the discussion was quite a friendly one and that Mr Meyers did not say `I am going to take action against Farmers' and Mr Faulkner agreed that Mr Meyers did not say `If you do not withdraw the goods from sale I am going to take proceedings against the company', or words to that effect. Indeed Farmers had been a customer of the defendant for a long time and Mr Meyers was no doubt anxious not to say things which would offend its officers and lose him custom and it is unlikely that he would have bluntly said, `If you don't withdraw the goods from sale I will in due course take proceedings against Farmers'.

▨▨▨▨▨ U and I Global Trading (Australia) v Tasman-Warajay *continued*

However, the absence of direct words by Mr. Meyers, saying that he would take action, does not involve in my view that no threat within the meaning of s 121(1) was made: cf *Luna Advertising Co Ltd v Burnham and Co* (1928) 45 RPC 258 at 260; *Willis and Bates Limited v Tilley Lamp Co* (1943) 61 RPC 8 at 11; *C and P Development Co (London) Limited v Sisabro Novelty Co Limited* (1953) 70 RPC 277 at 282.

I am of the opinion that what Mr Meyers said to the officers of Farmers was sufficient to indicate to them that if the goods were not withheld from sale Farmers would be infringing rights belonging to Mr Meyers' company for which subsequently Farmers would be legally liable to his company and that Mr Meyers did threaten Farmers with an action or proceeding for infringement within the meaning of s 121(1).

[501] It was not suggested, nor could it have been suggested, that the defendant could satisfy the court that the acts in respect of which proceedings were threatened would constitute an infringement of a patent or an infringement of rights within the provisions of s 121(1)(a) or (b). Accordingly the threats were unjustified."

This is an application for an interlocutory injunction. Accordingly it is only necessary that the applicant establish that there is a serious question to be tried and that the balance of convenience is in favour of the making of an order.

In my opinion there is a serious question to be tried that the letter amounts to an unjustifiable threat. The statement that the respondent reserves its right to sue does not save it. It is a threat to sue for infringement if the respondent obtains a right to do so in the future by virtue of s 57 of the Act. It is a threat to sue for infringement if the respondent is so minded on a future occasion. It is no less a threat that the respondent may not be so minded. The purpose of the letter is clearly to dissuade the recipients other than the applicant from buying tracking systems for conveyor belts from the applicant and to dissuade the applicant from offering such equipment for sale.

The threat is presently unjustified. It is not saved by the fact that rights may be obtained at some future time. Section 129 does not give a person a right to make threats if the circumstances provided for in paragraphs (a) or (b) of the section are made out; the section only operates as a statutory defence to proceedings against conduct which is otherwise unlawful (*Townsend Controls Pty Ltd v Gilread* (1989) 14 IPR 443 at 448; *Mechanical Services (Trailer Engineers) Ltd v Avon Rubber Co Ltd* (1977) RPC 66 at 74-75).

The onus of proving justification is on the patentee or the holder of the patent application. The onus of establishing invalidity of the patent, if such is alleged, lies on the applicant for relief. The respondent incorrectly, in my view, submits that:

"the respondent has a statutory defence to the claim of 'threats' pursuant to s 129(b) and s 57 of the *Patents Act 1990* in that the standard patent application has not been shown by the applicant to be invalid".

Likewise the submission that:

"It would be pointless for the Court to now grant an injunction against the continuance of any threats on the part of the Respondent as the Petty Patent has now been granted. Any relief claimed by the Applicant in relation to the alleged unjustified threats must now be limited to 'damages' of any loss suffered by it as a result of the alleged unjustified threats."

misunderstands the nature of the statutory cause of action and the operation of the onus on the respondent to negative the allegation that the threats are unjustifiable by establishing the circumstances in either (a) or (b) of s 129 of the Act.

▬▬▬▬   U and i Global Trading (Australia) v Tasman-Warajay *continued*

Because the market for this type of equipment in the coal industry is limited and because the threats have been made to all potential buyers, the impact of the threats is potentially very damaging. Further, the letter of 13 January must be placed in the context of express threats of proceedings for infringement in September, November and December 1994 which led to the undertaking being given on 16 December 1994. The reservation in that undertaking was "to notify persons of any pending patent application in respect of its training idler and the possible consequences of infringement". The letter of 9 January 1995 arguably goes substantially beyond that reservation and therefore is not saved by s 131 of the Act.

On the material before me it is not possible to determine the strength of any possible argument of justification. The expert evidence is divided as to whether the product sold by the applicant would infringe the claims of the invention claimed in Patent Application 645150 or Petty Patent 658110. Because of the nature of the market and the difficulty in obtaining evidence that purchasers would have dealt with the applicant but for the threats of the respondent, I am not persuaded that damages alone would be an adequate remedy. The conduct of the respondent has been to attempt to force the applicant out of the market or substantially limit its market share by threats and there is nothing on the material to persuade me that the respondent will not continue such conduct pending trial. The balance of convenience is in favour of making an order for interlocutory injunctive relief.

Note

[10.145] As to threats in relation to innovation patents see s 129A(1)-(2) .

The fact that the defendant honestly believed that the actions amounted to an infringement is not an excuse and the defendant must establish infringement unless the applicant can prove invalidity.

■ Exemplary damages in patent infringement

[10.150] Schedule 5 of the *Intellectual Property Laws Amendment Bill 2006* (Cth) proposes an amendment to s 122 of the *Patents Act* to allow exemplary damages to be awarded where the defendant has wilfully committed infringement. The proposal would provide an exemplary damages regime in patent law consistent with the approach found under the *Copyright Act 1968* (Cth), s 115 (4). In deciding whether to award exemplary damages a court must consider the flagrancy of the infringement, the need to deter similar infringements of the patents, the infringers conduct after the infringement or after being informed that he or she had allegedly infringed the patent, any benefit accruing to the infringer and any other relevant matters.

EXPLOITATION

■ Ownership

[10.155] Any person may make an application for a patent (s 29), but a patent can only be granted to a person who is the inventor, or is a person who would be entitled to have the patent assigned to them, derives title from the inventor, or is the legal representative of a deceased person entitled to the patent (s 15). The person to whom the patent is granted becomes the owner of a patent entered on the Patent Register.

Where a patent application is made nominating a person as an eligible person for grant, and that person is not in fact entitled to grant, the Commissioner has powers to deal with a number of possibilities which may arise in the course of the application, during opposition proceedings, arising from court proceedings or after revocation by the Commissioner to grant the patent to the person entitled (see ss 33-36). It is a ground of opposition to grant that the nominated eligible person is not entitled to the patent (s 59(a)).

Where a patent has been granted to a person who is not eligible for grant, the patent may be revoked under s 138(3)(a). The ground of revocation is referred to as "obtaining", where another has obtained the patent wrongfully.

Because inventions are frequently made by several people working together, there are provisions for co-ownership of patents. Two or more co-owners are each entitled to equal undivided shares of the patent. Each may exploit the patent without accounting to the others, but cannot grant a licence or assign an interest in the patent without the consent of the other (s 16(1)). Where one co-owner sells a product protected by a patent, the purchaser and successors in title may deal with the product as if it had been sold by all of the patentees (s 16(2)). The Commissioner has limited powers to give directions to co-owners in order to attempt to resolve disputes in relation to dealings with the patent, granting of licences and the exercise of exclusive rights (s 17).

A "person entitled to have a patent assigned" to them is most often an employer claiming the right to be granted a patent invented by an employee. In the absence of an agreement to the contrary, where a person is an employee, rather than an independent contractor, and the invention is made within the scope of the employees' duties, the employer will be entitled to the patent. This is usually explained by reference to an "implied term" in the contract of employment. See, for example, *Sterling Engineering Co Ltd v Patchet* [1955] AC 534. Another possibility is that the employee owes an obligation of good faith. Cf *Worthington Pumping Engine Co v Moore* (1902) 20 RPC 41 and *Charles Selz Ltd's Application* (1954) 71 RPC 158.

■ Assignment

[10.160] An assignment must be in writing and signed by or on behalf of the parties to the transaction (s 14(1)). Assignments of patent rights may be limited to a place or part of Australia (s 14(2)). The Act is silent as to "horizontal" dissection of rights (that is, splitting up the modes of exercising a patentee's rights; cf copyright). Assignments should be registered (reg 19.1) or the document is not admissible to prove the assignees interest, although exceptions exist in s 196.

■ Licences

[10.165] There may be exclusive licences, sole licences and non-exclusive licences. The *Patents Act 1990* (Cth) has no requirements as to formalities for a licence to be granted, but it is advisable for a licensee to register a licence in order to protect against the claims of a bona fide purchaser for value without notice, and to secure admissibility of evidence the agreement in court proceedings without difficulty (ss 187-189, 196).

Exclusive licence

[10.170] An exclusive licensee is defined in Sch 1, Dictionary to mean:

"a licensee under a licence granted by the patentee and conferring on the licensee, or on the licensee and persons authorised by the licensee, the right to exploit the patented invention throughout the patented area to the exclusion of the patentee and all other persons"

See *El Du Pont De Nemours v Commissioner of Patent (No 2)* (1989) 15 IPR 289, *Stack v Brisbane City Council* (1995) 32 IPR 69.

In a sole licence, patentee agrees to grant a licence to one person only.

Tying arrangements in licences

[10.175] *Patents Act 1990* (Cth), s 144 attempts to prevent tying arrangements requiring a licensee to deal exclusively with the licensor. The High Court has tended to take a restrictive view of s 112 (the equivalent of s 144 in the 1952 Act), but licensing arrangements must not fall foul of *Trade Practices Act 1974* (Cth), Part IV, and must not inhibit the Australian manufacturing industry: *Transfield Pty Ltd v Arlo International Ltd* (1980) 144 CLR 83. Too restrictive licensing arrangements may lead to the application of compulsory licences (s 133), or revocation for non-working (s 134).

Compulsory licences

[10.180] Chapter 12 of the *Patents Act 1990* (Cth) provides a regime of compulsory licences where a court may grant a licence on reasonable terms including remuneration. The patentee must have refused to grant a request for a licence and be failing to work the invention so as to meet the reasonable requirements of the public (see s 135). The system applies to standard patents and innovation patents. Courts have proved most reluctant to grant compulsory licences.

The orders must be in accordance with international agreements, and the TRIPs Agreement introduced a more complex approach to compulsory licence grant than obtained under the *Paris Convention*. The Declaration on the TRIPs Agreement and Public Health adopted by the WTO Fourth Session Ministerial Conference in Doha, Qatar on 14 November 2001, saw the grant of compulsory licences as a possible approach to the perceived difficulties with access to patented pharmaceuticals (para 5(b)), and the TRIPs Council was instructed to consider new arrangements for compulsory licences for WTO members with insufficient or no manufacturing capacities (para 6). A *Decision On The Implementation Of Paragraph 6 Of The Doha Declaration On Public Health The TRIPS Agreement And Public Health* was made on 30 August 2003 and published on 1 September 2003 at <www.wto.org/ English/tratop_e/trips_e/implem_para6_e.htm>.

The *Intellectual Property Laws Amendment Bill 2006* (Cth) proposes a new ground on which a person may apply for a compulsory licence. This is based on a new "competition test" to allow for the grant of a compulsory licence if the patentee has, in connection with the patent, engaged in anti-competitive conduct prohibited under Part IV of the *Trade Practices Act 1974* (Cth). Interestingly, this proposed amendment differs from the proposals on compulsory licences made in the IPCRC, *"Review of the Intellectual Property Legislation under the Competition Principles Agreement"* (the *"Ergas Report"*).

Other Intellectual Property Areas

PART **4**

CHAPTER 11

DESIGNS

INTRODUCTION

[11.05] For the past 100 years designs law has been the less glamorous cousin of other intellectual property regimes, protecting neither novel technology (the realm of patents) nor the products of our cultural lives (the realm of copyright). However, the role and status of design and designers in our lives has increased as academically trained designers have learned to fuse functionality with lifestyle to create, for instance, Philippe Starck kitchen utensils (manufactured by Alessi) or the Apple iPod with it's "golden mean" proportions (creating a design advantage over other MP3 players). "Design can be nothing more than eye candy, or it can change the world. Its reach is extraordinary and its imprint on our lives enormous. Design affects all of us, in one way or another, every day, even though we may fail to realise it most of the time".[1]

The Australian law governing rights in registered designs is contained in the *Designs Act 2003* (Cth). This Act replaces previous legislation, which was almost a century old. Although updated from time to time, with some significant changes made in 1981, for much of the 20th century designs law was not particularly relevant to design practice. For this reason, in 1995, the Australian Law Reform Commission (ALRC) published a report[2] (after an extensive review of designs law) and made recommendations for the enactment of a new designs regime to modernise and simplify existing legislation, and to remove difficulties that had arisen. The aim of this chapter is to give students of intellectual property an understanding of the scope of designs protection, an ability to recognise the subject matter, and the capacity to analyse the relationship with copyright law, particularly the Australian legislature's attempts to reduce "dual protection" which would otherwise confer a long term of copyright protection on mass-produced household and industrial items.

Historically, designs law is based on the *Patents, Designs & Trade Marks Act 1883* (46 & 47 Vict c 57), which in turn derived its design regulation aspects from a series of statutes, commencing with the *Designing & Printing of Linens (etc) Act 1787* (27 Geo 3, c 38), which initially conferred a two-month period of protection on designs for certain textiles. This precursor of the registered designs system began in response to England's loss of pre-eminence as a producer of industrial goods after the Industrial Revolution. Parliament, in an attempt to stimulate the local textile industry, conferred a "copyright" upon the owners of designs for linens, calicoes, cottons and muslins satisfying certain criteria of novelty and originality. This protection was extended to other textiles and in 1839 (2 & 3 Vict c 17) to any "article of manufacture" for the shaping and configuration thereof. The proprietors of the textile designs sought protection for their creativity, similar to that already conferred on the authors of books. In 1835 a parliamentary Select Committee was appointed to inquire into the best means of competing with the superiority of French industrial design, which was attributed to the encouragement and protection given by French law. The result of the Select Committee's findings was the Designs Acts of 1839 and 1842, influenced by French law and now forming the basis of the modern law. This emphasis on textile design is still important for developing economies and discussions surrounding the TRIPs Agreement have focused on designs for textiles. Quite apart from textile designs, clothing itself may be protected by designs legislation; indeed in 2005 the greatest number of design applications by any one company (103) were filed by fashion designers Scanlan&Theodore.[3]

The aim of design protection is to allow the designer to exclusively exploit their work for a period of time, while the community enjoys the benefits of having well-designed products, enhancing the beauty, safety and functionality of everyday life. The development of a marketable design may involve expense in developing prototypes, then tooling and laying down plant to produce the item. Not all good ideas succeed commercially, and as part of the cost of finished products reflects the risks taken by entrepreneurs, it is desirable to be able to

---

1   N Barraclough, SMH "Good Weekend" (16 June 2005), p 22.
2   ALRC, Designs, Report 74, (AGPS, 1995).
3   <www.ipaustralia.gov.au/>, "Design Statistics".

protect the investment made in producing a saleable design and prevent others moving straight into production of viable items. Product development and the design of new products is an important aspect of entrepreneurial effort in developed economies. Manufacturing has been identified as a key growth area for the Australian economy to complement the volatility of the market for primary sector exports from agriculture and mining. Manufactured products must appeal to the consumers who are going to buy them; design affects the "form, fit, feel and function of a product" and is not something that should be added on afterwards but paid attention from the outset. Important advantages that good design confers may be protected by registering new and distinctive designs.

Design registration may supplement patent rights but it is not a substitute, in that articles and technology as such are not protected, only the design features as explained above. On the other hand, design protection will be available for a product, which may not be patentable because it relies on known technology, but nevertheless has a new and distinctive appearance which can be monopolised by the owner of design rights. Recent examples of unpatentable but protected-design technology includes vacuum cleaner parts;[4] seals for pipes and equipment used in mining;[5] opaque glass bricks[6] and other accoutrement of everyday life such as light switches and power points, window locks, tapware, car parts and furniture.

The ALRC has stated that the primary objective of designs law is to encourage innovation in Australian industry for the country's net economic benefit, and is a key element in the innovation and marketing processes.[7] By way of illustration of how marketers regard effective design as important in selling a product, see the evidence in *Koninklijke Philips Electronics NV v Remington Products Australia Pty Ltd* (2000) 48 IPR 257, where electric shavers with a triple rotary head were sold on the basis of a "motoring theme"; "a 'masculine' association with a fantasy world of fast sports cars—Jaguars and Porches", with the three heads as three wheels.[8]

SUBJECT MATTER OF DESIGN REGISTRATION

■ Definition of "design"

▬▬▬ Designs Act 2003 (Cth), ss 5, 6 ▬▬▬

[11.10]

5 "design", in relation to a product, means the overall appearance of the product resulting from one or more visual features of the product.

...

6 (1) For the purposes of this Act, a thing that is manufactured or hand made is a product (but see subsections (2), (3) and (4)).

(2) A component part of a product may be a product for the purposes of this Act, if it is made separately from the product.

---

4   *Dyson Ltd v Qualtex (UK) Ltd* (2005) 65 IPR 188.
5   *Mining Equipment (Minquip) Pty ltd v Alfagamma Australia Pty Ltd* (2004) 64 IPR 237.
6   *Glass Block Constructions (Aust) Pty ltd v Armourglass Australia Pty Ltd* [2005] ADD 1 (6 Jan 2005).
7   ALRC, *Designs*, n 2, p 31.
8   At 279.

━━━━ Designs Act 2003 (Cth), ss 5, 6 *continued*

(3) A thing that has one or more indefinite dimensions is only a product for the purposes of this Act if any one or more of the following applies to the thing:
    (a) a cross-section taken across any indefinite dimension is fixed or varies according to a regular pattern;
    (b) all the dimensions remain in proportion;
    (c) the cross-sectional shape remains the same throughout, whether or not the dimensions of that shape vary according to a ratio or series of ratios;
    (d) it has a pattern or ornamentation that repeats itself.
(4) A kit which, when assembled, is a particular product is taken to be that product.

[11.15] The object of modern designs law is to protect the visual form ('overall appearance') of products (usually mass-produced goods) with exclusive rights for a limited term. The current definition borrows much of the language of the previous definition found in the *Designs Act 1906* (Cth) which was said to be specifically aimed at reserving "to the owner of the design the commercial value resulting from customers preferring the appearance of articles which have that design to that of those which do not have it": *AMP Inc v Utilux Pty Ltd* [1972] RPC 103 at 108 per Lord Reid. This appearance is created by the visual features of a product, defined as:

━━━ Designs Act 2003 (Cth), s 7 ━━━

[11.20]
7 (1) In this Act:
"visual feature", in relation to a product, includes the shape, configuration, pattern and ornamentation of the product.
(2) A visual feature may, but need not, serve a functional purpose.
(3) The following are not visual features of a product:
    (a) the feel of the product;
    (b) the materials used in the product;
    (c) in the case of a product that has one or more indefinite dimensions:
        (i) the indefinite dimension; and
        (ii) if the product also has a pattern that repeats itself—more than one repeat of the pattern.

[11.25] Designs law protects the look of a product, not the "fundamental form" of the product itself, which other manufacturers must be free to make and sell. Before 1981 there was considerable doubt as to whether any functional aspects of articles could be registered, even if they also had some "eye appeal", since there was deep suspicion of allowing monopolies to develop. Obviously protection of functionality may come close to protecting the basic form of a product and could be considered to extend the protection so as to monopolise the market for certain products. On the other hand, concentrating on protection of visual features is said to leave an "innovation gap" where some features of articles cannot get either patent or design protection—for example, pump parts or other machine components where the technology is not innovative enough for a patent (or the patent has expired) and the item, as part of a "cog" in a machine, lacks the visual features required for design registration. In some objects, the visual features may in fact constitute the functional features, for example key blanks; *Ramsay v Master Locksmiths Association of Australasia Ltd* (2004) 64 IPR 94.

The ALRC looked at the innovation threshold for design, which is confined to the *appearance* of an article, and decided against recommending extending the boundaries beyond visual appearance, in line with existing law: *Kestos v Kempat* (1935) 53 RPC 139; *Re Wolanski's Registered Design* (1953) 88 CLR 278; *Edwards Hot Water Systems v SW Hart & Co Pty Ltd* (1983) 49 ALR 605; *Weir Pumps Ltd & CML Pumps Ltd v Central Electricity Generating Board* (1983) 2 IPR 129. In an earlier version of the current Act (*Designs Bill 2001* (Cth)) "the mere colour of a product" was specifically excluded from being a visual feature, and the case law indicates that the colour of an article does not itself constitute a design: *Re Application by Bourjois Ltd* (1988) 11 IPR 625; *Application by Nigel Louez Graphic Design Pty Ltd* (1989) 15 IPR 570.

■ Designs must be new and distinctive

Designs Act 2003 (Cth), s 15(1)

[11.30]
15 (1)   A design is a *registrable design* if the design is new and distinctive when compared with the prior art base for the design as it existed before the priority date of the design.

[11.35] The novelty and distinctiveness is to be judged by looking at the overall impression in relation to the design. Section 19 sets out the factors to be considered in looking at the overall design. The previous case law prohibited from registration designs differing only in "immaterial details" (see *Re Calder Vale* (1934) 53 RPC 117 at 125 per Farwell J) or in "features commonly used in the relevant trade" (see *Dalgety Australia Operations Ltd v FF Seeley Nominees Pty Ltd* (1985) 5 IPR 97). However, the previous criteria of "new or original" were not onerous, thus "a small difference in appearance from the prior art is enough to give novelty": *Safe Sport Australia Pty Ltd v Puma Australia Pty Ltd* (1985) 4 IPR 120 at 125 per King J. The previous designs regime was criticised as having too low a standard of novelty and, correspondingly, infringement was therefore more difficult to establish where very minor changes were enough to take the copy outside of the scope of registration.

■ "New" designs have not been used or published

Designs Act 2003 (Cth), s 15(2)

[11.40]
15 (2)   The *prior art base* for a design (the *designated design*) consists of:
    (a) designs publicly used in Australia; and
    (b) designs published in a document within or outside Australia; and

━━━ Designs Act 2003 (Cth), s 15(2) *continued*

(c) designs in relation to which each of the following criteria is satisfied:
  (i)   the design is disclosed in a design application;
  (ii) the design has an earlier priority date than the designated design;
  (iii) the first time documents disclosing the design are made available for public inspection under section 60 is on or after the priority date of the designated design.

Note: For *document*, see section 25 of the *Acts Interpretation Act 1901*.

[11.45] The previous *Designs Act 1906* (Cth), s 20 provided for a statement of novelty which clarified what features or combinations thereof constitute novelty in the design. This was also useful in infringement proceedings to aid evaluation of the obviousness or fraudulence of an alleged imitation. The 2003 Act provides guidance on determining "substantial similarity of overall impression".

Prior publication or prior use of a design within Australia prevents it from being "new and distinctive" so as to be registrable. Section 15(2) (above) sets out the prior art base as including publication generally and through disclosure in an application for design registration.

What constitutes "publication" is not defined and has not always been clear even under the 1906 Act, however, the ALRC considered that advertising (and certainly selling) would amount to publication. In *Safe Sport Australia Pty Ltd v Puma Australia Pty Ltd* (1985) 4 IPR 120, it was suggested that showing a prototype to a buying organisation could amount to prior publication, in the absence of any suggestion of confidentiality. See also *Re Application by Baker & Priem (No 2)* (1989) 15 IPR 660; *Mining Equipment "Minquip" Pty Ltd v Alfagamma Australia Pty Ltd* (2005) 64 IPR 237; cf *Hall v Lewis* (2004) 64 IPR 61.

The *Designs Act 2003* (Cth), s 17 sets out previous disclosures of a design which are to be disregarded in deciding if the design is "new and distinctive". These include unauthorised publication and circumstances in which the design regulations exclude the publication from anticipating the rights. For example, some items are not registrable as designs, in which case it is left to copyright to provide protection. Typically items such as book jackets, calendars, labels, greetings cards, stamps and the like have copyright protection and do not require design registration.

━━━ **Designs Act 2003 (Cth), s 19** ━━━

[11.50]
19 Factors to be considered in assessing substantial similarity in overall impression
(1) If a person is required by this Act to decide whether a design is substantially similar in overall impression to another design, the person making the decision is to give more weight to similarities between the designs than to differences between them.
(2) The person must also:
  (a) have regard to the state of development of the prior art base for the design; and
  (b) if the design application in which the design was disclosed included a statement (a *statement of newness and distinctiveness*) identifying particular visual features of the design as new and distinctive:
    (i) have particular regard to those features; and

(ii) if those features relate to only part of the design—have particular regard to that part of the design, but in the context of the design as a whole; and

(c) if only part of the design is substantially similar to another design, have regard to the amount, quality and importance of that part in the context of the design as a whole; and

(d) have regard to the freedom of the creator of the design to innovate.

(3) If the design application in which the design was disclosed did not include a statement of newness and distinctiveness in respect of particular visual features of the design, the person must have regard to the appearance of the design as a whole.

(4) In applying subsections (1), (2) and (3), the person must apply the standard of a person who is familiar with the product to which the design relates, or products similar to the product to which the design relates (the "standard of the informed user").

(5) In this section, a reference to a person includes a reference to a court.

■ Designs law protects appearance, not the article itself

[11.55] Intellectual property laws are framed to allow competition in the marketplace while protecting that which is truly innovative. To this end, the distinction between a product and its appearance remains important under the 2003 legislation, but can be illustrated by an older case.

▰▰▰▰▰▰▰ Re Wolanski's Design ▰▰▰▰▰▰▰

[11.60] *Re Wolanski's Design* (1953) 88 CLR 278 High Court of Australia

KITTO J: **[279]** This is an application by motion on notice, asking that the registration of a design under the *Designs Act 1906-1950* (Cth) be cancelled. Several grounds are stated in the notice of motion, but the only jurisdiction of this court, as a court of first instance, to cancel the registration of a design is that which is created by s 28(a) of the Act, and under that section the only ground provided for is that the design has been published in the Commonwealth prior to the date of the registration, that is to say, prior to the date of the lodging of the application for registration: see ss 17, 26(2).

The design to which the application relates is registered in class 14 in respect of "neck-tie support", and the representation of it, appearing in the certificate of registration in evidence before me and consisting of drawings showing a front and rear view respectively depicts an article shaped so that, if covered with material of a kind of which ties are made, it will resemble the knot of a necktie which has been tied in the manner usually adopted by men. It is equipped with a projection at its back, sloping downwards from the top, by which it may be hooked on to the neckband of the wearer's shirt between the peaks of the collar. A piece of material is intended to be added so as to resemble the portion of a tie which normally falls from the knot. When the article thus produced is placed in position, the collar of the shirt will fall over and thus conceal the corner extremities of the pseudo-knot, and the illusion of a normally-tied tie will result.

Such is the function to be performed by the article for which the design is intended, but, for the purpose of deciding the case, I am not concerned with any question of function: *Hecla*

▰▰▰▰ Re Wolanski's Design *continued*

Foundry Co v Walker, Hunter & Co (1889) 14 App Cas 550. It is necessary to keep steadily in mind that that which is the subject of the impugned registration and is said to have been published before the date of registration is nothing but a design, applicable, as the definition in s 4 says, to the purpose of the ornamentation, or pattern, or shape, or configuration, of an article. It is not an article made according to a particular shape or pattern. Much less is it a method of making such an article, or a method of achieving an end by the use of such an article. It is a conception or suggestion as to shape, configuration, pattern or ornament: *Pugh v Riley Cycle Co Ltd* [1912] 1 Ch 613 at 619; and accordingly what the proprietor of a design gets by its registration is a monopoly for one thing only, and that is "one particular individual and specific appearance": Russell-Clarke on **[280]** *Copyright in Industrial Designs* (5th ed, 1930), p 17; *Kestos Ltd v Kempat Ltd* (1935) 53 RPC 139 at 151. In the present instance, the design is not one which is applicable to ornamentation or pattern; it is an idea of shape, or configuration, two words between which there is no need to draw.

APPLICATION FOR REGISTRATION

[11.65] The *Designs Act 2003* (Cth) deals with application and registration of designs in ss 20-61. An application will be examined to check compliance with formal requirements but, unlike the previous design regime, substantive examination on "new and distinctive" will only take place after registration unless requested earlier "by any person". The owner of the design will be "the entitled person" defined in s 13 as the creator (designer) or employer or other person to whom the rights have been assigned. "Designer" is not defined but is likely to be the copyright owner in the artistic work that is the basis of the design. The registration of a design by someone other than the owner is a ground for expungement of the registration. It may be difficult to decide the issue of ownership when the design is produced by co-operative effort or the question arises of authorship being exercised pursuant to an agreement for valuable consideration; see *Chris Ford Enterprises Pty Ltd v B H & JR Badenhop Pty Ltd* (1985) 4 IPR 485.

Co-ownership is dealt with in s 13 of the Act and in the event of a dispute the Registrar may make a determination as to who is entitled to the design (s 29). As with patents, the priority date is important in determining rights. The priority date is the date of application. The 2003 Act introduces an alternative to registration, which is publication, and an applicant must decide within six months whether to publish or obtain registration. Publication will not in itself provide protection against infringement but will prevent others subsequently registering the same design.

INFRINGEMENT

▰▰▰▰▰ **Designs Act 2003 (Cth), s 71** ▰▰▰▰▰

[11.70]
71(1)   A person infringes a registered design if, during the term of registration of the design, and without the licence or authority of the registered owner of the design, the person:

(a) makes or offers to make a product, in relation to which the design is registered,

━━ Designs Act 2003 (Cth), s 71 *continued*

> which embodies a design that is identical to, or substantially similar in overall impression to, the registered design; or
>
> (b) imports such a product into Australia for sale, or for use for the purposes of any trade or business; or
>
> (c) sells, hires or otherwise disposes of, or offers to sell, hire or otherwise dispose of, such a product; or
>
> (d) uses such a product in any way for the purposes of any trade or business; or
>
> (e) keeps such a product for the purpose of doing any of the things mentioned in paragraph (c) or (d).
>
> (2) Despite subsection (1), a person does not infringe a registered design if:
>
> (a) the person imports a product, in relation to which the design is registered, which embodies a design that is identical to, or substantially similar in overall impression to, the registered design; and
>
> (b) the product embodies the design with the licence or authority of the registered owner of the design.
>
> (3) In determining whether an allegedly infringing design is substantially similar in overall impression to the registered design, a court is to consider the factors specified in section 19.
>
> (4) Infringement proceedings must be started within 6 years from the day on which the alleged infringement occurred.

[11.75] In referring to "substantial similarity in overall impression", the *Designs Act 2003 (Cth)*, s 19 spells out in some detail guidance for the court in assessing this similarity (or otherwise). This is to address the perception that previously the scope of protection was construed extremely narrowly, with the result that only a minor variation in appearance is needed to avoid infringement of design rights: see *Foggin v Lacey* (2003) 57 IPR 225 at 231, where infringement "requires that there be no differences that the eye can detect" (per Moore and Bennett JJ).

Giving more weight to similarities than differences, even if they are only part of the product as a whole, may result in more findings of infringement than under the previous test of "imitation", obvious or fraudulent, where differences from a registered design may have been accorded too much weight in the view of some users who considered the previous test for infringement did not meet the needs of those seeking design protection.

In assessing the "new and distinctive" features, the court must apply the standard of "the informed user", being a person familiar with the product to which the design relates (s 19(4)).

The informed user standard is intended to introduce a more objective test for infringement. An example of the deficiencies of the previously narrowly applied test is *Koninklijke Philips Electronics NV v Remington Products Australia Ltd* (2000) 48 IPR 257 in which the features of a design (a "three wheeled" shaver) had been copied but due to differences of dimensions between the products, no infringement was found despite fairly blatant copying. Under the new test the distinctive aspects of the product would have to be given more weight in assessment of infringement. In fact, even under the previous legislation courts have on occasion been assisted by expert evidence in understanding design features in infringement cases: see *Dart Industries Inc v Décor Corp Pty Ltd* (1989) 15 IPR 403; *Gerard Industries Pty ltd v Auswide Import Export Pty Ltd* (1998) 40 IPR 119.

Section 71(1)(a) provides that infringement occurs if a person, without the "licence or authority" of the registered owner makes a product in relation to which the design is registered, which embodies a design that is identical to, or substantially similar in overall impression to, the registered design. Importing such a product into Australia for sale or any trade purpose, or using and keeping a product for a trade or business purpose, is also an infringement (s 71(1)). Action must be commended within six years of any alleged infringement (s 71(4)).

■ Spare parts defence

[11.80] A controversial defence to infringement has been included in the updated *Designs Act* to protect consumers by allowing reverse engineering of spare parts for motor vehicles. Section 72(1) provides that a registered design is not infringed if the product in relation to which a design is registered is a component part of a complex product; and the use of the design (or authorisation of use) is for the purpose of the repair of the complex product so as to restore its overall appearance in whole or part. A part that is custom designed to fit one make and model of car is usually "new and distinctive" enough to gain design protection. However, since this in fact allows monopolisation of the market for that part, the *Designs Act 2003* creates space for competing manufacturers. The background to the defence is discussed further below in the context of the design/copyright overlap debate, an area where the legislature and the courts have long grappled with issues of how to prevent domination of the market place by individual manufacturers.

JURISDICTION AND REMEDIES

[11.85] Jurisdiction to hear matters arising under the *Designs Act 2003* (Cth) is given to the prescribed courts by s 73(2), being the Federal Court (s 83) and State and Territory Supreme Courts (s 84). Remedies may include injunction, damages or account of profits but are not limited to these forms of relief (s 75(1)). The Court may reduce or refuse to award damages if the defendant was "innocent" in the sense of being unaware that a design was registered and had taken all reasonable steps to find out s 75(2). Additional damages are available for flagrant infringement (s 75(3)).

INTERNATIONAL PROTECTION

[11.90] Australia is a member of the *Paris Convention for the Protection of Industrial Property 1883*, which applies to industrial designs that are protected by countries in the Paris Union and provides for a "national treatment" of designs registered in member countries. There is provision under the *Hague Agreement concerning the International Deposit of Industrial Designs* for an international application for designs protection to be regarded as an equivalent to a national application. Australia is not a member of the Hague Agreement, but following the Singapore-Australia Free Trade Agreement 2003 where both countries agreed to comply with the powers of the Geneva Act of the Hague Agreement, the *Designs Regulations 2004* provide for recognition of an international deposit made pursuant to the agreement to be treated as an application made in Paris Convention countries which are party to it. Similarly, under the Australia-US Free Trade Agreement of 2005, each party committed to make its best efforts to comply with the provisions of the Hague Agreement.

OVERLAP WITH COPYRIGHT PROTECTION

■ Introduction

[11.95] One of the main issues in the design protection area is its relationship with copyright protection, as both regimes may protect the same subject matter, particularly where a "drawing" may be considered a design. The *Copyright Act 1968* (Cth), s 10 provides:

"'artistic work' means:
(a)   a painting, sculpture, drawing, engraving or photograph, whether the work is of artistic quality or not;
(b)   a building or a model of a building, whether the building or model is of artistic quality or not; or
(c)   a work of artistic craftsmanship whether or not mentioned in paragraph (a) or (b); but does not include a circuit layout within the meaning of the *Circuit Layouts Act 1989*."

In combination with the *Copyright Act 1968* (Cth), s 21(3) which provides that a version of an artistic work in another dimension will be deemed a reproduction of that work, the result is that the owner of copyright in an artistic work has, without the controls imposed by the *Designs Act 2003* (Cth), the power to control a large range of commercial applications of that work. This protection would arise at an indefinite point of time, and continue for the relatively long term given by the *Copyright Act 1968* (Cth), instead of the maximum 10 year period (dating from registration) allowed by the *Designs Act 2003* (Cth), s 46. Other advantages for the owner of copyright include the lack of formality required for protection and the international protection automatically acquired in other countries subscribing to intellectual property agreements to which Australia is a signatory. Remedies for infringement may be broader than those given under the *Designs Act 2003* (Cth), and include the possibility of damages for conversion in respect of infringing copies and exemplary damages. On the other hand, design protection confers a monopoly right on the owner of a design, thus avoiding the need to prove copying within copyright concepts.

The question of overlap and possible dual protection under both the designs and copyright regimes is partly philosophical, the issue being that one should not be allowed to exploit in an industrial setting the sort of artistic work normally afforded copyright protection. Other arguments against dual protection reflect the fact that intellectual property rights are an exception to a general rule. Since copyright protection is greater, and lasts almost indefinitely in terms of product marketing than design protection, it arguably confers too much power on design owners and their licensees. This may stultify progress and inhibit other designers and manufacturers from producing articles and new product lines (see the discussion in *Vacuum Cleaner Parts Dyson Ltd v Quiltex (UK) Ltd* (2005) 65 IPR 188). The sort of item which arguably begins life as an "artistic work" under the *Copyright Act 1968* (Cth) could include anything that can be registered as a design and obviously includes things of use and even importance in everyday life ranging from kitchenware and bathroom fittings, sporting goods, fashion accessories and apparel to furnishings and fabrics, toys as well as medical devices, hospital equipment, tools, spare parts and machinery, in fact, the whole range of manufactured articles.

■ Spare parts: Policy is against copyright protection

[11.100] Criticism of the effects of copyright law in protecting mass-produced items began with the House of Lords in *British Leyland Motor Corp v Armstrong Patents Co Ltd* [1986] FSR

221 where the majority decided that copyright protection should not be available for car exhaust systems. The original manufacturer of the exhaust systems had been able to ensure a lucrative market in spare parts by challenging the right of any other manufacturer to provide car owners and repairers with reverse engineered exhaust systems to fit Leyland cars. The reasoning of the Law Lords in *British Leyland* got around, rather than applied, the letter of copyright.

The Australian courts have not had a "spare parts exception" to copyright infringement case to decide, but the arguments are explored in *Warman International v Envirotech Australia Pty Ltd* ([**11.105**]). In that case a sales engineer working for a pump manufacturer had copied and used plans and information for pumps contained in certain publications, including the *Warman Data Book* and the *Warman Slurry Pumping Manual*. It was argued that any copyright in the drawings and manuals would not be infringed on the basis of the *British Leyland* case. The Court's response is set out below.

▬▬▬ Warman International v Envirotech Australia ▬▬▬

[11.105] *Warman International v Envirotech Australia Pty Ltd* (1986) 6 IPR 578 Federal Court of Australia

WILCOX J: **[598]** In relation to the merits of the copyright claim, counsel for the first, second and third respondents refer to the *British Leyland* case. That was an action by a manufacturer of motor cars to restrain the production by the defendant of replacement exhaust pipes designed to fit the plaintiff's cars. It was not suggested that the defendant had copied the original drawings, apparently it had followed a process of reverse engineering but it was said that the reproduction of the shape and dimensions of the original exhaust pipes indirectly infringed the plaintiff's copyright in the drawings from which they were produced.

The exhaust pipes were not registered under the *Registered Designs Act 1949* (UK) the members of the House of Lords apparently regarded the pipes as non-registrable because of lack of originality. The House proceeded upon the basis that the exclusion from copyright protection effected by the equivalent of our s 77 applied only to registrable designs. None the less, the defendant's appeal succeeded. By majority, the House upheld a submission that there was what Lord Edmund-Davies called a "spare parts exception" to the general rule protecting the copyright of a manufacturer. The exception was described by Lord Bridge of Harwich (2 WLR at 414) in these words:

> "The owner of **[599]** a car must be entitled to do whatever is necessary to keep it in running order and to effect whatever repairs may be necessary in the most economical way possible. To derive this entitlement from an implied licence granted by the original manufacturer seems to me quite artificial. It is a right inherent in the ownership of the car itself. To curtail or restrict the owner's right to repair in any way may diminish the value of the car."

Lord Templeman (at 421), with whom Lord Scarman expressly agreed, accepted a submission "that Parliament did not intend the protection afforded by copyright to a drawing should be capable of exploitation so as to prevent the reproduction of a functional object depicted on a drawing". But [he commented] there is a good deal of legislative and judicial history to be considered.

As Lord Templeman made clear, the problem confronting the House in *British Leyland* arose because of judicial decisions to the effect that it was an infringement of the copyright

▓▓▓▓▓▓ Warman International v Envirotech Australia *continued*

in a plan indirectly to copy that plan by the making of an article, combined with the failure of the UK Parliament to carry into effect a view expressed in 1952 by an expert committee the Gregory Committee that 'it should not be possible to protect under the *Copyright Act* more in the constructional or functional field than is protectable under the *Registered Designs Act*. His Lordship regarded it as anomalous that the owner of copyright in a drawing of a non-registrable article perhaps non-registrable because of the absence of novelty should be protected against the marketing by a competitor of a copy of that article, whilst the law denied copyright protection in a drawing of a registrable article. One method of eliminating this anomaly would have been to hold that the UK equivalent of s 77 of the *Copyright Act 1968* (Cth) applies to all unregistered articles, whether registrable or not. But the majority of the House took a different path, eliminating the anomaly within a limited area by creating an exception in respect of spare parts for durable goods.

The result achieved in *British Leyland* may fairly be described as remarkable; representing as it does a major qualification upon the scheme laid out wisely or unwisely under the UK copyright and designs legislation. If the relevant UK decisions commencing with *King Features Syndicate Inc v O & M Kleeman Ltd* [1941] AC 417, running through to *LB (Plastics) Ltd v Swish Products Ltd* [1979] RPC 551 and including *Dorling* were followed in Australia, the anomaly perceived by Lord Templeman would arise in this country. But it may be another matter whether there would be judicial intervention along the lines of *British Leyland*; especially having regard to the fact that parliament has dealt with the interrelationship between the *Copyright Act* and the *Designs Act* as recently as 1981. Whatever one may think of the adequacy of the solutions then adopted as to which see my comments in *Hutchence v South Sea Bubble Co Pty Ltd* (1986) 64 ALR 330 at 342-343 it cannot be denied that this inter-relationship is a matter to which Parliament has given its attention in recent times.

■ Legislative developments

[11.110] Despite the reluctance of Australian judges to apply a "spare parts exception", the Australian legislature has attempted to effect such a policy by eliminating the possibility of copyright protection for mass-market articles. This has resulted in an arcane, complex and uncertain legal regime due to the interaction of copyright and design law in preventing "dual protection". The issue of trying to remove copyright protection for the three dimensional form of a design is highly relevant to the issue of spare parts. During the *Designs* reference, the ALRC originally recommended a simpler regime, but with provision for referring potentially anti-competitive designs to the Australian Competition and Consumer Commission (ACCC) which would then assess whether the granting of design rights would have the effect of substantially lessening competition in a market. Potentially anti-competitive designs would have been identified by a number of characteristics; basically they would be components of a durable product—in other words, a spare part. These recommendations did not survive the public comment and government response following the ALRC *Designs Report*, and in any event the 2003 Act introduced the "spare parts defence" mentioned above whilst retaining the attempt to prevent dual protection through the interaction of designs and copyright concepts.

■ Prevention of "overlap" with design protection

[11.115] *Copyright Act 1968* (Cth), ss 74-77 are provisions to curtail what may be considered to be excessive copyright protection for designs (artistic works) which are mass-produced in a three-dimensional version. The *Designs (Consequential Amendments) Act 2003* was passed with the *Designs Act 2003* to amend the *Copyright Act* as necessary. The provisions apply mainly in the context of drawings that become the designs for manufactured articles, whether a hot water system pump, a spare part, a Harry Potter figurine, or any other manufactured item.

Copyright Act 1968 (Cth), s 74

[11.120] 74 Corresponding design
(1) In this Division:
"corresponding design", in relation to an artistic work, means visual features of shape or configuration which, when embodied in a product, result in a reproduction of that work, whether or not the visual features constitute a design that is capable of being registered under the *Designs Act 2003*.
(2) For the purposes of subsection (1):
"embodied in", in relation to a product, includes woven into, impressed on or worked into the product.

■ Copyright protection where corresponding design registered
[11.125] Subject to s 76, where copyright subsists in an artistic work (whether made before the commencement of this section or otherwise) and a corresponding design is or has been registered under the *Designs Act 1906* or the *Designs Act 2003* (on or after that commencement), it is not an infringement of that copyright to reproduce the work by embodying that, or any other, corresponding design in a product.

Copyright Act 1968 (Cth), s 77

[11.130] Application of artistic works as industrial designs without registration of the designs
77 (1) This section applies where:
    (a) copyright subsists in an artistic work (other than a building or a model of a building, or a work of artistic craftsmanship) whether made before the commencement of this section or otherwise;
    (b) a corresponding design is or has been applied industrially, whether in Australia or elsewhere, and whether before or after the commencement of this section, by or with the licence of the owner of the copyright in the place of industrial application; and
    (c) at any time on or after the commencement of this section, products to which the corresponding design has been so applied (the **products made to the corresponding design**) are sold, let for hire or offered or exposed for sale or hire, whether in Australia or elsewhere; and
    (d) that time, the corresponding design is not registrable under the Designs Act 2003 or has not been registered under that Act or under the Designs Act 1906.

(1A)   This section also applies if:

(a) a complete specification that discloses a product made to the corresponding design; or

(b) a representation of a product made to the corresponding design and included in a design application;

is published in Australia, whether or not paragraphs (1)(b) and (c) are satisfied in relation to the corresponding design.

(2) It is not an infringement of the copyright in the artistic work to reproduce the work, on or after the day on which:

(a) products made to the corresponding design are first sold, let for hire or offered or exposed for sale or hire; or

(b) a complete specification that discloses a product made to the corresponding design is first published in Australia; or

(c) a representation of a product made to the corresponding design and included in a design application is first published in Australia;

by embodying that, or any other, corresponding design in a product.

(3) This section does not apply in relation to any articles or products in respect of which, at the time when they were sold, let for hire or offered or exposed for sale or hire, the corresponding design concerned was excluded from registration by regulations made under the Designs Act 1906 or the Designs Act 2003 , and, for the purposes of any proceedings under this Act, a design shall be conclusively presumed to have been so excluded if:

(a) before the commencement of the proceedings, an application for the registration of the design under the Designs Act 1906 in respect of those articles, or under the Designs Act 2003 in respect of those products, had been refused;

(b) the reason, or one of the reasons, given for the refusal was that the design was excluded from registration under that Act by regulations made under that Act; and

(c) when the proceedings were commenced, no appeal against the refusal had been allowed or was pending.

(4) The regulations may specify the circumstances in which a design is, for the purposes of this section, to be taken to be applied industrially.

(5) In this section:

"building or model of a building" does not include a portable building such as a shed, a pre-constructed swimming pool, a demountable building or similar portable building.

"complete specification" has the same meaning as in the Patents Act 1990 .

"design application" has the same meaning as in the Designs Act 2003 .

"representation", in relation to a design, has the same meaning as in the Designs Act 2003.

━━━━━━━━━━ **Copyright Act 1968 (Cth), s 77A** ━━━━━━━━━━

[11.135] Certain reproductions of an artistic work do not infringe copyright
77A (1)It is not an infringement of copyright in an artistic work to reproduce the artistic work, or communicate that reproduction, if:
- (a) the reproduction is derived from a three dimensional product that embodies a corresponding design in relation to the artistic work; and
- (b) the reproduction is in the course of, or incidental to:
    - (i) making a product (the **non infringing product**), if the making of the product did not, or would not, infringe the copyright in the artistic work because of the operation of this Division; or
    - (ii) selling or letting for hire the non infringing product, or offering or exposing the noninfringing product for sale or hire.
(2) It is not an infringement of copyright in an artistic work to make a cast or mould embodying a corresponding design in relation to the artistic work, if:
- (a) the cast or mould is for the purpose of making products; and
- (b) the making of the products would not infringe copyright because of the operation of this Division.

━━━━━━━━━━━━━━━━━━━━━━━━━━━━━━━━━━━━━━

SUMMARY

[11.140] In summary the *Copyright Act 1968* (Cth), ss 74-77 setup the following regime; if a design is registered, the drawing that relates to the design (the "corresponding design": s 74) will lose copyright protection *when used as a design* (s 75). If a design is not registered, but is "industrially applied", that drawing will lose design protection and will not have copyright protection either (when used as a design) (s 77). The registration or use of the design must be done by or with the permission of the owner of the rights (ss 76, 77).

Another issue that affects the scope of design protection is not overlap but the "gap" in protection created when certain products are excluded from registration, such as designs, and also excluded from copyright protection through the underlying drawings (corresponding design). This is due to the operation of *Copyright Act 1968* (Cth), which disallows copyright protection for unregistered designs. If those designs are also unregistrable, there is no formal intellectual property protection. Functional innovations not sufficiently inventive under the patent system to warrant protection will fall into this category. It is expected that the innovation patent should help fill the "gap". However, there is no prohibition in Australia against copying another's product as such: *Parkdale Custom Built Furniture Pty Ltd v Puxu Pty Ltd* (1982) 42 ALR 1; see also *Koninklijke Philips Electronics v Remington Products Australia Pty Ltd* (2000) 48 IPR 257.

CHAPTER 12

CONFIDENTIAL INFORMATION

INTRODUCTION

[12.05] Valuable information may be difficult to protect unless it is packaged in a form recognised as intellectual property, given that Australian courts have resisted inventing new torts to protect privacy, personality or other rights not distinctly acknowledged as within the boundaries of copyright, patent or design law. However, an action based on confidential information may be available to protect a range of material, whether a "trade secret", personal, or otherwise sensitive information. Although it is true to say that the bulk of confidence cases involve trade secrets such as manufacturing techniques, customer lists, engineering designs and marketing procedures, the action developed around the protection of personal information although this is not to say it ever amounted to a positive right to privacy. However, recently developments overseas, for example, the introduction of human rights legislation in Europe, have required existing causes of action to evolve to embrace rights such a privacy not previously recognised by common law.

Apart from personal or business information, breach of confidence may protect government information and group interests such as sensitive or sacred knowledge. Beginning in the 1970s, legislation to protect "cultural heritage" was passed by some States[1] to protect heritage beyond that embodied in archaeological sites or artefacts. However, this and other legislation has been found to be inadequate in dealing with essential aspects of indigenous culture, such as the need for consultation with Aboriginal custodians of knowledge, the restrictions on information which are part of the preservation of the cultural heritage, and the aspects of spirituality and belief which require confidentiality[2] although in *Foster v Mountford* (1976) 14 ALR 71, the law of confidence was used to protect oral Aboriginal tribal secrets when copyright was unavailable in the absence of a recognised "work in material form".

There are some international obligations in respect of the protection of information although these obligations are framed in terms of existing protection and do not extend to "ideas" as such; these are generally under a general prohibition on "unfair competition". TRIPs Agreement, Art 39(1) requires members to provide protection against unfair competition and in doing so to protect undisclosed information and data submitted to government or governmental agencies. Paris Convention, Art 10*bis* is entitled "Unfair Competition" and prohibits conduct which would be described as passing off. Australia considers that it meets these obligations through a combination of laws.

Countries belonging to the English common law tradition generally provide protection for valuable information through a mixture of judge-made legal doctrines. A combination of the equitable action for breach of confidence, breach of fiduciary obligation, breach of contract and some other secondary actions are used. Recognition of a general tort of unfair competition was rejected by the High Court in *Moorgate Tobacco Co Ltd v Philip Morris Ltd* (1984) 156 CLR 414, 3 IPR 545; however, Australia's unfair competition laws include the common law actions of passing off, injurious falsehood, defamation (including what used to be called slander of goods and slander of title), unconscionability and the statutory enactments which prohibit misleading and deceptive conduct. The *Trade Practices Act 1974* (Cth) has a number of sections dealing with these matters.

It is now generally accepted that the action to restrain breach of confidence has borrowed from a number of areas to become a sui generis action, the basis of which is the principle that "A person ought to keep a secret if he has said that he will do so. In recent decisions English courts have translated this simple moral precept into a legal principle of considerable breadth".[3] The elements of the "moral precept" in the form of the action for breach of confidence are dealt with below and this chapter sets out how the law will provide protection against unauthorised use or disclosure of personal and private information where all of the traditional elements of the cause of action can be proven. However, the law of confidence does not operate as a general common law action against all invasions of privacy.

In the United Kingdom in a series of recent decisions the superior courts have been examining the interaction between the action for breach of confidence and the requirements of the *Human Rights Act 1998* (UK) which seeks to implement obligations under the European

---

1   For example, *Aboriginal Heritage Act 1972* (WA).
2   Evatt, E, "Review of the Aboriginal and Torres Strait Islander Heritage Protection Act 1996", cited in Sackville R, "Symposium: Traditional Knowledge, Intellectual Property and Indigenous Culture: Legal Protection of Indigenous Culture in Australia" (2003) 11 Cardozo J Int & Comp Law 711, 728.
3   Cornish and Llewellyn, *Intellectual Property: Patents, Copyright, Trade Marks and Allied Rights* (5th ed, Sweet and Maxwell, London).

Convention on Human Rights. These cases include *Douglas and others v Hello! Ltd* [2001] 2 All ER 289 CA; *Venables and another v News Group Newspapers Ltd and others* [2001] 1 All ER 908, *A v B* [2002] 3 WLR 542 CA and *Campbell v MGN* [2002] EWCA Civ 1373.

In *Douglas v Hello! Ltd* two celebrities objected to publication of "unauthorised" photos of their wedding. Selby LJ doubted that the surreptitious obtaining of personal information would always be protected by the action for breach of confidence even if the information were of a confidential nature. He was concerned about the requirement that an obligation of confidence should exist between the parties and, reflecting upon the artificiality of finding such a relationship in cases of snooping, paparazzi photographs or by way of found material, speculated that a more general tort of interference with privacy might be required. He said

> "I would conclude, at lowest, that [counsel for the plaintiffs] has a powerfully arguable case to advance at trial that his two first-named clients have a right of privacy which English law will today recognise and, where appropriate, protect. To say this is in my belief to say little, save by way of a label, that our courts have not said already over the years. ...
>
> What a concept of privacy does, however, is accord recognition to the fact that the law has to protect not only those people whose trust has been abused but those who simply find themselves subjected to an unwanted intrusion into their personal lives. The law no longer needs to construct an artificial relationship of confidentiality between intruder and victim: it can recognise privacy itself as a legal principle drawn from the fundamental value of personal autonomy."

The existence of such a tort was rejected in *Wainwright v Home Office* [2003] 4 All ER 969.

A majority the House of Lords in *Campbell v MGN Ltd* [2005] UKHL 61 found that where private or personal information was of a confidential nature it could indeed be protected from unauthorised publication even where it had been obtained in a surreptitious fashion. This was in keeping with the broad formulation of the equitable obligation by Lord Goff in *Attorney General v Guardian Newspapers Ltd (No 2)* [1990] 1 AC 109 at 281.

In *Australian Broadcasting Corporation v Lenah Game Meats Pty Ltd* (2001) 208 CLR 199, (2002) 54 IPR 161, the High Court of Australia declined to grant a remedy purely on the basis that information had been obtained through what might be considered "unconscionable actions" even involving allegedly unlawful conduct. In this case the plaintiff's were attempting to prevent the ABC from broadcasting film of the process used to slaughter possums for game meat. The film had been taken by animal rights activists and it was alleged that their activities were both surreptitious and involved a trespass and break in to plaintiffs property. However, the High Court found that there was nothing that was clearly information of a confidential nature to protect and so the action for breach of confidence did not apply. The judges observed that the plaintiff would need to ground an action in a general tort designed to protect against the invasion of the privacy and the case contains some speculation that it might be time for the common law to recognise such an action.

TYPES OF VALUABLE COMMERCIAL INFORMATION

■ Advances in technology

[12.10] A number of industries have little physical infrastructure but rely heavily on intellectual property as the main business asset; this is true of the biotechnology and computer industries. "Biotechnology" refers to the use of biological material having functions in industrial applications. Animal and plant cells, enzymes, plasmids and viruses as well as the use of genetic information provide the basis of many advances in safeguarding human and animal health and in agriculture. A type of monopoly right with regard to new plant varieties not used for food or animal fodder crops is allowed for in the *Plant Breeders Rights Act 1994* (Cth) but application of patent law to biotechnology has proven to be fraught for reasons ranging from questions of basic patentability to "concerns about exclusive licensing of patents related to genetic tests ... impact on costs, access to testing, the quality of testing, and innovation in the development of new or improved testing techniques."[4]

The Australian biotechnology industry comprises a mix of small, medium and large local firms and also multinational enterprises.[5] A typical aspect of the biotech sector is the small start-up company that develops a particular technology or application and is then bought by a larger concern.

Similarly to the biotech sector, key employees in computing industries often obtain access to an employer's confidential business information, and form a skilled and highly mobile work force sought after by competing firms to whom the previously acquired knowledge may be invaluable. Apart from the uncertainties of the operation of the *Copyright Act 1968* (Cth) in protecting software, the industry to date has relied upon innovation and development to retain a competitive lead. In such an environment rules protecting confidentiality are of greater importance than the clumsy operation of a statutory regime which is expensive to engage with and may even operate to destroy the intellectual property it is intended to protect.

Disclosure of the claimed invention is a feature of the patent system. Patent protection of biological material involving micro-organisms requires the deposit of the micro-organisms in a culture collection in order to disclose the invention so as to satisfy the requirement of patent legislation and that there be consideration moving to the public, being the revelation of a beneficial secret in exchange for a period of monopoly protection. *Patents Act 1990* (Cth), s 40(3) and (5) provide that where an invention involves the use, modification or cultivation of a micro-organism, and a person skilled in the art could not reasonably be expected to perform the invention without having a sample of the micro-organism, then the organism must be lodged with a prescribed depository institution, along with all relevant information about the characteristics of the organism known to the applicant for the patent. Such disclosure is regarded by some as too extensive, "super disclosure" in fact, leaving the owner of the micro-organism nothing to sell in the form of "know-how". Costs to second entrants to industries where know-how rather than equipment is a major ingredient are only a small percentage of the original developer's costs, which makes the information a valuable asset and requires firms to protect it while at the same time exploiting it and training personnel in the "secret" art.

The action for breach of confidence may be used to ensure that rivals do not obtain information of advantage to them on a competitive basis, and also to restrain employees setting up on their own account from using information "owned" by their former employer. Contractual provisions based on an understanding of confidentiality will be enforceable as long as the provisions do not amount to a restraint of trade. The dimensions of a permissible "non-compete" clause in a contract of employment are established by the principles discussed below in the *Ansell* case, see **[12.70]**.

■ Customer lists and business strategies

[12.15] It is not only high-tech industries which have secrets to protect. Historically, the most commonly litigated trade secret issues have involved customer lists, starting with cases from

---

4   ALRC, *Genes and Ingenuity: Gene Patenting and Human Health*, Report 99 (June 2004), p 21.
5   ALRC, *Genes and Ingenuity: Gene Patenting and Human Health*, Report 99 (June 2004), p 403.

the 19th Century. See, for example, *Robb v Green* [1895] 2 QB 315. Companies spend time and money developing and maintaining customer lists and obviously do not want departing employees taking these lists and using them in competition with the former employer by poaching customers: *NP Generations Pty Ltd v Feneley* (2001) 52 IPR 563. Other types of protectable business information may overlap with customer lists, for example, details of sales volume, but may also be independently valuable. A list that is supplied by one company but then added to through the efforts of another company's marketing campaign may become the property of the second party: *American Express v Thomas* (1990) 19 IPR 574.

Prices, sales forecasts, supply sources, merchandising data and relevant financial information may all be protected as trade secrets. The classic case on this is *Robb v Green* [1895] 2 QB 315 where the defendant copied a list of customer's names and addresses from his employer's order book, intending to and then using the list to solicit orders from those customers after he set up his own business. That case was decided on the basis that it was a breach of the obligation to observe good faith towards the employer under the contract of service to copy out a customer list while still employed. Neither does it matter that the list (or other information) is not written down but simply remembered as long as a conscious effort is made to retain the information. In *Coral Index Ltd v Regent Index Ltd* [1970] RPC 147, the plaintiff company alleged a former employee had wrongfully used lists of the plaintiff company's customers to solicit business for his new employer. Stamp J found that the names and addresses of a number of customers had become lodged in the defendant's memory as a natural result of having been the plaintiff's office manager for several years, and no conscious attempt to make a mental list of them had been made, in which case information had become part of the defendant's own knowledge and skill. Even when information in the list could have been obtained from other sources the rule is that former employees may not make use of the convenient compilation provided by the employer's business records: see *Roger Bullivant v Ellis* [1978] FSR 172; *Dowson & Mason Ltd v Potter* [1986] 2 All ER 418.

Sophisticated versions of "customer lists" such as marketing techniques and procedures or names of suppliers and supply chain strategies may also be trade secrets: see *Woolworths Ltd v Olson* (2004) 63 IPR 258. In *Thomas Marshall (Exports) Ltd v Guinle* [1978] 3 All ER 193, the plaintiff company was a manufacturer and marketer of textiles and clothing for supply to large chain stores in the United Kingdom. The defendant was the managing director of the company, and had solicited orders from the company's customers while filling those orders with goods from the company's suppliers, but none of the profits from these transactions went to the company. This behaviour amounted to gross and repeated breaches of the contractual obligation of fidelity owed to the company as a consequence of the service agreement with the defendant, which prohibited the disclosure of confidential information. Although he had "used" but not necessarily "disclosed" confidential information and was therefore not in breach of the express terms of the contract, Megarry V-C identified various forms of information which were capable of being confidential (at 210):

> "They are the names and telex addresses of the company's manufacturers and suppliers and their individual contracts; the negotiated prices paid by the company; the names of some overseas buying agents through whom the company deals; the company's new ranges, actual or proposed; information as to the requirements (such as styles) of the company's customers; details of the company's current negotiations; negotiated prices paid by customers to the company; the company's samples; and the company's current 'fast-moving' lines. ... Even in the Eastern European countries with state monopolies, a knowledge of the particular officials with whom business can most satisfactorily be done may be an important and confidential matter; and in the Far

East, with many rival sources of supply, a detailed knowledge of the cheapest, most reliable and most efficient sources must be something that a skilled buyer would firmly keep to himself as a valuable asset."

In recent years, the courts have been called upon to distinguish between so-called "marketing strategies" for which trade secret status has been claimed and a mere method of doing business which is not protected. A good example of this is *Independent Management Resources Pty Ltd v Brown* (1986) 9 IPR 1. In that case, the Victorian Metropolitan Fire Brigade (MFB) hired a public relations consultant (the plaintiff) to help persuade companies to install an improved fire alarm. The plaintiff set out its "marketing strategy" and employed two "project detailers" to implement the strategy. After some months the MFB decided to call for tenders as the plaintiff's plan was rather expensive (due to a 100% profit margin, as later became apparent). The defendant had been a "project detailer" under the plaintiff's scheme and she left the job and successfully tendered for the contract, upon which the plaintiff sued her for breach of duties of fidelity and/or confidence. It was held that she had not undermined her position of trust towards her employer, and the so-called confidential information lacked the necessary quality of confidence, being no more than the application of common sense to the tasks at hand, constituting only general knowledge, which could be used in competition against the former employer. Marks J had this to say about the marketing strategy (at 3-4):

"[T]he plaintiff's plan, although dressed up in the language of the public relations industry and stretched out with double spacing over several pages, amounted in its bare essentials to no more than personal contact by two persons with the MFB clients, diplomatic explanation aided, where appropriate, by ... visual aids ... and obtaining signatures to a contract. The so-called 'strategy' was thus of the simplest kind and required little or no expertise, merely selection of personable employees, supervision and monitoring per media weekly reports of progress. It was such an employee, which the defendant became, who received the somewhat fancy nomenclature 'project detailer'."

The dividing line between confidential information and the employee's natural accretion of knowledge and understanding will be discussed below.

■ Formulae and recipes

[12.20] One of the first English trade secret cases seems to have been *Newbery v James* (1817) 35 ER 1011, which concerned a secret formula for pills for the treatment of gout and rheumatism, as well as certain pills known as "Analyptic Pills". This formula was thought so valuable that the plaintiff tried to restrain the defendant from revealing the "secret, art or mystery of making or preparing any of the said medicines". In the event, no relief was granted as the pills had previously been the subject of a patent which had expired and since the patent specification revealed details of the invention there was no secret to protect.

As information becomes available on the internet and the formula for most things is easily obtained, the ingredients themselves may not be secret but the effort in thinking up and trialling the possible uses to which familiar components can be applied may require a period of market exclusivity for the originator in order to recoup the investment. For example, extensive litigation occurred concerning an arthritis cure using green mussels: *Aquaculture Corp v New Zealand Green Mussel Co Ltd* (1985) 5 IPR 353; (1988) 10 IPR 319; (1990) 19 IPR 527. This case may be regarded as a case protecting the technique (for making a preparation for treating rheumatoid arthritis from freeze-dried mussels) as well as protecting the "formula"; information about the process concerning the identification and isolation of the active ingredient.

■ Plans and machinery

[12.25] Improvements to machinery for making rubber gloves were protected in *Ansell Rubber v Allied Rubber Industries* [1967] VR 37 (see **[12.70]**) even though they may not have been patentable, being too slight an advance on the existing art to satisfy the requirements of patent legislation as to "novelty" and "non-obviousness" of inventions; however, patentable inventions may also be protected as confidential information. In *Seager v Copydex* [1967] 1 WLR 923, the defendants applied for a patent for a new type of carpet grip based partly on information provided by the plaintiff. In *Speed Seal Products Ltd v Paddington* [1986] 1 All ER 91, Mr Paddington, an engineer, had been employed by the plaintiff company on its coupling design committee. After leaving and setting up his own company Paddington applied for patents for couplings for use on pipes at oil rigs and jetties. There was no doubt that he was using confidential information acquired in the course of carrying out his duties on the committee.

Business manuals and drawings are prima facie suitable material for protection, particularly if the applicants for an injunction regarded them as valuable and confidential: *Warman International v Envirotech Australia Pty Ltd* (1986) 6 IPR 578. In that case there was also the possibility of copyright protection for drawings and manuals, as well as a serious question to the tried as to conduct contravening *Trade Practices Act 1974* (Cth), s 52, which prohibits corporations in trade or commerce engaging in misleading or deceptive conduct. Even if there are no other avenues of protection available, however, an obligation of confidence may arise from the delivery of drawings to a defendant for a particular purpose. In *Saltman Engineering Co Ltd v Campbell Engineering Co Ltd* (1948) 65 RPC 203, the plaintiffs had given the defendants drawings of tools so that the defendants could manufacture the tools for them. The defendants began making and selling these tools on their own account, breaking the obligation of confidence by using the drawing for purposes other than those for which they were confided to them.

■ Entertainment industry

[12.30] Ideas in the entertainment field may need protection at the "concept" stage before being "reduced to material form" suitable for copyright protection, notably in cases where ideas for programs (for various media, whether free-to-air television, subscription services or computer streaming) are developed and formats are increasingly being regarded as a form of valuable property which can be sold or licensed around the world, for example, docusoaps such as Popstars, and reality gameshows like Big Brother.[6]

A number of cases have found for plaintiffs whose ideas have been "pitched" to a media proprietor and subsequently used without their permission; see *Talbot v General Television* [1980] VR 224; *Fraser v Thames Television* [1984] QB 44; *Wilson v Broadcasting Corp of New Zealand* (1988) 12 IPR 173.

■ Personal relationships

[12.35] The recognition of a form of commercial "property" has been slower to develop than the concept of protection for individual secrecy and to a large extent, the elements of that action for breach of confidence have been framed in terms of personal relationships: see *Argyll v Argyll* [1967] Ch 302, discussed in *Coco v AN Clark* ([**12.45**]). This approach does not see information as a form of property in itself but stresses the impropriety of using or disclosing information learnt in the course of a relationship between the parties without the permission

---

6   See J Roscoe and G Hawkins, "New Television Formats" (2001) 100 *Media International Australia* 1.

of the person who is entitled to keep the information secret. In most of the cases in this model the courts are concerned with enforcing the conditions of the relationship between the parties. The issue of preventing publication of surreptitiously obtained material (such as photographs of celebrities in private or compromising situations) is discussed in recent English cases *Douglas and others v Hello! Ltd* [2001] 2 All ER 289 CA; *Venables and another v News Group Newspapers Ltd and others* [2001] 1 All ER 908, *A v B* [2002] 3 WLR 542 CA, and *Campbell v MGN* [2002] EWCA Civ 1373 and by the High Court in *Australian Broadcasting Corporation v Lenah Game Meats Pty Ltd* (2001) 208 CLR 199, (2002) 54 IPR 161.

ELEMENTS OF THE ACTION

[12.40] Because, perhaps, of the wide range of communication protectable by the action for breach of confidence the courts have had difficulty in framing the action according to the classifying of information by type (although some general outlines can be drawn up to identify the sort of information which may be "confidential") and have looked instead to the behaviour of the parties. The classic formulation of the conditions to be satisfied before an action can succeed is found in the following case.

▬▬▬▬▬▬▬▬   Coco v AN Clark (Engineers)   ▬▬▬▬▬▬▬▬

[12.45] *Coco v AN Clark (Engineers) Ltd* [1969] RPC 41 Chancery Division

[The plaintiff entered into negotiations with the defendant for the production on a joint venture basis of a moped designed by the plaintiff. The negotiations broke down and the defendants proceeded to produce mopeds on their own account which the plaintiff claims involved a breach of confidence.]

MEGARRY J: Mr Mowbray bases himself on the defendant company's misuse of information given to the company under circumstances of confidence. The essence of his case is breach of confidence. He expressly disclaims any contention that he could enjoin mere copying such as might have occurred if the Coco had been manufactured and put on the market by the plaintiff, and the defendant company had then bought one of them, dismantled it and slavishly copied it. Mr Mowbray says that what happened here was that the plaintiff supplied confidential information to the defendant company for one particular purpose, namely, a joint venture in producing the Coco, and that for the defendant company to use this information for its own purposes, without the plaintiff's consent is a breach of confidence. The argument before me has fallen under two main heads: first, whether there has been any breach of the obligation of confidence, and, secondly, whether the case is one where an injunction ought to be granted. I will consider these two heads in turn.

The equitable jurisdiction in cases of breach of confidence is ancient: confidence is the cousin of trust. The *Statute of Uses 1535* is framed in terms of "use, confidence or trust;" and a couplet, attributed to Sir Thomas More, Lord Chancellor avers that:

> "Three things are to be helpt in Conscience;
> Fraud, Accident and things of Confidence."

See I Rolle's *Abridgement* 274. In the middle of the last century, the great case of *Prince Albert v Strange* (1849) 2 De G & Sm 652; 64 ER 293 reasserted the doctrine. In the case before me, it is common ground that there is no question of any breach of contract, for no contract ever

▓▓▓▓▓ Coco v AN Clark (Engineers) *continued*

came into existence. Accordingly, what I have to consider is the pure equitable doctrine of confidence, unaffected by contract. Furthermore, I am here in the realms of commerce, and there is no question of any marital relationship such as arose in *Duchess of Argyll v Duke of Argyll* [1967] Ch 302. Thus limited what are the essentials of the doctrine?

In my judgment, three elements are normally required if, apart from contract, a case of breach of confidence is to succeed. First, the information itself, in the words of Lord Greene MR in the *Saltman* case (at 215), must "have the necessary quality of confidence about it." Secondly, that information must have been imparted in circumstances importing an obligation of confidence. Thirdly, there must be an unauthorised use if that information to the detriment of the party communicating it. I must briefly examine each of these requirements in turn.

First, the information must be of a confidential nature. As Lord Greene said in the *Saltman* case (at 215): "something which is public property and public knowledge" cannot per se provide any foundation for proceedings for breach of confidence. However confidential the circumstances of communication, there can be no breach of confidence in revealing to others something which is already common knowledge. But this must not be taken too far. Something that has been constructed solely from materials in the public domain may possess the necessary quality of confidentiality; for something new and confidential may have been brought into being by the application of the skill and ingenuity of the human brain. Novelty depends on the thing itself, and not upon the quality of its constituent parts. Indeed, often the more striking the novelty, the more common-place its components. Mr Mowbray demurs to the concept that some degree of originality is requisite. But whether it is described as originality or novelty or ingenuity or otherwise I think there must be some product of the human brain which suffices to confer a confidential nature upon the information: and, expressed in those terms, I think that Mr Mowbray accepts the concept.

The difficulty comes, as Lord Denning, MR pointed out in the *Seager* case (at 931), when the information used is partly public and partly private; for then the recipient must somehow segregate the two and, although free to use the former, must take no advantage of the communication of the latter. To this subject I must in due course return. I must also return to a further point, namely, that where confidential information is communicated in circumstances of confidence the obligation thus created endures, perhaps in a modified form, even after all the information has been published or is ascertainable by the public; for the recipient must not use the communication as a springboard: see the *Seager* case (at 931, 933). I should add that, as shown by *Cranleigh Precision Engineering Ltd v Bryant* [1965] 1 WLR 1293 at 1309-1310; [1966] RPC 81, the mere simplicity of an idea does not prevent it being confidential. Indeed, the simpler an idea, the more likely it is to need protection.

The second requirement is that the information must have been communicated in circumstances importing an obligation of confidence. However secret and confidential the information, there can be no binding obligation of confidence if that information is blurted out in public or is communicated in other circumstances which negative any duty of holding it confidential. From the authorities cited to me, I have not been able to derive any very precise idea of what test is to be applied in determining whether the circumstances import an obligation of confidence. In the *Argyll* case (at 330) Ungoed-Thomas J concluded his discussion of the circumstances in which the publication of marital communications should be restrained as being confidential by saying "If this was a well-developed jurisdiction doubtless there would be guides and tests to aid in exercising it." In the absence of such guides or tests he then in effect concluded that part of the communication there in question would on any reasonable test emerge as confidential. It may be that that hard-worked creature, the

▬▬▬▬ Coco v AN Clark (Engineers) *continued*

reasonable man, may be pressed into service once more; for I do not see why he should not labour in equity as well as at law. It seems to me that if the circumstances are such that any reasonable man standing in the shoes of the recipient of the information would have realised that upon reasonable grounds the information was being given to him in confidence, then this should suffice to impose upon him the equitable obligation of confidence. In particular, where information of commercial or industrial value is given on a business-like basis and with some avowed common object in mind, such as a joint venture or the manufacture of articles by one party for the other, I would regard the recipient as carrying a heavy burden if he seeks to repel a contention that he was bound by an obligation of confidence: see the *Saltman* case (at 216). On that footing, for reasons that will appear, I do not think I need explore this head further. I merely add that I doubt whether equity would intervene unless the circumstances are of sufficient gravity; equity ought not to be invoked merely to protect trivial tittle-tattle, however confidential.

Thirdly, there must be an unauthorised use of the information to the detriment of the person communicating it. Some of the statements of principle in the cases omit any mention of detriment: others include it. At first sight, it seems that detriment ought to be present if equity is to be induced to intervene; but I can conceive of cases where a plaintiff might have substantial motives for seeking the aid of equity and yet suffer nothing which could fairly be called detriment to him, as when the confidential information shows him in a favourable light but gravely injures some relation or friend of his whom he wishes to protect. The point does not arise for decision in this case, for detriment to the plaintiff plainly exists. I need therefore say no more than that although for the purposes of this case I have stated the propositions in the stricter form, I wish to keep open the possibility of the true proposition being that in the wider form.

Note

[12.50] The elements enunciated by Megarry J in *Coco v AN Clark* have gained general acceptance. In fact, one commentator has suggested that the judgment "assembled" ideas from earlier cases, particularly *Saltman Engineering Co v Campbell Engineering Co* (1948) 65 RPC 203 and *Seager v Copydex (No 1)* [1967] 2 All ER 415: Meagher, R P; Heydon, J D; Leeming, M J, *Meagher, Gummow & Lehane's Equity: Doctrines and Remedies* (4th ed, Lexis Nexis, 2002, para 4110). These elements will now be examined individually.

■ Information must be of a confidential nature

General
[12.55] The sort of information in the "trade secret" category was reviewed earlier in this chapter. However valuable it is, in order to be protected, the information must be actually confidential, although secrecy may be "imperfect" in relation to a communication given in confidence: *Interfirm Comparison Pty Ltd v Law Society of NSW* [1975] 2 NSWLR 104 at 118-119. If "relative secrecy" (*Franchi v Franchi* [1967] RPC 149) is maintained the confidence will still be protected. In deciding whether information is in the public domain or still confidential, the level of information, practices and usages in the relevant trade or industry will help determine the issue and the plaintiff's own efforts to maintain secrecy may be a guide to what

attitude to take towards the information: see *Print Investments Pty Ltd v Art-vue Printing Pty Ltd* (1983) 1 IPR 149; *Ansell Rubber v Allied Industries* [1967] VR 37; *Printers & Finishers v Holloway* [1965] RPC 239; *Mense v Milenkovic* [1973] VR 784; *IF Asia Pacific v Galbally* (2003) 59 IPR 43.

In the following case, the knowledge subject to protection was said to be names and addresses of manufacturers and suppliers and the terms of the contracts with the company, prices paid by and to the company, names of overseas agents, the company's new ranges, information as to the requirements of customers, details of current negotiations, and sales figures for successful products.

Thomas Marshall (Exports) v Guinle

[12.60] *Thomas Marshall (Exports) v Guinle* [1979] Ch 227

MEGARRY V-C: **[248]** If one turns from the authorities and looks at the matter as a question of principle, I think (and I say this very tentatively, because the principle has not been argued out) that four elements may be discerned which may be of some assistance in identifying confidential information or trade secrets which the court will protect. I speak of such information or secrets only in an industrial or trade setting. First, I think that the information must be information the release of which the owner believes would be injurious to him or of advantage to his rivals or others. Second, I think the owner must believe that the information is confidential or secret, ie, that it is not already in the public domain. It may be that some or all of his rivals already have the information: but as long as the owner believes it to be confidential I think he is entitled to try and protect it. Third, I think that the owner's belief under the two previous heads must be reasonable. Fourth, I think that the information must be judged in the light of the usage and practices of the particular industry or trade concerned. It may be that information which does not satisfy all these requirements may be entitled to protection as confidential information or trade secrets: but I think that any information which does satisfy them must be of a type which is entitled to protection.

[12.65] The following case sets out important principles as to the duty of confidentiality during employment and the duty surviving the end of an employment relationship. For a similar situation set in the Australian mining industry see *AIM Maintenance Ltd v Brunt* (2004) 60 IPR 572.

Ansell Rubber Co v Allied Rubber Industries

[12.70] *Ansell Rubber Co Pty Ltd v Allied Rubber Industries Pty Ltd* [1967] VR 37 Supreme Court of Victoria

[The plaintiff company, which manufactured rubber gloves, had devised a machine which would produce the gloves in a continuous automated process. The machine had been patented, but some improvements to it, including a dryer-blower and ancillary apparatus for flock lining the gloves, were not patented. The plaintiff had not made public or disclosed to any competitor the design, construction or operation of its equipment. It had been concerned to keep it private and had imposed a rule against the admission of unauthorised persons to its factory and its employees were informed of the confidentiality of the machine's operation.

▨▨▨▨ Ansell Rubber Co v Allied Rubber Industries *continued*

Two employees of the plaintiff, Grigg and Ashcroft, who knew of the plaintiff's secrecy policy joined with two others in a venture to manufacture rubber gloves in competition with the plaintiff. Griggs (a fitter) had been employed by the plaintiff for 12 years in the glove manufacturing department and knew of the company's secrecy obligations. Ashcroft (an engineer) had been the plaintiff's production manager for 15 months and also knew of the policy and his obligations. Injunctions were sought by the plaintiff to prevent the defendants from making rubber gloves using the trade secrets of the plaintiff.]

GOWANS J: **[39]** The point I have reached in the examination of the evidence is that Grigg, while in the employ of the plaintiff, assisted Ashcroft in the production of plant to be used by the defendant company in a venture in competition with his employer, and in the course of doing so made use of and communicated information about the plaintiff's No 2 glove-making machine which he had acquired in the course of his employment by the plaintiff, and in particular made use of and communicated to Ashcroft, for incorporation in the production of the plant, information so acquired about the batten assembly of that machine of the plaintiff; and about the dryer-blower; and the information so used by Grigg was the subject of a confidence, as he knew and Ashcroft knew; Ashcroft had, after he had ceased to be employed by the plaintiff, used, by incorporating it in the production of the plant, information about the glove-making machine and the dryer-blower which he and Grigg had acquired in the course of their employment by the plaintiff and which was the subject of a confidence, as he knew.

The defendants, however, contend that, even if this were so, the plaintiff is not entitled to protection for a further reason. Reliance is placed on the principle that the courts will refuse to prevent a man earning a living by using his knowledge, skill and experience he has acquired as his own and will refuse to treat its use as an actionable breach of contract or confidence. Any use made by either of these two defendants of information was, it is said, a use of knowledge and experience of that kind.

[40] In this field a distinction has to be maintained between information and knowledge acquired in confidence by a employee during his employment which he uses or discloses for his own advantage while he is still an employee, and information and knowledge so acquired which he uses for his own advantage after his employment is finished. A further distinction has to be drawn between information which forms part of the employee's stock of general knowledge, skill and experience, and that which should fairly be regarded as a separate part of the employee's stock of knowledge (whether it be identifiable as "particular" or "detailed" or "special") which a man of ordinary intelligence and honesty would regard as the property of the former employer. I will endeavour later to locate the line of this demarcation as it has been drawn in the legal authorities. It will be sufficient at present to indicate my conclusions that information made use of by Grigg and communicated by him to Ashcroft for incorporation in the production of the defendant company's plant, while Grigg was still an employee of the plaintiff, was of a kind which was not withdrawn from protection by the application of the principle relied upon by the defendants, and further that there was information made use of by Ashcroft in the production of the defendant company's plant which is not withdrawn from protection by reason of that principle.

The nature of the subject matter and the conflicts that have emerged on so many issues have involved me in this detailed, and I am afraid over-long, examination of the facts. I now turn to a consideration of the legal principles which have to be applied.

The starting point is said to be the equitable doctrine laid down in *Keech v Sandford* (1726) 2 Eq Ca Ab 741; 22 ER 629, that a trustee cannot be allowed to make a profit out of his trust, and its expansion to all persons standing in a fiduciary relation to another: *Keith Henry & Co*

▰▰▰▰ Ansell Rubber Co v Allied Rubber Industries *continued*

Pty Ltd v Walker (1958) 100 CLR 342 at 350. It has been applied to many different kinds of such relationships whether created by contract or otherwise: *Argyll v Argyll* [1965] 2 WLR 790, and to many different conceptions of property. It has been applied to rights in respect of the publication of works of art: *Prince Albert v Strange* (1849) 64 ER 293; and rights in secret formulae: *Morison v Moat* (1851) 68 ER 492.

It has been extended to breaches of confidence as well as breaches of trust or contract: *Abernethey v Hutchinson* (1825) 2 LJ Ch 219; 47 ER 1313, and the obligation of confidence may be express or implied: *Argyll v Argyll* (at 801). That obligation may come into existence by reason of the terms of an agreement, or what is implicit in them, by reason of the nature of the relationship between persons, or by reason of the subject matter and the circumstances in which the subject matter has come into the hands of the person charged with the breach.

At this stage I turn more particularly to the first way in which the plaintiff's claim to relief is put, and the law relating thereto. It is concerned primarily with Grigg's conduct during his employment. The doctrine I have referred to has been applied to the position of a servant **[41]** in relation to his master and his property, and to the obligations of the servant in relation to information obtained in the employment. "And where a person is by virtue of his employment charged with the duty of furthering his employer's interest, he is also charged with the duty of not using the information obtained by him as their employ to their detriment": *Prebble v Reeves* [1910] VR 88 at 108. What the obligation really involves is that the employee must not take advantage of his own profit of what he has learned confidentially in the service of his employer: Fridman, *The Modern Law of Employment*, p 455; and see *Halsbury* (3rd ed), Vol 25, p 462, s 894. In *Merryweather & Sons v Moore* [1892] 2 Ch 518 at 524; [1891-94] All ER Rep 563, Kekewich J, used the language: "an abuse of confidence necessarily existing between him and his employers—confidence arising out of the mere fact of employment, the confidence being shortly this, that the servant shall not use, except for the purposes of service, the opportunities which that service gives him of gaining information", and (at 522) "perhaps the real solution is that the confidence postulates an implied contract; that where the court is satisfied of the confidential relation, then it at once infers or implies the contract arising from that confidential relation a contract which thus calls into existence the jurisdiction to which I have referred". See also *Robb v Green* [1895] 2 QB 315; [1895-99] All ER Rep 1053; *Measures v Measures* [1910] 1 Ch 336; *British Reinforced Concrete Engineering Co v Lind* (1917) 34 RPC 101; *Reid & Sigrist Ltd v Moss & Mechanism Ltd* (1932) 49 RPC 461; *Wessex Dairies Ltd v Smith* [1935] 2 KB 80; [1935] All ER Rep 75 *Vokes v Heather* (1945) 62 RPC 135 at 141-142, and *Bent's Brewery Co Ltd v Hogan* [1945] 2 All ER 570.

These were cases concerned with conduct during employment in breach of the duty of fidelity which a servant owes to his master, and in breach of contract or confidence. In many of them the confidential nature of the information was apparent from the nature of the subject matter, eg names of customers, weekly sales, total wages; or from the circumstances in which it came into existence, eg a private conference. In most cases it was recorded in some tangible form the use of which could be enjoined and required to be delivered up. Where it was not, difficulty was sometimes felt and expressed as to what effective form of injunction could be granted against its use. But in *Amber Size & Chemical Co v Menzel* [1913] 2 Ch 239, Astbury J, considered that the use of a memorised secret process could not be restrained, and in *Printers & Finishers Ltd v Holloway* [1965] RPC 239; [1964] 3 All ER 731, an injunction was granted against the use of a machine improperly copied at the instance of a servant for the benefit of another. In that case Cross J, said (at 255):

"There mere fact that the confidential information is not embodied in a document but is carried away by the employee in his head is not of course, of itself a reason against

████ Ansell Rubber Co v Allied Rubber Industries *continued*

the granting of an injunction to prevent its use or disclosure by him. If the information in question can fairly be regarded as a separate part of the employee's stock of knowledge which a man of ordinary honesty and intelligence would recognise to be the property of his old employer, and not his own to do as he likes with, then, the court if it thinks that there is a danger of the information being used or disclosed by the ex-employee to the detriment of the old employer, will do what it can to prevent that result by granting an injunction. Thus an ex-employee will be restrained from using or disclosing a chemical formula or a list of customers which he has committed to memory."

Then after referring to the facts in **[42]** *Reid & Sigrist Ltd v Moss & Mechanism Ltd* (1932) 49 RPC 461, he added:

"It appears, indeed, that after the discussions, and while he was still in the plaintiff's employ, the defendant made and later took away with him drawings embracing the matters discussed. But even if he had not done so and relied simply on his memory of the confidential discussions I think that an injunction would still have been granted."

Given the kind of information described by Cross J, I think it is immaterial that it is not recorded in a tangible form.

The cases also show that anyone who aids, abets in or procures the breach of contract of confidence may be enjoined together with the servant against the use of the information.

The American *Restatement of the Law of Agency* (2nd ed), Ch 13, s 395, states the principle in terms which accord with the English authorities:

"Unless otherwise agreed, an agent is subject to a duty to the principal not to use or to communicate information confidentially given him by the principal or acquired by him during the course of or on account of his agency or in violation of his duties as agent, in competition with or to the injury of the principal, on his own account or on behalf of another, although such information does not relate to the transaction in which he is then employed, unless the information is a matter of general knowledge."

The "Comment" says: "The agent also has a duty not to use information ... acquired by him through a breach of duty to the principal, for any purpose likely to cause his principal harm or to interfere with his business." And again:

"The rule stated in this section applies not only to those communications which are stated to be confidential, but also to information which the agent should know his principal would not care to have revealed to others or used in competition with him. It applies to unique business methods of the employer, trade secrets, lists of names, and all other matters which are peculiarly known in the employer's business. It does not apply to matters of common knowledge in the community nor to special skill which the employee has acquired because of his employment."

I have applied these conceptions to the detailed knowledge of the plaintiff's batten assembly, and the knowledge of the dryer-blower, which I have found made its way through the medium of Grigg to use in the defendants' company plant, and have reached the conclusions that it does not represent the kind of skill which Grigg had acquired because of his employment, while it does represent a matter particularly known in the plaintiff's business, and that it was used by him in violation of his duty.

The conduct in which Grigg engaged, even if no confidential information had been shown to have been disclosed and used, would, having regard to his position with the plaintiff and

▬▬▬ Ansell Rubber Co v Allied Rubber Industries *continued*

the opportunities he possessed for passing on particular and detailed information of a confidential nature, constitute a breach of his duty to his employer not to act contrary to its interests. In *Hivac Ltd v Park Royal Scientific Instruments Ltd* [1946] 1 Ch 169; [1946] 1 All ER 350, that was held to be the position in a case which concerned a production engineer and his wife, a forewoman, and other skilled manual workers, who employed their spare time in helping a competitor of their employer make scientific instruments. The case (as reported) concerned the position of the manual workers, the production engineer and his forewoman wife having been summarily dismissed. The breach of duty on the part of those two could hardly have been in doubt.

"Conduct which in respect of important matters is incompatible with the fulfilment of an employee's **[43]** duty, or involves an opposition, on conflict between his interest and his duty to his employer, or impedes the faithful performance of his obligations, or is destructive of the necessary confidence between employer and employee, is a ground of dismissal": per Dixon and McTiernan JJ, in *Blyth Chemicals Ltd v Bushnell* (1933) 49 CLR 66 at 81.

In that case the learned justices went on to say that if a finding had been made that in all he did the manager concerned was actuated by one design, namely, to prepare a position to which he could retreat with a considerable part of his employee's [sic] business, the court would have been entitled, if not bound, to hold he had been guilty of misconduct.

Such misconduct must create a liability in damages. ... **[46]**

I turn now to the second way in which the plaintiff's claim for relief is put. In its formulation, it places emphasis on the conception of "trade secrets". But this is only a particular subject matter to which the principles relating to breach of confidence have been applied. It is a subject matter associated with what is loosely called "trade", and it might, as aptly, have been called "commercial confidence". The English authorities are more disposed to refer to "confidential information" and not to resort to definitions of the term "trade secret", while the American authorities tend to use the expression "trade secret" as a term of art.

This submission of the plaintiff is better understood as placing emphasis primarily on the conduct of Ashcroft after his employment with the plaintiff had ceased. Because his activities occupied a wider field than Grigg's, the scope of the matter dealt with is enlarged.

In *Helmore v Smith* (1887) 35 Ch D 449 at 456, Bowen LJ, said he could not "countenance the doctrine that the confidential information received by a servant to advance his master's business may be used afterwards by him to advance his own business to the injury of his master's interests. It is part of the implied contract between the master and the servant that such confidential information is not to be used to the master's disadvantage." See also *Kirchner & Co v Gruban* [1909] 1 Ch 413 at 422; [1908-10] All ER Rep 242.

I have found that at the commencement of his employment Ashcroft was told by More that the success of the plaintiff company was largely tied up with its dipping operations and the unique methods the plaintiff employed and which it had itself developed, and for that reason the secrets of those methods were jealously guarded; and that Ashcroft knew of the plaintiff's policy of keeping information about its glove-making machines private (including the No 2 glove machine and the dryer- blower); and he knew of its intention that there should not be any disclosure of information about their design, construction or operation. In my opinion, this is sufficient to justify the implied contract not to use the information to the detriment of the employer spoken of in **[47]** *Helmore v Smith* and *Kirchner v Gruban*. On the face of it, the information I have referred to was confidential information.

▬▬▬ Ansell Rubber Co v Allied Rubber Industries *continued*

But since the implied contract concerns the use of the servant's labour skill or talent, it is subject to the rule of public policy that a man is not to be restrained, either by contract or without it, from using after his employment his personal skill, knowledge and experience. That conception includes "the skill and knowledge in his trade or profession which he had no right to reveal to anyone else matters which depend to some extent on good faith ... it would be a breach of confidence to reveal trade secrets, such as prices etc. or any secret process or things of a nature which the man was not intended to reveal": per Farwell LJ, in *Leng v Andrews* [1909] 1 Ch 763 at 774. This was approved by Lord Atkinson in *Herbert Morris v Saxelby* [1916] 1 AC 688 at 704; [1916-17] All ER Rep 305, and he also (at 702-703) spoke of "trade secrets such as secret processes of manufacture" and "documents highly confidential" and "drawings of special machines", as being protected. Lord Parker (at 709) also referred to "such an acquaintance with his employer's trade secrets as would enable him, if competition were allowed, to take advantage of his employer's trade connection or utilise information confidentially advanced". Lord Shaw (at 714) said:

> "Trade secrets, the names of customers, all such things which in sound philosophical language are denominated objective knowledge these may not be given away by a servant; they are his masters property, and there is no rule of public interest which prevents a transfer of them against his master's will being restrained. On the other hand, a man's aptitudes, his skill, his dexterity, his manual or mental ability all those things which in sound philosophical language are not objective, but subjective they may and ought not to be relinquished by a servant; they are not his master's property they are his own property; they are himself."

It is in this way that the concept of "trade secrets" comes into the English authorities.

But what are the indicia of a "trade secret" or "highly confidential information" or "objective knowledge" so referred to by the learned law lords, and in particular can the terms be applied, and how do they apply to machines, particularly where there is no express contract of restraint?

In the first instance, at all events, I must endeavour to ascertain what English law says about these concepts, and particularly in the latter connection. There is nothing in the way of definition.

In *Amber Size & Chemical Co v Menzel* [1913] 2 Ch 239, the subject matter was a process, and it was found as a fact that the plaintiff possessed and exercised a secret process, but by reference to what criteria does not appear. There were however three observations made by Astbury J, in arguendo (at 241-242), which are of significance: "Surely if the servant is told it is a secret process and is employed on that footing, there is an implied obligation not to use or disclose it?"; and "Possession of tangible materials cannot be a sine qua non in the case of a secret which the employee can commit to memory?"; and again" None of these cases really touch the question of information as to a secret process acquired during the confidential employment. How can it possibly matter whether the servant learns the process by heart or writes it down? It is an equal breach of confidence to use or disclose it in either case?" In *BO Morris Ltd v Gillman* (1943) 60 RPC 20, it was found that information as to the details of a milling machine were confidential and a trade secret, and the property of the plaintiff, [48] but on what evidence does not appear except that the machine was capable of turning out a variety of products by trifling adjustments in the mechanism, that the plaintiff alone used it in England, and that it had been reproduced by the plaintiff from a machine imported by it from Germany. I have already referred to *Saltman Engineering Co Ltd v Campbell Engineering* (1948) 65 RPC 203, and to *Terrapin Ltd v Builders (Hayes) Ltd* [1960] RPC 128. In the latter case

▨▨▨▨▨▨ Ansell Rubber Co v Allied Rubber Industries *continued*

the subject matter was a modification of a design for making prefabricated folding houses consisting of a flat roof and a roof made of stressed (wooden) skin. It was held, notwithstanding an attack on its "novelty", that the conjunction of these two items was "something new if it were workable", and that the information about it was given in confidence.

In *Mustad (O) & Son v Dosen* [1964] 1 WLR 109; [1963] 3 All ER 416, the subject was information about the construction of a machine perfected by a Norwegian firm whose business was purchased by the plaintiffs. The machine was "an extremely unique and clever arrangement by which fish hooks can be produced at the rate of 75 per minute". There was an express agreement against disclosing information. Lord Buckmaster observed that "it might well be that, had nothing more happened, the circumstances connected with this case, would have been sufficient to support the claim which the appellant put forward". But it was held, the secret as a secret had ceased to exist by its having been precisely and fully disclosed in a specification for a patent applied for by the plaintiff.

In *Commercial Plastics v Vincent* [1964] 3 WLR 820; [1964] 3 All ER 546, the Court of Appeal, in deciding whether the plaintiffs had any trade secrets or confidential information in relation to the manufacture of sheeting for adhesive tape, held that even though it was difficult to classify any particular item of information in the plaintiffs' possession as being confidential (other than information contained in documents which could be protected by other appropriate legal remedies), the fact that the defendant could probably remember in general in relation to any matter concerning adhesive tape what was the problem and what was the solution, what experiments were made, and whether the results were positive or negative, meant that the plaintiffs had confidential information capable of being protected by a suitably drafted condition or covenant.

I have already referred to *Cranleigh Precision Engineering Ltd v Bryant* [1965] 1 WLR 1293; [1964] 3 All ER 289, where the subject matter, in the first action, was certain features of above-ground swimming pools. Roskill J, said:

> "I think the knowledge that the particular clamping strip was the right type of clamping strip to use for this particular purpose, coupled with the knowledge of how to define to a plastics manufacturer what was required for that particular purpose, and that a plastics manufacturer could readily supply the particular form of strip, is and was a trade secret of the plaintiff. I take the same view in relation to the interfit of the plate, which, it is worth noting, Bryant and the defendant company in their leaflet D3, have described as 'unique'."

Finally, in *Printers & Finishers Ltd v Holloway* [1965] RPC 239; [1964] 3 All ER 731, from which I have already set out some of the observations of Cross J, that learned judge observed (RPC at 253) that "not all information which is given to a servant in confidence and which it would be a breach of his duty for him to disclose to another person during his employment is a trade secret **[49]** which he can be prevented from using for his own advantage after the employment is over, even though he has entered into no express covenant with regard to the matter on hand". He gave an example of printing instructions given to the employee, many of which were not "trade secrets" at all, and which, in so far as they would not be called "trade secrets", and could be carried in his head, he was entitled to use for the benefit of a subsequent employer. One of the subject matters in the case was a piece of equipment for collecting surplus flock, called a cyclone. It was said (at 245):

> "Cyclones are well-known items of equipment, but how precisely any given cyclone should be shaped internally in order to carry out the particular job which it is to, is a matter which, unless you are told, you can only discover by trial and error. The

▬▬▬▬ Ansell Rubber Co v Allied Rubber Industries *continued*

plaintiff's cyclones were constructed in accordance with information given to them by United Merchants [an American firm] as modified in the light of experience of their own particular requirements. There is no doubt that in having his cyclone copied from that of the plaintiff's, Penny was saving Vita-Tex [one of the defendants] a certain amount of time, trouble and expense."

There was held to be a breach of duty by the employee during his employment and although no damages were given against the defendant Vita-Tex, for whose benefit the cyclone had been copied, because no use had been made of it (at 252), an injunction was granted against its use (at 257). On the other hand, an injunction was refused against use or disclosure of information about plant and processes, that was in the employee's head alone, and which in terms would have prevented him, when employed by others who used plant and machinery similar to the plaintiff's, from using his recollection of a corresponding piece of machinery of his former employers to resolve some difficulty.

There is very little in these English cases to enable one to identify a "trade secret". But some collation of the characteristics may be attempted, without trying to make it an exhaustive statement. Its subject matter may not be a process in common use, or something which is public property and public knowledge, but if it is the result of work done by the maker upon materials which may be available for the use of anybody, so as to achieve a result which can only be produced by somebody who goes through the same process, it will be sufficient. All of its separate features may have been published, or capable of being ascertained by actual inspection by any member of the public, but if the whole result has not been achieved, and could not be achieved, except by someone going through the same kind of process as the owner, it will not fail to qualify by reason of the publication. It may derive from a maker in another country without losing its character, if it is used, or entitled to be used, by the owner alone in the country in which the owner operates. There is no suggestion of the need for invention. Little can be gathered of the degree of secrecy required beyond what is implied in what is said. But it is a fair inference from what is said that the employer must have kept the matter to himself and from his competitors. The emphasis in the cases is on the confidence.

American law is rather more explicit. The *Restatement of the Law of Torts* (1st ed), Article 757, states in the "Comment":

"*Secrecy*. The subject matter of a trade secret must be secret. Matters of public knowledge or of general knowledge in an industry cannot be appropriated by one as his secret. Matters which are completely disclosed by the goods which one markets cannot be his secret. Substantially, a trade secret is known only in the particular business in which it is used. It is not requisite that only the proprietor of the business know it. [50] He may, without losing his protection, communicate it to employees involved in its use. He may likewise communicate it to others pledged to secrecy. Others may also know of it independently, as, for example, when they have discovered the formula by independent invention and are keeping it secret. Nevertheless, a substantial element of secrecy must exist, so that, except by the use of improper means, there would be difficulty in acquiring the information. An exact definition of a trade secret is not possible. Some factors to be considered in determining whether given information is one's trade secret are:

(1)   the extent to which the information is known outside of his business;
(2)   the extent to which it is known by employees and others involved in his business;

▰▰▰▰ Ansell Rubber Co v Allied Rubber Industries *continued*

(3) the extent of measures taken by him to guard the secrecy of the information;

(4) the value of the information to him and to his competitors;

(5) the amount of effort or money expended by him in developing the information;

(6) the ease or difficulty with which the information could be properly acquired or duplicated by others.

Novelty and prior art. A trade secret may be a device or process which is patentable; but it need not be that. It may be a device or process which is clearly anticipated in the prior art or one which is merely a mechanical improvement that a good mechanic can make. Novelty and invention are not requisite for a trade secret as they are for patentability. These requirements are essential to patentability because a patent protects against unlicensed use of the patented device or process even by one who discovers it properly through independent research. The patent monopoly is a reward to the inventor. But such is not the case with a trade secret. Its protection is not based on a policy of rewarding or otherwise encouraging the development of secret processes or devices. The protection is merely against breach of faith and reprehensible means of learning another's secret. For this limited protection it is not appropriate to require also the kind of novelty and invention which is a requisite of patentability."

Reference may also be made in this connection to the extracts from the American cases set out in Turner, *The Law of Trade Secrets*, Ch 2B, p 21 et seq; and in particular (for the resemblance to the circumstances of the present case) to the judgment of the Supreme Judicial Court of Massachusetts in *Junker v Plummer* 320 Mass 76; 165 Am LR 1449 (1946). The case was concerned with the combining machine evolved by the plaintiff after considerable experimental work: although it was of such simple mechanical principle and open construction that anyone possessed of average manual skill who had the opportunity to work with it and note its purpose could build a duplicate, the fact was that there was no other machine faintly resembling it in use anywhere, although other combining machines, using the same principle but differing in certain features and costing much more, were known; the plaintiff's employees had been told the machine was his idea, that nobody else had one and that he did not want its operation broadcast to the world and, although no contract of secrecy was required or mentioned, it was made plain to them that the plaintiff had an idea which he considered of value, unprotected by patent, and that it might cause loss to him if it got to others; although friends of the plaintiff's employees from time to time, came to the plaintiff's premises where the machines were in sight and in operation, there was no evidence that any of these persons interested themselves sufficiently to learn the details of the construction and operation of the machine so as to produce it. An employee of the plaintiff left his employment and went into competition with him building a machine which was "substantially a replica" [51] of his. Two others did the same using a machine "substantially similar" to his. All their knowledge of the plaintiff's machines had been acquired solely by reason of their employment by the plaintiff. They were found to have "appropriated the plaintiff's special knowledge, skill and brain child". It was held on appeal that the plaintiff had rightly been awarded an injunction and damages.

The general rule is stated in the *Restatement of the Law of Agency* (2nd ed), s 396, in these terms:

"Unless otherwise agreed, after the termination of the agency, the agent

(a) has no duty not to compete with the principal;

(b) has a duty to the principal not to use or disclose to third persons, on his own account or on account of others, in competition with the principal or to his injury, trade secrets, written lists of names, or other similar confidential matters

▰▰▰▰▰ Ansell Rubber Co v Allied Rubber Industries *continued*

> given to him only for the principal's use or acquired by the agent in violation of
> duty. The agent is entitled to use general information concerning the method of
> business of the principal and the names of customers retained in his memory, if
> not acquired in violation of his duty as agent."

This accords with the English authorities.

I have applied these principles of law as I understand them to the facts I have found, and, in my judgment, the design, construction and operation of the plaintiff's No 2 glove-making machine (including the flocking apparatus) and of the dryer-blower were trade secrets of the plaintiff, and Ashcroft's knowledge of them acquired during his employment was confidential information, and he knew that that was so. I have not had evidence that Ashcroft deliberately recorded or memorised this information during his employment for his own use afterwards, although I do not exclude it as a possibility. But I am not prepared to find that in creating the defendants' machines, he merely made use of what lay in his recollection. On the other hand, I have found that he had Grigg's assistance and made use of Grigg's opportunities in his employment for obtaining information of the plaintiff's plant, and in particular in relation to the particulars of the batten assembly and the blower-dryer. Ashcroft was, therefore, not merely using his personal skill, knowledge and experience. He used information of a special or particular nature belonging to the plaintiff. He committed a breach of confidence and breach of contract in making use, for the benefit of the syndicate and the defendant company, of trade secrets and confidential information which were the property of his former employer, the plaintiff. Grigg, of course, was party to this. On this basis, they are liable in damages and to be enjoined. So also is Palmer liable to be enjoined for substantially the same reasons as I have given in relation to the first submission. The defendant company is equally liable for the same reasons as before.

In my opinion, therefore, the plaintiff has succeeded, on both branches of its submission, in establishing its right to relief against all the defendants.

■ Relative secrecy

[12.75] As *Ansell Rubber* illustrates, it is not necessarily fatal to a claim that the information is known to others, even a substantial number of others, but as *Ansell* also shows information needs to be "looked after" so as not to enter the public domain through carelessness. See *Facienda Chicken Ltd v Fowler* (1985) 6 IPR 155; *IF Asia Pacific v Galbally* (2003) 59 IPR 43. The question is whether there is still sufficient secrecy to give commercial value to the plaintiff from the difficulty of acquiring the information without improper means.

The value of a "trade secret" depends (in part) upon the ease with which the information may be kept secret. A simple mechanical design incorporated into a product will not remain secret for long, as competitors may acquire the product upon its "publication" to the market place and reverse-engineer it. On the other hand determining the nature of a particular process by which an article of manufacture comes into being may be much more difficult. Examples of processes kept secret have included a method of concentrating sulphuric acid, and the General Electric Co's technique for the manufacture of artificial diamonds. The Pfizer Co reportedly maintained the secrecy of its process for the commercial production of citric acid for many years beyond the term of any patent.

The possibility of reverse engineering need not necessarily make the product/

information/idea public. It depends on the difficulty and whether others have in fact reverse engineered and learned the information through that process: *Yates Circuit Foil Co v Electrofoils Ltd* [1976] FSR 345. In cases where all information previously secret is revealed in a patent specification open for public inspection, the information has been made public and is no longer a trade secret. The controller of the former secret may rely upon breaches of trade secret until the date of publication of the specification, but after that date must rely upon the rights given by the patent claims.

■ Termination of secrecy

▬▬ Falconer v Australian Broadcasting Corporation ▬▬

[12.80] *Falconer v Australian Broadcasting Corporation* (1991) 22 IPR 205 Supreme Court of Victoria [This was the hearing of an interlocutory injunction for the restraint of the broadcast of a television program. The facts appear sufficiently from the decision below.]

ASHLEY J: **[206]** The plaintiff, Robert Falconer, seeks an interlocutory injunction which in substance will restrain the defendant, Australian Broadcasting Corporation from broadcasting on television any picture image or description of the person formerly known as Vlado Rajicic which could reasonably reveal the current identity or whereabouts of the person formerly known as Vlado RaJicic or any member of his family.

Rajicic was, it appears, a member of a drug trafficking group who turned informer. Over a period of some months he undertook this role of informer. It was very risky work. What he did, according to the police, played a very significant part in the arrest of a majority of the 16 persons who were eventually charged with offences arising out of the investigation. Eventually those charged were sentenced to imprisonment for terms of between three and 18 years. In addition, assets of or controlled by the accused and valued at nearly $2 million were seized, and the Australian Taxation Office raised assessments of over $2 million with penalties of $801,000.

Rajicic, his wife and two children were for a period of about one year following the arrest of certain of the accused in February 1988 under 24 hour police protection. Then Rajicic and his family were relocated and given a change of identity. This relocation and change of identity was effected in the course of the work of a group in the Victoria Police Force known as the Witness Protection Unit. Only very few persons in that group know the present identity and whereabouts of the man who was Vlado Rajicic.

The protection afforded Rajicic and his family was in consequence of assurances given him as to the safety of his family and himself if he was prepared to cooperate with the police and give evidence for the Crown. He took legal advice, it appears, before committing himself to the course of co-operation that he undertook.

Having account of the role played by Rajicic as an informer and witness, the police hold fears that, if his present identity and whereabouts become known, he and his family will be at risk to their safety.

The defendant runs a current affairs program entitled *The 7.30 Report*. On 11 September 1991 it commenced a series on the activities of the witness protection scheme. As a promotion of what was to be screened on 12 September it showed a photograph depicting three persons. One of them was the former Rajicic. His face was briefly highlighted. Material later filed by the defendant shows that Rajicic was to be the subject of considerable comment on the program of 12 September, had that program gone to air, and that the photo was to be shown in the course of the program on 12 September.

▅▅▅▅▅▅ Falconer v Australian Broadcasting Corporation *continued*

According to the affidavit of Sally Anne Neighbour, sworn 17 September:

"The defendant wishes to publish the segment as it deals with the giving of indemnity in controversial circumstances and the executive producer of *The 7.30 Report* and I believe it is in the public interest that the subject of indemnities in serious criminal prosecution be the subject of full and informed public discussion."

... [208]

It was common ground between the parties that equity will intervene to restrain the disclosure of confidential information.

That is the way in which the plaintiff frames his case.

The restraint which the court will impose in the appropriate circumstances is not auxiliary to the enforcement of a legal right: see, for example, *Prince Albert v Strange* (1849) 1 N & T 1 at 25; *Pollard v Photographic Co* (1888) 40 Ch D 348 at 349, 353-4 per North J; *Lord Ashburton v Pape* [1913] 2 Ch 469 at 457 per Swinfen-Eady J; *Argyll v Argyll* [1967] Ch 302 at 322 per Ungoed-Thomas J; *Attorney-General v Jonathon Cape Ltd* [1976] QB 572 at 617-8 per Lord Widgery CJ. It is not relevant to search for an interest protected in law—a task which chiefly occupied the members of the High Court in *Victoria Park Racing and Recreation Grounds Co Ltd v Taylor* (1937) 58 CLR 479, a case to which Mr Ruskin referred me. In the present case it is recognised that there is potentially an interest which equity will protect. The question is whether the particular facts call for equity to intervene.

Mr Ruskin raised a series of matters which, he submitted, led to a conclusion that the plaintiff's case was without foundation. But ultimately he made this submission, in answer to a question that I put him:

"I have conceded, I think, that if (the photographs) had never got into the public domain there would be an arguable case that they arose in confidence, and should not be given out to anybody. It seems to me to follow the fact that as they are in the public domain, that makes the difference."

His reference to the photographs being in the "public domain" was a reference to the fact that they were introduced into evidence at the committal hearing of May 1988.

... [210]

Both counsel referred me to *G v Day* [1982] 1 NSWLR 24. In that case the plaintiff was a man who believed he had seen, in the US, in 1982 another man named Nugan. The latter was thought to have committed suicide in 1980. He was a man thought to be involved in questionable dealings. The plaintiff communicated his belief that he had seen Nugan to officers of the Corporate Affairs Commission. Before doing so, he said that he feared for his safety and that he would only make a statement if his anonymity was preserved. He was given a suitable assurance. In reliance upon this statement a fresh inquest was held. In fact the plaintiff's belief was honest, but mistaken. Prior to the second inquest being held, a journalist employed by Truth newspaper contacted the plaintiff and said that he believed the plaintiff was the mystery witness. The plaintiff denied this. Later he was told by the journalist that the material emanated from the Corporate Affairs Office (there was no evidence of this) at which stage "speaking off the record" the plaintiff asked the journalist not to publish his name. There was evidence that the plaintiffs name had been mentioned on the television briefly. [211] On the television, the connection between the plaintiff's name and the Nugan affair was less than clear.

It was submitted for the defendants that the identity of the informant, as distinct from information conveyed, was not confidential in quality. Yeldham J, at 35, rejected that submission. The present case is stronger again from the plaintiff's standpoint. Identity is the confidential information.

It was argued for the defendants that confidentiality had been lost because the plaintiffs name had been mentioned on television. There, Yeldham J referred to cases dealing with loss of confidentiality by reason of prior disclosure—including *Interfirm Comparison (Aust) Pty Ltd v Law Society of New South Wales* [1975] 2 NSWLR 104 at 117-8 per Bowen CJ in Equity, *Commonwealth v John Fairfax & Sons Ltd* (1980) 55 ALJR 45 at 50 per Mason J, and he concluded at 40-1:

> "In the present case the references to the plaintiff on television were transitory and brief. His name was mentioned once only on each occasion. It was not recorded in any permanent form (other than in the script) and there is no suggestion that any reaction from any viewer was conveyed to the plaintiff. Probably his name would not be remembered by any who did not already know him. I regard these disclosures as being of a limited and impermanent nature. Any publication in a newspaper would, on the contrary, be in a permanent form for all its readers to note.
>
> Where, as here, there has been a limited publication of the plaintiff's name without his knowledge or approval, where he is entitled, to the knowledge of a newspaper publisher, to expect anonymity, and where any unauthorised publication of his identity will probably be to his detriment, I do not consider that the court should be astute to deprive him of relief merely by reason of that limited publication. Plainly, if disclosure had been in another newspaper, different considerations may well apply, and if the plaintiff had been party to or consented to any prior identification of himself, then his action would necessarily fail. But I see no reason why, in a case where it is likely that many readers of *Truth* would not have seen or learned of the telecasts, the plaintiff should not have the protection to which, but for such telecasts, he would have been entitled."

G v Day was a case, thus, where the confidential material itself was disclosed to a third party by the plaintiff, he being the party to whom the material was of principal concern. Despite these facts, and despite limited disclosure elsewhere, the court intervened to prevent further disclosure.

It may be said that the disclosure there was short, impermanent and effected by television; contrast disclosure by photograph tendered in court proceedings. On the other hand, that case involved prior disclosure of the confidential information itself. And the authorities to which his Honour referred underlined, I think, the need to look at the potential effect of prior disclosure on a case by case basis. In the present case it is true that the photographs were a court exhibit. But that was in 1988, and the litigation in which they were tendered is now long past. None of the photographs were, it seems, published in the press at the time. The extent of their circulation seems likely to have been magistrate, counsel, solicitors and the accused. That is a far cry from the circulation achievable by a national television current affairs program in 1991.

In the present case the confidential information existing between Rajicic and a few policemen is his present identity (I continue to assume at this **[212]** stage that the information contained in the photographs is not and was not itself confidential). The defendant knows that such information is, at least by intention of the parties privy to it, confidential. The defendant wishes to use two pieces of information which are said not to be confidential in a manner which is well capable of destroying the confidentiality of that which is held confidential. Those two pieces of information are: (1) the photographs; (2) the intimation that the photographs depict Rajicic.

In my opinion, where confidentiality attaches to information such that equity would

▆▆▆▆▆▆ Falconer v Australian Broadcasting Corporation *continued*

prevent its unauthorised disclosure, equity may also protect that information from disclosure by means of the use of non-confidential material. Particularly that should be so where the use of that material produces, as its inevitable outcome, not by some unintended sidewind, the means whereby the confidentiality of information may be breached. If equity did not give protection in such circumstances, the very thing that equity seeks to prevent would be effectively countenanced. Where equity has been cautious in saying, even where there has been some disclosure of confidential information, that this will destroy the protection which equity gives such material, there appears to me to be a stronger case again for restraining the use of non-confidential information which may well breach the confidentiality of information which has been otherwise carefully protected.

The plaintiff has satisfied me provisionally, that the principles of equity extend to prevent disclosure in the circumstances I have outlined.

... [213]

In my opinion the public policy considerations against disclosure of Rajicic's present identity are material to the exercise of my discretion, it having been once determined that there is confidential information. That is so whether the confidential information is conceived to include or exclude the photographs themselves.

Such public policy considerations tend in favour of the restraint which the plaintiff seeks. There is the need to ensure "a flow of intelligence about planned crime and its perpetrators". Anonymity of informers, and their [214] protection against those who would later wish them ill, are in my opinion matters of importance in the exercise of my discretion.

■ Circumstances importing an obligation of confidence

Contractual

[12.85] In a developed trade secret law here is no need for a contract between the parties to establish the existence of the relationship requiring confidentiality. Cases like *Saltman Engineering v Campbell Engineering* (1948) 65 RPC 203 make this clear. However, where a contract exists between the parties this can be important. The contract may specifically establish that between the parties the information is to be treated as secret, the contract may shape the scope of the duty, and it may be evidence that there is a relationship of confidence in existence.

In many cases an express term of confidentiality will exist, otherwise it can usually be implied. Obviously, in the context of a contract of service the existence of a contractual relationship between the parties imposes the obligation of confidence upon an employee. Employees are likely to learn their employer's trade secrets. A great many cases of trade secret or breach of confidentiality litigation are concerned with employers seeking to prevent their current employees or their former employees from divulging or using information learnt during employment. There is usually a difference between the obligations owed during employment and those owed after employment ceases.

The agreement may be express or implied from the fact of employment: see *Robb v Green* [1895] 2 QB 315; *Lamb v Evans* [1893] 1 Ch 218; *Amber Size & Chemical Co Ltd v Menzel* [1913] 2 Ch 239; *Lord Ashburton v Pape* [1913] 2 Ch 469; *Stevenson Jordan & Harrison v McDonald & Evans* [1952] 1 TLR 101 at 107; *Faccenda Chicken Ltd v Fowler* [1986] 1 All ER 617; *Printers & Finishers Ltd v Holloway* [1964] 3 All ER 731; *Ansell Rubber Pty Ltd v Allied Rubber*

Industries Pty Ltd [1967] VR 37; *Gilman Engineering Ltd v Ho Shek On* (1986) 8 IPR 313. The obligation of confidence, the second element of the test from *Coco* is thus present: *Fiscal Technology Co Ltd v Johnson* (1991) 23 IPR 555.

Employees and ex-employees present special problems, because of the common law principle that it is against public policy to prevent an employee, after leaving employment, from using general knowledge and skill acquired in the capacity of employee. One of the most difficult questions is to define the dividing line between general knowledge and skill, which an employee may legitimately exploit elsewhere, and confidential information. The issue is given prominence in a context of corporate failure or restructuring, and the practice of redundant employees using their redundancy payout to set up in business in the same line as their former employers. Employers may attempt to prevent the use of information after employment by specific contractual terms in the contract of employment which bind the employee after they have left employment. These are called restrictive covenants. These covenants may be expressed as agreements not to use or divulge certain information. They may also be agreements not to set up in competition with the employer, or work for a competitor for some years. The extract from *Ansell Rubber* above concerns not only the concept of secrecy of information but also some issues particularly relevant to the employment context, including: (i) the obligation of confidence arising from a contract of employment; (ii) the extent to which such an obligation survives the termination of the employment relationship; (iii) the general duty of fidelity owed by an employee to an employer.

The common law has a general principle of free movement of labour, and covenants, which improperly conflict with this principle, may be found to be void and unenforceable. Generally, a restrictive covenant may be justified only if it can be shown that the employer is seeking to protect a trade secret or relations with customers. The covenant must not be wider than is necessary to protect the employers' interests. So there will be a testing of which information is within the covenant, the length of time for which the restriction applies and the geographical area of the restriction.

Some information, which an employee would learn whilst working in the industry at large, must be regarded as part of the employee's general stock of skill and knowledge which they may take to another employer. Such information cannot be regarded as a trade secret and will not be protected by the general law of confidence. Nor can express contractual restriction of such information be justified. Not only is it not a trade secret but it cannot be fair to enforce the contractual term which would restrict the free flow of labour. Important cases illustrating these principles are *Printers & Finishers Ltd v Holloway* [1965] RPC 239; *Facienda Chicken Ltd v Fowler* (1985) 6 IPR 155; *ANI Corp Ltd v Celtite Australia Pty Ltd* (1990) 19 IPR 306 and *Wright v Gasweld Pty Ltd* (1990) 20 IPR 481. These issues are addressed in the extract from *Ansell Rubber* ([**12.70**]) and in *Print Investments Pty Ltd v Art-vue Printing Pty Ltd* (1983) 1 IPR 149.

Statutory

[**12.90**] There may be legislative sources of the obligation of confidence apart from the contractual or general one, for example, corporations law: see *AG Australia Holding Ltd v Burton* (2002) 58 IPR 268. The *Freedom of Information Act 1982* (Cth) protects from disclosure certain documents if the information contained therein is confidential or commercially valuable (ss 43, 45). The statute provides no definition of these concepts, however, and it is left to the Administrative Appeals Tribunal and the Federal Court to identify or define what is confidential or commercially valuable. Corporations seeking to safeguard trade secrets from competitors (not necessarily ex-employees) will want to know the limits of a request for information made pursuant to FOI legislation: see *Corrs Pavey Whiting & Byrne v Collector of Customs (Vic)* (1987) 10 IPR 53. It should also be noted, as discussed in *Ansell*, that the relevant features of a "trade secret" are codified in the American *Restatement of the Law of Torts* (1st ed), Art 737.

In some jurisdictions, the basic obligation to protect confidentiality comes primarily from a statute. One such model can be seen in an American approach. In 1980 the National Conference of Commissioners of Uniform State Laws proposed a uniform *Trade Secrets Act* which has been adopted by a number of States. This Act provides that information is property. A trade secret under the Act is information, (including a formula, pattern, compilation of data or information, program, device, method, technique or process), which derives economic value from not being generally known and which is the subject of efforts to keep it secret. A full range of civil remedies including injunctions, accounts damages and delivery up is available. The similarity between this Act and the description in the TRIPs Agreement is obvious.

An example of this type of trade secret statute is found in the Republic of Korea where in 1991 the *Unfair Competition Prevention Act* was amended to provide protection for trade secrets. The Korean Act was closely modelled on the Japanese *Trade Secret Law*, which itself draws upon the American model and the principles of the German civil tradition. Another statutory example containing some unusual elements is Indonesia's *Trade Secret Law*.

Privacy and confidence: Statutory basis

[12.95] While the common law has not yet formulated enforceable privacy obligations, there is a statutory regime, although it also does not create a general statutory tort of invasion of privacy. The *Privacy Act 1988* (Cth) applies to private sector organisations and Commonwealth agencies and establishes a number of principles which will apply unless the organisation has developed its privacy code approved by the Privacy Commissioner (also established by the Act). The Act provides principles relating to a range of privacy issues including collecting, storing, disclosing, securing and being accurate about private information, rights to anonymity in certain situations, and in particular, attention to information relating to political, religious or philosophical beliefs, membership of associations or trade unions, criminal records, health status and sexual preference. A person aggrieved by an infringement of these principles may lodge a complaint with the Privacy Commissioner seeking either a restraining order or compensation.

An important development is the introduction of the European Convention on Human Rights, Arts 8 and 9 and the *Human Rights Act 1998* (UK), s 12, introducing the right to respect for private and family life, albeit allowing for "jurisprudence which acknowledges different degrees of privacy": *Douglas v Hello! Ltd* [2001] 2 All ER 289 at 329. In the appeal of that case, which concerned the publication of unauthorised photographs of a celebrity wedding where the newlyweds had sold the rights to another magazine, Lord Justices Phillips, Clarke and Neuberger reluctantly formed the view that:

> "We conclude that, in so far as private information is concerned, we are required to adopt, as the vehicle for performing such duty as falls on the courts in relation to Convention rights, the cause of action formerly described as breach of confidence. As to the nature of that duty, it seems to us that ss 2, 3, 6 and 12 of the *Human Rights Act* all point in the same direction. The Court should, insofar as it can, develop the action for breach of confidence in such a manner as will give effect to both Art 8 and Art 10 rights." *Douglas v Hello! Ltd* (2005) 65 IPR 449 at 465.

Proprietary

[12.100] Is information property, or can it ever be? Some courts have moved away from the discussion and simply treat information as proprietary, for example, *Linda CL Koor v Lam Toi Hing* (1992) 23 IPR 607 (Supreme Court of Hong Kong). However, this has been the cause of much vigorous debate.

In the United States, in those States where a statute makes information property, there have been numerous prosecutions under the *National Stolen Property Act*. The Federal Courts have construed the words "goods and "things of value" to include intangible trade secrets. An example is *US v Bottone* 365 F 2d 389 (2nd Cir, 1966), where the information was in documents. The documents were taken, copied and the originals returned. The charge was transporting stolen goods, being the copies, worth $5000 or more interstate or in foreign trade. The case depended on the value. The Court found that the physical form of the goods was secondary to the matter recorded on them and that the information was "goods" which had a value of more than $5000. There are limits to this since the Court said that the rule would not apply to information which was memorised.

Equitable obligation

[12.105] In *Coco v AN Clark* (**[12.45]**), Megarry J proposed that the reasonable person be asked whether, in the shoes of the recipient of information, it should have been realised that the information was being given in confidence. The precise circumstances in which communication imports an obligation of confidence have not always been easy to state.

▀▀▀▀▀▀ Attorney-General (UK) v Heinemann ▀▀▀▀▀▀ Publishers Australia

[12.110] *Attorney-General (UK) v Heinemann Publishers Australia Pty Ltd* (1987) 75 ALR 353 Supreme Court of New South Wales

[This is an extract from the British Government's appeal against the finding by Powell J that the information Peter Wright, a former MI5 employee, wished to publish in his book *Spycatcher* was no longer confidential information.]

MCHUGH J: **[453]** Independently of contract, an enforceable equitable obligation of confidence may arise if confidential information is imparted in circumstances imputing an obligation to keep it confidential: *Saltman Engineering Co Ltd v Campbell Engineering Co Ltd* (1948) 65 RPC 203; *Prince Albert v Strange* (1849) 2 De G & Sm 652; 64 ER 293; *Coco v AN Clark (Engineers) Ltd* [1969] RPC 41. Sometimes the information may be conveyed with the express statement that it is confidential. But perhaps more frequently the obligation of confidence is to be deduced from the circumstances. In a business context, relevant circumstances will include the extent to which the information is known inside and outside the business, the measures taken to guard the secrecy, the value of the information to the person disclosing the information and his competitors, the amount of effort and capital invested in acquiring the information and the ease with which it can be acquired by others: see *Ansell Rubber Co Pty Ltd v Allied Rubber Co Pty Ltd* [1967] VR 37 at 50 per Gowans J. But that list is not exhaustive: *Deta Nominees Pty Ltd v Viscount Plastic Products Pty Ltd* [1979] VR 167 at 193 per Fullagar J. In other cases the obligation will arise simply from the common expectations or understandings of people in general. For this reason communications between husband and wife are confidential in respect of matters to whose publication either party might reasonably object: *Argyll v Argyll* [1967] Ch 302. In some cases an obligation of confidence is imposed to give effect to a more

▬▬▬▬ Attorney-General (UK) v Heinemann Publishers Australia *continued*

general obligation owed by the confidee. An employee owes a duty to act in good faith in the interests of his employer: *Robb v Green* [1895] 2 QB 315. Many statements can be found in the cases which indicate that this general obligation of fidelity imposes a specific obligation not to reveal information which is confidential: *Robb v Green* (at 10); *Measures Bros Ltd v Measures* [1910] 1 Ch 336 at 343. However, not all information which the employee obtains or receives in the course of his employment is impressed with an obligation of confidence. An employee is not precluded from disclosing employment information which did not have or has now lost the quality of confidentiality: cf *Bent's Brewery Co Ltd v Hogan* [1945] 2 All ER 570 at 576-577. Moreover, an employee may be entitled to publish or use employment information because, although the employer regarded the information as confidential, he has so acted that the employee was entitled to assume that he could use it or publish it: cf *Worsley & Co v Cooper* [1939] 1 All ER 290 at 306-310; *Aveley/Cybervox Ltd v Celltech Ltd* [1982] FSR 92 at 99-102. In these cases the implied duty of good faith is displaced, although it may be that it is displaced only to the extent that publication or use does not harm the employer's interests. Finally, it is well settled that an obligation of confidence owed by an employee does not cease with the termination of the employment: *Amber Size & Chemical Co Ltd v Menzel* [1913] 2 Ch 239.

Once it is established that a person without authorisation is proposing to publish confidential information imparted to him in confidence during a private or business relationship, little more need be proved for equity to restrain the publication. If **[454]** information imparted in confidence retains the necessary quality of confidence "in the sense that the preservation of its confidentiality of secrecy is of substantial concern to the plaintiff", then, subject to any special defences, equity will invariably restrain the publication: cf *Moorgate Tobacco Co Ltd v Philip Morris Ltd* (1984) 56 ALR 193; 156 CLR 414 at 438 per Deane J. Private concern or embarrassment is prima facie sufficient detriment to ground an injunction to restrain the threatened publication of confidential information acquired by one citizen in the course of his or her relationship with another.

However, when a question arises as to whether a person owes an obligation of confidence to a government in respect of information acquired in the course of his relationship with that government or a question arises as to whether a government or one of its departments or agencies owes an obligation of confidentiality to a citizen or employee, the equitable rules worked out in cases concerned with private relationships must be used with caution. This is especially so when the issue is whether the publication of information will be detrimental to the interests of the government in question or one of its agencies.

Courts of equity will protect the confidentiality of information imparted in confidence by governments: *Attorney-General (UK) v Jonathan Cape Ltd* [1976] QB 752; *Commonwealth v John Fairfax & Sons Ltd* (1980) 32 ALR 485; 147 CLR 39 at 50-52. The doors of the Chancery are not closed to governments or their agencies. Courts of equity will also protect the confidentiality of information given by citizens to governments and their departments and agencies: *Castrol Australia Pty Ltd v EmTech Associates Pty Ltd* (1980) 33 ALR 31; *Norwich Pharmacal Co v Commissioners of Customs & Excise* [1974] AC 133 at 189 per Viscount Dilhorne. But the relationship between the modern state and its citizens is so different in kind from that which exists between private citizens that rules worked out to govern the contractual, property, commercial and private confidences of citizens are not fully applicable where the plaintiff is a government or one of its agencies. Private citizens are entitled to protect or further their own interests, no matter how selfish they are in doing so. Consequently, the publication of confidential information which is detrimental to the private interest of a citizen is a legitimate concern of a Court of equity. But governments act, or at all events are constitutionally required to act, in the public interest. Information is held, received and imparted by

████████ Attorney-General (UK) v Heinemann Publishers Australia *continued*

governments, their departments and agencies to further the public interest. Public and not private interest, therefore, must be the criterion by which equity determines whether it will protect information which a government or governmental body claims is confidential.

In the absence of a claim based on a contractual or statutory obligation, equity will not protect the disclosure or use of what I shall call government information unless, at the time when the information was acquired, it was or would have been regarded by the government and the confidant as confidential, that it was imparted in circumstances which imposed an obligation of confidence, that it retains its confidentiality, and that it is in the public interest to treat it as confidential. In *Commonwealth v John Fairfax & Sons Ltd* (1980) 147 CLR 39 at 52; 32 ALR 485 at 493 Mason J said that:

> "The court will not prevent the publication of information which merely throws light on the past workings of government, even if it be not public property, so long as it does not prejudice the community in other [455] respects. Then disclosure will itself serve the public interest in keeping the community informed and in promoting discussion of public affairs. If, however, it appears that disclosure will be inimical to the public interest because national security, relations with foreign countries or the ordinary business of government will be prejudiced, disclosure will be restrained. There will be cases in which the conflicting considerations will be finely balanced, where it is difficult to decide whether the public's interest in knowing and in expressing its opinion, outweighs the need to protect confidentiality."

A decision by a judge sitting alone in the original jurisdiction of the High Court is probably not binding on this court. But binding or not, the views expressed by Mason J are in my opinion correct and should be followed. The law of England is the same: *Attorney-General (UK) v Jonathan Cape Ltd* (at 770-771).

I therefore reject the argument of the Attorney-General that, in an action by a government to restrain the breach of confidential information, it is enough that the publication of the information is a matter of "substantial concern" to the government or one of its agencies.

Notes

[12.115] The British Government appealed to the High Court from the finding of the majority of the New South Wales Court of Appeal, Kirby P and McHugh JA (Street CJ dissenting) that the appeal from Powell J's decision should be dismissed. The nature of the equitable obligation of confidence was not discussed in the High Court (nor by Street CJ in the Court of Appeal).

See *Minister for Mineral Resources v Newcastle Newspapers Pty Ltd* (1997) 40 IPR 403 for a further discussion of confidential government information. For comments on the law of confidence as compared with the law relating to fiduciary obligations, see *Lac Minerals Ltd v International Corona Resources Ltd* (1989) 16 IPR 27 at 45-46.

■ Misappropriation of information/third party users

[12.120] Information may be simply misappropriated rather than communicated, but the person obtaining it may still realise its secrecy and be placed under an obligation not to use it: *Franklin v Giddens* [1978] Qd R 72; see also discussion in *Douglas v Hello! Ltd* (2005) 65 IPR 449.

The second limb in *Coco v AN Clark* requires that the information in question has been received in circumstances importing an obligation of confidence. Difficulties arise where a third party uses trade secrets originally divulged in confidence to employees or others. If the third party is aware that the trade secret has been improperly obtained then liability appears to be uncontroversial: see *Printers & Finishers Ltd v Holloway* [1965] RPC 239 at 253. Where a trade secret is innocently obtained but the acquirer subsequently comes to learn that it was obtained in breach of confidence, that knowledge will impress that secret with the obligation of confidence in the hands of the third party: see *Stephenson, Jordan & Harrison Ltd v McDonald* [1952] 69 RPC 10.

Problems arise where an innocent third party obtains a purloined trade secret without knowledge of its theft. Kearney J in *Print Investments Pty Ltd v Art-vue Printing Pty Ltd* (1983) 1 IPR 149 at 153 suggested that the authorities left it an open question whether an injunction would lie against an innocent third party. The possibility of a bona fide purchaser's defence has been canvassed in a number of dicta. However, this possibility was strongly criticised by Helsham CJ in Eq in *Wheatley v Bell* [1982] 2 NSWLR 544. Statutory based systems which make information "property" may be able to deal with this issue more easily. Interestingly, the courts have found that unconscious use of information will be a breach of the duty to keep information confidential. An example is *Seager v Copydex Ltd (No 1)* [1967] 1 WLR 923.

■ Scope of the obligation of confidence

▬▬▬ Smith, Kline & French Laboratories (Aust) ▬▬▬ v Secretary, Department of Community Services & Health

[12.125] *Smith, Kline & French Laboratories (Aust) Ltd v Secretary, Dept of Comm Services & Health* (1991) 20 IPR 643 Federal Court of Australia

[This case concerned the drug cimetidine, a patented synthetic compound which was widely used for treating gastro-intestinal ulcers. Since its invention in the United Kingdom some 20 years before, it had gained a worldwide market. The drug was sold in Australia as "Tagamet" and "Duractin". The Australian patent expired on 15 February 1988, Alphapharm, the respondent, markets "generic" form of drugs and applied for approval of its version of cimetidine. This dispute concerned a variety of information contained in material sent by the appellant (SK & F) to the Federal Department of Community Services & Health which was responsible for allowing marketing approval in Australia.]

SHEPPARD, WILCOX and PINCUS JJ: **[645]** These two appeals, which were heard together, are against judgments of Gummow J relating to the use by Commonwealth health authorities of confidential information supplied by companies in the pharmaceutical business. His Honour dismissed an application by members of a group of such companies (the SK & F application), whose purpose was to restrict official use of such information. He granted an application by another pharmaceutical company (Alphapharm); it claimed declaratory relief affirming the authorities' right to use the confidential information in question. The appellants seek to support the proposition, rejected by Gummow J, that confidential information furnished to obtain governmental approval of the use of a pharmaceutical substance may not be resorted to in considering an application by another applicant, for approval of a version of the same substance. It is convenient to call the substance a "drug", despite the pejorative meaning that word has, in some contexts, acquired.

The appellants say that even if, as Gummow J held, the use of the appellants' confidential information in considering applications for approval by others generally operated to the

▰▰▰▰ Smith & Ors v Secretary, Department of Community Services & Health *continued*

detriment of those others, making their purpose of obtaining approval for their version of the drug more difficult to fulfil, still the appellants' confidential information cannot be so used. The, appellant which supplied the information is that first named in the proceedings' title (SK &F).

The drug in question is cimetidine, a patented synthetic compound which has proved to be of great value in treating gastro-intestinal ulcers. Since its invention in the UK about 20 years ago, it has been used around the world for that purpose and has earned large sums for the patentee (the second appellant) or companies associated with or licensed by the patentee. The drug has been sold in Australia under the trade names "Tagamet" and "Duractin". Many millions of dollars have been expended on the drug in this country. The Australian patent expired on 15 February 1988, but is the subject of an application for extension which has not yet been heard.

In July 1988, Alphapharm applied for approval of its version of the drug, but that application has not been dealt with, in consequence of an interlocutory injunction granted on 10 November 1987 in the proceedings in which the present appellants were applicants, and of Departmental reaction to that injunction. Alphapharm did not, of course, invent cimetidine, nor has it a licence from the patentee. Alphapharm took advantage of the expiration of the patent to attempt to introduce a formulation of cimetidine differing from the SK & F formulations; such a drug is called "generic" in the industry. The word "generic" implies in this context not merely that the drug is of the same kind as the patentee's, but also that there is no licence from the patentee, the patent having expired.

[646] The patentee does not, of course, seek to protect the information with respect to cimetidine disclosed in its patent specification. The dispute concerns a variety of other information, contained in material sent in support of a number of successive applications made for approval of cimetidine and compounds containing that substance. Those applications were made to the respondent Secretary of the relevant Department.

As amended, the SK & F application sought certain declarations and, as well, injunctions restraining the respondent from using certain confidential information for any purpose other than the exercise of statutory powers in relation to versions of cimetidine submitted by SK & F ... [654]

Gummow J found that when SK & F furnished the B1 data between 1975 and 1987, it did so on the implicit understanding that it would be:

> "kept [655] confidential in the sense that it would not be disclosed to any other pharmaceutical company lest use be made of it to the commercial disadvantage of the company which had supplied the information".

But if the submission on behalf of the appellants as to the test of the extent of confidentiality is accepted, that finding as to what was implied is of no consequence; for the appellants say that all that counts is the confider's purpose and that could not have gone beyond Departmental consideration of its own applications.

There is indeed some authority which, at least superficially, supports that view. One learned commentator has remarked:

> "The test which has found widespread acceptance is whether or not the information was disclosed for a limited purpose. If the information was disclosed for a limited purpose, the confidence crystallises around that limited purpose. The confidant will be bound by an obligation the content of which is not to use or disclose the information for any purpose other than the limited one for which the information was imparted":
> F Gurry in Finn, *Essays in Equity* (1985) at p 118.

▬▬▬▬ Smith & Ors v Secretary, Department of Community Services & Health *continued*

In many circumstances, that suggested test will produce a proper result, but the circumstances in which confidential information is supplied may vary widely. To determine the existence of confidentiality and its scope, it may be relevant to consider whether the information was supplied gratuitously or for a consideration; whether there is any past practice of such a kind as to give rise to an understanding; how sensitive the information is; whether the confider has any interest in the purpose for which the information is to be used; whether the confider expressly warned the confidee against a particular disclosure or use of the information—and, no doubt, many other matters. Confidential information is commonly supplied without payment: for example, by a prospective employee (or his referee) to support an application for employment. The understanding ordinarily would be that the prospective employer would not disclose the information to any third party; but it would hardly be expected that its use would necessarily be confined to the employment application itself. If that application were successful, the employee would not act on the assumption that material in the relevant file would be destroyed. He would surely be inclined to assume that it might be resorted to later to assist the employer in making decisions relevant to the employee—for example, as to whether the employee (rather than another) should be promoted, or dismissed.

The test of confider's purpose will not ordinarily be appropriate where each party's interest is quite different, and known to be so. Here, the confider's purpose is simple and narrow, the confidee's much broader. SK & F had only the purpose of having its applications approved. A person supplying confidential information to the government for the purpose of obtaining a licence (or a permission or concession) would ordinarily assume that the government would not destroy the application file after the confider had attained his purpose. The confider would probably expect that the information would be kept against the day when it might be needed to serve the government's legitimate interests: for example, to provide a record in case the decision is challenged as improper; to enable statistical information to be collected; or, acting directly against the interests of the confider, to compare the information supplied with the confider's subsequent **[656]** performance, in determining whether to cancel the licence. Gummow J referred to the reasons of McHugh JA (as his Honour then was) in *Attorney-General (UK) v Heinemann Publishers Australia Pty Ltd* (1987) 10 NSWLR 86 at 191; amongst other things, McHugh J said:

"But the relationship between the modern State and its citizens is so different in kind from that which exists between private citizens that rules worked out to govern the contractual, property, commercial and private confidences of citizens are not fully applicable where the plaintiff is a government or one of its agencies. Private citizens are entitled to protect or further their own interests, no matter how selfish they are in doing so ... (b)ut governments acts (sic), or at all events are constitutionally required to act, in the public interest".

Megarry J has suggested a broad test to determine whether an obligation of confidence exists. In *Coco v AN Clark (Engineers) Ltd* [1969] RPC 41, Megarry J said:

"It seems to me that if the circumstances are such that any reasonable man standing in the shoes of the recipient of the information would have realised that upon reasonable grounds the information was being given to him in confidence, then this should suffice to impose upon him the equitable obligation of confidence".

However, this test does not give guidance as to the scope of an obligation of confidentiality, where one exists. Sometimes the obligation imposes no restriction on use of the information, as long as the confidee does not reveal it to third parties. In other circumstances, the confidee may not be entitled to use it except for some limited purpose. In considering these problems, and indeed the whole question, it is necessary not to lose sight of the basis of the obligation to respect confidences: "It lies in the notion of an obligation of conscience arising from the circumstances in or through which the information was communicated or obtained". This is quoted from *Moorgate Tobacco Co Ltd v Phillip Morris Ltd (No 2)* (1984) 156 CLR 414 at 438 per Deane J, with whom the other members of the court agreed. A similar broad view has been taken in the US: *EI Dupont de Nemours Powder Co v Masland* (1917) 244 US 102:

> "Therefore the starting point for the present matter is not property or due process of law, but that the defendant stood in confidential relations with the plaintiffs, or one of them. These have given place to hostility, and the first thing to be made sure of is that the defendant shall not fraudulently abuse the trust reposed in him. It is the usual incident of confidential relations".

Similar expressions recur in other cases: *Seager v Copydex Ltd* [1967] RPC 349 at 368: "The law on this subject ... depends on the broad principle of equity that he who has received information in confidence shall not take unfair advantage of it".

To avoid taking unfair advantage of information does not necessarily mean that the confidee must not use it except for the confider's limited purpose. Whether one adopts the "reasonable man" test suggested by Megarry J or some other, there can be no breach of the equitable obligation unless the Court concludes that a confidence reposed has been abused, that unconscientious use has been made of the information.

[657] Here, SK & F supplied, in pursuit of its commercial interests, a mass of information, part of which was confidential. It did not trouble to identify that part when furnishing the information. Nor did it, until very late in the piece, make the assertion that was so much pressed upon us in this Court, namely that the Department could not make purely internal use of the information other than for SK & F purposes, not even when public health and safety made that necessary. In those circumstances, it appears to us that the primary Judge was correct in concluding as he did that no equitable obligation was breached, except as to the use of the sample for the government of Papua New Guinea.

We would add that, in our opinion, Courts exercising equitable jurisdiction should not be too ready to import an equitable obligation of confidence in a marginal case. There is the distinction between use of confidential information in a way of which many people might disapprove, on the one hand, and illegal use on the other. Not only the administration of business and government, but ordinary communication between people, might be unduly obstructed by use of too narrow a test, such as that which the appellants put forward here. This is amply illustrated by the facts of the present case in which the evidence clearly showed the substantial interference with vital functions of government, in protecting the health and safety of the community, which could ensue if the appellants' primary submission were accepted. It is our view that the "blanket" protection of the SK & F B1 data which the appellants sought, as well as the rather more limited protection suggested during the hearing in this Court, would go well beyond any obligation which ought to be imposed on the Secretary.

This conclusion is at least consistent with that arrived at in the High Court in New Zealand in 1988 and in the House of Lords in 1989: *Smith Kline & French Laboratories Ltd v AG* [1989] 1 NZLR 385, In *Re Smith Kline & French Laboratories Ltd* [1989] 2 WLR 397. We have, however, found it unnecessary to include in these reasons an analysis of either of those decisions.

Note

[12.130] The *Therapeutic Goods Act 1989* (Cth) was amended to allow the use of information to assess "generic" applications following this case. The TRIPs Agreement, Art 39(3) requires protection of undisclosed test data or other data which is required to be submitted for marketing approval of pharmaceutical or agricultural chemical products using new chemical entities. The data must be protected against unfair commercial use, and against disclosure unless disclosure is necessary to protect the public.

Unauthorised use to the detriment of the person communicating information

[12.135] The third aspect of Megarry J's classic formulation of the elements of an action for breach of confidence has been criticised as unnecessary. In any event, the common law courts have taken a very flexible attitude to what constitutes detriment. In trade secret cases, such factors as loss of exclusivity, loss of custom, having to face commercial competition, effect upon reputation and indeed anything that impinges upon the interests of the plaintiff will justify the granting of an injunction. Where the plaintiff wants compensatory damages, the actual harm or loss will have to be proved, and this may be a narrower requirement than mere detriment.

The detriment, if necessary, need not be financial but could be personal or social. Detriment may be necessary if the plaintiff is a government seeking to restrain publication of information: see *Attorney-General (UK) v Heinemann Publishers Australia Pty Ltd* (1987) 10 IPR 153 at 219-220 per Kirby J. Where the plaintiff is a "governmental plaintiff", the disclosure may need to result in probable prejudice to the workings of government before sufficient "detriment" is found: see *Minister for Mineral Resources v Newcastle Newspapers Pty Ltd* (1997) 40 IPR 403.

PARTLY CONFIDENTIAL INFORMATION—THE "SPRINGBOARD DOCTRINE"

[12.140] It is not always the plaintiff's information alone that is used, nor is the use necessarily fraudulent or unconscionable if a defendant mistakenly "mixes" the secret with his or her own ideas or expertise to achieve a certain result. The rule has emerged, however, that information may not be used as a "springboard" for activities detrimental to the plaintiff, even when all the information has reached the public domain or some of the information was not confidential to the plaintiff anyway. The "springboard' doctrine was formulated in *Terrapin Ltd v Builders Supply Co (Hayes) Ltd* [1967] RPC 375 by Roxburg J:

> "As I understand it the essence of this branch of the law, whatever the origin of it may be, is that a person who has obtained information in confidence is not allowed to use it as a springboard for activities detrimental to the person who made the confidential communication and spring board it remains even when all of the features have been published or can be ascertained by actual inspection by any member of the public ... the possessor of such information must be placed under a special disability in the field of competition in order to ensure that he does not get an unfair start."

This doctrine does not mean that information which has reached the public domain is still a trade secret. It means that care must be taken to determine whether the defendant is relying on the information which has genuinely reached the public as the public could do, or if the defendant is relying on the advantage of having had the secret before it was revealed and is now making unfair use of that previous access to the secret. Consider the examples of the *Terrapin Case* and *Aqua Culture Corp v New Zealand Green Mussel Co Ltd* (1985) 5 IPR 353; (1988) 10 IPR 319. This approach strongly reflects unfair competition principles rather than any notion of "property rights".

Seager v Copydex

[12.145] *Seager v Copydex Ltd* [1967] 1 WLR 923 Court of Appeal

[The plaintiff and the defendant had discussed the possibility of the defendant manufacturing and distributing carpet grips on a design developed by the plaintiff. After a breakdown of negotiations between the parties the defendant produced an alternative grip which the plaintiff alleged imported aspects of his design.]

LORD DENNING MR: **[931]** I have no doubt that Copydex honestly believe the alternative was their own idea; but I think that they must unconsciously have made use of the information which Mr Seager gave them. The coincidences are too strong to permit of any other explanation.

I start with one sentence in the judgment of Lord Greene MR in *Saltman Engineering Co v Campbell Engineering Co* (1948) 65 RPC 203 at 213; [1963] 3 All ER 413 at 414, CA:

"If a defendant is proved to have used confidential information, directly or indirectly obtained from the plaintiff, without the consent, express or implied, of the plaintiff, he will be guilty of an infringement of the plaintiff's rights."

To this I add a sentence from the judgment of Roxburgh J in *Terrapin Ltd v Builders' Supply Co (Hayes) Ltd* [1960] RPC 128 at 130, CA, which was quoted and adopted as correct by Roskill J in *Cranleigh Precision Engineering Ltd v Bryant* [1965] 1 WLR 1293 at 1317, 1319; [1964] 3 All ER 289:

"As I understand it, the essence of this branch of the law, whatever the origin of it may be, is that a person who has obtained information in confidence is not allowed to use it as a springboard for activities detrimental to the person who made the confidential communication, and springboard it remains even when all features have been published or can be ascertained by actual inspection by any member of the public."

The law on this subject does not depend on any implied contract. It depends on the broad principle of equity that he who has received information in confidence shall not take unfair advantage of it. He must not make use of it to the prejudice of him who gave it without obtaining his consent. The principle is clear enough when the whole of the information is private. The difficulty arises when the information is in part public and in part private. As, for instance, in this case. A good deal of the information which Mr Seager gave to Copydex was available to the public, such as the patent specification in the Patent Office, or the "Klent" grip, which he sold to anyone who asked. If that was the only information he gave them, he could not complain. It was public knowledge. But there was a good deal of other information he gave them which was private, such as the difficulties which had to be overcome in making a satisfactory grip; the necessity for a strong, sharp tooth; the alternative forms of tooth; and the like. When the information is mixed, being partly public and partly private, then the recipient must take special care to use only the material which is in the public domain. He should go to the public source and get it; or, at any rate, not be in a better position than if he had gone to the public source. He should not get a start over others by **[932]** using the information which he received in confidence. At any rate, he should not get a start without paying for it. It may not be a case for injunction or even for an account, but only for damages, depending on the worth of the confidential information to him in saving him time and trouble.

Applying these principles, I think that Mr Seager should succeed. On the facts which I have stated, he told Copydex a lot about the making of a satisfactory carpet grip which was not in the public domain. They would not have got going so quickly except for what they had learned in their discussions with him. They got to know in particular that it was possible to make an alternative grip in the form of a "V-tang," provided the tooth was sharp enough and strong enough, and they were told about the special shape which would produce this result. The judge thought that the information was not significant. But I think it was. It was the springboard which enabled them to go on to devise the "Invisigrip" and to apply for a patent for it. They were quite innocent of any intention to take advantage of him. They thought that, as long as they did not infringe his patent, they were exempt. In this they were in error. They were not aware of the law as to confidential information. They were not at liberty to make use of any confidential information he gave them without paying for it.

▬▬▬▬▬▬▬▬▬▬▬▬▬▬▬▬▬▬▬▬▬▬▬▬▬▬▬▬▬▬▬▬▬▬▬▬▬▬

▬▬▬▬▬▬ **Coco v AN Clark (Engineers)** ▬▬▬▬▬▬

[12.150] *Coco v AN Clark (Engineers) Ltd* [1969] RPC 41 Chancery Division

MEGARRY J: Before I turn to the second main head, that of interlocutory relief, I should mention one point on the substantive law that caused me some difficulty during the argument. This is what may be called the "springboard" doctrine. In the *Seager* case [1967] 1 WLR 923 at 931, Lord Denning quoted a sentence from the judgment of Roxburgh J in the *Terrapin* case [1960] RPC 128 at 130, which was quoted and adopted as correct by Roskill J in the *Cranleigh* case [1965] 1 WLR 1293 at 1317. It runs as follows:

> "As I understand it, the essence of this branch of the law, whatever the origin of it may be, is that a person who has obtained information in confidence is not allowed to use it as a springboard for activities detrimental to the person who made the confidential communication, and springboard it remains even when all the features have been published or can be ascertained by actual inspection by any member of the public."

Salmon LJ in the *Seager* case (at 933) also states: "The law does not allow the use of such information even as a springboard for activities detrimental to the plaintiff."

Quite apart from authority, I would recognise the principle enshrined in those words as being salutory. Nevertheless, I am not entirely clear how it is to be put into practical effect in every case. Suppose a case where there is a confidential communication of information which is partly public and partly private; suppose that the recipient of the information adds in confidence ideas of his own, improving the initial scheme; and suppose that the parties then part, with no agreement concluded between them. How is a conscientious recipient of the ideas to comply with the requirements that equity lays upon him? For in the words of Lord Denning (at 931) in the *Seager* case, he

■■■■■■ Coco v AN Clark (Engineers) *continued*

"must take special care to use only the material which is in the public domain. He should go to the public source and get it: or, at any rate, not be in a better position than if he had gone to the public source. He should not get a start over others by using the information which he received in confidence".

Suppose that the only confidential information communicated is that some important component should be made of aluminium instead of steel and with significant variations in its design and dimensions. The recipient knows that this change will transform a failure into a success. He knows that, if he had persevered himself, he might have come upon the solution in a week or in a year. Yet he is under a duty not to use the confidential information as a springboard or as giving him a start.

What puzzles me is how, as a law-abiding citizen, he is to perform that duty. He could, I suppose, commission someone else to make the discovery anew, carefully abstaining from saying anything to him about aluminium or the design and dimensions which will achieve success, but this seems to me to be artificial in the extreme. Yet until this step is taken and the discovery made anew, he cannot make use of his own added ideas for the further improvement of the design which he had already communicated in confidence to the original communicator, ideas which would perhaps make a success into a triumph. He cannot build his superstructure as long as he is forbidden to use the foundations. Nor is the original communicator in a much better case. He is free to use his own original idea, which converted into success; but he cannot take advantage of the original recipient's further ideas, of which he knows, until such time as he or someone commissioned by him would, unaided by any confidence, have discovered them.

For those who are not law-abiding and conscientious citizens there is, I suppose, a simple answer: ignore the duty, use the information, and then pay damages. This may be the course which Lord Denning envisaged in the *Seager* case: for after stating that the recipient should not get a start over others by using the confidential information, he continued on (at 932): "At any rate, he should not get a start without paying for it. It may not be a case for injunction or even for an account, but only for damages, depending on the worth of the confidential information to him in saving him time and trouble." I also recognise that a conscientious and law-abiding citizen, having received confidential information in confidence, may accept that when negotiations break down the only honourable course is to withdraw altogether from the field in question until his informant or someone else has put the information into the public domain and he can no longer be said to have any start. Communication thus imposes on him a unique disability. He alone of all men must for an uncertain time abjure this field of endeavour, however great his interest. I find this scarcely more reasonable than the artificiality and uncertainty of postponing the use of the information until others would have discovered it.

The relevance of this point, I think, is this. If the duty is a duty not to use the information without consent, then it may be the proper subject of an injunction restraining its use, even if there is an offer to pay a reasonable sum for that use. If, on the other hand, the duty is merely a duty not to use the information without paying a reasonable sum for it, then no such injunction should be granted. Despite the assistance of counsel I feel far from assured that I have got to the bottom of this matter. But I do feel considerable hesitation in expressing a doctrine of equity in terms that include a duty which law-abiding citizens cannot reasonably be expected to perform. In other words, the essence of the duty seems more likely to be that of not using without paying, rather than of not using at all. It may be that in fields other than industry and commerce (and I have in mind the *Argyll* case) the duty may exist in the more stringent form; but in the circumstances present in this case I think that the less stringent

▄▄▄▄▄ Coco v AN Clark (Engineers) *continued*

form is the more reasonable. No doubt this matter may be canvassed and resolved at the trial; but on motion, in a case where both the probabilities and the evidence support the view that the fruits of any confidential communication were to sound in monetary compensation to the communicator. I should be slow to hold that it was right to enjoin the defendant company from making any use of the information.

Notes

[12.155] The usual remedy where a defendant has used confidential information as a "springboard" will be a temporary injunction against the defendant to cover the period of headstart unfairly obtained, or damages to deprive the defendant of the fruits of the advantage. In *Titan Group Pty Ltd v Steriline Manufacturing Pty Ltd* (1990) 19 IPR 353 O'Loughlin J said (at 377):

> "The start (and finish) of a springboard cannot be determined from the cases, except by analogy, for the determination of the duration of the springboard is 'a question of degree depending on the particular case': *Franchi v Franchi* [1967] RPC 149 at 153 per Cross J. But in every case the period of the springboard will always be 'one of limited duration': *Harrison v Project & Design Co (Redcar) Ltd* [1978] FSR 81 at 87 per Graham J."

See also *British Franco Electric Pty Ltd v Dowling Plastics Pty Ltd* [1981] 1 NSWLR 448; *Ackroyds (London) Ltd v Islington Plastics Ltd* [1962] RPC 97; *Deta Nominees Pty Ltd v Viscount Plastic Products Pty Ltd* [1979] VR 167; *Speed Seal Products Ltd v Paddington* [1986] 1 All ER 91; *Aquaculture Corp v New Zealand Green Mussel Co (No 1)* (1985) 5 IPR 353; *(No 2)* (1988) 10 IPR 319; *(No 3)* (1990) 19 IPR 527; *US Surgical Corp v Hospital Products International Pty Ltd* [1982] 2 NSWLR 761.

DISCLOSURE IN THE PUBLIC INTEREST

[12.160] The publication or use of the information in breach of confidence is justified in the wider public interest to protect such things as national security, public health, the administration of justice and the fabric of society. Framed rather narrowly in Australia, it is unlikely that the defence will protect "whistleblowers" revealing information concerning inefficiency, irregularities or technical breaches of the law. The courts of the United Kingdom have taken a broader approach to the public interest defence and have instead adopted the broader proposition that disclosure should not necessarily be enjoined where the public interest in publication outweighs the public interest in confidentiality.

This concept of "balancing" competing interests is discussed by Rath J in the extract from *Castrol Australia Pty Ltd v Emtech Associates Pty Ltd* (1980) 33 ALR 31 ([12.165]) and is illustrated to some extent by an English case, *Lion Laboratories v Evans* (1984) 3 IPR 276. Lion Laboratories manufactured and sold a computerised instrument called the Lion Intoximeter 3000. The machine was used by the Police in breath testing drivers for blood alcohol levels and if the levels were above a defined limit the driver would be charged with a crime. Two former employees believed that there was doubt about the reliability and accuracy of the machine. They attempted to supply documents and information to national newspapers. Lion Laboratories applied for an injunction to restrain publication. The Court refused to grant an injunction to restrain information when there was public interest in securing proper evidence before the court in drink driving cases, and in safeguarding the civil liberties of the accused. One feature of this case was the lack of likelihood that the responsible government agency would pursue the truth in an unbiased fashion. The public interest outweighed the interest of Lion Laboratories in preserving secret information about its product.

In Australia a governmental plaintiff must show that disclosure would result in probably prejudice to the workings of government: see *Minister for Mineral Resources v Newcastle Newspapers Pty Ltd* (1997) 40 IPR 403. Insofar as confidences of the government are concerned, Mason J in *Commonwealth v John Fairfax & Sons Ltd* (1980) 147 CLR 39 at 52 explained:

> "The court will not prevent the publication of information which merely throws light on the past workings of government, even if it be not public property, so long as it does not prejudice the community in other respects. Then disclosure will itself serve the public interest in keeping the community informed and in promoting discussion of public affairs. If, however, it appears that disclosure will be inimical to the public interest because national security, relations with foreign countries or the ordinary business of government will be prejudiced, disclosure will be restrained. There will be cases in which the conflicting considerations will be finely balanced, where it is difficult to decide whether the public's interest in knowing and in expressing its opinion, outweighs the need to protect confidentiality."

Support for this approach is to be found in *Attorney-General (UK) v Jonathan Cape Ltd* [1976] QB 752, where the court refused to grant an injunction to restrain publication of the diaries of Richard Crossman. Lord Widgery LCJ said (at 770-771):

> "The Attorney-General must show (a) that such publication would be a breach of confidence; (b) that the public interest requires that the publication be restrained, and (c) that there are no other facts of the public interest contradictory of and more compelling than that relied upon. Moreover, the court, when asked to restrain such a publication, must closely examine the extent to which relief is necessary to ensure that restrictions are not imposed beyond the strict requirement of public need."

Although this statement has been criticised on the ground that it is contrary to principle and unduly restricts the right of government to restrain disclosure, his Lordship was correctly elaborating the principle so as to take account of the special character of the government and defining the detriment which it needs to show."

▬▬▬▬▬ Castrol Australia v Emtech Assoc ▬▬▬▬▬

[12.165] *Castrol Australia Pty Ltd v EmTech Assoc Pty Ltd* (1980) 33 ALR 31 Supreme Court of New South Wales

[For the purpose of developing a new lubricating oil the plaintiff submitted a number of oils to the first defendant for testing. The first defendant prepared a report for the plaintiff. The plaintiff subsequently consulted the Trade Practices Commission (now the ACCC) to ensure that its promotional material complied with the consumer protection provisions of the *Trade Practices Act 1974* (Cth). The Commission indicated that the plaintiff's promotional claims

██████ Castrol Australia v Emtech Assoc *continued*

might breach ss 52 or 53 of the Act in that it made possibly exaggerated claims for the performance of the oil. The Commission then served a notice under s 155 of the Act to discover the first defendant's test report. The plaintiff sought injunctions against the defendants to enjoin disclosure of the report. The defendant's responded by arguing either that the report was not protected by the law of confidence or that disclosure of the report was in the public interest.

The Court found on the evidence of the report that the promotional material of the plaintiff did not breach the Act. His Honour continued:]

RATH J: **[53]** Secondly, even if I thought that the results stated in the EmTech report did not support the advertised claims, I should not accept this circumstance as a sufficient reason for relieving the commission of its obligation of confidence in regard to the disclosure and use of the report. In taking this position, I am preferring expressions of judicial opinion that have laid stress on public policy in the preservation of confidence to expressions of like opinion that appear to be based on an expanded concept of public interest.

In *Gartside v Outram* (1856) 26 LJ Ch 113, the plaintiffs were suing to restrain the defendant, a former employee, from disclosing any of their dealings and transactions. The defendant in answer to the plaintiffs' bill said that the plaintiffs conducted their business in a fraudulent way. Wood V-C said (at 114):

> "But there are exceptions to this confidence, or perhaps, rather only nominally, and not really exceptions. The true doctrine is, that there is no confidence as to the disclosure of iniquity. You cannot make me a confidant of a crime or fraud, and be entitled to close up my lips upon any secret which you have the audacity to disclose to me relating to any fraudulent intention on your part: such a confidence cannot exist."

In *Weld-Blundell v Stephens* [1919] 1 KB 520, Bankes LJ (at 527) explained *Gartside v Outram* as one of a class of cases of confidential communications as to the proposed commission of a civil wrong on a person. Similarly, Warrington LJ said of it (at 534): "The fraud there alleged was a systematic fraud pursued by the plaintiffs in the course of their business, and the disclosure of the evidence in the defendants' possession would tend to prevent such frauds in the future." With these observations in mind, I think it is proper to refrain from giving an unduly wide meaning to the word "iniquity" in Wood V-C's famous dictum that "There is no confidence as to the disclosure of iniquity".

In *Initial Services Ltd v Putterill* [1968] 1 QB 396; [1967] 3 All ER 145, the defendant, in defence of his breaking confidence as a former employee, sought to plead that the plaintiff was a party to an agreement to keep up prices, which agreement had not been registered under the *Restrictive Trade Practices Act 1956*, and that the plaintiff had issued a circular to its customers that was misleading in its explanation of the plaintiff's increased charges. Thus the plaintiff's conduct, as alleged by the defendant, was similar to the "systematic fraud pursued by the plaintiffs in the course of their business" that Warrington LJ had found in *Gartside v Outram*. Lord Denning MR said of the exception to **[54]** confidence referred to in *Gartside v Outram* the following (at 405):

> "The exception should extend to crimes, frauds and misdeeds, both those actually committed as well as those in contemplation, provided always and this is essential that the disclosure is justified in the public interest. The reason is because 'no private obligations can dispense with that universal one which lies on every member of society to discover every design which may be formed, contrary to the laws of the society, to destroy the public welfare': see *Annesley v Anglesea (Earl)* (1743) LR 5 QB 317; 17 State Tr 1139."

███████ Castrol Australia v Emtech Assoc *continued*

The "exception" cannot universally be extended to crimes actually committed, as Bankes LJ pointed out in *Weld-Blundell v Stephens* [1919] 1 KB 520 at 527, 528; but the exclusion from the protection of confidence of designs formed "to destroy the public welfare" expresses a concept which is authoritatively expressed in modern terms in the following way by Viscount Finlay in *Weld-Blundell v Stephens* [1920] AC 956 at 965-966:

> "It would be startling if it were the law that an agent who is negligent in the custody of a letter handed to him in confidence by his principal might plead in defence that the letter was libellous. There may, of course, be cases where some higher duty is involved. Danger to the state or public duty may supersede the duty of the agent to his principal."

In *Fraser v Evans* [1969] 1 QB 349; [1969] 1 All ER 8, the plaintiff was a public relations consultant of the Greek government. He sought to restrain publication in a newspaper of an article based on a report he had made to the Greek government. His claimed based on breach of confidence failed at the threshold because, in the view of the Court of Appeal, only the Greek government had any standing to complain. Lord Denning advanced a possible additional ground in the following passage (at 362):

> "Even if Mr Fraser had any standing to complain, *The Sunday Times* say that in any event they have just cause or excuse for publishing. They rely on the line of authority from *Gartside v Outram* to the latest case, *Initial Services Ltd v Putterill*. They quote the words of Wood V-C that 'there is no confidence as to the disclosure of iniquity'. I do not look upon the word 'iniquity' as expressing a principle. It is merely an instance of just cause or excuse for breaking confidence. There are some things that require to be disclosed in the public interest in which event no confidence can be prayed in aid to keep them secret."

But Lord Denning felt that it might be difficult for *The Sunday Times* to make out that case in the circumstances. Accordingly the passage quoted would not appear to be a reason for the decision. It is thus unnecessary to consider the effect of the "entire agreement" of Widgery LJ with Lord Denning and Davies LJ: see, on this point, *Malone v Metropolitan Police Commissioner* [1979] 1 All ER 256; [1979] 1 WLR 700 at 715-716. The formulation, "just cause or excuse for breaking confidence", is of course unexceptionable, provided that it is not used to whittle down the obligation of confidence, and introduce exceptions that would not qualify under Viscount Finlay's "higher duty" criterion.

[55] *Hubbard v Vosper* [1972] 2 QB 84; [1972] 1 All ER 1023, is another decision of the Court of Appeal in which Lord Denning said, in relation to a claim of confidence, that "the information must be such that it is a proper subject for protection" (at 95) and went on to quote from *Fraser v Evans*: "There are some things which may be required to be disclosed in the public interest, in which event no confidence can be prayed in aid to keep them secret." The other members of the court agreed with Lord Denning. Wood V-C's "iniquity" has on this language become simply "public interest", with no further definition. The application was an interlocutory one, and no final decision on the facts was called for; but Lord Denning said (at 96) that there was good ground for thinking that the alleged confidential material (courses in "Scientology") contained "such dangerous material" that it was in the public interest that it should be made known. Thus the test actually applied was in effect danger to the public. Megaw LJ said, "there is here evidence that the plaintiffs are or have been protecting their secrets by deplorable means". He concluded that they did not come to the court with clean hands.

▬▬▬▬ Castrol Australia v Emtech Assoc *continued*

Ungoed-Thomas J in *Beloff v Pressdram Ltd* [1973] 1 All ER 241, expressed his understanding of Lord Denning's judgment in *Hubbard v Vosper*, and the defence of public interest, as follows (at 260):

"In *Hubbard v Vosper* Lord Denning MR treated material on scientology published in breach of confidence as susceptible to a defence of public interest on the ground that it was dangerous material, namely medical quackeries 'dangerous in untrained hands'.

The defence of public interest clearly covers and, in the authorities does not extend beyond, disclosure, which as Lord Denning MR emphasised must be disclosure justified in the public interest, of matters carried out or contemplated, in breach of the country's security, or in breach of law, including statutory duty, fraud, or otherwise destructive of the country or its people, including matters medically dangerous to the public; and doubtless other misdeeds of similar gravity. Public interest, as a defence in law, operates to over-ride the rights of the individual (including copyright) which would otherwise prevail and which the law is also concerned to protect. Such public interest, as now recognised by the law, does not extend beyond misdeeds of a serious nature and importance to the country and thus, in my view, clearly recognisable as such."

This passage, in my respectful view, expresses no more than a reasonable elaboration of Viscount Finlay's "higher duty" concept, and is an acceptable statement of the law as to the defence of public interest in an action for breach of confidence. In copyright law there may in Australia be a question as to whether there is a place for such a non-statutory defence: cf *Pacific Film Laboratories Pty Ltd v Federal Commissioner of Taxation* (1970) 121 CLR 154 at 166. What is particularly important in Ungoed-Thomas J's formulation of principle is his emphasis on the gravity of the conduct that may give rise to the defence. If there is to be a defence labelled public interest, some such confinement of its vague boundaries is in my view essential.

[56] In *D v National Society for the Prevention of Cruelty to Children* [1978] AC 171; [1977] 1 All ER 589, Lord Denning in the Court of Appeal had treated the court's power to compel disclosure of confidential information as the converse of the court's exercising its power to restrain breach of confidence. "To my mind", he said (AC at 190) "it is all a question of balancing competing interests." He was in the minority in the Court of Appeal, but in the House of Lords his decision was confirmed by a majority of the House. But though the House applied the criterion of public interest to the question of compelling disclosure in judicial proceedings of confidential information, there is no adoption in the speeches of their lordships of public interest as a test for refusing relief in an action to restrain the disclosure of confidential information.

In *Woodward v Hutchins* [1977] 1 WLR 760; [1977] 2 All ER 751, the Court of Appeal refused the plaintiffs an injunction to restrain disclosure of confidential information. The plaintiffs had issued a writ for libel against the defendants, and the defendants proposed to plead justification. The plaintiffs were a well-known group of singers, and one defendant was their former press relations agent. Lord Denning said (at 763-764):

"If a group of this kind seek publicity which is to their advantage, it seems to me that they cannot complain if a servant or employee of theirs afterwards discloses the truth about them. If the image which they fostered was not a true image, it is in the public interest that it should be corrected. In these cases it is a question of balancing the public interest in maintaining the confidence against the public interest in knowing the truth ... In this case the balance comes down in favour of the truth being told, even if it should involve some breach of confidential information."

Woodward v Hutchins is the spring tide mark of "public interest" as a criterion for refusing relief in confidence cases. If Lord Denning's quoted statement is taken literally the court will test the legitimacy of breach of confidence by its conception of the balance of public interest in the particular circumstances of the case. As in *Woodward v Hutchins* itself the balance may weigh down in favour of disclosure even if no "iniquity" either criminal or tortious, is involved. In no previous case has the obligation of confidence been weighed against the "public interest" in "truth being told". If this new test is right, then Viscount Finley's concept of "higher duty" no longer expressed the law. In my opinion the court, in considering whether just cause for breaking confidence exists, must have regard to matters of a more weighty and precise kind than a public interest in the truth being told. No doubt the plaintiffs in *Woodward v Hutchins* had gone to considerable lengths to present a favourable public image. In a sense their image was a matter of public interest, but not in the sense that as a matter of public policy the defendants were entitled, or required, to break confidence. The former press relations agent to the plaintiffs seems to me to have been in a position comparable to that of the accountant who, in *Weld-Blundell v Stephens*, was held to be negligent in leaving a libellous letter addressed to him in the office of the defamed persons.

[57] The actual decision in *Woodward v Hutchins* is supportable on the ground, given by the court, that the grant of an injunction on the basis of breach of confidence would frustrate the long standing principle that an injunction will not be granted to restrain publication of a libel where the defendant proposes to plead justification. This was the ground relied upon by Lawton LJ in that case. Bridge LJ in agreeing, as he did, with both judgments, was presumably agreeing with the common ground of decision.

Even if the view expressed by Lord Denning, as to one side of the balance being weighed down by the public interest in truth being told, is the ratio decidendi of *Woodward v Hutchins*, it would not be applicable to the present circumstances, for the following reasons. In that case the plea of justification involved the defendants in justifying the truth of the libel, or being liable to substantial damages. The defendants in other words had undertaken the task of showing that the plaintiffs deliberately fostered a public image which was a false one. But in this case none of the defendants has claimed that the plaintiff is guilty of an offence. In fact, as Mr Gilbert's affidavit in the Federal Court of Australia said, the commission had not decided to commence proceedings against the plaintiff. Nothing was disclosed in the present hearing indicative of any different decision being made. Further, although is was submitted on behalf of the commission that the EmTech report did not support the plaintiff's claims in advertising, I have found that, whilst this submission may represent the commission's view, there is substance in the contrary submission made on behalf of the plaintiff. Disclosure of the EmTech report therefore does not necessarily destroy the "image" that the plaintiff presented for GTX-FM in its advertising. There is here no simple balance with disputable truth on one side of the scales.

Taking such guidance as I can from the authorities I have reviewed on the principles applicable where a defendant seeks to excuse breach of confidence, I am of the opinion that no sufficient excuse, on the evidence at present before the court, has been shown for allowing the defendants to disclose or use the plaintiff's confidential information, in particular the EmTech report, and any information in explanation or elaboration of that report that the commission and its officers may have obtained from the second defendant.

CHAPTER 13

PROTECTION OF BUSINESS REPUTATION

INTRODUCTION

[13.05] Business reputation is protected from wrongful appropriation by the tort of passing off and by the closely related actions which may be brought under the *Trade Practices Act 1974* (Cth) prohibiting false, misleading or deceptive conduct or representations. The fair trading legislation of various States and Territories echoes the federal prohibition on misleading conduct; *Trade Practices Act 1974* (Cth), s 52 provides that "A corporation shall not, in trade or commerce, engage in conduct that is misleading or deceptive or is likely to mislead or deceive". This current emphasis on consumer protection sees injured traders more or less as incidental beneficiaries of regulation designed to ensure that the public does not suffer due to deceptive marketing practices. However, in the early stages of passing off, the emphasis was on preventing or punishing fraudulent business practices. The fact that this benefited merchants whose goodwill was damaged by such practices seems not to have been the dominant concern of the courts, and this goodwill came to be recognised as a form of property. While it is possible to distinguish between a statute with consumer protection focus in the form of trade practices and fair trading legislation, and a common law passing off action to protect traders, this section of the materials will draw on the common threads that have led to development of the notion that traders should be recognised as having some proprietary interest in the goodwill built up by their efforts, developing from the equity courts analysing the injured trader's interest as proprietary in nature.

The historical origins of the action in passing off are imprecise. In *Magnolia Metal Co v Tandem Smelting Ltd* (1900) 17 RPC 477 at 483, Lord Halsbury described the passing off action as "a well recognised cause of action, certainly for the last 250 years". He traced it back to the reign of Elizabeth I. This Elizabethan genesis is derived from a dictum of Doderidge J in a 1617 case, *Southern v How*. That case was first reported in *Popham's Reports* (1617) Pop 143; 79 ER 1243 published in 1656. The report stated (at 144, 1244):

> "Doderidge [sic] said, that 22 Eliz the action upon the case was brought in the Common Pleas by a clothier, that whereas he had gained great reputation for his making of his cloth by reason whereof he had great utterance to his benefit and profit, and that he used to set his mark on his cloth whereby it should be known to be his cloth: and another clothier, observing it, used the same mark to his ill-made cloth on purpose to deceive him, and it was resolved that the action did well lie."

Whatever the origins of passing off, the dimensions of the action became firmly fixed in the late Victorian period in England, contemporaneous with the extensive growth of industry and commerce at that time. At that time passing off was one of a number of "economic torts" available to protect business reputation, including the torts of injurious falsehood, defamation, deceit and negligent misstatement. The difficulties of making out the elements of these actions, including the bad motive of the defendant, led to passing off becoming more useful as it centred on the deception of consumers or the likelihood thereof, independent of any malice on the part of the defendant. The emphasis thus shifted, if not entirely away from the wrongful conduct of the deceptive trader, at least towards the concept of rights attaching to the reputation earned by a trader in the marketplace. Originally, this centred on "marks" used by traders to identify their goods. The British Parliament responded in 1875 to calls for greater protection against imitators by establishing a system for the registration of trade marks rather than by proscribing a wider range of competitive practices. The trade mark system, subsequently adopted in Australia, allows the proprietor of a distinctive mark to acquire a monopoly over its use and is the next topic covered in this casebook. Passing off, and the statutory versions of it found in fair trading legislation, are not confined to protecting a "sign"; they confer protection on a wider range of marketing efforts than the protection for signs allowed by the *Trade Marks Act 1995* (Cth).

Although the actions for passing off and for breach of *Trade Practices Act 1974* (Cth), s 52 are the principal ways in Australia in which business reputation is protected, a number of other actions, lying outside the traditional scope of industrial and intellectual property law, are available to assist in the protection of business reputation. The torts of deceit and negligent misstatement mentioned above are two obvious examples. In a number of cases, pleaded as associated actions under *Trade Practices Act 1974* (Cth), s 52, defamation and injurious falsehood have also been relied upon to protect a trading reputation. Trade mark legislation is the most obvious form of statutory protection for trading reputation, but from time to time other legislation becomes relevant. For example, the *Sydney 2000 Games (Indicia and Images) Protection Act 1996* (Cth) was passed to protect the Sydney Olympics ("the best ever", as it turned out) from "ambush marketing" which would have undermined the sponsorship income to be derived from licensing the valuable Olympic name, insignia and other symbols associated with the 2000 Olympics. This legislation followed an investigation into untoward marketing practices by a Senate Committee: *Cashing in on the Sydney Olympics—Protecting the Sydney Olympic Games from Ambush Marketing*, Senate Legal and Constitutional References Committee (March 1995). The Federal Government in April 2001 decided to extend the operation of the 1996 legislation (originally intended to cease effect on 31 December 2000) in respect of the unlicensed commercial use of the words "Olympic", "Olympic Games" and "Olympiad". This is in order to provide extra opportunities for AOC fundraising. Similar legislation exists in other jurisdictions to protect the IOC's marketing strategies: see *NZ Olympic and Commonwealth Games Association v Telecom NZ* (1996) 35 IPR 55.

Passing off and legislation have interacted in the last 40 years or so to protect the interests not just of individual traders and corporations, but of groups of producers, particularly those with trade names denoting geographic origins, of which the most obvious example is "champagne". Where the consumers in a particular jurisdiction have failed to recognise the geographic significance of a name, trade negotiations, both bilateral and under the TRIPs Agreement, have secured the rights independently. In 1981 the Federal Court found that, in Australia, "champagne" was a generic term for wine made with certain grapes and according to a certain method, and was not distinctive of wine from any particular locality, despite the strenuous arguments from a group of 12 French producers from the Champagne district that the name had a distinct geographic connotation: *Comite Interprofessionel Du Vin de Champagne v NL Burton* (1981) 38 ALR 664. However, by 1991 New Zealand consumers apparently would have been misled by the use of the name "champagne" on sparkling wine made by Penfolds in Australia and imported into New Zealand: *Wineworths Group Ltd v Comite Interprofessionel Du Vin De Champagne* (1991) 23 IPR 435.

The retrieval of "champagne" as a distinctive name has been achieved by litigation around the world, but also by the increased recognition of geographic indications as a form of intellectual property protected under trade mark law. More immediate protection has been achieved by the use of bilateral agreements whereby admission to overseas markets such as the European Community is made easier for products, particularly wine, where the geographic indicator is not used. See the *Australian Wine and Brandy Corporation Amendment Act 1993* (Cth) under which certain wine names indicating geographic origin, type of grape or other traditional expressions are to be phased out according to an agreed timetable. Apart from "champagne", other names forbidden to Australian wine producers will include "burgundy", "claret", "moselle", "port", "sherry", beaujolias, "vinho verde" (and "vino verde"), and others.

Having secured wine names for their exclusive use, the Europeans have now moved on to cheese. In October 2001 the European Court of Justice held that "Parmesan" for cheese can only be used by producers resident in Parma. It is unlikely that Australian consumers regard "Parmesan" as a geographic name, and the reservation of this name for producers in that town may not be readily agreed to during trade negotiations.

NATURE OF THE INTEREST PROTECTED IN PASSING OFF ACTIONS

Reddaway v Banham

[13.10] *Reddaway v Banham* [1896] AC 199 House of Lords

[From 1879 the appellant manufacturer of machine belting had described his product as "Camel Hair Belting". The respondent, who had been employed by the appellant, began to manufacture belting on his own account from 1889, which he sold from 1891 as "Camel Hair Belting". In exonerating the respondent's conduct the Court of Appeal had taken the view that all that the respondent had done was to tell the simple truth.]

LORD HERSCHELL: [209] I cannot help saying that, if the defendants are entitled to lead purchasers to believe that they are getting the plaintiffs' manufacture when they are not, and thus to cheat the plaintiffs of some of their legitimate trade, I should regret to find that the law was powerless to enforce the most elementary principles of commercial morality. I do not think your Lordships are driven to any such conclusion.

The principle which is applicable to this class of cases was, in my judgment, well laid down by Lord Kingsdown in *Leather Cloth Co v American Leather Cloth Co* (1865) 11 HL Cas 523 at 538; 11 ER 1435. It had been previously enunciated in much the same way by Lord Langdale in the case of *Croft v Day* (1843) 7 Beav 84; 49 ER 994. Lord Kingsdown's words were as follows:

"The fundamental rule is, that one man has no right to put off his goods for sale as the goods of a rival trader, and he cannot, therefore (in the language of Lord Langdale, in the case of *Perry v Truefitt* (1842) 6 Beav 66; 49 ER 749), be allowed to use names, marks, letters, or other indicia, by which he may induce purchasers to believe that the goods which he is selling are the manufacture of another person."

It is, in my opinion, this fundamental rule which governs all cases, whatever be the particular mode adopted by any man for putting off his goods as those of a rival trader, whether it is done by the use of a mark which has become his trade mark, or in any other way. The word "property" has been sometimes applied to what has been termed a trade mark at common law. I doubt myself whether it is accurate to speak of there being property in such a trade mark, though, no doubt some of the rights which are [210] incident to property may attach to it. Where the trade mark is a word or device never in use before, and meaningless, except as indicating by whom the goods in connection with which it is used were made, there could be no conceivable legitimate use of it by another person. His only object in employing it in connection with goods of his manufacture must be to deceive. In circumstances such as these the mere proof that the trade mark of one manufacturer had been thus appropriated by another, would be enough to bring the case within the rule as laid down by Lord Kingsdown,

▆▆▆▆▆ Reddaway v Banham *continued*

and to entitle the person aggrieved to an injunction to restrain its use. In the case of a trade mark thus identified with a particular manufactory the rights of the person whose trade mark it was, would not, it may be, differ substantially from those which would exist if it were, strictly speaking, his property. But there are other cases which equally come within the rule that a man may not pass off his goods as those of his rival which are not of this simple character—cases where the mere use of the particular mark or device which had been employed by another manufacturer would not of itself necessarily indicate that the person who employed it was thereby inducing purchasers to believe that the goods he was selling were the goods of another manufacturer.

■ "Reputation" may be more than protection for a "mark"

▆▆▆▆▆ ## AG Spalding & Bros v AW Gamage ▆▆▆▆▆

[13.15] *AG Spalding & Bros v AW Gamage Ltd* (1915) 84 LJ Ch 449 House of Lords

[The respondent scrap rubber merchants had sold a superseded line of the appellant's footballs as the appellant's latest product.]

LORD PARKER OF WADDINGTON: ... **[450]** There appears to be considerable diversity of opinion as to the nature of the right, the invasion of which is the subject of what are known as passing off actions. The more general opinion appears to be that the right is a right of property. This view naturally demands an answer to the question property in what? Some authorities say property in the mark, name, or get-up improperly used by the defendant. Others say, property in the business or goodwill likely to be injured by the misrepresentation. Lord Herschell in *Reddaway v Banham* [1896] 65 LJ QB 381; [1896] AC 199 expressly dissents from the former view; and if the right invaded is a right of property at all, there are, I think, strong reasons for preferring the latter view. In the first place, cases of misrepresentation by the use of a mark, name, or get-up do not exhaust all possible cases of misrepresentation. If A says falsely, "These goods I am selling are B's goods," there is no mark, name or get-up infringed unless it be B's name, and if he falsely says, "These are B's goods of a particular quality," where the goods are in fact B's goods, there is no name that is infringed at all. Further, it is extremely difficult to see how a man can be said to have property in descriptive words, such as "Camel Hair" in the case of *Reddaway v Banham* where every trader is entitled to use the words, provided only he uses them in such a way as not to be calculated to deceive. Even in the case of what are sometimes referred to as Common Law Trade Marks the property, if any, of the so-called owner is in its nature transitory, and only exists so long as the mark is distinctive of his own **[451]** goods in the eyes of the public or a class of the public. Indeed, the necessity of proving this distinctiveness in each case as a step in the proof of the false representation relied on was one of the evils sought to be remedied by the *Trade Marks Act 1875*, which conferred a real right of property on the owner of a registered mark. I had to consider the matter in the case of *Burberrys v Cording* (1909) 26 RPC 693 and I came to the same conclusion.

Note

[13.20] The *Spalding* case demonstrates a growing recognition of the proprietary rights in goodwill extending beyond rights in a name. Misrepresentation causing harm to the defendant can even result from "reverse passing off", where instead of suggesting that the defendant is the source of the plaintiff's goods or services, the misrepresentation results from the defendant claiming the plaintiff's product as their own. In *Bristol Conservatories v Conservatories Custom Built* [1989] RPC 455, the defendant designed and manufactured conservatories to be built onto existing houses; its sales people showed potential customers photographs of the plaintiff's work. It was held by the United Kingdom Court of Appeal that this amounted to a claim that the defendant's product was of the same quality as the plaintiff's. In *Parkdale Custom Built Furniture Pty Ltd v Puxu Pty Ltd* (1982) 149 CLR 191 the plaintiff complained of the use of photographs of the plaintiff's furniture range in the defendant's advertising, although that issue was not supported by sufficient evidence.

■ Development of passing off: Composition of goods and geographic indication protection

▬ Erven Warnink Besloten Vennootschap v J Townend ▬

[13.25] *Erven Warnink Besloten Vennootschap v J Townend & Sons (Hull) Ltd* [1979] AC 731 House of Lords

[The appellant manufacturers in the Netherlands of a liquor called "advocaat", which was exported to Britain, objected to the use by the respondents of that name for a drink which they manufactured and distributed in Britain. The main ingredients of the appellant's advocaat were eggs and an expensive spirit base, but no wine. The respondents produced their "Keeling's Old English Advocaat" using a mixture and dried eggs and Cypress sherry, which was wine-based and attracted a lower rate of excise, therefore making the product cheaper. The use of the respondent's name on their product would have tended to distinguish it from the imported Dutch advocaat; however, the issue was whether the name implied a certain geographic origin, and certain ingredients.]

LORD DIPLOCK: **[740]** ...The action for what has become known as "passing off" arose in the 19th century out of the use in connection with his own goods by one trader of the trade name or trade mark of a rival trader so as to induce in potential purchasers the belief that his goods were those of the rival trader. Although the cases up to the end of the century had been confined to the deceptive use of trade names, marks, letters or other indicia, the principle had been stated by Lord Langdale MR as early as 1842 as being: "A man is not to sell his own goods under the pretence that they are the goods of another man": *Perry v Truefitt* (1842) 6 Beav 66 at 73; 49 ER 749. At the close of the century in *Reddaway v Banham* [1896] AC 199, it was said by Lord Herschell that what was protected by an action for passing off was not the proprietary right of the trader in the mark, name or get-up improperly used. Thus the door was opened to passing off actions in which the misrepresentation took some other form than the deceptive use of trade names, marks, letters or other indicia; but as none of their Lordships committed themselves to identifying the legal nature of the right that was protected by a passing off action it remained an action sui generis which lay for damage sustained or threatened in consequence of a misrepresentation of a particular kind.

Reddaway v Banham, like all previous passing off cases, was one in **[741]** which Banham

■■■■■ Erven Warnink Besloten Vennootschap v J Townend *continued*

had passed off his goods as those of Reddaway, and the damage resulting from the misrepresentation took the form of the diversion of potential customers from Reddaway to Banham. Although it was a landmark case in deciding that the use by a trader of a term which accurately described the composition of his own goods might nevertheless amount to the tort of passing off if that term were understood in the market in which the goods were sold to denote the goods of a rival trader, *Reddaway v Banham* did not extend the nature of the particular kind of misrepresentation which gives rise to a right of action in passing off beyond what I have called the classic form of misrepresenting one's own goods as the goods of someone else nor did it provide any rational basis for an extension.

This was left to be provided by Lord Parker in *AG Spalding & Bros v AW Gamage Ltd* (1915) 84 LJ Ch 449 at 450. In a speech which received the approval of the other members of this House, he identified the right the invasion of which is the subject of passing off actions as being the "property in the business or goodwill likely to be injured by the misrepresentation" The concept of goodwill is in law a broad one which is perhaps best expressed in words used by Lord Macnaghten in *Inland Revenue Commissioners v Muller & Co's Margarine Ltd* [1901] AC 217 at 223-224:

> "It is the benefit and advantage of the good name, reputation, and connection of a business. It is the attractive force which brings in custom."

The goodwill of a manufacturer's business may well be injured by someone else who sells goods which are correctly described as being made by that manufacturer but being of an inferior class or quality are misrepresented as goods of his manufacture of a superior class or quality. This type of misrepresentation was held in *AG Spalding & Bros v AW Gamage Ltd* (1915) 84 LJ Ch 449 to be actionable and the extension to the nature of the misrepresentation which gives rise to a right of action in passing off which this involved was regarded by Lord Parker as a natural corollary of recognising that what the law protects by a passing off action is a trader's property in his business or goodwill.

The significance of this decision in the law of passing off lies in its recognition that misrepresenting one's own goods as the goods of someone else was not a separate genus of actionable wrong but a particular species of wrong included in a wider genus of which a premonitory hint had been given by Lord Herschell in *Reddaway v Banham* [1896] AC 199 at 211 when, in speaking of the deceptive use of a descriptive term, he said:

> "I am unable to see why a man should be allowed, *in this way more than in any other* to deceive purchasers into the belief that they are getting what they are not, and thus to filch the business of a rival."

I quote this passage, in which I have supplied the emphasis, because it was Lord Herschell who gave the leading speech in an earlier decision of this House in *Native Guano Co v Sewage Manure Co* (1889) 8 RPC 125 at 129 that was principally relied on by the Court of Appeal as justifying their reversal of the judgment of Goulding J in the instant case.

Spalding's Case (1915) 84 LJ Ch 449 led the way to recognition by judges of other species of the same genus, as where although the plaintiff and **[742]** the defendant were not competing traders in the same line of business, a false suggestion by the defendant that their businesses were connected with one another would damage the reputation and thus the goodwill of the plaintiff's business. There are several cases of this kind reported of which *Harrods Ltd v R Harrod Ltd* (1923) 41 RPC 74, the money lender case, may serve as an example.

Lord Parker's explanation of the nature of the proprietary right protected by a passing off action also supplied a new and rational basis for the two 19th century decisions of Page Wood

▇▇▇▇▇▇▇ Erven Warnink Besloten Vennootschap v J Townend *continued*

V-C in *Dent v Turpin* (1861) 2 John & H 139; 70 ER 1003, and *Southorn v Reynolds* (1865) 12 LT 75, in which one of two traders, each of whom had by inheritance acquired goodwill in the use of a particular trade name, was held entitled, without joining the other, to obtain an injunction restraining a third trader from making use of the name, despite the fact that the plaintiff's right of user was not exclusive. The goodwill of his business would be damaged by the misrepresentation that the defendant's goods were the goods of a limited class of traders entitled to make use of it, of whom the plaintiff was one and the defendant was not.

My Lords, *AG Spalding & Bros v AW Gamage Ltd* (1915) 84 LJ Ch 449 and the later cases make it possible to identify five characteristics which must be present in order to create a valid cause of action for passing off:

(1) a misrepresentation;

(2) made by a trader in the course of trade;

(3) to prospective customers of his or ultimate consumers of goods or services supplied by him;

(4) which is calculated to injure the business or goodwill of another trader (in the sense that this is a reasonably foreseeable consequence) and

(5) which causes actual damage to a business or goodwill of the trader by whom the action is brought or (in a quia timet action) will probably do so.

In seeking to formulate general propositions of English law, however, one must be particularly careful to beware of the logical fallacy of the undistributed middle. It does not follow that because all passing off actions can be shown to present these characteristics, all factual situations which present these characteristics give rise to a cause of action for passing off. True it is that their presence indicates what a moral code would censure as dishonest trading, based as it is upon deception of customers and consumers of a trader's wares but in an economic system which has relied on competition to keep down prices and to improve products there may be practical reasons why it should have been the policy of the common law not to run the risk of hampering competition by providing civil remedies to every one competing in the market who has suffered damage to his business or goodwill in consequence of inaccurate statements of whatever kind that may be made by rival traders about their own wares. The market in which the action for passing off originated was no place for the mealy mouthed; advertisements are not on affidavit; exaggerated claims by a trader about the quality of his wares, assertions that they are better than those of his rivals even though he knows this to be untrue, have been permitted by the common law as venial "puffing" which gives no cause of action to a competitor even though he can show that he has suffered actual damage in his business as a result.

Parliament, however, beginning in the 19th century has progressively **[743]** intervened in the interests of consumers to impose on traders a higher standard of commercial candour than the legal maxim caveat emptor calls for, by prohibiting under penal sanctions misleading descriptions of the character or quality of goods; but since the class of persons for whose protection the *Merchandise Marks Acts 1887-1953* and even more rigorous later statutes are designed, are not competing traders but those consumers who are likely to be deceived, the Acts do not themselves give rise to any civil action for breach of statutory duty on the part of a competing trader even though he sustains actual damage as a result: *Cutler v Wandsworth Stadium Ltd* [1949] AC 398 and see *London Armoury Co Ltd v Ever Ready Co (Great Britain) Ltd* [1941] 1 KB 742. Nevertheless the increasing recognition by Parliament of the need for more rigorous standards of commercial honesty is a factor which should not be overlooked by a judge confronted by the choice whether or not to extend by analogy to circumstances in which it has not previously been applied a principle which has been applied in previous cases

▓▓▓▓▓▓ Erven Warnink Besloten Vennootschap v J Townend *continued*

where the circumstances although different had some features in common with those of the case which he has to decide. Where over a period of years there can be discerned a steady trend in legislation which reflects the view of successive parliaments as to what the public interest demands in a particular field of law, development of the common law in that part of the same field which has been left to it ought to proceed upon a parallel rather than a diverging course.

Note

[13.30] Lord Diplock's formulation in *Spalding* of the five characteristics of a passing off action was not intended to be determinative of the circumstances in which the elements of the tort are present. Nevertheless, his formulation has almost become a "general proposition" of the law, despite the warning against this. In practice, certain of the elements are either assumed to exist or have been criticised as unduly restrictive and conveniently overlooked. The Australian courts, for example, have been prepared to allow passing off to be extended to protect images, characters and personalities per se without the necessity for public deception being shown. The next extract discusses this trend.

■ Not a proprietary right, but misrepresenting

▓▓▓▓▓▓ Telstra v Royal & Sun Alliance Insurance ▓▓▓▓▓▓

[13.40] *Telstra Corporation Limited v Royal & Sun Alliance Insurance Australia Limited* [2003] 57 IPR 453 Federal Court of Australia

MERKEL J: [454] ...

Introduction
The first applicant Telstra and the second applicant ("Sensis"), which is a wholly owned subsidiary of Telstra claim declaratory and injunctive relief, as well as damages or an account of profits, against the first respondent ("Royal") and the second respondent ("Wilson Everard") in respect of their advertising of car insurance to the public under the name of Shannons Insurance ("Shannons").

...

The *Yellow Pages* Goggomobil advertising campaign
... [455] ...
At the time of the campaign the Goggomobil, which was manufactured in the 1950s, was a rare, inexpensive and relatively unknown car. The first Goggomobil advertisement commences in the driveway of a suburban house, in which a yellow Goggomobil is parked on a jack with a man underneath it. The man, portrayed by the actor Tommy Dysart ("Dysart"), crawls out from underneath the car. He is middle-aged, heavy-set, dressed in overalls and wears a pendant. The car is leaking oil. The scene moves to inside the house where the man, with a heavy Scottish accent, tells his wife ""I've broken Fritz". He then flicks through a publication, picks up the telephone and, after dialling a number, asks "I was wondering if you

▬▬▬▬ Telstra v Royal & Sun Alliance Insurance *continued*

could help me" stating that "I've got a problem with my Goggomobil". He pauses, and slowly repeats the word "Goggo-mobil". He rings up another number and again says he has a problem with his Goggomobil. The man, becoming increasingly frustrated, is required to spell in his Scottish brogue, "G-O-G-G-O". He rings again to say he has a problem with his Goggomobil, pauses, and cautiously says "yeah, 1954" and, getting excited, says "Yeah, no not the dart. Not the Dart. They always think it's the Dart!". The Dart is a particular Goggomobil model of that era. The man, with his wife smiling at him, starts laughing uproariously and, simultaneously, the advertisement fades to the well-known yellow and black *Yellow Pages* walking fingers logo, with the man's laughter and joyous voice calling out in the background "It's a wee ripper".

The first Goggomobil advertisement featured a likeable and memorable character, an unusual and distinctive motor vehicle, the use of the telephone to help solve an obscure problem, and tells its story in a humorous manner.

... In 1998 Sensis produced a second advertisement using Dysart, who by then had become known as "Mr Goggomobil", his wife and the same yellow Goggomobil. This advertisement showed "Mr Goggomobil" and his wife, who was sitting with him in the Goggomobil, being prevented from driving the Goggomobil out of their driveway by two *Yellow Pages* directories placed under one of the rear wheels of the vehicle.

...[456] ...

The Shannons advertising campaign

In May 2000 Royal, a major general insurer, acquired Shannons, which had specialised in insuring vintage, veteran or classic motor vehicles since the early 1970s. After the acquisition Royal decided to expand the business conducted by Shannons by increasing the exposure of the Shannons brand to motoring enthusiasts who owned "special vehicles". In particular, in pursuit of its objective of marketing its policies to a broader cross-section of motoring [457] enthusiasts Shannons, acting through its marketing consultant Frank Moore Advertising Pty Ltd, engaged Wilson Everard to create the television, radio and print advertising for its campaign.

Late in 2001 Wilson Everard came up with the idea of using Dysart and a Goggomobil for Shannons advertising. It was thought that "using Tommy Dysart and a Goggomobil would be instantly recognisable for Shannons as people were aware of Tommy and his appearance in the *Yellow Pages* advertisement." The Goggomobil vehicle was attractive to Shannons as it had come to the public's attention in the *Yellow Pages* campaign and was the type of enthusiast's car that would be insured by Shannons. Also its rare and unique character would not offend the car brand loyalties of Shannons customers.

...

In January 2002 an animatic (ie a rough mock-up) of a proposed advertisement was produced by Wilson Everard in order to obtain the reaction of focus groups to the advertise-ment. The animatic started with a voice-over that stated that the advertisement would open on "the famous and instantly recognisable figure of Mr Goggomobil standing proudly by his car". The animatic was made up of stills from the first Goggomobil advertisement with a voice-over that revealed that "Mr Goggomobil" was now looking for insurance for his vehicle. The animatic concluded with the Shannons logo, rather than the *Yellow Pages* logo. At no point did the animatic make any reference to *Yellow Pages* or its logo.

Klein and Associates, a professional marketing group, was engaged by Shannons to show the animatic and another proposed advertisement to four selected focus groups comprising male motoring enthusiasts. One group comprised motor enthusiasts who insured with

Shannons. The other three groups did not insure with Shannons but were likely to have known of it. The research report prepared by Klein and Associates stated:

"All respondents in this study recognised `Goggomobile' as an historic, outstanding, iconic, talked about and much loved *Yellow Pages* TVC [television commercial], with estimates of the time since it was on air ranging from 5 to 15 years.

Among the majority and as a television commercial promoting Shannons insurance, 'Goggomobile' was exceptionally well received and well regarded.

Importantly, we highlight that: **[458]**

- the idea of borrowing (or ambushing) an old advertising icon for Shannons gain was considered to be a masterful act of cleverness and was variously described as 'quirky', 'clever', 'opportunistic', 'taking a free kick', 'smart', 'brilliant', 'cheeky', 'mad', 'fun', and so forth
- not a single interviewee in this study deemed it inappropriate or wrong (or held it against Shannons) for borrowing 'Goggomobile', with most admiring Shannons for being sufficiently cheeky and clever to do so:
- 'It's absolutely brilliant to have thought of it and such a clever idea.'
- 'Good on Shannons I reckon.'
- 'Goggomobile' was considered to be a perfect vehicle for promoting Shannons (for as interviewees themselves had done, Mr Goggomobile was now using the *Yellow Pages* and his telephone to shop for car insurance)
- no-one was alienated by a Goggomobile (which might have occurred among Holden people if a Ford had been featured or an American muscle car owner if a Jag had been utilised, etc.)"

... **[459]** ...

The approval of Pacific Access to the reproduction of parts of the first Goggomobil advertisement was sought. Pacific Access' response was that copyright subsisted in the first Goggomobil advertisement, the proposed advertisement was a reproduction of the first Goggomobil advertisement and Pacific Access was not prepared to allow its advertisement to be incorporated into Shannons' advertising campaign.

After Pacific Access' refusal Wilson Everard was instructed "to create a script that did not reproduce parts of the 1991 *Yellow Pages* advertisement". **[460]** Mr Lachlan Dunn ("Dunn"), an employee of Wilson Everard, was given the task of creating the new script. His evidence was that he was told to take "the Goggomobil concept a step further" and make it look "completely different to the *Yellow Pages* advertisement".

Dunn created three scripts dated 6 February 2002, but only the 30 second script, entitled "The Ol' Dart", was proceeded with. ...

[Following further consulation and objection from Pacific Access] the script was revised to remove the reference to Dysart's expression of the "G" after Goggomobil and Dysart's voice-over of the telephone number, with its emphasis on "O" "O", was also removed. With those changes, and some other less significant changes, the final form of the script was as follows:

"**Vision:** *We open on a sunny outdoor scene in the driveway of a typical suburban house. We see a man giving a final polish to a gleaming vehicle.*

We instantly recognize the man—it is Mr Goggomobil—and it is obvious a few years have past since we last saw him—he is graying and he is carrying an extra bit around the middle. The car is different too—instead of a yellow sedan up on blocks, his pride and joy is a gleaming, immaculate Goggomobil Dart (that's right, the Dart1) in flawless, shannons green.

▬▬▬ Telstra v Royal & Sun Alliance Insurance *continued*

>   *As he takes a step back to admire his handiwork, Mr Goggomobil pulls a mobile phone*
>   *form his pocket and beings punching in numbers before speaking ...*
>   [Dysart]: Hello ...I'd like to insure my Goggomobil...(pause)...(frustrated)... Go-go-
>   mob-il...
>   Vision: *Before he continues we fade to a later shot of the same scene—he is pacing around*
>   *the car impatiently while on another call. We fade again to another shot—these quick scenes*
>   *are simply to show him becoming more and more frustrated. We then...fade to a final shot—*
>   *he is sitting in the car, tapping his fingers impatiently on the steering wheel...*
>   MVO: Shannons Insurance shares the passion with car enthusiasts ...
>   [Dysart]: Aye that's right—it is the Dart—aye!!! (laughs)
>   Vision: *He is excited and very happy to have finally found what he's looking for. We fade to*
>   *final super...*
>   Super: Shannons (logo)—Share the Passion
>   1300 139 006
>   Agreed value. Choice of repairers.
>   Lifetime no claim bonus protection
>   MVO: ... so call Shannons for a special quote on your special vehicle."... [464] ...

The first Shannons advertisement is alleged to be an infringement of the copyright owned by Telstra in the first Goggomobil advertisement and in the script for that advertisement. However, the televising and broadcasting of all of the Shannons advertisements is alleged to constitute passing off and a contravention of ss 52, 53(c) and 53(d) of the TPA.

[His Honour found that there was no infringement of the literary or dramatic works related to the Telstra advertisement as the first Shannons advertisement does not use substantially the same dialogue and the setting or structure of the first Shannons advertisement is sufficiently different to fall well short of a "substantial" reproduction of the first Goggomobil advertisement.]

[468] ...

Passing off and misleading conduct

It appears to be common ground between the parties that, subject to the requirement of actual damage in the passing off claim, the applicants' passing off case is, in general, co-extensive with their case of contravention of ss 52, 53(c) and 53(d) of the TPA. Both cases depend on whether the Shannons advertisements represent that *Yellow Pages* was in some way associated or [469] connected with Shannons, the Shannons advertisements or the services Shannnons offers. If no such representation has been made the applicants' claims must fail. If any such representation was made it is untrue and a necessary prerequisite for the success of the passing off and misleading conduct claims will have been established.

Although the applicants made their claims in relation to the two television advertisements and the four radio advertisements broadcast as part of Shannons advertising campaign, in my view the only substantial case of misrepresentation is in respect of the first Shannons television advertisement.

[469] ... Advertising that conjures up a brand without referring to it was described in the evidence as "secondary" or "suggestive" brand advertising. By such advertising images can become established and so well-known that they create an impression of association or connection to a primary brand, notwithstanding that the name of the brand does not appear in the advertisement. The symbol, logo or image is referred to as secondary or suggestive branding as its expression gives a ready impression of association or connection with the

primary brand. Examples of such advertising include the Nike swoosh, McDonald's arches, the "Ronald McDonald" character, the Coca Cola bottle and the *Yellow Pages* "walking fingers" logo.

Secondary branding or suggestive brand advertising occurs when a word, **[470]** character, symbol or image creates, on its own, instant recognition or association with a particular product or business. The adoption of such characters, symbols or images by another advertiser will usually raise the question of whether that advertiser is representing that it, or its goods or services, have an affiliation, association or connection they do not have. In *R & C Products Pty Limited v S C Johnson & Sons Pty Limited* (1993) 42 FCR 188 at 194 Davies J observed:

> "if advertising or get-up has acquired special signification, then the adoption of elements of the advertising or get-up by another trader may give rise to a misrepresentation. Then the question will be whether other steps have been taken which sufficiently distinguish the one trader and its products from the other trader and its products."

Twentieth Century Fox Film Corporation v South Australian Brewing Co Ltd (1996) 66 FCR 451 ("the *Duff Beer* case") was concerned with the name "Duff", which had acquired a powerful secondary meaning in relation to "Duff Beer" as a result of the use of the name "Duff Beer" in the television program "The Simpsons". Tamberlin J concluded (at 470) that the use by the respondents of the term "Duff Beer" was misleading and deceptive as it is likely to lead to an assumption by consumers that permission had been given by "The Simpsons" to the respondents to produce "Duff Beer". His Honour found (at 467) that the respondents' intention was "to 'sail as close as possible to the wind' in order to 'cash in' on the reputation of 'The Simpsons' without stepping over the line of passing off or deceit". Tamberlin J observed (at 466):

> "Intention to take advantage of the goodwill of another, does not of itself establish a cause of action ... A court will, however, more readily infer where there is intention, that the promoters who know the field of business well, were justified in entertaining the hope or expectation that the attempt would succeed and it assists the conclusion that the public was so influenced: cf *Australian Guarantee Corporation Ltd v Sydney Guarantee Corp Ltd* (1951) 51 SR (NSW) 166 at 170-171, applied by Gummow J in *Telmak Teleproducts (Australia) Pty Ltd v Coles Myer Ltd* (1988) 84 ALR 437 at 445."

Of course each case must depend on its own particular facts. In the present case the evidence establishes that as a result of the first *Yellow Pages* advertisement Dysart's "Mr Goggomobil" had become a form of secondary branding for *Yellow Pages* when employed in the manner and context set out in the first Goggomobil advertisement... **[473]**

The real question for the Court in the present case is whether the manner and context in which Dysart and the Goggomobil were used by Shannons in the first Shannons advertisement represented that *Yellow Pages* had some association or connection with that advertisement or had endorsed or approved the services offered in it. It is to that question that I now turn.

[474] ...The *Yellow Pages* Goggomobil campaign was directed to the public at large or, at the least, that large part of the public capable of using the *Yellow Pages* directory. Although the first Shannons advertisement targeted motor enthusiasts it was shown on commercial television to a large segment of the viewing public over a number of timeslots and in the course of a variety of programs. As was said in *Parkdale Custom Built Furniture Proprietary Limited v Puxu Proprietary Limited* (1982) 149 CLR 191 at 199, consideration must be given as to the class of consumers likely to be affected by the conduct. That is of some importance in

▬▬▬ Telstra v Royal & Sun Alliance Insurance *continued*

a case such as the present as the initial question is whether the misconceptions, or deceptions, alleged to arise or to be likely to arise are properly to be attributed to "the ordinary or reasonable members" of the relevant segment of the viewing public: see *Campomar Societad Limitada v Nike International Ltd* (2000) 202 CLR 45 at [105] 86-87. In the present case the relevant class of the public likely to be affected by the conduct in question were viewers who saw the first Shannons advertisement and were aware of the *Yellow Pages* Goggomobil campaign. Plainly, that class constitutes a significant segment of the public.

As observed above, whether the use of Mr Goggomobil and his Goggomobil vehicle to solve a problem by use of the telephone would result in secondary or suggestive brand advertising for *Yellow Pages* depends upon the manner and context in which that subject matter is employed. The extensive and significant contextual similarities between the first Goggomobil advertisement and the first Shannons advertisement and the manner in which Dysart and his Goggomobil have been used to ensure "instant recognition" have led me to conclude that the first Shannons advertisement constitutes such secondary advertising. The difficulty that confronted Shannons is that it needed to appropriate the features that made the first Goggomobil advertisement both famous and popular, if it were to "cut through the 'clutter'" of advertising and gain the instant recognition and attention of the viewing public that it was seeking. Thus, the features that Shannons most desired to retain, and did retain, in the advertisement that was broadcast were the features that were most likely to result in the first advertisement being perceived by the relevant class of the public to be another *Yellow Pages* advertisement or to be in some other way connected or associated with *Yellow Pages*. Of course, the further Shannons moved away from those features (such as the other Shannons advertisements) the less likely its advertisement would be seen to have a connection with *Yellow Pages*. However, the problem for Shannons with that outcome is that it would lose the advantage of the instant recognition and response it was seeking from its first advertisement. That recognition and response was gained by Shannons recreating in its advertisement the features that gave the first Goggomobil [475] advertisement the "warmth, humour and familiarity" that made that advertisement so well-known, popular and memorable ... In particular, Shannons relied on re-creating the character of "Mr Goggomobil" in a similar problem solving context.

As was explained by Burchett J in *Pacific Dunlop Pty Ltd v Hogan* (1989) 23 FCR 553 at 584, in the analogous context of character advertising:

"The whole importance of character merchandising is the creation of an association of the product with the character; not the making of precise representations. Precision would only weaken an impression which is unrelated to logic, and would in general be logically indefensible. Yet the impression must be powerful to be effective. The only medium likely to convey the vague message of character merchandising, while giving it the force and immediacy of an exciting visual impact, is television."

In *Mark Foys Pty Ltd v TVSN (Pacific) Ltd* (2000) 104 FCR 61 ("*Mark Foys*") at 76-78 the Full Court explained why it is sufficient that "some form" of association or connection is conveyed notwithstanding that the precise form of the association or connection may not be articulated or identified. That is akin to the situation in the present case. I am satisfied that the overall impression created by the showing of the first Shannons advertisement upon a significant portion of ordinary and reasonable members of the relevant class of the public was that *Yellow Pages* is in some way associated or connected with the advertisement or with locating the services offered in it. Accordingly, I am satisfied that the advertisement made a representation to that effect. While there would be doubt as to the precise form of the

▟▟▟▟ Telstra v Royal & Sun Alliance Insurance *continued*

association or connection a significant segment of the relevant public would also be likely to conclude that the first Shannons advertisement is another *Yellow Pages* "Mr Goggomobil" advertisement, but that he is now using his telephone to look for Shannons insurance, rather than a repairer, for his vehicle. The representations of association or connection I am satisfied were conveyed by the first Shannons advertisement "cause more than mere wonderment or confusion [as to whether an association or connection exists] and travel into the areas of positive misrepresentation": see *Mark Foys* at 77.

The most compelling argument of the respondents against a connection or association between the first Shannons advertisement and *Yellow Pages* is the absence of any *Yellow Pages* branding, *and* the presence of Shannons' branding, in the advertisement. It was argued that those features would leave the public in little doubt that this was an advertisement for Shannons insurance and not for *Yellow Pages*. There may be force in that argument if the viewing public consisted solely of persons who had insured with Shannons or were aware of its specialised products. Those persons might have responded to the advertisement by regarding it as a clever use of the *Yellow Pages* advertisement in an advertisement by Shannons insurance. That view, however, is predicated upon those persons being well aware of Shannons and the unique role it plays in insuring "special" vehicles. The problem with that view is that such persons only constitute a small segment of the viewing public and therefore their likely response to the advertisement provides no answer as to how the larger section of the relevant viewing public, which would not have an awareness of Shannons, might view it. Indeed, the advertisement was primarily targeting a section of the viewing public that was not aware of Shannons.... [476] ...

For the above reasons I have concluded that the first Shannons advertisement misrepresents that it is also an advertisement by *Yellow Pages* or that *Yellow Pages* is in some way associated or connected with that advertisement or with locating the services offered in it. As *Yellow Pages* had no association or connection whatsoever with the advertisement or with those services, the making of the representation:

- contravened s 52 of the TPA because it was misleading or deceptive or likely to mislead or deceive;
- contravened s 53(d) of the TPA because it represented that Shannons had an "affiliation" with *Yellow Pages* (ie, an association: see *Mark Foys* at 76-77) which it did not have;
- established a critical element of the applicants' claim of passing off.

However, I do not regard the first Shannons advertisement as representing that the insurance services offered by Shannons are sponsored or approved by *Yellow Pages*.

[477]...The respondents argued that the applicants' claims are misconceived insofar as they seek to claim some proprietary rights or goodwill in the character of "Mr Goggomobil'. As explained above, I have not founded my decision in respect of the first Goggomobil advertisement on any such rights or goodwill. Indeed, my rejection of the applicants' claims in respect of the other Shannons advertisements is based upon my acceptance of the respondents' argument that the applicants do not have proprietary rights or goodwill in the character of "Mr Goggomobil". However, a different outcome attended the first Shannons advertisement because the context and the manner in which "Mr Goggomobil" was used in that advertisement resulted in a representation of association or connection that does not exist.

ESTABLISHING REPUTATION AND DECEPTIVE CONDUCT

[13.45] The three key elements in a passing off suit are the subsistence of some reputation or goodwill on the part of the plaintiff, deceptive conduct on the part of the defendant, and the existence or threat of damage to the plaintiff as a result of that conduct. There are many ways of trespassing on the reputation comprising the proprietary rights protected by passing off. Rather than provide a case on each "type" of passing off, the extracts below set out the general principles which lead to a finding that the vital elements of "misrepresentation ... made by a trader" as set out by Lord Diplock and also in the *Trade Practices Act* (Cth), s 52, and equivalent fair trading provisions in State legislation. The principles of establishing reputation are also relevant to understanding the concept of "distinctiveness" in trade mark law.

The most obvious form that passing off takes is to use another's name, whether a business name or product name. The difficulty of establishing reputation in descriptive material is emphasised by the following extracts, which also illustrate that the actual decision in any particular case will depend very much upon the particular facts and if the existence of a reputation can be shown to exist then even descriptive material will be protected. There may be limits on using even one's own name or family name if, in the circumstances, it could be taken to refer to another person or business: see *Noel Leeming Television Ltd v Noel's Appliance Centre Ltd* (1985) 5 IPR 249; *Gollel Holdings v Kenneth Maurer* (1987) 9 IPR 109. As the internet grows in importance as a means of obtaining goods and services, including information, conflicts between company and product names, and domain names, will lead to the possibility of trade mark infringement, discussed in the next chapter, but also more generally, to passing off. The general principles, of establishing reputation and then showing the defendant has misled consumers, will apply, albeit updated for the speed of communications and globalisation of reputation.

Apart from the use of names and descriptive terms, it is often convenient for defendants to "borrow" fictitious characters, copy the get-up or packaging of a product, or otherwise mislead the persons concerned to buy the relevant products or services into thinking the plaintiff is the supplier. The flexibility of the passing off action can be seen in the vast range of subjects sought to be protected, including the "theme" or particular scenes from movies: see, for example, *Hogan v Pacific Dunlop Ltd* (1988) 12 IPR 225. As mentioned in the *Goggomobile* case above **[13.40]**, in *Twentieth Century Fox Film Corp v South Australian Brewing Co Ltd* (1996) 34 IPR 225 an Australian brewer was prevented from selling beer using the name of an imaginary product, "Duff" beer, used by cartoon characters in the cult television program The Simpsons. Indeed even the facial make-up of a pop star has been the subject of an action: see *Merchandising Corp of America Inc v Harpbond Ltd* [1982] FSR 32. The passing off action, as the character merchandising cases illustrate, is often a last, but successful, resort, when other intellectual property actions are not available.

The following extracts cover different aspects of establishing reputation in passing off. Read the approach taken by the judges in terms of assessing the extent of reputation and how that is evidenced, location of reputation, effect on the purchaser of the defendant's behaviour and the expectations of consumers in regarding their own interests.

Australian Surf Life Saver v S & I Publishing

[13.50] *Australian Surf Life Saver Pty Ltd v S & I Publishing Pty Ltd* (1998) 43 IPR 595 Federal Court of Australia

MOORE J: **[596]**

Introduction

On 8 July 1998 Australian Surf Life Saver Pty Ltd (Life Saver) commenced proceedings against S & I Publishing Pty Ltd (S & I) seeking injunctive and other relief founded on the tort of passing off and an alleged contravention of ss 52 and 53 of the *Trade Practices Act* (the Act). The proceedings relate to the publication of a magazine by S & I with a masthead similar to that of a magazine now owned by Life Saver. ...

The following is the background leading to the proceedings. In July 1998 Life Saver purchased an interest in a magazine called "Triathlon Sports". The magazine had been published since 1984 as a specialist sports magazine. It is not entirely clear from the evidence the nature of the interest that Life Saver purchased but it included the masthead "Triathlon Sports". The most recent edition of that magazine is Vol 13 No 7 published in April 1998. In June 1998 S & I published a magazine called "Triathlon & Multi Sport Magazine".

The focus of "Triathlon Sports" magazine is the sport of triathlon which involves athletes competing in three types of athletic activity, namely running, swimming and cycling. Since 1984 it has been supplied, distributed, sold and marketed to the general public through newsagents and by subscription throughout Australia. Ten issues have been published each year. They have been published monthly except for the months of May, June, July and August in which it has been published bimonthly. This pattern of publication has reflected the seasons for triathlon competition which conclude each year at the end of April and resume in September. Thus the magazine has been published each month during periods in which triathlon competitions have been held and bimonthly during periods when they were not. Until February [597] 1988 "Triathlon Sports" magazine was distributed by Gordon and Gotch Ltd. Distribution figures disclose that for the nine editions before February 1998 between approximately 7,000 and 8,200 copies were distributed and between approximately 2,500 and 4,300 were sold. From February 1998 distribution has been undertaken by NDD Distribution Pty Ltd and a similar number of copies have been distributed and sold except in relation to the most recent edition where the number of copies distributed was only 5,400.

Until early 1997 the front cover of the magazine was typically in the form of annexure "A" to this judgment. The masthead was in the following form:

It can be seen that the word "Triathlon" is printed prominently and in upper case with the word "Sports" appearing less prominently below it but also in upper case.

The format changed in early 1997 and the new format can be illustrated by the most recent edition of the magazine published in April 1998. It had a front cover in the form of annexure "B" to this judgment. The masthead of that edition was in the following form:

It can be seen that the word "Triathlon" remained prominent in the masthead though it is in lower case. The word "Sports" remained in upper case though was less prominent and was off centre and above the word "Triathlon".

The first edition of the magazine published by S & I also contained as part of its masthead the word "Triathlon". The front cover of the first edition is annexure "C" to this judgment. The masthead adopted was: [598]

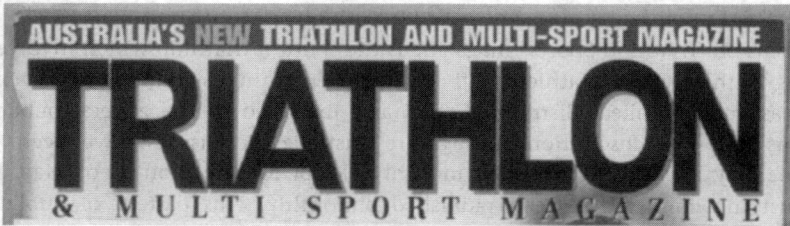

The evidence

The following discussion of the evidence is restricted to what I perceive to be the material evidence. It concerns the adoption of the name "Triathlon & Multi Sport Magazine" by S & I and the consequences of its adoption in the marketplace.

(i) The evolution of "Triathlon & Multi Sport Magazine" and S & I's intention

Mr Rod Cedaro, who is the editor of "Triathlon & Multi Sport Magazine" and Mr Silvio Morelli who is the managing director of S & I gave evidence about the development of "Triathlon & Multi Sport Magazine" including the adoption by S & I of its name. Their evidence was to the following effect.

...

Cedaro had a conversation with Morelli in which Cedaro proposed that Morelli consider publishing a triathlon magazine. ... [599] ... Cedaro noted in his letter that there were two specialist triathlon publications produced in Australia, namely "Australian Triathlete" and "Triathlon Sports". The latter was a reference to the magazine acquired by Life Saver. Cedaro said that that magazine had been around the longest, that is, for 14 years. He stated, however, that it had a bad name created by its then owner and had been run into the ground. Cedaro expressed in his letter the view that there was not enough advertising revenue in the sport of triathlon to support three specialist publications. He also said that his initial idea had been to purchase the magazine name "Triathlon Sports" and revamp and re-release it under a new banner "Triathlon Downunder". ... Morelli decided against the idea of acquiring "Triathlon Sports" magazine.

In October 1997 Cedaro accepted the position of editor of a new triathlon magazine. The working title for the new magazine was, for a period, "Triathlon Downunder". However it is

██████ Australian Surf Life Saver v S & I Publishing *continued*

relatively clear that by October 1997 Morelli was not happy with that name and another name was being considered, namely "Inside Triathlon". This name was proposed by Morelli though Cedaro told him there was a US magazine of the same name distributed in Australia. A letter from Cedaro to Morelli dated 9 October 1997 makes plain that this was the name then being proposed. However in November 1997 Cedaro had a conversation with a journalist working for "Inside Triathlon" and informed her of the proposed name to be published by S & I. This led to an email from a US corporation, Inside Communications Inc, (who publish "Inside Triathlon") indicating a preference that S & I not use the name "Inside Triathlon". This led to a decision by Morelli to abandon that name.

In November 1997 Cedaro suggested to Morelli the name "Multi Sport Magazine" though it was rejected by Morelli because it would confuse people by suggesting that it was predominantly a multi sport magazine which it was not. Multi sport is a reference to triathlon and sports containing several but not all of the elements of triathlon or variations of them. After abandoning the name "Inside Triathlon", Morelli considered the name "Triathlon Australia" as a possible title. However after discussions with a representative of Triathlon Australia, which appears to be a body formed to regulate the sport in Australia, Morelli abandoned this name as well. He also canvassed in December 1997 the name "Triathlon 2000" but that was abandoned after Cedaro observed that the magazine would become dated after the year 2000 had passed.

[600]... Morelli was then, as he described it, "very conscious" of the existence of "Triathlon Sports" and three other magazines in the market place dealing with the sport namely "Australian Triathlete", "Inside Triathlon" and "Triathlete". Morelli's evidence was that he deliberately picked a masthead style and layout that was very different from each of these magazines so as to maximise the distinctiveness of the new magazine in the marketplace.

I do not accept Morelli's evidence about the adoption of the name, "Triathlon & Multi Sport Magazine". He was not, in my opinion, a credible witness. In April or May 1998 Morelli became aware that Life Saver was going to purchase "Triathlon Sports" magazine. It was also at about this time that Morelli decided to use the title "Triathlon & Multi Sport Magazine" giving great prominence to the word "Triathlon". It is probable, in my opinion, that Morelli then decided that it would be open to him to effectively do what he had earlier rejected, namely acquire and use, in substance, the title "Triathlon Sports" though without purchasing it. He decided to do so by using a title that had many similarities both in language and format to the title of the magazine he then knew was being acquired by another. It is probable, in my opinion, that Morelli took a considered commercial risk of adopting a distinctively similar title at a time he believed was opportune.

(ii) Evidence concerning confusion

Evidence was led by Life Saver to demonstrate that purchasers and advertisers were misled. It is important to bear in mind, however, that evidence of this type, or evidence to the contrary, does not displace the duty a judge has to consider objectively the effect of the impugned conduct: see for example, the helpful discussion in the dissenting judgment of Davies J in *Brock v Terrace Times Pty Ltd* (1982) 40 ALR 97 at 105-106. The applicant called four witnesses who gave evidence about the effect of the similarities between the two magazines. The first was Mr Gerry Halaby who is a director and shareholder of Life Saver. He gave evidence about an incident on 8 July 1998 at a Cronulla newsagency. He observed on the news stands the magazine "Triathlon & Multi Sport Magazine". He picked it up and showed it to the person at the counter and asked whether it was "Triathlon Sports" magazine. The response was that it was. Halaby responded by saying that it was not "Triathlon Sports" magazine but "Triathlon

& Multi Sport" magazine to which the person at the counter said that the mastheads were virtually the same and he thought it was "Triathlon Sports" magazine. This evidence was not objected to save as to relevance and Halaby was not cross examined about it.

Evidence was given by Ms Vicki Nettle who is a part-time nurse and triathlete. Though she is not a professional triathlete she is a regular participant in triathlon events in New South Wales and has been participating for five years. For that period she has purchased on a regular basis the magazine "Triathlon Sports". On 13 July 1998 she went to a newsagent at Sylvania and looked at the news stand. She noticed the word "Triathlon" on the cover of a magazine and picked it out intending to purchase it. She thought the magazine was the magazine she regularly purchased, namely "Triathlon Sports". While she was waiting at the counter to purchase the magazine she flicked through it and could not see [601] sections on events that she normally read. On further examination she realised that it was a different magazine with the title "Triathlon & Multi Sport Magazine". She proffered the view in evidence that had she not looked at it in detail she would have believed it was the magazine owned by Life Saver. While she had an indirect connection with Halaby her evidence was credible and I accept it. The evidence she gave about being misled was not diminished in cross-examination.

To similar effect was the evidence Mr Jon Wilks who is an amateur triathlete and a member of the Cronulla Triathlon Club. ...

The last witness called by the applicant concerning the effect of the similarities was Susan Stevens. She is a director and shareholder of a company called Hot Designs Pty Ltd which sells and supplies sportswear clothing. She has dealt with the proprietor of "Triathlon Sports" magazine for over six years and, I infer, has advertised in it. Her evidence was that in mid to late June 1998 she received a copy of "Triathlon & Multi Sport Magazine" and thought it was the magazine published by Life Saver with another section added to it. She continued to believe that it was the magazine published by Life Saver until she received a phone call on 3 July 1998 by someone from that company who informed her that the magazine had not been published by Life Saver. Ms Stevens gave evidence about other matters which I do not view as material. Her evidence was not diminished in cross-examination.

The respondent relied on six witnesses on this issue and they were not cross examined on their affidavits. Mr Timothy Stevenson gave evidence that he has competed in the sport of triathlons for the last 13 years both in Australia and internationally. He purchases triathlon related magazines on a regular basis and is aware of the magazine "Australian Triathlete" as well as the magazines published by Life Saver and S & I. He has subscribed to "Australian Triathlete" for the last 18 months and buys "Triathlon Sports" occasionally. He first saw "Triathlon & Multi Sport Magazine" on sale at a Melbourne newsagency in July 1998. His initial reaction was that it was a new magazine bearing the words "Volume 1 No 1" and had a different masthead layout and included the word "Multi". He said that he was never under the impression that that magazine was "Triathlon Sports" in a revamped form or the same magazine.

Evidence of a slightly different character was given by Mr Benjamin Gachercole. He is an accredited triathlon coach. His evidence was that he was aware of four magazines in Australia incorporating the word "Triathlon" or "Triathlete". They are, apart from the magazines of Life Saver and S & I, "Australian Triathlete" and "Triathlete". The latter magazine is published in the US and he usually refers to it as the US Triathlon magazine.

Similar evidence was given by Ms Jennifer Alcorn who has been involved in [602] the sport of triathlon for the last 12 years. For the first nine years she competed as an elite triathlete both in Australia and internationally and for the last three years has worked, full time, as a triathlon coach. She also gave evidence about her reaction to "Triathlon & Multi

Sport Magazine" when she was first shown it by an athlete at her triathlon club. Her initial reaction was that it looked great and was a new magazine. She had earlier discussed with Mr Rod Cedaro, the editor of "Triathlon & Multi Sport Magazine", that a new magazine was to be published. When she first saw the magazine she was not sure who had published it as she thought the magazine to be published by Cedaro was to have a different name, namely, "Triathlon Downunder". However as a matter of first impression she knew that the magazine she saw was not "Triathlon Sports" because of its different title and layout. ...

Evidence was also given by Mr Ainsley Hart who has a business retailing bicycles and accessories in the inner city. He has competed in the sport of triathlon for the last six to seven years. He is aware of the various magazines earlier referred to and since November 1997 has advertised his business in the magazines "Australian Triathlete" and "Triathlon Sports". He reads "Triathlon Sports" and "Australian Triathlete" and "Triathlete" on a regular basis. The first two are regularly sent to him by the publishers because he advertises in them. He first became aware of "Triathlon & Multi Sport Magazine" when he was sent a circular and advertising rate card some time in May 1998. He says that when he received this material it was clear to him that it was a new triathlon related magazine and he was not under the impression that "Triathlon Sports" was involved in any way. He did not advertise in the first edition of "Triathlon & Multi Sport Magazine". He purchased a copy of the first edition of "Triathlon & Multi Sport Magazine" on the day it first came out. He says that he knew it was a new magazine because it looked nothing like "Triathlon Sports". He also thought it was not connected with "Triathlon Sports" because of differences in the layout and the masthead of the magazine. He proffered the view that no reader who buys triathlon magazines could be misled.

Evidence was also given by Professor Knight who holds a personal chair in the School of Science at Griffith University. He has had an interest in the sport of triathlon since 1991 and has participated in triathlon competitions since 1994. He describes himself as an avid reader of sporting publications and plainly has been involved in the development of sports and sports training in a substantial way. He has been aware of the magazine "Triathlon Sports" but has not been impressed by its contents. His opinion is that it lacks substantive articles providing in-depth technical information and advice about the three sports comprising triathlon. [603] However recently, with his son, his attention was drawn to "Triathlon & Multi Sport Magazine" at a local newsagency. He flipped through its pages and was impressed by its quality. He was prompted to send Cedaro an e-mail congratulating him on the first edition. He said that at no time did he consider "Triathlon & Multi Sport Magazine" to be a new edition or otherwise connected with "Triathlon Sports". This opinion appears to have been based on a consideration of the contents of the magazines and the extent to which advertising featured in both and the journalistic style of one and not the other. Nine other e-mails or letters to Cedaro are also in evidence and the tenor of them is that the writer was impressed by the first edition. Some of them indicated it was a superior publication to "Triathlon Sports".

Relevant legal principles

Many of the principles that govern proceedings such as these have recently been conveniently summarised by Goldberg J in *Betta Foods Australia Pty Ltd v Betta Fruit Bars Pty Ltd* (1998) ATPR 41-624. His Honour said (at 40,839-40,840):

> "The applicant puts its case on the basis of common law passing off and misleading or deceptive conduct in breach of s 52 of the *Trade Practices Act* 1974 (Cth) ('the Act'). Although it has been said that the precise definition of the elements of the tort of

■■■■■ Australian Surf Life Saver v S & I Publishing *continued*

passing off is elusive: *ConAgra Inc v McCain Foods (Aust) Pty Ltd* (1992) 33 FCR 302, 355 per Gummow J; *Dodds Family Investments Pty Ltd v Lane Industries Pty Ltd* (1993) 26 IPR 261, 268, the authorities show there is a need to establish reputation, misrepresentation and the likelihood of damage: *ConAgra Inc v McCain Foods (Aust) Pty Ltd* (supra); *Reckitt and Colman Products Ltd v Borden Inc* (1990) 17 IPR 1, 7; *Vieright Pty Ltd v Myer Stores Ltd* (supra) 40,486. What is accepted as the authoritative statement of the necessary elements to establish the cause of action of passing off is found in the judgment of Lord Diplock in *Erven Warnink Besloten Vennootschap v J Townend & Sons (Hull) Limited* [1979] AC 731 (the *Advocaat Case*) where at 742 his Lordship stated the five characteristics which needed to be present as:

'(1) a misrepresentation

(2) made by a trader in the course of trade

(3) to prospective customers of his or ultimate consumers of goods or services supplied by him

(4) which is calculated to injure the business or goodwill of another trader (in the sense that this is a reasonably foreseeable consequence) and

(5) which causes actual damage to a business or goodwill of a trader by whom the action is brought or (in a quia timet action) will probably do so."

This statement has been accepted in Australia: *Moorgate Tobacco Co Ltd v Philip Morris Ltd* (No 2) (1984) 156 CLR 414, 443-444 per Deane J; *ConAgra Inc v McCain Foods (Aust) Pty Ltd* (supra) 308-310. Although the law of passing off has been said to be capable of summary in one short general proposition—no man may pass of his goods as those of another: *Reckitt and Colman Products v Barden Inc* (supra) at 7—it is necessary as Lord Oliver said in that case, to establish three elements for passing off action: first, goodwill or reputation attaching to the relevant goods in the mind of the purchasing public by association with the identifying get-up. such that the get-up is recognised by the public as distinctive specifically of the applicant's goods; secondly a misrepresentation leading, or likely to lead, the public to believe that the respondent's goods are the goods of the applicant or a particular source; thirdly the suffering, or likely suffering, of damage by reason of the erroneous belief engendered by the misrepresentation. As the Full Court observed in *Vieright Pty Ltd v Myer Stores Ltd* (supra) 40,493 those elements gave rise to three questions: [604]

(1) Has the applicant proved that the get-up under which its [magazine] have been sold since [1984] has become associated in the minds of substantial numbers of the purchasing public specifically and exclusively with the applicant's [magazine]?

(2) If the answer to that question is in the affirmative does the get-up under which the respondent markets its [magazine] amount to a representation by the respondent that the [magazine]s which it sells are the applicant's products?

(3) If the answer to that question is in the affirmative, is it, on a balance of probabilities, likely that, if the respondent is not restrained a substantial number of members of the public will be misled into purchasing the respondent's [magazine] in the belief that they are the applicant's [magazine].

In *Equity Access Pty Ltd v Westpac Banking Corp* (1990) ATPR 40-994 Hill J at 50,950-50,951 set out a number of propositions which applied in relation to the ingredients of a cause of action under s 52 of the Act. The propositions can be summarised as follows:

(a) for conduct to be misleading or deceptive conduct it must convey, in all the circumstances, a misrepresentation;

(b) there will be no contravention of s 52 unless the error or misconception which occurs

▬▬▬▬ Australian Surf Life Saver v S & I Publishing *continued*

results from the conduct of the corporation and not from other circumstances for which the corporation is not responsible;

(c) conduct will be likely to mislead or deceive if there is a "real or not remote chance or possibility" of misleading or deceiving regardless of whether it is less or more than 50 per cent;

(d) conduct causing confusion or uncertainty in the sense that members of the public might have been caused to wonder whether the two products or services might have come from the same source is not necessarily co-extensive with misleading or deceptive conduct; [and]

(e) the applicant must establish that it has acquired the relevant reputation in the name, that is that the name has become distinctive of the applicant's business or products.

...

One specific issue emerging in these proceedings was whether the word "triathlon" was a descriptive word. This issue arises because of the observations of Stephen J in *Hornsby Building Information Centre Pty Ltd v Sydney Building Information Centre Ltd* (1978) 140 CLR 216 at 229-231. His Honour said at 229:

"There is a price to be paid for the advantages flowing from the possession of an eloquently descriptive trade name. Because it is descriptive it is equally applicable to any business of a like kind, its very descriptiveness ensures that it is not distinctive of any particular business and hence its application to other like businesses will not ordinarily mislead the public. In cases of passing off, where it is the wrongful appropriation of the reputation of another or that of his goods that is in question, a plaintiff which uses descriptive words in its trade name will find that quite small differences in a competitor's trade name will render the latter immune from action (*Office Cleaning Services Ltd v Westminster Window and General Cleaners Ltd* (1946) 63 RPC 39 at 42 per Lord Simonds). As his Lordship said (at 43), the possibility of blunders by members of the public will always be present when names consist of descriptive words—'So long as descriptive words are used by two traders as part of their respective trade names, it is possible that some members of the public will be confused whatever the differentiating words may be'. The risk of confusion must be accepted, to do otherwise is to give to one who appropriates to himself descriptive words an unfair monopoly in those words and might even deter others from pursuing the occupation which the words describe."

...[605] ...

However it is not necessarily simply a question, as submitted by counsel for S & I, of first determining whether the word or words are descriptive and, depending on the answer to that question, then ascertaining whether the words had acquired a secondary meaning: see *The Kettle Chip Company Pty Ltd v Apand Pty Ltd* (1993) 46 FCR 152 at 165-166. The characterisation of a word or words as descriptive and its effect may involve an inquiry of the type discussed by Hill J in *Equity Access Pty Ltd v Westpac Banking Corp* (1990) ATPR 40-994 at 50,956:

"Just as the distinction between descriptive and fancy names is not a distinction of law so too it is wrong to see the distinction in black and white terms. The reality is that there is a continuum with at the extremes purely descriptive names at the one end, completely invented names at the other and in between, names that contain ordinary English words that are in some way or other at least partly descriptive. The further along the continuum towards the fancy name one goes, the easier it will be for a

███████ Australian Surf Life Saver v S & I Publishing *continued*

plaintiff to establish that the words used are descriptive of the plaintiff's business. The closer along the continuum one moves towards a merely descriptive name the more a plaintiff will need to show that the name has obtained a secondary meaning, equating it with the products of the plaintiff (if a name admits of this—a purely descriptive name probably will not) and the easier it will be to see a small difference in names as adequate to avoid confusion."

This passage was cited with approval by a Full Court in *Dodds Family Investments Pty Ltd v Lane Industries Pty Ltd* (1993) 26 IPR 261. However even descriptive words may, through use in a particular way, become distinctive such as to enable the established user of them to restrain their use by others: see *Opals Australia Pty Ltd v Opal Australiana Pty Ltd* (1993) ATPR 41-264.

I should refer to two matters concerning the intention of a respondent in proceedings such as these. The first is that if an intention on the part of the respondent to mislead or deceive can be inferred then the Court can more readily hold the respondent to have engaged in conduct likely to mislead or deceive: see *Australian Home Loans Ltd (t/a Aussie Home Loans) v Phillips* (1998) ATPR 41-626. The second emerges from the judgment of Lockhart J in *Bridge Stockbrokers Ltd v Bridges* (1984) 4 FCR 460 at 474-475. His Honour noted that if the conduct of a corporation caused mere confusion or uncertainty in the minds of the public in the sense that they may be caused to [606] wonder whether two products may have come from the same source, the corporation would not have contravened s 52. If, however, a corporation set out on a course of conduct so as to create uncertainty in the minds of the public as to whether two products came from the same source then that constitutes conduct proscribed by s 52. These views were endorsed by Gummow J in *NSW Dairy Corp v Murray Goulburn Cooperative Co Ltd* (1989) 86 ALR 549 at 558. In an appeal from that judgment of Gummow J the Full Court did not express a contrary view: see (1990) 24 FCR 370 at 387-388. However, for reasons I shortly explain, it has been unnecessary to approach the matter on this footing.

Conclusion

I accept that the word "Triathlon" is descriptive in the sense that it describes a sport and when found on the cover of a magazine that was overtly a sports magazine, may be descriptive of the contents of the magazine and thus the type of magazine it is. It is not a word over which a monopoly of use can be asserted in the name of a magazine. However, in the present case, a singular feature of the magazine acquired by Life Saver has been its publication with a masthead featuring prominently the word "Triathlon". This characteristic did not alter when the word was printed in lower case and italicised in early 1987. Indeed I think the word, in both formats, could fairly be said to dominate the cover of the magazine because of both the size of the word in an absolute sense and, more significantly, its relative size to other text on the cover. The manner in which the word is portrayed renders it distinctive. Until the publication of "Triathlon & Multi Sports Magazine" in July 1998, the use of the word, portrayed in this way, distinguished "Triathlon Sports" from other magazines in the same field, that is, reporting on the sport of triathlon and other multi sports. While other magazines in the Australian market in this field have displayed a word in the masthead which is prominent, the word "Triathlon" has featured only on the cover of the magazine now owned by Life Saver. There is direct evidence that this characteristic is of significance to consumers and I think it may reasonably be inferred that the dominant use of the word "triathlon" provides a point of distinction at the time of purchase between the magazine owned by Life Saver and other magazines generally dealing with the same subject matter in the market. The adoption of the same word and its prominent display by S & I constitutes, in my opinion, a representation that its magazine is the magazine owned by Life Saver.

Australian Surf Life Saver v S & I Publishing *continued*

It may be accepted that there are points of distinction. The style in which the word "Triathlon" appears in the S & I magazine, that is, in upper case and not italicised is different. Moreover the masthead in the S & I magazine is framed at the top by a red flash containing a reference to the magazine as being a "New" (in yellow) triathlon and multi sport magazine. That it is new is also apparent by the reference to Vol 1 No 1 at the base of the masthead. The magazine published by S & I contains additional and different words qualifying the word "triathlon". However the word "sport" appears in both though as the singular in one and the plural in the other. Ultimately, however, the only substantial point of distinction in the collocation of words used in the title is the addition of the words "& Multi" in the magazine published by S & I.

In my opinion the prominent use of the word "triathlon" in the magazine published by S & I will create something more than mere confusion or uncertainty. There is a real possibility that purchasers of triathlon magazines will **[607]** and will continue to believe the magazine published by S & I is the magazine owned by Life Saver. In reaching this conclusion it has been unnecessary to rely on any inferences that might be drawn from a finding that S & I intended to mislead purchasers. However the finding I have made concerning the adoption of the masthead by S & I fortifies the conclusion I have reached. Counsel for S & I submitted that if the two magazines continue to be published in their present form then it would be obvious to consumers as they view them both being offered for sale, that they were two different publications. In those circumstances, it was submitted, attention would move from the dominant word "Triathlon" to the indicia of difference to which I have just referred. However one can readily conceive of situations where the two magazines are not displayed sufficiently close together to permit that comparison. Even if they were, a consumer may nonetheless view them as the same magazine but published in a slightly different format as different editions. Situations may also arise where a vendor stocks one but not the other or stocks both and sells all copies of Life Saver's magazine leaving on display and for sale only copies of the magazine published by S & I.

It is unnecessary to deal with the effect of the conduct of S & I on advertisers rather than consumers though the matters I have identified to this point are less likely, in my opinion and notwithstanding the evidence of Stephens to the contrary, to impact on advertisers who may well be more discerning in the comparisons they might make.

The applicant has made out grounds for injunctive relief under the Act. It is unnecessary to consider whether the tort of passing off is also made out.

■ Mimicking success: Can a competitor use a descriptive term?

Apand v The Kettle Chip Company

[13.55] *Apand Pty Ltd v The Kettle Chip Company Pty Ltd* (1994) 30 IPR 337 Federal Court of Australia

LOCKHART, GUMMOW AND LEE JJ: **[339]**

This is an appeal by leave from orders of a Judge of this Court (Burchett J) in which declarations were made that the appellant had engaged in passing off and in conduct that was misleading or deceptive in contravention of s 52 of the *Trade Practices Act 1974* (the Act).

███████ Apand v The Kettle Chip Company *continued*

The claim for damages or an account of profits was stood over until further order. His Honour's reasons are now reported as *Kettle Chip Company Pty Ltd v Apand Pty Ltd (formerly CCA Snack Foods Pty Ltd)* (1993) 46 FCR 152.

The nature of the dispute

The appellant manufactures potato chips which it markets under the brand "Smith's". "Smith's" is a longstanding and well-known brand name in the Australian market and the appellant is the largest manufacturer of potato chips in Australia.

On 21 July 1989, the respondent, which had been incorporated under another style, changed its name to The Kettle Cooked Chip Company Pty Ltd. On 3 August 1992, there was a further change of name, to The Kettle Chip Company Pty Ltd.

In 1989 the respondent began to manufacture and market potato chips in packets labelled "The Kettle Chip". In December 1991 the packet label was changed to "The Kettle Chip Co". From December 1990 and July 1991 respectively, two other companies, "Hawker" and "Frito-Lay", began to market potato chips manufactured and packaged for them by the respondent. The Hawker and Frito-Lay packets were labelled as "Kettle Chips" and "Kettle Crisps" respectively.

The respondent marketed its product in 100 gram packets of 4 types: Lightly Salted, Chilli Flavour, Thai Spice Flavours, and Herb and Spice Flavour. Hawker potato chips were marketed in 75 gram and later 150 gram packets of three types: Lightly Salted, Chilli Flavour, and Herb and Spice Flavour. Frito-Lay crisps were marketed in 75 gram packets as Lightly Salted, and Jalapino Chilli Flavour, and later in 50 gram, 100 gram and 200 gram packets.

Potato chips manufactured by the respondent were made by the batch-cooking method. The respondent obtained equipment and advice for the batch-cooking of potato chips from a corporation carrying on that business in the US. It was said that chips cooked by that method were known in the US as "kettle cooked chips" or "kettle chips". His Honour found that consumers in Australia had not heard of a commodity "kettle chips" before the respondent commenced manufacturing and marketing its product.

The batch-cooking of potato chips requires an operator to stir the chips in a vat of hot oil and to determine when the cooking process has been completed. The process produces a chip of distinctive flavour and texture.

The appellant manufactured its chips by mass production methods. It used a conveyor belt which took a continuous flow of potato slices through an oil-filled cooker.

At the time the respondent commenced manufacturing and marketing its chips it was a single enterprise corporation formed to obtain and utilise American know-how and to introduce a new product to the Australian market. The batch-cooking method of manufacture used by the respondent restricted the volume of chips that could be produced and caused the respondent to incur higher [340] production costs than the method used by the appellant. The respondent's chips were sold at a "premium price" at garages, greengrocers, delicatessens, bottle shops, newsagencies, cinemas and chemist shops, outlets described as the "route market". The route market does not include the major supermarket chains.

In the period between December 1989 and March 1992 the respondent sold over 12 million packages of its product. Sales commenced in New South Wales in December 1989 and expanded to Queensland in February 1990, Victoria in the following month, to Western Australia in June 1990, to South Australia in August 1990, and to Tasmania in November of that year. By May 1992 the respondent's product was sold at approximately 10,000 outlets.

Sales of the Hawker and Frito-Lay packets were more modest. Up to September 1992 over 2 million packages of each had been sold.

...

Apand v The Kettle Chip Company *continued*

In May 1992 the appellant introduced to the market potato chips produced by the multi-zone fryers. The chips were marketed in packets labelled "Country Kettle". The size of the lettering used for the label gave those words dominance in the get-up of the packaging. The diamond-shaped brand and logo "Smith's", usually a prominent feature in the appellant's packaging of its potato chip products, was present but of lesser size than usual. The launch was supported by extensive television advertising using a raucous commercial identified in the evidence as "Chippie Chippie Shake".

... **[341]** ...

The trial

At the trial, the respondent contended that the combination of the words "The Kettle Chip" and the get-up used in the packaging of the respondent's product distinguished the respondent's goods to a significant number of consumers and that the original and revised forms of packaging used by the appellant appropriated the respondent's reputation and constituted passing off and contravention of s 52 of the Act.

The learned primary Judge concluded that when the appellant launched its product in May 1992, the packaging of the respondent's product had acquired a considerable reputation. His Honour found (46 FCR at 164-165):

> "Even if (as the [appellant] contended) the word 'Kettle' and the symbol of a cauldron, although each was marked 'TM' for trade mark, did not in themselves exclusively identify the [respondent's] goods for 'a significant number of consumers in the relevant market' (*Johnson & Johnson Australia Pty Ltd v Sterling Pharmaceuticals Pty Ltd* (1991) 30 FCR 326 at 336, per Lockhart J), there can be no doubt on **[342]** the evidence that its packet, including that word and symbol together with all the other features I have mentioned, did identify its potato chips for a great many people. It had sold millions of packets so marked. The [appellant's] choice of a packet design so closely resembling the [respondent's] is eloquent and expert testimony to the attractive power of its combination of features. Once the [appellant] made that choice, even if it acted honestly in doing so (and in all the circumstances I do not think it did), it came under an obligation to take particular care to ensure that its product was adequately distinguished from that of the [respondent]. Lord Oliver of Aylmerton put the matter strongly, with reference to a not dissimilar context, in *Reckitt & Colman Products Ltd v Boden Inc* [1991] 1 WLR 419 at 507-508; [1990] 1 All ER 873 at 887 (a passage cited by Davies J in *R and C Products Pty Ltd v SC Johnson and Sons Pty Ltd* (1993) 42 FCR 188 at 194):
>
> > 'In the end the question comes down not to whether the respondents are entitled to a monopoly in the sale of lemon juice in natural size lemon-shaped containers but whether the appellants, in deliberately adopting, out of all the many possible shapes of container, a container having the most immediately striking feature of the respondent's get-up, have taken sufficient steps to distinguish their product from that of the respondents. As Roma LJ observed in *Payton & Co Ltd v Snelling, Lampard and Co Ltd* (1900) 17 RPC 48 at 56:
> > > "[W]hen one person has used certain leading features, though common to the trade, if another person is going to put goods on the market, having the same leading features, he should take extra care by the distinguishing features he is going to put on his goods, to see that the goods can be really distinguished ...
> > > "I stress the words "to see the goods can be really distinguished" ...'
>
> I have reached the clear conclusion that the [appellant] was guilty of passing off, as well as contravention of s 52 of the *Trade Practices Act*."

▆▆▆▆▆▆ Apand v The Kettle Chip Company *continued*

... the finding... of his Honour [was that] the appellant in all the circumstances had not acted honestly. It is sufficient for present purposes to note that this was so expressed in the above passage as to indicate that it was not essential to the ultimate findings that were made.

The primary Judge had given close consideration to the differences between the relevant packaging. He said (at 161):

> "Of course, a person who places the packets before him, side by side, can also see differences. But that is not how passing off by imitation of another trader's mark or get-up is to be tested. In general, and more particularly in the case of an item likely to be purchased for a small price without long consideration, the comparison which must be made is between the impression of the (respondent's) goods retained in a customer's mind and the impression made by the sort of consideration he is likely to give to the (appellant's) product before purchasing it. Only a rare potato chip consumer, who has previously studied the (respondent's) packets, is likely to go through that exercise again upon seeing a packet, some time later, on display in a service station or a corner shop. If, as he passes it, it appears to him to be the same 'Kettle' product he liked before, or another flavour put out by the same people, he is very likely to purchase it without further examination."

In reaching what he described as a "clear conclusion" that the case for passing off and contravention of s 52 of the Act had been made out, his Honour said "The packets speak for themselves" (at 165).

The appellant had submitted that the word "Kettle" was a descriptive word which the appellant was entitled to use in its packaging. The primary Judge said (at 166):

> "I have already expressed the conclusion that, taking all these features together, the (appellant's) packet deceptively reflects the (respondent's). It would not affect this **[343]** conclusion if I were to hold that the word 'Kettle', considered alone, would be a descriptive word. Nor would the conclusion be affected even if I were to hold that the word would have, considered alone, no secondary meaning distinguishing the (respondent's) product."

His Honour went on to say that in any case he would have great difficulty with the proposition that the word "Kettle" was relevantly descriptive. He pointed out that since a descriptive word may be distinctive, the context and circumstances of its use must be considered.

His Honour found that the word had little descriptive connection with the product manufactured and marketed by the respondent and, furthermore, that the manner in which it was used by the respondent, namely as an apparent brand name in conjunction with the display of a conventional cauldron in stylised form with other elements of get-up, gave the word a secondary meaning. As stated earlier, his Honour accepted that at the time the appellant introduced its batch-cooked product to the Australian market, the word "Kettle" was not a generic term descriptive of a type of potato chip sold in that market. His Honour appeared to be prepared to infer that the word "Kettle" as used in the respondent's labelling of its packets, with the strong symbols used on those packets, reinforced by the distinctiveness of the respondent's product, had caused the word "Kettle" to be part of a matrix of "memory hooks" which identified the respondent's potato chips for "a significant number of consumers in the relevant market" particularly the casual consumers who represented many of the purchasers of goods the in the "route market". (See *Johnson & Johnson Australia Pty Ltd v Sterling Pharmaceuticals Pty Ltd* (1991) 30 FCR 326 at 336.)

▓▓▓▓▓ Apand v The Kettle Chip Company *continued*

The primary Judge was satisfied that the manner in which the word "Kettle" was used by the respondent had resulted in the word acquiring a secondary meaning, namely, that of a brand name distinguishing the respondent's products. His Honour reached that conclusion by finding that the word "Kettle" neither naturally nor readily described a potato chip and the prominence of "Kettle" in the labelling of the respondent's packets associated with striking symbols was unlikely to convey a meaning other than that of a brand name. His Honour was left in no doubt by the evidence relating to get-up that the word "Kettle", supported by those symbols identified the respondent's product for a great many people.

The primary Judge also (46 FCR at 165) referred to a body of evidence which attempted to show instances of actual deception. He said that whilst much of it was in inadmissible form, it did include examples of actual deception which was not challenged. He referred, in particular, to the evidence of a marketing assistant of the respondent, that customers had complained to her on a number of occasions about "Country Kettle" potato chips, obviously on the assumption that these were the product of the respondent's manufacture.

Mr Ballard has been the Managing Director of the appellant since 1986. He agreed, in cross-examination, that he had much experience in reading the results of market research and in using it for the making of marketing decisions. Mr Ballard gave evidence that, in the present case, he considered the final packaging and at that time the packaging of all the known competitors.

Mr Ballard agreed that the respondent manufactured a distinctive style of potato chip, and attributed that distinctiveness to several features, including a crunchier texture and an irregular shape. He stated that the respondent's product represented a discrete segment of the potato chip market. Mr Ballard said that the word "Kettle" described that product and that consumers associated that word **[344]** with a different process of manufacture without consumers having detailed knowledge of the elements of that difference. He also said that the use of a stylised cauldron on the packaging led to the creation of an image which the public associated with that distinctive product.

In the brief for preparation of a design for the packaging (the Pack Design Brief) the appellant's Group Product Manager, Mr Guthrie, acknowledged that consumers held a "sound awareness" of the respondent's product and that the respondent had established "a rich image base" for that product. Mr Guthrie stated therein that the image had been established by the respondent through, inter alia, "product uniqueness" and "packaging", and that consumers attributed particular values to the product marketed by the respondent, namely a homemade style and the absence of mass production. According to Mr Guthrie a key attribute of the term "kettle chips" was the sense of care and hand-cooked attention that the term evoked.

The decision and the appeal
... **[345]** ...
The central point of the appellant's appeal, however, was whether the primary Judge erred in treating the word "Kettle" as a "key" word and one which had obtained a secondary meaning distinctive of the respondent's product at the time the appellant commenced to market potato chips under the name "Country Kettle".

As we have said, his Honour was satisfied that the combination of the use of strong symbols, the get-up and the use of the word "Kettle" in the appellant's packaging had appropriated sufficient elements of the distinctive labelling and get-up of the respondent's product to constitute the tort of passing off and an infringement of s 52 of the Act. His Honour stated that he was aided in reaching that conclusion by the absence of evidence from certain managerial staff employed by the appellant. However, it is apparent that the foundation for his Honour's findings rested upon a comparative assessment of the packaging and the

▰▰▰▰ Apand v The Kettle Chip Company *continued*

inferences of reputation in the respondent's product made available by the evidence before him, and that his Honour's willingness to make those findings did not depend in any degree upon the absence of evidence from executives involved in the design or selection of the label "Country Kettle" or the packaging of that product.

In dealing with the appellant's contention that the word "Kettle" was a descriptive word, his Honour noted that the appellant relied upon opinions expressed in qualitative market survey reports and upon evidence of Mr Ballard that "Kettle" signified a particular style of potato chip and not a name used by the respondent for its product.

Although the primary Judge found that Mr Ballard's evidence was not reliable, his Honour's opinion on Mr Ballard's credit was inessential to his Honour's **[346]** conclusion that the word "Kettle" had a secondary meaning. We will deal with the adverse finding on Mr Ballard's credit later in these reasons.

... **[348]**

Issues of honesty and credit

We turn now to his Honour's findings on the honesty of the appellant's conduct and the credit of Mr Ballard.

Certain propositions were not in dispute before us. They are discussed in authorities such as *Parkdale Custom Built Furniture Pty Ltd v Puxu Pty Ltd* (1982) 149 CLR 191; *Cadbury-Schweppes Pty Ltd v Pub Squash Co Pty Ltd* [1981] RPC 429; *ConAgra Inc v McCain Foods (Aust) Pty Ltd* (1992) 33 FCR 302; and *Levi Strauss v Kimbyr Investments Ltd* (1994) 28 IPR 149. First, merely to imitate the trade mark or get-up of another trader does not establish a case of fraudulent intent to attract custom by misleading purchasers of the goods of the defendant into the belief that they are acquiring those of the plaintiff, or goods with which the plaintiff is connected in the course of trade. The plaintiff must always show the necessary reputation in its name or get-up and if it fails to do so, then the existence of a fraudulent intent itself cannot supply that deficiency. Here, his Honour found, and we agree, that the necessary reputation was established. Further, the finding which followed as to passing off and contravention of s 52 was not dependent upon the supplementary finding as to dishonesty.

His Honour concluded that the appellant did not act honestly in choosing the name "Country Kettle" for its product and the design for the packaging in which the product was marked (46 FCR at 164, 170-174). He held that:

- the appellant set out to duplicate the characteristics of the respondent's product;
- it made a sophisticated analysis of the image which the respondent had created for its product in the market;
- it then set out to give its own product the same image in order to win back the customers who were buying the respondent's potato chips and thus regain lost market share;
- the appellant deliberately subordinated its name of "Smith's" in favour of adopting and emphasising a name that used the key word in the name under which the respondent had sold the same product and placed on its packets the pictures of potato chips, potatoes and a cauldron previously described, together with other details which fostered the impression of strikingly similar packaging;
- a considerable risk was taken by the appellant of an adverse court decision and that there was express evidence that the legal implications were "discussed"; [and]
- in these circumstances the inference was strong that the appellant's own executives considered there was much to gain from the use of so close an imitation of the name, symbol and get-up of the respondent's increasingly popular product.

His Honour's conclusion that the appellant did not act honestly was based on a number of findings which we shall state and consider in turn. Before doing so, however, we observe that

▣▣▣▣▣▣ Apand v The Kettle Chip Company *continued*

his Honour's findings about the appellant's conduct and of Mr Ballard's lack of credibility were intertwined. His adverse findings about Mr Ballard led him to find dishonest conduct by the appellant more readily.

The findings relating to Mr Ballard's credit were not necessary in order to decide the critical issues in the case, in view of the opinion of his Honour that there had been passing off and contravention of s 52, determined in accordance with the customary objective tests applicable to each cause of action.

... [356] ...

Conclusion as to fraudulent intent

Intent to mislead or deceive or to pass off is not an essential element in the proof of a contravention of s 52 of the Act or passing off although proof of intention to mislead or deceive may lead the Court to infer more readily that there has in fact been conduct which is misleading or deceptive or that passing off has occurred.

With respect to the primary Judge's decision, in our opinion the evidence does not support the finding that the appellant intended to mislead or deceive consumers into believing that its "Country Kettle" product was the product of the respondent, or emanated from it or was in some way associated with it.

There is, as the primary Judge found, a definite similarity between the name and get-up of the package of the two products. But, as we have said earlier in these reasons, mere proof of the fact that a person has deliberately copied the name or get-up of a trade rival does not of itself establish a contravention of s 52 or a passing off of goods or services.

The evidence supports the finding that the intention of the appellant was rather to promote an awareness in the mind of the consumer of "Country Kettle" as a new brand of chip to gain the benefit of the favourable impression shared by consumers that a "Kettle Chip" was a better chip produced by a different process [357] than most mass produced chips; but not to lead people to believe that the appellant's product was linked or associated with the respondent's product.

... [358] ...

Remedies

It remains for the respondent to elect between a remedy in damages or an account of profits. We have referred to the objective considerations which establish a finding of contravention of s 52 of the Act and leads to damages under s 82. It has not yet clearly been settled whether the width of s 87 of the Act includes a restitutionary remedy in the nature of an account of profits; see *Munchies Management Pty Ltd v Belperio* (1988) 84 ALR 700 at 713; *Wardley Australia Ltd v Western Australia* (1992) 175 CLR 514 at 525-527; *Dart Industries Inc v Decor Corp Pty Ltd* (1993) 179 CLR 101. We say nothing further upon that issue.

There remains for consideration the election between damages and an account of profits in aid of the passing off action. The relevance of fraud to recovery of damages in passing off is discussed in *ConAgra Inc v McCain Foods (Aust) Pty Ltd* (1992) 33 FCR 302. As to the remedy of an account, in *Dart Industries*, supra at 110-111, Mason CJ, Deane, Dawson and Toohey JJ said (omitting footnotes):

> "Damages and an account of profits are alternative remedies. An account of profits was a form of relief granted by equity whereas damages were originally a purely common law remedy. As Windeyer J pointed out in *Colbeam Palmer Ltd v Stock Affiliates Pty Ltd* (1968) 122 CLR 25 at 34, even now an account of profits retains its equitable characteristics in that a defendant is made to account for, and is then stripped of, profits which it has dishonestly made by the infringement and which it would be uncon-

▬▬▬ Apand v The Kettle Chip Company *continued*

scionable for it to retain. An account of profits is confined to profits actually made, its purpose being not to punish the defendant but to prevent its unjust enrichment. The ordinary requirement of the principles of unjust enrichment that regard be paid to matters of substance rather than technical form is applicable."

The reference to profits which have been "dishonestly made" requires further comment. It is not to be understood as requiring fraud sufficient for the purposes of an action in deceit. In *Colbeam Palmer*, supra at 34, Windeyer J spoke of profits made by the defendant "during the period he knew of the plaintiff's rights". In such a context what is involved is persistence after notice of the claims of the plaintiff which, when made good, found the successful action against the defendant; see *BM Auto Sales Pty Ltd v Budget Rent A Car System Pty Ltd* (1976) 51 ALJR 254 at 258; *US Surgical Corp v Hospital Products International Pty Ltd* (1983) 2 NSWLR 157 at 248-249 (rev'd on other grounds: 156 CLR 41); *ConAgra Inc v McCain Foods (Aust) Pty Ltd* supra at 362-364. Thus, in *My Kinda Town Ltd v Soll* (1983) RPC 15 at 47, Slade J **[359]** accepted that in principle the plaintiffs were entitled to an account of profits to run from the date of receipt by the defendants of the plaintiffs' solicitors' letter before action.

Note

[13.60] Despite the success of the Kettle Chip Co in the case extracted above, and indeed, the registration of KETTLE as a trade mark, the company lost an action against Frito-Lay, which sold "Thins" crisps with the slogan "kettle cooked potato chips" on the packet. This use of the name was held not to amount to trade mark infringement nor to passing off since the phrase described the process of production, rather than identifying the source of the chips: *Pepsico Australia Pty Ltd v Kettle Chip Co Pty Ltd* (1996) 33 IPR 161.

■ Conduct of the defendant must be misleading, not merely "unfair"

▬▬▬▬▬ **Parkdale Custom Built Furniture v Puxu** ▬▬▬▬▬

[13.65] *Parkdale Custom Built Furniture Pty Ltd v Puxu Pty Ltd* (1982) 149 CLR 191 High Court of Australia

[The respondent manufacturer of "Contour" furniture, had sought to prevent the appellant from imitating the design of its furniture, in the latter's "Rawhide" range. The respondent had sought an injunction under s 80 of the *Trade Practices Act 1974* (Cth) to restrict the appellant from engaging in misleading or deceptive conduct in breach of s 52 of that Act. Gibbs CJ and Mason J (Murphy J dissenting) did not consider that the appellant's conduct breached s 52. Brennan J, who also decided in favour of the appellant relied on passing off principles.]

BRENNAN J: **[219]** ... In my opinion, this is a case where common law principles are relevant to a true understanding of the scope and operation of s 52. The relevant principles prescribe the protection to which a manufacturer is entitled against the marketing of copies of his goods and the correlative (albeit incidental) protection of consumers who might be led by the appearance of a copy into believing that it is made by that manufacturer.

The protection afforded by the common law stops short of according to a manufacturer a monopoly right to the manufacture and sale of goods of a particular design unless he is the owner of a design validly registered under the *Designs Act 1906* (Cth) in respect of goods of that kind. The relevant principles in a passing off action were stated by Graham J in *Benchairs Ltd v Chair Centre Ltd* [1974] RPC 429, a case in which the plaintiffs' claim in passing off depended solely on the fact that the shape and design of the defendants' chair was so close to the shape and design of the plaintiffs' chair that its mere existence on the market would lead to confusion with the plaintiffs' chair. (An alternative claim for infringement of a registered design succeeded before Graham J, but failed before the Court of Appeal.) Graham J held (at 435):

> "The mere copying of the shape of the plaintiffs' article is not in itself such a representation ... [ie a representation by the defendant that his goods are those of the plaintiff] ... Anyone is entitled, subject to some monopoly or statutory right [220] preventing him, to copy and sell any article on the market, and false representation and passing off only arise when a defendant does something further which suggests that the article which he is selling is that of the plaintiff. This he may do by a direct representation to that effect such as by the use of the plaintiffs' name or mark, or by an indirect representation such as by imitation of get-up by enclosing the article in a distinctive package which is similar to that used by the plaintiff."

... [221] ...

The public freedom to manufacture and sell an article to which a particular design is applied is not taken away by the *Designs Act* except in favour of the registered owner of a registered design, and his prima facie monopoly will be defeated if the design was not novel or original when it was registered: *Macrae Knitting Mills Ltd v Lowes Ltd* (1936) 55 CLR 725. The validity of registration depends upon the novelty or originality of the design (see *Designs Act* s 17(1)); if it were otherwise the registered owner would acquire a monopoly without any compensating benefit being obtained by the public.

The design of the "Contour" suite was not registered under the *Designs Act*. Puxu acquired no statutory monopoly in the manufacture and sale of lounge suites of the "Contour" design; it acquired no right (either under the *Designs Act* or otherwise) to exclude others from manufacturing lounge suites of the "Contour" design. Therefore Parkdale was free to apply the design of the "Contour" [222] suite to suites of its own manufacture. Of course, Parkdale was not free to pass off the "Rawhide" suite as a "Contour" suite, but there is no evidence that it did so. It used its own trade name; it affixed its own distinguishing label. Nor did Parkdale get up the "Rawhide" suite for sale in a way which would induce anybody to think that it was the "Contour" suite. A distinction is drawn between the get-up of goods and the copying of the actual goods. Similarity in get-up may evidence passing off, but (statutory monopoly apart) all are free to copy the goods themselves. The distinction was stated by Fletcher Moulton LJ in *JB Williams Co v H Bronnley & Co Ltd* (1909) 26 RPC 765 at 773-774:

> "The get-up of an article means a capricious addition to the article itself, the colour, or shape, it may be, of the wrapper, or anything of that kind; but I strongly object to look at anything, that has a value in use, as part of the get-up of the article. Anything which is in itself useful appears to me rightly to belong to the article itself. For instance, supposing that a firm had been, say for 20 years, the only firm to sell wooden chairs in which the natural wood was simply varnished, and not painted at all, that would

▬▬▬▬ Parkdale Custom Built Furniture v Puxu *continued*

not give them the slightest right to complain of a person putting on the market chairs simply varnished, even though they had been the only persons who had sold them for so long that such chairs might at first be supposed to be their manufacture. The reason is that the newcomer has not in any way imitated the get-up; he has only reproduced the article."

■ **Reputation exists among "prospective customers or ultimate consumers of goods or services"**

[13.70] In *Weitmann v Katies Ltd* [1977] ATPR 40,041 it was alleged by the seller of expensive women's blouses using the mark "St Germain" that Katies, a store frequented by "value for money" shoppers, was deceiving customers by selling t-shirts with "St Germain" embroidered on the sleeve, and shown on a label. Franki J, who was dealing with a s 52 application, said at 17,442:

"Whether conduct is deceptive in the subject case must be examined in the light of what the alleged deceptive words mean to the relevant purchaser when used on the sleeve of the ladies T-shirts as they are to be sold. This involves two questions, first, who is to be considered as the relevant purchaser; and, second, what will the words mean to that purchaser? This seems to lead to two of the questions which arise in a passing off action, first, what is the appropriate class of purchasers to be considered and, secondly, have the words 'Saint Germain' acquired what is commonly called a secondary meaning, namely do they indicate to the appropriate class of purchasers that the goods have come from a particular source, whether the name of that source is known or not?"

As the *Triathlon* and *Kettle* cases illustrate, the way that consumers shop for casual purchases of small-value items will influence the view taken of the defendant's behaviour. The purchaser will be expected to look after their own interests to some extent, according to the majority view in the next extract.

▬▬▬▬▬▬ **Parkdale Custom Built Furniture v Puxu** ▬▬▬▬▬▬

[13.75] *Parkdale Custom Built Furniture Pty Ltd v Puxu Pty Ltd* (1982) 149 CLR 191 High Court of Australia

GIBBS CJ: **[199]** ... Section 52 does not expressly state what persons or class of persons should be considered as the possible victims for the purpose of deciding whether conduct is misleading or deceptive or likely to mislead or deceive. It seems clear enough that consideration must be given to the class of consumers likely to be affected by the conduct. Although it is true, as has often been said, that ordinarily a class of consumers may include the inexperienced as well as the experienced, and the gullible as well as the astute, the section must in my opinion be regarded as contemplating the effect of the conduct on reasonable members of the class. The heavy burdens which the section creates cannot have been intended to be imposed for the benefit of persons who fail to take reasonable care of their own interests. What is reasonable will of course depend on all the circumstances. The persons likely to be affected in the present case, the potential purchasers of a suite of furniture costing about $1,500, would, if acting reasonably, look

▰▰▰▰ Parkdale Custom Built Furniture v Puxu *continued*

for a label, brand or mark if they were concerned to buy a suite of particular manufacture.

The conduct of a defendant must be viewed as a whole. It would be wrong to select some words or act, which, alone, would be likely to mislead if those words or acts, when viewed in their context, were not capable of misleading. It is obvious that where the conduct complained of consists of words it would not be right to select some words only and to ignore others which provided the context which gave meaning to the particular words. The same is true of acts. In the present case the conduct of the appellant was not simply to manufacture and sell furniture that resembled that of the respondent. The appellant sold only furniture that had been labelled, in the ordinary way, so as to show the name of the manufacturer. If the appellant's conduct was likely to mislead possible purchasers, it is difficult to see why the respondent's conduct in selling its furniture would not also be likely to mislead. However that may be, in my opinion, the conduct of the appellant did not contravene s 52. Speaking generally, the sale by one manufacturer of goods which closely resemble those of another manufacturer is not a breach of s 52 if the goods are properly [200] labelled. There are hundreds of ordinary articles of consumption which, although made by different manufacturers and of different quality, closely resemble one another. In some cases this is because the design of a particular article has traditionally, or over a considerable period of time, been accepted as the most suitable for the purpose which the article serves. In some cases indeed no other design would be practicable. In other cases, although the article in question is the product of the invention of a person who is currently trading, the suitability of the design or appearance of the article is such that a market has become established which other manufacturers endeavour to satisfy, as they are entitled to do if no property exists in the design or appearance of the article. In all of these cases, the normal and reasonable way to distinguish one product from another is by marks, brands or labels. If an article is properly labelled so as to show the name of the manufacturer or the source of the article its close resemblance to another article will not mislead an ordinary reasonable member of the public. If the label is removed by some person for whose acts the defendant is not responsible, and in consequence the purchaser is misled, the misleading effect will have been produced, not by the conduct of the defendant, but by the conduct of the person who removed the label.

MASON J: [201] ... Keely J stated that it was necessary to consider whether the appellant's conduct was misleading or deceptive or likely to mislead or deceive "ordinary members of the public likely to be considering purchasing such an item from a retailer" noting that this included "the shrewd and the ingenuous, the educated and uneducated and the experienced and the inexperienced in commercial transactions": *CRW Pty Ltd v Sneddon* [1972] AR (NSW) 17 at 28; see also *World Series Cricket Pty Ltd v Parish* (1977) 16 ALR 181 at 203. However, his Honour gave detailed consideration to which of the differences between the "Contour" and "Rawhide" suite he considered "would be likely to be observed by an ordinary member of the public who had previously looked at the Post and Rail 'Contour' chair as a potential purchaser". Lockhart J considered that Keely J had applied too narrow a test in excluding those who may have seen pictures of the furniture in newspapers, magazines, or on television but not the actual chairs themselves. Whether or not Keely J did so err, Lockhart J is correct in stating that here "the relevant class of persons likely to be exposed to the alleged misleading or deceptive conduct would be anyone interested in purchasing lounge suites or chairs in the higher price range". As his Honour noted, the class protected by s 52 must vary according to the facts of each case. In furniture of this price range in the order of $1,500 for a three-piece lounge suite one would in the ordinary course expect persons within the admittedly wide range of potential purchasers to exercise somewhat more vigilance than may be the case with the purchase of items of less financial significance having less impact on the appearance of the home: cf *Jafferjee v Scarlett* (1937) 57 CLR 115 at 124.

Conduct does not breach s 52(1) merely because members of the public would be caused to wonder whether it might not be the case that two products come from the same source.

MURPHY J [dissenting]: **[214]** ... The prudent buyer may not be misled, but not all buyers are prudent. The Act aims to protect the imprudent as well as the prudent. What degree of imprudence is protected? In applying a similar provision of the *Consumer Protection Act 1969* (NSW) the Industrial Commission said that an advertiser's responsibility extended to readers both "shrewd and ... ingenuous, ... educated and ... uneducated and ... inexperienced in commercial transactions. ... An advertisement may be misleading even though it fails to deceive more wary readers". (See *CRW Pty Ltd v Sneddon* [1972] AR (NSW) 17 at 28, adopted by St John J in *Parish v World Series Cricket Pty Ltd* **[215]** (1977) 16 ALR 172 at 179; see also *Re Registered Trade Mark "Yanx"; Ex parte Amalgamated Tobacco Corp Ltd* (1951) 82 CLR 199 at 206, in relation to the *Trade Marks Act*.) In the US the standard adopted under the *Federal Trade Commission Act 1914* in relation to a somewhat similar provision takes into account "the ignorant, the unthinking and the credulous, who, in making purchases do not stop to analyse, but are governed by appearances and general impressions". (See *Florence Mfg Co v JC Dowd & Co* 178 F 73 at 75 (1910); also *Aronberg v Federal Trade Commission* 132 F 2d 165 (1942)). In *Federal Trade Commission v Standard Education Society* 302 US 112 at 116 (1937) [82 Law Ed 141] the Supreme Court pointed out that the fact that a false statement is obviously false (or an imitation obviously an imitation):

> "[T]o those who are trained and experienced does not change its character, nor take away its power to deceive others less experienced. There is no duty resting upon a citizen to suspect the honesty of those with whom he transacts business. Laws are made to protect the trusting as well as the suspicious. The best element of business has long since decided that honesty should govern competitive enterprises, and that the rule of caveat emptor should not be relied upon to reward fraud and deception."

The circumstances of this case have provoked judicial differences on the effect of the label. Without extending to extremes the reach of s 52, my view is that the case fits within it.

■ Deceiving how many consumers?

[13.80] The different conceptual approaches to this issue, in passing off and s 52 is referred to in the extract below.

▬▬▬▬▬ .au Domain v Domain Names ▬▬▬▬▬

[13.85] *.au Domain Administration Ltd v Domain Names Australia Pty Ltd* [2004] 61 IPR 81 Federal Court of Australia

FINKELSTEIN J: **[85]** ...

On the question of s 52, I am going to guide myself by the following principles. Most of them are uncontroversial:

1. Conduct will be misleading or deceptive if it conveys a false representation.
2. The question whether conduct is misleading or not is an objective question of fact which the court must determine for itself against the background of all relevant facts. Accordingly, while evidence of deception may be led it is not essential to the case.
3. Whether conduct is misleading does not, however, depend upon the defendant's intention, for a corporation which acts honestly and lawfully may contravene s 52. But if there is an intention to mislead the court may more easily infer that the conduct was in fact misleading. [86]
4. Conduct which does no more than cause confusion or uncertainty is not misleading or deceptive. Section 52 is directed to something else.
5. For there to be a contravention of s 52 the conduct must cause (in the sense explained in point 6) an erroneous assumption or misconception. That is, there must be a "sufficient nexus" between the conduct and the error or misconception.
6. Nevertheless, it is not necessary to show that anyone has in fact been misled. It is enough that the conduct is likely to mislead or deceive in the sense that there is a real chance or possibility of deception.
7. Where the conduct involves the making of a statement which is literally true or accurate the conduct may still be misleading. It all depends upon the circumstances.

The precise manner in which these principles are applied will differ from case to case. In particular, the way in which the court will determine whether certain conduct has the capacity to cause error or misconception will vary dependent upon the nature of the case before the court. Here I have in mind the two broad categories of case brought under s 52. The first is an action by a plaintiff who complains that he has been misled by the defendant's conduct and seeks redress. Section 52 appears in Pt V of the *Trade Practices Act*. Part V is headed "Consumer Protection" and it is with consumers that s 52 is principally concerned. In this type of case the plaintiff has the burden of proving that the impugned conduct was misleading and that he altered his position (that is, was induced) as a result. In most cases it will not be difficult to determine whether the defendant's conduct amounts to misleading conduct. Nor will it be difficult to determine whether the conduct induced the plaintiff to act to his detriment.

The second category is where the plaintiff has not been, and does not fear being, deceived or misled. Such a plaintiff brings a s 52 action for a different purpose. He may be in competition with the defendant and is seeking to protect his business from unfair competition (as he might in a passing off action). Or the plaintiff may be a statutory authority such as the ACCC which brings the action to vindicate the public interest. In this type of case the plaintiff usually alleges that the conduct is likely to cause a third party to be misled or deceived. The question whether the conduct is likely to mislead a third party cannot be resolved in the same way as in an action where the plaintiff seeks to establish that he personally has been misled. In such a situation it is necessary to keep in mind the two further classes of action identified by Deane and Fitzgerald JJ in *Taco Company of Australia Inc v Taco Bell Pty Ltd* (1982) 42 ALR 177, 202-203. The first concerns a case where there is an "express untrue representation made only to identified individuals". I take the judges' reference to the case of an "express representation" to refer to an action that is founded on the literal meaning of a representation about a fact (including the non-existence of a fact) or state of affairs. An express representation may be made by words, through the use of symbols for conveying information or by other conduct. An express representation must be distinguished from an implied or inferred representation—"[a]n implication is included in and part of that which is expressed: an inference is something additional to what is stated": *Lubrano v Gollin & Co Pty Ltd* (1919) 27 CLR 113, 118. Deane and Fitzgerald JJ said that as regards this first class of case, the task of deciding (1) whether a representation conveys a false representation and (2) whether the representation [87] has caused error or misconception, should be "uncomplicated". Most actions where the plaintiff alleges that he has been misled will fall into the first (express representation) class.

The second class identified by Deane and Fitzgerald JJ concerns a case where the alleged misrepresentation is not express and is not made to identified individuals, but is made to the public at large or to a section of the public. As regards this class, Deane and Fitzgerald JJ said that determining whether conduct may lead to error should involve the following process. First, it is necessary to identify the relevant section (or sections) of the public by reference to which the issue is to be tested. Second, once the section of the public is identified the issue is to be considered by reference to all who come within the section. This may include the astute and the gullible, the intelligent and the not so intelligent, the well educated and the poorly educated. Third, it is permissible (but not essential) to have regard to evidence that some person has in fact been misled, though this evidence will not be conclusive. Finally, it is necessary to enquire whether any proven misconception has arisen because of the misleading or deceptive conduct.

In *Campomar Sociedad, Limitada v Nike International Ltd* (2000) 202 CLR 45 the High Court (at 84) approved the observations of Deane and Fitzgerald JJ regarding the manner in which a plaintiff should go about establishing whether or not particular conduct has produced error or misconception. In addition, the High Court (at 85-86) laid down two further rules. First, where the persons allegedly misled are not identified individuals but are members of a class it is necessary to isolate "a representative member" of the class and enquire whether this hypothetical individual is likely to be deceived. Second, when considering the likely effect of the misrepresentation on this hypothetical person he (or she) should be judged as an "ordinary" or "reasonable" member of the class. In this way, reactions to the representation that are "extreme" or "fanciful" will be disregarded.

The High Court's decision in *Campomar Sociedad* has settled some issues arising out of s 52 and raised others. One unresolved issue concerns a matter of characterisation. How is one to distinguish between a case which involves a representation made to identified individuals and a case where the representation is made to the public or to a section of the public? I had occasion briefly to consider this problem in *Australian Securities and Investments Commission v National Exchange Pty Ltd* (2003) 202 ALR 24, at 27-28. There the defendant had made false representations to approximately 5,000 shareholders of a major public company. Each shareholder to whom the representations were made was identifiable by name and address. I treated the case as one where the representation had been made to identified individuals. If I were to adopt that approach in the instant case, it would be characterised as a case concerning representations to identified individuals, although the notices in issue were despatched to several hundred thousand businesses.

Upon further reflection I suspect I was probably in error in the *National Exchange* case, although the error was not one which could have affected the result. There can be no doubt that when the impeached conduct is directed towards an indeterminate group or to a group defined by general or collective criteria the case should be treated as one involving a representation to the public at large or to a section or class of consumer. It seems that the same approach should be followed when the case involves a representation to an identifiable [88] group and the plaintiff is alleging not that he was misled but that members of the group (whether great or small in number) were misled by the conduct. In *Elders Trustee and Executor*

■■■■■ .au Domain v Domain Names *continued*

Co Ltd v E G Reeves Pty Ltd (1987) 78 ALR 193, 241 Gummow J indicated that he would treat this type of claim as a "representation to the public" case. This approach, which is the approach I propose to adopt, invites attention to the nature of the claim and not the identity of the person to whom the representation is directed.

I appreciate that on one view the approach might be criticised for applying too fine a distinction. There will be cases where a person other than the representee brings the action and the group to whom the allegedly misleading representation was made is so small that it cannot sensibly be described as a class or a section of the public. In that circumstance it may be neither possible nor necessary to identify a hypothetical member of the group for the purpose of deciding the likely effect of the impugned conduct. If no hypothetical individual is identified the court must determine the likely effect of the conduct on the actual members of the group. There will also be cases on the margin where it will not be clear whether they should be treated as "representation to the public" cases. But the difficult cases are likely to be few and far between.

I also appreciate that the approach I am required to adopt has the potential of producing anomalous results, at least at the theoretical level. Let it be assumed that the proprietor of a business brings an action against a competitor complaining that one of the competitor's advertisements, sent only to a handful of customers, contained allegedly false statements about the origin of the competitor's products. In order to succeed the plaintiff would have to establish that a hypothetical member of the group of customers would have been misled by the advertisement. On the other hand, if a member of the group were to bring an action complaining that he personally had been misled by the advertisement, he would need to prove that only he had been misled. The anomaly is that by virtue of the different tests it is possible that the individual complainant might lose his action but the proprietor of the business may succeed, or vice versa. This would be a very strange result.

Another potential difficulty arises because the class to whom the impugned conduct is directed will often comprise a diverse group. That is, the members of the group might include the uneducated, the inexperienced, the ignorant and the unthinking as well as the educated, the intelligent and the informed consumer. How then is one to identify and give characteristics to *Campomar Sociedad's* hypothetical individual? Logic demands that if one is dealing with a diverse group then, for the purpose of determining whether particular conduct has the capacity to mislead, it is necessary to select a hypothetical individual from that section of the group which is most likely to be misled. If the court is satisfied that this hypothetical individual is likely to have been misled by that conduct, that would be sufficient.

The final point in relation to "representation to the public" cases concerns the requirement, which has been stated in many decisions both at first instance and on appeal, that for the representation to be actionable it must be shown that significant numbers of the group to whom the representation is directed are likely to have been misled or deceived. This requirement can be traced back to the decision of Franki J in *Weitmann v Katies Ltd* (1977) 29 FLR 336, an early s 52 case....[see **[13.70]**] The application failed because the judge held that the particular mark, the name of a geographic location, did not indicate that the clothing sold by the respondent originated from the applicant. In giving his reasons, however, the judge went further than the case required. He said (at 339) that in a s 52 case the principles relating to a passing off action were "in a general sense ... particularly relevant with regard to determining whether certain conduct is misleading or deceptive". He went on to say (at 343) that in such a case he was required to "consider whether a reasonably significant number of potential purchasers would be likely to be misled or deceived just in the same way as this question should be considered in a passing off action".

██████ .au Domain v Domain Names *continued*

Franki J was correct in stating that in a passing off action it is necessary for the plaintiff to show that a large number of consumers are liable to be deceived by the defendant's use of a particular name or get up: *Saville Perfumery Ltd v June Perfect Ld* (1941) 58 RPC 147, 175-176. This is hardly surprising. The basis for a passing off action is a proprietary right in goodwill established through the use of a name or get up in connection with the plaintiff's goods: *A G Spalding & Bros v A W Gamage Ltd* (1915) 32 RPC 273, 284; *Erven Warnink Besloten Vennootschap v J Townend & Sons (Hull) Ltd* [1979] AC 731 at 741-742, 754. The action is for damage done or threatened to be done to that property by the defendant. That is the reason the plaintiff must show that a significant number of people are likely to be misled. Unless many people are misled it is unlikely that the plaintiff's goodwill will be damaged.

In my opinion, however, *Weitmann v Katies Ltd* borrowed from the law relating to passing off without due regard to the difference between a passing off action and a claim based on s 52. In *Hornsby Building Information Centre Pty Ltd v Sydney Building Information Centre Ltd* (1978) 140 CLR 216, 226 Stephen J warned against such reasoning. He said that a s52 case is not (unlike in passing off) founded upon protection of a trader's goodwill, but is directed to preventing the very deception of the public which operates to injure that goodwill. Put another way, a passing off action is concerned with deception or confusion of the public as to the source of goods, whereas the policy behind Pt V of the *Trade Practices Act* is designed to prevent the deception of consumers of goods or services: cf *McWilliam's Wines Pty Ltd v McDonald's System of Australia Pty Ltd* (1980) 33 ALR 394, 410. Moreover, as Mason J said in *Parkdale Custom Built Furniture Pty Ltd v Puxu Pty Ltd* (1982) 149 CLR 191, 205: "[t]he operation of s 52 is not restricted by the common law principles relating to passing off".

It seems to me that there is simply no warrant for imposing a requirement that in a "representation to the public" case significant members of the public must be misled by the impugned conduct before there can be a contravention of s 52. First, s 52 does not prescribe this requirement. Second, there is no reason in principle why the requirement should exist. Third, it would be strange if a court were to determine that certain conduct had the capacity to mislead (and did in fact mislead a handful of people) but nevertheless held that the conduct was not actionable because an insufficient number of people were misled.

These reasons are not, of course, enough for me to disregard the previous case law on the topic because the position is that a number of Full Court decisions [90] have followed Franki J's dictum, albeit without any analysis. The decisions include, among others: *Snoid v Handley* (1981) 38 ALR 383; *10th Cantanae Pty Ltd v Shoshana Pty Ltd* (1987) 79 ALR 299; *Siddons Pty Ltd v Stanley Works Pty Ltd* (1991) 29 FCR 14. But there is a way out. I am of opinion that the dictum cannot survive the High Court's decision in *Campomar Sociedad*. By laying down the rule that in a "representation to the public" case the question whether conduct is misleading or deceptive is to be assessed by reference to the reaction of the hypothetical representative member of the class to whom the representation is directed, the High Court has left no scope for the operation of the requirement that it must also be shown that a significant number of members of the class have been misled. That is, the two requirements cannot sit side by side. I take the position now to be that the dictum imposed in *Weitmann v Katies Ltd* has been overtaken.

██

■ Source of reputation

[13.90] Traditionally, passing off protects traders against other traders and the defendant will inevitably be a business person or enterprise. *Trade Practices Act 1974* (Cth), s 52 prohibits "a corporation in trade or commerce" from engaging in misleading and deceptive conduct. On the other hand, plaintiffs may be individuals, sporting bodies, charities or churches, as long as the reputation they are trying to protect is sufficiently established in the public mind as "belonging" to the plaintiff. This does not mean that the actual identity and business address of the plaintiff must be known by the relevant consumers, as long as the public associates a product or service with a particular source which in fact, turns out to be the plaintiff. Even if the plaintiff is only one of a class of traders sharing a reputation, each will be entitled to protect their own interests against passing off by outsiders.

■ Location of reputation

[13.95] Reputation exists among customers or potential customers, those "attracted to do business" with the supplier. A series of older cases held that those customers and the trader must be within the same jurisdiction, as "mere reputation" does not by itself constitute property which the law protects: see, for example, *Anheuser Busch Inc v Budejovivky Budvar NP* [1984] FSR 413. A more modern approach has been to require customers within a jurisdiction, even if the goods or services come from elsewhere. In trade mark law the concept of a "well-known mark" has been introduced. The delineation between having reputation (as a form of property) and being "well-known" is not yet well understood, however it is a status that may not be "conferred lightly". See L Bently and B Sherman, *Intellectual Property Law* (OUP, 2001, p 689), citing *Microsoft Corp's Applications* [1997-1998] *Information Technology Law Reports* 361.

It would appear that reputation can be established more quickly, and travel faster when a financial product is involved, or an online newspaper, where customers deal with the supplier electronically. In *Al Hyat Publishing Co Ltd v Sokarno* (1996) 34 IPR 214 the publisher of a well-known Arabic language newspaper, Al Hyat, began negotiations to electronically transmit pages and have the paper published in hard copy by an Australian agent. When the enterprise proved too expensive to be viable, the defendant went ahead and applied for trade mark registration of the name, masthead and logo. Although interlocutory, Tamberlin J found that the evidence supported the conclusion that a substantial number of persons in Australia would have accessed the Al Hyat newspaper via the Internet, and would be likely to be misled by the proposed sale and publication of the Australian sourced newspaper under that name and logo. For an example of a reputation forged overnight due to press announcements of a new corporation, see *Fletcher Challenge Ltd v Fletcher Challenge Pty Ltd* [1981] 1 NSWLR 196, discussed in the *Healthy Choice* case (see further below).

Maxim's v Dye

[13.100] *Maxim's Ltd v Dye* [1977] 1 WLR 1155; [1978] 2 All ER 55 Chancery Division

[The plaintiff, an English company, had since 1907 owned the famous Parisian restaurant Maxim's which, it argued enjoyed extensive goodwill in England, being patronised by persons resident in England. In December 1975 the defendant had opened a restaurant in Norwich under the name Maxim's and decorated it in a style to give it a French atmosphere. The plaintiff sought an injunction to restrain the defendant from using the name Maxim's arguing that the lower standard of the defendant's restaurant would injure the plaintiff's goodwill.]

GRAHAM J: [1160] ... If it is in law correct to say that a plaintiff cannot establish that he has goodwill in England which will be protected by our courts without actually showing that he has a business in England, then of course, that is the end of the matter and the

▨▨▨▨▨ Maxim's v Dye *continued*

plaintiff cannot recover here, but in my judgment that is not the law. The true position is, I think as I stated in the *Baskin-Robbins* case [1976] 2 FSR 545 and I would like to quote my conclusion in that case on the point (at 548):

> "Some businesses are, however, to a greater or lesser extent truly international in character and the reputation and goodwill attaching to them cannot in fact help being international also. Some national boundaries such as, for example, those between members of the European Economic Community are in this respect becoming ill-defined and uncertain as modern travel, and Community rules make the world grow smaller. Whilst therefore not wishing to quarrel with the decisions in question, if they are read as I have suggested, I believe myself that the true legal position is best expressed by the general proposition, which seems to me to be derived from the general line of past authority, that that existence and extent of the plaintiff's reputation and goodwill in every case is one of fact however it may be proved and whatever it is based on."

If writing the passage again I would, for purposes of clarity, add the words "in his business" after the words "reputation and goodwill" towards the end of the quotation. In circumstances such as the present it also seems to me that a plaintiff's existing goodwill in this country, which derives from and is based on a foreign business, such as one in Paris or elsewhere in the common market, may be regarded as prospective but none the less real in relation to any future business which may later be set up by the plaintiff in this country.

[Graham J supported his conclusion by reference to the effect of Britain's accession to the European Economic Community.]

▬▬▬▬▬▬▬▬▬▬▬▬▬▬▬▬▬▬▬▬▬▬▬▬▬▬▬▬▬▬▬

▬▬▬▬▬▬ **Taco Bell v Taco Co of Australia** ▬▬▬▬▬▬

[13.105] *Taco Bell Pty Ltd v Taco Co of Australia Ltd* (1981) 60 FLR 60 Full Federal Court of Australia

[Since 1973 the plaintiff had conducted a Mexican food restaurant at Bondi under the name "Taco Bell's Casa". The defendant operated and franchised the operation of a large chain of Mexican food restaurants under the name "Taco Bell" in the US, Canada and Guam, but no restaurant or other business had been carried on in Australia by the defendant or its franchisees in Australia prior to September 1981. In that month the defendant opened Mexican food restaurants under the Taco Bell name in Sydney and Granville, a Sydney suburb. The plaintiff and defendant brought claims and cross-claims alleging passing off and misleading or deceptive conduct in breach of s 52 of the *Trade Practices Act 1974* (Cth).]

ELLICOTT J: [75] ... In *Athlete's Foot Marketing Associates Inc v Cobra Sports Ltd* [1980] RPC 343, Walton J considered most of the cases cited on behalf of the respondent and the applicant and decided that a plaintiff cannot sue for passing off if he has no customers or nobody who is in a trade relation with him in the jurisdiction. He summarised his views in the following passage (at 350):

> "[I]t would appear to me that, as a matter of principle, no trader can complain of passing off as against him in any territory—and it will usually be defined by national boundaries

although it is well conceivable in the modern world that it will not—in which he has no customers, nobody who is in a trade relation with him. This will normally [76] be expressed by saying that he does not carry on any trade in that particular country ... but the inwardness of it will be that he has no customers in that country; no people who buy his goods or make use of his services (as the case may be) there."

In that case Walton J refused to grant an injunction because the plaintiffs did not disclose "one single solitary transaction by way of trade with anybody in this country at all".

Having considered all the authorities cited, I agree in general terms with the conclusion which Walton J reached. In order to succeed in an action for passing off in relation to the Sydney metropolitan area a plaintiff must show that it has a goodwill here. This can usually be established by proof that there has been some prior business activity here involving the use of the name or mark or get-up in question in relation to the plaintiff's goods or services. The nature and degree of business activity will differ from case to case. It does not follow from what Walton J said that a single transaction will always suffice. In some cases it may. Nor is it necessary that a plaintiff has established a place of business here. Its goods may have been imported and sold here under the relevant name or mark by another. It may have licensed people to use its name or mark on products which are sold there. It may have advertised here to solicit orders by post from the public or to encourage the public to travel to do business at its premises in another country. In this time of fast communication it may even have solicited customers here to travel long distances to another country to use its services there. ... [78] ...

A business has goodwill attached to it in a particular place if there is an attraction among people there to do business with it. Even if it has no place of business there people residing there may, nevertheless, be attracted to do business with it. For example, by buying goods which it produces and are sold there by importers, or by ordering goods from it by mail or by travelling from their residence to its place of business in an adjoining country. This "attractive force" is usually created because there has been some business activity in that place on the part of the owner of the business or those dependent on it, intended to so attract people. One cannot, in logic, exclude the possibility that it could exist because people who live there are prompted to seek out the business by a knowledge gained by them whilst travelling or living in another country where the place of business exists (for example, a Hong Kong tailor). However, one thing, in my opinion, is clear, namely, knowledge by people in Sydney that a successful business is being conducted in the United States under a distinctive name does not give that business a reputation or goodwill here unless people in Sydney are attracted to do business with it despite the distance separating them. Only then could it be said that there existed in Sydney "the attractive force which brings in custom". In many cases distance or the nature of the business will make it highly improbable that anybody could be so attracted.

Here, the overseas business is operating or licensing the operation of fast Mexican food restaurants in the US under the name "Taco Bell". People living here have for some time been aware of that business because they have travelled or lived in the US. But neither the proprietor of the business nor any person [79] dependent on it has ever carried on business here. Nor have they sought by advertising or otherwise to attract customers from here to patronise its restaurants in the US. Indeed, the very nature of the business conducting fast-food outlets and the great distances separating Sydney from that place makes it highly improbable that they would ever attempt to do so. This case, in this respect, is quite unlike the case of Maxim's Ltd. It is possible that some of those people who have this knowledge, if they travel to the United States, might patronise "Taco Bell" restaurants there, but clearly enough it would be absurd to suggest that they would resort there for that purpose or while living in Sydney attempt to do business with it.

▬▬▬▬ Taco Bell v Taco Co of Australia *continued*

It follows, in my view, that the knowledge of this section of the public in Sydney of "Taco Bell" restaurants in the US is no evidence of relevant reputation nor of the existence of a goodwill here which the respondent or Taco Bell of California is entitled to protect by an action of passing off. Nor is it, in the circumstances of this case, any defence to an action for passing off by the applicant since, having regard to the evidence, it did not, in my opinion, prevent the applicant from establishing a reputation for its restaurant under the name "Taco Bell's Casa".

▬▬▬▬ ConAgra v McCain Foods (Aust) ▬▬▬▬

[13.110] *ConAgra Inc v McCain Foods (Aust) Pty Ltd* (1992) 23 IPR 193 Federal Court of Australia

LOCKHART J: **[195]**
This case raises two important questions of law in the field of passing off: first, is it necessary that a plaintiff carry on business or have a place of business in Australia to maintain an action for passing off; and second, what is the significance of fraudulent intention of a defendant?

The appeal is brought from the judgment of a Judge of the Court (Hill J), whose reasons are now reported in (1991) 101 ALR 461. The appellant, ConAgra Inc, is a company incorporated in the US which carries on business there in diverse areas but generally related to food. The appellant manufactures and markets in the US frozen foods under a number of brand names including the name relevant to this case, "Healthy Choice". The concept of the product Healthy Choice originated in September 1985 following a heart attack of the Chairman and Chief Executive Officer of the appellant who found himself unable to obtain food with a pleasant taste that fell within his restricted diet, that is to say, food low in fat, cholesterol and salt. A few years passed before Healthy Choice was marketed as a range of frozen dinners. The name "Healthy Choice" was the result of a "brainstorming session" in June 1987. The packaging design for the product was formulated so that the product would stand out from all other frozen food packaging, would communicate the twin ideas of pleasant taste and good health and prominently feature the nutritional claims of "low fat, low cholesterol and low sodium". The colour green was chosen as the primary background colour of the packaging to differentiate the Healthy Choice product from other products; and a small figure of a running man appeared on the packet to convey, so it was said, an image of health and vitality. Trademark registration was sought and obtained in the United States for the mark Healthy Choice in connection with a number of food items. Since the national launch of the product in January 1989 with an initial range of ten products, the range has expanded so that at the present time it consists of some 79 products.
...**[196]**
The appellant does not presently manufacture the Healthy Choice products other than in the United States but, due to the geographical position of the US, there is a spillover of the product both into Canada and Central America.

In March 1986 the appellant entered into a licence agreement with Wattie Frozen Foods Limited (Wattie) whereby Wattie was licensed to introduce and distribute ConAgra Frozen Foods in both Australia and New Zealand and in other Pacific markets. Subsequently, probably in January 1991, Australia was deleted from the agreement. This

▬▬▬ ConAgra v McCain Foods (Aust) *continued*

coincided with the view formed by Mr McNamara (Vice-President, International Business of ConAgra Frozen Foods) in December 1990 that Australia was a strategic market in which to do business. Some research into the possibility of commencing manufacture in Australia is presently being conducted, but no firm decision to do so has, it would seem, yet been made. It is Mr McNamara's present intention, however, to introduce the product range Healthy Choice to Australia by about June this year.

...

The respondent, McCain Foods (Aust) Pty Ltd, is the wholly owned subsidiary of a Canadian company. It estimates its sales turnover in Australia for 1990-1991 as $A206m. It commenced operations in Australia in 1968 selling imported French Fries, later turned to producing frozen pizzas and frozen vegetables, and in 1987, as a result of an acquisition, moved into manufacturing and marketing frozen food dinners. The respondent now has some 21% of the total frozen food market in Australia, second only to the food brands sold by the Petersville Group of companies and ahead of the competing brands of Nestle and Sara Lee. The respondent's estimated market share of the frozen dinner market in Australia is 23%.

The respondent had, in February 1989, commenced manufacturing and selling a low cholesterol range of French Fries. The success of that product prompted the research and development manager of the respondent to write in October 1989 a memorandum to the product manager of the [197] respondent, with a copy to Mr Boyle, the then marketing director of the respondent, that consideration should be given to producing low cholesterol dinners.

In October 1989, Mr Boyle travelled to the US and Canada and noticed the appellant's product on the shelves in supermarkets in various cities in Canada and the US. He was sufficiently impressed that he obtained five examples of the packaging and took them back with him to Australia along with packets of other products.

On Mr Boyle's return to Australia he prepared a report on his trip to the senior management of the respondent saying that, "The ... product 'Healthy Choice' (low cholesterol) is getting very favourable comments in the US. We should look closely at this one." Discussions ensued between Mr Boyle and the product manager. In early December 1989 Mr Boyle instructed a member of the respondent's staff to request the respondent's patent attorney to lodge an application for registration of the trade mark HEALTHY CHOICE. Subsequently in July 1990, after advice, the patent attorney lodged an application for registration of those words together with the McCain logo.

...[233]

On reputation

The Canadian and US cases seem to take a much broader approach but, as was pointed out in the Canadian case of *Orkin*, this may be explicable, at least in part, by the large elements of commonality within North America, not necessarily dependent upon national boundaries of the US and Canada. Similar considerations apply in my view as between Australia and New Zealand. There obviously must be some link with the forum and, it seems to me, reputation is the most appropriate link. There must be evidence of local reputation, but business activities need not be carried on within the forum.

The test for whether a foreign plaintiff may succeed in a passing off action is, according to most of the more recent English cases, not that he must have business activities or a place of business in the UK; but whether, as a question of fact, his business has goodwill or a reputation in England. This is a broader, though more uncertain and elastic, concept than its predecessors. In my view the approach to this question adopted by the Canadian, US and New

████████ ConAgra v McCain Foods (Aust) *continued*

Zealand courts, together with the English cases of which *Baskin Robins* is one example, are more in harmony with the realities of contemporary business.

The Australian authorities do not present an entirely clear picture. In *Taco Bell*, as mentioned earlier, the Judge at first instance and Franki J, a member of the Full Court on appeal, followed fairly closely *Athletes Foot*, although Deane and Fitzgerald JJ, after noting "a degree of inconsistency in the cases", did not find it necessary to decide the question whether any goodwill or reputation which the appellants possessed was sufficient to base their action for passing off because they disposed of the case on another ground. The High Court in *Turner*, in particular Isaacs J, and the High Court in *Budget* left open the point that arises in this case. However it was made clear by the High Court in *Budget*, that for a plaintiff to succeed, whether he conducts his business here directly or through agents or other intermediaries, the courts will often accept minimal evidence that a business is being carried on, though the cases do show that this may depend on the extent to which he has a substantial reputation there.

It is no longer valid, if it ever was, to speak of a business having goodwill or reputation only where the business is carried on. Modern mass advertising through television (which reaches by satellite every corner of the globe instantaneously), radio, newspapers and magazines, reaches people in many countries of the world. The international mobility of the world population increasingly brings human beings, and therefore potential consumers of goods and services, closer together and engenders an increasing and more instantaneous awareness of international commodities. This is an age of enormous commercial enterprises, some with budgets larger than sovereign states, who advertise their products by sophisticated means involving huge financial outlay. Goods and services are often preceded by their reputation abroad. They may not be physically present in the market of a particular country, but are well known there because of the sophistication of communications which are increasingly less limited by [234] national boundaries, and the frequent travel of residents of many countries for reasons of business, pleasure or study.

In my opinion, the "hard line" cases in England conflict with the needs of contemporary business and international commerce. A trader's reputation may be injured locally by many means. A trader may have a famous and well-known commodity, yet a person, totally unconnected with him, may in a country where the trader's goods are not sold and where he has no place of business nevertheless cause confusion in the marketplace and lead the consumers to believe that a business connection exists between the two. The local person may produce a product inferior in quality to the product of the overseas trader and this may taint irreparably the reputation of the original product and of its maker. The reality of modern international business is that contemporary consumers are not usually concerned about the actual location of the premises of a company or the site of its warehouse or manufacturing plant where the goods are produced, but they are concerned with maintenance of a high level of quality represented by internationally known and famous goods.

The requirement in some of the cases that a very slight form of business activity is sufficient is really a somewhat artificial concept. The real question is whether the owner of the goods has established a sufficient reputation with respect to his goods within the particular country in order to acquire a sufficient level of consumer knowledge of the product and attraction for it to provide custom which, if lost, would likely to result in damage to him. This is essentially a question of fact.

As I outlined in more detail earlier, it is still necessary for a plaintiff to establish that his goods have the requisite reputation in the particular jurisdiction, that there is a likelihood of deception among consumers and a likelihood of damage to his reputation. But reputation within the jurisdiction may be proved by a variety of means including advertisements on

▇▇▇▇▇ ConAgra v McCain Foods (Aust) *continued*

television, or radio or in magazines and newspapers within the forum. It may be established by showing constant travel of people between other countries and the forum, and that people within the forum (whether residents there or persons simply visiting there from other countries) are exposed to the goods of the overseas owner (see for example *C and A Modes*, *Orkin* and *Midas*).

Certainly the law of passing off does not confer protection on the owners of goods who have no reputation in a particular jurisdiction, otherwise they would have an international monopoly with respect to the name, get-up or mark applied to their goods (and services) and may never intend to exploit it in the particular jurisdiction. It is the likelihood of deception among consumers and of damage to reputation that are the critical requirements to establish a case of passing off and they prevent any such unauthorised international monopoly being granted to a plaintiff.

...[235]

For these reasons, I am of the opinion that it is not necessary in Australia that a plaintiff, in order to maintain a passing off action, must have a place of business or a business presence in Australia; nor is it necessary that his goods are sold here. It is sufficient if his goods have a reputation in this country among persons here, whether residents or otherwise, of a sufficient degree to establish that there is a likelihood of deception among consumers and potential consumers and of damage to his reputation.

What is the relevance of fraud
...[243]

As appears earlier in my reasons, fraud is significant in two respects. First, fraud in the sense of a deliberate intent to steal a plaintiff's business, goodwill or reputation as in the *Collins Company v Brown* case. Second, in the sense of "digging a commercial pit" in advance of the plaintiff who is proposing to commence business in the jurisdiction and thus cause injury or the probability of injury to the plaintiff. It is in this latter sense that one must read the observations of Isaacs J in *Turner* at 364-365 and the judgment of Needham J in *Olin*.

In my opinion, his Honour's findings of fact when considering the question of fraud have not been shown to be in error; but I must confess to having difficulty with the conclusion of his Honour that fraud "in the relevant sense" has been established. At the highest his Honour's findings mean that the respondent deliberately set out to copy or adopt the appellant's packaging and the name "Healthy Choice" to positively establish a relationship of some kind between the appellant and the respondent or their respective products, though this is not a finding specifically made by his Honour on the issue of fraud. More likely though is that his Honour's findings as to fraud mean that the respondent embarked upon a course of deliberately appropriating the name "Healthy Choice", the use of the words "low cholesterol, low fat, low sodium" and aspects of the appellant's packaging in such a way that the respondents knew could cause confusion between the two products or could cause some consumers to believe that the McCain product was in some way connected with the ConAgra product.

Merely to imitate the name of another trader or his product or his get-up does not establish a case of fraud. That appears clearly from the *Pub Squash* case. I have the distinct impression from my reading of the evidence in this case that what the respondent really set out to do was to apply to its own product and packaging so much of the name of the appellant's product Healthy Choice and get-up of its packaging as it could do, without contravening the law, not because it wanted to have its product confused with that of the appellant, but because it was most impressed by the striking success of the appellant's frozen food products in the US and sought to adopt it for its own products in Australia as a good idea ...

▬▬▬▬ ConAgra v McCain Foods (Aust) *continued*

GUMMOW J: **[244]**
I would dismiss the appeal and cross-appeal. The appellant should pay the respondent's costs of the appeal and the respondent should pay the appellant's costs of the cross appeal.

I turn first to the passing off issues.

[245] Putting to one side the necessity for a local trading goodwill, this is not a case of reliance upon a famous name or mark which over a substantial period has become well known in the forum. This was the position with "Selfridges" (*Selfridges Ltd v Selfridges (Australasia) Ltd,* Harvey CJ in Eq, *Sydney Morning Herald,* 6 April 1933); "General Motors" (*Turner v General Motors (Australia) Proprietary Ltd* (1929) 42 CLR 352 at 363) and "C and A" (*C and A Modes v C and A (Waterford) Ltd* [1978] FSR 126 at 137).

In cases where the courts have moved (whether on an interlocutory or final basis) to protect the potential exploitation, by the conduct of local trading, of an existing reputation in the forum, the plaintiff still has been required to make out (at the appropriate level for interlocutory or final relief) its case for the existence of that reputation. Examples are *Sheraton Corp of America v Sheraton Motels Ltd* [1964] RPC 202 at 203; *Globelegance BV v Sarkissian* [1974] RPC 603 at 612; *Metric Resources Corp v Leasemetrix Ltd* [1979] FSR 571 at 579; *Home Box Office Inc v Channel 5 Home Box Office Ltd* [1982] FSR 449 at 456; *Esanda Ltd v Esanda Finance Ltd* [1984] 2 NZLR 748 at 752-753 and *Orkin Exterminating Co Inc v Pestco Co of Canada Ltd* (1985) 19 DLR 4th 90 at 93-94. All of these judgments, save the last, were delivered upon applications for interlocutory relief. (See also *BM Auto Sales Pty Ltd v Budget Rent a Car System Pty Ltd* (1976) 51 ALJR 254 at 258.) Some caution is needed against treating findings as to reputation at the interlocutory level as if they were findings as to what would suffice to establish reputation at a trial.

...**[246]**
The failure of the appellant's case as to reputation spells doom for the appellant, whatever the position as to fraud. I agree that in a case such as the present a failure to establish a reputation in the forum cannot be overcome by proof of fraud on the part of the defendant. The role of fraud in the modern passing off action was debated before us and it is a topic to which I return later in these reasons. Another issue of law which arose on the appeal was the significance attached to the absence of local trade in the appellant's product.

Notwithstanding the failure of the appeal on the facts, the Court should express its conclusions upon these important issues in the law of passing off, there being no binding Australian appellate authority.

Passing off

Within the passing off action, there is an accommodation and adjustment of three competing interests. First that of the plaintiff in protecting the commercial advantages flowing from his efforts and investment, secondly that of the defendant in being free to attract purchasers for his goods and services by what appears to him to be an effective means, and thirdly that of consumers in selecting between competing goods and services without the practice upon them of misrepresentations.

Attempts to produce a definition of the tort which is both succinct and comprehensive have had mixed success. In *Erven Warnink Besloten Vennootschap v J Townend and Sons (Hull) Ltd* [1979] AC 731 at 742, Lord Diplock identified five essential characteristics of a passing off action, and Lord Fraser of Tullybelton [1979] AC 731 at 755-756, also identified, but in somewhat different terms, five such characteristics. There followed in the English Court of Appeal differences of opinion as to whether these two sets of criteria were distinct, overlapping, or cumulative and whether, in any event, either was comprehensive: *Anheuser-Busch Inc v Budejovicky Budvar NP* [1984] FSR 413 at 463, 472; *Bristol Conservatories Ltd* **[247]**

▦▦▦▦   ConAgra v McCain Foods (Aust) *continued*

v Conservatories Custom Built Ltd [1989] RPC 455 at 465-467; Morcom "Developments In the Law of Passing off" (1991) 10 EIPR 380 at 382. As Ralph Gibson LJ pointed out in the second of these cases (supra at 466) the probanda formulated by Lord Diplock and Lord Fraser would not, for example, allow for cases of "reverse" passing off.

In *Reckitt & Colman Products Ltd v Borden Inc* [1990] RPC 341 at 406, Lord Oliver of Aylmerton formulated the essential elements in a passing off action without referring specifically to earlier authority. Now, Nourse LJ (in *Consorzio del Prosciutto di Parma v Marks & Spencer plc* [1991] RPC 351 at 368-369) has said that the formulations by Lord Diplock and Lord Fraser had not in his experience given the same degree of assistance in analysis and decision as "the classical trinity" of (1) reputation (2) misrepresentation and (3) damage. Nourse LJ regards what was said in the *Borden* case as signalling a "welcome return to the classical approach".

It is neither necessary nor appropriate for us to comment upon these vicissitudes of the recent English case law. But it is to be observed that the law of passing off contains sufficient nooks and crannies to make it difficult to formulate any satisfactory definition in short form. However, "the classical trinity" does serve to emphasise three core concepts in this area of the law. This appeal is concerned with all of them, namely, the geographical requirements for a sufficient reputation, the nature of the interests damaged, and the significance of fraud in the making of the misrepresentation.

Fraud today
...[256]

What then is the present significance of fraud in the passing off action? There are various categories of case in which it will be significant if the defendant has embarked upon his activities fraudulently in the sense of the old common law cases. These categories are in addition to the class of case where there is some evidentiary assistance to be derived from those circumstances.

First, the absence or presence of fraud in the common law sense will be determinative of the plaintiff's equitable rights in cases where a charge of unclean hands is made out against the plaintiff; this is because whilst the plaintiff's unclean hands ordinarily would disentitle him to relief in equity, the existence of the fraud on the part of the defendant would give the plaintiff a right to damages at law. In that action the equitable defence would be of no effect. The plaintiff may then have an injunction to avoid the necessity of repeated actions at law, notwithstanding the plaintiff's unclean hands. That is what is established in *Kettles and Gas Appliances Ltd v Anthony Hordern & Sons Ltd* (1935) 35 SR (NSW) 108, with reference to the analysis of *Ford v Foster* (1872) LR 7 Ch App 611, by Isaacs ACJ in *Angelides v James Stedman Hendersons Sweets Ltd*, supra at 65-66.

Secondly, whilst there is some authority for the view that there is no passing off where the defendant does no more than carry on business under his own name, such user must be bona fide; *Clayton v Vincent's Products Ltd* (1934) 34 SR (NSW) 214; *Parker Knoll Ltd v Knoll International Ltd* [1962] RPC 265; *Parker and Son (Reading) Ltd v Parker* [1965] RPC 323.

Thirdly, in my view, in the ordinary passing off case (where the whole of the dispute is centred in the one jurisdiction) the failure of the plaintiff to show the existence of his reputation cannot be overcome merely by proof of a fraudulent design on the part of the defendant. The authorities bearing upon the question are collected in *Telmak Teleproducts (Australia) Pty Ltd v Coles Myer Ltd* (1988) 84 ALR 437 at 444-445. However, fraudulent conduct is important in the line of cases which I have described where the plaintiff and the defendant export their goods for sale in a foreign market and the plaintiff has no reputation with consumers in the jurisdiction in which the action is brought, although he does have a reputation in the foreign market where the goods of the defendant are sold.

▬▬▬▬ ConAgra v McCain Foods (Aust) *continued*

The present case is concerned with a variant of this third situation. The complaint of the appellant is not that the respondent is manufacturing in Australia goods for export to the appellant's markets in the US where the appellant has conducted activities on a large scale, but that the respondent seeks to pre-empt the entry of the appellant into the Australian market. In such a case is it necessary that the appellant establish a case of the existence in Australia of a reputation among consumers, or is it sufficient that the respondent is acting in the manner described by "digging a pit" in the path of the entry by the appellant into the Australian market? In my view, the appellant cannot succeed in such a case, even if fraud [257] be shown, unless the plaintiff can show a reputation in that market. Only if this be so will the activities of the defendant convey a misrepresentation to the public and the misrepresentation is the gist of the action.

Before returning to this issue, it is appropriate first to consider whether, in any event, the existence of such a reputation would be sufficient, or whether the appellant would also have to show (as it cannot do on the facts) the existence of a reputation attached to the present conduct of a business in Australia.

The answer to that question requires some further consideration of the development of the notion of the proprietary right which is said to be protected by the passing off action. ... [262]

Reputation and present business operations
The question for the Court is whether in this divided state of English authority we should adopt the approach that was accepted by the English Court of Appeal in the *Budweiser Case*, at the expense of the earlier Australian authorities.

...[263]

The preferred position
In my view, where the plaintiff, by reason of business operations conducted outside the jurisdiction, has acquired a reputation with a substantial number of persons who would be potential customers were it to commence business within the jurisdiction, the plaintiff has in a real sense a commercial position or advantage which it may turn to account. Its position may be compared with that of a plaintiff who formerly conducted business within the jurisdiction and has retained a reputation among its erstwhile customers, and with that of a plaintiff with a reputation which arises from its trade in the jurisdiction, but extends to goods or services which are not presently marketed by him. If the defendant moves to annex to itself the benefit of such a reputation by attracting custom under false colours, then the defendant diminishes the business advantage of the plaintiff flowing to it from the existence of his reputation.

This is so whether the plaintiff is a party which may expand into a new field of business or resume a former business conducted in the jurisdiction, or a party which may enter the jurisdiction to establish a business for the first time. The immediacy and intensity of the intention of the plaintiff to commence or resume business is, in my view, a question going not so much to the invasion of the plaintiff's rights as to the imminence of a threat sufficient to justify an injunction. The bad faith of the defendant will not be sufficient to confer rights upon a plaintiff where the necessary reputation in the jurisdiction is lacking. Further, in my view, in these cases the presence of bad faith on the part of the defendant is not an additional requirement [264] which is to be satisfied by the plaintiff; fraud in the sense of persistence after notice of the plaintiff's rights will suffice.

In *Ballarat Products Ltd v Farmers Smallgoods Co Pty Ltd* [1957] VR 104 at 108, Hudson J said:

"On behalf of the defendant it was contended that, as no business is being carried on by the plaintiff, there can be no goodwill of which the name can form part. I cannot

■■■■ ConAgra v McCain Foods (Aust) *continued*

accept this proposition. In my opinion goodwill may continue to exist despite the cessation of the business operations that have given rise to it. If a trader by his personality, skill or method of trading has acquired a reputation in a particular class of business and thereby established an extensive connection in that business, to say that upon his ceasing to trade his reputation will immediately disappear is contrary to fact. It remains as something of value which he can turn to account whenever he chooses."

To the same effect, but the setting of a claim based upon foreign reputation, is the decision of the Ontario Court of Appeal in *Orkin Exterminating Co Inc v Pestco Co of Canada Ltd* (1985) 19 DLR (4th) 90 (noted (1986) 76 TMR 173; (1986) 2 IPJ 375).

The plaintiff was an American company which had begun its operations in Georgia in 1901 and had built up one of the largest pest control businesses in the world. It did not carry on business in Ontario or elsewhere in Canada, but had a reputation there. This was held to be sufficient to support an action for passing off against a Canadian company which began using the plaintiff's name in the business it conducted in metropolitan Toronto. The judgment of the Court of Appeal was delivered by Morden JA. The decision has since been applied, at the interlocutory level, in *HIT Factory Inc v HIT Factory Inc* (1986) 12 CPR (3d) 287.

Morden JA made the following points which are of significance on the present appeal. First, he referred to *Harrods Ltd v R Harrods Ltd* supra and *Yale Electric Corp v Robertson* supra, together with *Stork Restaurant Inc v Sahati* 166 F 2d 348 (1948) in relation to the proposition (at 101):

"[A] plaintiff does not have to be in direct competition with the defendant to suffer injury from the use of its trade name by the defendant. If the plaintiff's trade name has a reputation in the defendant's jurisdiction, such that the public associates it with services provided by the plaintiff, then the defendant's use of it means that the plaintiff has lost control over the impact of its trade name in the defendant's jurisdiction."

Secondly, at 103-104, his Lordship referred to the significance attached in some of the English decisions to very slight business activities in the jurisdiction as "purely symbolic" rather than illustrative of the true principle, namely that the plaintiff was entitled to retain the possibility of exploiting its goodwill in England. Thirdly, he did not see it as imposing an unreasonable restraint on the defendant to enjoin it from using the name of the plaintiff, saying (at 105):

"The public are entitled to be protected from such deliberate deception and Orkin, which has laboured long and hard and made substantial expenditures to create the reputation which it now has, which reputation has spread to Ontario, is entitled to the protection of its [265] name for misappropriation. The spectre of Orkin having a monopoly in Ontario in its name and distinctive logo, even though it is not now carrying on business here, is considerably less troubling than the deceptive use of its name and symbol by another."

Fourthly, in response to the submission by the defendant that the circumstance that it had embarked upon deliberate deception was irrelevant, Morden JA said (at 106-107) that whilst the defendant's bad faith alone did not confer a cause of action on a foreign plaintiff, it was a relevant factor to take into account in framing the law so as to adjust the competing interests, the interests of a dishonest defendant being entitled to less weight than those of one which had acted bona fide.

■■■■■■   ConAgra v McCain Foods (Aust) *continued*

Finally, with reference to the meaning attached to the term "goodwill" in such English cases as the *Budweiser* Case, his Lordship observed (at 107-108) that this meaning appeared to be based on definitions assigned to "goodwill" in a tax case, namely *Muller's* Case, and continued:

"Virtually no words have a single fixed meaning, particularly goodwill, and, with respect, I do not think that the meaning appropriate in the *Muller* case is necessarily appropriate in a passing off case which involves issues of remote territorial use. In this kind of case I think the main consideration should be the likelihood of confusion with consequential injury to the plaintiff. Generally, where there is such confusion there is goodwill deserving of protection."

I would, with respect, accept all that was said for the Ontario Court of Appeal in those five propositions, save only that I would regard the dishonesty of the defendant as going more to the remedy than the right of the plaintiff.

What is said in the Canadian decision is consistent with an Australian decision, *Fletcher Challenge Ltd v Fletcher Challenge Pty Ltd* [1981] 1 NSWLR 196. Powell J (at 205) stated the relevant question as being "does the plaintiff have the necessary reputation?", rather than "does the plaintiff itself carry on business here?".

Where the intention of the defendant is to cause harm to the plaintiff by pre-empting the plaintiff's exploitation in the jurisdiction of its goodwill there, then, in my view, the charge of fraud is made out. In an otherwise appropriate case, damages may be awarded in addition to equitable relief. This is so even if, as in the present case, there may be insufficient grounds for holding that the defendant also had the objective of building up its goodwill in the jurisdiction by misleading the customers who dealt with it into believing they were getting the goods of the plaintiff.

In the present case, the primary Judge (101 ALR at 487) held that it was likely, in the sense of more probable than not, that the appellant would commence, at some time in the future, the manufacture and marketing in Australia of its "Healthy Choice" product; should it do so, then it was clear that the appellant would suffer damage by there being on the market another product with the name "Healthy Choice", and the probability of that damage was sufficient to found a passing off action, subject to the need to show a sufficient reputation in the jurisdiction.

However, whilst I would not disturb the finding of the primary Judge as to fraud, I should add that, like Lockhart J, my impression from the evidence is that there is much to be said for the view that the respondent acted as it did, not to filch the appellant's market or prospective market in Australia, but because it was impressed by the success of the appellant's product in the [266] US and thought that a similar product was likely to succeed here. That would not amount to fraud in the required sense. Deliberate copying does not necessarily indicate fraud. A notable example is provided by *Cadbury-Schweppes Pty Ltd v The Pub Squash Co Ltd* [1981] RPC 429 at 493-494. See also, in the field of registered trade marks *Aston v Harlee Manufacturing Co* (1960) 103 CLR 391 at 400-402; *Moorgate Tobacco Company Ltd v Philip Morris Ltd* (1980) 145 CLR 457 at 477.

Trade Practices Act

I agree with what has been said by Lockhart J as to the issues arising under this legislation.

■ Location of reputation: Sales by foreign websites?

▬▬▬▬▬ Ward Group v Brodie & Stone ▬▬▬▬▬

[13.115] *Ward Group Pty Ltd v Brodie & Stone Plc* (2005) 64 IPR 1 Federal Court of Australia

MERKEL J: [3]

Introduction
The applicant ("the Ward Group") is the Australian manufacturer and distributor of anti-greying hair creams and lotions marketed under the brand name "Restoria" ("the Australian Restoria products"). The Ward Group claims that similar hair creams and lotions manufactured and distributed by the respondents in the United Kingdom under the same brand name ("the UK Restoria products"), which were advertised for sale and sold on certain websites on the internet, infringed its trademarks and passed off the UK Restoria products as and for the Australian Restoria products.

...

At trial the issues arising for determination were:
(1) whether the advertising and sale of the UK Restoria products on the Internet by the website proprietors infringed the Ward Group's Australian trade marks or constituted a passing off of the UK Restoria products as and for the Australian Restoria products of the Ward Group; and, if so
(2) whether Brodie & Stone, as the manufacturer and distributor of the UK Restoria products in the United Kingdom, was liable as a joint tortfeasor in respect of the trade mark infringements and passing off of the website proprietors.

There are two special features about the claims in the present case. The first is that the advertising of the UK Restoria products, together with numerous other [4] products, for sale on the internet by the website proprietors was not specifically targeted or directed at customers in Australia. Rather, the advertising targeted potential purchasers anywhere in the world at large.

The second feature is that the case against Brodie & Stone is not based upon it having sold UK Restoria products to any of its customers intending or knowing that those goods were to be advertised for sale or sold by a customer on the Internet. Rather, the case was based upon the Ward Group informing Brodie & Stone that some of Brodie & Stone's customers were selling the UK Restoria products to entities or individuals who, in turn, were selling UK Restoria products on the Internet, and that the offering to sell and selling of those products to customers in Australia on the Internet constituted an infringement of the Ward Group's Restoria trade marks in Australia and passing off. The Ward Group contended that once Brodie & Stone became aware of those matters it was obliged to place restrictions on the resale of its UK Restoria products, and its failure to do so made it a joint tortfeasor in respect of the trademark infringements and passing off alleged against the website proprietors.

Plainly, the Ward Group's claims, if upheld, can have significant consequences for the sale of goods on the Internet.

Background
The Ward Group manufactures and distributes the Australian Restoria products in Australia and elsewhere under the brand name "Restoria". It is registered under the *Trade Marks 1995* (Cth) ("the TMA") as the proprietor of four trade marks bearing the mark "RESTORIA" in the class concerned with hair products and cosmetics ("the Australian Restoria marks"). It is also the registered proprietor of Restoria trade marks in over 70 other countries, but not in the United Kingdom.

███████ Ward Group v Brodie & Stone *continued*

The Ward Group has manufactured, advertised, marketed, distributed and sold the Australian Restoria products in Australia since its incorporation in 1957. It began exporting the products in 1965 and conducts a wide and extensive trade worldwide, although not in the United Kingdom, in the Australian Restoria products. It is clear that the Ward Group has established a substantial reputation and goodwill in relation to the Australian Restoria products and their brand name, Restoria.

...[5]

Selling the UK Restoria products on the internet

In the usual course persons searching in Australia for a particular product on the Internet are likely to obtain search results for web pages located around the world. For example, a person searching for Restoria products may carry out a Google or Yahoo search on the internet which will reveal, inter alia, the websites, including the Ward Group sites, that advertise those products under the Restoria name.

The UK Restoria products were advertised for sale on three websites (www.westons.com, www.beauty4you.co.uk, and www.auravita.com ("the websites")), which were owned or operated by one or other of the website proprietors...

The only evidence of sales of the UK Restoria products in Australia is the evidence adduced by the Ward Group of purchases of those products by its solicitors acting on its behalf ("the trap purchases"). ...[9]

Passing Off

The misrepresentation pleaded by the Ward Group is that the website proprietors passed off their businesses and products as and for the Ward Group's businesses and products, or as businesses or products endorsed or approved by the Ward Group. Although no such representation was expressly made by the website proprietors, the representation is said to be implied by the advertising and sale on the Internet by the website proprietors of the UK Restoria products under the Restoria brand name.

The representation expressly made by the website proprietors was that they were advertising the UK Restoria products for sale under their established brand name on the Internet. That was an accurate representation which, in the present context, only became capable of being a misrepresentation once the UK Restoria products were advertised for sale in Australia where the brand name Restoria had a repute and goodwill associated with the Ward Group. If Australian consumers had been targeted by the website proprietors for the marketing and sale of the UK Restoria products under the Restoria name, the fact that the representation, when made in the United Kingdom, was accurate would probably not save it from becoming a misrepresentation when the representation was made and received in Australia. The reason for that conclusion is that the cases to which I later refer treat such a representation as being made to and received by consumers in Australia, rather than a representation made to the world at large.

But that is not what occurred in the present case. Rather, the website proprietors did not target or direct their advertising at Australian consumers. ... There is also an additional issue arising from the fact that the trap purchasers, being the persons who procured the representations to be made in Australia and being the only persons in Australia to whom the representations were specifically directed, were well aware that the Restoria mark used on the websites was, and was intended to be, related to the UK Restoria products and not the Australian Restoria products.

■ Proving reputation: Admissibility of expert evidence

[13.120] Evidence needs to prove reputation and deception. In what circumstances is expert evidence relevant on these points?

Henschke v Rosemount Estates

[13.125] *Henschke & Co v Rosemount Estates Pty Ltd* (1999) 47 IPR 63 Federal Court of Australia

[Henschke, a South Australian boutique wine maker and owner of the "Hill of Grace" label and trade mark, objected to Rosemount Estate's marketing wines under the "Hill of Gold" label. Expert evidence from marketing experts, wine writers, and wine retailers was called by both parties on the points of reputation and confusion. Rosemount Estate disputed the admissibility of much of Henschke's expert evidence.]

FINN J: [83]
As to the first of these matters, reputation, I am prepared to accept that, for present purposes, these experts are able to venture opinions on facets of the wine's reputation especially as to quality. What I am far less inclined to accept is that, whatever their specialised knowledge based on experience might be: cf *Evidence Act 1995*, s 79; that knowledge would enable or qualify them relevantly to express opinions on the reputation of the wine amongst the segment of the wine consuming public with which this case is concerned ("uninvolved consumers": see below) ...

As to the opinions ventured on the issue of mistake, confusion etc resulting from the names a somewhat different issue presents itself. The respondent has submitted that this evidence is simply inadmissible. Reliance was placed upon the observations of Gummow J (with whom Black CJ and Lockhart J agreed) in (*Interlego AG v Croner Trading Pty Ltd* (1992) 111 ALR 577), at 617-618 on the admissibility of "consumer evidence" in cases of the present variety. His Honour observed (inter alia):

> "Secondly, the question whether a mark or get up so nearly resembles another as to be deceptive or likely to deceive is a question for the tribunal of fact and is not a matter for any witness to decide: *Kerly*, supra, p 425. The issue of whether consumers have been or are likely to be deceived was described by Lord Diplock as a 'jury question': *GE Trademark* [1973] RPC 297.
>
> ...
>
> Thirdly, evidence of consumers and retailers as to the likelihood of deception will be critical if a special market is involved.
>
> ...
>
> Fifthly, ... evidence as to the habits of purchasers does not include evidence of prospective purchasers that they would be deceived, or evidence of retailers that purchasers would be deceived."

This, it is said, is a case of the second and fifth propositions.

The applicants had submitted in contrast, relying upon (Co-Director, Wine Marketing Research Centre, SA) Professor Lockshin's evidence, that the wine market is relevantly a "special market" and [84] that the experts' opinions are admissible in consequence under the third proposition above. I have referred above to the essence of the Professor's evidence in this regard.

I am unable to agree with the applicants in this. The difference between the ordinary rule relating to evidence of deception or likely deception and the "specialised market" rule

▬▬▬ Henschke v Rosemount Estates *continued*

was, as Gummow J acknowledged, explained by Lord Diplock in *GE Trademark*, above, at 321-322:

> "[W]here goods are of a kind which are not normally sold to the general public for consumption or domestic use but are sold in specialised markets consisting of persons engaged in a particular trade, evidence of persons accustomed to dealing in that market as to the likelihood of deception or confusion is essential. A judge, though he must use his common sense in assessing the credibility and probative value of that evidence is not entitled to supplement any deficiency in evidence of this kind by giving effect to his own subjective view as to whether or not he himself would be likely to be deceived or confused. In the instant case this would apply to the large industrial electrical machinery sold under the Rondel Mark. But where goods are sold to the general public for consumption or domestic use, the question whether such buyers would be likely to be deceived or confused by the use of the trade mark is a 'jury question'. By that I mean that if the issue had now, as formerly, to be tried by a jury, who as members of the general public would themselves be potential buyers of the goods, they would be required not only to consider any evidence of other members of the public which had been adduced, but also to use their own common sense and to consider whether they would themselves be likely to be deceived or confused.
>
> The question does not cease to be a 'jury question' when the issue is tried by a judge alone or on appeal by a plurality of judges. The judge's approach to the question should be the same as that of a jury. He, too, would be a potential buyer of the goods. He should, of course, be alert to the danger of allowing his own idiosyncratic knowledge or temperament to influence his decision, but the whole of his training in the practice of the law should have accustomed him to this, and this should provide the safety which in the case of a jury is provided by their number. That in issues of this kind judges are entitled to give effect to their own opinions as to the likelihood of deception or confusion and, in doing so, are not confined to the evidence of witnesses called at the trial is well established by the decisions of this House itself."

See also *Polaroid Corp v Hannaford & Burton Ltd* [1974] 1 NZLR 368 at 378.

While the wine purchasing market may be special in the sense that it has unusual features (for example, over 16,000 brands and over 1000 producers), it is not "specialised" in the sense that participants therein have and are to be expected to have a particular knowledge, skill or experience that the general public relevantly does not. The wine market is one in which the general public participates directly: wine is sold to the public for consumption. In Lord Diplock's sense it is a market in which a judge "would be a potential buyer". A market is not to be made a "specialized" one merely because a feature (or features) within it differentiates it in some way from other consumer markets. Such a feature could probably be identified for many consumer markets. I would have to say in the present case, that the process of differentiation suggested by the applicants seemed to owe more both to the understandable desire to accentuate whatever differences were in fact available and to the scholars' desire to emphasise the distinguishing characteristics of their particular field of interest, than to the identification of a specialisation based upon differences of moment and substance. I should indicate that I do not regard Dr Hall's acceptance that the study of wine marketing is a specialist area of expertise is in any way inconsistent with the above conclusion. It merely means that a person with that expertise may [85] be able to be of assistance to the Court in explaining behaviour in that market. It does not make the market itself a "specialised market".

...

████████ Henschke v Rosemount Estates *continued*

... To the extent that the experts express an opinion of the likelihood of an association being made by the relevant section of the wine purchasing public (see below) in consequence of the shared words in the brand names of the two wines, I am not satisfied that, save possibly for Mr Forrestal (a well-known writer and wine judge), they have been shown to possess a specialised knowledge based on experience that would allow them to venture that opinion. In saying this I am not in any way doubting the particular respective experience of each in aspects of the wine industry. What I am questioning is their demonstrated possession of such specialised knowledge of consumer decision-making processes in this market as would admit of their expressing the particular opinion they have. Their experience would, at least in some cases, indicate a knowledge of the fact of actual mistake or confusion arising where there has been a particularly close similarity in brand names (for example, Moss Wood and Moss Brothers; Karrivale and Karriview; Wyndham Estate Bin 555 and Eden Valley TR 222). What it does not adequately suggest is a knowledge based on an experience of the factors that may be causative of, and the conditions that create the likelihood of, mistake or confusion in the decision-making of uninvolved wine purchasers as could found the opinion ventured: cf *Clark v Ryan* (1960) 103 CLR 486. At best some number of the opinions on mistake and confusion seem based on no more than conjecture or intuition. These experts in my view are being used to argue the applicants' case: *Clark v Ryan*, at 491.

...

With the possible exception of Mr Forrestal, I am not satisfied (a) that [86] these experts have the specialised knowledge to give an opinion on the likelihood of mistake, confusion, etc; or (b) that, in any event, their actual opinions are ones from which I might receive some assistance. Accordingly, Mr Forrestal apart, I do not admit their evidence insofar as it relates to the issue of mistake, deception etc caused by the Hill of Gold name. Even if admissible, and I here include Mr Forrestal, I have grave doubts that any weight could or can be attributed to this body of evidence. The opinions represent little more—if that—than a general statement of practical experience and then a conclusion by way of assertion on the issue in this case. The conclusion in my view merely invites further question. As Mr Shavin QC for the applicants acknowledged, to the extent the detailed processes of thought by which each reached their conclusions are not set out, there is an element of uncertainty as to how much reliance can be placed on them. I agree but would go much further. Without significant elaboration its reliability must be open to question—the more so when one has regard to the evidence of the academic experts, Professor Lockshin and Dr Hall, on the complex of factors affecting the making of consumer purchasing decisions.

Having ruled the applicants' expert evidence (a) on reputation admissible but to be accorded little weight unless otherwise indicated in a particular instance; and (b) on the issue of mistake, etc, inadmissible or else of little weight, I make like rulings for like reasons in relation to the same type of expert evidence adduced in response by the respondent.

[13.130] See also *Cadbury Schweppes Pty Ltd v Darrell Lea Chocolate Shops Pty Ltd* [2006] FCA 363. In this case Heery J rejected marketing expert evidence about the likelihood of consumer misassociations and errors being made because of similar uses of the colour purple by Darrell Lea Chocolates on the grounds that "ordinary human behaviour is not a matter to be proved in courts by opinion evidence, whether expert or otherwise".

PROVING REPUTATION: ADMISSIBILITY OF SURVEY EVIDENCE

[13.135] Evidence of "ordinary human behaviour" may be provided by survey evidence. There is a Federal Court practice note that establishes a procedure for obtaining this type of evidence. Compliance with the practice note is not a criterion of admissibility, however it can be argued that poor surveys should be excluded under s 135 of the *Evidence Act 1995* (Cth) because the probative value of the evidence is substantially outweighed by the danger that it might be unfairly prejudicial, be misleading or confusing, or result in undue waste of court time. If admitted, non-compliant surveys may be judged as lacking in probative value because of deficiencies in survey design. See *Cadbury Schweppes Pty Ltd v Darrell Lea Chocolate Shops Pty Ltd (No 2)* [2006] FCA 364; *Cadbury Schweppes Pty Ltd v Darrell Lea Chocolate Shops Pty Ltd (No 4)* [2006] FCA 446.

▰▰▰▰▰▰▰▰▰▰ Practice Note No 11 ▰▰▰▰▰▰▰▰▰▰

[13.140] *Practice Note No 11*, Chief Justice Black of the Federal Court, 1994.

11. Survey evidence
There are many problems in obtaining acceptable survey evidence including the use of relevant and unambiguous questions and whether the actual conduct of the survey (including methodology) is satisfactory.

The admissibility of surveys is always a matter for the trial Judge to determine but the risk of the survey being rejected or given little, if any, weight at the trial may be diminished if the following procedure when a party seeks to have a survey conducted. Subject to other directions of the Court in the particular case, the Court expects that this practice will usually be followed:

1. Notice should be given in writing by the party seeking to have the survey conducted to the other parties to the proceeding.
2. The notice should give an outline of:
    (a) the purpose of the proposed survey;
    (b) the issue to which it is to be directed;
    (c) the proposed form and methodology;
    (d) the particular questions that will be asked;
    (e) the introductory statements or instructions that will be given to the persons conducting the survey;
    (f) other controls to be used in the interrogation process.
3. The parties should attempt to resolve any disagreement concerning the manner in which the survey is to be conducted and any of the matters mentioned in 2 above.
4. The matter of the survey should be raised with the Court at the directions hearing as soon as possible after the steps mentioned above have been taken.

DAMAGE OR LIKELIHOOD OF DAMAGE

[13.145] Although this casebook is not intended to cover remedies for infringement of intellectual property, the "damage" element in passing off is addressed here more from the point of view of an essential aspect of the cause of action. In *Spalding* ([13.15]), Lord Diplock required, as one of the essential elements of passing off, injury to the goodwill of another trader, or probability of damage in the sense of it being a "reasonably foreseeable consequence". In *Pacific Dunlop Ltd v Hogan* (1989) 14 IPR 398, Beaumont J had this to say (at 428) about the "damage" element in passing off cases:

> "The substantive position is well settled. The cause of action for passing off is complete as soon as the relevant misrepresentation is made, even though no actual deception and damage to the plaintiff can be shown to have resulted from it: see Naresh, "Passing off, Goodwill and False Advertising: New Wine in Old Bottles" [1986] CLJ 97 at 103-104; see also *Erven Warnink BV v J Townend & Sons (Hull) Ltd* [1979] AC 731 (the *Advocaat* case); see also Morison, "Unfair Competition and 'Passing Off' " (1956) 2 Sydney L Rev 50 at 61. The position under s 52 is the same. Independently of these substantive questions, adjectival matters may call for separate consideration. For instance, the grant of an injunction is discretionary and a claim for more than nominal damages would require evidence because substantial damages are compensatory. But none of this is to say that passing off and a contravention of s 52 had not been established here.
>
>   I would dismiss the appeal."

In *Hogan v Koala Dundee Pty Ltd* (1988) 12 IPR 508 Pincus J summarised the position at 522:

> "The question of loss is relevant in two ways. First, at least some risk of loss, if not actual loss, is necessary in order to justify the grant of an injunction to restrain passing off: *Harrods Ltd v R Harrod Ltd* (1923) 41 RPC 74 at 81; *Taco Co of Australia Inc v Taco Bell Pty Ltd* (1982) 42 ALR 177 at 196. Secondly, the applicants want damages.
>
>   As to the first point, although the evidence is not strong, I think enough has been shown to satisfy the condition I have mentioned. The use of these images in two little shops would not make much of a dent in the marketing plans of the applicants. Nevertheless, the prospects of licensing another vendor of (for example) T-shirts would, one would expect, be a little diminished by the fact that Crocodile Dundee images have already been used in that connection. Apart from that, in this extended passing off field it is in my opinion enough, in order to justify an injunction, to show loss in the sense that the applicant has lost the chance of getting a fee from the respondent.
>
>   The second aspect of damage poses rather more difficult questions. The weight of authority is in favour of the view that 'fraud' is necessary in order to support a claim for damages for passing off, but precisely what fraud means in this connection is unsettled."

▬▬▬ BM Auto Sales v Budget Rent A Car System ▬▬▬

[13.150] *BM Auto Sales Pty Ltd v Budget Rent A Car System Pty Ltd* (1976) 12 ALR 363 High Court of Australia

GIBBS J: **[370]** It was further argued on behalf of the appellants that the award of damages could not be sustained because fraud was neither sufficiently alleged nor proved. It is unnecessary to consider whether proof of fraud was necessary to support the recovery of nominal damages. It is enough to say that fraud, for the purposes of an action of this kind, "is not necessarily such as would support an action of deceit, but would **[371]** be constituted by persistence after notice": *Turner v General Motors (Aust) Pty Ltd*, per Isaacs J, at 362.

▬▬▬ BM Auto Sales v Budget Rent A Car System *continued*

The evidence in the present case left no doubt that the appellants persisted in the use of the name with full knowledge that it had become distinctive of the respondent's business and that the use of the name was calculated to deceive. ... It is trite law that fraud should be distinctly and clearly alleged, and no relaxation of that requirement should be encouraged, but in an action of passing off, where fraud is not a necessary ingredient of the cause of action, it is not an inflexible rule that the court cannot find fraud unless it has been pleaded. ...

This passage suggests that the court regarded the element of fraud necessary to justify an award of damages as being at least akin to deceit in the ordinary sense. One may deduce that from the holding that "the use of the name was calculated to deceive" and the reference to the way in which fraud must be pleaded.

[The other members of the Court agreed.]

[13.155] The role of "fraud" in both a finding of misleading conduct and in creating the likelihood of awarding damages has been covered in a number of the cases in this chapter, notably in the *Healthy Choice* (**[13.110]**) and the *Kettle* (**[13.55]**) cases.

■ Common field of activity/confusion

[13.160] For some time, the courts were reluctant to find that the plaintiff could suffer any damage or likelihood thereof unless the parties were engaged in a "common field of activity" a phrase used by Wynn-Parry J in the following case.

▬▬▬▬▬▬ **Derek McCulloch v Lewis A May** ▬▬▬▬▬▬

[13.165] *Derek McCulloch v Lewis A May Ltd* (1947) 65 RPC 58 Chancery Division

[The presenter of *Children's Hour*, known as "Uncle Mac", objected to the sale of breakfast cereal under the name "Uncle Mac's Puffed Wheat". Further, the packaging proclaimed that "Uncle Mac loves children, and children love Uncle Mac!".]

WYNN-PARRY J: ... **[64]** ...It is of the essence of an action for passing off to show, first, that there has been an invasion by the defendant of a proprietary right of the plaintiff, in respect of which the plaintiff is entitled to protection, and, secondly, that such invasion has resulted in damage or that it creates a real and tangible risk that damage will ensue.

It is with the first part of that proposition that I am immediately concerned. It is established beyond argument that under the law of England a man is not entitled to exclusive proprietary rights in a fancy name in vacuo; his right to protection in an action for passing off must depend on his showing that he enjoys a reputation in that name in respect of some profession or business that he carries on or in respect of some goods which he sells. Further, he must show that the acts of the defendant of which he complains have interfered or are calculated to interfere with the conduct of his profession, business, or selling goods, in the sense that those acts of the defendant have led or are calculated to lead the public to confuse the profession, business or goods of the plaintiff with the profession, business, or goods of the defendant. The element of confusion is essential, but the element of confusion necessitates comparison.

...

■■■■■■ Derek McCulloch v Lewis A May *continued*

... [66] ... I have listened with care to all the cases that have been cited and upon analysis I am satisfied that there is discoverable in all those in which the court has intervened this factor, [67] namely, that there was a common field of activity in which, however remotely, both the plaintiff and the defendant were engaged and that it was the presence of that factor that accounted for the jurisdiction of the court.

...Upon the postulate that the plaintiff is not engaged in any degree in producing or marketing puffed wheat, how can the defendant, in using the fancy name used by the plaintiff, be said to be passing off the goods or the business of the plaintiff? I am utterly unable to see any element of passing off in this case. If it were anything, it were libel, as to which I say nothing. Passing off, in my judgment, it certainly is not. If I were to accede to the plaintiff's claim I should, as I see it, not merely be extending quite unjustifiably the scope of the action of passing off, but I should be establishing an entirely new remedy; and that I am quite unprepared to do.

I therefore conclude that the plaintiff in this case established no cause of action.

[13.170] For a long time, the requirement that there be a "common field of activity" between the business affairs of the plaintiff and the defendant in a passing off suit effectively denied pop stars, actors, and the owners of rights in fictitious characters any relief against unauthorised character merchandisers. In *Wombles Ltd v Womble Skips* [1977] RPC 99 the creator of the fictitious "wombles" characters who are famous for cleaning up Wimbledon Common objected to the use of the name for rubbish skips. Walton J said this at 100:

> "In the present case is there a common field of activity in the sense in which I have above-defined it between the plaintiff Wombles Ltd and the defendant Wombles Skips Ltd? I regret to say that in my opinion there is no such common field of activity. What the plaintiff is doing is to license people to use some of the copyright material comprised in and surrounding the Wombles. That in most cases, if indeed not in all of them, involved the use of a picture of one of the Wombles, whether it be a picture of Great Uncle Bulgaria, Tobermory, or one of the other well-known Wombles. But there is no such similar picture on any of the skips. Indeed Mr Robin Jacob, appearing for the defendant, protested that he was the only real Womble because he was the only person really carrying on the business of clearing up rubbish, and it may be that hereafter the defendant company's skips will be illustrated accordingly. I have nothing to do with that at all."

See also *Tavenor Rutledge Ltd v Trexapalm Ltd* [1977] RPC 275; *Lyngstad v Anabas Products Ltd* [1977] FSR 62.

In *Children's Television Workshop Inc v Woolworths (NSW) Ltd* [1981] 1 NSWLR 273 at 281, Helsham CJ expressly ruled that the plaintiffs (producers of the Sesame Street television programme and the creator of the "Muppet" characters appearing in the show) and the defendant (manufacturers and vendors of soft toys, including dolls of characters from Sesame Street) were operating in a common field. This was because the public was, by now, familiar with the licensing out of names and characters to manufacturers of a variety of products and so would see a connection between the originator of a character and the producer and seller of the merchandise:

> "In a relevant sense the defendants are acting in a way that will cause the public to believe that they are selling the plaintiffs' goods. In more refined terms, the deception is that the public will believe that the plaintiffs, or the first plaintiff, as a licensor are,

or is, associated with the defendants in putting these goods on the market for sale, or in permitting the defendants to sell them. That amounts to a connection, in respect of the marketing of these three character representations, between the business of the plaintiffs and the business of the defendants."

It is this somewhat artificial requirement, that there needs to be a connection between the licensor and the seller of merchandise, recognised by the public, that Pincus J found unnecessary in *Hogan v Koala Dundee Pty Ltd* (1988) 12 IPR 508.

Australian courts had previously rejected the necessity for the parties to be in a common field of activity, as the next case indicates.

■ Henderson v Radio Corp ■

[13.175] *Henderson v Radio Corp Pty Ltd* [1960] SR (NSW) 576 Supreme Court of New South Wales

EVATT CJ and MYERS J: [589]...This is an appeal by the defendant in a passing off suit in which it was restrained by injunction from selling, distributing, or supplying copies of a gramophone record cover entitled "Strictly for Dancing" having upon it a representation of a photograph of the plaintiffs in the suit.

[590] The respondents are husband and wife and are well-known professional ballroom dancers, particularly in professional dancing circles. They came to Australia from England in August 1957 and since that time have engaged in public performances, lectures and demonstrations. There is evidence that they are the best-known dancers of their type here. They are known professionally as "The Hendersons".

The appellant is a maker and distributor of gramophone records. On 6 March 1958 it placed on the market a gramophone record entitled "Strictly for Dancing: Vol 1". Three hundred and sixty-two copies of the record were made and 268 were sold to retailers in Australia. The number sold in New South Wales was not stated.

The record is one of music suitable for ballroom dancing and was described as strict tempo dance music. It was intended for the instruction of students in dancing and for use by dancing teachers, but might also be bought by the public.

The cover or container is blue and has upon it two black and white photographs of couples dancing. The background, as it were, to the photographs is a ballroom with a couple dancing and people seated at tables and is all in shades of blue. The background is printed in such a way that it is hardly distinguishable unless it is some distance from the eye. The result is that when the record cover is held in the hand, as one would read it, the figures in the black and white photographs are clear and sharp, but the figures in the background (viz the two Hendersons dancing) are blurred. However, when the cover is seen from a little distance, as it would be in a shop window, or on a shelf behind a counter, its appearance is altered. The background figures become quite distinct and striking, but the black and white figures, because of the distance, cannot be made out except as two couples executing a ballroom dance. The general effect in a shop display is to give prominence to the Hendersons and their dancing: which could easily lead to deception of possible purchasers.

On the back of the cover is a list of dances recorded and, in heavy type, a strong recommendation of the record by one Kingston, a professional dancer, who claims to be superior to all others and the world champion ballroom dancer. The background figure on the front is a reproduction of a photograph of the respondents, but their names do not appear anywhere on the cover. The photograph was taken in a television studio in England for a magazine

███████ Henderson v Radio Corp *continued*

called *Dance News*, which granted a licence to use it to a company manufacturing records in England. That company made the record "Strictly for Dancing" and designed the cover. Later it sent the metal master record with a copy of the cover to the appellant and gave to it a licence to reproduce the cover. The cover complained of is an exact copy of the English cover and the records were made by pressing them from the metal master. Until the respondents complained to the appellant, it was not aware of the identity of the background figures.

The appellant having refused to discontinue the use of the reproduction of the photograph of the respondents on the cover, the respondents commenced a passing off suit to restrain them. Sugerman J granted an injunction but refused an inquiry as to damages, because he found that any damage would have been represented by only a nominal sum. It is from that decree [591] that the appeal is brought, but there is no cross-appeal on the question of damages. The only question at the hearing and before us was whether there had been a passing off by the appellant which the respondents were entitled to have restrained....

Four witnesses were called on this issue on behalf of the respondents. They were the president of an association of dancing teachers, the secretary of another such association, a theatrical agent and the assistant secretary of the trade union to which the professional dancers belong. Each said in substance that when he saw the record he recognised either Henderson or Henderson and his wife and gathered from the fact that their pictures were on the cover, that they had sponsored ie, recommended or approved the record, or were associated in some way with it. The appellant called no evidence on this aspect. His Honour did not express any adverse view of these witnesses but he did not accept the view that buyers of the record would come to the same conclusion as the witnesses.

However, the facts relevant to this issue, including the evidence to which we have referred, are not in dispute. The only question is the proper inferences to be drawn from them, and in those circumstances we are entitled to form our own opinion: *Benmax v Austin Motor Co Ltd* [1955] AC 370.

Unaided by evidence, one might consider that the dancing figures merely indicate the type of music on the record and that it is not possible to come to the conclusion for which the respondents contend. But one is not unaided by evidence and, having regard to the fact that the record was primarily intended for professional dancing teachers, and to the uncon-tradicted evidence of four experts in that field, we are of opinion that the proper finding is that the class of persons for whom the record was primarily intended would probably believe that the picture of the respondents on the cover indicated their recommendation or approval of the record. The only rational purpose of the wrongful use of the respondents' photograph on the disc container was to assist the sale of the disc it contained.

[592] This false representation was not only made by the appellant, but would almost inevitably lead to a similar false representation on the part of every shopkeeper who might buy the records from the appellant and sell them or display them for sale.

It still remains to be considered whether that finding establishes the necessary element of deception, namely, that the business of the appellant was connected with the business of the respondents. In our opinion it does.

The representation that the respondents recommended the record is an inducement to buy it. The recommendation can only be attributed to the respondents in their capacity of professional dancers, that is, a recommendation made in the course of their professional activities, and means that as professional dancers they have associated themselves with the appellant in promoting sales of the record, and that amounts to a connection, in respect of the marketing of the record, between the business of the respondents and the business of the appellant ...

▬▬▬ Henderson v Radio Corp *continued*

In our opinion the evidence established a passing off by the appellant and, subject to proof of injury, as to which we will have something to say later, the respondents, were entitled to relief by way of injunction.

It has been contended, however, that the court has no jurisdiction to grant an injunction unless there is what has been called a common field of activity and in this case, it is said, there is none. The argument is based on a statement by Wynn-Parry J in *McCulloch v Lewis A May (Produce Distributors) Ltd* (1947) 65 RPC 58 at 66, 67:

> "I am satisfied", he said, "that there is discoverable in all those (cases) in which the court has intervened this factor, namely, that there was a common field of activity in which, however remotely, both the plaintiff and the defendant were engaged and that it was the presence of that factor that accounted for the jurisdiction of the court."

This principle was accepted by Sugerman J, who found a common field of activity in the capacity of the respondents to place their approval upon a record of ballroom dance music, which, he said, might be regarded as appurtenant or potentially appurtenant to the profession or business of ballroom dancing.

We have some difficulty in accepting the proposition stated in *McCulloch's* case. If deception and damages are proved, it is not easy to see the justification for introducing another factor as a condition of the court's power to intervene.

...

... [593] ...The remedy in passing off is necessarily only available where the parties are engaged in business, using that expression in its widest sense to include professions and callings. If they are, there does not seem to be any reason why it should also be necessary that there be an area, actual or potential, in which their activities conflict. If it were so, then, subject only to the law of defamation, any businessman might falsely represent that his goods were produced by another provided that other was not engaged, or not reasonably likely to be engaged, in producing similar goods. This does not seem to be a sound general principle.

■ Damages require actual damage

▬▬▬ Henderson v Radio Corp ▬▬▬

[13.180] *Henderson v Radio Corp Pty Ltd* [1960] SR (NSW) 576 Supreme Court of New South Wales

EVATT CJ and MYERS J: [594] ... Passing off is a wrong and is actionable at law. In such an action damage is presumed on proof of passing off and therefore a nominal sum by way of damages follows as a matter of course. General damages may, however, only be awarded if there is evidence of damage. Instead of proceeding at law a plaintiff may sue in equity for an injunction, as may be done in respect of other wrongful acts of a different nature. If he sues in equity, he takes advantage of the equitable principle that the court will interfere by injunction to restrain irreparable injury to property (per Romer LJ in *Samuelson v Producers Distributing Co Ltd* (1932) 48 RPC 580 at 593), and therefore he must go further than he need at law. He must show irreparable injury, that is that he has suffered injury which cannot be properly compensated by damages, or that he will probably suffer such injury.

If a plaintiff in equity succeeds in having the defendant enjoined, he may also have an

▰▰▰▰ Henderson v Radio Corp *continued*

account of profits or an inquiry as to damages. Formerly, he could only have had an account, because that was equity's only remedy, but since *Lord Cairns' Act*, he may have damages. If he elects to take an inquiry as to damages, he takes a common law remedy and his damages will be ascertained in the same way as they would have been ascertained at law.

With these considerations in mind, we turn to the arguments advanced on behalf of the respondents. First, it was said, it was unnecessary for the respondents to prove damage, because damage is presumed. That is clearly incorrect because the question is whether they have made out a case for an injunction and to do that they must show irreparable injury. We have been strongly pressed with some remarks of the Court of Appeal in *Draper v Trist* (1939) 56 RPC 429, to the effect that, upon proof of passing off, damage is presumed. But in that case the court was dealing with the assessment of damages pursuant to an inquiry, an order for an injunction having been made in the action with the consent of the defendant, and did not deal with the question under discussion here.

That a plaintiff in equity must prove damage is such a well-established principle that it is almost unnecessary to cite authority for it. We have already referred to the statement of Maugham J in *British Medical Association v Marsh* (1931) 48 RPC 565 at 574, that a plaintiff must prove either positive injury or, in a quia timet action, a reasonable probability of injury and will only add to it the remarks of Farwell J in *British Legion v British Legion Club (Street) Ltd* (1931) 48 RPC 555. He said (at 563):

"There must be evidence either of damage already committed, or the circumstances must be such as that the court can properly come to the conclusion that there is a serious risk, a real tangible risk, of damage in the future."

■ Establishing damage: Trap purchases

Ward Group v Brodie & Stone

[13.185] *Ward Group Pty Ltd v Brodie & Stone Plc* (2005) 64 IPR 1 Federal Court of Australia
The facts are discussed at **[13.115]**.

MERKEL J: **[6]** ... The only evidence of sales of the UK Restoria products in Australia is the evidence adduced by the Ward Group of purchases of those products by its solicitors acting on its behalf ("the trap purchases"). ... **[7]**

There was some controversy between the parties about the trap purchases. As was pointed out by Farwell J in *CC Wakefield & Co Ld v Purser* (1934) 51 RPC 167 at 171: **[8]**

"Test orders or, as the Defendant prefers to call them, trap orders are in a case of this kind, it seems to me, quite essential. I fail to see how the Plaintiffs can safeguard themselves or the public without having resort to some such method of testing the matter as is used in the present case; but, trap orders or test orders, whichever they may be called, are scrutinised by the Courts with some jealousy and rightly so because, if, as a result of a trap order or a test order, a person is to be charged with the very serious offence of fraudulently misrepresenting the goods which he is supplying to the public, to the detriment of the public as well as of the Plaintiffs, the Court must be satisfied that the offence has been proved strictly. Further, if a person is resorting to a test order

███████ Ward Group v Brodie & Stone *continued*

or a trap order, even in a case of this kind, where the necessity for such a device may be a real one, that person is bound to carry out the proceeding with the utmost fairness to the prospective defendant to the action. It is essential, if the plaintiff is to succeed in the action which he ultimately brings, that he should be able to satisfy the Court that he has acted throughout with the most exact fairness to the defendant and has given him every reasonable chance of investigating the matter for himself, so that he may be in a position to put forward in the action, if one follows, any and every defence properly open to him."

In the present case the trap purchases made on behalf of the Ward Group by its solicitors undoubtedly satisfied the criteria laid down by Farwell J. Nonetheless, Brodie & Stone contended that the trap purchases might convey a misleading impression. It was contended that because Restoria products are available from a large number of retail outlets in Australia and on the Ward Group's websites, it is unlikely that Australian consumers would seek out or become aware of the UK websites offering the UK Restoria products for sale. It was also contended that, even if a consumer in Australia became aware of the websites offering the UK Restoria products, it would make little economic sense for the consumer to purchase the UK Restoria products from the website proprietors at higher prices and higher postage costs than those applicable to the Australian Restoria products available for purchase either on the Ward Group's Australian websites or at retail outlets in Australia.

There was no evidence of any sales of the UK Restoria products in Australia apart from the trap purchases. Also, although the UK Restoria products continue to be available for sale on the Internet there is no reason to expect that sales in Australia were likely to occur. In that regard it is not disputed that it would be more expensive to purchase the UK Restoria products rather than their Australian counterparts. That is of some significance given that the Ward Group has accepted that "this is not a case where there are material differences in quality or standard" between the UK and the Australian Restoria products.

[10] ...I am satisfied that the Ward Group has failed to establish the fifth characteristic referred to by Lord Diplock, which requires the party seeking relief in a passing off action to establish some actual or probable damage: see *Taco Bell* at 196. In the present case the trap purchases were the only sales able to be established on the evidence. However, and importantly, the evidence also established that it was most unlikely that anyone else in Australia had searched on the Internet for, and then purchased, the UK Restoria products instead of, or in preference to, the Australian Restoria products. I would add that, as the UK and Australian Restoria products have a common origin and are not materially different in quality or standard, any sale of UK Restoria products in Australia is unlikely to harm the goodwill attaching to the Australian Restoria products. In that regard the circumstances of the present case may be analogous to those considered in *Revlon Inc* at 102-104. In any event, the issue of actual or probable damage is a question of fact and I am not satisfied that the Ward Group has established that any representations made by the website proprietors, or any other conduct engaged in by them, has caused actual damage to the Ward Group or will probably do so. Thus, I am not satisfied that the Ward Group has made out its cause of action in passing off against the website proprietors.

CHAPTER 14

TRADE MARKS

NATURE OF THE INTEREST PROTECTED

[14.05] The law of trade marks is an extension of the law of passing off, and like passing off and *Trade Practices Act 1974* (Cth), s 52, protects efforts directed at the marketing of goods and services. Very few products are sold without being labeled in some way, and protection for trade marks is defined in the *Trade Marks Act 1995* (Cth) in terms of protecting "signs" associated with a trader's reputation. Passing off also protects marks or signs that are associated with a particular company or trader, but can extend to wider manifestations of reputation. Having a system of registered marks overcomes a major hurdle of passing off litigation, which is the need to prove reputation; once a mark (or sign) is registered, it is the property of the registered owner. In a passing off action, the reputation being claimed must be demonstrated by much more cumbersome evidence, as discussed in the previous chapter.

The nature of the "property" in a trade mark was discussed in *Attorney-General (NSW) v Brewery Employees Union (NSW)* (1908) 6 CLR 469 (the *Union Label case*). The *Trade Marks Act 1905* (Cth) provided in Part VII for the registration of workers' marks. These marks were an indication that the goods to which they were appended were the product of "an individual Australian worker or association of Australian workers". The New South Wales Attorney-General sought, inter alia, a declaration that Parliament had no power or authority to enact Part VII of the Act. The Attorney-General argued that workers' marks were not trade marks. Griffith CJ in the High Court held:

"In my opinion it follows, from a consideration both of the statute law of England and the Australian colonies up to 1900 and of the authoritative expositions of the law with respect to trade marks in British Courts of Justice, that, whether the term 'trade mark' as used in s 51(xviii) of the Constitution is to be regarded as a term of art or as a word used in popular language, it did not in that year denote every kind of mark which might be used in trade or in connection with articles of trade and commerce, but meant a mark which is the visible symbol of a particular kind of incorporeal or industrial property consisting in the right of a person engaged in trade to distinguish by a special mark goods in which he deals, or with which he has dealt, from the goods of other persons.

This concept includes in my opinion five distinct elements:

(1) A right which is in the nature of property.

(2) The owner of the right must be a person, natural or artificial, engaged in trade.

(3) The right is appurtenant or incident to the dealing with goods in the course of his trade.

(4) The owner has such an independent dominion over the goods to which the mark is to be affixed as to entitle him to affix it to them; (it is not material whether this right is incident to his possession of the goods or arises under an agreement with the owner of them).

(5) The mark distinguishes the goods as having been dealt with by some particular person or persons engaged in trade; (I use the word 'particular' not as meaning that the person in question is indicated nominatim, but as indicating that he is a person who has an independent individual right with respect to the goods in question, and who is capable of ascertainment upon inquiry).

With regard to this species of property the power of the Parliament is absolute. They can prescribe the conditions on which it may be acquired, retained, or enjoyed; they may possibly even prohibit its enjoyment altogether; but they cannot, by calling something else by the name of 'trade mark', create a new and different kind of industrial property."

Collective marks, such as fair trade marks that indicate the goods were manufactured in accordance with particular labour conditions, are permitted under the TRIPS agreement. The external affairs power now provides a supplementary constitutional power to the intellectual property power under s 51(viii).

With the expansion of the internet, rights and obligations between trade marks, domain names, business names and company names start to overlap. The Advisory Council on Intellectual Property (ACIP) *Review of Enforcement of Trade Mark* (2002) noted that some confusion related to trade mark, business name, company name and domain name use could be addressed by more co-operation between IP Australia, responsible for trade marks; company names registered with the Australian Securities and Investment Commission (ASIC); business names registered to protect consumers in each State and Territory; and the Australian domain name register. This concern sparked a separate ACIP review in 2004 to examine how confusion in usage can be limited, and how to facilitate the streamlining of the application process for such names. Education about the particular "rights" that attach to registrations would clearly help matters. Other issues under discussion include abolishing business name registrations and making trade mark registration a condition of company or business registration. However, not all company names would be eligible for trade mark registration. Other proposals include the idea of centralising registers.

ACIP also sought comments on the effectiveness of Australian dispute resolution policies for disputes concerning cybersquatting and "bad faith" registrations of domain names. However, this is a policy area generally dealt with at the global level. Although the domain name system began as an electronic addressing system, without necessarily suggesting any proprietary rights inherent in the name used, domain addresses now also function as powerful marketing tools.

▬▬▬ Review of Intellectual Property Legislation ▬▬▬ under the Competition Principles Agreement

[14.10] Intellectual Property Competition Review Committee, *Review of Intellectual Property Legislation under the Competition Principles Agreement*, Final Report (September 2000) (References omitted.)

■ Trademarks/domain names

As the internet explodes in popularity and ecommerce becomes increasingly important to business, governments around the world are struggling to find a regulatory framework which provides the certainty of rights needed for the efficient operation of a market economy in which ecommerce plays a significant role while minimising administration and transaction costs. The main issue brought to the Committee's attention under its Terms of Reference that is relevant here is the conflict between domain names and trademarks.

Trademarks can be registered with IP Australia under the *Trade Marks Act* in one or more of 42 independent categories of goods and services. The same trademark could be used by different owners in different categories or territories, provided it does not cause confusion in the market place. Global co-ordination of trademarks is handled by WIPO through various treaties. Recent treaties aim to ban the use of "famous" trademarks between countries.

Domain names are electronic addresses used on the Internet, commonly on the world wide web. As they are the addressing arrangements for an integrated global network, they must be unique, worldwide. To enable multiple use of common words for easier address remembrance, various levels with different suffixes are allowed, for example, .com for commercial use, .au for Australia etc. Registration of domain names has, until recently, been handled by an informal network of delegates within the internet system. More recently, it is becoming better organised through a mixture of not-for-profit and for-profit companies. Internationally, the domain name registration system is coordinated by ICANN, a not-for-profit organisation that now includes international representatives.

After referral of the issue to WIPO by ICANN, the recent final WIPO report on the interaction of trademarks and domain names included recommendations on a variety of topics including the following:
*   best practices for registration authorities;
*   administrative procedure concerning abusive domain name registrations;
*   exclusions for famous and well-known marks;
*   new generic top level domain names (gTLDs).

The Uniform Domain Name Dispute Resolution Procedure (UDRP) was adopted by ICANN in Autumn 1999, and made applicable as of 1 January 2000 to those generic Top Level Domains ending in the .com, .org, and .net suffixes. As of 15 June 2000, all ICANN-accredited domain name registrars had adopted the UDRP and required that domain name registrants agree to abide by the terms of that policy. The policy replaces various other ad hoc policies of individual registrars, and has been praised for assisting with speedy and efficient resolution

▓▓▓▓▓▓ Review of Intellectual Property Legislation *continued*

of disputes. ... These include abusive registrations of trade names, geographical indications and other rights not based on trademarks.

... Submissions received in response to the Issues Paper and the Interim Report strongly supported the WIPO and ICANN dispute resolution initiatives. It was also suggested that Australia should consider passing domain name cybersquatting law similar to that passed by the USA.

A number of submissions expressed concern at the overlap between trade marks and domain names and business and company names which created confusion in the market.

A view was put to the Committee that a (gTLD) .tm for trademarks should be implemented as this should allow legitimate trade mark owners to apply for and own the domain name address in respect of their trade mark. This view was challenged by a submission which noted the domain name system has the potential to bring into conflict businesses which had previously coexisted in different product or geographic markets without dispute. It is not feasible to divide domain names into classes of goods or services like the trade mark register and such proposals to implement new domains such as .shop/ .store and .product or .tm will only exacerbate the problem.

... The Committee believes that resolving issues of cross-border disputes and domain name register standards will not be well served by an ad hoc approach, rather, they are best dealt with from an international perspective by ICANN and WIPO ... it urges the Government to speedily adopt the model dispute resolution procedures developed by WIPO and ICANN.

MEANING OF "TRADE MARK"

[14.15] "Trade mark" is defined in *Trade Marks Act 1995* (Cth), s 17 as a "sign" used or intended to be used to distinguish goods or services from those of other traders.

See s 6, "sign".

■ Conceptual issues

What is a sign?

[14.20] "A sign is something by knowing which we know something more." (Charles Sanders Pierce)

A sign is a form of compressed meaning. The trade mark conveys multiple suggestions about the goods and services with which it is associated. Consider the sign used by the Australian Broadcasting Corporation (ABC). It was originally commissioned in 1965, following a competition to design a symbol to identify the ABC's radio and broadcasting activities. The sign was created by Bill Kennard, for which he received £25.

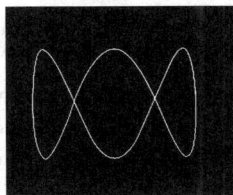

The symbol is known as the Lissajous figure, derived from an oscilloscope waveform for measuring radio and television frequencies. As a trade mark it has a signalling function. It indicates a corporate identity for ABC broadcasting, as well as communicating something about the nature of the service provided by the ABC. It suggests this kind of service comes from this unique source.

These signalling connotations of the trade mark are not all that has made it valuable. It has also proven a successful mark because of the simplicity and ease of its recognition and because of the ability to adapt the sign to meet new corporate ends. The sign can be applied in a range of advertising formats. Originally produced for black and white reproduction and used in television broadcasts and on the side of ABC Broadcast Kombi Vans, it is now used in various formats and for an extensive range of merchandising. The symbol has gone through various transformations over the years, but each remains readily identifiable and continues to fulfil the signalling function as desired by the corporation.

It is the underlying symbol that is crucial here and not the precise expression of it. As a matter of graphic representation, there is a world of difference between a two-dimensional vector line oscilloscope rendering of a broadcast signal, and a similar shape expressed as a three-dimensional rather abstract reflective object. Yet, though the expressions are graphically and technically quite different creations, the relation between them remains clear to the intended audiences.

In addition to a signalling function, a sign also has an expressive function. This refers to the emotional content sought to be communicated to the audience by use of the sign. It is a subjective message, and audiences do not necessarily read all the emotional connotations as intended.

The signalling and expressive functions of the ABC sign have evolved over the years and in relation to each other. One of the virtues leading to the choice of the original sign in addition to the signalling features already mentioned was its purported expressive function. The sign was taken as symbolic of the ABC's mandate to provide radio and television to as many Australians as possible. It was chosen to herald an organisation in charge of new broadcast technologies, disseminated on a grand scale. Under the controversial leadership of Jonathon Shier, a shiny new metallic computer-generated version of the sign was launched to signal the ABC's expansion beyond radio and television into digital broadcasting. The evocation of the original symbol today expresses continuity with the technological past and stability of service, as well as gesturing to the corporation's technological future.

Critics of Shier read much else into the expressive function of this new sign:

"The brutal symbol replaced the customer-connected 'Your ABC' with its relaxed musical mnemonic including personal delivery by fingertips as crayons. The cold new logo told what was left of the ABC audience 'You can go and get stuffed, it's my ABC now baby. Like it or lump it!'"[1]

---

1   Miller, *Ad News*, 22 June 2001.

What a sign's meaning is taken to be is not simply dictated by its creator or the investor in the sign to a passive, compliant viewer. The reader's experience, preferences, social values, interest in and exposure to the trade mark and its owner affect any significance that is attached to a sign. The departure of Jonathon Shier from the management of the ABC has been followed with the launching of a new, more organic-looking, computer-generated version of the corporate logo.

A successful sign will carry with it the connections or reputation recommended by the history of its use, but the meaning of a sign is not fixed. A sign is multi-layered. Its significance is contextual and the meaning attributed to it is ultimately determined by its many and varied audiences.

The politics of reading signs

[14.25] The development of marketing techniques has complicated the reading of signs. A few signs, such as an unknown artist's signature, remain a relatively unsophisticated reference to the unique producer of a particular kind of good. Most signs today however, serve the function of indicating an origin, as well as selling society on an ever-expanding horizon of goods or services. These marks are implicated in manufacturing a desire for the product as well as informing about the product, making it difficult to separate the signalling and expressive functions of the sign. Is the Calvin Klein sign telling me about the product to which it is associated, or in knowing and attaching value to the sign, does it say more about me and my receptivity to image marketing?

Photo: Nancy Bleck; Model Cayvan Econmi
Source: http://adbusters.org/spoofads/fashion/

Many cultural critics argue that the most successful examples of contemporary marketing eschew any real association with actual products or their origins. The marks are a form of social marketing. What is sold is a nebulous association with a particular lifestyle, set of ideas, philosophy or world view. A well-known mark, through licensing agreements, can be potentially applied to any product deemed capable of sustaining the supposedly unique lifestyle value suggested by it.

As Rosemary Coombe retells it:

"An apocryphal story circulates at marketing conferences: Coca-Cola executives, it is said, routinely visit bottling plants around the globe to monitor the size and proportions of the famous logo to ensure that it does not become distorted on the local product. Gathering together the staff from several plants, a senior Coca-Cola executive is reported to have declared that the company could lose all its staff, lose its access to the sources of its raw materials, lose its capital and its accounts, but as long as it had this (lights shine on a display board greatly enlarging the famous red and white script), it would be possible to walk into a bank and receive sufficient credit to replace the entire global infrastructure".[2]

The name once signalled a drink with ingredients of coca leaf and cola nut. Nowadays very few people can explain what the names stands for, but more can recognise it when it is shown in the correct ribbon script, than can spell it.[3] Coca-Cola™, along with brands such as Nike, Reebok, Virgin, Body Shop, McDonald's, Starbucks and Pepsi, tobacco advertisers, and fashion labels like Gap, Tommy Hilfiger and Benetton to name just a few, are often read as representing a "world-wide style culture".[4] In these examples it is the expressive function, the aspirational quality suggested by the use mark, that is the all-valuable signification. It is because the marks have strong expressive functions and weak signalling functions that makes them suitable for licensing in relation to a very wide range of goods or services.

Reading the legal meaning of a sign

[14.30] The law is not all that interested in the marketing choices or politics associated with the adoption and development of a particular sign. But legal protection of the mark might affect a corporate choice of whether to select it in the first place or not.

Lawyers and trade mark practitioners do not necessarily spend a great deal of time studying semiotics, but they do practice it in a specialist sense.

Trade mark law has, as a matter of legal history and policy, focused on maintaining a level playing field amongst all traders, allowing no-one to monopolise as a sign that might be a desired association by many, and preventing consumer confusion over competing goods in the marketplace through the use of misleadingly similar signs. This has led to the development of legal tests that require a mark to be "inherently distinctive" and not likely to cause deception or confusion in order to gain registration (see **[14.135]-[14.195]**).

From a semiotic point of view, the notion that any sign is "inherently" anything, that the meaning inheres in the sign itself, is meaningless. A sign, even a badly designed one, signals some association with a product circulating in a marketplace. It is not internally referent. The law is well aware of this, and what the legal shorthand of inherent distinctiveness refers to is the need for a level of abstract association or formal distance between the sign and the product in order to keep the most desired and obvious associations from being monopolised by any one trader. With this in mind, the law has inordinately focused on interpreting the signalling function of a sign, trying to read the meaning of the sign in terms of its most obvious, "objective" connotations given the chosen application. In reading the cases on distinctiveness, you will become familiar with reading marks without assuming any particular expressive content or context.

A difficulty arises, however, in reading signs abstractly and at a distance, when a sign, whether registered or not, has already obtained a level of reputation in the marketplace. The law needs to pay heed to the existing reputation of signs in order to fulfil its fair competition and consumer protection functions. Deceptive practices, that hurt traders and consumers alike, often involve cheap imitations and piracy of well-known reputable marks.

Once a consideration of existing reputation comes into the picture, it is extremely difficult to discern the existing connotation of the sign without being influenced by the marketing of the sign. Whilst the reputation of the sign can be determined with reference to the effect

---

2   *The Cultural Life of Intellectual Properties. Authorship, Appropriation and the Law* (Duke University Press, Durham, London, 1998), p 56.
3   P Mollerup, *Marks of Excellence: The History and Taxonomy of Trademarks* (Phaidon Press Inc, 1999), p 24.
4   N Klein, *No Logo: Taking Aim at the Brand Bullies* (Picador, New York, 2000).

of past marketing on its existing audience—what consumers make of the sign given their existing exposure to it—consumers are not of a homogenous mind. Some are more sophisticated readers of signs than others, some more likely to be open to expressive connotations, some more literal in interpretation. They do not necessarily form an "objective" audience capable of definitively determining the nature and extent of an existing mark's reputation and meaning. One of the most difficult tasks in trade mark law is determining the significance of an existing mark's reputation and its relation to other traders and their chosen marks.

Those investing in trade marks seek to maximise its economic value by seeking maximum protection of their mark. They are keen to use the law to protect and maintain the mark's distinctiveness, in order that it remain eligible for registration. However, they are also often motivated to use the protection offered by the law to commercial advantage. It is often hard to differentiate attempts to protect a trade mark from dilution from more strategic use of the law to expand market position and block competition.

In some cases, the owner of a mark is successful in convincing the law that the meaning of the sign simply corresponds with their corporate intention as expressed in past marketing campaigns, without proper reference to the actual comprehension of the sign by consumers. In such cases, the owner of the sign is able to co-opt the law into furthering their corporate agenda, without due regard to the law's original policy objectives and other beneficiaries— other traders' marketing needs and consumer's information needs.

In recent years, the level of legal protection awarded to the well-known sign, such as McDonald's™ or Nike™, has become one of the more controversial areas of trade mark law. The problem has been compounded by the development of global marketing and licensing practices, as discussed above. Where a trade mark has little signalling function outside of a link with a particular branded identity, and a strong expressive content, the sign can have endless possible significations, limited only by the imagination and licensing skill of the corporate owner. Protection of such a mark potentially involves protection against a broad range of a competitor's possible marketing opportunities.

To take a recent English example, is the reputation of the McDonalds™ sign so pervasive that consumers would assume an association between the giant and a small take-away restaurant called McChina? In deciding in favour of the owner of McChina™ Judge David Neuberger said, "It appears to me on analysis that McDonald's are virtually seeking to monopolise all names and words with the prefix 'Mc' or 'Mac'." However, using trade mark and equivalents to passing off and trade practices law, McDonald's were successful in stopping a "McAllan's" sausage stand in Denmark, a "McCoffee" cafe in San Francisco and a Scottish-themed sandwich bar, "McMunchies", in Buckinghamshire from using the "Mc" prefix. In Australia, McWilliam's Wines successfully defended the right to use the name "Big Mac" in connection with wines in *McWilliams Wines Pty Ltd v McDonalds System of Australia* (1980) 33 ALR 394.

E-commerce raises even more difficulties concerning protection of well-known marks. Trade mark law is territorial. Further, similar marks might be registered in a jurisdiction, if they are used in association with unrelated goods or services, where there is no likelihood of consumer confusion. Where there are multiple possible claimants to a name within a jurisdiction, and beyond, who should be entitled to exclusive use of a domain name that may include a trade mark reference?

When Australian swimwear company Absolut Beach sought to register their eponymous trade mark in Australia, Swedish liquor giant, Vin & Spirit, the makers of Absolut™ Vodka, opposed it. They believed that the "Absolut" brand had been the subject of such extensive promotion since 1981 that there was now a general public perception that any business carried on with reference to the "Absolut" name or mark would be assumed to be part of or associated with the liquor company. Whilst the "Absolut Beach" registration survived this opposition action in Australia, the mark was not registered as a trade mark offshore. When the Australian company set up its "Absolut Beach" website, Vin & Spirit filed trade mark infringement actions in the United Kingdom and United States, and sought to have the domain name handed over to them, accusing the Sydney-based retailer of "cyber-squatting". The Australian company lacked the financial backing to defend the actions, and gave up the domain name.

This chapter deals with the way Australian law resolves trade mark disputes, and therefore considers only the local impact of global marketing strategies and practices. However, it is important to remember that Australian legal practice also operates in the context of a global corporate reality. As Australian trade mark practitioners respond to the needs of their multi-national clients, pressure is put on the future development of our law. Further, as the "Absolut" swimwear example demonstrates, advising a small business can require an awareness of the global legal implications of the use of the trade mark.

The ACIP *Issues Paper* (2002) and *Review on Enforcement of Trade Marks* (2004) noted community concern about disadvantages facing small and medium enterprises in trade marks law. However, they found that the difficulties and disadvantages facing small businesses was primarily related to the time and financial resources required for managing rights. A separate proposal for special trade mark treatment of "national icons" such as Phar Lap, Ned Kelly, ANZACS, or Sir Edmund (Weary) Dunlop, was rejected by the Government in 2005.

Trade mark law is a mix of a specialist strand of semiotics, assisted by advertising and marketing knowledge in order to best protect investment in a sign, and an understanding of competition and consumer perspectives in order to stop a trade mark owner being granted excessive protection. The student will already be familiar with some of these concerns, from his or her knowledge of passing off law. However, trade mark law is statute-based law with its own specialist bureaucracy within IP Australia. This provides for a more particular and technical framework in which these similar principles operate.

■ "Used, or intended to be used"
[14.35] See ss 7, 8.

═══════ **Imperial Group v Philip Morris** ═══════

[14.40] *Imperial Group Ltd v Philip Morris & Co Ltd* [1980] FSR 146 Chancery Division

[The plaintiff cigarette manufacturers chose the name "Merit" for a projected brand of cigarettes. It was subsequently advised that the name was unregistrable under the *Trade Marks Act 1955* (Cth) but that it should obtain registration of the mark "Nerit". The mark, which was registered in 1974 was selected because it was as close as possible to the unregistered word. Any other person using the mark Merit could arguably be infringing the Nerit mark by using a confusingly similar mark. In 1975 the defendants launched the brand "Merit" cigarettes in the United States. In the same year the plaintiffs had a limited launch of the "Nerit" brand cigarettes to maintain the registration of the mark. In September 1976 the defendants launched its "Merit" brand in the United Kingdom. In January 1977 the plaintiffs made a more substantial launch of its Nerit brand. In March 1977 it commenced an infringement action against the defendants which responded with the defence, inter alia, that the plaintiff's mark should be expunged as it was registered without any bona fide intention for its use.]

BALCOMBE J: ... [156]..For the defendants to succeed under this head I must be satisfied:

(i) that "Nerit" was registered without any bona fide intention on the part of the plaintiffs that it should be used in relation to the goods in respect of which it was registered by the plaintiff; and

(ii) that there has in fact been no bona fide use of "Nerit" in relation to those goods by the plaintiffs up to 16 April 1977.

In my judgment the question under this head turns upon the meaning to be attributed to the words "bona fide" in the context in which they are used in the two limbs of para (a) of s 26(1). The plaintiffs say that they mean "honest" and that both their intention to use the mark "Nerit" and its actual use were honest. The defendants say that they mean "genuine" and that it is clear from the evidence that there never was any genuine intention to use the mark "Nerit" nor was there ever any genuine commercial use of the mark. [His Honour referred to the case of *Electrolux Ltd v Electrix Ltd* (1953) 71 RPC 23 (CA).]

... [157] In that case the plaintiffs were the proprietors of two registered trade marks "Electrolux" and "Electrux", the latter having been registered in 1928. (For the sake of simplicity I ignore a third registered mark "Elektrolux".) At all material times up to 31 March 1947 all the articles which were relevant to the proceedings before the court vacuum cleaners had been marketed under the name "Electrolux", and "Electrux" was never used at all. In 1947 the plaintiff started to market one of their cheaper models under the name "Electrux". The reason for this was because they had become aware of the defendants' use of the mark "Electrix", also in relation to vacuum cleaners, and they wished to be able to resist any application by the defendants for the removal of "Electrux" from the register under s 26 and to challenge the defendants' use of the mark "Electrix". In due course the plaintiffs did commence an action for the infringement of their mark "Electrux" by the defendants' mark "Electrix" and the defendants moved to expunge the mark "Electrux" from the register on the grounds that the plaintiffs' use of that mark had not been bona fide. The Court of Appeal held that the plaintiffs' use of "Electrux", although commenced with knowledge of the defendants' use of "Electrix" and for the purpose of enabling an action to be brought against them for infringement, had been genuine, substantial and bona fide in the sense of s 26 of the Act. The following passages from the judgments show the considerations which motivated the members of the Court of Appeal in that case.

Per Evershed MR (at 36, line 3):

"I do not propose to attempt any definition of what does or may constitute bona fide use within the terms of s 26. I find it sufficient to say, after much anxious thought and sympathy for the defendants, that I do not think it has here been established that the use by the plaintiffs of the word 'Electrux' was not bona fide because the occasion for adopting the policy of marketing their cheaper model under that name was a desire to gain an advantage in proceedings which I assume were then contemplated against the defendants. I have said I attempt no definition, but the use here shown does not seem to me in any real sense capable of [158] being described as a pretended use. ... Commercially speaking it is not shown that the use made by the plaintiffs of this mark was not an ordinary and genuine use, and it certainly was substantial."

Per Jenkins LJ (at 41, line 29):

"On the question of bona fide user, there is no doubt that from March 1947 onwards ... the plaintiffs consistently used their mark 'Electrux' to designate and distinguish one of their products, namely their cheaper type of vacuum cleaner. There is no doubt that such use was perfectly genuine and was substantial in amount. That being so, I

▦▦▦▦ Imperial Group v Philip Morris *continued*

feel difficulty in seeing how it can be held not to have been bona fide. The reason urged by Mr Shelley for holding it not to be bona fide is that the use of 'Electrux' was a manoeuvre directed against the use by the defendants of 'Electrix'; but, as my Lord has said, if in using 'Electrux' the plaintiffs indeed had that object in view, nevertheless they were doing no more than asserting and taking advantage of the rights accorded to them by the Act. In my view, the use of 'Electrux', being a real commercial use on a substantial scale and in that sense genuine, cannot on this account properly be regarded as other than bona fide user."

Per Morris LJ (at 42, line 21):

"In regard to the issue as to whether there has been bona fide user by the plaintiffs of the mark 'Electrux', it seems to me that in s 26 of the Act a contrast is being drawn between use, on the one hand, and non-use, on the other. The legislature, in my view, had in mind that someone could not gain immunity from attack by asserting use when there was really only some fictitious or colourable use and not a real or genuine use."

(He then refers to a passage from the speech of Lord Simon in *Palser v Grinling* [1948] AC 291 at 310 and continues):

"It is, of course, clear that when the phrase 'bona fide' is used, its context must be considered when deciding what is its meaning. In my judgment there was in the case bona fide user by the plaintiffs of the mark 'Electrux'. The evidence which is before us, to which I need not refer, relating to the volume and extent of the use of the mark since it was applied to one of the models manufactured by the plaintiffs is such as to put it, in my view, beyond all question that, judged by ordinary commercial standards, there was a genuine use by the plaintiffs of this mark."

In the instant case, both parties claim to derive assistance from the judgments of the Court of Appeal which I have quoted. The plaintiffs claim that the judgments establish that their motives for registering and using "Nerit" as a mark are irrelevant to the question of bona fides; indeed Mr Falconer went so far as to assert that "Electrux" in that case was a "ghost mark". Mr Leggatt relied on the repeated references to "commercial" and "genuine" use ... **[159]** ...

I need not here repeat the findings of fact set out earlier in this judgment; suffice it to say that it is clear from those findings that the plaintiffs never intended to, and never did, use "Nerit" as a genuine commercial trade mark for a brand of cigarettes; the sole purpose of registering and using "Nerit" was to acquire a monopoly right to use the unregistrable name "Merit" and to prevent anyone else from using that name. In my judgment such an intention, and such use, were not "bona fide" within the meaning of that phrase as used in the context of s 26 of the Act. The decision of the Court of Appeal in *Electrolux Ltd v Electrix Ltd* appears to me to support the defendants' case by the insistence throughout the judgments that the use of the mark "Electrux" was a genuine and commercial use, the inference being that if the court had been satisfied that the use was neither genuine nor commercial they would have considered it not to have been bona fide. The mark "Electrux" was there used genuinely and commercially in that it was used as a trade mark to identify one of the plaintiffs' particular models, and the fact that that use was prompted by a desire to prevent the defendants using the mark "Electrix" did not make the use of "Electrux" mala fide. To suggest that "Electrux" was a "ghost mark" comparable to "Nerit" in the present case indicates, in my judgment, misunderstanding of the decision in *Electrolux Ltd v Electrix Ltd*.

[14.45] The presumption that an applicant intends to use a mark is rebuttable by showing that there is no real possibility of the applicant being able to market the products or services in respect of which a mark is to be applied. It may happen that someone wishes to register a name or logo which is well-known overseas but not in use in Australia. This may be possible but can be successfully opposed by the overseas company: see, for example, *Michael Sharwood & Partners Pty Ltd v Fuddruckers Inc* (1989) 15 IPR 188; *Daimaru Pty Ltd v Kabushiki Kaisha Daimaru* (1990) 19 IPR 129. See also *Sizzler Restaurants International Inc v Sabra International Pty Ltd* (1990) 20 IPR 331; cf *Dunlop Olympic Ltd v Cricket Hosiery Inc* (1990) 20 IPR 475.

A proper intention to "use" a mark "in the course of trade" is the opposite of "trafficking" in trade marks. Previously, under the 1955 legislation, s 74(4) of the Act provided that the Registrar was not to register anyone as a user of a trade mark if this would "tend to facilitate trafficking in the trade mark". This potentially created a barrier for character merchandisers seeking to license marks for a wide range of goods, but also inhibited the activities of persons seeking to register marks and sell them, possibly to the overseas proprietor of the same mark.

In the *Holly Hobbie* case (below), the House of Lords discussed the widespread licensing of the cute "holly hobby" character for use on a wide variety of goods not manufactured by the trade mark owner, American Greetings Corp.

Re Trade Mark "Holly Hobbie"

[14.50] *Re Trade Mark "Holly Hobbie"* (1984) 1 IPR 486 House of Lords

LORD BRIGHTMAN: **[488]** My Lords, this appeal relates to commercial activity commonly called "character merchandising". The expression is used to signify the exploitation of a well-known invented name, whereby the author or promoter of the name licenses or purports to license its use on the goods of traders who have no other connection with the licensor. If the invented name is a registered trade mark of the licensor in respect of certain classes of goods, the licensor may wish to protect his position by obtaining registration of the mark in respect of the goods of the licensee. The question is whether, on the facts of the case before your Lordships, applications for the registration of the trade mark "Holly Hobbie" in respect of the goods of certain licensees were properly refused by the registrar on the ground that registration would tend to facilitate trafficking in a trade mark ... **[492]**

[After discussing previous authorities Lord Brightman continued:]

The law clearly did not recognise the entitlement of the owner of a trade mark to deal with it, like a patent, as a commodity in its own right. The same point was highlighted 15 years later in your Lordships' House in *Bowden Wire Ltd v Bowden Brake Co Ltd* (1914) 31 RPC 385, where Lord Loreburn said this (at 392):

> "The object of the law is to preserve for a trader the reputation he has made for himself, not to help him in disposing of that reputation as of itself a marketing commodity, independent of his goodwill, to some other trader. If they were allowed, the public would be misled, because they might buy something in the **[493]** belief that it was the make of a man whose reputation they knew, whereas it was the make of someone else. ... In this case the appellants parcelled out the right to us in their trade mark as if they had been dealing with a patent."

> ... To my mind, trafficking in a trade mark context conveys the notion of dealing in a trade mark primarily as a commodity in its own right and not primarily for the purpose of identifying or promoting merchandise in which the proprietor of the mark

▬▬▬▬ Re Trade Mark "Holly Hobbie" *continued*

is interested. If there is no real trade connection between the proprietor of the mark and the licensee of his goods, there is room for the conclusion that the grant of the licence is trafficking in the mark. It is a question of fact and degree in every case whether a sufficient trade connection exists. In my opinion, on the facts of these particular applications, the Assistant Registrar and the High Court were entitled to take the view that the registration of the licensee as a registered user, pursuant to s 28, would tend to facilitate trafficking in a trade mark."

[14.55] There is no express prohibition on "trafficking" anymore, but the requirement of "use" or "intention to use" requires some connection between the owner of the mark and any licensors. The nature of the intention to use was considered by Lord Hanworth MR in *Ducker's Trade Mark* (1928) 45 RPC 397 at 402 where he observed:

"I agree that the goods need not be in being at the moment, and that there is futurity indicated in the definition; but the mark is to be a mark which is to be definitely used or in respect of which there is a resolve to use it in the immediate future upon or in connection with goods. I think that the words 'proposed to be used' mean a real intention to use, not a mere problematical intention, not an uncertain or indeterminate possibility, but it means a resolve or settled purpose which has been reached at the time when the mark is to be registered."

That intention is presumed on the making of the application for registration: see *Aston v Harlee Manufacturing Co* (1960) 103 CLR 391 at 401.

■ "To distinguish"

[14.60] The words "to distinguish" have generated most trade mark litigation and an assessment of the distinctiveness of a sign is largely a matter of evidence, judgment, semantics and argument. The 1995 Act takes the route in s 41 of outlining what is *not* distinctive, whereas the 1955 *Trade Marks Act* instead tried to set out categories of what *is* inherently distinctive (s 24). Even under the 1955 legislation, an important aspect of the concept of distinctive marks was defined negatively, that is, *not* descriptive, *not* geographic, etc (s 24(d)). The cases on distinctiveness extracted below at **[14.135]** and **[14.195]**, mainly deriving from the 1955 legislation, will be discussed in the context of registration of marks/signs.

■ "Goods or services"

[14.65] See s 6 "goods of a person" and "services of a person" and s 19, certain trade marks may be registered.

Trade marks could only be registered in relation to goods until 1978. In that year the Act was amended to apply to marks in relation to services. The categories of service which can be registered are taken from the Nice Agreement concerning the *International Classification of Goods and Services for the Purposes of the Registration of Marks 1957.* See **[14.90]**. The way in which the Act was amended to extend its protection to services was, broadly, to apply the provisions relating to goods marks so far as feasible to service marks. See *Caterpillar Loader Hire (Holdings) Pty Ltd v Caterpillar Tractor Co* (1983) 1 IPR 265.

■ "Dealt with or provided in the course of trade"

[**14.80**] The definition of "trade mark" in *Trade Marks Act 1995* (Cth), s 17 requires that the sign be used to distinguish goods or services "dealt with or provided in the course of trade" from those of other traders. The previous Act in s 6(1) required that the mark sought to be registered "indicates a connection in the course of trade between the goods or services and a person who has the right, either as proprietor or registered user, to use the mark". This is another aspect of the general proposition that it is not possible to register what is not the property of the person using (or intending to use) the mark. The "dealing" with in the "course of trade" indicates the need for a proper connection between the trader and the mark.

In *Re Application by New York Yacht Club* (1987) 9 IPR 102 the club made an application to register in the mark AMERICA'S CUP for "Art galleries and the perpetual promotion of challenge sailing matches for friendly competition between foreign countries" being services included in Class 41. A number of objections to registration of the mark were raised; however, the main objection was that the words AMERICA'S CUP are not a trade mark within the meaning of the Act, on the grounds that the club did not have the right to organise the event, which privilege went to the winner each time. Events such as the Davis Cup, World Series Cricket and the Olympics are organised by one identifiable body.

REGISTRATION

■ Administration and Register

[**14.85**] *Trade Marks Act 1995* (Cth), Part 19 provides for a Registrar and Deputy Registrar of trade marks. Part 20 in s 207 provides that there shall be kept at the Trade Marks Office a Register of Trade Marks into which particulars of marks are inserted together with other relevant information about marks such as the goods or services in respect of which it is to be used, and "all other matters that were on the old register", which include any corrections, alterations, rectifications or amendments, any disclaimers, limitations or conditions to which a mark is subject, and notice of any assignments or transmissions. This no longer includes details of registered user agreements, and "trafficking" in marks is no longer disallowed, although it may be poor commercial practice.

The previous legislation provided that the Register be divided into four parts. Part A comprised marks registered under the 1905 Act together with marks registered as distinctive since the commencement of the 1955 Act. Part B comprised marks which were not distinctive but which were capable of becoming so. Part C comprised certification trade marks and Part D, defensive trade marks. The Register still provides for recording of "registered marks, certification trade marks and defensive marks" (s 207) but no longer divides registered marks into Parts A and B, although many cases on trade marks refer to this division and it is useful to understand the difference. Essentially, Part A was for "inherently distinctive marks" and Part B for those marks which needed some degree of "acquired distinctiveness" to function as a mark. The distinction is explained at [**14.135**]. Section 41 of the 1995 Act deals with the difference between inherent and acquired distinctiveness.

For administrative convenience goods and services are divided into classes and registration is required for each class. This classification is based upon that settled by the 1957 Nice Agreement to which Australia has acceded.

▬▬▬ Trade Marks Regulations 1995, Schedule 1 ▬▬▬

[14.90] *Trade Marks Regulations 1995* (Cth), sch 1: Classification of goods and services (Regulation 3.1)

Part 1	Classes of goods

Item No (Class No)	Class of Goods (Class Heading)
1	Chemicals used in industry, science and photography, as well as in agriculture, horticulture and forestry; unprocessed artificial resins, unprocessed plastics; manures; fire extinguishing compositions; tempering and soldering preparations; chemical substances for preserving foodstuffs; tanning substances; adhesives used in industry
2	Paints, varnishes, lacquers; preservatives against rust and against deterioration of wood; colourants; mordants; raw natural resins; metals in foil and powder form for painters, decorators, printers and artists
3	Bleaching preparations and other substances for laundry use; cleaning, polishing, scouring and abrasive preparations; soaps; perfumery, essential oils, cosmetics, hair lotions; dentifrices
4	Industrial oils and greases; lubricants; dust absorbing, wetting and binding compositions; fuels (including motor spirit) and illuminants; candles, wicks
5	Pharmaceutical, veterinary and sanitary preparations; dietetic substances adapted for medical use, food for babies; plasters, materials for dressings; material for stopping teeth, dental wax; disinfectants; preparations for destroying vermin; fungicides, herbicides
6	Common metals and their alloys; metal building materials; transportable buildings of metal; materials of metal for railway tracks; non-electric cables and wires of common metal; ironmongery, small items of metal hardware; pipes and tubes of metal; safes; goods of common metal not included in other classes; ores
7	Machines and machine tools; motors and engines (except for land vehicles); machine coupling and transmission components (except for land vehicles); agricultural implements, other than hand operated; incubators for eggs
8	Hand tools and implements (hand operated); cutlery; side arms; razors
9	Scientific, nautical, surveying, electric, photographic, cinematographic, optical, weighing, measuring, signalling, checking (supervision), life-saving and teaching apparatus and instruments; apparatus for recording, transmission or reproduction of sound or images; magnetic data carriers, recording discs; automatic vending machines and mechanisms for coin operated apparatus; cash registers, calculating machines, data processing equipment and computers; fire-extinguishing apparatus
10	Surgical, medical, dental and veterinary apparatus and instruments, artificial limbs, eyes and teeth; orthopaedic articles; suture materials
11	Apparatus for lighting, heating, steam generating, cooking, refrigerating, drying, ventilating, water supply and sanitary purposes
12	Vehicles; apparatus for locomotion by land, air or water
13	Firearms, ammunition and projectiles; explosives; fireworks

14	Precious metals and their alloys and goods in precious metals or coated therewith, not included in other classes; jewellery, precious stones; horological and chronometric instruments
15	Musical instruments
16	Paper, cardboard and goods made from these materials, not included in other classes; printed matter; bookbinding material; photographs; stationery; adhesives for stationery or household purposes; artists' materials; paint brushes; typewriters and office requisites (except furniture); instructional and teaching material (except apparatus); plastic materials for packaging (not included in other classes); playing cards; printers' type; printing blocks
17	Rubber, gutta-percha, gum, asbestos, mica and goods made from these materials and not included in other classes; plastics in extruded form for use in manufacture; packing, stopping and insulating materials; flexible pipes, not of metal
18	Leather and imitations of leather, and goods made of these materials and not included in other classes; animal skins, hides; trunks and travelling bags; umbrellas, parasols and walking sticks; whips, harness and saddlery
19	Building materials (non-metallic); non-metallic rigid pipes for building; asphalt, pitch and bitumen; non-metallic transportable buildings; monuments, not of metal
20	Furniture, mirrors, picture frames; goods (not included in other classes) of wood, cork, reed, cane, wicker, horn, bone, ivory, whalebone, shell, amber, mother-of-pearl, meerschaum and substitutes for all these materials, or of plastics
21	Household or kitchen utensils and containers (not of precious metal or coated therewith); combs and sponges; brushes (except paint brushes); brush-making materials; articles for cleaning purposes; steel wool; unworked or semi-worked glass (except glass used in building); glassware, porcelain and earthenware not included in other classes
22	Ropes, string, nets, tents, awnings, tarpaulins, sails, sacks and bags (not included in other classes); padding and stuffing materials (except of rubber or plastics); raw fibrous textile materials
23	Yarns and threads, for textile use
24	Textiles and textile goods, not included in other classes; bed and table covers
25	Clothing, footwear, headgear
26	Lace and embroidery, ribbons and braid; buttons, hooks and eyes, pins and needles; artificial flowers
27	Carpets, rugs, mats and matting, linoleum and other materials for covering existing floors; wall hangings (non-textile)
28	Games and playthings; gymnastic and sporting articles not included in other classes; decorations for Christmas trees
29	Meat, fish, poultry and game; meat extracts; preserved, dried and cooked fruits and vegetables; jellies, jams, fruit sauces; eggs, milk and milk products; edible oils and fats
30	Coffee, tea, cocoa, sugar, rice, tapioca, sago, artificial coffee; flour and preparations made from cereals, bread, pastry and confectionery, ices; honey,

■■■■■■ Trade Marks Regulations 1995, Schedule 1 *continued*

	treacle; yeast, baking-powder; salt, mustard; vinegar, sauces (condiments); spices; ice
31	Agricultural, horticultural and forestry products and grains not included in other classes; live animals; fresh fruits and vegetables; seeds, natural plants and flowers; foodstuffs for animals, malt
32	Beers; mineral and aerated waters and other non-alcoholic drinks; fruit drinks and fruit juices; syrups and other preparations for making beverages
33	Alcoholic beverages (except beers)
34	Tobacco; smokers' articles; matches

Part 2   **Classes of services**

Item No (Class No)	Class of Services (Class Heading)
35	Advertising; business management; business administration; office functions
36	Insurance; financial affairs; monetary affairs; real estate affairs
37	Building construction; repair; installation services
38	Telecommunications
39	Transport; packaging and storage of goods; travel arrangement
40	Treatment of materials
41	Education; providing of training; entertainment, sporting and cultural activities
42	Scientific and technological services and research and design relating thereto; industrial analysis and research services; design and development of computer hardware and software; legal services
43	Services for providing food and drink; temporary accommodation
44	Medical services; veterinary services; hygienic and beauty care for human beings or animals; agriculture, horticulture and forestry services
45	Personal and social services rendered by others to meet the needs of individuals; security services for the protection of property and individuals

[14.95] The classes of registration set out as an administrative tool are not definitive in deciding if goods or services are the same or similar (s 14) or "closely related" (s 44) for the purposes of deciding whether signs conflict with or infringe existing registered signs. See, for example, *Coleman Company Inc v Igloo Products Corp* (1999) 48 IPR 158.

■ Eligibility for registration
[14.100] *Trade Marks Act 1995* (Cth), s 27(1) provides that "A person may apply for the registration of a trade mark in respect of goods and/or services" if they claim to be the owner of the mark (and are using or intending to use the mark, authorising or intending to authorise another to use it, or intending to assign the mark to a company about to be formed, which corporation will use the mark). *Trade Marks Act 1995* (Cth), s 28 allows the possibility of joint proprietorship. Section 58 provides for opposition to registration on the ground that the applicant is not the owner of the mark.

Authorship as the basis of proprietorship

███████████████████ **Aston v Harlee Manufacturing** ███████████████████

[14.105] *Aston v Harlee Manufacturing Co* (1960) 103 CLR 391 High Court of Australia

[On 14 May 1952 the applicant sought registration of the mark "Tastee Freez" in respect of iced milk. The respondent was a US franchisor of dairy and ice cream products which were franchised under the name "Tastee Freez". The respondent had applied for registration of that name as a trade mark in the US on 5 August 1950. The registration was effected on 27 April 1954. In December 1951 the applicant had had discussions with the respondent about operating as a franchisee. On 10 February 1956 notice of opposition to the applicant's registration was lodged by the respondent which on 3 April 1956 applied itself for the Tastee Freez mark.]

FULLAGAR J: **[398]** ... The case seems to me to be one of considerable difficulty. What s 27 doubtless primarily contemplates is the case where two or more rival claimants for the same mark, or nearly identical marks, assert a title acquired by user. In the present case there has been, even up to the present time, no relevant user of the mark in question by either party in Australia, but it does not follow that neither party is entitled to register the mark. Section 32 of the Act provides that any person claiming to be the proprietor of a trade mark may apply to the Registrar for the registration of his trade mark. The right to registration depends, therefore, on proprietorship of a mark. The conception of proprietorship, other than proprietorship acquired by a user which has made the mark distinctive of the applicant's goods, is a difficult conception, but it has been **[399]** explained by Dixon J in *Shell Co of Australia Ltd v Rohm & Haas Co* (1949) 78 CLR 601 at 625ff, where his Honour (at 626) refers to the history of the English legislation. His Honour quotes Cotton LJ as saying in *Re Hudson's Trade Marks* (1886) 32 Ch D 311 at 319, 320:

> "The difficulty is this: Is a man to be considered as entitled to the use of any trade mark when he has never used it at all? That is a difficulty, but I think the meaning is this. If a man has designed and first printed or formed any of those particular and distinctive devices which are referred to in the first part of s 10, he is then looked upon as the proprietor of that which is under that Act a trade mark, which will give him the right so soon as he registers it."

Dixon J then sums up the position by saying (at 627):

> "It is clear enough from the course of legislation and of decision that an application to register a trade mark so far unused must, equally with a trade mark the title to which depends on prior user, be founded on proprietorship. The basis of a claim to proprietorship in a trade mark so far unused has been found in the combined effect of authorship of the mark, the intention to use it upon or in connection with the goods and the applying for registration."

"Authorship", says his Honour a little later (at 628), "involves the origination or first adoption of the word or design as and for a trade mark".

The passages quoted above require careful consideration in relation to the present case. In the first place, I do not think that the requirement of "authorship" means that the applicant must be the true and first inventor: he has not to establish anything analogous to what an applicant for letters patent for an invention must establish. I do not think that an opponent of an application for registration of a trade mark could succeed by saying merely "I thought

▬▬▬▬ Aston v Harlee Manufacturing *continued*

of it first", or even "I thought of it first, and communicated it to the applicant". It is otherwise if the opponent has used the mark in relation to goods. In *Re Hick's Trade Mark* (1897) 22 VLR 636 at 640, Holroyd J, speaking for a Full Court, said:

> "In order to substantiate his application to be placed on the register for this word he must have claimed to be the proprietor, and the word 'proprietor' must be taken to mean the person entitled to the exclusive use of that name. If there is anyone else who would be interfered with by the registration of the word 'Empress' in the exercise of a right which such person has already acquired to use the same word in application to the same kind of thing, then Hicks **[400]** ought not to have been put on the register for that trade mark."

The reference in this passage to a "right acquired" does not, of course, mean that an opponent, or a person aggrieved on a motion to expunge, must show that he has acquired such a right to the mark at common law as would enable him to maintain an action for passing off.

In the second place, it would appear that an applicant may be the "author" of a trade mark, although he has deliberately copied or adopted a mark registered in a foreign country in respect of the same description of goods. In *Re Registered Trade Mark "Yanx": Ex parte Amalgamated Tobacco Corp Ltd* (1951) 82 CLR 199 at 202 Williams J said: "To try and register in Australia a word which the applicant to the knowledge of the respondent is using elsewhere on its cigarettes is sharp business practice. But it is not in itself fraudulent or a breach of the law." (I would think myself that it may or may not, according to circumstances, constitute "sharp business practice".) Again, it is otherwise if the opponent or person aggrieved has used the mark, for prior user by the foreign proprietor negatives the claim of the Australian applicant to "authorship". But the user must be user in Australia: the most extensive user by another person in foreign countries will not avail by itself to defeat an applicant for registration in this country. It has been said, however, that the courts frown on these borrowings from abroad, and very slight evidence of user in Australia has been held sufficient to protect the proprietor of a foreign trade mark: *Seven Up Co v OT Ltd* (1947) 75 CLR 203 at 211. A good example is *Blackadder v Good Roads Machinery Co Inc* (1926) 38 CLR 332. That was clearly, I think, not a case of fraud. The vital fact was that, as the court held, the goods were to be regarded as having "come into the Australian market" bearing the trade mark "Winner". Another good example perhaps an extreme example is the *Yanx* case (1951) 82 CLR 199. But, where there has clearly been no user at all in Australia, an applicant for a trade mark identical with a mark registered in a foreign country is entitled to be regarded, so far as Australia is concerned, as the "author" of the mark. I can see no reason why this should not be so. In *Seven Up Co v OT Ltd* (1947) 75 CLR 203 at 211, Williams J, after citing certain English authorities, said:

> "In my opinion the effect of these cases is that in the absence of fraud it is not unlawful for a trader to become the registered proprietor under the Trade Marks Act of a mark which has been used, however extensively, by another trader as a mark for similar goods in a foreign **[401]** country, provided the foreign mark has not been used at all in Australia at the date of the application for registration."

Latham CJ quoted this passage with approval (at 216) on an appeal from Williams J, which was dismissed.

There is another element mentioned by Dixon J in the *Shell Co's* case (1949) 78 CLR 601 at 627, which is stated as essential to the proprietorship of an unused trade mark. That

■■■■■■   Aston v Harlee Manufacturing *continued*

element is the intention of the applicant for registration to use it upon or in connection with goods. As to this I need only say that I do not regard his Honour as meaning that an applicant is required, in order to obtain registration, to establish affirmatively that he intends to use it. There is nothing in the Act or the Regulations which requires him to state such an intention at the time of application, and the making of the application itself is, I think, to be regarded as prima facie evidence of intention to use. I cannot think that the Registrar is called upon to institute an inquiry as to the intention of any applicant, and I think that, on an opposition or on a motion to expunge, the burden must rest on the opponent, or the person aggrieved, of proving the absence of intention. Again, I do not think that "intention" in this connection ought to be regarded as meaning an intention to use immediately or within any limited time. A manufacturer of (say) confectionery would, I should suppose, be entitled to register three trade marks in relation to confectionery, though he intended only to use two of them and had not made up his mind as to which he would use. If he in fact does not use any of them for the period specified in s 72, the unused mark or marks may be expunged under that section. On the other hand, a manufacturer of confectionery, who had no intention of ever manufacturing motor cars, might be held disentitled to register a mark in relation to motor cars: the effect of *Re Registered Trade Marks of John Batt & Co* [1898] 2 Ch 432; [1899] AC 428, is, I think, correctly stated in the first paragraph of the headnote to the report of the case before Romer J and the Court of Appeal.

A claim to proprietorship of a trade mark will be defeated if it is proved that to give effect to it would be to involve a fraud upon another person. A recent example is the case of *Farley (Aust) Pty Ltd v JR Alexander & Sons (Qld) Pty Ltd* (1946) 75 CLR 487, where Williams J held (at 492) that a registration had been fraudulently obtained, on the ground that a promise not to use the mark after existing stocks **[402]** had been disposed of had "lulled the applicant" (sc. for expungement) "into a state of false security". It would appear that something short of fraud may suffice to defeat an application for registration, or support an applicant for expungement. Thus Latham CJ in the *Seven Up* case (1947) 75 CLR 203 at 215 said: "User in Australia would be relevant. So also would facts establishing a breach of confidential relations or any fraud."

I have now stated the facts which I regard as relevant and the principles which I think I have to apply, and I now come to the first question which I have to determine. That is the question whether Aston is entitled, for the purposes of his application of 14 May 1952, to be regarded as the proprietor of the trade mark "Tastee Freez".

Prima facie he is, in my opinion, so entitled. Before the date of his application for registration neither Harlee nor anybody else had used the mark in Australia, and it follows that, so far as Australia is concerned, he was the author or originator of it.

... **[404]** ...

It may well be that a scrupulous businessman would not have done what Aston did without informing Harlee beforehand that he intended to make the application, or at least informing Harlee afterwards that he had done so. But I cannot find enough in this case to distinguish it from the *Seven Up* case (1947) 75 CLR 203. When once it is conceded, as a matter of law, that a person may apply for and obtain in Australia a valid registration of a trade mark registered and used in a foreign country but not used in Australia, I do not think that exceptions and qualifications should be introduced which are based merely on conceptions of commercial ethics. Aston's action may or may not be what Williams J in the *Yanx* case (1951) 82 CLR 199 at 202 called "sharp business practice", but what he did was done without active deception, without the saying or doing of **[405]** anything misleading and without, as I think, any breach of any confidence reposed in him.

■■■■■■ Aston v Harlee Manufacturing *continued*

For the above reasons I am of opinion that Aston is entitled to be treated as the proprietor of the trade mark in question. Since his application for registration is poor in time to that of Harlee, it follows that Harlee is not entitled to be treated as the proprietor of the mark. I propose to make a declaratory order accordingly.

Notes

[14.110] There are numerous examples of local traders adopting marks which have been registered and used overseas. In fact, it has been said that it is a "well established principle of Australian trade mark law that it is no offence to copy a foreign trade mark": *Sizzler Restaurants International Inc v Sabra Int Pty Ltd* (1990) 20 IPR 331 at 342. See also *Michael Sharwood & Partners Pty Ltd v Fuddruckers Inc* (1989) 15 IPR 188; *Jamieson v American Dairy Queen Corp* (1989) 18 IPR 101; *Riviera Leisurewear Pty Ltd v J Hepworth & Son Plc* (1987) 9 IPR 305; *Daimaru v Kabushiki Kaisha Daimaru* (1990) 19 IPR 129; *Dunlop Olympic Ltd v Cricket Hosiery Inc* (1990) 20 IPR 475. Proprietorship in Australia can be established by overseas trade mark owners by "a very small amount of use of the foreign mark": *Seven Up Co v OT Ltd* (1947) 75 CLR 203 at 211.

The *Trade Marks Act 1995* (Cth) introduced the concept of a "well-known mark" whereby a mark used overseas may be regarded as "known" to the Australian public, even if not "used" in this country in a trade mark context. This concept of being "well-known" does not, however, extend to protecting any prior use.

■ On what date does protection commence? (s 72)

See s 72.

Proprietor's use as criterion

■■■■■■■■■■■■■■■■ **Moorgate Tobacco v Philip Morris** ■■■■■■■

[14.115] *Moorgate Tobacco Co Ltd v Philip Morris Ltd* (1984) 156 CLR 414 High Court of Australia

[Philip Morris manufactured and distributed cigarettes in Australia under the trade mark KENT which it was licensed to use by Loew's Incorporated the owner of the mark in Australia. Between 1975 and 1976 there were discussions between Loew's and Philip Morris on the question of extending the scope of the licence agreement to embrace the proposed marks KENT'S GOLDEN LIGHTS and KENT'S SPECIAL MILD. Advertising material and cartons of the cigarettes displaying the proposed marks which had been test marketed in the United States and Belgium were sent to Philip Morris.

In June 1977 the appellant entered into an agreement with Loew's to purchase its international cigarette business, including the Australian KENT mark. On 12 July 1977 Philip Morris applied for registration in Australia of the mark GOLDEN LIGHTS, the appellant argued that pursuant to the agreement between Philip Morris and Loew's, which the appellant had purchased, it was entitled to the GOLDEN LIGHTS mark.]

DEANE J: [431] …The starting point of the first argument is the proposition that, at the time when Philip Morris applied for registration of the trade mark GOLDEN LIGHTS Moorgate had "the right in Australia to the trade mark [432] KENT GOLDEN LIGHTS". It is conceded that, unless that proposition is made good Moorgate can obtain no protection in respect of the mark GOLDEN LIGHTS from the provisions of the licence agreement protecting the "Trademark Rights" of the licensor. The only basis upon which Moorgate seeks to make good its claim to such a "right" in Australia is that Loew's had become the proprietor of the trade mark KENT GOLDEN LIGHTS where for the purposes of s 40(1) of the *Trade Marks Act 1955* (Cth) with the result that it was entitled to apply for registration of the mark and to resist the application of any one else who purported to apply for registration of it as "the proprietor". It was conceded by Moorgate that it could not claim to have become the proprietor of the mark as an unused mark during the currency of the licence agreement since it did not apply for registration of the mark until more than two weeks after the licence agreement had expired. That being so, Moorgate's claim to have become "the proprietor" of the mark KENT GOLDEN LIGHTS must, of necessity, be based upon prior use: see *Kendall Co v Muslyn Paint & Chemicals* (1963) 109 CLR 300 at 304-305.

The prior use of a trade mark which may suffice, at least if combined with local authorship, to establish that a person has acquired in Australia the statutory status of "proprietor" of the mark, is public use in Australia of the mark as a trade mark, that is to say, a use of the mark in relation to goods for the purpose of indicating or so as to indicate a connection in the course of trade between the goods with respect to which the mark is used and that person (see, generally, *Shell Co of Australia Ltd v Esso Standard Oil (Aust) Ltd* (1963) 109 CLR 407 at 423-424: *Re Registered Trade Mark "Yanx"; Ex parte Amalgamated Tobacco Corp Ltd* (1951) 82 CLR 199 at 204-205; and the definition of "trade mark" in s 6(1) of the *Trade Marks Act*). The requisite use of the mark need not be sufficient to establish a local reputation and there is authority to support the proposition that evidence of but slight use in Australia will suffice to protect a person who is the owner and user overseas of a mark which another is seeking to appropriate by registration under the *Trade Marks Act*. In such a case, the court "seizes upon a very small amount of use of the foreign mark in Australia to hold that it has become identified with and distinctive of the goods of the foreign trader in Australia": see *Seven Up Co v OT Ltd* (1947) 75 CLR 203 at 211; [1947] ALR 436 at 437; *Aston v* **[433]** *Harlee Manufacturing Co* (1960) 103 CLR 391 at 400. In so far as the trade mark KENT GOLDEN LIGHTS is concerned, Loew's was the author, owner and user of that mark in the US. Assuming, in its favour, that evidence of but slight use in the course of trade in Australia would suffice to establish its status as proprietor of the mark, as distinct from merely precluding another from establishing local authorship, the question arises whether there was evidence of even such slight use. For Philip Morris, it is submitted that there was no evidence at all of any relevant use.

To establish prior use of the mark in Australia, Moorgate relies upon evidence that, during or in connection with discussions between Loew's and Philip Morris about the introduction of the low tar and nicotine cigarette in Australia, packets of cigarettes and associated advertising material displaying the name KENT GOLDEN LIGHTS were handed personally, or in one instance sent by mail, to representatives of Philip Morris in Australia. That evidence indicates that there were at least three occasions on which such cigarette packets and advertising material were so delivered. At the times when those items were so delivered, there was no intention on the part of Loew's that it would itself trade in the goods in Australia. Nor, for that matter, had it been decided what name would be used if Philip Morris were, under licence from Loew's, to commence to manufacture and market the goods in Australia at some indefinite future time.

The court was referred to a large number of cases and to some administrative decisions in which consideration has been given to what constitutes a use or user of a trade mark for the

▬▬▬▬ Moorgate Tobacco v Philip Morris *continued*

purposes of the statutory notion of proprietorship of the mark before registration. The cases establish that it is not necessary that there be an actual dealing in goods bearing the trade mark before there can be a local use of the mark as a trade mark. It may suffice that imported goods which have not actually reached Australia have been offered for sale in Australia under the mark (*Re Registered Trade Mark "Yanx"; Ex parte Amalgamated Tobacco Corp Ltd* (1951) 82 CLR 199 at 204-205) or that the mark has been used in an advertisement of the goods in the course of trade: *Shell Co of Australia v Esso Standard Oil (Aust) Ltd* (1963) 109 CLR 407 at 422. In such cases, however, it is possible to identify **[434]** an actual trade or offer to trade in the goods bearing the mark or an existing intention to offer or supply goods bearing the mark in trade. In the present case, there was not, at any relevant time, any actual trade or offer to trade in goods bearing the mark in Australia or any existing intention to offer or supply such goods in trade. There was no local use of the mark as a trade mark at all; there were merely preliminary discussions and negotiations about whether the mark would be so used. The cigarette packets and associated material were delivered to Philip Morris to demonstrate what Loew's was marketing in other countries and what Philip Morris might market, under licence from Loew's, if it decided to manufacture and trade in the goods in Australia and to use the mark locally at some future time. There was no relevant trade in the goods in Australia and the delivery of the cigarette packets and associated material to Philip Morris did not, in the circumstances, constitute a relevant user or use in Australia of the mark KENT GOLDEN LIGHTS for the purpose of indicating or so as to indicate a connection in the course of trade between the new cigarettes and Loew's. It follows that Moorgate has failed to establish proprietorship of the mark KENT GOLDEN LIGHTS either at the time Philip Morris applied to register the mark GOLDEN LIGHTS or at the time when the licence agreement expired. It is unnecessary to consider whether, if Moorgate had succeeded in establishing such proprietorship, its rights in respect of the mark KENT GOLDEN LIGHTS would have been protected by the provisions of Article VI of the licence agreement, notwithstanding that the new low tar and nicotine cigarettes were not "Licensed Products" under that agreement or whether, even if its rights in the mark KENT GOLDEN LIGHTS were within the protection of Article VI, that protection extended to preclude Philip Morris from applying for registration of the mark GOLDEN LIGHTS. It should, perhaps, be mentioned that Moorgate did not argue in this court that the fact that advertisements of the US' KENT GOLDEN LIGHTS cigarettes came into Australia via American magazines meant that there had been a relevant use or user of the name in Australia: see *Seven Up Co v OT Ltd* (1947) 75 CLR 203 at 211; [1947] ALR 436 at 437.

[Gibbs CJ, Mason, Wilson and Dawson JJ concurred.]

▬▬▬▬▬▬▬▬▬▬▬▬▬▬▬▬▬▬▬▬▬▬▬▬▬▬▬▬▬▬▬

■ What kind of "use" is sufficient?

▬▬▬▬▬▬▬▬ **Lomas v Winton Shire Council** ▬▬▬▬▬▬▬▬

[14.120] *Lomas v Winton Shire Council* (2002) FCAFC 413 Federal Court of Australia, Full Court

COOPER, KIEFEL AND EMMETT JJ:

The proceeding
2. On 20 November 1997 ("the Priority Date"), Ms Lomas lodged Application No 749100 ("the Application") for registration, under the Act, of the trade mark "Waltzing Matilda" in respect

of various goods and services in classes 29, 30, 31, 35 and 42 ("the Trade Mark"). Insofar as is presently relevant, the following goods and services were specified in relation to classes 29, 30 and 42:

- Class 29: Prepared foods included in this class;
- Class 30: Prepared foods included in this class;
- Class 42: Services in class 42 namely, the establishment, operation and conduct of outlets, venues and facilities for the supplying and provision of meals and refreshments, including restaurants, cafes, food outlets, meal rooms, dining venues, eateries, cafeterias, canteens, snack bars, takeaway stores and fast-food outlets; providing foodstuffs and beverages to the said outlets, venues and facilities; catering services; advisory and consultancy services pertaining to the said services.

3. On 7 September 1999 notices of opposition were lodged by the respondents to the application for leave to appeal, Winton Shire Council ("Winton") and The Waltzing Matilda Centre Limited ("the Company"). Winton is a local governmental authority. The Company was established under the auspices of Winton and two of its directors are representatives of Winton.

4. On 17 August 2000, a delegate of the Registrar of Trade Marks ("the Registrar") determined that the oppositions by Winton and the Company failed on all grounds. The delegate decided that the Application should be registered and directed that registration proceed unless, within 30 days, the Registrar was served with a copy of a notice of appeal. The delegate directed that, in the event of such an appeal, registration not occur before the appeal was decided or discontinued.

5. Winton and the Company appealed to the Federal Court from the decision of the delegate. The grounds of appeal, as specified by Winton and the Company in their particulars, were as follows:

(i) Ms Lomas is not the owner of the Trade Mark as she is not the first user of the Trade Mark in Australia on or in connection with the goods and/or services specified in the Application;

... the primary judge concluded that ... (i), which is based on s 58 of the Act, had been made out....

The Factual Background

20. In April 1895 the song "Waltzing Matilda" ("the Song"), the words of which were written by A B "Banjo" Patterson, was first performed in the town of Winton. The words to the Song had been composed at Dagworth Station, about 100 kilometres from the town of Winton. In April 1995 Winton hosted celebrations, in the town of Winton, of the centenary of the first performance of the Song. The celebrations consisted of a programme of special events, entertainment, historical displays and exhibitions over twelve days. The programme featured different elements of the themes of the Song, its history and the connection between the Song and the town of Winton.

21. A central feature of the marketing and publicity campaign for the celebration was the use of a logo as follows:

6 APRIL 1995

▬▬▬▬ Lomas v Winton Shire Council *continued*

The logo shows a figure of a swagman with an animal over his shoulder in a swag, with the words "1895 Waltzing Matilda Centenary 1995" in a scroll across the figure of the swagman, the words "Waltzing Matilda Centenary" above the logo and the words "Winton Queensland" and the date "6 April 1995" below it. Food and beverages provided during the celebrations included damper, billy tea and food cooked in camp ovens by a person employed by Winton dressed in the character costuming of a swagman.

22. From about March 1995 to April 1995, a store was established in the main street of Winton offering a range of products, brochures and material promoting the celebrations and the town of Winton. Products available for sale included stubby holders, pannikin or tin cups, tea towels, T-shirts, teaspoons, postcards and caps. The tin cup, for instance, had "Waltzing Matilda Centenary Winton Queensland 1895-1995" printed on the outside of it, and the tea towel had a stylized swagman set against a depiction of the Southern Cross constellation under which the words "Waltzing Matilda Centenary Winton Queensland 1895" appeared.

23. In March 1995 plans for the design and development of a permanent attraction in the town of Winton celebrating the Song, to be known as the Waltzing Matilda Centre ("the Centre"), were prepared. In October 1996 Winton decided to construct and operate the Centre. In February 1997 the foundation stone for the Centre was laid. On 28 August 1997 a logo for the Centre was finalised and it has been used since then. From October 1997 Winton conducted pre-opening advertising and publicity for the Centre.

24. In particular, in October 1997, Wintonh circulated a brochure calling attention to "The Waltzing Matilda Centre". The brochure contains the following reference to an aspect of the proposed activities of Winton at the Centre:

"Savour old fashioned, home baked bush fare at the Country Kitchen"

25. Winton also caused an advertisement ("the Advertisement") to be published in the 1 November 1997 edition of the Accommodation and Touring Guide of the Royal Automobile Club of Queensland ("the RACQ Guide"). The Advertisement was headed "THE WALTZING MATILDA CENTRE". Next to a representation of a rural scene the words "Outback Qld's Newest Attraction Open Easter 1998" appear in a starburst.

26. The following text then appears:

"Travel the Matilda Highway to Winton, the home of the Waltzing Matilda legend then visit the outback's exciting new attraction—the Waltzing Matilda Centre.

This national centre combines history and creative technology to present the Waltzing Matilda legend, life in the bush, interactive displays with exhibitions which capture the true spirit of the Australian character as well as the famous QANTILDA Museum collection.

Visit the Waltzing Matilda General Store for unique souvenirs and the Waltzing Matilda Country Kitchen for a traditional homestead meal.

Open 7 days: 9.00 am-5.00 pm.
For information: Winton Shire Council.
PO Box 228
Winton QLD 4730".

27. Immediately under the Advertisement in the RACQ Guide, the following entry appears:

"WALTZING MATILDA CENTRE, WALTZING MATILDA CENTRE AND QANTILDA MUSEUM.

[Telephone Number] Winton, the home of WALTZING MATILDA, will open the WALTZING MATILDA CENTRE based upon our national song during Easter 1998. Plan to be part of the opening celebrations from 9-13 April 1998. Include the WALTZING MATILDA CENTRE and QANTILDA MUSEUM in your next outback trip."

28. In March 1998 Winton began operating the Centre. Despite the suggestion in the Advertisement, at no time since the publication of the Advertisement has there been any use of the name "Waltzing Matilda Country Kitchen", whether in connection with the Centre or otherwise. On the other hand, from the time when the Centre began operating, there has been an eating establishment conducted in the Centre under the name "Coolibah Country Kitchen".

29. The Company was formed in January 1999. Since its formation, it has operated the Centre, including the eating establishment called the "Coolibah Country Kitchen".

The Decision of the Primary Judge

30. The primary judge considered that the publication of the Advertisement was evidence of "an existing intention to offer or supply goods bearing the mark in trade" and concluded that there was, in November 1997, a genuine intention to offer to supply food stuffs and restaurant services bearing the mark "Waltzing Matilda". His Honour considered that the use of the words "Country Kitchen" did not defeat that conclusion, in the same way that the description "Waltzing Matilda Restaurant" or "Waltzing Matilda Café" would be a use by Ms Lomas of the Trade Mark in relation to goods or services within the classes in respect of which the application was made.

31. His Honour found that Winton used the Trade Mark in relation to the Centre and rejected the contention of Ms Lomas that the relevant marks were "The Waltzing Matilda Centre" and "Waltzing Matilda Centenary Celebrations". Consistently with that conclusion, his Honour considered that, in the Advertisement, the Trade Mark was used rather than the mark "Waltzing Matilda Country Kitchen".

32. His Honour concluded that the goods and services of that prior use of the Trade Mark by Winton were the same as those in the Application, or were at least "the same kind of thing", referring to In *Re Hicks' Trademark* (1897) 22 VLR 636 at 640. Accordingly, his Honour found that, since Winton had used the Trade Mark before the Priority Date, Winton was the owner of the Trade Mark as at the Priority Date and that, therefore, Ms Lomas was not the owner of the Trade Mark. Accordingly, his Honour held that the opposition should succeed in so far as it was based on s 58 of the Act.

Grounds of Appeal

33. The questions that would be raised on appeal are limited to the operation of s 58 of the Act. Ms Lomas formulated four so-called errors on the part of the primary judge as follows:

(1) His Honour erred in concluding that there was use of the Trade Mark in relation to country kitchen services since, if there was use of a trade mark by Winton before the Priority Date, the trade mark used was "Waltzing Matilda Country Kitchen".

(2) Any such use as was made of the Trade Mark in the Advertisement was not use of the Trade Mark such as would give ownership of that trade mark to Winton.

(3) Contrary to his Honour's conclusion, an inference should not be drawn that there was an intention to use the Trade Mark as at the Priority Date since Winton's intention as at the date of publication of the Advertisement had changed by the time of commencement of the operation of the Centre in March 1998.

(4) The only services in Class 42 in respect of which there was prior use of the Trade Mark in relation to country kitchen services were:

▓▓▓▓▓ Lomas v Winton Shire Council *continued*

"The establishment, operation and conduct of outlets, venues and facilities for the supplying and provision of meals and refreshments, including restaurants, cafes, food outlets, meal rooms, dining venues, eateries, cafeterias, canteens, snack bars, take away stores and fast food outlets."

Accordingly, any prior use by Winton found by the primary judge was not such as to extend to the following services in Class 42:

"Providing food stuffs and beverages to the said outlets, venues and facilities; catering services; advisory and consultancy services pertaining to the said services."

Use of the Trade Mark by Winton

34. It is clear that the Company has never used the Trade Mark in any sense. The question is whether, by causing the Advertisement to be published in the RACQ guide, Winton used the Trade Mark in such a way as to become the owner of it within the meaning of the Act.

35. On questions of fact and degree involving matters of judgment and impression, minds may differ. Thus, in a doubtful case, respect and weight should be given to the views of a primary judge. That approach should not, however, be a fetter on an appellate court in giving effect to its own conclusion where it is definitely of a contrary view to that taken by a primary judge—see *SAP Australia Pty Ltd v Sapient Australia Pty Ltd* [1999] FCA 1821 at [38].

36. The legislative scheme relating to opposition proceedings ... indicates that an opponent has the onus of establishing the ground of opposition relied on. In the present context, that means that Winton and the Company must establish that Ms Lomas was not the owner of the Trade Mark as at the Priority date, at least on the balance of probabilities. On one view, they may be required to establish that she was clearly not the owner ....

37. The basis of any claim to ownership of a trade mark so far unused is to be found in the combined effect of authorship of the mark, the intention to use it upon or in connection with goods or services and applying for registration of the mark—*Shell Company of Australia Ltd v Rohm and Haas Company & Anor* (1949) 78 CLR 601 at 627 ("Shell Company Case"). Authorship in that sense involves the origination or first adoption of the word as and for a trade mark—*Aston v Harlee Manufacturing Company* (1960) 103 CLR 391 at 399.

38. Thus, if the Trade Mark had not been used prior to the Priority Date in connection with the goods and services specified in the Application, Ms Lomas should be treated as the owner of the Trade Mark. On the other hand, if Winton is able to establish that, as at the Priority Date, it was the owner of the Trade Mark and not Ms Lomas, the opposition based on s 58 would succeed. The only basis advanced by Winton in support of its opposition is that it became the owner of the Trade Mark by reason of the publication of the Advertisement and the inferences that can be drawn from such publication.

39. The question of substance that is raised by the proceeding is what constitutes a use or user of a trade mark for the purposes of the statutory concept of ownership of the mark prior to registration. It is not necessary that there be an actual dealing in goods bearing a trade mark before there can be said to be use of that mark as a trade mark in Australia. For example, there may be use where goods intended to be imported into Australia have not actually reached Australia but have been offered for sale in Australia under the mark. It may even be possible to establish use where the mark has been used in an advertisement of goods in the course of trade in circumstances where there is an existing intention to offer or supply goods bearing the mark in trade or there is an actual trade or offer to trade in the goods bearing the mark—*Moorgate Tobacco Co Ltd v Phillip Morris Ltd and Anor* [No. 2] (1984) 156 CLR 414 at 433-4. However, where there is no actual trade or offer to trade in goods bearing the relevant mark in Australia or any existing intention to offer or supply such goods in trade, but merely preliminary discussions and negotiations about whether the mark would be so used, there is

no use so as to constitute ownership of the mark (see *Moorgate Tobacco* (No.2) at 434). In reaching his conclusion, the primary judge clearly had regard to those principles.

40. The evidence indicates that there have been three uses by Winton of the expression "Country Kitchen": first on its own in the brochure of October 1997, then in conjunction with "Waltzing Matilda" in the Advertisement and finally in conjunction with "Coolibah" in the operation of the Centre. That tends to suggest that the expression may be descriptive of a kind of service, being an outlet, venue or facility for the supply and provision of meals and refreshments that can be characterised as a "country kitchen". On the other hand, the use of capital letters is more indicative of a trade name.

41. The Advertisement was headed "THE WALTZING MATILDA CENTRE" and invited tourists to visit "the outback's exciting new attraction - the Waltzing Matilda Centre". It referred twice to "the Waltzing Matilda Legend". It also invited tourists to visit "the Waltzing Matilda General Store for unique souvenirs". Thus, the Advertisement was drawing attention to the proposed facilities of the Centre, which were to include a general store, for unique souvenirs, and a country kitchen, for traditional homestead meals.

42. The absence of any reference in the brochure to "Waltzing Matilda" in mentioning of the country kitchen, and the fact that, when it commenced operation in April 1998, the country kitchen was called the "Coolibah Country Kitchen", suggests that the reference to "Waltzing Matilda" in connection with a country kitchen in the Advertisement was no more than a reference to the proposed facility within the Centre. The lack of constancy in the usage by Winton of the expression "Country Kitchen" gives rise to an inference that Winton took some time in forming a settled intention as to the name under which the proposed country kitchen facility would trade.

43. The Court should not hasten to find that a name given to a centre or business superstructure is automatically given to every actual or proposed facility within it. The fact that Winton, in the Advertisement, separated the proposed facilities such as the "country kitchen" and the "souvenir shop" and then subsequently named the country kitchen the "Coolibah Country Kitchen" suggests that the "Waltzing Matilda" name applied to the Centre rather than to every component within it.

44. The Advertisement does not signify that Winton was intending, in November 1997, to offer services using the Trade Mark. Nor does it signify that Winton was, in November 1997, offering to provide country kitchen services at some later time under the Trade Mark. Winton had no intention of providing country kitchen services in November 1997, whether in connection with the Trade Mark or otherwise. It did not intend to provide any such services before April 1998.

45. We are not persuaded, on the balance of probabilities, that the Advertisement by itself can be characterised as a use of the Trade Mark in relation to country kitchen services in the course of trade, such that it is possible to identify an intention, existing before the Priority Date, to offer or supply country kitchen services using the Trade Mark. That is the only basis advanced by Winton and the Company in support of the contention that Winton and not Mrs Lomas was the owner of the Trade Mark as at the Priority Date within the principles of the Shell Company Case. Further, we are certainly not persuaded that the Application should clearly be rejected on the ground that Ms Lomas was not the owner of the Trade Mark as at the Priority Date.

Specification of Goods and Services

46. In any event, while the services of a country kitchen may be characterised as "the establishment, operation and conduct of an outlet, venue or facility for the supplying and provision of meals and refreshments", conducting an outlet, venue or facility, which can

▰▰▰▰▰ Lomas v Winton Shire Council *continued*

properly be characterised as a country kitchen providing traditional homestead meals, does not involve:

- providing foodstuffs and beverages to outlets, venues and facilities for the supplying of meals and refreshments;
- catering services; or
- advisory and consultancy services pertaining to the establishment, operation and conduct of outlets, venues and facilities for the supplying and provision of meals and refreshments.

It follows that, even if the opposition based on s 58 succeeded, the primary judge erred insofar as his Honour directed that the specification of services in Class 42 be deleted entirely.

...

Conclusion

48. In the light of the conclusion that Winton had not used the Trade Mark so as to deprive Ms Lomas of ownership as at the Priority Date, the opposition should fail.

■ Processing applications

[14.125] Following lodgment of an application in the approved form the examiner is required by *Trade Marks Act 1995* (Cth), s 31 to ascertain and report whether the application meets the prescribed requirements and the trade mark is capable of registration under the Act. Where an adverse report ensues, the applicant is permitted by s 33(4) to amend the application to remove the objection. An appeal lies to the Federal Court from the Registrar's refusal to accept an application or from the imposition of any conditions by the Registrar (s 35). Part of the art of getting a trade mark registered is engaging in dialogue with the examiner as to the registrability of signs for which registration is sought. Clients will frequently want to register something too descriptive, or otherwise lacking distinctiveness and a well argued debate may secure success even if queries are raised. In *Blount Inc v Registrar of Trade Marks* (1998) 40 IPR 498 the court determined that the effect of s 33 is that where "the Act requires the Registrar to be '*satisfied*' of any matter, it is to be understood as requiring that he or she be persuaded of the matter according to the balance of probabilities (*Rejfeck v McElroy* (1965) 112 CLR 517 at 521)." See also *Registrar for Trade Marks v Woolworths PLC* (1999) 45 IPR 411.

Acceptance of an application is advertised in the *Official Journal* (s 34). A three-month period then commences during which a notice of opposition may be lodged (s 52). Any person may oppose the registration of a mark. The grounds are the same grounds on which an application may be rejected and those commonly relied upon include lack of distinctiveness of a mark; earlier conflicting registration, mark confusing, scandalous or contrary to law and lack of intention to use the mark in good faith. Opposition proceedings require a minimum of eighteen months to conclude, with most taking more than two years. Section 39 restricts from registration marks that are excluded by regulation, and s 40 requires that a mark must be able to be represented graphically, so that smells and sounds have to be capable of description in words or diagrams.

If no notice of opposition is lodged the mark becomes registered. Registration is for an initial period of ten years from the date of application. Further renewals of ten years may be obtained indefinitely. Where a notice of opposition has been lodged, the opponent is required to lodge evidence in support, to which the applicant is permitted a reply.

■ Convention applications

[14.130] Where an application for registration is made in Australia within six months after the first application for the mark in a "Convention country" (most countries are signatories to the relevant intellectual property conventions) *Trade Marks Act 1995* (Cth), s 29 deems the date of application for Australian purposes to be the date of lodging the convention application.

REGISTRABLE MARKS

■ Distinctiveness: Inherent and acquired

[14.135] *Trade Marks Act 1995* (Cth), s 41 sets out the grounds for rejecting a mark on the basis that it is not "capable of distinguishing the applicant's goods or services in respect of which the trade mark is sought to be registered". There are two aspects to being "capable of distinguishing"; the mark is either "inherently adapted" to do so, or has or will acquire distinctiveness. Before 1995, the register used to be divided into Part A for inherently distinctive marks, and Part B for those which had to be used and acquire reputation before being seen as distinctive of the applicant's goods or services. However, every mark had to have some "inherent adaptability" about it. Under the 1995 Act, there is a "scale" of registrability beginning with marks that are inherently adapted to distinguish (s 41(3)) and contemplating a mix of inherent and factually distinctive criteria, including use of the mark and other circumstances (s 41(5)). A totally "unadapted" to distinguish mark may be registered, but only if the Registrar is convinced that the mark has been used enough to achieve recognition in the market place (s 41(6)).

The following cases discuss the concept of distinctiveness, both inherent and acquired. A note to s 41 indicates that marks will generally not be "inherently adapted to distinguish" if they consist of a sign normally referring to kind, quality, quantity, intended purpose, value, geographical origin, or some other characteristic of the goods or services including time of production of goods or rendering of services. The requirement of distinctiveness applies to all "signs", not only word marks, but artwork, pictures, illustrations or logos can all be registered. However, if amounting to little more than an illustration of a product or some description of it, the mark will not be "distinctive".

The new types of signs highlighted in the *Trade Marks Act 1995 (Cth)* (that is, shapes, colours, smells, sounds and aspects of packaging) have caused some confusion in terms of how such marks can be distinctive. The ACIP, *Review of Enforcement of Trade Marks Issues Paper* (2002) noted perceptions that such applications were being treated unfairly by examiners, who refused to accept them on the same grounds applied to traditional word or logo marks. How a "shape" mark and a "colour" mark can be considered distinctive is considered in the cases below.

■ General principles/geographic names

▬▬▬ Clark Equipment v Registrar of Trade Marks ▬▬▬

[14.140] *Clark Equipment Co v Registrar of Trade Marks* (1964) 111 CLR 511 High Court of Australia

[The applicant sought to register the trade mark MICHIGAN in respect of tractor shovels, front end loaders and other heavy earth moving equipment. Registration was refused by the Registrar.]

▬▬▬ Clark Equipment v Registrar of Trade Marks *continued*

KITTO J: **[512]** On the evidence before me I am satisfied that in Australia the word MICHIGAN has been extensively used by the appellant for more than 20 years as a mark to distinguish its goods of the description in respect of which registration is sought, and that its use of the word for that purpose, in advertisements and upon its products themselves, has resulted in a widespread recognition of the word, among persons concerned with products of the kind, as distinguishing the appellant's goods from the goods of other persons. But s 26 makes it plain that that is not enough to entitle the appellant to the registration it seeks. I need not dwell upon **[513]** the point that the word "registrable" in s 25(1) is appropriate to allow for, and at least does not displace, the view often expressed or implied in judgments of the courts that the Registrar has a discretion to refuse registration even where the express requirements of the Act appear to be satisfied. I am concerned more with the fact that s 26, having in subs (1) denied registrability unless the mark is "adapted to distinguish" the applicant's goods, by subs (2) dissects the expression "adapted to distinguish" so as to show that two inquiries are relevant not only an inquiry concerning acquired distinctiveness but an inquiry concerning the inherent fitness of the mark for the purpose of distinguishing the applicant's goods from those of other persons. It is undeniable that a mark which, considered by itself, would seem unadapted to that purpose, because its natural signification is against a notion that goods to which it is applied are the goods of the applicant and of no one else, may yet come by actual use or by virtue of special circumstances to be so closely associated with the applicant's goods in the minds of the relevant public that its apparently disqualifying signification is effectively obscured, and distinctiveness in fact is thus achieved. But although such a measure of practical success with the mark may well provide a sufficient foundation for a passing off action, the *Trade Marks Act* does not accept it as necessarily sufficient for the special protection which it affords to registered trade marks. True, the Act does not say that a mark which has any degree of natural unsuitability to distinguish an applicant's goods shall be refused registration notwithstanding that it has acquired a degree of distinctiveness in relation to his goods; but it does require that if the mark is to any extent inherently unadapted for the purpose that fact shall be weighed in the scales against the degree of acquired distinctiveness in determining the ultimate question whether the mark is registrable as being "adapted to distinguish" the applicant's goods.

That ultimate question must not be misunderstood. It is not whether the mark will be adapted to distinguish the registered owner's goods if it be registered and other persons consequently find themselves precluded from using it. The question is whether the mark, considered quite apart from the effects of registration, is such that by its use the applicant is likely to attain his object of thereby distinguishing his goods from the goods of others. In *Registrar of Trade Marks v W & G Du Cros Ltd* [1913] AC 624 at 634, 635 Lord Parker of Waddington, having remarked upon the difficulty of finding the right criterion by which to determine whether a proposed mark **[514]** is or is not "adapted to distinguish" the applicant's goods, defined the crucial question practically as I have stated it, and added two sentences which have often been quoted but to which it is well to return for an understanding of the problem in a case such as the present. His Lordship said:

> "The applicant's chance of success in this respect [ie in distinguishing his goods by means of the mark, apart from the effects of registration] must, I think, largely depend upon whether other traders are likely, in the ordinary course of their businesses and without any improper motive, to desire to use the same mark, or some mark nearly resembling it, upon or in connection with their own goods. It is apparent from the history of trade marks in this country that both the legislature and the courts have always shown a natural disinclination to allow any person to obtain by registration under the *Trade Marks Act* a monopoly in what others may legitimately desire to use."

The interests of strangers and of the public are thus bound up with the whole question, as Hamilton LJ pointed out in the case of *RJ Lea Ltd* [1913] 1 Ch 446 at 463; (1913) 30 RPC 216 at 227; but to say this is not to treat the question as depending upon some vague notion of public policy: it is to insist that the question whether a mark is adapted to distinguish be tested by reference to the likelihood that other persons, trading in goods of the relevant kind and being actuated only by proper motives in the exercise, that is to say, of the common right of the public to make honest use of words forming part of the common heritage, for the sake of the signification which they ordinarily possess will think of the word and want to use it in connection with similar goods in any manner which would infringe a registered trade mark granted in respect of it.

The fact that this is the test is the basic reason for the frequent refusal, exemplified in this court by the case of *Thomson v B Seppelt & Sons Ltd* (1925) 37 CLR 305, to register as a trade mark a word of prima facie geographical signification. It is well settled that a geographical name, when used as a trade mark for a particular category of goods, may be saved by the nature of the goods or by some other circumstance from carrying its prima facie geographical signification, and that for that reason it may be held to be adapted to distinguish the applicant's goods. Where that is so it is because to an honest competitor the idea of using that name in relation to such goods or in such circumstances would simply not occur: see per Lord Simonds in the *Yorkshire Copper Works* case (1954) 71 RPC 150 at 154. This is the case, for example, where the word as applied to the relevant [515] goods is in effect a fancy name, such as "North Pole" in connection with bananas: *A Bailey & Co Ltd v Clark Son & Morland Ltd* (the *Glastonbury* case [1938] AC 557 at 562; (1938) 55 RPC 253 at 257) (see also the *Livron* case (1937) 54 RPC 327 at 339), or where by reason of user or other circumstances it has come to possess, when used in respect of the relevant goods, a distinctiveness in fact which eclipses its primary signification. Compare in the case of a descriptive word: *Dunlop Rubber Co's Application* (1942) 59 RPC 134. But the probability that some competitor, without impropriety, may want to use the name of a place on his goods must ordinarily increase in proportion to the likelihood that goods of the relevant kind will in fact emanate from that place. A descriptive word is in like case: the more apt a word is to describe the goods, the less inherently apt it is to distinguish them as the goods of a particular manufacturer. This may seem at first blush a paradox, as Lord Simonds and Lord Asquith suggested in the *Yorkshire Copper Works* case (1954) 71 RPC 150 at 154, 156, but surely not when Lord Parker's exposition of the subject is borne in mind.

The consequence is that the name of a place or of an area, whether it be a district or a county, a state or a country, can hardly ever be adapted to distinguish one person's goods from the goods of others when used simpliciter or with no addition save a description or designation of the goods, if goods of the kind are produced at the place or in the area or if it is reasonable to suppose that such goods may in the future be produced there. In such a case, the name is plainly not inherently ie in its own nature, adapted to distinguish the applicant's goods; there is necessarily great difficulty in proving that by reason of use or other circumstances it does in fact distinguish his goods; and even where that difficulty is overcome there remains the virtual if not complete impossibility of satisfying the Registrar or the court that the effect of granting registration will not be to deny the word to a person who is likely to want to use it, legitimately, in connection with his goods for the sake of the geographical reference which it is inherently adapted to make. The leading authorities on the subject include the *Yorkshire Copper Works* case (1954) 71 RPC 150 (the judgment of Lord Evershed in that case when it was in the Court of Appeal (1953) 70 RPC 1 contains a valuable discussion of the topic), the *Glastonbury* case [1938] AC 557; (1938) 55 RPC 253 and the *Liverpool Electric*

Cable Co case (1928) 46 RPC 99. These cases show, as the Registrar said in *Dan River Trade Mark* [1962] RPC 157 at 160 in a decision which was **[516]** endorsed by Lloyd-Jacob J, that there is a category of words which are so adapted for descriptive purposes that no amount of acquired distinctiveness can justify their registration, and that among such words are the names of large and important industrial towns or districts, and also of smaller towns or districts if they are a seat of manufacture of the goods for which registration is sought.

The principles to which I have referred appear to me to conclude the present case against the appellant. Michigan is the name of a State of the USA. The appellant produces there goods of the kind for which it uses the name as its mark in Australia as well as in America. It is true that there is no evidence before me that any other manufacturer produces similar goods in Michigan at present, but it is a matter of common knowledge, of which I take judicial notice, that in the State there are important manufacturing centres, and it is well within the bounds of reason to suppose that persons other than the appellant may in the future produce there goods similar to some or all of the goods comprised in the category for which the appellant now seeks trade mark registration. There are only two circumstances which may be considered as tending to diminish the normal likelihood that another manufacturer of for example power cranes in Michigan, sending his goods to Australia, may fairly wish to use the word Michigan in respect of them in this country in a manner which a trade mark registration would prevent. One circumstance I have mentioned already: it is that the word has at present a reputation here as referring specifically to the appellant's goods. The other I have not mentioned: it is that in the US the appellant has obtained registration of the word MICHIGAN as a trade mark in respect of such goods as those described in its present application. No evidence has been tendered as to the effect of trade mark registration according to US law, but I shall assume for the purposes of the case that apart from the appellant no manufacturer of the relevant goods, not even a Michigan manufacturer, is free to use the word Michigan in the manner of a trade mark for his goods in the US. The appellant submits that for that reason no such manufacturer will be very likely to want the word for use in Australia in any manner which would infringe a registered trade mark consisting of the word, especially if he knows, as he almost certainly will, of the distinctiveness the word has come to have in this country. But even allowing for the cumulative effect of these considerations it seems to me impossible to conclude that there is no likelihood of other traders, in the **[517]** ordinary course of their businesses and without any desire to get for themselves a benefit from the appellant's reputation, wishing in advertisements and otherwise to describe, for example, their power cranes from Michigan as Michigan power cranes. They may well wish by such means to take legitimate advantage of a reputation which they believe or hope that the State of Michigan possesses among Australians for the quality of its manufacturing products, and it would be contrary to fundamental principle to grant a registration which would have the effect of denying them the right to do so by using the name of the State. It is no answer to say that if registration be granted such a manufacturer may nevertheless describe his goods as "made in Michigan" or in some other ways indicate that Michigan is their place of origin. He is not to be excluded by the registration of a trade mark from any use of the word Michigan that he may fairly want to make in the course of his business.

For these reasons I am of opinion that MICHIGAN is not adapted, and is not capable of becoming adapted, to distinguish goods of the relevant kinds with which the appellant is or may be connected in the course of trade from goods in respect of which no such connection subsists, and is therefore not registrable in Part B as being or as capable of becoming distinctive of goods in respect of which registration is sought and with which the appellant is or may be connected in the course of trade.

■■■■■■ Clark Equipment v Registrar of Trade Marks *continued*

Accordingly, I hold that the Assistant Registrar was right in refusing to accept the application in this case, and I dismiss the appeal.

Note

[14.145] As with passing off, geographic names are unlikely to be distinctive. See *Re Application by Sakata Rice Snacks Pty Ltd* (1998) 43 IPR 378 (Sakata is the name of a city in Japan, a major seaport housing large national stores of government rice holdings). See, however, *Chancellor, Master and Scholars of the University of Oxford (t/a Oxford University Press) v Registrar of Trade Marks* (1988) 15 IPR 646, where there was discussion of the fact that even if the publisher OUP could sue in passing off to protect their reputation as a supplier of prestige books, the *Trade Marks Act 1955* (Cth) would have prevented registration on the grounds that "OXFORD" can never be adapted to distinguish. See also *Re Waterford Glass Group Ltd* (1987) 9 IPR 339; *Re Chubb Australia Ltd* (1990) 20 IPR 175; *Re Willow Lea Pastoral Co Pty Ltd* (1990) 20 IPR 180.

In the *Trade Marks Act 1995* (Cth), one ground of rejection of a mark is that is contains or consists of a false geographical indication (s 61). Protection for geographical indications, particularly wine names, was upgraded in the 1995 Act as part of Australia's international obligations to give proper protection to such geographic names.

Geographic name: Not necessarily "the name of any place"

■■■■■■■■■■ **Magnolia Metal Co's Trade Mark** ■■■■■■■■■■

[14.150] *Magnolia Metal Co's Trade Mark* [1897] 2 Ch 371 Court of Appeal (UK)

RIGBY LJ: **[392]** The objection to the word "Magnolia", as being a geographical name within the meaning of the section, in our opinion fails as to both the marks (2) and (3). It is no doubt shewn by the evidence that there are places in the US called by the name "Magnolia", and if "geographical name" in s 64, subs (e), were equivalent to "the name of any place", "Magnolia", as the name of the places mentioned in the **[393]** evidence, would fall within the exception. But, in our judgment, the phrase "geographical name" in s 64, subs (e), ought not in general to receive so wide an interpretation. It must, we think, in the absence of special circumstances, be interpreted so as to be in accordance in some degree with the general and popular meaning of the words, and a word does not become a geographical name simply because some place upon the earth's surface has been called by it. For example, we agree with Kekewich J that the word "Monkey" is not proved to be a geographical name by shewing merely that a small and by no means generally known island has been called by that name. If, indeed, in its primary and obvious meaning the word has reference to locality, as the word "Melrose" in *Van Duzer's* case (1887) 34 Ch D 623, or the word "Eboli" in *Sir Titus Salt Co's* case [1894] 3 Ch 166 (from which Chitty J declined to distinguish the derivative "Eboline"), it may well be a geographical name within the meaning of the subsection. Even when the primary signification is not geographical, if the name is really a local name (however little known the locality may be), and the name is given because of the connection of the article with the locality, whether that be real or imputed only by those who give the name, it may well be a geographical name within the meaning of the subsection. An instance of this is to be found in the case of the word

▬▬▬ Magnolia Metal Co's Trade Mark *continued*

"Apollinaris", given to the water from a spring known as the Apollinaris Spring. So, if "Magnolia" had been the name of a place where the metal was manufactured, we should have been by no means inclined to say that it would not be a geographical name when applied to the article manufactured in the place having the name. In mark No (2) the word "Magnolia" is so associated with the device of the flower as to shew on the fact of the mark what its origin was. But, as to both marks, the evidence shews that the word "Magnolia" was adopted, not as the name of or in connection with any place, but after the flower, which again was named, as pointed out by Lindley LJ during the argument, after a French botanist, Magnol, and we should not have been prepared to say that it was a geographical name within the meaning of the section, if that were the only objection to the trade marks.

■ General principles/entirely descriptive

▬▬▬ The College of Law ▬▬▬

[14.155] *The College of Law Pty Ltd* (1999) 47 IPR 404 Decision of the Delegate of the Registrar of Trade Marks

D NANCARROW: [405] On 10 March 1997, The College of Law Pty Ltd (the applicant) filed an application to register a series of word trade marks, THE COLLEGE OF LAW and THE AUSTRALIAN COLLEGE OF LAW in class 41 in respect of "educational and training services".

In his first report on the application, the examiner of trade marks raised a ground for rejecting the application under s 41 of the *Trade Marks Act 1995* (the Act). He said that the trade mark was not capable of distinguishing the applicant's services from the services of others, because other traders are likely to need the words to indicate their similar services. He also raised a ground of rejection under s 51, that the two marks did not constitute a series. The applicant chose to delete the second mark, to overcome the series difficulty, and to submit evidence of use in an attempt to overcome the ground for rejection under s 41. The examiner and a Principal examiner found the evidence insufficient to overcome this objection. The applicant was informed of this position in the examiner's second report. In response, the applicant raised further issues that it wished the examiner to consider in connection with the ground for rejection under s 41. When the examiner, after considering this material, maintained this ground for rejection in his third report, the applicant requested to be heard in the matter.

... [406]

Discussion

As the examiner had maintained that the trade mark was "not capable of distinguishing" the applicant's goods from those of other traders, I must consider it under Section 41 of the Act.

... The expression "inherently adapted to distinguish", as found in s 41(3), has been discussed in *Blount Inc v Registrar of Trade Marks* (1998) 40 IPR 498 (the *Oregon* case) by Branson J. Her Honour confirms that the expression is to be understood under s 41(3) of the Act in the same way as under s 26(2) of the *Trade Marks Act 1955* with the words at 506:

"The notion of a trade mark being inherently adapted to distinguish the designated goods was of primary significance under the 1955 Act. There is no reason to think that the phrase "inherently adapted to distinguish the designated goods from the goods of

▬▬▬ The College of Law *continued*

other persons" appearing in s 41(3) of the Act is not intended to be understood in the light of decisions under the 1955 Act, and comparable UK legislation which includes references to inherent adaptability."

[407] ... So the question to be resolved in the present case is, "what is the likelihood that other persons, offering educational and training services, particularly in matters of law, and being actuated by proper motives, will think of the phrase THE COLLEGE OF LAW and want to use it in connection with their services".

I note that the specification for this application claims "educational and training services". The applicant's services are offered at a college and entail subjects encompassing Law. I do not believe that the mark is inherently adapted to distinguish the services of the applicant from the services of other traders offering similar educational programs. I find, then, that the mark is not acceptable under s 41(3) of the Act.

In her written submissions, Ms Gourley had not argued for acceptance under s 41(3) but had submitted that the mark could be accepted under either s 41(5) or s 41(6). ...

Ms Gourley submitted that a number of factors should be considered to allow the application acceptance under s 41(5) of the Act. These factors included a list of more than ten choices available to traders who wish to describe their own [408] educational and training services, such as INSTITUTE OF LEGAL TRAINING, ACADEMY OF LEGAL TRAINING and LAW SCHOOL. The attorney added that it was only necessary that the mark have a "scintilla of inherent adaptation to distinguish" in order to qualify for consideration under s 41(5). In addition, Ms Gourley cited two previous trade mark decisions, for THE SOUND, and for ORIGINAL JAZZ CLASSICS and ORIGINAL BLUES CLASSICS. In these decisions, the delegate of the Registrar had determined that the marks possessed sufficient "inherent adaptability to distinguish", and thus allowed the provisions of s 41(5) to be applied to the applications. Ms Gourley argued that the present application should be allowed the same consideration.

(a) Section 41(5)

(1) Other descriptions available

Although the material put to me indicated that there were many different descriptive terms available for other traders to use to describe their similar services, this factor does not change the test to be passed for this trade mark, if the provisions of s 41(5) are to be applied. It is still required that the mark must be, to some extent, inherently adapted to distinguish the applicant's services from the services of other traders.

The words of King J in *Seven Up Co v Bubble Up Co, Inc* (1987) AIPC 90-433 at 37,810 are pertinent on this point, where he said:

"The fact that there are other words customarily used to identify the class of goods concerned would not render it less likely that other traders would wish to use a term which, although it would not appeal to an official as an apt description, would nevertheless be thought to appeal to the general public. ... I think that the mark applied for is so likely to interfere with 'the common right of the public to make honest use of words forming part of the common heritage, for the sake of the signification which they ordinarily possess' that it should be regarded as unregistrable in Part B of the Register."

Despite the list of alternatives provided by Ms Gourley in her submissions, I believe that the words THE COLLEGE OF LAW provide nothing more than a description of the applicant's business. It is a phrase that readily conveys the nature of the applicant's educational and

▰▰▰▰▰ The College of Law *continued*

training services. As such, I cannot accept that this argument is helpful in showing that the mark has any inherent capability to distinguish the applicant's services, or, therefore, is helpful in providing reason to consider the application under s 41(5).

(2) The earlier acceptances

Ms Gourley referred me to two earlier decisions. These cases were *Re Application by Eltham Woodwind (Importing Pty Ltd)* (1996) 34 IPR 668 for the trade mark THE SOUND and *Re Application by Fantasy Inc* (1997) 39 IPR 381 for the marks ORIGINAL JAZZ CLASSICS and ORIGINAL BLUES CLASSICS. The three trade marks involved in these decisions were found to be "to some extent inherently adapted to distinguish the designated goods or services" for their respective goods. They were all given consideration under s 41(5) of the Act. I have reproduced these marks below for convenient comparison.

[409] In the *Fantasy Inc* decision (supra), at 384, the delegate commented on his reasons for considering the applications under s 41(5) with the following words:

> "I am of the opinion that the words contained in the subject marks, viz 'original jazz classics' and 'original blues classics', respectively, are not, by themselves, capable of distinguishing the applicant's goods from those of others in the marketplace. All of the words are well-known, and their respective combinations have clear meanings, which add nothing to the trade marks' capacity to distinguish.
>
> However, I believe that the get-up of the respective combinations does give to the trade marks a low level of inherent adaptation to distinguish."

These comments lead to the logical conclusion that, had the applications been simply ORIGINAL JAZZ CLASSICS and ORIGINAL BLUES CLASSICS in block capitals, then the delegate would have decided that they had no "inherent adaptation to distinguish".

Similarly, in the *Eltham Woodwind* decision (supra), at 670 and 671, concerning THE SOUND trade mark, the delegate made the following comments:

> "[T]he present combination of words is not in the same class as laudatory words, ... The combination of words, the subject of this trade mark, does have a degree of descriptiveness but does, in my opinion have a low level of inherent adaptation to distinguish.
>
> ...
>
> The trade mark does have some degree of 'get-up', evidence from the 'segno' device forming the 'S' in the word 'Sound', the quaver device forming the letter 'd' in that word and the curlicues in the type face in which the trade mark is presented."

Here, although the delegate found that the words did have "a low level of inherent adaptation to distinguish" because the words "THE SOUND" were not in the same category as "the best sound" or "the ultimate sound", the trade mark also contained a degree of "get-up" in the device elements. These elements also provided assistance to decide that the mark had "a low level of inherent adaptation to distinguish".

In relation to the present application, the words THE COLLEGE OF LAW are all well-known and produce a clear meaning, in combination, as denoting services of an educational

▰▰▰▰ The College of Law *continued*

or training body in providing legal courses. The present mark has no device elements and it has no "get-up" by way of stylisation of lettering. It clearly lacks the factors that existed in the above trade marks that allowed them to be considered for registration in terms of s 41(5).

I am of the opinion that the mark THE COLLEGE OF LAW is entirely descriptive of the applicant's services and lacks any inherent adaptation to distinguish these services from the similar services of other traders. ... The result of such a conclusion is that the mark can only be considered for registration under the provisions of s 41(6).

[410] (b) Section 41(6)

... The evidence of use submitted by the applicant consisted of a Statutory Declaration from Brian Keith Thomas, Company Secretary of the applicant, dated 3 September 1998. The declaration claimed use of the mark in relation to legal education and training services from February 1975. Mr Thomas further declares that the applicant is the largest provider of profes-sional legal training programs in the Southern Hemisphere and offers approximately 90 continuing legal courses annually with approximately 10,000 students registered to attend such courses. In addition, he also states that approximately 15,000 students have graduated from the Graduate Diploma in Legal Practice course since 1975. The exhibits provide examples of the applicant's advertising material, various information booklets, course handbooks and a sample graduation certificate. The applicant has also promoted its services by means of distribution of material to universities, contact with members of the legal profession and displays at career fairs and exhibitions.

In applying the provisions of s 41(6) in *Blount* (supra), Branson J commented, at 508, that:

> "The question to be considered under s 41(6) is whether the applicant has established that, because of the extent to which the applicant has used the trade mark before the filing date ... it does distinguish the designated goods as being those of the applicant.
>
> The above question is, in my view, entirely one of fact. It does not involve consid-eration of the question whether the word 'Oregon' is one 'which other traders are likely, in the ordinary course of their businesses and without any improper motive, to desire to use upon or in connection with their goods'.
>
> ...
>
> Section 41 is concerned with capacity to distinguish. As s 41(6)(a) makes plain, a trade mark which is not to any extent inherently adapted to distinguish may nonetheless be treated under the Act as capable of distinguishing if, by reason of past use, it does in fact distinguish."

These words direct me to ignore the concept that other traders may require use of the words in the mark. I must simply consider whether the use made of the mark by the applicant (prior to the date of filing) is sufficient to enable me to believe that the trade mark does, in fact, distinguish the applicant's educational and training services from the similar services of other traders.

I note that in the evidence submitted, the applicant's mark is always used with a device. The form of this mark is as shown below.

[411]

THE
COLLEGE
OF LAW

▓▓▓▓▓ The College of Law *continued*

The device is sometimes used alone, but the mark THE COLLEGE OF LAW does not appear, in the evidence, apart from the device. In addition, the words are used in a descriptive sense, as being the college where the education and training is conducted, within the written information contained in the brochures in the evidence. These factors tend to reduce the effectiveness of the evidence of use in providing a reputation for the words alone as operating as trade mark, and thus providing proof that the mark THE COLLEGE OF LAW does distinguish the services as being those of the applicant.

Although Ms Gourley had submitted that the applicant's mark did distinguish its services in the relevant market, no clear indication was made to isolate the elements that constituted that "relevant market". I do not believe that this relevant market, in this instance, could be considered only those who have enrolled or could enrol in the legal courses provided. A significantly high proportion of the entire general public has had, at some stage of their lives, a need to obtain legal advice or has the need to use professional representation in a legal matter. The applicant seeks registration of this trade mark through this Office on a national register. I conclude, therefore, that the relevant market for determining whether or not the mark does, in fact, distinguish the applicant's services must be the Australian public at large.

Given the highly descriptive nature of this mark, I believe that the amount of use shown is not sufficient to produce the level of recognition, at the date of filing, in the minds of the general Australian population that the mark does, in fact, distinguish the applicant's services in the manner that is required by the Act.

... [412]

This material (submitted) indicates to me that the applicant's courses clearly have a major application to those who intend to practise in New South Wales. Given that the population of the state was approximately 5.4 million in 1986 and 5.7 million in 1993, the figure of 220,000 is quite considerable in respect of that state only. If approximately one person in each 25 in New South Wales has registered for courses at the College of Law, between 1975 and 1997, then the exposure of the mark to a much larger percentage of the population, such as families and friends of these enrolled students, cannot be ignored.

Although for the entire population of Australia I am not convinced that the mark had achieved the desired level of recognition, the situation in respect of New South Wales provides a different scenario.

I do believe that the evidence submitted provides sufficient notoriety in New South Wales alone to enable me to accept this application for a registration limited to that jurisdiction.

Conclusion

From the foregoing, I have found that the trade mark THE COLLEGE OF LAW is not to any extent inherently adapted to distinguish the applicant's services from similar services of other traders. I have also found that the evidence submitted is not sufficient to enable me to accept this application for registration, in terms of s 41(6) of the Act, in respect of the applicant's present claim for the use throughout Australia. However, as I believe that the evidence is sufficient to show that the mark does, in fact, distinguish the applicant's services from those of other traders throughout New South Wales.

Under the present circumstances, subject to an appeal from this decision I intend to refuse this trade mark application. However, if the applicant advises me, in writing, within one month of the date at the foot of this decision that it is prepared to limit its claim for registration to New South Wales, I am prepared to accept the application with the standard endorsements involving evidence and the geographical restriction.

■ Names of persons

[14.160] Personal names lack inherent distinctiveness as many people can share a name. The Trade Marks Office conducts a search of Australian surnames to assess whether a "name" trade mark is too common. In *Re Application by Glenleith Holdings Ltd (Patent Office)* (1989) 15 IPR 555, the applicant sought to register the name ROBBIE BURNS (with a small picture of the poet) for Scotch Whisky. The Senior Examiner of Trade Marks (J Hooton) said:

> "In order to qualify as a registrable mark under s 24(1)(a) the name of a person must be rendered in a special or particular manner. The applicant's submission that 'Robbie Burns' is not the name of a person being the name of a deceased Scottish poet does not overcome the objection in terms of s 24(1)(a) because the names 'Robbie' and 'Burns' did not die with that famous Scottish poet. 'Burns' is in fact a very common surname occurring 7584 times in the Standard Search for Australian Surnames and 'Robbie' is a well-known form of Robert. There is therefore a reasonable probability that persons with the name of 'Robbie Burns' exist."

In *Re Application by Lee Kum Kee (Patent Office)* (1988) 12 IPR 212 the name Lee Kum Kee in Chinese characters could not be registered for sauces, condiments and spices, as it constituted a surname recognised by purchasers. However, the transliteration of the Chinese name into the three English words was registrable (in Part B, at that time) although the name "LEE" on it's own was too common to achieve registration. Similarly a name written in Arabic was refused registration where it conveyed primarily "surnomial significance": *Avedis Zildjian Co* (1990) 18 IPR 474.

A person's signature is usually regarded as inherently distinctive, and one type of mark allowed registration under the *Trade Marks Act 1955* (Cth) was "the signature of the applicant for registration or some predecessor in the business", unless the signature was in too commonplace a style of writing. See *"Barry Artist" Trade Mark* [1978] RPC 703; cf *Parison Fabrics Ltd's Application* (1949) 66 RPC 217.

Registering a name that is not very unusual in its own right requires it to be written in such a way that makes it "distinctive".

Name of a person represented in a special or particular manner

▬▬▬▬▬▬▬ Fanfold Ltd's Application ▬▬▬▬▬▬▬

[14.165] *Fanfold Ltd's Application* (1928) 45 RPC 325 Court of Appeal (United Kingdom)

LORD HANWORTH MR: [329] ...The facts can be stated quite shortly. There is a company which carries on its business as Fanfold Ltd, and they applied for the registration in Part A, of the register of a trade mark, which consists of their name written in a particular manner somewhat arched so that the word "Limited" can be written in rather smaller letters underneath it and below the word "Limited", and making a tangent to the arch there is a scroll or ribbon pattern somewhat faintly indicated.

The matter went before the Registrar, and he decided that the company were not entitled to register the mark. I have read his judgment carefully, and I think that he decided two things ... The Registrar set out the description of the mark, and then said:

━━━ Fanfold Ltd's Application *continued*

"The name is represented in relatively very heavy type which at once impresses the eye and rivets the attention; while the scroll, when looked at from a short distance, loses its identity if it does not wholly disappear. So far, therefore, as the features of the proposed trade mark go, the learned Registrar comes to the conclusion that it does not consist of more than the name of Fanfold Ltd, because the accompanying ribbon or scroll does not arrest the eye, and loses its identity, if it does not wholly disappear ... The type employed in the representation of the name is quite ordinary; and it does not appear to me that the slight arching of the name (which in itself is a common form of display) and the addition of the indistinctive scroll device are so special or particular as to fit the whole mark to distinguish the applicants' goods."

... [332] ...

In order to be registrable under para (1) you must, first of all, have a name which is represented in a special or particular manner; but (it may be either superadded or interpreting what is meant by "special or particular manner") there must be distinction, and that distinction is required so that there may be an indication that the goods on which the mark is put are the goods of the proprietor, and the distinction must be one which is adapted to distinguish those goods of the proprietor for the purpose of enabling the definition of a trade mark to be fulfilled.

━━━

━━━ Standard Cameras Ltd's Application ━━━

[14.170] *Standard Cameras Ltd's Application* (1952) 69 RPC 125 Chancery Division

LLOYD-JACOB J: ... [128] ... [I]t appears that the main ground upon which registration was sought was that the representation attached to the application form was of a distinctive mark within the meaning of that phrase in s 9(1)(e) of the *Trade Marks Act*. As Mr Whyman very rightly says, if the representation is looked at the conclusion is obvious that in the ordinary circumstances of trade goods bearing this mark would be known as, and asked for under the name, "Robin Hood". Accordingly, he was induced thereby to consider that the real decision in this matter turned upon whether the name "Robin Hood", or the words "Robin Hood" as such, wholly unembellished or added to, could properly be regarded as conveying the distinctiveness necessary to justify registration under the Act.

He goes on to point out that although the name "Robin Hood" is attached to a legendary or possibly historical character, none the less the surname "Hood" is by no means uncommon in this country and that, as the proper name "Robin" is also familiarly used in these days, the combination of the two is not altogether unexpected and, as the trade and commerce of this country is open to everybody, it is only right that the tribunal should have in mind the possibility that the male son of Mr and Mrs Hood, to whom the proper name "Robin" may have been given at his christening, may find himself eventually engaged in trade in the manufacture or distribution of photographic apparatus, and in that connection it is at any rate not unlikely that he may desire or make use of his own name.

It has always to be borne in mind when considering that sort of approach that, in connection with the registration of surnames upon evidence of distinctiveness, the court has said on a number of occasions that the uncommonness of the name itself is a factor to be borne in mind when considering registrability. Where the danger to be guarded against requires the combination of a number of circumstances, including, firstly, the accident of the surname being the same, secondly, the event that the proper name is the same, thirdly, that the trade engaged upon by this person shall be the same, and fourthly, that the desire to use the name upon the goods should also have presented itself to the mind of this hypothetical person, quite obviously the possibilities of confusion are correspondingly diminished the more factors it is necessary to add together in order to arrive at the probability.

The Act specifically provides for the safeguarding of a bona fide use of a person's own name or of the name of his place of business. Therefore generally, in considering the propriety of permitting applications such as the present to proceed to registration, the tribunal must always have in mind the likelihood or otherwise of the events which ingenuity can so readily formulate having any real relation to what can be expected in practice. On the whole, I should be inclined to share his view that, if in practice this mark were to come to be understood by the trade and public as amounting to no more than the name "Robin Hood", it would be a mark that could not properly fall to be registered under the provisions of s 9(1), but would require to have evidence of its distinctiveness before it could properly be entered upon the register....

[129] ... As I see the matter, it is therefore incumbent upon a tribunal judging the propriety of this application to look at that which is applied for and if it appears, as it does, that it is the name of an individual, namely, "Robin Hood", then to consider whether that is represented in a special or particular manner as the section requires. No one, I think, would seriously contend that to any ordinary eye the representation of the words "Robin Hood" set out on this application would not be accepted by everybody as being out of the common. Having come to the conclusion that it is out of the common, I have to look at it to see whether it is sufficiently out of the common to strike the eye as being peculiar, and by "peculiar" I mean not likely to occur to somebody who merely wishes to represent the word.

I myself entertain no doubt that it is an unusual representation, which does strike the eye as uncommon, and which I should suppose is so unlikely as to be substantially impossible for any ordinary man wishing to represent the name "Robin Hood" to arrive at. Accordingly, were the matter before me, sitting as the Registrar of Trade Marks, I should have accepted this application for registration under the provisions of s 9(1)(a) of the *Trade Marks Act*.

■ An invented word

▅▅▅▅ Howard Auto Cultivators v Webb Industries ▅▅▅▅

[14.175] *Howard Auto Cultivators Ltd v Webb Industries Pty Ltd* (1946) 72 CLR 175 High Court of Australia

DIXON J: [180] ... A rotary hoe is a familiar agricultural implement and the appellants whose business consists in the manufacture and sale of machines for agriculture and horticulture, trade largely in them. The respondent's application is to register in respect of cultivating implements the wordmark "Rohoe". It is clear that it is not registrable as a trade mark unless it is an invented word within the meaning of s 16(1)(c) of the Commonwealth *Trade Marks*

▨▨▨▨▨ Howard Auto Cultivators v Webb Industries *continued*

Act 1905-1936. The Registrar, who dismissed the appellants' opposition and granted registration, **[181]** held that it does amount to an invented word and the question is whether that decision is right.

The fact that a word is not included in the dictionaries is not enough to show that it is an invented word, nor is the fact that it has been newly constructed: *Re Yalding Manufacturing Co's Application* (1916) 33 RPC 285 at 289. The materials from which such a word has been fashioned cannot be neglected and if it is compounded of elements of which the source is manifest and the intended meaning is transparent, it becomes a question whether there is anything more than a colourable attempt at reproducing some of the sounds and all the sense of an expression belonging to common speech. Misspellings, variations and distortions of ordinary words do not amount to invention, and it has been held that to write a proper name backward is not to invent a word: *Re George Cording Ltd's Application* (1916) 33 RPC 83. Novelty is, of course, looked for and that means more than giving existing words or a combination of words a disguise, whether phonetic or graphic, which the mind of the hearer or reader at once penetrates. In the words of Lord Shand (*Eastman Photographic Materials Co v Comptroller-General of Patents, Designs & Trade Marks* [1898] AC 571 at 585; 15 RPC 476 at 487):

> "There must be invention, and not the appearance of invention only. It is not possible to define the extent of invention required; but the words, I think, should be clearly and substantially different from any word in ordinary and common use. The employment of a word in such use, with a diminutive or a short and meaningless syllable added to it, or a mere combination of two known words, would not be an invented word; and a word would not be 'invented' which, with some trifling addition or varied trifling variation, still leaves the word one which is well-known or in ordinary use, and which would be quite understood as intended to convey the meaning of such a word."

On the other hand the new word need not be wholly meaningless and it is not a disqualification "that it may be traced to a foreign source or that it may contain a covert and skilful allusion to the character or quality of the goods". This is the expression of Lord Macnaghten (at 583), who also said "the word must be really an invented word. Nothing short of invention will do. On the other hand, nothing more seems to be required". No one now supposes that the *Trade Marks Act* requires that a word or words, although invented, shall not contain or suggest any reference to the character or quality of the goods or that it imposes any further requirement which must be **[182]** fulfilled for the word to be registrable. But, though, as appears from Lord Macnaghten's statement, some signification or indication of meaning is not inconsistent with invention, yet in deciding whether what is put forward is an invented word or is but an old word or words masquerading under some thin disguise of orthography, abbreviation or pronunciation, the fact that it is effectual in conveying the same meaning cannot be disregarded. It is not surprising, the subject matter being trading goods, that more often than not the meaning discernible in a word said to be newly devised relates to the character or quality of the goods. But logically the circumstance that it is this particular kind of meaning that is signified rather than some other should not weigh against the claim for invention, notwithstanding that, in the case of an existing word, such a meaning would disqualify the word as the essential particular of a registrable mark.

The real difficulty lies in the recognisable features of a word said to be new and invented. If in its features there is an immediate disclosure of the origin and meaning of the elements of which it has been formed, the question must arise whether it is anything more than a version or perversion of an existing word or words. Lord Herschell (at 581) thought that an invented word had no meaning until one has been attached to it. He made a qualification,

▬▬▬▬ Howard Auto Cultivators v Webb Industries *continued*

not now material, with reference to combinations of foreign words little known to Englishmen. He stated his opinion that a combination of two English words was not an invented word, even although the combination might not have been in use before, and that a mere variation in orthography or termination of a word would not be sufficient to constitute an invented word if to the eye or ear the same idea would be conveyed by the word in its ordinary form. The same thing had been put by Lindley LJ in the course of his dissenting judgment in *Re Farbenfabriken Application* [1894] 1 Ch 645 at 652, the decision of the majority in which was overruled by the House of Lords in the *Solio* case (*Eastman Photographic Materials Co v Comptroller-General* [1898] AC 571). He said (at 652, 653):

> "Any word which is in fact new, and not what may be called a colourable imitation of an existing word, is, in my opinion, an invented word. ... Again, I do not think that a word can fairly be called an invented word if it is so nearly like a known word in spelling or sound as to be an obvious imitation of it and is in substance that word though spelt or sounded a little differently."

In Lord Parker's summary in *Philippart v William Whiteley Ltd* [1908] 2 Ch 274 at 279 the two things, viz that the word must **[183]** be new and that it must not be connotative, are expressed as separate conditions: "To be an invented word, within the meaning of the Act, a word must not only be newly coined in the sense of not being already current in the English language, but must be such as not to convey any meaning, ... to ordinary Englishmen. It must be a word having no meaning, or no obvious meaning, until one has been assigned to it." He employed the expression "ordinary Englishmen" because "it is not enough that it might suggest a meaning to a few scholars." Lord Greene MR in *Re Boots Pure Drug Co* [1938] Ch 54 at 65, in pointing out that Lord Parker had stated two considerations as essential before a word could be an invented word, transformed the "ordinary Englishmen" into "an ordinary educated Englishman" and proceeded to restate and illustrate the requirement as follows:

> "But the next question would be whether, although not a word current in the English language, it was a word which would convey an obvious meaning, as might well happen if the word was by some sort of a jingle, of the presence of some element in it, one which suggested an obvious meaning to the English hearer."

Examples of words which, although new in formation, have failed because of these principles, to qualify as invented words are, "Orlwoola" (1909) 26 RPC 683 at 850, "Absorbine" (*Christy v Tipper* [1905] 1 Ch 1; 21 RPC 755), "Arsenoid" (*Re Yalding Manufacturing Co's Application* (1916) 33 RPC 285), "Eanco", scil "E and Co" (*Re Eisman & Co's Application* (1920) 37 RPC 134), "Uneeda" (*Re National Biscuit Co's Application* [1902] 1 Ch 783; 19 RPC 281), "Panoram" (*Re Kodak Ltd's Trade Mark* (1903) 20 RPC 337), "Aluminox" (*Re Salter's Application* (1923) 40 RPC 402), "Trakgrip" (at all events so I read the judgment of Simonds J in *Re Dunlop Rubber Co's Application* (1942) 59 RPC 134). On the other hand "Yeastvite" has been accepted into the category of invented words (*Irving's Yeast-Vite Ltd v Horsenail* (1934) 150 LT 402), and so has "Sardovy", from sardines and anchovy (*Re Brown, Wills & Nicholson's Application* (1923) 41 RPC 171), and "Oxo" (*Re Liebig's Extract of Meat Co's Trade Mark* (1902) 22 NZLR 165) ...

... **[185]** ... The question, though in a very small compass, is not an easy one, as the division of opinion it has provoked shows. But my conclusion is that the word formed bears a face value for those for whom it is meant and to them has an obvious meaning based upon an obvious structure, one element in which is a plain English word and the other a transparent abbreviation. It is very different from a covert and skilful allusion to the character

▰▰▰▰ Howard Auto Cultivators v Webb Industries *continued*

of the goods. I therefore think that it is not an invented word within the meaning of s 16(1)(c) of the *Trade Marks Act 1905-1936*.

I think that the appeal should be allowed and the application for registration refused.

[Rich, Starke and McTiernan JJ delivered judgments to like effect; Latham CJ and Williams J dissented.]

Notes

[14.180] "Foreign" words having some meaning in English will be refused registration if the meaning is too readily apparent. In *Re Applications by Maxam Food Products Pty Ltd (Patent Office)* (1991) 20 IPR 381 the mark "LA DELIZIOSA" was refused registration on the basis that it amounted to a laudatory expression in relation to the goods, a range of pasta products. It was argued that the expression was "a nonsensical combination which would not be used by Italian speakers"; however, even if not grammatically correct, it still had a transparent meaning.

A good example of an "invented word", one with no meaning apart from when applied to the goods or services is found in the word FUDDRUCKERS, used with respect to hamburgers: see *Michael Sharwood & Partners Pty Ltd v Fuddruckers Inc* (1989) 15 IPR 188.

Manufacturers may give a new product a distinctive name which then becomes the industry term for the item and therefore descriptive: for example, "Beta movie" in *Re Sony Kabushiki Kaisha* (1987) 9 IPR 466. In that case BETA was refused registration because it had already become generic before the application. See *Trade Marks Act 1995* (Cth), s 24.

While most traders prefer their mark to have something descriptive or complimentary to suggest about their goods, the general rule of unregistrability of descriptive words, devices or phrases is subject to the proviso in the previous legislation that words not have a "direct" reference to the character or quality of goods or services, and the note to s 41 states that marks are not inherent adapted to distinguish if they are "ordinarily" used to indicate characteristics of goods or services.

Words not having direct reference to or not ordinarily used to indicate characteristics of goods/services

▰▰▰▰▰▰▰▰▰▰▰ **Mark Foy's v Davies Coop** ▰▰▰▰▰▰▰

[14.185] *Mark Foy's Ltd v Davies Coop & Co Ltd* (1956) 95 CLR 190 High Court of Australia

[The appellant was the registered proprietor of the mark "Tub Happy" in respect of articles of clothing. It brought infringement proceedings against the respondent which in an advertising campaign used the slogan "Exacto Cotton Garments Tub Happy Cotton Fresh Budget Wise". The respondent resisted the infringement action by claiming, inter alia, that the appellant's trade mark was not registrable since it was a reference to the character or quality of goods falling within s 16(1)(d) of the 1905 Act.]

DIXON CJ: **[194]** It is, I think, a mistake first to assume that words like "tub happy" do convey a meaning either to people in general or to a particular class of persons and then on that assumption to inquire what exactly the meaning is. Indeed to institute a search for a meaning almost necessarily implies that in ordinary English speech the words do not possess

Mark Foy's v Davies Coop *continued*

a connotation sufficiently definite to amount to a direct reference to the character or quality of the goods. And that is true even when to standard English usage is added all the figurative idiomatic and slang phraseology that may be currently in use. Once, however, the question is asked what do the words mean and there is started a search for a meaning, a process of analysis and of reasoning by exclusion of alternatives is begun. No doubt such a search may, without any sacrifice of logic, end in construing the words as meaning that the garments will emerge happily from the washtub. But if they are so interpreted, the interpretation is chiefly the consequence of failure to find another meaning. I venture to think, however, that a man, or for that matter a woman, hearing for the first time the words used in combination and in connection with cotton garments, would not so understand the words at once. Certainly such a person would not so understand them intuitively and without stopping to reflect and ask himself or herself what meaning the words could really possess.

The fallacy of asking what is the meaning of the phrase lies in the basal assumption that the words are intended to convey some definite meaning and perhaps the further assumption that the meaning has reference to the garments or the cottons. The assumption is fallacious because it overlooks the fact that language is not always used to convey an idea. Many uses of words are purely emotive. A word or words are often employed for no purpose but to evoke in the reader or hearer some feeling, some mood, some mental attitude. This is true of much advertising, which common experience shows to be full of meaningless but emotive expressions supposedly capable of inducing a generally favourable inclination in the almost subconscious thought of the passing auditor or hasty reader. Words put forward as trade marks are very likely indeed to be chosen in the same way. **[195]**

Though Mr Holmes for the respondent did of course put forward the claim that "tub happy" means washable, it was a meaning it was necessary to suggest. It was not a meaning that had sprung unaided to the mind and it was not one which he was able to establish by reference to instances of known usage.

It is easy to say that the words are addressed to persons who are accustomed to speak an idiom to which courts are strangers and who are more sensitive than judges to allusive forms of speech, which, it is claimed, possess a greater efficacy in the lively communication of more or less definable ideas. But if the claim is that the words possess a meaning which courts might not be expected to know, it would have been easy enough to adduce evidence of the meaning; a thing which was not attempted.

The reason for introducing the word "direct" into the provision from which s 16(1)(d) comes was to check the tendency which had been disclosed by certain decisions to find a sufficient reference to the character or quality of goods in expressions from which it could only be spelled out. The test must lie in the probability of ordinary persons understanding the words, in their application to the goods, as describing or indicating or calling to mind either their nature or some attribute they possess.

I cannot think that the words now in question go further than, if as far as, suggesting in a vague and indefinable way a gladsome carelessness propos of the tub. They may have an emotive tendency, but they do not appear to me to convey any meaning or idea sufficiently tangible to amount to a direct reference to the character or quality of the goods. ...

WILLIAMS J: **[201]** Any reference that the words "tub happy" have to the character or quality of articles of clothing is very remote. They are in the nature of a coined phrase. Inanimate objects including articles of clothing cannot have the character or quality of happiness whether they are in a tub or not. But the defendants' case is that the common metaphorical use of the adjective would convey to prospective buyers of the fabrics that the cotton emerged from the wash tub more attractive than ever in appearance with fibres and colours as good if not better than ever. Therefore, so it is said, the words are a description of the character or quality of the goods and moreover are not entitled to registration. This claim gives far too specific a meaning to the vague figurative use of the word "happy" in connection with "tub". Like so many expressions used in advertisements no definite or actual meaning seems to belong to the combination "tub happy". There is a cloudy suggestion only about it that all will be well in a wash tub but that is all. The attitude of mind of those who glance at such advertisements may be affected favourably by some sort of vague association of ideas but it falls a long way short of conveying any meaning to them. To say that articles of clothing are tub happy is in the ordinary use of English meaningless. The words contain at most a "covert and skilful allusion" to the quality of washability which is characteristic of articles of clothing made of some kinds of material including cotton. At most they create an impression that this is what they are intended to convey. They do not trespass upon the rights of other traders to use any ordinary English words or phrases referring to the washable qualities of their goods. They do not attempt to "enclose and appropriate as private property certain little strips of the great open common of the English language". No doubt the words are intended to "contain a meaning—a meaning is wrapped up in them if you can only find it out": see the speech of Lord Macnaghten in the *Solio* case [1898] AC 571 at 583. And it may not be hard to find out that meaning but the words do not refer in any ordinary sense, laudatory or otherwise, to any character or quality of articles of clothing, still less do they do so directly.

[Kitto J dissented.]

■ Distinctiveness of shape marks

▬▬▬▬▬ Kenman Kandy v Registrar of Trade Marks ▬▬▬▬▬

[14.190] *Kenman Kandy Australia Pty Ltd v Registrar of Trade Marks* [2002] 56 IPR 30 Federal Court of Australia, Full Court

Image for Trade Mark 783465

FRENCH J: **[31]**

Introduction

Kenman Kandy Australia Pty Ltd ("Kenman Kandy") has applied for and been refused registration of the shape of its "millennium bug" sweet as a trade mark under the *Trade Marks Act 1995* (Cth). An appeal to a judge of this Court against the decision of the Registrar of Trade Marks was dismissed and the company now seeks leave to appeal to the Full Court.

The law relating to the registration of shape trade marks in Australia is still relatively new, such registration only having been possible with the coming into operation of the 1995 Act. Its application is not without difficulty. The criteria of registrability applicable to quite different kinds of "signs" under trade marks law as it stood prior to 1995 must now be applied to shapes. In this case the central issue is whether the shape of the goods in question is inherently adapted to distinguish them from the goods of other traders.

...

▄▄▄▄▄▄ Kenman Kandy v Registrar of Trade Marks *continued*

The Essential Features of a Trade Mark

[42] In July 1992, the Working Party to Review Trade Marks Legislation established by the Minister for Science, Customs and Small Business in 1989 presented its report entitled *Recommended Changes to the Australian Trade Marks Legislation.*

...On the question of distinctiveness the working party proposed that, in accordance with Article 15.1 of the TRIPS Agreement, a trade mark should be [43] defined as "any sign capable of distinguishing the goods or services of one person from those of other persons". The basic test for registrability, it was suggested, should be defined in a way that provided guidance on its application. The working party's recommendation in this respect (Rec 5) was, in substance, though not in precise wording, reflected in s 41 of the 1995 Act.

At the beginning of the Report the Working Party observed that, under the law as it stood in 1992, registrable marks had largely been confined to signs consisting of words, letters, numerals, figurative elements of combinations of one or more of these. The registration of colours, shapes, sounds, tastes or smells as marks was "either difficult or impossible under these provisions". (par 1.1) The Working Party said:

> "Developments in marketing and technology throughout the world indicate that the Australian legislation should now cater for a wider range of "signs" than have hereto been considered capable of functioning as trade marks. These developments have been recognised in the General Agreement on Tariffs and Trade (GATT) discussions and by the European Communities (EC) and the United Kingdom (UK) in the Draft Final Act, Directive and White Paper, and more recently by New Zealand (NZ) and South Africa (SA) in the NZ Proposed Recommendations and the SA Draft Trade Marks Bill respectively." (Report p 35)

The changes proposed to the definition of trade mark were therefore placed in the context of international developments. In relation to the shape and packaging of goods it was said by the Working Party:

> "There is majority support for the proposition that if the sign constitutes some element of the shape or the packaging of the product, and if the applicant can demonstrate that that element is not necessary for the proper functioning, or does not result from the nature of the product or its packaging, then it should be capable of registration." (Report p 37)

The Criteria of Registrability for Shapes

[44] It is necessary to inquire what the Act requires of shapes that would be trade marks. To be a trade mark, a shape must be used to distinguish goods or services dealt with or provided in the course of trade by a person from goods or services so dealt with or provided by any other person. That definition is entirely consistent with the idea of "shape" as an attribute of goods which distinguishes them from others. It is not to be read down to cover only some aspect of the physical configuration of goods. The shape which distinguishes the goods may be their shape taken as a whole. The inclusion of "shape" in the definition of "sign" stands against the suggestion that it can never be an attribute separate from the goods to which it relates. It mandates consideration of shape as a distinctive attribute although not a necessary feature of the particular goods. Where shape serves function, then it may not bear that character of a distinctive attribute. Like the three headed shape of the Philips Rotary Shaver it would not be capable of registration—*Koninklijke Philips Electronics NV v Remington Products Australia Pty Ltd*. As Stone J observes in her reasons for judgment, the separation issue in that case was at least in part an element of the capacity to distinguish. I respectfully agree with the

▬▬▬▬▬ Kenman Kandy v Registrar of Trade Marks *continued*

observations of Burchett J in   that a shape that goods possess because of their nature or the need for a particular technical result could not operate as a trade mark. I respectfully also agree with the analysis of Stone J in this regard and with her Honour's conclusion that there is no suggestion in this case that the shape of the millennium bug has any functional significance other than aesthetic.

...

The ultimate question in applying this test is whether the mark, considered apart from the effects of registration, is such that by its use the applicant is likely to attain its object of thereby distinguishing its goods from the goods of others—*Clark Equipment Co v Registrar of Trade Marks* at CLR 513. This does not involve adventures in the Aristotelian taxonomy of form and substance. It requires a practical evaluative judgment about the effects of the relevant mark **[44]** in the real world. Kitto J, in *Clark Equipment*, referred to the way in which the question was approached by Lord Waddington in *Registrar of Trade Marks v W & G du Cros Ltd* [1913] AC 624 at 634-635, when he said:

> "The applicant's chance of success in this respect [ie in distinguishing his goods by means of the mark, apart from the effects of registration] must, I think, largely depend upon whether other traders are likely, in the ordinary course of their businesses and without any improper motive, to desire to use the same mark, or some mark nearly resembling it, upon or in connection with their own goods."

...The shape of the millennium bug involves a symmetrical disposition of projections ("legs") and recesses ("eyes"). Theoretically it may be the case that the number of possible symmetrical arrangements of projections and recesses is not infinite. Assuming that to be so, it is speculative, absent evidence, to draw conclusions about that number and whether the particular arrangement has any significant impact upon the access of other traders to the use of insect like shapes as trade marks. In that connection it is necessary to bear in mind that this trade mark is still at the registration stage. It enjoys the benefit of the presumption of registrability mandated by s 33. To the extent that critical criteria upon which registration might be rejected are in doubt, the application should be accepted. Closer adversarial scrutiny may occur in opposition—*Registrar of Trade Marks v Woolworths* at CLR 377. In my opinion the appeal should be allowed.

LINDGREN J (dissent): [49]

Section 41 generally seeks to strike a balance between two public interests: the public interest in the general body of traders and consumers having available a vocabulary of signs to facilitate communication about a class of goods (for convenience, I will refer to "goods" and not to "services"), and the public interest in a particular trader being able to use a sign to communicate a "packet of information" about the source of that trader's goods. The balance is struck by ensuring that in exchange for a narrowing of the vocabulary of signs available to be used by traders as trade marks, the public obtains a benefit through the receipt of special information about the goods of a particular trader.

...

"Inherently adapted to distinguish"

[52] What is the notion conveyed by the expression "inherently adapted to distinguish" within subs 41(3) of the Act?

...While inherent adaptation to distinguish requires attention to be focused on the mark itself, and is intended to stand in sharp contrast to a mark's capacity to distinguish arising from use, the notion of "the mark itself" does not exclude from consideration the nature of

▰▰▰▰ Kenman Kandy v Registrar of Trade Marks *continued*

the range of goods within the class or classes in respect of which registration is sought, or the various ways in which the mark might, within the terms of the registration, be used in relation to those goods. Indeed, those matters must be taken into account. But in the present case, all that falls for consideration in these respects is the proposed use of the Bug shape as the shape of items of confectionery. Whether the Bug shape is inherently adapted to distinguish can be tested by assessing how it would be perceived and [53] understood by members of the public seeing items of confectionery of that shape for the first time, because this test excludes the possibility of a trade mark significance arising from use.

... [56]

I ask myself whether the Bug shape, as the shape of items of Kenman's confectionery, would, immediately following registration and without any prior education of the public that it has a trade mark significance, be able to do the job of distinguishing Kenman's confectionery from the confectionery of others.

The relationship between a trade mark and goods

...Prior to the introduction of shape marks in the 1995 Act, it was accepted that a trade mark must be capable of being described and depicted as something apart from the goods in relation to which it is to be used; cf *Smith Kline and French Laboratories (Australia) Ltd v Registrar of Trade Marks* (1967) 116 CLR 628 at 639 per Windeyer J (citing Lindley LJ in *In re James's Trade Mark* (1886) 33 Ch D 392 at 395: "A mark must be something distinct from the thing marked. A thing cannot be a mark of itself"). A similar view was taken in the United Kingdom prior to the introduction of shape marks in that country; cf *Re Coca-Cola Co* (1986) 6 IPR 275 (*Coca-Cola (UK)*) at 277 per Lord Templeman.

Philips v Remington (Aust, Lehane J) was a case in which it was alleged that the marketing of three-headed rotary electric shavers infringed two marks registered under the 1955 Act. Both marks represented a three-headed rotary shaver, one being a stylised "plan" showing three rings triangularly arranged within a rounded triangle circumference, and the other being a "perspective" giving the appearance of some depth, that is, of a third dimension. Lehane J concluded (at [26]) that "shape" in the definition of "sign" in the 1995 Act included "the shape of goods, or of part of them".

[57] ... In dismissing the appeal in *Philips v Remington* (Aust, FC) Burchett J, with whom Hill and Branson JJ agreed, stated (at [12]) that merely to produce and deal in goods in a shape which was a functional shape of the thing (the three-headed rotary shaver) depicted by a registered two-dimensional trade mark, was not to engage in use of the mark "upon, or in physical or other relation to, the goods" within subs 7(4) of the Act, or to use it "in relation to the goods" within subs 20(1) of the Act. His Honour said that it is to be assumed that goods in the market are "useful" and that "it follows that a mark consisting of nothing more than the goods themselves could not distinguish their commercial origin, which is the function of a mark" (also at [12]).

Burchett J observed that since the introduction of shape marks had made no radical change in the principles of trade mark law, it followed that a shape dictated by the nature of goods or by a particular technical result to be obtained from the goods ... could not function as a trade mark. But his Honour continued (at [16] and [17]):

"*It does not follow that a shape can never be registered as a trade mark if it is the shape of the whole or a part of the relevant goods, so long as the goods remain distinct from the mark.* Some special shape of a container for a liquid may, subject to the matters already discussed, be used as a trade mark, just as the shape of a medallion attached to goods might be so used. A shape may be applied, as has been said, in relation to goods, perhaps by moulding or impressing, so that it becomes a feature of their shape, though

■■■■■■ Kenman Kandy v Registrar of Trade Marks *continued*

it may be irrelevant to their function. Just as a special word may be coined, a special shape may be created as a badge of origin. But that is not to say that the 1995 Act has invalidated what Windeyer J said in *Smith Kline*. The special cases where a shape of the goods may be a mark are cases falling within, not without, the principle he expounded. For they are cases where the shape that is a mark is 'extra', added to the inherent form of the particular goods as something distinct which can denote origin. The goods can still be seen as having, in Windeyer J's words, 'an existence independently of the mark' which is imposed upon them.

The conclusion of this discussion is not that the addition of the word 'shape' to the statutory definition calls for some new principle, or that a 'shape' mark is somehow different in nature from other marks, but that *a mark remains something 'extra' added to distinguish the products of one trader from those of another*, a function which plainly cannot be performed by a mark consisting of either a word or a shape other traders may legitimately wish to use. That proposition has commonly been stated in connection with marks that seek to appropriate the actual name of the product or an apt description of [58] it; but *the principle equally applies in the case of a shape or picture representing the very form and appearance in which another trader might legitimately wish to make the product."* (my emphasis)

The facts of the present case are different from those which Lehane J, and on appeal Burchett J, had in mind. The Bug shape is not required by the nature of the goods or by the objective of obtaining a particular technical result. The nature and purpose of confectionery require only that it be able to be eaten. The shape of the individual pieces is a matter for each manufacturer, which can be expected to be guided by considerations of visual appeal. Importantly, there is no shape or category of shapes which can be regarded as "natural", "usual" or "inherent" for items of confectionery to which the Bug shape would be regarded as foreign. On the contrary, the Bug shape is entirely typical of the caricaturistic real or imaginary animal shapes which manufacturers of confectionery are disposed to use.

Therefore, the Bug shape as the entire shape of entire items of confectionery would be perceived by consumers, seeing it for the first time, as simply another member of the well known family of shapes that confectionery manufacturers chose for their visual appeal. Seeing Bug-shaped confectionery for the first time, the consumer would not understand at all that the shape was being used "in relation to" the confectionery for the purpose of saying something about its origin.

For the above reasons, the Bug shape as the shape of items of confectionery is not inherently adapted to distinguish Kenman's confectionery from the confectionery provided by others and the present appeal should be dismissed.

STONE J: [61]

... the current state of the authorities suggests that there is a particular problem concerning the registrability of a shape trade mark, namely whether it is necessary that a trade mark be able to be described and depicted as something separate and apart from the goods in relation to which it is to be used and, if so, whether this is possible for a shape which is the whole shape of a good (the "separation issue"). This issue sometimes appears to be quite separate from the issue of inherent adaptation and sometimes an element of that issue.

Separation of trade mark from goods

The separation issue was articulated by Windeyer J in *Smith Kline and French Laboratories (Australia) Limited v Registrar of Trade Marks* (1967) 116 CLR 628 (*Smith Kline*). This was an

▬▬▬ Kenman Kandy v Registrar of Trade Marks *continued*

appeal from a decision of the Registrar of Trade Marks refusing to accept for registration certain applications relating to medicinal capsules, one half of which was opaque and coloured and the other half, transparent and colourless. The capsules contained different coloured [62] granules or pellets that gave a speckled appearance to the transparent part of the capsule. According to Windeyer J, the applicant wanted to register "the total appearance of its capsules" and thus obtain a monopoly for the sale of "parti-coloured capsules containing pellets of different colours". In an ex tempore judgment his Honour said this (at 639 - 640):

> "A trade mark is defined in the [*Trade Marks Act 1955*] as 'a mark used or proposed to be used in relation to goods' for the purposes stated. This definition assumes, it seems to me, that the mark is something distinct from the goods in relation to which it is used or to be used. It assumes that the goods can be conceived as something apart from the mark and that the mark is not of the essence of the goods. The goods are assumed to have an existence independently of the mark. ... A thing can always be described and distinguished in appearance by any visible characteristic which it has, its shape, colour or any mark which it bears. But the test is not—Can the goods be described or depicted without reference to their markings? As I see it, a mark for the purposes of the Act must be capable of being described and depicted as something apart from the goods to which it is to be applied, or in relation to which it is to be used. ... It accords ... with the various things included in the definition of "mark". That list is not expressed as exhaustive but it is certainly illustrative. I do not think that a mere description of goods simply by shape, size or colour can be a trade mark in respect of those goods."

It would seem from Windeyer J's subsequent comments that his Honour regarded the separation issue as distinct from the issue of capacity to distinguish. In the context of legislation that, at the time, did not permit the registration of shape trade marks this is not surprising.

Did the 1995 Act effect a radical change to trade mark law?

Burchett J stated, [in *Philips v Remington (Aust)*] at [15], that the changes in the 1995 Act were not intended to effect a radical change in trade mark law and concluded that a shape that goods possessed "because of their nature" or because of the need for a "particular technical result" could not function as a trade mark because such a shape could not distinguish the trade source. His Honour went on to say, at [16], that he did not regard this as precluding the shape of goods being registered as a trade mark where the shape is the whole or part of the relevant goods, but added,

> "But that is not to say that the 1995 Act has invalidated what Windeyer J said in *Smith Kline*. The special cases where a shape of the goods may be a mark are cases falling within, not without, the principle he expounded. For they are cases where the shape that is a mark is 'extra', added to the inherent form of the particular goods as something distinct which can denote origin. The goods can still be seen as having, in Windeyer J's words, 'an existence independently of the mark' which is imposed upon them.
>
> The conclusion of this discussion is not that the addition of the word 'shape' to the statutory definition calls for some new principle, or that a 'shape' mark is somehow different in nature from other marks, but that a mark remains something 'extra' added [63] to distinguish the products of one trader from those of another, a function which plainly cannot be performed by a mark consisting of either a word or shape other traders may legitimately wish to use."

▦▦▦▦ Kenman Kandy v Registrar of Trade Marks *continued*

...The issue of function was of great significance in the dispute between Philips and Remington that surfaced in a number of jurisdictions. In *Philips v Remington (Eng)*, Jacob J was quite explicit about this aspect. His Honour accepted that it was possible to make an effective rotary shaver that would be outside the scope of the trade mark protection but stated, at 287-288:

> "However, it is also the case that the engineering scope for variation outside the trade mark is very limited. Moreover the three-headed shape of the present Philips design is one of the best ways possible of making a rotary shaver. ...
>
> So, if Philips are right, they will have obtained a permanent monopoly in respect of matters of significant engineering design by virtue of a trade mark registration."

The concerns expressed in both *Philips v Remington (Aust)*, FC and *Philips v Remington (Eng)* about the prospect of trade marks creating monopolies related only to the registration of trade marks that would restrict access to functional features or innovations, and for this reason were well founded. It is this concern that finds expression in the requirement that a trade mark be something added to the inherent form of goods. The "inherent form" of goods, in my view, can only refer to those aspects of form that have functional significance. Were the 1995 Act to enable the registration of a trade mark that would give the owner a monopoly over functional features it would indeed have made a radical change to trade mark law. There is nothing in the 1995 Act or in the discussions that preceded it to suggest that this was intended.

[64] ... I agree that the 1995 Act was not intended to make the radical change of providing for registration of a trade mark that would have the effect of restricting access to functional features or innovations. The policy concerns expressed by Burchett J were relevant to the issues considered in *Philips v Remington (Aust)*, FC, because that case was concerned with functional features. There is however, no suggestion, that in this case, the appellant's bug shape has any functional significance unless one regards having an attractive shape as functional. For reasons expressed below .., I do not regard the fact that a sign may evoke a positive emotional response as having functional significance for present purposes. ... [65]

Inherent adaption

The authorities give very little guidance as to what is necessary for inherent adaption either generally or with respect to shapes. It is clear that words (ordinary or technical) which are descriptive of the character or quality of the goods are not inherently adapted to distinguish; *Burger King Corporation v The Registrar of Trade Marks* (1973) 128 CLR 417 ("Whopper" as descriptive of large hamburgers); *Eutectic Corporation v Registrar of Trade Marks* (1980) 32 ALR 211 ("eutectic" as descriptive of machines and tools used in welding); *FH Faulding & Co Limited v Imperial Chemical Industries of Australia and New Zealand Limited* (1965) 112 CLR 537 ("Barrier" in respect of hand cream). This is so even if the word or words are contractions or corruptions of ordinary words; *Tastee Freez's Application* [1960] RPC 255 ("Tastee Freez" used in connection with ice cream [66] and water ices); *The Registrar of Trade Marks v Muller* (1980) 144 CLR 37 ("Less" in respect of pharmaceutical products); *Bausch & Lomb Inc v Registrar of Trade Marks* (1980) 28 ALR 537 ("Soflens" in respect of contact lenses); *Advanced Hair Studio of America Pty Ltd v Registrar of Trade Marks* (1988) 12 IPR 1 ("hairfusion" in respect of a service for fixing hairpieces to the head). The same principle applies to pictorial descriptions of goods; *Eclipse Sleep Products Incorporated v The Registrar of Trade Marks* (1957) 99 CLR 300 (a six-sided border having circular ends, as in the shape of a spring, used in connection with a "Springwall Mattress"). It is also well established that the name of a geographical location is not inherently adapted to distinguish goods because another trader may legitimately wish to use the name in connection with goods made in or associated with that place; *Thomson v B Seppelt & Sons Limited* (1925) 37 CLR 305 (use of the words, "Great Western" in respect of still and sparkling wines produced from grapes grown in the Great Western region of Victoria); *Clark Equipment* (use of the name "Michigan" in respect of earthmoving and the like equipment); *Blount Inc* (use of name "Oregon" inside an oval device in respect of power tool accessories); *Oxford University Press v Registrar of Trade Marks* (1990) 24 FCR 1 (use of name "Oxford" in respect of printed publications); *A Bailey and Company Limited v Clark, Son and Morland* [1938] AC 557 (use of name "Glastonburys" in connection with sheepskin slippers).

Signs that are descriptive of the character or quality of the relevant goods or which use a geographical name in connection with them cannot be inherently distinctive because the words have significations or associations that invite confusion and because registration of a trade mark using such words would preclude the use by others whose goods have similar qualities or which have a connection with the relevant areas...

...In my opinion it is the absence of these associations and significations that makes a sign inherently adapted to distinguish one trader's goods from those of another. In other words the concept is negative not positive. Support for this [67] view can be found in the cases in which a trade mark has been found to be inherently adapted to distinguish. In *Mid Sydney Pty Ltd v Australian Tourism Co Ltd* (1998) 90 FCR 236 it was argued that the registration of a trade mark consisting of the words "Chifley Tower", registered by the owner of a large office and retail building of that name, in respect of property management services and retail and office leasing services should be cancelled because, inter alia, it lacked the capacity to distinguish the services in respect of which it was registered. The Full Federal Court, applying the principles formulated by Kitto J in *Clark Equipment*, rejected this argument, stating at 251:

> "The Chifley Tower is not part of the common heritage in the sense that a town, suburb or municipality is. ... There is not public policy against [the building owner] restricting those who have come to occupy space within its building as to the way in which they use its name in connection with goods they produce or services they provide. That being so, it is not easy to see, in our view, why any separate public policy, of a kind identified by Kitto J, should apply so as to deprive the name selected by [the building owner] of a capacity to distinguish, in circumstances where there could be no legitimate reason for persons other than those carrying on business within The Chifley Tower to use its name in connection with their goods or services."

It is the absence of association and signification that accounts for invented words often being found to be inherently adapted to distinguish a trader's product. A good example of the invented word that has no meaning and therefore is inherently adapted to distinguish is the word "Fuddruckers" used in respect of services rendered by restaurants and other similar establishments; *Sharwood v Fuddruckers Inc* (1989) 15 IPR 188.

[69] ... It was accepted by the respondent's delegate that the bug shape was not a shape in common use. The delegate stated:

> "It is a stylised six-legged 'creature'. It does not represent a recognisable animal or insect or other living or mythical thing of which I am aware, and no ready descriptive word comes to mind in viewing it. It is, in my view, an invented shape. It strikes the eye as distinguishable from other shapes, being not so amorphous or ordinary as to be unmemorable, even though no name readily attaches it. It could be said that it carries the stamp of an individual imagination."

▬▬▬ Kenman Kandy v Registrar of Trade Marks *continued*

The delegate distinguished such an invented shape from ordinary well-known shapes which, in relation to confectionery, could include:

* "easily recognisable shapes that occur in nature (for example animals, flowers, insects, people, teeth);
* reproductions of common man-made objects (for example pillows, buildings);
* shapes familiar to everyone because they are commonplace solid geometric forms (for example cubes, globes, rectangular solids); and
* shapes neither natural nor geometric that form part of our common mythologic heritage (for example mermaids, angels, dragons)."

Despite the delegate accepting that the bug shape did not fall into any of these categories but was an invented shape and was not a shape that others need to use, he ultimately rejected the claim that it was inherently adapted to distinguish the appellant's confectionery because their shape did not appear, at first instance, to have trade mark significance.

The learned primary judge ...accepted the respondent's submissions that registration of the trade mark with the consequent grant of exclusive use of that trade mark to the appellant would narrow the "great common" of shapes available to traders generally. His Honour stated, at [33],

> "I have reached the conclusion that the subject mark is not inherently adapted to distinguish Kenman's confectionery from that of others. I agree that the mark is concocted; so far as I am aware, no real insect has this shape. However, the shape [70] is reminiscent, to a greater or lesser degree, of a variety of insects. That fact is important, especially when it is remembered that the mark is intended to be registered in respect of confectionery. Children constitute a significant part of the confectionery market; and children relate spontaneously and strongly to animals and animal-like creatures. Moreover, confectionery is highly malleable. Taken together, these factors make it likely that confectionery manufacturers will, from time to time, wish to put out products in shapes reminiscent of animals. To allow registration, for confectionery, of the shape of a real or readily-imagined animal would be to commence a process of 'fencing in the common' which would speedily impose serious restrictions upon other traders."

Conclusion

The delegate's conclusion implies a view that the test of inherent adaptation has a positive aspect as well as a negative. This view is also inherent in his Honour's reasons along with the concern expressed as 'fencing in the common'. For reasons already explained, it is my opinion that the test propounded by Kitto J in *Clark Equipment* .. sets out the necessary and sufficient criteria to determine whether a mark is adapted to distinguish one trader's goods from those of another. Applied here, the question is whether, if the bug shape were to be registered as a trade mark, other persons trading in confectionery and 'being actuated only by proper motives' would think of this shape and want to use it connection with their goods in any manner that would infringe the appellant's trade mark. That question must be answered bearing in mind that infringement would include using as a trade mark in relation to confectionery, not only the bug shape but also any 'sign that is substantially identical with, or deceptively similar to' the bug shape; s 120 of the 1995 Act. A subsidiary and difficult question is whether the appellant's bug shape, by virtue of it being recognisable as a 'bug', has associations that deprive it of the inherent capacity to distinguish the appellant's confectionery from that of other traders.

▨▨▨▨ Kenman Kandy v Registrar of Trade Marks *continued*

A shape (or word) that is entirely concocted does not have the associations that would lead to confusion. I do not regard such a shape as being part of the 'great common' any more than does a concocted word or a novel combination of common words; see for example *Mark Foy's* and *Wella*. The learned primary judge drew a distinction between concocted words, which, he said, were possibly infinite in number and the possibilities for concoction of animal-like shapes, which, he said were finite. With respect, I do not see the justification for this distinction. If there is any distinction I would have thought the advantage of greater variety lay with the category of three dimensional shapes which may involve any number of combinations of planes, arcs, angles and so forth.

Although the bug shape is suggestive of insect life it is not the shape of any specific insect or bug. Indeed, were it not for the description given by the appellants, it might as easily be seen as some extra-terrestrial object or space equipment such as a modified lunar landing module. Registration of the bug shape as a trade mark would not give the appellant a monopoly over all bug or insect shapes—only this particular shape and any substantially identical or deceptively similar shape. I see no reason in principle or policy why this should be so.

In my opinion the appeal should be allowed and the decision of the primary judge set aside.

Distinctiveness of colour marks

Woolworths Limited v BP

[14.195] *Woolworths Limited v BP plc* [2006] FCAFC 132 Federal Court of Australia, Full Court

Image for Trade Mark 676547

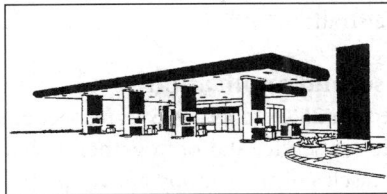

HEEREY, ALLSOP & YOUNG JJ:

Introduction

1. The respondent BP plc made two applications for registration of the colour green in association with service stations. The appellant Woolworths Ltd opposed registration. A delegate of the Registrar of Trade Marks refused the applications on the ground that the marks were not capable of distinguishing BP's goods and services: *Trade Marks Act 1995* (Cth), s 41(2), (5) and (6). The primary judge allowed an appeal and directed that the applications proceed to registration: *BP plc v Woolworths Ltd* (2004) 212 ALR 79. A Full Court of this Court granted Woolworths leave to appeal: *Woolworths Ltd v BP plc* (2006) 150 FCR 134.

2. Woolworths does not challenge the primary judge's conclusion that the colour green as such is not inherently adapted to distinguish BP's goods and services but is capable of acquiring distinctiveness through usage as a trade mark. The appeal concerned three main

▬▬▬▬ Woolworths Limited v BP *continued*

issues. Broadly stated, the first is whether the trial judge erred in finding that the amendments to the endorsements of each of the applications were not made contrary to s 65 of the Act; the second is whether each of the marks does distinguish BP's goods or services by reason of its prior use and whether the trial judge erred in finding that BP's trade mark applications should be registered pursuant to s 41(6) of the Act; and the third concerns this Court's power to grant relief.

Application 559837 (the first application)

3. ... [A square of green material was affixed, each side being about 3.5 cm]

The trademark is limited to the colour green as shown in the representation attached to the application form."

4. It was common ground that what was "affixed to the Schedule of this application" and what was "attached to the application form" was the same thing: the green square under the heading "The Schedule".

5. After the commencement of the Act in 1995 the three applications were consolidated into one application, numbered 559837. Class 1 goods were deleted.

6. At the time of making the consolidated application on 17 July 1997 the respondent amended the endorsement by inserting the following:

"The trade mark consists of the colour green as shown in the representation on the application as applied to a significant proportion of the exterior surface of the buildings, canopies, pole signs and other component parts of service stations used for the sale of the goods and the supply of the services covered by the registration."

7. On 30 October 1997, the endorsement was re-amended to the following form:

"The trade mark consists of the colour GREEN as shown in the representation on the application applied as the predominant colour to the fascias of buildings, petrol pumps, signage boards – including poster boards, pole signs and price boards – and spreaders, all used in service station complexes for sale of the goods and supply of the services covered by the registration."

Application 676547 (the second application)

8. The second application, filed on 25 October 1995 in respect of services in class 42, attached a schedule containing a sketch of a service station together with a convenience store and a car wash in the background. The fascias of the canopy above the petrol pumps, the convenience store and car wash, the front and back of the tanks, the rubbish bin, the poster board, the price board and the spreaders (the area on the petrol pump immediately above the glass display area) were all coloured green.

9. When first filed the schedule contained the endorsement:

"The mark consists of the colour green applied to the exterior surfaces of the premises used for the supply of the said services as exemplified in the representation attached to the application"

10. In July 1997 this was amended to:

"The trade mark consists of the colour GREEN applied to a significant proportion of the exterior surface of the buildings, canopies, pole signs and other component parts of service stations used for the supply of the services covered by the registration, as exemplified in the representation attached to the application form."

And ultimately in October 1997 to:

> "The trade mark consists of the colour GREEN applied as the predominant colour to the fascias of buildings, petrol pumps, signage boards – including poster boards, pole signs and price boards – and spreaders, all used in service station complexes for the supply of the services covered by the registration, as exemplified in the representation attached to the application form."

Use of colour by service stations

11. In his reasons for judgment the primary judge described the historical usage of colours and logos by major participants in the retail petrol industry in Australia and the events leading up to the changes in BP's use of colour which has led to these proceedings. In the passages which follow we have summarised the more important background facts. None of them was in dispute.

12. The emergence of service stations led oil companies to apply their colours and logos to parts of the structures in an effort to identify themselves and distinguish themselves from their rivals. From 1920 BP in the United Kingdom had a logo consisting of the letters "BP" in upper case on a background in the shape of a shield. At first the letters were in red within a black shield, but in 1923 the colours were changed to green and yellow.

13. BP has used the letters "BP" and the green and yellow shield logo in Australia since 1954 when it entered the Australian market on its own account. About this time oil companies began aggressive promotion of their brands. Petrol rationing had ended and the motor car was becoming the principal means of transportation for most people in the industrialised world.

14. In the late 1950s BP decided to standardise the image of its service stations around the world. It retained the French design firm Compagnie D'Esthetique Industrielle who produced a "New Look" involving white, yellow, green and red. Photographs of BP service stations in Australia between the early 1960s and the late 1980s show the canopy above the dispensing islands was generally painted white with a green and yellow horizontal parallel stripe on the fascia. In one photograph the canopy is painted white and has no stripes. The poles holding the canopy are painted white.

15. In 1986 BP decided to change the appearance of its service stations. Its existing get-up had been applied inconsistently around the world and its main competitors had changed or were in the process of changing the appearance of their own service stations. This project was dubbed "Project Horizon". Addison Design Consultants and MAS Research Marketing & Consultants Ltd were retained.

16. In early 1989 a design and colour were approved. The green shade Pantone 348C was chosen. This was to become the predominant colour applied to BP's service stations.

17. BP devised a strict procedure for the implementation of Project Horizon. The implementation occurred in two stages. First, there was the re-imaging of existing service stations. Then there was the building of new sites. Three levels of re-imaging for existing stations were laid down. Level 3 was the top re-imaging standard. Service stations in this level adopted a new bullnose canopy edge, stand alone petrol pumps with larger spreaders, back lighting, and a new identification sign. Level 3 was applied to key company-owned sites in prime, highly visible locations. Service stations re-imaged to level 2 had flat faced canopies and stand-alone petrol pumps with spreaders above the main identification sign as well as additional signage. Level 2 was applied to small towns and rural sites which did not have such a substantial patronage to justify the cost of top level re-imaging. Level 1 was for smaller sites and was confined principally to re-painting. All levels had the following common features: the colour green was to be applied to the canopy, fascias, main identification sign, all auxiliary signage,

━━━━ Woolworths Limited v BP *continued*

the car wash and convenience store fascia; the fuel dispensing area in the service station was also to be predominantly green; and the main identification sign would be between five to ten metres high to attract the eye of the motorist.

18. Between July 1989 and July 1991 approximately 1200 BP service stations in Australia adopted the new get-up. By December 1995, a total of 1356 retail service stations had been re-imaged. The amount BP spent on the project, inclusive of capital works, was substantial: between July 1989 and September 1996 it spent $50,564,909 with a further $91,898,317 being spent since then. The worldwide budget for Project Horizon was US$500 million.

19. BP widely promoted its new image. Every television advertisement screened in Australia since late 1988 has ended either with a green BP flag or a road which turns into green. In the print media, BP's "Easy in, Easy Out" advertisement referred to "BP's new green stations". A later "Easy In, Easy Out" advertisement had the following text: "At BP the new green stations keep the wheels turning for more and more motorists every day". The "Stop at the green light" advertisement advised motorists that there was more "to our petrol stations than their new green look". The advertisement invited motorists to pull in "[n]ext time you see the green light".

20. Woolworths entered the Australian retail petrol market in June 1996. By December 1998 there were 83 Woolworths service stations, of which 58 were located in car parks adjacent to shopping centres in which a Woolworths supermarket was situated. Different trading names were used:

- "Woolworths Plus Petrol"—New South Wales, Australian Capital Territory, Queensland, Western Australia, South Australia and the Northern Territory;
- "Safeway Plus Petrol"—Victoria;
- "Purity Plus Petrol" and "Roelf Vos Plus Petrol"—Tasmania.

In 2000 some Woolworths service stations began incorporating convenience stores.

21. The Woolworths service stations used the Woolworths supermarket logo as well as the colours red, green and white as part of their get-up. The canopy was painted green with the words "Woolworths" and "+ Petrol" painted in white. The poles holding up the canopy were white. The pay point that was located at the premises was painted green. From October 1996 to April 2001 the green colour was Pantone 347C. In April 2001 the shade was changed to Pantone 354C, which is the same green as is used in the supermarket logo.

22. 7-Eleven stores were set up in Australia in 1977. Two years later 7-Eleven began to establish combined "format stores" (self-service drive-in service stations which incorporated a convenience store). As at 31 August 2002, 7-Eleven had 276 stores operating in Australia, 149 of which were in the combined format. 7-Eleven stores have a distinctive get-up. It comprises a band of three horizontal colours (orange, green, and red) on a white background which appears on the canopy of the service stations and on the building façades.

23. Caltex has operated in Australia since 1941 as a refiner, distributor and marketer of fuels and lubricants. In the early 1980s Caltex established its service stations and from the mid-1980s began incorporating "Star Mart" convenience stores into those stations. Initially the colours incorporated in the Caltex livery were primarily white, red and black. The canopy was painted red with the word "Caltex" written in white. The canopy also incorporated the Caltex logo which comprised a white circle with a red star cut out. The poles holding up the station were white. The logo was encased on a black signage board.

24. In February 1999 Caltex adopted a new colour scheme for its service stations and convenience stores. A "deep ocean green" appears as part of the Caltex logo, on the price board and on the numbers appearing above each pump. A "turquoise" green together with orange and yellow appears on the "Star Mart" logo and on the awnings of "Star Mart" convenience stores. Caltex also markets fuel under the "Vortex" brand. "Vortex" service

stations, of which there now are five in the Sydney metropolitan area, use the colour green on their logo and canopy. The Vortex logo consists of two halves of a green oval which is encased on a white background. Between the two halves the word Vortex appears in black. ...

Distinctiveness and the operation of s 41

... 65. His Honour noted (at [16]) that the Act does not suggest that the registrability of a colour mark is to be approached any differently from that of any other mark.

66. His Honour held (at [19]-[23]) that, for the purposes of s 41(3) and (5), the colour green, in the shade shown in the applications, was not inherently adapted to distinguish BP's goods and services. Accordingly, his Honour had to consider whether use of the marks before the filing of the applications distinguished the goods and services of BP. As his Honour put it (at [23]), BP had to establish:

"first, that it has used the particular shade of green as a trade mark and, second, that in the minds of the public the primary significance of that shade of green, when used in connection with the supply of petroleum products or the provision of petroleum services, identifies the source of those goods or the provider of those services as originating from a particular trader, though not necessarily from an identified trader."

67. His Honour noted (at [24]) that since most objects have some colour, merely applying a colour to a product will not act as an identifier for that product. For colour to function as a trade mark the colour must be used to distinguish products, and not as mere ornamentation or decoration. The question is whether the trader has used the colour in a way that informs the public that the product emanates from a particular source.

68. There was no issue on appeal about the correctness of the primary judge's view that the colour green was not inherently adapted to distinguish the designated goods and services for the purposes of s 41(3) and (5) of the Act. Thus, the only issue was the application of s 41(6).

69. It is convenient to set out the key paragraphs of the trial judge's reasoning on s 41(6), at [62]-[65] of his reasons for judgment:

"From all of the evidence there is at least one inescapable conclusion. It is that each major oil company that retails petroleum products through service stations has adopted a get-up for its stations which is distinctive of that company's products. The same is true of a non-oil company retailers, such as Woolworths and 7-Eleven, whose own evidence (the 7-Eleven witness was called by Woolworths) speaks eloquently of the distinctiveness of their own styles. So far as BP is concerned, there is simply no doubt in my mind that its get up, with its predominant use of green, is a badge of origin. Not only do consumers know that a predominantly green (in a particular shade) service station signifies a source, for the most part they also know that source to be BP. I am quite satisfied that this was as true in 1991 as it was in 1995. At the time of the first group of applications, the new get up had been in existence in some areas for upwards of three years and in almost all areas of Australia for at least a short time. Although short it was of sufficient duration to establish distinctiveness, in my opinion.

Here, however, we have a problem of a different order. BP's get-up consists of more than one feature. It comprises the shield, the letters BP, the use that is made of the colour yellow, as well as the colour green. It is true that as a result of its green program, green was regarded as BP's dominant corporate colour. Yet green is only one aspect of its total image. The question that arises in these circumstances is whether it is possible to dissect that total image and obtain trade mark registration of only one component of the whole image.

■■■■■ Woolworths Limited v BP *continued*

I have not found any English or Australian authorities which provide any guidance on this issue. On the other hand the matter has been extensively considered in the US. Most, but not all, of the cases have arisen when an attempt has been made to register as a trade mark the background design for a word, letter or device mark. ... The relevant principles to be extracted from these cases, principles which I intend to apply, are these: Separate components of a single get-up or design may qualify for registration as a mark. They will be capable of registration if each feature considered separately distinguish the goods or services in question. If the get-up or design creates "a separate and distinct commercial impression" then the separate parts will not be registrable. However, if each separate part creates an impression which is totally separate from the others and is distinctive, that is it performs the trade mark function of identifying the source of the goods and services to customers, that will suffice. J McCarthy, McCarthy on *Trade Marks and Unfair Competition Vol 1* at SS 7.28 puts it this way: "The design must emerge out of the 'background' and 'hit the buyer in the eye' such that it is likely to guide the buyer in purchasing decisions."

Customers identified BP's service stations by the colour green alone, independently of the shield. These are the reasons. First BP is the only service station that used green as the predominant colour on its get up when the applications were filed. Second BP has made extensive use of the colour green in its get up – not only with the implementation of Project Horizon but as early as 1956 when green was adopted as one of BP's corporate colours in Australia. Third the colour green has featured prominently in the company's advertising. On the evidence which I have, much of which was not before the examining officer, I am bound to reach the conclusion that the colour green in the shade depicted in the applications had acquired a secondary meaning and had become distinctive of BP's goods and services in the classes for which registration is sought when the applications were filed in 1991 and 1995 respectively."

70. There were two related strands to Woolworths' arguments on appeal. The first strand was that the primary judge's focus was not directed to the full scope of the mark. Woolworths stressed that the use of the word predominant in the endorsements meant that the mark was not for the colour green alone, but was wider—green as the predominant colour with any other (unspecified) colour. Thus, Woolworths submitted, the primary judge erred by considering the distinctiveness of green alone and not the distinctiveness of the mark in its full scope. The second strand was that, by relying on the results of the survey that was put into evidence, the trial judge confused the fact that green was associated with BP and its get-up with the more specific question of whether green had been used by BP in the manner claimed in the application as a badge of origin.

71. Bound up in both strands of the argument were the propositions that the evidence was inadequate to establish trade mark usage of green alone prior to 1991 or 1995 and that the analysis was not to be undertaken by looking to the get-up of BP's service stations. Woolworths submitted that the questions posed by s 41(6) ought to have been addressed by examining the evidence which showed the extent to which BP had actually used the trade mark it had applied for, as a trade mark, in order to assess the distinctiveness called for by s 41(6).

The requirements of s 41(6) and use as a Trade Mark

...81. One of the difficulties with the approach of the primary judge is that one does not find any analysis expressed in the terms of s 41(6), although his Honour referred to the statutory questions posed by s 41(6) early in his reasons. The primary judge proceeded to analyse the evidence and draw his conclusions by reference to the get-up of the service stations: at [62]-

[65]. Apart from those conclusions his Honour made no express finding about what had been used as a trade mark. Certainly, one can recognise the discussion of what may be a very similar issue in the United States of disaggregating get-up for the purposes of individual trade mark registration. However, s 41(6) calls for a more precise analysis. In *Philmac Pty Ltd v Registrar of Trade Marks* (2002) 126 FCR 525 at 548 [71], Mansfield J said that for the purposes of applying s 41(6) to a colour mark two issues needed to be addressed. The first is whether the use of the colour in the manner described in the application has, prior to the date of the application, constituted use of the colour as a trade mark. The second issue is whether the trade mark applied for does in fact distinguish the applicant's products, having regard to evidence concerning the actual use of the colour as a trade mark. We agree with that approach. Thus, s 41(6) requires specific consideration of the extent to which BP has used each of the marks applied for as a trade mark before the date of filing and whether that use was sufficient to distinguish the designated goods and services as being those of BP: *Blount v Registrar of Trade Marks* (1998) 83 FCR 50 at 60.

82. In our view, there are obvious dangers in approaching these issues by reference to the get-up of the service stations. The foremost danger, perhaps, is that the inquiry will be diverted into an examination of the distinctiveness of the colour green alone, and away from the questions posed by s 41(6). That danger must be heightened where the evidence clearly showed that BP had used the colour green in ways, and as part of other trade marks, that did not correspond with the trade marks that were the subject of the applications in suit. For the purpose of s 41(6), the focus of the inquiry should be the use of the marks applied for, rather than use of colour as part of the get-up or packaging of goods generally: cf *British Sugar plc v James Robertson & Sons Ltd* [1996] RPC 281 at 302. Woolworths submitted that the primary judge was diverted in this way, and as a result incorrectly concluded that the trade marks the subject of the applications had been used by BP, either at all or to such an extent that they did distinguish BP's goods and services. We agree with this submission.

The evidence of use

...99. Taking all the evidence together the following can be said. First, in the context of the oil industry in which a small number of companies had for many years used colours to distinguish their goods and services from the goods and services of competitors, before 1989 BP used green and yellow to distinguish its service stations, goods and services from those of its competitors.

100. Secondly, by 1989, BP made a deliberate decision to change what might be called the colour branding of BP. Green was to be, and was, used more extensively than yellow in the livery of service stations and in advertising. It continued, however, to be used with yellow.

101. Thirdly, on the fascias of buildings, petrol pumps, signage boards, (including poster boards, pole signs and price boards), and spreaders in service stations (the parts of service stations referred to in the endorsements), green was used as the predominant colour, but only with yellow. This use of green as the predominant colour, with the use of yellow, can be understood as trade mark use, replacing the use of green and yellow given approximately equal weight and prominence as the company's brand colours before 1989.

102. Fourthly, the question arises whether, after 1989, the advertising reveals not only the use of predominantly green with yellow as the company's colours and as a trade mark, but also the use, as a trade mark, of green alone. This question cannot be answered simply by attempting to find an advertisement without yellow present, although there is no such advertisement in evidence. For the conclusion to be drawn that green alone was being used by BP as a trade mark prior to 1991 or 1995, one must understand the material as stating to the ordinary person that

━━━━━━ Woolworths Limited v BP *continued*

green alone was being used as a badge of origin to distinguish BP's goods and services from those of its competitors.

103. Some of the print media referring to "green stations" and the "green light" clearly sought to use green in this way. Overall, however, it is difficult to conclude that the colour green was used by BP before 1991 and 1995 as a trade mark other than by its use of green as the predominant colour in conjunction with yellow. Certainly, on the evidence, in relation to the parts of the service station referred to in the endorsements, green has always been used in conjunction with yellow.

104. The fact that from a distance the predominant green of the colour of the service station (in particular the fascias of the canopy and buildings and any pole sign) would be noticed, and would assist the motorist in identifying the existence of a BP service station, is not sufficient to transform the use of green predominantly with yellow into the use of green as a trade mark. The fact is that the fascias had yellow logos and marks prominently placed on them, the main identification signs had the green and yellow logo and mark, as well as yellow script, the price boards had a green background and yellow writing, the pumps and spreaders had yellow logos and marks.

105. After the change brought about by "Project Horizon", green predominated in the colour scheme of the service station, but at all times it was used with yellow as the subsidiary, but ever present companion. Looking at all the advertisings, print, television and point of sale material, we conclude that the colours used to distinguish BP's goods and services from those of its competitors in the parts of the service stations referred to in the endorsements were its existing brand colours, green and yellow, with a marked and clear predominance of green. Green, alone, was not used as a trade mark in the parts of the service stations referred to in the endorsements. BP stressed, however, the educative role of that part of the advertising which stressed green – that told the reader of the "Green BP stations" and to "stop at the green light". But even if it be assumed that there was some trade mark use of green alone in the particular print advertisements to which we have referred, the evidence is inadequate to elevate that to the point where it establishes the matters referred to in s 41(6).

106. Taking all of the evidence into account, including the absence of evidence as to the frequency of specific print or television advertising, we are unable to conclude that any trade mark use of colour by BP at the relevant times has been other than green as the dominant colour in conjunction with yellow as the subsidiary colour.

The survey evidence

107. BP relied heavily on the results of a survey that was admitted into evidence. The survey was professionally and competently done under the supervision of a person qualified to undertake and to assess the survey and its results, a Dr Bednall. The appellant did not seek to impugn Dr Bednall's evidence, so far as it went. However, the appellant challenged the trial judge's reliance on the survey evidence to support his Honour's conclusions as to the distinctiveness of BP's use of green as a trade mark.

108. BP sought to prove two things by the survey: that the colour green had become distinctive of BP and of the goods and services of BP, and that this conclusion was indicative of the perception by the public before 1991 and 1995 of BP's use of the colour green being trade mark use. ...

121. We are satisfied that the primary judge fell into error in the key paragraphs of his reasons at [62] and [65]. First, his Honour erred by directing his attention to the "get-up" of the service stations, as opposed to the use before 1991 or 1995 of colour as a trade mark, whether green, or green and yellow, in respect of the parts of the service station claimed in

████ Woolworths Limited v BP *continued*

the application. Given BP's use of the colours green and yellow in its trade marks and in other ways, we do not think that BP's total image could be dissected so as to support these applications in the manner suggested by the primary judge. Secondly, his Honour did not consider whether BP's use of the colour green prior to 1991 and 1995 constituted trade mark use of the marks claimed in the applications, such that they had become distinctive of BP's goods and services. In particular, his Honour did not consider the full scope of each of the marks by asking whether BP had used the colour green as the predominant colour with yellow or any other (unspecified) colour: cf *Campomar Sociedad, Limitada v Nike International Ltd* (2000) 202 CLR 45 at 76 [72]. Thus, in our view, his Honour's conclusion on BP's use of green prior to 1991 and 1995 did not support his finding of distinctiveness under s 41(6). Thirdly, his Honour erred in treating the survey as evidence that the trade marks the subject of the applications must have been in use as trade marks before the priority dates, so as to distinguish BP's goods and services. In reality, the survey respondents were directed to the use of green alone, which was not the mark the subject of the applications. As a result of these errors, the primary judge did not properly address the statutory questions posed by s 41(6).

122. Thus, we do not accept the proposition that the survey itself or the survey together with the other evidence of use, proves that before 1991 or 1995 there was trade mark use of the colour green alone on the parts of the service station that are referred to in each endorsement. Nor do we accept that it proves trade mark use of the colour green as the predominant colour on the parts of the service station that are referred to in each endorsement, with any other accompanying colour.

123. In our view, BP failed to establish as at July 1991 or October 1995 that it had used each of the trade marks it had applied for, that is green as the predominant colour of the parts of the service station referred to in the endorsements with any other (unspecified) colour. Nor in our view did BP establish as at July 1991 or October 1995 use as a trade mark of the colour green alone in respect of the parts of the service station referred to in the endorsements.

124. Thus, in our view, on the evidence, BP failed to establish the matters provided for in s 41(6) of the Act.

125. Even if the submission of BP were to be accepted that it had established trade mark use of the colour green on the parts of the service station referred to in the endorsements before 1991 or 1995, the two applications do not claim any such trade mark use of colour. They do not claim the use of green alone in the trade mark, nor do they claim the use of predominant green with yellow. Rather the applications claim green as the predominant colour to the various parts of the service station identified, with the subsidiary colour or colours of the trade mark unidentified. That was not the use of green before 1991 or 1995. The trade mark use before 1991 and 1995 in relation to the parts of the service station referred to in the endorsements was predominantly green with yellow as the subsidiary colour or, assuming contrary to our view, green alone. ...

RESTRICTIONS ON REGISTRATION

[14.200] Apart from the general prohibitions on non-distinctive marks (s 41), false geographic indicators (s 61), generic marks (s 24), marks which cannot be represented graphically (s 40) and marks excluded by regulation (s 39), the *Trade Marks Act 1995* (Cth) addresses overriding concerns about marks which are deceptive, contrary to law, or already registered for the goods or services in question. These are scandalous/contrary to law (s 42); trade mark likely to deceive or cause confusion (s 43) and where a trade mark is identical to or deceptively similar to an existing mark (s 44). These objections were covered by ss 28 and 33 of the 1955 Act. An assessment of the issue as to whether marks are "substantially identical with or deceptively similar to" each other (s 44) is also relevant in deciding infringement (s 120).

■ Prior use/prior registration

▬ Southern Cross Refrigerating v Toowoomba Foundry ▬

[14.205] *Southern Cross Refrigerating Co v Toowoomba Foundry Pty Ltd* (1954) 91 CLR 592 High Court of Australia

[The appellant had sought registration of the trade mark SOUTHERN CROSS in respect of gas absorption and electric refrigerators and parts thereof. The application was opposed by the respondent which had registered trade mark SOUTHERN CROSS in respect of well-drilling machinery, milking machines, engines and windmills. The opposition was based on s 114 of the 1905 Act (equivalent to s 43 of the 1995 Act) and s 25 of that Act (equivalent to s 44 of the 1995 Act). Kitto J at first instance had held s 25 not to be applicable and held that the registration would not cause confusion and hence breach s 114.]

DIXON CJ, MCTIERNAN, WEBB, FULLAGAR and TAYLOR JJ: **[606]** The fact that examination of the nature of the applicant's goods may, by itself, induce an observer to conclude that they are different in character from those of an opponent, and designed to serve different purposes, is by no means conclusive. Nor is the fact that the applicant's goods are not specified by the regulations as being within the same class of goods: see *Re The Australian Wine Importers Ltd* (1889) 41 Ch D 278 at 291 and *Reckitt & Colman (Aust) Ltd v Boden* per Latham CJ (1945) 70 CLR 84 at 90. There may be many matters to be considered apart from the inherent character of the goods in respect of which the application is made and some indication of what matters are relevant to this inquiry was given by Romer J in *Re Jellinek's Application* (1946) 63 RPC 59. Romer J thought it necessary to look beyond the nature of the goods in question and to compare not only their respective uses but also to examine the trade channels through which the commodities in question were bought and sold. Shortly after the decision in *Jellinek's* case (1946) 63 RPC 59 the Assistant-Comptroller elaborated on the observations of Romer J in the following manner:

> "[I]n arriving at a decision upon this issue the reported cases show that I have to take account of a number of factors, including in particular the nature and characteristics of the goods, their origin, their purpose, whether they are usually produced by one and the same manufacturer or distributed by the same wholesale houses, whether they are sold in the same shops over the same counters during the same seasons and to the same class or classes of customers, and whether by those engaged in their manufacture and distribution they are regarded as belonging to the same trade. In the case of *Jellinek's Application*, Romer J classified these various factors under three heads, viz, the nature of the goods, the uses thereof, and the trade channels through which they are bought and sold. No single consideration is conclusive in itself, and it has further been emphasised that the classifications contained in the schedules to the Trade Marks Rules are not a decisive criterion as to whether or not two sets of goods are 'of the same description': *Re an Application by John Crowther & Sons (Milnsbridge) Ltd* (1948) 65 RPC 369 at 372. Much the same considerations are evident in the observation of Dixon J (as he then was) in *Reckitt & Colman (Aust) Ltd v Boden* (1945) 70 CLR 84 at 94 when he said:

▬▬▬ Southern Cross Refrigerating v Toowoomba Foundry *continued*

'What forms the same description of goods must be discovered from a consideration of the course of trade or business. One factor is the use to which the two sets
of goods are put. Another is whether they are commonly dealt with in the same
course of trade or [607] business. In the present case, the goods are quite different,
their uses are widely separated and they are not commonly sold in the same kinds
of shops or departments.'"

Giving full weight to all of these matters we are satisfied that s 25 has no application to this
case. The goods to be compared and their respective uses are vastly different and, though the
evidence shows that in the course of marketing and distribution there may be substantial
points of contact, the evidence does not lead to the conclusion that the goods of the appellant
are of the *same description* as those of the respondent.

We have thought it necessary to make some references to the matters proper for consideration in relation to this issue under s 25 for the argument of the appellant seizes upon them
and asserts that once these matters have been considered and the relevant issue answered in
favour of an applicant it is impossible to say that the use by him, with respect to his goods,
of the trade mark in question would be "likely to deceive" within the meaning of s 114.
Whilst conceding that the likelihood of deception is not as great where, in no sense, can it be
said that an applicant's goods are the same or of the same description as those of an
opponent, it is quite clear that the latter finding by no means disposes of the relevant inquiry
under s 114. To suggest that it does really confuses the nature of the inquiry which arises
under s 25 for it is not sufficient in order to reach the conclusion that an applicant's goods
are of the same description as those of an opponent, merely, to find that in the course of
marketing there is a likelihood of deception taking place; the inquiry is much more limited
and must be answered in favour of the applicant unless upon an examination of the material
matters the conclusion is justified that the applicant's goods ought to be regarded as being of
the same description as those of the opponent. This is far from saying that if the evidence
shows a probability or likelihood of deception such a conclusion would be justified. Indeed,
if it were not a distinct and separate inquiry it would be impossible to reconcile the multitude
of cases—of which *Re Jellinek's Application* (1946) 63 RPC 59 and *Reckitt & Colman (Aust) Ltd v
Boden* (1945) 70 CLR 84 are themselves examples—in which it has been thought necessary to
consider the likelihood of deception notwithstanding a finding that the respective goods of
the applicant and the opponent were not the same or of the same description.

The question whether it is likely that deception will result from the use of a mark which
is the same as, or which closely resembles, [608] a trade mark already in use may, and
frequently will, require the consideration of matters additional to and distinct from those
which are relevant to an inquiry under s 25. It may be of importance to see whether the
registered mark is general or special in character and to ascertain the extent of its reputation.
Again, it may be important to see whether the goods in respect of which it is registered
constitute a narrow class or a wide variety of goods as also will be the question whether the
goods of both the applicant and the opponent will be likely to find markets substantially in
common areas and among the same classes of people. It is, of course, for the person applying
for registration to establish that there is no likelihood of confusion and we agree with Kitto J
that registration should be refused if it appears that there is a real risk that "the result of the
user of the mark will be that a number of persons will be caused to wonder whether it might
not be the case that the two products came from the same source"; it is, of course, not
necessary that it should appear that the user of the mark will lead to passing off: see Morton
J (as he then was) in *Re Hack's Application* (1940) 58 RPC 91 at 103. Further, it is not enough
for the applicant:

■■■■■■ Southern Cross Refrigerating v Toowoomba Foundry *continued*

"to negative the likelihood of confusion in relation to the actual trade carried on by the opponent at the time of registration and to the manner in which the latter then uses his mark. The applicant must also take into account all legitimate uses which the opponent may reasonably make of his mark within the ambit of his registration" (*Reckitt & Colman (Aust) Ltd v Boden* per Dixon J (as he then was) (1945) 70 CLR 84 at 94, 95.)

The second branch of the appellant's argument asserted that the question of fact under s 114, which was decided adversely to him, should, upon the evidence, have been decided otherwise. In our opinion, there was, however, abundant evidence to justify his Honour's conclusion; there was evidence which his Honour found "entirely convincing" and we find it of equal cogency. Not only was there evidence which established the probability of confusion but, also, quite substantial evidence of actual confusion. But the appellant claims that any actual or probable confusion had proceeded or would proceed from a belief that the respondent had a monopoly of the "Southern Cross" mark. This mistaken belief, it was said, alone had led to the actual confusion deposed to and this circumstance operated to strip the evidence of real weight. We do not agree. In part the confusion resulted from the use by the appellant of a mark which had long and widely been used by the respondent, in part from the fact that it was a mark which had been used by the latter [609] with respect to such diverse objects as both manual and power well-drilling and boring machinery, milking machines and engines and windmills, in part from the fact that in the course of business those articles frequently are and have, for a long time, been sold in country stores where, side by side with them, domestic refrigerators are stocked and sold, and last, but not least, from the circumstances that the name "Southern Cross" is a mark of a general character and—as appears from what we have already said—of a wide and varied significance. A careful scrutiny of the evidence convinces us that the respondent made out a clear case, not only that a user of the mark by the appellant for the purposes proposed by it would be likely to deceive, but that it has already done so in a not inconsiderable number of cases. In those circumstances we do not propose, nor do we think it necessary to traverse the whole of the facts again.

■ Deceptive or confusing (s 43)/Conflicting reputation (s 60)

■■■■■ **Torpedoes Sportswear v Thorpedo Enterprises** ■■■■■

[14.210]   *Torpedoes Sportswear Pty Limited v Thorpedo Enterprises Pty Limited & Anor* (2003) 59 IPR 318 Federal Court of Australia

BENNETT J: **[319]**

This is an appeal from the decision of the Delegate of the Registrar of Trade Marks ("the Delegate") to accept the application made by the first respondent, Thorpedo Enterprises Pty Limited ("Enterprises" or 'the respondent") on 17 March 1999 to register the trade mark THORPEDO ("the THORPEDO mark").

...

The parties

Australian Trade Mark Registration No 585117, being PARADISE LEGENDS TORPEDOES ("the Paradise Legends mark"), was registered by Paradise Legends Pty Ltd ("Paradise") in 1992 in

▨▨▨▨▨ Torpedoes Sportswear v Thorpedo Enterprises *continued*

class 28: protective paddings, protective paddings for sporting shorts, therapeutic protective padding. Paradise assigned the Paradise Legends mark on 24 February 1998 to Torpedoes International Pty Limited ("International"). Paradise was placed into liquidation on 1 October 1998.

International filed a trade mark application on 7 September 1998 in class 25: clothing including headgear and footwear, which is Australian Trade Mark Registration No 772346 ("the T device mark") as follows:

I shall refer to the large, stylised T that precedes the word Torpedoes as "the T device".

International was placed into liquidation on 6 December 1999. On 9 December 1999, Sportswear acquired the assets of International, including the Paradise Legends mark and the T device mark (together, "the Sportswear marks") for $25,000. ...

[320] Mr Ian Thorpe describes himself as "an Australian swimming representative".

The first occasion on which Mr Thorpe was called "Thorpedo" was, apparently, on 17 March 1997, when it was used in an article in the Daily Telegraph newspaper. Since then, on numerous occasions, in both the print and electronic media and in advertisements the word "Thorpedo" has been referred to in connection with Mr Thorpe. On each occasion, according to the evidence, Mr Thorpe's name and/or his likeness have appeared when the word was used.

In early 1998, Mr Thorpe instructed his financial adviser, Mr Sheridan, to incorporate a company to enter into commercial arrangements on his behalf, to be called Thorpedo Enterprises Pty Ltd. Mr Thorpe chose the "Thorpedo" part of the company name because he liked the name that the media had used to describe him. In 2001, he instructed Mr Sheridan to incorporate Thorpedo International Pty Limited ("Thorpedo International").

Enterprises applied for the THORPEDO mark on 17 March 1999 ("the relevant date").

While some goods are not within the registered classes for both the Sportswear marks and the THORPEDO mark, there are common classes of goods for which the competing marks are registered. ... [329]

Relevant principles

The question of deceptive similarity involves a number of different and additional considerations. The question is whether the normal use of the THORPEDO mark in relation to the class of goods specified in the application would be likely to cause deception and confusion in the face of Sportswear's normal use of its marks.

A different comparison is made than that for substantial identity. Here the question is one of impression based on recollection of the mark (*Shell* at 415). While it is not necessary to prove actual deception, neither is a mere possibility of confusion sufficient: *Southern Cross Refrigerating Co v Toowoomba Foundry Pty Ltd* (1954) 91 CLR 592 (*Southern Cross*); there must be real, tangible danger of confusion occurring (*Woolworths*). It is sufficient if, by reason of use of the mark, a number of people would wonder if two products came from the same source (*Southern Cross*). In *Australian Woollen Mills Ltd v FS Walton & Co Ltd* (1937) 58 CLR 641 (*Woollen Mills*), Dixon and McTiernan JJ apparently considered both the visual and aural use of the marks there in question; the reference by their Honours to the effect produced in the course of the ordinary conduct of affairs would include aural use, where the evidence was that the mark was applied to goods that were regularly referred to orally by name (at 658).

▮▮▮▮▮ Torpedoes Sportswear v Thorpedo Enterprises *continued*

The task is one requiring the application of common sense and impression, which can depend on a combination of visual and aural impression and the estimation of the effect likely to be produced in the ordinary conduct of affairs (*Anheuser-Busch Inc v Budejovicky Budvar* (2003) 56 IPR 182 at 217.

I was referred to a number of cases in which words were compared and conclusions drawn as to whether or not there was deceptive similarity. It is, of course, helpful to see the process of reasoning applied in each case but, of necessity, much turns on the individual words under consideration. It is not necessarily helpful to trawl through decided cases to examine how different decision makers have formed conclusions, based on their own impressions, as to whether or not confusion or deception arises when two specific words are compared visually and aurally. In this regard, I refer to the words of Windeyer J in *Re Bali Brassiere Co Inc's Registered Trade Mark* and *Berlei Limited's Application* (1968) 118 CLR 128 at 139:

> "Cases were cited to me from passages in judgments dealing with marks held to be, or held not to be, by reason of similarities, deceptive or confusing. I have read these cases, and others. I do not think I need discuss them. The governing principles are not in dispute; and little is to be gained by the quotation of enunciations and elaborations of them in other cases. The difficulty is always in their application to the facts of the case in hand."

Much depends on the words themselves, their origins and meanings and the surrounding circumstances of their use. What an examination of the cases where similar words are compared visually and aurally show, is that each such comparison depends on matters such as the pronunciation of the words, their meaning and the categories of goods to which the marks are to be applied.

[330] There is little dispute as to the principles to be applied although it must be remembered that previous decisions frequently turned on the question of onus, which has changed under the Act. [The opponent bears the onus to establish deception and confusion, and opposition should only be upheld if the court is satisfied that the mark should clearly not have been registered See *Registrar for Trade Marks v Woolworths* (1999) 45 IPR 411; *Lomas v Winton Shire Council* (2003) AIPC 91-839].

Those principles, as relevant to this case, can be summarised as follows and are largely drawn from the very well known and regularly cited cases *Pianotist Company Ltd's Application* (1906) 23 RPC 774 (*Pianotist*) per Parker J; *Woollen Mills*; *Cooper Engineering Co Pty Ltd v Sigmund Pumps Ltd* (1952) 86 CLR 536 (*Cooper Engineering*) (which specifically adopted Parker J in *Pianotist*); *Southern Cross*; *Shell* and other cases to which I shall refer:

- The rights of the parties are determined as at the date of the application (*Woolworths* at 383).
- The two words are considered by look and by sound but not side by side. An attempt must be made to estimate the effect or impression produced on and retained by customers and potential customers (*Shell* at 415; *Woollen Mills* at 658).
- What is to be compared with one mark is the impression based on recollection of the other mark that persons of ordinary intelligence and memory would have (*Shell* at 415; *MID Sydney Pty Ltd v Australian Tourism Co Limited* (1998) 90 FCR 236 (*MID Sydney*) at 245).
- Consideration is given to the goods to which the marks are to be applied and the nature of the customer, as well as all the surrounding circumstances when the marks are used in a normal way as a trade mark (*Pianotist* at 777).
- In considering the look and sound of the marks, the goods, the customers and all the surrounding circumstances, it is also important to look at the whole of the marks (*Mars GB Ltd v Cadbury Ltd* [1987] RPC 387 at 395).

▬▬▬▬ Torpedoes Sportswear v Thorpedo Enterprises *continued*

- If a mark in fact or from by its nature is likely to be the source of some name or verbal description by which buyers will express their desire to have the goods, then similarities both of sound and of meaning may play an important part. The usual manner in which ordinary people behave must be the test of what confusion or deception may be expected (*Woollen Mills* at 658).
- The question is whether there will be confusion in the mind of the public which will lead to confusion in the goods (*Pianotist* at 777); that a number of persons will be caused to wonder whether it might not be the case that the two products come from the same source (*Southern Cross* at 595 and 608). This involves estimating the effect or impression produced on the mind of potential customers (*Woollen Mills* at 658).
- Deceptiveness must result but from similarity; a likelihood of deception is judged by the effect of the similarity in all of the circumstances (*Shell* at 416).
- It is not necessary to prove actual probability of deception leading to a passing off but mere possibility of confusion is not enough; there must be a real, tangible danger of it occurring (*Southern Cross* at 595). The court would need to be satisfied that there was a reasonable likelihood of deception or confusion before denying acceptance of the application for registration (*Woolworths* at 381). [331]
- When the sounds of two words are being compared, it is generally a matter of first impression, because a person familiar with the two words will be neither deceived nor confused. It is not a question of meticulous comparison and allowance must be made for imperfect recollection and bad or careless pronunciation (*Aristoc Ltd v Rysta Ltd* (1944) 1B IPR 467 (*Aristoc*) at 472).
- In making an aural comparison, one has regard to what appears to be the natural and ordinary pronunciation, although evidence is admissible to establish a pronunciation that departs from the normal fashion, such as evidence of those in the trade or consumers (*Wingate Marketing Pty Ltd v Levi Strauss* (1994) 49 FCR 89 at 129 per Gummow J; *Pacific Publications Pty Ltd v IPC Media Pty Ltd* (2003) 57 IPR 28 at 56).
- The fact that two marks convey the same idea is not sufficient in itself to create a deceptive resemblance between them and a proprietor of a mark is not entitled to a complete monopoly of all words conveying the same idea as that mark (*Cooper Engineering* at 539). This fact can, however, be taken into account in deciding whether two marks which really looked alike or sounded alike were likely to deceive (*Cooper Engineering* at 539). The presence of a common idea may be a determining factor because the idea is more likely to be recalled that the precise details of the mark (*Jafferjee v Scarlett* (1937) 57 CLR 115 (*Jafferjee*) at 121-2) but the suggestion of differing ideas may serve to reduce the risk of confusion (*Johnson & Johnson v Kalnin* (1993) 26 IPR 435 (*Johnson & Johnson*) at 440). The idea that is relevant is the idea that the mark will naturally suggest to the mind of one who sees it (*Jafferjee* at 121).
- Where an element of a trade mark has a degree of notoriety or familiarity, it would be artificial to separate out the physical features of the mark from the viewer's perception of them. The question of resemblance is about how the mark is perceived (*Woolworths* at 386).
- It is sufficient if persons who only know one of the marks and have perhaps an imperfect recollection of it are likely to be deceived (*Cooper Engineering* at 538; *Aristoc* at 472).
- Consideration must be given of all goods or class of goods in respect of which registration is desired (*Pianotist* at 777-778).
- The comparison is between marks, not uses of marks, although use is not irrelevant as a circumstance. The consideration is not only actual use but also the extent of the statutory

▨▨▨ Torpedoes Sportswear v Thorpedo Enterprises *continued*

monopoly by reference to the full extent of the goods or services in respect of which the mark is registered (*MID Sydney* at 245).

- Onus of proving that there is or is not a reasonable probability of deception may be a deciding factor (for example *Aristoc*).

The test of "resemblance" for the purposes of s 6(3) of the *Trade Marks Act 1955* was summarised by Lindgren J in *Gardenia Overseas Pte Ltd v The Garden Co Ltd* (1994) 29 IPR 485 (*Gardenia*) at 493:

> "'Resemblance' with s 6(3) of the [1955] Act involves an assessment by the court of the visual and aural impressions made by the two marks when compared, but the likelihood of deception or confusion referred to in that subsection involves an [332] assessment of what would be the probable visual and aural impressions on customers and potential customers which would arise if the marks were being used properly and within the scope of the registration, that is to say, it involves the concept of 'notional normal and fair use'."

This was approved by the Full Court in *The Coca-Cola Company v All-Fect Distributors Ltd (t/as Millers Distributing Company)* (1999) 47 IPR 481 at 496 in respect of the Act. In *Gardenia*, Lindgren J found sufficient difference in the words "garden" and "gardenia", including differences in "syllabic structure and pronunciative emphases" of the respective words, bearing in mind that the test of aural impression is not one of supposing the two words are said one after the other. I have already noted the slight difference in "pronunciative emphasis" of "Thorpedo" and "Torpedoes". His Honour concluded in *Gardenia* that it may be possible that a person would be caused to wonder but that there was no "real tangible risk" of confusion occurring.

Decision

...

Visual impression

I accept the respondent's submission that, by reason of the visual differences between the T device mark and the THORPEDO mark, the visual impression of the marks is different. There is no evidence that consumers would [333] ignore the T device. Even if I were to disregard the typeface and the joinder of the letters in "Torpedoes", that device would convey an impression of dissimilarity.

Aural comparison

I am prepared to accept that goods may be ordered by the relevant members of the public over a counter or by telephone by the spoken word. It is then necessary to balance the relative importance of the aural use of the marks and their visual appearance. It is not the case, however, (as in *Woolworths* at 421) where marks used in relation to services would not be displayed on goods. In those circumstances, as the Full Court noted, the aural impression might be more important than the manner of visual presentation.

One may have regard to the likelihood of careless pronunciation (*Eno v Dunn* (1890) 1B IPR 391) but there is no evidence as to what the consequence of such carelessness would be. It is, of course, possible to pronounce "Thorpedo" and "Torpedoes" in a very similar fashion. One could ignore the "th" and pronounce it as a "t"; one could then, simultaneously, ignore the "es". However, in ordinary use, "th" functions as a different letter and different sound to "t". The presence of the "es" not only adds to the end of the word, it also serves to shift to some extent the emphasis on the syllables of "Torpedoes" compared to "Thorpedo". In the latter there is slightly more emphasis on the middle syllable; in the former the emphasis is more evenly distributed throughout the word.

The respondent again submits that the comparison aurally is between "Tee Torpedoes" and "Thorpedo", the "tee" being necessary to take account of the essential feature, the T device. I do not accept that a consumer would speak of the T device mark in this way and would not include the "tee". However, if the consumer did so, that would further lessen the likelihood of deception or confusion. I am not persuaded that, aurally, the words themselves are sufficiently similar to cause confusion but that is not an end to the matter.

Confusion as to the origin of the goods

... The evidence establishes a linkage between "Thorpedo" and Mr Thorpe. Bearing in mind Mr Thorpe's sporting ability, that linkage would reasonably extend to the mind of a customer for sporting goods and clothing. In the absence of evidence of actual confusion, I am of the view that it is unlikely that customers would attribute a "Torpedoes" origin to goods bearing the THORPEDO mark, especially when the test is not one of mere possibility of confusion but of real, tangible danger that a number of persons will be caused to wonder whether the products come from the same source (*Southern Cross* at 595 and 608).

Imperfect recollection

Is THORPEDO sufficiently close to the T device mark to cause confusion, particularly in terms of imperfect recollection? ... [334] When comparing two words which are both well known, one as a word used in ordinary parlance and the other a word associated with a particular person, it is more difficult to establish a likelihood of mistaken impression.

In *Johnson & Johnson*, the court dealt with a submission that, with a famous mark, the likelihood of imperfect recollection should be discounted. The evidence there did suggest that perception and recognition do not involve the whole word so much as certain features which are then matched to that which is contained in the memory, so that the word is then recognised. There is no such evidence in this case and the situation is reversed, in that the evidence leads to the conclusion that, as between "Thorpedo" and "Torpedoes", the former was, at the relevant date, the more well known and, it could be said, famous.

The idea behind the marks

...In *Sports Café Ltd v Registrar of Trade Marks* (1999) 42 IPR 552 (*Sports Café*), the Full Court considered deceptive similarity and the relevance of the idea behind a mark. The Court there affirmed the principle that, rather than a side by side comparison, regard is had to the impression carried away as well as the effect of spoken description. Citing *Cooper Engineering* which, in turn, approved the principles summarised by Parker J in *Pianotist* at 777, the Full Court adopted the test of judging the look and the sound, together with the goods to which the marks are to be applied and the nature and kind of customer likely to buy those goods and the surrounding circumstances. In *Cooper Engineering* the High Court observed (at 539):

> "[t]he fact that two marks convey the same idea is not sufficient in itself to create a deceptive resemblance between them, although this fact could be taken into account in deciding whether two marks which really looked alike or sounded alike were likely to deceive".

"Thorpedo", while an invented word, is based upon Mr Thorpe's name. The evidence is that it was a name by which Mr Thorpe was known and referred to; it connotes Mr Thorpe rather than a torpedo, the connotation of the T device mark. Use of the opposed mark, not

▬▬▬ Torpedoes Sportswear v Thorpedo Enterprises *continued*

necessarily as a trade mark, before the filing date of the application may serve to distinguish goods of Sportswear from the goods of another person (*Blount* at 508-510) and this would lessen the likelihood of confusion. While I am of the view that the marks are not visually similar, visually similar marks can engender different meanings which provoke [335] independent ideas, for example by reason of surname significance. That is the case here so that, even if they were visually similar, the marks can exist side by side without confusion (*Sporoptic Pouilloux SA v Arnet Optic Illusions Inc* (1995) 32 IPR 430 at 436.

It has been put that the idea behind each of the words is a torpedo. Again, of course, there was no evidence to establish this point. The evidence points the other way. "Thorpedo" is associated with Mr Thorpe, as a play on his name. While it may well have been coined to bring in the connotation of a torpedo that is not, according to the evidence, the primary association of the word. The words "Thorpedo" and "Torpedoes" are used separately and distinctly and in different contexts in the evidence. In any event, the presence of some common idea (a torpedo) may tip the scales because the idea is more likely to be recalled than the precise details (*Jafferjee* at 121-2; *Johnson & Johnson* at 439) while the suggestion of different ideas (Mr Thorpe versus a torpedo) may serve to reduce the risk of confusion (*Johnson & Johnson* at 440). To give a proprietor of a mark a monopoly over any mark which conveyed an idea would contravene the *Cooper Engineering* principle (*Sports Café* at 559).

In any event, a registered trade mark does not give a complete monopoly of all words conveying an idea. Even if it were to be accepted that both words only conveyed the idea of a torpedo, the fact that a common idea is conveyed becomes relevant only if the marks themselves look or sound alike and then might tip the balance (*Sports Café* at 557). In looking at questions of aural similarity, it is not sufficient to look at similarities of sound alone; similarities of meaning must also be considered (*Woollen Mills* at 658). There is no evidence that the public would attribute the same or a similar meaning to the two words; the evidence is to the contrary.

Rights under s 60 of the Act
Reputation
[336] ... Even if I were to find that the words are deceptively similar, Sportswear would need to establish that "Torpedoes" had acquired a reputation in Australia and that, because of the reputation, the use of the THORPEDO mark would be likely to deceive or cause confusion.

[337] ... The test for reputation required under s 60, as set out by Kitto J in *The Kendall Co v Mulsyn Paint and Chemicals* (1963) 109 CLR 300 at 305 is that any substantial number of persons likely to be concerned in the purchasing of goods must either infer that the goods have come from the same source or at least be caused to wonder whether that might be so but it is necessary for a party relying on reputation to establish it by evidence.

Sportswear submits that, where a holder of a mark has obtained a reputation but is not advertising or selling products at the time the respondent enters the market, the likelihood of confusion may be increased due to the inability of a consumer to conduct a side by side comparison of the marks or to analyse them from a standpoint of having a fresh recollection of Sportswear's mark. Sportswear says that "it is possible that confusion ... would occur". A mere possibility is not sufficient and there is, of course, no evidence of actual confusion in which the reputation of "Torpedoes" played a part which, while not necessary, would support Sportswear's case.

Sportswear also submitted that it can rely on the combined reputation arising from use of the Paradise Legends mark, which placed prominence on the word "Torpedoes" in a relatively unstylised presentation, the use of the T device mark and the use of the word "Torpedoes" alone. This ignores the words of s 60 which require a link between the mark, to which the THORPEDO mark is said to be deceptively similar and the reputation of that mark. It also draws attention to the lack of evidence directed to the reputation of the word "Torpedoes" alone. Sportswear has not established the link.

Even if I were to assume that I can take account of the combined use of the Paradise Legends mark, the T device mark and the word "Torpedoes" as giving rise to a reputation in the word alone, and taking no account of the status of Sportswear and its predecessors in title, the evidence, including that of advertising and sales does not establish reputation. The evidence does not lead to the conclusion that, because of the reputation of "Torpedoes", the use of the THORPEDO mark would be likely to deceive or confuse.

Reverse confusion

Acceptance of the notoriety of the THORPEDO mark and its association with Mr Thorpe gives rise to the question whether the public may be confused and wonder whether "Torpedoes" has a connection with the THORPEDO mark and/or Mr Thorpe ("reverse confusion"). Where a name or a word is clearly associated in the public mind with a particular person, such as Mickey Mouse and Minnie Mouse with Walt Disney, their use by another as trade marks would be likely to deceive, as suggesting that the goods are somehow connected with that person (*Radio Corporation Pty Ltd v Disney* (1937) 57 CLR 448).

[338] ... The question is whether the reputation of the mark for which application is made is relevant in the question of deceptive similarity in s 44. This raises the question whether s 44 is 'directional', that is, whether the deceptive similarity is determined only by making the comparison as against the registered mark. This involves determining whether a consumer would be caused to wonder whether goods with the proposed mark come from the registered mark's source. Alternatively, the non directional construction would include consideration as to whether a consumer would be caused to wonder whether goods bearing the registered mark come from the source of the proposed mark. The language of the section "an application for the registration of a trade mark ... must be rejected if the applicant's mark is ... deceptively similar *to* a trade mark registered by another person" (emphasis added) may indicate that a directional approach is mandated. The section does not say, for example, that as a result of registration there is deception, which would indicate a non-directional approach. This is in contrast to the more neutral language, in a directional sense, of s 28 of the *Trade Mark Act 1955* (Cth) which refers to "a mark ... the use of which would be likely to deceive or cause confusion ... shall not be registered as a trade mark".

Section 44 directs reference to s 10 of the Act for deceptive similarity. Section 10 provides that "a trade mark is taken to be *deceptively similar* to another trade mark if it so nearly resembles that other trade mark" as to deceive or cause confusion. This language is somewhat more consistent with a directional approach. Further, the Working Party Report, in dealing with permissible grounds of opposition (at page 47) spoke in terms of the prior reputation in Australia of the registered mark whereby use of the proposed mark would be likely to deceive or confuse and did not refer to the reputation of the proposed mark.

Combining the effect of s 44(1)(a)(i) and s 10, the registration of the THORPEDO mark must be rejected if the THORPEDO mark is substantially identical *with* the Sportswear marks or if it *so nearly resembles the Sportswear marks* that it is likely to deceive or cause confusion (emphasis added).

[339] ... it must be borne in mind that what is being compared for the purposes of deceptive similarity are the marks themselves. To focus on an issue of whether there is established a reputation sufficient to support a business goodwill for a passing-off action

▅▅▅▅▅ Torpedoes Sportswear v Thorpedo Enterprises *continued*

diverts attention from the real issues that arise under s 44 (*Pioneer Hi-Bred* at 439; *Carnival Cruise Lines Inc v Sitmar Cruises Ltd* (1994) 31 IPR 375 (*Carnival Cruises*) at 383). Reputation is only relevant as one of the surrounding circumstances affecting an evaluation of whether consumers would be likely to be deceived or confused. Reputation of the proposed mark is then a factor which may mean that resemblance to the registered mark will still not result.

... Does s 44 mandate a consideration whether, by reason of the reputation of the opposed mark (the THORPEDO mark), purchasers of the goods with the registered mark (the T device mark), may be caused to wonder whether the source of those goods is Mr Thorpe or Enterprises? In my opinion, the answer is no. The reputation of the THORPEDO mark is relevant, in the way I have dealt with it. As I have said, that reputation, relevant as a circumstance to be taken into account in considering deceptive similarity under s 44, indicates that purchasers of goods would be less likely to be deceived or confused. In any event, there is no evidence that purchasers of Sportswear's goods would be confused as to the source of those goods.

... I am not satisfied that any of the grounds of opposition have been made out.

▅▅▅

■ Marks becoming deceptive at a later date: Continuing operation of s 43

[14.215] See also ss 85-89.

▅▅▅▅▅▅▅ **Campomar Sociedad v Nike International** ▅▅▅▅▅▅▅

[14.220] *Campomar Sociedad Limitada v Nike International Ltd* (2000) 202 CLR 45 High Court of Australia

GLEESON CJ, GAUDRON, McHUGH, GUMMOW, KIRBY, HAYNE AND CALLINAN JJ: [53]

The nature of the dispute

"Nike" is not an invented word. In Greek mythology, Nike was the goddess of victory. The *Oxford English Dictionary* discloses that the term was also used to describe a range of surface to air guided missiles, developed by the US from 1951.

On both sides in the present litigation, the term "NIKE" has been [54] adopted as a trade mark. On one side, that of the appellants, which are Spanish corporations, the trade mark is registered in respect of cosmetics and toiletries, particularly perfume, and on the other side, that of the respondents, whose headquarters are in the US, the trade mark is registered and used for sporting footwear and clothing. There has been litigation between them in Hong Kong and in the UK with respect to subject matter similar or substantially similar to that which arises for determination in the present appeals.

These appeals are concerned with the working out of the legal consequences in Australia of this double use of the name "NIKE". This does not involve the operation of any tort of unfair competition. In *Moorgate Tobacco Co Ltd v Philip Morris Ltd [No 2]*, this Court held that the existence of an action in unfair competition would be "inconsistent with the established limits of the traditional and statutory causes of action which are available to a trader in respect of damage caused or threatened by a competitor". Indeed, as a general proposition, the law of torts values competitive conduct between traders to keep down prices and improve products.

Here, neither side has marketed goods in Australia of the same description as the other. Nevertheless, the essence of the complaint of the US concern is that the appellants, in putting their goods on the Australian market in 1993, had sought to "cash in on [the 'NIKE'] reputation, which they [had] done nothing to establish". However, in *Victoria Park Racing and Recreation Grounds Co Ltd v Taylor*, Dixon J said that in "British jurisdictions" courts of equity have not:

> "thrown the protection of an injunction around all the intangible elements of value, that is, value in exchange, which may flow from the exercise by an individual of his powers or resources whether in the organization of a business or undertaking or the use of ingenuity, knowledge, skill or labour. This is sufficiently evidenced by the history of the law of copyright and by the fact that the exclusive right to invention, trade marks, designs, trade name and reputation are dealt with in English law as special heads of protected interests and not under a wide generalization."

This passage was approved by this Court in *Moorgate Tobacco Co* [55] and should be regarded as an authoritative statement of contemporary Australian law.

On the other hand, the gist of the complaint of the appellants, the Spanish corporations, is that the US concern seeks to "swamp" their Australian registrations by exploiting a false belief—a belief built up by advertising and promotional expenditure that, in Australia, the only goods that are or will be marketed under the mark "NIKE" are those of the respondents.

It is against that background that issues arise respecting the law of registered trade marks, principally under the *Trade Marks Act 1955* (Cth) (the 1955 Act), that of misleading or deceptive conduct under s 52 of the *Trade Practices Act 1974* (Cth) (the TP Act) and the common law of passing off. Questions also arise respecting the interrelationship between the two statutory regimes and between those regimes and the common law.

... [68]

Deception and confusion

The 1955 Act established a system which, in various respects, involved a prospect of deception and confusion. Those provisions dealing with licensing and assignment "in gross" and honest concurrent user are examples. Provisions with respect to licences by way of registered user and to assignments without goodwill had been introduced by the *Trade Marks Act 1948* (Cth) and were continued respectively by Parts IX (ss 73-81) and X (s 82) of the 1955 Act. Of these registered user provisions, Fullagar and Taylor JJ said in *Heublein Inc v Continental Liqueurs Pty Ltd*:

> "It may, of course, be said that the provisions as to registered users, contemplating, as they do, the use by one person of another person's mark, sanction what would have been regarded under the earlier legislation as a form of deception but the deception which would result from the use by the appellant of the mark in question here could not [69] by any means be described in the language of the Report of the Goschen Committee as 'no material deception' (*Kerly on Trade Marks*)."

Later, in *Riv-Oland Marble Co (Vic) Pty Ltd v Settef SpA*, Bowen CJ referred to the provisions in the 1955 Act for the assignment of trade marks without goodwill and to the concurrent user provisions of s 34 of the 1955 Act as indicating that "inherent in the system" established by that statute there was "some degree of deception and confusion". A similar point was made by McHugh J in *Murray Goulburn*. His Honour referred to the House of Lords decision in *Eno v Dunn* with respect to the 1883 UK Act. This often is referred to as indicating that the purpose of a provision such as s 28 is the protection of the public. McHugh J then continued:

> "But the [1955 Act] has other competing purposes. Since the decision in *Eno v Dunn*, the scope of the legislation has changed. Thus, while the [1955 Act] has the purpose of protecting the public by indicating the origin or nature of goods or services, it also

has the purpose of protecting the valuable rights which a proprietor acquires in relation to a trade mark. Since the decision in *Eno v Dunn*, the enactment of provisions with respect to registered users (ss 73-81) and assignment of trade marks without goodwill (s 82) has changed the focus of the [1955 Act]. The registered user provisions, the assignment provisions and the limited indefeasibility given to registered proprietors tend to suggest that, after registration, the interests of traders are preferred to the competing interests of consumers in being protected from the use of marks which are likely to deceive or confuse. Thus, the presence in the [1955 Act] of ss 73-82 tends to neutralise the inference to be drawn from s 28 standing alone."

Provisions respecting honest concurrent use, whereby identical or nearly identical trade marks for the same goods or description of goods might be registered by more than one proprietor, subject to possible imposition of conditions, had first been made in Australia by s 28 of the 1905 Act. Of the concurrent use provision in s 34 of the 1955 Act, Bowen CJ observed in *Riv-Oland*:

"No doubt this provision had its origin in the situation that [70] traders in different parts of the country might be circulating goods within their particular region under marks which were similar and doing so quite honestly. In such circumstances expansion of the respective markets might tend to bring the likelihood of deception or confusion. Notwithstanding this the policy of the legislation was to enable honest concurrent users to register their marks."

Further, the 1955 Act contemplated that two or more persons might be proprietors of registered trade marks which were substantially identical or deceptively similar. This was so, even where, as in the present litigation, the registrations were not for the same goods or services. Section 58(3) provided that in such a case:

"[R]ights of exclusive use of either of those trade marks are not (except so far as their respective rights have been defined by the Registrar or a prescribed court) acquired by any one of those persons as against any other of those persons by registration of the trade marks but each of those persons has otherwise the same rights as against other persons (not being registered users) as he would have if he were the sole registered proprietor".

The statute thus recognised the continued registration of trade marks which were substantially identical or deceptively similar and regulated the rights of those proprietors inter se.

Another instance of a degree of deception or confusion inherent in the system established by the 1955 Act was provided by s 118. It stated:

"The use of a registered trade mark in relation to goods or services between which and the person using the trade mark a form of connection in the course of trade subsists shall not be deemed to be likely to cause deception or confusion on the ground only that the trade mark has been, or is, used in relation to goods or services between which and that person or a predecessor in title of that person a different form of connection in the course of trade subsisted or subsists."

This section was designed to immunise a trade mark from a claim of likelihood of deception or confusion where a change of user of the trade mark occurred. The provision followed upon the adoption by the Dean Committee of para 93 of the *Report of the Knowles Committee*. This in turn had referred to what had been said on the [71] subject in the UK in 1934 by the Goschen Committee. That Committee had said:

■■■■■ Campomar Sociedad v Nike International *continued*

"We think that, in the present state of the law, any change in the nature of the user of a registered trade mark might be held by the Courts to be likely to lead to deception and consequently to invalidate the registration, and that there is force in the representations made to us that the law in this respect should be altered. The theory underlying our recommendations for relaxing some of the present restrictions on the assignment of trade marks, and for making provision for the registration of users of registered trade marks, is that greater elasticity in our trade mark system is urgently required by the conditions of modern commerce and that this can be introduced without any serious risk of deception or other results contrary to the public interest."

Enough has been shown to demonstrate that, in varying ways and to varying degrees, the 1955 Act, by its express provisions, established and sanctioned a system the operation of which involved a measure of likely deception or confusion. The construction of s 28 of the 1955 Act should be approached with this in mind and not from a vantage point which abhors the prospect of any such deception or confusion. The operation of s 28 on its proper construction should not be so strained to avoid that prospect.

In *Murray Goulburn*, Mason CJ observed that it was curious that a mark, the use of which is deceptive, should remain in the Register and lead to the availability of relief against a registered proprietor by way of passing off or perhaps under s 52 of the TP Act, thereby restricting the exercise by the registered proprietor of his statutory rights. However, as the matters referred to above indicate, there is no curiosity in a state of affairs under which Campomar may retain its registrations. This is because, as it is expressed in the *Restatement Third, Unfair Competition*:

"The substantive scope of trademark rights [has gone beyond the initial emphasis on fraud and property rights and] now reflects the recognition of numerous interests, including the trademark owner's claim to the benefits of its good will, the interest of consumers in reliable indicia of source and sponsorship, and the right of other sellers to compete vigorously with the trademark owner in the marketplace."

It is also significant that, as Taylor J remarked in *FH Faulding & Co Ltd v Imperial Chemical Industries & Ltd*, [72] s 56 of the 1955 Act, which had been modelled on s 15 of the 1938 UK Act, was to be seen:

"as a provision intended to define exhaustively what manner of use after registration of a registered trade mark which is a word mark shall or shall not operate to invalidate the mark. It is not to be invalidated 'by reason only of the use, after the date of the registration, of a word or words which the trade mark contains or of which it consists, as the name or description of an article or substance'. But if there is 'a well-known and established use of a word as the name or description of an article or substance by a person or persons carrying on a trade in that article or substance, not being use in relation to goods connected in the course of trade with the proprietor or a registered user of the trade mark', the registration of the trade mark, so far as regards registration in respect of the article of any goods of the same description, 'shall be deemed for the purposes of section twenty-two of [the 1955 Act] to be an entry wrongly remaining in the Register'."

The other members of the Court in that case decided that the mark in question, "Barrier", in relation to skin protective creams had not been distinctive at the time of its registration and so did not deal with the precise point made by Taylor J. The same may be said of the decision in *Berlei Hestia Industries*.

The analysis by Taylor J in *FH Faulding & Co* is important in demonstrating the weak foundation in legislative history for any proposition that, unless s 28 be given a continuing or secondary operation, there will be continued in the scheme of the 1955 Act a weakness which was well recognised in the earlier legislation. In 1933, in the *Pyrex Case*, Mann J had held that this registration under the 1905 Act should be expunged on the ground that "Pyrex" had become a generic term to describe a product with particular physical characteristics. In *FH Faulding & Co*, Taylor J doubted that the provisions of the 1905 Act allowed for such a result and saw s 56 of the 1955 Act as designed to overcome this particular limitation.

The forerunners of s 28 were s 114 of the 1905 Act and s 11 of the *Trade Marks Act* 1905 (UK) (the 1905 UK Act). Before the enactment of the 1955 Act, what Deane J later described as "the only convincing analysis in judgments of persuasive authority" **[73]** was that of Eve J in the *Gripe Water Case*. Eve J had refused to give s 11 of the 1905 UK Act a secondary or continuing operation. The 1955 Act did not enact, alongside s 56, a further provision in terms which would overcome the result in the *Gripe Water Case*.

In *Murray Goulburn*, Deane J said, in a passage which we would adopt:

"It is true that there are considerations of policy which favour removal from the register of any registered mark whose use is likely to deceive or cause confusion. Those considerations are, however, modified by the availability of ordinary criminal or civil procedures to prevent dishonesty, fraud and passing off and by the fact that registration of a trade mark does not ordinarily constitute a licence for what would otherwise be unlawful conduct: see, for example, *Lyle and Kinahan Ltd's Application*; *Van Zeller v Mason, Cattley & Co*; and note the narrowness of the trade mark exception in s 51(3)(c) of the [TP Act]. On balance, it appears to me that the policy considerations favouring a construction of s 28 which would make the section directly applicable to prohibit the continued registration of any duly registered mark which was brought within par (a) by subsequent events are outweighed by the considerations militating against the lessening of the effective protection of a mark which due registration was, in my view, intended to provide."

... [75]

The construction of s 28

It is convenient now to come to the immediate issue respecting the construction of s 28. The text is set out earlier in these reasons. Section 28 appeared in Part IV (ss 24-39) which was headed "REGISTRABLE TRADE MARKS".

... Within Part IV, the criteria which had to be satisfied to supply a capacity for registration in Part A or Part B were expressed in positive and negative form. A trade mark with specified characteristics "[was] registrable" in Part A (s 24) or Part B (s 25) as the case may be. On the other hand, a mark which met one or more of the four adverse criteria listed in s 28 "shall not be registered as a trade mark". The result was that, even if a trade mark, being, say, an invented word within the meaning of s 24(1)(c), was registrable as a distinctive mark, it was not to be registered as a trade mark if its use "would be likely to deceive or cause confusion" (s 28(a)). It was for the applicant for registration to show that there was no such likelihood.

The circumstances which render the mark deceptive or confusing in this sense may, of course, stem from the prior commercial activities of others, not the inherent character of the mark. In this way, by denying to any other trader registration of the same or a similar mark, s 28 provided what might be described as a "negative protection" for a well-known mark, even one not already registered and not used in relation to the same goods or services as those in respect of which the application for registration was made. The result was that, to a degree, s 28 operated as an "anti-dilution" device.

Further, the phrase in s 28(a), "would be likely", involved a particular prospective inquiry. The question whether there was a likelihood of confusion was not to be answered by reference to the manner in which the applicant for registration had used its mark in the past. Rather, regard was to be had to the use to which, within the ambit of the registration, the applicant could properly put the mark if the application were to be granted. The onus to show that there was no such likelihood was to be discharged by the applicant in respect of [77] all of the goods coming within the specification in the application, not only in respect of those goods on which the applicant proposed to use the mark immediately. Thus, if registration were sought in respect of particular goods and there would be a likelihood of deception if the mark were used upon such goods marketed as expensive products, it was no answer that the applicant proposed to use the mark only upon goods to be sold as inexpensively produced items. But that is not to give s 28(a) the secondary or continuing operation for which the respondents contended on these appeals.

Where it applied to preclude registration, s 28 required the provision of an adverse report by the Examiner under s 41(b) as to whether the trade mark the subject of the application in question was capable of registration, and refusal by the Registrar of the application (s 44), even if the trade mark otherwise was registrable in Part A (s 24) or Part B (s 25). Although otherwise capable of registration, the mark was not to be registered as a trade mark if it displayed one or more of the negative characteristics listed in s 28. Further, even if registered despite the barrier imposed by s 28, that original registration would have been "wrongly made" and thereafter be liable to expungement under s 22(1)(b).

If the structure and purpose of the 1955 Act are understood in this way, there is no reason to depart from the apparent and ordinary meaning and effect of s 28. Further, to fail to do so and to give s 28 a continuing or secondary operation, thereby prescribing conditions for the continued registration of a trade mark, which had been capable of registration when registered, would lead only to confusion worse confounded. The doctrine, if it be that, of "blameworthy conduct" is an example; it is a gloss on the text of s 28 to mitigate what would appear to be the harsh consequences of a construction of s 28 which accommodates such a continuing or secondary operation.

The difficulties to which this in turn gives rise are exemplified in the differences of judicial opinion, both in the *Murray Goulburn* litigation and the present case in the Federal Court, as to what particular facts must be shown to support a holding of "blameworthy conduct". It is unnecessary to peer further into this overgrowth upon the statutory structure because, as we have indicated, the occasion for any such doctrine disappears once the terms of s 28 be allowed their ordinary meaning in the setting in which they are found in Part IV of the 1955 Act.

The result for the present appeals is that the Campomar registrations were not wrongly remaining in the Register within the meaning of s 22(1)(b) of the 1955 Act and thus their automatic registration under the 1995 Act was not liable to attack on that ground.

The primary operation of s 28

There remains the question whether the Campomar registrations nevertheless are liable to expungement under s 22(1) because they are entries [78] which were "wrongly made". This involves the application of s 28 in its primary, and, as indicated above, its sole operation as a barrier to the Campomar registrations at their respective deemed dates of registration in 1986 and 1992.

■■■■■ Campomar Sociedad v Nike International *continued*

Sheppard J made no findings on these issues. Nor did the majority of the Full Court. It was unnecessary for their Honours to do so in order to uphold the orders made by Sheppard J. However, it was necessary for Burchett J, who would have allowed the appeals, to deal with these issues. He did so and found that the Campomar registrations were not to be impeached for contraventions of s 28.

Burchett J pointed out that the evidence had concentrated upon "the rapidly growing reputation of Nike International in the period up to trial". He noted that the Campomar registrations had been effected without opposition by Nike International and, in the case of the first registration in 1986, after correspondence with Nike Inc in which that corporation had indicated to Campomar that perfume and cosmetic products were not part of its "image".

Burchett J concluded:

"In my opinion, it would not be right to make a finding that Campomar's trade marks, particularly the earlier mark, offended s 28(a) at the date of their registration. Of course, this conclusion is stronger, on the evidence I have been discussing, in relation to the 1986 registration; but, given the validity of that, I do not think the slight extension of it involved in the later registration could be regarded as in itself involving any likelihood of deception or confusion.

It is clear that the remedy of expunction is a remedy to be granted or withheld in the court's discretion. The trial judge did not advert to this discretion because the weight he gave to the brand extension argument caused him to devote no separate consideration to the rights conferred by registration on Campomar in respect of the marketing of fragrances and cosmetic products generally, without any overt link to sports. At least in the case of the 1992 registration, assuming the 1986 registration was valid when granted, I think that, even if the 1992 registration offends s 28(a), the court's discretion should be exercised in favour of [Campomar]. In reaching that conclusion, I take into account s 34 and the matters of principle in relation to it which I have already discussed."

Section 34 was addressed to honest concurrent use. The matters of principle of which Burchett J spoke appear to be the need to recognise as points going to the exercise of discretion the special circumstances [79] that arise from "the collision of marks through the invasive effect of brand extension" across national boundaries in an age of expansion in international commerce.

Nike Australia has been the exclusive Australian importer, distributor and manufacturer of "NIKE" products since 1 June 1992. In the immediately preceding period from January 1989, the exclusive Australian importer and licensee had been John D Trading Pty Ltd. From about August 1984 to January 1989, the exclusive Australian importer and licensee had been a Victorian company, Impression Sports Pty Ltd (Impression), which operated a division under the trading style "Nike Australia". There was an issue on the pleadings and not resolved at the trial as to the degree to which the sales and promotion in Australia of "NIKE" footwear and athletic clothing was extensive between 1972 and 1986. In this period, the growth of sales of "NIKE" footwear had been inhibited by a system of import quotas. The initial investment in the new division of Impression had included $1.582 million to purchase import quotas. Shoes imported outside the quota system incurred a penalty duty of $15 per pair. The evidence suggests that "NIKE" footwear had been sold in Australia since about 1972 and "NIKE" products were advertised and promoted to a significant degree in the early 1980s. In the period 1 July to 31 December 1985, Impression spent $200,000 on promotions and advertising. The "Nike Australia" division of Impression was not trading profitably at the beginning of 1986. In the period between July 1984 and November 1985, approximately $280,000 in royalties were due to Nike International.

It was for Campomar to satisfy the Registrar, or, as it transpired, the Federal Court, that on 29 August 1986 there was no reasonable probability of confusion, that is to say a real, tangible danger of it occurring. It would be enough if the ordinary person had entertained a reasonable doubt that perfumery products branded "NIKE" would come from the same source as footwear and athletic clothing products; a determination of that issue would involve the consideration of all the surrounding circumstances, including those in which the marks would be used and those in which the goods would be bought and sold, and the character of the probable purchasers of the goods. The propositions are well settled and derive from the compelling reasons of Kitto J in *Southern Cross Refrigerating Co v Toowoomba Foundry Pty Ltd*.

In their written submissions in this Court, the respondents referred to various items of evidence which, it was submitted, if taken together, would found a conclusion resolving in their favour the issue respecting [80] the application of s 28(a) on 29 August 1986 to the first Campomar registration. We have reviewed that evidence, in addition to the matters referred to above. We have concluded, even allowing, as must be the case, for the onus to negative the application of s 28(a), that there was no reasonable probability of confusion in the sense required by the authorities. The case at trial appears largely to have been conducted by reference to the state of affairs in 1994 rather than that in 1986. Given the relative strength of the evidence as to the state of affairs at the two dates, that is not surprising. Accordingly, Burchett J was correct in his conclusion that the first Campomar registration was not registered in contravention of s 28.

There remains the second appeal. This concerns the second Campomar registration in respect of which the relevant date for the primary application of s 28(a) is 2 August 1992. This registration, as Burchett J pointed out in the Full Court, involved a "slight extension" from "perfumery products" to "soaps". However, the registration was also in respect of "[b]leaching preparations and other substances for laundry use; cleaning, polishing, scouring and abrasive preparations".

As we have indicated, the thrust of the evidence was to establish, as found by Sheppard J, at the time of the institution of the actions in the Federal Court in 1994 an extensive reputation of "NIKE" for athletic footwear and sporting gear. The evidence demonstrated a reputation which grew in the late 1980s. The respondents, or their US affiliated companies, sponsored major international sporting events after 1986 and in 1985 arrangements had been made with Michael Jordan, the US National Basketball Association's 1985 Rookie of the Year, for him to endorse and promote "NIKE" products. The "Air Jordan" line promoted and endorsed by Michael Jordan was a great success. The evidence thus showed a rapidly growing reputation, not only internationally but in Australia, in the period up to trial. Given the onus borne by Campomar and the strength of this evidence, we would not be sufficiently satisfied that, on 2 August 1992, there was not the reasonable probability of confusion referred to in the authorities.

However, that is not the end of the matter. The power to expunge the registration involves the exercise of a discretion. That is to say, the term "may" in s 22 is not to be read as meaning "must". In *Murray Goulburn*, Brennan J pointed out that, in the exercise of a discretion, it may be relevant to consider not only the public interest but also the respective contributions to the state of affairs made by the parties involved. This aspect of the matter was adverted to by Burchett J in the Full Court in the manner described earlier in these reasons. His Honour would have exercised the discretion favourably to [81] the appellants. Rather than return the second appeal to the Federal Court, the discretion should be exercised by this Court.

The correspondence culminating in the communication of 9 June 1986 would not, as

▪▪▪▪▪ Campomar Sociedad v Nike International *continued*

Sheppard J pointed out, have supported any belief by Campomar that Nike International regarded it as entitled to market its goods in such a way as to give the impression they were or might be connected with Nike International. However, Campomar had been told that Nike International did not believe that perfumes and cosmetic products were part of that company's image. This was given as the reason which had led Nike International to decide against participating in the project put forward by Campomar. Further, Nike International had also written in the same communication that it understood that Campomar had "registered the name 'NIKE' in the class covering 'Perfume and Essences'". Thereafter, Nike International had opposed neither of the Campomar registrations which then were made in Australia. So far as the second Campomar registration also included "soaps", it was nevertheless within the assumption upon which the earlier correspondence reasonably had led Campomar to act.

Finally, as has been indicated earlier in these reasons, it does not necessarily follow that such registration by Campomar of "NIKE" for "soaps" may be turned to account only by the marketing of goods in such a way as to give an impression that they are or might be connected with Nike International. The trial judge found, with respect to the marketing after the commencement date of the second Campomar registration of "NIKE SPORT FRAGRANCE", that this conduct was engaged in so as "to take advantage of the goodwill and reputation of Nike International". On the assumption that this is a matter to be taken into account in the exercise of the discretion conferred by s 22, it does not eclipse the other considerations favouring the exercise of the discretion to refuse an order for expungement.

Nevertheless, the wide description of goods included in the second Campomar registration, in so far as it goes beyond "soaps", lies outside the subject matter of the earlier correspondence. It appears that Burchett J would have exercised the discretion in favour of retaining the whole of the second registration. However, the orders to be made on the second appeal should provide for the automatic registration under the 1995 Act to be limited.

The entry in the Register for the second Campomar registration should be rectified by amending the goods in respect of which the trade mark is registered to read "soaps, being goods in class 3".

Section 52

The result is that, even if they otherwise were minded to do so, Nike **[82]** International and its related corporations may not, without the licence of Campomar, expand their business in Australia by having "NIKE" on products the subject of the Campomar registrations. There remains for consideration the submissions by the appellants in the first appeal in which they seek the discharge of the injunctive orders made by Sheppard J restraining their marketing of perfume and other products under or by reference to the name "NIKE" or any other name or marks substantially identical with or deceptively similar thereto. The orders were founded both in ss 52 and 80 of the TP Act and, in the accrued jurisdiction of the Federal Court, in the tort of passing off.

Before considering the submissions with respect to s 52 and passing off, it is convenient to recapitulate the conclusions reached respecting the construction of s 28 of the 1955 Act and to contrast the scope of its operation and that of s 52 and passing off.

Section 28(a) barred the registration of a mark the use of which would have been likely to deceive or cause confusion. The issue was to be determined at the date of the application for registration and with respect to all of the goods for which registration was desired, not only those for which there was proposed an immediate use. A state of confusion falling short of an actual probability of deception leading to a passing off would not negative the operation of s 28 and would not lift the bar to registration.

▨▨▨▨ Campomar Sociedad v Nike International *continued*

By this prophylactic operation of s 28, an applicant might be denied registration for certain goods even though the subsequent use of the mark on those goods would not mislead or deceive or be likely to have that result, and would not found an action against the applicant for contravention of s 52 or passing off. Thus, there could be a field of activity in which, whilst the applicant was denied registration of the mark and the rights against other traders which this would have given, use of the mark by the applicant could not be enjoined by those traders.

The first appeal concerns a significant variant of that situation. The Campomar registrations were not barred by s 28 and their existence on the Register will support an infringement action against other traders. However, the registrations would not answer actions against Campomar and Nike Cosmetics based on either s 52 or passing off if, as Sheppard J found to be the case, the ingredients for those actions were made out.

... [87]

In the present case, evidence was given of the marketing of the "NIKE SPORT FRAGRANCE" products in pharmacies. Sheppard J said:

> "Some of the evidence establishes that this product was found displayed in pharmacies beside or underneath other sports fragrances, including a sports fragrance marketed under the name 'Adidas'. Evidence establishes that the well-known sporting [88] organisation Adidas does either itself, or through other companies which it authorises, market a sports fragrance bearing its name."

Further, an examination of the affidavit and oral evidence of the witnesses shows that in the assumption they made as to the extension of "NIKE" sportswear business into a sports fragrance, they were aware of and influenced by the activities of the Adidas company in introducing a range of Adidas fragrance products. In those circumstances, looking at the matter objectively, there was nothing capricious or unreasonable or unpredictable in Sheppard J's conclusion that the placing of the "NIKE SPORT FRAGRANCE" product in the same area of pharmacies with other sports fragrances was likely to mislead or deceive members of the public into thinking that the "NIKE SPORT FRAGRANCE" product was in some way promoted or distributed by Nike International itself or with its consent and approval.

INFRINGEMENT

[14.225] *Trade Marks Act 1995* (Cth), s 20 gives the registered owner the exclusive rights to use the mark, authorise others to use it and obtain relief in respect of infringement. Infringement is defined in s 120.

■ Section 120: Use as a mark

▨▨▨▨ Mark Foy's v Davies Coop ▨▨▨▨

[14.230] *Mark Foy's Ltd v Davies Coop & Co Ltd* (1956) 95 CLR 190 High Court of Australia

WILLIAMS J: [202] The remaining question is whether the rights conferred on the plaintiff by s 50 have been infringed. The defendants have used the exact words of the plaintiff's trade mark so that the plaintiff need not rely on s 53. It is contended that the plaintiff's rights have

▬▬▬▬ Mark Foy's v Davies Coop *continued*

not been infringed because the defendants have not used the words as a trade mark at all, but only descriptively as a laudatory [203] or puffing expression to extol the goods. They rely on the speech of Lord Tomlin, concurred in by Lord Atkin and Lord Russell of Killowen, in the *Yeast-Vite Case* in the House of Lords (1934) 51 RPC 110. The Act there in question was the English *Trade Marks Act 1905-1919* and the particular section under review was s 39, which corresponds to s 50 of the *Commonwealth Act*. The definition of "trade mark" in the English Act was the same as the definition in the *Commonwealth Act 1912*. There was no section in the English Act corresponding to s 53 of the *Commonwealth Act*. The plaintiffs were the proprietors of the registered trade mark "YEAST VITE" and it was held that this mark was not infringed by the defendant selling in his shop a preparation labelled "Yeast Tablets a substitute for Yeast-Vite" which was not the plaintiff's preparation. Lord Tomlin said (at 115):

> "Now the act which the appellants contend amounts in law to an infringement of their exclusive right as registered proprietors of the trade mark is the use by the respondent upon the bottles in which he sells his preparation of the phrase 'Yeast Tablets, a substitute for Yeast-Vite'. This is clearly a use of the word 'Yeast-Vite' on the respondent's preparation to indicate the appellant's preparation and to distinguish the respondent's preparation from it. It is not a use of the word as a trade mark, that is, to indicate the origin of the goods in the respondent by virtue of manufacture, selection, certification, dealing with or offering for sale."

His Lordship continued (at 116):

> "The question therefore here … is, what is the property right of the appellants and has it been infringed? It is true that the language of the definition of a trade mark contained in s 3 of the Act of 1905 cannot without some change of form be read directly into s 39, but it is equally true that the language of s 39 must carry with it some implied limitation, unless it is to be given a meaning extending its operation altogether outside the scope of the Trade Marks Acts. The phrase 'the exclusive right to the use of such trade mark' carries in my opinion the implication of use of the mark for the purpose of indicating in relation to the goods upon or in connection with which the use takes place, the origin of such goods in the user of the mark by virtue of the matters indicated in the definition of 'trade mark' contained in s 3."

[204] … If the defendants in the present case had advertised that their Exacto cotton frocks washed as well as the plaintiff's Tub Happy frocks it could not be said that the words "Tub Happy" were used by the defendants in relation to goods to indicate a connection in the course of trade between the goods and themselves. They would only be used in support of a claim that their cotton goods washed as well as the plaintiff's Tub Happy goods. In such a case the words "Tub Happy" would not be used as a trade mark within the meaning of the present definition. Section 50 states that the proprietor of a registered trade mark has the exclusive right to the use of the trade mark upon or in connection with the goods in respect of which it is registered. This appears on its face to mean that no one but the proprietor can use the trade mark upon or in connection with the goods in respect of which it is registered for any purpose. One purpose within the section would appear to be the use of the trade mark by an opponent for the purpose of claiming that his goods were a substitute for those of the proprietor. It does not matter that the identity of the proprietor of the trade mark is unknown to the public. It is the trade mark which identifies the goods and the sale of goods that have acquired a reputation could be seriously prejudiced by an opponent offering his goods as substitutes for them. But in the *Yeast-Vite Case* the House of Lords narrowed the meaning of s 50 by implying after the words "the exclusive right to the use of the trade mark" the words "as a trade mark". Their

Mark Foy's v Davies Coop *continued*

Lordships held that the exclusive rights of the registered proprietor are only infringed if the trade mark is used as a trade mark for the purpose mentioned in the definition. This construction must be applied to s 50 of the *Commonwealth Act* and the presence of s 53 in that Act can make no difference. Section 53 is really an appendage to s 50 and its function is to widen the definition of infringement so as to include cases where the defendant does not use the identical trade mark but uses a mark substantially identical with it or so nearly resembling it as to be likely to deceive. But the alleged infringement must still be the use of the plaintiff's trade mark or some mark substantially identical with it as a trade mark.

But the *Yeast-Vite Case* does not assist the defendants. They are not using the words "Tub Happy" in the same way as the defendant was using the words "Yeast-Vite" in that case. They **[205]** are advertising the words "Tub Happy" and emphasising them in relation to their own cotton garments for the purpose of indicating a connection in the course of trade between the goods and themselves. The public are not being invited to compare the "Exacto" goods of the defendants with the "Tub Happy" goods of the plaintiff. They are being invited to purchase goods of the defendants which are to be distinguished from the goods of other traders partly because they are described as "Tub Happy" goods. In *Aristoc Ltd v Rysta Ltd* [1945] AC 68 at 94, Viscount Maugham cites the following appropriate passage from the judgment of Lord Green MR in *Saville Perfumery Ltd v June Perfect Ltd* (1941) 58 RPC 147 at 161:

> "In an infringement action, once it is found that the defendant's mark is used as a trade mark, the fact that he makes it clear the commercial origin of the goods indicated by the trade mark is some business other than that of the plaintiff avails him nothing, since infringement consists in using the mark as a trade mark, that is, as indicating origin".

Needless to say, if the defendant uses the words of the plaintiff's trade mark as indicating origin it is still an infringement notwithstanding that the defendant always adds his own name: *Kerly on Trade Marks* (7th ed, 1951), p 445.

For these reasons the appeal should be allowed.

■ Descriptive use of a mark: Not infringement

[14.235] See s 122.

Shell Co v Esso Standard Oil

[14.240] *Shell Co Australia Ltd v Esso Standard Oil (Aust) Ltd* (1963) 109 CLR 407 High Court of Australia

KITTO J: **[420]** This appeal is from a judgment given in favour of the plaintiff upon the trial of an action brought in this court for infringement of two trade marks. The trade marks are registered in respect of "products and preparations for lubricating, heating, illuminating, and fuel and power generating purposes". One mark consists of a grotesque drawing of a person with a head in the shape of a drop of oil which has just fallen from a container and by reason of its viscosity is drawn out to an asymmetrical peak at the top. A face is suggested by lines indicating eyebrows, eyelids and mouth (but no nose or ears), all so curved and disposed as to give the impression that the being depicted is immensely pleased with himself. There is no neck. The body is about as long as the head but narrower; and it is bifurcated to create **[421]**

▌▬▬▬▬▬▬ Shell Co v Esso Standard Oil *continued*

a suggestion of short legs, each with a foot turned outwards. Arms and hands are indicated, and they assist the impression of self-satisfaction by being drawn as if the thumbs were hooked into braces near the armpits, though no braces, and indeed no indication of clothes, are to be seen. The other trade mark is identical, save that the figure displays an oval badge suspended immediately below the head and bearing the word "Esso", which is a name used by the respondent for some of its products.

... The conduct of the appellant which the learned primary judge held to have constituted infringement consisted in causing two advertising films, of the animated cartoon variety, to be exhibited to the public in the course of television programmes. ... In each film a "humanised" oil drop is made to personify the appellant's "Shell" petrol, and to perform a series of exuberant antics designed, in conjunction with some letterpress and the spoken word, to create in the minds of viewers a feeling of pleasure at recognising desirable attributes in Shell petrol. In the course of his merry pranks, the Shell Eulenspiegel constantly changes in shape and expression. He always has a head in the shape of an oil drop drawn to a peak at the top, and generally the head is supported, without a neck, by a body bifurcated to indicate short legs with feet turned outwards. Arms and hands take up varying positions, and what passes for a face expresses varying emotions. On some occasions the figure, in the course of its mutations, approaches fairly closely in appearance to the respondent's trade marks; but the name "Esso" is never [422] seen, and the changes of appearance follow one another so swiftly that the viewer can hardly gain more than a general impression of a Protean creature who could be, having regard to some of his manifestations at least, the man whom the respondent has registered as its trade mark, but could equally be another member of the same tribe. It may be assumed for present purposes, however, that in the course of each film the figure takes on, at least for a moment or two now and then, an appearance substantially identical with that of the trade marks.

The question, then, is whether such a user of the oil drop figure as takes place by the exhibition of the films on television involves infringement of the trade marks. It is a question not to be answered in favour of the appellant merely by pointing to the brevity of the occasions when substantial identity is achieved. The assumption I have made means, of course, that if the oil drop figure as appearing in some of the individual frames of the films were transferred as separate pictures to another context the use of the pictures in that context could be an infringement. But the context is all-important, because not every use of a mark which is identical with or deceptively similar to the trade mark, in the course of trade, in relation to property which the proprietor of the mark possesses in virtue of the registration.

... The crucial question in the present case seems to me to arise at this point. Was the appellant's use, that is to say its television presentation, of whose particular pictures of the oil drop figure which were substantially identical with or deceptively similar to the respondent's trade marks a use of them "as a trade mark"? [425] With the aid of the definition of "trade mark" in s 6 of the Act, the adverbial expression may be expanded so that the question becomes whether, in the setting in which the particular pictures referred to were presented, they would have appeared to the television viewer as possessing the character of devices, or brands, which the appellant was using or proposing to use in relation to petrol for the purpose of indicating, or so as to indicate, a connection in the course of trade between the petrol and the appellant. Did they appear to be thrown on to the screen as being marks for distinguishing Shell petrol from other petrol in the course of trade?

Clearly they were used so that the figure in all its varying forms would be understood as representing Shell petrol for the purposes of the disjointed tale that is told. But the connection in the films between the oil drop man and the petrol he symbolises is a connection limited

■■■■■■ Shell Co v Esso Standard Oil *continued*

by the purpose of the occasion. At every point of the exhibition, whether the resemblance to the respondent's trade marks be at the moment close or remote, the purpose and the only purpose that can be seen in the appearance of the little man on the screen is that which unites the quickly moving series of pictures as a whole, namely the purpose of conveying by a combination of pictures and words a particular message about the qualities of Shell petrol. This fact makes it, I think, quite certain that no viewer would ever pick out any of the individual scenes in which the man resembles the respondent's trade marks, whether those scenes be few or many, and say to himself: "There I see something that the Shell people are showing me as being a mark by which I may know that any petrol in relation to which I see it used is theirs." And one may fairly affirm with even greater confidence that the viewer would never infer from the films that every one of the forms which the oil drop figure takes appears there as being a mark which has been chosen to serve the specific purpose of branding petrol in reference to its origin. No doubt if, later, the viewer were to come across the respondent's trade mark used in relation to petrol his recollection of the films might lead him to think that the appellant, taking advantage of a reputation created for the oil drop figure by means of the films, had adopted the figure, in one of its forms, as a mark for its petrol. But that would be quite a different matter from inferring, while sitting in front of his television set, that the figure in one or more, some or all, of its exhibited forms was being placed before him there as a trade mark for Shell petrol.

In my opinion this case is covered in principle by the English decisions I have cited. One or two may be particularly mentioned. **[426]** In *JB Stone & Co Ltd v Steelace Manufacturing Co Ltd* (1929) 46 RPC 406 (CA), a registered trade mark which consisted of the word ALLIGATOR was held infringed by a use of the expression "alligator pattern"; but the judgments make it plain that if the second word had been clear enough in meaning to make the whole expression signify only that the goods were of a type of which ALLIGATOR goods were an example there would have been no infringement, because the context would then have shown that the word "alligator" was being used otherwise than as a trade mark. The *Yeast-Vite Case* is a striking example of a context precluding a conclusion that a use complained of as an infringement was a use as a trade mark. The case of *Edward Young & Co Ltd v Grierson Oldham & Co Ltd* (1924) 41 RPC 548 is perhaps the case most usefully to be compared with the present. There the use complained of was a use of a static picture; here it is of a series of pictures. The only purpose served by the use of the single picture there was, as the only purpose of the use of all the pictures here is, to convey a particular message to those who should see it. There the purpose became apparent when the single picture was considered in the light of a usage common in the relevant trade; here it appears when each picture is considered in the light of all the other pictures amongst which it has a place in the sequence and of the accompanying letterpress and spoken word. There the message was simple: that the goods came from Portugal; here it is simple also, though the method of conveying it is complicated and incoherent; it is that the chemical composition of Shell petrol gives it advantages over its rivals. There, once the "purpose and nature" of the use were understood that is the expression of Sargant LJ (at 579) the action for infringement failed. In my opinion the purpose and nature of the use complained of in the present case are such that this action should fail also.

For these reasons I would allow the appeal.

[Dixon CJ, Taylor and Owen JJ concurred; McTiernan J dissented. See also *Montana Wines Ltd v Villa Maria Wines Ltd* (1984) 2 IPR 203.]

■ Use in Australia: Infringement by foreign internet sales?

▬▬▬▬▬ Ward Group v Brodie & Stone ▬▬▬▬▬

[14.245] *Ward Group Pty Ltd v Brodie & Stone Plc* (2005) 64 IPR 1 Federal Court of Australia

The facts of this case are found at **[13.115]**.

MERKEL J: **[11]**

Trade Mark Infringement

In *Hoffman-La Roche* at 45 [145]-[146] I considered the question of when a statement originating outside of Australia is made and received in Australia:

> "In a different context, Mason CJ, Deane, Dawson and Gaudron JJ in *Voth v Manildra Flour Mills Pty Ltd* (1990) 171 CLR 538 observed at 567-568:
>
> > 'In some cases an act passes across space or time before it is completed. Communicating by letter, telephone, telex and the like provide examples.'
>
> However, after also observing that generally the tort of negligent misstatement is committed where the statement is received and acted upon their Honours pointed out that the statement may be received in one place and acted upon in another. They stated:
>
> > 'If a statement is directed from one place to another place where it is known or even anticipated that it will be received by the plaintiff, there is no difficulty in saying that the statement was, in substance, made at the place to which it was directed, whether or not it is there acted upon.'
>
> See also *Sydbank Soenderjylland A/S v Bannerton Holdings Pty Ltd* (1996) 68 FCR 539 at 547-548 and *Diamond v Bank of London and Montreal Ltd* [1979] 1 QB 333 at 345-346. This principle has been applied to conduct found to contravene Pt V of the TPA: see *No 1 Raberem Pty Ltd v Monroe Schneider Associates Inc* (unreported, Federal Court, No G10 of 1989, von Doussa J, 8 February 1991)."

In *Norbert Steinhardt & Son Limited v Meth* (1961) 105 CLR 440 at 442 Fullagar J stated that a groundless threat of patent infringement "is to be regarded as made at the time when, and at the place where, it is received by the person to whom it is addressed". In that case, a letter containing the relevant threats was written in the USA and received in England, and his Honour found that the threats were made in England.

A similar approach has been taken in relation to publications or statements made on the Internet. When such publications or statements are made to the world at large, and not to persons or subscribers in a particular jurisdiction, there is some difficulty in regarding them as having been made by a website in a particular jurisdiction. However, where the publication or statement is directed or targeted at persons or subscribers in a particular jurisdiction there is no difficulty in treating them as having been made and received in that jurisdiction: see *Zippo Manufacturing Company v Zippo Dot Com Inc* 952 F Supp 1119 (WD Pa 1997) at 1125-1127, *New Zealand Post Ltd v Leng* [1999] 3 NZLR 219 at 225 and 230-231 and *Mecklermedia Corp v DC Congress GmbH* [1998] Ch 40 at 51-52. That question arose in *Australian Competition and Consumer Commission v Chen* (2003) 132 FCR 309 (*Chen*), which concerned false representations of an association or connection between certain American websites (which used the name of the Sydney Opera House) and the Sydney Opera House, which were intended to be made to, and were directed at, Australian consumers. The representations were found to have been made in Australia by the website proprietors when the intended downloading in Australia occurred.

[12] On the facts of the present case the first occasion on which the website proprietors would be considered to have intended to use and used the RESTORIA mark in Australia was when they accepted the orders placed by the trap purchasers in respect of the UK Restoria products in terms that used the RESTORIA mark. The reason I have arrived at that conclusion is that prior to that time the trap purchasers were downloading a representation made on the Internet to the world at large, and not a representation intended to be made to, or directed or targeted at, them in Australia. Thus, I do not accept the contention made by the Ward Group that the use of the RESTORIA mark by the website proprietors on the Internet, without more, was a use of the mark by them in Australia.

In summary, the use of a trade mark on the Internet, uploaded on a website outside of Australia, without more, is not a use by the website proprietor of the mark in each jurisdiction where the mark is downloaded. However, as explained above, if there is evidence that the use was specifically intended to be made in, or directed or targeted at, a particular jurisdiction then there is likely to be a use in that jurisdiction when the mark is downloaded. Of course, once the website intends to make and makes a specific use of the mark in relation to a particular person or persons in a jurisdiction there will be little difficulty in concluding that the website proprietor used the mark in that jurisdiction when the mark is downloaded.

[His Honour found that because the only evidence of infringement of the trade mark via downloading in Australia were 'trap purchases' this conduct involved implicit, if not explicit, consent to the infringing use of the trade mark.]

▪ Substantial identity and deceptive similarity

▬▬▬▬▬ Polaroid v Sole N ▬▬▬▬▬

[14.250] *Polaroid Corp v Sole N Pty Ltd* [1981] 1 NSWLR 491 Supreme Court of New South Wales

[The plaintiffs were registered proprietor and registered user of the trade mark POLAROID registered in 1945 in Part A of the Act in respect of "transparent organic plastic material in the form of sheets or blocks". The defendants in 1979 embarked on an advertising campaign for the sale of its window insulating material "Solaroid". The plaintiff brought an action for infringement.]

KEARNEY J: [494] On the question as to whether there is substantial identity or deceptive similarity between the registered mark and the defendant's mark, guidance is provided by the consideration of this point by Windeyer J in *Shell Co of Australia Ltd v Esso Standard Oil (Aust) Ltd* (1963) 109 CLR 407 at 414, 415. His Honour there points out that they are independent criteria, and are to be judged in different ways. His Honour then formulates the manner in which such criteria are to be considered in relation to such marks in the following terms:

"In considering whether marks are substantially identical they should, I think, be compared side by side, their similarities and differences noted and the importance of these assessed having regard to the essential features of the registered mark and the

███████ Polaroid v Sole N *continued*

total impression of resemblance or dissimilarity that emerges from the comparison. 'The identification of an essential feature depends' it has been said, 'partly on the court's own judgment and partly on the burden of the evidence that is placed before it': *de Cordova v Vick Chemical Co* (1951) 68 RPC 103 at 106. Whether there is substantial identity is a question of fact: see *Fraser Henliens Pty Ltd v Cody* (1945) 70 CLR 100, per Latham CJ (at 114, 115), and *Ex parte O'Sullivan; Re Craig* (1944) 44 SR (NSW) 291, per Jordan CJ (at 298), where the meaning of the expression was considered. ...

On the question of deceptive similarity a different comparison must be made from that which is necessary when substantial identity is in question. The marks are not now to be looked at side by side. The issue is not abstract similarity, but deceptive similarity. Therefore the comparison is the familiar one of trade mark law. It is between, on the one hand, the impression based on recollection of the plaintiff's mark that persons of ordinary intelligence and memory would have; and, on the other hand, the impressions that such persons would get from the defendant's television exhibitions."

His Honour further commented with respect to the question of deceptive similarity (at 416):

"When the Act speaks of marks being 'deceptively similar' to the registered mark, it propounds, I think, the same test as in the former Act was expressed by the phrase 'so nearly resembling it as to be likely to deceive'. The deceptiveness that is contemplated must result from similarity; but the likelihood of deception must be judged not by the degree of similarity alone, but by the effect of that similarity in all the circumstances."

While these propositions are accepted as being applicable, there is a difference of approach between the parties as to the manner in which at least the test of deceptive similarity should be applied to the circumstances of this case. The plaintiffs, in reliance upon the decision of Wootten J in *Marc A Hammond Pty Ltd v Papa Carmine Pty Ltd* [1976] 2 NSWLR 124 at 127, 128, emphasise that s 62(1) is concerned with a deceptively similar mark as distinct from a deceptive use of a mark. The plaintiffs further point to the defence under s 62(2) which is referable to the use rather than to the mark. The necessity to distinguish between the use of the mark itself is basic to the plaintiff's approach. The defendants contend that in order to determine "the effect of that similarity in all the circumstances" it is necessary to consider features other than the respective marks alone. On this topic the plaintiff's first proposition is that in the light of Wootten J's decision in relation to the test of "deceptively similar" under s 62(1) it is not to the point to inquire whether or not the defendants by their use of the first defendant's mark are deceiving anyone or causing confusion. This raises the wider question of the ambit of the inquiry to be made in applying the test of deceptive similarity under s 62(1), which is the principal point on which the parties differ.

Before dealing further with this point, certain other propositions of the plaintiff may be mentioned as to which there is no substantial disagreement:

(a) that it is not to the point for the purposes of s 62(1) that the defendant has added other material to the trade mark, such as in the present instance the addition of the word "Solaroid" of the words, "Auto-Tint": *Lever Bros Port Sunlight Ltd v Sunniwite Products Ltd* (1949) 66 RPC 84 at 89; *Mark Foy's Ltd Davies Coop & Co Ltd* (1956) 95 CR 190 at 204, 205;

(b) that it is irrelevant whether a defendant is acting fraudulently, or whether he has acted in good faith and is merely continuing to persist in such action after receiving notice: *Kerly's Law of Trade Marks* (10th ed), p 336; **[496]**

(c) that s 62 is in a different form from the equivalent English section (s 4) of the 1938 English *Trade Marks Act*. Indeed, the significance of this difference was pointed out by Windeyer J in the *Shell Co* case (1963) 109 CLR 407 at 414, his Honour stating that infringement under the English section involves: "the use of a mark identical with the registered mark, or so nearly resembling it as to be likely to deceive or cause confusion", adding the comment that such provision says nothing expressly about substantial identity whereas, of course, the Australian Act specifies this element as a test in considering infringement;

(d) that where s 62(1) speaks of the use of a mark, reference must be to the definition section, s 6(2), which while confining user to the use of a printed or other visual representation of the mark, thereby omitting reference to oral use, extends the use of the mark, beyond use upon the subject goods to use in physical or other relation to such goods, thus comprehending material such as brochures and other promotional material, which has been tendered in evidence in this case;

(e) that it is ultimately for the judge to determine as a matter of impression whether the requisite degree of resemblance exists to satisfy either or both of the criteria of substantial identity or deceptive similarity: *McWilliam's Wines Pty Ltd v McDonald's System of Australia Pty Ltd* (1980) 33 ALR 394 at 399.

Reverting to the principal point, the plaintiff's mode of applying the criteria as analysed by Windeyer J ((1963) 109 CLR 407 at 414, 415) requires the exclusion of elements which might be described as passing off considerations and confines the inquiry accordingly.

On the other hand the defendants contend that while passing off considerations are not relevant under s 62(1) in a direct sense, nevertheless, in a case under s 62(1), it is permissible to look to the use of the mark. They further submit that, notwithstanding the distinction between subs (1) and subs (2) of s 62, which is so strongly emphasised by the plaintiffs, the use to which such mark is put is not irrelevant under subs (1). The defendants rely upon the long-established terminology adopted in trade mark law, both on the early authorities and in the statutory provision, and submit that the wording of s 62(1) should not be given a radically different effect without a clear indication to that effect in the Act.

Thus, the defendants submit that the test of "deceptively similar" takes one back to the definition section, s 6(3), which provides:

"For the purposes of this Act, a trade mark shall be deemed to be deceptively similar to another trade mark if it so nearly resembles that other trade mark as to be likely to deceive or cause confusion."

The defendants then say that therefore the inquiry concerning deceptive similarity under s 62(1) necessarily encompasses factors and considerations outside the marks themselves.

Further support for this approach on the part of the defendants is sought to be derived from such decisions as that of *Southern Cross Refrigerating Co v Toowoomba Foundry Pty Ltd* (1954) 91 CLR 592. The defendants point to the passage in the judgment of Kitto J (at 594, 595) setting out the matters to be taken into account in considering the question of the likelihood to deceive, or associated questions of confusion. In effect, the defendants submit that the tests which were so formulated in relation to an application for registration under s 114 of the former Commonwealth Act apply also in relation to the question of deceptive **[497]** similarity arising to be determined under s 62. The defendants also refer on this point to the decisions of the House of Lords in *Berlei (UK) Ltd v Bali Brassiere Co Inc* [1969] 1 WLR 1306; [1969] 2 All ER 812 and of the Privy Council in *Hannaford & Burton Ltd v Polaroid Corp* [1976] 2 NZLR 14. These cases were not, of course, cases of infringement, but applied criteria appropriate to applications for expungement or registration where the wide-ranging inquiry

▬▬▬▬ Polaroid v Sole N *continued*

embraces inter alia, the risk of confusion in the minds of a substantial number of persons and other factors mentioned in the *Southern Cross Refrigerating* case (1954) 91 CLR 592 at 608.

It seems to me that this proposition of the defendants is not a valid approach to the question raised for determination under s 62. The definition in s 6(3) is not directed to a case such as the present of a contest between a registered mark and another mark. It is concerned only with a competition between two trade marks, and is limited to that situation. It is directed rather to situations necessitating comparison of trade marks under such sections as s 33, s 34, s 58(3) and s 82(2) of the Act: see also *Smith Kline & French Laboratories Ltd's Trade Mark Applications* [1976] RPC 511 at 532, per Lord Diplock. So far as the authorities are concerned to which the defendants refer, I do not consider that they have significant bearing on the matters raised for consideration and determination in dealing with the question of infringement under s 62. They were concerned, as previously mentioned, with different situations involving wider considerations that are admissible under s 62(1).

As counsel for the plaintiff phrased it, these cases involve a different universe of discourse from that involved when the court is measuring the monopoly of a party already on the register and thus entitled to the protection and assistance provided by the Act in aid of the right so held.

Therefore, I uphold the plaintiff's first proposition coupled with its contention as to exclusion of passing off elements in limiting the inquiry called for under s 62(1). The defendants further submitted that it was proper to look at the market, and in this regard suggested that the products of the plaintiffs are in a more expensive range, and also that they are provided to a different class of customer from that applicable in the case of the defendant's goods. For the same reasons as outlined above, I do not consider that matter of this kind is appropriate to be considered under the tests stated in s 62. The same comment is to be made as to the defendants' submission that the absence of evidence of actual confusion is to be taken into account. Here again, this question is completely outside the range of the inquiry required under s 62.

In further answer to these further submissions of the defendants, it might be added that it is not a question of the manner in which the plaintiffs use their marks, but rather a question of which market, and the extent of the market which the plaintiffs are to be treated as free to use. The only question posed under s 62 is whether the defendants have trespassed into any part of that area reserved to the plaintiffs by virtue of their proprietorship of the registered marks. This question is to be determined by reference to potential use in such area by the defendants of the first defendant's mark: see *Marc A Hammond Pty Ltd v Papa Carmine Pty Ltd* [1976] 2 NSWLR 124 at 128; *Berlei Hestia Industries Ltd v Bali Co Inc* (1973) 129 CLR 353 at 362, per Mason J.

[498] Applying the tests referred to by Windeyer J ((1963) 109 CLR 407 at 414, 415, 416) to the two subject marks, the plaintiffs point to the fact that, viewed as a whole, the only difference upon which the defendants can rely is in the first letter of the subject words, and that, so far as substantial identity is concerned, both in respect of essential features and total impression, the similarity is such as to constitute substantial identity. On this point the defendants contend that the words have different connotations, the word "solar" involving a concept of sun; whereas "Polaroid" or "Polar" evoke an entirely different concept; so that ordinary people would not think of any connection between the two words. The plaintiffs assert that there is a common concept evoked by both words, namely that of light; whereas the defendants suggest that this would not occur to the ordinary person, considering the two words side by side, as creating substantial identity. The defendants further rely strongly upon the fact that the differences in the one letter between the two words are highly significant, because it is the first letter of each word, and it is located in the accented syllable in each of the words.

It seems to me that, considering the two marks side by side, they are not substantially identical in regard to the essential features of the marks. Nor do I have a total impression of resemblance between them to the extent of substantial identity. The first letter in each word conveys to my mind a difference between the words which constitutes an essential feature of each of them, so as to preclude a finding that the registered marks and the defendants' mark are substantially identical.

As to deceptive similarity, the impression here to be considered is of course different from that of the impression to be considered in viewing the two marks side by side. As emphasised by Windeyer J ((1963) 109 CLR 407 at 415) it is an impression based on recollection which may be an imperfect recollection of the plaintiffs' marks that persons of ordinary intelligence and memory would have, and on the other hand, the impression that such persons would get from the defendants' mark. It seems to me that, in applying this test, the similarity between the two marks is such as to qualify as deceptive similarity. The deceptiveness, I consider, flows not only from the degree of similarity itself, but also from its effect considered in relation to the circumstances of the goods, the prospective purchasers and the market covered by the plaintiffs' monopoly. The two words are in the general impression created, so alike that I consider that there is a strong likelihood of confusion arising from the deception created by such similarity.

Accordingly, I would uphold the plaintiffs' claim that an infringement has occurred in the use of the defendants' mark.

While the evidence clearly shows such infringement on the part of the first defendant, there is also evidence indicating that the second defendant has been privy to the commission of infringing acts in the use of the defendants' mark. It is apparent that he is the managing director of a small private company, in which the only other director is his wife. It is also apparent that he actively participates in the day-to-day conduct of the first defendant's business activities. I consider that accordingly he is to be treated as being privy to and authorising the infringing acts on the part of the first defendant. Therefore, I conclude that relief ought to be given against both defendants: *Reitzman v Grahame-Chapman & Derustit Ltd* (1950) 67 RPC 178 at 185.

© Council of Law Reporting for New South Wales (1981)

Sections 120(1), (2) and (3)

Coca-Cola v All-Fect Distributors

[14.255] *Coca-Cola Co v All-Fect Distributors Ltd* [1999] 47 IPR 481 Federal Court of Australia

BLACK CJ, SUNDBERG and FINKELSTEIN JJ: [483]

The appellant is the manufacturer and distributor of Coca-Cola. It is the proprietor of a trade mark registered under the *Trade Marks Act 1955* (the 1955 Act) and the *Trade Marks Act 1995* (the Act), namely a contour drawing of the glass bottle in which Coca-Cola has traditionally been sold. The trade mark is registered in class 32 in respect of beverages and syrups for the manufacture of such beverages. At first instance two other registered trade marks were in issue—the word marks COCA-COLA and COKE. Those marks are no longer in issue. The contour drawing mark is depicted below.

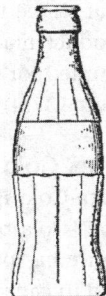

▨▨▨▨ Coca-Cola v All-Fect Distributors *continued*

The respondent is a confectionery wholesaler which imports and distributes, amongst other products, a cola flavoured confectionary which is shaped somewhat [483] like the contour bottle. When fresh the confectionary is soft and gelatinous and lies curled or rolled up in its container. However, when laid out flat it looks like this—

... [485]

It was common ground before the primary judge that

- since 1938 the appellant has carried on the business of manufacturing, promoting and selling non-alcoholic carbonated beverages known as Coca-Cola throughout Australia under and by reference to the marks COCA-COLA and COKE and the contour bottle, which was a bottle of distinctive appearance
- since at least 1938 the appellant has widely advertised its business and beverages in Australia by reference to the word marks COCA-COLA and COKE and the contour bottle
- the appellant's business and goods have become widely and favourably known and identified in the minds of the general public throughout Australia by means of the word marks COCA-COLA and COKE and the contour bottle
- the appellant's business and goods have a substantial, exclusive and valuable reputation and goodwill throughout Australia by reference to the word marks COCA-COLA and COKE and the contour bottle
- members of the public who have acquired or propose to acquire goods or services from, or otherwise transact or propose to transact business with, any person carrying on business under or by reference to the word marks COCA-COLA and COKE and the contour bottle, expect to be dealing with persons associated with or licensed or approved by the appellant, and rely upon the reputation acquired by the appellant in Australia.

The appellant contended that the extensive use, including the licensing, of the contour bottle as a trade mark has resulted in the bottle being so well known in Australia that it is understood by the public to be used exclusively in connection with products made by, for, or with the approval of the appellant. As a consequence, it was claimed that any product with that shape would be identified and recognised by the public as the appellant's product or a product made for it or with its approval. The respondent denied all the claims, and cross claimed for the loss and damage it had suffered as a result of the seizure of the consignments. See s 137(4) of the Act.

Coca-Cola

Coca-Cola is one of the most extensively advertised products in Australia. In Australia the Coca-Cola beverage is sold in glass bottles, aluminium cans and plastic bottles. The contour bottle has been used extensively in Australia since 1938. From the 1960s the drink has been sold in cans as well as in the contour bottles. Since the 1970s Coca-Cola has been sold mainly in plastic bottles. Notwithstanding this, the contour bottle has remained a mark or sign which is readily recognised by its shape alone as the COCA-COLA or COKE bottle. Since 1994 a significant proportion of the marketing of the Coca-Cola beverage in Australia has used or promoted the image of the contour bottle. Cans of the drink include a pictorial representation of the contour bottle, and Coca-Cola advertisements regularly feature the bottle as a distinctive identifier of Coca-Cola products. In 1994 the appellant modified some of the plastic bottles to use the contour bottle design. Further, since 1994 certain of the advertising has used the contour bottle alone, whereas previously the bottle had almost invariably been used in advertisements in conjunction with the words COCA-COLA or COKE. The applicant has developed a comprehensive merchandising program to exploit **[486]** the goodwill associated with its trade marks in relation to a wide range of products which are unrelated to the original beverage. Examples in Australia of products which feature the contour bottle are a bottle opener, a tin container, a drinking mug, a fridge magnet, an ornament, a key chain, and salt and pepper containers.

The confectionary

The confectionary is made in Germany by Efruti GmbH & Co KG and is distributed in Australia by the respondent. It is gelatinous and cola flavoured, and when laid out flat bears some resemblance to a Coca-Cola contour bottle. As appears from the representation set out earlier in this judgment, when compared with the contour bottle mark the confectionary is slightly elongated and somewhat distorted in shape. The bulk of the respondent's sales are from warehouses where tubs of the confectionary are presented in cardboard boxes for purchase. About 90% of the respondent's sales of the confectionary are made to small wholesalers who in turn supply retailers. The remaining 10% of sales are direct to retailers.

The transparent plastic tubs in which the confectionary is sold contain one hundred sweets. Because of their gelatinous content the sweets lie curled or rolled up in the tub. The primary judge considered that until a piece is removed from the tub and straightened out it does not look much like a contour bottle. The tub is clearly labelled as containing "Efruti" cola bottles. The label on the tub shows two cola bottles reclining in the sun on a desert island sipping cola. The primary judge thought the bottles on the label similar to, but not recognisable as, contour bottles. His Honour was of the view that the confectionary, whether in its edible form or as represented on the label, was plainly intended to convey a "fun version" of the contour bottle. The colour scheme, get up and pictorial representations on the tub do not suggest any association with Coca-Cola or the appellant. Retailers usually sell the confectionary from the Efruti tub or from their own containers. It is sold in milk bars, convenience stores, newsagents, petrol stations and other similar outlets.

The cola bottle confectionary had been on the market in Australia for some time before the respondent started selling it in 1992. The respondent has sold the product in Australia since that time. A sales brochure for the confectionary shows the bottles standing up in a tub and prominently features the Efruti label. The primary judge considered that even when the bottles are standing up they are not easily recognised as having a shape similar to that of the contour bottle. His Honour thought the brochure consistent with the "fun" representation on the tub labels.

On the respondent's evidence the bottles were referred to by its employees as "Cola bottles", "Cola bottle lollies" and "Cola lollies", and no reference was made to the sweets as "Coca-Cola lollies" or "Coca-Cola bottles". Despite some inconclusive evidence to the contrary from a private investigator retained by the appellant, the primary judge was not satisfied that the respondent or its employees, in marketing or distributing the confectionary, identify it as associated or connected with COCA-COLA or COKE, or use those names. His

▮▮▮▮▮ Coca-Cola v All-Fect Distributors *continued*

Honour said that putting to one side the shape and appearance of the bottle, nothing in the get up, labelling or manner of presentation of the confectionary indicates any such association or connection. ... [487]

The legislation
Section 120 of the Act deals with infringement of a trade mark.

Primary judge's reasoning
The appellant's case before the primary judge under s 120(2) was that the respondent had used as a trade mark a sign substantially identical with, or deceptively similar to, the contour bottle mark in relation to goods of the same description as the goods in respect of which the mark was registered (beverages [488] and syrups for the making of beverages). Under s 120(3) it was contended that the respondent had used as a trade mark a sign substantially identical with, or deceptively similar to, the well known contour bottle mark in relation to unrelated goods (confectionary), which use was likely to indicate a connection between the confectionary and the appellant. The parties joined issue on two main points, common to both s 120(2) and (3). The first was whether the importation, distribution and sale of the cola bottle confectionary constituted use of the confectionary "as a trade mark". The second was whether the cola bottle confectionary was substantially identical with, or deceptively similar to, the appellant's mark.

The primary judge decided both points in the respondent's favour. He also decided in the respondent's favour an issue that does not appear to have been in dispute, and is not described as one of the matters in contention. This was whether for the purposes of sub-s (2) the confectionary is "goods of the same description as that of goods ... in respect of which the trade mark is registered", namely beverages and syrups for the manufacture of such beverages. His Honour dealt with that point in the course of considering the claim that the respondent had infringed the COCA-COLA trade mark. He said:

> "The applicant relied upon the ingredients of confection ('a sweet preparation (liquid or dry) of fruit or the like, as a preserve or sweet meat') and the Coca-Cola beverage, which share sugar, colour, flavour and acids. However, having some overlapping ingredients does not, in my view, make the cola bottle confectionary goods of the same description [or closely related goods] as required. Further, the fact that both categories of goods may be sold through the same or similar trade channels, such as convenience stores, is of limited assistance to the applicant when one considers the wide range of unrelated goods sold in outlets that sell beverages, such as Coca-Cola and the cola bottle confectionary. The use to which the goods in respect of which the mark is registered are put, for example, using concentrates, extracts etc or ingredients in beverages or drinking a beverage and eating confectionary, are quite different. In my view, the cola bottle confectionary is basically a good of a different description to the registered goods [and is not a closely related good] for the purposes of s 120(2)."

His Honour adopted these reasons when he came to consider whether the confectionary was goods of the same description as those in relation to which the contour bottle trade mark was registered. (It is not clear why his Honour used the expressions we have placed in brackets— closely related goods.)

The primary judge regarded the appellant's "real case" of infringement to have arisen under subs (3)—the use by the respondent of a sign substantially identical with, or deceptively similar to, the contour bottle mark, in relation to unrelated goods, in a manner which is likely to be taken as indicating a connection between the unrelated goods (the cola bottle

▰▰▰▰ Coca-Cola v All-Fect Distributors *continued*

confectionary) and the registered owner of the trade mark. The two issues peculiar to s 120(3) that arose in connection with this claim were whether the cola bottle confectionary had been used as a trade mark, and if so, whether that use was likely to be taken as indicating a connection between the confectionary and the appellant. The first issue turned on the words in subs (3)(b)—"uses as a trade mark"—and the second on those in subs (3)(c)—"likely to be taken as indicating a connection between the unrelated goods ... and the registered owner of the trade mark". His Honour concluded that:

- "the cola bottle confectionary, as such, does not indicate or connote origin of the goods and hence application or use of the contour bottle (represented by the confection) as a trade mark or, to put the matter in terms of s 17 of the Act, the [489] confectionary does not distinguish the goods so as to indicate they were goods dealt with or provided by any particular person;
- whilst the cola bottle confection is recognisable as having the shape of the contour bottle, consumers would not be likely to believe or expect it to have a commercial or trade connection of some kind with the applicant by reason of having that shape; [and]
- consumers would not be led to wonder whether it might be the case that the confectionary comes from the same source as Coca-Cola."

After observing that use as a mark requires that the mark be used in such a way as to indicate or connote origin of the goods, his Honour gave four reasons for concluding that the confectionary does not indicate or connote origin:

- The inscription "Cola" and the colour of the confectionary are descriptive of the flavour rather than the origin of the goods.
- The elongated and distorted form and appearance of the confectionary, although generally recognisable as having the shape and basic markings of the contour bottle, is dissimilar to it in significant respects and is far from an exact copy of it. Thus the product itself does not present as indicating or connoting its origin.
- Insofar as the packaging, labelling and get up of the tub containing the confectionary feature a shape similar to that of the contour bottle, they do not do so in a manner that indicates or connotes origin. To the extent origin is indicated, the predominantly blue and green label points to "Efruti" as the origin of the product.
- His Honour's "impression and estimate" was that the confectionary is presented as a fun product, perhaps cheekily imitating the contour bottle, but not as representing any other connection with it.

The primary judge concluded by saying:

> "Thus, the cola bottle confectionary is merely recognisable as having the well known shape of the contour bottle but would not be likely to be believed or expected to have a trade or commercial connection of some kind with the applicant by reason of having that shape. Likewise consumers would be unlikely to be led to wonder whether it might be the case that the confectionary comes from the same source as Coca-Cola."

His Honour dismissed the trade practices and passing off claims because, for the reasons he had given in relation to the trade mark claim, the appellant had not established any misrepresentation as to the existence of a trade or commercial connection between it or its confectionary and the respondent or its products.

"Uses as a trade mark"

Under the 1955 Act a registered mark was infringed by someone who "uses a mark which is substantially identical with, or deceptively similar to, the trade mark, in the course of trade".

Coca-Cola v All-Fect Distributors *continued*

In *Shell Co of Australia Ltd v Esso Standard Oil (Aust) Ltd* (1963) 109 CLR 407 it was said to be implied in both s 58(1) and s 62(1) of the 1955 Act that the "use" there referred to is limited to use "as a trade mark". Section 120 of the current Act expressly incorporates that requirement. Counsel for the respondent submitted that whether the respondent was using the sign as a trade mark depended on the answer to the question—"Do I, just by looking at the confectionary, conclude that the shape is put there to tell us that the Coca-Cola Co is the manufacturer of those goods?" This formulation, it was said, was an adaptation of what Kitto J had said in *Shell*. In our view counsel's formulation is not a correct adaptation and does not ask the right question. Use "as a trade mark" is use of the mark as a "badge of origin" **[490]** in the sense that it indicates a connection in the course of trade between goods and the person who applies the mark to the goods. See *Johnson & Johnson Aust Pty Ltd v Sterling Pharmaceuticals Pty Ltd* (1991) 30 FCR 326 at 341, 351. That is the concept embodied in the definition of "trade mark" in s 17—a sign used to distinguish goods dealt with in the course of trade by a person from goods so dealt with by someone else.

The authorities provide no support for the view that in determining whether a sign is used as a trade mark one asks whether the sign indicates a connection between the alleged infringer's goods and those of the registered owner. Cases such as *Mark Foy's Ltd v Davies Coop & Co Ltd* (1956) 95 CLR 190 at 204-205, the *Shell* case at 425, *Johnson & Johnson* at 347-348, 351, *Wingate Marketing Pty Ltd v Levi Strauss* (1994) 49 FCR 89 at 134-145 and *Musitor BV v Tansing* (1994) 29 IPR 203 at 213, 216 show that the question is whether the sign used indicates origin of goods in the user of the sign; whether there is a connection in the course of trade between the goods and the user of the sign. Thus in *Shell* at 424-425 Kitto J, with whom Dixon CJ, Taylor and Owen JJ agreed, said:

> "Was the appellant's use, that is to say its television presentation, of those particular pictures of the oil drop figure which were substantially identical with or deceptively similar to the respondent's trade marks a use of them 'as a trade mark'?
>
> With the aid of the definition of 'trade mark' in s 6 of the Act, the adverbial expression may be expanded so that the question becomes whether, in the setting in which the particular pictures referred to were presented, they would have appeared to the television viewer as possessing the character of devices, or brands, which the appellant was using or proposing to use in relation to petrol for the purpose of indicating, or so as to indicate, *a connection in the course of trade between the petrol and the appellant*. Did they appear to be thrown on to the screen as being marks for distinguishing Shell petrol from other petrol in the course of trade?"

And later his Honour said:

> "no viewer would ever pick out any of the individual scenes in which the man resembles the respondent's trade marks, whether those scenes be few or many, and say to himself: 'There I see something that the Shell people are showing me as being a mark by which I may know that *any petrol in relation to which I see it used is theirs*."

The emphases are ours.

[492] ... The confectionary has three features that are not descriptive of the goods. They are the silhouette, the fluting at the top and bottom, and the label band. It is not necessary for the respondent to adopt any of those features in order to inform consumers that its product is a cola flavoured sweet. It could do so by using the cola colour, the word COLA and the shape of an ordinary straight-walled bottle. The silhouette, fluting and band are striking features of the confectionary, and are apt to distinguish it from the goods of other traders. The

■■■■■ Coca-Cola v All-Fect Distributors *continued*

primary function performed by these features is to distinguish the goods from others. That is to use those features as a mark. It is true, as the respondent said, that the fact that a feature is not descriptive of goods does not necessarily establish that it is used to distinguish or differentiate them. But in the present case we are compelled to the conclusion that the non-descriptive features have been put there to make the goods more arresting of appearance and more attractive, and thus to distinguish them from the goods of other traders. ... [495]

"Substantially identical"

A person infringes a registered trade mark within s 120(2) by using as a trade mark a sign that is substantially identical with or deceptively similar to the trade mark. The primary judge did not deal expressly with the first of these alternatives, though his conclusion that consumers would not be led to wonder whether it might be the case that the confectionary comes from the same source as Coca-Cola (ie the confectionary was not deceptively similar to the contour bottle mark) may well carry with it that the features of the confectionary are not substantially identical with the mark. In order to determine whether marks are substantially identical they should be compared side by side, their similarities and differences noted and the importance of these similarities and differences assessed having regard to the essential features of the registered mark and the total impression of resemblance or dissimilarity that emerges from the comparison. See *Shell* at 414 per Windeyer J; *Powell v Glow Zone Products Pty Ltd* (1996) 36 IPR 343 at 364; *Carnival Cruise Lines Inc v Sitmar Cruises Ltd* (1994) 120 ALR 495 at 513. There are significant differences [496] between the confectionary and the contour bottle mark. Even when the confectionary is laid out flat, it does not have the pronounced waisting effect that there is in the bottom quarter of the mark. There is a space for the label on the confectionary, but it is of a different shape from that on the mark. The confectionary has COLA written in the label area. The only close similarity is in the fluting. A total impression of similarity does not emerge from a comparison of the two marks, and accordingly the shape of the confectionary is not substantially identical with the contour bottle mark.

"Deceptively similar to"

Section 10 of the Act provides that a trade mark is taken to be deceptively similar to another trade mark if it so nearly resembles that other mark as to be likely to deceive or cause confusion. No intention to deceive or cause confusion is required: *Re Bali Brasserie Co Inc's Registered Trade Mark* (1968) 118 CLR 128 at 139. The distinction between "likely to deceive" and "likely to cause confusion" lies not in some element of culpability in the user to be inferred from the word "deceive", but in the effect of the mark on prospective purchasers. In *Pioneer Hi-Bred Corn Co v Highline Chicks Pty Ltd* [1979] RPC 410 at 423 Richardson J, in the New Zealand Court of Appeal, said:

"'Deceived' implies the creation of an incorrect belief or mental impression and causing 'confusion' may go no further than perplexing or mixing up the minds of the purchasing public .... Where the deception or confusion alleged is as to the source of the goods, deceived is equivalent to being misled into thinking that the goods bearing the applicant's mark come from some other source and confused to being caused to wonder whether that might not be the case."

...

In the *Shell* case at 414-415 Windeyer J said:

"On the question of deceptive similarity a different comparison must be made from that which is necessary when substantial identity is in question. The marks are not

████████ Coca-Cola v All-Fect Distributors *continued*

now to be looked at side by side. The issue is not abstract similarity, but deceptive similarity. Therefore the comparison is the familiar one of trade mark law. It is between, on the one hand, the impression based on recollection of the plaintiff's mark that persons of ordinary intelligence and memory would have; and, on the other hand, the impressions that such persons would get from the defendant's television exhibitions. To quote Lord Radcliffe again: 'The likelihood of confusion or deception in such cases is not disproved by placing the two marks side by side and demonstrating how small is the chance of error in any customer who places his order for goods with both the marks clearly before him .... It is more useful to observe that in most persons the eye is not an accurate recorder of visual detail, and that marks are remembered rather by general impressions or by some significant detail than by any photographic recollection of the whole': *de Cordova v Vick Chemical Co* (1951) 68 RPC 103 at 106."

Whether one device mark "resembles" another involves an assessment of the visual impression made by the two marks when compared. In contrast, the likelihood of deception or confusion involves an assessment of what would be the probable visual impression on customers or potential customers which would be produced as a result of the "notional normal and fair use" of the marks. See *Gardenia Overseas Pty Ltd v The Garden Co Ltd* (1994) 29 IPR 485 at 493. The **[497]** notional normal and fair use of the confectionary is as an item acquired on impulse by consumers in a retail environment such as a convenience store, a milk bar, a newsagent, a petrol station or other similar outlet. Those who buy the confectionary are children and teenagers, especially teenage girls. Coca-Cola is also sold at some of those outlets to a similar type of purchaser.

As Dixon and McTiernan JJ said in *Australian Woollen Mills Ltd v F S Walton & Co Ltd* (1937) 58 CLR 641 at 659, whether a mark is deceptively similar to another depends on a combination of visual impression and judicial estimation of the effect likely to be produced in the course of the ordinary conduct of affairs. In many cases it is a question to which different answers can reasonably be given. Taking into account the "imperfect recollection" that customers may have of the contour bottle mark, and the fact that the "idea" suggested by the mark is more likely to be recalled than its precise details, the factors that have led us to conclude that the features of the confectionary are likely to cause confusion in consumers, that is to say, cause them to wonder whether it might be the case that the confectionary comes from the same source as Coca-Cola, are these:

- the contour bottle is extremely well known
- there are similarities between the features of the confectionary and the contour bottle mark:
  - both have curved rather than flat sides
  - both have a top portion with longitudinal fluting, a central portion without fluting and a lower portion with fluting
  - the upper and lower portions have the same number of flutes
  - the fluting on the confectionary closely resembles that on the contour bottle mark
  - both have a flat base and a banded neck
- to a greater or lesser degree depending on the feature, the respondent has taken all significant features of the contour bottle mark
- the word COLA on the confectionary, though not itself a mark, reinforces the link between the confectionary and Coca-Cola that is conveyed by the shape of the confectionary
- when fresh, the lower half of the confectionary is the same colour as Coca-Cola, again reinforcing the link referred to.

▆▆▆▆▆ Coca-Cola v All-Fect Distributors *continued*

"Not likely to deceive or cause confusion"

Section 120(2) concludes with the words:

"However, the person is not taken to have infringed the trade mark if the person establishes that using the sign as the person did is not likely to deceive or cause confusion."

As Lord Evershed MR said in *Taverner Rutledge Ltd v Specters Ltd* [1959] RPC 355 at 359-360:

"Though it may generally be as you say a mark likely to cause confusion, in fact in the way I have used it and in the circumstances and environment in which I have used it, it is not likely to cause confusion."

Whether the respondent can establish that the use of the features of the confectionary is not likely to cause typical consumers to wonder whether it might be the case that the confectionary comes from the same source as Coca-Cola should be remitted to the primary judge. As will appear, other issues will also be remitted to his Honour.

[498] Section 120(3)

In view of the respondent's concession at trial, to which the appellant held it on appeal, that the confectionary was goods of the same description as the registered goods, there is no need to consider whether the primary judge was correct in concluding that no infringement under s 120(3) had been made out. Sub-sections (2) and (3) are mutually exclusive—the former dealing with "goods of the same description ..." and the latter with "goods ... that are not of the same description ...".

■ Parallel imports

[14.260] Whilst the importation of goods bearing counterfeit Australian trade marks obviously constitutes an infringement, it is less certain whether the unauthorised importation of goods bearing a mark applied by the registered proprietor constitutes an infringement. In *Champagne Heidsieck et Cie Monopole Societe Anonyme v Buxton* [1930] 1 Ch 330 the French manufacturer of wine intended for the French market objected to the importation of that wine into Britain. Clauson J (at 341) ruled that the importation of the plaintiff's wine was not an infringement since as he noted that "the use of a mark by the defendant which is relied on as an infringement must be a use upon goods which are not the genuine goods, ie, those upon which the plaintiff's mark is properly used, for anyone may use the plaintiff's mark on the plaintiff's goods, since that cannot cause the deception which is the test of infringement".

▆▆▆▆ Wingate Marketing v Levi Strauss ▆▆▆▆

[14.265] *Wingate Marketing Pty Ltd v Levi Strauss Pty Ltd* (1994) 16 ATPR 41-303 Federal Court of Australia

[The issue arose as to whether the importation of substantially altered Levi jeans, sold as second hand goods, amounted to trade mark infringement. It was held that use of a mark on repaired clothing was not infringement.]

SHEPPARD J: [42,045] ... A second hand shop or a charity shop selling second hand clothing which included worn or used Levi Strauss jeans would not without more infringe any of the

━━━━━ Wingate Marketing v Levi Strauss *continued*

Levi Strauss marks by selling the second hand garments although they might bear one or more of those marks. Members of the public acting reasonably are not misled or confused by the fact that in countless cases second hand products have attached to them original labels, many of which will consist of or contain the trade marks of a variety of manufacturers and distributors. Certainly they will not think that the second hand shop with which they deal is an offshoot of, or has some connection with, the original supplier of the product when new. They may think that a substantially altered garment bearing a trade mark is a second hand garment manufactured or distributed by the company whose name appears on the label affixed to the goods, but if that be so, it will not be because the mark is being used as a trade mark, but because of other factors, which taken together, may well warrant the conclusion that the person marketing the goods is passing them off as having been originally made or produced in the form in which they then are. That really is the essence of the Levi Strauss complaint in relation to this aspect of the case. But, in my opinion, it is properly dealt with in the context of misrepresentation and passing off and not in the context of infringement of trade mark.

━━━

━━━ Review of Intellectual Property Legislation under ━━━ the Competition Principles Agreement

[14.270] Intellectual Property Competition Review Committee, *Review of Intellectual Property Legislation under the Competition Principles Agreement*, Final Report (September 2000) (References omitted.)

Parallel importation and the Trade Marks Act

Background

Use of a trade mark in relation to goods or services will not infringe the *Trade Marks Act* provided that the registered mark has been applied to the goods or services by, or with the consent of, the Australian owner of the mark [see the *Montana* case below]. The *Trade Marks Act* therefore adopts the principle of international exhaustion, whereby placing the goods onto the market exhausts the owner's ability to control subsequent dealings with the goods or services.

The Federal Court in March 1999 consolidated the consistent approach of Australian courts in rejecting the rights of an international trade mark owner to control the distribution channels of its goods through trade mark rights, affirming the exhaustion of rights doctrine.

However, there appears to still be uncertainty surrounding the situation where goods are imported from overseas after an assignment of the Australian trade mark to the Australian distributor.

Views for and against

The Committee received submissions on parallel importation and the *Trade Marks Act* which point out the uncertainty of the position where the overseas owner of a trade mark conditionally assigns the trade mark to an Australian distributor. The assignment is made on the condition that once the distributorship arrangement between the owner of the overseas trade mark and the Australian trade mark comes to an end, the Australian trade mark must be reassigned to the overseas owner. The purpose of such an arrangement is to permit the Australian distributor to prevent the parallel importation of trade marked goods from overseas that would compete with the Australian distributor. Even despite questions about the legality of these arrangements there are various transactional costs involved in setting up these assignments aimed at giving the distributor the right to control the flow of the trade marked goods.

If the overseas trade mark owner retained the Australian ownership of the trade mark and retained the Australian distributor merely as an authorised user, neither the Australian distributor nor the overseas trade mark owner could prevent parallel importing. This would be due to the impact of s 123 of the *Trade Marks Act* and the various case law concerning parallel importation that was decided pursuant to the *Trade Marks Act 1955* (Cth).

Section 123(1) of the *Trade Marks Act 1995* provides that a mark applied to the same or similar goods "with the consent of" the registered owner does not infringe. There are doubts as to what "consent" means in this context, although the section is presumed to introduce into trade mark legislation the concept of exhaustion of rights. However, before the introduction of s 123 into the present trade mark legislation, arrangements preventing parallel importation of trade marked goods were effected through the mechanism of foreign companies assigning their Australian trade marks to local distributors in order to assist the local distributor to prevent parallel importation.

In the *Fender Guitar Case, Fender Australia v Bevk* [(1989) 15 IPR 257] Justice Burchett held that a local distributor, to whom the foreign owner had assigned its trade mark in Australia, was entitled to prevent the parallel importation of goods bearing the trade mark. On the facts before him, the Judge found that the local company had developed an independent reputation in the trade mark by virtue of its selection of the goods it imported and the after sales service which it provided to the public. There was no challenge to the validity of the assignment of the trade mark from the foreign company to the local company. Following this case it became common for foreign companies to assign their Australian trade marks to local distributors in order to assist the local distributor to prevent parallel importation.

A recent case, *Transport Tyre Sales Pty Ltd v Montana Tyres Rims & Tubes Pty Ltd* (1999) 43 IPR 481 (the *Montana* case) has cast doubts upon the "Fender Guitar" arrangements, where an international manufacturer assigned its Australian trade marks to a local distributor, in order to use trade mark rights to challenge parallel importation. This case consolidates the consistent approach in Australian courts in rejecting the rights of an international trade mark owner to control the distribution channels of its goods through trade mark rights, affirming the "exhaustion of rights doctrine". However, the appeal judgment leaves unanswered some of the most important issues arising out of the facts in the *Montana* case. In relation to the recordal of assignments, the Court did not consider the issue of "sham" transactions, and there remains a question whether in some circumstances involving "Fender" assignments, where the assignment document does not on its face reflect the real agreement between the parties, the lodgment of the document could amount to a false suggestion thereby invalidating the assignment.

A submission by Mr Mark Davison states that there are some difficulties and inefficiencies associated with the present position. They include:

• the situation is uncertain. Neither authorised Australian distributors nor the parallel importer are certain of the legality of the parallel importer's activity.

• trade mark owners and their Australian distributors will be entering into assignments and related agreements purely for the purpose of preventing parallel importing. There are various transactional costs incurred in these activities such as liability for capital gains tax and legal fees every time the trade mark is assigned and reassigned. There is no benefit derived to consumers from these transactional costs which will be passed on to consumers.

- parallel importers can have their trading activities ended by the stroke of a pen although there is no real change in the trade activities of the overseas owner, the Australian distributor or the parallel importer. The appropriateness of parallel importing from the policy perspective is not altered in any way by the mere conditional assignment of Australian ownership to an Australian distributor but the legality of parallel importing may hinge on it.

He therefore concludes:

"What is clear is that the type of artificial arrangements that have lead to the *Montana* case and *Fender v Bevk* should not impact on the legality of parallel importing of trade marked goods. Whatever policy position is taken on the issue of parallel importing, that position should not be capable of being altered by the formation of artificial arrangements in which an Australian distributor which was previously acting as an authorised user becomes the owner of the Australian trade mark in circumstances which demonstrate that it will simply continue to perform its role as an authorised user. Section 123 of the Act needs to be amended or a new subsection introduced to clarify that issue of what is included within the concept of 'consent' by the trade mark owner to the application of the trade mark to goods. Such an amendment should make it clear that a registered owner who is, in effect, the authorised user of the overseas owner of the same trade mark is consenting to the application of the trade mark to goods made by or under the control of that overseas owner."

Submissions also pointing out the restrictions on competition of this issue were also received from the ACCC and Mr Leslie Aldor acting on behalf of Holstar Cycles Pty Ltd.

Committee considerations

The Committee accepts that the current situation imposes costs, including creating uncertainties that inevitably affect the competitive process.

As a general matter, the Committee believes that suppliers should be able to enter into exclusive dealing arrangements except when these will substantially lessen competition in a market. The Committee accepts that the contractual assignment of trade marks is one of the means by which exclusive dealing arrangements may be established.

However, in line with its broader approach to parallel importation, the Committee does not believe that contracts of trade mark assignment should serve as a means of triggering statutory provisions that protect a supplier from import competition. Rather, the Committee takes the view that contractual provisions should be enforced in this area, as they are in others, by means of proceedings against breach.

Recommendations

The Committee recommends that the *Trade Marks Act* should be amended so as to ensure that the assignment provisions are not used to circumvent the intent to allow the parallel importation of legitimately trade marked goods.

OTHER ASPECTS OF TRADE MARK REGISTRATION

■ Certification trade marks

[**14.275**] *Trade Marks Act 1995* (Cth), Part 16 provides for the registration by organisations or associations of marks which they apply as attesting to a particular standard or quality. Applications for registration are accompanied by the rules which will govern the use of the mark.

The wrongful use of a certification mark, such as approved by the Standards Association of Australia, will also breach *Trade Practices Act 1974* (Cth), s 53: see *Hartnell v Sharp Corp of Australia Pty Ltd* (1975) 5 ALR 493.

■ Defensive registration

[**14.280**] Certain marks, because of their considerable reputation, could cause confusion if registered by other than their originators in respect of novel categories of goods or services. *Trade Marks Act 1995* (Cth), Part 17 permits registration of such marks to prevent their use for goods or services not covered by the registration. Examples of marks registered as defensive marks in Australia include HOLDEN, LEVI'S, CHANEL, GILLETTE, KLEENEX and VICKS.

For Part 17 registration it is not necessary for the applicant to intend to use the mark for goods or services in respect of which registration is obtained.

■ International trade mark conventions

[**14.285**] Australia is a member of the union established by the *Paris Convention for the Protection of Industrial Property 1883* under which the members of the union enjoy the same rights in each union country as that country's nationals, as well as certain Convention rights.

The principal Convention right is a right of priority. Following the filing of an application for registration of a trade mark in a union country, a person has a period of six months during which he has priority in filing for registration in any other union country. This priority is given effect to by *Trade Marks Act 1995* (Cth), Part 17A.

Australia is also a member of the *Nice Agreement concerning the International Classification of Goods and Services for the Registration of Marks*. This provides for a common classification of goods or services for the purpose of registration of marks.

INDEX